cmagvold

The Undeclared War

THE WORLD CRISIS AND

AMERICAN FOREIGN POLICY

The

Undeclared War

1940-1941,

by

WILLIAM L. LANGER

and

S. EVERETT GLEASON

Published for the Council on Foreign Relations

BY

HARPER & BROTHERS PUBLISHERS NEW YORK

Library of Congress catalog card number: 53-7738

LIBERIS · NOSTRIS · AMATIS

CONTENTS

CONTENTS

CONTENTS

CONTENTS

PREFACE

The surprise attack of the Japanese on Pearl Harbor, followed by the precipitate declaration of war on the United States by Germany and Italy, brought to an abrupt end a prolonged period of uncertainty and indecision in American public sentiment and foreign policy. The fall of France, more than a year before, and the subsequent threat of a Nazi invasion of England had, to be sure, convinced a majority of Americans of their great stake in the survival of Britain. That conviction had been expressed in the widespread approval of the famous Destroyer-for-Bases Deal of September, 1940, despite the fact that the transaction was tantamount to the abandonment of American neutrality. During the ensuing months it was reaffirmed by popular support for the policy of all aid to the embattled British, short of war. As embodied in the Lend-Lease Act, this policy clearly involved active American participation in the European conflict on Britain's behalf.

Yet most Americans still cherished the fervent hope that unstinting provision of military and other aid to the opponents of Hitlerism might spare their country involvement in actual hostilities. They clung to this hope for another full year, despite the fact that militarily the democratic cause fell on ever more evil days. France and Spain, so it seemed, would soon succumb to Nazi pressure and open the way to Axis conquest of Gibraltar, which in turn might well prove the prelude to Axis control of North and West Africa and possibly to a Nazi assault upon the bulge of Brazil.

Though Britain withstood the ferocious air attacks of 1940, Hitler elsewhere scored one signal triumph after another. In the eastern Mediterranean the situation was particularly threatening in the spring of 1941. General Wavell's initial victory over Graziani's Fascist forces in Libya was soon undone by Rommel's spectacular advance on Egypt. This coincided with the dramatic Nazi Blitzkrieg which engulfed the Balkans and came to a halt only on Crete and at the portals of European Turkey. Even when, in June, 1941, the Fuehrer overreached himself in the effort to liquidate his erstwhile Soviet ally, neither London nor Washington felt that much consolation was to be derived from this astounding reversal of Nazi policy. Hitler's victory over Stalin seemed a foregone conclusion and there was every reason to suppose that the Nazis, once they had secured their rear, would again throw the full weight of their military power against the west.

The situation at sea was equally depressing. Nazi submarine wolf packs were taking a heavy toll of British and Allied shipping, thus threatening to defeat the very purpose of the Lend-Lease program. Mr. Churchill no longer seriously attempted to conceal his conviction that nothing short of actual American naval and air participation could keep Britain's life lines open. President Roosevelt and his advisers, though like their compatriots reluctant to face the stark realities, were gradually being driven to the same conclusion. For months on end they repeatedly approached the crucial issue only to shy away from it. The well-known aversion of the American people to war seemed an insuperable barrier to intervention, despite a growing realization that the national interest left no real alternative. Not until the autumn of 1941 did the unrelenting pressure of ugly facts lead the American people to at least tacit acceptance of undeclared and limited war against Germany in the Atlantic.

During these agitated and fateful months the Administration was deterred from intervention also by the difficulties and delays encountered in the program of war production and national rearmament, and perhaps even more by the continued aggravation of the crisis in the Far East. The clash of American and Japanese interests and objectives was of long standing and had, by 1941, led to so complete a deadlock that in retrospect it is difficult to believe that the conflict could have been resolved otherwise than by war. Ever since Japan's adherence to the Berlin-Rome Axis through the Tripartite Pact of September, 1940, the United States was forced to recognize the high probability that the outbreak of hostilities with Germany would entail a Japanese attack on British, Dutch or American possessions in the Pacific. Furthermore, the President and his associates had to reckon with the ever-present possibility that Hitler would succeed in persuading the Japanese to attack Malaya or the Dutch Indies while by-passing the Philippines. In that event the American Government would have been faced with a serious and difficult dilemma. Since American statesmen and military authorities were agreed that Nazi Germany constituted the primary threat to the national security, it was a matter of great moment to stave off hostilities with Japan as long as possible and to avoid at all costs a military commitment in the Pacific of such magnitude as to hamper eventual operations in the Atlantic or Europe.

The agonizing problems presented by American public opinion, by the inadequacy of American military power, by the rapid deterioration of the democratic position in Europe, by the prospect of a Nazi conquest of Soviet Russia, and by the standing menace of Japanese aggression in the Pacific, all contributed to the anxiety, perplexity and vacillation of American foreign policy in the years 1940 and 1941.

It is this period and this extraordinarily complicated situation which we review and analyze in the present volume. Our study, the second part of our treatment of "The World Crisis and American Foreign Policy," follows logically and chronologically upon our earlier volume, *The Challenge to Isolation, 1937-1940,* published in 1952. The nature and purpose of the whole effort, as well as the materials upon which our account rests, have been described at some length in the preface of the earlier volume. It is superfluous, therefore, to restate them here.

Completion of the present study has been somewhat retarded by the fact that in the course of the year 1950 we were both recalled to government service, to which thenceforth we were, naturally, obliged to devote most of our time and effort. However, the text of *The Undeclared War* had already been completed in draft form and consequently only the necessary work of revision and the final polishing of the manuscript were delayed by the intrusion of other responsibilities.

We have been fortunate in retaining the interest and support of the Council on Foreign Relations, which sponsored the entire project, and also of many other organizations, agencies and individuals of whom mention has been made in our earlier preface. To the list should be added the name of Brigadier General John Magruder (Ret.), who made available to us certain papers dealing with his mission to China. We gladly take this opportunity to express once again our deep gratitude for the kindness and generosity shown us on all sides, and more particularly to thank Dr. Stetson Conn, of the Historical Division of the Department of the Army, who, despite heavy personal as well as official responsibilities, found time to read the whole manuscript and give us the benefit of his great knowledge and critical acumen. Our secretaries, Miss Frances Douglas and Miss Ina Holtzscheiter, have been unflagging in their interest and devotion, while our respective wives have been not only tolerant and long-suffering, but ever helpful in the preparation of the manuscript, the reading of proof, and the compilation of the index.

It should perhaps be stated once again that this study, like its predecessor, is in no sense a work of official or even semiofficial history. The Department of State, which has reviewed the manuscript, has done so solely in the interest of national security. The few changes it has suggested have been of a minor character and have in no case involved anything to which we, as conscientious historians, felt that exception must be taken. Above all, we should like to emphasize that neither officials of the Government nor any other persons have ever made the slightest effort to influence our interpretations or conclusions. These, like the plan, content and arrangement of the volume, are exclusively our own and we assume sole and complete responsibility for them.

Much thought and effort have gone into this account of the world crisis and the development of American policy in its global setting. We can only hope that the contents will prove reasonably commensurate with the climactic developments they describe and analyze, namely, the tortured emergence of the United States of America as leader of the forces of light in a world struggle which even today has scarcely abated and is still undecided.

WILLIAM L. LANGER
S. EVERETT GLEASON

The Undeclared War

CHAPTER I

The Tripartite Pact

1. THE INTERNATIONAL SETTING

During the entire summer of 1940 the fate of Britain and of European democracy hung in the balance. The Nazi conquest of Norway in the face of greatly superior sea power had been followed almost at once by the triumphant sweep of German forces through the Low Countries. At Dunkirk the Allied troops had, to be sure, been in large measure evacuated, but only with the loss of much essential equipment. Early in June the French had made a valiant but forlorn effort to hold on the Somme. In ten days their resistance had been broken, and on June 17 the new Cabinet headed by the aged Marshal Pétain had sued for an armistice. Thereafter Britain stood alone, awaiting the assault of the Nazi power which now controlled much of western Europe, was allied with Italy, and could still count on the cooperation of Soviet Russia. During the summer Britain's cause seemed hopeless. Hitler, while preparing for an amphibious invasion of England on the grand scale, loosed his air squadrons against British shipping, ports and industrial centers. It was a moot question how long the British, almost completely unprepared on the ground, could fight off attack from the air. Though the Royal Navy commanded the seas, it too was suffering heavy losses from submarine and air attack, and there was no assurance that it could prevent a concerted and determined Nazi attempt to reach the shores of southern England.

Throughout the world the crucial importance of the struggle between Germany and Britain was fully recognized, and those governments which still retained freedom of action plotted their policies according to their estimates of the outcome. The American people, long wedded to isolation and long deluded by hopes of avoiding involvement in foreign conflicts, had fallen into near panic when at last it recognized the magnitude of Nazi power and realized the threat to its own way of life as the British bastion and

1

British Fleet seemed doomed to disaster. President Roosevelt, who for some time had been warning of the dangers inherent in the European situation, had at once (June 10) proclaimed the Charlottesville program, committing the material resources of the nation to the opponents of aggression. Since, however, these resources had not yet been harnessed for war, the amount of assistance afforded Britain during the summer of 1940 was extremely limited. Not until Hitler seemed on the verge of invading England did the President finally consent to trade fifty over-age American destroyers for base rights in Britain's American possessions. Therewith the British secured substantial reinforcement for defense and, what was perhaps more important though less tangible, added assurance that the United States would throw ever greater weight behind resistance to the Nazis. After the Destroyer Deal American neutrality was hardly more than a technicality; the United States had clearly aligned itself with resistance to Nazi aggression.

But many months were still to pass before American support could become fully effective. War production was only getting under way and as yet no conclusive measures had been taken to raise an army even for national and hemisphere defense. In these circumstances it was but natural that the chief concern of the Administration should have been the protection of its own and neighboring shores, and that it should have staked its hopes on Britain's capability to withstand unaided the shock of invasion, should that come. Furthermore, Washington could not overlook the fact that the crisis confronting the nation was not a European, but a world crisis. Asia, like Europe, was in turmoil, for since 1937 Japan had been engaged in undeclared war against Nationalist China and had, with increasing effrontery, been challenging the Far Eastern position and interests of the United States as well as those of the European powers. The British, the French and the Dutch were none of them capable of withstanding Japanese pressure. The first two powers had been obliged to close the supply routes into China through Burma and Tonkin, while the latter was confronted with Japanese demands on the Netherlands Indies which seemed to presage an early advance into the southwest Pacific. In China itself European nationals were exposed to obloquy and abuse; foreign interests—American as well as European—were blandly disregarded or flagrantly violated by the Japanese military.

In the summer of 1940 the only hope of restraining or obstructing the Japanese seemed to lie in a strong American policy, for which, in fact, there was much clamor throughout the land. But the Administration, while willing to resort to half measures in the hope of deterring the Tokyo extremists, refused to take decisive steps. The President and his advisers were quite aware that the problem of the Pacific could not be considered apart from that of the Atlantic, but they had decided that the more formidable and menacing of the two great expansionist powers was Germany, not Japan.

Consequently they resisted whatever temptation they may have felt to throw the weight of American sea and industrial power against Japan, and determined, so far as possible, to avoid a major crisis in the Far East until the situation in Europe had been clarified. However, the course of events in the Far East depended more upon Japan than upon its opponents. It is therefore essential to analyze developments in the Pacific area in order properly to understand and evaluate the over-all American policy.

2. Triumph of the Activists

Ever since 1937 the Japanese militarists, who had engineered the attack on China, had been eager to join hands with the Nazis. Both powers regarded Communist Russia as an enemy and looked upon the great European colonial nations—Britain and France—as obstacles to the realization of their dreams for domination in Europe and Asia. But a German-Japanese coalition, which might well have led to war with the European sea powers and would inevitably have estranged the United States, held little attraction for the Japanese imperial court and was generally opposed by Japanese naval authorities, by most of the bureaucracy, and by important commercial-industrial interests. For many months Japanese official circles had engaged in violent controversy over this issue, until in August, 1939, Hitler's unceremonious conclusion of his pact with Stalin brought the conflict in Tokyo to an abrupt end. During the winter and spring of 1939-1940 the Japanese Government had pursued a cautious and inconclusive policy, awaiting like many other Governments the outcome of the war in Europe.

Hitler's resounding victories of the spring and summer of 1940 stirred the Japanese expansionists as nothing before. Their campaigns in the vastness of China had not forced the Nationalist regime of Chiang Kai-shek into submission and there was little prospect of subduing China so long as foreign powers—notably Soviet Russia, Britain and the United States—continued to give the Chungking Government material support. As against the dreary outlook in China, alluring vistas opened before the Japanese in southern Asia and the Pacific. Defeated France was the possessor of the rich states of Indo-China, while the vanquished Netherlands held the East Indies, from which Japan could hope to secure oil and other much-needed strategic materials. To many Japanese it seemed almost criminal to let slip so golden an opportunity for assuring the present and future needs of the national economy. Britain was hardly in a position to obstruct Tokyo's plans for a Greater East Asia Co-Prosperity Sphere, and there was at least doubt whether the United States would offer determined opposition. On the other hand Germany, as the victor over France and the Netherlands, would clearly have something to say with respect to French and Dutch colonial possessions. All the more reason for the Japanese activists to seek an arrangement with the master of Europe.

Even the moderate Yonai-Arita Cabinet, which had governed Japan from January until July, 1940, had been forced by military and other pressures to take steps toward reopening negotiations for a military alliance with Germany. But apparently the Army had no faith in an Administration which had systematically opposed the German connection. On July 16 the High Command engineered the downfall of the Cabinet and arranged for a new Government under Prince Fumimaro Konoye, with General Hideki Tojo as Minister of War and Yosuke Matsuoka as Minister for Foreign Affairs. Prince Konoye, related to the imperial family, was a well-known and popular politician, apparently well intentioned, but naïve and notoriously weak. At the time of his appointment he was much enamored of totalitarianism and much preoccupied with the transformation of Japan into a single-party state. Such ideas were certainly not antipathetic to the Army, which banked heavily on Konoye's prestige and popularity.

Most members of the Konoye Cabinet had been associated with the armed forces or the administration in Manchuria, and therefore reflected the views and aspirations of the so-called Kwantung clique. General Tojo was well known as a dynamic Army leader and one of the deepest-dyed expansionists. Foreign Minister Matsuoka, on the other hand, was just about to come into his own. He had spent his youth and had obtained most of his education in the United States, and liked to pose as an exponent of friendly relations between Tokyo and Washington. The development of his policy warrants grave doubt on this score, though in truth it is not easy to follow the gyrations of this extraordinary person. Matsuoka proved himself a man of nimble mind and unbridled energy, but unaccountable, unreliable, and erratic. To quote one of his subordinates, Konoye was like a shy squirrel sheltered in the deep forests, while Matsuoka was a stormy petrel, delighting to spread its wings over the foaming sea.[1] As the executive agent of the Japanese High Command the new Foreign Minister was to have a rare opportunity to display his "brilliance." Being extremely loquacious, he could not long keep his counsel. To an American correspondent he proclaimed that democracy was finished, that totalitarianism was bound to win, and that there was no room in the world for two systems. He left no doubt whatever that the new Japanese Cabinet was going "hell bent for the Axis and for the New Order in Asia," and that it would ride roughshod over British and American interests.[2]

The Konoye Cabinet lost no time in drafting a program for action, a program which was enshrined, on July 26 and 27, 1940, in two key documents. The first of these was entitled *Outline of Basic National Policy,* and the second *Gist of Main Points in regard to Dealing with the Situation to Meet the*

---

[1] Toshikazu Kase: *Journey to the "Missouri"* (New Haven, 1950), 40-43.
[2] *Grew Diary (MS.),* July 21, 1940, reporting Matsuoka's remarks to Wilfred Freischer; also Joseph C. Grew: *Ten Years in Japan* (New York, 1944), 324; Sir Robert Craigie: *Behind the Japanese Mask* (London, 1946), Chapter XVIII.

Change in World Conditions. Main points of these plans provided for the establishment of "an unshakable national structure such as conforms to the new world situation," on which Japan could "march forward toward the realization of the national policy by mobilizing the total strength of the nation." As usual, settlement of the China Incident was given first priority among the objectives of foreign policy. The Cabinet decided that this end, so important to the establishment of the New Order in Asia, could be accomplished only by cutting Nationalist China's supply lines from the outside world. This in turn involved the "settlement" of southern problems: "to strengthen policies towards French Indo-China, Hongkong and the Settlements, to check assistance to the Chiang regime and root out the feeling of enmity toward Japan." "The diplomatic policy" toward the Netherlands East Indies was also to be reinforced, so that Japan might obtain important raw materials.

Since, obviously, this program was bound to meet with opposition from other powers, the Konoye Cabinet was obliged to provide for that eventuality. It therefore decided "to foster a strong political tie with Germany and Italy, and to take active steps in the adjustment of diplomacy towards the Soviet Union while maintaining a firm front towards the United States." Apparently there was considerable discussion of this last item, but Matsuoka succeeded in persuading Konoye and others of his colleagues that the threat of an American embargo on supplies essential to Japan obliged the Tokyo Government to seek alternative sources of such supplies in the southern regions and that, in order to secure a free hand in the south, it was necessary not only to ally with Germany and Italy and to reach agreement with Soviet Russia, but to take a "resolute position" with respect to the United States. These important decisions having been reached, the Government on August 1, 1940, issued a public announcement foreshadowing the introduction of a totalitarian system and proclaiming, in more or less veiled terms, its international program:

Japan's foreign policy, which aims ultimately at the construction of a new order in Greater East Asia, will be directed, first of all, toward the complete settlement of the China affair, and to the advancement of the national fortune by taking a farsighted view of the drastic changes in the international situation and by formulating both constructive and flexible measures to meet these changes.[3]

3. JAPAN ON THE MARCH

The policies elaborated by the Konoye Government on July 26-27, 1940, were not to be taken up seriatim, but to be pursued concurrently. It was

[3] Text in *Documents on American Foreign Relations*, III (1940), 253 ff. The texts of the key documents are to be found in the *Tokyo War Crimes Documents*, Exhibits 541 and 1310. They were discussed in detail by General Tojo in his defense memorandum (Exhibit 3655, pp. 36, 181 ff.). See also Feis: *The Road to Pearl Harbor* (Princeton, 1950), Chapter XI.

therefore inevitable that their impact should be felt throughout the Far East and that the situation in that area should rapidly become more tense. In China itself Japanese commanders reverted to their earlier high-handed methods in dealing with foreign interests. At the end of July they arrested a number of British subjects on what appeared to be a very flimsy pretext, thereby creating in London the feeling that matters were fast reaching the breaking point.[4] Even though British fears proved exaggerated, the London Government did, in mid-August, finally decide to yield to Japanese pressure and withdraw its forces from the international settlements at Shanghai. The local authorities thereupon proposed to assign one of the British sectors to the United States and the other to Japan, a solution which the Japanese promptly vetoed. There ensued a long dispute between Washington and Tokyo, punctuated by much bitterness and recrimination. The scope of the present study makes it impossible to consider such specific issues in detail, though they are worth mentioning as reflections of the aggressive and uncompromising attitude adopted by the Japanese authorities toward foreign rights and interests. Mr. Matsuoka's repeated expressions of desire for a settlement of differences carried little conviction and Ambassador Grew was probably correct when he pointed out, in mid-September, that the Japanese were determined to take advantage of the situation in Europe and exploit the restrictions which that situation imposed on American action.[5]

In London it was feared that, beyond China, the Japanese would act first against the Netherlands East Indies. The British, Dutch and Australians were alike concerned lest the American embargo on the export of aviation gasoline and lubricants to Japan (July 26, 1940) result "in bringing matters to a head in the Far East" by forcing the Japanese to turn on the Indies so as to assure themselves of an adequate supply of oil.[6] Since the Netherlands Government was dependent on British support and since the Churchill Government was intent on avoiding war with Japan, concerted and repeated efforts were made by London to induce the United States to take a strong, positive line by warning Tokyo or even opposing militarily eventual Japanese moves against the Indies. But Washington was disgusted by the yielding attitude of the British toward Japan and distinctly irritated by London's

[4] Statement of Lord Halifax in the House of Lords, July 30, 1940; telegram from Kennedy (London), July 31, 1940.

[5] For details see *Foreign Relations of the United States: Japan*, I, 862 ff., 877 ff., which we have supplemented with the following: tels. to Grew, August 23, September 10; tels. from Grew, September 4, 12; memo of conversation between Mr. Ballantine and Mr. Morishima, of the Japanese Embassy, August 30; memo of conversation between Under Secretary Welles and Ambassador Horinouchi, September 13, 1940.

[6] Memo from Mr. Dunn to Mr. Welles, July 29, 1940, reporting the anxiety of the British Embassy; memo of conversation between Mr. Ballantine and the Netherlands Minister, July 31, 1940; tel. from Kennedy, reporting a memo from the Netherlands Government in London. See also Churchill's letter to the Prime Ministers of Australia and New Zealand, August 11, 1940 (in Winston S. Churchill: *Their Finest Hour*, Boston, 1949, 435 ff.).

decision to close the Burma Road and withdraw from Shanghai. Mr. Hornbeck, the State Department's chief adviser on Far Eastern affairs, was convinced that the Japanese would not make a sudden attack on the Indies or Singapore unless driven to desperation, and perhaps not even then. If they advanced at all, he held, they would do so in a series of steps designed to safeguard their flank. Evidently Secretary Hull and the President accepted this estimate, for the Administration refused to go beyond the public declarations of April, 1940, in favor of the *status quo* in the Indies. In reply to Dutch pleas for postponement of any further oil embargo, Under Secretary Welles remarked that even Dutch interests would not be served by "an [American] attitude of complete supine acquiescence in the continuing and ever-enlarging policy of Japanese aggression in the Pacific region." [7]

These remarks were hardly called for, since the Netherlands authorities were determined to resist Japanese pressure to the best of their ability. At the end of July, 1940, the Netherlands Minister in Tokyo, General Pabst, was informed by the Japanese Foreign Office of Japan's intention to increase substantially its demands for oil from the Indies and to send an imposing delegation to Batavia to negotiate a general settlement. The Dutch agreed, but managed to delay the arrival of the mission for some weeks. Not until the end of August was the appointment of Mr. Kobayashi, the Japanese Minister of Commerce and Industry, as head of the mission announced, and not until September 12, 1940, did he arrive in the Indies with his large and impressive staff. [8]

From the Japanese records now available it is reasonably clear that Tokyo naval authorities were much opposed to the use of force against the Netherlands Indies at this time, feeling as they did that Japan was not yet prepared to face a conflict at sea with the United States and Britain. [9] Under the circumstances the Kobayashi Mission was not authorized to press its demands to the limit. The Netherlands authorities persisted in evading all proposals or suggestions for political agreements and even for general economic arrangements. They took the stand that Japanese demands for oil should be discussed with the oil companies, but that Japanese desires for a share of control in those companies could not be met. After his first conversations in Batavia, Minister Kobayashi reported to Matsuoka in great discouragement:

[7] Tel. from Kennedy, August 6, 1940; memo from the Australian Minister in Washington, with comments by Mr. Hornbeck, August 14, 1940; memo of conversation between Mr. Welles and the Netherlands Chargé d'Affaires, September 24, 1940. We have used also a memo of conversation between Secretary of the Treasury Morgenthau and Sir Andrew Agnew, Chairman of the British Petroleum Board, September 3, 1940 (in *Morgenthau Diaries, MS.*, Vol. 302, p. 152), and the *Stimson Diary (MS.)*, September 11, 1940, reporting a conversation with Mr. Hornbeck.

[8] Hubertus van Mook: *The Netherlands Indies and Japan* (New York: 1944), 44-46; *Grew Diary (MS.)*, August 3 and 24, 1940.

[9] "Kido Diary," August 10, 1940 (*Tokyo War Crimes Documents*, No. 1632HH).

The [Dutch] Governor General does not realize that the present situation is so serious that if he remains so old-fashioned as to be concerned with diplomatic formulas only, the existence of the Dutch East Indies will be in danger, and he can not keep pace with the changing situation. He openly tried to do his utmost to evade political problems. He evinced not the slightest sign of fervor to try to sound out the true intention of the Japanese Government towards the Dutch East Indies. In as much as he does not understand our real idea of friendly relations between the two countries, it is no use for us to continue the negotiations with such a Governor General. It has made me feel that I have come all this way in vain.[10]

The details of the ensuing long and tedious discussions need not detain us here. Kobayashi remained at his post until the outlines of an oil agreement were reached on October 16, 1940, but the details of this agreement were left for further negotiation. The Japanese had begun by asking for 3,000,000 tons of oil annually, a fivefold increase over what they had theretofore been getting. The Dutch had declared such quantities beyond their productive capacity and eventually the Japanese had been obliged to compromise on much more modest figures. They were promised a spot sale of 33,000 tons of aviation gasoline, as against the 400,000 tons annually that they had proposed. Furthermore, their demand for 1,100,000 tons of aviation crude was scaled down to 120,000 tons, and their demand for 1,000,000 tons of other crude oil was reduced to 540,000 tons. Nothing came of their efforts to secure a measure of control over the oil industry, while their suggestions for "friendly coöperation" in the larger sphere were politely ignored.[11]

The State Department estimate that the Japanese would not for the present attack the Netherlands Indies thus proved sound. The Tokyo Government did succeed in securing some additional oil from the Indies, but it had not forced the issue of "friendly coöperation," which the Netherlands authorities knew only too well was designed as the first step toward the integration of their Pacific possessions in the Greater East Asia Co-Prosperity Sphere. Evidently the Japanese did not as yet feel the need for extreme measures and furthermore considered themselves too unprepared to risk conflict with the great sea powers. Before taking further action against the Indies they undoubtedly thought it necessary to secure their flank. Tokyo's main effort, therefore, was directed toward French Indo-China, where in fact the Japanese secured their first resounding and fateful success.

[10] Tel. from Kobayashi to Matsuoka, September 13, 1940 (*Toyko War Crimes Documents*, No. 2748A[6]).

[11] Van Mook: *The Netherlands Indies and Japan*, 49 ff., reviews the negotiations in some detail. We have used also a long review despatch of November 27, 1940, by Mr. Achilles, American Chargé d'Affaires assigned to the Netherlands Government-in-Exile; a memo by the President of the Standard Vacuum Oil Company, September 27, 1940 (*Morgenthau Diaries, MS.*, Vol. 318, pp. 155 ff.); and the news reports in the *New York Herald Tribune*, August 16 and 29, 1940, and *The New York Times*, August 30, September 13 and 25, 1940.

4. THE INDO-CHINA CRISIS

Northern Indo-China was of the utmost strategic importance to Japan, partly because one of the most practicable supply routes into southern China originated in Tonkin and partly because this region was the natural gateway to southeast Asia, much coveted for its rice, rubber and tin. Hardly had the French Government asked Hitler for an armistice (June, 1940) when the Japanese demanded and secured from the Governor General of Indo-China the closing of the so-called Yunnan Railroad to shipments of war materials into China, as well as permission to station in the colony a Japanese control commission. The French obviously had no choice, in such a time of crisis, but to yield to Japanese pressure, despite the fact that they were well aware that compliance would probably lead to further demands. General Georges Catroux, at that time Governor General, hoped to soften the anticipated shock by carrying on informal discussions with General Nishihara, chief of the Japanese control commission. What Catroux suggested was that the French Administration might grant the Japanese further facilities for carrying on their campaign against southern China, provided Tokyo would guarantee the territorial integrity and French sovereignty over Indo-China. However, this unauthorized proposal filled the Vichy Government with concern and Catroux was at once recalled. Actually he did not surrender his authority until July 20, 1940, at which time Admiral Jean Decoux assumed control.[12]

Meanwhile the Konoye Cabinet had come into power as the agent of Japanese militarist and expansionist elements. Among other things, Tokyo's decisions of July 26 and 27, 1940, provided for further action with regard to Indo-China, both to cut off the supply route to China and to strengthen the economic position of Japan by preparing the way for the incorporation of Indo-China in the East Asia Co-Prosperity Sphere.[13] In accord with these decisions Foreign Minister Matsuoka on August 1, 1940, submitted to the French Ambassador, M. Arsène Henry, an *aide-mémoire* demanding the right of transit for Japanese forces through Indo-China, the construction of airfields in the colony, and agreement in principle to an economic arrangement which would bind Indo-China securely to the Japanese sphere. These demands were accompanied by verbal threats and permitted of little delay on the part of the Vichy Government. M. Baudouin, the French Foreign Minister, had long been connected with the *Banque de l'Indo-chine* and was therefore able to speak with some authority on the problem. While Ad-

[12] Amiral Decoux: *A la barre de l'Indochine* (Paris, 1949), 68 ff.; *The Private Diaries of Paul Baudouin* (London, 1948)), 171, 184; André Gaudel: *L'Indochine française en face du Japon* (Paris, 1947), 75 ff.; and the detailed treatment in Albert Kammerer: *La vérité sur l'armistice* (2 ed., Paris, 1945), 351-62.

[13] Memo of the Tokyo Foreign Office reviewing the development of the issue (*Tokyo War Crimes Documents,* No. 985A) and the "Tojo Memorandum" (*ibid.*).

miral Decoux was instructed to resist any attempt by the Japanese to land forces, the Vichy Government decided to pick up the threads of the Catroux-Nishihara conversations, that is, to accept discussion of Japanese requirements, but only in return for Tokyo's recognition of French sovereignty and of Indo-China's territorial integrity. It was Vichy's hope that by this approach some time could be bought during which American support might be enlisted.[14]

On August 5, 1940, concurrent with the despatch of the French reply to Tokyo, the Vichy Foreign Office instructed Count Saint-Quentin, the Ambassador in Washington, to inform the United States Government confidentially of the Japanese demands and indicate that "the resistance of the French Government to the Japanese demands would necessarily depend to a large extent on the nature and effectiveness of the support which the American Government would be disposed to give it." Apparently this important matter was referred at once to the President. Of the discussions in the White House nothing is known, but on August 6, 1940, Mr. Dunn, Political Adviser of the State Department, gave the French Ambassador an oral reply. To quote Mr. Dunn's notes:

I told the French Ambassador that we have been doing and are doing everything possible within the framework of our established policies to keep the situation in the Far East stabilized; that we have been progressively taking various steps, the effect of which has been to exert economic pressure on Japan; that our Fleet is now based on Hawaii, and that the course which we have been following, as indicated above, gives a clear indication of our intentions and activities for the future. I also raised with the French Ambassador the question whether it would be practicable for the French to delay discussions with the Japanese with respect to Indo-China for a period.

Saint-Quentin at once remarked that this reply would probably not enable the French Government to resist the Japanese demands and that it would in all likelihood be impracticable to delay the negotiations:

He went on to say that in his opinion the phrase "within the framework of our established policies," when associated with the apparent reluctance of the American Government to consider the use of military force in the Far East at this particular time, meant that the United States would not use military or naval force in support of any position which might be taken to resist the Japanese attempted aggression on Indo-China.

Mr. Dunn made no effort to gainsay this interpretation of his words, whereupon the Ambassador reported to his Government that there was no prospect of active American aid against Japan.[15]

[14] Private Diaries of Paul Baudouin, 187-88; François Charles-Roux: Cinq mois tragiques aux Affaires étrangères (Paris, 1949), 250-51; Decoux: A la barre de l'Indo-chine, 94.
[15] Tel. from Murphy (Vichy), August 4, 1940, reporting the coming French démarche; aide-mémoire from the French Embassy in Washington, August 6; memo from Mr. Dunn

Although the State Department scrupulously avoided holding out hope of armed assistance to the French, Ambassador Grew was at once instructed to call on Matsuoka and point out to him that the United States Government was "seriously perturbed" by the reports of Japanese demands on Indo-China. The Ambassador was to recall Secretary Hull's statements of April 17 and May 11, 1940, regarding the maintenance of the *status quo* in the Netherlands Indies, and to indicate that in the view of the Washington Government the same doctrine applied also to Indo-China. Matsuoka declined to discuss the matter, but suggested that the newspaper reports were greatly exaggerated. He then remarked confidentially that the French Government had already accepted the Japanese demands in principle. While this observation was perhaps technically correct, it certainly conveyed an erroneous impression and may well have prejudiced the State Department against the French policy.[16]

Despite Ambassador Saint-Quentin's remarks to Mr. Dunn, the Vichy Government decided to do everything possible to stall off the Japanese, and so informed Washington. Furthermore, an effort was made by the French to enlist German support against Tokyo.[17] The Germans expressed sympathy but refused to intervene, so the Vichy Government had to manage as best it could. On August 9 and 10 the French Ambassador in Tokyo had several conversations with officials of the Japanese Foreign Office. The latter were somewhat more conciliatory but nonetheless insistent. They evaded French demands for political guarantees and refused to be pinned down by concrete specifications as to the numbers of troops and types of airfields they envisaged.[18]

At Vichy the reports of Tokyo's obduracy provoked a minor crisis. General Weygand, the Minister of Defense, initially favored out-and-out resistance, relying on figures produced by the Chief of Staff of the Colonial Forces to prove that such resistance was feasible. M. Lémery, the Minister for Colonies, and other members of the Cabinet took the same stand. But M. Baudouin challenged the figures of the military, contended that resistance was simply impossible, pointed out that in any case resistance would

---

to Under Secretary Welles, August 6, 1940; *Private Diaries of Paul Baudouin*, 188, 193; Charles-Roux: *Cinq mois tragiques*, 251-52, giving the text of Saint-Quentin's report, which corresponds completely with the American record.

[16] *Foreign Relations of the United States: Japan*, II, 289-90; tel. to Grew, August 6, and tel. from Grew, August 7, 1940; memos of conversation between Mr. Hamilton and M. Truelle of the French Embassy, August 7, 8, 1940. London and Chungking were informed of the American *démarche* in Tokyo, which was followed a few days later by a similar British step (tel. to Johnson, August 14; tel. to Kennedy, August 15, 1940).

[17] Conversation of General Huntziger with General Stülpnagel, August 8, 1940, in *La délégation française auprès de la Commission allemande d'Armistice* (Paris, 1947), pp. 106 ff.

[18] Japanese Foreign Office memo (*Toyko War Crimes Documents*, No. 985A); *Private Diaries of Paul Baudouin*, 193, 198-99; Charles-Roux: *Cinq mois tragiques*, 252-53.

lead to the total loss of Indo-China, and pleaded that some sort of agreement was imperative.[19] The Foreign Minister had his way; on August 15 the Vichy Government despatched new proposals to Tokyo. These proved highly irritating to Matsuoka, who threatened to drop the negotiations "and execute military actions." As the crisis approached its climax, both Tokyo and Vichy turned to the Germans for support, but neither was given encouragement.[20]

On the evening of August 16, 1940, the French Cabinet concluded that further resistance was inadvisable, and on the following day M. Baudouin explained to the American Chargé d'Affaires that "in the absence of any material support from Great Britain and the United States as distinguished from the enunciation of principles" France felt obliged to yield. He warmly disclaimed German pressure on Vichy and declared the entire episode "a terrible blow." The Chargé d'Affaires, according to the French version, expressed his deep understanding of France's plight and stated that "it would be vain to expect from the American Government anything other than a verbal condemnation of Japanese initiatives." M. Baudouin thereupon suggested that Washington warn Japan that the military occupation of Indo-China must be purely temporary. This suggestion was then transmitted to Washington and on August 21 elicited from Under Secretary Welles a statement to the French Ambassador, which the latter reported as follows:

We understand the situation of the French Government and, since we are not in a position to come to its assistance, we do not feel that we have the right to reproach it for according military facilities to Japan. But, if we were to recommend to Tokyo that its occupation be temporary, we would be accepting the principle of it. But this would be a violation of the *status quo,* the maintenance of which we shall continue to insist upon.[21]

For the purposes of the present study it is unnecessary to review all phases of the final negotiations. The French stood by their demand for political assurances and did what they could to delay and restrict their concessions to the Japanese. Matsuoka, in turn, maintained his threatening attitude and let it be understood that it was the High Command of the Canton Army which insisted on Indo-Chinese facilities as necessary to promote its cam-

[19] *Private Diaries of Paul Baudouin,* 198-99; Général Maxime Weygand: *Mémoires: Rappelé au service* (Paris, 1950), 336-39; Charles-Roux: *Cinq mois tragiques,* 253; Maurice Martin du Gard: *La carte impériale* (Paris, 1949), 427.

[20] Tel. from Ambassador Ott to the German Foreign Office, August 15, 1940 (*Tokyo War Crimes Documents,* No. 4029E); *La Délégation française auprès de la Commission allemande d'Armistice,* 131.

[21] Text in Charles-Roux: *Cinq mois tragiques,* 255; summary in *The Private Diaries of Paul Baudouin,* 203-4, 211. These statements were referred to in detail in a French memorandum reviewing the Indo-China crisis, transmitted in a tel. from Matthews, September 19, 1940. The tel. from Murphy, August 17, 1940, is in the State Department files, but we have been unable to locate any record of Mr. Welles's conversation with Ambassador Saint-Quentin on August 21, 1940.

paign against China. Finally, on August 29, 1940, Matsuoka and Ambassador Arsène Henry signed a political accord, under the terms of which the Tokyo Government recognized the "permanent French interest in Indo-China," while the Vichy Government in its turn recognized the "preponderance of Japanese interest in that area." This agreement, however, was to go into effect only after the conclusion of a military arrangement, to be negotiated at Hanoi, the capital of Tonkin.[22]

Almost before the ink was dry on the political agreement, General Nishihara on August 30, 1940, presented Governor General Decoux with the text of a military accord, requesting or rather demanding French signature by September 2 (midnight) at the latest. The Japanese emissary and his aides were "insolent, haughty and angry," and insisted that negotiations be opened forthwith. Decoux replied that he needed time to decode the text of the Tokyo agreement and that he had no instructions from Vichy, whereupon Nishihara told him "to stop sleeping, to get busy, or take the consequences."[23] The Governor General, however, was not to be intimidated. He had in fact been urging Vichy to refuse military concessions on the plea that they would make Indo-China a Japanese satellite, and had been arguing that Japan would not dare use force, in view of the attitude of other powers. Supported by the local military commander, General Martin, Decoux was quite prepared to offer armed resistance, though he had only a few planes and some antiquated tanks.[24]

Acting on his own, the Governor General on September 2 rejected the Japanese ultimatum, whereupon Nishihara announced that the military occupation of Indo-China would begin on September 5. Meanwhile, however, Vichy had appealed to Tokyo, which disavowed Nishihara. The situation was somewhat eased and by September 5 an agreement in principle was arrived at, the details to be discussed by the respective military staffs. The French negotiators exerted themselves to delay these discussions as long as possible, in the hope that support from the western powers might yet serve to deter the Japanese. In the interval the situation again grew tense. The Japanese Canton Army was on the frontier, eager to advance on the colony; the Chinese Government, for its part, was threatening to send in forces if the French Government permitted the Japanese to use Indo-China as a base of attack on Yunnan; finally, the Siamese Government was pressing long-standing claims to Indo-Chinese territory west of the Mekong River.[25]

[22] Japanese Foreign Office memo (*Tokyo War Crimes Documents*, No. 985A); *Private Diaries of Paul Baudouin*, 211-23; tel. from Matthews (Vichy), August 17, 1940.

[23] Report of Mr. Nicholson to Secretary Morgenthau, quoting Decoux's account, September 21, 1940 (*Morgenthau Diaries, MS.*, Vol. 308, pp. 239 ff.); Decoux: *A la barre de l'Indochine*, 103.

[24] Decoux: *A la barre de l'Indochine*, 98-101; du Gard: *La carte impériale*, 428; testimony of General Martin (*Procès de M. Pétain*, Paris, 1945, p. 277).

[25] Decoux: *A la barre de l'Indochine*, 107 ff., 132 ff.; Charles-Roux: *Cinq mois tragiques*, 260 ff.; tels. from American representatives at Hanoi, August 31; Saigon, September 4; Chungking, September 3; and Tokyo, September 6, 1940.

Decoux's great hope was to secure planes and other munitions from the United States, or preferably from nearby Manila. On various occasions he appealed to American representatives for such aid. Similarly the Vichy Government, though it had little faith in the idea that Indo-China could be defended, renewed its efforts to induce American diplomatic action in Tokyo. Within familiar but narrow limits Washington was prepared to give support. On September 3, evidently before the terms of the Tokyo agreement of August 29 were known in Washington, Ambassador Grew was instructed to call Matsuoka's attention to current reports and point out the unfortunate effect which, if true, they would have on American public opinion. On the following day Secretary Hull publicly stated the American position in substantially the same terms. It was unlikely, however, that the Japanese would attach much weight to mild remonstrances. Matsuoka admitted that Japanese troops would pass through Indo-China, but added that there would be no permanent occupation.[26]

It was at this juncture (September 5) that M. Baudouin informed the American Chargé d'Affaires at Vichy of the terms of the Tokyo accord and of the pressure that was being exerted by the Japanese at Hanoi. He furthermore took occasion to repeat that Indo-China could not resist without American and British material support. This news led to further American (and British) remonstrances in Tokyo on behalf of the *status quo* in Indo-China, but more importantly to the development of ill-feeling between Washington and Vichy. Mr. H. Freeman Matthews, the American Chargé d'Affaires, was instructed to complain to M. Baudouin of Vichy's failure to keep the United States Government fully informed and to express the shock felt in Washington by France's submission. Two days later (September 11) Secretary Hull called the French Ambassador's attention to "the surprise and disappointment" felt in Washington. France's recognition of Japan's preponderance of interest in Indo-China was a severe blow to American policy.[27]

Irritation with Vichy's policy did not, however, blind the State Department to the danger of Tokyo's activities. Representations and protests were repeatedly lodged with the Japanese Government, but since none of these contained even a suggestion of American action as distinguished from mere words, Japanese authorities felt safe in disregarding them and even in retorting with thinly veiled insults. At the time it was believed, probably with justice, that the Japanese Canton Army was the driving force behind Matsuoka's demands, and that Tokyo was helpless in the face of military pres-

---

[26] *Foreign Relations of the United States: Japan*, II, 291 ff.; *The Memoirs of Cordell Hull* (New York, 1948), I, 903. See also the Japanese statements in *Documents on American Foreign Relations*, II, 275 ff.

[27] Tel. to Matthews, September 9, 1940; State Department memo of December 19, 1940, reviewing the Indo-China negotiations; Hull: *Memoirs*, I, 904; *Private Diaries of Paul Baudouin*, 231, 234; Charles-Roux: *Cinq mois tragiques*, 259.

sure. Whatever the truth, it was obvious that the Japanese would not long tolerate the dilatory tactics of Governor General Decoux. On September 19 Matsuoka informed the French Ambassador that on September 22 Indo-China would be militarily occupied, with or without an agreement. Vichy ordered Decoux to resist, but in the interval Nishihara disclaimed the ultimatum and reduced his demands. There was a final flurry of argument until, on September 22, 1940, the accord was finally signed. Under its terms the French made available to the Japanese three airfields in Tonkin (as against six originally called for); granted permission for the stationing of 6000 Japanese troops (as against 25,000 or 32,000 at first demanded); agreed to permit the eventual passage of Japanese forces (never to number more than 25,000 men) through Tonkin to Yunnan; and consented, subject to further negotiation, to allow a division of the Canton Army to be evacuated through Tonkin. Actually the Canton Army did not await further arrangements. On September 23 a Japanese force crossed the frontier at Langson. The French resisted, but took such a beating that the outlook became extremely dark. Nevertheless, thanks to Decoux's brave stand, the Japanese advance was halted on September 25, after which the situation quieted down.[28]

While American exasperation with Vichy reached new heights with the issuance, on September 23, of a French statement suggesting that Washington had approved the Tokyo agreement of August 30, the American Government at this late date began to consider seriously the possibility of providing material aid to Indo-China. A purchasing commission from the colony had been in the United States for some time, but had been unable to accomplish anything. On September 23 the so-called Liaison Committee, consisting of Under Secretary Welles, General Marshall and Admiral Stark, discussed the problem of sending arms, if only a few rifles. The Committee agreed that the planes for which the French had been clamoring were out of the question. However, there would be no objection if the French made use of the American planes immobilized aboard the carrier *Béarn* at Martinique. Apparently the Vichy Government at once inquired of the Germans whether it might employ these planes for the defense of Indo-China. But the Germans, at that very time engaged in negotiating the Tripartite Pact with Japan, made no reply. In the end, Indo-China received no substantial American support. After its initial spurt, Washington presently decided against selling arms or munitions, partly because it had few to spare, partly because it distrusted the use that might be made of them.[29]

[28] Decoux: *A la barre de l'Indochine*, 109 ff.; *Private Diaries of Paul Baudouin*, 243-46; Hull: *Memoirs*, 905-7, for details of American protests to Tokyo.

[29] The State Department memorandum of December, 1940, reviewing the Indo-China issue, deals with the negotiations for arms at some length. On October 7, 1940, M. Chauvel, chief of the Far East Division of the Vichy Foreign Office, told Mr. Matthews that the Germans had no objection to the supply of arms and munitions by the United States, but refused to allow use of the planes at Martinique. Actually the Germans appear to have given no definite reply to the French inquiry (*La Délégation française auprès de la Commission Allemande d'Armistice*, II, Paris, 1950, pp. 113, 205, 241).

5. Defense and Retaliation

To gain their objectives in Indo-China the Japanese had chosen the moment when the fate of Britain hung in the balance. If for almost two months they put up with the tergiversations and delays of the French, it was certainly not from fear of British reprisals or of military action on the part of the United States. Tokyo paid little if any attention to the oft-repeated admonitions of Washington and must have noted with pleasure that the American protests amounted to little more than pleas for the maintenance of the *status quo* and the employment of peaceful means to settle international issues. Under the circumstances the Japanese Army leaders must have felt quite safe in recommending and pressing for ruthless action. But the Government preferred to attain its ends by negotiation rather than force, for it certainly recognized that Washington still had a deadly arrow in its shaft, and that the relatively innocuous economic sanctions decreed against Japan on July 26, 1940, might well be followed by more drastic measures of the same type. That danger was far from imaginary.

The apparent weakness of American policy toward Japan during August and September, 1940, was merely a reflection of the dilemma that plagued the President and his advisers. They had already concluded that the dangers which threatened from Europe were greater and more immediate than those looming in Asia, and they were therefore determined not to challenge Japan militarily while Hitler seemed on the threshold of decisive victory. Having denied themselves the application of force, they were bound, nevertheless, to consider what means of pressure, other than mere words, they might employ to deter or obstruct the Japanese advance.

Mr. Churchill appears to have been more confident of Britain's future than most others. He had no faith in appeasement of Japan and, because he realized that Britain itself could do little in the Far East, strongly favored stiff opposition on the part of the United States.[30] Hardly had the Destroyer Deal been closed when, on September 5, 1940, Lord Lothian, in the company of his Australian colleague, broached the Far Eastern problem in conversation with Secretary Hull. The Ambassador indicated particularly the desirability of a strong American stand with respect to the East Indies, but evoked little response from the Secretary, who carefully evaded a definite statement.[31] Nonetheless, the Ambassador soon returned to the charge, hinting that the United States might take some action to prevent the Japanese occupation of Indo-China. On this occasion Secretary Hull pointed out the difficulty of giving support to countries so remote. He recalled that the

[30] See his messages to Halifax, July 20, 26, 1940, and his message to the Prime Ministers of Australia and New Zealand, August 11, 1940 (Churchill: *Their Finest Hour,* 435-36, 647, 650).

[31] Memo of conversation between Mr. Hull, Lord Lothian, Mr. Casey and Sir Andrew Agnew, September 5, 1940.

United States "had gone almost to the limit of resisting step by step Japanese aggression without the very serious danger of a military clash." The Secretary's record then continues:

I said that this Government expects to continue its protests and its opposition to Japanese aggression, and to this end it plans to render further financial aid to China and to impose more and more reprisals and retaliation of a commercial and economic nature on Japan. I expressed the view that it would not be wise, even from the British standpoint, for two wars to be raging in the East and the West at the same time; that if this country should enter any war, it would immediately result in greatly cutting off military supplies to Great Britain.

Lord Lothian suggested that Britain, Australia and the United States join in some arrangement regarding bases and general defense in the Pacific, but to this Mr. Hull replied that the Japanese undoubtedly knew that such arrangements could be made at short notice and that therefore no need existed for perfecting them at the moment.[32]

It is clear, from these conversations, that the Secretary refused to be drawn into any policy that might lead to military conflict with Japan. On the other hand, Mr. Hull indicated what further measures of retaliation his Government was considering. One was increased financial support for the Chinese Nationalist regime, the other extension of the embargo on exports to Japan.

The question of a further loan to China had been under debate for many weeks, but, for technical and other reasons, had not been brought to a conclusion. On September 5, 1940, a message reached Washington from General Chang Chung, the trusted adviser of Chiang Kai-shek, who reported the situation in Nationalist China as so desperate that further aid from the United States was imperative. In return for assistance Chungking offered the lease of certain bases.[33]

This message, evidently inspired by the Destroyer Deal, was clearly intended to jog Washington into action. At any rate it served that purpose, for the decision was now quickly reached to grant China a further loan through the Export-Import Bank, repayment to take the form of Chinese shipments of tungsten ore. The loan was publicly announced on September 25, 1940, on the very eve of the conclusion of the Tripartite Pact.[34]

Of even greater significance was the question of further economic sanctions against Japan. The first step had been taken on July 26, 1940, with the embargo on aviation gasoline and high-grade iron and steel scrap. But this measure represented a compromise between the two factions in the

[32] Memo of conversation between Mr. Hull, Lord Lothian and Mr. Casey, September 16, 1940; Hull: *Memoirs*, I, 906-7.

[33] Messages of September 5, 6, 1940 (*Morgenthau Diaries, MS.*, Vol. 303, pp. 73, 297).

[34] *Morgenthau Diaries, MS.*, Vol. 305, p. 237 (September 13); Vol. 307, p. 294 (September 23, 1940).

Roosevelt Cabinet which took widely different views about the advisability of bringing real pressure upon Japan. To the protagonists of severe sanctions it was clear that the regulations of July 26 were ineffectual. The Japanese were believed to have petroleum stocks to meet requirements for six or seven months, and they could produce the needed aviation gasoline by using tetraethyl, obtainable from Germany, Italy, Russia, or Mexico. Actually, during the month of August, 1940, licenses were issued for the export to Japan of $21,000,000 worth of American petroleum products, somewhat more than the total for the entire first six months of the year. In short, American oil was still flowing freely to Japanese storage tanks.[35]

As to iron and steel scrap the situation was similar. Only the highest grade was embargoed by the regulations of July 26, 1940, and the Japanese were importing most of the remaining seventy-five grades as fast as they could. In August, 1940, over 300,000 tons were licensed for export to Japan, an amount just about equal to the total for the first half of the year. What was to be done under the circumstances? If all scrap were put under license, it was difficult to see how it could be exported to Britain without the American Government's inviting charges of discrimination. In the State Department all conceivable schemes were being analyzed while Secretary Morgenthau, ever the champion of bold action, urged upon the President a total embargo on all scrap. If the Japanese, he argued, should protest against the sale of such materials to the British, the State Department could reply that such sale was in the national interest. But Secretary Hull still had his reservations. Like the Japanese, he was awaiting the outcome of the Battle of Britain before deciding his policy.

This whole darn thing is hanging in the balance [he telephoned to Morgenthau]. If the British go down, then the Japs will probably spread out over all the Pacific just like wild men. If the British hold on, why we'll be able to restrain them [the Japs] and put on additional impediments to them and a loan to China. And now for a very few days until we see just a little further on that British thing, my judgment is that, glad as I am to go along on this, it would be better to let it remain just on a day-to-day basis.[36]

News of the Japanese military demands on Indo-China, together with increasing pressure within the Cabinet, undoubtedly contributed, along with the growing chances of Britain's survival, to bring about a change of attitude. On September 10, 1940, Secretary Hull instructed Ambassador Grew

[35] Morgenthau's report of a conference with Secretary Knox, Secretary Ickes, and representatives of American oil companies, August 14, 1940 (*Morgenthau Diaries, MS.,* Vol. 294, p. 121; Vol. 295, p. 228); State Department memos by the Division of Controls, August 30 and September 10, 1940.

[36] *Morgenthau Diaries (MS.),* Vol. 303, p. 250 (September 6); Vol. 305, pp. 52, 126 (September 11 and 12, 1940); also memo by the State Department Division of Controls, August 30, 1940, and memo by the Division of Far Eastern Affairs, September 5, 1940.

to state to the Tokyo Foreign Office that if Japan continued to violate American rights, it might become necessary for the United States to take measures of defense: "If the United States must take positive measures for self-defense in its relations with Japan, such retaliatory measures will be amply warranted and will have been brought about by Japanese disregard, persistent and continued, of the rights of the United States."[37]

By this time Mr. Grew, who had long distinguished himself by his patient and understanding attitude, was obliged to admit that with the Konoye Cabinet things had taken a turn for the worse. He found his discussions with Matsuoka "completely frustrating," and had to acknowledge that the Japanese were determined to take advantage of the situation in Europe and make the most of the restrictions which that situation imposed on America's freedom of action. In a now famous telegram of September 12, 1940, he recorded his considered opinion that the Japanese were waiting breathlessly for Britain's defeat and that their rate of progress was being influenced more by Hitler's successes than by any other factor. Apparently the only way to check Japan and preserve the *status quo* in the Far East was to apply greater economic pressure. Grew rehearsed his former objections to sanctions and pointed out that such measures might always call forth retaliation, if not by the Tokyo Government, then "by some sudden stroke by the Navy or Army without prior authorization or knowledge of the Government." Nevertheless, he and his military and naval attachés felt that the point had been reached when stronger measures were necessary:

Japan is today one of the predatory powers; having submerged all ethical and moral sense, she has become unashamedly and frankly opportunist, at every turn seeking to profit through the weakness of others. American interests in the Pacific are definitely threatened by her policy of southward expansion, which is a thrust at the British Empire in the East. Admittedly America's security has depended in a measure upon the British Fleet, which has been in turn and could only have been supported by the British Empire. If the support of the British Empire in this her hour of travail is conceived to be in our interest, and most emphatically do I so conceive it, we must strive by every means to preserve the *status quo* in the Pacific, at least until the war in Europe has been won or lost. This cannot be done, in my opinion, nor can we further protect our interests properly and adequately merely by the expression of disapproval and carefully keeping a record thereof. Clearly, Japan has been deterred from the taking of greater liberties with American interests only because she respects our potential power; equally it is clear that she has trampled upon our rights to an extent in exact ratio to the strength of her conviction that the people of the United States would not permit that power to be used. It is not impossible that once that conviction is shaken, the uses of diplomacy may again become accepted.[38]

[37] Tel. to Grew, September 10, 1940.

[38] Tel. from Grew, September 12, 1940, printed in part in *Peace and War* (Washington, 1943), 569 ff., and in full in *Pearl Harbor Attack*, II, 635 ff. See also Grew's testimony in *Pearl Harbor Attack*, II, 584 ff., and the telegrams from Peiping which gave rise to the discussion (*ibid.*, IV, 1712 ff.).

This "Green Light" message, though concerned primarily with the violation of American rights in China, must have been read in the context of
Japanese activities in Indo-China and the Netherlands Indies. The whole
issue of sanctions was warmly debated in a Cabinet meeting on September
19, the very moment at which the Japanese were addressing their latest
ultimatum to Governor General Decoux. In the course of the discussion
Secretary Hull expatiated on the Japanese advance in Indo-China and declared that it had become necessary to extend the embargo on scrap iron
and steel, as well as to give further aid to China. Secretaries Morgenthau
and Stimson at once seized the opportunity to advocate an embargo on all
oil products, which the President also seemed to favor. But Mr. Hull reiterated his fears lest such a measure serve only to drive the Japanese into attacking the Indies. Though Mr. Stimson retorted that it would be harder
for the Japanese to get oil from the Indies than from the United States and
that their long supply line would be exposed to British naval threat, Mr.
Hull carried his point.[39]

The last ten days of September were thus a particularly critical and anxious period. Japanese-American discussions about the future of the Shanghai
settlements had become extremely acrimonious, so much so that on September 20 Under Secretary Welles had a long and plain-spoken interview with
the Japanese Ambassador. To quote his record:

I said it must be evident to him, as it was to me, that no matter how much men of
good will in both countries might try to prevent it, if this situation continued, no one
could prophesy with any assurance that the result might not be of a very serious
character.

Then, referring to Japan's highhanded course in Indo-China, Mr. Welles
reminded the Ambassador of American policy to assist the victims of aggression:

I said that I would be lacking in candor if I did not make clear to the Ambassador
that, consistent with its policy with regard to Great Britain, the United States would
likewise feel it necessary to furnish such means of assistance in the way of supplies,
munitions, etc. for these victims of aggression in the Pacific area as might be required.[40]

At that time it was really intended that support should be provided the
Indo-Chinese authorities.[41] Eventually it proved impossible or inexpedient to
do so, but the conclusion of the military convention between France and
Japan on September 22 certainly raised the temperature in Washington.
On September 24 the complete embargo on all types of iron and steel scrap

[39] *Stimson Diary* (*MS.*), September 19, 1940; *Morgenthau Diaries* (*MS.*), Vol. 307,
pp. 65 ff., 76, 141 (September 19, 20, 1940).
[40] *Foreign Relations of the United States: Japan*, II, 881 ff.; tel. to Grew, September
20, 1940.
[41] *Minutes of the Liaison Committee*, September 23, 1940; memo of conversation between Mr. Welles and the French Ambassador, September 24, 1940.

was decided upon; on September 25 the new loan to China was announced; and on the following day the new regulations on scrap were published.[42]

Noting in his diary the imposition of the embargo, Secretary Stimson wrote: "This is a direct hit at Japan, a point which I have hoped we would hit for a long time."[43] And so it was, for it cut off the main source of supply for one of Japan's key war materials. But the satisfaction of Mr. Stimson, as well as of Secretary Morgenthau, was tempered by the sense of "too little and too late." The thing should have been done months ago, before the Indo-China affair, remarked Morgenthau to one of his friends.[44] Furthermore, something should be done at once with regard to an even more important item: oil. That seemed to be the really crucial sanction, yet it continued to be neglected. The argument sounds plausible, but even in retrospect it is impossible to determine whether imposition of an oil embargo in September, 1940, would have been wise. At the time both the State and Navy Departments were convinced that Japan, if denied the oil of the United States, would seize the Indies in revenge. Whether, in fact, that would have happened cannot, of course, be demonstrated. The British, Dutch and Australians were all highly nervous on the subject and never tired of pleading against such drastic action as an embargo on all oil. On the other hand, it may be recalled that the Japanese Navy was opposed to occupation of the Indies because it felt unequal to a conflict with Britain and the United States. Yet oil was absolutely indispensable to the Japanese and they might well have felt impelled to take action against the Indies, if only as a move of desperation. When, in July, 1941, the embargo on oil was finally decided on, American-Japanese relations deteriorated at a phenomenal rate. Considering the state of American unpreparedness in September, 1940, it may well have been the part of wisdom not to resort to the ultimate sanction. For the time being the embargo on scrap served the double purpose of braking Japanese war production and threatening even more drastic action.

6. Negotiation of the Pact

The imposition of further economic sanctions, America's response to Japanese expansion southward, happened to coincide with a development of infinitely greater importance to the United States and the world at large, namely the conclusion of the Tripartite Pact between Germany, Italy and

[42] Memo by the Division of Far Eastern Affairs, September 23, 1940; letter of Secretary Hull to the President, September 24, 1940; *Morgenthau Diaries (MS.)*, Vol. 308, pp. 42 ff., 220 ff. (September 24, 1940); Herbert Feis: *The Road to Pearl Harbor* (Princeton, 1950), 96 ff. The regulations and orders are printed in *Foreign Relations of the United States: Japan*, II, 222 ff.

[43] *Stimson Diary (MS.)*, September 26, 1940.

[44] *Morgenthau Diaries (MS.)*, Vol. 308, p. 42.

Japan. The negotiation of this famous and fateful agreement had been carried on during September in the utmost secrecy and its impending signature became known to Ambassador Grew only as the last important decisions were being taken. Little is known even now of the discussions that led up to the pact. Since the negotiations took place in Tokyo, the captured German Foreign Office records throw little light on them. On the other hand, the Japanese records have for the most part disappeared, presumably destroyed in the great bombings of Tokyo in 1945. The historian, then, is thrown back on fragmentary evidence and is obliged to piece together such disjointed scraps as have survived the vicissitudes of war.[45]

During 1938 and 1939 Hitler and Ribbentrop had made Herculean efforts to draw Japan into a military alliance, which on their side was envisaged as a sure means of neutralizing both Soviet Russia and the western democracies. The Japanese Army and its ardent spokesman, General Oshima, the Ambassador to Berlin, had been quite ready to make a deal on that basis, but after many months of debate and argument the negotiations foundered on the opposition of the Japanese Court, Government and Navy circles to any pact which might expose Japan to conflict with the great sea powers. When the Konoye-Matsuoka Cabinet was formed in July, 1940, the project had been dormant for almost a year. Meanwhile Hitler's amazing successes in Europe had opened to Japan bright prospects of Dutch, French and perhaps British colonial spoils in the Far East. The Japanese military were more eager than ever to ally their country with a victor who appeared invincible, and the risks, too, seemed smaller than they had previously been. France was out of the running and Britain appeared certainly doomed. As for the United States, it seemed reasonable to suppose that that power would be unwilling to challenge a German-Japanese coalition singlehanded. The moment was most opportune and the new Foreign Minister, with his military supporters, was determined to make the most of it.

Hardly had Matsuoka taken over his post when he let it be known that he meant to hitch the Japanese wagon to the Nazi star. One of his first moves was to institute a major purge of the foreign service which involved the removal of many diplomats known to oppose a pact with Germany or to favor close relations with Britain or the United States. That having been done, the Foreign Minister appointed Chuichi Ohashi, a member of the Manchurian clique and a confirmed champion of the alliance with Germany, as Vice Foreign Minister, and Toshio Shiratori, former Ambassador to Rome and a persistent advocate of the pro-Axis policy, as special adviser.

[45] Among the lost documents one is to be particularly regretted. This was a Japanese Foreign Office memorandum of 156 pages entitled "Outline of the Process of Drafting Various Drafts and of the Internal Procedure pertaining to the Tripartite Pact of Japan, Germany, and Italy, and Pertaining Documents" (see *Tokyo War Crimes Documents, Defense Document 1656A*).

General Oshima, at that time living in retirement, was passed over for reasons still unknown.[46]

At the same time the new Cabinet laid down the important policy decisions of July 26 and 27, 1940, which provided the setting for what was to follow. These decisions, it may be recalled, looked to the settlement of the China Incident and especially to the expansion of Japanese control over Indo-China. In other words, the new Government proposed, for the time being, to divert its attention from Soviet Russia in order to garner the fruits of Hitler's victories. Since Soviet Russia and Germany were partners, it was believed that, through alliance with Germany, Japan could obtain insurance against Soviet attack. An important item in Matsuoka's program was, indeed, the establishment of closer relations with the Kremlin. But the crucial point was to secure the alliance with Germany for immediate purposes. If Japan was to acquire the Asian heritage of the Netherlands, France and possibly Britain, Hitler as the conquerer of those countries could hardly be left out of account. To obtain German recognition of Japan's extensive claims, the Fuehrer's terms would have to be met. But, after all, commitment of Japan against Britain would no longer be the hazardous proposition it had been in 1939, and there was every likelihood that the United States, far from taking a stronger line, could actually be deterred from further opposition.

This line of reasoning emerges clearly from the records which have come down to us, and will be seen to have colored the diplomatic exchanges. These began on August 1, 1940, when Matsuoka had his first conversation with General Ott, the German Ambassador. The Foreign Minister made plain that he desired a deal with Germany and hoped to construct the Greater East Asia Co-Prosperity Sphere, which, he added, would involve neither subjugation nor exploitation. Apparently the Ambassador was none too responsive to these advances, nor was the German Foreign Office much impressed with the Japanese offer of aid in the hour of Nazi victory.[47] But the Japanese could hardly take "no" for an answer. Ambassador Kurusu was instructed to raise the question directly with Foreign Minister Ribbentrop, who in 1938 and 1939 had been the driving force behind the negotiations. Of the details nothing is known beyond the fact that Kurusu pressed for German recognition of Japan's Far Eastern sphere and that Ribbentrop received the idea of a belated conclusion of the alliance with his usual exuberance. Judging from remarks he made somewhat later to Count Ciano,

---

[46] Kido deposition (*Tokyo War Crimes Documents,* Defense Document 2502), and tel. from Ott to the German Foreign Office, August 2, 1940 (*ibid.,* Document No. 4029C).

[47] Tel. from Ott to Berlin, August 2, 1940 (*Tokyo War Crimes Documents,* Nos. 1590A and C). According to the *Halder Diary,* July 11, 1940, the Germans were by no means pleased by the Japanese policy toward Indo-China. See also Matsuoka's explanations to his colleagues, September 19, 1940 (*Tokyo War Crimes Documents,* No. 1202).

one may conclude that he saw the proposition chiefly in terms of its propaganda value: the coalition with Japan would impress the whole world, would discourage Soviet Russia from drifting away from the pact of August, 1939, and above all would strengthen isolationist sentiment in the United States and prevent President Roosevelt from aligning his country more closely with the British.[48]

Such further discussion as may have taken place between Ribbentrop and Kurusu it is impossible to recapture, but it is noteworthy that the Berlin Government, contrary to Washington's conviction, did nothing during August and September, 1940, to support the Japanese demands on the French with respect to Indo-China. Evidently Hitler was biding his time to see what terms could be extracted from the impatient Matsuoka. It is altogether likely that the reports of American correspondents during this period were well founded. On August 10, 1940, Hallett Abend reported from Shanghai:

> Diplomats arriving here from Germany declare that Hitler is intensely annoyed that Japan has not formally adhered to the Axis . . . and is even more intensely annoyed that Japan is trying to enrich herself by attempting to obtain ascendancy over the colonial possessions of France and the Netherlands.

Somewhat later another American newspaperman wrote that the Germans in Tokyo were taking the stand that Japan would have to pay for expansion by making appropriate arrangements with Berlin. No wonder, then, that as late as August Ambassador Grew should have shared the conviction that relations between Japan and Germany were growing worse.[49]

Though it cannot be proved, it seems highly probable that Hitler's decision was influenced by news of the American-Canadian Agreement at Ogdensburg (August 17) and Churchill's announcement (August 20) of the forthcoming lease of bases to the United States. In Berlin it was at first thought that this transaction involved bases in the Pacific (like Singapore) as well as in the Atlantic. Matsuoka, for his part, was greatly exercised by the thought that the United States might obtain bases in Australia and New Zealand and must have been immensely relieved to learn that Ribbentrop had decided to despatch General Heinrich Stahmer as Minister Plenipotentiary to Tokyo. Stahmer was a confidential adviser of the Nazi Foreign Minister and had been actively involved in the negotiations of 1938-1939. There was every reason to suppose that his coming meant business.[50]

[48] Conversation between Ribbentrop and Ciano, September 19, 1940 (*Ciano's Diplomatic Papers,* London, 1948, p. 390). For Kurusu's *démarche* we have used a German Foreign Office memo for Ribbentrop, August 7, 1940 (*Tokyo War Crimes Documents,* No. 4029).

[49] Hallett Abend in *The New York Times,* August 11, 1940; reports of A. T. Steel, August 31, as printed in *Pearl Harbor Attack,* IV, 1712 ff.; Grew: *Ten Years in Japan,* 348 ff.; Craigie: *Behind the Japanese Mask,* Chapter XVIII.

[50] *Halder Diary,* August 23, 1940, notes the departure of Stahmer and the news of the Anglo-American pact in the same entry. On the conclusion of the Tripartite Pact

In anticipation of Stahmer's arrival the four most important Japanese ministers (Konoye, Matsuoka, General Tojo and Admiral Yoshida) met in conference to block out their proposals. They agreed that the time had come for strengthening the bonds with Germany and Italy to ensure mutual coöperation in establishing the new order in Europe and Asia, and they concurred in the opinion that if need be Japan should be ready to take any action, including the use of armed force. It was thought that Germany might not immediately require Japan's military coöperation against Britain and that, in such event, the main objective would be the United States. In any case, it was agreed that talks with Stahmer would be futile unless Japan were prepared to employ armed force if necessary. The record of the conference, a truly remarkable and revealing document, then continued:

> Japan and the two countries of Germany and Italy will mutually coöperate in order not to allow the United States to interfere in regions other than the Western Hemisphere and the United States possessions, and also in order to safeguard the political and economic interests of both contracting parties in this connection. Further, in the event of either contracting party entering upon a state of war with the United States, the other contracting party will assist that party by all possible means. Japan and the two countries of Germany and Italy will closely coöperate with respect to the action to be taken in regard to Central and South America.

Mutual support in settling the China Incident and in bringing pressure to bear upon Britain was to be provided, and with regard to Japan's "sphere of living" in East Asia it was specified:

> The sphere to be envisaged in the course of negotiations with Germany and Italy as Japan's Sphere of Living for the construction of a Greater East Asia New Order will comprise: the former German Islands under mandate, French Indo-China and Pacific Islands, Thailand, British Malaya, British Borneo, Dutch East Indies, Burma, Australia, New Zealand, India, etc., with Japan, Manchuria and China as the backbone.

Recognizing that this was a rather tall order and more than the Germans might be willing to accept, the conference decided that in the forthcoming negotiations only the area from Burma eastward (including the Netherlands East Indies) and from New Caledonia northward should be mentioned and that, for immediate purposes, India might be assigned to the Soviet sphere. Finally, with respect to the use of armed force, the conference determined that if the China Incident were nearly settled, force should be employed if the situation were favorable, but "in the event that the China Incident has not yet been settled, it will be Japan's guiding principle to take action within limits short of war. If, however, domestic and foreign condi-

---

the official Nazi press emphasized that it was intended to forestall an Anglo-American agreement on Pacific bases (*The New York Times,* September 28, 1940). Japanese fears on this score were revealed by Matsuoka in his explanations to the Imperial Council (*Tokyo War Crimes Documents,* No. 1202); they were recognized also by Ambassador Grew (*Grew Diary, MS.,* September 30, 1940).

tions take a decidedly favorable turn, or if it is deemed that, irrespective of whether our preparations are complete or not, the development of the internal situation permits of no further delay, Japan will resort to armed force."[51]

This forthright blueprint goes a long way toward explaining the further course of Japanese policy down to the attack on Pearl Harbor. It provides incontrovertible proof of the extent of Japanese ambitions and of Japanese determination to attain them, if need be by the use of armed force. Matsuoka must have been deeply gratified, however, when he learned that the German price for recognition of Japanese claims in Asia and the Pacific was far lower than he was prepared to offer. Stahmer arrived in Tokyo on September 7, 1940, and, together with Ambassador Ott, held important conferences with Matsuoka on September 9, 10 and 11. The Foreign Minister's colleagues and subordinates have testified that Matsuoka kept the whole matter in his own hands and personally conducted all negotiations without further consultation with Konoye or Tojo, which, in all truth, was hardly necessary.[52] Although no record of the discussions appears to have survived, the summary of the German proposals leaves little doubt that Hitler and Ribbentrop were prepared to recognize the Japanese sphere, so far as they were told about it, and that they concentrated their effort on one thing: to bring Japan into alliance with Germany and Italy in the hope of thereby deterring the United States from active intervention on Britain's behalf. It is apparent that the Destroyer Deal had profoundly disturbed the Nazi leaders. It was greatly in their interest to defeat Britain before the United States threw its weight into the scales. The prospect of an early invasion of England had by this time become dimmed, and it was therefore all the more important for the Fuehrer to make provision against American interference.

In this sense Stahmer explained to Matsuoka that the German Government, far from desiring to expand the existing conflict into a world war, was eager to terminate it as soon as possible and was therefore especially anxious to keep the United States out of it. For the time being Germany did not look to Japan for military assistance, but simply wanted Japan to restrain and prevent the United States from intervening. Germany did not expect war with the United States in the near future, but regarded an American-Japanese conflict as eventually unavoidable. A close understanding between Germany, Italy and Japan offered the only hope of avoiding the entrance of the United States into the war or of forestalling an American clash with

[51] Record of the Four Ministers Conference, September 4, 1940 (*Tokyo War Crimes Documents,* No. 2137D).

[52] Affidavit by Stahmer (*Tokyo War Crimes Documents,* Exhibit 2744); statement by Prince Konoye (*ibid.,* Defense Document 1580); "Tojo Memorandum" (*ibid.*); testimony of Shiratori (*ibid.,* Defense Document 2878); deposition of Saito, adviser of the Foreign Office (*ibid.,* Defense Document 332); affidavit of Ishii, staff member of the Military Affairs Section (*ibid.,* Defense Document 2786).

Japan. If the three powers took "a strong and determined attitude, unequivocal and unmistakable," they might succeed. "A weak, lukewarm attitude or declaration at this juncture will only invite danger." Germany was prepared to promise to do everything possible to restrain the United States in the Atlantic, and would send Japan as much equipment—planes, tanks—as it could.

As for the matters dear to the hearts of the Japanese, Stahmer made no difficulties: "Of course, Germany recognizes and respects Japan's political leadership in Greater East Asia. All she wants in these regions is of an economic nature, and she is ready to coöperate with Japan to further her aims." Germany was likewise ready to contribute to the improvement of relations between Soviet Russia and Japan, but suggested that this matter be broached only after conclusion of the Tripartite Pact, at which time Germany would gladly act as "an honest go-between." In conclusion the Nazi emissary urged the need for agreement between Germany, Italy and Japan before the war with Britain came to a close. Taking the long view, he pointed out that the struggle might prove a protracted one, against the entire Anglo-Saxon world. But he ended on a note of assurance: "Despite the fact that the Axis (including Japan) must be thoroughly prepared to meet the worst emergency, Germany will, on the other hand, make use of every means in her power to prevent a clash between the United States and Japan, and even to improve relations between the two, if it is humanly possible."[53]

The Japanese Foreign Minister must have been surprised and deeply gratified to find that, in return for recognition of Japan's far-reaching aspirations and the good offices of Germany in effecting better relations with Soviet Russia, Japan was asked only to sign up with Germany and Italy and to take a "strong and determined attitude" toward the United States. On this basis the negotiators came to agreement in record time, the more so as both sides were exceedingly anxious, for different reasons, to seal the pact. Texts were quickly drawn for clearance with the respective Governments. Ribbentrop appears to have received the draft while on a visit to Rome (September 19) and to have taken this opportunity to inform Mussolini, for the first time, that Italy was about to have another partner. The German Foreign Minister was clearly elated by his prospective diplomatic victory:

. . . The formation of an alliance of that nature should have the advantage of reinforcing the isolation reaction against Roosevelt's interventionist policy. When presenting the event to world opinion, it would be necessary to stress that a world bloc against the spread of the conflict is being formed.

It remains to be seen what reactions that event will produce in Russia. Some think that the formation of the Tripartite Alliance might throw the Soviets into the arms of the democracies. Ribbentrop does not think so—for two reasons. Firstly, because the

[53] Summary of discussions between Matsuoka, Stahmer and Ott on September 9 and 10, 1940 (*Tokyo War Crimes Documents,* No. 1129).

Soviets are still too weak, and know that a large part of the German land forces are now concentrated on their frontiers. In the second place, because Russia is a land power, and no help could reach her through the agency of the English and American fleets, while the hostility of Japan would bring upon her the immediate burden of the Japanese Army in Manchuria.

The Duce raised no objection, in fact seems to have been wholly convinced that a brilliant propaganda move would intimidate the American Government and public. According to the record:

The Duce expresses his complete agreement with the plan for an alliance with Japan which will have the effect of paralyzing American action. One must bear in mind that the Americans are very much afraid of Japan and of her fleet in particular, since the American fleet, while being quantitatively large, must be considered an amateur organization like the English army.[54]

Matsuoka seems to have had somewhat greater difficulty in persuading the Emperor, some of his Cabinet colleagues, and members of the Privy Council. The extant Japanese records are not entirely clear as to the sequence of conferences. Apparently the chief Ministers (Liaison Conference) met on September 16 to consider the matter. There was some anxiety lest the pact lead to greater American economic pressure against Japan and that, in case of war, Japan might run short of essential materials. But Matsuoka gave assurances that preparations had already been made to procure supplies from the South Seas and other places, and General Tojo explained:

It is the United States that is encouraging the Chungking Government or anti-Japanese movement at the present time. Should a solid coalition come to exist between Japan, Germany and Italy, it will become the most effectual expedient to restrain the United States. The more effectually we restrain the United States, the more possibly and quickly we shall be able to dispose of the Sino-Japanese conflict. On the other hand, if we can bring about a *rapprochement* between the Soviet Union and our country as a result of the Tripartite coalition and through the good offices of Germany and Italy, especially Germany, we shall be able to spur the quick ending of the Sino-Japanese conflict.[55]

A few days later (September 19) the Imperial Conference met in the presence of the Emperor to review the draft treaty. Matsuoka gave an account of the negotiations, noting that the Germans, excepting Hitler and Ribbentrop, had at first been cool to the Japanese advances and that no progress had been made until Stahmer arrived in Tokyo. He had, so he explained, expected that the Germans would demand recognition of their sphere in Africa as well as in Europe, but this point had not been raised.

[54] Record of conversation between Mussolini, Ribbentrop and Ciano, September 19, 1940 (*Ciano's Diplomatic Papers*, 389-93). See also the *Ciano Diaries* (New York, 1946), 293. A tel. from Kirk (Berlin), September 28, 1940, reflects the same arguments.
[55] *Tokyo War Crimes Documents*, No. 1259.

As for Japan's claims, the Germans had been told that they included Indo-China, Burma, Thailand, the Straits Settlements, oceanic islands like the Netherlands East Indies, New Guinea, and New Caledonia. India had not been mentioned, but the Germans had been informed that later Japan might want to expand to Australia and New Zealand. The Germans had raised no objections. They had accepted the Japanese sphere as the latter defined it.

There was much discussion of the phrase about any member of the coalition being "publicly or secretly" attacked by another power not as yet involved in the war. According to Matsuoka, Stahmer had explained that "secretly attacked" referred to such situations as the use by the United States of important British bases in the Pacific, or the appearance of the United States fleet at Singapore, or the grant to the United States by the British of bases near the European battlefields, especially in the Mediterranean. Summing up, Matsuoka explained: "Germany and Japan have a common aim in concluding this pact. Germany wants to prevent America's entry into the war, and Japan a Japanese-American conflict." Ever since the conclusion of the American-Canadian agreement the United States attitude had become unbearable and he, Matsuoka, had feared that the United States would try to secure bases in Australia, New Zealand, India, Burma or elsewhere, and might be preparing "a battle array for encircling Japan." There was no longer any room for improving relations by courtesy or friendship. Japan must be firm and join with as many nations as possible. He hoped President Roosevelt would reconsider.[56]

On September 26, 1940, when the drafts were ready for signature, the Privy Council met in almost all-day session to scrutinize every point of the proposed agreement. Certainly it cannot be said that the Tokyo Government embarked upon its new course without scrupulous consideration of all factors involved. The Ministers were asked many searching questions. One member of the Council pointed out that thus far the United States had been holding back, lest pressure on Japan drive that country into alliance with Germany. Thus the proposed pact, far from serving as a warning to the United States, might stiffen that country's attitude and lead to war. Matsuoka challenged this view and maintained that experience had proved that nothing could be achieved by friendly means:

If there is any means by which to check the deterioration of relations, and if possible, to improve them at all, that will be to assume what Minister Stahmer called a "determined attitude." For that purpose, it will be of the utmost importance to make as many allies as possible, and to proclaim it before the world as soon as possible, thus strengthening our position against the United States. While keeping ever vigilant eyes upon any repercussions which may arise from such a move on our part, I will try at

[56] Ambassador Grew learned of this meeting (tels. from Grew, September 19, 20, 1940; Grew: *Ten Years in Japan,* 354). *Tokyo War Crimes Documents,* No. 1202, is undated but appears to be a record of this conference.

the same time not to overlook any opportunity of restoring our relations with America to a more normal basis. The important point is, first of all, to show unmistakably a firm stand against the United States.

Despite this reassurance, the Privy Council expressed great anxiety about the state of Japan's preparations for war. General Tojo explained that only part of the Army would be used against the United States and that therefore "there is nothing to worry about." Similarly other Ministers, including the Minister of the Navy, assured the Council that Japan already had large supplies of war materials, especially oil, and that in the event of a long war more could probably be secured from the Netherlands East Indies. Eventually the Council accepted the draft, but admonished the Government to avoid incitement of the United States or Britain, to do its utmost to improve relations with Soviet Russia, and not to neglect preparations for the worst possible eventualities. At 9:40 P.M. the Council met with the Emperor and recommended approval of the treaty, which Hirohito gave rather reluctantly at 10:15 P.M.[57]

At the insistence of the Germans, the signature of the treaty took place in Berlin on September 27, 1940, with Ribbentrop, Ciano and Ambassador Kurusu in the key roles. In view of the great importance of the agreement to the development of American policy, it seems best to quote the text in full:

The Governments of Germany, Italy and Japan consider it the pre-requisite of a lasting peace that every nation in the world shall receive the space to which it is entitled. They have, therefore, decided to stand by and coöperate with one another in their efforts in Greater East Asia and the regions of Europe respectively. In doing this it is their prime purpose to establish and maintain a new order of things, calculated to promote the mutual prosperity and welfare of the peoples concerned.

It is, furthermore, the desire of the three Governments to extend coöperation to nations in other spheres of the world who are inclined to direct their efforts along lines similar to their own for the purpose of realizing their ultimate object, world peace.

Accordingly, the Governments of Germany, Italy and Japan have agreed as follows:

Article 1. Japan recognizes and respects the leadership of Germany and Italy in the establishment of a new order in Europe.

Article 2. Germany and Italy recognize and respect the leadership of Japan in the establishment of a new order in Greater East Asia.

Article 3. Germany, Italy and Japan agree to coöperate in their efforts on aforesaid lines. They further undertake to assist one another with all political, economic and military means if one of the three Contracting Powers is attacked by a Power at present not involved in the European War or in the Chinese-Japanese conflict.

Article 4. With the view to implementing the present pact, joint technical commis-

[57] Minutes of the Privy Council meeting, September 26, 1940 (*Tokyo War Crimes Documents,* Nos. 1215 and 1461), and Prince Konoye's memorandum on the Tripartite Alliance (*ibid.,* Defense Document 1580).

sions, to be appointed by the respective Governments of Germany, Italy and Japan, will meet without delay.

Article 5. Germany, Italy and Japan affirm that the above agreement affects in no way the political status existing at present between each of the three Contracting Parties and Soviet Russia.

Article 6. The present pact shall become valid immediately upon signature and shall remain in force ten years from the date on which it becomes effective.

In due time, before the expiration of said term, the High Contracting Parties shall, at the request of any one of them, enter negotiations for its renewal. . . .[58]

The text of the pact is so clear as to require no particular comment. Ambassador Grew and many others were impressed at the time by the ostensible advantages the agreement brought Germany as compared with those that seemed to accrue to Japan.[59] This viewpoint was no doubt based on the proposition that Japan committed itself to come to the assistance of Germany if the latter were attacked by the United States, an eventuality certainly feared at the time by Hitler. Japan, it could be argued, was invoking the hostility of the United States to no good purpose. It should be remembered, however, that Matsuoka's principal aims were to secure German recognition for Japan's prospective Greater East Asia Sphere and to obtain the good offices of Germany in effecting an understanding with Soviet Russia that would permit Tokyo to turn south without running the risk of attack in the north. True, the Germans were in no position to prevent the expansion of Japan into Dutch, French or British territory, but it nevertheless meant a good deal to the Japanese to buy off the chief claimant, and it should be remembered also that at the time there still seemed to be a good possibility, if not a probability, that Hitler would subdue Britain and secure control of the British Fleet.

A further point connected with the text of the pact deserves attention. During the last phase of the negotiations between Japan and the United States, that is, in the autumn of 1941, Washington made great efforts to secure assurance that Japan was not absolutely bound to support Germany in the event of a German-American conflict. The Japanese negotiators insisted that Japan had retained a certain freedom of action in this respect and there has consequently continued to be some doubt as to just what Article 3 of the Treaty involved. The Japanese sources throw some light on this important point. On September 16, 1940, Matsuoka explained to the Liaison Committee that if the issue arose, it would be solved by consultation between the contracting parties: "In this regard [i.e., choice of time to start a war] the standpoint of our Empire will be held independent, as a matter of fact." Similarly he answered questions at the meeting of the Privy Council

[58] Authorized English version as published by the German Government (*Documents on American Foreign Relations,* III, 304-5).
[59] *Grew Diary (MS.),* September 27, 1940; Grew: *Ten Years in Japan,* 332.

ten days later: "the decision upon whether an action or a chain of actions by America or another third power would be regarded as constituting 'attack' shall only be decided by a consultation among us three powers."[60] It was probably some leak of this discussion that led Ambassador Grew to think that there was some *procès-verbal* connected with the treaty.[61] Actually there was much discussion between Matsuoka and Stahmer on this point, eventuating in an exchange of letters (September 27, 1940) providing for consultation as described by Matsuoka.[62] There can no longer be any doubt, therefore, that Japan did retain a certain freedom of action, though of course the whole purpose of the treaty, to deter the United States from intervening against Germany, would have been detsroyed if the proviso attached to Article 3 had become known.

The signature of the Tripartite Pact took place in Berlin with the accustomed pomp and show, and amidst an outpouring of eloquence. In both the German and the Japanese capital the idea of the New Order was heavily stressed and the pact represented as a great step toward peace, based upon a just distribution of the world's resources. Ribbentrop proclaimed: "This pact is not directed against any other people. It is aimed exclusively against those warmongers and irresponsible elements in the rest of the world who, contrary to the real interests of all nations, strive to prolong and extend the present conflict." Matsuoka in turn indicated that the elements in question were ". . . the countries which attempt to obstruct, directly or indirectly, our construction of a New Order in Great East Asia, and even those who resort to all sorts of stratagems in order to block the path of Japan's advance toward the fulfillment of her great historic mission—that of establishing world peace."[63] No effort was spared to impress the United States with the strength of the coalition now formed to keep America from throwing in its lot with Britain. The warning had been sounded; it remained only to see whether or not the will of America could be broken by high-sounding threats.

[60] *Tokyo War Crimes Documents*, Nos. 1202, 1259.

[61] *Grew Diary (MS.)*, October 7, 1940; see also the interesting analysis by Tolischus, in *The New York Times*, November 10, 1941.

[62] *Tokyo War Crimes Documents*, Exhibit 555.

[63] Various declarations are printed in *Documents on American Foreign Relations*, III, 305 ff., and in *Foreign Relations of the United States: Japan*, II, 166 ff.

CHAPTER II

America, Britain and the Japanese Challenge

1. DEFIANCE WITHIN LIMITS

Secretary Hull set the tone of the American response to the publication of the Tripartite Pact by issuing an official statement, approved by the President, and released without delay:

The reported agreement of alliance does not, in the view of the Government of the United States, substantially alter a situation which has existed for several years. Announcement of the alliance merely makes clear to all a relationship which has long existed in effect and to which this Government has repeatedly called attention. That such an agreement has been in process of conclusion has been known for some time, and that fact has been fully taken into account by the Government of the United States in the determining of this country's policies.[1]

Armed with the assurance of the Government that everything had been foreseen and that actually nothing had changed, commentators and newspaper editors generally adopted a stiff line. The country, which had openly defied Hitler by committing itself to all-out support of Britain, was in no mood to cringe before Japan, or to be frightened by what Senator Claude Pepper termed an "international squeeze play." News of the additional loan to China and of the imposition of an embargo on the shipment of scrap to Japan evoked strong popular support; a public opinion poll of September 30, 1940, indicated that 57 percent of those queried thought the United States should take steps to keep Japan from becoming more powerful, even if it meant the risk of war.[2] Public sentiment in general took the line that if the dictators of Europe and Asia were going to coöperate, that was all the

[1] Press release of September 27, 1940 (*Foreign Relations of the United States: Japan*, II, 169). See also Hull: *Memoirs*, I, 909.
[2] Feis: *The Road to Pearl Harbor*, 122.

more reason for the United States to stand by Britain and perhaps conclude an out-and-out alliance with that power.[3]

In official circles, however, something less than the equanimity suggested by Secretary Hull prevailed. It is of course true that a military alliance between Germany and Japan had been bruited for years, but the fact remains that the Tripartite Pact, when finally concluded, came as a surprise and a shock. Furthermore, the explicit commitments of the agreement were decidedly more impressive than the vague community of interest underlying the Anti-Comintern Pact of earlier days. The State Department, like the British Foreign Office, suspected that the new alliance contained secret clauses giving Japan a free hand in Indo-China and the Netherlands Indies, and that it might be followed shortly by new aggressive moves. Secretary Hull is reported to have told the President that the pact probably presaged quick action on Tokyo's part, action that might force the United States into war.[4] The Administration was therefore confronted with the question whether it should acquiesce in the loss of Indo-China or the Indies, or take immediate steps to forestall such a calamity. In the latter case there arose the further question whether or not to act in concert with the British and Dutch.

The reader may recall that for some time a group of Cabinet officers, including Secretaries Stimson, Knox, Morgenthau and Ickes, together with Mr. Harry Hopkins, had been vehemently urging an embargo on oil shipments to Japan as the most effective deterrent measure available to the United States. Thus far they had lost their case, but news of the Tripartite Pact gave them an admirable opportunity to reopen it. Secretary Stimson thus recorded his thoughts in his private diary:

It is a very serious proposition of course, but it is so evidently evidenced by fear on the part of the Axis and so clearly represents only what they would do without a treaty, that I personally have not been much worried by it and I don't think the President has. If it should come to a showdown, at present and so long as the British Fleet lasts, the Axis in Europe could not help Japan if she got into trouble with us, and Japan could not help Germany or Italy if they got into trouble with us. So in substance the new arrangement simply means making a bad face at us. It will be pretty useful, I think, however, in waking up our people to the effect that at last they have got what they have been talking about—isolation. The United States is isolated except for one great power and that's the British Commonwealth, and I already see signs of a realization of this among the thoughtless. Clamors are being made for an alliance with Great Britain already.[5]

In short, Mr. Stimson was convinced that the Tripartite Pact was a bluff, that the gun pointed at the United States was not loaded. He had long been

---

[3] See the editorials in *The New York Times* and *New York Herald Tribune*, September 30, 1940, and the review of opinion on the West Coast in *The New York Times*, October 13, 1940.

[4] Feis: *The Road to Pearl Harbor*, 123.

[5] *Stimson Diary (MS.)*, September 27, 1940.

persuaded that force was the only weapon Tokyo understood and respected, and that therefore only a policy of firmness promised success. To him, as to Secretary Ickes, the deterrent measures thus far taken were altogether inadequate and the oil embargo therefore imperative. To quote Mr. Ickes:

> We didn't keep Japan out of Indo-China by continuing to ship scrap iron, nor will we keep Japan out of the Dutch East Indies by selling it our oil. When Japan thinks that it can safely move against the Dutch East Indies, and is ready to do so, it will go in, regardless. It will make it all the more difficult for it to go in if it is short on oil and gasoline.[6]

Even Secretary Hull, who had consistently advocated a policy of caution, appears to have been momentarily assailed by doubt. Some of his closest advisers, notably Mr. Norman Davis and Mr. Stanley Hornbeck, took the view that Japan could not and would not strike back and that therefore expediency dictated that the United States act before it was too late. Quite possibly Mr. Hull was influenced also by Ambassador Grew's argument that Japan could no longer be viewed as an individual nation. It had become a "member of a team" and henceforth would have to be treated like the team as a whole.[7]

In contrast to these civilian leaders, the military advisers of the President were firmly opposed to all measures of retaliation likely to provoke the Japanese to make war. General Marshall and Admiral Stark recognized that a conflict with Japan in the near future was altogether probable, but they insisted that the United States was as yet unprepared for hostilities in the Pacific and that in any event it was more in the American interest to arm against Hitler and support Britain than to devote a major effort against Japan.[8]

Only the President could decide between these conflicting views and recommendations. That he found the issue perplexing is indicated by his rebuff to Secretary Morgenthau, whose pleas for a strong policy were put aside by Mr. Roosevelt with the acid remark that he himself and Secretary Hull were "handling foreign affairs."[9] His perplexity had not been dispelled by the time of the October 4 Cabinet meeting, as revealed by Secretary Stimson's record. There was, he noted, a "red hot debate on the Far East":

[6] Letter of Secretary Ickes to the President, October 17, 1940 (*Roosevelt Papers: Secretary's File*, Box 58). We have used also the *Stimson Diary (MS.)*, October 1, 1940, and the *Morgenthau Diaries (MS.)*, October 2, 1940 (Vol. 318, pp. 148 ff.). See further Henry L. Stimson and McGeorge Bundy: *On Active Service in Peace and War* (New York, 1947), 385, and the inspired account of Forrest Davis and Ernest K. Lindley: *How War Came* (New York, 1942), 154 ff.

[7] Grew: *Ten Years in Japan*, 349.

[8] The argument was effectively developed in the Strong Memorandum of September 25, 1940, which is discussed in greater detail in the following chapter. See also the report of Edgar Mowrer in the *Chicago Daily News*, October 1, 1940, and Mark S. Watson: *Chief of Staff: Prewar Plans and Preparations* (Washington, 1950), 115 ff.

[9] *Morgenthau Diaries (MS.)*, October 2, 1940 (Vol. 318, pp. 127 ff.).

President spoke very seriously on the situation that confronts us with the agreement between Japan and Germany and Italy. Japan has already begun to checkmate and we had a long discussion of what our action should be. Everybody agreed that the purpose of the three Axis powers was to scare us out of giving material aid to Great Britain, but the general consensus was that we make no reply—we should do no talking, but do some straight acting which will show Japan that we mean business and that we are not in the least afraid of her. Various plans were discussed.[10]

Though no decision was arrived at and Secretary Morgenthau therefore felt that he and his friends had been "suppressed," the temper of the activist group was clearly expressed in Secretary Knox's public address at Washington on October 5, 1940. According to Mr. Knox the Tripartite Pact was aimed directly at the United States, and the American way of life was threatened as never before. Under the circumstances the Secretary recalled and commended the famous words of Captain Parker at Lexington Green: "Don't fire unless fired upon. If they want war, let it begin here."[11]

Yet no drastic measures were adopted by the Administration. From the records presently available it is impossible to trace the reasons for the President's indecision. It may safely be assumed, however, that he was swayed by the arguments of his military advisers. Furthermore, Secretary Hull probably relapsed into his customary caution and used his influence to head off risky moves. Finally, the White House and State Department may have been impressed by the initially threatening attitude of Japan. Prime Minister Konoye announced publicly that "should the United States refuse to understand the real intentions of Japan, Germany and Italy, and persist in challenging them in the belief that the pact among them represents a hostile action, there will be no other course open to them than to go to war." Hard upon this statement came a declaration by Matsuoka that American insistence on the *status quo* in the Pacific could result only in war.[12]

No less menacing was the Japanese response to the American embargo on the export of iron and steel scrap. On October 5 Matsuoka pleaded with Ambassador Grew to urge his Government not to impose further restrictions on trade which, he asserted, "would intensely anger the Japanese people." Three days later Ambassador Horinouchi handed Secretary Hull Tokyo's formal statement, repeating the warnings publicly uttered by Konoye and Matsuoka: "In view of the high feeling in Japan, it is apprehended that, in the event of continuation by the United States Government of the present attitude toward Japan in matters of trade restriction, future relations between Japan and the United States will be unpredictable." The Ambassador took the occasion to notify Mr. Hull that the Tokyo Government was not

[10] *Stimson Diary* (*MS.*), October 4, 1940.
[11] *Vital Speeches,* VII, 34 ff.
[12] These statements are printed, respectively, in *Documents on American Foreign Relations,* III, 280 ff., and in *Foreign Relations of the United States: Japan,* II, 171 ff. See also Hugh Byas, in *The New York Times,* October 5, 1940.

deceived by American efforts to disguise economic sanctions as measures of rearmament and defense. The embargo on scrap, he declared, was clearly discriminatory, and therefore constituted "an unfriendly act."

Mr. Hull's temper rose as he listened to these minatory words. There was no excuse, he said, for Japanese doubts of the sincerity of the American statement, the more so as he himself had consistently opposed even harsher measures against Japan. Then, growing angrier and correspondingly more candid, the Secretary expressed his amazement that Japan of all nations should question the right of the United States to do what it deemed necessary for its own defense:

> The least objection to our taking issue with Japan with respect to the foregoing matters would be called an unfriendly act, and, as Premier Konoye said recently to the press, it would be the occasion for war so far as Japan was concerned. I added that of course if any one country is sufficiently desirous of trouble, it can always find any one of innumerable occasions to start such trouble. In brief, it is not left to the other country to participate in such decision.

> . . . .

> I reiterated the view that it was unheard of for one country engaged in aggression and seizure of another country, contrary to all law and treaty provisions, to turn to a third peacefully disposed nation and seriously insist that it would be guilty of an unfriendly act if it should not cheerfully provide some of the necessary implements of war to aid the aggressor nation in carrying out its policy of invasion.[13]

The Ambassador took his leave, having nothing more to say and, one senses, less opportunity to say it. However, he had made his point and, to all appearances, the Japanese warnings struck home. For all his stinging arraignment of Japanese policy, Mr. Hull resumed his vigorous opposition to further retaliatory measures. He dissuaded the President from declaring an embargo on oil, pointing out that such a step would almost certainly lead to greater Japanese pressure on the Dutch and possibly to an invasion of the Indies. Mr. Roosevelt was in fact so completely converted to this view that he would not even permit interference with Japanese vessels loading cargoes of goods already under embargo. In the words of a Treasury official, Mr. Roosevelt did not want "to gum the works on any shipment to Japan. Everything was to be kept as 'normal' and 'regular' as possible." In the same spirit the President wrote to Mrs. Roosevelt somewhat later in response to an inquiry about an oil embargo:

> The real answer that you *cannot* use is that if we forbid oil shipments to Japan, Japan will increase her purchases of Mexican oil and, furthermore, may be driven by actual necessity to a descent on the Dutch East Indies. With this writing we all regard such action on our part as an encouragement to the spread of war in the Far East.[14]

[13] *Foreign Relations of the United States: Japan,* 223 ff.; Hull: *Memoirs,* I, 912 ff.
[14] Letter to Mrs. Roosevelt, November 13, 1940 (now printed in *F.D.R.: His Per-*

For the time being, then, nothing more was done to impair Japan's war-making capability. From fear of provoking an unwanted conflict in the Far East, the Administration decided to pick its way with the utmost caution. No doubt the President and even Secretary Hull on occasion itched to do something really drastic, for they, like the forward members of the Cabinet, burned with resentment at Japanese attempts to intimidate the United States. But when it came to a showdown the Government invariably fell back on words and demonstrations. Thus, on October 8, 1940, the State Department announced to the press that it had issued its first major warning to American nationals in the Far East to return home unless obliged to remain by urgent business. Even on this occasion, however, great efforts were made to strike the right note: firmness without sensation or alarm. The announcement referred to the "abnormal situation continuing in the Far East," but closed by pointing out that the warning was merely "a continuation of the policy inaugurated in regard to the Far East in 1937 and in regard to Europe last year." Ambassador Grew was convinced that the gesture was highly effective, inasmuch as it led to realization on the part of many Japanese that the decision as to peace or war might not rest solely with Tokyo. If this was so, the impression could hardly have been more than transitory. The course of Japanese policy suggests that no punitive measures short of the oil embargo imposed in July, 1941, had anything approaching a seriously deterrent effect.[15]

2. BRITISH PROPOSALS

The British Prime Minister, ever alert to his country's interest and ever ready to exploit any possibility of strengthening the ties that already bound America to the British cause, evidently looked upon the Tripartite Pact as a welcome opportunity to score another point. The opening note of a new move on his part was struck by Lord Lothian on September 29, 1940, while lunching with Major McHugh (U.S.M.C.), until recently American Assistant Naval Attaché at Chungking. In the course of conversation the British Ambassador pointed out that a German invasion of Britain was no longer likely and that therefore the British command of the Atlantic was assured for at least another ten months. This, he argued, gave the United States time for "necessary action" in the Pacific. Under the Tripartite Pact coöperation of the three signatory powers could hardly extend beyond the sphere of diplomacy. But even if Gibraltar, Suez and Hongkong should fall, an American fleet based on Singapore could control the trade routes to the

sonal Letters, 1928-1945 (New York, 1947-48), II, 1077). For the rest we have used a memo of the Division of Controls to the Administrator of Export Control, October 10, 1940, and the Morgenthau Diaries (MS.), October 8, 1940 (Vol. 320, pp. 21 ff.), and October 14, 1940 (Vol. 321, p. 215).

[15] The text of the statement is printed in Foreign Relations of the United States: Japan, II, 114. Grew's comments are from his MS. Diary, October 11, 1940.

east and so prevent Germany and Italy from obtaining supplies from that area. More importantly, an American fleet could cut the Japanese trade routes and by its presence prevent a Japanese attack on the Dutch Indies, which would entail a division of the Japanese naval forces.[16]

With such thoughts in mind, the Ambassador must have been agreeably surprised by his discussion with Secretary Hull about the significance of the Tripartite Pact on September 30, 1940. Mr. Hull, having restated his belief that the pact simply formalized a situation long existing, ranged further afield than was his wont. In these first days after the signature of the treaty he was disposed to entertain proposals for effective countermeasures. He reflected "that Japan would, as a most ordinary precaution, find it necessary to assume that whether or not the United States and Great Britain have express or definite agreements with regard to naval and air bases across the Pacific to and including Singapore, the special relations between these two countries are such that they could overnight easily establish coöperative relations for the mutual use of these bases." He then inquired whether the British and Dutch and other South Pacific Governments had conferred on the matter of pooling their defense forces in case of danger; what the size of such forces might be; and what size fleet the Japanese would require to overcome them.

Lothian disclaimed knowledge of these technical matters, but seized his chance to inquire what the American attitude would be if the British reopened the Burma Road on October 17, 1940. This was a sore point with the Secretary, who had made no secret of his disapproval when in July, 1940, the London Government had decided, under pressure from Tokyo, to close the road for three months. He made it fairly clear, however, that Washington would welcome the reopening and in this connection rehearsed the various steps already taken by the United States to deter the Japanese from further action. His notes of the conversation read:

I added that I did not undertake to predict, much less to make commitments, as to how fast or how far this Government may go in following up the various acts and utterances in which it has been indulging; that, of course, the special desire of this Government is to see Great Britain succeed in the war and that its acts and utterances with respect to the Pacific area would be more or less affected as to time and extent by the question of what course would, on the part of this Government, most effectively and legitimately aid Great Britain in winning the war.[17]

It goes almost without saying that Lothian's report of this conversation was grist for Mr. Churchill's mill. For some time he had been wrestling with the question whether or not to announce the reopening of the Burma Road and thus to defy Tokyo. Even though he persuaded himself that the Japanese, who

[16] Memo of conversation between Major J. M. McHugh and Lord Lothian, dated September 30, 1940.

[17] Memo of conversation between Hull and Lothian, September 30, 1940. Extracts of this record are printed in *Peace and War*, 574 ff., and in Hull: *Memoirs*, I, 911.

had not made war on Britain in the desperate month of July, would be unlikely to do so at a time when Britain had withstood the first Nazi assault,
there was always a serious chance that the Japanese would fight on an issue
which bore so directly on the successful conclusion of the China Incident.
Mr. Churchill clearly rated highly the deterrent effect of the American Fleet
at Hawaii and had on various occasions proposed that at least part of the
American naval forces be sent to Singapore, his conviction being that under
such conditions the Japanese would not dare move, either against Britain or
against the Dutch Indies.[18] He was therefore much elated by Secretary
Hull's suggestions. On October 4 the British Cabinet decided to reopen the
Burma Road on October 17 and the Prime Minister took the opportunity,
in transmitting this news to President Roosevelt, to develop the theme of an
American naval visit, "the bigger the better," to Singapore. Such a simple
action, he pointed out, might speak louder than words. Furthermore, the
occasion might be used to initiate technical discussions of naval and military
problems, in which the Dutch might be invited to participate. "Anything in
this direction," he concluded, "would have a marked deterrent effect upon
a Japanese declaration of war upon us over the Burma Road opening. I
should be very grateful if you would consider action along these lines, as it
might play an important part in preventing the spread of the war."[19]

The British proposals were considered on October 5 at a meeting of the
Liaison Committee (Under Secretary Welles, General Marshall and Admiral Stark), which decided to recommend against a naval visit to Singapore, for the already well-established reasons that such a move might
precipitate hostilities and that the western Pacific was in any case a theater
of war second in importance as compared to the Atlantic.[20] But it was by no
means a foregone conclusion that this recommendation would be accepted,
for, as it happened, the related question whether the United States Fleet
should remain at Hawaii or return to its customary Pacific coast base was
at that very time the subject of heated debate among American officials. In
general, the naval authorities wanted the Fleet brought back to San Diego.
They recalled that it had been sent to Hawaii in the first place only for
maneuvers and that there were excellent technical reasons for returning it
to its usual base. But the State Department, notably Mr. Hornbeck, was
convinced that the presence of the Fleet at Pearl Harbor was a genuine
deterrent to the Japanese and that it should therefore not be withdrawn
during the critical period following the announcement of the Tripartite
Pact.[21]

[18] Churchill: *Their Finest Hour,* 497-98, 667-68.
[19] Tel. from Mr. Churchill to the President, October 4, 1940 (full text in Churchill:
Their Finest Hour, 497-98).
[20] Watson: *Chief of Staff: Prewar Plans and Preparations,* Chapter IV.
[21] See especially Hornbeck's memo of September 21, 1940, in *Pearl Harbor Attack,*
XVI, 2007 ff.

Admiral J. W. Richardson, the Commander in Chief of the Fleet, had been summoned to Washington in connection with this issue and arrived in the capital on October 7. To his great dismay he found, from preliminary conversations with Secretary Knox and Admiral Stark, that current talk was not of bringing back the Fleet, but rather of detaching part of it for a visit to Singapore and of reinforcing Admiral Hart's much smaller Asiatic Fleet at Manila.[22] How serious this "talk" was appeared when, on October 8, Admiral Richardson lunched at the White House with the President and Admiral Leahy, the former Chief of Naval Operations. Mr. Roosevelt opened the discussion by inquiring of Admiral Leahy whether he considered a reinforcement of Admiral Hart would serve to deter the Japanese. Leahy thought it might have such an effect temporarily, but, holding that war with Japan was in any case all but inevitable and that the Asiatic Fleet might be lost, warned against sending to Manila more than a few of the least valuable combatant ships.

Admiral Richardson opposed even a minor gesture of this kind. His chief concern was to have the main Fleet brought back to the Pacific coast, a move in favor of which he adduced many excellent reasons. Among other things, he argued, the Fleet was unprepared for war and could not be used for offensive operations until provided with a "train" of auxiliary vessels. If, he continued, war with Japan was imminent, the Fleet should be brought back to be properly prepared for such an eventuality. It was beyond his comprehension how a fleet that was unready for war could be a serious deterrent to Japan and he did not hesitate to argue with the President on this score. But Mr. Roosevelt stuck to the contrary view, summing up his position thus: "I can be convinced of the desirability of retaining the battleships on the West Coast if I can be given a good statement which will convince the American people and the Japanese Government that in bringing the battleships to the West Coast we are not stepping backward."[23]

Richardson's dejection over the President's attitude was deepened by his subsequent discussions with Admiral Stark and Mr. Hornbeck. Stark sympathized with the arguments for bringing the Fleet back to the West Coast, but apparently did not regard them as conclusive. The Commander of the Fleet was thus obliged to assume responsibility for incurring risks in order that the Fleet might be used, not as a weapon of war, but as a weapon of diplomacy. Indeed, the President had left no doubt that the issue had acquired strong political overtones: even though the presence of the Fleet at Pearl Harbor might not be an effective deterrent to Japan, its withdrawal to the West Coast would be interpreted at home and abroad as a step back-

[22] Richardson's testimony, in *Pearl Harbor Attack,* I, 264 ff.

[23] *Pearl Harbor Attack,* I, 265, 268 ff. Admiral Richardson's summary was set down in a memo to Admiral Stark of October 9, 1940 (printed in *Pearl Harbor Attack,* XIV, 962). On Leahy's feeling about the likelihood of war with Japan see *Pearl Harbor Attack,* I, 342 ff.

ward on the part of the United States. Under the circumstances the President felt he had no other course but to keep the Fleet at Hawaii.[24] Whether or not its presence there did serve to deter Japan is a question that will probably be argued till Doomsday without conclusive evidence ever being adduced one way or another. Mr. Churchill, as noted above, rated its effect highly and it is only fair to say that the Japanese, even though they realized the Fleet was not prepared for action, appear to have been profoundly disturbed by its presence. After all, Japan's great gamble, on which it based its hope of victory, was the later attempt to destroy the Fleet on December 7, 1941.[25]

The decision to leave the United States Fleet at Pearl Harbor did not necessarily preclude the despatch of an American naval contingent to Singapore, as proposed by Mr. Churchill. It will be recalled that Admiral Stark, General Marshall and Under Secretary Welles were at one in opposing such a move. Secretary Hull, though genuinely apprehensive of Japanese reaction to the announcement of the reopening of the Burma Road, shared Welles's feeling that further aggressive moves by Japan might be designed as "a baited trap" to draw the United States into hostilities in the Pacific and so cut down American support of Britain. In the State Department only Mr. Hornbeck held to the view that the defense of Singapore was a vital interest of the United States and that the crux of the international situation lay in the Far East.[26] Outside the State Department it was particularly Secretary Stimson, probably influenced by his friend Hornbeck, who pleaded for acceptance of the British invitation, in conjunction with a total embargo on trade with Japan. An American naval force at Singapore, he emphasized, would strengthen British morale and establish command of the Japanese sea lanes: "By closing those lanes and, at the same time, cutting off all American commerce with Japan, we should eventually reduce that country to comparative impotency." China would be strengthened and could provide air bases for possible operations against Japan. Australia, New Zealand and the French Pacific Islands would be safeguarded.[27]

During his luncheon discussion with Admiral Richardson on October 8 the President had made no mention of the proposal for a visit of American naval forces to Singapore. There is, in fact, no evidence that Mr. Roosevelt at any time viewed such a visit as feasible or desirable. But he was apparently impressed by Stimson's argument and told Secretary Knox that if the Japa-

[24] Richardson's description of his interviews with Hornbeck, Knox and Stark on October 9 and 10, 1940, are given in *Pearl Harbor Attack*, I, 298, 305 ff.

[25] Admiral Leahy, even after hearing Richardson's testimony at the Pearl Harbor Inquiry, continued to hold that the Fleet at Pearl Harbor was a real deterrent. See *Pearl Harbor Attack*, I, 352 ff.

[26] *Moffat Diary* (*MS.*), October 6-10, 1940. Mr. Moffat, at that time Ambassador to Canada, records in detail his conversations with Hull, Welles, Berle and Hornbeck during a visit to Washington in October.

[27] *Stimson Diary* (*MS.*), October 8 and 12, 1940; letter of Stimson to the President, October 12, 1940 (*Roosevelt Papers:* Secretary's File, Box 63).

nese took "drastic" action in response to the reopening of the Burma Road, he was considering a total embargo on trade with Japan, and, in addition, was thinking of establishing a naval patrol consisting of two lines of ships, one extending from Hawaii west to the Philippines, and the other from Samoa west to the Netherlands Indies.[28] At the same time he requested a chart showing British and French bases or possible bases for surface ships, submarines and aircraft in the Pacific, east of the international date line.[29]

Admiral Richardson, completely dumfounded by these projects, which went far beyond the proposal to reinforce Admiral Hart's Asiatic Fleet, at once asked Secretary Knox whether the President was contemplating a declaration of war on Japan. Surely, he remarked, if American patrol ships intercepted Japanese commerce, war was bound to ensue. The American Fleet, he reiterated, was not prepared for war, indeed not even prepared to maintain a patrol such as the President suggested. Secretary Knox, who probably sympathized with Stimson's views, had no answer to Richardson's objections, but replied with some asperity that if the Admiral did not like the President's plans, he and Admiral Stark could draw up their own "to accomplish the same purpose."

The further development of the President's plan is obscure. Mr. Roosevelt discussed it with Mr. Welles as a "plan or project" in the interest of national security, but then seems to have dropped the idea after further consideration with his naval advisers. On October 23 Secretary Knox wrote the President that he had talked with Mr. Stimson about the latter's proposal to send a force to Singapore and that he had "gathered the impression that he (Stimson) was satisfied that a demonstration in that quarter in less strength than he suggests would meet all requirements."[30] The "demonstration in less strength" turned out to be a modest program for reinforcing the defenses of the Philippines, which involved a revision of the long accepted view that in the event of war those islands could not be held. In reply to questions at a press conference Secretary Knox stated categorically on October 23: "We can defend anything and are not indifferent to the security of land anywhere under the American flag. As long as these territories [the Philippines] fly the American flag, the Navy is ready to defend them." On the same day the War Department announced that it was sending two squadrons of pursuit planes to the Philippines, and three weeks later (November 12) it was decided to base ten additional submarines in the islands. At about the same time the Australian Government agreed to make fifty additional planes available for the defense of Singapore. This alternative

[28] Knox's account to Admirals Stark and Richardson, October 10, 1940 (*Pearl Harbor Attack*, I, 305 ff., 316 ff.; XIV, 1006 ff.).

[29] Memo of Captain D. J. Callaghan to the President, transmitting such a chart, October 17, 1940 (*Roosevelt Papers*: Secretary's File, Box 52).

[30] Letter of Knox to the President, October 23, 1940 (*Roosevelt Papers*: Secretary's File, Box 59).

program for deterring Japan had been worked out with the full approval of the State Department and gratified even the most ardent advocates of strong action: "At least we have got this far with regard to that vital point of defense, Singapore," noted Secretary Stimson in his diary.[31]

Actually these issues had, by mid-October, become less pressing, for the Japanese reaction to the British announcement of the reopening of the Burma Road (October 8, 1940) was unexpectedly guarded. This may have been due, at least in part, to the strong language used by Mr. Churchill and Mr. Roosevelt in rapid succession. On October 8 the Prime Minister struck a clearly defiant note in announcing the Cabinet's decision:

This Three Power Pact is, of course, aimed primarily at the United States, but also in a secondary degree it is pointed against Russia. Neither of the branches of the English-speaking race is accustomed to react to threats of violence by submission, and certainly the reception of this strange ill-balanced declaration in the United States has not been at all encouraging to those who are its authors.

In his Columbus Day Address (October 12) the President was no less forceful:

The Americas will not be scared or threatened into the ways the dictators want us to follow. No combination of dictator countries of Europe and Asia will halt us in the path we see ahead for ourselves and for democracy. No combination of dictator countries of Europe and Asia will stop the help we are giving to almost the last free people now fighting to hold them at bay.[32]

In view of these warnings Konoye and Matsuoka could hardly delude themselves into thinking that action taken against either Britain or the United States, or against their interests in the Far East, would be met by anything less than combined resistance. There can be no doubt that even the extremists among the Japanese did not at that time feel prepared to throw down the gauntlet. The Foreign Minister therefore deemed it expedient to strike an apologetic note. His statement of October 10 read in part:

Lastly, I might add that the Tripartite Pact was not entered into with the intention of directing it "against" the United States, but it was, I should say, directed, if at all, "for" the United States. To state frankly, the parties to the Pact wished earnestly that such a powerful nation as the United States, in particular, and all other nations at present neutral would not be involved in the European War, or come by any chance into conflict with Japan because of the China affair or otherwise. Such an eventuality, with all the possibility of bringing an awful catastrophe upon humanity, is enough to

[31] *Stimson Diary* (*MS.*), November 6 and 12, 1940; memo of conversation between Hull and the Australian Minister, November 12, 1940; memo by Hornbeck, November 5, 1940 (copy in the *Norman Davis Papers, MS.*, November 20, 1940).

[32] Churchill: *Blood, Sweat and Tears* (New York, 1941), 390; *The Public Papers and Addresses of Franklin D. Roosevelt*, IX, 466.

make one shudder, if one stops to imagine the consequences. In short, the Pact is a pact of peace.

A few days later (October 13) Matsuoka began a speech in Tokyo by inviting the United States to join the Tripartite Pact and, in the spirit of *hakko ichiu,* to assist the Axis partners in making the world one family. Further on, however, he characteristically told his audience that Japan was "firmly determined to eliminate any nation that obstructed the New Order." If the war in Europe took a turn unfavorable to Germany and Italy, Japan must be prepared to assist its new allies.[33]

Americans showed little disposition to analyze the double talk of the Japanese Foreign Minister. The big thing to them was that Tokyo gave no indication of resort to war. Throughout the country there was much elation and some outright bravado. Japan's "bluff" had been called and, according to Secretary Knox's newspaper, the *Chicago Daily News,* "conversationally, at least, Japan has executed one of the most precipitous backdowns in diplomatic history." Washington, too, was relieved and gratified to learn from Ambassador Grew that Matsuoka was "deeply disturbed" by America's reaction to the Tripartite Pact.[34] Mr. Morgenthau considered that reaction a "great victory" for the advocates of strong measures and was more than ever convinced that the moment had arrived "to put up a big fight . . . about the gasoline thing," the oil embargo. Mr. Stimson, in turn, urged upon the President that the moment was opportune for "bold and affirmative action in the Pacific.[35]

Actually the President took no further steps, probably for fear of pressing his advantage too far. The existing measures, notably the retention of the Fleet at Hawaii, the projected reinforcement of the Philippines, the embargo on iron and steel scrap, were evidently serving the purposes of the moment. To send the Fleet farther west, or to impose an embargo on oil, might well provoke Japan to action and result in the loss of the Dutch Indies. Above all, it might involve the United States as well as Britain in hostilities in a theater which, by common consent, was regarded as secondary to Europe. It seemed best to leave well enough alone, to gain what time was possible, and to wait and see whether the deflation of the Tripartite Pact might lead to a change in Tokyo's policy. If any weight is to be given statements by the Japanese Foreign Minister, the President's decision was probably a wise one. Early in November Matsuoka remarked to the British Ambassador that the possibility of war could be dismissed "unless the United States should enter

[33] *Documents on American Foreign Relations,* III, 272 ff.; *The New York Times,* October 14, 1940.

[34] Grew: *Ten Years in Japan,* 346 ff.

[35] *Morgenthau Diaries (MS.),* October 14, 1940 (Vol. 321, pp. 324 ff.) ; *Stimson Diary (MS.),* October 12, 1940.

the war or give some serious provocation such as would be involved if a powerful American squadron were to visit Singapore."[36]

3. THE ISSUE OF ANGLO-AMERICAN STAFF CONVERSATIONS

Pursuing the suggestion thrown out by Secretary Hull to Lord Lothian on September 30, 1940, Mr. Churchill had included in his message to the President (October 4) a proposal for staff conversations at Singapore between British, American and Dutch naval authorities. There was nothing particularly novel about the suggestion, except the locality, for ever since the Far Eastern situation had become acute in 1937 it had been recognized on both sides of the Atlantic that in the event of war the two Anglo-Saxon powers would have to coöperate in defense against Japan. From time to time there had been exchanges of information and discussion of strategic problems; on the American side, in fact, plans for eventual hostilities in the Pacific were based squarely on the proposition that the United States would have allies in such a contingency.[37] When, in August, 1940, Admiral Ghormley had been sent to London as Special Naval Observer, he had continued conversations on these problems with British naval authorities. But the discussions were carefully restricted by the American Government. They were "informal," involved no detailed joint planning, and above all carefully excluded any "commitment."

Since June, 1940, Mr. Churchill had pressed, as strongly as he decently could, for the inauguration of formal staff conversations on the highest military level. Such had, in fact, been established between the United States and Canada as a result of the Ogdensburg Agreement of August 17, 1940. Obviously the signature of the Tripartite Pact at the end of September provided an ideal opportunity for proposing once again that, in view of the projected reopening of the Burma Road and the generally increased danger of Japanese aggression, definite arrangements should be made for the military coöperation which on both sides was taken for granted.

The full development of the projected staff conversations is not clear from presently available records, but the American decision not to send a naval force to Singapore naturally ruled out the possibilities of high-level talks at that base and led to consideration of formal discussions in Washington. On October 7, 1940, Secretary Hull took up the matter with Lord Lothian. He expressed surprise that Admiral Ghormley had not long since discussed with Sir Dudley Pound, the First Sea Lord, the naval problems of the Far East, and readily agreed to a "conference of experts" to be held as soon as possible either in Washington or London. Apparently, however, the Secretary was still thinking in terms of purely technical discussions, for he went on

---

[36] *Grew Diary (MS.)*, November 11, 1940.

[37] Captain Tracy S. Kittredge: *United States-British Naval Coöperation, 1939-1942* (MS. study of the Office of Naval History); see also Samuel E. Morison: *The Rising Sun in the Pacific* (Boston, 1948), 48 ff.; and Watson: *Chief of Staff: Prewar Plans and Preparations,* 113 ff.

to say that nothing in the way of formal staff conversations should take place prior to the presidential election.[38]

The Ambassador and his Government fully understood the political considerations and readily agreed to Mr. Hull's proposal "to send service representatives unobtrusively to Washington to continue to explore military-naval problems with United States Army and Navy Staffs." Almost at once rumors got about that "important conversations" were to take place with the British on Pacific defense. In view of the fact that the White House confirmed these rumors and that British Under Secretary Butler announced in the House of Commons that the two Governments were exploring possibilities for coöperation in the Pacific, it seems likely that the leakage of information was intentional and meant as an additional warning to Japan.[39] It may well have served that purpose, but at the same time it gave rise to exaggerated and quite unwarranted talk of secret American commitments to Britain. In the election campaign the President's opponents charged him with leading the country along devious paths toward war. As a result the Administration had to backtrack. On October 16 Mr. Welles informed the British Chargé d'Affaires that the United States Government desired that for the time being Ghormley's conversations in London be confined to exchange of information, without commitments, direct or implied, as to the course the United States would pursue in the Far East. However, he added, the situation "might alter in two or three weeks' time."[40]

In this way the President left himself free, during the election campaign, to refute all charges that he had made or was making secret commitments. As a practical matter, however, Admiral Ghormley continued to examine with his British counterparts the existing plans for British-Dutch coöperation in the Far East and to discuss what relations should be established between their forces and the American forces in that area in the event of war. Furthermore, arrangements were made to have Commander Thomas (U.S.N.) stop off at Singapore on his way to his post at Bangkok. This he did early in November, when preliminary Anglo-American discussions at the local level were initiated in the Far East.[41]

The stage was thus set for the staff conversations, which, as soon as the presidential election was over, were arranged for the winter of 1940-1941.

[38] Memo of conversation between Mr. Hull and Lord Lothian, October 7, 1940. See also Admiral Richardson's testimony in *Pearl Harbor Attack*, I, 268 ff.; Watson: *Chief of Staff: Prewar Plans and Preparations*, 117 ff.

[39] The White House statement was printed in the *Christian Science Monitor*, October 10, 1940. We have used also a British memo to the Department of State, October 16, 1940.

[40] The British proposals had been submitted on October 14. The details are given in Kittredge's MS. study on *United States-British Naval Coöperation*, Chapter XII. We have used also a memo of conversation between Mr. Welles and Mr. Butler, October 18, 1940, and a memo of conversation between Mr. Berle and Mr. Casey, the Australian Minister, October 21, 1940.

[41] Memo of conversation between Mr. Hornbeck and the British Chargé d'Affaires, October 28, 1940. By far the fullest account of these developments is in the Kittredge

They provide perhaps the most eloquent and conclusive evidence of the mistake committed by Ribbentrop and Matsuoka in supposing that the Tripartite Pact, by raising the specter of war in the Pacific, would distract the American Government from its efforts to support and strengthen Britain. The immediate result, certainly, was to evoke defiance on both sides of the Atlantic and to reinforce the American determination to stand by Britain come what come may. The Tripartite Pact, if anything, brought Americans to the realization that the forces threatening in Europe and Asia were leagued in a common purpose, and that the attainment of their objectives endangered American as well as British interests and security. As such, it was one more factor in bringing the two great democracies closer. Presently they were to approach, directly and frankly, the inescapable problem of military coöperation, which to many influential Americans already appeared as an eventual necessity.

4. JAPAN: COUNSELS OF CAUTION

From Tokyo's point of view one of the most important items in the negotiations for the Tripartite Pact was the one assuring Japan of German aid in furthering an agreement with Soviet Russia. Since the Japanese militarists were itching to capitalize on the German victory over the Netherlands and France by expanding Nippon's control over Southeast Asia and the Dutch Indies, a settlement of the long-standing and highly dangerous differences with the Soviet Union was recognized as indispensable before the advance to the south could be safely pressed. Ribbentrop did in fact exert himself to bring Moscow and Tokyo together, but by the autumn of 1940 the Kremlin had already become so suspicious of Nazi moves that it was anything but eager to fall in with Axis plans. Discussion of the course of Soviet policy as it affected both the British and German positions must be left to a later chapter. In the present context it is enough to point that by the time of Molotov's notable visit to Berlin (November 12, 1940), Tokyo's hope of an understanding with the Kremlin had already paled. Soviet obduracy, combined with the defiant attitude of the democracies, had drained the Tripartite Pact of much of the promise which, in September, had dazzled and deluded Matsuoka and his Army supporters.

A brief review of the development of Japanese policy in the six weeks between the ostentatious ceremonies in Berlin and the appearance of Molotov in the Nazi capital will provide the essential counterpart to the preceding discussion of British and American reaction to the pact. An appropriate point of departure is the *Tentative Plan for Policy towards the Southern Regions*, a Japanese memorandum dated October 4, 1940.[42] This exposition of Tokyo's objectives was based squarely on the expectation that Chiang

---

MS. study on *United States-British Naval Coöperation*, Chapter XII, but see also *Pearl Harbor Attack*, IV, 1931 ff.

[42] *Tokyo War Crimes Documents*, No. 837A.

Kai-shek and Nationalist China, duly impressed with the hopelessness of continuing the struggle against the prospective coalition of Japan, Germany, Italy and Soviet Russia, would accept Japanese terms and in fact participate in the construction of the Greater East Asia Co-Prosperity Sphere. Under these auspicious circumstances, and on the theory that the United States would be paralyzed by fear, Japan expected to have relatively little difficulty in establishing control over the entire Pacific west of Hawaii, with the exception of Guam and the Philippines, which could be left for later treatment. In Indo-China an independence movement was to be sponsored and the French forced to renounce sovereignty. A similar movement was to be launched in British Burma, after which Chiang Kai-shek, secretly supported by the Japanese Army, was to stage an invasion. Siam (Thailand) was to be brought into alliance with Japan, which could then use that strategically situated country to mount an attack on Singapore. Finally, during the battle for Singapore, the Japanese were to present demands on the Netherlands Indies which, if rejected, would serve as a pretext for military seizure. The chief demand was to be for the severance of the Indies from the Dutch Crown, and the acceptance of independence under Japanese aegis. Hongkong was to be turned over to a compliant China.

Tokyo could not be accused of failure to plan well in advance, for the captured Japanese records teem with documents of this kind. If nothing more, they convey a vivid sense of the extravagance of imperialist hopes and the urgency with which the national objectives were pursued. On the other hand, even the Japanese militarists were a fairly hardheaded lot; they calculated their capabilities carefully and, when the occasion demanded, were willing to step back and, albeit reluctantly, stay their hand. Had it been otherwise, they would have struck when France fell in June, 1940, or at least when the Nazis turned on Russia a year later, instead of waiting several more months before steeling themselves for the Pearl Harbor strike. Apparently the response to the Tripartite Pact induced Tokyo to bide its time. During the critical month of October, 1940, while Churchill dauntlessly proclaimed the reopening of the Burma Road and both London and Washington watched anxiously for the next Japanese move, there was no significant reaction from Tokyo. Neither Indo-China nor Singapore was attacked, nor were the Netherlands Indies occupied. On the contrary, Japanese activity all along the exposed southern front was surprisingly circumspect.

With regard to Indo-China the French themselves, and particularly the Governor General, Admiral Decoux, were convinced that the agreement of September 22, 1940, concluded amidst so much saber rattling, would be followed almost at once by demands for military bases in the southern part of the colony, or at least by demands that would result in exclusive Japanese control of the colony's economy. Again and again Admiral Decoux warned Washington of further Japanese designs and appealed for munitions to strengthen his feeble defenses. Nothing came of these pleas, partly because the American Government had little if anything to spare and feared that valuable matériel sent to Indo-China would eventually fall into Japanese hands, and partly because it thought the Vichy Government might well, as evidence of firm purpose, send to Saigon the ninety planes that were going to rack and ruin at Martinique. Unhappily Vichy could do nothing about the planes without German permission, which was not forthcoming.[43] The British, on their part, were so distrustful of Vichy that they intercepted a transport carrying four battalions of Senegalese troops from Jibuti to Indo-China, and refused to permit these reinforcements to reach Decoux, despite American representations to the Admiralty.[44]

Meanwhile the Indo-Chinese Government was confronted with a more immediate and direct military threat from Siam (Thailand), which had for some time been pressing its claims to two small territories on the right bank of the Mekong River. The French were convinced that the Bangkok Government was acting under the inspiration of Tokyo and that it aimed at the acquisition of all Laos and Cambodia. They therefore rejected the Siamese demands and, when the Siamese forces began military operations at the end of September, denuded the defenses of Tonkin in order to check if not prevent a Siamese advance to the Mekong.[45]

London and Washington, equally convinced that the Bangkok militarists were the tools of Tokyo, were much concerned by what seemed the impending doom of Indo-China, but took utterly divergent views about how best to save the situation. The American Minister at Bangkok, Mr. Grant, argued that if the Siamese acquired even a bit of Indo-Chinese territory, Japan would soon be in control not only of the French possessions, but of Siam as well. He therefore urged the State Department emphatically to use all its influence to moderate the Siamese demands. At the very least, he thought, the United States should point out to Bangkok the desirability of regaining its lost territories by direct and peaceful negotiation with Saigon, rather than through Japanese benevolence. At home, however, Mr. Hornbeck counseled that the most efficacious way to save Siam from Japanese control was to warn Tokyo that an assault on that country would result in armed support of the victim by the United States and Britain. Such advice was, as usual, postulated upon the idea that the Japanese would recoil before a firm attitude on the part of the democracies. Since Secretary Hull was by no

[43] See above, Chapter I. In addition to the sources there referred to, we have used memos of conversation between Mr. Welles and Ambassador Henry-Haye, October 9, November 25, December 11 and December 17, 1940, and a forty-page memo by the Division of Far Eastern Affairs (December, 1940) reviewing the development of the situation in Indo-China from September 19 to December, 1940. See further André Gaudel: *L'Indochine française en face du Japon* (Paris, 1947) and especially Admiral Decoux: *A la barre de l'Indochine*, 136 ff.

[44] Decoux, *A la barre de l'Indochine*, 136.

[45] Decoux: *A la barre de l'Indochine*, 132 ff.

means convinced of this and since it was difficult to envisage effective aid to a country as remote as Siam, nothing came of Hornbeck's exhortations.[46]

It is doubtful whether in any case the British Government would have adopted a firm policy on this issue. Sir Josiah Crosby, the British Minister at Bangkok, held strongly to the view that the French should acquiesce in the modest demands of the Siamese Government, if only to avoid much more costly sacrifices later. To oppose the Siamese claims would simply drive the country further into dependence on Japan and eventually provide Japan a base for attack on Singapore. Unless the United States and Britain were prepared to use military force to frustrate Japanese designs on Indo-China and Siam, Sir Josiah could see no alternative to a policy of appeasing the Siamese and so keeping Bangkok out of the Japanese camp even if Indo-China itself were doomed.[47]

The strangest thing about the Siamese imbroglio, and by far the most significant in the present context, was the fact that initially Tokyo appears to have had no hand in Bangkok's reclamations. According to the Japanese archives it was the Siamese leaders who, in September and October, sent delegates to Tokyo to solicit Japanese support. Not until November 5, 1940, did the Japanese decide to aid, and then on condition that Siam coöperate politically and economically in the establishment of the New Order in East Asia. Furthermore, Tokyo's decision seems to have been based in part at least on fear lest the Americans and British secure an alliance with Siam and use it as a base from which to threaten Japanese operations to the south. In any case, the Siamese Prime Minister, Pibul, accepted the Japanese terms and on November 11, 1940, it was agreed that Siam should moderate its demands in some respects, while Japan should act as mediator in negotiations with Indo-China.[48] Important though this agreement proved to be in the sequel, it can hardly be said that in the autumn of 1940 the Tokyo Government interjected itself precipitously into the Siamese-Indo-Chinese conflict.

Japanese negotiations with the Netherlands Indies, discussed in some detail in the preceding chapter, were perhaps more revealing of Tokyo's caution than any other episode of the month of October. While both London and Washington remained on tenterhooks for fear of Japanese aggression against these valuable and all but helpless possessions, the Dutch authorities resolutely refused to entertain the demands of the Japanese mission and referred it to the private interests (partly British and American) which controlled the production and exportation of such important commodities as oil.

[46] Tels. from Grant (Bangkok), October 4 and 11, 1940; memo of Hornbeck to Welles, October 28, 1940, suggesting a reply to British notes on Siam of October 25, 1940.

[47] British memos to the State Department, October 18 and 31, 1940; *Grew Diary* (*MS.*), November 13, 1940, recording the Ambassador's abhorrence of Crosby's attitude. See also Decoux's bitter remarks in his *A la barre de l'Indochine*, 132 ff.

[48] Excerpts from *Business Report of the South Seas Section* (*Tokyo War Crimes Documents*, No. 1411); tel. from Ambassador Ott to the German Foreign Office, November 21, 1940 (*ibid.*, No. 4042A).

While the Dutch Governor General successfully evaded all suggestions of a political nature, the oil companies refused to consider proposals for Japanese control and in fact drove a hard bargain even in the negotiation of new oil contracts. Mr. Kobayashi left Batavia after a preliminary agreement had been reached on October 16. The final contracts were signed on November 12, 1940, though they assured Japan only about one half of what it had originally demanded. True, the Japanese Cabinet had on October 25 again outlined its plans for the Indies, which were to be weaned of their economic ties with the west and made to accept membership in the Greater East Asia economy. But, like other Japanese programs, this one represented an ideal and little more. Not even London or Washington could complain of the outcome of the first round of negotiations at Batavia. The Dutch authorities had done a really noteworthy job.[49]

The Dutch achievement was the more remarkable because the local authorities could hope for little more than moral support from the British and Americans. Secretary Hull counseled them against acceding to Tokyo's demands, on the theory that if they yielded, they would be inviting attack.[50] But he did not suggest, even remotely, the possibility of American armed support in the event of invasion. Nor would the British make a firm commitment to assist the Indies against attack. Nevertheless, the Dutch gave assurance that they would resist invasion, even alone, if necessary.[51] Failing full and unequivocal assurances of support they preferred that the British and Americans abstain from measures so drastic as to provoke Japan and yet not drastic enough to deter that power. Had the British project for combined defense conversations at Singapore materialized, the picture would have been altered. But when Churchill's efforts to draw the United States naval forces into the western Pacific foundered, the Dutch had to rely on their own tact, skill, firmness and courage. Admirable as these qualities were, however, they produced success only because the Tokyo Government was not at the time prepared to force the issue. To the Japanese the Indies were perhaps the finest pearl in the prospective colonial booty. They had carefully mapped their objectives, but they were by no means foolhardy in pursuit of them. Not until the attack on Singapore had begun did they plan to send the Dutch an ultimatum. When, in late September, 1940, they set their hand to the pact with the victorious Nazis, their most extravagant desires seemed near fulfillment. But by mid-November disillusionment had set in. Tokyo still recoiled from open challenge of the democracies and for the time being, at least, held in abeyance its ambitious designs.

[49] See Hubertus van Mook: *The Netherlands Indies and Japan* (New York, 1944), 49 ff. We have used also the long review despatch of Mr. Achilles, dated November 27, 1940. The Japanese Cabinet decision of October 25, 1940, is in *Tokyo War Crimes Documents*, No. 2137G.

[50] Tel. to Foote (Batavia), October 5, 1940. See also Hull: *Memoirs*, I, 895 ff.

[51] Memo of conversation between Mr. Hornbeck and the Netherlands Minister Counselor, October 14, 1940; memo of conversation between Mr. Welles and the Dutch Minister, October 28, 1940.

CHAPTER III

Hitler and the West

1. A FATEFUL SETBACK

During the late summer and early autumn of 1940 Hitler concentrated his military effort on the subjugation of his one remaining enemy, Great Britain. At first it had seemed to him incredible that the British, once their French ally had sued for an armistice, could fail to recognize their cause as hopeless. It was only with great reluctance that he faced the problem of invading England, a problem which, because of British command of the seas, was patently a difficult if not impossible one. As the Nazis elaborated their plans, violent disagreements developed between the High Commands of the Navy and the Army as to how the operation should be mounted. Eventually Hitler himself intervened and saw to it that preparations were pushed with the utmost vigor. By early September the plans were ready and the key decisions made. There was to be a first assault wave of some 90,000 men, equipped with 4500 horses, 3900 carts, 2311 motorcycles, 26,000 bicycles, 650 tanks, 1500 automobiles and trucks, and 2600 mortars and guns. To transport this force 550 barges, 185 tugs and 370 motorboats were to be assembled in the Ostend area, and 45 steamers, 90 barges and 180 motorboats in the Le Havre-Cherbourg area. In addition the German Air Force (*Luftwaffe*) required 52 antiaircraft batteries, which involved an additional 800 barges, 35 steamers and 250 motorboats and tugs. With great difficulty the major part of this transport was assembled and concentrated in Belgian and French ports, where it soon became an alluring target for the Royal Air Force. Nonetheless, on September 3 Hitler tentatively fixed the date of the invasion as September 21, when there was a reasonably good chance of fair weather and a calm sea.[1]

[1] *Fuehrer Conferences on Matters Dealing with the German Navy* (Washington, 1947), 1940 (2), 1 ff., 5 ff., 9 ff.; statement of Prime Minister Atlee to Parliament, November 18, 1946 (*Fighting Forces*, February, 1947); Churchill: *Their Finest Hour*, Chapter XV; Anthony Martienssen: *Hitler and His Admirals* (New York, 1949), 69 ff.; Kurt Assmann: *Deutsche Schicksalsjahre* (Wiesbaden, 1950), 182 ff.

Though Prime Minister Churchill appears to have remained unconvinced that Hitler would actually embark upon so difficult and risky an enterprise, the British Chiefs of Staff evidently questioned his confidence and the British people throughout September definitely expected an invasion. On September 7 the "invasion imminent" signal was flashed to all British military units, and on September 11 Mr. Churchill himself warned the country that "no one should blind himself to the fact that a heavy, full-scale invasion of this Island is being prepared." However, British leaders were exuberantly confident of their ability to ward off the attack if it came. All possible defense preparations had been made and the Germans themselves were aware that they would meet vigorous resistance on the beaches and throughout the countryside. Considering the great superiority of the British at sea, the odds were heavily against the would-be invader. Mr. Churchill and his colleagues actually hoped, under the circumstances, that Hitler would take the chance. According to Ambassador Kennedy, they desired an invasion attempt "first, because they feel it will furnish a major setback for Hitler," and further "because it will give some clear indication of whether Hitler has a power beyond anything Britain can cope with." But by September the Prime Minister was persuaded that unless the Germans came very soon, they could not possibly do so during the autumn. On October 4 he cabled President Roosevelt in jocular vein: "The gent has taken off his clothes and put on his bathing suit, but the water is getting colder and there is an autumn nip in the air."[2]

Actually Hitler was convinced, as Churchill suspected, that the invasion could not be undertaken until the Nazi *Luftwaffe* had attained air superiority over southern England. Marshal Goering, the German air chief, was fully persuaded that his efficient and fanatically Nazi Air Force could subdue the British without an invasion, by which he therefore put little store. Since mid-August the *Luftwaffe* had applied its full resources to the task, first attacking British shipping and ports, then concentrating on crucial airfields, and finally (September 7) opening a vast and sustained assault on London and other industrial centers. In the course of September and October the attacks grew ever larger and more frequent. The valiant defense by the numerically inferior Royal Air Force and Anti-Aircraft Defence Command is a matter of history, but should not be allowed to obscure the fact that the margin between victory and defeat proved dangerously narrow. Experts are now generally agreed that if Goering had concentrated the German effort on the destruction of British airfields and fighter forces, he might have succeeded.

---

[2] Telegram of Churchill to the President, October 4, 1940; telegrams from Kennedy, September 11, 20, 1940; Atlee statement, as cited above; Churchill: *Blood, Sweat and Tears* (New York, 1941), 367 ff. (speech of September 11, 1940); Churchill: *Secret Session Speeches* (New York, 1946), 21 (speech of September 17, 1940); Churchill: *Their Finest Hour,* 310 ff., 457, 498. On German estimates of British strength see Martienssen: *Hitler and His Admirals,* 81, and Assmann: *Deutsche Schicksalsjahre,* 182 ff.

The constant change of German objective was certainly an important factor in Britain's salvation. But probably even more significant was the weather factor. During the critical six weeks from mid-August till the end of September the weather continued abnormally unfavorable for flying. Both Hitler and Goering were certain that ten days or two weeks of really good conditions would clinch the defeat of the British. Day by day they waited for a turn of fortune, but it did not come and eventually the rains and fogs of autumn set in. By the end of September the Germans had suffered such heavy losses at the hands of the R.A.F. that they had to resort to less effective night bombing attacks. At about the same time (October 1) the British were able to put the first radar warning systems into operation. Despite terrific punishment, the R.A.F. was able to maintain air superiority over southern England, and London and other important centers had managed to survive the harrowing ordeal of constant bomb and fire attacks.[3]

Pending the outcome of the epic air battle over southern England, Hitler again and again deferred action on the projected invasion, until finally he became convinced that no decision could be achieved during the current year. On October 12 the operation (*Sea Lion*) was postponed until the spring of 1941, though preparations were to be maintained as a matter of deception. Submarine attacks on British shipping, however, continued with unabated vigor and with astounding success, while air attacks on British cities were also maintained until the end of the year. It seems likely that Hitler was unwilling for some time to admit that his plans had gone awry. Until well into October he apparently deluded himself with the hope that the air attacks would yet force the British to their knees. Again and again he assured his Italian friends that Britain was to all intents and purposes already defeated. On October 4 he declared that the British people could not possibly endure the ordeal indefinitely, and on October 28 he expressed the conviction that British resistance would be broken even without an invasion: "When even the hopes on which England bases her propaganda have come to naught, we shall see an English collapse as rapid and complete as that which broke France." No doubt statements like this eventually came to be reflections of wishful thinking rather than rational estimates. But there is abundant evidence to show that the Fuehrer never really understood why the British refused to recognize and concede their defeat. It seemed to him the height of folly for Churchill and his colleagues to continue a struggle which was so patently hopeless.[4]

[3] Among numerous accounts J. M. Spaight's *The Battle of Britain* (London, 1941) is still one of the best. Churchill's account in *Their Finest Hour,* Book II, Chapter 1, is authoritative and dramatic, and rests upon the German records which became available with the end of the war. Of great interest and importance are also the official despatches of Air Chief Marshal Sir Hugh C. T. Dowding: *The Battle of Britain,* dated August 20, 1941 (supplement to the *London Gazette* of September 10, 1946), and of General Sir Frederick A. Pile: *The Anti-Aircraft Defence of the United Kingdom,* dated October 21, 1946 (supplement to the *London Gazette* of December 16, 1946).

[4] The records of German-Italian conversations (*Ciano's Diplomatic Papers,* London,

Whether or not Britain would be forced to submit continued to be the all-absorbing question during the dramatic weeks of September. On September 7, as the first great bombing attack was made on London, Ambassador Kennedy reported laconically: "There's hell to pay here tonight." The Ambassador was willing to admit that the London Government was "keeping a stiff upper lip," but he could not believe that Britain had either the leadership or the productive capacity to withstand the punishment meted out by the Nazis. He was sure that Mr. Churchill and his friends were hoping and praying every minute that something would happen to bring the United States into the war, and he was tortured by the thought that in such an eventuality the American people would have to carry the whole burden of an essentially hopeless conflict.[5]

Major General Delos C. Emmons, of the United States Army Air Forces, carried away from his inspection trip to England an almost equally depressing conviction. He considered the Royal Air Force the finest in the world, but thought it too weak to prevent an invasion. Since General Emmons felt that the United States could not possibly permit Britain to go under, it seemed to him inescapable that America should be in the war at an early date. On the other hand, Brigadier General George V. Strong, who in June had been highly skeptical of Britain's future, returned to Washington on September 20 after many conferences with Mr. Churchill and other British leaders. He reported them supremely confident, though frank to admit their dependence on American aid: "They are going about their job coolly, calmly and a bit grimly, with a firm determination that if they cannot win out they will go on fighting to the bitter end and then go down with the flag flying." Public morale was high and the R.A.F. in good shape, despite the lack of combat crews. Though the shipping situation was serious and the financial position bad, production was holding up and might well improve during the winter. All told, General Strong was persuaded that if the invasion did not take place by October 15, the situation would probably take a turn for the better.[6]

These divergences of view among competent American observers with authoritative information from the British side are the best evidence of the uncertainty and doubt that clouded the international scene as the fury of the Nazi air attack threatened Britain with defeat and ruin. The United States Government, of course, had long since been committed to aid Britain

---

1948, pp. 386, 389 ff., 395 ff., 403) reflect the gradual but never complete German disillusionment. The record of Hitler's conference with his generals on September 14, 1940 (*Halder Diary*), is also revealing.

[5] Tels. from Kennedy, September 7, 11, 19, 20, 27, 1940.

[6] Strong report, dated September 25, 1940, copy of which was sent to the State Department on October 5, 1940. A summary of the report was published at the time (see *Bulletin of International News,* XVII (2), 1335-36); *Stimson Diary (MS.),* September 23, 1940.

to the best of its ability and had only recently demonstrated its hope and faith by turning over fifty destroyers to the Royal Navy. On the other hand, the Japanese Government, when it concluded the Tripartite Pact with Germany and Italy (September 27), must have done so in the conviction that Britain was doomed and that it was high time for Japan to assure itself of an adequate share of the imperial spoils. In contrast to these great powers there were others, notably Soviet Russia, Vichy France and Franco's Spain, whose policy remained fluid. The two latter, in particular, were obliged as a matter of urgency to arrive at an estimate of Britain's chances and of Hitler's probable further courses of action. Neither France nor Spain felt free to commit itself fully one way or the other. The story of their maneuverings is as important as it was dramatic, for together these two powers were to inflict yet another setback on the then supposedly invincible Hitler.

2. The Nazi Plan for a Flank Attack

Like other European conquerors before him, Adolf Hitler thought essentially in continental terms. He laid his plans and pursued his preparations for the invasion of England without inner conviction and, instead of devoting himself entirely to that compelling problem, turned his thoughts to an eventual attack on the Soviet Union. Given this state of mind, it is not surprising that the Fuehrer was slow to grasp the tremendous importance of the submarine war, or that he staked such high hopes on the subjugation of Britain through air attack.

Nonetheless, Hitler could hardly overlook the importance of solving the British problem, the more so as it became ever more obvious that the United States intended to give all possible material support to the British cause. Though fully convinced that the full weight of American aid could not be brought to bear for at least another two years, Hitler thought it expedient to engineer the Tripartite Pact, which he and Ribbentrop were persuaded would serve as a deterrent to active American intervention in European affairs. In like fashion he hoped to nip in the bud any idea of Soviet support for Britain by rapidly concentrating some forty German divisions along the Eastern Front.[7]

In keeping with the policy of political intimidation as embodied in the Tripartite Pact, Hitler planned to associate all or most of the remaining "independent" governments of Europe with the great coalition under Nazi leadership. His hope was that when once countries like Spain, Yugoslavia, Bulgaria, Rumania and even Soviet Russia had been bound together in one inclusive pact, the British could not help but recognize that the continent was united against them and that further resistance would be futile. Better than anything else, this fine-spun scheme reveals Hitler's inability to under-

[7] All this was fully explained to Mussolini and Ciano at the Brenner Pass meeting of October 4, 1940 (*Ciano's Diplomatic Papers*, 395 ff.).

stand the psychology of other nations, more particularly that of the Anglo-Saxons.[8]

Admiral Raeder and the High Command of the German Navy were much better schooled than Hitler in the principles and problems of global conflict. Again and again they warned of the almost insuperable difficulties involved in an invasion of England in the face of vastly superior naval power, and stressed to the Fuehrer the urgent need for building more submarines so as to expand the campaign against British shipping. As the prospects for *Sea Lion* grew dim, Raeder redoubled his efforts to convince the Fuehrer that the British position must be attacked indirectly and that precautions should be taken against the day when the United States openly joined forces with Britain, which was and would remain Germany's chief enemy. The Admiral's thoughts ranged far and wide. He foresaw eventual British or American occupation of the Spanish and Portuguese Atlantic islands (Azores, Canaries, Cape Verdes) and urged that steps be taken to forestall such seizure and at the same time secure for Germany certain bases essential for the interdiction of British commerce from South America and South Africa. To the same end he argued the great importance of French West Africa and particularly the admirable port of Dakar. Above all, he pleaded the necessity of resolving the Mediterranean question in the near future. The Mediterranean, he reminded Hitler, was considered by the British to be the pivot of their world empire, and they would no doubt soon concentrate their efforts on attempting to knock out Italy and secure complete control of the area. It was therefore imperative that the Axis drive the British from that sea:

Control of the Mediterranean area is of vital importance to the position of the Central Powers in southeastern Europe, Asia Minor, Arabia, Egypt and the African area. Unlimited sources for raw materials would be guaranteed. New and strategically favorable bases for further operations against the British Empire would be won. The loss of Gibraltar would mean crucial difficulties for British import traffic from the South Atlantic. Preparations for this operation must be begun at once, so that they are completed before the U.S.A. steps in. It should not be considered of secondary importance, but as one of the main blows against Britain.

Therefore Gibraltar must be taken and control of the Suez Canal secured:

An advance from Suez through Palestine and Syria as far as Turkey is necessary. If we reach that point, Turkey will be in our power. The Russian problem will then appear in a different light. Fundamentally, Russia is afraid of Germany. It is doubtful whether an advance against Russia from the north will be necessary.[9]

By the end of September, as hopes for an invasion of England were fad-

---

[8] *Halder Diary*, October 8, 15, 1940.
[9] *Fuehrer Conferences*, 1940 (2), 17 ff. (conference of September 6, 1940); 24 ff. (conference of September 26, 1940). See also Kurt Assmann: *Deutsche Schicksalsjahre*, 340 ff.

ing, Hitler felt obliged to agree with "the general trend" of Raeder's thought. But he was acutely aware of the many obstacles that beset this new strategy. For one thing, the Germans had recognized the Mediterranean as the Italian sphere of activity, and the Italians, after countless delays, had just executed the first operations of their campaign against Egypt. The British, greatly outnumbered, had fallen back, and on September 16 Marshal Graziani had advanced to Sidi Barrani. The Germans doubted whether their Fascist partners could ever get to Suez under their own steam, and suspected that the Italians would reject German aid. The question of the eastern Mediterranean and Egypt therefore necessitated further negotiations with Mussolini. Gibraltar, in turn, involved Spain, as did the projected acquisition of bases in the Canaries, while Dakar and West Africa called for some sort of settlement with Vichy France. How and in what order to approach these various issues was itself a problem of some magnitude.

Hitler was at his best when, by threats of military force, he could dragoon lesser powers into doing his bidding. When confronted with more delicate and complicated situations he was often at a loss as to how to proceed. The rather extensive records of his diplomatic maneuverings during the autumn of 1940 reflect the confusion of mind and deed that plagued him and leave the historian in a quandary as to how to unravel the tangled skein.

Apparently Hitler and his generals were first attracted by the idea of capturing Gibraltar and securing bases on the Canary Islands through air operations. The second of these undertakings seemed relatively simple in view of the power and achievements of the *Luftwaffe,* while the first provided a challenge worthy of the masters of land warfare. Gibraltar was poorly defended and the Germans had no doubt that through air attack and the use of special troops they could repeat, on a larger and more spectacular scale, their dramatic assault on the Belgian fortress of Eben Emael. As early as July 31 the Fuehrer had decided on such an attack and to this decision he was to cling tenaciously throughout the following months.[10]

The Gibraltar plan entailed an agreement with Spain, whose consent to the occupation of the Canary Islands by German air forces was also desirable, if not absolutely necessary. Hitler therefore prepared himself for discussions with Generalissimo Franco. Since the latter had expressed willingness to enter the war on the Axis side, and since Hitler was perfectly ready eventually to hand over Gibraltar to the Spaniards, there was every reason to suppose that the necessary arrangements could be made. True, the Spaniards had advanced extensive, not to say extravagant, colonial claims, but Hitler felt no compunction about promising them what was necessary, even though in the end he might not want to live up to his promises.[11]

The actual course of events proved profoundly disappointing to the

[10] *Fuehrer Conferences,* 1940 (2), 12 ff.
[11] *Halder Diary,* September 14, 1940 (record of a conference with Hitler).

Fuehrer, who was presently persuaded by Admiral Raeder and others that an arrangement with conquered France might be easier and more profitable. Eventually that line of action also proved abortive and the entire plan went bankrupt. Hitler was to learn that the world at large was not misled by his confident utterances about the complete but unacknowledged defeat of Britain. To many it appeared that the war might be long and that ultimately Britain, supported by the United States, might emerge as victor. Caution and procrastination were in order and wisdom dictated that irrevocable commitments be avoided. Franco Spain and Vichy France both provide instructive examples of crafty maneuvering in the midst of conflict. Incredible though it may seem, Franco and Pétain inflicted on Hitler setbacks so serious that, indirectly at least, they helped to provoke a shift of the war from the West to the East.

3. THE TEMPTATION OF FRANCO

Although it is impossible, for lack of evidence, to speak of Spanish policy in this period with any degree of finality, it is certain that Franco's sympathies lay with Nazi Germany and Fascist Italy. The Caudillo knew that his country, worn out by the civil war and in dire economic distress, was unequal to further military operations, yet he and his Falangist supporters cherished ambitious designs for territorial expansion which included Gibraltar, French Morocco, the Oran Department of Algeria, and various lesser areas of West Africa. On the defeat of France, the Spanish Government had promptly taken control of the International Zone of Tangier and had opened a brisk diplomatic campaign to extract concessions from France in Morocco. These latter efforts had met with no significant success and Franco must have realized that it was not enough for his purposes to have Spain's enemies defeated by others. To acquire a suitable share of the spoils, Spain would have to take active part in the conflict. Like Mussolini earlier, Franco was therefore intent on entering the war on Germany's side, but only when satisfied that the end was drawing near and that no great military effort would be involved. As conditions for intervention he would, of course, require advance assurance that Spanish claims would be satisfied, as well as the provision of munitions and food without which hostilities were simply impossible. Actually Spain was heavily dependent for essential imports on Britain, the United States and other countries. In order to prevent a rupture of this trade, it was imperative to act with the utmost circumspection, not to say duplicity.

In the summer of 1940 it seemed to Franco that the moment for action had come. Britain's fate seemed already sealed and a recasting of colonial empires was clearly at hand. In early August the Caudillo therefore renewed with urgency his earlier suggestions to both Hitler and Mussolini that Spain enter the war in order to attain its national objectives. The Fuehrer, however, was well aware of Spain's weakness and ill-impressed by Franco's craving for territory. Since at the time he had no particular need of assistance, he looked upon Spanish intervention as a liability rather than an asset.[12]

The Nazi attitude underwent a change as the plan for invading England was abandoned and the strategy of a flank attack on British trade routes was being evolved. Hitler therefore agreed to a visit to Berlin by Señor Serrano Suñer, brother-in-law of the Caudillo, chief of the Spanish propaganda machine, and leader of the extremist element of the Falange. Serrano Suñer was a fanatical nationalist, an enemy of democracy and an ardent admirer of totalitarianism. He made no secret of his violent Anglophobia, nor did he hesitate to avow his devotion to Nazi Germany. These sentiments were not, of course, in conflict with his patriotic hopes. He expected Hitler to help his friends, and he was not unmindful of the fact that the Fuehrer, if Spain failed him, might take advantage of his military strength and position to reduce Spain as he had reduced France.[13]

Serrano Suñer, with a large entourage, was received in Berlin on September 16, 1940, with the usual pomp. For ten days he carried on discussions with Hitler and Ribbentrop, after which he proceeded to Italy to await the outcome of conferences between the Fuehrer and the Duce with regard to Spanish claims. Ribbentrop, bland as ever, began the conversation by assuming that Spain would intervene in the war whenever called upon to do so. But his visitor carefully avoided setting a date and concentrated on the exposition of Spanish colonial claims and requirements in the way of munitions, food and fuel. The German Foreign Minister countered by setting forth Germany's own aspirations in Africa, which included a couple of bases on the Moroccan coast and another base in the Canary Islands. These suggestions met with a cold reception and no meeting of minds was achieved. Hitler, in his own conversations with Serrano Suñer, confined himself to an analysis of military questions connected with the seizure of Gibraltar and carefully abstained from controversial territorial issues. It seemed to him incredible that Spain should fail to appreciate the rare opportunity to join the victor and attain an appropriate place in the new European and African order. All in all, the spectacular visit of the Falangist leader left both sides with disagreeable impressions.[14]

[12] This phase of the Spanish situation is treated at some length in the preceding volume of this series, *The Challenge to Isolation,* Chapter XXI.

[13] In his apologia: *Entre les Pyrenées et Gibraltar* (Geneva, 1947), 145 ff., Ramon Serrano Suñer makes much of this consideration.

[14] *The Spanish Government and the Axis* (Washington, 1946), No. 4 (German record of Serrano Suñer's conference with Hitler on September 17, 1940); No. 5 (Franco's letter to Hitler of September 17, 1940); on the German side see further *Nazi Conspiracy and Aggression,* IV, No. 1842-PS, and Paul Schmidt: *Statist auf diplomatischer Bühne* (Bonn, 1949), 497. On the Spanish side Serrano Suñer's own account (*Entre les Pyrenées et Gibraltar,* Chapter X) generally confirms the German records. The episode is systematically treated in Herbert Feis: *The Spanish Story* (New York, 1948), Chapters XIII and XIV.

Initially Hitler seems to have been willing to grant such Spanish demands as seemed necessary, if only in order to get on with the Gibraltar operation which, incidentally, he had discussed in great detail with Franco's emissary. But on second thought indignation got the better of him. Spain was so weak and could offer so little, yet Franco's demands were beyond all reason. Besides, he reflected that satisfaction of Spanish claims might conflict with Italian demands and French interests. De Gaulle, supported by the British, had just attempted an assault on Dakar, only to meet with vigorous and effective resistance from the Vichy Governor. Evidently the French were determined to defend their empire against the British. If they were to learn that Morocco and part of Algeria were to be turned over to the Spaniards, they might well decide to throw in their lot with the British and face the consequences. All in all, it was hard to see how the clash of interests between Italy, France and Spain could be resolved through anything but a grandiose fraud. The Fuehrer was undecided as to the best course. Obviously the first step was to review the problem with his Italian partner. To that end the two dictators arranged to meet at the Brenner Pass on October 4, 1940.[15]

While the special trains stood in the snow-clad Alpine pass, the two dictators conferred for hours on their future strategy. Hitler made the most of his opportunity to lecture his colleague on the military situation. Britain, he assured him profusely, was already defeated. Nonetheless, it was important to press operations in the Mediterranean and in Africa. Germany would be ready to aid the Italians with tanks and dive bombers in their further campaign against Egypt. At the same time, the attack on Gibraltar must be arranged. Germany would do what it could to meet the Spanish requirements, but Hitler left no shadow of doubt that he considered Spanish colonial claims outrageous. For one thing, they conflicted with Germany's own need for bases in Morocco. Furthermore, satisfaction of Spanish claims by the Axis would undoubtedly precipitate a British occupation of the Canary Islands and the defection of French North Africa to de Gaulle and the British: "that would be serious and would involve the Axis in the extension of its own operational fronts." On balance, it might become necessary to undertake the Gibraltar operation without Spanish coöperation. In fact, it might be more advantageous to attempt an agreement with Vichy France, which had shown some inclination to participate in the war against Britain and might be brought into the great continental coalition which for the moment was the Fuehrer's dazzling vision.

Mussolini was given little opportunity to dissent. He, too, was estranged by the exorbitance of the Spanish demands, but his chief preoccupation was clearly with Hitler's proposal to seek an arrangement with France. He re-

---

[15] The *Halder Diary*, September 23, October 2 and 3, 1940, reflects Hitler's changing mood. See further *Ciano's Diplomatic Papers*, 389 ff. (conference of Ribbentrop, Mussolini and Ciano on September 19, 1940); the *Ciano Diaries*, 293 ff.; and *The Spanish Government and the Axis*, No. 6 (interview of Hitler with Ciano, September 28, 1940).

minded the Fuehrer that Italy hoped to secure French territory around Nice, the whole of Tunisia, Corsica and French Somaliland, and suggested that the only solution was to conclude peace with France. Obviously the aspirations of Italy and Spain, both burning with zeal to dismember the French Empire, presented the Fuehrer with a hopeless problem of reconciliation. The Brenner meeting ended on an inconclusive note. Hitler was to make an effort to reduce the Spanish and French problems to a common denominator. He was to try to arrange Spanish intervention in the war and at the same time persuade the French to make the necessary concessions to Italy and to join the grand alliance against Britain. This undertaking was indeed Herculean.[16]

Hitler's plan was to meet personally with Franco and Pétain and work out a deal along these lines: France was to be brought into the Axis in return for a guarantee of Algeria, Morocco and West Africa. On the other hand, France was to accept the cession of at least Corsica and Tunisia to Italy, and the loss of Alsace-Lorraine and various territories in Equatorial Africa to Germany. How Spain's demands were to be met is not revealed by the record. Evidently Hitler hoped to secure Spanish intervention and cooperation against Gibraltar in return for that much desired fortress and for the assurance that in the final peace settlement other Spanish aspirations would be realized. Recognizing that these proposals would probably not appeal to Franco, Hitler virtually made up his mind to act against Gibraltar on his own.[17]

During the next two weeks attention was focused on plans for the Fuehrer's coming conferences. The original arrangement provided that discussions be opened with Spain, after which conversations should be initiated with the French—first with M. François-Poncet, former French Ambassador to Berlin and currently French Red Cross representative in Paris, and thereafter with Marshal Pétain himself. A little later it seems to have been decided that Hitler should confer first with Pétain, then with Franco, and then again with Pétain. Finally, however, arrangements were made for the Fuehrer to meet Franco at the Spanish border soon after October 20, and to confer with Pétain immediately thereafter.[18]

Meanwhile the Caudillo took an important step in preparation for the coming negotiations. On October 17 London and Washington were shocked to learn that the Spanish Foreign Minister, Juan Beigbeder, had been suddenly replaced by Serrano Suñer, fresh from his visits to Germany and Italy. Beigbeder had been well regarded by the democracies and was credited with having faith in the eventual victory of Britain. It was he who had been carrying on the delicate negotiations by which Spain hoped to assure itself

---

[16] *Ciano's Diplomatic Papers,* 395 ff. (record of the Brenner conference). The *Halder Diary,* October 7, 8, 15, 1940, throws much light on the discussions.

[17] *Halder Diary,* October 8, 11, 15, 1940.

[18] *Halder Diary,* October 8, 15, 16, 1940.

of vital supplies of food and fuel, in return for which London and Washington hoped the Madrid Government could be kept from intervention in the war on the Axis side. Serrano Suñer's views were well known and his advent to power as Foreign Minister could be taken only as presaging the identification of Spain with the Nazi cause. At the very least it could be predicted that a new phase of the Spanish question was about to open. Pending the outcome of the meeting of Hitler and Franco, the western capitals waited anxiously for indications of future developments.

4. The Enigma of Pétain

Despite its defeat and consequent military impotence, France came to play an important role in international politics during the autumn of 1940. This was so largely because the French, even after the British attack on their Fleet at Mers-el-Kebir on July 3, 1940, retained considerable sea power, and perhaps even more because France possessed a huge and strategically important colonial empire in Africa. The North African territories were obviously vital to the control of the western Mediterranean, while the West African possessions lay on the flank of some of the most active trade routes. The Equatorial colonies, in turn, were indispensable for the development of new air lines from West African bases to the Sudan and Egypt.

Had Hitler grasped the full strategic significance of North Africa in June, 1940, it is altogether likely that he would have pushed his advance through Spain and across the Straits of Gibraltar. Having failed to do so, he was soon obliged to grapple with the problem of rectifying his earlier error and more particularly of preventing the British, supported by the United States, from taking advantage of the situation. There was certainly danger that they might do so, for American authorities were keenly aware of the closeness of West Africa to the bulge of Brazil and were as much concerned about the Azores as they were about Greenland and Iceland.[19] In August, 1940, the decision had been made to reopen the American consulate at Dakar, chiefly for the purpose of watching over the activities of supposed German agents in that important town. Consul Thomas C. Wasson had arrived at his post on September 15, 1940, on the eve of the Gaullist-British attack.[20]

Mr. Churchill, for his part, needed no indoctrination on the significance of West Africa and the Mediterranean. He did everything possible to build up the defense of Egypt, even at a time when men and material were badly

[19] Replying to Professor S. E. Morison, who had written urging that the Azores be included in the Western Hemisphere, the President remarked: "You are dead right about the Azores, but, though I, as a former officer of the American Geographical Society, have tried to put them into the Western Hemisphere, they insist on missing out by several hundred miles. Diplomatically you are dead wrong—practically you are dead right." (*Roosevelt Papers:* Secretary's File, Box 66—letter of September 6, 1940.)

[20] Thomas C. Wasson: "The Mystery of Dakar" (*American Foreign Service Journal,* April, 1943).

needed for protection of the mother country. Furthermore, the British lent all aid and comfort to General de Gaulle in his efforts to bring about the defection of the French African colonies and supported his plans for an attack on the crucial Dakar base. A British estimate, which was communicated to Admiral Ghormley, the American "Special Observer" in London, recognized that the Germans might at any time attack through Spain and seize bases like Gibraltar, Casablanca, Dakar and even the Atlantic islands. Somewhat later General Strong reported, on his return from London, that the British assumed that sooner or later the Axis powers would move into both Spain and Portugal.[21]

While the British and Germans both cast covetous eyes on the Atlantic islands, neither dared move for fear of provoking action by the other and even more of driving Spain and Portugal into the opposing camp. Meanwhile the Free French under de Gaulle had succeeded in establishing their control over the French colonies of Chad, Cameroon and Equatorial Africa. Plans were already far advanced for the attack on Dakar, where it was believed, erroneously, that the Germans were entrenching themselves. At first success seemed almost certain. Mr. Churchill was already dreaming of extending the Gaullist movement to North Africa, which was to be put under the command of General Catroux, deposed Governor General of French Indo-China, who arrived in London on September 17.[22] President Roosevelt was fully informed of the Dakar project and, according to Lord Lothian, was enthusiastic about it, saying that he hoped the British could establish themselves firmly in West Africa before it was too late.[23]

The attack on Dakar took place on September 23-25, 1940, and resulted in a complete victory for the defenders. Governor General Pierre Boisson turned a deaf ear to all proposals that he join the Free French. Through leakage of the news in London he had been forewarned of the operation and had been reinforced by three cruisers and three destroyers which the British, through failure to coördinate intelligence, had permitted to pass through the Straits of Gibraltar on September 11. Although General de Gaulle, personally in command of the operation, was inclined to break off the action when it became clear that he would have to fight his compatriots, the British insisted on an attempt to wring victory from what was already a hopeless situation. But two days of a heavy artillery duel between sea and land proved so costly that the enterprise had to be given up. One result of the

---

[21] The estimate presented to Admiral Ghormley was dated August 29, 1940 (Kittredge MS. study on *United States-British Naval Coöperation*); General Strong's report was dated September 25, 1940.

[22] Churchill: *Their Finest Hour*, 474, 665; General Georges Catroux: *Dans la bataille de Méditerranée* (Paris, 1949), 23 ff.

[23] Letter of Lord Lothian to Sir Samuel Hoare, October 19, 1940 (quoted in Hoare: *Complacent Dictator*, New York, 1947, p. 81); see also Churchill's message to Roosevelt, September 23, 1940 (quoted in Churchill: *Their Finest Hour*, 487-88); Jacques Soustelle: *De Londres à Alger* (Paris, 1947), 163.

unfortunate episode was the development of friction between de Gaulle and his British supporters. The Free French leader did not return to England, but departed for Equatorial Africa, where he devoted himself to the establishment of a Free French territorial state in the hope that thereby the dissident French could acquire a more independent status.[24]

The combined British-Free French attack on Dakar had the important effect of deepening the cleavage already existing in the Vichy Government between the violently anti-British faction and those who still hoped to salvage something of the old alliance. Laval and his adherents had for some time been predicting the victory of Germany over Britain and preaching the necessity of winning the good graces of the victor even at the expense of substantial sacrifices. The Vice Premier had been doing his utmost to establish his own contacts with the Germans and had evidently given Abetz, the German representative in Paris, unauthorized assurances that Vichy France was prepared to join in the war against Britain, at least to the extent of military operations in Africa. The defection of the French colonies in Central Africa and particularly the attack on Dakar were adduced by him as conclusive evidence that the British were intent on taking over the French colonial empire, and much was made of the danger that the Germans themselves might take countermeasures if the Vichy Government failed to take a strong line. After Dakar Laval's demands, reinforced by Admiral Darlan, proved irresistible. For two days (September 24, 25) French planes from North Africa bombed Gibraltar. Had Laval had his way, the Vichy Government would have declared war on Britain in reprisal for the attempt to seize West Africa.[25]

Although Laval pursued his policy aggressively, the opposing forces at first succeeded in maintaining themselves. M. Baudouin, the Foreign Minister, and the Foreign Office staff almost without exception, favored an effort to improve relations with London. General Weygand, the Minister for Defense (until September 5), M. Bouthillier, the Minister for Finance, and a number of other government officials supported this policy. These men feared that Hitler might succeed in arriving at a settlement with Britain at France's expense. They were well aware of Italy's claims and were unwilling to overlook the harshness of Nazi action in Alsace-Lorraine and the northern

---

[24] Of the numerous accounts of the Dakar affair see Churchill: *Their Finest Hour,* Book II, Chapter IX. On the French side see Vice-amiral Muselier: *De Gaulle contre le gaullisme* (Paris, 1946), Chapter XI; Soustelle: *De Londres à Alger,* Chapter IV; Maurice Martin du Gard: *La carte impériale* (Paris, 1949), Chapter VI; François Charles-Roux: *Cinq mois tragiques aux Affaires étrangères* (Paris, 1949), 323 ff.; General Catroux: *Dans la bataille de Méditerranée* (Paris, 1949), 20 ff., states that even before the attack on Dakar, Churchill was dissatisfied with de Gaulle's leadership and tried to induce Catroux to head the movement.

[25] The earlier phases of the Laval policy are discussed in the preceding volume, *The Challenge to Isolation.* See further Charles-Roux: *Cinq mois tragiques,* 206 ff., 302, 328 ff.; *The Private Diaries of Paul Baudouin,* 224, 246, 249; *Pétain et les allemands: mémorandum d'Abetz* (Paris, 1948), 14 ff.

départements. In short, they saw little prospect of ever being well treated by the Germans and firmly believed that France's future depended on a victory of Britain, supported by the United States. Since some of them were by no means convinced that Britain was doomed, they were willing to ignore hostile acts dictated by the necessities of war. France's urgent need for imports from the African colonies and the related need for securing some relaxation of the British blockade provided them further arguments.[26]

The position of Marshal Pétain between these conflicting groups may never be completely clarified. The aged Chief of State regarded the domain of policy as peculiarly his own. He was extremely jealous of his prerogatives and notoriously secretive toward all his advisers, none of whom could ever be sure that he enjoyed full confidence. So much, however, seems fairly certain: that Pétain had initially expected Britain to be quickly defeated and had therefore looked upon the armistice as a purely temporary agreement. Despite the grievances against the British which he had voiced so volubly in June and July, the Marshal appears to have been unwilling to take the initiative toward a complete break. German disregard of some clauses of the armistice and particularly the expulsion of the French population from Lorraine probably ended any illusions of a peace "between gentlemen and soldiers" that he may have originally envisaged. We may take it that Pétain, while intensely disliking the maneuvers of Laval, felt the need for seeking some adjustment with the Germans, without the intention, however, of allowing relations with Britain and by derivation with the United States to become irreparable.[27]

Initially Laval was unable to report much progress in negotiations for the simple reason that the Germans showed little interest or trust in his program. When, at the end of August, the Vice Premier succeeded in securing an interview with General von Brauchitsch, the Commander in Chief of the German Army, he met with nothing but contempt in response to his offer of French aid against the British.[28] But the defection of the French Central African colonies, together with the growing Nazi realization of the importance of Africa and the Mediterranean for the further conduct of the war against Britain, soon brought a change. It is hardly necessary to recall that by September, 1940, Admiral Raeder was making an issue of the French African colonies, warning that the British or Americans might occupy the Atlantic islands and even take over West Africa:

[26] Charles-Roux: *Cinq mois tragiques,* 178 ff., 206 ff., gives the best exposition of this viewpoint, but see also Louis-Dominique Girard: *Montoire: Verdun diplomatique* (Paris, 1948), 137 ff.

[27] On Pétain's attitude see Charles-Roux: *Cinq mois tragiques,* 185; Général Maxime Weygand: *Mémoires: Rappelé au service* (Paris, 1950), 382; Girard: *Montoire,* 109 ff., 137 ff.

[28] *The Private Diaries of Paul Baudouin,* 224; Charles-Roux: *Cinq mois tragiques,* 301.

In the French possessions in Equatorial Africa there is an open break with Pétain's Government and a swing over to General de Gaulle. There is danger that unrest and revolt might spread to the French West African colonies. The economic situation in the colonies, particularly as regards foodstuffs, is used by Britain as a means of exerting pressure. An agreement between the colonies and Britain, and revolt against France, would jeopardize our own chances of controlling the African area; the danger exists that strategically important West African ports might be used for British convoy activities and that we might lose a most valuable source of supplies for Europe. The danger of an attack on the part of the U.S.A. is not entirely out of the question, in view of the possibilities for such action.

Far-sighted measures are necessary to counteract any development of this kind. Therefore the Naval Staff agrees in principle to sending French naval forces to the areas threatened; to the resumption of merchant traffic between the colonies and neutral countries by means of French and neutral vessels, in order to alleviate economic difficulties; and to attempt to re-establish merchant shipping between France and her colonies.[29]

Somewhat later, just as the attack on Dakar drew to its end, Raeder returned to the charge:

The question of Northwest Africa is also of decisive importance.

All indications are that Britain, with the help of de Gaulle's France, and possibly also of the U.S.A., wants to make this region a center of resistance and to set up air bases for attack against Italy. Britain will try to prevent us from gaining a foothold in the African colonies.

In this way Italy would be defeated.

Therefore action must be taken against Dakar. . . . The possibility of action on the part of France against the British is therefore very promising. It is desirable that support be given to the French, possibly by permitting use of the *Strasbourg*.

It would be expedient to station air forces in Casablanca in the near future. In general, it appears important to coöperate with France in order to protect Northwest Africa—after certain concessions have been made to Germany and Italy. The occupation of France makes it possible to compel her to maintain and defend the frontiers advantageous to us.[30]

Apparently the Dakar episode clinched the matter so far as Hitler was concerned. He agreed with Raeder's reasoning and, according to the record:

He will have to decide whether coöperation with France or with Spain is more profitable; probably with France, since Spain demands a great deal (French Morocco), but offers little. France must guarantee beforehand to fulfill certain German and Italian demands; an agreement could then be reached regarding the African colonies. Britain and the U.S.A. must be excluded from Northwest Africa.[31]

The flaw in this program was that Italy's claims upon France would have to be settled if Germany were to escape the danger of losing one friend in

---

[29] *Fuehrer Conferences,* 1940 (2), 17 ff. (conference with Hitler on September 6, 1940).

[30] *Fuehrer Conferences,* 1940 (2), 24 ff. (conference of September 26, 1940).

[31] *Ibid.*

the process of seeking another. Hence the meeting of the two dictators at the Brenner Pass (October 4, 1940). On that occasion Hitler did his best to convince his colleague that to grant the Spanish demands would mean a British occupation of the Canary Islands and the defection of North Africa to de Gaulle. He assured Mussolini that there were indications that France could be brought into the anti-British coalition, and that he had no intention of according France a role of primary importance in the new Europe. The Duce offered no direct opposition, but made clear that Italy stood by its territorial demands and suggested that the best solution might be a formal peace settlement with the French.[32]

It remained to be seen, then, whether the Vichy Government would accept a peace settlement which, while guaranteeing French possession of certain African colonies, would involve the cession of Nice, Corsica and Tunisia to Italy and the loss of Alsace-Lorraine, two bases in Morocco, the former German colonies (Togo and Cameroon), and Equatorial Africa to Germany. Abetz, the German representative in Paris, reported that such a deal could probably be made with Laval, especially if the Germans held out the hope of eventual compensation from the British spoils. True, Abetz suspected that French requests for permission to rearm part of the Navy and build up the North African forces might conceal eventual hostile designs. He also suspected collusion between Vichy and the Free French organization in London. But on balance he held that an agreement could be advantageously made without too much risk. Hitler himself seems to have felt that France would never be Germany's friend, that the dream of revenge would revive on the earliest possible occasion, and that eventually France and Britain would join forces again. But the chance had to be taken, and so arrangements were made for a conference between Hitler and Pétain toward the end of October.[33]

For weeks before and after the Dakar episode the Vichy Foreign Office was tortured by anxiety over French relations with Britain. The British blockade raised the specter of serious want during the coming winter, while British support of de Gaulle in bringing about the defection of the French colonies brought real danger that the Germans might insist on taking over the defense of North and West Africa themselves. Through contacts between the French and British Embassies at Madrid, M. Baudouin had several times warned the British of the probability of German occupation of the colonies if London continued to encourage the spread of Gaullist dissidence.[34] These efforts proved futile, but the successful defense of Dakar served the purpose of convincing the Germans that Vichy fully intended to

---

[32] *Ciano's Diplomatic Papers*, 395 ff.; *Halder Diary*, September 28, 1940; October 8, 11, 1940.

[33] *Pétain et les allemands: mémorandum d'Abetz*, 14 ff. (Abetz's report of October 8, 1940); *Halder Diary*, October 15, 1940.

[34] *The Private Diaries of Paul Baudouin*, 228 (September 2) and 234 (September 8, 1940).

defend its African possessions against British attack. The question remained, however, whether Laval's clamor for reprisals might lead to further weakening of Vichy relations with London, which in turn would almost automatically enhance French dependence on Germany.

In the critical last days of September Baudouin and the pro-British faction at Vichy attempted once more to reëstablish better relations with London. The South African, Canadian, Irish and Portuguese Governments were appealed to for good offices and the Madrid conversations were renewed. Baudouin's chief argument was that if the Vichy Government were not to be driven into the arms of Germany, the British must relax the blockade on shipments from the colonies to unoccupied France and must desist from attacks on the colonies. It is unnecessary to follow these negotiations in detail. As they developed, Mr. Churchill appears to have taken the stand that only through firmness could Vichy be brought into line. Lord Halifax, on the other hand, seems to have been more conciliatory. At first there was much recrimination between London and Vichy. The British made clear that they would not withdraw their support from de Gaulle; only if Vichy provided assurance that the French colonies would not fall under German or Italian control would London consider relaxation of the blockade. Pétain in turn was irritated by British support of de Gaulle, whom he regarded as a traitor. The French reply was therefore cool. Nonetheless, both sides continued to reiterate their desire for an understanding and some agreement regarding the colonies and the blockade was well under way when news of the forthcoming conference of Hitler and Pétain threw the entire French-British relationship once more into jeopardy.[35]

The objectives of Baudouin and his associates were clearly to forestall German interference in North Africa and secure some alleviation of the British blockade. But undoubtedly Vichy was deeply concerned also by the attitude of Washington, which was, if anything, more suspicious and severe than London's. Leaving aside American discontent over France's surrender in June, 1940, and particularly over Pétain's refusal to send the French Fleet to British or American ports, more recent developments had enhanced Washington's distrust of Vichy. The President and his advisers found it impossible to forgive the French submission to Japan's demands on Indo-China, which was taken as clear evidence that Vichy was dancing to Hitler's tune. No doubt the British attitude and Free French propaganda also played a part in shaping the convictions of the Administration. It was only natural that Mr. Churchill should have painted the prospect in somber hues and made the most of reports of German activities in West Africa. At the time of the Dakar action he warned Mr. Roosevelt: "It would be against our

[35] Memos from the British Embassy in Washington, October 1 and 21, 1940, reviewing the Madrid conversations. See also Sir Samuel Hoare: *Complacent Dictator,* 70 ff., and Churchill: *Their Finest Hour,* 502, 526; and on the French side *The Private Diaries of Paul Baudouin,* 253-56, and Charles-Roux: *Cinq mois tragiques,* 342-55.

joint interests if strong German submarine bases were established there," and suggested that American warships be sent to Monrovia and Freetown. Above all, he bespoke the President's intervention to forestall a Vichy declaration of war on Britain:

> What really matters now is that you should put it across to the French Government that a war declaration would be very bad indeed for them in all that concerns United States. If Vichy declares war, that is the same thing as Germany, and Vichy possessions in the Western Hemisphere must be considered potentially German possessions.[36]

In this connection it should be remembered that American military leaders were deeply concerned lest the Nazis launch a direct or indirect attack on Latin America. The French Antilles or French Guiana, if Hitler were to get control of them, would provide bases for Nazi submarine operations. Despite the provisional arrangements already made to insure against the use of French ships, planes and gold on Martinique, every rumor of plans or activities in that area aroused suspicion and apprehension in Washington. During October, 1940, the Martinique question was to be a significant item in Franco-American negotiations.

The official American view of the world situation was set forth in a memorandum of October 1, 1940, originally drafted by General Strong and the Army planners (probably on the basis of estimates brought from London), then revised with the assistance of the State Department for submission to the President.[37] In this document it was recognized that Hitler would probably not attack the United States until he had achieved "strategic freedom" in Europe by disposing of Britain and the Soviet Union. With each day of postponement the invasion of England became less likely, but as that menace faded, the German threat to Gibraltar and the Italian threat to Suez increased. While it was conceivable that the British might continue to use the Mediterranean even if Gibraltar were lost, there was but cold comfort for the United States in that thought. For the seizure of Gibraltar would be followed by German occupation of North Africa. Dakar would then serve the Axis as an air and naval base and the way would be clear to attack South America. Furthermore, there was danger that both Spain and Portugal would presently be drawn into the Axis orbit. If this became imminent, the British or Americans might find themselves obliged to take steps to prevent the Germans from seizing the Canaries, Azores and Cape Verdes.[38]

[36] Churchill's message to Mr. Roosevelt, September 23, 1940 (quoted in Churchill: *Their Finest Hour*, 487-88).

[37] Memo entitled: *The Problem of Production of Munitions in Relation to the Ability of the United States to Cope with its Defense Problems in the Present World Situation.* We have used a copy of this memo from the *Morgenthau Diaries* (MS.), Vol. 321, pp. 113 ff. On its provenance see Watson: *Chief of Staff: Prewar Plans and Preparations,* 115.

[38] This review of probable developments in the Atlantic was, of course, only a small part of the memo, which was addressed primarily to the question of American munitions requirements. See infra, Chapter III, Section 2. Secretary Hull's remarks to a group of

Since it is clear that Washington had an excellent grasp of the African problem and a generally accurate understanding of Hitler's objectives, it need not be wondered at that the State Department followed every move on Vichy's part with sharp and suspicious eyes. The President had approved the Free French-British attack on Dakar and, in reply to Mr. Churchill's request, had instructed Under Secretary Welles to speak at once to the French Ambassador. Mr. Welles pointed out that the only hope for an independent France lay in the victory of Britain, and added that the Ambassador could imagine the effect which a Vichy declaration of war would have on American opinion. Such a move, he suggested, might require that French possessions in the New World be placed under Pan American trusteeship. Certainly, he concluded, the American people did not believe that German control of Dakar could be either in their own or in France's interest.[39] However, the President seems to have passed over in silence Mr. Churchill's proposal that American warships be sent to the West African coast.

Further negotiations between Washington and Vichy during October took their departure from reports that the French were appropriating large sums of money to the development of naval facilities, including a submarine and air base, on Martinique. Since such expenditures seemed hardly reasonable, the Navy Department feared lest the new facilities be intended for later use by Germany.[40] The President must have been quite disturbed by this news, for he summoned the French Ambassador at once, warned him against any changes in the *status quo* of Martinique and suggested that the Vichy Government declare publicly that it would neutralize all its possessions in the Western Hemisphere. In return, the United States Government might release sufficient funds from the frozen French account to enable Vichy to defray the expenses of its diplomatic and consular establishments in the New World.[41]

While Henry-Haye was communicating with his Government, the American naval observer at Martinique reported that, although before the war the French Government had studied certain military and naval projects, no work had ever been undertaken.[42] On October 7, 1940, Ambassador Henry-Haye gave Mr. Welles assurances on this point and expressed the Vichy Government's willingness to coöperate in every way to satisfy the United States "that the French possessions in this Hemisphere will in no event become a source of danger to the security of the United States." Vichy was

---

Army and Navy officers on October 12, 1940 (quoted in William L. Langer: *Our Vichy Gamble,* New York, 1947, p. 79), appear to have been based on this memo.

[39] Memo of conversation between Mr. Welles and Ambassador Henry-Haye (September 24, 1940); see also Henry-Haye's report, in Charles-Roux: *Cinq mois tragiques,* 340-41.

[40] Letter from the Navy Department, October 1, 1940.

[41] *Morgenthau Diaries (MS.),* Vol. 319 (October 4, 1940); memo of conversation between Welles and Henry-Haye, October 7, 1940.

[42] Letter from the Navy Department, October 4, 1940.

prepared to have official American observers stationed in French Guiana, Guadeloupe and St. Pierre-Miquelon as well as at Martinique. These observers would be given every opportunity to find out what was going on and to convince themselves that nothing was in progress that would endanger the security of the United States. Vichy undertook further to instruct Admiral Robert, the commander of all French possessions in the Western Hemisphere, to receive a high ranking American officer and study with him the military measures to be taken to dispel uneasiness in Washington. In view of France's present position, Vichy desired to avoid any written contract or treaty, but promised that any arrangements arrived at with Admiral Robert would be complied with meticulously.[43]

There was nothing unusual in what Mr. Welles described as "the friendly and coöperative reaction" of Vichy on this occasion, for the French Government was profoundly worried lest, after the Havana Conference, the American Governments insist on setting up a trusteeship for the French possessions in the New World. However, Mr. Welles was pleased and promised to consult the President, who readily concurred in the French proposals and dropped his request for a public declaration of neutralization. On October 16 Mr. Welles informed the French Ambassador that Vichy's proposals had been accepted and that the Navy Department would soon designate officers for duty as observers in the French possessions. French funds were to be released for the purpose specified, but only on a month to month basis. This latter provision was probably designed to meet the objections of both Secretary Hull and Secretary Morgenthau, both of whom were highly suspicious of Vichy. With respect to the release of French funds Mr. Hull had remarked tartly to his Treasury colleague: "I think that the French are playing the German game one hundred percent over there at Vichy and I'm not concerned about helping them to do it."[44]

The Martinique agreement was clearly a business proposition, advantageous to both parties. It cannot therefore be taken as a reflection of mutual good relations. Such did not actually exist during October, 1940. Americans and British alike were aware of the activities of Laval and strongly suspected that before long that energetic politician would carry the day at Vichy. On October 11, 1940, Marshal Pétain broadcast a long message to the French people in which he declared that France was ready to seek collaboration in all fields and with all neighbors. Germany, he continued, had the choice, in the hour of victory, between imposing a traditional, oppressive peace settlement and granting a new peace of collaboration. It is impossible, even now, to state

[43] Memo of conversation between Welles and Henry-Haye, October 7, 1940; memo by the Division of European Affairs, October 10, 1940.

[44] *Morgenthau Diaries (MS.)*, Vol. 319 (October 4, 1940). The further development of the agreement is recorded in a memo of conversation between Welles and Henry-Haye, October 16, 1940, and in the *Morgenthau Diaries (MS.)*, Vol. 323, pp. 120 ff. (October 18, 1940).

definitely what was intended by this utterance, but it seems likely that Pétain was making a move to inject himself into the Franco-German problem, which thus far Laval had succeeded in managing in his own way. More important, perhaps, was Pétain's growing realization that the war might continue for a long time and that France must seek a peace settlement with Germany so as to put an end to the harsh terms of the armistice, with special reference to the vast number of French prisoners still in German hands, the administrative disruption of France, and kindred matters.[45]

Whatever Pétain's motive, it was almost inevitable that his address should have been read in London and Washington as a bid to the Germans to accept French collaboration. On October 19 Mr. Matthews, the American representative at Vichy, reported that Laval

. . . had staked his position so openly and definitely on a German victory and co-operation with Germany that he could hardly turn back and retain his prominent place in French political life. Darlan has quoted Laval as having stated literally to him at lunch several days ago "the only way to save France or what can be saved of France is to do for the Germans what the United States is doing for England."[46]

Whether and when London or Washington learned of the forthcoming conference between Pétain and Hitler does not appear from the record, but on October 20 Mr. Churchill cabled President Roosevelt rumors that Vichy was preparing ships and colonial troops to aid the Germans against Britain. Though the Prime Minister added that he himself did not believe these rumors, he took occasion to point out again that if the French Fleet were turned over to the Germans, it would be a very heavy blow. As a wise precaution he suggested that the President speak in the strongest terms to the French Ambassador and emphasize the disapprobation with which the United States would view such a betrayal of the cause of democracy and freedom.[47] At the same time Mr. Churchill delivered a radio appeal to the French people, warning them that Hitler was resolved on nothing less than the complete destruction of the French nation, assuring them that Britain would fight on, and calling upon them to rearm spiritually.

Mr. Roosevelt was evidently willing and eager to meet all British appeals for support. He summoned the French Ambassador without delay and told him that a Government, because it is a prisoner of war of another power, is not thereby justified in serving its conqueror against a former ally. He reminded Henry-Haye of Pétain's earlier assurances regarding the French Fleet and stated that the United States Government viewed these pledges as covering also any action by the French Fleet against the British. Turning to the rumors of an imminent Franco-German agreement, Mr. Roosevelt remarked that, if France were to assist Germany "actively" in the war, the

---

[45] On the Marshal's speech see particularly Girard: *Montoire,* 159 ff.
[46] Tel. from Matthews, October 19, 1940.
[47] Quoted in Churchill: *Their Finest Hour,* 513; Hull: *Memoirs,* I, 849.

American Government could make no effort, when the proper time came, to insure that France retained its overseas possessions.[48]

It is impossible to determine how sincere were the expressed British fears of an agreement between Vichy and Berlin. Considering the representations of men like General Smuts and Prime Minister Mackenzie King on behalf of better Franco-British relations; considering the fact that in these very days London and Vichy were on the point of reaching a mutually satisfactory arrangement about the blockade and the future of the French colonies; and considering, finally, that a special Vichy agent, Professor Louis Rougier, was about to arrive in London, one can hardly believe that British fears were altogether genuine. It does seem, however, that Mr. Churchill was pursuing a policy of calculated toughness in the hope of bringing France, or at least the important French colonies, back into the war on Britain's side, and that he made the most of Mr. Roosevelt's readiness to throw his influence into the scales. In any event, on the eve of Hitler's conferences with Franco and Pétain, the democracies on either side of the Atlantic stood shoulder to shoulder. Surely it may be assumed that this formidable alignment, documented before the world by the Destroyer Deal, was taken into consideration by the Spanish and French Chiefs of State. The invasion of England was evidently off for the immediate future. There was a fair chance that the war might drag on indefinitely and indecisively, and that eventually the weight of American power might seal the fate of Nazi Germany:

The story is not yet finished, but it will not be so long [Mr. Churchill told the French people on October 21]. We are on his track, and so are our friends across the Atlantic Ocean, and your friends across the Atlantic Ocean. If he cannot destroy us, we will surely destroy him and all his gang, and all their works. . . . Remember, we shall never stop, never weary, and never give in, and that our whole people and Empire have vowed themselves to the task of cleansing Europe from the Nazi pestilence and saving the world from the new Dark Ages . . . We seek to beat the life and soul out of Hitler and Hitlerism. That alone, that all the time, that to the end.[49]

5. HENDAYE AND MONTOIRE

There is no evidence that Hitler's thinking on Spain and France progressed much in the three weeks following his meeting with Mussolini on the Brenner Pass, or that he set out on his projected conferences with Franco and Pétain with a clean-cut program. He and Ribbentrop had arranged to travel by rail to the Spanish frontier and to receive Franco and Serrano Suñer in the Fuehrer's special train on October 23, 1940. En route a stop was made at Montoire, on the Loire River, where Hitler and his Foreign Minister received M. Laval on October 22. This preliminary meeting seems

[48] Tel. from the President to Mr. Churchill, October 24, 1940, summarized in Churchill: *Their Finest Hour*, 514.
[49] Churchill: *Their Finest Hour*, 511-12.

to have been devised by Otto Abetz, the German representative in Paris, with whom Laval had for some time been discussing the future of Franco-German relations. Laval later maintained that he had expected to see only Ribbentrop, and that he and Abetz had almost reached Montoire by motor before he learned that Hitler would receive him. The conference lasted for more than an hour, during which, according to the German record, Laval expressed his hope that Germany would not abuse its victory and reminded the Fuehrer that he, Laval, had favored collaboration even before the war. Hitler, on his part, made a point of the fact that the outcome of the conflict was certain and that Frenchmen who still hoped for a favorable turn in the situation were utterly deluded. Laval agreed and declared that, as a Frenchman, "he desired the defeat of Britain with all his heart." He was sure that many of his compatriots favored collaboration with Germany and were prepared to share the costs of war if only the Fuehrer would agree to a fair settlement. To this Hitler replied that a final settlement could come only with the end of the war, but that, if France agreed to collaborate, French interests might be safeguarded. Perhaps Britain rather than France could then be made to pay for German, Italian and Spanish claims in Africa. He suggested that if Pétain were ready to accept collaboration in principle, he would be glad to confer with him.[50]

Laval hurried back to Vichy to break the news of his reception by Hitler and to make arrangements for the Hitler-Pétain conference. He met with general consternation. Pétain himself was probably not averse to a conference with Hitler, if only in the hope of alleviating the burdensome provisions of the armistice. But he had long looked askance at Laval's secret confabulations in Paris and was evidently much concerned because the Germans had chosen the Vice Premier as their intermediary. Among other things he seems to have feared lest Hitler call upon him to take France into the war against Britain. In the end, however, he was persuaded that he could not afford to give offense. After a Cabinet meeting on October 23 it was agreed that the Marshal and Laval should go to Montoire on October 24, 1940.[51]

Meanwhile, on October 23, 1940, Hitler spent several hours with Franco and Serrano Suñer at Hendaye. As was his wont, the Nazi leader began by expatiating on the forthcoming defeat of Britain and forecasting the situation that would then emerge. If Spain would coöperate, Africa could be closed to the British, who, after the capture of Gibraltar, could be excluded from the Mediterranean as well. He therefore proposed an immediate alliance between Spain and the Axis, with the provision that Spain should enter

[50] The German record, as summarized in Langer: *Our Vichy Gamble*, 89-90; *The Diary of Pierre Laval* (New York, 1948), 57 ff.; Fernand de Brinon: *Mémoires* (Paris, 1949), 25 ff.; Paul Schmidt: *Statist auf diplomatischer Bühne*, 500 ff.

[51] Langer: *Our Vichy Gamble*, 93; *The Private Diaries of Paul Baudouin*, 261-63; Charles-Roux: *Cinq mois tragiques*, 373; Yves Bouthillier: *Le drame de Vichy* (Paris, 1950), 194 ff.

the war when the Germans were ready to attack Gibraltar, in January, 1941. That coveted fortress would then be turned over to Spain, along with certain Moroccan territories. With regard to the larger Spanish colonial claims, the Fuehrer was frank. He hoped, so he said, to bring France into the war and consequently could not ask Pétain to make huge sacrifices. Furthermore, if Morocco and part of Algeria were ceded to Spain, French North Africa would undoubtedly revolt and the British might secure a foothold there. Of course, once Britain were defeated, France could be otherwise compensated, and then Spain's claims might be met.

The Caudillo was unmoved by Hitler's eloquence. Slouched in his seat, he marshaled countless objections. In a vague way he agreed to sign a secret protocol of adherence to the Axis, but a military alliance, he said, would be impossible unless all Spanish claims were accepted. As for intervention in the war, that might expose the Canary Islands and Spanish coasts to British attack. Furthermore, Spain was in dire need of food, fuel and modern armaments. In any event, it would be a matter of pride for the Spaniards to conquer Gibraltar themselves. Hitler readily offered aid in defense of the Canaries and Spanish Morocco, but these offers were ignored. After several hours of argument, the meeting broke up without firm commitments. The discussions were resumed the following day between Ribbentrop and Serrano Suñer, but again without producing agreement. Hitler had every reason to be disappointed and irritated. A few days later he was to tell Mussolini that rather than go through such a conference again, he would prefer to have three or four teeth drawn.[52]

The Fuehrer's conference with Pétain and Laval at Montoire on the late afternoon of October 24, 1940, was more pleasant if not more profitable than the Hendaye colloquium. Hitler and his military entourage were visibly impressed by the aged hero of Verdun, who bore himself with reserve and dignity. Even Laval, in the presence of the Marshal, spoke little and only with caution. The conversation throughout was general. Hitler made no specific offer and Pétain assumed no definite commitment. Presumably the results of the Hendaye meeting seemed to the Fuehrer so disappointing that he no longer felt he had a firm foundation for further transactions. What emerged from the conference was the draft of a *procès-verbal,* for which Hitler undertook to secure Mussolini's concurrence. After some discussion of France's responsibility for the war, Hitler indicated his readiness to conclude a peace of reconciliation provided France helped defeat Britain. Pétain

---

[52] There is an incomplete record of the discussion in *The Spanish Government and the Axis,* No. 8. For a summary based on the German record, see Langer: *Our Vichy Gamble,* 91-92, which reflects also the reports of the American Ambassador in Madrid, October 24 and 31, 1940. Hitler's account to Mussolini is to be found in *Ciano's Diplomatic Papers,* 399 ff. For recent accounts of importance see Schmidt: *Statist auf diplomatischer Bühne,* 500 ff., and the entries in the *Halder Diary,* October 24, 29, November 1, 1940, which were based on reports from the German Foreign Office.

accepted the principle of collaboration, while Laval digressed to point out the importance of this concession and urge that Vichy be given time to prepare French opinion for its role in the struggle against Britain. Apparently the Fuehrer did not suggest actual French intervention against Britain. According to the *procès-verbal,* he manifested his determination to see France occupy, in the New Europe, the place to which it was entitled. With respect to the French colonial empire, France was to recognize certain changes as inevitable in order to harmonize the reciprocal interests of Germany, Italy, France and Spain. However, at the end of the war France was to be compensated for its losses at Britain's expense, so that in the final settlement the French domain in Africa would be substantially as large as before. Pétain, for his part, joined in recognizing that "the Axis Powers and France have an identical interest in seeing the defeat of England accomplished as soon as possible. Consequently the French Government will support, within the limits of its ability, the measures which the Axis Powers may take to this end."[53]

The real significance of the Montoire discussions and agreement will undoubtedly be disputed for many years to come. The narrative of subsequent developments in Franco-German relations will provide the soundest basis for judgment, but one point at least calls for immediate consideration. Hitler throughout attempted to act as the agent of the Axis in organizing a grand coalition against Britain. He knew from his discussions with Mussolini at the Brenner (October 4) that the Duce favored a deal with Spain, which, like Italy, was ravenous for French spoils. But the Hendaye conference demonstrated that little was to be expected from Franco, and Hitler felt inhibited from pressing for an agreement with Pétain for fear of estranging his Italian colleague. Evidently Mussolini wrote Hitler immediately after the Montoire meeting expressing anxiety lest collaboration with France endanger the realization of Italian claims.[54] Hitler thought it expedient to hurry off at once with Ribbentrop to dispel the Duce's apprehensions.

The two dictators met once again at Florence on October 28, 1940. It stands to reason that the Fuehrer's account of the Hendaye and Montoire conferences was slanted to suit his listener. Nevertheless, there is evidence in other sources to suggest that his remarks were sincere. The Spanish claims, he said, were of such scope that their acceptance would cause the immediate alignment of the French colonial empire with the Gaullists. Hence nothing was to be gained beyond the secret adherence of Spain to the Tripartite Pact. As for Pétain and France, Hitler expressed his conviction that the rift

[53] Full text in Langer: *Our Vichy Gamble,* 93-96, and in *Pétain et les allemands: mémorandum d'Abetz,* 23 ff. On the meeting see, from the German side, Schmidt: *Statist auf diplomatischer Bühne,* 503 ff.; *Halder Diary,* October 27, 29, 1940; and, from the French side, Laval's account in *Procès de M. Pétain,* 194-97; *The Private Diaries of Paul Baudouin,* 267; Bouthillier: *Le drame de Vichy,* 194 ff.; de Brinon: *Mémoires,* 34 ff.; Girard: *Montoire,* 210-14.

[54] *Halder Diary,* October 29, 1940.

between Vichy and de Gaulle was genuine. It was in the Axis interest, he continued, that Vichy retain control of North Africa and it would be best to let France itself defend that crucial area. He was, he confessed, well impressed with Pétain, though Laval seemed to him "a dirty, democratic politician, a man who doesn't believe in what he says, who turns to us only to save himself." All told, Mussolini was induced to admit that the Pétain regime was probably the best, though he persisted in his view that no more than "passive coöperation" was to be desired. Reluctantly he agreed that when Britain was defeated, France might be compensated for its colonial losses to Italy and Spain. But Hitler had to assure him that if the war ended in a compromise, France would have to pay for everything.[55]

In view of this exchange, it could almost have been predicted that the Hendaye-Montoire policy would have but little future. Hitler's friends and would-be friends were little consolation to him. They eagerly awaited his defeat of Britain, but they did little or nothing to aid him in that great task.

6. END OF THE GIBRALTAR DREAM

Hitler refused to believe that Franco had spoken his last word at Hendaye. From mid-October German military planners had been working out the details of the attack on Gibraltar, from which the Fuehrer hoped so much. To the Germans the operation seemed simple enough. Hitler, indeed, deluded himself into thinking that the retention of Gibraltar was essentially a question of prestige for the British. He thought it not impossible that the defenders, once they realized what was in store for them, would abandon the rock, since voluntary withdrawal would be less damaging to British prestige than expulsion by force.[56] To clinch the matter, however, the operation was carefully worked out: first there was to be an attack by dive bombers and paratroops, after which troops would arrive from the French frontier and from Italian ports to consolidate the conquest and perhaps carry the campaign across the Straits into Africa. The assault was first planned for mid-December, but was finally fixed for January 10, 1941.

It seemed to the Nazi dictator quite incredible that Franco should refuse to coöperate, considering that Gibraltar, the long-wished for, was eventually to be turned over to the Spaniards. Despite reports of German agents that Franco and his Government were apprehensive of British action against the Canary Islands and against Spain itself, and despite warnings that the internal situation of Spain was so wretched that the country was dependent on British food and other supplies, Hitler pushed on with his plans for including Spain in the Tripartite Pact and reverted to his earlier resolution to force Spain into the war, if necessary.[57] In conference with his military ad-

[55] *Ciano's Diplomatic Papers*, 399 ff.
[56] *Halder Diary*, October 16, 1940.
[57] *Halder Diary*, November 2 and 4, 1940.

visers on November 4, 1940, the Fuehrer expressed the belief that Spain would enter the war within a short time. The transfer of German troops to the Spanish frontier should therefore begin at once and, as soon as they were in position, air attacks should be loosed upon the British Fleet at Gibraltar. Furthermore, the Canary and Cape Verde Islands were to be occupied, and three German divisions sent to the Portuguese frontier as a deterrent to hostile Portuguese action. To these far-reaching plans Admiral Raeder at once raised objections. The Cape Verdes, he pointed out, could hardly be occupied except from French West Africa. They were not of great value and to seize them would only provoke British or American action against the Azores or against Portugal itself. In sum, it would be most advantageous to Germany to leave Portugal and its possessions out of account. In view of these considerations, Hitler ordered further study of this aspect of the problem.[58]

After further examination it proved impossible for the *Luftwaffe* to undertake operations against the Atlantic islands. It was therefore decided to aid the Spaniards to fortify the Canaries and to encourage Portugal to build up the defenses of the Azores. Hitler was most reluctant to abandon his plans for securing control of the Azores, which, he argued, "would afford him the only facility for attacking America, if she should enter the war, with a modern plane of the Messerschmidt type, which has a range of 12,600 km." German occupation of the islands would also force the United States to build up its own antiaircraft defenses, instead of aiding Britain. But the operation against the Azores would be difficult, and any breach of Portuguese neutrality might lead to the immediate seizure of Portuguese possessions by the British or Americans.[59]

Following these decisions, Serrano Suñer was invited to Berchtesgaden to sign the documents admitting Spain to the Tripartite Pact and providing for Spain's entry into the war. According to Serrano Suñer's account, his departure was preceded by a meeting of Franco with his generals, at which all agreed that Spain was in no condition to go to war. Under the circumstances Ribbentrop and Hitler wasted their eloquence in attempting to demonstrate that the operation against Gibraltar would bring the war to a rapid close. Serrano Suñer pleaded that Spain needed more time and that above all action must be postponed until expected food shipments from Britain and the United States had arrived.[60]

---

[58] *Fuehrer Conferences,* 1940 (2), 32 ff. Details for the operation against Gibraltar were laid down in the important directive of November 14, 1940 (*Nazi Conspiracy and Aggression,* III, 444-PS). See also F. H. Hinsley: *Hitler's Strategy* (Cambridge, 1951), 104 ff.

[59] *Fuehrer Conferences,* 1940 (2) 37 ff. (report of the conference of November 14, 1940, with annexes); also *Halder Diary,* November 14, 18, 30, 1940.

[60] *Ciano's Diplomatic Papers,* 405 ff. (record of the Ribbentrop-Ciano conference of November 4, 1940) and 409 (record of Hitler's conference with Serrano Suñer); Serrano Suñer: *Entre les Pyrénées et Gibraltar,* Chapter XII; *Halder Diary,* November 18, 1940.

This was bad news indeed, which moved Hitler to cast his troubles upon his friend Mussolini. In an exceptionally long letter of November 20 he drew a bleak picture of the military and political outlook, with particular reference to the ill-advised Italian attack on Greece. As for Spain, the Fuehrer argued that intervention must be effected within six weeks in order to eliminate Gibraltar, block the Straits, and transfer at least two German divisions to Spanish Morocco as insurance against the defection of French North Africa to the British. The Mediterranean problem was one of highest priority, and must be resolved before the end of the winter.[61]

Mussolini agreed and suggested that he himself might visit Franco in a further effort to make him see the light. Nothing came of this proposal, so Hitler was left with the problem of bringing the Caudillo into line. In early December he despatched Admiral Canaris, Chief of the German Military Intelligence Service, on special mission to Madrid. But Canaris returned with empty hands. Franco told him without adornment that Spanish intervention by the date suggested (January 10, 1941) was utterly impossible and that it would result only in the loss of the Spanish and Portuguese islands to the British. As for the attack on Gibraltar, Franco would neither support nor permit it.

It takes but little imagination to picture Hitler's indignation on receiving Canaris's report. He could hardly proceed with his plans despite the Caudillo, whom in private he covered with obloquy. For he had by this time convinced himself that such action would precipitate the defection of French North Africa to de Gaulle and the British. He therefore gave thought to the possibility of denouncing the tenuous agreements with Spain and thus regain freedom of action for an understanding with Vichy France. Among other things, he was tired of considering Italian susceptibilities in this matter. But, as though to blast his last hope, Pétain dismissed Laval at this crucial moment (December 13, 1940), and the Fuehrer had no immediate alternative to shelving his favorite plan. It is easy to believe that he never forgave Franco his refusal to assist in the assault on Gibraltar, possession of which, according to Hitler, would have denied Britain and the United States access to the Mediterranean and might thereby have decided the war in Germany's favor.[62]

It is probably safe to conclude that for a time, in the summer of 1940, Franco was prepared to intervene in the war on the German side, just as Mussolini had taken the plunge on the assumption that the conflict would soon be over. At the time it did indeed seem that Britain could not long survive. The Caudillo would have chanced brief participation had he been guaranteed satisfaction of all Spanish claims. But by the time of the Hendaye

---

[61] *Les lettres secrètes échangées par Hitler et Mussolini* (Paris, 1946), 81 ff.

[62] State Department interrogation of Dr. Paul Schmidt, October 22, 1945. For the rest see *Halder Diary*, December 2, 5, 8, 9, 1940; Assmann: *Deutsche Schicksalsjahre*, 348; and Hinsley: *Hitler's Strategy*, 121-22.

conference it was no longer certain that the war would soon be terminated. In addition, Hitler felt unable to accept all the Spanish demands. From that time on the matter was fairly settled so far as the Spanish dictator was concerned. He and his associates were convinced that Spain could under no conditions engage in a prolonged conflict. The economic situation of the country would not permit it. Germany was unable to supply Spain's extensive requirements for food and fuel, while imports from abroad were dependent on British good will, in view of the blockade. Despite their strong dislike of the British and their many grievances, real or imagined, Franco and Serrano Suñer, in dealing with Hitler, could never exorcise Churchill and his American supporters from their minds.

The British Ambassador at Madrid, Sir Samuel Hoare, had long since convinced his Government that Spain's economic needs could be exploited to hold the Franco Government to its policy of nonbelligerency. Just enough food and fuel were permitted to pass through the blockade to keep the country viable, but not enough to allow preparation for war. The American Government, in turn, had been persuaded by London of the wisdom of this policy and had adopted it, though reluctantly and suspiciously. American liberal opinion was extremely hostile to the Fascist dictatorship of Franco and took the view that to supply economic assistance was simply to relieve the regime of a major threat to its existence. However, early in October President Roosevelt had agreed to send Spain a Red Cross shipment of food, the Madrid Government having promised that full publicity should be given to this humanitarian gesture, that Red Cross officials should be permitted to supervise the distribution, and that in no event should any of the food find its way to Germany. Indeed, the Administration had gone further, and had offered to discuss a credit of $100,000,000 to Spain, provided Franco gave assurance that Spain would not intervene in the war against Britain.[63]

At this crucial moment came the appointment of Serrano Suñer as Foreign Minister, followed almost immediately by the Hendaye conference. The British appear to have viewed these developments with considerable equanimity and Ambassador Weddell, too, held to his conviction that the Spanish economic situation alone would make the country's entry into war impossible. Franco, the Army and the majority of the population, he reported, were opposed to abandonment of nonbelligerency. It seemed unlikely that Spain would voluntarily depart from that policy, and equally unlikely that Hitler would take action to force such departure.[64] But Secretary Hull, ever fearful of public reaction and therefore hesitant about aiding Franco, decided that for the time being, at least, relief should be deferred.

[63] For the earlier history of this policy see the preceding volume: *The Challenge to Isolation*, Chapter XXI. We have used further tels. to Weddell (Madrid), October 12, 18, 19, 1940, and tel. from Weddell, October 16, 1940. See also Hull: *Memoirs*, I, 876, and Feis: *The Spanish Story*, 61-62.

[64] Tel. from Weddell, October 24, 1940.

Mr. Weddell had an opportunity, on October 31, 1940, to inquire of Serrano Suñer whether the Hendaye conference portended a change in Spanish policy. The Foreign Minister was evasive, but made no secret of Spain's sympathy with the Axis. He spoke of his country's "political solidarity" with Germany and Italy, of its determination to rid itself of the "subordinate position" so long imposed on it, and of its insistence henceforth on "a voice in European affairs." The Ambassador's attempt to stress the friendly feeling of the United States for Spain provoked a sarcastic inquiry about the projected Red Cross shipment, which led Weddell to state that no further action could be taken until he had received personal assurances from Franco respecting the future course of Spanish policy. Reporting to Washington, the Ambassador felt obliged to recommend that in the future aid to Spain "should be largely based on political rather than upon humanitarian or commercial considerations." Supplies, if sent at all, should be limited, holding out the hope of larger amounts as a "bait to keep Spain out of war."[65]

The decision of Washington went beyond anything the Ambassador recommended or deemed wise. On November 5 Weddell was instructed to abandon his effort to see Franco and was told that in view of Serrano Suñer's remarks and the existing state of American public opinion, no help would be given Spain if the latter sided with Germany against Britain. But this decision, again, brought remonstrances from the Ambassador and, perhaps more importantly, from the British. Sir Samuel Hoare seemed satisfied with assurances from Franco that Spain would not enter the war on Germany's side and would resist with arms any German attempt to cross the frontier. The British urged that the United States proceed with its relief shipments, advancing the starkly realistic argument that famine was so imminent in Spain that failure to secure food from Britain and the United States might compel Franco to throw in his lot with the Nazis. This estimate was probably not far from the truth, for even the uncompromising Serrano Suñer felt impelled to make a conciliatory gesture. On November 12 he explained to Weddell that Spain's position with respect to Germany was identical with that of the United States toward Britain, except that Spain had nothing to give the Axis. When asked whether Spain would resist by force a German attempt to invade, he replied "yes, to the last man," which in fact appears to have been the Spanish position, known to Hitler.[66]

The State Department was certainly influenced by British pleas, but Secretary Hull made haste slowly and on every occasion stressed the hostility of the American public to any program of aid. Finally, on November 29, 1940, Ambassador Weddell was granted a long interview by Franco, who was

[65] Tel. from Weddell, October 31, 1940; Hull: *Memoirs*, I, 876; Feis: *The Spanish Story*, 100 ff.
[66] Tel. to Weddell, November 5; tel. from Weddell, November 8, 1940; memo of conversation between Mr. Welles and Mr. Butler, of the British Embassy, November 11, 1940. For further detail see Hull: *Memoirs*, I, 877, and Feis: *The Spanish Story*, 101 ff.

probably driven by sheer necessity to make this momentous concession. The Ambassador explained in detail the conditions on which the American Government would resume its program of relief and begin negotiations for a substantial credit. These included not only private assurances, but a public declaration by Franco that Spain would not depart from the policy of non-belligerency. The Ambassador expatiated also upon the American policy of supporting Britain and stressed his conviction of Britain's ultimate victory. Any aid given Spain would have to be in keeping with this policy and this conviction.

Franco listened, but avoided a clear and simple reply. He declared it impossible for him to deceive the President and made no effort to conceal his sympathies for the Axis. On the other hand he pointed out that even if Spain wished to aid Germany and Italy, it was in no position to do so. As for the future, who could tell what might eventuate? The Ambassador was satisfied that these general statements were all that could be extracted from the Caudillo by way of assurance. Reporting to the State Department he said it was obvious to him that Franco had come to the conclusion that the war was likely to end in stalemate rather than in German victory. Furthermore, the Caudillo seemed genuinely concerned by the danger of German invasion, since there were some fifty idle German divisions near the frontier, through no fault of Spain's, according to Franco. Weddell thought the wise course would be to resume at least the relief program, for Franco would probably refuse to make a declaration as to future Spanish policy, if only for fear of the German reaction.[67]

Meanwhile the British had proceeded to conclude with Madrid an exchange agreement making possible triangular trade between Spain, Portugal and Morocco.[68] Furthermore, they informed the Madrid Government on December 1 that they were prepared to grant a credit of £2,000,000 and to issue navicerts for the importation of as much as one million tons of grain from Canada and Argentina during the ensuing twelve months. It is quite likely that the British knew of the Canaris mission and of Hitler's pressure on Spain to enter the war. At any rate they not only made the above generous offer, but continued to exert all possible influence on Washington to participate in the aid program. Since the main objective of the United States in this matter was to support the British position, the President in mid-December decided to despatch the relief shipment and open discussions for a credit, provided Madrid gave adequate assurances as to its future intentions. Actually even the food shipment was delayed until January, 1941,

[67] Tel. from Weddell, November 29, 1940; Hull: *Memoirs,* I, 879; Feis: *The Spanish Story,* 104 ff. In his apologia, Serrano Suñer makes much of the threat of German invasion, which must in fact have weighed heavily on Madrid, considering Hitler's strenuous efforts to bring Spain into the war.

[68] Text in "Les accords concernant l'Afrique du Nord française" (*Cahiers d'histoire de la guerre,* October, 1949); see also Hoare: *Complacent Dictator,* 80 ff.

because the British suspended their own program in protest against the high-handed Spanish procedure in Tangier. In view of the highly vocal opposition in the United States even to the relief of Spanish hunger, there seemed no reason to act until the British were prepared to do so. The projected credit was, in fact, shelved completely because of what Mr. Hull described as the "terrific" outburst of public indignation when news of the project transpired.[69]

The amount of British and American aid given Spain prior to Franco's decision to reject the Nazi advances was certainly far too small to have been of much importance. It is, in fact, impossible to demonstrate that Franco's policy was influenced by it one way or the other. This much, however, appears certain: Spain could not possibly embark on anything but a very short war or in fact avoid serious famine without securing food from abroad. Hitler was in no position to supply food and Spain was therefore dependent on Britain and the United States. Franco probably made his decision partly because his territorial claims were not satisfied and partly because he recognized that the war would in all likelihood be protracted. Once the latter conclusion had been reached, there could be no further thought of intervention. On the contrary, Franco, for all his antipathy to the British and the democracies generally, was thenceforth obliged to cultivate the good will of Britain and the United States. At a minimum the economic power of the western states was an important contributory factor in keeping Spain from closer identification with the Axis.

7. France, Britain and the United States

In the eyes of Mr. Churchill, as of Hitler, the position of Vichy France was more important by far than that of Franco's Spain, for a substantial part of the French Fleet was still intact and Vichy still commanded the allegiance of most of the French Empire. The British had helped engineer the defection of the Equatorial colonies and had tried, at Dakar, to initiate the Gaullist acquisition of the crucial West and North African possessions. The Dakar attack had failed, however, and had severely strained relations between the British and the Free French. De Gaulle had gone to Brazzaville to organize an independent Free French state in Africa. The British in turn had taken a new tack and had attempted, through negotiations at Madrid, to strike a bargain with Vichy which, it was hoped in London, would forestall an agreement between Pétain and Hitler and at the same time provide assurance against German control of North and West Africa. General Weygand had assumed his new post as Delegate General of the Vichy Govern-

[69] Tel. to Weddell, December 18; tel. from Weddell, December 20, 1940. The entire American position was succinctly restated in a telegram to Weddell of December 20, 1940. The British policy was expounded in an *aide-mémoire* from the British Embassy, December 21, 1940. See further Hull: *Memoirs*, I, 881-82; Feis: *The Spanish Story*, 106.

ment for all the African territories, with the special mission of reconstituting their armed forces and assuring their defense. Despite Weygand's role at the time of the armistice, he appears to have been held in high regard by the British, who began to cherish hopes that he might play the part previously assigned to de Gaulle. Washington shared these hopes and already during October there had been conversations in the State Department looking toward British-American agreements with the French authorities in Morocco that would enable the latter to secure much needed supplies of fuel, textiles, sugar and tea.[70]

Under the circumstances the Montoire conference came as a terrible shock to both London and Washington. It seemed to indicate clearly that Laval had succeeded and that Vichy was about to align itself with the Axis against Britain. The British Foreign Office learned from an "absolutely sure source" that the Fuehrer had not only made demands involving the partial dismemberment of the French Empire, but had insisted also on the right to make use of the French Fleet and French bases in North Africa.[71] In the moment of crisis, Mr. Churchill drafted a personal message from King George to Marshal Pétain, assuring him of Britain's continued good will and begging him not to injure France's former ally by making concessions to the Germans beyond those called for in the armistice, or by taking sides against Britain.[72] At the same time the Prime Minister appealed to President Roosevelt to address a warning to Pétain not to surrender the Fleet or make African bases available to the Germans.[73]

Mr. Roosevelt required no prodding. The American Chargé d'Affaires at Vichy, Mr. H. Freeman Matthews, had just reported that friendly officials of the French Foreign Office were saying that Laval had won over Pétain to full collaboration with Germany. Secretary of War Stimson was convinced that France was about to turn over to the Axis both the Fleet and the African bases, and that there was nothing for the British to do "except attack and seize the Fleet before it can join Italy and Britain's other enemies."[74] In view of what seemed so acute a danger, the President had acted even before Mr. Churchill's suggestion reached him. On October 25 he had despatched a message to Pétain repeating in substance what he had said a few days earlier to Ambassador Henry-Haye. He recalled the Marshal's previous as-

[70] Langer: *Our Vichy Gamble,* 104-5, on the early phases of the economic negotiations. See also Hull: *Memoirs,* I, 853, on the hopes aroused by Weygand's assignment.

[71] Tels. from Johnson (London), October 26, 27, 1940.

[72] The text of this message, which was dated October 25 and was transmitted through American channels, is officially printed in a White Paper: *Despatch to H.M.'s Ambassador in Paris regarding Relations between H.M.'s Government in the United Kingdom and the Vichy Government in the Autumn of 1940* (Cmd. 6662-July 13, 1945).

[73] Mr. Churchill to the President, October 26, 1940 (full text in Churchill: *Their Finest Hour,* 514).

[74] Tel. from Matthews, October 26, 1940; *Stimson Diary (MS.),* October 25 and 26, 1940.

surances regarding the French Fleet and pointed out that if, nevertheless, the Fleet were put at the disposal of the Germans, "such action would constitute a flagrant and deliberate breach of faith with the United States Government." It would furthermore "most definitely wreck the traditional friendship between the French and American peoples, would permanently remove any chance that this Government would be disposed to give any assistance to the French people in their distress, and would create a wave of bitter indignation against France on the part of American public opinion." Finally, if France pursued such a policy, "the United States could make no effort when the appropriate time came to exercise its influence to insure to France the retention of her overseas possessions."[75]

It so happened that in these tense days a special Vichy emissary, Professor Louis Rougier, appeared in London. Rougier had offered in mid-September to undertake the mission in an attempt to secure a relaxation of the British blockade and an understanding about the French colonies. His project had been enthusiastically received by Foreign Minister Baudouin and had been approved by Pétain. Beyond these two men, only General Weygand appears to have been in the secret. Weygand, already appointed to his new post in Africa, had urged Rougier to impress on the British that unless they ceased their attacks on the French colonies, the Germans would probably insist on sharing in their defense. Thereby an indispensable base for a future reconquest of Europe would be lost. According to Rougier, Weygand remarked: "If the British arrive with four divisions, I will fire on them; if they come with twenty divisions, I will welcome them."[76]

Rougier was received by Lord Halifax on October 23 and by Mr. Churchill on October 24, the very day of the Montoire conference. He explained that the Vichy regime reflected many different views, extending all the way from extreme collaborationism to genuine resistance. No doubt he gave assurances regarding Pétain's position and that of Baudouin. As a result of the discussions, Rougier drew up a memorandum (October 28) on which British Foreign Office officials noted certain emendations. This memorandum stated that Britain would make no compromise peace and that Britain was already enjoying substantial American support. The war would last only another year if North Africa were to revolt and thus provide Britain with bases in Tunisia. On the other hand, if Britain were to lose Egypt and be excluded from the Mediterranean, the struggle might continue for ten years. A great deal therefore depended on France. Britain would restore the integrity of France if the latter abstained from aiding the Axis and especially if it assisted Britain. Furthermore, Britain would permit food shipments

[75] Tel. to Matthews, October 25, 1940 (full text in *Peace and War*, 580 ff., and in Langer: *Our Vichy Gamble*, 97).

[76] Louis Rougier: *Les accords Pétain-Churchill* (Montreal, 1945), Chapter III; Weygand: *Mémoires*, 471; *The Private Diaries of Paul Baudouin*, 241, 246; Girard: *Montoire*, 170 ff.

from North Africa to France, and would agree not to countenance further Gaullist attacks on the French colonies if Vichy promised not to attempt reconquest of the already dissident colonies. British radio attacks on Marshal Pétain would also cease if France engaged itself not to cede bases to the Germans and agreed to reënter the war against Germany as soon as Britain gave proof of sufficient power to equip and land colonial forces. France was to give assurance that the Fleet would be scuttled rather than allowed to fall into German or Italian hands. According to one of the British emendations: "If General Weygand will raise the standard in North Africa, he can count on the renewal of the whole-hearted collaboration of the governments and peoples of the British Empire, and on a share of the assistance afforded by the United States."[77]

At the time of the Pétain trial in 1945 the Marshal's counsel adduced this memorandum, which had been approved by Pétain, as evidence of the existence of a gentleman's agreement between Britain and France. Mr. Churchill at once took issue, denying that any agreement had been arrived at or that Rougier had been authorized to submit any proposals to Pétain. The British, according to the Prime Minister, had intended only an approach to Weygand in the hope of inducing him "to enter of his own initiative into direct and secret negotiations with His Majesty's Government, with the object of bringing North Africa back into the war on the Allied side when the time was ripe."[78]

It is impossible even now to resolve all the questions connected with this negotiation. It seems, however, that Rougier, in his eagerness, tended to exaggerate or at any rate to misinterpret the character of the draft memorandum. Evidently Churchill was thinking less in terms of an agreement with Pétain, who was suspected of being under Laval's thumb, than of enlisting Weygand's aid. This interpretation is supported by the fact that Rougier returned to Vichy by way of Algiers, that Weygand was informed through the British Consul General at Tangier that Rougier had been fully instructed by the Prime Minister, and that further British messages were transmitted to the General. In sum, Churchill at this time made every effort, through Rougier, through direct correspondence, and through General Catroux, to prove to Weygand that Britain could and would hold out and that the con-

[77] The document is reproduced in Rougier: Les accords Pétain-Churchill, 131 ff., 416 ff. It is summarized also in The Private Diaries of Paul Baudouin, 274-75, and in Bouthillier: Le drame de Vichy, 185 ff.

[78] Churchill's statement in Parliament, June 12, 1945, and the later Foreign Office statements (The New York Times, June 13, July 17, 1945), together with the Despatch to H.M.'s Ambassador in Paris regarding Relations between H.M.'s Government in the United Kingdom and the Vichy Government in the Autumn of 1940 (Cmd. 6662-July 13, 1945). Rougier replied with a statement in The New York Times, July 21, 1945, and with a privately printed Reply to the British White Paper (1946). See also the revised edition of his book (1946). Churchill, in Their Finest Hour, 508, barely mentions the matter.

flict could be greatly shortened if French North Africa aligned itself with Britain. The gist of the argument was contained in these words:

Mr. Churchill does not understand what prevents the French leaders, at least some of them, from seceding in Africa, where they would have an empire and at the same time have command of the seas and of all the French financial resources presently in the United States. The Prime Minister is convinced that the opportunity presented is the most brilliant ever presented to bold men.[79]

Weygand treated these advances with the utmost reserve. Quite apart from his conviction that premature action would compromise everything, he was estranged by the suggestion that he, a soldier, should lend himself to political maneuvers. He therefore forwarded copies of the correspondence to Pétain, who replied at length on November 9, 1940, in a letter which is of considerable interest for the light it throws on his policy. Among other things the Marshal assured Weygand that at Montoire collaboration had been accepted only in principle. If the issue were reopened he, Pétain, would make certain that it remained confined to the economic sphere and to the defense of the African empire, excluding any idea of aggression against Britain: "I am firmly resolved not to associate myself, for this purpose, either with the Italians or with the Germans." As for Rougier, the Marshal remarked that at Vichy he was regarded as a British agent. In conclusion he stated: "The situation of our country requires the maintenance of a careful equilibrium between collaboration with Germany (inevitable in the economic sphere) and what the British and Americans propose. This obligation I shall not lose from sight."[80]

By the time Rougier reached Vichy (November 8) the situation in French Government circles had become extremely complex. The Foreign Office had had no part in the Montoire conference. Laval had, in fact, refused flatly to have Baudouin included in the French party. Thereupon Baudouin resigned, though at Pétain's special request he remained in the Government as an adviser to the Marshal. At the same time M. Charles-Roux, the experienced Secretary General of the French Foreign Office and one of the chief exponents of close relations with Britain, withdrew from office. Laval was appointed Foreign Minister for reasons that are still obscure, but probably to impress the Germans.[81] In any event, his appointment did not signify the Marshal's acceptance of the Laval policy. On the contrary, Pétain was much frightened by the prospect that Laval might provoke a rupture with Britain and serious difficulties with the United States. At Baudouin's suggestion he

[79] The texts of the various messages are given in full in Weygand: *Mémoires*, 470 ff. Catroux's appeals, drafted in collaboration with Mr. Eden, during the latter's mission to Cairo, were of the same tenor, but did not reach Weygand until two weeks later. See Catroux: *Dans la bataille de Méditerranée*, 70 ff.

[80] This letter is photostatically reproduced in Weygand: *Mémoires*, Appendix X.

[81] *The Private Diaries of Paul Baudouin*, 264, 267, 268; Charles-Roux: *Cinq mois tragiques*, 374.

therefore sent a message to Churchill through Prime Minister Salazar of Portugal assuring the British that France would take no hostile action and that collaboration would never extend to military operations.[82]

In line with these efforts to relieve tension were Pétain's replies to the appeals of King George and President Roosevelt, replies which reiterated that France would make no "unjustified attack" on its former ally, and that the French Fleet would never be surrendered to the Axis.[83]

These assurances, however, were not enough for Secretary Hull. On November 4 he summoned the French Ambassador to a long conference, on which occasion he stated that the United States Government had "thus far" retained its high regard for Marshal Pétain and appreciated France's unhappy position as a captive nation. But he complained bitterly of the obscure attitude and sharp practice of the Vichy Government which, he emphasized, would not get it ahead "two inches" in its relations with the United States. The American Government proposed to remain on guard against Laval's efforts to appease Hitler by aiding him militarily through "supplying of naval and air bases, or other help given by the land, sea, or air forces of France." The Vichy Government should understand clearly the "supreme and firm purpose [of the United States] to have no relations with any Government, such as that of Vichy, which would give the slightest encouragement to Hitler either directly or indirectly." The United States Government was "too concerned about possible future attacks by Hitler to acquiesce in the slightest with acts of the French Government that would aid or encourage Hitler in still wider conquest, especially in the direction of this hemisphere."[84]

Washington certainly took a somber view of the Montoire conference. While concerned about Africa and the French Fleet, it was even more directly and immediately exercised about Martinique and the ships and planes stationed there. Secretary Knox convinced himself, if not the President, that American forces should occupy Martinique at once, and the Navy Department requested the War Department to prepare a force of 5000 men within seventy-two hours to garrison the island. Secretary Stimson and General Marshall, however, opposed this plan as "half-baked" and argued with Mr. Hull and Mr. Welles (who had known nothing about it) that the seizure of Martinique would probably result in the remaining French colonies going "head over heels" into the arms of Germany. The scheme was held in abeyance while Mr. Welles warned the French Ambassador that the United States Government "could under no conditions permit any indirect alien control to be exercised in Martinique or in any other French colonies in the

---

[82] *The Private Diaries of Paul Baudouin,* 268, 272-73 (October 30, 1940).

[83] Tel. from Matthews, November 1, 1940, published in *Peace and War,* 391 ff. See also Hull: *Memoirs,* I, 850-51.

[84] Memo of conversation between Mr. Hull and Ambassador Henry-Haye, November 4, 1940, published in full in *Peace and War,* 592 ff.

Western Hemisphere, and that it most decidedly could not agree to any modification of the existing agreement regarding the movement of French naval vessels nor the transfer of French gold and other assets on the island so that these assets could pass into German hands." At the same time Admiral John W. Greenslade was sent on a second mission to Admiral Robert (November 2-3, 1940) and a carrier and patrol planes were despatched to observe ship movements near the island. As it turned out there was no reason for all this anxiety. The French Ambassador unhesitatingly reaffirmed earlier assurances and Admiral Robert, for his part, agreed to such measures of surveillance as were deemed necessary.[85]

American preoccupation with the French Fleet and possessions afforded Mr. Churchill repeated opportunities to exert further pressure on Vichy. On November 10 he notified the President of reports that the French were planning to bring the battleships *Richelieu* and *Jean Bart* from Casablanca and Dakar to Toulon. The British, he stated, were bound to prevent such a move, but he begged the President to warn Vichy against attempting it. Mr. Roosevelt did so at once, adding an offer to buy the two ships. Pétain replied that the armistice prevented such sale and that in any case the Germans would never permit it. He took the opportunity, however, to restate once more his "most solemn assurances" with regard to the French Fleet and to promise that it would never be used against the British unless the latter attacked. Furthermore, he seized the occasion to point out that the policy of collaboration seemed to be much misunderstood in the United States. By it he meant "only economic collaboration and in no sense military aid to Germany in her war against Britain, nor cession of bases." The Marshal spoke critically of the British, who were still supporting "the traitor de Gaulle," but he admitted that they were fighting the good fight and would never yield. That being so, he realized that France must hope for a British victory. Yet he did not see how this could be achieved, in view of the inability of the British to invade the Continent. Therefore, a drawn peace appeared the best solution, and the sooner it came, the better.[86]

In keeping with British efforts to persuade Weygand to assume leadership of a dissident movement in North and West Africa were the American plans to strengthen that region economically and so loosen its dependence on metropolitan France. The first discussions of this program had taken place with French officials in Morocco even before the Montoire meeting. The subject was then pushed vigorously by the appropriate officers of the State

[85] *Stimson Diary* (MS.), October 26, 1940; tel. to Matthews, October 29, 1940; instructions from Admiral Stark to Admiral Greenslade, October 30, 1940; memo of conversation between Welles and Henry-Haye, October 31, 1940; tel. to Matthews, November 6, 1940. See also Amiral Georges Robert: *La France aux Antilles* (Paris, 1950), 85 ff.

[86] Tel. from Johnson (London), November 10, 1940; tel. to Johnson, November 13, 1940; tel. to Matthews, November 13, 1940; tel. from Matthews, November 16, 1940. See also Churchill: *Their Finest Hour*, 516-18; Hull: *Memoirs*, 871, and, for details, Langer: *Our Vichy Gamble*, 100-2.

Department, who argued that "from our larger defense interests it is important that French Morocco should not fall into hostile hands, and anything done to bolster the morale of the authorities and people of that area and to avoid collapse, whether economic or political, of French Morocco is all to the good." A long memorandum entitled *The Political Implications of American-Moroccan Trade* was completed in the Department on November 12 and Consul General Felix Cole, at Algiers, was instructed to open negotiations with Weygand. But the entire project at once provoked opposition from the economic experts of the Department, who distrusted everything and everybody connected with Vichy and refused to believe that aid sent to North Africa would not eventually redound to the advantage of the Axis. The result of this split in the Department was a delay extending over several weeks. Only in December, 1940, was the memorandum of November 12 sent to Mr. Cole and arrangements made for a special mission of investigation into conditions in North Africa.[87]

Meanwhile Mr. Churchill had taken a new tack in dealing with the French situation. The Prime Minister was keenly aware of the hostility of Laval and Darlan and suspected them of trying to provoke naval incidents that would lead to war with Britain. On the assumption that this collaborationist clique was or would soon be in control at Vichy, London had sent a warning that any aggressive French action would result in hostilities and that in such event the British would bomb Vichy itself.[88] But by mid-November a shift had begun. It is impossible, with the presently available evidence, to establish the reasons for the change, but it may well be that realization of Weygand's unwillingness to act against Vichy and news of Pétain's reaction to the Rougier negotiations played an important part. Rougier had arrived at Vichy on November 8 and the Marshal had received his report with great satisfaction. Laval, though now Foreign Minister, was not informed at all about this matter, and Pétain's unreserved approval of the Rougier memorandum was communicated to London through Prime Minister Salazar of Portugal.[89]

Even though the British may not have intended to give the Rougier memorandum the importance attached to it by Vichy, the Marshal's approval of it was at least symptomatic. Churchill was now hopeful that a *modus vivendi* could be arrived at and informed de Gaulle frankly of his determination to try. At the same time the Prime Minister reviewed the French situation in a memorandum to his Cabinet colleagues. He still argued for a stiff policy, to make Vichy feel that the British, as well as Hitler, had teeth, and he still held by his suspicions of the French collaborationists:

[87] For details see Langer: *Our Vichy Gamble,* 105-8; to be supplemented by Weygand: *Mémoires,* 483 ff.

[88] *Despatch . . . Regarding Relations between H.M.'s Government . . . and the Vichy Government in the Autumn of 1940* (Cmd. 6662), 18 ff.; Churchill: *Their Finest Hour,* 516-17.

[89] *The Private Diaries of Paul Baudouin,* 274-75.

Laval is certainly filled by the bitterest hatred of England and is reported to have said that he would like to see us "crabouillés," which means squashed so as to leave only a grease-spot. Undoubtedly, if he had had the power, he would have marketed the unexpected British resistance with his German masters to secure a better price for French help in finishing us off. Darlan is mortally envenomed by the injury we have done to his Fleet. Pétain has always been an anti-British defeatist, and is now a dotard.

To build on such men, argued Churchill, would be vain:

They may, however, be forced by rising opinion in France and by German severities to change their line in our favour. Certainly we should have contacts with them. But in order to promote such favourable tendencies we must make sure the Vichy folk are kept well ground between the upper and nether millstones of Germany and Britain. In this way they are most likely to be brought into a more serviceable mood during the short run which remains to them.[90]

In consonance with this new departure, Lord Halifax informed the American Chargé d'Affaires that Britain attached "enormous importance" to the maintenance of "all possible" contacts with Vichy and hoped particularly that the appointment of Mr. Pierre Dupuy as Canadian Chargé d'Affaires at Vichy would create a useful channel.[91] Under the circumstances the British must have been deeply gratified by President Roosevelt's decision to send an Ambassador of high rank to France. On November 13 he had offered the post to General John J. Pershing, writing: "Your personal prestige with the French people would prove of the greatest value in this endeavor and your close relationship with Marshal Pétain would undoubtedly make it easier for the views of this Government to be expressed to him through you in a friendly way but without reserve." Pershing would certainly have been the ideal man for the assignment, but for reasons of health he was obliged to decline. Thereupon Mr. Roosevelt wrote Admiral William D. Leahy, former Chief of Naval Operations and at the time Governor of Puerto Rico:

We are confronting an increasingly serious situation in France because of the possibility that one element in the present French Government may persuade Marshal Pétain to enter into agreements with Germany which will facilitate the efforts of the Axis powers against Great Britain. There is even the possibility that France may actually engage in the war against Great Britain and in particular that the French Fleet may be utilized under the control of Germany.

We need in France at this time an Ambassador who can gain the confidence of Marshal Pétain, who at the present moment is the one powerful element in the French Government who is standing firm against selling out to Germany.

Leahy at once accepted the appointment, but it was to be some time before he could take over the post. The President's letter to him is, however, an ex-

---

[90] Memo of November 14, 1940 (Churchill: *Their Finest Hour,* 526-27); Churchill message to de Gaulle, November 11, 1940 (*ibid.,* 516-17).
[91] Tel. from Johnson, November 20, 1940.

cellent brief statement of the official American view of the situation as it existed in November, 1940.[92]

The new British policy bore fruit early in December, 1940, with the conclusion of a secret agreement closely following the lines of the earlier Rougier memorandum. It so happened that Professor Jacques Chevalier, appointed Minister of Public Instruction in the Vichy Government in September, 1940, was a boyhood friend of Lord Halifax. The latter, through the new Canadian representative, Mr. Dupuy, sent Chevalier a letter, which was delivered on December 4. This recognized that, in order to deceive the Germans, a state of ostensible tension between France and Britain would have to be maintained, but proposed a secret understanding. Pétain, informed of this development, agreed at once, suggesting only one minor change in the proposed draft. Dupuy thereupon went to Madrid, whence he telephoned the agreement to Halifax. On December 9, 1940, he cabled Chevalier that it had been approved by the Foreign Office.

In the case of this agreement, as in that of the Rougier memorandum, the British and particularly Mr. Churchill have been most reluctant to acknowledge its existence, allegedly so as to spare the sensibilities of postwar French Governments. But the evidence is fairly conclusive that the agreement was accepted by both sides and was scrupulously observed in all respects. It provided that a state of artificial coolness (*froideur,* as suggested by Pétain, rather than *tension* as originally proposed by Halifax) be maintained; that the dissident French colonies be left provisionally in their existing status and that an effort be made, at an appropriate time, to reach an understanding about them; that with regard to the Fleet and the colonies, Marshal Pétain should renew his assurance not to deliver them to the Axis at any price or on any pretext; that the British radio should abstain from interference with the internal affairs of France; that the British Government should regard as coastal trade all transport needed for the food supply of Africa and metropolitan France; that the French troops in the colonies should resist any attempt at invasion, from whatever quarter; and finally, that the accord be kept rigorously secret.[93]

Although almost every aspect of Vichy policy is bound to remain controversial, it seems reasonably clear that the purpose of the Montoire meeting, so far as Pétain was concerned, was, firstly, to deprive Laval of his monopoly of relations with the Germans; secondly, to achieve such relief of the armistice terms as might be possible; and, thirdly, to forestall German ef-

[92] The letters to Pershing and Leahy are now printed in *F.D.R.: His Personal Letters,* II, 1079-81.

[93] Chevalier's account, in *Procès de M. Pétain,* 254-55; *The Private Diaries of Paul Baudouin,* 282-83. The fullest account of this matter, written in collaboration with M. Chevalier, is that of Prince Xavier de Bourbon: *Les accords secrets franco-anglais de décembre 1940* (Paris, 1949). The authors have benefited also from their correspondence with M. Chevalier on this subject.

forts to interfere with the African colonies. The old Marshal had, by the end of October, convinced himself that the British would fight on and that the United States would give them increasing support. He failed to see how the British could win, but he had to envisage a long struggle. His great objective was to avoid France's falling completely under German control and having to intervene against Britain. He therefore tried to maintain a precarious balance between the two opponents, at least until the British were in a stronger position. If this analysis is correct, it stands to reason that with regard to Laval and the collaborationists, Pétain had to do what he could to frustrate their avowed plans. To understand the situation fully it is therefore necessary to trace at least briefly the further development of the Franco-German relationship.

8. COLLABORATION: THE FIRST PHASE

Laval regarded the Montoire conference as the first fruit of his secret Paris negotiations and as the starting point for the policy of collaboration which he so ardently advocated. Having succeeded Baudouin as Foreign Minister, he acted as master of Vichy and promptly proceeded to arrange with Abetz for the implementation of the policy which Pétain had agreed to "in principle." It is perhaps unjust to accuse Laval of having been eager to sell his country to Hitler. Actually his policy seems to have been based squarely on the proposition that a German victory was certain and that it behooved France to win the good graces of the Fuehrer in order to secure alleviation of the armistice requirements and ensure a favorable peace settlement. His immediate objective was to demonstrate to the Germans that France was prepared to collaborate sincerely, but that the victors, on their side, must be patient and conciliatory. They must realize that the French public could but gradually be brought to recognize the wisdom and advantage of collaboration. This could be done by returning substantial numbers of war prisoners, by relaxing the line of demarcation between occupied and unoccupied France, by reducing the costs of occupation, by returning the northern departments to French administration, etc. Furthermore, in view of the widespread sympathy in France for the British cause, the Germans must appreciate that the best way to bring the country into the war on Germany's side was to attempt to reconquer the dissident colonies and so provoke the British to attack.[94]

Few members of the Vichy Government were prepared to support the Laval policy. Admiral Darlan, of whom Churchill was so suspicious, was to be sure violently anti-British and subscribed to the policy of economic collaboration with Germany on the theory that France could not hope to exist on

[94] See especially Bouthillier: *Le drame de Vichy,* 194 ff., 209. At the Pétain trial in 1945, Laval reaffirmed his stand: "Do you think that in 1940 any man of sense could imagine anything but a German victory?" (*Procès de M. Pétain,* 195).

any other basis. But Darlan was determined that the Germans should never get control of the Fleet. Neither was he willing to see the Germans get a foothold in North Africa. While eager to repay the British tit for tat, he desired to avoid an open break with the British lest France lose island possessions like the Antilles, Madagascar and Réunion.[95] Others, like General Huntziger, the Minister of War, and M. Bouthillier, the Minister of Finance, were associated with Laval in his negotiations with the Germans, but not so much out of sympathy with his policy as in the hope of extracting concessions from the victor. When the time came, both joined in the cabal that led to Laval's downfall. The other members of the Government were little if at all involved in the Laval policy and most of them, notably the Foreign Office staff, favored France's orientation toward the democracies. However, they followed the Marshal's lead in accepting the policy of collaboration "in principle." Pétain is said to have remarked: "It will take six months to discuss this program and another six months to forget it."[96] No doubt many Vichy officials shared this attitude and agreed that some gesture must be made in the German direction if only to forestall drastic action before the international situation had become clearer.

Laval, however, lost no time in following up the Montoire agreement. His first concrete aim was to reconquer the dissident colonies, so as to make a real impression on Hitler. On October 31, 1940, he, General Huntziger and M. Bouthillier conferred in Paris with Abetz, General Stülpnagel and a number of German military and economic experts. Laval seized this occasion to make an impassioned speech: the Montoire conference, he declared, was an event of impressive historical importance:

The offer of collaboration on the part of the German Chancellor is a gesture of magnanimity without historical precedent. The Chancellor of the Reich did not ask us to declare war on Britain. He asked us to enter a European coalition against Britain and, within the framework of this coalition, in the first place to work out military collaboration in Africa. The Ambassador [Abetz] and myself believe it necessary to arrive as quickly as possible at an agreement on ways and means of realizing the policy decided upon at Montoire. . . . I am able to report particularly that the French Council of Ministers has unanimously approved the policy of collaboration and that we are firmly determined to follow it.

Thereupon he entered a plea for German assistance: there were, he alleged, still many Frenchmen, including some perfectly decent people as well as the adherents of the Popular Front, Jews and Freemasons, who still staked their hopes on British victory. These people must be convinced that, in view of the complete defeat of Britain, salvation could be found only in collaboration with Germany: "All good Frenchmen must desire a German victory.

[95] Bouthillier: *Le drame de Vichy,* 227 ff., 301 ff., especially Darlan's memorandum to Pétain of November 8, 1940.
[96] *Procès de M. Pétain,* 313.

Britain must pay the costs of the war. Only then will a peace guaranteeing European collaboration for the future become possible."

The German negotiators had been instructed not to make an offer, but to hear what the French were willing to bid. Actually, however, Laval argued that the Germans must make substantial concessions in order to win over French opinion, and General Huntziger presented a memorandum asking for permission to increase considerably the French forces in North Africa and advancing various other desiderata of a military nature. These, he argued, were all necessary to meet further British aggression and organize an offensive against the Gaullist colonies.[97]

The German attitude was one of reserve, but from the record it appears that Hitler and his associates were persuaded that Pétain and Laval were sincere and that, given time, they would act against the Gaullist colonies and eventually perhaps against Britain itself. The Germans therefore granted many of the French requests for permission to reinforce the armies in North and West Africa. But the Germans were reluctant to make further concessions. They regarded the prisoners of war as the best guarantee of France's good behavior and took the attitude that they must await further evidence of French willingness to collaborate. When Laval conferred with Goering on November 9, the Nazi Marshal was perfectly frank about these matters, reminding his visitor that the first job was to defeat Britain and that France could hasten this defeat by reconquering its dissident colonies.[98]

Hitler's directive for the further prosecution of the war (November 12, 1940) reflected qualified optimism in the highest Nazi quarters:

> The aim of my policy towards France is to coöperate with this country in the most effective way for the future prosecution of the war against England. For the time being France will have the role of a "nonbelligerent power"—she will have to tolerate German military measures on her territory, especially in the African colonies, and to give support, as far as possible, even by using her own means of defense. The most pressing task of the French is the defensive and offensive protection of their African possessions (West and Equatorial Africa) against England and the de Gaulle movement. From this initial task France's participation in the war against England can develop fully.[99]

It is worth noting that this same directive was concerned primarily with Spain and the Gibraltar project. In other words, Hitler was not pressing the issue of French collaboration because Spain was more immediately important to him. Furthermore, the Italian attitude toward France was a constant drag on the development of collaboration. The details are lacking, but the

[97] On this conference see especially Bouthillier: *Le drame de Vichy*, 205 ff., and particularly Annexe II (Abetz's report of October 31) and Annexe III (Hemmen's report of October 31, 1940), from which the above quotations are taken.

[98] *Halder Diary*, October 31, November 1, 1940; Bouthillier: *Le drame de Vichy*, 214 ff.; *The Private Diaries of Paul Baudouin*, 275; *La Délégation française auprès de la Commission allemande d'Armistice* (Paris, 1947), II, 352-53, 389 ff.

[99] *Nazi Conspiracy and Aggression*, III, 444-PS.

German records leave little doubt that Mussolini continued to frown upon closer relations with France, being deeply concerned lest eventually France overshadow Italy in the Fuehrer's favor.[100]

Under the circumstances collaboration bore less fruit than Laval hoped and wished for. At the end of November he was still angling for a meeting with Ribbentrop. This project fell through, but on November 29 and December 10 Laval, Darlan and Huntziger were invited by the Germans to confer on military plans. General Warlimont, the chief German delegate, made clear on these occasions that the French were to organize an attack on the Lake Chad region and, having recovered that dissident colony, to extend their attack to neighboring British colonies, thus cutting the air route across Africa to Egypt and at the same time provoking British counteraction that would make France's intervention in the war logical. Laval was fully prepared to embark upon this hazardous course, but General Huntziger advanced many objections. Among other things, he noted, the Germans would have to give assurance that they would not attempt later on to take over the colonies. Furthermore, they would have to release many of the colonial troops still in captivity. In any event, it would be impossible to undertake such a campaign before the spring of 1941 at the very earliest. In short, the War Minister adroitly evaded concrete propositions when the Germans finally made them.[101]

The German proposals and Laval's acquiescence were too much for Pétain, who had long viewed the Vice Premier's activities with distrust and fear. On hearing of the November 29 conference, the Marshal is reported to have exclaimed: "We are near an explosion!"[102] Supported by most of his Ministers, Pétain was trying to restore good relations with Britain. Yet here was Laval busily engaged in plotting the involvement of France against Britain. Baudouin, Bouthillier and Peyrouton (Minister of the Interior) were bringing pressure upon the Chief of State to dismiss Laval and appoint as Foreign Minister M. Pierre-Etienne Flandin, who would be more agreeable to the British. This solution appealed to Pétain, who conferred with Flandin on December 7 and filled his ears with complaints of Laval's machinations. No doubt the conclusion of the Halifax-Chevalier agreement (December 6-9) made a change all the more attractive. Yet to dismiss Laval was of necessity a daring challenge to the Germans as well as to the formidable Vice Premier himself. The old Marshal was clearly fearful of so drastic a measure and as late as December 13 felt obliged to yield to Laval's importunities. Laval and Abetz had cooked up a scheme by which the remains of

---

[100] *Halder Diary*, November 11 and 18, 1940, the latter entry recording the German-Italian conferences at Innsbruck.

[101] *Pétain et les allemands: mémorandum d'Abetz*, 40 ff.; Bouthillier: *Le drame de Vichy*, 225, 243; *The Private Diaries of Paul Baudouin*, 280, 283; *Halder Diary*, December 2 and 15, 1940; de Brinon: *Mémoires*, 46 ff.

[102] *The Private Diaries of Paul Baudouin*, 280.

Napoleon's son (l'Aiglon) should be returned by the Germans from Vienna to Paris, on which occasion Pétain was to appear in the capital for the ceremonies. The end result was to be a striking demonstration of German generosity and a consecration of the policy of collaboration.

The aged Marshal was spared this humiliation through the determination of his associates, almost all of whom, including Darlan, insisted that Laval be removed. Peyrouton took all possible police precautions to forestall disturbances. Thereupon, on the afternoon of December 13, Pétain called for the resignations of all his Ministers, of which he accepted only that of Laval. The victim was as angry as he was surprised, but had no means of resistance. Under police escort he was taken to his estate, while Flandin assumed the post of Foreign Minister. This highly dramatic episode was carried off with consummate skill. It brought to an abrupt end the first phase of Vichy history and the first essay at collaboration. At the same time it marked the victory of those forces in the French Government which, if they did not all favor the reëstablishment of close relations with Britain, at least advocated a policy of cautious balance between the two great antagonists in the European conflict.[103]

News of Laval's fall must have come to Hitler as a severe shock. He was tortured by fear lest French North Africa desert to the British, an eventuality which, as he wrote Mussolini, must be prevented at any price. Abetz, probably inspired by Laval, had fostered grave suspicions of Weygand's activities and intentions, and the question of demanding his recall had already been raised in Nazi councils. While Laval and Warlimont were planning the reconquest of the dissident colonies, Hitler as a precaution had issued a directive (December 10, 1940) stating that, "should revolts occur in parts of the French Colonial Empire now under command of General Weygand, preparations must be made for the speedy occupation of the territories of the French motherland which are still unoccupied."[104]

Pétain's courageous action of December 13 threatened to put the quietus on a crucial part of the Nazi plans. On December 9 the British had opened a counteroffensive from Egypt which was to blast all German hopes that the Italians might secure control of the eastern Mediterranean. On the very next day Franco had made clear that Spain could not and would not intervene in

---

[103] For a detailed account of the highly complicated circumstances leading to Laval's downfall see Langer: *Our Vichy Gamble*, 108 ff., now to be supplemented by Girard: *Montoire*, 296 ff.; *Pétain et les allemands*, 44 ff. (Abetz's report); Bouthillier: *Le drame de Vichy*, 216 ff., 245 ff., 253 ff.; *The Private Diaries of Paul Baudouin*, 280 ff., 284 ff.; *Le procès Flandin* (Paris, 1947), 164 ff.; Colonel Groussard: *Chemins secrets* (Paris, 1948), Chapter III; *The Diary of Pierre Laval*, 66 ff.; de Brinon: *Mémoires*, 49 ff.

[104] Cited in Martienssen: *Hitler and His Admirals*, 97. For the rest see Hitler's letters to Mussolini of November 20 and December 5, 1940 (*Les lettres secrètes échangées par Hitler et Mussolini*, 81 ff., 96 ff.); *Pétain et les allemands*, 42 ff. (Abetz's report of December 12, 1940); *Halder Diary*, December 8, 1940.

the war for some time, or countenance Nazi operations against Gibraltar. The untimely disappearance of Laval from the Vichy scene was therefore the last of a series of setbacks—in a sense the most ominous, inasmuch as it seemed to signify the collapse of collaboration and forecast the dissidence of French North Africa. It was a foregone conclusion, therefore, that Hitler would do his utmost to have Laval reinstated. Abetz hurried to Vichy, secured Laval's release from police surveillance, and obliged Pétain to recall the ex-Minister to Vichy for conference. Nothing, however, came of these efforts. Pétain insisted that Laval's dismissal was entirely a domestic matter and that he proposed to adhere to the policy of collaboration. He was willing to agree to almost anything but the return of Laval to power. Abetz continued his pressure for some time, but without effect.[105]

The Germans took no comfort from the Marshal's assurances and were rightly convinced that Laval had been dismissed for his plan to get rid of Weygand and steer France into war against Britain. Reviewing the whole episode in a letter to Mussolini (December 31, 1940), Hitler wrote that the official explanations given by Vichy were false:

I do not doubt for a moment that the real reason [for Laval's dismissal] lies in the fact that General Weygand made demands which amounted to a deal, and that the Vichy Government was not in a position to resist these demands without risking the loss of all North Africa. I think it probable also that at Vichy itself there is a whole clique of people who approve the Weygand policy, at least tacitly. I do not think that Pétain is personally disloyal. But one never knows.[106]

Flandin's appointment provided little solace, for even though he was supposedly inclined toward friendship with Germany, he was also suspected of aiming at closer relations with Britain and was, in fact, altogether welcome to Churchill. The Germans therefore saw no alternative to putting their money on Darlan, whose Anglophobia was notorious. Darlan no longer believed in the early collapse of Britain, but could not see how the British could ever win the war. Within limits, therefore, he was willing to collaborate with the Germans, in the vain hope, shared by many Frenchmen, that in a German-dominated Europe France could succeed in playing an important role, especially after Hitler disappeared from the scene. On Christmas Eve, Darlan presented himself to Hitler with a letter from Pétain. He explained Laval's fall as the result of a "personal row" and begged the Fuehrer to continue the policy of collaboration. But Hitler, though ready to work with Darlan if possible, especially with an eye, as Pétain put it, "of embracing him and his ironclads," refused to commit himself for the time being. The events of December and the blasting of so many fond hopes had

---

[105] Langer: *Our Vichy Gamble*, 111; *Pétain et les allemands*, 44 ff. (Abetz's report of December 18, 1940); *The Private Diaries of Paul Baudouin*, 292 ff.; *Le procès Flandin*, 169 ff.
[106] *Les lettres secrètes*, 103 ff.; *Pétain et les allemands*, 44 ff.

left him disillusioned and bitter. Darlan himself had to admit that all he had gotten for his pains was "an explosion of bad temper."[107]

By the end of the year, then, Hitler's far-flung plans for flank attacks on Britain in the Atlantic and Mediterranean had ended in failure. It would, however, be a gross exaggeration to credit British or American policy with this result. At the root of these developments lay the one great and compelling fact that Britain had withstood the Nazi assault and that the prospect of an early termination of the war had faded. The outlook for a British victory was still extremely faint, but the British, with command of the seas, still had valuable cards to play. Above all else, they could point to the ever increasing support of the United States, politically as well as materially. All governments, including the Nazi Government, recognized the potential power of this combination. The great question, therefore, was whether Hitler could still oblige Britain to yield before the odds against him became too great.

[107] *The Private Diaries of Paul Baudouin,* 298-99; for the German record of the interview see Langer: *Our Vichy Gamble,* 122-23. Darlan's views and policies were rather frankly expounded by him in conversation with Matthews and Admiral Leahy (*ibid.,* 116-17, 123).

CHAPTER IV

Mussolini and the Mediterranean

1. THE ADVANCE ON EGYPT

The Suez Canal is the eastern gateway to the Mediterranean, as Gibraltar is the western. In the strategy adopted by Hitler for a flank attack on the British it was therefore equated in importance with the capture of the famous rock. In principle this aspect of the Mediterranean problem presented less difficulty than the Gibraltar operation, since in place of the recalcitrant Franco the Nazis had to deal only with a willing and loyal ally, Benito Mussolini. In practice, however, the plans for an assault on Egypt proved just as abortive as the project for the intervention and coöperation of Spain. Indeed, Mussolini was to reveal himself as a liability rather than an asset, and the Germans were soon to rue the day when they had agreed that the Mediterranean should be Italy's sphere of influence. Not only did the Duce fail dismally to carry out his assignment to invade Egypt, but by his stupid attack on Greece at the end of October, 1940, he contributed generously to the expansion of the war to the Balkans and to involvements which were eventually to cost the Axis whatever chance of victory it might have had in a protracted war.

Having had no military success in the campaign against France, the Duce's chief remaining opportunity to share in the anticipated victory against Britain, and so establish a strong claim to colonial spoils, lay in the attack on Egypt from Libya and the ultimate conquest of Suez. In the summer of 1940 the odds seemed all in his favor, for the Italian forces available for the operation outnumbered the British forces in Egypt by more than four to one. Marshal Italo Balbo had been entrusted with the conduct of the campaign and is reputed to have had secret plans for an attack to begin in mid-July, 1940. But Balbo was killed in an airplane accident at the end of June and his successor, Marshal Rodolfo Graziani, hero of the war against Abyssinia, was utterly dissatisfied with the preparations as he found them.

He used what influence he had to postpone the decision to march, but the Duce had little patience with professional hesitancy and insisted that at least a limited offensive be launched against Egypt, to coincide with the projected German invasion of England in August or September. In this matter, as in his decision to attack France in June, 1940, the Italian dictator's chief consideration was to have some conquest in hand before appearing at the peace table. The expulsion of the insignificant British defense forces from Somali-land in early August, 1940, could hardly be regarded as sufficient for the purpose. Despite Graziani's objections, therefore, the Duce notified Hitler in late August that all preparations were complete and that the Italian forces in Libya had been ordered to attack on the day when the Germans launched their cross-Channel operations.[1]

German military men were highly skeptical of the ability of the Italians to defeat the British, no matter what the odds, and therefore concerned themselves more and more with the problem of applying their own forces to the operation.[2] As the prospects for a direct assault on England grew dim, the importance of the Mediterranean became increasingly obvious. The Germans must therefore have been much gratified when, on September 13, 1940, Graziani began his advance into Egyptian territory. In less than a week he had progressed sixty miles and had taken Sidi Barrani. But this operation proved nothing, for the greatly outnumbered British rolled with the punch and fell back. They noted that the Italian campaign was slow, unenterprising and even timid, and that no real effort was made to proceed beyond the fortified position at Sidi Barrani.[3]

Mr. Churchill, meanwhile, was keenly aware of the importance of Egypt and Suez to the further conduct of the war and was determined to hold this crucial area at all reasonable cost. He insisted that British forces in Kenya, Palestine and other parts of Africa be concentrated in Egypt, on the theory that one could not hope to be secure in all areas. Furthermore, he worked out plans for an air route from West Africa (Takoradi) to Khartum and, despite the acute threat of German invasion, began to send reinforcements of men, guns and tanks from the home country. The risk he was taking was a grave one, but perfectly sound, as the sequel was to show. In his own words: "The decision to give this blood-transfusion while we braced ourselves to meet a mortal danger, was at once awful and right."[4] Just as Graziani com-

[1] Letter of Mussolini to Hitler, August 27, 1940 (*Les lettres secrètes échangées par Hitler et Mussolini,* 77 ff.). For more detail see Rodolfo Graziani: *Africa settentrionale, 1940-1941* (Rome, 1948), 18 ff., and the same author's *Ho difeso la patria* (Cernusco, 1948), 225-95.

[2] The initial German attitude is well reflected in the *Halder Diary,* July 31, 1940.

[3] In addition to the books of Graziani see General Sir Archibald P. Wavell: *Operations in the Middle East from August, 1939, to November, 1940* (despatch dated December 10, 1940, published as a supplement to the *London Gazette,* June 11, 1946); Field-Marshal Lord Wilson of Libya: *Eight Years Overseas* (London, 1948), 43 ff.; and Churchill: *Their Finest Hour,* Book II, Chapter VI.

[4] Churchill: *Their Finest Hour,* 428.

pleted his occupation of Sidi Barrani the first British reinforcements began
to reach the defenders. From that time on, through October and November,
more and more troops and matériel were concentrated in Egypt, progressively shifting the balance of military power to the disadvantage of the
would-be invaders.

By the end of September German strategy for the Mediterranean had
been generally established. Admiral Raeder had convinced the Fuehrer that
the Mediterranean question must be cleared up during the coming winter:
Suez must be taken, and there must be an advance from Egypt through
Palestine and Syria as far as Turkey. This program was, admittedly, beyond
Italian capabilities; consequently German assistance would have to be provided.[5] This was one of the issues which Hitler therefore discussed with the
Duce at the Brenner Pass meeting of October 4. Mussolini explained that
shortly the Italians would initiate the second phase of the offensive, which
would take them to Marsa Matruh, the terminus of the Egyptian railroad
from Alexandria. Finally, in late November or December, there was to be a
third phase, which would lead to the Nile Delta and end with the occupation of Alexandria. Hitler, in turn, took the opportunity to offer his colleague specialist forces for these operations, but the Duce assured him that
he would need nothing more than some armored cars, a number of heavy
tanks and some formations of dive bombers (*Stukas*). Possibly troops might
be needed for the third phase, but that matter could be discussed later.[6]

Hitler understood that it was a matter of prestige for Mussolini to win a
victory without German aid, and for that reason abstained from pressing the
issue. He did, however, send General von Thoma, Chief of the German
Mobile Forces, on special mission to Rome and Libya to consult and report.
Von Thoma returned at the end of October with a most depressing report
on the state of affairs. He found the Italian High Command and Graziani's
headquarters at loggerheads, Rome pressing constantly for action, while the
Commander in Chief sought to avoid further operations. The Italians revealed no desire at all for German assistance, realizing doubtless that before
long they would be under complete Nazi domination. Yet, according to von
Thoma, they could not possibly do the job alone. They were simply no good
as soldiers; in fact, one Englishman was better than twelve Italians. If the
operation against Egypt was to succeed, no less than four German armored
divisions would have to be provided. By this time the British, according to
German reports, had concentrated 200,000 men in Egypt. Obviously the
job confronting the Axis had become a formidable one. Indeed, Hitler and
his generals had already come to the conclusion that, without awaiting

[5] Report of Admiral Raeder to Hitler, September 26, 1940 (*Fuehrer Conferences,
1940,* Part 2, pp. 24 ff.).

[6] *Ciano's Diplomatic Papers,* 398; *Ciano Diaries,* October 4 and 5, 1940. A tel. from
Matthews (Vichy) of October 14, 1940, gave a fairly accurate report of these conversations. We have used also the *Halder Diary,* October 8 and 15, 1940.

Italian moves, Crete ought to be seized so as to secure a suitable base for German air attacks on the British Fleet and the Suez Canal.[7]

At the end of October, then, the Italian forces were still immobilized at Sidi Barrani, while their opponents were rapidly building up their forces and supplies. Hitler and his military advisers were in a quandary. They had come to see the immense importance of attacking the British, on land and on sea, of getting control of the Suez Canal, and if possible advancing into the Middle East so as to secure access to the raw materials of that region. Yet they felt helpless in the face of Italian vanity and incompetence. But the cup of Hitler's frustration was not yet full. As he returned from his disappointing conferences with Franco and Pétain, he learned to his dismay that Mussolini had decided to make war on Greece on October 28.

2. AGGRESSION AGAINST GREECE

Ever since the Italian occupation of Albania in April, 1939, there had been good reason to fear that Greece was slated as the next victim of Fascist imperialism. Certainly the Greeks themselves put no store by the assurances lavished upon them by Mussolini and Ciano, while the western capitals assumed that the Duce would turn on Greece at an opportune moment, unless he decided that Yugoslavia was the more suitable prey. No useful purpose would be served by reviewing all the alarums and excursions provoked by Italian designs. The important point is that Ciano and a majority of Fascist leaders were bent on annihilating the inconvenient Greek state as a necessary step in the extension of Fascist power over the eastern Mediterranean. War seemed inevitable in mid-August, 1940, when the Greek warship *Helli* was torpedoed by an "unknown" submarine. At that time Britain seemed effectively neutralized and Mussolini had every reason to expect that his longed-for victory could be secured at little cost. But he was quickly reminded by Ribbentrop that the Nazis were intent on maintaining peace in the Balkan area and would therefore find an attack on Greece most unwelcome. Somewhat later, however, Ribbentrop committed the error of assuring the Duce that Italy should have a free hand in disposing of both Yugoslavia and Greece. This statement was made in response to Mussolini's exposition of a plan to liquidate Greece after a further advance against Egypt and after the expulsion of the British Fleet from the Mediterranean. The Italians never fulfilled these conditions, but took full advantage of the opening given them by the Nazi Foreign Minister to launch one of the most harebrained exploits of the entire war.[8]

[7] On von Thoma's mission we have used the *Halder Diary*, October 24 and 26, 1940, but see also B. H. Liddell Hart: *The German Generals Talk* (New York, 1948), 155 ff., and Desmond Young: *Rommel* (London, 1950), 80-81.

[8] The most important sources for the background of the Italian attack are *The Greek White Book: Diplomatic Documents relating to Italy's Aggression against Greece* (Eng. transl., London, 1942); the memoirs of the Italian Minister to Athens, Emanuele Grazzi:

The actual decision to launch the assault from Albania into Epirus was taken on October 15, 1940, and appears to have been provoked by news of the unexpected mission of Nazi troops to Rumania. It may be assumed that Mussolini felt impelled to action also by Graziani's inability to fill the bill in North Africa. But the crucial thing was that Hitler, completely ignoring his ally, had by his occupation of Rumania taken a step which was clearly a disturbance of the *status quo* in the Balkans. The Duce was enraged by this affront and, according to Ciano's diary, gave vent to his temper in these words: "Hitler always faces me with a *fait accompli*. This time I am going to pay him back in his own coin. He will find out from the papers that I have occupied Greece."[9]

The records of the Fascist council of October 15, 1940, provide eloquent proof, if any is needed, of the utter irresponsibility with which the modern would-be Caesar arrived at his fateful decisions. The oft-repeated warnings of the Italian Minister in Athens that the Greeks would resist were brushed aside with the argument that such resistance would be ineffective if the aggression were sudden and vigorous. The Italians reckoned that they had a numerical superiority of two to one and that they could overrun Epirus in two to three weeks. After that the rest of Greece could be quickly occupied and the strategic island of Crete could be seized. It was hoped that the British Air Force could be held in Egypt and that the British would not attempt to despatch ground forces to the aid of the Greeks. Ciano gave his solemn promise that a suitable pretext for aggression could be arranged; beyond that nothing further was required. In the early hours of October 28, 1940, the Italians confronted the Greek Government with a short-term ultimatum, accusing it of unneutral acts and more particularly of aid to the British. The ultimatum was rejected at once and before the day was out the Italian forces were on the march.[10]

Actually the Duce did not quite dare to have Hitler learn these tidings from the newspapers. He wrote him an explanatory letter several days before the event, but saw to it that the news should not reach him immediately. Hitler was en route to his meetings with Franco and Pétain and did not receive his colleague's message until after the Montoire conference. It was later to be the fashion in German circles to describe the Fuehrer as so thunderstruck by the news of the coming attack on Greece that he at once

---

Il principio della fine (Rome, 1945); of the Italian Military Attaché in Athens, Colonel Luigi Mondini: *Prologo del conflitto italo-greco* (Rome, 1945); and of Marshal Pietro Badoglio: *L'Italie dans la guerre mondiale* (Paris, 1946). See further the critical accounts of Raymond Klibansky, editor, in *Mussolini: Memoirs* (London, 1949), 261 ff.; Wiskemann: *The Rome-Berlin Axis*, 225 ff.; and Gaetano Salvemini: "Pietro Badoglio's Role in the Second World War" (*Journal of Modern History*, December, 1949, pp. 326-33).

[9] *Ciano Diaries*, October 12, 1940.

[10] Mussolini's own account of the conference of October 15 is given in *Mussolini: Memoirs*, 177 ff., but this should be read in conjunction with the analyses of Klibansky, Salvemini and Wiskemann, as cited above.

had his special train diverted to Italy, where he met with Mussolini and
Ciano at Florence on October 28, 1940. The fact of the matter seems to
have been that Hitler had intended all along to report to Mussolini at an
early date on his negotiations with Spain and France, and that the news of
the attack on Greece simply induced him to advance the date of the meeting in the hope of yet forestalling action. Writing to Mussolini on November
20, 1940, after the onset of the Italian reverses, Hitler explained that he had
hoped to induce his partner to postpone the operation against Greece until
a more favorable season and especially to persuade him not to launch the
attack until Crete had been seized in a lightning attack. He had, so he said,
wanted to offer Mussolini for this purpose a parachute division and a division of airborne infantry.[11]

That there was at least a measure of truth in these asseverations is shown
by the notes of the Florence meeting. The astonishing thing about that record, however, is the fact that it contains nothing about the attack on Greece
beyond Hitler's offer of support, as needed.[12] The lengthy discussions on this
occasion concerned primarily Spain and France, and other European questions. One can only conclude, therefore, that the Duce's transgression did
not at the time appall Hitler. However low his opinion of Italian military
capabilities, he undoubtedly did not envisage a disaster of such magnitude
as the Duce was preparing for himself. He probably felt that if Mussolini
would abstain from too great opposition to German plans to pamper Vichy,
it would be unseemly that he himself should be too outspoken in condemnation of the Italian aggression. Besides, there was always the chance that
Greece would collapse and that the Axis would secure possession of Crete.
It was only in retrospect that Hitler let himself go in reproaches. Mussolini's
crime was not that he attacked Greece, but that he failed to conquer it. Bemoaning the past, the Fuehrer wrote the unfortunate Duce in December,
1944: "If in 1940 Italy, instead of attacking Greece, had together with Germany resolved the Spanish problem, the development of the war might have
taken a different course."[13]

The Italian campaign against Greece was ill-starred from the beginning.
The Greek armies were stronger and better prepared than their opponents
realized. As soon as they had mobilized they succeeded in holding the invaders and before long were able to assume the offensive. Furthermore,
Italian hopes that Bulgaria would join in the fray and seize Saloniki came
to naught when the Turkish Government warned Sofia that intervention on
Bulgaria's part would entail immediate counteraction by Turkey.[14] Perhaps
an even more serious miscalculation on the Duce's part was his estimate
that Britain could or would do nothing of importance. Graziani remained

[11] Les lettres secrètes échangées par Hitler et Mussolini, 81 ff.
[12] Ciano's Diplomatic Papers, 399 ff.
[13] Quoted by Klibansky, in Mussolini: Memoirs, 282.
[14] Tel. from MacMurray (Ankara), October 31, 1940.

at Sidi Barrani and would hear nothing of a further offensive toward Marsa Matruh. Consequently the British had some latitude of action. They made the most of it. Indeed, before long it appeared likely that the United States, too, would throw its weight into the scales to the extent of providing the Greeks needed munitions and supplies. These developments far transcended anything that Mussolini and perhaps even Hitler had envisaged. They involved fundamental changes in the east and helped give a turn to the war that was to prove calamitous to Hitler as well as Mussolini.

3. Repercussions of the Greek Conflict

The British Government had, on April 13, 1939, offered Greece a guarantee of assistance in the event of aggression by a third power. It therefore went without saying that Mr. Churchill, when appealed to by the Greek Prime Minister, General Metaxas, at once promised all possible support. As a matter of fact, the Italian attack gave the British a much desired opportunity to secure control of Crete, the importance of which as an air and naval base was as obvious to Mr. Churchill as to Hitler. On the invitation of the Athens Government, British forces were landed at Suda Bay on November 1, 1940. Soon afterward the island of Lemnos was also occupied. In return the British despatched to Greece five squadrons of bomber and fighter planes from Egypt. Advanced elements of these forces arrived on November 6 and soon took part in the bombardment of Albanian ports and Italian communications. There can be no doubt that they helped substantially to redress the balance of air power and that they interfered seriously with Italian efforts to reinforce the front.[15]

Had Mr. Churchill had his way, troops as well as planes would have been sent to support the Greek resistance. Among other things the Prime Minister considered such aid essential to maintain Turkish confidence in the sincerity of British promises. But General Wavell, commanding the British forces in the Middle East, objected to sending any of his forces across the Mediterranean, on the theory that it would in any case be impossible to provide enough troops to affect the outcome. In addition, Wavell was already hatching plans for an offensive against Graziani and so felt loath to part with any of his forces. For security reasons his plans had not yet been communicated to London. Mr. Churchill learned of them only on November 8, when Mr. Eden returned from an extended special mission to the Middle East. The idea of turning the tables on Graziani made a real appeal to the Prime Minister and therefore little more was heard of the transfer of troops from Egypt to Greece. The British contented themselves with the occupation of Crete and the provision of limited air power.[16]

[15] Churchill: *Their Finest Hour*, 533 ff.; Air Vice Marshal J. H. D'Albiac: *Air Operations in Greece, 1940-1941* (despatch dated August 5, 1941, now printed as a supplement to the *London Gazette*, January 9, 1947).

[16] Churchill: *Their Finest Hour*, 538 ff.; General Sir Archibald P. Wavell: *Operations*

Though modest in scope, British support of Greece was of great importance, particularly for its effect on German plans. Even before the Italians had embarked upon their foolhardy adventure, Admiral Raeder had been worrying about a possible British occupation of Crete, which, he noted, "would be of great importance for naval supremacy in the eastern Mediterranean and for defense against an Italian offensive in Egypt." It may well be imagined, then, how disconcerted Hitler and his military advisers were when they learned that the British had anticipated them. The occupation of Lemnos was regarded by Hitler as an even more grievous development, for it gave Britain an advanced position from which to encroach on the mainland, enabled Britain to influence and support Turkey, and gave Britain facilities for launching air attacks on the Rumanian oil fields. As early as November 4, 1940, the Fuehrer decided that antiaircraft reinforcements, fighters and fighter-bombers should at once be sent to Rumania. Furthermore, he decided that Italy would have to be supported by at least two German divisions, which were to advance from Rumania through Bulgaria in the direction of Saloniki, with or without the consent of the Bulgarians. Finally, he ordered that Bulgaria should be supported militarily against any attack by Turkey. By November 12 these plans had been expanded. Ten divisions were to be used, partly in order to hold Turkey in check, but chiefly to occupy northern Greece and secure positions from which German planes could reach the British bases threatening the Rumanian oil fields.[17]

Thus the Italian aggression obliged Hitler to devise countermeasures which, in turn, were to involve more and more of the Balkans in hostilities, with results to be chronicled later. Originally, the Fuehrer planned his military intervention to take place within a few weeks, but various considerations obliged him to postpone action until the early spring of 1941. Meanwhile the Greeks stopped the Italian advance and launched an offensive of their own. To make matters even worse for the aggressors, the British on November 11 delivered a spectacular carrier plane attack on Italian warships lying in the harbor of Taranto. Several battleships were hit and about half of the vaunted Italian Fleet was crippled. By this single stroke, writes Mr. Churchill, "the balance of naval power in the Mediterranean was decisively altered."[18]

As they saw the tables being turned on the Axis, the Germans were chagrined beyond words by their ally's stupidity. They discerned at once that

---

in the Western Desert from December 7, 1940 to February 7, 1941 (despatch dated June 21, 1941, printed as a supplement to the London Gazette, June 26, 1946).

[17] Fuehrer Conferences, 1940 (2), 32 ff., 44; and the Hitler directive for further military operations, November 12, 1940 (Nazi Conspiracy and Aggression, III, 442-PS).

[18] Churchill: Their Finest Hour, 544 ff.; Admiral Sir Andrew Cunningham: Fleet Air Arm Operations against Taranto on November 11, 1940 (despatch dated January 16, 1941, printed as a supplement to the London Gazette, July 22, 1947).

events in Greece and the Mediterranean would react on the projected conquest of Egypt. To quote a memorandum of the German Naval Staff:

> The Italian offensive against Greece is decidedly a serious strategic blunder; in view of the anticipated British counteractions it may have an adverse effect on further developments in the eastern Mediterranean and in the African area, and thus on all future warfare.
>
> The enemy clearly has supremacy in the eastern Mediterranean at present, and it is possible that his position in the eastern Mediterranean area will become so consolidated that it will no longer be possible to drive the British Fleet from the Mediterranean.
>
> The Naval Staff is convinced that the result of the offensive against the Alexandria-Suez area and the development of the situation in the Mediterranean, with their effects on the African and Middle Eastern areas, is of *decisive importance for the outcome of the war*.
>
> . . . .
>
> The Italian armed forces have neither the leadership nor the military efficiency to carry the required operations in the Mediterranean area to a successful conclusion with the necessary speed and decision. A successful attack against Egypt by the Italians alone can also scarcely be expected now. The Italian leadership is wretched. They have no understanding of the situation; above all they have not yet perceived in what manner their offensive against Greece primarily damages *Italy's* powers of endurance.

According to the German Naval Staff the only remedy, in these circumstances, was for the Germans themselves to take a hand. Greece must be occupied, the advance from Libya must be supported, and an offensive through Turkey on Suez must be seriously considered.[19]

These notes apparently provided Hitler the ammunition for a long and plaintive letter to the unhappy Duce, despatched on November 20, 1940. The ill-considered attack on Greece, he pointed out, had already seriously impaired Axis prestige and drawing power. Militarily the British had secured bases from which to bomb not only the Rumanian oil fields, but the ports of Albania and southern Italy. It was therefore urgently necessary to bring Spain into the war and win over Turkey and the Balkan states, while at the same time trying to divert Soviet Russia from the Balkans and Middle East. Furthermore, the Italians must push their advance to Marsa Matruh as quickly as possible, so as to secure an air base from which German bombers could attack the British Fleet and the Suez Canal. This objective was to be given first priority, and the Mediterranean question to be solved in the course of the winter. Judicious employment of Axis air forces would turn the Mediterranean, within three or four months, into the grave of the British Fleet, after which the German land offensive against Greece could begin in early March, 1941.[20]

[19] *Fuehrer Conferences, 1940* (2), 50-52 (undated, but evidently of November 14, 1940).
[20] *Les lettres secrètes échangées par Hitler et Mussolini*, 81 ff.

To Hitler's homily Mussolini replied but briefly, saying that he had had his black week but that he was preparing thirty divisions for operations against Greece and was determined to destroy that presumptuous little nation. Most of the other questions raised by Hitler he either ignored or glossed over. The Duce certainly knew that it would be impossible for Graziani to stage a further advance without German help, which he devoutly hoped he could escape. He felt unable, however, to deny that closer coöperation between German and Italian air forces was necessary, with the result that Hitler promptly despatched General Milch to Italy to work out the necessary agreements. By early December the Fuehrer was fully prepared to launch his *Stukas* against Alexandria. That he felt sure of success is indicated by a further message to Mussolini, saying that the German air contingents would have to be returned by February.[21] But the situation was even worse than Hitler realized, for within a matter of days the British themselves loosed an offensive from Egypt which was to blast all hopes so carefully nurtured by the Germans.

General Wavell and the staff of the Army of the Nile had been elaborating their plans in greatest secrecy ever since mid-October. The attack on the Italian positions had been first scheduled for the end of November, but actually commenced on December 6, when some 30,000 British troops, all motorized, advanced from Marsa Matruh forty miles over the desert and encamped thirty miles from the front, unobserved by the Italians. The assault began on December 9 and Sidi Barrani was taken on the following day. Of the large Italian forces (about 80,000) many were surrounded and some 38,000 taken prisoner ("about five acres of officers and two hundred acres of other ranks"). British losses in killed and wounded totaled hardly 500. Within a week the Italians were driven from Egyptian territory and forced back on Sollum and Bardia. There ended the first phase of the "desert victory," which inspired Mr. Churchill to cable General Wavell: "It looks as if these people were corn ripe for the sickle."[22]

The British offensive of December, 1940, which was to be only the prelude to greater conquests in the opening months of the New Year, was quite as stunning a blow to the Germans as to the Italians. Admiral Raeder's Naval Staff viewed the situation "with grave misgivings" and pointed out that "apart from the considerable prestige gained by Britain, the military and strategic success must not be underestimated. The threat to Egypt, and thus to Britain's position in the entire eastern Mediterranean, in the Near East, and in the North African area, has been eliminated with one stroke." Hitler, for his part, bemoaned the "complete lack of leadership in Italy," and agreed that it was "no longer possible to drive the British Fleet from

[21] *Lettres secrètes échangées par Hitler et Mussolini,* 93 ff.

[22] Wavell: *Operations in the Western Desert from December 7, 1940, to February 7, 1941;* Lord Wilson of Libya: *Eight Years Overseas,* Chapter II; Churchill: *Their Finest Hour,* Book II, Chapter XVI.

the Mediterranean."[23] The Fuehrer, clearly worried lest opposition elements in Italy undermine Mussolini's position, wrote his colleague consolingly that great powers often make the mistake of attacking small states with insufficient forces. Although no major counterattack in Africa would be possible for some months, the situation was by no means desperate, for in the west Britain was to all intents and purposes already defeated and the position of the Axis was strong also in the Balkans. In any event, he concluded, the Duce could always count on Nazi support.[24] How sincerely he meant this assurance is shown by the record of his conference with his military leaders on January 8 and 9, 1941, when he expressed his firm determination to prevent the collapse of the Italian position. Substantial German forces and matériel were to be sent to North Africa as well as to Albania, and the attack on Greece through Bulgaria was to be expedited in all possible ways.[25]

Whatever the resolutions and plans of Hitler for the future, the fact remained that the year 1940, period of the most resounding Nazi successes, ended for the Axis in disappointment and gloom. Within one week in early December the Fuehrer learned that Franco refused to intervene in the war or even permit Nazi operations against Gibraltar; that Pétain had unceremoniously dismissed Laval, the apostle of collaboration between France and Germany; and that Wavell's offensive had all but destroyed five Italian divisions, driven the Fascists from Egyptian soil and blasted Axis plans for control of the eastern Mediterranean. Meanwhile the valiant Greeks, allied with Britain and diplomatically supported by the Turks, had carried their offensive into Albania and threatened to destroy the utterly demoralized Italian forces.

4. THE POSITION OF TURKEY

Axis plans for depriving the British of control of the eastern Mediterranean and the Suez Canal necessarily attracted attention to the position and probable future policy of the Turkish Republic. Technically speaking the Ankara Government, bound by treaty to Britain and France, should have entered the war against Italy when that power intervened in June, 1940. The Allies had not, however, pressed the point, for Turkey was militarily neither equipped nor organized for war and there was grave danger that Turkish intervention might have little other effect than to turn the Nazi armies into the Balkans and Middle East. The British were therefore content to have their ally maintain a policy of friendly neutrality against the day when active participation in the war would be more desirable and practicable.[26]

---

[23] *Fuehrer Conferences, 1940* (2), 68.

[24] *Les lettres secrètes échangées par Hitler et Mussolini*, 103-13 (letter of December 31, 1940).

[25] *Fuehrer Conferences, 1941* (1), 1 ff.

[26] Sir Hughe Knatchbull-Hugessen: *Diplomat in Peace and War* (London, 1949),

   This situation naturally did not meet Hitler's requirements as well as it did the British, and the Ankara Government consequently found itself under constant pressure from the German Ambassador, the notorious Franz von Papen, to throw in its lot with the future masters of Europe. For a time the Turks were able to resist such pressure, but by the autumn of 1940 they were confronted with the problem of their own future in the light of Nazi activities in Rumania and in the Balkans generally. Von Papen's frank avowal that Hitler was about to "rearrange the Balkans" was bound to occasion uneasiness in Ankara and raise the question whether something could not still be done to organize the Balkan states for common defense. The idea was by no means new. It was known to bristle with difficulties, and was hardly likely to succeed unless backed by powers stronger than Turkey. It seemed important to the Turkish statesmen, therefore, to mend their relations with Soviet Russia and if possible bring Britain and Russia together in a common front opposed to changes in the Balkan *status quo*. If, reasoned the Turks, the United States also could be induced to throw the weight of its influence into the scales, so much the better.

   The Kremlin, as deeply disturbed as Ankara by German activities in Rumania, was by no means averse to improving its relations with Turkey, which had been cool, to say the least, since Foreign Minister Saracoglu had visited Moscow in October, 1939, and refused an agreement which at that time had been pressed upon him.[27] The Kremlin therefore recalled Alexis Terentiev, its envoy to Ankara, and despatched a new Ambassador, Sergei Vinogradov, who was received by President Inönü of Turkey on October 3, 1940. A few days later (October 8) the Turkish Ambassador to Moscow, who had been absent from his post for two months, returned to duty, announcing after a conversation with Molotov that relations between the two countries were normal and friendly.[28]

   The British Government certainly welcomed any moves that might accentuate the Soviet-German antagonism in the Balkans and strengthen opposition to Nazi designs in that area. Furthermore, it would certainly have received with enthusiasm any American contribution to the same end. Unlikely though it was that Washington would take a hand in these geographically remote issues, the Turks decided at least to make the effort. On October 9, 1940, Mr. Ertegün, the Turkish Ambassador in Washington, had a long conversation with Assistant Secretary Berle on the general inter-

---

166; despatch from MacMurray (Ankara), October 29, 1940, reviewing at length the evolution of Turkish policy from March to October, 1940. The Turkish position is discussed in detail in David J. Dallin: *Soviet Russia's Foreign Policy* (Boston, 1942), 305 ff.; in Harry N. Howard: "Germany, the Soviet Union and Turkey during World War II" (*Department of State Bulletin*, XIX, July 18, 1948, pp. 63-78); and in Cevat Açikalin: "Turkey's International Relations" (*International Affairs*, XXIII, 1947, pp. 477 ff.).

[27] See *The Challenge to Isolation*, Chapter IX, Section 1.

[28] *Bulletin of International News*, XVII (2), 1400.

national situation. He began by pointing out that Soviet-Turkish relations were satisfactory and that the two powers respected each other. But the appearance of German forces in Rumania indicated "that the tide was coming very close." Turkey was prepared for every eventuality and proposed to resist any attempt at invasion. But, he continued, "each of the European nations had been handling its affairs as though it were buying a ticket in the sweepstakes: if the number turned up, the nation might win, or preserve itself. Actually, it had meant disaster." The Ambassador thought there was still "the nick of time" to build a bloc of certain remaining countries, which might save the situation. If Soviet Russia, Turkey, possibly Greece and Bulgaria could be brought together, and if they could count on the support of the United States, there might be a reasonable chance of avoiding further catastrophe.

Mr. Berle admitted that Nazi-Soviet relations seemed to be drifting into crisis and that Soviet national interest and expediency would seem to lead the Kremlin toward coöperation with powers not dominated by Germany. On the other hand, since it was clearly the Soviet policy to avoid involvement in the war, the Kremlin would probably continue to collaborate with Germany, at least in appearance, until forced to do otherwise. As for the immediate future, Mr. Berle thought it not unlikely that the Germans might stage an attack on Suez through Syria and Palestine. To this idea the Turkish Ambassador heartily subscribed, explaining that for that very reason he was suggesting the possibility of an opposition bloc. There the discussion ended, for obviously the Assistant Secretary could say nothing more than that he would consider the Ambassador's suggestions.[29]

These were not empty words, for Mr. Berle at once referred to the Division of Near Eastern Affairs such questions as whether, if nothing further were done, the Turks would resist the Germans, or permit them passage to Syria; and whether, if the Turks resisted the Germans, the Soviets would support them or stab them in the back. The general conclusion of the appropriate officials in the Department was that the Turks would probably fight if the Germans attempted to move on the Dardanelles and that Soviet Russia would probably not take military action on either side. As to the problem of American support of Turkey, it was pointed out that facilities had already been given the Ankara Government for the purchase of military supplies and that this was about the only measure open to the United States, short of war, to encourage the Middle Eastern countries to resist aggression.[30]

That Turkish apprehensions in October, 1940, were not exaggerated can be demonstrated from German sources. Perusal of the *Halder Diary* leaves no doubt that Hitler and his military advisers were much incensed by

[29] Memo of conversation between Mr. Berle and Ambassador Ertegün, October 9, 1940.
[30] Memo of Mr. Berle to Mr. Alling, October 11, 1940; memo of the Division of Near Eastern Affairs, October 16, 1940.

Turkey's attitude. They seriously considered the possibility of attacking Suez in a land campaign through Turkey, Syria and Palestine and were at times tempted to use force against the Turks to secure the right of transit.[31] In this situation the Ankara Government could do little more than declare its determination to resist and encourage the Balkan states to stand together in the face of common danger.[32]

One deterrent to a German advance through the Middle East was of course fear of antagonizing Soviet Russia and thereby perhaps provoking a Soviet-British coalition. Hitler meant to discuss this particular problem when Molotov came to Berlin in mid-November. Meanwhile the Italian attack on Greece gave the eastern Mediterranean situation an entirely new turn. Though the Ankara Government decided not to intervene militarily on the side of Greece, it at once informed the British and Greeks that if Bulgaria joined in the attack, or if the Italians moved on Saloniki, Turkey would consider itself threatened and would act accordingly. In the National Assembly President Inönü proclaimed that Turkey regarded the ties with Britain as solid and unshakable, and made the added point that relations with the Soviet Union had been restored to those of normal friendship.[33] The Turks did not share the prevalent opinion that Greek resistance was hopeless and calculated rightly that by their own firm stand they would enable the Greeks to withdraw their forces from eastern Thrace for use in Albania. Without a doubt the Turkish policy contributed substantially to the successes of the Greeks, as the outbreak of the Greek conflict itself served to define and strengthen the Turkish position. In other words, Mussolini's adventure cost Hitler whatever chance he may have had of forcing the Turks into an agreement that would permit him to send troops through the Middle East against Suez.

Perhaps even more serious for the Fuehrer was the patent *rapprochement* between Turkey and Soviet Russia resulting from the growing Balkan crisis. As Hitler saw it, the way to forestall further development of such an entente was to offer the Kremlin coöperation in the realization of its traditional aims with respect to the Straits. If the German terms had been sufficiently attractive, there can be little doubt that Stalin and Molotov would have listened attentively, for the evidence indicates that Molotov cautiously avoided too close a relationship with Turkey until he had had an opportunity to explore the possibilities with Hitler during his visit to Berlin on November 12. On that occasion the issue was in fact discussed and German offers made. But, as will be shown in the following chapter, the Nazi proposition was regarded by Moscow as inadequate. After mid-November the Kremlin evidently estimated that it would be more advantageous to the Soviet Union to have

[31] See, e.g., the *Halder Diary*, October 26, 1940.

[32] *Bulletin of International News*, XVII (2), 1400-1402.

[33] Tel. from MacMurray, October 31, 1940; Knatchbull-Hugessen: *Diplomat in Peace and War*, 167; *Bulletin of International News*, XVII (2), 1520.

Turkey, backed by Britain, serve as a barrier to Nazi expansion in the east than to exploit the tense international situation to secure specific concessions with regard to the Straits. In the last analysis, then, the developments of October and November in the eastern Mediterranean involved a distinct weakening of the Axis position.

5. SAD EPILOGUE: AMERICAN "AID" TO GREECE

The American reaction to the Italian aggression against Greece was immediate and violent, but was otherwise simply a variation on the theme first played when the Nazis overwhelmed Poland and the Soviets invaded Finland. Popular sympathies went out to the small nation victimized by the armed might of a ruthless neighbor. But in the case of Greece, as of Finland, it proved impossible to devise ways and means of translating sympathy into concrete aid.

The exhilarating news that the Athens Government had chosen to defy an Italian ultimatum, worded and presented with a cynicism rare even in those degenerate days, was greeted throughout the United States with paeans of praise, interspersed liberally with references to the heroic Greeks of the classic age. But there was, at the outset, no thought that anything further would be expected of the great democracy of the New World. Few, if any, could guess that Greek resistance would last more than a few weeks, or that the armies of General Papagos could do more than disturb the timetable of Axis victory. British aid to the stricken country was loudly applauded, but again there was no reason to suppose that such aid could be brought to bear in sufficient time or magnitude to affect the outcome materially. Only when it became apparent that Greek capacity for resistance had been underrated did hope spring up. Thenceforth American comment abandoned the elegiac for the martial note.

On November 23, less than a month after the outbreak of hostilities, the Greeks captured the Albanian town of Koritza, from which the Italians had launched their invasion. Americans suddenly realized that General Metaxas' hope of destroying the enemy might after all be realized. Enthusiasm over the "miracle of Greek resistance" was boundless. No longer could Greek appeals for support be easily dismissed on the assumption that resistance would collapse before aid could reach the scene of battle. Accordingly, when King George of Greece addressed a personal appeal to President Roosevelt (December 3, 1940), it was impossible to evade the issue. The King requested moral and material assistance, which General Metaxas spelled out as a loan to buy munitions and planes.[34]

There were, however, serious obstacles to any program of aid to Greece, quite apart from the strategic decisions involved in sending matériel to a

[34] *Documents on American Foreign Relations,* III, 314; tel. from MacVeagh (Athens) transmitting an appeal from Prime Minister Metaxas, December 9, 1940.

country likely before long to be attacked by Germany. Unfortunately the American Government, having decided that the effect on Greece of a proclamation of a state of war between Greece and Italy would be "negligible," had on November 15 invoked the provisions of the Neutrality Act. Thenceforth it was all but impossible, without recourse to Congress, to make available to Greece funds for the purchase of munitions. No doubt popular sentiment favored a loan to Greece, but seasoned observers recalled the sorry spectacle of Congressional bungling of the loan to Finland earlier in the year and gave little hope of a more favorable outcome.[35]

Assuming that these formidable legal and political obstacles could have been surmounted, there remained the all but insuperable barrier to aid for Greece presented by the lack of instruments of war, not only for the British, Chinese, and Latin Americans, but for the defense of the United States itself. The plain truth was that every plane, every gun, and every ship, existing or contracted for, was already earmarked for delivery to the American forces or to those of the nations on which the security of the United States was held to depend. If these priorities were to be abruptly revised in deference to the needs of Greece, the change could be justified only by a painstaking examination of the gains and losses in terms of overall strategy. True, the advocates of assistance to Greece could advance realistic as well as sentimental arguments. They could point to the oft-reiterated American promise to extend all possible support to countries resisting aggression. The Greeks were certainly giving an unexampled demonstration of heroic and successful resistance. If they were let down, how could it be expected that other small nations, in the Balkans or elsewhere, would act as hurdles in the Nazi path?

Had the Administration made its decision in the light of these cogent factors, it would be hard to quarrel with whatever decision was finally reached. There is every evidence, however, that the President first resolved to send aid to Greece and only then began to consider the pros and cons of his decision. On December 5, 1940, he replied to King George with the assurance that "steps were being taken" to extend assistance. This message was presently followed by a reply to Prime Minister Metaxas which, while emphasizing that existing legislation made it impracticable to lend money to Greece for the purchase of munitions, promised that "special consideration" would nevertheless be given to facilitating the acquisition of the needed matériel.[36]

What the President meant by "special consideration" soon became painfully apparent to his harassed advisers. Peremptory instructions were given Assistant Secretary of State Berle to make available to the Greeks immediately thirty of the new P-40 pursuit planes. This gesture was to mark only

[35] Memo of the Division of Controls, November 5, 1940; Hull: *Memoirs*, I, 886. Public opinion polls registered 60 per cent in favor of a loan to Greece at the end of November, 1940 (*Public Opinion Quarterly*, March, 1941, p. 158).

[36] *Documents on American Foreign Relations*, III, 315; tel. to MacVeagh, December 18, 1940.

the first step in a tragicomedy of attempted aid to Greece which ended only when the German invasion of the spring of 1941 mercifully rescued the Administration from its embarrassment. In effect, there were no P-40 planes not already earmarked, as the President ought to have known when he promised them. To give such planes to Greece would have meant to take them from U.S. Army and Navy stores, or from the British. In the effort to save the situation, such maneuvers were in fact tried, with the result that serious recriminations took place between Government departments and between American and British agencies. The Greeks never secured any P-40's. As the Greek Minister made clear, a proposal to stage *Panama Hattie,* a current Broadway success, with the President in attendance, in the interests of Greek War Relief, could hardly be regarded as an acceptable substitute![37]

No useful purpose would be served by following the hectic course of the ensuing negotiations. The President himself finally tired of the controversy he had precipitated and was willing, in the end, to let the matter drop, as the War and Navy Departments urged. Mr. Hull, for his part, was goaded to fury by the spectacle of some half dozen agencies meddling in foreign policy, and is alleged to have issued orders in the State Department that no one was even to mention the subject of planes for Greece. To be sure, voices continued to be raised pointing out the incalculable damage to American prestige that must result from a failure to live up to the President's promise, but even these voices were stilled when Hitler cut short the debate by his spectacular invasion and conquest of Greece.[38]

The Greeks, then, derived no material benefit from the sympathy and generous impulse of the President and the American people. Nonetheless, they bore no ill will. On the contrary, they evidently drew strength from the realization that not only the British but the great democracy beyond the seas were identified with their cause. By the same token, Americans saw more clearly than ever before how immediate was the threat of totalitarian aggression and how urgently needed was a major effort to support resistance before it was too late. While rejoicing in the successes of the Greeks and British, Americans came to appreciate the importance of Middle Eastern and Balkan problems and to understand their bearing on the overall development of the conflict. With the new year they were to become nationally as well as emotionally involved in issues which only recently had seemed to be those of another, alien world.

[37] *Morgenthau Diaries (MS.),* December 9, 1940, to February 11, 1941 (Vols. 337 ff.) ; *Berle Diaries (MS.), passim.*

[38] *Morgenthau Diaries (MS.),* January 31, 1941 (Vol. 353, pp. 184 ff.) ; *Berle Diaries (MS.),* February 14, 1941.

CHAPTER V

Stalin and the East

1. THE KREMLIN AND THE TRIPARTITE PACT

The two thoughts expressed by Hitler with utter monotony during the autumn of 1940 were, firstly, that Britain was already defeated, and secondly, that what kept the British from recognizing this obvious fact was the hope that the United States and Soviet Russia would intervene to save them from perdition. The Tripartite Pact between Germany, Italy and Japan was designed primarily to frighten the United States with the specter of a Pacific war and consequently to distract America from support of Britain. For this purpose, the more imposing the Axis coalition, the better. An integral and important part of the Nazi plan was therefore to associate as many powers as possible in a world-embracing alliance. Spain, France and the various Balkan states were all envisaged in the dream of Hitler and Ribbentrop. By far the most important candidate, however, was Soviet Russia, which, if it could be drawn into the new combination, would deprive Britain of a last remaining hope.

The Japanese, in turn, had an equal or even greater interest in bringing the Kremlin into the pact, for Soviet Russia and Japan were confirmed enemies who, as recently as the summer of 1939, had been engaged in what amounted to undeclared war on the Manchurian frontier. So long as a huge and self-contained Soviet Army was in position on the borders of the Japanese possessions, it was unsafe for the Japanese to embark on their program of southern expansion. In the course of the negotiations leading to the Tripartite Pact, the Germans had agreed to use their influence with Moscow to bring about a settlement of Soviet-Japanese differences and associate the Soviet Union with the new power combination. It will be recalled that the published text of the pact stated explicitly that the agreement "affects in no way the political status existing at present between each of the three contracting parties and Soviet Russia."

The German representative in Moscow informed Foreign Commissar Molotov of the alliance with Japan only on the evening of September 26, 1940, less than twenty-four hours before its actual signature. The Soviet statesman evinced immediate interest and insisted that his Government was entitled, under the Soviet-German nonaggression pact of August, 1939, to see and comment on the text, including all secret articles, before the actual signature of the agreement. It was not, however, until October 2 that the Germans responded to his request, pointing out that there were no secret clauses and that, since the relationship of the contracting powers to Soviet Russia was specifically excluded from the pact, the Kremlin had no valid claim to be consulted.[1]

It is likely that Molotov already knew more than the German Chargé d'Affaires could tell him, for a Soviet spy ring was at the time operating in Tokyo with unbelievable success. Richard Sorge, one of the most remarkable spies of the entire war period, had for years posed as a Nazi journalist and had ingratiated himself with General Ott, the German Ambassador to Japan. There appears to be little doubt that Sorge was fully informed of the German-Japanese negotiations and that he reported them promptly to Moscow.[2] This fact must be kept in mind in considering the Kremlin's reaction to the proposals presently submitted to it by the Germans. Commissar Molotov could therefore listen with some equanimity to the lavish assurances proffered by both the Germans and Japanese. The world at large knew nothing of the Soviet position beyond what could be deduced from an editorial in *Pravda* of September 30, 1940. This took almost exactly the line marked out by Secretary Hull a few days before: the pact was "in effect an embodiment of the relations already formed between Germany, Italy and Japan on the one hand, and the United States and Britain on the other," but, in the Soviet view, it signified "the advent of a new and more extensive phase of the war." "The Soviet Union, on its part, true to its policy of peace and neutrality, can confirm, in so far as this will depend on it, that this policy remains and will remain unalterable."[3]

So far as most commentators could detect, what *Pravda* meant to say was that the lines between the opposing forces were being ever more sharply drawn, but that the Kremlin still aimed to stand aloof. This could be interpreted to mean that the Soviet Government was well content to see the two opponents fight it out, provided always that Soviet Russia could itself be spared the ordeal of conflict. This cool attitude was naturally far from what the Japanese had anticipated. The Tokyo press had been celebrating the

[1] *Nazi-Soviet Relations, 1939-1941*, edited by Raymond J. Sontag and James S. Beddie (Washington, 1948), 197-99, 201-3.
[2] Department of the Army: *The Sorge Spy Ring*, a report released on February 10, 1949.
[3] *The New York Times*, September 30, 1940.

forthcoming agreement with Soviet Russia as though it were already a reality.[4]

But weeks passed without word from Moscow. It was not until the end of October that General Tatekawa, newly despatched Japanese Ambassador to the Soviet Union, was able to impress on Molotov the great desire of his Government for a treaty of friendship and nonaggression, this to be followed by negotiations on specific issues such as the Japanese oil concessions in northern Sakhalin, fishery rights, frontier incidents, and Soviet aid to Nationalist China. To Ambassador Steinhardt General Tatekawa stated that the Japanese were willing to make great concessions to attain their end: Japan was ready to recognize Soviet control of Outer Mongolia and Soviet special interests in Sinkiang, and trusted that in return the Kremlin would recognize the Japanese position in Manchuria and at least publicly renounce aid to Chiang Kai-shek. However, the Japanese Ambassador had no opportunity to present the Japanese terms, for Commissar Molotov waved the whole matter aside with the remark that the question of an agreement with Japan was "under study."[5]

Molotov was, at the time, about to undertake a journey to Berlin, during which, as he already knew, the Germans would broach the question of Soviet adherence to the Tripartite Pact. Furthermore, the Japanese offer had not been the only one to reach the Kremlin in the weeks following conclusion of the Axis-Japanese agreement. The British, too, had been active, with the result that Stalin and Molotov found themselves back in the position they had occupied in the summer of 1939. All sides were wooing the Kremlin, which quite naturally concluded that, if it were to shift its position at all, it could command a high price. For the moment Moscow did not even inquire as to the Japanese terms, which in any case it would want to compare with those of other suitors. Before examining the Nazi-Soviet conferences in Berlin, it is therefore essential to consider what other possibilities Stalin and Molotov had before them.

2. The Lure of the West

Prime Minister Churchill, as Hitler suspected, never abandoned hope that the Soviet Union would come to see that its own interest lay in reducing aid to Germany and drawing closer to Britain. He who ran should be able to

---

[4] Wilfrid Fleisher in the *New York Herald Tribune,* October 2, 1940; *The New York Times,* October 3, 1940.

[5] Tel. from Steinhardt, November 8, 1940, reporting a conversation with Tatekawa. Hugh Byas, in *The New York Times,* October 22, 1940, reported somewhat similar terms from Tokyo. See further a U.P. despatch from London, in *The New York Times,* November 5, 1940. According to a British report the Japanese were prepared to sell South Sakhalin to the Soviets, and to provide them with a corridor through Manchuria to Dairen (letter of Mr. Nevile Butler of the British Embassy to Mr. Hornbeck, November 5, 1940).

read the handwriting on the wall, thought the British statesman. Once Britain had gone under, the Nazi drive was bound to turn east and attempt the realization of the land-grabbing program so brutally expounded in *Mein Kampf*. Hardly had Mr. Churchill come to office when he addressed Stalin on this matter and sent Sir Stafford Cripps to Moscow to press the argument. In conversation with the new Ambassador on July 1, 1940, Stalin had in fact conceded the cogency of British reasoning, but had made it very clear that in his opinion the Kremlin would do best to remain aloof from the conflict as long as possible, even if eventually it would have to oppose Hitler singlehanded. His calculation turned on the thought that though the Nazis might subdue Britain, they would be so weakened by the operation that they would be less formidable foes, particularly as the Soviet Union would in the interval have had time to advance its preparations.[6]

Under the circumstances there was nothing for Sir Stafford Cripps to do but bide his time while Nazi-Soviet relations became increasingly strained by Balkan issues. But the Ambassador's letters leave no doubt that he was profoundly bored by his enforced inactivity and gradually came to the conclusion that the prospect of the much-desired Anglo-Soviet alliance had grown dim indeed.[7] So discouraged was the British diplomat that initially he envisaged only ill effects from the Tripartite Pact. The published reaction of the Kremlin evidently revived his hopes, for he presently cabled the British Foreign Office suggesting that the psychological moment had come for making another effort to induce the Kremlin to line up against Japan and the Axis. The principal bait was to be an offer to release the funds of the three Baltic States, which were still blocked in London.[8]

Neither Britain nor the United States had recognized the absorption of the Baltic states by the Soviet Union, and the action of the two Governments in blocking Baltic funds was one of the manifold grievances which the Kremlin professed to hold against the western powers. Assuming, then, that concessions on this point might influence the Soviet leaders, the British sounded out Washington as to the American attitude toward the proposed move. Heretofore the State Department had taken a stiffly negative position. The British must consequently have been agreeably surprised to learn that while Secretary Morgenthau had doubts of the wisdom of the step, Secretary Hull voiced no objection. Thus encouraged, Lord Lothian presently approached Mr. Hull to find out whether the United States itself might conceivably contemplate a similar concession. Again the response was not unfavorable. The Secretary reminded Lothian that the Administration had steadfastly refused to recognize the acquisition of territory by force. But, he

---

[6] On this see *The Challenge to Isolation,* Chapter XIX, Section 1, and Chapter XXI, Section 4.

[7] Eric Estorick: *Stafford Cripps* (London, 1949), 263 ff.

[8] Memo of conversation between Mr. Dunn and the Counselor of the British Embassy, Mr. N. M. Butler, October 1, 1940.

added, if the Soviet Union showed a real disposition to move in the desired direction, he would be willing to deal with Baltic funds and ships under American control "on a reciprocal basis rather than to adhere inflexibly to our nonaggression policy."[9]

In view of Mr. Hull's known aversion to negotiations with Soviet Russia and his but recently reiterated conviction that the Soviets "couldn't be trusted for a minute," his reaction to the British suggestion was truly surprising.[10] The explanation is obviously to be found in the fact that, during the first days after the conclusion of the Tripartite Pact, the Secretary was deeply concerned lest war ensue quickly. Momentarily, at least, he seems to have overcome his distrust of the Kremlin and to have been willing to have a further go at a policy of conciliation. Lord Lothian took full advantage of the situation to request that Ambassador Steinhardt be instructed to impress on the Soviet leaders the obvious community of interest of the United States and the Soviet Union in the face of Japanese expansion.[11]

Sir Stafford Cripps lost no time in pressing his suit. In conversation with Commissar Molotov he announced Britain's intention to reopen the Burma Road and harped on the dangers presented by Tokyo's policies. On the plea that the American reaction would no doubt be influenced by Moscow's stand, he suggested that consultation and coöperation between the Soviet Union, Britain and the United States might be in order. But Molotov was evidently worried by this suggestion. His reply was anything but encouraging: since the three powers were unable to agree on small matters, he failed to see that consultations on major issues such as the Far East would serve a useful purpose.[12]

But Sir Stafford was not to be easily daunted. In mid-October the Kremlin agreed to renew trade negotiations with the British, and the Soviet press began to write appreciatively of British pluck in fighting off the Nazi air offensive. "There is obviously a complete change in outlook due to Germany's occupation of Rumania, which has upset people very much following on the Japanese alliance," reported the British Ambassador. "Everything for us is much easier and the press is more sympathetic."[13] He therefore advised Mr. Churchill that Britain had a chance to influence the Kremlin and outbid Germany for Soviet support, outlining the terms that might be submitted. The Cabinet decided to make the try. The State Department was informed at once and requested to assure the Soviet Government that the

[9] *Morgenthau Diaries (MS.)*, October 1 and 2, 1940 (Vols. 317, p. 226, and 318, pp. 15 ff.); memo of conversation between Mr. Hull and Lord Lothian, October 14, 1940.

[10] Hull's attitude was forcefully expressed at a Cabinet meeting on September 27, 1940, recorded in the *Stimson Diary (MS.)* of that date.

[11] Tel. from Steinhardt, October 12, 1940.

[12] Tel. from Steinhardt, October 5, 1940.

[13] Estorick: *Stafford Cripps*, 263.

United States would see to it that Japan did not become a source of danger to the Soviet Union.[14]

Cripps was once again to be disappointed when he attempted to see Molotov and submit his handsome offer. No explanation was given, but Ambassador Steinhardt shrewdly surmised that Molotov's assignment was to deal with the Germans and that the Kremlin did not want him compromised by negotiations with the British. After all, arrangements were just being made for the Foreign Commissar to visit Berlin.[15] The British Ambassador had to content himself, therefore, with an interview with Molotov's deputy, Andrei Vishinsky, who received him on October 22, 1940. Sir Stafford prefaced his remarks by expressing Britain's conviction of ultimate victory over Germany, particularly in view of the ever increasing flow of American aid. He then proceeded to set forth the British proposals: the British Government would promise not to conclude peace without prior consultation with the Soviet Union; neither would it make agreements with third powers aimed at the Soviet Union; neither would it attack Baku or Batum. Furthermore, the British Government would conclude with the Soviet Government a trade agreement providing for the supply of rubber, tin and other commodities. In return the Kremlin was to observe genuine neutrality in the current war; to adopt a policy of benevolent neutrality toward Turkey or Iran if either became involved in hostilities with the Axis; to continue aid and support of Nationalist China; and to sign a nonaggression pact with Britain at a propitious moment after conclusion of the trade agreement. In conversation Cripps evidently enlarged the British offer to include *de facto* recognition of the Soviet acquisition of the three Baltic states, eastern Poland, Bessarabia and northern Bukovina, pending final disposition of these matters at the end of the war.

Vishinsky, like Molotov, was not one to betray enthusiasm even over the most alluring offer. He asked a few questions to satisfy himself that Cripps's proposition was more than a personal one, and inquired whether Washington was privy to the British proposals. Cripps replied in the affirmative and assured Vishinsky that the British Government recognized that the Kremlin could not presently take steps apparently incompatible with its agreements with Germany, but that it would like an understanding looking to the future. The Ambassador, only too eager to be satisfied, took no umbrage at Vishinsky's noncommittal attitude. It was enough for him that his interlocutor appeared to take the matter seriously.[16]

[14] Memo of conversation between Mr. Welles and Mr. Butler, October 18, 1940.

[15] Tel. from Steinhardt, October 23, 1940.

[16] On this episode see also John Scott: *Duel for Europe* (Boston, 1942), 148 ff.; David J. Dallin: *Soviet Russia's Foreign Policy, 1939-1942* (New Haven, 1942), 321 ff.; W. P. and Zelda Coates: *A History of Anglo-Soviet Relations* (London, 1943), 651; Max Beloff: *The Foreign Policy of Soviet Russia*, II (New York, 1949), 357 ff. We have used also tels. from Steinhardt, October 23 and 28, 1940.

The British policy which culminated in the Cripps proposals was viewed with mixed feelings by American officials. The State Department had just completed another grueling round of conversations with the difficult and offensive Soviet Ambassador, Oumansky. Some progress had been made toward the settlement of minor issues, but from Secretary Hull down there was little disposition among Department officials to trust Soviet policy or to put faith in the possibility of establishing really friendly relations.[17] In conversation with the Turkish Ambassador, who had suggested the desirability of supporting Soviet attempts to build a Balkan bloc in opposition to Hitler, Assistant Secretary Berle pointed out that firm relations with Russia would never be really established until two matters had been cleared up:

The first was the cessation of Russian revolutionary propaganda in the United States, directed against the Government. The second was the Russian assertion of the right to take and seize territory by violence, as she had done in Latvia, Lithuania and Estonia and had attempted to do, with some success, in Finland, despite the fact that she herself had played a large part in setting these countries free. The United States had definitely set its face against that kind of thing; and we would find it difficult to establish really cordial relations with a country which pursued a policy of this kind. This was an objection of principle; but if we abandoned our principles in this matter, we had very little to stand on.[18]

Yet the Department, like the British Foreign Office, could not entirely ignore the dangers involved in eventual Soviet adherence to the Tripartite Pact. Through anti-Nazi members of the German Embassy in Moscow it had learned of the rift that had opened in the Nazi-Soviet pact as a result of conflicting interests in the Balkans, and recognized the possibility of exploiting this new development.[19] It has already been noted that Secretary Hull himself had raised no objection to British plans for appeasement of the Kremlin. Mr. Welles, in turn, had made an effort in the same direction when on October 8 Oumansky, on instructions from Molotov, reopened the tiresome negotiations on outstanding issues. For once the Ambassador appeared in a relatively amiable mood. He abandoned his previous insistence that the United States Government release the machine tools and war matériel which the Soviet Government had ordered prior to July 2, 1940, and which had been taken over by the United States under the provisions of the President's proclamation placing war materials under the licensing system. Oumansky did, however, press for irrevocable export licenses for future purchases of war materials in the United States.[20]

As a result of this conversation, the State Department made a substantial

[17] See *The Challenge to Isolation,* Chapter XXI, Section 4.
[18] Memo of conversation between Mr. Berle and the Turkish Ambassador, October 9, 1940.
[19] Memo of conversation between Mr. Berle and Secretary Morgenthau, October 1, 1940 (*Morgenthau Diaries, MS.,* Vol. 317, p. 22).
[20] Tel. to Steinhardt, October 9, 1940.

concession to the Soviets. On October 12 it revoked its earlier decision and announced that all suspended shipments of machine tools should be released forthwith. It was assumed in Washington that negotiations would thenceforth make better progress.[21] Ambassador Steinhardt, however, was highly critical of British as well as American attempts to court the Soviets. He recognized the change that had come over the Nazi-Soviet relationship, but insisted that the Kremlin was still motivated primarily by the desire to keep out of the European war, that is, out of the war with Germany. Stalin, he held, would do anything to avoid such an eventuality. All British efforts to get the Soviet Government to take positive action involving real risk of war with Germany would fail so long as the Germans themselves required of the Kremlin nothing more than neutrality.[22]

On the subject of unilateral American concessions to save the Welles-Oumansky conversations Mr. Steinhardt was even more vehement. In personal letters to friends in the State Department he expounded his views in detail. The idea that the Soviet Union could be influenced to change its policy and enter any kind of "Anglo-American-Soviet alliance in-the-making" was essentially childish, he declared, since the Kremlin could take such a course only at the risk of German invasion. No amount of "appeasing" would change the Soviet attitude toward Germany, which would remain what it was until the German Army ceased to be the principal threat to the Soviet Union. Actually, continued Steinhardt, recent approaches to the Kremlin by Britain and the United States were regarded by the Soviets simply as signs of weakness.

The Ambassador reserved his bitterest criticism for British attempts to involve the United States in their own particular "appeasement policy." Such efforts to make the United States a "wet nurse" in weaning Soviet Russia from Germany were destined to failure. Furthermore, newspaper talk of British plans was bound to react unfavorably on the Kremlin because of its effect on the Germans.

Steinhardt realized that State Department support of the Cripps program stemmed from anxiety to prevent a *rapprochement* between Soviet Russia and Japan, which could prove highly dangerous to American interests in the Far East. Even so, he felt extremely pessimistic about the chances of achieving anything in that direction. He thought it obvious that the Soviet Union would welcome war between the United States and Japan, and believed the Kremlin had decided that its purposes would best be served by a Soviet-Japanese nonaggression treaty. Once the Far Eastern conflict had begun, however, the Kremlin would probably withhold assistance from Japan in the hope that that power would be defeated by the United States and that the Soviet Union could reap the harvest without military effort on its part. "It is

[21] *Morgenthau Diaries (MS.)*, October 9, 1940 (Vol. 321, p. 196).
[22] Tels. from Steinhardt, October 2 and 8, 1940.

difficult," concluded the Ambassador, "to envisage a Japanese-American naval war, the ultimate outcome of which will not be of material value to the Soviet Union."

As for resumption of the Welles-Oumansky conversations and the concessions recently made by the State Department, Steinhardt believed he had conclusive proof of their effect on the Kremlin. In the past few weeks, he pointed out, Soviet authorities had been particularly recalcitrant and uncoöperative. They were not offering the United States any significant *quid pro quo*. Oumansky undoubtedly represented to Molotov that Washington was seeking the good graces of Moscow in anticipation of war with Japan. In any case, the Soviets were now gloating over the supposed American "need" of their friendship, and were becoming increasingly difficult. All told, concluded the Ambassador, there was no use whatever in imagining that the Kremlin "responds to kindness or evidence of goodwill." To base American policy on such notions would result only in lowering the national prestige. It would be "dead wrong."[23]

Although high officials of the State Department knew through Steinhardt that Molotov was going to Berlin, they felt obliged to heed the British request that American influence be used in support of Cripps's efforts. Steinhardt was instructed, if he should succeed in seeing Molotov, to explain to him that the Welles-Oumansky conversations were evidence of America's "sincere desire" to improve relations with Russia and that the State Department was much pleased with the results already achieved and hoped for further success "in broader and more important fields." Signature of the Tripartite Pact emphasized the new dangers to be expected from the aggressors; accordingly, the United States hoped that peace-loving nations would resist the pressure to make commitments incompatible with maintenance of their independence. Even great powers, momentarily outside the scope of aggression, should not ignore these considerations. Such powers—i.e., Soviet Russia—should remember that if they assumed obligations to the Axis limiting their freedom of action, these engagements would tend to isolate them from other free nations, and to "mortgage their future to the powers of aggression." The United States Government, therefore, welcomed the opportunities afforded by the Welles-Oumansky conversations to relieve friction between the two countries, and believed that if the way toward closer association continued to be prepared, such association could help to prevent hostilities from spreading.[24]

Steinhardt, like Cripps, was given no opportunity to confer with Molotov and had to content himself with Vishinsky, whom he saw on October 30. The Ambassador began by alluding to the pleasing progress of the Welles-

[23] Memo from Mr. Atherton to Mr. Welles, November 26, 1940, quoting excerpts from a letter of Steinhardt's of October 20, 1940.
[24] Tel. to Steinhardt, October 26, 1940.

Oumansky conversations, only to meet with professions of astonishment on Vishinsky's part. He knew nothing, said the Deputy Commissar, of any achievements in the Washington negotiations. Nevertheless, he added, the Soviet Government had decided, as a matter of principle, and irrespective of any so-called concessions by the United States, to grant certain requests long urged by the Ambassador. The United States was to be allowed to open a consulate at Vladivostok and was to be provided with further housing for the embassy staff in Moscow!

This effort to magnify compliance with routine American requests into magnanimous concessions was certainly familiar to the Ambassador and was probably assessed by him at its true worth. When it came to discussion of really vital matters of high policy, Vishinsky vouchsafed nothing more than what Steinhardt himself described as a "stereotyped" Soviet statement of policy. The Soviet Government, so Vishinsky averred, had always opposed aggression and recognized that in certain cases it was limitless. The furtherance of peace was a "consistent aspect" of Soviet foreign policy. The Kremlin sought "friendship" with all states, and in so doing had neither restricted its freedom of action nor isolated the Soviet Union from other countries. Hence its policy was demonstrably "correct." In any event, Soviet Russia could protect itself from aggression from whatever source. To the point-blank question whether the Soviet Union was contemplating a non-aggression pact with Japan, Vishinsky declined to answer, leaving the Ambassador convinced that this was indeed the case.[25]

Having cherished no illusions, Steinhardt could hardly have suffered disappointment. Sir Stafford Cripps, by contrast, waited hopefully if not patiently for the reply to his lavish proposals. Weeks passed, yet no word came from the Kremlin. Instead, the announcement was made about November 10 that Commissar Molotov was shortly to depart for Berlin. This was a terrible blow to Sir Stafford, who hurried at once to Vishinsky to relieve his feelings. "I pointed out," he wrote, "that we (i.e., the British) must assume the visit amounted to a rejection of our proposals unless I had the assurance to the contrary, which I got in a very ridiculous form, i.e., that Molotov's visit had nothing to do with their relations to us, was only a return of Ribbentrop's visit, etc., etc."[26]

Even in historical perspective it is difficult to add much to Ambassador Steinhardt's contemporary estimate of Soviet policy in the weeks following the conclusion of the Tripartite Pact, except perhaps to question his conviction that the Kremlin desired an American-Japanese conflict. It seems more likely that the Soviet leaders looked upon the situation created by Japan's association with the Axis as another providential opportunity to exploit the international tension in the Soviet interest. They found them-

[25] Tel. from Steinhardt, October 30, 1940.
[26] Estorick: *Stafford Cripps,* 266; tel. from Steinhardt, November 9, 1940.

selves in the enviable position of having their traditional Japanese enemy pressing for an agreement and eager to offer highly attractive terms. At the same time the British, supported by the Americans, were figuratively falling over their own feet in their efforts to deter the Kremlin from closing the deal with Tokyo, and submitting exceedingly generous concessions in the process.

It is most unlikely that the Kremlin had even the slightest intention of striking a bargain with either side for, as Steinhardt never tired of pointing out, the controlling factors in Soviet policy were the relationship with Germany and the desire to see the current conflict waged on as nearly equal terms as possible, so that both sides might exhaust themselves while the Soviet Union stood aside. As the situation had developed by October, 1940, it may be assumed that Stalin and Molotov saw less need for or advantage in Soviet intervention than ever before. The offers of the British on the one hand, and the eagerness of the Germans and Japanese to bring Soviet Russia into the Tripartite Pact on the other, afforded the Kremlin a most unusual bargaining position. The Soviet leaders were determined to make the most of it. When Molotov set out for the Nazi capital it was to extract from Hitler concessions which, from the Soviet standpoint, were of much greater immediacy and of infinitely greater importance than any the British could possibly provide.

3. Nazi-Soviet Altercations

The steady deterioration of Nazi-Soviet relations subsequent to Hitler's unexpectedly rapid success against France is a subject of vital importance and interest. In the international setting of the summer and autumn of 1940 it was a development no less significant than Hitler's abortive effort to force the British into submission. The full story, however, is long and complicated, involving the affairs of eastern Europe and the Balkans, all the way from Finland in the north to Turkey in the south. The scope of the present study does not permit a full analysis of all factors in the situation; only the broad outlines can be given, with particular reference to the impact of Nazi-Soviet relations on the position of Britain and by derivation on the course of American policy.[27]

When the Germans and Japanese, in signing the Tripartite Pact, pro-

---

[27] Developments in the eastern European states are treated in considerable detail in Dallin: *Soviet Russia's Foreign Policy,* which is still decidedly worth reading. Among later accounts, most of them based on documentary material, may be mentioned Grigoire Gafencu (former Rumanian Foreign Minister): *Prelude to the Russian Campaign* (London, 1945); DeWitt C. Poole: "Light on Nazi Foreign Policy" (*Foreign Affairs,* October, 1946); Harold C. Deutsch: "Strange Interlude: The Soviet-Nazi Liaison" (*The Historian,* Spring, 1947); A. Rossi: *Deux ans d'alliance germano-soviétique* (Paris, 1949); Max Beloff: *The Foreign Policy of Soviet Russia,* II (New York, 1949); Kurt Assmann: *Deutsche Schicksalsjahre* (Wiesbaden, 1950). Nothing of consequence has been published in Soviet Russia.

jected the inclusion of Soviet Russia in the new global combination, they were hardly choosing an auspicious moment for proposing to Stalin and Molotov that they identify themselves fully with Axis policy. By the end of September Hitler had become highly impatient with his eastern partner, while the Kremlin, in turn, had become deeply suspicious and fearful of Nazi designs and activities. There is not the slightest reason to suppose that the Fuehrer had abandoned the program laid down years before in *Mein Kampf*.[28] Apparently his ultimate objective was always to conquer living space in the east, and his conflict with Britain an unwelcome diversion. When the Soviet Government, alarmed by the sudden fall of France and the prospect of the early defeat of Britain, hastily began to concentrate troops along the frontier, Hitler at once shifted forty divisions to the east. By the end of July, 1940, he was already talking of the necessity for disposing of the Soviet threat once and for all. Presently he ordered that preliminary studies for a campaign be taken in hand. There is reason to suppose that for a time he dreamed of initiating operations in the autumn of 1940 and that he was dissuaded only with difficulty by his military advisers and especially by Admiral Raeder, who kept stressing that Britain was the chief enemy and that all effort should first be centered on the Atlantic and Mediterranean.[29] Only in the context of these designs and nascent plans can the course of discussions between Berlin and Moscow be rightly understood.

The Fuehrer certainly reckoned that the presence of imposing German forces in Poland would be enough to ensure Germany against a Soviet surprise attack. "Soviet Russia is ruled by men of sense," he was wont to say.[30] But he evidently feared lest the Soviets, having already capitalized on Nazi victories by appropriating Bessarabia and northern Bukovina, steal another march on him. Various indications suggested that the Kremlin was planning a second war against Finland and there was evidence also of Soviet activity in Yugoslavia and Bulgaria. Hitler and Ribbentrop strongly suspected that Stalin's policy was "to exploit to the maximum eventual complications, thrusting forward, with the complicity of Bulgaria and Yugoslavia 'as far as the Straits, the Aegean and even the Adriatic.' "[31]

It was undoubtedly the underlying fear of such developments that led Hitler to interfere drastically in Balkan affairs, as he did in settling the

---

[28] His remarks about the future of Russia, as recorded in Henry Picker: *Hitlers Tischgespräche, 1941-1942* (Bonn, 1951), were little more than a repetition and elaboration of his earlier views.

[29] B. H. Liddell Hart: *The German Generals Talk* (New York, 1948), 170 ff.; F. H. Hinsley: *Hitler's Strategy* (Cambridge, 1951), Chapter V. Of particular interest is a memo of Admiral Raeder, dated January 10, 1944 (*Nazi Conspiracy and Aggression*, VI, C-66).

[30] See his remarks to Mussolini during the Brenner Pass meeting, October 4, 1940 (*Ciano's Diplomatic Papers*, 395 ff.), and the *Halder Diary*, October 15, 1940.

[31] *Ciano's Diplomatic Papers*, 386, 389 ff. (conferences of August 29 and September 19, 1940, with Hitler and Ribbentrop).

Hungarian-Rumanian dispute by the Vienna Award (August 30, 1940). Basically he desired nothing more than preservation of the *status quo* in the Balkans, so that Germany could draw needed supplies from that area. But as the prospects of defeating Britain faded and the Nazis had to envisage a long war, local disorder became intolerable to them. One thing led to another: the loss of half of Transylvania and then of the Dobrudja (to Bulgaria) resulted in an overturn in Rumania. General Ion Antonescu, later to become one of Hitler's most trusted friends, took over control of the country, while King Carol fled abroad, leaving the throne to his young son, Michael. Germany and Italy guaranteed the independence and integrity of the rump state, but before long Hitler felt impelled to take further precautions. The Rumanian oil wells were of vital importance to Germany's conduct of the war. Fearing a possible Soviet attack on the Balkans, Hitler therefore decided to despatch military "instructors" to train the Rumanian forces. Their real task, however, was very different, namely, to protect the oil fields against destruction or seizure by a third power, "to enable Rumanian forces to fulfill certain tasks in German interests," and lastly "to prepare for deployment from Rumanian bases of German and Rumanian forces in case a war with Soviet Russia is forced upon us."[32]

Similar preventive measures were taken with respect to Finland, where the Germans thought it necessary to protect the nickel mines near Petsamo and the iron-ore mines of northern Norway against possible attack. Growing Soviet interference in Finnish affairs and ever recurring demands (including the demand for transit rights to the Soviet base at Hangö) had convinced the Helsinki Government that another attack was imminent. Evidently disappointed in their efforts to secure assurances of Swedish aid, the Finns turned to Berlin for support. This time they met with a reception quite different from that of November, 1939. Hitler was firmly determined not to countenance further Soviet expansion in the Baltic and arranged for the Finnish purchase of arms and munitions in Germany. In return the Finns agreed that the Germans might transport equipment and service personnel across Finland to the Kirkenes area of northern Norway. On September 22, 1940, the military arrangement was followed by a political understanding, and a few days later the first German troops disembarked in Finnish ports.[33]

These German moves were all made without prior consultation with the Kremlin, which, in fact, was usually informed of them just as they were about to take place. The result was an ominous exchange of recriminations

[32] Directive of September 20, 1940 (*Nazi Conspiracy and Aggression*, VI, C-53).

[33] John H. Wuorinen, editor: *Finland and World War II* (New York, 1948), 84 ff.; tels. from Sterling (Stockholm), August 2; Thurston (Moscow), August 19; Kirk (Berlin), September 25; and Schoenfeld (Helsinki), September 26, 1940. See also Dallin: *Soviet Russia's Foreign Policy*, 293-96, and Beloff: *The Foreign Policy of Soviet Russia*, II, 342.

between Berlin and Moscow, culminating in pointed criticism in the inspired press of both countries. The rather monotonous *Tass* description of German statements that the Soviet Government had been notified in advance as "not corresponding to the facts" infuriated Hitler and his associates, who, while never hesitating to charge their opponents with prevarication, did not relish being themselves publicly branded as liars.[34]

By late September and early October, and especially after the news broke that a German mission and "instructional staff" had arrived in Rumania (October 7), the Nazi-Soviet relationship had soured to the point where there was talk in Berlin of "undeclared hostility."[35] Correspondingly the Kremlin seems to have envisaged the possibility of a German attack at an early date. The pronouncements of Soviet leaders suggested imminent danger as well as determination to resist aggression. Thus Molotov had said in his speech of August 1: "We must keep our entire people in a state of mobilization, preparedness in the face of the danger of military attack, so that no 'accident' and no tricks of our foreign enemies could catch us unawares." In the same vein Marshal Timoshenko had addressed the graduates of the Military Academy on October 5, stressing that while the Soviet Union stood aloof from the imperialist war, "this does not mean that we are safe from any provocation that may threaten our borders . . . We must be ready for any emergency and further strengthen the Red Army's fighting capacity." A few weeks later, at the celebration of the October Revolution, Timoshenko sounded an even more ominous note. He spoke of the "exceptionally dangerous and alarming international situation," which he characterized as "pregnant with various surprises," and which therefore must be watched with "the utmost vigilance." "The Red Army," he boasted, "is always ready at the first call of the Party and the Government to give a crushing rebuff to anyone who may dare an attempt on the sacred borders of our Socialist State."[36]

Hitler and Ribbentrop were evidently not troubled by incongruity and certainly did not lack confidence in their ability to manipulate things to suit their ends. Otherwise they would hardly have tried, in the prevailing atmosphere of suspicion and animosity, to realize their grand design of including Soviet Russia in the great world combination of which the Tripartite Pact was to be the nucleus. Their first effort was to convince the Kremlin that this pact was intended primarily to prevent the expansion of the European war by frightening off the United States, and that it was in no sense directed

[34] The charges and countercharges, interlarded with Molotov's insistent demand to see the full text of these agreements, are given in full in *Nazi-Soviet Relations,* 188 ff.

[35] Tel. from Kirk, October 4, 1940.

[36] Beloff: *The Foreign Policy of Soviet Russia,* II, 335; *Bulletin of International News,* XVII (2), 1403; *Daily Worker,* November 8, 1940. The *Halder Diary,* September 30, 1940, speaks of increasing reports that the Soviets expected war with Germany in 1941.

against the Soviet Union.[37] At the same time Count von der Schulenburg, the German Ambassador in Moscow, was visiting Berlin and exerting all his influence in favor of a more conciliatory attitude toward Moscow, especially on Balkan issues. Hitler decided to link these various matters and to invite Molotov to Berlin for broad general discussions. Without much inner conviction he was willing to make a try for a further deal, involving at least fulfillment of his obligation to Tokyo to work for a Soviet-Japanese agreement. On October 13, therefore, Ribbentrop addressed to Stalin a lengthy epistle consisting of the well-worn Nazi version of the events of the war and explaining all the recent German moves, to which the Kremlin had taken such strong exception, as measures necessary to forestall British action or to frustrate British attempts to draw other nations into the struggle.

The Tripartite Pact, according to Ribbentrop, fell into the same category:

The conclusion of this pact is the logical result of a conception of foreign policy—long adhered to by the Reich Government—in which both friendly German-Soviet coöperation and friendly German-Japanese coöperation have a place side by side and undisturbed. Beyond that, however, friendly relations between Germany and Soviet Russia as well as friendly relations between Soviet Russia and Japan, together with the friendship between the Axis Powers and Japan, are logical elements of a natural political coalition which, if intelligently managed, will work out to the best advantage of all the powers concerned. . . . In summing up, I should like to state that, in the opinion of the Fuehrer, also, it appears to be the historical mission of the Four Powers—the Soviet Union, Italy, Japan, and Germany—to adopt a long-range policy and to direct the future development of their peoples into the right channels by delimitation of their interests on a worldwide scale.[38]

Thus did Ribbentrop lay the Nazi cards on the table, indicating that in order to enlist Soviet membership in the grandiose Tripartite Pact, Hitler was prepared to examine the conditions for further German-Soviet collaboration.

The reader will realize that it is impossible to speak of specific Soviet motives and reactions with any degree of confidence, for the Kremlin has not seen fit to publish official documents; neither is it a practice for Soviet statesmen to publish their memoirs. At best, therefore, the historian can suggest probable Soviet objectives, drawing on known facts as they support or fail to support one interpretation or another. In the present case it is

[37] *Nazi-Soviet Relations,* 195, 197-98, 201-2.

[38] *Nazi-Soviet Relations,* 207-13 (letter of October 13, 1940). We have used also the *Halder Diary,* September 30 and October 8, 15, 1940. It is interesting to note that on October 17, 1940, Ambassador Steinhardt reported that a member of the German Embassy in Moscow, who had accompanied von der Schulenburg to Berlin, stated that while the Ambassador had in general succeeded in inducing his Government to adopt a more conciliatory policy, "the conviction remained strong in Germany that war with Russia was ultimately inevitable, and that an abrupt change in German policy would not be improbable. Much would depend on the results of the impending talk between the Ambassador and Molotov."

reasonably safe to assume that the Kremlin had already learned, through its espionage service in Tokyo, of Japan's burning desire for a nonaggression pact, and of the Nazi promise to exert every effort to further this end. Furthermore, Stalin and Molotov almost certainly knew that the Tripartite Pact was in fact not aimed at the Soviet Union, but was largely designed to divert the United States from lending effective aid to Britain. On the face of it, then, the Kremlin may well have argued that the Tripartite Pact served Soviet interests. It was bound to accentuate the tension already existing between Britain and the United States on the one hand, and Japan on the other. At the same time American official announcements left little doubt that the United States was determined to support Britain whatever the consequences. Britain itself threw down the challenge to Japan by reopening the Burma Road. Above all, the signature of the pact had led to the pathetic efforts of the British, abetted by the United States, to wean the Soviets from their German connection by offering extravagant concessions. The Kremlin, by keeping both Japan and Britain at arm's length during October, retained full freedom of action with respect to German advances, while the Germans in turn were certainly troubled by the talk of an Anglo-Soviet *rapprochement* which ran through the British press.

There is no reason to suppose that Stalin and Molotov had any intention of doing business with the British. Their hope was probably that Nazi Germany would exhaust itself in the struggle with an enemy which was constantly receiving increased aid from the United States. The Kremlin was in all likelihood quite truthful in its reiterated statements that Soviet Russia desired to remain aloof from the "imperialist" war. This meant that the Soviet Government had a genuine interest in prolonging the Nazi-Soviet Pact. But the situation created by the Tripartite Pact provided the Kremlin an unforeseen opportunity to make capital of the new developments. If Japan desired a nonaggression pact, it would have to pay dearly. If the Nazis, by the same token, wished to include the Soviet Union in the Axis front against the democracies, they could attain their end only at great sacrifice. Molotov could be relied upon to make the most of these opportunities.

A revealing light is thrown on the relative positions of Germany and Soviet Russia at this time by the fact that Count von der Schulenburg handed Ribbentrop's letter to Molotov in the belief that a request for an audience with Stalin would be refused.[39] Stalin, however, replied cordially on October 21, agreeing that further improvement in the relations between Germany and the Soviet Union was entirely possible "on the permanent basis of a long-range delimitation of mutual interests" (Ribbentrop's sug-

---

[39] *Nazi-Soviet Relations,* 214-15, revealing Ribbentrop's irritation on this point. The letter was not delivered to Molotov until October 17, 1940, because Schulenburg thought it best to translate it first into Russian.

gestion had been a long range policy of the four powers based on delimitation of their interests). Stalin accepted the invitation for Molotov to visit Berlin, but as to discussions including Italy and Japan he remarked that, while not opposed in principle, he believed this question would have to be examined further.[40] In a word, Stalin at the very outset shifted the base of discussion: the delimitation of mutual interests was to take place between Germany and Soviet Russia, and the question of Soviet adherence to the Tripartite Pact was reserved.

It is not clear from the documents whether the Germans sensed the implications of the Soviet reply. Ribbentrop was uncritically exultant over the news that Molotov would arrive soon after November 10 and wished to trumpet the tidings to the whole world without delay. Molotov, however, threw cold water on the idea and insisted that nothing be announced until the very eve of his departure.[41] Ribbentrop's pride was hurt but, nothing daunted, he elaborated a program for discussion which, he felt sure, would lead to the conclusion of a pact within a few weeks. On November 4 he expounded his ideas to Count Ciano, who was to elicit Mussolini's views. In the light of what developed during the Molotov visit, the Ribbentrop program, as a reflection of German aims and hopes, is of the highest interest and may therefore be quoted at some length:

The first problem, both in time and in importance, is that which concerns Russia's relations with the Axis and with Japan. Although activity to this end has hardly begun, Herr von Ribbentrop considers it possible to negotiate an agreement between the Tripartite Powers and Russia after Molotov's visit to Berlin, which will take place on the 11th of this month. During the negotiations he will keep in close contact with the Italian and Japanese Governments. Since the possibility of reaching a military agreement with Russia is ruled out, Ribbentrop considers that a political and economic pact should be made based principally on mutual recognition of the territorial situation, on an undertaking by each party never to give aid to the enemies of the other and finally on a broad collaboration and friendship clause. To this Pact two Secret Protocols should be added. The first of the Secret Protocols should fix the areas of expansion of each of the interested Powers: Russian dynamism to be directed towards the South, to be anti-British in character and aiming at safeguarding the position of Afghanistan and Persia as far as possible; Italian dynamism, towards Mediterranean Africa and the Red Sea; German dynamism, towards Equatorial Africa. Ribbentrop stressed that he made no mention of the Balkans; that was on set purpose since he does not intend to discuss the Balkan problems with Russia, considering them to be internal questions for the two Axis Powers. The second Secret Protocol should concern Russia's position with regard to the Dardanelles and the Black Sea. Ribbentrop considers that it would be necessary in practice to go the length of abolishing the Montreux Convention and give Russia two things: (1) a declaration that the Black

[40] Nazi-Soviet Relations, 216.
[41] Die Beziehungen zwischen Deutschland und der Sowjetunion, 1939-1941, edited by Alfred Siedl (Tübingen, 1949), Nos. 179, 181, 182. This collection contains a few documents not included in Nazi-Soviet Relations.

Sea is considered to be an internal Russian Sea, (2) free passage through the Dardanelles. In that way, Ribbentrop considers that it should be possible to avoid any Russian attempt to establish herself territorially and militarily on the Dardanelles themselves, a fact to which the Axis Powers would not be able to remain indifferent. In exchange for free passage through the Dardanelles, the four Powers participating in the future agreement would pledge themselves to give Turkey a guarantee to maintain the territorial *status quo.* . . . Once an agreement has been drawn up with Russia, Ribbentrop would propose certain steps with Turkey aimed at producing a *rapprochement* with the Axis.[42]

Although Hitler must have approved the Ribbentrop program, it is doubtful whether he shared in full the naïve self-confidence of his Foreign Minister. Such of his utterances as have come down to us from these days reveal his customary ambivalence toward Soviet Russia. At his meeting with Mussolini at Florence (October 28) he stated quite baldly: "the distrust on my side towards Stalin is matched by Stalin's distrust towards me." At the same time he admitted his desire to align the Kremlin in the coalition that was to isolate Britain: "with Russia's rapprochement to the Axis, a front will be created which will stretch from Japan to Spain."[43] His interest in this imposing combination was certainly compelling at the time, but he found it quite impossible to repress his deeper feelings. To his generals he observed: "Russia remains *the* European problem. Everything must be done to be prepared for the great reckoning."[44] His important directive for the further conduct of the war, dated November 12 (the day of Molotov's arrival in Berlin), reflects considerable confusion of spirit: "Political discussions have been initiated with the aim of clarifying Russia's attitude for the time being. Irrespective of the results of these discussions, all preparations for the East which have already been verbally ordered will be continued."[45]

4. MOLOTOV IN BERLIN

In the forenoon of November 12, 1940, Molotov got out of his train at the Anhalter Station in Berlin, to be greeted by Ribbentrop, General Keitel and a select group of other distinguished Nazis. The weather was chilly and there was a drizzling rain, but the Foreign Commissar's reception was no less impressive than that accorded Ribbentrop on the occasion of his own historic visit to Moscow a year before. There was, it is true, no such colorful and exuberant celebration as Berlin reserved for full-fledged members of the Axis family, but everything was pitched on a note of cordiality and for the rest fitted Molotov's desire to keep the occasion subdued and business-

[42] Conversation between Ciano and Ribbentrop at Schönhof, November 4, 1940 (*Ciano's Diplomatic Papers,* 405-07).
[43] *Ciano's Diplomatic Papers,* 402 ff.
[44] *Halder Diary,* November 1 and 4, 1940.
[45] *Nazi Conspiracy and Aggression,* III, 442-PS.

like. Yet piquancy was not entirely lacking, for the red flag of the proletarian revolution was given due prominence and flew side by side with the Nazi swastika banner atop Bellevue Castle, where Hitler housed his distinguished guest.

The Berliners themselves had to look sharply for a glimpse of the Soviet notable, for there was much to talk about and little time for parade. With the exception of the hours devoted to the inevitable official luncheons and dinners, the two days of the visit were taken up completely by almost uninterrupted conferences, lasting far into the night. It could well be said that when Molotov was not closeted with Ribbentrop, he was consulting with Hitler. It was really a marvel that any man should survive so heavy a bombardment of words and ideas. But on such occasions the Foreign Commissar proved that he, like Stalin himself, was a man of iron. At no time could his hosts detect signs of weariness or flagging attention. Molotov struck them like a professor of mathematics—keen, factual, logical, a man of plain words and no smiles.[46]

It is quite unnecessary in the present context to analyze in detail the long and complicated discussions that took place on November 12 and 13, 1940. The full German records of the conferences, captured at the end of the war, have been published by the United States Government, and are readily available.[47] Only the salient points of the argument will therefore be considered.

The conference hours of the first day (November 12) were consumed almost entirely by lectures on the part first of Ribbentrop, then of Hitler. The now well-worn theme that Britain was already defeated and that it was merely a matter of time before it would concede its defeat, was exploited to the full, while every effort was made to play down the importance of American aid to Britain. "Because of the extraordinary strength of their position, the Axis Powers were not, therefore, considering how they might win the war, but rather how rapidly they could end the war which was already won." That was the whole point of the Tripartite Pact, which it was hoped Soviet Russia would join, so that all four powers could divide the available living space between them. In the process the Soviet Union could thus ob-

[46] The most vivid, intimate account of the conferences is that of Paul Schmidt: *Statist auf diplomatischer Bühne*, Chapter XXI.

[47] *Nazi-Soviet Relations*, 117 ff. The account in James F. Byrnes: *Speaking Frankly* (New York, 1947), 287 ff., was based on the State Department's interrogations of Paul Schmidt and Gustav Hilger, of whom the latter was the official German interpreter. Further material derived from these interrogations may be found in DeWitt C. Poole: "Light on Nazi Foreign Policy" (*Foreign Affairs*, October, 1946). The only contribution from the Soviet side is to be found in a report of the press conference of Vice Commissar S. A. Lozovsky, replying to Hitler's speech of October 3, 1941 (*Soviet Information Bulletin*, October 9, 1941), and in the Soviet refutation of the German records, published as *Falsificators of History* (Soviet Embassy, Washington, D. C., February, 1948).

tain a settlement of the historic Straits question more in keeping with its requirements. If the Kremlin agreed to such a policy, the details could be worked out through diplomatic channels and eventually the German, Italian and Japanese Foreign Ministers could meet in Moscow to conclude the epoch-making pact.

Thus ran the exposition of Ribbentrop, which was really nothing more than an elaboration of the message sent to Stalin in mid-October. During the afternoon Hitler went into action, discoursing pontifically on long-term planning of international relations and on the possibilities of further developing the Nazi-Soviet system of collaboration. The shadows that had lately fallen upon German-Soviet relations were all explained by the fact that Germany was obliged to frustrate the wily efforts of the British to extend the war. To hear Hitler, the Nazis deserved every kind of consideration, as they were waging the great struggle for a New Europe. France and Spain allegedly had already been brought into line, albeit with difficulty. If the Kremlin, too, were to take a liberal view of pending issues, a fortune was to be gained by all partners:

Much greater successes could then be achieved, provided that Russia did not now seek successes in territories in which Germany was interested for the duration of the war. The future successes would be the greater, the more Germany and Russia succeeded in fighting back to back against the outside world, and would become the smaller, the more the two countries faced each other breast to breast. In the first case there was no power on earth which could oppose the two countries.

Reverting again and again to this basic thesis, Hitler sketched an alluring future for the Soviet Union, as for the Axis: "After the conquest of England, the British Empire would be apportioned as a gigantic world-wide estate in bankruptcy of forty million square kilometers. In this bankrupt estate there would be for Russia access to the ice-free and really open ocean." But to make the most of the situation, "all the countries which could possibly be interested in the bankrupt estate would have to stop all controversies among themselves and concern themselves exclusively with the partition of the British Empire. This applied to Germany, France, Italy, Russia and Japan." Hitler described his plan as the creation of "a world coalition of interested powers which would consist of Spain, France, Italy, Germany, Soviet Russia and Japan and would to a certain extent represent a coalition —extending from North Africa to Eastern Asia—of all who wanted to be satisfied out of the British bankrupt estate." This great moment was obviously not the time to engage in altercations about "insignificant revisions" of existing arrangements. For Stalin and Molotov these trifles should be as nothing compared with the opportunities to settle the vital question of the Turkish Straits and to advance to the Persian Gulf and British India.

These few paragraphs telescope the record of hours of discussion, during which, in consonance with their intent throughout, the Nazi leaders applied themselves to convert Molotov to their far-flung schemes for a world coalition, which at times Hitler represented not only as a move to force Britain to submit, but as a necessary precaution against eventual American imperialism. But Molotov steadfastly refused to fall in with this beguiling proposition. As soon as the wordy Ribbentrop had drawn to the end of his breath at the first conference, the Soviet Commissar, conceding that "an exchange of ideas regarding the great problems concerning not only Germany and Soviet Russia but also other states as well might, indeed, be useful," complained that such phrases as "the New Order in Europe" and "the Greater East Asian Sphere" were vague and not entirely comprehensible. He thought it important to obtain "more accurate definitions of these concepts." In any case, these matters would require much more discussion of details.

Rather than lose himself in hypothetical partitions of the world, Molotov advocated attention to the delimitation of spheres of influence as between Germany and Russia. "The establishment of these spheres of influence in the past year was only a partial solution, which had been rendered obsolete and meaningless by recent circumstances and events." The Kremlin, he stated, therefore desired first of all to come to an understanding with Germany, and only later with Italy and Japan, after securing "precise information" as to the significance, nature and aim of the Tripartite Pact. This stand Molotov maintained with the utmost obstinacy, resisting all Hitler's blandishments. The Kremlin, he said, had no objection in principle to associating itself with a world coalition, but first "there were issues to be clarified regarding Russia's Balkan and Black Sea interests with respect to Bulgaria, Rumania and Turkey." It was not clear to him why these specific issues, which were already adversely affecting the Nazi-Soviet Pact, should not be disposed of before the grandiose plans of the Fuehrer were examined.

Hitler must have realized, at the end of the first day, that if anything was to be accomplished, he and Ribbentrop would have to submit to difficult discussions of immediate, concrete issues. These took place on the second day and were marked by many rancorous exchanges. Finland proved to be a particular source of controversy, since Molotov asked explanations of the transit of German troops through Finland and demanded to know whether in respect to that country the pact of August, 1939, which assigned it to the Soviet sphere, was still valid. The Fuehrer explained that it was necessary for him to ensure against the establishment of British bases in Finland or Sweden. He was willing to concede that Finland remain within the Soviet sphere, and promised not to send any more troops when the current operation was completed. On the other hand, he insisted over and over again that Germany could not tolerate another attack by the Soviets on Finland, for Germany required peace in the Baltic. Molotov evaded a direct answer to the question whether the Kremlin contemplated another Finnish War, but indicated that if the Germans kept their hands off, the Soviet Government could reach a satisfactory agreement with Helsinki.

Bitter words were exchanged also about Soviet action in seizing part of Bukovina, about the Axis guarantee to Rumania (clearly directed against the Soviet Union, as Molotov did not fail to point out), and about the presence of German forces in Rumania. The Foreign Commissar was by no means satisfied by the bland explanation of the Germans, which he had heard before. He wanted to know whether Hitler would agree to a Soviet guarantee of Bulgaria similar to the Axis guarantee of Rumania. To this the Fuehrer retorted with the testy question whether the Bulgarians had requested such a guarantee. Clearly it did not suit the Germans to have the Soviets in direct or indirect control of Bulgaria at a time when they were planning to march their forces through that country in a spring campaign against Greece.

From the Soviet standpoint Bulgaria was important as a base for operations against Turkey in the event that Ankara rejected Soviet demands regarding the Straits. Ribbentrop had outlined German views on this question: the Montreux Convention was to be scrapped and Germany, Italy and Soviet Russia were to work together to secure Turkish consent to free passage through the Straits, for the Soviet Union and other Black Sea powers. Thereafter Turkey was to be detached from its alliance with Britain and included in the grand Axis coalition. Molotov's response to these schemes was to point out that his Government could not be content with mere "paper" guarantees, but required "real" security. A guarantee given to Bulgaria would help and, for the rest, the Kremlin was sure it could reach a satisfactory arrangement with Turkey. In short, if the Soviets were established in Bulgaria, they would be able to bring sufficient pressure on the Turks to oblige them to grant whatever the Kremlin considered necessary for its security against attack through the Straits.

The last of the conferences took place between Ribbentrop and Molotov, in the Foreign Minister's well-appointed air raid shelter, after the "already defeated" British had sent their bombers over Berlin and broken up a dinner at the Soviet Embassy. On this final occasion Ribbentrop did what he could to pour oil on the troubled waters. In fact he fetched from his brief case the draft agreements which ten days before he had read to Ciano. He did not, he said, expect his guest to express an opinion on these drafts until after he had had a chance to consider them with Stalin, but he once more conjured up the great coalition to carve up the world. Furthermore, he stressed the fact that the Japanese were prepared to pay a generous price for a non-aggression treaty with Soviet Russia. But Molotov's replies remained far from heartening. The Commissar wanted no misunderstanding, and so restated quite emphatically the Soviet interest not merely in Bulgaria, Rumania and Hungary, but in Greece and Yugoslavia as well. With scant respect for his host's sensibilities, he cast doubt on the validity of the German argument that Nazi infringements of the 1939 agreement were merely temporary expedients to hasten the defeat of the British. Indeed, he charged that the Germans were merely "assuming" that the war with Britain was as good as won. He left no shadow of doubt that while he approved Soviet participation in the Tripartite Pact "in principle," he could not retreat from the position "that all these great issues of tomorrow could not be separated from the issues of today and the fulfilling of existing agreements. . . ." Useful though the talks had been, it would be necessary to pursue consideration of these unsettled questions through diplomatic channels.

The following morning Molotov and his retinue entrained for Moscow. The famous visit, which the world had watched in hushed suspense, was a thing of the past. According to the final communiqué, the exchange of views between the German and Soviet statesmen had taken place "in an atmosphere of mutual confidence," and had resulted "in agreement by both sides on all important questions of interest to Germany and the Soviet Union." To this a circular telegram to German diplomatic missions abroad added: "The result clearly proves that all conjectures regarding alleged German-Russian conflicts are in the realm of fantasy and that all speculations of the foe as to a disturbance in the German-Russian relationship of trust and friendship are based on self-deception." The reader will judge for himself the value to be attached to these reassuring statements.

5. AFTERMATH OF THE BERLIN CONVERSATIONS

The Molotov debacle, coming after Hitler's luckless conferences with Franco and Pétain, and after Mussolini's ill-considered attack on Greece, must have been the crowning disillusionment to the Fuehrer. Since he had already made up his mind that sooner or later Soviet Russia must be eliminated, he had embarked upon the conversations halfheartedly and fully determined not to discuss with the Soviet emissary German policy in the Balkans. The later testimony of his associates suggests that Hitler was positively alarmed by Molotov's attitude respecting Finland, Bulgaria and Turkey. No doubt reading his visitor's mind correctly, he believed the Kremlin intended to establish control over these countries and feared lest, having done so, the Soviets, in conjunction with the British, attempt to encircle the Nazi Reich.[48]

To forestall his competitor's expected moves, the Fuehrer decided to waste no further words but push on with his plans for the inclusion of the Balkan states in the Tripartite Pact. Hungary, though by no means pro-

[48] DeWitt C. Poole: "Light on Nazi Foreign Policy" (*Foreign Affairs*, October, 1946); Schmidt: *Statist auf diplomatischer Bühne*, (Bonn, 1949), Chapter XXI; Rossi: *Deux ans d'alliance germano-soviétique*, 182. On November 20, 1940, Hitler told the Hungarian statesman, Count Teleki: "Russia looms on the horizon like a threatening cloud" (*Die Beziehungen zwischen Deutschland und der Sowjetunion*, No. 191).

German, was first to bow to the inevitable: on November 20 Count Csaky signed the pact on behalf of his country.[49] Rumania, with German troops and aviation units already on its soil, and with its Government committed to close coöperation with Nazi Germany, presented no difficulties and adhered to the pact on November 23. On the contrary, Yugoslavia and Bulgaria held out. Prince Paul of Yugoslavia, though under considerable pressure from pro-Axis members of the Government and much disposed to be fatalistic, nevertheless managed to evade the proposals of Berlin. Hitler, on the other hand, was most anxious to keep Yugoslavia quiet until the Greek problem was disposed of, and so decided not to force the issue. In like manner he accepted temporary failure of his efforts to bring Bulgaria into camp. On November 17 he argued for three hours with King Boris, whom he had invited to Berchtesgaden for purposes of intimidation. Boris countered by stressing the known hostility of Soviet Russia to any association of Bulgaria with the Axis and Hitler himself recognized that undue pressure might lead to conflict with the Kremlin.[50] In Bulgaria's stead, Slovakia was taken into the grand coalition and the Nazi press announced that this move "ended the present series."

Of the reaction of Stalin and the Politburo to Molotov's report of the Berlin discussions nothing is known. A few facts may, however, be advanced as of at least symptomatic value. Thus, on November 15 the Soviet press agency, *Tass,* denied newspaper reports that the Soviet Union and Japan had reached an agreement regarding spheres of influence in the Far East and that the Kremlin had agreed to suspend its aid to the Chungking Government.[51] If this official comment had any ulterior purpose, it was either to reassure Britain and the United States, or to dampen Ribbentrop's hopes.

A much greater stir was occasioned by a diplomatic leak in London involving the revelation of the Cripps offer to the Kremlin of October 22, 1940, and giving a fairly accurate tabulation of the terms. Cripps himself was furious and laid the whole business to alleged anti-Soviet elements in the Foreign Office or the British Broadcasting Corporation. The Foreign Office, however, was inclined to believe that Soviet Ambassador Maisky was at the bottom of the affair and that his objective was to provide the Kremlin with a decent excuse for dropping the entire negotiation. In retrospect it seems more likely that if in fact Maisky was responsible for the leak, the Kremlin's purpose was to exploit a proposal it had never intended to accept. By publishing the far-reaching offer made by Cripps, it may well have aimed to demonstrate to Berlin how easily it could do business with Britain and how profitable the transaction could be. If this was actually the Soviet

---

[49] Despatch from Montgomery (Budapest), November 23, 1940. See also the Minister's later interpretation of developments in Hungary: John F. Montgomery: *The Unwilling Satellite* (New York, 1947).

[50] Tel. from Lane (Sofia), December 2, 1940.

[51] *The New York Times,* November 15, 1940.

objective, the British press contributed to its success by hailing the offer as "sensible" and as proof perfect that the British Government was not insincere in its efforts to promote better relations with Moscow. Lord Halifax, by announcing in the House of Lords that the offer was in effect still open, must have added to Stalin's satisfaction. The Kremlin, incidentally, maintained a prolonged and altogether deafening silence on this episode.[52]

If the above conjectures have any validity, it may be assumed that the Kremlin was at one and the same time attempting to impress Hitler and mend its relations with the democracies. In this connection two other events may have significance. On November 16, 1940, the American Communist Party Convention voted unanimously to sever all connections with the Comintern, while on November 27 Ambassador Oumansky called on Under Secretary Welles and, in reply to a request of Mr. Welles's of October 31, presented a statement of Soviet foreign policy. The reports of Molotov's negotiations in Berlin, he asserted, had been gravely distorted. He, Oumansky, was authorized to state "that the foreign policy of the Soviet Union remained completely independent . . . and would continue to be a policy of complete neutrality and avoidance of war." Nor was this all. Queried by Mr. Welles on the Soviet attitude toward China, the Ambassador replied that he was likewise authorized to say that Soviet policy toward China was "identical" with that of the United States. Far from anticipating a conflict of objectives between the Soviet Union and the United States in the Pacific, the Soviet Government held these objectives to be "similar."[53]

These straws in the wind, if they had any significance at all, pointed toward the daring step taken by the Kremlin in replying to the Hitler-Ribbentrop proposals. On the evening of November 25 Molotov called in the German Ambassador and gave him the following message for his Government:

The Soviet Government is prepared to accept the draft of the Four Power Pact which the Reich Foreign Minister outlined in the conversation of November 13, regarding political collaboration and reciprocal economic support, subject to the following conditions:

1) Provided that the German troops are immediately withdrawn from Finland, which, under the pact of 1939, belongs to the Soviet Union's sphere of influence. At the same time the Soviet Union undertakes to ensure peaceful relations with Finland and to protect German economic interests in Finland (export of lumber and nickel).

2) Provided that within the next few months the security of the Soviet Union in the Straits is assured by the conclusion of a mutual assistance pact between the Soviet Union and Bulgaria, which geographically is situated inside the security zone of the

---

[52] Tels. from Steinhardt, November 17 and 27, 1940. *The New York Times,* November 16, 1940; London *Times* and *Manchester Guardian,* November 18, 1940. See also the article by Harold J. Laski in the *Providence Evening Bulletin,* November 24, 1940.

[53] Memo of conversation between Mr. Welles and Ambassador Oumansky, November 27, 1940.

Black Sea boundaries of the Soviet Union, and by the establishment of a base for land and naval forces of the USSR in the vicinity[54] of the Bosporus and the Dardanelles by means of a long-term lease.

3) Provided that the area south of Batum and Baku in the general direction of the Persian Gulf is recognized as the center of the aspirations of the Soviet Union.

4) Provided that Japan renounces her rights to concessions for coal and oil in Northern Sakhalin.[55]

Molotov amplified this statement by saying that the two secret protocols suggested by Ribbentrop should be expanded to five. If Turkey voluntarily accepted the above terms and joined the Four Power Pact, Germany, Italy and the Soviet Union should guarantee Turkish independence and integrity. If Turkey refused to join, then the three powers were to agree "to work out and carry through the required military and diplomatic measures."

In the absence of reliable evidence it is easy to construct a variety of hypotheses to explain the Kremlin's considered reaction to the Berlin proposals. The simplest and most obvious one seems also the soundest and most reasonable. The Soviet leaders, knowing how anxious the Germans and Japanese were to include Soviet Russia in the world coalition and so commit it against Britain and the United States, were willing to go along, but only at a price and a high price. They demanded a free hand in Finland and refused to be excluded from the Balkans. If the Germans were to have Rumania, the Soviets required equivalent control of Bulgaria and above all of the Straits. There is no reason to suppose that Molotov submitted these terms to the Germans in the expectation that they would be rejected. On the contrary, he later expressed surprise at the Germans' failure to reply. If one tries to read Stalin's mind, one might venture the opinion that he probably believed a firm stand would bring its reward. In any event, to set forth Soviet demands would not worsen the Kremlin's position. The partners would then simply agree to disagree. Obviously, if the Germans fell in with Soviet desires and the Soviet Union eventually found itself at war with Britain, its defensive position would have been greatly strengthened by control over Finland and the Straits. The same would be true, though in a somewhat lesser degree, in a struggle with Germany, if it came.

Of Hitler's reaction to the Soviet note little can be said with certainty. However, the uncompromising attitude he had taken during his talks with Molotov leaves little doubt that he never had the slightest intention of accepting such terms. According to the later testimony of his associates, the Soviet demands convinced him that the Kremlin was actually plotting an

---

[54] In *Nazi-Soviet Relations,* 258, this phrase reads "within range of." The original German is "im Rayon" and from the further text of the Soviet message it is perfectly clear that what was meant was "at," that is, in the vicinity of the Bosporus.

[55] *Nazi-Soviet Relations,* 258-59; German text in *Die Beziehungen zwischen Deutschland und der Sowjetunion,* No. 192.

attack.[56] Even though this may be something of an exaggeration, contemporary records demonstrate that the Fuehrer felt the time had indeed come for the great decision. He knew full well that the Kremlin, without awaiting his reaction to the note of November 25, was moving heaven and earth to induce the Bulgars to accept a treaty of mutual assistance.[57] If successful, the Soviets might well obstruct Nazi plans to invade northern Greece from Rumania. Hitler was absolutely determined to go on with his Balkan plans and was more than ever convinced that sooner or later the Soviet threat to Nazi designs must be eliminated. On December 5, 1940, he instructed his generals to go ahead full speed with preparations for a campaign against the Soviet Union, to be launched at the end of May, 1941. The Finns and the Rumanians were to participate and the effort was to be made to destroy the Soviet armies west of the Dnieper.[58] This instruction was followed, on December 18, 1940, with the first directive for operation *Barbarossa,* calling for the completion of all plans and preparations by May 15, 1941.[59]

It can be argued, of course, that the Fuehrer's decision was not irrevocable and that he still had five months to change his mind before ordering the initiation of hostilities. As a matter of fact both Marshal Goering (Commander of the Air Forces) and Admiral Raeder (Commander of the Fleet) tried repeatedly to dissuade their chief from an eastern campaign and to convince him that Britain should first be subdued by air and submarine attack, and by operations in the Atlantic and Mediterranean. Raeder especially warned of the rapidly growing flow of supplies from the United States to Britain and urged that German war production be focused on planes and submarines: "Britain's ability to maintain her supply lines is definitely the decisive factor for the outcome of the war." Hitler promised to do something responsive to these views, but his interest shifted elsewhere. "Considering present political developments, i.e., Russia's inclination to interfere in Balkan affairs," he remarked, "it is necessary to eliminate at all cost the last enemy remaining on the continent before he [i.e., Soviet Russia] can collaborate with Britain. For this purpose the Army must be made sufficiently strong. After that, everything can be concentrated on the needs of the Air Force and the Navy."[60]

A little later the Fuehrer expounded his views in a succinct and revealing passage:

[56] DeWitt C. Poole: "Light on Nazi Foreign Policy" (*Foreign Affairs,* October, 1946, pp. 150 ff.).

[57] *Halder Diary,* December 3, 1940; *Les lettres secrètes échangées par Hitler et Mussolini,* 98-99 (letter of December 5, 1940). On Soviet activity in Bulgaria we have used also a tel. from Earle (Sofia), December 9, 1940. See also the detailed account in the London *Times,* December 11, 1940.

[58] *Halder Diary,* December 5, 1940. See also *Nazi Conspiracy and Aggression,* IV, 1799-PS; Hinsley: *Hitler's Strategy,* Chapter VI.

[59] *Nazi Conspiracy and Aggression,* III, 446-PS.

[60] *Fuehrer Conferences, 1940* (2), 68 ff. (conference of December 27, 1940).

Stalin must be regarded as a cold-blooded blackmailer: he would, if expedient, repudiate any written treaty at any time. Britain's aim for some time to come will be to set Russian strength in motion against us. If the U.S.A. and Russia should enter the war against Germany, the situation would become very complicated. Hence any possibility for such a threat to develop must be eliminated at the very beginning. If the Russian threat were nonexistent, we could wage war on Britain indefinitely. If Russia collapsed, Japan would be greatly relieved; this in turn would mean increased danger to the U.S.A.[61]

So Hitler determined to drive out the devil by calling in Beelzebub. The decision was a fateful one, but altogether characteristic. Having failed to subdue the British in the summer of 1940, the Fuehrer had allowed himself to be talked into complicated schemes for cutting British supply lines and driving the British from the Mediterranean. His diplomatic efforts with Franco and Pétain had proved thoroughly disappointing, and his colleague, Mussolini, had made matters worse by inviting defeat in Greece and Libya. At the same time the Tripartite Pact, far from distracting and frightening the United States, had tended only to cement the unwritten alliance between the two great democracies. If Soviet Russia had joined the Axis coalition, Japan's hands would have been freed for an advance to the south, and Britain would have been deprived once and for all of any prospect of Soviet support. Hitler sensed only too keenly that if the war were prolonged, American aid to Britain might become decisive, or the Kremlin might eventually consider that its interests demanded intervention to forestall British defeat. If, then, he could have bound Soviet Russia to Germany and its partners, he would have scored an important success. But Stalin refused to sell the imperial Russian heritage for a mess of potage. Undazzled by the prospect of empire in the Persian Gulf and India, he and Molotov stuck by the time-honored Russian claims in eastern Europe and the Middle East. To accept the Soviet demands would have been, for Hitler, tantamount to surrendering his nearest and dearest objectives. He was through with diplomacy and would let the cannon speak. Why, after all, should he allow two hundred divisions to stand idle? If properly used they could clean up the Greek and Mediterranean messes left by Mussolini and thereafter turn to the broad plains of the Soviet Union. There, after all, were the great expanses of which Hitler dreamed as the future German living space.

[61] *Fuehrer Conferences, 1941* (1), 4 (conference of January 8 and 9, 1941).

CHAPTER VI

One for All, All for One

1. Defense of the Panama Canal

The chief motive behind American policies toward Spain and Portugal was, in the final analysis, much the same as that which dictated strong support of Britain. French West Africa, the Canaries, the Azores, and the Cape Verde Islands constituted, together with the British Isles themselves, the first line of defense of the Western Hemisphere. It will be useful, therefore, to turn now to the hemisphere itself, and trace the course of American efforts to put the two continents in condition to resist attack if the first line were actually to give way.

This will involve, first, an analysis of American efforts to shore up the military bastions of the hemisphere fortress, and, thereafter, an examination of the policy of strengthening the economic foundations upon which inter-American defense ultimately rested. The delicacy of Washington's relations with the Latin American Republics made great demands on the Government's resources. Not less significant from the standpoint of hemisphere defense, however, was the progress of negotiations, first with Britain looking toward the rapid creation of American bases in the areas designated in the Destroyer Deal; then with Canada, carrying out the Ogdensburg Agreement; and finally, with Greenland and Iceland to insure against their use as stepping stones for attack on the North American continent.[1]

Japan's adherence to the Axis pact naturally spurred the United States Government to even more vigorous efforts to translate the hopeful resolutions of the Havana Conference (July, 1940) into concrete defense measures. If Washington had no intention of permitting the Japanese action to reverse the priority assigned to the Atlantic over the Pacific theater, the Administration had now to contemplate added burdens deriving from the legitimate fears of the Latin American Republics. While the immediate effect of

[1] The general military-strategic problem is treated by Hanson W. Baldwin: *United We Stand* (New York, 1941).

Japan's joining the Axis was to strengthen the voices of those Latin American neighbors who sympathized with the policy of hemisphere solidarity, it likewise added weight to the arguments of those who were lukewarm or hostile. To fall in openly and speedily with the inter-American program might provoke Japanese attack across the Pacific, as well as German attack in the Atlantic.[2]

President Roosevelt, in greeting the first contingent of Latin American officers invited at the beginning of October, 1940, by General Marshall and the War Department to see for themselves the progress of American rearmament, struck an urgent but hopeful note. He described the inter-American defense program as a matter of "one for all and all for one." The amenities of such occasions were duly observed, and the Latin American visitors, through their spokesman, General Felipe Rivera of Bolivia, pledged wholehearted support of American ideals.[3] They enjoyed an excellent dinner and on the morrow began a conducted tour. What these officers would report to their Governments about production in American arsenals and factories would have significant bearing on Mr. Roosevelt's hemisphere ideal of one for all and all for one. Meanwhile, Washington assumed the initiative in the solution of various problems.

By all odds the most critical hemisphere problem reëmphasized by the conclusion of the Tripartite Pact was the protection of the Panama Canal. More than ever after September 27, 1940, this waterway was the key to the defense of the western continents. The joint responsibility of the American and Panamanian Governments to provide additional protection for the Canal, when necessary, had been recognized by the agreements of March 2, 1936. Since then, but with particular intensity after July, 1940, the United States Government had been negotiating with Panama with a view to obtaining base sites within the territory of the Republic which would provide the added air protection now deemed absolutely essential for the Canal. No agreement, however, had been reached by the end of the summer on such thorny issues as jurisdiction, length of lease, and appropriate remuneration. Fortunately the Army had earlier negotiated a private lease for a large air base at Rio Hato, and had also despatched forces, with the consent of the Panamanian authorities, to the small islands of Taboga and Tabogiullia.[4]

Understandably, American military authorities, both in Washington and in the Canal Zone itself, urged the State Department and Mr. William

[2] Roland H. Sharp in the *Christian Science Monitor,* September 30; John W. White in *The New York Times,* October 20, 1940.

[3] *The New York Times,* October 2, 1940.

[4] Despatch from Dawson (Panama City), August 11, 1939; letter of Welles to Dawson, September 14, 1939; tel. from Dawson, July 11, 1940; despatch from Dawson, September 20, 1940; tels. to Dawson, July 13, September 25, 1940. For an excellent review see Almon R. Wright: "Defense Sites Negotiations between the United States and Panama, 1936-1948" (*Department of State Bulletin,* August 11, 1952).

Dawson, the American Ambassador to Panama, to secure in their negotiations the maximum defensive advantage for the United States, particularly with respect to exclusive jurisdiction and long-term tenure of the areas to be leased. The State Department, on the other hand, aware that Panama constituted a test case for the Good Neighbor Policy in the eyes of all other American Republics, counseled a moderation with which the military at times became impatient. But to Mr. Welles it would have been a poor bargain if, in obtaining from Panama all that General Daniel Van Voorhis, the American Commander at Panama, might rightly deem necessary for defense of the Canal, the United States sacrificed the confidence of Latin America, which it was so anxious to protect. In any case, despite a reduction of the War Department's initial demands, agreement with Panama on the terms of the leases was still far from consummation when, in October, 1940, the Administration of President Boyd was succeeded by that of President Arnulfo Arias.[5]

The new President's initial broadcast tended to arouse doubt about an individual who had formerly been Panamanian Minister to Rome, and who had been accused in liberal circles of entertaining sympathy for the Axis. Whatever his motives, Arias's speech of October 2, 1940, complained that American forces had occupied the Rio Hato field and other defense sites in the Republic's territory without waiting for the conclusion of a binding agreement with the Government of Panama. This was technically accurate, but it overlooked the fact that the "occupation" (by lease from a private owner) had been negotiated with the full knowledge and consent of the preceding Administration.[6] Furthermore, rumor had it that a deleted sentence of the presidential broadcast contained the threat that if the United States maltreated Panama, the latter would make concessions "to other powerful countries."[7]

Despite Arias's unpromising debut, Ambassador Dawson was not inclined to make an issue of the Rio Hato reference, or of the current charge that the President sympathized with the Axis. The Ambassador believed that the new Chief Executive intended eventually to grant the bases, but was determined to strike the best possible bargain before doing so. Nevertheless, Mr. Dawson could predict no early conclusion of the negotiations, and General Van Voorhis proceeded with the development of the Rio Hato base even at the risk of friction.[8]

[5] Letter of Secretary Woodring to Secretary Hull, June 20; letter of Welles, Acting Secretary, to Assistant Secretary of War Johnson, July 3; letter of General Van Voorhis to General Marshall, November 12, 1940.

[6] Letter of General David L. Stone to Laurence Duggan, January 5, 1941; despatch from Dawson, September 20, 1940.

[7] Despatch from Dawson, October 5, 1940. On the supposed attitude of President Arias, see R. O. Boyer in the newspaper PM, December 26, 1940; H. B. Murkland, "The Hispanic American Scene," in Events, January, 1941, p. 68; and, more recently, the article of Almon R. Wright, as cited above.

[8] Despatches from Dawson, October 14, 25, November 22, 1940.

Ambassador Dawson's estimate proved, unhappily, to be quite justified. A Joint Investigating Board was presently set up to examine and report on the base sites desired by the United States, some seventy-one tracts of land, exclusive of the Rio Hato base. During the balance of the year proposals and counterproposals flew back and forth between the two capitals. Panama refused to commit itself to leases longer than the term of a single presidential administration plus one year (seven years in all). The United States, having already climbed down from its original request for much longer leases, now declined to budge from the position that anything less than a ninety-nine-year lease would fail to provide adequately for the defense of the Canal or justify the cost of the installations. The United States Government had already signified acceptance of the principle that when the emergency was over, the leased tracts would revert to Panama. That, Washington believed, was as far as it could go.[9]

Similar exchanges characterized the negotiations as to jurisdiction, payment for sites, and most of the remaining issues. While Presdient Arias steadfastly refused to name a price, he made it abundantly clear that any notion of using the current market value of the sites as a basis for compensation was altogether unfitting, not to say niggardly, in a wealthy Government like that of the United States.

So matters rested throughout the autumn and winter of 1940-1941. The American Government argued, cajoled, and warned. Time and again Washington cited the urgency of the situation and Panama's joint responsibility under the terms of the 1936 conventions. No satisfactory response was forthcoming, particularly as the Arias Administration was increasingly disposed to insist that solution of the problem of base sites should be preceded by satisfaction of many other Panamanian demands upon the United States. By the end of the year it seemed that Washington was headed for a showdown with the Government of Panama. The United States could not avoid insisting upon adequate facilities for the protection of its vital interests and those of the entire continent, regardless of the obstructive tactics of the Panamanian Government. The risk that a firm attitude would occasion talk about sovereignty, which could be used to effect in the other American Republics, would have to be run. The Administration was confronted with a real emergency "in which practical considerations should prevail over theoretical ones."[10]

[9] Despatches from Dawson, November 9, December 7, 9, 30; tels. from Dawson, November 26, December 23; letters from Dawson to Welles and Duggan, November 12, 13; letter of Marshall to Welles, November 15, enclosing a letter from Van Voorhis; tels. to Dawson, November 23, December 28, 1940.

[10] Informal memo of the Division of American Republics, December 17, attached to despatch from Dawson, December 7; United States aide-mémoire, December 30, 1940, and Panama's reply (tel. from Dawson, January 7, 1941). We have also used a letter of General Van Voorhis to General Marshall, January 3, 1941, of which a copy was sent to the State Department.

2. THE USE OF LATIN AMERICAN BASES

Happily, the American Government managed to avoid an open struggle with the Arias Administration. The protracted negotiations with Panama illustrate, however, the delicacy of Washington's relations even with an American Republic which had signed a specific defensive treaty. It was only to be expected that negotiations with other hemisphere governments would also run upon difficulties. While the general tone of Washington's relations with its Latin American neighbors was now more cordial than ever before, the United States faced a formidable task in attempting to induce all the Governments of the hemisphere to fall in with what it deemed essential arrangements for the defense of the two continents without resorting to methods which would jeopardize the very solidarity which Washington sought to cultivate.

In early October reports began to appear in the press that since July, 1940, United States Army and Navy officers had been engaged in informal and secret conversations with their opposite numbers in the other American Republics. According to the account of *The New York Times* correspondent in Buenos Aires, these "confidential agents" of the United States had been sounding out the major South American Governments on their capabilities for self-defense, their willingness to put bases at the disposal of the United States, their requirements by way of assistance, and their readiness for staff conversations looking toward plans for joint defense. Except for the proposal involving staff conversations, the reports went on to say, "Washington's overtures" had not been received with notable warmth. There was widespread hostility to any idea of the unilateral lease of bases to the United States and, according to the reports, the possibility of a more favorable reception for "Uruguay's proposal that whatever bases are established should be open to use by all American nations."[11]

These premature and probably locally inspired reports had unfortunate repercussions. They provoked controversies, both inside and outside the chancelleries of the hemisphere, which for a time threatened to undo whatever favorable results had initially derived from the visits of United States officers. Since, however, the end product was a genuine clarification of the United States position respecting inter-American base arrangements, it is worth pursuing the story to its reassuring conclusion.

As the reader may recall, there was nothing in the instructions issued to United States officers to justify the charge that the United States was seeking to lease bases for its exclusive use in any South American states.[12] Washington had already declared that the bases leased from Britain would be open to the use of the other American Republics. Moreover, the initial de-

[11] John W. White in *The New York Times,* October 4, 13, 14, 1940.
[12] *The Challenge to Isolation,* Chapter XVIII, Section 3.

fense conversations were of an exploratory nature and any agreement reached at the military level would have been as a matter of course subject to approval at the governmental level. In any event, no defense arrangements with the Governments of Latin America were contemplated that would have involved an infringement of their sovereignty. Whether the representatives on mission of the War and Navy Departments invariably succeeded in making this clear in their conferences with their Latin American counterparts is not certain. The instructions for the guidance of the United States officers were of necessity couched in general terms, leaving a certain latitude for interpretation. The officers in question were naturally more interested in practical arrangements which would enable America's neighbors to ward off an attack than in nice formulas designed to protect every detail of national sovereignty. The Latin American officers, in turn, tended to view the issue of bases from the angle of concrete advantages to their own military establishments. The result in some cases was to obscure the exact scope of the staff conversations and their true objectives. Unhappily this confusion gave Axis agents and Communist sympathizers a golden opportunity to misrepresent the purposes of the United States Government. They were not slow to seize and exploit that opportunity.[13]

The initial reports of an impending agreement between the United States and Uruguay on the use of the latter's existing base facilities were presently followed by others from "unimpeachable diplomatic sources" in Buenos Aires stating that Brazil and Chile had agreed to lease bases to the United States, and that Uruguay would presently follow suit.[14] Washington at first refused to comment on these reports, but the story evoked much unfavorable criticism in South American and Axis capitals. Official quarters in Chile, admitting that since the Havana Conference there had been discussions with the United States on a variety of defense questions, quite correctly denied that the lease of bases to the United States had ever been on the agenda. The Brazilian Foreign Minister, Señhor Aranha, a firm friend of hemisphere coöperation, similarly refuted the allegation on behalf of his own country. So, also, did the Foreign Minister of Argentina.[15]

It was in Uruguay, however, that revelation of the alleged content of the defense discussions occasioned the maximum mischief. Newspaper reports that the Uruguayan Government was about to grant the United States a base on the River Plate coincided almost exactly with the scheduled opening of the military conversations between Uruguayan and American officers on October 22.[16] These reports were seized upon by nationalist forces as a providential opportunity to embarrass the Administration and, in particular,

[13] H. Fernandez Artucio: *The Nazi Underground in South America* (New York, 1942), 116 ff.; Hull: *Memoirs*, I, 813 ff.

[14] *The New York Times*, October 14, 1940.

[15] *The New York Times*, October 15, 16 and 17; tel. from Armour (Buenos Aires), October 15, 1940.

[16] Tels. from Wilson (Montevideo), October 15, 22, 29; despatch from Wilson, October 22, 1940; Fernandez Artucio: *The Nazi Underground in South America,* 117.

its Foreign Minister, Dr. Guani. The resulting struggle, in which the issue of bases soon became hopelessly engulfed in the crosscurrents of domestic politics, provides a striking and characteristic example of the difficulties attending American efforts to solve the problems of adequate military defense for the southern continent.

As in other cases, the staff conversations between officers of the United States and the Uruguayan armed forces were primarily technical in character. They had as their major objective agreement on the use of existing base facilities and the development of further sites required for the defense of the Uruguayan coast and ports. Determined not to be intimidated by the opposition, Foreign Minister Guani insisted that the conversations be held as scheduled. In a week's time they were successfully concluded. Since some degree of secrecy was for a time maintained, Dr. Guani's opponents, both at home and abroad, were able to pour out a flood of charges that the Government was deliberately sacrificing Uruguay's sovereign rights to the demands of United States "imperialists." The Uruguayan agreement, and indeed the agreements about to be reached with other Latin American Governments, were all alleged to involve the lease of national territory for the exclusive use of the armed forces of the United States.

Groundless though these charges were, newspaper reports of the staff conversations were such as to arouse deep suspicion. The Uruguayan officers, it was said, had first been presented with a memorandum outlining the position of the United States. This they had allegedly rejected on the plea that the whole question of bases should be considered from a Pan American point of view and worked out in agreement with the other River Plate countries. The American officers, it was further reported, had accepted the Uruguayan position and the staff conversations had thus established the principle that bases in Uruguay were to be placed at the disposal of all American Republics in case of emergency.[17]

From such accounts it was easy to draw the false inference that the initial American proposal was for bases in Uruguay (and presumably elsewhere in Latin America) of which the United States would have exclusive jurisdiction and use during the emergency. That inference was drawn and skillfully exploited both by the opposition party in Uruguay and by Axis propagandists abroad. The Axis press solemnly warned the Latin American Republics that United States policy was substituting a "marriage of force" for the "generous lover" of Europe. The reaction of the Spanish press in particular was so bitter and violent as to elicit a strong statement from the Uruguayan Minister at Madrid. Secretary Hull's quick insistence that this Government's hemisphere defense plans did not conflict in any way with the sovereignty or integrity of any nation did little to blunt these propaganda shafts.[18] The

[17] John W. White in *The New York Times,* November 10, 1940.
[18] *The New York Times,* November 8, 10, 22; December 7, 1940; *Documents on American Foreign Relations,* III, 138.

Uruguayan Foreign Office likewise attempted to answer its critics by issuing an official communiqué stating that no foreign power would have control of Uruguay's projected bases, and that, furthermore, these facilities would, in case of need, be placed at the disposal of all American Republics. Nevertheless, the hue and cry continued and spread.[19]

Both the United States Legation at Montevideo and Mr. Welles as Acting Secretary of State made every effort to clarify the policy of the American Government and thus ease the heavy pressure on Foreign Minister Guani. On November 13 Mr. Welles gave his press conference what he believed to be an unequivocal statement of the American position:

I want to make it very clear that the United States Government has never sought directly or indirectly to obtain the lease or cession of air and naval bases in Uruguay. As Secretary Hull has frequently stated, in none of our conversations with any of the other American Republics has there ever been involved the possibility of any suggestions on our part which would affect in any sense the sovereignty of any other American nation.[20]

Even the Welles statement, however, failed to clear the atmosphere. Intended as a disavowal of negotiations for exclusive United States rights in South American bases, it could be interpreted as a denial that bases had ever been the subject of negotiations of any kind between the United States and the Latin American Governments. Since this was obviously not the case, Dr. Guani's foes pounced upon the Welles statement as final proof of the Uruguayan Foreign Minister's duplicity. The latter's situation soon approached the point of genuine crisis and the prospects for a successful outcome of United States policy for inter-American defense appeared seriously jeopardized.

Other Latin American leaders promptly took steps to forestall similar complications in their respective countries. The President of Chile, Pedro Aguirre Cerda, felt obliged to deny that his Government had ever discussed with the United States the subject of bases, or that Chile was building or indeed planning bases, even for Pan American use. President Ortiz of Argentina was more restrained, but could not bring himself to voice more than a mild endorsement of the ideal of hemisphere defense (press interview of November 19). The attitude of Argentina, and its great concern over the possibility of any bilateral agreement between the United States and Uruguay for River Plate bases, were plainly set forth in a statement of the Argentine Ministry of Foreign Relations on November 22, 1940. This statement revealed that opposition to Dr. Guani was by no means merely domestic, and that Argentina, too, had been discussing the subject of River Plate bases. "The problems of the River Plate," concluded the statement, "in which are bound the permanent interests of Argentina and Uruguay,

---

[19] *Documents on American Foreign Relations,* III, 136.
[20] *Ibid.,* 137.

must be considered henceforth among the proposals of continental defense inspired by the resolutions of the last Pan American Conference."[21]

Thus Argentina made clear that it was decidedly interested in any arrangements between the United States and Uruguay, a country with which Argentina considered itself closely linked. Nor could the American Ambassador at Buenos Aires, Mr. Norman Armour, record any evidence of readiness on Argentina's own part to resume the staff conversations with United States officers which had ended without significant results early in October.[22]

In the face of concerted attack by the opposition in the Uruguayan Senate and of evidence of Argentine concern over any arrangements which did not take careful account of that power's interest in the River Plate estuary, Dr. Guani elected to pursue the bold course. In a fighting speech before the Senate, he threw down the gauntlet to his opponents: "I am authorized to state," said the Foreign Minister, amidst heckling of the opposition group, "that the Government will not permit party political intervention in the direction of the grave problems that the Government is facing in its handling of international affairs. The Government is determined to protect national security and nothing and nobody can alter that determination."[23]

The Foreign Minister served notice on the opposition of his determination to pursue a coöperative hemisphere policy and proceed with plans for an agreement with Washington regardless of consequences. The United States Minister at Montevideo, reporting the course of the six-hour debate which followed, was pessimistic about the probable outcome. Mr. Wilson pointed out that there was no reason to doubt the overwhelmingly friendly sentiments of the Uruguayan people or their general approval of the program for inter-American defense. The danger lay rather in the likelihood that continental defense policy would become entangled with purely domestic issues of democracy and constitutional reform. The constitution of Uruguay enabled the opposition party to hold half the seats in the Senate, though it had secured only one third of the popular vote in the most recent elections. Wilson believed the issue of constitutional reform would presently have to be fought out. He devoutly hoped, however, that the aggressive tactics of Dr. Guani would not produce a constitutional crisis and wreck the entire program which the Uruguyan Administration was sponsoring in the interests of hemisphere defense.[24]

For a time it appeared that this would in fact be the result of the Foreign Minister's fighting stand. After six hours of violent debate the Senate passed

[21] President Cerda's statements are quoted in the *New York Herald Tribune*, November 16, 1940. The Argentine statements are printed in *Documents on American Foreign Relations*, III, 138 ff.; tel. from Armour (Buenos Aires), November 24, 1940.

[22] Despatch from Armour, November 20, 1940; memo of conversation between Welles and Ambassador Espil of Argentina and Vice Admiral José Guisasola, May 30, 1941.

[23] *The New York Times*, November 22, 1940.

[24] Tels. from Wilson, November 22 and 25, 1940.

a vote of censure against him and registered its opposition to the construction of any bases "jeopardizing Uruguayan sovereignty." In great haste Mr. Welles on November 22 repeated with renewed emphasis and greater precision his earlier assurance that the United States had never, in the case of Uruguay or any other American Republic, proposed an agreement which would have infringed in any degree the sovereignty of those countries.[25]

The outcome was a resounding vindication of Foreign Minister Guani and his policies. On November 27 the Uruguayan Chamber of Representatives, by a vote of fifty-three to twenty-one, expressed the nation's full confidence in the Government's policy. Thereafter, the principle of Uruguay's coöperation in the military program of hemisphere defense, including the allocation of bases for the use of all the Republics in case of emergency, gradually ceased to be a significant issue in that country.[26]

Argentine opposition to Dr. Guani's program took somewhat longer to overcome. Dr. Roca, the Foreign Minister, stuck by his Government's original plan for a regional defense pact among the River Plate countries— Argentina, Uruguay, and Paraguay. The problem presented to Uruguay was, thus, to work out an arrangement with Argentina which would give that country the necessary assurance without adversely affecting Uruguay's agreement with the United States. Washington, aware of Argentine dissatisfaction with Uruguayan policy, made every effort to promote a satisfactory understanding between Buenos Aires and Montevideo. The United States Government's position with respect to regional defense agreements among Latin American states had in the past been distinctly negative. As Mr. Welles had earlier informed the Chilean Foreign Minister, Washington believed the most effective method of coöperation for defense lay in united action of all the Republics, rather than in local arrangements among specific states. So the United States, said Mr. Welles, interpreted the resolutions of the Havana Conference.[27]

Nevertheless, the State Department did not actively oppose Argentine plans for a defense pact with Uruguay and Paraguay. The American Government undoubtedly hoped that such a development might prevent the growth of friction between Uruguay and Argentina comparable to that between Peru and Ecuador, a situation which was then regarded as the most dangerous chink in the armor of the hemisphere.[28]

Thus, by the end of December the greatly exaggerated Uruguayan "base

[25] *Documents on American Foreign Relations,* III, 137; John W. White in *The New York Times,* November 23, 1940.

[26] *Documents on American Foreign Relations,* III, 138; tel. from Wilson, November 25, 1940.

[27] Tel. to Bowers (Santiago), November 12, 1940, containing a message apropos of rumors of impending conferences among the River Plate Republics, the Amazon River states, and those countries of the Pacific coast of which Chile was the natural leader.

[28] Tels. from Armour, November 27, 28; tel. to Armour, November 29; memo of Captain W. O. Spears, U.S.N., of the Office of the Chief of Naval Operations, to Mr. Chapin, State Department, November 23, 1940.

incident" had been reduced to its proper proportions. With this key Republic of South America the United States had finally reached an agreement which it hoped would pave the way for those sought from other Governments of that continent. To be sure, the agreement was still on paper only. As Minister Wilson had pointed out at the very beginning of the negotiations, future developments would depend in large measure on the ability of the United States to make essential war materials available to Uruguay. Many months were to elapse before the United States, having secured the agreement, found itself in a position to supply the matériel needed by Uruguay to carry out its part of the bargain.[29]

The chief significance and the major achievement of the Uruguayan negotiations lay in the final clarification of American policy respecting inter-American defense agreements. After some pain and anguish Washington succeeded in making clear to all well-disposed Governments that its formula for bases, and for all related defense arrangements, was not the formula upon which the Destroyer Deal with Britain was based. Washington was willing to help finance the development of Latin American bases and certainly desired to use them in case of emergency. Jurisdiction, however, was to remain with the state within whose boundaries the bases were located, and access was to be granted not only to the United States, but as needed to other American Republics. As this was the original objective of the United States Government, the negotiations with Uruguay serve as an illustration of the unexpected difficulties involved in attaining it, and of the extraordinary tact required to achieve results even in the case of a government particularly friendly toward the United States and devoted to the ideal of hemisphere solidarity.[30]

Space does not permit examination of kindred defense negotiations conducted during these months with other Governments of Latin America. Nor would such examination provide additional light on the hemisphere defense policy of the United States. Agreements in principle, similar to that arrived at with Uruguay, were worked out with most of the other states. Some Governments proved more coöperative than others. Argentina remained aloof. Brazil was friendly. All except the Central American Republics were cautious and acutely sensitive to any impairment of their sovereignty. In nearly every case the American Government encountered difficulties not unlike those met with at Montevideo. There was the invariable problem of negotiating with Governments in which the "outs" did their best to sabotage the efforts of the "ins." Washington had constantly to recognize the legitimate fears of its Latin American friends lest, by falling in with American plans, they invite the foreign aggression against which all were trying to defend. Washington had likewise to guard against the small but often aggressive and influential groups of pro-Nazis and Communists who deliberately

---

[29] Tels. from Wilson, October 29 and December 2, 1940.
[30] Tel. from Armour, November 27, 1940.

conspired to obstruct every effort of their own Governments to coöperate. The rate of progress was inevitably disappointing. It worried some officials of the War and Navy Departments as it puzzled plain citizens not conversant with the complications of Latin American politics. Nevertheless, by the end of 1940 the Army and Navy had concluded defense agreements with every country of South America except Argentina. The Good Neighbor Policy promised to be equal to the demands placed upon it by the threat of war.

3. A FRESH START WITH MEXICO

Washington's relations with Mexico City during the autumn and winter of 1940 call for special attention. In the case of America's immediate neighbor to the south, the facts of geographical proximity and of recent history made the achievement of defense objectives at the same time more desirable and more difficult than elsewhere in the hemisphere with the possible exception of Panama and Argentina.[31]

Preliminary staff conversations with Mexico had been completed early in August, 1940, with results in general highly satisfactory to the United States. Owing principally to the fact that the new Administration of President-elect Avila Camacho was to take over from President Cárdenas in December, the military agreements had not yet been approved at the governmental level. Washington had reason to hope, however, that the new regime would prove even more coöperative than its predecessor. The United States Government was, moreover, considering a broad plan for settling the whole "Mexican problem" in all its aspects. There was little hope of action, however, until the new President was so firmly established in office that he could safely run the political risks involved in a vigorous pro-American policy.[32]

The general objective of the first staff conversations between representatives of the War and Navy Departments and the Mexican military authorities was identical with that pursued in the South American Republics: an arrangement by which, with United States assistance, the Mexican Government could defend itself against external attack or internal subversion in the event that the Axis powers elected either course. Such an arrangement required, among other things, an agreement that, in case of emergency, United States armed forces would be invited by Mexico to use its naval and air bases. In the case of this neighbor, however, it seems clear that not only the Navy Department but President Roosevelt himself originally hoped that any agreement on Mexican bases—as at Magdalena Bay or Acapulco— might be modeled on the British base agreement. The Navy Department

[31] Maurice Halperin: "Mexico Shifts Her Foreign Policy" (*Foreign Affairs*, October, 1940).

[32] *Morgenthau Diaries* (*MS.*), October 23, 1940 (Vol. 324, p. 171); memo of Mr. Boal, U.S. Counselor of Embassy, Mexico City, September 17, 1940.

believed it necessary to obtain from the Mexican Government long-term leases and extensive jurisdiction within the base areas, though sovereignty would, as in the British case, remain with the home Government. The Army, thanks to arrangements permitting the development of airfields in Mexico and elsewhere in Latin America, felt no need for such long-term leases. General Marshall asked merely for the establishment of three staging fields which the Mexican Government had conditionally agreed to allow American combat aircraft to use in flights to Panama or elsewhere in Latin America.[33]

It was a foregone conclusion that the Navy Department's proposals would be no more acceptable to incoming President Avila Camacho than to outgoing President Cárdenas, particularly after the furor created by the Uruguayan incident. In Mexico as elsewhere it was the rule that all elements hostile to the United States, native or foreign, should make capital of the allegation that the use of bases was the first step in a course which would surely end in the destruction of the national sovereignty over such areas.[34] It was not surprising, therefore, that Ambassador Castillo Najera, in outlining the position of his Government to Mr. Welles early in November, proposed a different solution of the bases problem.

In its essentials the Mexican pattern was the "Pan American" pattern as it emerged in Uruguay. Mexico would agree with the United States and other interested American Republics on sites to be developed as bases. Once these sites had been selected, facilities would be built by Mexican engineers and laborers. The construction would be financed by the interested Governments in the proportion determined by their interest and economic capability, and their possible use of the bases. There could, of course, be no question of the slightest diminution of Mexican sovereignty over these ports and bases. They would remain under the control of the Mexican police and Army, subject to the same legal and administrative control as existed in all parts of the Republic. Mexico, in turn, would permit the bases to be used by any American state which officially declared itself in imminent danger of becoming involved in war with a non-American power.[35]

[33] Letter of Secretaries Knox and Stimson to Secretary Hull, October 24, 1940, furnishing a statement of their requirements. Earlier, Mr. Roosevelt had broached to Mr. Welles a scheme for a loan or gift to Mexico from the President's special fund "in return for certain naval rights in places like Magdalena Bay, Salina Cruz, and possibly something near the northeast corner of Yucatan" (Memo of the President to Welles, September 28, 1940).

Arrangements for the improvement of commercial airfields throughout Latin America, so as to make them suitable for emergency use by military planes, are discussed in the *Stimson Diary (MS.),* October 28, November 8, 9, 1940; and the *Morgenthau Diaries (MS.),* November 8, 1940 (Vol. 330, pp. 136 ff.). We have used also a letter from General Marshall to Mr. Welles, October 23, 1940.

[34] The efforts of the Cárdenas Administration to counter these charges are described in despatches from Daniels (Mexico City), October 17 and 30, and November 2, 1940.

[35] Informal memo of the Ambassador to Mr. Welles, without date or signature, but presumably of early November; *Christian Science Monitor,* October 3, 1940.

Although Mr. Welles suggested to General Marshall and Admiral Stark, at a meeting of the Liaison Committee on November 12, that the War and Navy Departments work out their proposed bases arrangements along the lines desired by the Mexican Government, the Navy Department at least was not disposed to accept these proposals without demur. Secretary Knox, in a letter to Mr. Hull, argued that the Mexicans were, in effect, inviting the United States to finance the building of the facilities without offering any commensurate return. Mr. Knox expressed no objection to the use of the bases by any and all the American Republics if need arose, since it was unlikely that any but Mexican or United States forces would ever need to use them. Nor had the Secretary any designs on Mexico's sovereignty. He held out, however, for a long-term lease similar to that enjoyed by the United States at Guantánamo Bay in Cuba. He likewise clung to his earlier view that for the duration of the lease the United States Government should enjoy virtually exclusive jurisdiction within the bases, as in the case of the recently acquired British sites.[36]

Realizing eventually that his position was difficult to reconcile with the views of the Mexican Government, Secretary Knox proposed to Secretary Hull that a mixed Mexican-American Commission be set up not only to study the problem of suitable arrangements for naval bases, but also to review all the understandings reached in the earlier staff conversations. In point of fact, Mr. Welles and Ambassador Castillo Najera had anticipated the Secretary of the Navy in recognizing that the solution of such issues as bases in Mexican territory could be arrived at only in the context of broader defense plans, and only through negotiations on a level higher than that of staff conversations. A model already existed in the Joint American-Canadian Defense Commission. In his conversations with Mr. Welles, the Ambassador suggested that a similar board be set up with Mexico.[37] By November 12 Mr. Welles was able to inform General Marshall and Admiral Stark that President Roosevelt had given his consent to the immediate establishment of a Mexican-United States Defense Commission.[38]

At this point the promising development of defense arrangements with Mexico was abruptly stopped. There was clearly a considerable gulf between what the Navy Department still regarded as minimum requirements for the adequate protection of Mexico against aggression and what the

[36] Memo of Mr. Welles to Orme Wilson, Secretary of the State-War-Navy Liaison Committee, November 12; letter of Knox to Hull, November 19; Duggan's memo to Mr. Welles, October 23, 1940, opposing Navy Department suggestions that the leased area at Guantánamo Bay be extended, and that U.S. Marines be stationed at certain points outside its existing limits.

[37] Tel. to Daniels, November 26, 1940.

[38] Memo of Mr. Welles to Mr. Orme Wilson, November 12; tel. to Daniels, November 26, 1940. The President hinted at the impending creation of the commission at his press conference of November 8, 1940 (*Public Papers and Addresses,* IX, 564). Letter of Mr. Welles to the President, November 22, 1940, submitting for his approval the names of the U.S. members of the Joint Commission.

Mexican Government believed it practicable to offer in view of the domestic political situation. General Almazán's refusal to admit the validity of President Avila Camacho's election involved the possibility of armed insurrection. The year ended, therefore, without even an announcement of the Joint Defense Commission, to say nothing of a solution of the several issues which motivated its creation. President Avila Camacho indicated his desire to delay the announcement of the new board. Unfriendly voices in Mexico were already insinuating that the new Administration had made territorial concessions to the United States in return for American recognition of the new regime. Many months were therefore to elapse before the Joint Mexican-American Defense Commission became an acknowledged reality.[39]

Though progress in the negotiation of defense agreements with Mexico was slow, Mr. Welles, who was in charge of this as of other Latin American problems, had reason for taking an optimistic view. For one thing, the prediction that President Avila Camacho would be favorably disposed to the United States had proved sound, even if the new Chief Executive felt obliged to proceed with circumspection. At his inauguration on November 30, he stressed Pan American solidarity and pledged adherence to "the international Pan American doctrine, which is the only hope for the salvation of civilization and international rights." The hearty reception accorded Vice President Wallace, who represented Mr. Roosevelt at the inauguration and later addressed the Mexican Congress, contributed to the belief that it would presently be possible to resolve all outstanding differences between the two Governments and enable them to work together in the interests of hemisphere solidarity.[40]

Similarly, Under Secretary Welles had reason to believe that his efforts to educate the public in general, and the military in particular, on the necessity for discreet treatment of the Latin American Republics were gaining recognition. It was not easy to counter the arguments of the War and Navy Departments on the urgent need for defense installations on Mexico's Pacific coast, as at the bulge of Brazil or at other important areas in South America.[41] Mr. Welles and the State Department, however, stuck to their conviction that any infringement of the Good Neighbor Policy in the interests

[39] Memo of conversation between Mr. Welles and the Mexican Ambassador, December 14, 1940. The American members of the new commission, as telegraphed to Ambassador Daniels on November 26, included, for the Army: Brig. Gen. J. N. Greely, Lt. Col. Donald Wilson of the Air Corps, and Lt. Col. M. B. Ridgway; and for the Navy: Capt. W. O. Spears, Commander K. B. Bragg, and Commander C. T. Durgin. On the hesitations of the Mexican Government, see tel. and despatch from Daniels, December 6, 13 and despatch from Boal (Mexico City), December 20, 1940.
[40] Bulletin of International News, XVII (2), 1658; cf. Events, January, 1941, pp. 66 ff.
[41] On the Galapagos Islands, we have used the minutes of the State-War-Navy Liaison Committee for September 23, 1940. The President's interest is attested in the Stimson Diary (MS.), October 18 and November 8, 1940; see also Samuel F. Bemis: The Latin American Policy of the United States (New York, 1943), 381 ff.

of immediate gain would be certain to result in eventual loss. If there was some complaint in the American press at the end of 1940 about the slow progress of the program of inter-American defense, such complaint was now accompanied by frank recognition of the delicacy of the problems faced by the Government. Only in rare instances was there any suggestion that the Big Stick replace the Good Neighbor.[42]

4. HEMISPHERE REARMAMENT AND ECONOMIC DEFENSE

Minister Wilson's warning that the real success of any defense arrangements made at Montevideo would depend in large measure upon America's ability to supply Uruguay with the munitions and materials for the construction of base facilities was a timely reminder that America's neighbors were not the only ones guilty of procrastination. To put the hemisphere in a posture of defense plainly required expenditures far beyond the existing capacity of the Latin American nations. For the necessary increase in their armaments as, indeed, for the mere maintenance of their peacetime economies, all the nations south of the Rio Grande now depended in varying degrees on the United States.[43]

The initial efforts of the Latin American nations to acquire munitions from the United States can be briefly summarized. There were no serious legal or psychological barriers to making munitions available to the American Republics, such as those which complicated the Administration's efforts on behalf of Britain and China. Mr. Hull had followed up the solemn pledges of the President's Columbus Day address on hemisphere solidarity by reaffirming that surplus war equipment belonging to the United States War and Navy Departments was indeed available to all Latin American countries "in keeping with the policy of continental defense."[44]

The root of the difficulty lay in the embarrassing lack of war matériel sufficiently modern to meet the stated requirements of the Latin American Governments. To be sure, many of the Attachés of the various Republics in Washington had trouble in deciding upon their most pressing armament needs. Likewise most of them found the intricacies of United States government procedure beyond the power of the ordinary intellect to grasp. But even when the preliminary hurdles were successfully cleared, the Latin American representatives were almost invariably exposed to ultimate frus-

[42] Hanson Baldwin in *The New York Times,* October 21, 1940.

[43] Tel. from Wilson (Montevideo), October 29, 1940. Since space prevents any detailed consideration of this aspect of American policy, the reader's attention is invited to the following accounts: Bemis: *The Latin American Policy of the United States,* especially Chapters XVII, XIX, and XX; Percy Bidwell: *The Economic Defense of Latin America* (Boston, 1941); *The Economic Defense of the Western Hemisphere* (Washington, 1941), a symposium of the Latin American Institute; *History of the Office of the Coördinator of Inter-American Affairs* (Washington, Government Printing Office, 1947), especially Chapters I, II and III.

[44] *Christian Science Monitor,* October 22, 1940.

tration. The United States had no modern planes, destroyers, or antiaircraft guns to spare from the meager supply then available for its own use or that of Great Britain. The hemisphere Governments, in turn, would accept no surplus, obsolescent substitutes.

Nothing better adorns this dismal tale than the report by Secretary Morgenthau in mid-December on the activities of the President's Committee, appointed a year earlier to facilitate the purchase of munitions in the United States by foreign governments. Mr. Morgenthau found much to praise in the first year's activity of this body, of which he was the chairman. But with respect to Latin America he was exceedingly reserved: "The Advisory Commission to the Council of National Defense has apparently given little heed to the requirements of foreign buyers other than British. In most instances it has been impossible to find sources of supply which are free to fill Latin American requirements."[45]

The Secretary of the Treasury went on to assure Mr. Roosevelt that this situation would presently be corrected. The Committee was even then engaged with the State Department and with Mr. Nelson A. Rockefeller's new agency in working out ways and means to give the Latin American states "some tangible evidence" of our Good Neighbor Policy. The decision, however, lay beyond the powers of Mr. Welles, Mr. Rockefeller, or Mr. Morgenthau himself. There were always the War and Navy Departments and the Advisory Commission to be won for any program involving the release of precious defense materials, not to mention Britain's reluctance to countenance any significant diversion of munitions from its desperately needed allotment.

The attitude of the War and Navy Departments was bluntly but sincerely expressed at a meeting on December 23, 1940, attended by their heads, as well as by Secretary Morgenthau, General Marshall, Admiral Stark, and Mr. Bonsal, Chief of the Division of American Republics of the State Department. The conference was occasioned by the necessity for agreement on the allocation of a certain number of pursuit planes which, in point of fact, were to become available only in August, 1941. A statement of the unfortunate political and military effects to be expected from failure to allot at least some of these planes to the American Republics left Secretary Stimson cold. South America was not a theater of war. Therefore, no planes could be sent there. He regretted this, but if our Latin American friends were unable to grasp the most rudimentary requirements of strategy, they must lack intelligence. The rest of the Committee generally agreed with the Secretary of War.[46]

Mr. Stimson's viewpoint was logical enough and even a cursory examination of the critical situation of Great Britain in the autumn of 1940, as well

[45] *Morgenthau Diaries* (*MS.*), December 19, 1940 (Vol. 341, pp. 219 ff.).
[46] *Stimson Diary* (*MS.*), December 23, 1940.

as of the slow pace of American munitions production, will suffice to explain his intransigence. At the same time, Mr. Welles could with equal justice urge upon his colleagues of the War and Navy Departments that they in turn could ill afford to be impatient over the delays encountered in reaching concrete defense agreements with the virtually unarmed nations of Latin America.

There was, indeed, no real solution for this dilemma save in a vast expansion of the national rearmament program. Until this began to show results, late in 1941, the twenty other American Republics had to content themselves with hopes that ultimately the United States would redeem its promises to help them obtain the wherewithal to defend themselves against the aggression they were constantly warned to expect. Under these circumstances it is less remarkable that the progress of inter-American defense was slow than that the Latin American states were willing to take significant risks at all, as they did in electing, at least in principle, to follow the policies laid down at Havana. One can only conclude that those Latin American officers who in October had started their conducted tour of American defense plants reported home that the United States military potential was far greater than was suggested by the quite inconsequential amount of military equipment actually shipped to Latin American countries by the end of 1940.

If the American Republics had little more than a lick and a promise from the scanty munitions cupboard of the United States, neither did American economic assistance provide a Lucullan banquet. The policy of strengthening the economic base of the hemisphere followed a course generally similar to that of military coöperation. There was no significant change in the principles of mutual aid enunciated at Havana. But here again, after the collapse of the grandiose cartel scheme for disposing of hemisphere surpluses, the Administration encountered the greatest difficulty in translating its stated policy into concrete programs of assistance.[47] This was true of efforts to devise practical expedients for tiding the Latin American states over the dislocation resulting from the loss of their European markets, and it was true also of efforts to assure them access to America's stores of scarce and strategic materials, growing ever scarcer as the demands of the defense program increased.[48] Most difficult of all was the fundamental problem presented by the peculiar economies of many of the Latin American nations. The State Department clearly recognized that a program of economic assistance to these states, if it was to succeed, would have to take account of long-range as well as short-term requirements. One or two typical examples must, however, suffice to suggest the magnitude of the problem.[49]

[47] See *The Challenge to Isolation,* Chapter XVIII, Section 5.
[48] United States policy governing the export of such materials was conveyed to the other American Republics in a circular telegram of December 12, 1940.
[49] Speech of Laurence Duggan before the Foreign Policy Association in New York

Of the larger Latin American states, Chile was perhaps in the most desperate straits. That country's representatives in Washington had been pleading for speedy assistance ever since the Havana Conference. Copper and nitrates had made up approximately three quarters of Chile's exports, and of these Germany and other blockaded nations had formerly absorbed about one half. The British were now taking their copper from within the Empire. The United States likewise imported little or none. Since Japan was the only other market, the Santiago Government was faced with the necessity of either persuading the United States to buy materials for which it thought it had no need, or of supplying them in significant quantity to a potential enemy. Here, indeed, was a critical problem in hemisphere solidarity, quite as difficult as those presented by Mexico's surplus oil, Argentina's beef, or Brazil's coffee.[50]

The Chilean Ambassador, in explaining this dilemma to Secretary of Commerce Jones, asked the United States to help solve it by buying copper and nitrates, and by lending $25,000,000 for exchange stabilization, $7,000,000 for construction of a hydroelectric iron and steel plant, and $2,000,000 for the immediate import of 100,000 tons of coal from the United States. The State Department, to which Secretary Jones turned for advice, recommended credits to Chile of $17,000,000. Negotiations continued for many weeks in an effort to relieve a situation for which no really satisfactory solution was apparent. President Roosevelt had recently directed that, wherever possible, priority be assigned to Latin American products in the United States program for the purchase of strategic and critical materials. The Advisory Commission did, in fact, recommend stock-piling of 300,000 tons of Chilean nitrates, but there was no prospect, it then thought, for the use of much copper. The final and bleakest aspect of Chile's plight was that it already owed United States exporters some $6,000,000. Unless the American Government advanced the dollars necessary to liquidate this debt, there was small chance that Chile could purchase coal or much else from private American firms. Washington finally made commitments for a credit of nearly $20,000,000. This, together with the extraordinarily rapid revision upward in 1941 of estimated American requirements for copper, enabled Chile to avoid what Mr. Welles described as the "most desperate repercussions" of the situation it faced at the end of 1940.[51]

City, November 2, 1940 (*Vital Speeches,* VII, 124 ff.). For Mr. Nelson Rockefeller's similar position see H. B. Hinton in *The New York Times,* October 13, 1940. On the difficulties of devising a workable trade program for the Western Hemisphere at this stage, see Percy W. Bidwell and Arthur Upgren: "A Trade Policy for National Defense" (*Foreign Affairs,* January, 1941); John W. Evans: "Economic Policy and Latin America" (*Yale Review,* Spring, 1941); Alvin H. Hansen: "Hemisphere Solidarity" (*Foreign Affairs,* October, 1940).

[50] Memo of Secretary of Commerce Jesse Jones to Mr. Morgenthau October 15, 1940 (*Morgenthau Diaries, MS.,* Vol. 322, pp. 35 ff.).

[51] Sumner Welles: *The Time for Decision* (New York, 1944), 218; *Morgenthau Diaries (MS.),* October 3, 1940 (Vol. 318, p. 283). On loan policy in Latin America, see Bemis: *The Latin American Policy of the United States,* Chapters XIX, XX.

Chile's difficulties illustrate many of the serious problems this Government encountered in the course of redeeming President Roosevelt's generous promise of 1939 that America's neighbors to the south should never suffer economic privation as a result of endorsing hemisphere solidarity. But Argentina, too, was an important and instructive case. As of October 1 that country had weathered what Assistant Secretary of State Berle described as a "difficult political crisis," had come through "nicely," and now had what looked like a regime markedly friendly to the United States. Anxious to assure Argentina of American economic support, and of willingness to stand by the "hemisphere line," Mr. Berle suggested that credits of some $50,000,000 be extended. Secretary Morgenthau quickly assented provided that Secretary Hull and Secretary Jones concurred.[52] When it came, however, to working out arrangements for a loan to finance increased trade between the United States and Argentina, difficulties at once emerged. The task fell initially to President Warren L. Pierson of the Export-Import Bank, then concluding a visit to South America in the interests of determining on the wisest use of the recently increased capital resources of the bank. He conferred directly with the Argentine Finance Minister, but when it developed that Pierson was not empowered to make firm commitments, the Argentines concluded that they could expect no economic assistance whatever from the United States. Washington received somewhat pessimistic accounts of the effect of Mr. Pierson's mission. Buenos Aires was complaining that as usual the United States helped Brazil but not Argentina, a reference to the fact that the Export-Import Bank had recently authorized further extensive credits to Brazil.[53]

Argentine pessimism proved unwarranted. In mid-November an Argentine financial delegation reached Washington for conferences which resulted on December 11, 1940, in the public announcement by Secretary Jones of a loan of $60,000,000 to Argentina. Two weeks later Secretary Morgenthau and Argentine Ambassador Espil were able to issue a joint statement on a currency stabilization agreement between the two nations involving another $50,000,000. The failure of Argentina to pass the necessary enabling legislation deprived the Buenos Aires Government for some time of the advantages thus obtained. At least, however, Washington had given evidence of willingness to aid even that Latin American state which was least enthusiastic about the ideals of hemisphere solidarity and most skeptical of United States objectives.[54]

These decisions do not by any means exhaust the list of items to be credited to the progress of economic solidarity when the books for 1940 were

[52] *Morgenthau Diaries* (*MS.*), October 1, 1940 (Vol. 317, pp. 28 ff.).
[53] *Morgenthau Diaries* (*MS.*), October 25, 1940 (Vol. 325, pp. 209 ff.); Paul Mallon in the *New York Journal-American,* November 27, 1940.
[54] The text of the joint statement of Morgenthau and Espil is printed in *Documents on American Foreign Relations,* III, 120.

finally closed. As of December 31, 1940, the United States had made credit commitments to the American Republics totaling $255,608,000, of which $45,659,000 had actually been disbursed.[55] The Inter-American Coffee Agreement, negotiated by the Inter-American Development Commission to assist in the disposal of another surplus commodity, was signed in Washington on November 28, 1940. On December 2 a special maritime conference, called by the Inter-American Financial and Economic Advisory Committee, ended its first session, reaching agreements which were to prove valuable subsequently in arranging the disposition of Axis and Danish vessels interned in the harbors of the hemisphere. Finally, a financial agreement had been reached with Colombia and a contract had been signed to purchase Bolivian tin for smelting in the United States—a palliative if not a cure for Bolivia's economic ills.[56]

This spate of agreements went far beyond the mere promises Washington was able to give in the matter of munitions and war materials. Taken together with the continuing labors of the various committees set up after the Havana Conference, they marked concrete progress toward mitigating the acute distress occasioned in Latin American states by the sudden loss of European markets. This is not to say that even the "temporary" dislocation (it had now lasted over a year) had been completely rectified. Above all, scarcely a dent had been made in the grand dilemma which ever loomed behind the problems immediately occasioned by the outbreak of war. There was no quick and simple formula by which the United States could assist its Latin American neighbors to diversify their economic life, to raise living standards, and thus to create a home market for their produce. American officials were well aware that genuine and permanent coöperation between the states of the Western Hemisphere depended ultimately on their ability to achieve a greater degree of economic as well as political stability. They also knew that such a program would require even greater economic concessions by the United States than those represented by Mr. Hull's trade agreements program, which had recently been renewed for a three-year period.[57]

Mr. Laurence Duggan, in an address of November 2, 1940, on hemisphere solidarity, pleaded with American businessmen not to take advantage of Latin America's current dependence on the American market to extract exorbitant prices for their goods. On the contrary he urged the advance of private credits at the lowest possible interest rates. He emphasized that the long-range program of United States economic assistance to the twenty

---

[55] Percy W. Bidwell: *Economic Defense of Latin America*, 74 ff.

[56] The texts of these and other statements and agreements are to be found in *Documents on American Foreign Relations*, III, Chap. II; cf. Bidwell: *Economic Defense of Latin America*, 59 ff.

[57] On the status of our trade agreements with the other American Republics, see Bemis: *The Latin American Policy of the United States*, Chapter XVII, and especially pp. 304 ff.; Hull: *Memoirs*, II, 1139 ff.

Republics was not merely a matter of Government policy. The attainment of American objectives, and indeed of all the manifold aspects of hemisphere solidarity which were dependent upon it, was conditional upon greater North American knowledge of, and interest in, Latin America. Mr. Duggan pointed straight to the heart of the problem: "When the people of this country know as much about the other countries of this hemisphere as they do of certain European countries, then we will have advanced a long way along the road to real understanding, without which the structure of inter-American solidarity will never be complete."[58]

Limitations of space prevent more than a mention of the manifold, not to say occasionally bizarre, efforts of the United States Government to pioneer in the field of cultural relations, which until a few years before the outbreak of the war had been largely left to private agencies and to foundations like the Pan American Union. To the activities of the State Department's older Division of Cultural Relations was now added the more elaborate program of Mr. Nelson A. Rockefeller's Office for Coördination of Commercial and Cultural Relations between the American Republics. On November 6 the President allocated $3,000,000 of his special defense funds to this program. By the end of 1940, however, the new agency's cultural projects were just getting under way, and its relations with the State Department and private organizations were still being defined. Only in 1941 did it become apparent that the combined efforts of the old and new, the public and the private organizations, were producing results even beyond what the Administration might reasonably have expected. Latin American culture was to become not merely an object of respectful interest to intelligent Americans; it was, as Professor Bemis has pointed out, by way of becoming a universal fad and craze.[59]

The rate of progress along the road of hemisphere solidarity seemed painfully slow and the road itself strewn with obstacles, but Mr. Hull, Mr. Welles, Mr. Duggan and their associates could take comfort from one solid fact: at no time in the history of the twenty-one Republics did the most powerful among them show greater restraint and understanding toward the others than it manifested in these anxious months. At no other period could the United States have so plausibly resorted to the Big Stick on the plea of overriding necessity to defend both itself and its neighbors. Washington stuck to its carrots, but even though the hemisphere response was decidedly favorable, the Roosevelt Administration had still little enough concrete evidence at the end of 1940 that its cautious and considerate policy was safe and sound. Only the passage of time could provide that. Meanwhile, how-

---

[58] *Vital Speeches,* VII, 124 ff.

[59] *History of the Office of the Coördinator of Inter-American Affairs,* 9 and 91 ff. On the general subject and background, see Bemis: *The Latin American Policy of the United States,* Chapter XVIII, 319 ff.

ever, the cheerful acquiescence of the American people in their Government's wooing of its Latin American neighbors indicated that they too were mastering the first and most difficult lesson in the new course on hemisphere coöperation: the lesson of method.

5. THE NORTHERN APPROACHES AND ATLANTIC OUTPOSTS

Canada, the recently leased British bases, Greenland and Iceland all presented problems of hemisphere defense more urgent than those of the Latin American countries. Though none of these problems were quite as complicated or delicate as those of Latin America, the United States Government was called upon to exercise in each case a high degree of tact in reconciling the necessities of hemisphere defense with the continued good will of its neighbors.[60]

American relations with Canada were in a special category, inasmuch as the Dominion was the only nation of the hemisphere actually engaged in hostilities. This fact did not of itself invariably and automatically smooth rough roads. It did suffice, however, to instill in the Canadians a sense of urgency which induced Prime Minister Mackenzie King's Government to be less suspicious of proposals for joint defense than was frequently the case with the Republics of Latin America. In implementation of the Ogdensburg Agreement (August 17, 1940), the Joint Canadian-American Defense Board conducted its third plenary session at Boston and Halifax early in October; its fourth at New York City in mid-December, 1940.

No details of these meetings or, indeed, of the almost continuous defense consultations between the two Governments were given out. Accordingly, there was a certain amount of popular dissatisfaction over the apparent lack of concrete coöperation between the United States and Canada. Actually the autumn meetings of the Defense Board were highly productive. Its report, approved by the President on November 19, 1940, recommended against the acquisition of American bases in the Dominion, but urged the Canadian Government to build at once facilities which could be used by United States planes and ships in the event of an attack on Canada. The Board likewise agreed to recommend forthwith the preparation of a detailed joint plan for the defense of North America. Thanks to this recommendation, such a plan was not only drawn up, but was approved by President Roosevelt and Prime Minister Mackenzie King well before Pearl Harbor.[61]

[60] On the subject of Canadian-American relations at this stage, the reader may consult, among others, the following useful accounts: C. P. Stacey: *The Military Problems of Canada* (Toronto, 1940); P. E. Corbett: "Canada in the Western Hemisphere" (*Foreign Affairs*, July, 1940); "Canada and Foreign Policy" (*Queen's Quarterly*, Winter, 1940); E. P. Dean: "Canada's New Defense Program" (*Foreign Affairs*, October, 1940).

[61] "ABC-22" was approved by the President on August 29, 1941 (*Pearl Harbor Attack*, III, 997).

Perhaps the most significant aspect of the Board's report was implied rather than stated. Throughout, it assumed that each of the two countries would immediately go to the assistance of the other in case of major attack, although the decision as to when such an attack had occurred and what form the assistance should take was left to the decision of each Government. The American Government was not prepared to include British members on the Board lest the single purpose of the Joint Board—the protection of the United States and Canada—be thereby altered.[62]

Even had the American and Canadian public been aware of the Board's general attitude and specific recommendations, few voices would have been raised in disapproval. Indeed, the *Chicago Tribune,* a well-known advocate of coöperation with Canada in defense of the hemisphere, now took great credit to itself for inspiring the current efforts.[63] Such minor difficulties as were occasioned between the Dominion and United States Governments derived largely from popular Canadian fear of alienation from Britain and of excessive dependence upon, or even annexation to, the United States. That the Canadian Government itself was relatively free of such worries was perhaps best indicated by its attitude toward American proposals affecting the Rush-Bagot Agreement of 1817, which forbade either Government to maintain significant naval strength on the Great Lakes. Both Governments were prepared to reinterpret this symbol of mutual good will and trust in such fashion as to permit each to take full advantage of Great Lakes shipyards for the construction of naval vessels and for other purposes not foreseen in 1817.[64] American-Canadian defense arrangements thus went ahead, if not rapidly, at least without any of the periodic misunderstandings and anxieties which slowed the pace of negotiations with America's southern neighbors.

Oddly enough, the American Government ran into more snags in working out with the British the details of the bases leased in September, 1940. The first difficulty arose almost immediately after consummation of the deal, in the shape of a British request for access to the projected naval bases on the same terms as Washington promised the other American Republics. In stating the position of his Government to Mr. Hull, Lord Lothian also requested access to the bases, under certain circumstances, for British commercial planes. This was a poser. On the one hand the Administration had engineered the Destroyer-Bases Deal in the interests of Great Britain almost as much as in its own. On the other, the United States and the twenty other American Republics had issued a manifesto of their joint determination to defend themselves against any foreign belligerent activity which threatened the hemisphere. Obviously, quite apart from the matter of

[62] Memos of Hickerson to Hull, October 16, 23, 1940; the former transmitted the report of the recent meeting, dated October 9, 1940.

[63] *Chicago Tribune* editorial, October 8, 1940.

[64] The relevant correspondence between the two Governments is reproduced in *Documents on American Foreign Relations,* III, 169 ff.

principle and appearance, to grant Britain, a non-American power, rights in these bases might well invite an incident involving Axis warships or planes. Finally, for technical reasons, the Navy Department opposed British military access to these bases and there was some anxiety in Washington to protect American airlines against competition from British companies operating between South America and the United States by way of Trinidad and Bermuda.

The initial reaction, as shown in the first draft of the reply to Lord Lothian, was to comply with the British request. Even Mr. Welles, who yielded to none in his concern for both the appearances and the realities of relations with the American Republics, approved the concession to Britain. Almost immediately, however, opposition developed within the State Department and elsewhere. On December 9 Mr. Welles, in response to a British inquiry as to how this Government would regard the construction of a purely British base on the island of Trinidad, indicated the new direction of official thinking. The Under Secretary pointed out that the proposed British action "would be a clear and flagrant violation of the letter as well as the spirit of the Declaration of Panama." It would almost certainly pave the way for German activity within the Neutrality Zone, the absence of which thus far had been of such great assistance to the British convoy system.[65]

This proved to be in essence the justification for Secretary Hull's final reply to the British Government on December 30, 1940, refusing to admit any "general right" of Great Britain to use of the facilities about to be constructed in the leased bases. This applied both to military and commercial aircraft. An effort was made, however, to coat this bitter pill. Specific British requests to use the bases might be considered, if and when they arose, even if the Government found it impossible to concur in any general right of use for British war planes and naval vessels. As for commercial aircraft, Mr. Hull assured the British Government that America itself did not contemplate allowing commercial airlines to use the bases. If Washington changed its mind on that subject, it would also reconsider its refusal to extend rights to British commercial planes.[66]

As between offending America's Latin American neighbors and at the same time inviting Axis activities in the Neutrality Zone, and wounding the British, the Administration clearly regarded the latter as the lesser evil.

[65] Memo of conversation between Mr. Welles and Mr. Butler of the British Embassy, December 9, 1940.

[66] Memo of Lord Lothian to Mr. Hull, September 26, and of Mr. Hull to the British Chargé d'Affaires, December 30, 1940. The President himself shared the anxiety of many leading Government officials to eliminate foreign, especially Axis, airlines in Latin America, and to replace them with United States, or wholly native-owned lines (*Stimson Diary, MS.,* October 28, 30, and November 8, 1940; *Morgenthau Diaries, MS.,* November 8, 1940, Vol. 330, pp. 136 ff.). On this subject see Melvin Hall and Walter Peck: "Wings for the Trojan Horse" (*Foreign Affairs,* January, 1941), and W. A. M. Burden: *The Struggle for Airways in Latin America* (New York, 1943).

Reasonable as this policy may have been, it rendered no easier the solution of the multifarious problems which presently arose in working out the details of the leases which were to govern occupancy of the British bases. In retrospect, these details seem unimportant. Washington was naturally eager to get on with the business, to construct the facilities as quickly as possible, and to base the operations of the Neutrality Patrol upon them. This seemed to the War and Navy Departments no less advantageous to the British than to ourselves.

The British Government, on the other hand, could not overlook the fears expressed by local Governments, in particular Bermuda's, lest the lease terms desired by the United States lead to a weakening of the ties that bound them to the British Crown, or, indeed, lest bathing facilities be impaired by impending American activities in adjacent base areas! Such worries were altogether natural and understandable, as was the general British appeal to the United States to be as "indulgent" and "lenient" as possible in working out details. This the Administration was anxious to do. It was not aided, however, by periodic demands from American isolationists and chauvinists for outright American acquisition of both the British and French islands in the Caribbean. Mr. Roosevelt never wavered in his determination not to saddle the United States with permanent liabilities. The friendly press also disclaimed sinister designs on British sovereignty over the base areas. Nevertheless, at the end of the year the United States and British Governments had made virtually no progress in working out the leases even though, as Secretary Knox announced on November 20, 1940, United States patrol planes were already operating out of Bermuda, Newfoundland and Trinidad.[67]

Not until early January, 1941, in response to a personal appeal from Prime Minister Churchill, did the President agree to send an American commission to London to expedite the conclusion of the lease arrangements. Even then, it did not prove easy to reach agreement.[68]

Similarly, American planning for possible future bases in Greenland and Iceland had scarcely gone beyond the exploratory stages by the end of 1940. Another visit to Greenland by the United States Coast Guard vessel, *Northland,* in October, confirmed earlier impressions that existing defense facilities—in effect one three-inch antiaircraft gun—even though supplemented by the efforts of the Danes and Greenlanders themselves, were altogether inadequate to defend the island against possible German landings. Since

[67] Memo of conversation between Mr. Hull and Mr. Butler, British Chargé d'Affaires, December 13, 1940. Hamilton Fish suggested on November 23 that the United States cancel the British and French World War I debts in return for full possession of British and French colonies (*The New York Times,* November 24, 1940). In an editorial of December 24, condemning this and similar proposals, *The New York Times* remarked sarcastically that if there must be a horse trade with Britain, it had better be a real one. We could afford no more liabilities, such as the Virgin Islands.

[68] Tel. to London, January 11, 1941; Mark S. Watson: *Chief of Staff: Prewar Plans and Preparations* (Washington, 1950), 477-85.

Washington wanted neither the Canadians nor the British to build bases in Greenland, it was finally compelled to do something itself. In November, Governor Svane of Greenland, accompanied by American Consul Penfield, came to the United States for consultations. From the American point of view, the Governor's attitude left little to be desired. He wanted a completely frank discussion of the problem of Greenland's place in the defense of the Western Hemisphere. His own inclination was to maintain Greenland's neutrality as long as possible, but he realized that Greenland in an emergency would be almost completely dependent on the United States and was therefore inclined to follow the American lead in international relations. Should the United States get into the war, the Greenland Administration would coöperate in every way it could.[69]

Under the circumstances the United States Government could probably have secured without difficulty an arrangement granting it base facilities in Greenland. But at this time no such proposal was made. The War and Navy Departments contented themselves with a discussion of further measures to prevent German meteorological activities in the east coast area. Air and ship patrols appeared a more suitable means of achieving this objective than the landing of United States garrisons or the development of bases. The current United States war plan (Rainbow IV) did not envisage military defense of Greenland. Newfoundland was as yet the most northerly outpost of hemisphere defense. Accordingly no action was taken on Greenland bases until January, 1941, when the Canadian Government brought up the subject and obliged Washington to clarify its own plans or else permit Canada to assume primary responsibility for defending Greenland.[70]

Iceland was handled just as gingerly by the American Government, despite the great concern American officials professed to feel for its security against German attack. Indeed, the Administration leaned over backward in its efforts to avoid commitments to the Icelandic Government. At the end of December Iceland's Foreign Minister called in the American representative at Reykjavik, Mr. Kuniholm, to ascertain from him whether the United States would send forces to Iceland if requested to do so by its Government. The island was, of course, at this time garrisoned by British forces, actually mostly Canadians. Although Foreign Minister Stefansson stressed the fact that Iceland would prefer any fate to Nazi occupation, Mr. Kuniholm made it clear that if the United States were ever to heed an Icelandic appeal for armed assistance, it would have to be assured that this reflected the genuine desire of all Icelanders.[71]

[69] Memo of conversation between Consul Penfield and Governor Svane, outlining agenda for conversations in Washington, dated November 6, 1940.

[70] Memo for Mr. Welles, describing the meeting of November 25 between Governor Svane and representatives of the United States Army, Navy and Coast Guard, filed with Berle memo of November 16, 1940; Watson: *Chief of Staff: Prewar Plans and Preparations*, 485 ff.

[71] Despatch from Kuniholm (Reykjavik), December 24, 1940.

There the matter rested. Mr. Hull showed no inclination to take advantage of the favorable opening provided by these overtures. He instructed Mr. Kuniholm to refrain from encouraging or discouraging the Icelanders on the subject of future assistance by United States forces. Washington wanted to face this decision, when and if the emergency arose, without prior commitments.[72]

On the whole, the United States Government had at the end of 1940 more reason to feel reassured about the safety of the northern approaches to the hemisphere than of the southern. In its dealings with the Canadians and British, with the Icelanders and with the Greenlanders, the American Government encountered less a reluctance to meet its demands than impatience at the excessively cautious manner in which it was developing its hemisphere defense plans. This is not hard to explain. Canada was, of course, a belligerent. Iceland and Greenland were confessedly almost wholly dependent, in case of serious attack, upon American support. Under the circumstances, these Governments felt that the United States could never do too much for them. The American Government, on the other hand, saw their needs as part of a very much larger problem. The development of concrete plans for the creation of bases and garrisons in Iceland or Greenland, or for joint defense with Canada, was conditioned by the over-all strategic plan for defense of the hemisphere and of the North Atlantic in particular. What were the limits of the hemisphere? Were these limits to be defined by the usage of the geographers, by the conventions of diplomats, or by what the War and Navy Departments deemed vital to the defense of the United States? Were the activities of the American Navy and Air Force to be limited to patrol within the confines of the Neutrality Zone, or extended so far into the Atlantic as to exceed any previous definition of defense requirements for this hemisphere?[73]

Until the Administration had answered these questions, it could scarcely proceed with far-reaching plans involving Canada, Greenland, Iceland or the British Isles. The answers to these questions depended, in turn, on assurances that the American people would accord the same enthusiastic support to a daring, positive concept of hemisphere strategy as they had hitherto given to measures of more strictly passive defense of the western continents. Meanwhile these exploratory negotiations at least confirmed the the Government's expectation of the full coöperation of the other North American Governments, if and when it felt able to embark on a new and more daring course.

[72] Memo of Berle to Hull and Welles, January 17; tel. to Kuniholm, January 18, 1941; Hull: *Memoirs,* II, 946.
[73] On this problem see V. Stefansson: "What Is the Western Hemisphere?" (*Foreign Affairs,* January, 1941).

CHAPTER VII

Defense Demands and Campaign Promises

1. A Momentary Respite

Hitler's momentous decision to defer indefinitely his plans for an invasion of Britain had induced the nonbelligerent governments of Europe and Asia to question seriously the hitherto accepted axiom that the Axis would soon win the war. The effect of the new uncertainty was quickly visible in the elusiveness which began to characterize the policies of Vichy, Madrid, and Moscow. The Fuehrer's decision was likewise fraught with significance for American policy and action. Without interruption since the spring of 1940 the Roosevelt Administration had been acting or reacting to an unprecedented succession of crises. There had been no breathing spell in which the President could take stock of the long-term implications of his summer gamble on Britain's chance of survival. He had found scarcely a moment in which to consider for himself and for the American people the destination to which his actions, so largely grounded in faith or intuition, would ultimately carry the nation. The apparently successful defense of Britain against the assaults of the *Luftwaffe* seemed at the summer's end to have offered tentative proof that the President's gamble would pay off. With the overwhelming sense of relief, however, came the simultaneous realization that the American Government faced questions of high policy which could now no longer be postponed or simply sublimated in action. To what extent was the national security of the United States dependent not merely on Britain's survival, but on Britain's victory over Hitler? What would be required of the United States to assure such ultimate victory? Even if this objective could be achieved short of American entry into the war, it was likely to require the transformation of the nation's economy to a full wartime basis. It remained to be seen whether the American people, only now

175

recovering from the effects of the great depression, would be willing to accept the requisite sacrifice.

The almost imperceptible interval between the waning Battle of Britain and the waxing Battle of the Atlantic provided the first opportunity to pass judgment on the steps the Administration had been taking since spring. It likewise afforded a respite which Washington could use to plot a future course with firmer convictions as to the final destination of the ship of state. That something should be done with this opportunity was demanded not merely by the exigencies of national security but also by the inescapable fact that on the fifth of November, 1940, the people of the United States would be voting for the President of the United States.

The pages which immediately follow will attempt, first, to summarize the Administration's estimate of the situation resulting from Britain's success in withstanding the fury of the Nazi assault. It will then be necessary to examine the measures contemplated or set in motion to quicken the tempo of American rearmament and, with it, the scope and volume of American assistance to Great Britain. Since this scrutiny will reveal a discrepancy between the President's estimate of the danger confronting the nation and the policies he deemed it politically feasible to ask Congress and the people to endorse, a survey of popular opinion will help to explain this discrepancy, as well as to illuminate the much-debated problem of the President's leadership. Finally, a brief account of the 1940 election, insofar as it related to issues of foreign policy, will provide an appropriate conclusion to a short period of American policy in which, whether they realized it or not, the American people were becoming committed to the proposition that Britain must be saved and the Axis powers defeated whatever the cost.

2. Washington's Autumn Estimate

Naturally the precise details of Hitler's new strategy were unknown to the United States Government as, indeed, they were to the British. An invasion of England, if not in the winter of 1940, then in the spring of 1941, continued to be regarded in Washington as a probability. Yet, by and large, at the beginning of October American officials, military as well as civilian, were beginning to doubt the likelihood of a direct assault on Britain in the near future, and to sense the change in Axis strategy occasioned by the Fuehrer's decisions. Such was the burden of the reports of American Military and Naval Attachés. Such also were the conclusions to be drawn from the reports of the Chargé d'Affaires in Berlin, Mr. Alexander Kirk. These suggested that the Germans were abandoning their earlier blueprints for the new economic order in Europe in favor of hastily constructed schemes to bolster Europe's economy to withstand a long war.[1]

The most impressive evidence of Washington's grasp of the general direction of the new Axis strategy, together with a considered view of its impli-

---

[1] *Stimson Diary (MS.)*, October 3; tel. from Kirk, October 11, 1940.

cations for the national security, is provided by a lengthy memorandum of September 25, 1940, prepared for the guidance of the President and his chief military and civilian advisers.[2] Initially drafted in the War Plans Division (WPD) of the General Staff, this estimate was actually the work of many minds and many hands. To it Brigadier General George V. Strong, Chief of WPD, and Major General Delos C. Emmons of the Air Corps, who had just returned from weeks of consultation and observation in England, brought the latest strategic concepts of the British Chiefs of Staff, as well as those of Rear Admiral Robert L. Ghormley, who had remained behind in London.[3] Subsequently the memorandum passed through the hands, among others, of General Marshall, Admiral Stark, Secretaries Stimson and Knox, and Under Secretary Welles. Whether or not President Roosevelt actually read the paper remains uncertain, but in any case it represented the best official opinion available to him. It constituted a worthy complement to the *Basis for Immediate Decisions* which had guided American action during the summer of 1940, and set forth with equal clarity the considerations which its authors believed to govern the future.

Faced with uncertainty in every theater of the war, this carefully considered estimate really reduced itself to a choice of the least improbable moves to be anticipated from the Axis powers. It was conceded that Hitler was unlikely to open hostilities against the United States until he had inflicted a serious defeat on Britain and insured himself against a Soviet stab in the back. While the likelihood of a Nazi invasion of the British Isles lessened with each day of its postponement, the German threat to Gibraltar and the Italian threat to the Suez Canal increased commensurately. Even if the British somehow managed to operate in the Mediterranean though Gibraltar fell and Spain and Portugal slid into the Axis orbit, there would be small consolation for the United States in such an eventuality. With the Axis powers in control of French North Africa and of the Atlantic islands of Spain and Portugal, the vital Anglo-American command of the Atlantic would be challenged. The way would lie open to at least aerial penetration of South America, and the United States would be called upon to assist in the defense of northeast Brazil.

The framers of the Strong memorandum, as this report came to be called, did not, of course, anticipate that all these threats would materialize at once. But even if serious Axis aggression against the Western Hemisphere need not be envisaged for perhaps a year after the surrender or withdrawal

---

[2] "The Problem of the Production of Munitions in Relation to the Ability of the United States to Cope with Its Defense Problems in the Present World Situation" (*Morgenthau Diaries, MS.*, Vol. 321, pp. 113 ff.). On the origins and content of this document see Mark S. Watson: *Chief of Staff: Prewar Plans and Preparations* (Washington, 1950), 115 ff.

[3] The fullest account of this mission is in the Kittredge MS.: *United States-British Naval Coöperation,* but see the excellent summary in Watson: *Chief of Staff: Prewar Plans and Preparations,* 113-15.

of the British Fleet, this relatively long period of immunity could be drastically shortened if Japan attacked the United States. With major units of
the United States Fleet involved in the Pacific, an Axis assault on the
Western Hemisphere would become an immediate and dangerous possibility. The estimate section of the Strong memorandum therefore concluded
that grave difficulties confronted this nation in all four quarters of the globe.
The immediate task was to hasten rearmament until the nation was prepared for any eventuality from Gibraltar to Singapore. Greatly increased
aid to Britain must be part and parcel of the strategy of national defense.
Yet Britain's situation remained so perilous that, despite General Strong's
hopeful views, it was considered prudent to calculate America's future defense not only on the assumption of Great Britain's continued survival but
also on the assumption of its impending defeat.

By way of specific conclusions the estimate warned, in the first place, that
war with Japan was to be anticipated in the near future. Since the United
States was not prepared for hostilities in the Pacific, it would be compelled,
in the event of war, to confine its initial efforts to minor operations. Thus
the priority of the Atlantic over the Pacific was again confirmed. Secondly,
if the British Fleet were surrendered or destroyed, the United States would
be obliged within three months to defend all Atlantic outpost positions from
Greenland to the bulge of Brazil. Thirdly, the nation might be called upon
at any moment to employ United States armed forces to assist in forestalling
Axis-inspired uprisings against the governments of the Latin American
Republics. Finally, considerations of national security might at any time,
even prior to the capture or surrender of the British Fleet, dictate a preventive occupation of Dakar and the Azores.

There was no mistaking the seriousness of the danger confronting the
Republic as the authors of the Strong memorandum depicted it. The sense
of urgency was heightened by the second section of the report, which examined the readiness of the nation's forces to confront the estimated danger. In general terms, the defensive capabilities of the United States as of
the moment were deemed wholly inadequate. That was the verdict even
when these capabilities were calculated in terms of purely passive defense of
the hemisphere against direct attack. The discrepancy was, of course, much
more serious if the calculation were based on a positive strategy of defense
calling for vigorous measures to assure Britain's survival.

Getting down to facts and figures the Strong memorandum pointed out
that America needed as quickly as possible the fully equipped, well-balanced
Army of 1,400,000 men agreed upon the previous summer. At present, due
to serious shortages in virtually every type of equipment, but particularly
in ammunition and powder, the War Department would find it difficult to
maintain in the field a balanced force of even 55,000 men, if circumstances
suddenly required it. Even this diminutive force could be supplied and

equipped only by depriving the new Selective Service personnel and the National Guard units of equipment sorely needed for training. At current rates of production there was no hope of reaching the Army's goal earlier than April 1, 1942.

The status of the Navy afforded grounds for greater optimism. Though still, of course, a one-ocean affair, the United States Fleet was considered ready for immediate operations save for slight deficiencies in personnel, which could be remedied quickly by calling reservists to active duty.

As for aircraft, the Air Corps' objective of some 13,000 planes could not be met, on the basis of current or predicted rates of production, earlier than April 1, 1942. At the moment the Air Corps had on hand only 49 bombers equipped for daylight operations and but 140 suitable pursuit planes. The demands of foreign powers, especially Britain, had created a critical situation. On July 23, 1940, the Defense Advisory Commission had agreed with the British Purchasing Commission that American productive capacity would be sufficient to provide aircraft for Britain in numbers almost as great as those estimated to be needed by the American armed forces by April 1, 1942. No provision whatever had been made to satisfy the demands of Latin America.[4]

It was obvious that the aircraft goals of July, 1940, let alone any higher requirements, could not be met under existing production schedules. It was essential not only to increase output, but equally to induce the British to agree to standardize equipment in the interest of speeding output. Admittedly this would be difficult, if only because of the immense contribution to aircraft plant expansion made by British orders and by British capital.[5]

Having thus succinctly weighed the nation's military assets and found them wanting, the third and final section of the Strong memorandum culminated in a series of recommendations for national action, simple, direct, and unsullied by any taint of politics. In the first place, the existing productive capacity of the United States should be raised to the maximum through the increase of work hours and the addition of labor shifts in plants and factories. Foreign—mostly British—orders should not normally be disturbed without the consent of the Governments concerned. Henceforth, however, productive capacity available to foreign powers should be rationed so as to prevent hamstringing American rearmament. Plant expansion already financed by the British should be reserved for their use as long as required unless considerations of national security actually compelled the American Government to take over such facilities. But foreign purchase of critical items and of materials required for the manufacture of munitions should be accommodated to the procurement program of the American armed forces.

[4] According to this agreement, productive capacity in the period up to April 1, 1942, would have been allocated as follows: U.S. Army, 12,884 planes; U.S. Navy, 6208; Great Britain, 14,000.

[5] See the preceding volume: *The Challenge to Isolation,* Chapter XX, Section 2.

Exports of machine tools, except as needed to maintain the level of Britain's production, should be banned.

Finally, the Strong memorandum urged the establishment of a committee, consisting of high officials of the War, Navy, and Treasury Departments and the Defense Advisory Commission, to commence at once the implementation of the recommendations contained in the report.

Such, in outline, was Washington's best official estimate of the situation at the beginning of the autumn of 1940, together with recommendations, from the military point of view, as to what the United States must prepare to do in order to meet it. If not explicitly, then by the most obvious implication it challenged the major assumptions upon which the Administration had thus far based its national defense program and indeed its foreign policy. A mere six weeks before the national election, Mr. Roosevelt was soberly warned that he could not simultaneously rearm America and adhere to a business-as-usual philosophy. Clearer still was the consensus that there was no hope whatever, within the scope of the current effort, of providing Great Britain with the means of survival in a protracted war. Echoing publicly the verdict of the Strong memorandum were the voices of many influential editors and columnists. Mr. Walter Lippmann urged the President to face the facts, declare a state of national emergency, and by virtue of the wide authority he would thus obtain, "to mobilize the entire manpower, machine power, and money power of this country, letting everything else take second place." But with the election just around the corner, Mr. Roosevelt's reluctance even to read the Strong memorandum, let alone to act decisively on its recommendations, is at least understandable.[6] How far he felt able to move in the direction indicated may best be judged by a brief examination of the national rearmament program and of its vital adjunct, the program of all-out material aid to Great Britain. The autumn lull on the fighting fronts reaffirmed the fact that the effectiveness of American foreign policy, vis-à-vis both the nonbelligerent and the hostile powers, would depend upon American ability to meet commitments and back up threats.

3. The Choice Between Guns and Butter

In reviewing the progress of American rearmament since June, 1940, it may be noted at the outset that specialists in the subject, including its official historians, have made anything but extravagant claims to achievement throughout the entire course of the year 1940.[7] One fault, common to virtually every phase of the now widely ramified national defense effort, remained uncorrected even in face of the mounting perils confronting the

[6] Watson: *Chief of Staff: Prewar Plans and Preparations,* 118.

[7] The reader's attention is again invited to the following treatments of the subject: *Industrial Mobilization for War* (Washington, 1947), Vol. I; Donald M. Nelson: *Arsenal of Democracy* (New York, 1946); and Edward R. Stettinius, Jr.: *Lend-Lease: Weapon for Victory* (New York, 1944).

nation in the autumn of that critical year. This was the now notorious failure of the Chief Executive to provide an effective, centralized administrative organization either for the rearmament program as a whole or for any one of its several parts. The top organization for coördinating the defense effort, the Council of National Defense, consisting in theory of Cabinet officers with defense functions, remained an administrative fiction. Neither the Cabinet as a whole nor those members of it who constituted the Council provided effective guidance in defense matters. The Council did not meet at all; and rarely indeed did the President make use of his Cabinet as an instrument for coördinating the defense program, or, for that matter, any other significant national policy. At best, that body's stated Friday meetings suggested a forum or discussion group. Decisions were generally reached, when they could not be postponed, through private conversations between Mr. Roosevelt and individual members of the Cabinet.

The President had managed, throughout the summer of 1940, to preserve intact his own direct control over the defense program, acting with the advice of the seven members of the Advisory Commission to the Council of National Defense. This National Defense Advisory Commission (NDAC) was thus the sole agency upon which in practice the President's authority to place the nation in posture of defense had devolved. To define this body's powers and responsibilities, as they had developed since its inception in May, 1940, represented a problem in metaphysics which had thus far defied solution. Accordingly, there was chronic friction over jurisdiction between the Advisory Commission and the normal procurement and programming agencies of the Government, the War, Navy, and Treasury Departments.

To add to its woes, the Advisory Commission, whose members were all individuals of reputation and competence, had not succeeded in getting itself a chief. NDAC was thus not merely "defense by advice," it was that administrative anomaly, advice formulated by a body of theoretical equals. October came and went, but the NDAC remained without a responsible head, as Secretary Stimson complained, "except the President who has not the time to run it." The Secretary of War, by temperament not inclined to give undue weight to political considerations in what he regarded as an emergency, would have liked the President "to aggrandize the headless Defense Commission into a full-blown ministry of munitions." Secretary Morgenthau, more accustomed to the President's bizarre administrative practices, would probably have been glad to settle for a much more modest reform, as, for instance, vesting of responsibility for the defense program with the appropriate Cabinet officers, who would then form a genuine Council of National Defense.[8]

[8] *Stimson Diary* (*MS.*), October 14, 15, 16, 17, 1940; Henry L. Stimson and McGeorge Bundy: *On Active Service in Peace and War* (New York, 1947), 354-55.

The President, however, continued adamant against any change, alleging inability to find a single individual suitable to be "czar" of a centralized defense organization, and fearing that, even if the paragon could be found, his appointment would raise more problems, particularly in the field of labor relations, than it would solve. Accordingly, the top organization of the defense effort limped on through the 1940 election without significant change. Nearly all who had firsthand knowledge of the agency would probably agree with Mr. Donald Nelson's verdict that Mr. Roosevelt's failure to respond to pleas for a clearer definition of the powers of NDAC, or even to provide it with a single responsible head, was a cardinal error of administration from which stemmed the most serious weaknesses of that body.[9]

The President's motives for persisting in his views were doubtless mixed. He was probably disinclined, for elementary political reasons, to risk possible loss of labor support in the approaching election by appointing an eminent industrialist to control defense production. On a higher plane, he may well have feared a slowing down of production for defense by further emphasizing the issues between management and labor. Such caution certainly was in line with the general concept which up to this point had governed the defense effort as a whole. This was the doctrine that defense production was to be superimposed upon normal production for civilian purposes, rather than displacing it. There were at this date still several millions of unemployed workers, as well as scores of idle plants and facilities abandoned in the wake of the depression. The policy of the Administration had been consciously shaped to take up this slack before resorting to more drastic methods of increasing production. It was a policy that promised all things to all men—adequate national defense, full employment, higher living standards, the recovery of business, and the consolidation of labor's New Deal gains, in short, both guns and butter.[10]

Allied to these cogent reasons for clinging to a business-as-usual philosophy was the widespread confusion as to the real objectives of American rearmament. Was the purpose of that rearmament merely to enable the armed forces to ward off direct aggression against the United States or the Western Hemisphere, or did it envisage a more active defense role, namely, by continued and massive aid to the surviving democracies, notably Britain, to prevent Hitler from organizing Europe for attack against the New World? Thus far the President had given no final answer to this significant question. Perhaps he could scarcely have been expected to do so until the autumn had produced evidence justifying his earlier gamble on Britain's chances of survival, as well as his convictions as to the nature of the Axis threat to the United States.[11]

By October, however, as the Strong memorandum had emphasized in

[9] Nelson: *Arsenal of Democracy*, 21, 82 ff. Cf. *Industrial Mobilization for War*, I, 17, 23, 29 ff.; and Stimson and Bundy: *On Active Service in Peace and War*, 354.

[10] *Industrial Mobilization for War*, I, 32, 58, 79.

[11] Nelson: *Arsenal of Democracy*, 4.

calling for maximum production, it was becoming apparent that the guns-and-butter concept of national defense would presently have to go by the board. It was "high time," as Secretary Stimson put it, that "we got this country onto a basis of appreciating the danger and not wasting our energies going ahead with ordinary . . . peace industry which cuts into our war plans." Enthusiastically backed by Secretaries Knox and Morgenthau, Stimson succeeded in getting the President's consent to the first and, as they now seem, mincing steps away from the business-as-usual methods of defense production.[12]

Stimson and his War Department colleagues, Judge Robert P. Patterson and Mr. Robert A. Lovett, appealed for what seemed then quite radical changes: three shifts and longer working hours in defense plants, particularly aircraft factories; drastic curtailment of commercial plane production; and the abandonment of annual models by the automobile companies. The President agreed only to the last of these expedients and eventually the not very enthusiastic Mr. Knudsen secured the consent of the decidedly reluctant automobile industry to the scrapping of annual models and the use of the facilities and labor thus saved for defense purposes.[13]

This faint indication that the President was at last becoming convinced that the United States would probably have to give up some butter in order to have enough guns was presently followed by another and more substantial concession to his vociferous critics. On October 21 an executive order established within NDAC a Priorities Board. Mr. Donald M. Nelson was appointed to administer it, and to him Mr. Roosevelt presently entrusted his power to determine the order in which contracts for defense supplies should be filled, as well as to assign priorities to essential civilian items. This was tardy recognition of Mr. Bernard Baruch's insistence, based on long experience in the First World War, that priorities were the "synchronizing force" of any war production program. Baruch, whom the President had consulted regularly on the problems of the Advisory Commission, assured him that if he entrusted final decision on priorities to Nelson, on production to Knudsen, and on raw materials to Stettinius—all subject to appeal to the President—the result would be greater efficiency, while at the same time the President could avoid, "at least for the present," the appointment of the dreaded production czar.[14] In any event, it could no longer be gainsaid that large sums of money appropriated by Congress for national defense remained unexpended, among other reasons because the nation's industrial capacity was insufficient to produce everything required for both military and civilian use. Indeed, there was now critical competition between con-

[12] *Stimson Diary* (*MS.*), October 1, 4, 1940; *Morgenthau Diaries* (*MS.*), October 1, 1940.

[13] *Stimson Diary* (*MS.*), October 16, 1940.

[14] Memo to the President from Bernard Baruch, November 18, 1940. This, together with other communications from Baruch on the subject, is in *Roosevelt Papers:* Secretary's File, Box 64.

tracts for military items themselves. It was no longer enough, as in past months, for a haphazard priorities system to accord a rough general precedence to military over civilian orders.[15]

The creation of the Priorities Board coincided in time with the Administration's reluctant admission, in mid-October, that its July, 1940, goal of a fully equipped Army of a million and a half men and a two-ocean Navy, all to be reached by April 1, 1942, would not be attained at existing production rates. The dilemma thus presented might have been solved, of course, by a decision to revise downward the estimates of munitions required and to extend dates of delivery, rather than by recourse to the drastic remedy which constituted the only alternative. The crucial factor in the decision to take the strenuous course rather than to admit defeat in the battle of production was the simultaneous receipt of new and quite overwhelming British requests for additional war matériel. Any dim hope that both national needs and these new British requirements could be met under the current rearmament policy immediately flew out the window.[16]

The facts, in sum, were these. Sir Walter Layton, special envoy from the British Ministry of Supply, arrived in Washington at the beginning of October, with what purported to be an analysis of Britain's own war production and an overall statement of future requirements from the United States. For the first time, remarked an envious Secretary Stimson, the British were presenting "the whole sheet," a feat of calculation which Washington itself had scarcely dared essay. Other emotions doubtless replaced admiration when the Secretary of War discovered that Layton's request amounted to sufficient matériel from the United States in 1941 to equip fully, with British types of weapons, ten projected divisions![17]

Nor was this all. In submitting the request for general munitions, Sir Walter promised to return presently with a similar overall statement of specific British aircraft needs. The Administration anticipated a heavy demand. Mr. Churchill had already cabled the President that although the British position in the air was growing steadily stronger, the need for more aircraft was critical, much more so than the shortage of pilots which had earlier threatened to be the limiting factor. Even so, no one in the Admin-

[15] The text of the executive order establishing the Priorities Board, and related documents, is published in *Documents on American Foreign Relations,* III, 663 ff. Cf. Nelson: *Arsenal of Democracy,* 90; *Industrial Mobilization for War,* I, 28-30, 66 ff. On the conflict between the Army, the Navy, and the British both for production and the means of production, see Watson: *Chief of Staff: Prewar Plans and Preparations,* 312-16.

[16] *Industrial Mobilization for War,* I, 54; Watson: *Chief of Staff: Prewar Plans and Preparations,* 314-18.

[17] *Morgenthau Diaries (MS.),* October 4, 11, 15, 1940 (Vol. 319, p. 39; Vol. 321, pp. 95 ff.; and Vol. 322, pp. 153 ff.). Among other items the request included 1800 pieces of field artillery, 1,000,000 rifles, 1600 heavy and 1800 light antiaircraft guns. See *Industrial Mobilization for War,* I, 47-54, for a discussion of the problems created by the British proposal.

istration was quite prepared to contemplate Layton's request, submitted on October 25, 1940, for permission to place orders for some 12,000 additional planes to be produced in American factories.[18]

The problems emphasized and the decisions taken during the hectic discussions which followed upon these latest British appeals were of the highest significance not only for the policy of aid to Britain, but equally for national rearmament and defense.

Once they had recovered from the shock of Layton's request for munitions, both Secretary Morgenthau and Secretary Stimson determined to make strenuous efforts to meet the demand and, at the same time, to seize the opportunity thus presented to tackle and solve hitherto neglected problems of overall American requirements. Stimson feared that the Advisory Commission and the American people generally might look unfavorably on a British request which added a load estimated at approximately seven billion dollars to the existing demands on American production. While he hated to say "no," Secretary Stimson was convinced that the "whole question of the United States attitude toward the English" should be discussed with the heads of the departments and agencies involved, and their decisions reported to the President. Mr. Stimson had the heartiest support from Mr. Morgenthau, whose anxiety over the British orders had been increased by a further frank warning of Britain's probable inability to pay for what was needed. As early as October 14, the British Ambassador, Lord Lothian, had told him that after the American election Sir Frederick Phillips of the British Treasury was coming to Washington to "raise the red light signal in connection with our finances."[19]

To the great relief of Secretaries Morgenthau and Stimson, upon whom chiefly fell the burden of convincing the members of the Advisory Commission that it was to the advantage of the United States to try to meet the British requests for munitions, General Marshall at once showed himself sympathetic. He promised to assist in winning over Mr. Knudsen and his associates who had, as might have been expected, informed Layton and his indefatigable colleague, Mr. Arthur Purvis, that to provide equipment for ten British divisions was simply not "within the facilities of the American Government." As Secretary Stimson himself summed up the dilemma in conversations with his chief War Department subordinates, it was not a question of willingness to give the British everything possible. "The difficulty

---

[18] Winston S. Churchill: *Their Finest Hour* (Boston, 1949), 337-40; tel. from the Prime Minister to the President, October 4, 1940; *Stimson Diary (MS.)*, October 25, 1940. The new orders for planes, if placed, would bring up the total number of planes on order for Britain to approximately 26,000. The total number actually produced in the United States in October, 1940, was under 1000. Since September 1, 1939, only about 1600 American-made planes had been sent to Britain (*Morgenthau Diaries, MS.,* October 18, 1940, Vol. 323, p. 110).

[19] *Morgenthau Diaries (MS.)*, October 14, 1940 (Vol. 321, pp. 245 ff., 324).

is simply that we haven't got capacity enough in this country at this stage of the game."[20]

Refusing to admit that the Advisory Commission's statement of fact constituted sufficient reason to reject the British orders, Secretary Stimson cast about desperately for ways and means of modifying the orders to the point of feasibility. One of the most obvious steps was to induce London to revise its plans and accept ordnance and equipment of American instead of British design. Accordingly, Secretary Stimson and Secretary Morgenthau rehearsed the arguments in favor of standardization of American and British weapons which had met with but indifferent success in the past. On this occasion, however, it was a matter of take it or leave it. The upshot was Layton's decision to try to get his Government's consent to the substitution of American for British-type weapons, in return for Stimson's promise to do what he could to complete the rearmament of the ten projected British divisions at the earliest possible date.[21]

Secretary Stimson was elated, General Marshall relieved. As Stimson put it, Layton's conversion to the use of American weapons, or at least of weapons susceptible of being used by American forces in an emergency, made for a "much better program as far as we are concerned, and a much quicker program as far as he is concerned." And, getting at the heart of the matter, the Secretary added, "It will also create greater facilities for us to carry on our program."[22]

Useful as such expedients were, those officials of the Administration who were putting their full weight behind the British orders were painfully aware that the verdict of the Advisory Commission with respect to the limitations of American industrial capacity was an honest one. Thus, acceptance of anything approaching the full demands of the British Government would require a fundamental policy decision, indeed a series of them, in the realm of national security. Was the United States Government so completely convinced of the relevance of Britain's survival to America's own security that it was prepared to commit itself at this point to material assistance on so vast a scale? If the answer to this question was in the affirmative, the Administration must prepare to assume responsibility for putting the American economy on what could hardly be less than a full war footing.

[20] *Stimson Diary (MS.)*, October 18, 21, 1940; *Morgenthau Diaries (MS.)*, October 15, 1940 (Vol. 322, pp. 129 ff.); Stimson and Bundy: *On Active Service in Peace and War*, 355 ff.

[21] *Stimson Diary (MS.)*, October 24, 1940. Efforts to standardize equipment with the British, while earnest enough, ran into snags on both sides. A notable reason for failure in the category of aircraft was American unwillingness to release to the British the Norden bombsight, which required special construction in bombing planes. On grounds that the United States had obtained from the British far more such secrets than it had given, including radar, Secretary Knox and many others urged release of the highly secret American bombsight (*Morgenthau Diaries, MS.,* October 9, 1940). On this problem see Watson: *Chief of Staff: Prewar Plans and Preparations*, 316-18.

[22] *Stimson Diary (MS.)*, October 24, 1940; Stimson and Bundy: *On Active Service in Peace and War*, 359.

Such questions, and the corollaries that flowed from them, could evidently be answered only by the President of the United States. Secretary Stimson insisted, moreover, that he ought to answer them quickly. Accordingly, Mr. Morgenthau presently broached them to the President at Cabinet meeting. He suggested that Mr. Roosevelt air the entire issue before the American people by informing them in general terms just what Great Britain had purchased in the United States since the war began, what London wanted to order now, and what the Government planned to do with respect to these new orders. He proposed, in short, at long last to clarify the scope and timing of the Administration's policy of extending all aid to Britain short of war.

To Secretary Morgenthau's intense satisfaction, the President not only accepted the challenge but even suggested that he release the figures in the campaign address he was to make to the "Boston Irish" on October 30, a mere two days hence. It would, added Mr. Roosevelt, "do them good." Mr. Morgenthau accordingly undertook to see that the British Purchasing Commission, the Advisory Commission and all other government agencies involved in the problem of British orders get together and agree on the text of a statement to be incorporated in the President's Boston speech.[23]

Whether or not he was wholly aware of the magnitude of his commitment, the President, by this decision and timing, effectually forced his own subordinates and the representatives of the British Government, Messrs. Layton and Purvis, to arrive at a statement endorsing maximum material aid to Britain short of war—aid, indeed, far beyond the estimated capacity of the current production program to provide, or of the British purse to pay for. Hastily Secretary Morgenthau summoned for the next day, October 29, an official conclave to produce the desired agreement and the stipulated text. Early in the afternoon he convened in his office, among others, Messrs. Layton and Purvis of the British Purchasing Commission; Secretaries Stimson and Knox; General Marshall and Admiral Stark; Messrs. Knudsen and Nelson of the Advisory Commission; and Jesse Jones, Secretary of Commerce and head of the Reconstruction Finance Corporation. The ensuing discussion was, in Mr. Morgenthau's phrase, "an historical one." To those American representatives who had arrived early, Secretary Knox revealed his own state of mind in altogether forthright terms. "I should like to say," remarked the Secretary of the Navy, "in this crowd before the English get here, I can't escape saying that the English are not going to win this war without our help, I mean our military help." Mr. Forrestal, then Assistant Secretary, expressing agreement, Knox went on: "I mean, they cannot win alone. You might as well face that. Just as sure as I sit in this chair. . . . We needn't talk of it outdoors, but I think it is true."[24]

There is no record of the response to Secretary Knox's honest if indiscreet

[23] *Morgenthau Diaries* (*MS.*), October 28, 1940 (Vol. 325, pp. 126 ff.).
[24] *Morgenthau Diaries* (*MS.*), October 29, 1940 (Vol. 326, pp. 59 ff.).

expression of views, though it is a safe guess that Secretary Stimson and
many another Government official inside that office and "outdoors" probably agreed with it. Seasoned observers of the Washington scene had already noted, apropos of American entry into the war, that the question was
more often "when" than "whether," when government officials discussed
it.[25]

The ensuing debate was difficult, not to say painful, both for the British
and the Americans. It was not easy for individuals like Morgenthau, Stimson and Knox, who, whether they believed that we would get into the war
or not, were certainly convinced that Britain's cause was our own, to impose severe conditions on requests for assistance. Nevertheless, Secretary
Morgenthau felt impelled to state flatly that he would henceforth refuse to
approve the creation of new production facilities at American expense unless the weapons to be manufactured were of American design, or at least
of a type which General Marshall and Admiral Stark could conscientiously
certify as usable by the American Armed Forces.[26]

With equal force, though not in the presence of the British representatives, the Secretary of the Treasury expressed himself on the now emerging
problem of how the British Government was to pay for future orders placed
in the United States. "The only statement that I have made," said Mr.
Morgenthau, "is that as long as I was Secretary of the Treasury I would
never be part or parcel of lending them money again, and if it got to the
place that they couldn't pay, I would recommend that we give it to them."[27]

The British members of the conference naturally stressed the hardships
which a sudden shift from British to American weapons would occasion.
They could also point to the large part hitherto played by British capital in
the expansion of American plane production. Actually, however, they had
no alternative but to accept the American conditions. This they did at the
end of an exhausting afternoon, after which the conferees delegated to the
Secretary of War power to agree with Messrs. Layton and Purvis on what
types of American weapons could and would be supplied for the ten British
divisions, and on what dates delivery might be possible. At the beginning of
November these negotiations eventuated in the notable Layton-Stimson
Agreement, which represented a very considerable degree of British acquiescence in the American demand for standardization of munitions and
matériel, and a major step forward in the American defense program.[28]

Subject to this British concession, the Advisory Commission and the other
American representatives accepted in principle the British aircraft and
ordnance program. Together they worked out an agreed draft of the state-

[25] Turner Catledge in *The New York Times,* October 6, 1940.
[26] *Morgenthau Diaries (MS.),* October 29, 1940 (Vol. 326, pp. 50 ff., and 221 ff.).
Stimson Diary (MS.), October 29, 1940.
[27] *Morgenthau Diaries (MS.),* October 29, 1940 (Vol. 326, pp. 225 ff.).
[28] *Stimson Diary (MS.),* October 31, November 1, 1940.

ment for the President to make in Boston, the next day, announcing this consummation. At 6:15 P.M. Mr. Morgenthau left his office and hurried to the White House. The President, engaged in putting the final touches on his speech, expressed complete satisfaction with the statement handed him. He proposed to incorporate it without significant change in the body of his speech. And so, on the night of October 30, 1940, the "Boston Irish," among millions of others, heard Mr. Roosevelt proclaim the determination of the United States to assist the British Empire on a scale hitherto unimagined. Revealing, with British permission, that after the savage air attacks of August and September, the R.A.F. was actually stronger than ever, the President went on:

Tonight I am privileged to make an announcement, using Boston instead of the White House; the British within the past few days have asked for permission to negotiate again with American manufacturers for 12,000 additional planes. . . .

When those additional orders are approved, as I hope they will be, they will bring Britain's present orders for military planes from the United States to more than 26,000.

And we must remember that those orders will require more new plant facilities so that the present program of building planes for military purposes both for the United States and Britain will not be interrupted.

With that request have come orders, large additional orders, negotiated for artillery, for machine guns, for rifles, for tanks with equipment and ammunition. And again the plant capacity necessary to produce all of this military equipment is and will be available to serve the need of the United States in any emergency.

The productive capacity of the United States that I have talked about, which has made it the greatest industrial country in the world, is not failing now. It is going to make us, it is making us, the strongest air power in all the world. . . .[29]

It is not easy to exaggerate the importance of President Roosevelt's statement at Boston, either as it affected the policy of aid to Britain or the American program of defense production. It represented, as far as any single event could do so, the President's public acknowledgment of the doctrine that the survival of Great Britain was essential to America's national security, and that every assistance to that country short of war now constituted an integral part of the Administration's national defense program. In support of this doctrine, the Boston statement virtually pledged the United States to a program of aid to Britain which would thrust a new load of many billions of dollars on the nation's inadequate production facilities.

The effect of the statement on the Government's own defense program was perhaps more significant than the clarification it afforded on the degree of support the Administration proposed to render Great Britain. It need not be imagined that the addition of these immense British orders quickly transformed the character and tempo of American rearmament, or produced the

[29] *The New York Times,* October 31, 1940; *Morgenthau Diaries (MS.),* October 29, 1940 (Vol. 326, p. 145).

long-overdue reforms in its administration. Not until after the election did the Government really come to grips with the problems created by the President's decision; and even thereafter, for many months, the business-as-usual philosophy maintained its hold. At least, however, the Government agencies responsible for planning production and estimating needs had been given a solid basis on which to build. If the goals of the nation's rearmament were still goals of "defense," no plans or schedules could longer assume that such defense was to be passive and confined to the Western Hemisphere. From now on Britain was the first line of America's defense, or would be if Mr. Roosevelt were reëlected. For the first time since the start of hostilities it had become possible to appraise realistically America's productive capacity in terms of future needs. Such appraisal could have but one result: the conviction that far more strenuous efforts would have to be made by the American Government and people if the new objectives were to be met. The choice between guns and butter could be postponed, but no longer evaded.

4. PREËLECTION HESITANCIES

Mr. Roosevelt's decision to permit the British Government to place new orders for billions of dollars' worth of military equipment was the most significant preëlection step taken by the President in the sphere of national defense. His remaining responses to the criticisms and recommendations on American rearmament during these weeks can only be touched upon lightly. In the aggregate they were scarcely commensurate with the magnitude of the danger which the President himself believed confronted the country in the autumn of 1940.

Thus, in the highly important realm of those activities which, taken together, constituted economic defense or economic warfare, progress was at best routine and at worst almost imperceptible. Export control, freezing of foreign funds, purchase and stock-piling of strategic materials, shipping controls and the like were all, of course, related aspects of the total process of economic defense against total war, and were clearly and early recognized as such. The first suggestions that their interrelationship should logically result in their union under some form of centralized administration, or at least of centralized policy control, came at least as early as June, 1940. The Secretary of the Treasury was a timely and vigorous advocate of something like a board of economic defense. By October 1 the State Department was itself admittedly reaching a point where, in Mr. Berle's words, we were "quite frankly directing our economics where they will do the most good, and withholding them where it might be more dangerous."[30]

For a variety of reasons, legitimate or otherwise, these efforts to integrate the policy and direction of economic defense came to little at the time, or, indeed, for many months afterward. Obviously the State Department could and did claim a large, if not a dominant, voice in the determination of

[30] *Morgenthau Diaries* (MS.), October 1, 1940 (Vol. 317, pp. 16ff.).

policies to implement economic defense or wage economic warfare, since it quite properly regarded foreign economic policy as part and parcel of American foreign relations in general and was aware that economic sanctions should be pursued with caution by governments not ready to follow them with a shooting war if necessary. On the other hand, the State Department was scarcely equipped to administer what amounted to a ministry of economic defense. The Treasury was willing and claimed to be able to undertake this function, described by Mr. Morgenthau frankly as one of economic sanctions, "let us call it by its right name." Finally, the War Department, too, apparently cherished some hopes that its own claims to administer an economic defense agency might ultimately achieve recognition.[31]

The rivalry of these established agencies and the Advisory Commission, each with reasonable claims to a voice in the determination of economic defense policies, went on unchecked throughout the autumn. No real progress was made in the achievement of integrated effort. The various functions, though all related, continued to be exercised by different agents and agencies with only the most primitive arrangements to insure that each pursued the same ultimate objectives. Under the circumstances it is not surprising that they were often at cross-purposes.[32]

Responsibility, if not power, to direct the acquisition and stock-piling of certain raw and semifinished materials, deemed "strategic" and "critical" for national defense, rested primarily with the Advisory Commission's Industrial Materials Division, headed by Mr. Edward R. Stettinius, Jr. Admittedly the task of deciding how much of these materials to acquire and what prices to pay for them was excessively difficult in view of the prevailing uncertainty as to whether the United States was preparing simply to defend the hemisphere against attack, or was contemplating eventual global warfare against Germany and Japan. Having discarded as unsatisfactory older peacetime estimates inherited from the Army-Navy Munitions Board, Mr. Stettinius and his colleagues were spending a disproportionate amount of time and energy in an attempt to produce new ones satisfactory to the War and Navy Departments and responsive in general to the changing strategic situation. The effort met with the indifferent success that could have been expected in view of the Administration's inability or unwillingness to provide a clear answer to the question of what the nation was arming against.

It was this fact which must explain the absurdly optimistic progress reports which emanated at this juncture from Mr. Stettinius's office. Had not the conclusions been frequently challenged by the very officials responsible for them, the country could have entertained the comfortable assurance that it was well on the way to solving a problem vital to the national security.

[31] *Ibid.,* October 11, 1940 (Vol. 321, pp. 167 ff.).

[32] For extended discussions of this subject the reader should consult the relevant sections of *Industrial Mobilization for War,* and Donald M. Nelson: *Arsenal of Democracy.* See also Percy W. Bidwell: "Our Economic Warfare" (*Foreign Affairs,* April, 1942).

However, as Mr. William J. Batt, deputy to Mr. Stettinius, frankly admitted in a speech of October 22 at the Herald Tribune Forum in New York, there was a vast difference between planning to acquire strategic materials and having them on hand in stock piles. "Let no one suppose," concluded Batt, "that we have in the course of a few months completely solved our raw materials problem."[33] Quite apart from faulty administration and lack of clear policy guidance, the stock-piling program was encountering all the difficulties inherent in the prevailing business-as-usual attitude. If the Government was slow to import the strategic materials that were lacking, and not much speedier in expanding domestic production of others in short supply, there was decidedly less excuse for allowing civilian demands to eat away such small stocks as were being accumulated. As yet, however, the voices favoring civilian rationing, even of rubber, were the merest whispers.[34]

The uncoördinated efforts to stock-pile strategic materials were duplicated in the related economic warfare function of export control. The sphere of activity of its Administrator, Colonel Maxwell of the State Department, involved not only the obvious one of preventing the export of scarce materials required for national defense, but also the licensing of exports as a means of exerting economic pressure on foreign powers. It was difficult enough for the Administrator of Export Control to operate with the sole or even primary objective of restricting or preventing the export from the United States of materials deemed vital to rearmament. Exceptions to the general rule had constantly to be made in the interests of Great Britain and other friendly powers whose defense was deemed relevant to American security, or whose good will served the same end. When, however, there was superimposed on this aspect of export control the practice of granting or withholding export control licenses for the primary purpose of influencing the policy of foreign powers, Colonel Maxwell's task involved most delicate and complicated decisions.

A gradual tightening of the licensing process with the avowed object of preventing or minimizing export of critical materials continued throughout the summer and autumn of 1940. On October 10, for example, the President signed an Act of Congress authorizing him to requisition any and all war material manufactured for export but denied an export license, if such seizure was deemed in the public interest. As the White House explained the measure a few days later, it said nothing of the added power to permit or withhold exports as a means of bringing pressure on foreign nations. Indeed, the first notable exercise of this new power on October 17, when the Administration requisitioned some hundred planes ordered by the Swedish

[33] *Vital Speeches,* VII, 119 f.
[34] *Morgenthau Diaries (MS.),* October 18, 1940 (Vol. 323, pp. 130 ff.). A lively account of the early efforts to acquire stocks of rubber is provided by Herbert Feis: *Seen from E. A.* (New York, 1947), 3-93.

Government, was doubtless a relatively pure instance of seizure in the interest of national defense. Subsequent invocations of the requisitioning power, however, often betrayed a mixed inspiration. Desperate as was the lack of certain varieties of machine tools during 1940, some could perhaps have been spared to the Soviet Union, for example, had the policies of the Kremlin shown a stronger tendency to conform to American national interests.[35]

Disagreement between the State and Treasury Departments, which contributed to the difficulties of administering export control, was even more notable in the last of the major economic defense activities here considered: the control of foreign funds in the United States. Here, at least, the Treasury Department had a clear responsibility for assuring that the assets of the Axis powers in the United States or under its control, or those of nations overrun by the Axis powers, were not expended in a fashion detrimental to the security of the United States, as, for instance, to finance fifth column activities.

For many months the Treasury had been engaged in "freezing" the assets of European states overrun by the Axis, both as a means of manifesting displeasure with these acts of aggression, and of depriving the Axis powers of access to the American assets of their victims. The Secretary of the Treasury, however, regarded the blocking of funds of individual countries as insufficient and, as early as June, 1940, pressed Mr. Hull to adopt general measures of exchange control which would encompass virtually the entire world. When the State Department alleged the unfavorable repercussions which would be occasioned in friendly or sensitive areas, such as Latin America, the Soviet Union and the British Empire, Mr. Morgenthau stood his ground and insisted that in practice such areas could be exempted from the general controls. The true object was to frustrate the designs of Germany, Italy, and Japan.[36]

Throughout October arguments between Treasury and State Department officials over what opponents of extended exchange controls recoiled from as "financial sanctions" and what advocates described as "economic defense" proliferated. In retrospect, each side seems to have had strong arguments to support its position, and it would certainly be possible even now to defend a presidential decision in favor of either. No such decision, however, was forthcoming, with the result that discussion of the complicated pros and cons of general exchange control tended to degenerate into mere arguments between the State and Treasury Departments over their respective jurisdictions and prerogatives.[37]

[35] The relevant documents on the Act of October 10, 1940, are printed in *Documents on American Foreign Relations*, III, 744 ff.

[36] *Morgenthau Diaries (MS.)*, October 1, 1940 (Vol. 317, pp. 16 ff.). On this subject see Judd Polk: "Freezing Dollars Against the Axis" (*Foreign Affairs,* October, 1941).

[37] *Morgenthau Diaries (MS.)*, October 8, 1940 (Vol. 320, pp. 25 ff., 36 ff.).

Whether or not it was wise to wait many months, for instance, before proceeding to freeze German and Japanese assets in the United States is still debatable. Many uncertain factors had to be weighed: Hitler's intentions; the intentions, and above all the capabilities, of the United States; the effect on American opinion of such a step on the eve of the 1940 election; and others. Allowing for these legitimate grounds for difference between Mr. Morgenthau and Mr. Hull, the reader is still entitled to wonder that significant decisions involving national policy were often simply postponed for lack of any authority or mechanism, short of the President himself, to reconcile differences between the government agencies concerned. Not until the creation of the Board of Economic Warfare in the summer of 1941 did Mr. Roosevelt take serious steps to rationalize and integrate the separate but related forms of economic warfare.

If, thus, the Administration moved cautiously, not to say sluggishly, in implementing its program for economic defense, Mr. Roosevelt showed both courage and energy in moving to strengthen the nation's military position. On October 4 he assigned to Secretary Stimson the sum of $25,000,000, from funds under the immediate control of the White House, to commence the task of fortifying the Atlantic bases just acquired from Great Britain. The next day, in prompt response to a recommendation of the Strong memorandum, Naval and Marine Corps reserves were called to active duty. Secretary Knox followed this move with an announcement that the Fleet in the Pacific would be brought up to full personnel strength by the addition of some four thousand officers and enlisted men.[38]

The President really confounded the cynics, however, by the display of equanimity with which he discharged the politically unattractive duties which fell to him in connection with the recently enacted Selective Service Act. On October 16, the day set for registration under the new law, Mr. Roosevelt issued a personal message to the registrants informing them that the task confronting the nation was "as compelling as any that ever confronted our people, and I would add that each of us must willingly do his bit if we are to hold fast our heritage of freedom and our American way of life—our national existence itself. . . ." This personal message was followed by a radio address to the nation on the significance of the day. "We propose," said the President, "to keep the peace in this New World which free men have built for free men to live in. . . . Today's registration for training is the keystone in the arch of our national defense. . . ."[39]

While the President gave no hint in these messages that these potential soldiers and sailors might one day be compelled by the exigencies of na-

---

[38] *Stimson Diary* (*MS.*), October 4, 1940; *Bulletin of International News*, XVII (2), p. 1401. The President's very cautious views respecting increases in authorized personnel for the Navy were communicated to Secretary Knox in a memo of December 23, 1940 (*Roosevelt Papers:* Secretary's File, Box 59).

[39] *The Public Papers and Addresses of Franklin D. Roosevelt*, XI, 473 ff., 510 ff.

tional defense to serve outside the hemisphere, he neverthless adhered to the schedule which set the drawing of lots for the first group of selectees a week before Election Day. Though, as Secretary Stimson pointed out, "everyone was hinting around a while ago that it would not be done until after election," the ceremony was duly performed on October 29. It was the opinion of the Secretary of War that Mr. Roosevelt's "brave" speech had transformed the draft from a political liability into a political asset. This was neither the first nor last time that the President, overcoming doubts about the political effects of a bold decision, discovered the nation prepared to follow his leadership.[40]

Nevertheless, after this survey of the Administration's record of preëlection action in the realm of national defense, it is impossible to avoid the conclusion that, for one reason or another, Mr. Roosevelt was unwilling or felt unable to take the harsh measures which so many of his own advisers considered necessary to prepare the nation against the dangers confronting it. The best professional opinion available to the President, from the State Department as well as from the highest military quarters, agreed that in October, 1940, the United States faced real danger and was inadequately prepared to meet it. Mr. Roosevelt's advisers had not reached unanimous agreement on what additional measures of national defense should be undertaken, but there was little doubt in any of their minds that the existing effort, at least, was not truly commensurate with the danger. Before attempting an explanation of the President's reluctance to discard outmoded philosophies of national defense and plunge into a program which promised really to rearm and prepare the United States for the emergency, it will be useful to consider in subsequent sections the trend of popular opinion and the impact of the election campaign of 1940.

5. Public Opinion Before the Election

Spokesmen for the Roosevelt Administration have generally tried to explain away the manifest shortcomings of the rearmament program by insisting that the President went as fast in preparing the nation for the emergency as public opinion permitted. He repeatedly warned the people and the Congress that they faced a deadly peril, particularly after conclusion of the Tripartite Pact. He pointed out the necessity for wider comprehension of the danger, for greater zeal in making sacrifices, and for deeper national unity if the hemisphere was to resist aggression, and if Great Britain was to stand as its first line of defense. It was not primarily, they argue, failure of presidential leadership which accounts for the lagging tempo of rearmament or explains continued public confusion over the role of Britain in the national security. By implication, at least, they attribute major re-

[40] *Stimson Diary* (*MS.*), October 29, 1940; Robert E. Sherwood: *Roosevelt and Hopkins* (New York, 1949), 190.

sponsibility for these shortcomings to the American people. Afflicted with a kind of schizophrenia, sedulously developed by a strong isolationist minority, not even the events of the summer of 1940, to say nothing of the Administration's warnings, could shock them into a realization of their stake in the outcome of the wars in Europe and Asia.

Hostile critics of Mr. Roosevelt's policies, on the other hand, have tended to lay the blame for lack of popular conviction and national unity, then as later, firmly on the doorstep of the White House. They point out that the fall of France and the subsequent ordeal of Britain had removed the issue of national defense, as such, from the realm of political controversy. All factions, in Congress and outside, save only an insignificant minority of cranks, Communists, and Nazis, were united on the necessity for a defense program "adequate" to cover the whole, or at least the larger part, of the Western Hemisphere. That a business-as-usual atmosphere continued to play havoc with American rearmament, that Americans plainly remained of two minds on the wisdom of including Britain in plans for national defense, were faults for which the Administration was responsible. At best the President feared to assert genuine leadership; at the worst he deliberately played politics with the gravest issues of national security. Either he lacked real confidence in the good sense of the common man or he regarded frank discussion of his foreign policy as tantamount to defeat in his bid for a third term.

If the reader has not already sensed from the record that the truth is not nearly so simple as these views would suggest, a glance at the state of mind of the American people on the eve of the 1940 election should suffice to enlighten him. To begin with, it cannot be denied that after the summer of 1940 only an insignificant minority of Americans questioned the wisdom of taking precautions to ensure adequate defense against any likely combination of enemies. There was, however, a notable difference between passive acquiescence in the desirability of large-scale rearmament and the dynamic will to accept the sacrifices it entailed. Similarly, while the vast majority of Americans had now come to concur in the need for placing the national security beyond question, this by no means signified agreement either on the methods or the magnitudes involved in the task. It was certainly not axiomatic to all Americans that Britain's survival was vital to their security. Nor did they all agree perfectly on the degree of danger inherent in the Tripartite Pact.

It may be stated at the outset, with greater certainty than is possible with most of the complicated judgments involving public sentiment, that American opinion had not remained static since the fall of France. Mr. Roosevelt had no reason to despair of convincing his fellow citizens of the reality of the dangers confronting them in the autumn of 1940. It is not even certain that he would have suffered defeat at the polls if he had publicly advocated the measures of national defense and of aid to Britain which his military and civilian advisers were privately urging upon him. The stirring events of the summer had left their mark on the public, and even though popular grasp of America's stake in the war may not have been all that the President could have wished, it was a good deal firmer than it had been in the spring.[41] There were encouraging signs that the people of the United States had the wit to realize that rearmament on a scale and at a speed sufficient to meet the threat of an Axis victory could not be accomplished without some readjustments, indeed, some actual dislocation of the American standard of living. It is notable, for example, that a goodly majority had expressed approval of the Selective Service Act. An equal number professed to believe that adequate goals of national defense could not be attained without widespread revisions in the social legislation of the New Deal.[42]

It must be confessed that recognition of the need for sacrifice was tempered by widespread hostility to the objectives of the New Deal itself. Side by side with the affirmation that these objectives would have to be curtailed must be placed the belief of a sizable group that it was quite possible to rebuild America's defenses without notably lowering living standards or reducing civilian production. Neither labor nor industry nor the public at large could be brought to endorse the one obvious method of reaching defense production goals: the lengthening of working hours. There was a strong preference for simply hiring more men and women. Only a minority, though a growing one by autumn, contemplated with equanimity the prospect of price controls if the rearmament program were to result in still sharper price rises. A still smaller minority approved of raising revenue to finance rearmament by resort to excess profits taxes on the "munitions makers." However, if taxes had to be increased, it was thought better to levy them on this special group, still the object of wide public suspicion, than to exact sacrifices from the population at large by a more generalized imposition.[43]

In sum, acceptance of the proposition that the American people had by the autumn of 1940 embraced with near unanimity the necessity for wholesale rearmament needs to be qualified by evidence that the country was neither wholly aware of the cost of such an effort nor very eager to pay for it. To galvanize confused acquiescence into vigorous determination required courage and energy on the President's part, but the nation seemed susceptible to real leadership on this vital issue.[44]

Popular sentiment with respect to the scope and magnitude of the pro-

[41] Quincy Howe: "American Foreign Policy and Public Opinion" (*Yale Review,* Winter, 1942, pp. 315 ff.).

[42] *Public Opinion Quarterly,* March, 1941, p. 162. In October, 1940, only some 21 percent of Americans polled on the question professed belief that the nation could prepare for total war without "seriously amending" such legislation.

[43] Public opinion polls during the autumn of 1940 on these and related issues of U.S. rearmament are summarized in *Public Opinion Quarterly,* March, 1941, pp. 160 ff.

[44] Stimson and Bundy: *On Active Service in Peace and War,* 352 ff.

gram presented much the same challenge to the Administration. While Americans were almost unanimous in professing a desire that larger amounts of food and arms should go to Britain if it appeared that otherwise that country would be defeated, a majority still opposed changes in the Neutrality Law to permit American ships to transport these supplies. Again, though willing to see revision of the Johnson Act so as to enable the British to borrow money in the United States to finance the purchase of munitions, the majority which in midsummer had thought it more important to assist Britain than to avoid war was by autumn again tending to diminish in size. By October's end the American people were probably about evenly divided on the wisdom of taking this risk. The momentary cessation of spectacular action on European battlefields after the Battle of Britain evidently produced a rapid increase in the number of those who felt that somehow, after all, the British would win.[45]

Opinion on the issue of aid to Britain in the preëlection weeks may therefore be described as firm at the two extremes and fluid in the middle. At one extreme was a small, vocal, and determined minority, including many influential citizens, who favored an outright alliance with Britain. They urged supplying money, materials, and, if necessary, men. They were prepared to face a war if this program rendered war inevitable. At the other extreme was a still smaller minority of diehard isolationists, together with a scattering of pro-Nazis and pro-Communists, who were for ending at once assistance to Britain of any description whatsoever.

In between these two extremes, and comprising roughly three quarters of the American people, was a mass of opinion favoring at the very least no significant diminution in the prevailing scale of American aid to Britain and, indeed, advocating on the whole any increase in such assistance as could safely be contemplated without involving the United States itself in hostilities. But when confronted with the point-blank question of whether or not to go to war now, American opinion was still overwhelmingly in favor of remaining out.[46]

Behind these evidences of profound indecision with which Americans were confronting the issue of aid to the democracies remained two deeply ingrained popular sentiments. One was the natural desire to avoid war if possible or, at least, as long as possible. The other was the fatalistic assumption that, willy-nilly, the United States would find itself in the war before the conflict ended. Perhaps, therefore, the sooner the better.

These two patterns of thought and feeling had been firmly set in the American mind even before the actual outbreak of hostilities in Europe. Ever since September, 1939, they had been clashing with increasing vio-

---

[45] *Public Opinion Quarterly,* March, 1941, pp. 158 ff.

[46] *Ibid.,* p. 159. In mid-October a poll indicated 83 percent of Americans registering "no" in response to the question whether the United States should enter the war against Germany and Italy at once.

lence, but without decisive result. By the autumn of 1940 the battle lines were beginning to be very tightly drawn, and the issues were becoming more clearly discernible. For this development the American public was indebted primarily to the much-maligned pressure groups. The largest and most effective of these was unquestionably the Committee to Defend America by Aiding the Allies. However, its activities, hitherto opposed by ephemeral and ill-assorted groups of isolationists, had by autumn at last engendered a worthy foeman. By the beginning of October a student in the Yale Law School, Mr. R. Douglas Stewart of Chicago, had organized the America First movement, which quickly became the outstanding vehicle for the expression of generally isolationist opinion as against the influential cohorts of Mr. William Allen White. A glance at the programs and utterances of these warring groups will complete this brief appraisal of the state of American opinion on the war in so far as it had crystallized in the preëlection period.[47]

A good sample of the views represented in the emerging America First Committee was the speech on foreign policy delivered in Chicago on October 4, 1940, by the Committee's acting chairman, General Robert E. Wood. Wood began by pointing out the wide areas of agreement between the so-called isolationists and interventionists. Excepting what he called the "lunatic fringe" on both sides, General Wood found the rest in agreement on the necessity for a strong defense of the United States and the Western Hemisphere, as well as on the desirability of permitting Britain access to our industrial plant, provided that nation could pay for and transport the munitions it ordered.

Beyond this point, continued General Wood, the area of agreement on American foreign policy ended. He charged the Administration, a majority of newspaper editors and columnists, and the "very influential body of opinion" represented by the White Committee with promoting the free gift of munitions to the British and with other dangerous plans which certainly compromised America's neutrality, if they did not actually involve an alliance with Great Britain. As for himself, he shared none of these beliefs. He was sure you could not destroy an ideology, like that of the Nazis, by waging war on it. He doubted, in any case, whether England could be defeated, or her Fleet put out of commission. Even, however, if proved wrong on these points, it was inconceivable to him that a victorious Germany would invade the United States, or that the American way of life could not ultimately compete successfully against a victorious totalitarian system.

Reacting to the widespread hostility of interventionist groups against his

---

[47] On the role of the pressure groups, see Sherwood: *Roosevelt and Hopkins*, 165-68. No adequate study of the America First movement exists, but for evidence of the harsh feelings it engendered the reader is referred to J. R. Carlson: *Under Cover* (New York, 1943); Michael Sayers and Albert E. Kahn: *Sabotage* (New York, 1942); and Henry Hoke: *Black Mail* (New York, 1944).

own, Wood commented bitterly on the confused and illogical position the public in general was taking. "We have the anomalous situation of the polls showing a majority of the people favoring a course that is bound to get us into the war (increased aid to Britain), while the same polls show 86 per cent of the same people oppose actual entry into the war." The speech ended with a demand for prompt clarification. "The issue should be honestly presented to the people. If we aid Britain, short of war and beyond the limits of the Neutrality Act, it ultimately means war and should mean war. If we enter the war, we must enter it with all our strength in men and money. That is the only way to win a war."[48]

It would be a cardinal error to attribute to the White Committee the unanimity of view and conspiratorial singleness of purpose which General Wood believed he could detect. Now boasting some 750 local chapters, in which approximately ten thousand persons were active workers, it was becoming increasingly difficult for the Committee to merge its manifold shadings of opinion into a meaningful yet coherent program. In point of fact the Committee to Defend America by Aiding the Allies began in October to fall victim to internal stresses and strains which seriously weakened its efficiency throughout the rest of 1940 and eventuated in the resignation of William Allen White in January, 1941.[49] Mr. White was already at odds with many influential members of his central committee. He disapproved of its effort to amend or repeal the Neutrality Law and the Johnson Act. He disliked its use of the term "nonbelligerency" to describe the desirable American attitude.[50] He confessed to being profoundly worried by the "emanations from Room 2940," that is, by the outspokenly interventionist broadsides of the so-called Century Group. The influential leaders comprising this circle were in most cases also members of the White Committee. Their ardent partisanship, Mr. White felt, could not but reflect on the motives of the larger Committee, making it appear more war-minded than was desirable. Mr. White wished the Committee to Defend America by Aiding the Allies "to keep fairly abreast of public sentiment and not to get too far out in front."[51]

Above all, as Election Day approached, White, a major prophet of the Republican Party, believed his Committee should eschew partisan politics as a matter of principle. He therefore disapproved of the efforts of many of his colleagues to line up the Committee behind the campaign to prevent the reëlection of isolationist Congressmen and Senators, most of whom were Republicans. In this conflict White was certainly moved by the highest mo-

[48] *Vital Speeches*, VII, 130 ff.

[49] Walter Johnson: *Battle Against Isolation* (Chicago, 1944), 136 ff.

[50] Walter Johnson, ed.: *Selected Letters of William Allen White* (New York, 1947), 415.

[51] On the activities of the Century Group, and Mr. White's growing caution, see Johnson: *Battle Against Isolation*, 114 ff., 136, 176 ff. Room 2940 was the New York office number of Mr. Francis P. Miller, executive secretary of the Century Group.

tives. His personal relations with the President continued close and cordial, and both Mr. Roosevelt and Mr. Hull privately shared White's concern over the zealots in the Committee, though willing enough to allow them to raise trial balloons.[52] Nevertheless, his increasingly cautious approach to vital issues of foreign policy, and his growing sensitivity to the charges of warmongering hurled at him by the isolationists, combined to occasion discontent with his leadership among the more radical individuals and chapters of the Committee.

As one surveys the programs and activities of these pressure groups, the sense of confusion in the public mind is actually heightened. Even the organized advocates of increased aid to Britain, in close touch with the President, with leading members of the Administration, and with eminent British personalities, could not agree on the lengths they were prepared to go in support of their position. Among their opponents in America First there was scarcely more certainty about the limits which prudence should set to the policy of all-out assistance to Britain short of war. Nevertheless the heated controversies within and between these groups made at least one invaluable contribution to the democratic process. They kept bringing to the surface the fundamental questions which the average citizen of the United States would have clearly preferred to avoid answering. Was the survival of Great Britain vital to the security of the United States of America? If so, were Americans prepared to underwrite that survival even if it involved not merely a limitless investment of the national wealth, but quite possibly, before it ended, of the lives of their sons?

The attitude of the American people toward the Administration's policy of all aid to the democracies short of war was, in the preëlection weeks, much like their reaction to the rearmament program. It was by no means firm in either case; it was highly receptive to leadership in both. American hatred of war was still very real. The strength of the isolationists made them emphatically a force to be reckoned with. Their vocal powers, particularly on Capitol Hill, were undiminished. Nevertheless, fear of war was by no means so fixed that Americans, even isolationists, were prepared to commit suicide in order to avoid being murdered. The sentiment of the people in the final weeks of the presidential election campaign thus offered a direct challenge to President Roosevelt and to Mr. Wendell Willkie. Could the President afford to take the electorate into his confidence and admit that it might well prove impossible for them to have their cake and eat it too; to increase assistance to Britain, and avoid war; to make this hemisphere impregnable, and enjoy undiminished living standards? Such frankness might lose the election and jeopardize such progress as the President had been able to make since the crisis had deepened in the previous May. Warned by

[52] Records of Mr. Francis P. Miller, and conversation of the authors with Mr. Miller, October, 1947.

such veteran politicians as Fiorello La Guardia that "anti-third term would cease about the middle of October, and a concentrated drive be made on anti-war,"[53] the President faced a singularly difficult decision. The record of the last three weeks of the campaign best indicates how Mr. Roosevelt decided.

6. THE 1940 ELECTION

It will be recalled that in his acceptance speech to the Democratic Convention on July 19, the President had warned his audience and the nation that he was going to undertake no personal campaigning. He would stand on his record and would intervene in the campaign only if he were confronted by "deliberate or unwitting falsification of fact." With his superior sense of timing, the President refrained from justifying his foreign and defense policies before the electorate from July 19 until October 23, 1940—with two exceptions, only one of which clearly infringed the rule.

On September 11, addressing the Teamsters Union Convention, Mr. Roosevelt did take cognizance of what he described as the efforts of "those who seek to play upon the fears of the American people." He was sure that the people would "reject that kind of propaganda of fear" as they had rejected other varieties of election-time propaganda. Concluding his few remarks on the subject of foreign policy in a speech primarily devoted to national defense and the role of labor in it, the President reasserted his determination to preserve the nation's peace in words that were innocent of qualification:

I hate war, now more than ever. I have one supreme determination—to do all that I can to keep war away from these shores for all time. I stand, with my party, and outside of my party as President of all the people, on the platform . . . that was adopted in Chicago less than two months ago. It said: "We will not participate in foreign wars, and we will not send our army, naval, or air forces to fight in foreign lands outside of the Americas, except in case of attack."[54]

The President's only other violation of his rule was, on the whole, distinctly less palatable to those Americans who desired a foreign policy involving absolutely no risks. Speaking on Columbus Day, October 12, in Dayton, Ohio, he expounded his views on the subject of hemisphere defense. The address was deliberately pitched on a high, nonpolitical plane. It was a rallying cry to the Americas for solidarity in the face of common peril. The President did not minimize the dangers. They were, he said, "unprecedented." Japan's adhesion to the Tripartite Pact had left its mark. "Let no American in any part of the Americas question the possibility of danger from overseas," warned Mr. Roosevelt. "Why should we accept assurances

[53] Message of La Guardia to the President, October 1, 1940 (*Roosevelt Papers:* Secretary's File, Box 65).
[54] *Public Papers and Addresses,* IX, 407 ff.

that we are immune?" He gave, moreover, no hint of appeasement. On the contrary, he was defiant: "No combination of dictator countries of Europe and Asia will halt us in the path we see ahead for ourselves and for democracy." Likewise he refused to be intimidated into any diminution of aid to the British. "No combination of dictator countries of Europe and Asia will stop the help we are giving to almost the last free people now fighting to hold them at bay."

It is true that this address was a calculated homily on hemisphere solidarity, the one policy upon which Americans of both parties were now all but unanimously agreed.[55] It is also true that the President reiterated his devotion to peace as uppermost in his mind—"the objective for which I hope and work and pray." Yet, even as he rallied the people of the Americas to the banner of hemisphere defense, the President reminded his audience that in protection of the hemisphere "we include the right to the peaceful use of the Atlantic and Pacific Oceans." This, he declared, had been America's traditional policy, and to prove it he cited the exploits of the renowned American ships, *Constitution, Constellation,* and *United States,* which "drove the armed vessels of Europe out of the waters to the south of us. . . ." Thus, if the theme of this address was, as critics of Mr. Roosevelt point out,[56] merely hemisphere defense, no candid reader can ignore the fact that the President wove around that theme a reasonably full and forthright exposition of his foreign policy as a whole. He did not linger over the dangers involved in a positive policy of American aid to Britain or China, but those who heard him on Columbus Day were at least warned again of the general danger threatening the United States. Finally, the course which the President proposed to follow was not left wholly to the imagination of his listeners. "Our course is clear. Our decision is made. We will continue to pile up our defense and our armaments. We will continue to help those who resist aggression, and who now hold the aggressors far from our shores. . . ."[57]

The American people might indeed wonder whether the President who had spoken to the Teamsters Union on September 11 was the same architect of American policy who spoke at Dayton a month later. There was, however, to be more confusion before there was more clarity. The Republican candidate had taken no vows of silence. During the long and exasperating interval of his rival's self-enforced abstention, Mr. Willkie had carried his campaign throughout the length and breadth of the land. Woefully handicapped in his discussion of Mr. Roosevelt's foreign policy by his general agreement with its objectives, and by a strong sense of responsibility for national unity in the face of foreign danger, Mr. Willkie's attack on the

[55] Sherwood: *Roosevelt and Hopkins,* 185.
[56] For example, Charles A. Beard: *American Foreign Policy in the Making: 1932-1940: A Study in Responsibilities* (New Haven, 1946), 312.
[57] *Public Papers and Addresses,* IX, 460 ff.

Administration had done little to clarify the issues. He was compelled by and large to campaign not against the objectives of the Administration's foreign policy or defense program, but simply against the President's methods of implementing them. He had delivered some telling blows, particularly on the issue of the errors and shortcomings of the Administration's record on rearmament. In this, however, he was ever beset by the record of the Republican Party, whose enthusiasm for national defense was manifestly of recent date.

Mr. Willkie likewise dilated on the reluctance of the President to share with the people his real views on foreign policy, an accusation made the more effective by Mr. Roosevelt's continued refusal to speak out. Again, however, Mr. Willkie was confronted by a record of Administration measures for which majority approval was reasonably clear. Finally, the Republican nominee's own agreement not to attack the Destroyer Deal seemed to set his seal of approval, mildly qualified, on the most bitterly criticized instance of the President's habit of doing good by stealth. That decision, which, in the light of postelection events, quickly appeared as the measure of Mr. Willkie's patriotism and principle, really deprived him of his single most effective weapon.

During the final weeks of the campaign, therefore, Mr. Willkie permitted his discussion of foreign issues to descend to depths which he himself subsequently was willing to defend only as "campaign oratory." Having himself been prodigal in making mutually incompatible pledges of all-out material aid to Britain and assurances that he would never lead the country into war, the Republican candidate was, by early October, accusing his opponent of insincerity for having given identical assurances. Speaking on October 8 in the Bronx, a Democratic stronghold, Mr. Willkie scornfully asked if there were anyone in his audience "who really thinks that the President is sincerely trying to keep us out of war? . . . I want to ask the President," he went on, "and I demand an answer: Are there any international understandings to put America into the war that we citizens *do not* know about? . . ."[58] At St. Louis, on October 17, and consistently thereafter, he returned to these charges, urging his audience not to choose "a government for which peace is just a word. . . . Let them choose rather a government that will make peace a reality."[59]

The President professed hot indignation at these last-minute tactics of his Republican rival. It was not tempered by the growing conviction that Willkie's energetic campaign was producing results. Robert S. Allen, the columnist, privately confirmed Mayor La Guardia's earlier prediction that the third term issue would count for little. On the other hand, warned Allen, the Middle West would be irrevocably lost unless Mr. Roosevelt cam-

[58] *The New York Times,* October 9, 1940.
[59] *The New York Times,* October 18, 1940.

paigned there, and unless from "now on until election day you pound away with all your eloquence that *you are for peace*."[60] "Your suggestion that I stress peace," replied the President, "is excellent and I shall continue to do it with even greater emphasis. . . ."[61] As a matter of principle he professed to find it impossible to leave Washington for intervals of more than twelve hours, but floods of advice like Allen's confirmed his feeling that silence had ceased to be golden. On the morning after Mr. Willkie's St. Louis speech, the President solemnly informed the press that the point had been reached, foreseen by him at Philadelphia in July, when he must break his vows of silence in order to correct his opponent's "deliberate falsification of fact." In the remaining three weeks, he added, he would make five speeches.[62]

Mr. Roosevelt delivered the first of his five addresses at Philadelphia on October 23, the day after Mr. Willkie, speaking in Chicago, had again derisively challenged the good faith of his opponent's assurances that he would keep the country out of war. The Philadelphia speech was an effective piece of campaigning, but it ended abruptly any faint hope that Mr. Roosevelt's long-postponed rebuttal would illuminate the major issues of foreign policy. Asserting that his rival's constant reiteration of untrue charges against the Administration resembled the Nazi propaganda technique of repeating lies so consistently that they came to be accepted as truth, the President branded as complete falsehood the allegation that he had entered into secret commitments with foreign nations which endangered the national security or pledged the United States Government to participate in the war:

> I give to you and to the people of this country this most solemn assurance: There is no secret treaty, no secret obligation, no secret understanding in any shape or form, direct or indirect, with any other Government or any other nation in any part of the world, to involve this nation in any war or for any other purpose.[63]

The reader may judge from the record, so far as the authors have been able to reconstruct it, the President's veracity in making this statement. Having forcefully made it, Mr. Roosevelt devoted most of the Philadelphia speech to domestic political issues. However, before finishing he took occasion to denounce as another Republican falsification the charge that he wished to lead the country into war. Asserting that on this point he stood firmly on the plank of the Democratic Party's platform (repeating it word

---

[60] Letter of Mr. Robert S. Allen to the President, October 19, 1940 (*Roosevelt Papers: Secretary's File*, Box 64). The italics are Mr. Allen's.

[61] *F.D.R.: His Personal Letters, 1928-1945* (New York, 1950), II, 1073.

[62] *Public Papers and Addresses*, IX, 480 ff. On the circumstances of this decision and its results, see the realistic account in Sherwood: *Roosevelt and Hopkins*, 185 ff. The account in Basil Rauch: *Roosevelt from Munich to Pearl Harbor* (New York, 1950), 263 ff., stresses the element of principle as opposed to political expediency. Beard's analysis in *American Foreign Policy in the Making* (New Haven, 1946), 266 ff., dismisses all suggestions of principle in the campaigns of both candidates.

[63] *Public Papers and Addresses*, IX, 485 ff.

for word), the President ended with the words: "It is for peace that I have labored; and it is for peace that I shall labor all the days of my life."

In view of the abundant evidence supporting Mr. Roosevelt's assertion of his abhorrence of war and his anxiety to maintain peace, provided peace was compatible with the national security, it was fitting that he should have repudiated the oft-repeated imputation that he deliberately courted war. But this was scarcely the essence of the issue. Insofar as Mr. Willkie's charges had any validity, they reduced themselves to the accusation that the methods the President used to carry out his foreign policy, and particularly the scope of the program for assisting Britain by all means short of war, involved the evident risk of ultimate American involvement in the hostilities. On this, the crucial issue, Mr. Roosevelt had nothing to say to the American people at Philadelphia or anywhere else.

It would be monotonous to recount in detail the charges and countercharges which the two rivals exchanged day by day, almost hour by hour, in the final stage of the campaign. Wendell Willkie, having long since exhausted his substantial themes, abandoned the last vestiges of restraint in denouncing the good faith of his opponent. He recklessly invited those of his fellow citizens who regarded the survival of Britain as absolutely vital to American security, as well as those who were certain that peace for the Americas was the supreme objective of American policy, to unite on him as President. He left no lingering suspicion in the minds of his audience that he might conceivably fail to achieve both these objectives concurrently. The Republican nominee reached his climax at Baltimore on October 30, when he told his audience that if the President were reëlected, "you may expect we will be at war."[64]

The President, who had replied in kind to each challenge offered by his opponent, was speaking in Boston on the same day that Mr. Willkie spoke at Baltimore. As we have seen, he had, to the great satisfaction of his professional advisers on foreign policy, determined to make the Boston speech the occasion for informing the American people of his decision to permit the British Government to place billions of dollars' worth of new munitions orders in the United States. This announcement was to incorporate the wording agreed upon in advance by the appropriate members of his Cabinet and by the British as well. By clear implication, therefore, Mr. Roosevelt would publicly commit the United States to a program of aid to Britain which could with difficulty be reconciled with positive assurance that the United States would not engage in foreign wars.

Moreover, other minds than those of Messrs. Hull, Morgenthau, Stimson and Knox were to have a part in the drafting of the President's Boston address. The party politicians were now importuning Mr. Roosevelt. If he did not once and for all give a categorical promise to the electorate that

[64] *The New York Times,* October 31, 1940.

America's young men would not be sent to fight in foreign wars if he were reëlected, the election was lost. This urgent plea was dinned into the President's ears even on the train to Boston. Mr. Roosevelt at first objected strenuously to the inclusion of any such promise in the text of his speech. What, he asked, is a foreign war? Does it mean we will fight only in a civil war? In the end, however, convincing himself that the proposed phraseology was sufficiently obscure and meaningless, he consented to insert it as the only sure antidote to Willkie's poison about American boys being already on the transports.[65]

Accordingly, at Boston, on the night of October 30, 1940, the President capped Mr. Willkie's climax with words which, if they seemed meaningless to him, doubtless seemed sufficiently clear to his nationwide audience:

And while I am talking to you mothers and fathers I give you one more assurance. I have said this before, but I shall say it again and again and again:

Your boys are not going to be sent into any foreign wars.

They are going into training to form a force so strong that, by its very existence, it will keep the threat of war far away from our shores.

The purpose of our defense is defense.[66]

This was indeed categorical assurance to the American people, beside which the President's subsequent reference to the vast program of aid to Britain scarcely seemed to the man in the street a significant qualification. Nothing that Mr. Roosevelt was to say from then until Election Day approached the forcefulness of this unqualified commitment to the American people. The "Champ" had decisively outplayed Willkie at the latter's own game. There would be leisure to repent that in resorting to devices against which his own sound political instinct rebelled, the Chief Executive seriously weakened the cause he sought to advance and added no luster to his reputation for sincerity.

In any case, this was about the maximum enlightenment the American electorate was to receive from either candidate before going to the polls on November 5. Authorized spokesmen for the Administration could contribute little to dispel the greatly compounded confusion in the public mind. The Secretary of War clung steadfastly to his decision to refrain, as a Republican, from taking any part in the campaign.[67] Mr. Hull had been telling his intimates at the State Department that he would resign at the end of the current term, since he felt that his work was done, that he could not approve a third term, and that the President preferred the advice of Sumner Welles to his own.[68] The Secretary of State had therefore himself been

[65] Conversation of the authors with Mr. Robert E. Sherwood (who helped to write this speech), April, 1948; Sherwood: *Roosevelt and Hopkins,* 190-92.

[66] *Public Papers and Addresses,* IX, 514 ff.

[67] *Stimson Diary (MS.),* October 26, 1940.

[68] *Moffat Diary (MS.);* October 6-10, 1940.

silent, until the President finally persuaded him to make one nonpolitical address at the National Press Club in Washington on October 25. A few days later Mr. Hull endorsed the third term as necessary to assure continuity at a critical juncture in America's foreign relations.[69]

The Secretary's speech to the Press Club was a useful summary of the Administration's doctrine of the right of self-defense. Mr. Hull insisted that in the face of the Axis threat to the hemisphere and Hitler's repeated violations of international law, America's defense could no longer be based upon strict neutrality. The country was obliged by danger, and was justified by inalienable right, in undertaking to follow any course it deemed desirable to protect itself against attack.

In an early draft of this speech, its authors had inserted a paragraph suggesting that while no responsible American official had ever even intimated in Mr. Hull's hearing that national defense might require the Government to send "land forces" to fight outside the Western Hemisphere, this did not mean "that our Navy shall be denied the right at all times to sail any of the seven seas as a messenger of peace . . . without the permission of the would-be world conquerors."[70] But prudence apparently dictated the suppression of so provocative a statement. While the Secretary of State told his audience that the United States intended to continue giving aid to Britain and other countries defending themselves and so the United States against barbaric attack, there was no hint that such aid might eventually bring the nation into the conflict. While the Secretary's address left little to be desired as a warning of the reality of the dangers threatening the nation, the American voter could still assume that if the President were reëlected he was altogether likely to overcome these dangers by methods short of war. The purpose of defense was defense!

Still more reassuring was the message delivered to the American people by another influential spokesman for the Administration, the Ambassador to Great Britain, Mr. Joseph P. Kennedy. According to Mr. Morgenthau's testimony, the President had been much annoyed by his Ambassador's alleged sympathy for the Chamberlain appeasement policies of an earlier period, and by the pessimistic estimates of Britain's chances that Mr. Kennedy had since relayed to him. This, however, was conveniently overlooked in the desire to make use of the Ambassador's influence to check the last-minute surge of the Willkie campaign. This "Boston boy, beloved by all of Boston, and a lot of other places," as Mr. Roosevelt now described him, did yeoman service to the President's cause by his speech of October 29. He had returned to the United States, he said, with renewed conviction that the country must and would stay out of the war. There were simply no valid

[69] Hull: *Memoirs*, I, 864 ff.

[70] *Berle Diaries* (*MS.*), October 25, 1940. (This paragraph appeared in a draft of October 22.)

arguments, he assured his audience, for getting into it. If Americans did, they might quite possibly themselves be compelled to embrace totalitarian methods, thus defeating the very purposes for which they would have taken up arms. The Emergency Powers Act, passed by the British Parliament in May, 1940, so Mr. Kennedy implied, contained the potentiality of converting Britain itself into a totalitarian state.

Moreover, Mr. Kennedy felt justified in assuring his audience that American entry into the war, far from assisting Great Britain to final victory, would actually do that country a disservice. America at war would require for its own immediate use the very munitions that it was now able to send Britain. Coming from a source presumably so well informed, these views could not but exert an immense influence on American opinion. The burden of this, as of other election speeches, was that if the nation rearmed fast enough, it could stay out of the war and still secure the desired outcome.[71]

These campaign pronouncements constitute a reasonable sample of the quality of the debate through which the American people were supposed to resolve the mental confusion which had made it so easy for them simultaneously to advocate increased aid to Britain and avoidance of war. In effect, the only conclusion the voters were logically entitled to draw from the campaign of 1940 was their right, on the very highest authority, to persist in incompatible courses of action. On the eve of the election the differences between the foreign policy pronouncements of the presidential campaign had been reduced to the merest nuance.

It is impossible to attempt here an analysis of the contribution of the President's foreign policy to the narrow victory which he secured over Mr. Willkie on November 5, 1940. It seems likely that he owed his comparatively small margin in popular votes primarily to the influence of his words and, above all, to his record on foreign affairs. "It is amazing," he wrote to Carl Sandburg, "that the independent voters of America—an increasing number of them—many of them without real education—do have that final ability to decide our fate and the country's fate 'in the deep silence of their own minds.' "[72] It was in all probability the factor which turned the scales in his favor against the advantage derived by Mr. Willkie from the third-term issue and the growing opposition to New Deal domestic policies. If the influence of these foreign policy considerations seems paradoxical in view of the near identity of views of the Republican and Democratic nominees, it

[71] *The New York Times,* October 30, 1940. Cf. Henry Morgenthau, Jr., "The Morgenthau Diaries, Part IV" (*Collier's Weekly,* October 18, 1947, p. 16). The President wanted Kennedy home on or about October 21 (tel. to Kennedy, October 11, 1940). Conversation of the authors with Mr. Kennedy, June, 1949, in which he reaffirmed these views.

[72] Letter to Carl Sandburg thanking him for his support during the campaign (*Roosevelt Papers:* Secretary's File, Box 68), now printed in *F.D.R.: His Personal Letters,* II, 1086. See also Rauch: *Roosevelt from Munich to Pearl Harbor,* 270, and Sherwood: *Roosevelt and Hopkins,* 200 ff.

must be recalled that the record of their parties presented a very striking contrast. This the President most effectively exploited in that well-nigh perfect example of a campaign harangue, the Madison Square Garden address of October 28—the "Martin, Barton and Fish" speech.

Thanks to the record of the Republican Party on aid to the democracies, and its recent and not altogether convincing conversion to a strong program of national defense, Mr. Roosevelt won the votes of many Republican "interventionists," who entertained doubts about Mr. Willkie's capacity, if elected President, to wean his party from its isolationist predilections. Such votes were perhaps enough to counteract the undoubted defection of many conservative Democrats, who opposed the President on the third-term issue and the New Deal.

The character of the election and the comparatively narrow margin of the President's victory had profound repercussions, both abroad and at home. Outside the United States, in friendly as in hostile nations, Mr. Roosevelt's victory was considered a mandate to him to continue and, indeed, develop his announced policies of rearming the United States, defending the Western Hemisphere, and, above all, increasing assistance to Britain and other nations resisting the aggressors. The London *Economist* (November 2, 1940) commented that the known vices of Mr. Roosevelt were to be preferred to the unknown virtues of Mr. Willkie, a sentiment shared, it may be added, by many Americans as well. Elsewhere in Britain the exultation over Mr. Roosevelt's reëlection was less restrained. The Prime Minister described it as "a message from across the ocean of great encouragement and good cheer," to which, however, he added words of appreciation of Wendell Willkie's support of Britain.

As for the Axis, disappointment was temporarily disguised by the pretense that the result was foreordained and, in any case, could make no difference. Nevertheless, German official opinion did its best to emphasize the fact that both candidates had pledged themselves to keep the United States out of war. Therefore, Axis comment on the reëlection of the President remained on the whole discreet and cautious, in the hope of avoiding statements which could be deemed provocative to the United States. This strategy, of course, could not hide the fact that both in Berlin and Tokyo the President's victory was interpreted as insuring strenuous measures of aid to Britain and China.[73]

Similarly, the first American reaction to Mr. Roosevelt's reëlection was to view the result as a demonstration of support of the Administration's foreign policy record. For all the continuing misgivings over the third term and the President's domestic program, there was a widespread demand that the ranks should now be closed in the face of foreign peril. Wendell Willkie himself sponsored this move by pledging himself at once "to work for the unity of our people in the completion of the defense effort, in sending aid to

[73] *The New York Times,* November 7, 1940.

Britain, and in insistence upon the removal of antagonisms in America. . . ."

The American press, whose support of Mr. Willkie was out of all proportion to the popular vote, likewise rallied, with some notable exceptions, to the view that in the foreign field, at least, the President had won a mandate for his policies and that these policies now merited united support. *The New York Times,* which had opposed a third term, spoke for the majority of the press in its lead editorial of November 10. "One issue," said the *Times,* "which might have divided us we may with thankful minds set aside. We are in agreement as to the necessity for this country to defend its interests, its territories, and its way of life against all possible enemies; as to the necessity for rearming to make the defense certain; as to the desirability of doing all we lawfully and peaceably can to help Britain defend a cause that is also ours. . . ."[74]

All this was doubtless comforting to the President and his chief advisers on foreign policy, but as one of the shrewdest and most balanced commentators on international affairs, Mrs. Anne O'Hare McCormick, was quick to point out, "the most important effect of the election was on Mr. Roosevelt himself."[75] Could the President, mindful of the campaign pledges he had made, notably at Boston, really regard his reëlection as the mandate he needed to chart American policy along the course he thought necessary to insure the national security?[76] Within certain limits the answer was certainly in the affirmative. Mr. Roosevelt felt safe in announcing on November 8 that henceforth the Administration would apply a fifty-fifty "rule of thumb" in dividing munitions production with Great Britain. Various concrete measures of aid to Britain, held in escrow during the final weeks of the campaign, were, as will appear, quickly released at the signal of the President's reëlection.

Nevertheless, if Mr. Roosevelt could and did assume that the mandate of the people provided clear endorsement of what he had done for Britain since the previous spring, there could be no assurance that it could be stretched to cover the far riskier measures which he well knew would have to be undertaken in the near future if Britain's resistance was to be sustained. This was the price he had to pay for his belief, right or wrong, that to plead the case for his foreign policy in a manner calculated to produce clarification rather than confusion in the public mind would have cost him the 1940 election.

Be that as it may, Mr. Roosevelt's decision to leave the edges of his future intentions blurred entailed serious disadvantages. It laid him open to the charge, which the present authors believe unfounded, that he was deliberately misleading the American public by holding out promises of peace

---

[74] *The New York Times,* November 10, 1940.

[75] *The New York Times,* November 9, 1940.

[76] On this point see the President's own analysis in letters to King George VI and to Mr. Samuel I. Rosenman (*F.D.R.: His Personal Letters,* II, 1078 ff., 1083 ff.). Cf. Sherwood: *Roosevelt and Hopkins,* 200 ff.

while actually plotting measures to lead the nation into war. It placed a brake on many measures which he really believed urgently necessary to bolster Britain's position. It prolonged unduly the slow tempo of American rearmament. Most of all, it permitted the American people yet a while to cherish the agreeable illusion that they could both eat their cake and have it.

Serious as these liabilities were, there were evident compensations. Disguise it as they would, the Axis leaders felt the President's reëlection as a severe blow. For all Mr. Willkie's protestations of anxiety to assist Britain (as it turned out altogether sincere), Hitler could judge Mr. Roosevelt's intentions by his record. If the Fuehrer might still hope that by swallowing his pride and avoiding acts of provocation he could forestall American intervention, there was no hope that these tactics would induce or oblige Mr. Roosevelt to confine his measures of assistance to Britain within the limits of international law. The Nazi dictator could only continue to pray that he might overwhelm Britain before decisive American assistance could reach it.[77]

In sum, then, the effect of the 1940 election on the general form and direction of American foreign policy was negative, almost to the point of anticlimax. The great decision, the decision as to America's true stake in the war, was postponed another interval. As far as the popular attitude to the war was concerned, it is difficult to discern any significant change deriving from the floods of oratory during the last three weeks of October. A whole set of circumstances had contributed to rob the election of its potency as an agent for identifying real issues of foreign policy. There was the lull on the fields of battle, Hitler's shrewd decision to avoid provocative actions or words, the near identity of the candidates' promises to the people respecting defense and foreign policy, and above all the closeness of the race between the two candidates. All these factors, and others as well, combined to obscure rather than illuminate the foreign issues presented to the people.

Under the circumstances, and at this stage of appraisal, the reader will perhaps share the writers' reluctance to agree either with Mr. Roosevelt's admirers that public incomprehension offers the fundamental explanation of the President's failure to press more energetically for adequate measures of national defense and aid to Britain, or yet with his critics that it was the President's own failure to offer courageous and honest leadership that largely explains the continued popular indecision on American policy. A large element of truth is to be detected in both claims, and perhaps the only sure lesson to be drawn from the 1940 election is the truism that a political campaign offers a singularly poor means of public enlightenment. In any case, for what seemed to him (and perhaps was) good and sufficient reason, the President again deemed it more advantageous to stay in step with public opinion than to stake everything, including his own reëlection, on a gamble with his powers of leadership.

[77] Tel. from Morris (Berlin), October 22, 1940.

CHAPTER VIII

Origins of Lend-Lease

1. In Peril on the Sea

Lord Lothian's last address, read for the stricken Ambassador at Baltimore on December 11, 1940, presented a forthright analysis of the significance for Americans of the pending decision on the magnitude of their aid to Britain. 1941, he predicted, would be the critical year. Britain had survived the great air battle of 1940. If it could now withstand Hitler's fast-developing onslaught by sea and air against its life lines, and assure the uninterrupted flow of American supplies, Hitler's defeat was certain. But, warned the Ambassador, Britain could not accomplish this alone: "It is for you to decide whether it is in your interest to give us whatever assistance may be necessary to make certain that Britain shall not fail. . . . If you back us you will not be backing a quitter. The issue now depends largely on what you decide to do. Nobody can share that responsibility with you."[1]

Informed opinion throughout the world, friendly or hostile, largely shared the Ambassador's belief that the survival of Britain, not to say the defeat of the Axis, depended at the end of 1940 on the magnitude and timeliness of American aid. Hitler was noisily boasting that Britain fought on only in the forlorn hope of being saved by the United States and the Soviet Union. Franco and Pétain were weighing every move toward Berlin or London with an eye cocked on Washington. Tokyo was in an agony of indecision as to whether or not it was safe to assume that the United States would stand aside while Japan plundered Britain's Far Eastern empire. Although Adolf Hitler's revised strategy for bringing Britain to its knees had met with serious reverses, in at least one phase it was rolling along with unhoped-for success in the closing weeks of 1940. Admiral Raeder's grand design for starving Britain into submission by concerted sea and air attack against its vital lines of communication was giving evidence of fulfilling the

[1] *Documents on American Foreign Relations,* III, 370 ff.

213

highest expectations of its proponents. As the Battle of Britain waned, the Battle of the Atlantic waxed.[2]

The American public, distracted by such spectacular developments as the whirlwind series of conferences between Hitler and the European chiefs of state, the Italian attack on Greece, and most recently the desert offensive of the British Army in Libya, had paid but slight attention to the laconic reports of mounting British shipping losses. The words "Northwest Approaches" had not yet acquired here their subsequent grim significance. But American officials were quite prepared for Mr. Churchill's warning to the President on December 8, 1940, that if the danger of British defeat by a "swift over-whelming blow" had for the time being receded, the new danger which had replaced it was "equally deadly." "This mortal danger," explained the Prime Minister, "is the steady and increasing diminution of sea tonnage."[3] Ever since the November election official circles in Washington had been indulging in pessimistic speculation about a "ninety-day crisis." Admiral Stark professed to see no hope for Britain's survival beyond the next six months without American assistance on a much vaster scale. A growing number of Administration leaders were becoming convinced that in order to be decisive such assistance must presently transcend measures short of war, if it did not actually entail armed American intervention in the near future.[4]

Thanks to the evasions of the election campaign, these grave implications of the President's policy of assuring Britain's survival had remained obscure in the public mind. Important decisions, involving not merely the scope and pace of American aid to Britain, but the looming problem of London's in-ability to pay for this aid, had been side-stepped. As the Battle of the Atlantic entered the crisis stage and Britain's dollar assets allegedly approached the vanishing point, President Roosevelt was finally left with no alternative but to explain to the Congress and the people the realities and risks behind such reassuring formulas as "all aid short of war." The stages by which Mr. Roosevelt emerged from the fog of his campaign speeches to the compara-tive clarity of his Arsenal of Democracy address (December 29, 1940) sig-naled the birth of Lend-Lease and with it another absorbing installment in the Great Debate on American policy. The words and actions of the few crowded weeks following the election by no means wrote finis to the con-troversy over America's stake in Britain's survival. They did, however, give the American Congress and people the balance sheet of Britain's assets and liabilities, both moral and material. Accordingly, the means were available

[2] *Fuehrer Conferences* (1940), II, 37 ff. (November 14). For U.S. military opinion see Watson: *Chief of Staff: Prewar Plans and Preparations,* 368 ff.

[3] Tel. from the Prime Minister to the President, December 8, 1940, printed in full in Churchill: *Their Finest Hour,* 558 ff. Cf. *ibid.,* 598 ff., for statistics on British shipping losses October-December, 1940.

[4] *Stimson Diary (MS.),* December 13, 16, 1940; Watson: *Chief of Staff: Prewar Plans and Preparations,* 368 ff.

by which in a democracy the popular judgment could be formed and the will of the people expressed.

2. THE POSTELECTION SLUMP

The doubts, hesitations, and confusion respecting the Administration's program of aid to Britain, enhanced rather than diminished by the 1940 election campaign, lingered on for several weeks after Mr. Roosevelt's reelection. The interval was accurately described by Mr. Arthur Krock as the postelection slump.[5] This is not to say that these weeks recorded no progress in the rate of American assistance to Britain. Although the President kept his counsel, his chief military and civilian advisers proceeded on the assumption that whatever the precise scope of the mandate given the President by the people on November 5, 1940, it at least implied greatly increased aid to the British. Admiral Stark was the spokesman for much of official Washington when, after the election, he predicted that Mr. Roosevelt would now be freed of the "political preoccupations which had necessarily influenced him during the political campaign."

It was in this mood of eager anticipation that their long-deferred problems would presently be solved that the members of his official family greeted the President upon his triumphal return to Washington on the morning of November 7, 1940. The indefatigable Secretary of the Treasury had taken Mr. Roosevelt's reëlection as the cue for announcing his own renewed determination to get war matériel to England. He was now bent on finding some means or other by which the British could obtain categories of aircraft which they did not even have on order, but which offered some hope of enabling them to reduce their heavy shipping losses through submarine action. Specifically he had in mind the new Liberators (B-24's). Since these—and very few they were—had been produced for the United States Army only, the Chief of Staff would once again be confronted with the onerous responsibility of certifying that all these planes were not essential to the national defense and that some could be released to Britain.[6]

It was possible, thought Mr. Morgenthau, to make a case which would permit General Marshall to do the necessary certification. After all, he argued in presenting his idea to Knox, Stimson and the military, the British had done no "horse trading" with the United States. On "secret stuff," as Mr. Morgenthau described it, they had given ten times as much as had been given them, including radar, which was every bit as secret and significant as the Norden bombsight, with which American bombers were now being equipped. In any case, the Destroyer-Bases Deal offered a precedent. The British had released the secret of the "1820" airplane engine, which had enormously facilitated the output of the Liberators. This gift provided a

---

[5] The New York Times, December 15, 1940; Sherwood: Roosevelt and Hopkins, 222.
[6] Morgenthau Diaries (MS.), November 6, 1940 (Vol. 328, pp. 271 ff.); Stimson and Bundy: On Active Service in Peace and War, 359.

possible basis for permitting General Marshall, in good conscience, to allow transfer of a vital few of the completed planes to the British. The Secretary of the Treasury announced that if his colleagues disagreed with his reasoning, he was willing to go before Congress to seek enabling legislation —a significant illustration of Mr. Morgenthau's state of mind.

Legal restrictions were indeed becoming an ever more exasperating obstacle to the implementation of the aid-to-Britain policy, but Secretaries Stimson and Knox were quick to point out even more serious ones. Stimson emphasized what all the others so keenly felt, and none more than General Marshall, namely, the terrible risk of gambling on Britain's survival. No one, not even Mr. Morgenthau or the President, exceeded Mr. Stimson in enthusiasm for assisting the British. But, as he pointed out, the Secretary of the Treasury's proposal involved "very deep and basic questions, such as whether or not we can afford to take this risk—that is, whether the planes will probably be more valuable to American national defense in the hands of the British now than later in our hands." Secretary Knox thought that two months' time would reveal whether or not the British would pull through. Both Knox and Stimson were favorably inclined to Morgenthau's proposal, but it was agreed that General Marshall, who must certify the bombers, would have to make the final decision. The Chief of Staff expressed himself as favoring help to the British "as far as possible without hindering ourselves." Certainly, however, the decision was so hazardous as to require first a thorough investigation of the facts.[7]

To these doubts Secretary Morgenthau replied that he had already broached his plan to the President, who was favorably disposed to giving some of the B-24's to Britain and had ended the conversation with the remark that he thought it "about time that we got on that one and one basis" with the British. This portended the application of Mr. Roosevelt's fifty-fifty "rule of thumb" for the allocation of American-built planes between Britain and America's own armed forces.

On the same day (November 7), shortly after this discussion with his Cabinet colleagues, Secretary Morgenthau went to the White House for lunch with the President. Taking along Mr. Arthur Purvis of the British Purchasing Commission, Mr. Morgenthau adverted in the ensuing conversation to the President's announcement at Boston on October 30 permitting the British to order 12,000 planes in the United States. Mr. Roosevelt reaffirmed his desire that Britain share American-made munitions on a fifty-fifty basis, and stated that this would apply not only to the Flying Fortresses (B-17's), but even to newer types of bombers as they came off the line. The President furthermore revealed his rule of thumb to the public at a

[7] *Morgenthau Diaries* (*MS.*), November 6, 1940 (Vol. 328, pp. 271 ff.); *Stimson Diaries* (*MS.*), November 7, 1940; Watson: *Chief of Staff: Prewar Plans and Preparations,* 306-9.

press conference on the morning of November 8, and explained it to his Cabinet on the afternoon of the same day.[8]

This was not the only significant decision to issue from the President's lunch with Secretary Morgenthau and Mr. Purvis. The Secretary of the Treasury managed to focus his host's vagrant attention on a number of other problems. None seemed so pressing at the moment as the alarming increase in sinkings of British and Allied merchant vessels. The British Government acknowledged that unless the trend were reversed it could not even replace its losses, let alone build up shipping to adequate levels. Accordingly, the highest priority in the expanding list of Britain's needs would now have to be assigned to maintaining the minimum of cargo ships required to feed the population of the United Kingdom and provide the wherewithal for continuing the war. Listening to Mr. Purvis's gloomy disquisition, the President interrupted with an inquiry: Was it not possible, he asked in effect, for the United States to build cargo vessels and lease them to Great Britain?[9]

This characteristic bit of rumination marked another stage in the mental processes out of which the grand concept of Lend-Lease was gradually to emerge. As was his habit, Mr. Roosevelt delegated to others the problem of discovering ways and means of surmounting the legal and other obstacles which stood between the idea and the reality. When he discussed with his Cabinet on November 8 Britain's peril on the seas and broached his notion of having a vast number of merchant vessels built in the United States for lease to the British, the difficulties presented by the Neutrality Act and the question as to what flag these vessels would fly were quickly raised. Most of them Mr. Roosevelt dismissed as details. He supposed that the Attorney General would somehow solve these problems as, presumably, General Marshall would hit upon some scheme which would enable him to certify that the Flying Fortresses and other heavy bombers so desperately needed by the British were not essential to America's own defense.

Secretaries Knox and Stimson listened with satisfaction, not unmixed perhaps with irritation, as the President went on to emphasize to the Cabinet the expedients he envisaged for accomplishing this purpose within the framework of existing law and policy. Both these members of the Cabinet already entertained the most serious misgivings as to whether the President's ingenuity would enable him to avoid recourse to more fundamental measures to insure the volume of assistance Britain needed to weather the Battle of the Atlantic. Nevertheless, Stimson and Knox felt obliged to continue along the line the President was following until such time as he himself became

[8] *Public Papers and Addresses,* IX, 563; *Stimson Diary (MS.),* November 8, 1940; Hull: *Memoirs,* I, 870; Watson: *Chief of Staff: Prewar Plans and Preparations,* 308, 368. For the British view of Mr. Arthur Purvis's mission in Washington, see W. H. Hancock and M. M. Gowing: *British War Economy* (London, 1949), 229 ff.

[9] *Morgenthau Diaries (MS.),* November 8, 1940 (Vol. 33, pp. 135 ff.).

convinced that the policy of aid to Britain must be reappraised and the obstacles to its implementation faced in more forthright fashion.

The Secretary of War had his turn with the President at lunch on November 12. Mr. Stimson had not talked alone with his chief for many weeks.
He had a long and involved agenda and, aware of the President's inclination to dart from one idea to another, he had small hope of pinning him
down to the points on which his approval was essential. He was agreeably
surprised when, for an hour and a half, he managed to keep the President's
mind on the obstacles which stood in the way of giving the British half the
production of the latest American heavy bombers. He was able to report
that General Marshall had found it possible to earmark for Britain a number of B-24's as soon as they were completed. He could certify these aircraft
because the United States would receive a valuable *quid pro quo* in the
shape of airplane engines to be released by the British. The Flying Fortresses, however, seemed to present an insurmountable obstacle to the conscience of the Chief of Staff. Since the British had no such aircraft on order
here, it was impossible to "defer" to their program by exchanging bombers
on hand against future production for British account.

Obviously Secretary Stimson agreed with Mr. Morgenthau's recent conclusion that the time was approaching when all such problems would have
to be solved by requesting Congress to repeal the Walsh Amendment and
other restrictive legislation. The President, however, was not yet ready for
this. In the midst of Mr. Stimson's recital, he picked up a pad and pencil
and jotted down his own recipe for solving the problem of the bombers.
This involved submitting to the Attorney General the question of sending
Flying Fortresses to England accompanied by Air Corps personnel, with the
alleged purpose of seeing the planes tested under combat conditions. This
seemed to Mr. Roosevelt "the only peg on which we could hang the proposition legally."[10]

Since the President's penciled memorandum stipulated that Mr. Stimson
clear this scheme with Secretary Hull, the former sought out his colleague
as soon as he left the White House. Together Hull and Stimson lamented
the rigid language of the law which prevented the transfer of American-
owned munitions "even in cases where the transaction," said Stimson, "is
manifestly—in the broad view—for the interest of the defense of the United
States." The Secretary of State agreed that an effort must be made to secure
the repeal of the Walsh Amendment.[11]

Leaving Mr. Hull, Secretary Stimson next called on Attorney General
Jackson. Finding the latter out of town, he outlined the President's aircraft
scheme to the Assistant Attorney General. It did not take Judge Townsend
long to come up with an opinion. On the very next day he informed Secre-

[10] *Stimson Diary (MS.)*, November 12, 1940; Watson: *Chief of Staff: Prewar Plans
and Preparations*, 307 ff.

[11] For Secretary Hull's general attitude see his *Memoirs*, I, 872-73.

tary Stimson that the Administration could not give the British any of the B-17's—even for test purposes—without going to Congress, which had "entire dominion" over the property of the United States. It might be possible, however, to rig up an exchange of existing B-17's for other types of bombers which London had on order and which were to be furnished later. General Marshall reluctantly agreed that this device offered the only means of carrying out the President's wishes without recourse to Congress. Finally, on December 5, it was announced that negotiations for the release to Great Britain of twenty B-17 bombers had been completed. The United States Army had relinquished them. One had already been delivered.[12]

Similar involvements and vexations overtook nearly every other attempt of the Administration to find ways and means, within the law, to meet the mounting German pressure on Britain's life line. Early in November the President had informed Secretary Morgenthau and Mr. Purvis of his decision to permit the British to build 120 cargo ships in American yards, to purchase 63 more from the Maritime Commission and to acquire some hundred others from private firms. There was no assurance that this arrangement would have a decisive effect on the Battle of the Atlantic, but at least it might tide the British over the immediate crisis. Yet when Secretary Morgenthau, Secretary Knox and Admiral Land of the Maritime Commission sat down to work out the details, they encountered so many obstacles that all three emerged with the conviction that only much more drastic measures would save the situation. Knox, who had been urging Mr. Roosevelt to exert pressure on Prime Minister De Valera to grant Britain bases on the west coast of Ireland, now announced his conversion to an idea long entertained by Secretary Morgenthau: seizure of all Axis shipping immobilized in the ports of the Americas. Morgenthau welcomed Knox's support, but also urged the merits of President Roosevelt's newest suggestion that American shipyards build a vast number of cargo vessels and lease them to the British.[13]

At every turn the signs indicated the approaching end of stopgap devices for implementing the Administration's policy of assistance to Britain. Each new expedient pointed up the need for eventual recourse to Congress for a national decision on the limits of such assistance, or else for action by the Administration which, like the seizure of merchant shipping in American harbors, could scarcely be construed by the Axis powers as anything but an act of war. It is plain that many of the President's advisers, both civilian and military, had confidently expected that the election would precipitate a decision by the President to have done with half measures and evasions. It had not. Mr. Roosevelt showed scant disposition during November to face the

[12] *Stimson Diary (MS.)*, November 12, 13, 1940; *Bulletin of International News,* XVII (2), 1603, 1665 ff.; *The New York Times,* November 20, 21; December 5, 6, 1940.

[13] *Morgenthau Diaries (MS.)*, November 28, 1940 (Vol. 332, pp. 252 ff.).

facts. Publicly he disclaimed any intention even to revise the Johnson Act and the neutrality legislation, to say nothing of asking Congress to get rid of them altogether.[14]

There were other vital areas in which the President's reluctance to take immediate advantage of his reëlection occasioned great anxiety and disappointment to his more impatient aides. While the officers of the War and Navy Departments were trying to find ways and means of meeting the President's desire to send greater supplies of munitions to Britain, and the service chiefs were wrestling with their consciences in order to release planes and ships, domestic production continued to lag. Plagued on the one hand by strikes in vital plants, and on the other by the reluctance of manufacturers to reduce the level of civilian production, the rearmament program reacted sluggishly indeed to the immense new effort demanded of it by the President's election pledges simultaneously to rearm America and assure Britain's needs.[15]

No one exceeded the Secretary of War in the conviction that all-out aid to Britain was the surest means of safeguarding the security of the United States. Even so, Mr. Stimson was not blind to the fact that of late the British had been securing a disproportionate share of American munitions production, particularly of aircraft. The Secretary and his good friend and assistant, Judge Patterson, had framed the War Department's formula for the allocation of aircraft to Great Britain under the President's fifty-fifty rule of thumb. It was an arrangement as generous as prudence could conceivably permit. Judge Patterson would have given the British virtually everything they required subject only to two minimum conditions: America's own productive capacity must be enhanced by their orders; their orders must leave in American hands enough planes and armament for training, as distinct from final equipment. Secretary Stimson himself added one further condition: The United States must also retain enough planes, particularly long-range bombers, to meet a great emergency, such as would be precipitated by a sudden collapse of Britain.[16]

Secretary Stimson feared that even these minimum conditions were not being observed, and General Marshall heartily agreed with him.[17] The solution, however, was not to clamp down on further allocations to Britain, but rather to step up America's own production to the point where it would prove adequate for both its own and Britain's needs. The Secretary of War was more than doubtful whether these levels could be reached in a nation not actually at war. He was convinced, however, that much more could be achieved in rallying both industry and labor to a sense of the realities, and

[14] On Stimson's impatience with the legal restraints imposed on aid to Britain at this stage, see Stimson and Bundy: *On Active Service in Peace and War*, 359 ff.

[15] Secretary Stimson was particularly concerned with strikes in aircraft plants and by the reluctance of certain producers to cut production of commercial aircraft (*Stimson Diary, MS.*, November 22, 26, 27, 1940).

[16] *Stimson Diary (MS.)*, November 9, 1940.

[17] Watson: *Chief of Staff: Prewar Plans and Preparations*, 314-15.

he complained with some asperity of Mr. Roosevelt's unwillingness to come to grips with the menace represented by an industrial program and a labor policy still seemingly based on the old assumption that American rearmament could somehow be achieved without significant sacrifices by labor, management or the public. "The President's ideas," he observed, after a meeting at the White House with Secretary Knox, Mr. Sidney Hillman and the Attorney General, "were not at all crystallized on how to handle the priorities question or the labor question, but we threshed out a program that may work for a while."[18]

Secretary Knox and Admiral Stark were not far behind the procession led by their opposite numbers in the War Department. The Secretary of the Navy, in an address at Boston on November 14, appealed for greater national unity, and described the war as an "irreconcilable conflict which must be fought out to a finish." The only hope of avoiding involvement lay in strict devotion to the task of national defense. In that connection, America would not only appease no one on earth, but would give Great Britain "every possible degree of aid short of leaving ourselves defenseless."[19]

The Secretary of the Navy, together with General Marshall and Admiral Stark, had himself conferred with the President almost immediately after his return to Washington, in anticipation that Mr. Roosevelt's reëlection would at last permit staff conversations with the British in Washington on a more formal basis than it had been possible for Admiral Ghormley and the other American "Special Observers" to assume in their informal discussions with the British in London since August. In asking the President's consent for reviving this project, which, like so many others, had been temporarily shelved during the election campaign, General Marshall and Admiral Stark both informed the President that the whole basis for War and Navy Department defense planning was in need of thorough revision prior to further military consultation with the British. The fundamentals of such defense planning had not been the subject of a clear Presidential decision since they had been outlined after the fall of France. Unless the Chief of Staff and the Chief of Naval Operations could provide their planners with answers to basic questions of policy, particularly with respect to the scope of assistance to Britain, a firm defense strategy could not be mapped. Only the President could give these answers. He had been officially unresponsive when the Strong memorandum had been used to elicit them prior to the election.[20] It now became the turn of Admiral Stark to try his hand. On November 12 he forwarded to the President a memorandum on *National Defense Policy* which advanced the now famous Plan Dog concept. Drafted in the first instance by the Navy's planners, the document was being reviewed by General Marshall and Secretary Stimson, whose comments were subsequently

[18] *Stimson Diary (MS.)*, November 26, 1940.
[19] *The New York Times*, November 15, 1940.
[20] *Supra*, Chapter VII, Section 4.

sent to the White House and incorporated with the Navy memorandum.[21]

The Plan Dog memorandum set forth the world situation and examined the several alternative courses of action open to the United States in the light of it. It concluded that America's best hope for the successful defense of the Western Hemisphere lay in the survival of Britain. Hence, military planning should proceed on the assumption that all measures, including if necessary military measures, would be taken to avert Britain's defeat. Admiral Stark wrote:

I believe that the continued existence of the British Empire, combined with building up a strong protection in our home areas, will do most to assure the *status quo* in the Western Hemisphere, and to promote our principal national interests. As I have previously stated, I also believe that Great Britain requires from us very great help in the Atlantic, and possibly even on the continents of Europe and of Africa, if she is to be enabled to survive.

Plan Dog reiterated the now widely accepted view of the Army as well as of the Navy that future strategic planning, whether America or Anglo-American, should be based on an assumption that if and when the United States became involved in war against the three Axis Powers, the wisest course would be to anticipate "an eventual strong offensive in the Atlantic as an ally of Britain and a defensive in the Pacific." Accordingly, Admiral Stark recommended to the President that he authorize the secret and formal staff conversations with the British respecting both oceans, for which Lord Lothian had thus far been pressing in vain. Presidential approval of Plan Dog would not, of course, commit the United States to entrance into the war at some future date as an ally of Britain. Nevertheless, the Chief Executive would, if he agreed with Admiral Stark's memorandum, at least assure the War and Navy Departments that it was reasonable for their planners to assume as national policy that all measures, including ultimate armed intervention, would be taken to prevent the defeat of Britain.

Mr. Roosevelt shied away from immediate and formal approval of Plan Dog and its implications. Nevertheless, before the end of the year Admiral Stark's memorandum, after various revisions, secured the approval of the Secretaries of War and the Navy, as well as the endorsement of the Army-Navy Joint Board. The latter on December 21 endorsed a detailed memorandum on *National Defense Policy* which included in revised form much of the substance of the original Plan Dog. While the Secretary of State, fearful, perhaps, of weakness in the Pacific, withheld formal approval of the new policy, it became in fact the authorized basis upon which the

---

[21] The fullest account of this memorandum is provided in the Kittredge MS. on *United States-British Naval Coöperation,* but see Watson: *Chief of Staff: Prewar Plans and Preparations,* 119 ff. On the War Department planning mechanism, see Ray S. Cline: *Washington Command Post: The Operations Division* (Washington, Department of the Army, 1951), 34-37.

strategic planning of the nation's defense was developed during the spring of 1941 (Rainbow Plan V). In particular it became the point of departure for the preparation of the American position in the approaching Washington staff conversations with the British, to which the President had likewise given tacit assent.[22]

Mr. Roosevelt's cautious and indirect response to the efforts of his military advisers to secure the national policy guidance requisite for the vital task of planning a realistic strategy of defense was in line with other manifestations of his anxiety to avoid overt and clear-cut decisions in the post-election weeks. Although public opinion polls still indicated that only half the people of the United States were willing to contemplate recourse to methods of assisting Britain which risked American involvement in hostilities, there was certainly a widespread conviction that much more could and should be done to save Britain by action short of war. The disappointment and impatience at the inexplicable reluctance of the President to interpret his election mandate boldly was summed up in an editorial in the *New York Herald Tribune* (November 20) which warned that "one course more disastrous than having no policy at all is to decide upon a policy and then fail to apply it. The United States had decided upon its policy—all aid to Britain short of war. The time has come to implement it."

Spearheading public pressure in favor of a daring course was the advanced wing of the Committee to Defend America by Aiding the Allies, who redoubled their efforts on behalf of Britain as soon as the President's reëlection offered them an opportunity to regroup their forces irrespective of party affiliations. Mr. White himself conferred with the President and other Administration leaders shortly after the election with the object of preventing his policy committee from taking a position, as he put it, "cross-ways with the White House on national policies." He found much to confirm his own anxiety that the bolder spirits in the White Committee were planning to support a position at variance with that of the Administration. As he later recalled, the President, Secretary Hull, and Secretary Knox all "protested that they did not want us to agitate for convoys at that time, and that they were not ready to send troops, largely because they didn't have any trained nor equipped, and that at the very time when he [the President] was being abused as a hothead he was trying to put on the brakes and slow us down until we could catch up with ourselves by a trained and equipped army of a million men."[23]

[22] A succinct account of the developments in connection with Plan Dog is provided in Watson: *Chief of Staff: Prewar Plans and Preparations*, 120-25. On the President's views, see Sherwood: *Roosevelt and Hopkins*, 271 ff. Plan Dog was shown informally to the British on November 18, 1940, and approved by Mr. Churchill on November 21 (*Their Finest Hour*, 690). A compact outline of U.S. war plans of the period 1939-1941 is provided by Cline: *Washington Command Post: The Operations Division*, 55 ff.

[23] Letter of White to Clark Eichelberger, July 29, 1941 (Johnson: *Selected Letters of William Allen White*, 430-31). Cf. Johnson: *Battle Against Isolation*, 170 ff.

Nevertheless, against the judgment of Mr. White, the statement issued on November 26 by the Committee to Defend America by Aiding the Allies urged on the President and the people a program to assist the British which could only with difficulty be brought within the limits of measures short of war. Calling for vast increases in American defense production and in material assistance to the Allies, the Committee's statement importuned the President to accomplish this, if necessary, by declaring a state of national emergency. There was no explicit demand for convoying of American munitions, but the statement insisted that the life line between Britain and the Western Hemisphere must "under no circumstances" be cut and that the United States "must be prepared to maintain it." America should therefore build the maximum possible number of merchant vessels, as rapidly as in the days of the First World War, for rent or lease to Britain. Shipping pools should be established in order to permit the substitution of American for British cargo vessels in the Pacific and Indian Oceans, thus releasing British shipping for service in the Atlantic.

The Committee's statement further insisted that the time had come when Congress should assume a larger share of responsibility for the formulation of the policies and methods of aiding the Allies. Consequently, without citing the Johnson Act or the neutrality legislation by name, it called on Congress for a "wholesale revision" of American policy to get rid of statutes which hampered assistance to Britain and made difficult coöperation with countries defending themselves against attack by nations engaged in war in violation of treaties with the United States.

As for the Pacific, the manifesto called for the immediate imposition of an embargo on the shipment of all war materials to Japan. It likewise appealed for a clear naval understanding with Great Britain which would permit the American and British Fleets to be so disposed as to secure maximum advantages both in protecting the Atlantic and in checking the spread of the war in the Pacific. "The world's future," said the statement, "is secure if the British and American Fleets control the seas."[24]

However useful as a trial balloon Mr. Roosevelt may have regarded this broadside from the White Committee, he made no immediate move in the direction to which it pointed. From Hyde Park he announced his conviction that American aid to Britain was already at its peak, although he added that he would welcome any further assistance that could be given "under present circumstances."[25] He refused to involve the Executive Branch in the proposal for modification of the Johnson Act and the neutrality legislation. At his press conference of November 26 he had little to say about the labor problem, strikes, and the subversive activities of the Communists. While he manifested some concern over the inroads on combat aircraft construction

[24] Johnson: *Battle Against Isolation*, 170 ff.
[25] Arthur Krock in *The New York Times*, November 24; *Stimson Diary (MS.)*, November 25, 1940. For Mr. Hull's views, see his *Memoirs*, I, 872.

occasioned by the continued manufacture of commercial planes, he denied any intention of putting an end to a situation which so greatly alarmed his Secretary of War. Certainly there was little sense of urgency in the words with which the Chief Executive summed up the general policy which was to shape the budget for the next fiscal year. It would be, he said, "cut to the bone on non-military public works, because we believe that in the course of the coming summer the defense program is going to use the greatest number of people who are out of work . . . in other words, cutting down on the total number of employable needy unemployed."[26]

At the end of November, so far as the public was concerned, it was hard to detect the birth pangs of the "new phase" in rearmament and aid to Britain which had been so widely anticipated after Mr. Roosevelt's reëlection. There was no hint of daring measures or major innovations to meet the developing crisis in the Battle of the Atlantic. There seemed no likelihood that the President would put an end to the postelection slump by some dramatic appeal to the Congress or the people. Instead, the public learned that the President was about to take a cruise. Eventually the log jam was broken only by a series of decisions and actions which followed swiftly upon the return to the United States of the British Ambassador, who had tactfully absented himself during the final weeks of the election campaign. Stepping from the plane which had brought him from London, Lord Lothian, without prior consultation with American officials, informed the press that Great Britain's financial plight was now becoming desperate, and that in a few days Sir Frederick Phillips, of the British Treasury, would arrive to discuss the matter with United States officials.

3. BRITAIN'S FINANCIAL PLIGHT

Lord Lothian's blunt statement to the reporters upon his return was regarded in Washington as a most undiplomatic *faux pas*. Both the President and Mr. Morgenthau feared that it would arouse the suspicions of Congress and jeopardize such prospects as there were for approval of increased assistance to Britain. Mr. Hull was not only annoyed, but also skeptical as to whether the British financial picture was as black as Lothian painted it.[27] Actually, however, the Ambassador's indiscretion marked the beginning of the end of the postelection slump. By revealing to Congress and the public another aspect of Britain's plight, hitherto known only to a few government officials, Lord Lothian was instrumental in bringing the President to accept the conclusion which his own advisers had been urging on him: that he had no recourse but to go to the Congress and the people for a fresh and unequivocal mandate on the program of assistance to Britain and other nations

---

[26] Press conference of November 26, 1940 (*Public Papers and Addresses*, IX, 577 ff.).
[27] *Morgenthau Diaries* (*MS.*), November 25, 1940 (Vol. 332, pp. 266 ff.); *Moffat Diary* (*MS.*), December 3, 1940; Hull: *Memoirs*, I, 872.

whose resistance to the Axis could be regarded as contributing to the security of the Americas.

Specifically, it was the attempt of London to close the two billion dollar deal placing orders to equip ten British divisions which led to the recognition that Britain did not have the dollars to pay for these munitions and that the American Administration lacked authority to provide these dollars. On November 28 Secretary Stimson sent Secretary Morgenthau for approval the draft of a letter to Sir Walter Layton confirming the War Department's agreement that the British should place the orders, since Layton had accepted the stipulation that the matériel must be of an American type. Stimson, however, was unable to give Layton any assurance that London would not be expected to provide a considerable portion of the dollars required to finance the plant expansion necessary to produce these weapons. On reading Mr. Stimson's draft letter, the Secretary of the Treasury was himself so doubtful of Britain's ability to find the requisite dollars that he felt unable to take the responsibility for approving the agreement.[28]

At the meeting of the Cabinet on November 29 Mr. Morgenthau listened sympathetically while Mr. Stimson rehearsed the familiar arguments for permitting London to place orders not only for equipping the ten divisions, but for aircraft and cargo vessels as well. Even if, said the Secretary of War, these British orders should slow down the flow of matériel to American armed forces, the country would ultimately benefit by the immensely expanded production facilities which would result. There was, of course, no certainty of British survival, but the Administration was proceeding on the assumption that it was safe to postpone for an interval the date when the national forces were to be completely equipped. Present losses would be offset by much larger gains in the near future from the increased production stimulated by British orders.[29]

With most of this reasoning Secretary Morgenthau was in hearty agreement. The crucial problem, however, was the financing, and Mr. Morgenthau was but little impressed with his colleague's suggestion that the American Government pay the cost of the new production facilities through loans to Great Britain. Regardless of the political dynamite in the proposal, it was already clear that existing restrictions on the size of the national debt would have to be raised. After brief conferences with Democratic leaders of Congress and with Sir Walter Layton, Secretary Morgenthau decided that the proper place for the problem of financing the British orders was the lap of the President of the United States.[30] Accordingly he drafted a letter to Mr. Roosevelt enclosing Sir Walter Layton's formal statement of his Gov-

[28] Morgenthau Diaries (MS.), November 28, 1940 (Vol. 332, pp. 206 ff.).

[29] Stimson Diary (MS.), November 29, 1940. On the effect of the British orders, see Industrial Mobilization for War, I, 52 ff.

[30] Morgenthau Diaries (MS.), November 29, 30, 1940 (Vol. 334, pp. 83 ff.; Vol. 333, pp. 213 ff.); Hull: Memoirs, I, 873.

ernment's desire to place orders for aircraft, ships, and munitions amounting to over two billions of dollars. These orders would require an estimated capital investment (to create new capacity) of $700,000,000. "As you know," continued Mr. Morgenthau, "the British claim they have no funds to meet these payments." The Secretary of the Treasury concluded by signifying his desire for instruction.[31]

He did not have long to wait. The President summoned him and two of his assistants to meet at the White House at 2:30 P.M. the next day (December 1). Looking over Layton's statement Mr. Roosevelt promptly agreed that the crux of the problem was the capital investment required to enlarge existing American plants and build new ones. Mr. Morgenthau handed the President a brief statement, also prepared by the British, listing their available assets. After a hasty glance at these figures Mr. Roosevelt remarked cheerfully: "Well, they aren't bust . . . there's lots of money there." He then reiterated his desire that London be permitted to place the orders, and that American plants be built to fill the British orders as "stand-by capacity."

The question was how, and on it the rest of the discussion centered. It was finally suggested that the Reconstruction Finance Corporation finance the plant expansion upon certification from the Advisory Commission that the additional industrial capacity was essential to the national defense. The British could shoulder a proportionate share of the costs by the simple device of paying a surcharge on the price of each finished item manufactured for them. The President quickly agreed to this solution but Mr. Morgenthau, as an experienced observer of the uncertain fate of oral decisions by the Chief Executive, pressed for something in writing to place the decision beyond argument. Momentarily, Mr. Roosevelt hesitated. Glancing again at Layton's breakdown of the British orders, he came to the item of cargo ships. At once he reverted to his earlier leasing concept and remarked that "the ships can be done by the loan idea." There is nothing in the record, however, to suggest that on this occasion it occurred either to the President or to his advisers that if the United States Government could build and lease cargo ships to Britain, it could build and lease aircraft or any other weapons of war. In any case, the President complied with Secretary Morgenthau's request and wrote on the bottom of his memorandum the words: "Use United States R.F.C. funds for plant capital on United States orders." Queried as to what he meant by United States orders, Mr. Roosevelt explained that the American Government would place the orders, the R.F.C. would advance the capital to build the plants, and the British would pay, on delivery, for the items produced.

By 3:15 P.M. the elated Secretary of the Treasury had left the White House. It had taken no more than a few minutes with the President to secure the requisite authority to allow the British to place orders for some

[31] *Ibid.,* November 30, 1940 (Vol. 333, pp. 213 ff.).

two billions' worth of munitions. Hastening to telephone the good news to Secretary Stimson, Mr. Morgenthau found further cause for satisfaction. Mr. Stimson quoted the President as having told him in effect that "we have just got to decide what we are going to do for England. He says doing it this way is not doing anything." It seemed that Mr. Roosevelt was finally on the verge of initiating the expected new phase of all-out material assistance to Great Britain.[32]

4. A Message from Mr. Churchill

On December 3, 1940, President Roosevelt embarked on the U.S.S. *Tuscaloosa* for his first real opportunity to recover from the exertions of the campaign, and to collect his thoughts on the problems which his chief aides had in turn submitted to him for decision. Even as the President was boarding the *Tuscaloosa,* Secretary Hull called in his colleagues of the War and Navy Departments for a serious discussion. He was in his usual form, eloquent of phrase but a prey to gloom. He expatiated on the precarious situation of the British, the horrors of air bombardment, and the shocking losses among recent British convoys. After lengthy discussion the three men concluded that there were but two courses of action that gave real promise of enabling Britain to counter the alarming successes of the combined German air and submarine attacks on its life lines. One was to send the British more American planes and destroyers but, because of the crucial time factor and the dangerously low level of American stocks, the service Secretaries felt compelled to embrace the second course. "So although nobody else but Knox and I," wrote Mr. Stimson, "seem to face it fairly, I believe that the only thing that can be done, and the thing we eventually shall do, will be to convoy that lifeline from Canada across the Atlantic to Great Britain with our own destroyers."[33]

Although the cautious Mr. Hull could not yet bring himself to share the conviction of his colleagues that escort of convoys by American naval vessels offered the only firm assurance of Britain's survival, he agreed with them that all measures of material assistance to Britain would prove futile unless the American productive efforts were enormously expanded. "We all agreed," said Mr. Stimson of this meeting, "that we should do our best to try to stir the country—the business people of the country—who are still asleep." To this end the Secretary of War convened at his home on the same day (December 3) the members of the Advisory Commission, together with Secretaries Hull and Knox. At this luncheon meeting Messrs. Knudsen, Nelson and Stettinius undertook, in Mr. Stimson's words, to start "teams to go through the key people of business, beginning with the meeting of the American Manufacturers Association this coming week in New

[32] *Morgenthau Diaries (MS.),* December 1 (Vol. 334, pp. 1 ff.).
[33] *Stimson Diary (MS.),* December 2, 3, 1940.

York." For his part, Secretary Hull promised to make every effort to instill the same sense of urgency among his associates in the Administration and his friends in Congress.[34]

From the lunch table at Woodley the group hastily adjourned to the meeting called by Secretary Morgenthau to map the action required by the President's decision to permit the British to place their two billion dollars' worth of munitions orders. Virtually all the key figures of the Roosevelt Administration were present. Mr. Morgenthau described briefly his conversation with the President on December 1 and the resulting go-ahead order on the British contracts. He then turned the meeting over to his subordinates, Treasury experts on British finances, with the request that they explain a bewildering array of figures copied on the blackboard. With respect to its liabilities these figures indicated that the British Government would be required to pay out close to $3,000,000,000 on or before June 1, 1941. After some discussion of Britain's dollar resources, it emerged that as of that date the British Government would be a billion dollars shy, according to London's estimate. American Treasury officials, however, thought the British "should have enough to meet these payments."[35]

For some little time the argument surged about the blackboard. Its conclusion was perhaps best summarized by an exchange between two of the principals present. Secretary Knox, turning from the blackboard to Secretary Morgenthau, remarked: "We are going to pay for the war from now on, are we?" Mr. Morgenthau replied: "Well, what are we going to do, are we going to let them place more orders or not?" Mr. Knox ended it with the words: "Got to. No choice about it." With this verdict there was scant disagreement. Mr. Knudsen, speaking for the Advisory Commission, brushed aside worries about industry's capacity. "We can make it," he said, "if it could be financed." All agreed that this was the essence of the problem, and Mr. Jesse Jones of the R.F.C. confessed to feeling very disturbed at the prospect of authorizing the expenditure of $700,000,000 to build the plant capacity needed to fill the British contracts. It was Secretary Stimson, however, who went directly to the heart of the matter. While expressing himself as wholly convinced that the President's decision was the only one consonant with the national security, he admitted that he was shocked by the financial "depth we are getting into." All this, he insisted, pointed clearly to a thorough showdown on aid to Britain. "Can we take measures," he asked, "that are going to put us into a position where eventually we will be committed to going to war just to save our investment, or to save the pur-

---

[34] *Stimson Diary (MS.)*, December 3, 1940; Hull: *Memoirs*, I, 910 ff.

[35] *Morgenthau Diaries (MS.)*, December 3, 1940 (Vol. 335, pp. 97 ff.). The Treasury estimate of British dollar resources was drawn up in anticipation of the approaching visit of Sir Frederick Phillips of the British Treasury. For the British account, see Hancock and Gowing: *British War Economy*, 232 ff., and Churchill: *Their Finest Hour*, 555 ff. and 572 ff.

pose for which we made the investment, unless you have the consent of Congress?"[36]

The Secretary of War answered his own question with a firm negative. He insisted that "Congress ought to be taken into the confidence of the Executive—that the Executive should not go ahead on such an enormous project alone. . . . We had no right to do so until we had authority from Congress and to that there was no answer. . . ." Mr. Stimson had probably spoken for all who heard him. Secretary Morgenthau agreed that there was indeed no other answer. Pointing out that Sir Frederick Phillips would arrive in Washington in a day or two, he suggested that the meeting be prorogued until the additional data which the British Under Secretary of the Treasury was expected to bring could be considered.[37]

Mr. Morgenthau's subsequent conversations with Sir Frederick Phillips were among the most painful in the long span of his strenuous efforts to assist Great Britain. Wholly convinced that Britain's cause was also America's cause, the Secretary of the Treasury nevertheless felt obliged by the responsibilities of his office and by the demands of public opinion to take a firm, even a harsh line with the representative of the British Treasury. He insisted from the outset that London "come clean" on the status of its financial resources. The first conversation also revealed that the major bone of contention would be the disinclination of the British Government to sell rapidly and in their entirety British investments in the United States in order to secure dollars. The British-owned American Viscose Company symbolized this issue. When Mr. Morgenthau broached the question of its sale, Phillips replied that this would give the United States a monopoly of the manufacture of rayon. Denying that he entertained any selfish motive, the Secretary of the Treasury tried in a few sentences to explain his objectives:

After all, the business is here. But what is in the mind of the ordinary citizen is that England yet hasn't gone far enough that she is willing to part with these businesses in the United States in order to pursue the war. . . . It is a matter of—well, convincing the general public of the determination, of just how far the English businessman is ready to go. It is a psychological matter as much as anything else. I think you ought to know about it.[38]

It was not easy, explained Mr. Morgenthau to Mr. Hull over the telephone, to take this line with Phillips, but the fact remained that many Americans imagined that the British Isles were populated largely by dukes and earls of fabulous wealth, and only a few could distinguish between Britain's not inconsiderable sterling assets and its critical lack of dollars.

---

[36] Morgenthau Diaries (MS.), December 3, 1940 (Vol. 335, pp. 97 ff.); Stimson Diary (MS.), December 3, 1940.

[37] Stimson Diary (MS.), December 3, 1940; Hull: Memoirs, I, 873.

[38] Morgenthau Diaries (MS.), December 6, 1940 (Vol. 336, pp. 163 ff.). For British views of the dollar problem, see Hancock and Gowing: British War Economy, 232 ff., and Churchill: Their Finest Hour, 555 ff.

Accordingly, the Secretary of the Treasury did not deviate from his position in subsequent discussions with the British representatives. Only if the British emptied their pockets, only if they gave the United States Government a complete statement of their resources, both in America and elsewhere, would the Congress and people of the United States offer effective aid. "It gets down," concluded the Secretary, "to the question of Mr. Churchill putting himself in Mr. Roosevelt's hands with complete confidence. Then it is up to Mr. Roosevelt to say what he will do."[39]

Actually the Prime Minister had anticipated this advice. On December 8, 1940, he had sent the President his own lengthy analysis of his country's present position and future prospects. The President, still on his cruise, had an unusual opportunity to ponder one of the most significant documents in the long record of Anglo-American relations.[40]

The Prime Minister, reviewing the current situation, found much to be thankful for. The last five months of 1940 had seen a remarkable recovery by Britain from the disasters of the first six months. The danger of defeat by a single blow had faded with the *Luftwaffe's* failure in the Battle of Britain. The German industrial effort had reached its peak, Britain's was only getting into high gear, while America's was just beginning. Above all, the British were buoyed up by growing evidence that the United States regarded its own security as bound to Britain's survival. While there could be no suggestion of any relaxation, victory in two years' time was a possibility.

To achieve it, Mr. Churchill propounded to the President a general strategy which was long to remain the British program for the defeat of the Axis. This involved, in brief, a grand staying operation. Britain must avoid a direct onslaught on Hitler's Europe until such time as the ratio of strength of the Axis and the Allies had been largely reversed. When Britain had grown strong, through its own and American efforts, and Germany was staggering under the weight of bombs and blockade, that was the time to return to the continent and deliver the *coup de grâce*. Meanwhile Britain must conserve what it had, build up its strength, and avoid a decisive encounter with an enemy who at the moment held most of the cards.

In carrying out this strategy, continued Mr. Churchill, Britain would not require any large expeditionary force from the United States. While this left an implication that other types of American military manpower would be welcome, the Prime Minister did not enlarge on this sensitive subject. Instead he plunged into a description of the "mortal danger" which faced his country in the shape of mounting losses of merchant tonnage. These had now reached a scale approximating the worst months of the First World War. If the rate of loss continued, not only would ultimate victory be un-

[39] *Morgenthau Diaries (MS.)*, December 9, 1940.

[40] This message, received in Washington on December 7, is in the State Department archives and in *Morgenthau Diaries (MS.)*, December 7, 1940 (Vol. 337, pp. 15a ff.). It is printed in full in Churchill: *Their Finest Hour,* 558 ff.

attainable, but imminent defeat might not be avoided. So acute was the shortage of escort vessels that the battleship *Rodney* had had to be risked to protect a recent convoy. Germany had two battleships at least as good as Britain's best, and the Prime Minister scarcely dared contemplate the possibility of Vichy's Fleet joining the Axis, or of a renewal of Japan's southward drive. The Royal Navy had no forces in the Far East capable of dealing with the Japanese.[41]

Having thus sketched the present situation and future prospects of Great Britain, the Prime Minister came to the point of confiding in the President. In view of the magnitude of the task of building up the arsenal of weapons needed to avoid defeat in 1941 and to lay the foundation for ultimate victory, Mr. Churchill felt not merely entitled but indeed compelled to list the means by which the United States could render vital assistance to what was in so many respects "the common cause."

The overriding need clearly was to check the critical shipping losses on the Atlantic approaches to the British Isles. This could be attempted, first, by a revision of the American neutrality laws and a reassertion of the doctrine of the freedom of the seas. These steps could be followed by the immediate resumption of American commerce with all countries against which there existed no effective and legal blockade. American merchant shipping engaged in such commerce would be escorted by United States naval vessels and planes. Such a "decisive act of nonbelligerency," as the Prime Minister so tactfully labeled the proposal, would not provoke Hitler to a declaration of war on the United States. He could be counted upon not to repeat the Kaiser's mistakes and would surely not attack the United States until he had disposed of Britain. If, even so, the President felt he could not adopt these measures, the Prime Minister hoped at least for the gift or loan of additional American naval vessels, particularly destroyers.

Second, Mr. Churchill asked the President to use American influence to induce Prime Minister De Valera to grant the British use of desperately needed bases on the southern and western coasts of Ireland, whence the Royal Navy and Air Force might operate westward into the Atlantic against Axis submarines. The Prime Minister was in all probability aware that Washington had already indicated to Dublin its hope that De Valera's policy on bases would be reversed.[42] For his own part, Mr. Churchill revealed a willingness to placate the Irish by every expedient short of compelling Northern Ireland to join Eire.

All the foregoing measures of American assistance, the Prime Minister

[41] In an appendix to this message Mr. Churchill indicated that the grand total of shipping losses—British, Allied, and neutral—from June 2, 1940, through November 24, 1940, amounted to 569 vessels of 2,401,192 gross tons.

[42] The recent efforts of the State Department in this direction were set forth in a memo of conversation between Mr. Welles and the Irish Minister, November 9, 1940; in a tel. from Gray (Dublin), November 19, 1940; and in a memo of conversation between Mr. Hull and Lord Lothian, November 25, 1940. See Hull: *Memoirs*, I, 872.

emphasized, were designed to forestall a British collapse. To ensure final victory would require much more: three million tons of additional ship-building capacity; some 7000 combat aircraft by the spring of 1942; an equal number of training planes; and, finally, proportionate amounts of other military matériel. Of these demands on the American arsenal, in general, Mr. Churchill felt emboldened to say: "We ask for an unexampled effort, believing that it can be made."

This was coming clean with a vengeance, but the memorable message was not yet concluded. There remained the matter of payment. Mr. Churchill was not disposed to disguise his thought on this problem either. The moment was approaching, he declared, when the British Government would be unable to pay cash for the enormous supplies it required. Accordingly, he placed himself in Mr. Roosevelt's hands with closing paragraphs in which the integrity of his moral position was matched by his mastery of the written word:

While [he wrote] we will do our utmost and shrink from no proper sacrifice to make payments across the exchange, I believe that you will agree that it would be wrong in principle and mutually disadvantageous in effect if, at the height of the struggle, Great Britain were to be divested of all saleable assets so that after victory was won with our blood, civilization saved, and time gained for the United States to be fully armed against all eventualities, we should be stripped to the bone. . . .

If, as I believe, you are convinced, Mr. President, that the defeat of the Nazi and Fascist tyranny is a matter of high consequence to the people of the United States and to the Western Hemisphere, you will regard this letter not as an appeal for aid, but as a statement of the minimum action necessary to the achievement of our common purpose.[43]

While the President was studying the Prime Minister's letter aboard the *Tuscaloosa,* Secretary Morgenthau, to whom a copy was soon made available, decided that the matter was too urgent to permit deferment of action even for the week's interval before Mr. Roosevelt's return to Washington. Convinced that Mr. Churchill's message was the "real thing," a "complete statement," he reconvened in his office, on December 10, the same group of officials who had considered the problem of assistance to Britain a week earlier. The Secretary of the Treasury opened the meeting with a résumé of his grueling conversations with Sir Frederick Phillips. He was, he said, not yet quite satisfied that the Treasury had obtained all the information on the British position that was required. Among other reasons, the British Government was reluctant to reveal in its entirety the desperate condition of Britain's finances, to the Americans, to the Germans, or even to the British people themselves. Such disclosure might occasion despair in Britain, as well as fortify the isolationist argument in this country that the United States was

[43] It is noteworthy that certain of the Prime Minister's strategic concepts were closely akin to those advanced in Plan Dog.

on the point of making itself receiver for a bankrupt British Empire. Nevertheless, continued Mr. Morgenthau, Sir Frederick Phillips had revealed enough to confirm the gravity of his country's financial plight. The total cost of Britain's needs seemed likely to run to $5,000,000,000, and whatever its actual assets, they would prove hopelessly inadequate for an expenditure of that magnitude.

In their comments Secretary Stimson and General Marshall were somewhat more reassuring. As requested at the earlier meeting, they had once again examined the value of the British contracts to the defense of the United States in the event of a sudden collapse of resistance. General Marshall felt he could state that in the main, and quite apart from any question of London's ability to pay, the proposed British orders and the additional plant capacity required by them would be of high value to the national defense.

To Secretary Morgenthau, with the Churchill message as background, this verdict seemed clear enough to permit the Reconstruction Finance Corporation to proceed at once to the next step. Let its chief, Secretary of Commerce Jones, grant the credits necessary to create a portion of the new plant without waiting for presidential approval of the entire program. Mr. Morgenthau encountered no disagreement on the urgent need for action, but little support for this specific proposal. Mr. Jones in particular felt it would be illegal for him to extend credits to begin construction of the plants even though this course had been generally approved by the President. The R.F.C. could use its funds to build plants for the War Department, but not for Great Britain. Neither the R.F.C. nor the War Department could properly place orders for Britain in such plants. Only the British could place the orders, but the companies would not accept them without assurance that the British could pay. Plainly the British could not pay. Accordingly, Secretary Jones offered another solution: "I think," he told his colleagues, "the program is so big and so important that you ought to outline it; and if we can get agreement among ourselves . . . then the sooner you get to Congress, the better. I would first put it up to the President for his O.K. . . . then to Congress."

In short order the entire group was won to Secretary Jones's proposal for combining immediate action to assist the British with ultimate Congressional approval for the detailed program. Their decision was cabled to the President by Secretary Morgenthau on the evening of December 10. The total figure for British orders already placed or proposed, said the message, amounted to over $5,000,000,000. Against this London alleged that it possessed in cash or other quickly available dollar assets something less than $2,000,000,000. Therefore, continued the message, the Secretary of the Treasury and his colleagues had proposed to the British that evening the following plan. The British were themselves to advance fifty millions for the construction of new munitions plants. The R.F.C. would advance the remaining funds necessary to complete the new facilities, $150,000,000. London would also be required to make an advance payment of $200,000,000 to the manufacturers. As for the rest of Britain's vast orders, that problem must be placed before the Congress. "If," concluded Secretary Morgenthau, "the English will accept this proposal, all of us feel that this will tide them over until Congress meets in January, at which time it is the unanimous feeling of this group that we should present the entire matter to Congress."[44]

The President had three more days at sea in which to think through the many-sided problem of aid to Britain which, thanks to Prime Minister Churchill's letter and Secretary Morgenthau's message, had been posed with such clarity and force as to make a decision imperative. As the *Tuscaloosa* approached American waters, bearing, as the Administration leaders hoped, Mr. Roosevelt's answer, an attitude of lively expectation gripped Washington. The feeling quickly spread across the nation when, after December 11, Lord Lothian's address at Baltimore alerted the American people to the question of their stake in Britain's survival. The pitch was raised yet higher as the big guns, manned by Secretary Stimson and other Administration leaders in the prearranged campaign to awaken America from its lethargy, began to fire their salvos. Speeches were made by Stimson himself as well as by Judge Patterson of the War Department, and by Mr. Knudsen and Mr. Nelson of the Advisory Commission. Particularly notable was the address at Boston by Mr. Winthrop W. Aldrich of the Chase National Bank, urging his fellow businessmen to support all-out aid to Britain. "Let us meet the issue head-on without subterfuge or evasion," he insisted, "and put it directly up to Congress to provide Britain with the funds she will urgently need in the future."[45]

Not least of the founts of wisdom to which Americans were able to turn for guidance in this hour of decision was Adolf Hitler himself. In a speech to the workers of a Berlin munitions plant, the Fuehrer openly provided the most cogent arguments to free the American people of their confusion and apathy. On this occasion, providentially, Hitler undertook to explain the precise meaning of the struggle in which the German people was involved. It was, he proclaimed, a struggle to the death between the democratic and totalitarian worlds, one of which must "break asunder." As was widely understood, Hitler had thereby repudiated, so far as he could with words, those Americans who had so insistently argued that the outcome of the war in Europe could make no difference to the Americas.[46]

Concurrently with the outburst of speeches and newspaper headlines, Washington officialdom labored behind closed doors in a last-minute effort to get ready for the President's return. On the diplomatic front, Secretary

---

[44] *Morgenthau Diaries (MS.)*, December 10, 1940 (Vol. 338, pp. 35 ff.); *Stimson Diary (MS.)*, December 10, 1940; Henry Morgenthau, Jr.: "The Morgenthau Diaries," Part IV, "The Story Behind Lend-Lease" (*Collier's*, October 18, 1947).

[45] *The New York Times*, December 13, 14, 1940.

[46] Arthur Krock in *The New York Times*, December 15, 1940.

Hull and Under Secretary Welles made one more fruitless attempt, through the Irish Minister in Washington, to change the mind of Prime Minister De Valera on the issue of allowing the British to use bases in Eire. Not only did Minister Brennan cite once again all the familiar arguments for refusing the British request, but added that "tactless" efforts on the part of private citizens to enlist Irish-Americans in this cause were likely to have the opposite of the intended effect. Such efforts threatened all the recent gains in Anglo-Irish understanding. In the circumstances there was nothing State Department officials could do but to make clear to the Irish that America's national defense needs were likely to prevent much amelioration of Eire's own difficulties. Mr. Brennan's observations cast doubt on the possibility of any success attending the forthcoming mission of Colonel William J. Donovan to London and Dublin.[47]

While the State Department was thus attempting in vain to carry out one of Mr. Churchill's recommendations on measures of American assistance, most of the Administration's highest talent was concentrating on the even more difficult problems raised by the Prime Minister's appeal for "a decisive act of nonbelligerency by the United States." In order to have a position prepared for the President's consideration, Secretary Hull called to his office a few days before Mr. Roosevelt's return Secretaries Stimson and Knox, General Marshall and Admiral Stark, as well as Mr. Welles, Mr. Hornbeck, and Mr. Hamilton of his own staff. Together this group reviewed the situation. After Admiral Stark had reiterated his belief that at the current rate of shipping losses Britain could not survive longer than six months, Secretary Hull called for recommendations. Every variety of suggestion was tossed into the ring. Britain should be urged to strengthen Singapore and release planes to Chiang Kai-shek to obstruct the withdrawal of Japanese troops for eventual use against Malaya. The United States should itself hasten to send modern planes to the Philippines. The "Administration," meaning the President, should certainly consider escorting merchant shipping as far as the west coast of Ireland.

It again proved impossible to reach full agreement on these and other suggestions, but Secretary Stimson, at least, left a clear record of his position. The Secretary of War informed the company that experience compelled him to conclude that it would be impossible to expand American defense production to the levels necessary to safeguard America's security and prevent Britain's defeat "until we got into the war ourselves." Referring to a statement of General Marshall that out of the November plane production of the United States 400 aircraft had gone to the British as opposed to perhaps six for the Army Air Corps, Stimson lamented that whether in the

[47] Memo of conversation between Mr. Welles and the Minister of Eire (Mr. Brennan), December 9; memo of conversation between Mr. Hull and Mr. Brennan, December 16, 1940. Eire's record on this issue is conveniently outlined in "The Present Position of Eire" (*Bulletin of International News,* XVIII, 1941, pp. 132 ff.). See also R. M. Smythe: "Unneutral Neutral Eire" (*Foreign Affairs,* January, 1941).

Atlantic or the Pacific theaters the same woeful shortages prevailed. "We couldn't get any initiative until we were willing to take warlike measures."[48]

Turning to Admiral Stark as the meeting concluded, Mr. Stimson asked point-blank what measures the Chief of Naval Operations could suggest for the relief of Britain in the Atlantic. The latter replied that it would be necessary to repeal the Neutrality Act so as to permit American merchant vessels to carry supplies through the war zone directly into British ports. Upon being pressed, Stark was forced to admit that such a course would certainly lead to naval escort of convoys, and ultimately, in all likelihood, to American entry into the war. Accordingly, the meeting ended, in Secretary Stimson's words, "nowhere in regard to affirmative action."[49]

Such was the atmosphere of confusion and expectancy, hope and despair, into which President Roosevelt was plunged when he disembarked from the *Tuscaloosa* at Charleston, South Carolina, on December 14, 1940. Scarcely more than the Congress and the people could the leaders of the Administration agree on the wise and necessary measures to be recommended to the President in the interests of the nation's defense and Britain's salvation. At least, however, they had thoroughly explored Britain's crisis—material, moral, and financial—and they agreed that the decisive hour was striking. At few times in his career was Mr. Roosevelt to be more squarely confronted by an urgent and universal demand for the exercise of presidential leadership. As his own closest advisers had now demonstrated, nobody could share that responsibility with him.[50]

5. Ten Decisive Days

Mr. Roosevelt moved so swiftly and vigorously in the interval immediately following his return to Washington, that veteran observers of the political scene quickly reported the end of the postelection slump. One correspondent even ventured to prophesy that these "ten hectic days" would mark a turning point in history, so stiffened was the country's approach to "world and defense problems."[51] History has confirmed this judgment, although the first notable public utterance of the returning Chief Executive scarcely suggested so significant a change. Entraining at Warm Springs on his leisurely return to the capital, the President waved good-by to the crowd and promised to return in the spring for a longer visit "if the world survives." This typical specimen of Mr. Roosevelt's humor was at once pounced upon by the isolationist opposition as evidence of the frivolous fashion in which the Chief Executive was leading the Republic down the garden path to destruction.

[48] *Stimson Diary (MS.)*, December 13, 1940.

[49] *Stimson Diary (MS.)*, December 13, 1940. On the following day Stimson expressed almost identical views to Mr. Bernard Baruch in the course of a discussion of the defective organization of the Advisory Commission (*ibid.*, December 14, 1940).

[50] The President's cruise, and what little is known of his immediate reaction to the Churchill message, are described in Sherwood: *Roosevelt and Hopkins*, 221 ff.

[51] R. I. Strout in the *Christian Science Monitor*, December 23, 1940.

Whether tactful or not, this wisecrack indicated that the President had made up his mind to choose the bold course and to challenge the isolationists. Several last-minute developments fortified this resolution. It was doubtful that London could accept the proposals made by Mr. Morgenthau and cabled to the President on December 10. Instead, Sir Frederick Phillips had formally asked for an American loan to finance the British orders.[52] Also Mr. Churchill had cabled the President again just as he reached American waters. The Prime Minister was exultant over the initial British successes in the Libyan campaign, but could report no improvement in the shipping crisis. De Valera remained adamant; indeed, was content, said Mr. Churchill, "to sit happy and see us strangled."[53] Britain's fundamental position was unaltered and the question of the hour was what the President could do.

The first of Mr. Roosevelt's official family to get a partial answer was once again the Secretary of the Treasury. At a White House luncheon on December 17 the President turned to Morgenthau and the British guests and said: "I have been thinking very hard about what we should do for England. It seems to me the thing to do is to get away from a dollar sign. I don't want to put the thing in terms of dollars or loans." That being the case, the President continued, America's immediate course was to increase its production, then say to England: "We will give you the guns and the ships you need, provided that when the war is over you will return to us in kind the guns and ships we have loaned to you."[54]

Secretary Morgenthau attributed this notable formula, the essence of Lend-Lease, to one of the President's "brilliant flashes." Perhaps in view of the number of recent occasions (notably with respect to the problem of cargo vessels) on which Mr. Roosevelt had almost produced his idea, it may better be ascribed to what has been called the President's gift for "combinations."[55] If it was possible to build and lease cargo vessels to Britain, why not, the President had finally asked himself, guns, tanks, and planes? However and whenever the idea of Lend-Lease was conceived, it was definitely born on the occasion when Mr. Roosevelt framed and answered his own revolutionary question.

A few hours after the President had informed the Secretary of the Treasury of the manner in which the United States must meet Britain's financial crisis, he sketched the proposal to the American press and people. As he faced the large and impatient group of reporters at his press conference of

[52] *Morgenthau Diaries* (*MS.*), December 12, 1940 (Vol. 339, p. 208).

[53] Tel. from the Prime Minister to the President, December 13, 1940 (printed in Churchill: *Their Finest Hour*, 606-7).

[54] *Morgenthau Diaries* (*MS.*), December 17, 1940 (Vol. 340, pp. 342 ff.; Vol. 341, pp. 56 ff., 63 ff.). See further: Henry Morgenthau, Jr.: "The Morgenthau Diaries," Part IV: "The Story Behind Lend-Lease" (*Collier's Magazine*, October 18, 1947).

[55] On this see the speculation of Messrs. Alsop and Kintner in the *New York Herald Tribune*, December 26, 1940.

December 17, the President was at his fittest. His skillful blending of humor and solemnity, of candor and evasion, together with the high import of the news he dispensed, made the occasion memorable.[56]

Archly disclaiming that there was "any particular news," Mr. Roosevelt opened the conference with a ringing statement on the vital role which Great Britain was playing in the defense of the United States:

Of course, there is no doubt in the minds of a very overwhelming number of Americans that the best immediate defense of the United States is the success of Great Britain in defending itself; and that, therefore, quite aside from our historic and current interest in the survival of democracy in the world as a whole, it is equally important from a selfish point of view of American defense, that we should do everything to help the British Empire to defend itself.

This was the theme. Before inviting questions the President went on to elaborate it. In bantering language he made light of the "nonsense" he had been hearing about the "traditional" methods of financing war. The Axis powers had confounded the traditionalists by proving that one could wage war without money. They could be similarly confounded by new methods of assisting Britain. There was no reason to follow the argument of the traditionalist, "the narrow-minded fellow" who insisted that first the Neutrality Act and the Johnson Act be repealed and then loans made to Britain. Hardly less banal was the proposal to make outright gifts to the British. Instead, said the President, as though he were improvising, we could either "lease or sell' to Britain such portions of our munitions production as the course of events indicated would be wise, always assuming that the defense of Great Britain was the best defense of the United States.

In short, concluded Mr. Roosevelt, he was merely trying to get rid of the "silly, foolish, old dollar sign." Sensing that this would strike others than traditionalists as a highly novel idea, the President hastened to adduce analogies to illustrate his meaning and cushion the shock. Particularly inspired was his choice of the now famous parable of the garden hose. If one's neighbor's house was on fire and one had a hose, one didn't say to him: "Neighbor, my garden hose cost me $15; you have to pay me $15 for it." No, one connected the hose, helped put out the fire, and got the hose back afterward. So it should be with the munitions so desperately needed by Britain. The President said he could not now give details. The procedure was still under study and there was no use asking legal questions about it. It did, however, substitute for the dollar sign a "gentleman's obligation to repay in kind." The President was sure that all his listeners would "get" the idea.

Mr. Roosevelt then braced himself against the inevitable deluge of ques-

[56] Public Papers and Addresses, IX (1940), 604 ff.; Sherwood: Roosevelt and Hopkins, 225.

tions. Would this scheme take the country closer to war? The answer was, "No, not a bit." Even though the British waged war with "goods that we own"? The President thought not. Suppose we were to carry our own goods abroad and deliver them to Britain? Didn't the "whole theory" require amendment of the Neutrality Act? Mr. Roosevelt curtly dismissed any idea of sending the American flag into a war zone, but as to revision of the neutrality legislation, the reporter was right. Would the plan require Congressional approval? "Oh, yes," answered the President, "this would require various types of legislation, in addition to appropriations."

The questions then turned from the garden hose to the hydrant. The reporters asked the President if he had any plans for building up the stocks which might thus be siphoned to the British. Could the President do anything more than he was now doing, inasmuch as Mr. Knudsen was publicly insisting that the matter was crucial?

Mr. Roosevelt quickly reverted to the defensive, as he invariably did when confronted with criticism of the Administration's production program and of the Advisory Commission. He rehearsed his familiar argument against production czars. He parried questions about the role of labor unions in defense projects. It was premature, he insisted, to generalize about a longer work week in defense plants. All he would say in a positive sense was that the objective was "to keep all the machines that will run seven days a week in operation seven days a week."

Late though the hour, Mr. Roosevelt had clearly not yet outlined in his mind anything like so definite a program for expanding American production as he had just indicated for supplying Britain with munitions. Yet the latter was obviously dependent on the former. Even so, the significance of the President's press conference of December 17, 1940, can scarcely be exaggerated. It has been asserted, with much reason, that the garden-hose analogy assured the success of the Lend-Lease fight.[57] The occasion was regarded, alike by those who sympathized with the President's policy and those who opposed it, as fulfilling the expectations with which his return to the capital had been anticipated. The issue of aid to Britain had finally been presented to the people with some adumbration of its real implications. In short order, the President had promised, the issue would be presented to the Congress, which could be trusted to ensure that no aspect of the problem would long remain obscure.

On the next day it was already possible to gauge the preliminary world reaction to the President's new proposal for relieving Britain's financial plight: in this country general satisfaction, in London sheer relief, in Berlin a deafening silence. Meanwhile, Secretaries Stimson and Knox, who were to talk with the President on December 18, were preparing to lay before him two problems requiring decisions no less difficult than the one Mr.

[57] Sherwood: *Roosevelt and Hopkins,* 225.

Roosevelt had just made. Even though Britain were assured that lack of dollars would not deny it access to the American arsenal, the President would presently have to make sure that this arsenal produced sufficient matériel to satisfy the demands both of Britain and the United States. Thereafter he would have to determine what steps to take to ensure safe delivery of this matériel to Britain's armed forces.

Thinking over this latter issue during the interval since the indecisive meeting of December 13 with Hull, Knox, Marshall and Stark, Secretary Stimson had become more firmly convinced than ever that the United States would eventually become involved in the war and ought to plan in accordance with this eventuality. To his satisfaction Knox, Marshall, and Stark all indicated, in the course of deciding what to say to the President, general agreement with the Secretary of War's position. They also concurred with him specifically that "the eventual big act will have to be to save the life line of Great Britain in the North Atlantic."[58]

Secretary Stimson had also taken the lead in paving the way for a presidential move to provide a shot in the arm for the ailing defense production effort. Talking the problem over with Mr. Bernard Baruch, he found that the head of the War Industries Board of the First World War agreed heartily with him in principle that the most obvious need was to reorganize the Advisory Commission, giving it a single head. Realizing that the President's opposition to such a plan was undiminished, Mr. Baruch proposed as an alternative at least a clear delineation of the powers and responsibilities of the seven members of the Commission.[59] Stimson himself had now come to have some doubts, if not of the wisdom, at least of the practicality, of a production czar. Accordingly, after further consultation, he and his associates finally settled on a compromise plan for reorganization of the Advisory Commission. It avoided on the one hand lodging final authority in a single head, but on the other concentrated sufficient responsibility in Mr. Knudsen as Director to end the dangerous lack of coördination among the headless group of seven, who had thus far supervised the rearmament program.

Fully aware of the crosscurrents into which he was launching his new plan, Stimson had done his utmost to enlist support in every influential quarter before approaching the President. Jesse Jones had promised to help by enlisting President Green of the American Federation of Labor. Justice Frankfurter had in turn contracted to tackle Sidney Hillman of the C.I.O. Both Green and Hillman agreed to support the Stimson plan, though Hillman expressed some doubt as to Knudsen's organizing ability. Thus, by Wednesday noon, just before his appointment with Mr. Roosevelt, Secretary Stimson had in hand an outline for what was to become the Office of Pro-

[58] *Stimson Diary (MS.)*, December 16, 1940; Stimson and Bundy: *On Active Service in Peace and War,* 366.
[59] *Stimson Diary (MS.)*, December 14, 1940.

duction Management (OPM), along with promises of support from most of his Cabinet colleagues in his forthcoming struggle to convince the President that the Advisory Commission, as well as the character of the defense program it symbolized, must be replaced.[60]

At 2:45 P.M. on December 18, Secretaries Stimson and Knox, accompanied by their respective aides, Judge Robert P. Patterson and Mr. James V. Forrestal, were ushered into the President's study. Mr. Stimson entered with his usual trepidation. There was much ground to be covered: high strategy and policy respecting the salvation of Britain and the defense of the United States, on which the State, War, and Navy Departments had not yet reached complete agreement; the entire reorganization of the nation's rearmament program, upon which a somewhat precarious accord had been achieved. But final decisions must be made by the President, and conferences with him were often "difficult." "His mind does not follow easily a consecutive chain of thought, but he is full of stories and incidents, and hops about from suggestion to suggestion." Actually, Mr. Stimson was again to be agreeably surprised. He found the President quite as prepared for the business in hand as Secretary Morgenthau had found him the previous day. Not only had Mr. Roosevelt been thinking about reorganization of the rearmament program; he had even been thinking of aspects of it which had escaped the others. He insisted that there must be no boom of rising prices as industry expanded, and no depression after the war—"If there is a war."

As for Stimson's concrete proposal for reforming the Advisory Commission, the President expressed ready agreement with its major objective of concentrating greater responsibility in whatever new body emerged to direct defense production. Indeed, he informed his visitors that Mr. Harold Smith, Director of the Budget, had just called his attention to an old statute, "which nobody seemed to know about," which authorized the Chief Executive to create "a managing bureau for all kinds of emergencies." This the President thought might well provide the means for creating a new board which would substitute Knudsen, Knox, and Stimson for the old seven-man Advisory Commission. Speed, moreover, was essential. Mr. Roosevelt wanted to announce the great reorganization not later than the following Sunday!

To his listeners all this seemed too good to be true. In scarcely more time than he had required to launch the Lend-Lease project Mr. Roosevelt had now seemingly assented to the reorganization of the rearmament program along the very lines to which in the past he had been adamantly opposed. The decision gave promise that if Congress accepted the Lend-Lease formula for assuring Great Britain "unlimited resources," American industry would prove capable of producing them. It was a triumph for Stimson and the "all-outers," and with it for the moment they were content.[61]

[60] Stimson Diary (MS.), December 17, 18, 1940; Morgenthau Diaries (MS.), December 17, 1940 (Vol. 340, pp. 320 ff.).
[61] Stimson Diary (MS.), December 18, 1940.

The President then turned to the subject of Lend-Lease, Britain's perilous situation on the sea and in the air, and the appropriate American course of action. At the first opportunity Stimson and Knox introduced Admiral Stark's suggestion "about landing United States supplies in Ireland." While this proposal was certainly one with which Mr. Roosevelt was familiar, his reaction was negative. It quickly became apparent that he was not committing himself on the inevitability of war, on the possibility of escorting convoys, or on the extension of the neutrality zones to the Irish coast. Great Britain, he pointed out in allusion to Mr. Churchill's latest message, "already had a hold over Ireland in that she was sending a lot of supplies which Ireland could not get elsewhere."

With this lame argument the subject was dismissed. For the time being, at least, Mr. Roosevelt felt that escort by American naval vessels was out of the question. Consideration was therefore given to rather less dangerous expedients. At the Cabinet meeting next day there was further discussion of ways and means by which Axis, Danish, and French vessels immobilized in American ports might be legally taken over to ease the strain. It was also announced that the London Government had been permitted to place orders for the construction of sixty cargo vessels in American yards. True to form, Secretary Stimson was impatient with such halfway measures. Seizing foreign ships or even building new ones was merely to pour water into a leaky tub. The real need was rather to plug the leaks. Stimson told the President and Cabinet that "we ought forcibly to stop the German submarines by our intervention." Mr. Roosevelt smilingly replied "that he hadn't quite reached that yet."[62] This, if anything, was an understatement.

On December 20, two days earlier than the deadline set by the President, came the public announcement of the creation of the Office of Production Management. Stimson, Knox, Forrestal and Patterson had, after their talk with the President, worked frantically to iron out the remaining difficulties. Chief of these was to insure direct representation at the top for labor, without jeopardizing the vital principle of concentration of power. Secretary Stimson proposed as a compromise the creation of a "collateral board," headed by Sidney Hillman, to stand beside the triumvirate of Knudsen, Knox, and Stimson and safeguard the interests of the workers. When the plan was shown the President, its authors discovered that he had himself spent considerable time and thought on the problem and had "gone further than we had." The President had enlarged the original triumvirate by adding Mr. Hillman and giving him the title of Associate Director, with Mr. Knudsen as Director.[63]

There were some initial misgivings as to the manner in which Knudsen

[62] *Stimson Diary* (*MS.*), December 19, 1940; *Morgenthau Diaries* (*MS.*), December 17, 1940 (Vol. 340, pp. 382 ff.) ; *The New York Times,* December 20, 1940; Stimson and Bundy: *On Active Service in Peace and War,* 367.

[63] *Stimson Diary* (*MS.*), December 20, 1940; *Morgenthau Diaries* (*MS.*), December 20, 1940 (Vol. 342-A).

and Hillman would take the President's amendment. It had in it potentialities for conflict that might prove fatal to the basic reform sought by its original architects. On the other hand, Mr. Roosevelt was persuasive in his remarks on the necessity, political and otherwise, for adequate labor representation in directing the rejuvenated production effort. In any case the confidence of the architects of OPM in the patriotism and tact of Knudsen and Hillman was amply justified by their reaction to the President's decision. Mr. Knudsen took it, as Secretary Knox reported, "in a fine way," coupling his acceptance of the job with a new plea to the American people "to pull off their coats and roll up their sleeves." The Office of Production Management, he told them, had been born of the realization that the issues which had produced this war were "irreconcilable in character" and could not be "terminated by methods of appeasement." Secretary Stimson took the same line in stressing to Sidney Hillman the "predominant position" of organized labor not only in production, but "in the great basic issue before the country." This was the issue between the policy of appease and compromise and the policy of an "irreconcilable moral issue." Stimson now envisaged labor taking the same position in America as in Britain, as the "backbone of defense."[64]

6. ARSENAL OF DEMOCRACY

The rapid-fire decisions and announcements made by the President following his return to Washington might well have seemed to him good and sufficient response to the charges of inaction leveled at him since his reëlection. The public reaction to his moves was certainly favorable enough to permit such a deduction. Even ex-President Hoover, one of Mr. Roosevelt's most effective and consistent critics, had admitted in a New York speech that there were "new forces behind this war that were not present in the last war." Moreover, he had added, we wanted our industries "to function for Britain, China, and Greece."

If the President, however, was inclined to rest for a time on his oars and await Congressional action on his new programs, he was quickly confronted by pleas and demands for further manifestations of political leadership. Professing great alarm at the growth of the "appeasement movement headed by General Wood and Lindbergh," Secretary Stimson had already stressed that Mr. Roosevelt's recent demonstration of vitality lacked one significant element to carry complete conviction. That element was a full-dress speech making explicit the implications for American policy of all his recent actions. "I told the President," wrote Stimson, "that the only person that the American people took their information on foreign affairs from was the

[64] *The New York Times*, December 22, 1940; *Stimson Diary (MS.)*, December 21, 1940. The texts of the official announcements and orders setting up OPM are presented in *Documents on American Foreign Relations*, III, 668 ff. On the general subject see *Industrial Mobilization for War*, I, 54 ff.

President of the United States, and pretty soon he would have to get into action."[65]

Press and radio comment certainly seemed to bear out Secretary Stimson's warning. Mr. Knudsen's speeches, and Mr. Hull's patient labors to convert Senators and Congressmen, were all well and good. So were the manifestos of the William Allen White Committee. But, as Arthur Krock took occasion to point out, there were still great questions clamoring for answers. Churchill had not succeeded in convincing many still reluctant Americans that their own security was bound up with the survival of Britain. What did F.D.R. think of this? If the United States made the necessary sacrifices, did the President believe Britain could win? What would happen if the Axis won? There still was no clear answer to these questions, and the country still lacked what Mr. Krock called a master plan of defense. The President could and, Mr. Krock predicted, soon would sweep away the "doubts and confusions" which gave rise to all such queries.[66]

Mr. Roosevelt may well have determined to speak to the country without benefit of advice originating outside it. However, once again it was Adolf Hitler who provided the President a most favorable climate of opinion if he now chose to solicit the support of his fellow citizens for the new directions of his policy. The Fuehrer contrived this by permitting himself the luxury of some very forceful comment on Mr. Roosevelt's latest actions. The German High Command, whatever its judgment of the President's ultimate intentions as to entry into the war, was increasingly worried by the implications of American assistance to Britain short of war. Summing these up in a report to the Fuehrer at the end of December, Admiral Raeder warned that unless the new program were checked, it could be anticipated that United States naval vessels would presently take over all British patrol and escort duties in American waters. Britain's entire armament industry was being "shifted to America."[67]

While unwilling to heed Raeder's pleas to concentrate on the strategy and weapons which could alone bring Britain to its knees quickly, the Fuehrer had been sufficiently aroused by the news from Washington to permit relaxation of the rule forbidding provocative official criticism of American policies. On December 21 a "Wilhelmstrasse spokesman" boiled over with virulence. "We are watching with great interest," he said, "the attitude of a nation which has shown only restraint and friendliness towards one warring nation [Britain], but whose attitude towards the other has consisted of a policy of pinpricks, challenges, insults, and moral aggression which has reached a point at which it is insupportable." To turn over to Britain the 70,000 tons of German shipping in American ports, warned the spokesman, would be a "warlike act."[68]

[65] Stimson Diary (MS.), December 19, 1940.
[66] The New York Times, December 22, 1940.
[67] Fuehrer Conferences, 1940 (2), 68 ff. (December 27, 1940).
[68] The New York Times, December 21, 22, 1940.

This statement was doubtless intended to stir up American isolationists by indicating the depths of Berlin's resentment over the Administration's "provocations." The effect, however, was just the reverse. The scarcely veiled threat moved some of the President's most violent critics to shift their ground. Hamilton Fish, leader of the isolationist bloc in the House of Representatives, was a notable example. "The Government of the United States," he was quoted as saying, "will decide on what action to take to protect American interests regardless of complaints emanating from Berlin." For the most part the press followed the line taken by the *New York Herald Tribune* to the effect that the German threats were clumsy words not involving a remote chance that they would be followed by a declaration of war against the United States.[69]

Neither the President nor any Administration leader deigned to reply directly to the Wilhelmstrasse spokesman. The response was to come, instead, in the form of a fireside chat by the President, the first since May, 1940. Precisely when Mr. Roosevelt determined to take advantage of the favorable atmosphere created by Berlin is not clear. By December 23, however, rumors abounded that he would speak to the nation on foreign policy on the evening of December 29, 1940. Some correspondents ascribed the decision to the visit of Mr. Philip Murray of the C.I.O. to the White House on December 23, and to the demand of Senator Vandenberg for a full and frank report to the people on the progress of American rearmament. The Senator spoke for many Americans who did not share his isolationist sympathies, but who did agree with his stinging denunciation of "cryptic assurances that all is well with the defense program when clearly it isn't." Certainly, the popular response to OPM was much less enthusiastic than to Lend-Lease, and the suspicion would not down that Mr. Roosevelt's appointment of Sidney Hillman as Associate Director of OPM was a political move which sacrificed Knudsen's authority in order to placate organized labor.[70]

At any rate, on or about December 23 the President made his decision to speak and outlined the general tenor of his remarks to Harry Hopkins, Robert Sherwood and Judge Rosenman, who were soon at work on the first draft.[71] In the meantime the President sent up one more of the White Committee's trial balloons to test the latest changes in the intensity and direction of the winds of opinion. He released a telegram, signed by one hundred and seventy prominent citizens, pledging unqualified support for the Lend-Lease plan, urging that everything necessary be done to insure defeat of the Axis, and calling upon the Chief Executive to "clarify the

---

[69] December 23, 1940.

[70] Joseph Driscoll in the *New York Herald Tribune,* December 24, 1940; Arthur Krock in *The New York Times,* December 22, 1940; *Morgenthau Diaries (MS.),* December 27, 1940 (Vol. 334, pp. 1705 ff.).

[71] Sherwood: *Roosevelt and Hopkins,* 226 ff.

nature of the conflict" and inform the people clearly and boldly as to the possibilities and consequences of a British defeat.[72]

The balloon descended without recording any remarkable variations in the political climate. The isolationists, in and out of Congress, grew more vocal as they diminished in numbers. Senator Vandenberg was proposing one more resort to the discredited expedient of a negotiated peace, but coupled with it the counsel that if the Axis rejected a "just and realistic formula," America should go in at once for powerfully enlarged activity.[73] If this could be interpreted as a break in the isolationist ranks, Senator Wheeler's comment on the trial balloon telegram served to remind the President that there were still stalwarts to reckon with. "This is the same old crowd," complained Wheeler, "that from the inception of the war has been urging us, step by step, into the war. It does not take any courage for a lot of college professors and bankers who are too old to go into the front line trenches, to urge a war that someone else is going to have to fight, that the youth of America be loaned to Great Britain to do her fighting."[74]

Thus Mr. Roosevelt completed preparations for going before the microphone in the face of strong pressures from both extremes of opinion. Reviewing the final text with the President on Sunday morning, Secretary Stimson made one more attempt to urge his own view that "we were long past the stage of diplomacy when we could curry favor with any of the Nazi nations." It seemed to him impossible that once young Americans appreciated the issue between right and wrong, they would not be willing "to fight as well as make munitions." Mr. Roosevelt's precise reaction to this familiar argument is not recorded, but in general it was negative. "The President," wrote Stimson, "went as far as he could at the present time." The projected speech was characteristic in the highest degree of the President's instincts and temperament, and Stimson did not conceal his satisfaction with it.[75]

As the hour for delivery struck, Mr. Roosevelt commenced on a solemn yet reassuring note. This was not to be a "fireside chat on war," but on "national security." It was still his "whole purpose" to keep the country out of war. Yet the situation was critical, more critical than when he first assumed office in 1932, when the banks were closed, and when American industry was grinding to a stop. Not since Jamestown and Plymouth Rock had American civilization faced such dangers as at the present moment.

Mr. Roosevelt explained this peril by an analysis of the philosophy and objectives of the dictatorships. On the strength of their own appraisal—and here the President made the most of the Fuehrer's recent speech—the gulf

---

[72] *Berle Diaries* (*MS.*), December 29, 1940; Kluckhohn in *The New York Times,* December 27; Alsop and Kintner in the *New York Herald Tribune,* December 26, 1940.

[73] Quoted in *The New York Times,* December 27, 1940.

[74] Quoted in the *Christian Science Monitor,* December 28, 1940.

[75] *Stimson Diary* (*MS.*), December 29, 1940; Stimson and Bundy: *On Active Service in Peace and War,* 366.

between the totalitarian and democratic states could not be bridged. It was, therefore, neither right nor reasonable for the United States to encourage false hopes of a negotiated peace. That this country even now was being spared the horrors of war was attributable to the valor of the British and the Greeks in Europe and the Chinese in Asia. This fact had induced some people to imagine that wars on those continents were of no concern to Americans. Nothing could be more mistaken. If we need not seriously fear attack "while a free Britain remains our most powerful naval neighbor in the Atlantic," it was equally obvious "that we could not rest easy if the Axis powers were our neighbors there." It was not less foolish to imagine, as did the "continentalists," that if other continents fell to the totalitarians, we could organize a satisfactory way of life in the Western Hemisphere. In such a "new and terrible era," America would be living at the point of a gun, and would end up, if it survived at all, as a military dictatorship not unlike those it was now resisting.

Having thus disposed of two of the major arguments of his opponents, Mr. Roosevelt took on the third and most serious: the risk of direct military involvement latent in the policy of aiding Britain and its allies:

I make the direct statement to the American people that there is far less chance of the United States getting into the war, if we do all we can now to support the nations defending themselves against attack by the Axis than if we acquiesce in their defeat, submit tamely to an Axis victory, and wait our turn to be the object of attack in another war later on.

There is small reason to doubt that Mr. Roosevelt was honestly convinced of the truth of this affirmation, which, in fact, he had stated many times before. The novelty came rather in the further comment:

If we are to be completely honest with ourselves, we must admit that there is risk in any course we may take. But I deeply believe that the great majority of our people agree that the course I advocate involves the least risk now and the greatest hope for world peace in the future.

At long last the President had braced himself to call the attention of the people of the United States to one of those unpalatable truths which both he and Mr. Wendell Willkie had avoided during the campaign. Even so, he hastened to reassure his audience that the British sought from them only the implements of war. They asked no expeditionary force and the Administration had no intention of sending one. "You can, therefore, nail any talk about sending armies to Europe as a deliberate untruth."

Turning from the foreign to the home front, Mr. Roosevelt used the same technique in appraising requirements to fulfill the policy of all-out aid to Great Britain and its fighting allies. Just as there were dangerous risks inherent in that policy, so great sacrifices must attend the domestic production effort. He paid tribute to the splendid coöperation which had thus far characterized the relationships of the Government, industry and labor. The results were nothing to be ashamed of, but they were not enough. "We must have more ships, more guns, more planes—more of everything." We could have them only if we discarded the notion of "business as usual." The job couldn't be done merely by superimposing national defense requirements on existing production facilities. While the President coated this pill with the assurance that the Government proposed to do its best to protect the economic well-being of its citizens during the emergency, he did warn the nation that labor could not interrupt defense production by strikes. Nor could management block progress through fear of the consequences of "surplus plant capacity."

The fireside chat drew to its conclusion with an eloquent appeal to all Americans, to plant owners, managers, workers, and government employees, to devote themselves wholeheartedly to the great tasks that lay ahead:

We must be the great arsenal of democracy. For us this is an emergency as serious as war itself. We must apply ourselves to our task with the same resolution, the same sense of urgency, the same spirit of patriotism and sacrifice as we would show were we at war. . . .

I believe that the Axis powers are not going to win this war. I base that belief on the latest and best information. . . .

I call upon our people with absolute confidence that our common cause will greatly succeed.[76]

The response to the fireside chat of December 29, 1940, both at home and abroad, far surpassed the expectations of the President. The messages which presently poured into the White House were running, according to the President's secretary, Mr. Stephen Early, 100 to 1 in approval. It was the greatest response Mr. Roosevelt had ever had to any speech, and he was "immensely pleased."[77]

The Republican *New York Herald Tribune* described the fireside chat as one of the greatest speeches of the President's career, predicting that if he translated into action the leadership he had displayed, he would find the people of the United States unanimous in support of every measure he took. According to the *Christian Science Monitor,* "by ten o'clock on the night of December 29 . . . all the world knew that uncertainty no longer ruled. For President Roosevelt's fireside chat had clarified and crystallized America's choice, a choice really made long ago." "Candor," wrote Arthur Krock, "emerging at last from the camouflage of the campaign, has been received with a calmness which adds to the regret that this approach was delayed at the expense of six months of vital preparation. . . . Everyone seemed relieved to have had clearly posed an issue that has been forming since Munich."[78]

[76] *Public Papers and Addresses,* IX (1940), 633 ff. On the speech, see Sherwood: *Roosevelt and Hopkins,* 227 ff., and Rauch: *Roosevelt from Munich to Pearl Harbor,* 296-300.

[77] *The New York Times,* December 30, 31, 1940, contains a wide coverage of the national reactions to the speech.

[78] The *New York Herald Tribune,* December 30; *Christian Science Monitor,* December 30; *The New York Times,* December 31, 1940.

Certainly the moderation and firmness of the President's words brought their reward and proved the sagacity of his decision not to mock or castigate the isolationists. A number of them, including Congressman Fish and Senator Capper, expressed approval of the fireside chat.[79] Although the dyed-in-the-wool variety reacted with anger and scorn, it was not difficult to detect in their attacks the admission that the President's appeal had been extraordinarily successful. Norman Thomas thought it hard to imagine a more "clever" performance. To Senator Wheeler, the whole speech was "satanically clever propaganda" designed to appeal to "warmongers," "sordid romanticists," and "reckless adventurers," with the object of leading the country into war. While the eclipse of the isolationists was only temporary, Senator Wheeler's full-dress reply to the President over the radio, on the evening following the fireside chat, revealed once again the poverty of the isolationist resources for constructing a positive program. While rich in invective, Wheeler had nothing to offer as a substitute for the President's program except the chimera of a negotiated peace.[80]

Equally plain was the essentially negative character of the ties which united the heterogeneous groups opposing the Administration's foreign policy. Tagging along at the end of a motley procession which included honest pacifists, intellectual continentalists, constitutionalists, professional Anglophobes, and a few convinced pro-Nazis was one group more influential than its small numbers would indicate. This was the Communist Party, U.S.A. Far more effectively than the Bundists or other exotic specimens in the isolationist ranks, its disciplined leaders had learned the technique of using unlikely allies. The *Daily Worker* denounced the President's "bogey-man act," ridiculed the idea that for the "common people" there was any difference between the aims of Hitler and those of American bankers, and invited everyone to join its giant antiwar demonstration to be staged in Washington over the coming week end.[81]

Overseas reaction to the President's speech betrayed no startling departure from normal. Widespread enthusiasm in Britain was tempered by sober realization of the lateness of the hour and of the immense difficulties which faced the United States as it geared itself to achieve in time the necessary production goals.[82] The night on which the President spoke his momentous words had been selected by the Nazis for the devastating fire-bombing of the City of London. The sufferings of its citizens, endured with such surpassing fortitude, was somewhat lightened by the certainty that American indignation would be translated into enthusiasm for Mr. Roosevelt's program.

Official Axis comment was guarded, perhaps as a result of the boomer-

[79] *The New York Times,* December 30, 1940.
[80] *Vital Speeches,* VII, 203 ff.; Cf. D. F. Fleming: "Roosevelt's Call to Arms" (*Events,* February 1941, pp. 98 ff.).
[81] December 31, 1940.
[82] Samples printed in the *Chicago Daily News,* December 31, 1940. For Mr. Churchill's message to the President, see *Their Finest Hour,* 573.

anging of the previous week's effort. This time the Foreign Office spokesman confined himself to the Delphic utterance that the Roosevelt speech constituted such a momentous challenge that "political circles" would be very surprised if a direct and comprehensive reply were not made shortly.

Perhaps the most significant European reaction was also the most circumspect. The neutral and nonbelligerent capitals had little to say, but the mere publication of the speech in the press of Vichy, Madrid, Lisbon, and Moscow was momentous. The fundamental attitude of these Governments toward the war was influenced in the highest degree by their estimate of American intentions and capabilities. The latter might conceivably still be a matter for argument, but after December 29, 1940, America's intention to prevent an Axis victory over Britain was sufficiently clear.[83]

Mr. Roosevelt had again reluctantly gambled on his qualities of leadership and again had won. It is only natural, therefore, that at the time and ever since, voices should have been raised in regret that he was not willing to play for even higher stakes—for popular support of whatever steps might prove necessary if the Arsenal of Democracy proved inadequate to defeat the Axis. It is still too early to pass judgment on an issue which leads directly into the still unexplored recesses of an elusive mind. Suffice it to observe that the Arsenal of Democracy address at least stands as an authentic expression of the President's approach to the problem of political leadership. In it Mr. Roosevelt told the American people just as much and no more than he calculated was safe to tell them without jeopardizing the hearty support he required of them. If his words did not convey all the simplicity and grandeur of Mr. Churchill's similar demands upon the British people, they nevertheless testify to the President's keen insight into the mind of the American people—still only spectators in the somber arena of conflict. As an effort to reconcile the facts of his position as the elected leader of an uncertain nation with his constitutional responsibility for safeguarding that nation's security, the Arsenal of Democracy speech is still, in retrospect, entitled to the high repute it achieved at the moment it was delivered.

Long challenged to tell his fellow citizens the course he had charted, the President had at last accepted that challenge and had outlined the steps he believed the American people should take—not every step, for the President himself probably did not know every step—but at least the next steps. If they now took them, they would mark the most significant advance made since the outbreak of hostilities. Prior to the end of 1940 the American people had committed themselves to aiding the democracies by all means short of war. They were being asked in 1941 to commit themselves to aiding the democracies even at the risk of war. The issue, as Lord Lothian had said, now depended on them. If the initial response to the fireside chat was a true index of public sentiment, the result was scarcely in doubt.

[83] *Bulletin of International News,* XVIII (1941), 39, 44, 51, 52.

CHAPTER IX

Underwriting Victory: Lend-Lease

1. THE STATE OF THE UNION, JANUARY 1, 1941

On January 6, 1941, it was the President's solemn duty to send to the Congress his annual message on the State of the Union. Still uplifted by the surging response of the American people to his recent fireside chat, the President on this occasion repeated and even augmented the note of forcefulness which had resounded so impressively the week before. His annual message, said the Chief Executive, was "unique in our history," for the reason that the American past offered no precedent for the peril which at this hour confronted the Republic. After summarizing what the downfall of the democratic nations would mean to the United States, the President, discharging his constitutional obligations, reported to the Legislature that unhappily "the future and the safety of our country are overwhelmingly involved in events far beyond our borders."[1]

Proceeding to a brisk but not vindictive attack on those who belittled the peril or urged acceptance of a "dictator's peace," Mr. Roosevelt presented in capsule form the foreign policy for which the Administration believed it now had a mandate. "Our national policy," said Mr. Roosevelt, "is this:

First, by an impressive expression of the public will and without regard to partisanship, we are committed to all-inclusive national defense.

Second, by an impressive expression of the public will and without regard to partisanship, we are committed to full support of all those resolute peoples, everywhere, who are resisting aggression and are thereby keeping war away from our Hemisphere. By this support, we express our determination that the democratic cause shall prevail; and we strengthen the defense and the security of our own nation.

Third, by an impressive expression of the public will and without regard to partisanship, we are committed to the proposition that principles of morality and considerations for our own security will never permit us to acquiesce in a peace dictated

[1] *Public Papers and Addresses*, IX (1940), 663 ff.

by aggressors and sponsored by appeasers. We know that enduring peace cannot be bought at the cost of other people's freedom.

It was the President's judgment that the response of the American people to his words and actions, particularly since the November election, amounted to endorsement of a program which now called for nothing short of a declaration of economic warfare on the Axis. At the conclusion of several passages devoted to concrete measures, past and future, designed to carry out this program, the President even alluded to the dire possibility that economic warfare alone might not suffice to ensure success. The nations at war with aggression needed not man power, but "billions of dollars worth of weapons." To give them these was not an act of war "even if a dictator should unilaterally proclaim it so to be." In any case, concluded the President, the risk was going to be taken: "The happiness of future generations of Americans may well depend upon how effective and how immediate we can make our aid felt. No one can tell the exact character of the emergency situations that we may be called upon to meet. The Nation's hands must not be tied when the Nation's life is in danger."

The millions who heard these words might still entertain doubts as to whether and when Mr. Roosevelt thought it might become necessary for America to resort to war in order to carry through the national policy he enunciated. The President refrained from attempting to resolve such doubts. He had, however, under circumstances of traditional significance, affirmed his belief in the irreconcilable character of the conflict in Europe and his renewed conviction of America's obligation to assure the ultimate triumph of the democratic cause. With an eye to isolationist critics who carped at the failure of the democracies to define their cause, Mr. Roosevelt, again in capsule form, produced the formula which was destined to become the symbol of the aims of the warring democracies:

In the future days, which we seek to make secure, we look forward to a world founded upon four essential human freedoms.

The first is freedom of speech and expression—everywhere in the world.

The second is freedom of every person to worship God in his own way—everywhere in the world.

The third is freedom from want—which, translated into world terms, means economic understandings which will secure to every nation a healthy peacetime life for its inhabitants—everywhere in the world.

The fourth is freedom from fear—which, translated into world terms, means a world-wide reduction of armaments to such a point and in such a thorough fashion that no nation will be in a position to commit an act of physical aggression against any neighbor—anywhere in the world.[2]

If the address on the State of the Union was less enthusiastically received

[2] *Public Papers and Addresses,* IX (1940), 672.

than the fireside chat, the discrepancy is to be explained by the simple proximity of date of two closely related speeches, not to mention the President's further message accompanying the 1942 budget, which called for seventeen and a half billions of expenditures, 60 percent for national defense. As 1941 opened, therefore, there was much to reassure the President that the people would follow him on the course he had now outlined to them with reasonable clarity. Certainly this was the verdict of the public opinion polls. Whereas prior to the November election the country seemed evenly divided on whether to keep out of the war or assist Britain to win even at the risk of involvement, by mid-January those professing to favor the latter alternative had reached some 70 percent.[3]

On the other hand, the caution and hedging which alternated with candor and defiance in the President's statements on foreign policy were not without political justification. When confronted in the opinion polls with the direct question whether to enter the war now, a very large majority were still opposed. As Arthur Krock analyzed the state of public opinion at this precise moment, the American people, for all their growing comprehension of their stake in the war, "had not yet apparently abandoned their resolution neither to be pushed nor to descend into it, if they can still safely keep their footing on the rim."[4]

The true measure of popular response to the President's appraisals and appeals at the beginning of the new year would have to await the test of time. He had presented the issues to the Congress and the people with a frankness and force in marked contrast to the disingenuousness which had characterized many of his campaign speeches on foreign policy. He had posed the great question for 1941: Would the American people follow him in a program dedicated to the defeat of the aggressor states even at the risk of war? The first really satisfactory answer to that question came only after two months of nationwide debate on the first great step in the Administration's 1941 program: Lend-Lease.

2. DRAFTING THE LEND-LEASE BILL: H.R. 1776

The President had lost no time in translating the Lend-Lease scheme into legislative form. Realizing that Mr. Morgenthau's knowledge of Britain's financial position was both profound and sympathetic, he had assigned the task of drafting legislation to the Treasury Department. On January 2, 1941, actual work on the Lend-Lease bill began at a meeting called by Secretary Morgenthau and attended by the representatives of the British Purchasing Mission, as well as by the Treasury's legal advisers, Edward H. Foley and Oscar Cox, who thenceforth bore the brunt of the drafting. As the

[3] The Budget Message is printed in *Public Papers and Addresses,* IX (1940), 651 ff. The record of the public opinion polls for January, 1941, may be found in *Public Opinion Quarterly,* June, 1941, 320 ff.

[4] *The New York Times Sunday Magazine,* January 12, 1941.

Secretary enlarged upon the President's intentions, it developed that Messrs. Foley and Cox had already in mind a tentative plan. They suggested that a precedent and model existed in the Pittman-Bloom Act of June 15, 1940, authorizing the Secretaries of War and of the Navy to sell to the Latin American Republics certain types of war materials constructed in arsenals or shipyards under War or Navy jurisdiction. Why not, they asked, extend this statute to meet the present need?[5]

Mr. Morgenthau's response established at once that the forthcoming battle was to take place on a plane of principle. While, said the Secretary, the President had not yet thought through the form of the legislation, he wanted a virtually free hand in the allocation of American defense production. Moreover, he did not wish to obtain the needed authority by virtue of specious devices or indirection. Mr. Morgenthau quoted him as saying: "We don't want to fool the public; we want to do this thing right out and out." The President apparently deemed the issue too vital for the employment of subterfuges and intended that all questions springing from the concept of lend and lease should be hammered out in open debate.[6]

The broad outlines of the authority sought by the President were not difficult to discern. In Mr. Morgenthau's words, he was "groping for legislation which would give him a free hand to have the Army and Navy place orders for the material that they need, and adding to these orders as much more of a particular commodity as they think we will be called upon to lend to England, or to China, or to Greece." In the interests of efficiency and speed Mr. Roosevelt wanted blanket discretion, so that defense products could be apportioned without continuous reference to Congress and without the risk of time-consuming controversy. As for eventual repayment, the President likewise sought authority to determine the recompense. The British, said Mr. Morgenthau, "would just have to trust Mr. Roosevelt" on this score. So, for that matter, would the American people. These questions of delegating authority to the Executive to allot production and to determine compensation subsequently occasioned almost as hot a debate as did the issue of increased risk of war for the United States. As a matter of tactics as well as of principle, the Secretary of the Treasury instructed his subordinates to make the bill as broad as possible, on the assumption that Congress would certainly pare it anyway.[7]

The Treasury lawyers, Messrs. Foley and Cox, at once plunged into the

[5] *Morgenthau Diaries (MS.)*, January 2, 1941 (Vol. 344, pp. 67 ff.); H. Morgenthau, Jr.: "The Morgenthau Diaries," Part IV, "The Story Behind Lend-Lease" (*Collier's Magazine*, October 18, 1947). Cf. Hull: *Memoirs*, I, 873 ff., and Edward R. Stettinius, Jr.: *Lend-Lease: Weapon for Victory* (New York, 1944), 67 ff.; Robert E. Sherwood: *Roosevelt and Hopkins* (New York, 1948), 228; Basil Rauch: *Roosevelt, from Munich to Pearl Harbor* (New York, 1950), 289 ff.

[6] *Morgenthau Diaries (MS.)*, January 2, 1941 (Vol. 344, pp. 67 ff.).

[7] *Morgenthau Diaries (MS.)*, January 2, 3, 1941 (Vol. 344, pp. 67 ff., 149 ff., 237 ff., and 261).

work of drafting a joint resolution along the lines of the Secretary's instructions, and also to devise an interim plan which would permit the British to resume placing orders in the United States pending the passage of the Lend-Lease bill. By midnight of January 2 they had finished a first draft in the form of an amendment to the Pittman-Bloom Act. Thereafter they conferred with Secretary Stimson; Mr. Green Hackworth of the State Department; Speaker Rayburn and his Legislative Counsel, Mr. Beaman; Justice Frankfurter; Mr. Benjamin V. Cohen; and others. Almost all of them put in an oar. The War Department had already prepared a draft of its own, chiefly the handiwork of Mr. John J. McCloy.[8] The criticisms of Messrs. Frankfurter and Cohen were particularly significant. Cohen suggested that the British be permitted to repair and outfit their ships in American navy yards. Frankfurter advised against particularization of the powers to be granted the President and against specification of the countries to receive Lend-Lease aid. The Justice also proposed the eventual title of the bill.[9]

By January 6 the draft resolution was ready for submission to the President. At this juncture the belligerent countries which were to receive aid were still specified. Mr. Foley had also insisted upon making "darn sure" that certain portions of the neutrality legislation would be repealed by the new law, though without specifying precisely which provisions.[10]

The need for speed had meanwhile been reëmphasized by the receipt of a further message to the President from Mr. Churchill. Accepting Mr. Roosevelt's offer to send an American warship to bring to the United States from South Africa gold to the value of thirty million pounds sterling, the Prime Minister solemnly assured the President of his willingness to reveal his country's total assets as well as its total requirements:

> We shall be entirely ready for our part to lay bare to you all our resources and liabilities around the world, and we shall seek no more help than the common cause demands. We naturally wish to feel sure that the powers with which you propose to arm yourself will be sufficiently wide to deal with these larger matters, subject to all proper considerations. Without prompt and effective solution of these problems Hitlerism cannot be extirpated from Europe, Africa and Asia.[11]

What particularly worried the Prime Minister at this point was ways and means by which Britain could pay for orders already placed or to be placed during the interval prior to the passage of the new legislation. "It is not only

[8] Watson: *Chief of Staff: Prewar Plans and Preparations,* 323.

[9] *Morgenthau Diaries (MS.),* January 2-7, 1941 (Vol. 344, pp. 149 ff.). The growing influence of Justice Frankfurter in the sphere of foreign policy is noted in the *Moffat Diary (MS.),* January 31, March 31, 1941.

[10] "The Morgenthau Diaries" (*Collier's Magazine,* October 18, 1947); *Stimson Diary (MS.),* January 4, 1941.

[11] Tel. from Churchill to the President, December 31, 1940 (*Morgenthau Diaries, MS.,* January 2, 1941, Vol. 344, pp. 262 ff.); printed in full in Churchill: *Their Finest Hour,* 374-75.

a question," he wrote, "of total amounts, but of how we are to live through a period which may perhaps extend to February 15th. . . ."

Spurred on by Mr. Churchill's anxiety, Messrs. Morgenthau, Foley and Cox completed a revision of the bill on January 7, incorporating the President's comments of the previous day. The revised draft was then taken to Mr. Hull's office for another going over. The Secretary of State had two important criticisms. He thought it unwise to specify the countries to receive aid, possibly having in mind the future problem of the Soviet Union. Furthermore, like Mr. Stimson, he believed that the legislation should be submitted to the Congress as an independent measure rather than in the form of an amendment to the Pittman-Bloom Act, a device by which its authors had hoped to steer the bill into Congressional committees likely to be coöperative. It was decided to change the form, but to retain the list of the countries to receive aid. General approval was then given to the draft.[12]

As the draft of the bill was thus approaching its final form, the problem of legislative tactics increasingly claimed the attention of its sponsors. Secretaries Hull and Morgenthau, agreeing that Vice President Garner had permitted the Senate Foreign Relations Committee to be "packed" with isolationists, at first hoped to steer the bill into some other Senate committee, perhaps Finance. Secretary Stimson, who had already warned the President against sending the measure to Foreign Relations, recommended the Appropriations Committee, "where it would not be debated all winter." Mr. Roosevelt himself was anxious that the bill should at least have the "look" of originating in the House, though subsequently he recommended that it be introduced simultaneously in both houses. A final strategy conference, held on January 8 in Mr. Hull's office, led to the decision, subject to Speaker Rayburn's approval, to "kick" the bill into the House Military Affairs Committee. At the same meeting, attended by Congressmen McCormack and Rayburn, and Senators Barkley and Harrison, it was finally decided to drop mention of particular recipients, and to alter the title as suggested by Justice Frankfurter: "To Promote the Defense of the United States and for Other Purposes."[13]

Final clearance was accorded the projected bill on January 9 at a large White House conference following a Cabinet meeting. Senators Barkley, Connally, Harrison and George; Representatives Rayburn, McCormack, Bloom and Luther Johnson were present, together with the members of the Cabinet who had chiefly sponsored the bill, and Mr. Knudsen. Secretary Morgenthau had urged the President to invite the Congressmen, so that they might feel personal responsibility for the fate of the measure. On this

---

[12] *Morgenthau Diaries (MS.)*, January 7, 1941 (Vol. 344, pp. 91 ff.); *Stimson Diary (MS.)*, January 7, 1941; "The Morgenthau Diaries" (*Collier's,* October 18, 1947).

[13] *Morgenthau Diaries (MS.)*, January 3, 6, 7, 8, 1941 (Vol. 344, pp. 149 ff.; Vol. 345, pp. 89 ff., 265; Vol. 346, pp. 1 ff.).

occasion Mr. Roosevelt again stressed the necessity for speed, as well as his desire that the amount to be made available for foreign aid remain unspecified. Furthermore, he did not wish his power to lease and lend restricted to new matériel. Finally, he outlined the course to be taken to assist the British during the interval between the bill's introduction and its enactment, within which period the British would be unable to place new orders. Plant expansion was to begin immediately, financed in part by the Federal Loan Agency. By reshuffling current appropriations for the Army and Navy, continued the President, orders over and above their immediate needs could be placed. When the Lend-Lease bill became law, these products could be turned over to the British, Greeks or Chinese. Since this plan for interim aid followed an outline suggested earlier by Mr. Morgenthau and concurred in by Messrs. Stimson, Knox, Knudsen, Hillman and Jesse Jones, the President encountered no opposition.[14]

The Congressional leaders, however, did deal a blow to the Administration's hope of circumventing the Senate Foreign Relations Committee. Senator Barkley acknowledged that committee's hostility and the likelihood of delay, but he feared grave consequences if the majority leaders tried to force the bill artificially into the Military Affairs or some other committee. Speaker Rayburn and his associates had likewise concluded that in the House the bill would have to go to the Committee on Foreign Affairs. While there were no Republican members of Congress present on the occasion, despite the urging of Congressman Wadsworth that the President consult them, it developed that the House Minority Leader, Congressman Joseph Martin of Massachusetts, believed that the Republicans would coöperate provided the minority members of the committee were permitted full freedom to question Cabinet witnesses. To eliminate controversy over committee jurisdiction, it was finally decided that the majority leaders, rather than the committee chairmen, should introduce the bill—an unusual procedure. The President likewise signified his willingness, at the urging of Senator Barkley, to discuss the bill with influential Republicans who might be expected to favor its purposes—perhaps Senators Austin of Vermont and White of Maine, but not "Ham" Fish.[15]

The Lend-Lease bill was accordingly introduced simultaneously in both Houses on January 10, 1941, by Congressman McCormack and Senator Barkley. Outspoken criticism of H.R. 1776, as it was so happily designated, followed at once. It came almost entirely from isolationist Republicans, though a sprinkling of conservative Democrats, who usually supported the Administration's foreign policy, also questioned the wisdom of giving such wide authority to the Chief Executive. The bill "to destroy the Republic"

[14] "The Morgenthau Diaries" (*Collier's,* October 18, 1947); *Industrial Mobilization for War* (Washington, 1947), I, 123; *Morgenthau Diaries (MS.),* January 7, 1941 (Vol. 345, p. 265).
[15] *Morgenthau Diaries (MS.),* January 8, 9, 13, 1941 (Vol. 346, pp. 39 and 222 ff.; Vol. 347, pp. 158 ff.); *Stimson Diary (MS.),* January 10, 1941.

was bitterly denounced by the *Chicago Tribune,* which, however, was even at this point pessimistic about the likelihood of its defeat. Senator Wheeler descended to notable depths in stamping H.R. 1776 as a "triple-A foreign policy; it will plough under every fourth American boy." His was the only criticism which provoked a response from the President. Mr. Roosevelt promptly branded it for history as "the rottenest thing that has been said in public life in my generation."[16]

Republican reaction ranged all the way from the violent denunciation of Hiram Johnson and Hamilton Fish through the more reasoned objections of Alfred Landon to the endorsements—with various qualifications—of Congressman Wadsworth, Senator Austin, and Wendell Willkie. The latter's support had been foreshadowed a few days earlier when he warned his party that if it blindly opposed the bill and presented itself to the American people as the isolationist party, it would "never again gain control of the American Government." Encouraged by his good friend, Secretary Stimson, Mr. Willkie not only endorsed the bill, with mild reservations, on January 11, but three days later announced his plan to visit England for a firsthand view of the situation. This was heartening news to an Administration which was already committed to keeping friction at a minimum by itself adopting a conciliatory attitude. The President made his first public bid for Congressional collaboration at his press conference on January 10. He called for swift action, but left the method for providing it up to the Congress. He disclaimed any sinister desire for the power conferred by the bill, and denied that its provisions would nullify the neutrality laws and the Johnson Act. At his next conference he simply declined to comment further on the resolution. It was now in the hands of the Congress and the people.[17]

At this stage the British Government faced what seemed to be a Hobson's choice. In dire straits, it was now obliged to lay bare to the United States Government the most confidential information on the Empire's resources, an act as unprecedented as the peril which compelled it. Mr. Churchill virtually put his country at the mercy of Mr. Roosevelt. British representatives took part in the preliminary conferences to draft H.R. 1776. Mr. Arthur Purvis, in whom Secretary Morgenthau had such deserved confidence, and the Financial Counselor of the British Embassy, Mr. Puisent, submitted to the Treasury detailed schedules of British requirements and assets. Prime Minister Churchill was fulfilling his promise, and the available stocks of gold, of dollar exchange, and of readily marketable securities appeared increasingly inadequate in the face of Britain's requirements.[18]

Understandably, the British experienced the greatest difficulty in provid-

[16] Hinton in *The New York Times,* January 12, 1941; Kluckhohn in *The New York Times,* January 15, 1941; Dana Fleming: "Roosevelt's Call to Arms" (*Events,* February, 1941); Rauch: *Roosevelt, from Munich to Pearl Harbor,* 304 ff.

[17] *Stimson Diary (MS.),* January 8, 11, 13; Turner Catledge and Arthur Krock, in *The New York Times,* January 11, 12, 15, 1941.

[18] *Industrial Mobilization for War,* I, 53, 122 ff.; Forrest Davis and Ernest K. Lind-

ing full and accurate figures on their direct investments, as well as a quite reasonable reluctance to sell hastily what they regarded as a foundation of Britain's financial structure. For weeks, before and after H.R. 1776 was introduced, Mr. Morgenthau prodded them to deplete their holdings farther, on the perhaps shortsighted principle that the British should exhaust their own resources before receiving American aid. Early in January Sir Frederick Phillips obtained permission from London to sell direct British investments in the United States, with the result that weekly sales of British securities were stepped up from approximately $2,000,000 to $10,000,000. Even so, Mr. Morgenthau was not wholly satisfied that the British were doing all they could justifiably be expected to do. Subsequently, therefore, Sir Edward Peacock of the Bank of England was sent to this country to expedite the sale of such British-controlled enterprises as the American Viscose Company.[19]

Secretary Morgenthau and his Treasury associates remained convinced that H.R. 1776 would fail of enactment unless the entire dismal picture of Britain's financial position were revealed to the Congressional committees and, thus, to the world. Mr. Roosevelt himself was dubious of the wisdom of so complete an exposé, but Treasury strategists insisted that the first question in Congress would be: "How much have they got?" The effect of the proposed disclosure on public opinion both in Great Britain and the United States was anxiously, painfully weighed. Would these facts discourage the American people from helping Britain? Worse, would they discourage the British people from helping themselves? Mr. Morgenthau, sick at heart over this dilemma, was nevertheless sure that they would not. Honestly informed of Britain's true condition, Congress would provide for its survival at whatever cost. Though the responsibility for making these revelations weighed heavily upon the Secretary of the Treasury, he consoled himself with the argument that to disguise the facts would be dangerous. Hitler probably knew the worst anyway. The British eventually resigned themselves to the disclosure and placed themselves in the Secretary's hands. Sir Frederick Phillips warned him, however, that if the legislation were defeated after such vital information had been broadcast, the British would be "through."[20]

As finally revealed, the British picture was so dark as probably to have made inevitable a degree of incredulity even within the Cabinet. The principal doubts revolved around the problem of total imperial holdings outside the United States. These were estimated to be in the neighborhood of $10,000,000,000, but only a portion of them could be speedily realized. The

ley: *How War Came* (New York, 1942), 111; *Morgenthau Diaries* (*MS.*), January 2, 7, 8, 1941 (Vol. 344, pp. 67 ff.; Vol. 345, pp. 265 ff.; Vol. 346, pp. 51 ff.).

[19] *Morgenthau Diaries* (*MS.*), January 14, 1941 (Vol. 347, pp. 233 ff.); Davis and Lindley: *How War Came*, footnote, p. 113; *Stimson Diary* (*MS.*), January 14; W. H. Hancock and M. M. Gowing: *British War Economy* (London, 1949), 233 ff.; Churchill: *Their Finest Hour*, 573.

[20] *Morgenthau Diaries* (*MS.*), January 13, 1941 (Vol. 347, pp. 158 ff.).

British were by no means bankrupt; they were, however, rapidly running out of United States exchange. Vice President Garner refused to admit the distinction, and it required all of Sir Frederick Phillips's powers of persuasion to convince even the well-disposed Secretary Knox that his Government was proposing to liquidate all possible assets. Neither the President nor the Secretary of the Treasury succeeded in disabusing Mr. Hull of a fixed idea that Britain had actually some $18,000,000,000 worth of assets. It seemed, Mr. Morgenthau complained, that no one outside the Treasury believed the British figures.[21]

Although all four were basically agreed that Britain should use every available dollar to pay for what she required, Secretaries Stimson and Morgenthau split with Hull and Knox on the issue whether or not the British should be compelled to put up collateral for materials lend-leased. There was something to be said on both sides. Mr. Hull emphatically believed it would be a mistake to convey the impression that Britain was at the end of its resources. As an earnest of willingness to do its share, let it offer to put up such collateral as was required! Secretary Knox, agreeing, felt that otherwise the American public would think it had been "out-traded." It was certain, he added, that Congress would expect Lend-Lease to be on a "banking basis."

Stimson and Morgenthau disagreed. The issue, they insisted, was too critical to permit a "sharp trade." As it appeared to the Secretary of War, "we were not paying the money to Great Britain because we were investing, but we were paying it to her to secure a certain military advantage which she gave us by keeping up her defense." In the role of "pawnbroker" the United States would gradually take away everything which was making it worth while for the British to fight on. Finally, Mr. Stimson added prophetically, if the United States demanded the last pound of flesh, the postwar position of a victorious Britain would present problems scarcely susceptible of solution. Secretary Hull nevertheless thought Congress would insist upon guarantees and collateral, while Mr. Morgenthau held that Congress wouldn't give a "damn" for them.[22]

The President's views on these issues, which he proposed to transmit to Mr. Churchill in response to the latter's message of January 2, were in between those of his advisers. Mr. Roosevelt believed the total value of British assets in the United States amounted to about a billion and a half dollars, of which perhaps a billion could be liquidated. Whatever assets Britain possessed in countries other than the United States he realized would have to be used

[21] *Morgenthau Diaries* (*MS.*), January 8 and 13, 1941 (Vol. 346, pp. 51 ff.; Vol. 347, pp. 7 ff.); Hull: *Memoirs*, II, 923 ff.; *Stimson Diary* (*MS.*), January 13; "The Morgenthau Diaries" (*Collier's*, October 18, 1947). The President's views were given in a memo to Mr. Hull dated January 11, 1941 (*Roosevelt Papers*: Secretary's File, Box 78), now printed in *F.D.R.: His Personal Letters*, II, 1103-5.

[22] *Morgenthau Diaries* (*MS.*), January 13, 14, 1941 (Vol. 347, pp. 7 ff. and 233 ff.); *Stimson Diary* (*MS.*), same dates; Hull: *Memoirs*, II, 923.

to pay for purchases in those countries. On the other hand, he did agree with Mr. Hull that the British ought to put up some security for future payments, if for no other reason than to assist in getting Lend-Lease through. He even speculated on the possibility that such security might consist of sovereignty over certain British colonies in this hemisphere, doubtful though he remained whether these colonies would prove anything but a liability. "If we can get our naval bases," he wrote to Mr. Hull, "why, for example, should we buy with them two million headaches, consisting of that number of human beings who would be a drag on this country?"[23]

Congress itself was about to settle all these arguments concerning British collateral and, incidentally, to match what has been aptly described as an Administration "fertile of suggestions to the British for stripping themselves bare."[24]

3. CONGRESSIONAL HEARINGS

The House Committee on Foreign Affairs, with Congressman Sol Bloom in the chair, began hearings on H.R. 1776 on January 15, 1941. At the personal request of the President and at the urging of Secretary Morgenthau, Mr. Hull reluctantly assumed executive leadership of the fight for its passage. The Secretary of State felt strongly that since the Treasury had so far taken the lead and since his own influence had counted for so little, Mr. Morgenthau should appear as the chief sponsor of H.R. 1776. The President and Morgenthau, however, argued that presentation of the bill as a strategic and political instrument, as well as a financial measure, afforded it the best chance of speedy passage. Messrs. Hull, Morgenthau, Stimson and Knox had all previously agreed on how to divide discussion of the most important facets of the bill. Hull, appearing first, would discuss the diplomatic and international aspects. Morgenthau would confine himself rigidly to financial statements, while Stimson and Knox would devote their testimony to the military and strategic factors in favor of the legislation.[25]

For all his private misgivings and irritation, Secretary Hull proved a convincing opening witness. In a prepared statement, some preliminary portions of which had been written by the President, he announced that he would discuss "the controlling facts relating to the manner in which the dangers that now confront this hemisphere, and therefore this Nation, have arisen,

[23] Memo of the President to Secretary Hull, January 11, 1941 (*Roosevelt Papers:* Secretary's File, Box 78), now printed in *F.D.R.: His Personal Letters*, II, 1103-5. It may be noted that the President was more optimistic about the practical value of certain British islands in the Pacific, but even these, he reflected, would be difficult to defend against Japan.

[24] Hancock and Gowing: *British War Economy*, 233.

[25] Hull: *Memoirs*, II, 923. For Mr. Hull's alleged views we have also used *Moffat Diary* (*MS.*), January 31, 1941; "The Morgenthau Diaries" (*Collier's*, October 18, 1947); *Morgenthau Diaries* (*MS.*), January 13, 1941 (Vol. 347, pp. 7 ff.). Hull gave sufficient vent to his feelings to disclaim at several points in his testimony knowledge of answers, since "the bill was prepared in the Treasury."

and the circumstances which render imperative all possible speed in preparation for meeting these dangers." He then outlined the policies which the United States had long supported in the interests of peace and world order, and retraced the aggressive steps of Japan, Italy, and Germany. As for America's present dilemma, affirmed the Secretary of State:

. . . it has become increasingly apparent that mankind is today face to face, not with regional wars or isolated conflicts, but with an organized, ruthless and implacable movement of steadily expanding conquest. We are in the presence of forces which are not restrained by considerations of law or principles of morality; which have fixed no limits for this program of conquest; which have spread over large areas on land and are desperately struggling now to seize control of the oceans as an essential means of achieving and maintaining their conquest of the other continents.

The Secretary expounded the importance of continued Anglo-American control of the Atlantic and Pacific Oceans: "The most serious question today for this country is whether the control of the high seas shall pass into the hands of the powers bent on a program of unlimited conquest. It is in this light, above all, that we should order our present-day thinking and action with respect to the amount of material assistance which our country is prepared to furnish Great Britain."[26]

Hostile committee members, particularly the arch-Anglophobe, Mr. Tinkham of Massachusetts, baited Mr. Hull on the increased possibility of war which might result from passage of the bill. The Secretary answered succinctly: "I want you to know that in my view there is danger in either direction." On the whole, however, enactment of Lend-Lease was "the safest course."

Against charges that the bill was a violation of neutrality and contrary to international law, the Secretary vigorously invoked the right of self-defense and the demands of common sense. Germany and Italy had flaunted their contempt for all accepted concepts of law and neutrality and therefore we couldn't let such considerations "chloroform us into a policy of inactivity in the way of preparing our national defense." As had the President before him, the Secretary denied that the Lend-Lease law would cancel out the Johnson Act, for the reason that this law against loans to debt-defaulting nations did not "apply to this Government or to a public corporation." Several provisions of the Neutrality Act, however, would admittedly be superseded.[27]

The Secretary of State was followed by the Secretary of the Treasury, whose proposed course had likewise been cleared in advance by the President.

[26] *Hearings before the Committee on Foreign Affairs, House of Representatives, Seventy-seventh Congress, First Session on H. R. 1776* (Washington, Government Printing Office, 1941), 2 ff., hereinafter cited as *House Hearings. Hull: Memoirs,* II, 924; *Morgenthau Diaries (MS.),* January 15, 1941 (Vol. 348, p. 32).

[27] *House Hearings* (Hull testimony). Cf. Charles A. Beard: *President Roosevelt and the Coming of the War* (New Haven, 1948), p. 33.

Mr. Roosevelt, in a jocose mood, had telephoned Morgenthau not to be too definite, and above all not to let the country in for any of Great Britain's West Indian islands by way of compensation.[28] Aware that his long championship of aid to Britain made him a highly controversial figure, Mr. Morgenthau handled the Committee with kid gloves. He sat flanked by Treasury aides and spoke in an unemotional and businesslike fashion, scrupulously avoiding comment on foreign policy or other matters outside his own province. He spoke extemporaneously, but the mass of figures he submitted was difficult for the members to refute on the spot. In support of his argument he gave the Committee four separate statements on British finances: (1) a table of estimated Empire expenditures and receipts, excluding Canada, from January 1, 1941 to January 1, 1942; (2) a prospectus entitled *United Kingdom's Available Dollar Assets on January 1, 1941;* (3) a sketch, *Estimated Long-term Foreign Investments of the United Kingdom Outside the United States;* and (4) a comparison of British and American taxes.

In line with his firm decision, Mr. Morgenthau made no bones about stating the British position: "I have come here prepared to give you all the information which the British Treasury has furnished to me, and I give it to you with their consent. . . . And so far as I know, this is the first time in history that one government has put at the disposal of another figures of this nature." Naturally enough there was skepticism over the smallness of the figure on British dollar assets in the United States: $3,000,000,000. Mr. Morgenthau, however, denied that these assets amounted, as claimed, to $12,000,000,000, and again attempted to correct an error which derived chiefly from failure to distinguish between Britain's dollar and sterling assets. He went on to state that since the declaration of war the British Purchasing Commission had paid for and taken delivery of supplies amounting to $1,337,000,000. They had on order another $1,400,000,000 worth, for which they could probably pay in dollars if given the remainder of 1941 to do it. "But," warned the Secretary, "when it comes to finding the dollars to pay for anything like what they need in the future, they just have not got it." Nor did Morgenthau claim precise knowledge of the ultimate cost to the United States if Lend-Lease passed.[29]

After Mr. Morgenthau's testimony, Britain's dire predicament became public property, and, as Mr. Arthur Purvis commented, it was with "a sense of relief" that the British learned that the die had been cast. The

[28] *Morgenthau Diaries (MS.)*, January 15, 1941 (Vol. 348, p. 32).

[29] *House Hearings* (Morgenthau testimony), pp. 51 ff. On January 21, 1941, in a letter to Committee Chairman Bloom, Morgenthau revised his estimate of the British dollar position upward, the British Government having supplied more recent figures. These increased by $36,000,000 British dollar and gold assets available in the United States. In the course of the hearing, Secretary Morgenthau claimed justifiably that the bill was the product of many minds, and somewhat rashly made the point that it had not been initiated in the Treasury. For the use made of this to prove Administration efforts to conceal authorship, see Beard: *President Roosevelt and the Coming of the War*, 24-30. Cf. Rauch: *Roosevelt, from Munich to Pearl Harbor*, 305-6.

Chancellor of the Exchequer congratulated Mr. Morgenthau. It now lay beyond British powers to do more than await the verdict of the Congress on the gamble they had made in thus revealing Britain's weakness to the world.[30]

Fortunately Secretary Stimson, who followed Morgenthau on the witness stand, proved the most effective member of the Administration "team" though, as a "renegade" Republican and suspected interventionist, he was the target of especially heavy fire from the isolationist opposition. Proceeding, as did all other members of the team, on the axiom that the effective defense of the United States depended largely upon adequate and timely aid to Britain, the Secretary of War divided his argument into three major parts. In his prepared statement he dwelt upon the importance of the legislation in expediting American arms production, in establishing rational, orderly procurement of munitions for all countries concerned, and finally, in assuring America's own defense as well as that of friendly nations through the distribution of arms from the American arsenal. After pointing out that the situation was infinitely more serious than in 1917 because the arsenals of former Allied states were now producing for Germany, Stimson emphasized that under the bill the United States would become the sole purchasing agent for war materials and would be able to apportion them strategically. This centralization of control would eliminate competition among prospective purchasers and foster efficiency in the placing of contracts. Stimson believed that far from being a surrender of America's rights (of disposition) to other interests, the acquisition of discretion in purchasing would concentrate power and responsibility in American hands.[31]

Questioned closely and sometimes offensively by the Committee, Mr. Stimson sturdily defended the Administration's version of the bill. He opposed Congressman Fish's suggestion that Britain put up the West Indies as collateral, and refused to predict the sum needed to finance Lend-Lease. He denied that the President would abuse the authority delegated to him. He would certainly not give away the United States Navy. Experience had shown "that to defend ourselves against war or the danger of war it is necessary temporarily to concentrate our means of self-defense and make them more effective than we are accustomed to do in time of peace." If Congress wanted to specify the countries, it could do so, but this might mean constant amendment, since the situation changed so often. He emphasized that "a government or law which is so constructed that you cannot trust anybody will not survive the test of war." In response to a suggestion that a board be set up to determine what transfers of matériel should be made, Stimson paraphrased George Washington: If one man can perform a duty satisfactorily, the adequate performance of that duty is much im-

[30] *Morgenthau Diaries* (*MS.*), January 16, 1941 (Vol. 348, pp. 172 ff.).
[31] *House Hearings* (Stimson testimony), pp. 134 ff.

paired if it is delegated to two; and is still further impaired and sometimes rendered impossible if delegated to three or more.

As for United States unpreparedness, Mr. Stimson laid the blame nowhere. Although the nation's line of defense ran out into the middle of the Atlantic, America's Army was not yet as large as the Belgian forces in May, 1940. British orders, however, had stimulated United States production, and would continue to do so. In the end the United States would pick up "whatever lag we may have in their [the British] getting the first chance at the weapons, as contrasted with the situation we would have been in if they had not been getting munitions here."

The opposition tried constantly to induce Mr. Stimson to discuss inflammable issues not directly connected with the bill: escort of convoys, or the sending of United States vessels into the forbidden areas. He believed that none of these measures should be specifically prohibited by amendment, because "no one can foresee what situations might arise," and the country should not "tie its hands behind its back." He refused to acknowledge that the British position was without hope, and that it would eventually be necessary to send United States man power abroad. He warned, however, that he believed a crisis possible within the following three months, and urged speedy approval of the bill.[32]

Secretary Knox, who followed Stimson, pointed out that the British Fleet had served the United States as one half of a two-ocean navy. The United States had been successful in maintaining the Monroe Doctrine largely because the British Fleet had prevented aggression from Europe. Conversely, if that fleet were now destroyed, "we could not project our strength across two wide oceans." Continued British resistance was essential, therefore, to allow the United States time to prepare its defenses in both oceans. The Secretary concluded his statement by furnishing a table to emphasize the disturbing fact that if Britain's sea power were destroyed, the Axis navies would exceed the strength of the American.[33]

The questions asked of Knox were similar to those with which the Committee confronted Stimson. While less forthright, his answers generally paralleled those of his colleague. Knox admitted, as had Stimson, that the continental United States was not in immediate danger of attack. He also opposed amendments to the bill, as, for example, to forbid escort of convoys, on the familiar ground that it would be unwise to tie the Administration's hands in advance. On the other hand, the Committee was able to extract from him a statement opposing escort of convoys as an act of war and, more

[32] House Hearings (Stimson testimony); Beard: President Roosevelt and the Coming of the War, pp. 35-37; Bulletin of International News, XVIII (1), 120; Stimson and Bundy: On Active Service in Peace and War, 360-62. Stimson himself was dismayed and saddened by the ignorance and blind partisanship of most of the Republican members of the Committee: "It augured sadly for the country if they represent any very large percentage of our population" (Stimson Diary, MS., January 17, 1941).

[33] House Hearings (Knox testimony), 155-59.

serious, a flat negative on aid to Britain in the shape of "man power" if the moral and material assistance contemplated in H.R. 1776 proved insufficient.[34]

William S. Knudsen was the last member of the Government's "first team" to testify. The committee dealt with him rather considerately; its Republican members had perhaps been nettled by the sarcastic comments which the President had made at his press conference of the previous day: "The President—being very fond of the American Navy—did not expect to get rid of that navy." The bill, Mr. Roosevelt had added, "did not prevent the President . . . from standing on his head, but the President did not expect to stand on his head."[35] In any case, the Committee mostly repeated earlier questions and managed to corner Knudsen only on the problem of whether the contemplated aid to Britain would arrive in time to meet the crisis so freely predicted to occur within the next sixty to ninety days. Knudsen avoided making a categorical statement to the contrary, but admitted that significant matériel would not reach Britain until the end of 1941 unless adjustments were quickly made.[36]

Considering the highly partisan atmosphere of the hearings, the Administration spokesmen acquitted themselves on the whole with success. Following the President's own lead, they had emphatically presented the Lend-Lease bill as a measure preëminently designed to protect the nation's security without recourse to military intervention. In Secretary Stimson's own words, H.R. 1776 represented, in fact, "about the last call for lunch on that kind of procedure." Their tactics in refusing to enlarge upon the risk of war which was plainly inherent in the legislation has, of course, exposed them, along with the President himself, to the charge of having virtually perpetrated a fraud upon the Congress and people of the United States. It is still widely implied, if not categorically stated, that Mr. Hull and his three colleagues consistently misrepresented H.R. 1776 as a measure to ensure the security of the United States without recourse to a "fighting war," whereas in fact, it is argued, they were well aware that passage of the Lend-Lease bill would usher in a sequence of steps ending inevitably in American military participation in the war.[37]

Certainly there were already grave doubts, among the Government spokesmen who pleaded for passage of the bill, as to the likelihood that Lend-Lease alone would suffice to defeat the Axis. There is, however, no evidence to support the charge that the President and his advisers were

[34] *House Hearings* (Knox testimony), 160 ff.; Rauch: *Roosevelt, from Munich to Pearl Harbor,* 306-8.

[35] *The New York Times,* January 17, 18, 1941.

[36] *House Hearings* (Knudsen testimony), 189 ff.

[37] Beard: *President Roosevelt and the Coming of the War,* Chapter II (Representations of Lend-Lease Aid to the Allies), *passim;* J. T. Flynn: *The Roosevelt Myth* (New York, 1948), 295 ff. On the other side, see Rauch: *Roosevelt, from Munich to Pearl Harbor,* 303 ff.

either cynical or dishonest in their advocacy of the legislation. On the contrary, the record suggests that the Government team testified honestly to its belief that the best hope, such as it was, of achieving America's dual objectives of defeating Hitler and avoiding a shooting war lay precisely in the speedy passage of H.R. 1776. Events, at least, vindicated their belief that Hitler would not make the Lend-Lease Act a *casus belli.* However, the Government spokesmen for the bill preferred to allow the opposition to point up the dangers unquestionably involved in this as in any other plan by which America's security could have been effectively safeguarded.

The opposing witnesses eagerly shouldered that burden. The attack was spearheaded by the recently resigned Ambassador to Great Britain, Mr. Joseph P. Kennedy, who testified on January 21. Kennedy had already outlined his position in a radio address on the evening of January 18. Both his speech and his statement to the Committee attempted to reconcile such contradictory points of view as to detract seriously from his effectiveness as an opponent of H.R. 1776. Clearly torn between allegiance to the President and doubt as to the wisdom of so broad a grant of powers to him, Kennedy opposed the bill in its current form but advocated aid to Britain short of war and within the limits of the Constitution. At one moment he could state categorically that this was "not our war," and at another insist that England was waging war "against a force which seeks to destroy the rule of conscience, and reason, a force that proclaims its hostility to law, to family life, even to religion itself." He expressed confidence in Mr. Roosevelt's competence to determine foreign policy and acknowledged that efficiency demanded concentration of power. Mr. Kennedy did not, however, wish to see Congress "a mere rubber stamp," and believed it should play a part in the administration of Lend-Lease. His principal motivation was an extreme dread of war for which the United States was not prepared. In this, at least, he was altogether consistent. "I am," he summed up, "primarily interested in the proposition that I do not want to see this country go to war under any conditions whatever unless we are attacked. And I would like to see the Congress of the United States still have a hand so that they can represent the feeling of the people in the legislation."[38]

It was doubtless something of a shock to the opposition members of the Committee to hear the ex-Ambassador, who had been "smeared" as an arch-appeaser, refuse to describe himself offhand even as an isolationist. Greater consistency characterized the observations of Charles A. Lindbergh, who took the stand on January 23, 1941. Lindbergh stubbornly and courageously maintained the position he had long since taken. He advocated the immediate creation of a modern air force, the construction of bases, and other measures to assure adequate hemisphere defense, but insisted that

[38] *House Hearings* (Kennedy testimony), 221 ff. The text of Mr. Kennedy's radio address is included on pp. 259 ff.

when these measures had been completed there would be no danger of invasion. He went on to emphasize that long-term responsibility for the war was almost evenly divided, and claimed that he himself was absolutely neutral. Accordingly, he preferred to see neither side victorious. A negotiated peace, which he was sure the United States could readily secure if it would but try, was greatly to be preferred. He believed, he said, "a complete victory on either side would result in prostration in Europe such as we have never seen."

In the teeth of overwhelming public sentiment, Lindbergh went on to argue that it would be positively disadvantageous both to the United States and to Britain itself to persist in seeking a conclusive victory over the Axis. Even armed American intervention would not render probable a successful invasion of Europe. It would increase the bloodshed without being truly effective. Aid to Britain short of war was a policy thoroughly wrong at its inception but, since it had been initiated, argued Lindbergh, it should not now be dropped.

Specifically, Lindbergh opposed H.R. 1776 for two reasons: it was another step away from democracy and another step closer to war. In sum, he held that "we are strong enough in this Nation and in this hemisphere to maintain our own way of life regardless of what the attitude is on the other sides. I do not believe we are strong enough to impose our way of life on Europe and on Asia. Therefore, my belief is that the only success for our way of life and our system of government is to defend it here at home and not to attempt to enter a war abroad. . . ."[39]

Once Mr. Lindbergh had nailed the flag firmly to the ramparts of the isolationist fortress, subsequent testimony served chiefly to emphasize the diverse sources and inspiration of the opposition group, and to reveal how seemingly hopeless was the task of uniting them on any workable program. Norman Thomas, perennial presidential candidate of the Socialist Party, spoke eloquently for the non-Communist left wing. He took the position, familiar among liberal continentalists, that to enter the war would simply endorse the death warrant of America's own ailing democracy. Such faith did he profess in the contagious power of example as to hazard the opinion that the mere spectacle of a healthy American democracy might induce Adolf Hitler to abandon his policies of force and aggression.[40]

John Bassett Moore and Professor Edwin Borchard, distinguished constitutional lawyers, registered their objections on the ground that the bill required Congress to abdicate several of its most vital prerogatives to the Chief Executive.[41] The convictions of such men, and of other opponents of H.R.

---

[39] *House Hearings* (Lindbergh testimony), 371 ff. The mystery, if indeed there be one, at the core of Mr. Lindbergh's beliefs has not been wholly clarified by his reflections in *Of Flight and Life* (New York, 1948).

[40] *House Hearings,* 348 ff.

[41] Their letters, dated January 21 and 25, 1941, are printed in *Hearings before the Committee on Foreign Relations, United States Senate, Seventy-seventh Congress, First*

1776 on constitutional grounds, could obviously have little in common with the virulent hatred of "Britannia" and all her works displayed in the lurid rhetoric of Mr. William J. Grace, who represented the Citizens Keep Out of War Committee of Chicago, much less with the doctrines of the Reverend Gerald L. K. Smith, appearing for what he described as the Committee of One Million of Detroit. In truth, such diverse spokesmen could, as has been pointed out, agree on but one thing, namely, that "This is a war bill which grants to the President almost dictatorial power over the human and material resources of the United States and will, if enacted, lead inevitably to participation in the war on a world scale."[42]

This, as it proved, was both too tall and too narrow a tower to withstand the assaults of those who favored H.R. 1776, and who, though likewise divided in their views on the lengths to which the United States should go in support of Britain, found the Lend-Lease bill spacious enough to accommodate them all. The Commitee thus heard favorable comment on the bill from an imposing battery of private citizens: William Green of the American Federation of Labor; William C. Bullitt; General John F. O'Ryan; Miss Dorothy Thompson; and Mrs. J. Borden Harriman, American Minister to Norway at the time of the Nazi assault. Mr. Bullitt drew a characteristically hair-raising parallel between the current American state of mind and the complacent trust which prewar France had put in the Maginot Line. General O'Ryan, an exponent of immediate intervention, served the cause effectively by stressing a valid point that he felt was being overlooked: "People seem to believe that it takes two to make a war, while others, seemingly more astute . . . say no, it requires two or more, but the fact is that it requires only one to make a war, namely, the aggressor." Finally, Mr. Ernest W. Gibson, recently elected successor to William Allen White as head of the Committee to Defend America by Aiding the Allies, was able to rally that schism-rent but still powerful organization to a point which permitted him to lay before the Committee an emphatic and lucid statement in support of the Lend-Lease bill.[43]

The arguments within the Committee were echoed throughout the nation, where the Lend-Lease bill was pondered, praised and denounced, on cracker barrels, pulpits, and platforms the length of the land and beyond it. Influential private citizens differed sharply. President Hutchins of the University of Chicago, giving his own twist to the continentalist theory, sponsored the perfectionist argument that the "moral and intellectual" short-

---

Session, on S. 275 (Washington, Government Printing Office, 1941), 652 ff., hereafter referred to as *Senate Hearings.* For a development of their thesis, see E. S. Corwin: *Total War and the Constitution* (New York, 1947).

[42] Beard: *President Roosevelt and the Coming of the War,* 39.

[43] *House Hearings,* 636, 678 ff. On the circumstances surrounding Mr. White's resignation, see Walter Johnson: *Battle Against Isolation* (Chicago, 1944), Chapter VIII. On the President's reaction, see his letter to Mr. White of January 16 (*F.D.R.: His Personal Letters,* II, 1106).

comings of American democracy disqualified it for world leadership against totalitarian forces. He denounced H.R. 1776 as suicidal. Thomas Lamont spoke equally firmly in favor of the bill, while Henry Ford had meanwhile mellowed to the point of professing absolute neutrality. *The New York Times* noted a cleavage within the New York C.I.O.: the right wing, led by Sidney Hillman, supported Lend-Lease; while the left wing, following Joseph Curran of the National Maritime Union (and also the current Communist Party line), opposed it. Secretary Morgenthau was forced to note ruefully that his "fan mail" on H.R. 1776 was almost uniformly antagonistic.[44]

Meanwhile overseas comment did not promote harmony. Proponents of the bill seized with gusto on Berlin's ill-advised pronouncement of "Hats Off!" to Lindbergh for his courageous testimony in the face of the "moral terrorism" of the interventionists. Hitler personally made another contribution to the success of the legislation when, in the course of a speech of January 30, he promised to torpedo every ship carrying goods to England. The best the isolationists could produce to match these Axis contributions was to insist that when Mr. Churchill at Glasgow, in the presence of Mr. Harry Hopkins, stated that England would not require large armies from overseas *in 1941,* he surely inferred that America would have to send them *in 1942.*[45]

The Committee of the House concluded its public hearings, described by Mr. Arthur Krock as "briefer, more orderly and less emotional than had been expected," on January 29, and then reconvened briefly in executive session. Secretary Hull had already been heard in a closed meeting. He was followed by General Marshall and General George H. Brett of the Army Air Corps. Mr. Hull's secret testimony was substantially the same as he had given earlier in the public hearings, but more frankly and bluntly expressed. German dive bombers had since been seen over the Mediterranean, and there were persistent rumors of Axis demands on Vichy for facilities at Bizerte. The Secretary of State deduced that the long-expected onslaught on Britain was about to commence. The Secretary of War at least shared the fear that Britain's newly achieved position in North Africa was already "tottering."[46]

What course of action the United States should take in case the Axis powers actually initiated hostilities against this hemisphere had been considered and decided by Messrs. Hull, Stimson, and Knox together with General Marshall and Admiral Stark at a White House conference with Mr.

[44] *Vital Speeches,* VII, 258 ff., and 261; *The New York Times,* January 24, 1941; *Morgenthau Diaries (MS.),* Vol. 353, pp. 287 ff.

[45] *The New York Times,* January 25, February 16, 1941; *Bulletin of International News,* XVIII (1) (1941), 138 ff.; Winston S. Churchill: *The Unrelenting Struggle* (London, 1942), 22 ff.

[46] *The New York Times,* January 28, 1941; *Stimson Diary (MS.),* January 26, 28, 1941.

Roosevelt on January 16, 1941. The conclusions then reached followed closely the general reasoning of Plan Dog and the developing Rainbow V. The President issued a directive which, in case of war, called for a defensive posture in the Pacific and preparations for naval escort of shipping in the Atlantic. The Army would have to eschew offensive action until its strength could be built up. Meanwhile every effort was to be made to continue American shipments of munitions to England, since the President believed that Hitler's chief motive for involving the United States in war at this juncture would be to curtail such supplies. Thus, in effect, Mr. Roosevelt approved the Plan Dog concept and authorized planning on that basis.[47]

Presumably Mr. Stimson more than agreed with the President's views. Shortly after the significant White House meeting, the Secretary, assisted by Knox, Marshall, and Stark, prepared for the President "a sombre paper" on the relation of H.R. 1776 to America's increasingly critical position. He admitted that the chief immediate advantage to be expected from the passage of the Lend-Lease bill would be a boost to British morale. Significant material benefits could not be expected to flow from it much before 1942, particularly in view of the fact that Britain had been forbidden to place new orders in this country since October. Arguing for prompt passage of the bill, Mr. Stimson declared that such action probably offered "the last possible opportunity of . . . contributing more fully to the defense of this country by aid to Britain which is short of military action." He concluded, however, with a strong expression of doubt that the United States could long avoid escort of convoys, which the President had been quoted by reporters as saying the day before was something he had never "considered." Wrote Mr. Stimson:

I therefore think that the President should consider whether the American Government has not reached the time when it must realize that the policy it has thus far followed of limiting its aid to measures which are short of military action will not probably secure a British victory. It is my belief that consideration should be given to measures which will at the same time secure the life line of British supplies across the Atlantic and relieve their convoy duty units . . . which are sorely needed elsewhere.[48]

Stimson believed the President had been favorably impressed by his statement on the urgency of passing H.R. 1776, and was otherwise cheered by a heart-to-heart talk in which Mr. Roosevelt touched on his own plans "in regard to a possible break with the Axis and in regard to the possible necessity of convoying troops." The Chief Executive had likewise reassured Stimson by taking steps to permit the British to resume placing orders in this

---

[47] Watson: *Chief of Staff: Prewar Plans and Preparations,* 124-25. On the development of Navy plans for Atlantic convoys, see Samuel E. Morison: *The Battle of the Atlantic* (Boston, 1947), 44-45.

[48] "Résumé of Situation Relative to Bill 1776," January 22, 1941 (*Pearl Harbor Attack,* XX, 4275 ff.). For the President's press comment on convoying, see *The New York Times,* January 22, 1941.

country. Meanwhile, moreover, the President and the Administration leaders had grasped the fact that if the Lend-Lease bill was to become law within the interval suggested to Prime Minister Churchill (February 20 to March 1), some ground would now have to be sacrificed, as had been anticipated when the legislation was introduced.[49] Accordingly, on January 26 Mr. Hull summoned a conference to discuss the amendments which the House Committee on Foreign Affairs might recommend. Speaker Rayburn, Senator George, and Representatives McCormack, Bloom and Johnson were present, as were Secretary Morgenthau and others. They decided to recommend to the President acceptance of the following four amendments: first, a limit should be placed upon the period during which the President could authorize the War and Navy Departments to enter Lend-Lease agreements; second, provision should be made for frequent reports to Congress; third, the President should consult with the Chief of Staff and the Chief of Naval Operations before authorizing release to foreign nations of defense materials already on hand; finally, a provision should be inserted stating that nothing in the Act was to be construed as conferring on the President power to escort merchant ships with units of the American Navy.[50]

At Speaker Rayburn's reiterated suggestion the President summoned a bipartisan group to the White House the next day to go over the proposed amendments. Senator McNary of Oregon and Representative Martin of Massachusetts were present, as well as the Democratic leaders. Mr. Roosevelt, still adhering to his prearranged "hands off" policy, told the assembled company that he was "perfectly willing to accept any amendments by Congress that were desirable." He had implied as much in his press conference of January 24. As Secretary Morgenthau was to note later, the bipartisan conference went far to spike the guns of the opposition. Editorials applauded the President's gambit and, because the press recognized that the Administration already possessed votes sufficient to pass the bill on its own terms, the President's concessions were interpreted as magnanimous.[51]

The wisdom of the President's move was further vindicated by the receipt in the White House on January 28 of messages from Prime Minister Churchill and Harry Hopkins, who had now been with Churchill for two weeks, engaged in assessing England's most pressing necessities. The Prime Minister had just received Wendell Willkie, to whose introductory letter,

[49] *Stimson Diary (MS.)*, January 21-23; tel. from the President to Hopkins, January 26, 1941 (*Roosevelt Papers:* Secretary's File, Box 80); tel. from the President to the Prime Minister, January 16, 1941 (*F.D.R.: His Personal Letters*, II, 1107). On Stimson's efforts to prevail upon Jones and Morgenthau to let the British place orders pending the passage of Lend-Lease, we have used *Stimson Diary (MS.)*, January 18, 22, 23. The final arrangements were made by Secretary Jones and Mr. John J. McCloy (*ibid.*, February 3, 1941).

[50] *Morgenthau Diaries (MS.)*, January 26, 1941 (Vol. 351, pp. 42 ff.).

[51] *Morgenthau Diaries (MS.)*, January 26, February 10, 1941. Turner Catledge in *The New York Times*, January 28; Alsop and Kintner in the *New York Herald Tribune*, February 12, 1941.

given Mr. Willkie by the President at their meeting of January 19, 1941, the latter had appended in his own hand Longfellow's lines beginning, "Sail on, O Ship of State!" After expressing his emotion over this "mark of our friendly relations which have been built up telegraphically but also telepathically under all stresses," the Prime Minister weighed the immediate prospects in these terms:

All my information shows that the Germans are persevering in their preparations to invade this country and we are getting ready to give them a reception worthy of the occasion. On the other hand, the news from the East shows that a large army and air force are being established in Rumania and that the advance parties of the German air force have already to the extent of several thousands infiltrated themselves into Bulgarian airdromes with the full connivance of the Bulgarian Government. It would be natural for Hitler to make a strong threat against the British Isles in order to occupy us here and cover his eastern designs. The forces at his disposal are, however, so large that he could carry out both offensives at the same time. You may be sure we shall do our best in both quarters.[52]

Hopkins's message of the same date, his first lengthy communication on Britain's plight, contained, as its "most important, pertinent, single observation," the opinion of all British military leaders and of most of the Cabinet that invasion was imminent and certainly would come not later than May 1. Hopkins could not urge "too strongly" that any American action to be taken in response to Britain's immediate needs should be based on the assumption that the invasion was coming prior to that date. Everything available should be turned over at once.[53]

In the face of these fresh evidences of the "ninety-day crisis," the Administration felt justified in once again resorting to covert action. In secrecy the President and the War Department arranged to give the British 250,000 Lee-Enfield rifles and 50,000,000 rounds of ammunition.[54] The greatest relief must, therefore, have been occasioned by the promptness with which the House Committee on Foreign Affairs now wound up its labors with the discussion of nineteen proposed amendments to H.R. 1776. Of these it

[52] The President's message to Churchill, January 19, in *F.D.R.: His Personal Letters*, II, 1109; tel. from the Prime Minister to the President, January 28, 1941 (printed in full in Winston S. Churchill: *The Grand Alliance*, Boston, 1950, 25-26). The fullest account of Mr. Roosevelt's meeting with Willkie prior to his trip to England is given in Alden B. Hatch: *Citizen of the World: Franklin D. Roosevelt* (London, 1948), 218 ff. Stimson urged such a meeting on both Willkie and Roosevelt (*Stimson Diary, MS.*, January 17, 1941). On Mr. Willkie's meeting with the President, we have also used a memo of the President dated January 19, 1941 (*Roosevelt Papers:* Secretary's File, Box 82).

[53] Tel. from Hopkins to the President and Hull, January 28, 1941. Most of this message is quoted in Sherwood: *Roosevelt and Hopkins*, 256 ff. The reader is referred to the full and highly readable account of the Hopkins mission to England given by Mr. Sherwood in Chapter XI of his book.

[54] *Morgenthau Diaries (MS.)*, February 10, 1941 (Vol. 371, pp. 29 ff.). The arrangement was consummated during the absence of Secretary Morgenthau on vacation (*Stimson Diary, MS.*, February 5, 1941).

adopted only the four presented at the President's bipartisan conference. By a margin of seventeen to eight, which pleased Secretary Morgenthau immensely, the Committee on January 30 voted to report the amended bill to the House, and to recommend its passage. The dissenting members filed a minority report, professing sympathy for Britain and urging as an alternative to Lend-Lease a straightforward grant of $2,000,000,000 credit. Congressman Tinkham, representing the handful opposing all aid to Britain, declined to sign even the minority report.[55]

4. ENACTMENT OF LEND-LEASE

Formal debate on the bill began in the House on February 3, and continued until February 8. From the beginning there was little doubt of its prompt passage. The isolationists had neither the resources nor the self-confidence to put up a serious fight. The majority of the Republicans, under the Minority Leader, Congressman Martin, were united with a minority of dissident Democrats. A few, nevertheless, were prepared to bolt and follow the lead of Congressman Wadsworth of New York, who never flagged in his efforts to unite the Republican group supporting H.R. 1776 with those who endorsed all aid to Britain provided Congress retained absolute control of the purse strings.[56]

On February 8 the House of Representatives passed the bill, with additional amendments, by a vote of 260 to 165. The most important of these amendments was a provision that the President's powers might be terminated at any time before the expiration of the Act by a resolution of Congress. As the result of a surprise move on the part of the Democratic leaders, a ceiling of $1,300,000,000 was set on the value of military and naval equipment, in existence or under appropriation, which might be transferred to other governments. No limit, however, was placed on future aid.[57] The voting, as

[55] *The New York Times*, January 30, 31, February 1, 1941; *Morgenthau Diaries (MS.)*, January 31, 1941; *Report to Accompany H. R. 1776*, 77th Congress, 1st session, Report No. 18, January 30, 1941. This report analyzes the bill, section by section, and summarizes the affirmative arguments. Secretary Morgenthau has stated that it was written *in toto* in the Treasury (*Morgenthau Diaries, MS.*, Vol. 353, pp. 174 ff., January 31, 1941). *Minority Views to Accompany H. R. 1776*, 77th Congress, 1st session, Report No. 18, Part 2, January 31, 1941, submitted by Mr. Fish. This is a brief, reasonable summation of the dissenting opinions, and outlines the alternative program. *Documents on American Foreign Relations*, III, 715-17, gives a clear picture of the appearance of the Lend-Lease bill as it left the House Committee on January 30.

[56] Alsop and Kintner in the *New York Herald Tribune*, February 5; *The New York Times*, February 6, 1941. Cf. *Analysis of H. R. 1776*, prepared by the America First Committee, no date. On public sentiment toward the bill, see *Public Opinion Quarterly*, June, 1941, pp. 322 ff. Charles A. Beard, in *President Roosevelt and the Coming of the War*, pp. 44-68, selected from the *Congressional Record* a number of passages effectively illustrating the debate on Lend-Lease in the House and Senate.

[57] *The New York Times*, February 7, 9, 1941; *Documents on American Foreign Relations*, III, 717-20. For the President's reaction, see *F.D.R.: His Personal Letters*, II, 1133, and his memorandum to the Attorney General (March 17, 1941) in *Roosevelt Papers: Secretary's File*, Box 81.

anticipated, largely followed party lines, with 236 Democrats and 24 Republicans in favor; and 25 Democrats, 135 Republicans and Mr. Marcantonio of the American Labor Party opposed to the measure. Despite this, the House had, by reason of its fair, prompt and orderly action on legislation of the greatest significance, turned in a performance which reflected credit on the democratic process. Mr. Lindbergh himself felt moved to express to Chairman Sol Bloom his appreciation of the "tact and consideration" accorded him personally. The Senate, however, was not to move so expeditiously.[58]

The Senate Foreign Relations Committee, under the chairmanship of Senator Walter F. George, had, on January 27, opened its hearings on the Lend-Lease bill. Secretary Hull submitted the same statement he had read to the House Committee, and then induced the Senate Committee to meet in executive session. (He had previously confided to Stimson his concern that his vital information on the perilous situation would be noised about.)[59] Mr. Hull was followed by Secretary Morgenthau, whose testimony also closely paralleled that which he had given the House. He again offered his detailed figures on British resources, with the revisions necessitated by receipt of more recent data. As before, his attitude was cautious and almost deferential, even in the face of the brusque questionings of Senator Nye of North Dakota and Senator Clark of Missouri. He now maintained that $1,811,000,000 in gold and dollar exchange assets was all that the British regarded as available for purchases in the United States.[60]

Secretary Stimson appeared twice before the Senate Committee, on January 29 and 30—on the latter occasion in executive session. By this date not only Stimson, but many members of the War and Navy Departments and the Cabinet had come to realize that the question of escorting convoys carrying United States goods to areas held by the British loomed closer than had been generally anticipated. The Secretary of War, seconded by the Judge Advocate General of the Army, held that power to order United States Navy ships to escort duty was vested in the President, as Commander in Chief, by the Constitution. Testifying that he favored escort by the American Navy if "necessary" to get munitions to Britain, and believing that the issue, full blown, would soon be apparent to the country, Stimson was particularly anxious to prevent the inclusion in the Lend-Lease bill of a provi-

[58] The Autobiography of Sol Bloom (New York, 1948), 240-42. Messrs. Alsop and Kintner, favorably disposed to the President, point to the House debate as proof that Mr. Roosevelt avoided exerting pressure on Congress. They contend that during the debate Rayburn and his lieutenants accepted or rejected amendments without specific reference to the White House, and that Administration leaders made no great effort to whip Congressmen into line (New York Herald Tribune, February 12, 1941).

[59] Stimson Diary (MS.), January 24, 1941.

[60] Senate Hearings, 9 ff. According to Mr. Morgenthau, Senator Taft—who was not even on the Committee—was responsible for some of the opposition's irascible "grilling" ("The Morgenthau Diaries" (Collier's, October 18, 1947).

sion forbidding the President to order Navy ships to escort. His testimony was similar to but even stronger than that which he had given before the House Committee. He also opposed, in the interest of speed and efficiency, the amendment which required certification by the Chief of Staff prior to the disposal of any defense article.[61]

Secretary Knox, who followed Stimson, similarly enlarged upon his earlier statements before the House Committee. He took issue with Lindbergh's views on strategy, and criticized the dilatory attitude which the country in general was taking toward the war. He produced on behalf of the Navy Department—as Stimson had for the War Department—a statement of the effect of the passage of Lend-Lease on existing statutes relating to his Department. He also adduced the same argument for the building of ships that Stimson had used for planes: that British orders were valuable in increasing United States capacity to build. The Committee questioned him closely on the issue of escorting convoys and Knox again admitted his belief that employment of naval forces in convoying munitions would be "substantially" an act of war. Having been previously coached by Stimson, however, Knox contended that the President as Commander in Chief already had the power to order naval escort. He refused to be drawn out by Senator Nye on the subject of what steps beyond Lend-Lease the United States might have to take to prevent British collapse, but summed up his general position in these words: "I am not going to shut the door in the face of national defense, no matter what may come. If vital interests of the United States are at stake, we have to fight. . . . And when the time comes when we will not do that we will cease to have a country."[62]

Members of the Committee who opposed the bill summoned up a more imposing cloud of witnesses than had supported their position in the House hearings. The new roster likewise covered a wider range of ideological conviction. Among the newcomers were General Robert E. Wood, Chairman

[61] *Senate Hearings* (Stimson testimony), 85 ff.; *Stimson Diary (MS.)*, January 21, 27, 29, 1941. Some of Stimson's testimony, given in executive session, January 30, on the desperate airplane situation, leaked out. Senator Wheeler publicized it in a statement charging that five sixths of United States plane production was going to the British, and that the United States had not a single plane capable of combat in a European war, and alleging that Stimson had told the Foreign Relations Committee that the United States had on hand as of January 1 a total of 639 warplanes. The President remarked that the revelation of such figures would be a great comfort to the "Reich Dictator" (*The New York Times,* February 5, 1941). Figures sent to the President by Secretary Morgenthau indicated that during the period from July 7, 1940, to February 1, 1941, the United States had produced a total of 2251 combat aircraft and 2491 training planes. Of these, 607 combat planes and 1643 trainers had gone to the Army and Navy, while the British received 1512 combat planes and 486 training planes (*Morgenthau Diaries, MS.,* February 10, 1941, Vol. 371, pp. 93 ff.). According to Stimson's own figures, the U.S. Army Air Corps had on hand 287 combat planes as of February 1, none of which was equipped with armor or leakproof fuel tanks (*ibid.,* February 14, 1941, Vol. 372, p. 297); *Stimson Diary (MS.),* January 30, February 4, 1941.

[62] *Senate Hearings* (Knox testimony), 177 ff.; *Stimson Diary (MS.),* January 27, 1941.

of the American First Committee; Colonel Robert R. McCormick of the *Chicago Tribune;* Charles A. Beard; James S. Kemper, President of the Chamber of Commerce of the United States; Merwin K. Hart; and Joseph Curran of the National Maritime Union. The Communist-dominated American Youth Congress sent in an altogether characteristic statement, as did the successor to Father Coughlin. No views, however wise or foolish, were excluded.

Charles A. Beard, the intellectual leader of American isolationism, was content with only brief allusions to the "continentalism" which lay behind his violent opposition to Lend-Lease and which informed his plea to the Committee "to preserve one stronghold of order and sanity even against the gates of hell." Leaving to Senator Hiram Johnson the task of reading back passages from his own prolific writings on the follies of the interventionists' foreign policy, Mr. Beard confined himself to the specific dangers inherent in the legislation in question. He confessed that he had been "profoundly impressed by the magnificent way in which President Roosevelt had attacked that depression, his courage and . . . his fine public spirit." Nineteen forty-one, however, was not 1932, nor, indeed, 1917, when Mr. Beard had strenuously urged American participation in the First World War. As for the present bill to promote the defense of the United States, its title was "unprecise." It should read, he insisted, as follows:

All provisions of law and the Constitution to the contrary notwithstanding, an Act to place all the wealth and all the men and women of the United States at the free disposal of the President, to permit him to transfer or carry goods to any foreign government he may be pleased to designate, anywhere in the world, to authorize him to wage undeclared wars for anybody, anywhere in the world, until the affairs of the world are ordered to suit his policies, and for any other purpose he may have in mind now or at any time in the future, which may be remotely related to the contingencies contemplated in the title of the Act.[63]

Such a blast from the academic grove could not avoid making the words of dwellers in the market place, even those of Colonel McCormick, seem prolix and tame. And, indeed, there was little novelty (though often much honest conviction) in the sentiments of those who followed Mr. Beard into the arena. Dr. Charles Clayton Morrison, editor of the *Christian Century,* took issue with the "angry and futile sentimentalism" which had moved the Reverend Reinhold Niebuhr to speak of this as a war to preserve Christian civilization. "How could civilization," asked Morrison, who claimed to be no pacifist, "be more utterly destroyed than by modern war?" The cudgels for international law were wielded this time by Professor Herbert Wright of The Catholic University of America, whose opposition to the bill was based also on distrust of Soviet Russia. Philip Murray of the C.I.O., though not hostile, was frankly worried over the danger to labor's recent social

---

[63] *Senate Hearings* (Beard testimony), 307 ff.

gains, while Joseph Curran was certain that the proposed legislation was "downright Fascist." As for the brasher, pro-Communist, American Youth Congress, its written statement contained the slogan adapted from Senator Wheeler: "Don't lease or lend our lives. Defeat this bill."

While it should be borne in mind that a large proportion of these spokesmen concurred in the desirability of some assistance to Britain short of war, it was again quite impossible for them to agree on the point where risk of war clearly outweighed the advantage of British survival. Moreover, any practical agreement reached among the soberer isolationists was in constant jeopardy from the lunatic fringe, left and right. In this respect, the isolationists continued to labor under a burden far heavier than that of their opponents.

Differences of opinion, however, also characterized the testimony of those who spoke or wrote in favor of the bill, among whom were Wendell Willkie; former Ambassador James W. Gerard; Mayor Fiorello La Guardia; and President James B. Conant of Harvard University, who was shortly to undertake his first mission to Britain in the interests of scientific and technical collaboration.[64] Yet such men found it easier to agree on a Lend-Lease bill, even at the risk of war, than did their opponents on a program of effective aid to Britain short of war. Significantly, Dr. Conant, a lifelong exponent of the scientific method, encountered none of Dr. Charles Morrison's difficulties in accepting the Niebuhr thesis that the conflict in Europe was one in which religious values were at stake. In any event, added the President of Harvard, "fear of war cannot be the sole basis of national policy, if we as a people would be free." Nor did Mr. Charles Warren share the misgivings of other lawyers who, while willing to assist Britain, doubted the authority of the Commander in Chief to institute naval escort of convoys.[65] Michael Williams, an editor of *The Commonweal,* made it clear that many distinguished Roman Catholics did not share the political views expressed by Father Curran of Brooklyn or even by Cardinal O'Connell.

It remained, however, for Wendell Willkie, who had returned from England in order to testify, to render the Administration's cause the most effective service. Speaking before a capacity crowd on February 11, the head of the Republican Party declared his support of the modified bill and his approval of the amendments adopted by the House. Willkie pointed out that the opposition to the bill was not directed at the policy of aid to Britain. The country, with a high degree of unanimity, had embarked upon that policy. It was, therefore, already in the war, "if aid to Britain is what is going to get us into war." Under the circumstances, the obvious course was to ensure that American aid was effective. Feeble assistance would give

[64] On this mission see James P. Baxter, 3rd: *Scientists Against Time* (Boston, 1946).
[65] See the exchange of letters between Mr. Warren and Professor Corwin in *The New York Times,* February 13, 23, 1941. Professor Quincy Wright lent his vigorous support to the bill (*American Journal of International Law,* April, 1941, pp. 305 ff.).

Hitler a *casus belli* without appreciably helping Britain. Admittedly the bill involved the risk of war, but Hitler, as his record showed, would make war on the United States whenever he deemed it advantageous to himself. While Britain stood, however, he was far less likely to move against the United States. Willkie also confirmed the argument which Mr. Churchill made in his moving "give us the tools and we'll finish the job" broadcast of February 9, from London. The Prime Minister specifically repudiated the necessity for an American expeditionary force in 1942, or any other foreseeable date. Willkie stated that men in key positions with whom he had talked in England concurred in this judgment. He refused to commit himself on the convoy issue, but did say that it need not arise if the United States provided enough ships. He even proposed, to the consternation of the Secretary of the Navy, that the United States allocate to Britain five to ten destroyers a month! Taxed with the criticisms he had heaped on Mr. Roosevelt's foreign policy during the campaign, he brushed them aside for what they mostly were: "campaign oratory." Mr. Roosevelt was, now, "his President."[66]

Mr. Willkie's impressive support presumably deflated the opposition, because two days later, on February 13, the Senate Committee approved the Lend-Lease bill in substance. Again the vote, 15-8, approximated party lines: only Senator White of Maine deserted the Republicans and voted for the bill. Isolationist Democrats Gillette of Iowa and Clark of Missouri joined the Republicans and the Progressive, La Follette of Wisconsin, in disapproval. The committee upheld the amendments suggested by the House, and added another important one of its own. This had been sponsored by Senator James F. Byrnes, and provided that defense articles shipped or other aid rendered to any foreign nation should be limited by Congressional appropriations or contract authorizations.[67]

At this juncture there was already a marked swing in the nation's press toward acceptance, and editorial approval had become general. Only a handful of newspapers remained hostile to the measure itself, although a considerable number still urged restrictions on the authority delegated to the President. The restriction most strongly advocated was that recommended by Willkie and others: that the countries to be aided should be specified. This was apparently motivated in large part by the wish to exclude Soviet Russia. It had gradually been borne in on the press that the President's

[66] *Senate Hearings* (Willkie testimony), 870 ff. The President received Mr. Willkie for a private conversation on the evening of February 11 (*Stimson Diary, MS.,* February 11, 1941). Willkie stated privately that he had the President's own authority on the British request for destroyers and his support of their plea (*ibid.,* February 13, 1941). Cf. Mr. Roosevelt's letter to Senator Tobey of February 17 (*F.D.R.: His Personal Letters,* II, 1122). On this point we have also used a memo of Mr. McCloy to Secretary Knox, February 12, 1941 (*Roosevelt Papers:* Secretary's File, Box 73).

[67] *The New York Times,* February 14, 16, 1941; *Documents on American Foreign Relations,* III, 720-21. The report of the minority of the Senate Foreign Relations Committee is printed in full in *The New York Times,* February 19, 1941.

powers as Commander in Chief were given him by the Constitution, and not by the Lend-Lease bill. This "belated understanding" had pricked the "dictator" argument, used frequently in the initial attacks. That line of approach, however, was still pursued by the *Chicago Tribune* and the *Daily Worker* ("the Yanks are not coming"). Otherwise, because the majority of newspapers approved of aid to Britain as a fundamental United States policy, opposition was temperate. It was confined to expressions of fear that the bill would lead to war, of doubt that Britain was actually at the end of its dollar resources, and of lingering suspicion that America was being swindled. Secretary Morgenthau's comparison of United States and British income taxes had, however, hit its mark, and most editorials now urged against squeezing the British too vigorously.[68]

On February 17 Senator Barkley opened the debate on the floor of the Senate. Owing to the failure of the isolationists to secure any considerable support in public opinion, their speeches, though long and denunciatory, lacked the vital punch and spirit born of genuine hope of success. Nevertheless, every opposition Senator had his day and the oratory dragged on for more than two weeks. By implied threats of a filibuster, Senator Wheeler managed to stave off until March 1 Senator Barkley's motion to lengthen the duration of the Senate's sessions until the bill was disposed of. Senators Nye, Wheeler, Clark and their sympathizers in the small but militant isolationist minority spoke, comparatively, for a total period several times as long as did the bill's proponents. Reynolds of North Carolina wasted precious hours denouncing Britain's millionaires (particularly numerous, he thought, in India). Not until these had stripped themselves of their castles, horses, dogs and jewels, should the "one-gallused, overall-clad farmer or laborer" of this country be called on to pay. Thus did the archisolationists wage their desperate battle in the vain hope that the American people would suddenly rise up against Lend-Lease, as they had during the Supreme Court fight. No flood of angry condemnation materialized, not even after Secretary Jones "let the cat out of the bag" by blurting out before the House Banking Committee: "We are in the war, or at least we are nearly in the war. We are preparing for it."[69]

Although toward the end tempers grew short and tongues sharp, only two out of the welter of suggested amendments seriously threatened the objectives of the Administration. The most important of these was proposed by Democratic Senator Ellender of Louisiana. It ran:

[68] "Summaries of Editorial Opinion," by Alan Barth (*Morgenthau Diaries, MS.,* February 10 and 14, 1941); *Public Opinion Quarterly,* June, 1941, pp. 320 ff.

[69] *The New York Times,* February 21, 22, 23, 25; March 1 and 2. Paul Mallon in the *New York Journal-American,* February 22; *PM,* March 6; Alsop and Kintner in the *Washington Post,* March 29, 1941. To offset Senator Reynolds, Harry Hopkins, just back from England, urged Churchill to release a statement citing the increased taxes and other financial sacrifices occasioned by the war (tel. from Hopkins to Churchill, February 18, 1941).

Nothing in this Act shall be deemed to confer any additional powers to authorize the employment or use of persons in the land or naval forces of the United States at any place beyond the limits of the Western Hemisphere, except in the territories or possessions of the United States, including the Philippine Islands.

Secretary Hull quickly and vigorously expressed to several Congressmen his dismay over this proposal. The President was sufficiently alarmed to deviate from his "hands off" rule, and at his press conference of February 25 struck indirectly at the Ellender proposal, emphasizing that he opposed any amendment which would hamper the Government in extending all possible aid to Britain.[70] Senators Barkley and George, and Representatives Rayburn and McCormack, acknowledging that the proposal would carry great weight, discussed with the President and with Vice President Wallace methods of eliminating it. Ultimately the Administration threw its influence behind an innocuous substitute, drawn up by Mr. McCloy, Senator Byrnes and the Democratic leaders.[71] This watered-down revision merely stated:

. . . nothing in this Act shall be construed to change existing law relating to the use of the land and naval forces of the United States, except in so far as such use relates to the manufacture, procurement and repair of defense articles, the communication of information, and other noncombatant purposes enumerated in this Act."[72]

The second significant effort to alter the Administration's original concept of Lend-Lease was advanced by Senators Byrnes and Byrd, with the active assistance of Senator Robert A. Taft. Their various plans amounted to an effort to assure to Congress final discretion as to the production and transfer of supplies by retaining for it close control of appropriations. Senator Taft and his supporters argued that the President could lend or lease defense articles manufactured from funds granted for the Army and Navy. This would leave Congress no real alternative but to vote more funds to replace the articles for the United States armed forces. Soon after the Senate debate opened, Byrnes announced his intention to offer an amendment which would make clear that with respect to the transfer of any defense articles authorized by future appropriations, the President would have to secure Congressional authorization before disposing of them. The Foreign Relations Committee had earlier tried to stipulate this, but Byrnes had then believed their qualification unnecessary. Senator Byrd's subsequent proposal went even further: to specify that aid to foreign governments must be supplied out of funds exclusively for that purpose and not out of funds voted for supplying the United States armed forces.[73]

Some of the President's advisers were greatly disturbed by the Byrd

[70] The New York Times, February 26, 1941.
[71] Stimson Diary (MS.), March 7; New York Herald Tribune, March 8; Alsop and Kintner in the Washington Post, March 29, 1941.
[72] Documents on American Foreign Relations, III, 723.
[73] The New York Times, February 14, 20, 27; March 2, 1941.

amendment, which, Morgenthau insisted, would destroy the flexibility of the "Arsenal of Democracy philosophy" by forcing the adoption of separate British and American production programs. The Secretary of the Treasury hastily drew up a statement, eagerly signed by Stimson and Knox, warning the President that the suggested modifications would take all the stuffing out of the law. Working through Harry Hopkins, they prevailed upon Mr. Hull once again to use his great influence on Capitol Hill. Following a hurried conference at Mr. Roosevelt's bedside (he was down with the grippe), Mr. Hull reluctantly agreed to invite Senators Byrnes, George and Barkley to a meeting at which Stimson outlined the ill effects of the projected amendments. At a second meeting (March 4) General Marshall spoke earnestly on how aid to Britain had already assisted the United States. Morgenthau, Hull, Stimson and Forrestal added their arguments and eventually persuaded the Senate leaders to advance a compromise approved by the Cabinet officers and by Budget Director Harold Smith.[74]

Nevertheless, the Byrnes-Byrd modifications were in substance part of the bill when it was finally passed by a weary Senate on March 8, 1941, by a wide margin of 60-31. They were indeed the only vestiges of serious opposition which the supporters of the Administration failed to withstand. There was some indecision among the House leaders as to whether to accept the amendment or send the bill to joint conference. The President, however, reluctant to interfere again, let it be known that he would sign the bill as it was. With Bulgaria already in the Axis camp and Yugoslavia teetering on the edge, it was time to stop talking and face Hitler's spring offensive. The House, therefore, concurred in the Senate's amendments and overwhelmingly approved the bill on March 11, 1941. "Our blessings from the whole British Empire," cabled Churchill to the President, "go out to you and the American nation for this very present help in time of trouble."[75]

Although "all-outers," inside and outside the Government, showed anxiety and irritation over the undue length and poor quality of the Senate debate, there is, in retrospect, much to be said in favor of Mr. Roosevelt's decision to withhold his hand. If Senators Byrnes, Barkley and George ignored the precedent established by Congressmen Bloom and McCormack of holding daily strategy conferences during the progress of the bill through the House, Byrnes nevertheless was widely credited with shrewdness and tact in steering Lend-Lease along its more difficult Senate course. Even impatient critics would probably now concede that speed was not the only vital factor in the passage of this legislation. A high degree of unanimity was equally important and a gratifying measure of this was achieved when the

[74] *Stimson Diary (MS.)*, February 28, March 1, 2, and 4; *Morgenthau Diaries (MS.)*, Vol. 377, pp. 100 ff.; Vol. 378, pp. 9 ff. and 264 ff.

[75] Tel. from the Prime Minister to the President, March 9 (text in Churchill: *The Grand Alliance,* 128); *The New York Times,* March 9, 10, 11, 12; *New York Herald Tribune,* March 9, 1941; *Documents on American Foreign Relations,* III, 720 ff.

Senate finally passed the bill and the House subsequently concurred. Ten Republican Senators, headed by Austin of Vermont and McNary of Oregon, voted in favor. Only thirteen Democratic Senators, with seventeen Republicans, voted nay. The final tally in the House, 317-71, was a still more impressive testimonial to the wisdom of the Administration's tactics. Seasoned observers believed that on the whole the long Senate debate had enhanced public comprehension of the issues involved, even if steady harping by the isolationist minority on the refrain that Lend-Lease was intended as a war measure did slightly weaken at the end the majority sentiment among the public at large. As Senator Barkley summed up the Senate debate in a letter to Secretary Morgenthau: "It took a little longer than it should, but on the whole I think it is better to have given them a little extra time than to have created bad feeling by an effort to coerce the opponents of the bill. . . ." Once the die was cast, at any rate, a "close ranks" atmosphere immediately manifested itself. Congressman Martin and Senator Vandenberg, whose isolationist tendencies had already moderated, spoke for most of the minority in pledging their coöperation. Thus only a handful of diehards, led by Senator Wheeler and Senator Nye, pledged themselves to continue the fight.[76]

At ten minutes to four o'clock on the afternoon of March 11, the President signed the Lend-Lease Act. Before evening he sent to the British and Greek representatives lists of available weapons, prepared well in advance. On the next morning Congress received his request for an appropriation of $7,000,000,000 to implement the new law. Three days later he made his first appraisal of the Act when he spoke at the annual dinner of the White House correspondents. Resisting the impulse to indulge in recriminations, Mr. Roosevelt summed up the long battle of H.R. 1776 in words which simultaneously illumined the objectives he had sought and the methods he had chosen to reach them: "Let not the dictators of Europe or Asia doubt our unanimity now. . . . Yes, the decisions of our democracy may be slowly arrived at. But when that decision is made, it is proclaimed not with the voice of any one man, but with the voice of one hundred and thirty millions. It is binding on us all. And the world is no longer left in doubt. . . ."[77]

[76] Arthur Krock in *The New York Times*, March 11; *Morgenthau Diaries (MS.)*, March 13 (Vol. 381, p. 254). Summaries of press opinion prepared for the Secretary of the Treasury by Alan Barth noted a slight decline in public support of the bill, from the 58 percent of February 14, to 55 percent at the end of February (*ibid.*, Vol. 379, pp. 331 ff.). On the role of Senator Byrnes, see his *Speaking Frankly* (New York, 1947); Sherwood: *Roosevelt and Hopkins*, 264; and Alsop and Kintner in the *Washington Post*, March 28, 1941.

[77] *Public Papers and Addresses*, X (1941), 51 ff., 60 ff. Cf. Sherwood: *Roosevelt and Hopkins*, 265 ff. On the speed with which the President moved to implement the new law: *Stimson Diary (MS.)*, March 11, 12; *Morgenthau Diaries (MS.)*, February 25, 26, 1941 (Vol. 375, pp. 310 ff.; Vol. 376, pp. 56 ff.).

5. THE WASHINGTON STAFF CONVERSATIONS

In the midst of the national debate on Lend-Lease the President, without the knowledge even of Mr. Hull, had quietly slipped away from Washington to greet the new Ambassador of Great Britain as he reached Annapolis (January 24, 1941). The American public subsequently manifested great satisfaction over this deliberately ostentatious welcome to Lord Halifax. Writing to the President next day, Herbert Bayard Swope described it as a "stroke of genius" in which "you personified the nation."[78] The public, however, was quite unaware that the new battleship, *King George V*, which brought Lord Halifax from England, also carried other distinguished passengers: the representatives of the British Chiefs of Staff, appropriately disguised as military advisers to the British Purchasing Commission in Washington.

Invited by Admiral Stark the previous December with the approval of the President, these British officers were to meet secretly with their American counterparts in formal military staff conversations which lasted until March 29, 1941.[79] The purpose of these highly significant meetings was, in the words of their concluding report:

(a) To determine the best methods by which the armed forces of the United States and the British Commonwealth . . . could defeat Germany and the Powers allied with her, should the United States be compelled to resort to war [*be compelled* changed from *decide* by the President]; (b) to coördinate on broad lines, plans for the employment of the forces of the Associated Powers; and (c) to reach agreements concerning the methods and nature of Military Coöperation of the two nations, including . . . areas of responsibility, the major lines of military strategy to be pursued . . . the strength of the forces . . . and the determination of satisfactory command arrangements. . . .[80]

The first plenary session of the Washington staff conversations was held on January 29, 1941, against the somber background of the Battle of the Atlantic, as yet unrelieved by the passage of Lend-Lease. Both the President and Secretary Hull had determined in advance not to be present nor even to receive the British delegates, in order to emphasize that the discussions were to be at the technical and not at the governmental level. Thus, no binding commitments could be made by the American delegates. The open-

[78] Letter of Swope to the President, January 25, 1941 (*Roosevelt Papers:* Official File 48, Box 2); *Moffat Diary (MS.),* January 31, 1941.

[79] The most detailed account of the staff conversations is provided in the Kittredge MS.: *United States-British Naval Coöperation,* but all the main points are covered by Watson: *Chief of Staff: Prewar Plans and Preparations,* 374-91. On the preparations see *supra,* Chapter VIII, Section 2. The role of the State Department in facilitating the conversations is depicted in Secretary Hull's memos of conversation with Lord Lothian on November 25, 1940, and with the British Chargé d'Affaires, Mr. Butler, December 13, 1940; and in Mr. Welles's memos of conversation with Mr. Butler on December 14 and 23, 1940 (*Pearl Harbor Attack,* XX, 4072 ff.).

[80] "Report of the United States-British Staff Conversations" (short title "ABC-1"), March 27, 1941 (*Pearl Harbor Attack,* XV, 1485-1550).

ing statement of Admiral Stark (speaking also for General Marshall), which had the President's approval, was designed to the same end of insisting that any military agreements reached must remain contingent upon future political action by the Governments of Great Britain and the United States. While, ran this statement, it was self-evident that it would be advantageous to both countries if they were to become "associates" (changed by the President from "allies") in the event of war, it was at present the manifest desire of the American people to confine their assistance to Britain within the limits of material and economic aid.[81]

Having thus clarified at the outset the boundaries of profitable discussion, the American representatives outlined current United States national defense policy. Its primary feature remained the determination to secure the Western Hemisphere against attack. Next, the United States had committed itself to affording maximum material assistance to Britain against Germany, and, thirdly, it was opposing by all diplomatic means the extension of Japanese rule over additional territories. In the light of these fundamentals it seemed self-evident to the American delegates that if the United States did eventually become an active belligerent, it would serve its own as well as British interests best if the principal effort were exerted in the Atlantic and "naval-wise" in the Mediterranean. (This last was yet another presidential emendation.) Every effort should be made by both Governments to keep Japan out of the war, but if it proved impossible to forestall this eventuality, American operations in the Pacific should not be initially on such a scale as to jeopardize the success of the principal effort in the Atlantic.

With much of this now firmly established American strategic doctrine, the British staff officers found themselves quickly in agreement, since Admiral Ghormley had been expounding it in informal discussion with the Admiralty throughout the closing weeks of 1940. The British reply to the American opening statement therefore admitted that a decision would have to be sought first in the most vital theater: Europe. The British officers similarly recognized America's paramount concern for the security of the Western Hemisphere. However—and here differences emerged—the British insisted upon the vital importance to them of their Far Eastern position, including the security of Australia and New Zealand. If this position were lost —and the key to it was Singapore—the whole cohesion of the British Commonwealth would be lost with it. Singapore was, in their eyes, essential to the success of a joint Anglo-American war effort. While not denying this, the American delegates insisted that the British must assume responsibility for the defense of Singapore.

The Americans found themselves unable to accept the British rejoinder

---

[81] The opening statement (*Pearl Harbor Attack,* XIV, 1422), approved by the President on January 26, was based on the Joint Army-Navy Board's recent reformulation of United States national defense policy (*supra,* Chapter VIII, Section 2).

that they lacked adequate forces for this purpose, and, in the course of sub-sequent sessions, it developed that the specific disagreement over Singapore and the South Pacific area really illustrated a more general as well as a more profound difference between the British and American approach to a joint strategy for victory. As forecast earlier in the Prime Minister's letter to the President (December 8, 1940), the preferred British strategy continued to be of a delaying and defensive type. It contemplated no grand assault on *Festung Europa* until such time as blockade and air bombardment (as well, conceivably, as Soviet assistance in the east) had so reduced Germany's power to wage war that a return to the continent could be achieved without an appalling loss of life. This might, the British admitted, consume months or even years. In the meantime, however, Great Britain would attempt to maintain its peripheral positions in Malaya, North Africa, the Mediter-ranean, and the Middle East, thereby adding to the drain on Hitler's re-sources, and preparing some of these areas as jumping-off places for an assault on Europe.[82]

The American planners, well aware of the country's immense potential superiority in both matériel and man power, disagreed with portions of the British concept. If the United States became involved in the war, the Amer-ican strategic plan was to concentrate at once upon the creation of a vast striking force which as rapidly as possible was to be prepared to invade the continent. Only there could Hitler be decisively defeated. Accordingly, the American officers were skeptical of too great expenditure of men and ma-tériel in the defense of Britain's emplacements around the continent of Europe, save, of course, the United Kingdom itself. They refused to budge from the position they had long maintained, with the President's if not the State Department's support, with respect to Singapore.[83]

The Secretary of the Navy had announced early in January that the United States Fleet would on February 1 be divided into three forces: the Pacific Fleet, the Atlantic Fleet, and the Asiatic Fleet. In making this an-nouncement, Knox had implied that if there were to be any significant with-drawal of strength from the Pacific Fleet under Admiral Husband E. Kimmel, Admiral King's new Atlantic Fleet would be the beneficiary. Spe-cifically he had stated that the United States Asiatic Fleet would not be reinforced.[84] Therefore, to all British warnings that they themselves could

---

[82] The development of the discussion is outlined in Watson: *Chief of Staff: Prewar Plans and Preparations,* 375 ff.

[83] Watson: *Chief of Staff: Prewar Plans and Preparations,* 391 ff.

[84] *The New York Times,* January 9, 10; letter of Admiral Stark to Admiral Kimmel, January 13, 1941 (*Pearl Harbor Attack,* XVI, 2144 ff.). The testimony of Kimmel's predecessor, Admiral Richardson, on these changes is found *ibid.,* I, 281 ff.; cf. S. E. Morison: *Battle of the Atlantic,* 49 ff. Corresponding with the Navy's announcement of stronger concentration in the Atlantic was Secretary Stimson's move to combine three hitherto separate Army commands, viz., the Canal Zone, Puerto Rico, and Trinidad, into one command under General Van Voorhis (*The New York Times,* January 10, 1941).

not spare the capital ship strength to defend Singapore, and to their pleas that sufficient American strength be diverted from Pearl Harbor or elsewhere to assure Singapore's impregnability, the Americans turned a deaf ear. Upon this rock the conversations almost foundered. In the end, however, the military technicians sagely decided to submit their disagreements to the arbitration of political authority. Thereafter, since the areas of Anglo-American agreement were wider than the differences, progress was rapid. The upshot was the completion on March 27, 1941, of the now well-known joint report, "ABC-1."[85]

Thus, on the same day that Congress appropriated the seven billions necessary to assure Lend-Lease aid to Great Britain, the American-British staff conversations ended with the first major Anglo-American agreement on the strategy best calculated to make such aid effective. Admiral Stark and General Marshall presently approved ABC-1, and were followed by Secretaries Knox and Stimson. Mr. Hull, however, preferred to remain in ignorance of the details of the agreement. The President likewise withheld his formal, though not his tacit assent to the ABC-1 report and to the Joint Army-Navy War Plan (Rainbow No. V), based upon it, when both documents were officially presented to him in June. His decision was motivated again by a desire to make clear to all concerned, including the British Government, that the theoretical course of action sketched in ABC-1 was for the most part contingent upon America's actual entry into the war. If and when this occurred the President would implement both ABC-1 and Rainbow No. V.[86]

Most of the actions contemplated under ABC-1 were designed for a future state of American belligerency. Nevertheless, the staff conversations immensely facilitated the wise allocation of immediate responsibilities and available resources in prudent preparation for such an evident possibility. Thanks to the ABC-1 agreement, Admiral Stark could push ahead rapidly with the project of a Support Force within the Atlantic Fleet, in the event that the Administration decided to escort merchant vessels through the forbidden areas.[87] He could likewise send officers and technicians to Scotland and Northern Ireland to inspect sites for possible American bases in the same contingency, a task made more pressing because of Prime Minister De Valera's stubborn refusal to make bases available in Eire.[88] Knox could

[85] Kittredge MS.: *United States-British Naval Coöperation*. The report is printed *in toto* in *Pearl Harbor Attack*, XV, 1485-1550.

[86] *Pearl Harbor Attack*, IV, 1936 ff. For Stark's report on the President's reaction to ABC-1, see his letter to Admiral Kimmel, April 4, 1941 (*Pearl Harbor Attack*, XVI, 2160 ff.), and his letter of April 3 to Kimmel, Hart and King, April 3, 1941 (*ibid.*, XVII, 2462 ff.).

[87] For these preparations see S. E. Morison: *Battle of the Atlantic*, 49 ff.

[88] *Ibid.*, p. 53. Not even the persuasive arguments of Wendell Willkie, or Colonel Donovan's eloquence, supplementing the efforts of the American Minister, could move De Valera. Accordingly the United States Government firmly refused to supply Eire

further put Admiral Kimmel on notice to expect a transfer of some of his ships to the Atlantic Fleet. Lastly, but by no means least, ABC-1 made provision for continuing high level consultation between the British and American Chiefs of Staff. Not only did Admiral Ghormley return to his post in London accompanied by Major General James E. Chaney, but British staff officers remained in Washington to constitute the permanent British Joint Staff Mission, destined one day to form the British section of the Combined Chiefs of Staff. It was as a result of these close associations, and in the sense of mutual understanding rather than concrete commitments that, in Mr. Sherwood's phrase, the "common law alliance," publicly entered into through Lend-Lease, was privately consummated through the Anglo-American staff conversations in Washington.[89]

---

with Lend-Lease armaments (despatch from Gray, Dublin, February 6; tel. from Donovan to Knox, March 11; memo of conversation between Welles and the Irish Minister, Mr. Brennan, and the Irish Minister of Defense, Mr. Aiken, March 20; tel. to Gray, March 28, 1941).

[89] On the permanent staff arrangements see Watson: *Chief of Staff: Prewar Plans and Preparations*, 384 ff., and Cline: *Washington Command Post: The Operations Division*, 48-49. See also Admiral Stark's letter to Admiral Kimmel, February 25, 1941 (*Pearl Harbor Attack*, XVI, 2149 ff.). For efforts to prove or imply that Anglo-American war plans involved binding political commitments to Britain, see Beard: *President Roosevelt and the Coming of the War*, 420 ff.; and George Morgenstern: *Pearl Harbor: The Story of the Secret War* (New York, 1947), Chapter VIII.

CHAPTER X

Tokyo: Frustration and Retreat

1. SOVIET NONCOÖPERATION

Before launching its advance to the south, the Tokyo Government needed more than German recognition of the Japanese sphere, as accorded by the Tripartite Pact. If at all possible, it must free itself of the self-imposed incubus of the China Incident and above all liquidate the Soviet-Japanese antagonism, so as to feel secure in the north while it pursued its objectives in the south. Actually, the Chinese and Soviet problems were closely linked, for the Kremlin had, since 1937, been lending aid and comfort to the resistance of Nationalist China, for the obvious purpose of keeping its traditional Far Eastern enemy, Japan, engaged in an exhausting struggle. If, then, Tokyo were to succeed in settling outstanding issues with the Soviet Union, it might hope that Soviet aid to Chungking would end and that Chiang Kai-shek might be driven by desperation to accept Japanese terms. It will simplify the problem, therefore, to consider first the projected agreement between Tokyo and Moscow, to the achievement of which the German Government had promised to contribute in every way possible.

The Japanese objective could have been attained in one of two ways: either by the adherence of Soviet Russia to the Tripartite Pact, in which case the Kremlin would have joined the antidemocratic front in return for recognition of a sphere of influence or interest in Asia; or by the conclusion of a nonaggression pact between Soviet Russia and Japan, for which Tokyo was prepared to pay a substantial price. In the absence of official records from either side it is, of course, hazardous to speak positively of Japanese or Soviet policy in respect to this problem. However, it is known that in October, 1940, General Tatekawa had been sent to Moscow as Ambassador with the specific mission to negotiate a deal. From this it may be concluded that the Tokyo Government was not sanguine about the chances of Soviet Russia's abandoning its position merely in return for prospective gains at the expense of Britain and its friends. Before Ribbentrop had an opportunity to dangle that carrot before Molotov, General Tatekawa had already taken the first steps toward submitting the proposal for a nonaggression pact to the Kremlin. The Soviet Commissar had, however, shown great wariness and had made no effort to discover what Tokyo's specific terms might be. Clearly he was unwilling to do business until he had discovered what Hitler and Ribbentrop had to offer. During his visit to Berlin (November 12-14, 1940) he was to learn that the Germans were indeed eager for a settlement of Soviet-Japanese differences and that, according to the proposed Quadripartite Pact, the Soviet sphere of influence was to be to the south "in the direction of the Indian Ocean," while the Japanese sphere was to be "an area of eastern Asia to the south of the Island Empire of Japan."[1]

Of the further evolution of the Soviet-Japanese relationship almost nothing is known. It is reasonable to suppose that the Kremlin approached it not as a matter to be decided on its own merit, but as part of the larger problem of adherence to the Tripartite Pact, which in turn was synonymous with the problem of Soviet Russia's position in relation to the antagonists in the world struggle. Significantly, the *Tass* news agency on November 15, just after Molotov's return to Moscow, denied reports supposedly emanating from diplomatic circles in the Far East that the Soviet Union and Japan had reached agreement on their spheres of influence in the Orient, and that the Soviet Union had promised to discontinue its aid to Nationalist China.[2] At about the same time Ambassador Steinhardt reported that the Kremlin was demanding that Japan surrender its concessions in North Sakhalin as the price of an agreement. According to somewhat later information the Soviet demands were even more extensive and included the cession of Japanese (southern) Sakhalin and certain of the Kurile Islands, as well as rectification of the Siberian-Manchurian frontier. These terms were evidently too stiff for the Tokyo Government and the negotiations lapsed.[3]

This little-known chapter of wartime diplomacy may be said to have ended with the Soviet response to the conclusion of the treaty between Japan and the puppet Nanking Government on November 30, 1940. On December 5, 1940, the *Tass* agency announced "that the policy of the Soviet Union towards China remains unchanged," and that the Soviet Ambassador in Tokyo had so informed the Japanese Government.[4] Ten days

---

[1] See above, Chapter V. The earlier phases of the Soviet-Japanese negotiations were recounted in an article in *Pravda* of April 19, 1941, following the conclusion of the Soviet-Japanese neutrality treaty (tel. from Steinhardt, April 19, 1941).

[2] *The New York Times,* November 15, 1940; Max Beloff: *The Foreign Policy of Soviet Russia,* II (New York, 1949), 370.

[3] Tel. from Steinhardt, November 20, 1940; despatch from Grew (Tokyo), April 21, 1941, reviewing the history of the Soviet-Japanese negotiations.

[4] *Bulletin of International News,* XVII (2), 1667; Beloff: *The Foreign Policy of Soviet Russia,* II, 370. David J. Dallin: *Soviet Russia and the Far East* (New Haven, 1948), 159-60, is very inadequate on these matters.

later the Soviet Ambassador in Washington informed Under Secretary Welles officially that "the character of the Soviet Union's relations with China remains invariably good neighborly and is guided by the spirit of the Chinese-Soviet nonaggression pact of 1937."[5] Reviewing the entire problem of Soviet-Japanese relations at the end of the year, Ambassador Steinhardt concluded that an agreement was not imminent because of Tokyo's unwillingness to meet the Kremlin's exorbitant demands. The Ambassador thought the Kremlin genuinely desirous of an agreement, but believed "that the Soviet Government has sought and is seeking to exploit for its own immediate self-interest, as a means of exacting a higher price from Japan, the present situation in the Far East and in particular the existing tension between the United States and Japan."[6]

This estimate seems as reasonable now as when it was written. It was patently in the Soviet interest, as the relations between Moscow and Berlin became strained, to secure itself against attack in the Far East and in general to divert Japanese energies to the south. On the other hand, the Kremlin was definitely unwilling to sign the Tripartite Pact unless Germany conceded Soviet claims in eastern Europe; it was equally unwilling to conclude a nonaggression pact with Japan unless it could derive substantial gains from the transaction. By continuing its aid to China the Soviet Government could hamper Japanese freedom of action. At the same time it could safely calculate that if the Tokyo militarists were really determined to turn southward, they would eventually meet the Soviet terms.

To the Japanese the failure of the negotiations must have been a great disappointment. Tokyo's hopes that the Germans could bring Soviet Russia into the grand alliance were probably never high, but the evidence indicates that there was real expectation that Japan could on its own secure a nonaggression treaty at reasonable cost. These hopes had been blasted. So, by the end of 1940, had Japanese expectations that Nationalist China could be brought to see the hopelessness of its situation. Examination of this related subject will show that, so far as Japan was concerned, the Tripartite Pact provided little more than continuous disillusionment.

2. CHINA: A THORN IN THE FLESH

In the period following the Japanese attack on China in 1937 every Japanese Cabinet, on taking office, announced "settlement" of the China Incident as the first and foremost objective of its policy. Progress toward this end had, however, proved extremely limited, for the Chinese Nationalist regime, under Chiang Kai-shek, refused steadfastly to entertain any terms at all acceptable to Japan. By the autumn of 1940 the Japanese armies had

[5] Memo of conversation between Mr. Welles and Ambassador Oumansky, December 16, 1940.

[6] Tel. from Steinhardt, December 27, 1940.

secured control of practically all Chinese seaports and had overrun the rich-
est parts of the country. Yet the Nationalists, driven back on Chungking,
showed no inclination to abandon the struggle. In March, 1940, Tokyo had
engineered the establishment of the puppet regime of Wang Ching-wei at
Nanking, but even this drastic move had failed to make the expected impression on Chungking. The Japanese continued to win victories, but the
much-desired "settlement" still eluded them. With huge armies tied up in
China, it was hard to see how the Imperial Government could afford to
embark on further campaigns of expansion in southeast Asia. In short, there
was real danger that the golden opportunity presented by Hitler's successes
in Europe would have to be missed through Tokyo's inability to extricate its
forces from the gigantic involvement known as the China Incident.

The program underlying the Tripartite Pact seemed to promise a new approach to the problem, inasmuch as it was hoped in Tokyo that Britain
and the United States might be deterred from further aid to Chungking,
that Soviet Russia might be brought into the Axis, and that Germany might
exert sufficient pressure on Chiang Kai-shek to compel him to accept a compromise settlement. All these expectations were doomed to disappointment
before the close of the year 1940. In fact, the end result was exactly the opposite of what Tokyo had envisaged. The United States and Britain increased their support of Chungking, the Soviet Union refused to abandon
its policy of aiding China, and Germany failed in its efforts to make Chiang
Kai-shek see the light. It must be confessed that information on many aspects of this problem is exceedingly scant, but the main lines can be drawn
with considerable assurance and the American policy, at least, can be traced
in some detail.

Foreign Minister Matsuoka, when he concluded the Tripartite Pact, had
boundless confidence in the future. On October 7 he appealed publicly to
China to align itself with the Axis powers, instead of "playing a role in the
front line of European and American capitalism."[7] This appeal was presently followed by the communication to Chungking of Japan's proposed
terms for a negotiated peace.[8] The moment seemed altogether opportune,
for the Chungking regime was in a worse plight than at any time since the
beginning of hostilities in 1937. The Japanese had forced the closing of the
Yunnan Railroad and the Burma Road, and only limited supplies could be
brought from Soviet Russia by the overland route. Cut off from the outside
world, China was suffering from shortages of every kind. Inflation was
reaching dangerous dimensions and it was becoming exceedingly difficult to
maintain the armies in the field. Furthermore, the Japanese had sent new
and faster planes to China in August. These had driven the Nationalist Air
Force from the skies and were bombing Chungking and other Chinese cities

[7] *The New York Times,* October 8, 1940.
[8] *Pearl Harbor Attack,* XX, 4292.

with impunity. Though the British announcement of the reopening of the Burma Road afforded some prospect of relief, systematic Japanese air attacks on the road soon darkened this prospect also.

Chiang Kai-shek, beset by countless internal problems and rapidly coming to the end of his tether, was naturally much disturbed by Molotov's visit to Berlin and by the possibility that the Kremlin might undertake a radical revision of its Far Eastern policy. He must also have been troubled by the public announcement on November 13, 1940, that the Japanese Imperial Council had met in the presence of the Emperor and had reached "complete agreement" with respect to Japanese policy in the China affair.[9] Japanese records have since revealed that the Imperial Council had accepted an "Outline for Settlement of the China Incident," the main point of which was that a final effort should be made to induce Chiang Kai-shek to accept the merger of his Government with that of Wang Ching-wei. In case of refusal, Tokyo was determined to sign further agreements with the Nanking Government and, to all intents and purposes, make that puppet regime its agent in China.[10]

In support of this "final" Japanese effort, Ribbentrop also went into action. On the eve of Molotov's arrival in Berlin the Nazi Foreign Minister called in the Chinese Ambassador and attempted to frighten and cajole him into acceptance of the Japanese terms. He warned the Ambassador that Japan was about to recognize the Nanking regime officially and urged him to convey to Chungking the German view that Chiang Kai-shek would be well advised to yield.[11] Evidently elated by his ensuing conferences with Molotov, Ribbentrop followed up his first *démarche* by a second diplomatic move. The German Government, he told the Chinese Ambassador, was more than ever convinced that it was in China's interest to come to terms with Japan. Germany had won the war in Europe. Obviously, therefore, China could no longer expect much assistance from Britain or the United States. If China failed to take advantage of what Ribbentrop described as "the last chance," Japan would recognize Wang Ching-wei and Germany and Italy would follow suit. As a final inducement, Ribbentrop expressed the hope that China would join the Axis and promised that Germany would guarantee fulfillment of the Japanese terms of peace, if China accepted them.[12]

Neither the Japanese nor the Germans succeeded in moving Chiang Kai-shek by pleas and arguments. It may be recalled that on November 15, 1940, the Soviet official news agency, *Tass*, had announced that reports that Soviet Russia would discontinue aid to China were contrary to fact. Further-

[9] *Bulletin of International News,* XVII (2), 1596.

[10] "Tojo Memorandum" (*Tokyo War Crimes Documents,* Proceedings, 36,206); see also *Tokyo War Crimes Documents,* No. 837A.

[11] *Nazi-Soviet Relations,* 224.

[12] Tel. from Johnson (Chungking), November 20, 1940.

more, Chiang had by this time seen that the Japanese had not taken up the challenge thrown down by the British when they reopened the Burma Road, and he had received ample assurance that the United States would continue and even increase its aid. Since there was not the slightest danger that Britain, the United States or even Soviet Russia would recognize the legality of the Nanking regime, Chiang felt safe in standing his ground. A last minute appeal by Wang Ching-wei himself was ignored and the Japanese offers were turned down.

Tokyo's reply was the conclusion of a treaty defining the "basic relations" between Japan and the Nanking regime, and the issuance of a joint declaration of Japan, Manchukuo and "China" (November 30, 1940). These agreements provided for close collaboration in the political and economic spheres, and for common action against communism. In order that Japan might aid in the defense against communism, it was to be permitted to station troops in specified areas of Inner Mongolia and North China until after the "warlike operations" should have been brought to a close.[13]

Chungking's response to Tokyo's maneuver was utterly uncompromising. An official statement of the Chinese Foreign Office read in part as follows:

The National Government of the Republic of China has repeatedly declared, and desires to reiterate most emphatically, that Wang Ching-wei is the arch-traitor of the Republic and that the puppet regime at Nanking is an illegal organization whose acts of whatever character are null and void in respect of all Chinese citizens and all foreign countries. The so-called treaty just signed at Nanking is totally devoid of legality and has no binding force whatever.

Should any foreign country choose to accord recognition to the puppet organization, the Government and people of China would consider it a most unfriendly act and would be constrained to discontinue their normal relations with such a country.

Whatever Japan may attempt or conspire to do in China or in the Pacific, China is determined to fight on till victory is won, and she is confident of victory because to freedom and right and justice victory inevitably belongs.[14]

It is hardly worth making the point that in fully recognizing the "National" Government of Wang Ching-wei, the Japanese by no means solved their problem or reached a "settlement" of the China Incident. In fact, the Nanking regime was so far from being a solution that it is hard to believe that the Japanese themselves regarded it as anything more than a threat to Chungking. No one could suppose that Nanking would be able to subdue the rest of the country. Japan would have to keep troops there, as before, to fight the Communists, with whom Chiang was temporarily allied. Tokyo might flatter itself that it now had a "legal" basis for its "warlike operations" in China, and it eventually induced its German and Italian allies to

---

[13] Texts of these agreements are printed in *Foreign Relations of the United States: Japan*, II, 117 ff.

[14] Statement of December 1, 1940 (*Foreign Relations of the United States: Japan*, II, 122-23).

recognize the fact. But the rest of the world ignored the claim and refused to be misled by Japan's devious arrangements. Indeed, it is perfectly clear in retrospect that the Japanese recognition of the Nanking regime served only to harden the resistance of Nationalist China and to clinch the determination of the United States, Britain and Soviet Russia to support Chungking in every possible way, both to frustrate the Japanese effort to conquer China and to keep Japan so involved on the mainland that it would be unable to embark upon major operations elsewhere.

3. AMERICAN AID TO CHINA

The reopening of the Burma Road on October 17, 1940, came in the nick of time so far as Chiang Kai-shek and the Chungking Government were concerned. Their situation had already become desperate and they were now confronted with the likelihood that the Tripartite Pact would bring about fundamental changes in the power balance of the Far East. On October 18 the Generalissimo discussed his problems for fully two hours with the American Ambassador, Mr. Nelson Johnson, and requested him to inform President Roosevelt of the crisis which China was facing. The problems, he said, were not new, but he was convinced that President Roosevelt was not aware of the degree to which they had recently been exacerbated. China's economy was literally on the verge of collapse. Worse, the Communists were quietly taking advantage of the situation to undermine the prestige of the Nationalist Government and lower the morale of the Chinese people, already at the breaking point. True, the reopening of the Burma Road might afford some relief. It might even result in the resumption of supplies from Soviet Russia which, the Generalissimo revealed, had been suspended when the Burma Road was closed in July. If, however, the Japanese were to attack and block the road, conditions would become worse than ever. Communist influence would increase and the Kremlin might well divert its assistance to the Communist groups. While extremely grateful for past American loans, Chiang begged that Washington consider one large loan for the future. Mr. T. V. Soong, who was in Washington, could inform the President of China's needs and plans. Suffice it to say that for the defense of the Burma Road and of Chinese cities, planes were the supreme necessity. Volunteer crews to man them would be of incalculable value, but time was of the essence: "If American planes could not arrive before the road was closed [i.e., by Japanese bombardment] or before the Japanese stopped the sea routes by occupying Singapore, it would be too late and China's position would be extremely if not hopelessly critical."[15]

Ambassador Johnson subscribed in full to the Generalissimo's grim diagnosis and argued emphatically that assistance to China was essential to the defense of American interests in the Far East. The United States, he thought, should

[15] Tel. from Johnson (Chungking), October 18, 1940.

send help at once, and make it "genuine." He was bitterly critical of the kind of "flimsy" aid that had been given under the rubric of "all aid short of war." This, in his opinion, was futile and obnoxious. By forcing the Chinese to pay for supplies the United States was draining off what little money and resources remained and thus contributing to the already tragic inflation. The net effect was to discourage the Chinese in a war they were fighting in the American as well as in their own interest. It was time to end such "callous and dangerous smugness" and to send aid on a large scale and without delay. Badly needed were 500-1000 planes, of which 500 ought to be sent within three months if possible. There were, according to the Ambassador, excellent airfields in Chekiang, from which Formosa and Japan could be bombed. Adoption of such drastic measures might eventually make war between Japan and the United States unnecessary.[16]

There was no disposition in Washington to quarrel with the Ambassador's recommendations. Aid to Nationalist China had long been an accepted American policy. But it had, to date, been on a modest scale partly because of the shortage of important military supplies and partly because of technical difficulties of financing and transportation.[17] It was certainly important that the Chungking Government be enabled to continue the struggle against Japan, yet no good purpose would be served by raising extravagant hopes. In his reply to the Generalissimo (October 24), President Roosevelt struck a sympathetic, albeit cautious note. Chiang's veiled plea for an alliance was gently rejected: the Generalissimo must appreciate the traditional American policy of eschewing alliances except possibly in wartime. But this did not mean that the United States was precluded from supporting other nations by peaceful means if such support advanced American interests. Certainly Chinese and American interests ran on parallel lines and it was a premise of American policy that China was capable of setting up an effective democratic state.

Leaving these generalities and turning to Chiang's specific requests, Mr. Roosevelt expressed sympathy for China's plight and admiration for Chinese fortitude. He reiterated his desire for a just peace in the Far East, but hastened to warn the Generalissimo that Japan's military leaders would hardly subscribe to such a peace at the present time. The United States was therefore preparing to support China with further loans and was hoping to send more planes. In the first eight months of the year 115 planes had been licensed for export to China and of these 48 had actually been despatched. The President carefully avoided a firm commitment to send more, but pointed out that American armament production was mounting daily and that the outlook for the future was much rosier. Besides, he argued, it was

---

[16] Tels. from Johnson, October 20 and 23, 1940.

[17] Memo of the Division of Far Eastern Affairs, October 23, 1940, supporting Chinese requests for more loans and for planes.

doubtful whether the Japanese could seal the Burma Road by bombing attacks. As for Singapore, there was indeed a danger of Japanese attack, but it did not seem to him imminent. The Japanese, he opined, must realize the difficulties of such an operation and "would not lightly embark upon such a venture while Great Britain is still strong in Europe and the American Fleet is at Hawaii." In conclusion Mr. Roosevelt assured the Generalissimo that his proposals would be further discussed in Washington with the Chinese Ambassador and Mr. T. V. Soong. The United States Government would explore every means of aiding China within the limits of the law.[18]

Chiang Kai-shek did not conceal his gratification at learning of American plans to advance more money and perhaps provide more planes.[19] But for the rest the President's message fell short of the strong moral support which the Generalissimo felt necessary if the Chinese people were to be rescued from the despair and sense of abandonment which were overtaking it. He therefore took another, less direct tack. On November 2 he handed certain proposals to the British Ambassador which, a week later, he communicated to Ambassador Johnson also. These proposals called, in the first instance, for a joint declaration by China, Britain and the United States reaffirming the Open Door and the Nine-Power Treaty, and opposing Japan's attempt to establish a New Order in East Asia. This declaration was to be followed by another, by Britain and the United States alone, announcing that a free and independent China was a prerequisite for peace not only in the Far East but in the entire Pacific area. Thereupon a treaty of alliance was to be concluded between Britain and China, to which the United States would be invited to adhere. If Washington found it impossible to go so far, Chiang hoped it would at least indicate full approval and support.

The Generalissimo's proposals included also suggestions for concrete measures of mutual support. Britain and the United States were to lend China between two and three hundred million dollars. The United States was to "lend" China between 500 and 1000 planes, of which 200 to 300 were to be delivered before the end of 1940. Both Britain and the United States were to engage themselves to send military, economic and financial missions to China. In return China would promise that, in the event of war between Japan, Britain and the United States, the entire Chinese Army would participate and all Chinese airfields and ports would be placed at the disposal of the Allied forces.[20]

What Chiang was proposing, in the very days of Molotov's visit to Berlin, was that Britain and the United States should ally themselves outright with China, in what would have amounted to another Tripartite Pact. But, despite the danger that the Chungking regime might succumb to the pressure of Tokyo, reinforced by action on the part of Germany and perhaps

---

[18] Tel. to Johnson, October 24, 1940.
[19] Tel. from Johnson, October 31, 1940.
[20] Tel. from Johnson, November 9, 1940.

Soviet Russia, there could be no question of Washington's accepting such far-reaching commitments as the Generalissimo suggested. For the moment Acting Secretary Welles could only restate the American position with regard to alliances and entanglements and reiterate his Government's determination to do everything possible, within the established laws and policies, to help China.[21] At the same time every effort was made to reassure Chiang with respect to the Hitler-Molotov meeting. This, according to Washington, was primarily a move in psychological warfare, designed to intimidate various peoples and governments. There could be no doubt that Germany was doing its utmost to bring about a *rapprochement* between the Soviet Union and Japan, but there was little likelihood of an agreement between Germany, Soviet Russia and Japan which would prove really inimical to China, or even induce the Kremlin to sacrifice China.[22]

The Generalissimo was not easily comforted. Quite possibly he was taking advantage of the general world situation to press his plan for a new Tripartite agreement to counterbalance the Axis, but Ambassador Johnson was convinced that his appeals were those of a man "who has lost confidence in his ability to contend longer with a domestic situation which he feels he cannot control."[23] He had by this time learned that Japanese recognition of the rival Nanking regime was impending. Even though he refused to bargain with Tokyo, he had every reason to fear the worst, and therefore urged that the United States try to prevent Japanese recognition of Nanking or, failing that, adopt the plan proposed on November 9, 1940.[24] In a new message to Washington he explained:

We are well aware of America's traditional policy that no alliance is to be concluded with any country. But the present situation in the Far East requires from America consideration of the following two points:
I. Support by America of Chinese-British mutual assistance and alliance.
II. Issuance by America of a declaration jointly with Great Britain affirming their common stand in the Far East and their readiness to render all possible assistance to China, thereby enabling her to maintain her sovereignty and territorial and administrative integrity so as to restore international peace and order in the Pacific.

These two measures should be simultaneously carried out if the danger that now confronts China is to be averted, armed resistance is to be further strengthened, and Japan's Far Eastern new order and Wang Ching-wei's intrigue, centered round the creation of a puppet regime, are to be frustrated. Otherwise China's domestic and international difficulties will be dangerously worsened. Our economic and military affairs have already been very bad, and Japan's recognition of Wang Ching-wei's puppet regime will have a tendency to accelerate the collapse of our armed resistance.

I would be lacking in frankness if I did not communicate the foregoing to our friend, America. I hope that the American Government will be good enough to let me

[21] Tel. to Johnson, November 18, 1940.
[22] Tel. to Johnson, November 23, 1940, with a message for Chiang Kai-shek.
[23] Tel. from Johnson, November 27, 1940.
[24] Tel. from Johnson, November 21, 1940.

know as soon as possible whether it can support the concrete measures for assistance marked IV in my proposals and the suggested Chinese-British mutual assistance and alliance.[25]

At the very time this message was being transmitted President Roosevelt dropped the following note to Mr. Welles: "I have a hunch that we ought to do something in regard to the Chinese loan quickly or not at all—because I have real fear that the domestic situation in Free China will deteriorate unless we do something fast. Will you work on this?"[26] Actually efforts were already well under way to drum up more money and supplies for China. The contribution of additional planes had been blessed by Mr. Hull, whereupon Secretaries Stimson and Morgenthau, rejoicing that the Secretary of State was for once in agreement with them, were displaying ingenuity as well as zeal in trying to find the goods which, unhappily, did not exist. There simply were no planes not already earmarked for purposes of the highest priority: the defense of the British Isles and of the Western Hemisphere. A small shipment of pursuit planes, which had been ordered by Sweden, had already been taken over for use in the Philippines. Even so, Mr. Stimson considered switching them to China, until General Marshall declared it impossible to certify them as surplus. Thereupon Mr. Hull and Mr. Stimson bethought themselves of some sixteen planes at the time lying on the docks at Manila, en route to Siam. Mr. Morgenthau hastily "cooked up" a plan for diverting these to Chungking, but this promising scheme, too, came to nothing when it was learned that the planes lacked engines.[27]

The projected loan made little progress until the President intervened in late November. In view of the coming Japanese recognition of the Nanking Government it seemed to Mr. Roosevelt imperative that something be done, not only to fortify the morale of the Chinese but also to challenge the Japanese. He therefore telephoned Secretary Morgenthau (November 28) and informed him that China was to be given a loan of one hundred million dollars. The Export-Import Bank was to supply half this sum and Morgenthau was to get the other half from the Treasury's Stabilization Fund. This the President wanted done within twenty-four hours.

The "twenty-four hour policy," as Mr. Morgenthau described it, produced a flurry of excitement. The Secretary of the Treasury had pledged his word to Congress not to use any part of the Stabilization Fund to assist any country in prosecuting war. Neither his strong and unwavering sympathy for China, nor his profound loyalty to the President could induce him to authorize use of the fund without prior consent of Congress. Mr. Hull argued with him that "an emergency situation existed," while the President pleaded: "If you don't do it today, it may mean war in the Far East. . . .

[25] Tel. and despatch from Johnson, November 22, 1940.

[26] Note of November 22, 1940 (*Roosevelt Papers:* Secretary's File, Box 69).

[27] *Stimson Diary (MS.)*, October 18, 1940; *Morgenthau Diaries (MS.)*, October 23, 1940 (Vol. 324, pp. 196 ff.).

It is a matter of life and death." The trouble was that it was Friday and it would be impossible to convene the appropriate Congressional committees until the following Monday. The President personally telephoned the chairmen of the Senate and House committees, only to find that the latter insisted on regular Congressional approval.

Meanwhile Secretary Hull was drafting a statement announcing the loan. No one knew whether the President would go on with it or wait until Secretaries Morgenthau and Hull had been to "the Hill." Happily a way was found to overcome the curse of the week end, to meet the requirements of the situation, and to salve Mr. Morgenthau's conscience, all in one. Mr. Welles revised the State Department announcement in such fashion as to suggest a total of one hundred million dollars without committing the Treasury in advance to draw on the Stabilization Fund. On November 30, concurrently with Tokyo's announcement of its treaty with Nanking, Mr. Roosevelt gave out news of the "contemplated credit" to the Chinese Government. One half of this credit had already been arranged for; the other half was "in process of consultation with the appropriate committees of Congress."[28]

News of the loan was received with much satisfaction in Chungking and with widespread enthusiasm in the United States. Contrary to his expectation, Mr. Morgenthau, appearing with Mr. Hull in joint executive session of the Senate Banking Committee and the House Committee on Coinage, Weights and Measures, met with a friendly reception. Secretary Hull briefly reviewed American policy in the Far East since 1937 and explained China's need for funds. Among other things he stressed that "the continued resistance of China is of great importance to the continued resistance of Great Britain, and the continued resistance of both is of great importance to the ultimate peace and security of the United States." Asked whether he thought the loan would be regarded by Japan as an unfriendly act, the Secretary hotly denounced Japanese aggression and termed the proposed loan an act of self-defense: "If to act in self-defense is an unfriendly act—then we are proposing to do something that is unfriendly." Appeasement, he stressed, would be useless. The nations being overrun by the aggressors had no more chance of placating them "than a squirrel would of appeasing a boa constrictor." The committees then heard Mr. Morgenthau state that he did not think the proposal to use the Stabilization Fund involved assistance to China to win the war, after which Senator Glass, implying that it was all much ado about nothing, moved approval and adjournment.[29]

The financial commitments thus undertaken were not actually translated

---

[28] The text in *Documents on American Foreign Relations,* III, 282. The account above is based on the detailed record in the *Morgenthau Diaries* (*MS.*), November 29 and 30, 1940 (Vol. 333, pp. 31 ff., 228 ff.).

[29] *Morgenthau Diaries* (*MS.*), December 2, 1940 (Vol. 334, pp. 85 ff.).

into firm agreements until some months later.[30] Neither was much progress made in satisfying the other requirements of the Chungking Government, which the Generalissimo had advanced with such insistence. On December 4 Messrs. Hornbeck and Hamilton, in behalf of Secretary Hull, presented the Chinese Ambassador and Mr. T. V. Soong with the American reply to Chiang's "plan" of November 9. This reply reiterated the impossibility of an American-Chinese alliance and likewise of American pressure on Britain to conclude an alliance.[31] Furthermore, it deprecated the idea of a fresh declaration of principles, jointly or otherwise. Such a declaration, remarked Mr. Hornbeck, had been prepared for publication on November 30 but had been replaced by the announcement of the loan. There was no particular merit, he observed, in focusing attention on Japan's treaty with Nanking. The American attitude toward the Nanking regime had been made clear when it was first set up in March, 1940. Announcement of the loan left no doubt that the American attitude remained unchanged.

As for specific needs, Mr. Hornbeck promised the early delivery of fifty planes, to be followed by as many more as could be made available. The disappointment of the Chinese at this great reduction of the original request may have been tempered somewhat by Mr. Hornbeck's suggestion that the State Department might issue passports to American citizens who wished to serve as "aviation instructors" in China, a suggestion that foreshadowed the creation of Colonel Claire Chennault's Flying Tigers of later date.[32]

Secretary Morgenthau, for one, appears to have been unwilling to let the matter of air support for the Chinese rest there. He had evidently been intrigued by an idea bruited from time to time and suggested in Chiang's "plan," namely, that, with relatively few bombers, the Chinese could attack Japan itself and thus give an entirely new turn to the Far Eastern situation. On December 8 he broached the matter to Mr. T. V. Soong as they were both returning from lunch with the President. Mr. Morgenthau remarked that to ask for 500 planes, as the Generalissimo had done, was like asking for 500 stars. It might be more feasible for the United States to supply the Chinese a few long-range bombers and experienced crews. Since the Sec-

[30] The agreements, dated April 1, 1941, were not signed until April 25, 1941 (State Department memo by Richardson Dougall: *Financial Aid to China, 1939-1943,* dated 1 February, 1944).

[31] The British felt that since a "full-blown alliance" of Britain, the United States and China was impossible, an Anglo-Chinese alliance would only irritate Japan without providing much advantage to China. The British did, however, advance the Chinese five million pounds sterling for stabilization of the currency, and another five million for purchases in the sterling area (tel. from London to the British Embassy, December 3, 1940, communicated to the State Department; copy in *Morgenthau Diaries, MS.,* Vol. 335, p. 144).

[32] Memo of Mr. Hornbeck and Mr. Hamilton to Secretary Hull, outlining the proposed reply to the Chinese, December 3, 1940; memo of conversation between Mr. Hornbeck and Mr. Hamilton on the one side, and Ambassador Hu Shih and Mr. T. V. Soong on the other, December 4, 1940. The Joint Army-Navy Board considered the Chinese request for planes on December 11, 1940.

retary intimated that such was also the President's idea, it goes without saying that Mr. Soong responded enthusiastically. He agreed that the bombing of Tokyo would have a "very decided" effect on the Japanese people and might change the entire Far Eastern picture. He would, so he said, communicate at once with the Generalissimo with regard to this proposal.

While awaiting word from Chungking, Mr. Morgenthau undertook a bit of educational work among his colleagues. To his intense surprise he found Secretary Hull sympathetic with the scheme. On the other hand, there was reason to suppose that Secretary Stimson might object to releasing the bombers, for General Marshall was repeatedly warning Mr. Soong that the United States was simply not in a position to supply many planes of any type. However, at first the prospects for the Morgenthau program appeared reasonably bright. Chiang sent a message to President Roosevelt saying that he had authorized Soong to discuss the matter. In a less guarded message to Mr. Morgenthau the Generalissimo stated that he had received intelligence that in the spring the Axis powers would launch synchronized attacks on Gibraltar, Suez and Singapore. In order to forestall the attack on Singapore, it would be necessary "to carry the war into Japan proper," and for that purpose long-range bombers would be necessary. He hoped Flying Fortresses could be provided and along with them a proportionate number of medium bombers and pursuit planes "so that the air force thus constituted could also support the counteroffensive which I am preparing with a view to retaking Canton and Hankow."

It may be assumed that Mr. Soong lost no time in laying the proposed plan before the President. Among the latter's papers is an unsigned memorandum, dated in pencil as of December, 1940, which may well be the notes left at the White House by Mr. Soong. The memorandum set forth the situation in China and all that could be done with 500 planes (200 modern bombers and 300 pursuit planes) to hold the Japanese in China, to block a Japanese advance on Malaya and Singapore, and even to threaten the Japanese in Hainan and Formosa. There were, according to this paper, 136 airfields in China on which the "Special Air Unit" could be based.[33]

Provided with Chiang's message, Mr. Morgenthau at once requested an opportunity to discuss the whole matter with the President. The latter, when told that the Generalissimo was prepared to attack Japan, is reported to have exclaimed: "Wonderful!" After the Cabinet meeting on December 19 Mr. Roosevelt raised the issue with Secretaries Hull, Stimson, Knox and Morgenthau and requested them "to work out a program." Everything seemed to be going swimmingly and Mr. Morgenthau even reached the point of arranging with Mr. Soong about the monthly pay of the pilots who

[33] *Roosevelt Papers:* Secretary's File, Box 72. The substance of this memo is almost identical with remarks made by Mr. Soong to Secretary Morgenthau on December 18 and it is quite possible that it was Mr. Morgenthau who left the notes with the President.

would fly the bombers and of discussing with Colonel Chennault various operational details. But difficulties were not slow to crop up.

On Sunday afternoon, December 22, 1940, Secretary Stimson entertained Mr. Knox, Mr. Morgenthau and General Marshall at his home for an informal discussion preliminary to a conference on the following morning. The entire plan was gone over in some detail, General Marshall reporting on his various conversations with Mr. Soong. According to Mr. Stimson's notes:

As usual, the demand boils down to land planes—planes for our Army—and threatens to deplete us more. The proposition as it was made to us the other day was rather half-baked. It hadn't been thought out. It was the product of Chinese strategists rather than well-thought-out American strategy and I called this meeting to try to get some mature brains into it, before we got committed to it.

The "mature brains" were those of General Marshall, who examined the project with officers of the Air Corps. Marshall questioned the advisability of letting the Chinese have American bombers, the more so as they would have to be given at Britain's expense. At the formal meeting on Monday morning (December 23) the General made clear, in a long exposition, that he thought the idea "impractical." Evidently he convinced those present and Secretary Morgenthau undertook to report to the President the consensus of the group. Therewith the project was dropped, though, as a solatium to the Chinese, arrangements were finally worked out with the reluctant British by which about 100 pursuit planes (chiefly for protection of the Burma Road) should be made available over the first three months of 1941.[34]

American efforts to aid China call to mind the Chinese saying: "There is much noise on the stairs, but no one enters the room." Considering the magnitude of Chungking's problem, American assistance was meager and slow. Despite all assurances of sympathy and interest, the arms and munitions sent during the entire year 1940 amounted in value to only nine million dollars.[35] It must be said, however, that it was not the will to do better that was lacking. The American public had long held China in real affection and the Government had never wavered in its policy of supporting China against Japanese aggression. The obstacles to really effective aid were almost exclusively of a practical nature: problems of transportation on the one hand and the tremendous demands made on American industry by the requirements of Britain on the other. These difficulties continued to plague Washington in its efforts to relieve the Chinese crisis—a crisis which was soon to become endemic. Nonetheless, it must be recognized that the conclusion of the Tri-

[34] The records of the bomber project form a special volume (No. 342A) of the Morgenthau Diaries (MS.), covering the period from December 2 to 23, 1940. The final phases are treated in the same collection, Vols. 342 and 344, pp. 12, 46, 86, 171. Additional light is thrown on the matter by the Stimson Diary (MS.), December 10, 13, 22, 1940.

[35] State Department memo: An Appraisal of United States Policy towards China, 1937 to April 17, 1941.

partite Pact, the pressure of Germany on China to conclude peace with Japan, and the fear of a possible Soviet-Japanese agreement all emphasized the importance of Chinese resistance and consequently served to stimulate the American effort. And the moral effect, if not the material, was considerable. American and British statements of solidarity and the obvious readiness of the democracies to do whatever possible no doubt helped save China from the demoralization and collapse that threatened in October, 1940. Conceivably the Soviet Government, too, was thereby influenced to resume shipment of supplies to China. Matters of this sort are not susceptible of definite proof, but it seems reasonably clear that one result of the Tripartite Pact was to bring the conflict in China into focus and to close the ranks of Japan's opponents in support of Chinese resistance.

4. THE ISSUE OF COMBINED ACTION

President Roosevelt's reëlection was the signal for the British, supported by the Australians, to renew their earlier pressure for common action by the British Commonwealth, the Netherlands and the United States in both the economic and military spheres. According to the British there was imminent danger that the Japanese would soon take over all of Indo-China and perhaps the Netherlands East Indies, after which an attack on Malaya and Singapore could be expected. It was essential, therefore, to prevent Tokyo from building up large stores of strategic materials. Britain and the Commonwealth nations, it was pointed out, had attempted to reduce their exports of key commodities to amounts normal for peacetime. The United States, on the other hand, had imposed a moral embargo and had completely cut off exports of a restricted number of items to Japan. It was highly desirable and indeed necessary that the economic policies of the Americans, British and Dutch be coördinated and that efforts be made to cut down the shipment of essential commodities, especially raw materials, from Latin American countries. The British therefore proposed secret conferences in London to examine all aspects of this problem and recommend a common line of action.[36]

The State Department at no time countenanced the idea of a secret conference and evaded all suggestions for a common policy. The chief reason for its attitude was no doubt the fear of leaks and the consequent political ructions, but in addition the consideration that problems of economic warfare were the concern of several United States Government agencies. These agencies, notably the State Department and the Treasury, were so much at loggerheads that it was extremely difficult to arrive at agreement on specific measures. A common American policy, which was still little more than a

---

[36] Tels. to and from the British Embassy and London, October 19 and 24, 1940 (*Morgenthau Diaries*, MS.).

pious hope, would have been a prerequisite for any profitable discussion with other powers.

Nevertheless, there was much sentiment in Government circles for more extensive and drastic economic sanctions against Japan. Secretaries Stimson, Knox and Morgenthau all advocated such a policy and Secretary Hull was not altogether opposed. Mr. Hull's point was simply that an embargo on all petroleum products, or even a comprehensive embargo on key exports, would have the effect of driving Japan to desperation and perhaps precipitating the war which everyone in his own way hoped to forestall. He therefore continued to put the quietus on suggestions for full-blown economic warfare. Unobtrusively, however, more and more restrictions were imposed on the export of important items, including those particularly stressed by the British. The Japanese found that American firms refused to sell without license goods for which under the law licenses were not required. Or again, they discovered that licenses were necessary for the purchase of machine tools for which there was no market in the United States—even for some which had been designed specially for Japanese machinery. Their protests, however, were put aside with statements that all exports had to be considered in connection with the American defense production effort and that only the officials of the Government could judge what might or might not be spared.[37]

The particular matter of machine tools was clinched on December 10, 1940, when the White House issued the following statement:

The President announced today that national defense requirements for iron and steel have increased to such an extent that it has become necessary to subject, as of December 30, 1940, iron ore, pig iron, ferro alloys, and certain iron and steel manufactures to the licensing requirement. Licenses will be granted for exports to the British Empire and the Western Hemisphere; and for the present, so far as the interests of national defense permit, for exports to other destinations in quantities approximating usual or pre-war exports.

The date of this order had been carefully chosen to follow hard upon the announcement of the loan to China, and was clearly designed as an additional warning to Japan in reply to the conclusion of Tokyo's treaty with Nanking.[38] Nor was this all. In rapid succession there followed a whole series of executive orders, extending the licensing system to certain chemicals, abrasives, measuring and testing machines and equipment for the production of aviation lubricating oil (December 20, 1940); to many kinds of copper, brass, zinc, nickel and potash products (January 10, 1941); to aluminum foil (January 29, 1941); and to well and refining machinery,

[37] *Foreign Relations of the United States: Japan,* II, 229 ff. (protest of November 19 and reply to November 30, 1940).

[38] Hull: *Memoirs,* I, 915. See also Herbert Feis: *The Road to Pearl Harbor* (Princeton, 1950), 136 ff.

radium, uranium, calf and kip skins (February 4, 1941), etc.[39] Concurrently efforts were made to induce other American Republics to coöperate in the restriction of exports to Japan.[40]

No good purpose would be served by examining the technical details of these various regulations. They were intended, as the Japanese quickly pointed out, to prevent the Tokyo Government from getting materials of which it stood in serious need—materials, more particularly, which were essential to Japan's warmaking capacity. The American policy was, however, carefully trimmed to fit the frame of safety. That is, sanctions were applied piecemeal so as to avoid provocation yet produce a cumulative impact. The effect was, in fact, considerable. Exports to Japan, which in December, 1940, amounted to more than nineteen million dollars in value, dropped in the following month to eleven and a half. The decline was to continue as more and more items were put under the licensing system. With the imposition of the crucial oil embargo in July, 1941, American trade to Japan was to disappear completely.

With respect to Anglo-American staff conversations it had already been decided in October that these should be initiated in both London and Singapore, but that they should be confined to exchange of information on respective plans, with the explicit understanding that the United States would not thereby be committed to any specific course of action in the event of war with Japan. During the ensuing weeks Admiral Ghormley, the American Special Naval Observer in London, did carry on informal discussions with high Admiralty officials, while Captain Purnell, Chief of Staff of Admiral Hart's Asiatic Fleet, engaged as an observer in exploratory conversations with British authorities at Singapore.[41] From these preliminary talks it emerged that more general conferences on Anglo-American strategy were desirable, and a secret meeting was to be formally arranged in Washington. As for the defense of southeast Asia, there was, for the moment, little more to be done, since the Dutch authorities were afraid that military conversations with the British might provoke a Japanese attack at a time when the British forces in the area were decidedly weak. The British, in turn, were reluctant to promise the Dutch support in the event of attack unless there were some reason to believe that the United States also would take a hand.[42]

[39] The orders and detailed specifications are printed in *Foreign Relations of the United States: Japan,* II, 232 ff.

[40] Circular despatch to United States missions to the other American Republics, December 9, 1940.

[41] *Pearl Harbor Attack,* IV, 1931 ff. By far the most detailed and authoritative account of the staff conversations is the one in Captain Tracy B. Kittredge's MS. study: *United States-British Naval Coöperation, 1939-1942.*

[42] Memo of conversation between Mr. Welles and the Netherlands Minister, October 28, 1940; memo of Admiral Hart to Admiral Stark, November 13, 1940, arguing that the British in fact would only court disaster if they attempted to help the Dutch, and that the only effective deterrent to Japanese attack would be the certainty that the

In anticipation of formal Anglo-American staff conversations, as noted in an earlier chapter, Admiral Stark had initiated a study of all possible American courses of action in the event of the country's becoming involved in the war.[43] His Plan Dog, which obtained the approval of the highest American authorities in the course of December and January, argued that the fate of Britain would be decided in the Atlantic rather than in the Pacific. The wisest course for the United States would therefore be to plan for a strong offensive in the Atlantic and for a defensive in the Pacific. This meant that every effort must be made to avoid war with Japan until the conflict in Europe had been decided. This in turn signified that the United States would not be in a position to exert strong pressure upon Japan. On the other hand, Admiral Stark did not recommend that the United States Fleet be moved from Hawaii into the Atlantic. That move did not as yet appear necessary, and the Fleet, so long as it remained in the Pacific, was deemed a deterrent to Japanese expansion.[44]

This strategy fitted in well with the policy advocated by the Administration, which had been for some time based on the proposition that Hitler constituted the greatest and most immediate danger to the United States and that the country could therefore not afford to divert a major part of its military strength to the Pacific. On November 29, 1940, Mr. Hull met in conference with Mr. Stimson and Mr. Knox to consider the Japanese problem. Once again he defined American Far Eastern policy: "This was the policy of slowing Japan up, so to speak, as much as we could by fighting a rear guard diplomatic action, without doing it so stringently as to drive her to get her supplies by making an attack on the Netherlands." At a Cabinet meeting later on the same day the situation was once again reviewed. It was the day before the official announcement of Tokyo's treaty with Nanking, and therefore a critical moment. Apparently the President and his Cabinet were, with the possible exception of Mr. Hull, in agreement that the basic ideas laid down in Plan Dog were sound and that future American policy and strategy in the Pacific should be guided by them.[45]

Meanwhile Lord Lothian had returned from a stay of some weeks in England. He reported his Government most pessimistic about the Far Eastern situation and apprehensive of a Japanese attack on Singapore. He therefore urged that high level staff conversations be initiated at an early date and renewed his plea for the basing of an American Fleet at Singapore. To all this Mr. Hull responded with his usual circumspection:

I did not undertake to specify just what future plans of this Government in that area

United States would act; memo of conversation between Mr. Welles and the Netherlands Minister, December 5, 1940, in which the latter reported the attitude of the Dutch Governor General of the Netherlands East Indies.

[43] Chapter VIII, Section 2, above.
[44] Kittredge MS., as cited above.
[45] *Stimson Diary (MS.)*, November 29, 1940.

would or might be from month to month and week to week, but added that he [the Ambassador] knew the various steps in our program thus far, which contemplated a firm and resolute policy toward Japan, both diplomatically and militarily, and aid to China at the same time.

With regard to the staff conversations, the Secretary noted:

Of course, there could be no agreements entered into in this respect, but that there should undoubtedly be collaboration with the view of making known to each other any and all information practicable in regard to what both might have in mind to do, and when and where, in case of a military movement by Japan in the South or in some other direction.

But the question of basing American ships at Singapore the Secretary evaded with the remark that this was a question for experts to pass on. To this the Ambassador replied by expressing the hope that all phases of the Pacific situation would be discussed by the naval authorities on both sides.[46]

There was still much difference of opinion in American official circles about the wisdom of sending part of the United States Fleet westward, if not to Singapore, then at least to the Philippines. The President was certainly interested in the idea from time to time and was apparently entertaining it at the end of November.[47] In the State Department Mr. Hornbeck, who had already been so influential in the decision to leave the Fleet at Hawaii, argued at length that the loss of Singapore would mean severance of the life lines between the United Kingdom and the Pacific Dominions, and would entail a serious weakening of the British position in the critical eastern Mediterranean area. Thus it would gravely jeopardize Britain's chances of withstanding the Nazi attack and by derivation would imperil America's first line of defense.[48] Nonetheless, the question was allowed to hang fire, probably because American naval authorities were aware of the weakness of Singapore's land defenses and the inadequacy of its facilities for repairing capital ships, to say nothing of Admiral Stark's objection to any proposal involving dispersal of the Fleet. The British were encouraged to do all they could to strengthen the defenses of Singapore, and the United States itself undertook to reinforce the Philippines. Even this latter decision was kept quiet, on recommendation of the State Department, on the theory that it would impress Japan just as much if it gradually transpired, while formal publication might provoke Tokyo.[49]

[46] Memo of conversation between Mr. Hull and Lord Lothian, November 25, 1940 (now printed in *Pearl Harbor Attack*, XX, 4072 ff.). See also Hull: *Memoirs*, I, 914.

[47] *Morgenthau Diaries* (*MS.*), November 29, 1940 (Vol. 333, p. 31).

[48] Memo entitled "The Importance of Singapore to the Defense of the British Isles and the British Empire and to the Interests of the United States" (December 4, 1940). This memo was sent to the President on December 10, 1940 (*Roosevelt Papers:* Secretary's File, Box 62).

[49] Memo of Hornbeck to Hull, December 7, 1940; Hull tel. to President Roosevelt (at sea), December 9, 1940; *Stimson Diary* (*MS.*), December 13, 16, 1940; Hull: *Memoirs*, I, 915.

Meanwhile preparations for the forthcoming staff conversations were being completed. On December 2 the British were invited to send a delegation of officers to Washington and on December 23 they announced that, in addition to high naval officers, a representative of the Army General Staff and a member of the Air Force Command would arrive toward the end of January. These officers were to act as a subcommittee of the General Staff, and the discussions were to be based on a revised version of Plan Dog.[50] The project for staff conferences at Singapore also made progress. The Dutch, having surmounted the most immediate danger by concluding an economic agreement with Japan, now agreed that high officers of the Netherlands command should consult with the British at Singapore. It was the hope of American authorities that the British and Dutch could first work out their mutual obligations, after which American officers could compare notes and examine possible courses of action with the British alone. However, Admiral Hart was formally authorized on December 12 to send representatives to Singapore for consultation with the Dutch as well as with the British, if necessary. At the same time he was warned to maintain utmost secrecy, particularly with regard to any contact with the Dutch.[51]

Before the end of the year, then, arrangements had been completed for the general conferences in Washington and the special conversations at Singapore. These conferences, already discussed in the preceding chapter, were to begin in January, 1941, and naturally were to constitute an important landmark in the development of the war situation. The President's reëlection made it possible for him and his advisers to adopt a somewhat more positive line. But the impetus toward this coördination of plans with the British and the Dutch came from the conclusion of the Tripartite Pact between Germany, Italy, and Japan, and the consequent danger that Japan might move southward at an early date. True, in all the discussions concerning the staff talks, it was explicitly stated that they could involve no commitment on the part of the United States Government to adopt any specific course in the event of war. On the other hand, it stands to reason that consultations of this nature invariably lead to better understanding of the interests and policies of the conferring parties. The British and Dutch could thenceforth assume that in the event of war in the Far East the United States would do something. Otherwise debate on plans and operations would be nonsensical. It is safe to conclude, therefore, that as the Japanese girded themselves, both diplomatically and militarily, for expansion over southeast Asia, they also provoked counteraction on the part of their op-

[50] Kittredge MS., as cited above; memo of conversation between Mr. Welles and Mr. Butler of the British Embassy, December 23, 1940; Admiral Stark's testimony in *Pearl Harbor Attack*, XI, 5239 ff.

[51] Note from the British Embassy, December 9, 1940; instructions from Admiral Stark to Admiral Hart, December 12, 1940 (*Pearl Harbor Attack*, IV, 1929 ff.); *Stimson Diary (MS.)*, December 13, 1940; memo of conversation between Mr. Hull and Mr. Butler, December 13, 1940.

ponents. Even though written agreements and commitments were as yet out of the question, the solidarity of the United States, Britain and the Pacific Dominions, the Netherlands and China was becoming a fact. It can hardly be supposed that the Japanese were entirely oblivious of this significant development.

5. The Enigma of Japanese Policy

The history of these affairs calls for some analysis of the impact of American and British policy on the further evolution of Tokyo's plans. Unfortunately, however, a conclusive treatment is impossible. The Japanese Foreign Office and other papers submitted at the Tokyo War Crimes Trials contain little evidence for the period here considered and certainly do not permit the formulation of firm conclusions. At the time Ambassador Grew was quite willing to concede that there were moderates in Japan who thoroughly disapproved of their Government's course and cast about for ways and means of averting the catastrophe of war between Japan and the United States or Britain. Mr. Grew was impressed particularly by a project submitted to him by Mr. Teikichi Toda, a prominent member of the Japan Economic Federation and former secretary of the Japan-America Trade Council. This gentleman stated that Mr. Tetsuma Hashimoto, leader of the Black Dragon Society, proposed to visit the United States to gather information about American opinion on Far Eastern affairs. He reported further that Japanese industrial, business and financial leaders were unanimous in their opposition to the Konoye Cabinet. Matsuoka, he continued, was losing his mind and even influential Army circles were against his project for an agreement with Soviet Russia, feeling that such an agreement would ruin the last hopes for better relations with the United States. According to Mr. Toda, Prince Konoye, the War and Navy Ministers and even General Muto, President of the Military Affairs Bureau of the War Ministry, desired that Mr. Hashimoto visit the United States and if possible confer with President Roosevelt, Secretary Hull, Congressmen and editors. Hashimoto was by no means pro-American, and for that very reason his report would be highly valued in Tokyo.

These preliminary soundings were followed by a letter from Mr. Hashimoto himself. The writer confessed that, if he were an American, he would feel as Americans did about Japan's conclusion of the Tripartite Pact. Nevertheless, it was imperative to make an effort to forestall a war that would mean disaster and would settle nothing. He therefore appealed to American generosity and argued that if there were no improvement in relations between the two countries in the near future the extremists on the Japanese side would plunge their country into measures of desperation. Only understanding and patience could save the situation, and he (Hashimoto) was anxious to go to Washington and see what could be done.

Ambassador Grew, though at first suspicious and skeptical, convinced himself that Hashimoto's visit might have some value. Secretary Hull agreed with him and promised that if Hashimoto came, officers of the State Department would be glad to receive him. Hashimoto thereupon undertook the journey, which was given no publicity. From mid-January to mid-February, 1941, he conferred a number of times with State Department officials. On these occasions he maintained that War Minister Tojo sympathized with his ideas and stated that the immediate objective of his group was to get rid of Matsuoka. The burden of his message was that, if the United States would adopt a more conciliatory attitude, the objectionable features of Japanese policy might disappear. He suggested, among other things, the signature of a Pacific Pact assuring the continuance of the *status quo;* an American proposal for peace in both Europe and Asia; and the use of American influence to induce Chiang Kai-shek to make peace. At the same time he intimated that the United States should recognize Japanese leadership in East Asia, support commercial equality for Japan, assist Japan to secure a fair share of undeveloped natural resources, conclude a new trade treaty, and promise Japan a loan. This was a large order and one which fitted ill with the realities of the Far Eastern situation. Since nothing came of the Hashimoto talks, it is unnecessary to analyze them further. It may be remarked, however, that no one on the American side appears to have felt that they were anything but well-intentioned efforts to overcome a dangerous situation.[52]

It was Ambassador Grew's impression, in December, 1940, that many Japanese were worried by America's refusal to be intimidated by the Tripartite Pact, and by America's readiness to aid China. But he did not believe that the moderate elements could make themselves heard or effect any important change in policy. Even if the Konoye Cabinet were overturned, its successor would be obliged to follow the same course: "It would be utterly unthinkable for any leader or group of leaders in Japan at present to advocate withdrawal from China and abandonment of their dreams of southward advance."[53] Regretfully the Ambassador wrote President Roosevelt that American diplomatic efforts had been defeated by trends and forces utterly beyond control. All constructive work had been "swept away as if by a typhoon, with little or nothing remaining to show for it." The fact was that "Japan has become openly and unashamedly one of the predatory nations and part of a system which aims to wreck about everything that the United States stands for." Consequently the principal point at issue was not whether the United States would have to call a halt to the Japanese program, but when.[54]

[52] Tels. from Grew, December 7, 8, 14, 1940; memos of conversation between Mr. Hashimoto and Messrs. Hornbeck, Hamilton, Ballantine and Berle, January 18, 19, 22 and February 14, 1941. See also Grew: *Ten Years in Japan,* 355 ff.

[53] Grew: *Ten Years in Japan,* 357 (December 7, 1940).

[54] Letter from Mr. Grew to President Roosevelt, December 14, 1940 (Grew: *Ten Years in Japan,* 359 ff.).

The Ambassador's lugubrious conclusions were based largely on the fact that no real hope could be derived from either the words or the actions of responsible Japanese statesmen. Whenever a promising development took place, or a friendly word was spoken, it was invariably nullified by some counteraction or some reiteration of the aggressive program. For example, in early November, 1940, the Tokyo Government had inquired in Washington whether Admiral Nomura, the former Foreign Minister, would be acceptable as a successor to Ambassador Horinouchi. The suggestion was warmly received, for Nomura was known to have opposed the pact with Germany and in general enjoyed the reputation of being honest and sincere in his desire to improve relations with the United States. Nomura accepted the appointment only after long hesitation and then, as he said, "rather in the heroic spirit of a common soldier who is called to the colors." His departure was celebrated at a luncheon of the America-Japan Society, at which Matsuoka delivered one of his long, facile and enigmatic speeches. After propounding the familiar thesis that Japan was not engaged in an imperialist war of conquest in China, but rather in "a moral crusade," and after reiterating the contention that the United States willfully or otherwise misunderstood Japan's intentions, the Foreign Minister drew a lurid picture of the destruction of culture which would result from armed conflict. Then, in one and the same breath, he combined appeal and warning:

I do beseech my American friends to think twice, thrice, nay ten, hundred or thousand times before they take a leap that may prove fatal to all Humanity. In this connection, I wish to leave no doubt whatever in the mind of any American citizen of the fact that Japan is, and will remain, loyal to her Allies; that Japan's foreign policy will revolve in the future around the Three Power Pact as its pivot, as it did around the pivot of the Anglo-Japanese Alliance in the past when that Alliance was in force. This, of course, implies no threat. It is a simple statement of truism, made in order to prevent possible misapprehension. For an illusion on an issue like this will bring no good to anyone.

Yet, according to Matsuoka, Admiral Nomura's mission was "to usher in a happier period of mutual trust and better understanding" between Japan and the United States. The new Ambassador, in reply, stated that he and the Foreign Minister were agreed on "the necessity of improving drastically the relations between Japan and America, which have deteriorated so much of late."[55]

Admiral Nomura, then, was to effect an improvement—a "drastic improvement"—in Japanese-American relations, without the Tokyo Govern-

[55] The texts of these addresses are printed in *Foreign Relations of the United States: Japan*, II, 123-29. The appointment of Nomura was first broached to the American Government early in November, at which time Mr. Welles urged the President to approve (letter of Welles to the President, November 9, 1940, in *Roosevelt Papers: Official File, Box 197*).

ment's giving up one tittle of its program or in any way retreating from its association with Germany and Italy. As though to underline this last item, it was announced at about the same time that General Hiroshi Oshima, notorious advocate of military coöperation with Germany, would return to Berlin as Ambassador, replacing Saburo Kurusu, a professional diplomat. Furthermore, it was reported that German experts had arrived in Tokyo and that Japanese military and naval missions, as provided for in the Tripartite Pact, would soon depart for Berlin.[56]

It is only in the light of these circumstances that one can hope to evaluate the initiation of private negotiations looking toward a settlement of the Japanese-American conflict. Some time in December, 1940, Bishop James E. Walsh, Superior General of the Catholic Mission Society at Maryknoll, New York, and Father James M. Drought were in Tokyo investigating the state of their missions. In the course of their business they came in contact with Mr. Paul Wikawa, an official of the Coöperative Bank of Japan. The latter was evidently much impressed with what the Americans had to say about Japanese-American relations and arranged an interview with Foreign Minister Matsuoka. After much discussion, the two priests were asked to carry an unofficial communication to Washington which allegedly could not be sent through official channels for fear of its becoming known to the extremist group. The emissaries agreed on the understanding that the message was to be from Prince Konoye himself. As it turned out later, the message consisted of a secret proposal to nullify the Tripartite Pact, if not formally at least in practice; to recall all Japanese troops from China and to restore China's geographical and political integrity; and to explore the chief economic problems confronting Japan and the United States.[57]

Since there is no evidence whatever to suggest that Matsuoka at any time even remotely considered such a program desirable or feasible, one can only conclude that he consented to play a part in this transaction only under pressure from Prime Minister Konoye. It is quite likely, as Ambassador Grew believed, that Konoye had never been enthusiastic about the Tripartite Pact and that he was disturbed by the turn which Japanese-American relations had taken as a result of that agreement.[58] Konoye had taken Baron Hiranuma, former Premier and well-known opponent of the alliance with Germany, into his Cabinet as Minister for Home Affairs, and he may well have been responsible for Admiral Nomura's appointment as Ambassador to the United States. From the meager evidence available it seems that the

[56] Tel. from Grew, December 24, 1940.

[57] In 1941 Prince Konoye assured Bishop Walsh that this proposal did in fact originate with him. See the affidavit of Bishop Walsh (*Tokyo War Crimes Documents,* Defense Document No. 2579) and the "Memoirs of Prince Konoye" (*Pearl Harbor Attack,* XX, 3985 ff.). The authors have used also a memo entitled "The Japanese Negotiations, 1941" in the papers of Postmaster General Walker.

[58] Tel. from Grew, December 24, 1940.

Prime Minister had substantial support in the Cabinet for an effort to improve relations with Washington. Not only the Navy Minister but War Minister Tojo also appears to have favored this course and General Muto, the influential Director of the Central Bureau of Military Affairs, personally assured Father Drought that the Army would support the proposals about to be transmitted. Furthermore, during the ensuing weeks influential political leaders took advantage of the meetings of the Diet to interpellate Matsuoka and privately to criticize his policy. Former Foreign Minister Hachiro Arita played a leading part in heckling his successor, while former Prime Minister Koki Hirota went so far as to charge that the policy of the Tripartite Pact was ill-considered and might prove fatal to Japan.[59]

The opposition to Matsuoka, as reflected in the pilgrimage of Mr. Hashimoto, in the proposals to Bishop Walsh and Father Drought, and in the parliamentary maneuvers of Arita and Hirota, was clearly based on the fear that the American reaction to the Tripartite Pact had created a situation likely to result in war. Yet, impressive though the opposition was, Ambassador Grew could not bring himself to believe that it could overthrow the Konoye Cabinet or that any succeeding government would dare follow a different policy. One can only conclude that Matsuoka had very powerful backing in Army circles and that the military extremists, wedded to the alliance with Germany as an essential part of their program for the southward advance, were determined to push that program regardless of the risks involved.

The developments of January, 1941, provide substantial evidence that such was in fact the case. Particularly illuminating were Matsuoka's defiant outbursts in speeches to the Diet, for which Secretary Hull's statement of American foreign policy to the House Committee on Foreign Affairs (January 15, 1941) provided a convenient springboard. Speaking in support of the Lend-Lease bill, Mr. Hull had reviewed the evolution of Japanese policy in China and warned once again of the implications of the projected "New Order" in East Asia:

It has been clear throughout that Japan has been actuated from the start by broad and ambitious plans for establishing herself in a dominant position in the entire region of the Western Pacific. Her leaders have openly declared their determination to achieve and maintain that position by force of arms and thus to make themselves masters of an area containing almost one half of the entire population of the world. As a consequence, they would have arbitrary control of the sea and trade routes in that region.

. . . .

It should be manifest to every person that such a program for the subjugation and ruthless exploitation by one country of nearly one half of the population of the world

[59] Grew: *Ten Years in Japan,* 369. We have also used tels. from Grew, December 24, 1940, and February 18, 1941.

is a matter of immense significance, importance, and concern to every other nation wherever located.[60]

These remarks provoked a storm of indignation and protest in the Tokyo press but, according to what Ambassador Grew learned, Matsuoka was restrained by the opposition and perhaps by the Emperor himself from making immediate reply. In his opening address to the Diet (January 21, 1941) the Foreign Minister made no mention of Mr. Hull's statement, but devoted himself to a lengthy review of Japanese policy. He left no doubt that the Government would continue to adhere to the Tripartite Pact, that there would be no change in the status of Manchukuo and China, and that, "as leader of East Asia," Japan was determined to realize its program for a Greater East Asia Co-prosperity Sphere. He regretted America's "inadequate understanding" of Japan's aims and adjured Washington "to liquidate the state of things created by the force of past interests," and exert its great power for peace and civilization.[61]

But Matsuoka could not be held in check for long. On January 26 he loosed the full fury of his attack on Mr. Hull. A few samples will suffice to give the flavor of his retort:

Since the United States has no correct understanding of Japan's thoughts and actions we have no recourse but to proceed toward our goal. We cannot change our convictions to accommodate the American viewpoint. There is nothing left but to face America, though we shall continue without disappointment or despair to try to correct the fundamental misconceptions held by that nation. . . . Japan must dominate the Western Pacific, not for the sake of Japan, but for the sake of humanity. Japan must demand America's reconsideration of her attitude, and if she does not listen, there is slim hope for friendly relations between Japan and the United States.[62]

Even more ominous than these defiant and menacing remarks were the reports reaching Washington which indicated that the Japanese advance to the south was about to be resumed. On January 16, 1941, the Japanese mission to the Netherlands Indies renewed a number of demands for special privileges which the Dutch authorities had earlier rejected. As before, the Governor General resorted to highly developed tactics of delay. Furthermore, the Dutch Minister at Tokyo, General Pabst, lost no time in challenging the suggestion contained in Matsuoka's speeches that the Netherlands Indies were part and parcel of the Japanese sphere. The details are unimportant for present purposes, but it should be noted that neither Dutch courage and obduracy nor Japanese unwillingness to force the issue pro-

[60] Text in *Foreign Relations of the United States: Japan,* II, 131-33. See also Hull: *Memoirs,* II, 982.

[61] Text in *Documents on American Foreign Relations,* III, 260 ff. See also *Bulletin of International News,* XVIII (1), 109 ff.

[62] The first passage is from the text as given in *Foreign Relations of the United States: Japan,* II, 133-35; the second from the text in *Bulletin of International News,* XVIII (1), 174.

vided any firm assurance that Tokyo would not, at an early date, undertake the "settlement" of the Indies' future.[63]

With respect to Indo-China, Tokyo showed less patience and less reserve. It will be recalled that in December, 1940, hostilities had broken out along the frontier of Indo-China and Siam, the latter country attempting by force to satisfy its claims to certain territories on the right bank of the Mekong River. The French forces had proved unable to hold their own, but on January 17 a French naval detachment all but destroyed the Siamese Navy at Koh-Chang, off the Siamese coast. This was too much for the Japanese, who had committed themselves to support the Siamese claims. On January 18 the Japanese military commander presented the Indo-China Government with demands for the conclusion of an armistice and made clear that refusal would result in an ultimatum. On January 22, 1941, Vichy cabled its acceptance in principle of Japanese mediation. Negotiations began on January 28 aboard a Japanese warship and within three days both parties had been forced to accept Japanese proposals for an armistice. A week later, on February 7, French and Siamese delegations commenced a month-long conference in Tokyo which was to produce a settlement of the dispute under Japanese auspices.[64]

Neither Washington nor London could interpret this Japanese intervention as anything but the prelude to further Japanese advances in southeast Asia. It seemed altogether likely that Tokyo would presently demand bases in southern Indo-China and that Siam would pay for Japanese support by accepting the status of a puppet. Thereafter the Japanese military would be able to use their new facilities to launch attacks on Burma, Malaya or the Netherlands Indies. Worse, there was reason to suppose that Tokyo was embarking on this new phase of expansion with the encouragement of Germany, which had an obvious interest in further weakening the British position and distracting the United States from the policy of aiding Britain.[65]

That these misgivings were not unwarranted can now be demonstrated from the Japanese records, which reveal that the objectives of the mediation between Indo-China and Siam were agreed to at a Liaison Conference, including the highest civilian and military officials of the Japanese Government, on January 30, 1941. The decision of the conference was to form "a

[63] Memos supplied by the Dutch to the State Department, January 22 and February 3, 1941. See also Hubertus van Mook: *The Netherlands Indies and Japan* (New York, 1944), 80 ff.; Feis: *The Road to Pearl Harbor*, 150-51. Matsuoka's statement on the Netherlands Indies in the Diet (January 29, 1941) is printed in *Foreign Relations of the United States: Japan*, II, 306 ff.

[64] *Bulletin of International News*, XVIII (1), 161, 171, 173. The fullest account is to be found in Admiral Decoux: *A la barre de l'Indochine* (Paris, 1949), 141-44, but see also Hull: *Memoirs*, II, 985, and Feis: *The Road to Pearl Harbor*, 151 ff.

[65] Tels. from Grew, January 2 and 12, 1941; tel. from Grant (Bangkok), January 9, 1941; tels. from Leahy (Vichy), January 23 and 27, 1941. See also Grew: *Ten Years in Japan*, 365, 369 ff., and Admiral Leahy's testimony in *Pearl Harbor Attack*, I, 351.

close, inseparable union with both nations, militarily, politically and economically, for the sake of self-existence and self-defense." Naval and air
bases were to be demanded as the price of mediation.[66] Furthermore, the
conference decided to intensify the effort to forge closer bonds with the Axis
and to try once again for an agreement with Soviet Russia which would
provide security for Japan in the north while operations were being conducted in the south. Matsuoka had already appealed to the Germans to
bring pressure on Vichy to yield, arguing that an advance on Singapore
clearly required passage through Indo-China and Siam. The Germans, intent on encouraging an attack on Singapore, had already begun to put
the screws on Vichy.[67]

In further development of their policy the Japanese authorities decided,
on February 3, 1941, to approve a visit of Matsuoka to Moscow and Berlin.
He was to attempt once more to induce the Kremlin to join the Tripartite
Pact or, failing that, to conclude an agreement with Japan. Tokyo was prepared to recognize the Soviets' special position in Outer Mongolia and
Sinkiang, in return for which the Kremlin was to sell the northern (Soviet)
part of Sakhalin to Japan, discontinue aid to Chiang Kai-shek, guarantee
transportation for goods in Japanese-German trade, negotiate the settlement
of specific issues such as boundaries and fishing rights, and recognize Japan's
special position in North China, Manchuria and Inner Mongolia, as well as
its general position as leader of the Greater East Asia Sphere.[68]

As chance would have it, Hitler conferred with his generals on the very
next day (February 4) and devoted the meeting largely to the problem of
relations with Japan. Ambassador Ott had telegraphed from Tokyo that the
debates in the Japanese Diet proved unmistakably the unity of the Japanese
Government and people behind the Tripartite Pact. To be sure, the Government thus far had merely tried to frighten the United States from participation in the war, but "activist circles," led by Ambassador Shiratori and
Admiral Suetsugu, were pressing for an attack on Singapore.[69] That being so,
Admiral Raeder argued, in the conference with Hitler, that even as a neutral
Japan could render immense services to Germany by providing support short
of war. If such measures led to hostilities with the United States, so much
the better, at least if Japan participated vigorously in Axis strategy. In any

[66] "Outline of Policy with respect to French Indo-China and Thailand" (*Tokyo War
Crimes Documents,* Defense Document No. 2812); also the "Tojo Memorandum" (*ibid.,*
Proceedings, 36, 236 ff.).

[67] Memo of Weizsäcker to Ribbentrop, January 23, 1941 (*Tokyo War Crimes Documents,* No. 4025E-5); tel. from Leahy, January 28, 1941. The German attitude toward
Japan's role is indicated in Hitler's comments to his commanders, January 8 and 9,
1941 (*Fuehrer Conferences,* 1941 (1), 1 ff.).

[68] "Outline for Negotiations with Germany, Italy and the Soviet Union," February 3,
1941 (*Tokyo War Crimes Documents,* No. 2811).

[69] Tel. from Ott to Ribbentrop, January 31, 1941 (*Tokyo War Crimes Documents,*
No. 4032B).

event, the time had come for Germany to urge Japan to take measures to tie down American forces in the Pacific and reduce American aid to Britain. The latter country's weakness clearly invited an attack on Singapore, which Raeder, like the British themselves, regarded as the key to the British position in the Far East.[70]

Although Hitler reserved his final decision, he and his associates must have been delighted to learn from Ambassador Ott that Matsuoka was presently coming to Berlin. In breaking these glad tidings to the Ambassador, Matsuoka had reiterated Japan's "unconditional loyalty" to the Tripartite Pact and had assured him that if America's entry into the war appeared inevitable, the Japanese Government considered a "preventive attack" on Singapore the best method of minimizing the effectiveness of American operations in the Pacific, as well as of increasing Britain's difficulties. But, added the Foreign Minister, so serious a step could obviously be taken only in complete agreement with the Reich.[71]

It is unnecessary, in the present context, to develop this theme further. The point to be made is simply that Matsuoka, with the approval of the Cabinet and high military authorities, was about to make a major effort to square the Kremlin and ensure the support of Germany before the great advance to the south was launched. In his public statements he had left no doubt of Japanese loyalty to the Tripartite Pact or of his hopes for an agreement with Soviet Russia. The forced mediation of Japan in the Indo-Chinese-Siamese dispute appeared to be so much more evidence that grave events were in the offing. No wonder, then, that Ambassador Grew, reviewing the situation at the beginning of February, 1941, should have concluded that hope of effective opposition within Japan was vain. The extremists, he was convinced, were firmly in the saddle and fully determined to press on. The Germans were clearly encouraging them, and they either did not anticipate American intervention or, if they did, tended to discount it. "The outlook for the future of relations between Japan and the United States," concluded the Ambassador, "has never been darker."[72]

6. THE FEBRUARY WAR SCARE

In the midst of the alarums and excursions of January, 1941, the Washington Administration had preserved a marked degree of equanimity. Its policy had been fairly fixed: not to appease but also not to provoke Japan; to reject Tokyo's claims to leadership in East Asia and gradually tighten the restrictions on the export of war materials, but at the same time to stop short of the crucial oil embargo and the despatch of American warships to

[70] *Fuehrer Conferences,* 1941 (1), 5 ff.

[71] Tel. from Ott to Ribbentrop, February 10, 1941 (*Tokyo War Crimes Documents,* No. 4037B).

[72] Grew: *Ten Years in Japan,* 369.

Singapore. In his reply to Ambassador Grew's letter of December 14, 1940, President Roosevelt pointed out that the primary American concern was to support Britain and that therefore action against Japan would have to depend on circumstances and capabilities: "I must emphasize that, our problem being one of defense, we cannot lay down hard-and-fast plans. As each new development occurs, we must, in the light of the circumstances thus existing, decide when and where and how we can most effectively marshal and make use of our resources."[73]

In pursuance of this course, the President steadily enlarged the number of items under the license system and pressed on with the policy of aiding China. At the same time, every effort was made to avoid involvement in the dangerous issues that seemed to be coming to a head in the Far East. For example, the State Department steadfastly rejected all British pleas that American influence be brought to bear on the French to cede at least some of the disputed territory demanded by Siam. The State Department reasoned that the British suggestion would entail a violation of the basic American premise that the *status quo* in the Far East should not be altered by force, and that, furthermore, Siam was so clearly under Japanese control that it would be absurd to strengthen its position. The Department therefore restricted itself to fruitless attempts to preach self-denial to the Bangkok Government and warn it of the danger of Japanese domination.[74]

On the other side, the Administration continued deaf to Vichy's frantic pleas for assistance to Admiral Decoux. The State Department consistently urged Vichy to resist the Japanese demands "officially and diplomatically," but was far from convinced that the French really intended to stand up to Tokyo. Besides, there were no available munitions. The French were told that in any event nothing could be done until the hundred planes rotting at Martinique had been sent to the Far East. Since the Germans apparently refused to permit the transfer of these planes, the matter rested there. Throughout the long negotiations connected with the Japanese mediation between Siam and Indo-China the American Government carefully maintained a hands-off policy.[75]

In the same spirit of circumspection, the State Department demonstrated complete willingness to discuss American-Japanese relations with such un-

[73] Letter of the President to Ambassador Grew, January 21, 1941. Though drafted by Mr. Hornbeck of the State Department, this rather illuminating letter was hardly more than a paraphrase of a letter to Mr. Francis B. Sayre, High Commissioner to the Philippines, which, dated December 31, 1940, may have been written by the President himself (text in *F.D.R.: His Personal Letters*, II, 1093-95).

[74] Memo of conversation between Mr. Hull and the Siamese Minister, January 18, 1941; see also Hull: *Memoirs*, II, 985.

[75] Tels. from Grew, January 12, February 13 and 23; tels. to Grew, January 14, February 24, 1941; tels. from Leahy, January 9, 13, 23, 27, 1941; memo of conversation between Mr. Hull and the French Ambassador, January 10, 1941; Leahy's testimony, in *Pearl Harbor Attack*, I, 351.

official emissaries as Mr. Hashimoto on the one hand, and Bishop Walsh and Father Drought on the other. On their arrival in the United States in mid-January the two clerics had made contact with Postmaster General Walker, a prominent Catholic layman. Mr. Walker, in turn, had taken up the matter with Secretary Hull, who had arranged a conference with the President. The White House discussions, which took place on January 23, 1941, lasted for more than two hours, after which it was decided that Bishop Walsh and Father Drought should continue their informal contact with the Japanese Embassy and, through Mr. Walker, with Secretary Hull. However, the strictly confidential memorandum which Bishop Walsh had brought along did not seem very promising. What the Japanese proposed was that they let their obligations under the Tripartite Pact stand, but apply them also in reverse; that is, support the United States in the event of a German attack. Furthermore, they suggested that the United States coöperate in settling the China Incident "on the basis of the secret truce terms offered last October by Chiang Kai-shek." More generally, the United States and Japan should join in proclaiming a Monroe Doctrine for the Far East, guaranteeing to check attempts by any third power to alter the political status of the Philippines, Hongkong or Malaya, or the establishment of autonomous governments in Indo-China and the Netherlands Indies. In the economic field the Open Door policy was to be recognized and the United States was to give economic assistance to both Japan and China.[76]

The President, not rightly knowing what to do with this memorandum, gladly fell in with Secretary Hull's suggestion that the whole matter be held in abeyance until the arrival of the new Ambassador, Admiral Nomura. The State Department was frankly skeptical of the possibility that any Japanese Government could implement such proposals. It would hardly be feasible for Tokyo to withdraw its forces from China and, even if it did, the extremists would probably feel freer than ever to press for an advance to the south.[77] In general the President seems to have shared the feeling of the State Department, and particularly of Mr. Hornbeck, that the danger of a clash in the Pacific was not as great as Matsuoka's statements appeared to indicate. After all, Germany and Italy could not lend Japan effective support in a Pacific war and it was unlikely that Tokyo would be easily misled by Berlin's blandishments.[78] Mr. Hornbeck, indeed, went so far as to characterize the loud noises in the Japanese Diet and press as portending the very reverse of military action in the South Pacific. History, he argued,

[76] *Pearl Harbor Attack*, XX, 4291-93.

[77] *Pearl Harbor Attack*, XX, 4284 ff.; the affidavit of Bishop Walsh (*Tokyo War Crimes Documents*, Defense Document No. 2579); Hull: *Memoirs*, II, 985. We have used also the memo in the *Walker Papers* (*MS.*).

[78] This line of reasoning was fully developed in instructions to Ambassador Grew, January 2, 1941.

showed that when Tokyo was about to take action, it stopped talking. Matsuoka was simply bluffing, hoping to paralyze the United States and diminish American aid to Britain. If Washington permitted itself to be intimidated, Japan and Germany would gain their objective without war. The time had therefore come to call the Japanese bluff: "We should keep all the time in mind one big, outstanding fact, that Japan is not prepared to fight a war with the United States."[79]

The President was especially anxious to avoid trouble while the debate on the all-important Lend-Lease bill was being carried on in Congress, but the evidence suggests that Mr. Churchill took quite the opposite view. The British had all along purported to take Japanese intentions more seriously than the Americans, possibly in the hope of committing the United States to common action in one part of the world, if not in another. The Prime Minister therefore tended to argue that a strong stand by the United States was the best method of preventing Japanese action that might lead to dire consequences. Conceivably he may also have thought that the acuteness of the Far Eastern situation, if properly stressed, would favorably influence Congress with respect to the Lend-Lease legislation. Much of this is admittedly speculation, but some such reasoning seems to have underlain the war scare which broke at the beginning of February, 1941.

The first "flurry of excitement" occurred on February 4, when a message arrived from the American Naval Attaché in London reporting that he had been told officially that the Japanese were apparently planning a large-scale offensive, presumably against Indo-China, the Malay Peninsula or the Netherlands Indies, and that this action was no doubt to be coördinated with a German attack on Great Britain, to take place about February 10. Furthermore, there was intelligence that Japanese shipping was being recalled to home ports and that Japan would demand bases on the west coast of Siam from which the communications with Singapore could be cut.[80]

Evidently on the strength of this report, the President at once summoned Secretaries Hull, Knox and Stimson, together with General Marshall and Admiral Stark, to the White House. There, for more than two hours, the "general strategy of the situation, ranging from the Far East at one end and to Iceland at the other," was debated. Unfortunately Secretary Stimson's diary, from which this passage is taken, reveals nothing more specific. Only from a letter written by Admiral Stark to Admiral Kimmel a few days later does it appear that among other things Secretary Hull advocated sending more warships to the Far East. Stark, as usual, opposed the suggestion and

[79] Memo by Hornbeck, January 28, 1941. In this connection it is interesting to note that Admiral Stark, by whose opinion the President put great store, likewise did not believe that Japan would attack Singapore earlier than June, 1941 (Stark memo to the President, February 5, 1941, in *Pearl Harbor Attack*, XVI, 2152).

[80] Memo of the Office of Naval Intelligence to the State Department, February 4, 1941.

was supported by Mr. Stimson. Eventually, after "vehement" debate, the President stood by Stark.[81]

This was only the opening phase of the crisis. In rapid succession came further reports from both London and Tokyo stating that a substantial Japanese naval force was being concentrated off Saigon, that Tokyo would demand bases in southern Indo-China and on the Siamese coast, that large naval forces and an expeditionary force were being assembled at Hainan, and that military operations against Singapore must be expected in a matter of weeks.[82] On February 7 Ambassador Grew cabled similar rumors and urged the importance of American assistance if the morale of the British, Dutch and Chinese was to be upheld: "As I have said in the past, we are faced with a momentous question, which is not whether we should check Japan's southward advance, but when? . . . The Japanese, in our opinion, are relying on the passiveness of our country. We believe that if definite action is to be taken, it may have to be taken before long."[83]

Before Washington could take any decision, the British seized the initiative. On February 7 Foreign Secretary Eden called in the Japanese Ambassador, Mr. Mamoru Shigemitsu, and did some plain talking. He pointed out that Anglo-Japanese relations were deteriorating rapidly, that Japan was more and more following the Axis line, and that evidently Tokyo was preparing for further action. Britain, he continued, had no aggressive intentions, but did not propose to sacrifice British possessions in the Far East at the bidding of any power. Neither was the British Government prepared to agree that Japan alone was entitled to control the destinies of the peoples of the Far East. If British territories were attacked, they would be defended with the utmost vigor.[84] In reporting what Mr. Eden had told him, Mr. Harry Hopkins added that the Foreign Secretary was anxious to find a way for the United States Government to make clear its determination to prevent Japan from making further encroachments. The British believed the Japanese moves were taken under German influence and feared that for a time at least the Japanese might be able to cut the sea routes around the Cape of Good Hope, thus interdicting supplies from Australia and New Zealand.

This theme had been frequently sounded by the British, doubtless in the hope that it would make an appropriate impression in Washington. And so

[81] Letter of Stark to Kimmel, February 10, 1941 (*Pearl Harbor Attack*, XVI, 2147). For the rest, *Stimson Diary* (*MS.*), February 4, 1941.

[82] Memo from the Office of Naval Intelligence to the State Department, February 5, 1941; memo of conversation between Mr. Butler of the British Embassy and Mr. Hamilton of the State Department, February 7, 1941 (the latter in *Pearl Harbor Attack*, XIX, 3442 ff.).

[83] Grew: *Ten Years in Japan,* 369 ff.

[84] Tel. from Harry Hopkins to the President, February 8, 1941; tel. from Eden to Ambassador Craigie, February 9, 1941, copy of which was left with the State Department.

it did. On February 9 Mr. Hornbeck, in conference at the State Department, revived the proposal that American warships be sent to the Orient to check prospective Japanese moves.[85] Again this thorny issue was debated at the White House (February 10), with the result that the President now inclined toward some such action. According to Admiral Stark, Mr. Roosevelt said "he might order a detachment of three or four cruisers, a carrier and a squadron of destroyers to make a cruise to the Philippines, perhaps going down through the Phoenix and Gilbert or the Fiji Islands, then reaching over into Mindanao for a short visit and on to Manila and back." This was, of course, a much less drastic move than the despatch of ships to Singapore or the assignment of further forces to Admiral Hart's Asiatic Fleet. Nonetheless, Admiral Stark thought it politically objectionable.[86]

Actually the President did not persist in even this fairly innocuous program. He was definitely not in a heroic mood, for at the White House conference of February 10 he proposed nothing but a few "moral steps, or steps of action without any eventuality," the effectiveness of which he himself doubted. Among them were a second warning to Americans in the Far East (in Malaysia and the Philippines, as well as in China) to return home, and a decision that he and Secretary Hull should receive the new Japanese Ambassador and "pull very long faces and give him a very serious talk."[87] One can hardly explain this apparent timidity except in terms of the President's skepticism regarding Japanese plans or his anxiety to avoid public alarm while the Lend-Lease legislation was still pending. In any case, the new warning to Americans in the Far East was couched in mild terms and the President, when queried at a press conference (February 11) as to the likelihood of war, replied with a flat negative, adding, however, that if it did occur, it would not hamper continued American aid to Britain.[88]

British purposes could not possibly be served by any such milk-and-water program as the President expounded. Lord Halifax wrote to Mr. Hull: "I need not emphasize how greatly my Government hope that the United States Government will feel able to take some effective action in the very near future to deter the Japanese." He suggested a "joint declaration by the United States and the British Empire that any attack on the Netherlands Indies, or on British possessions in the Far East, would involve Japan in war immediately and irreparably with both the United States and the British Empire." While admitting that such a proposal might present "certain difficulties," Halifax suggested further that the President talk to Ambassador Nomura in terms similar to those employed by Mr. Eden in his discussion

[85] *Berle Diaries (MS.)*, February 9, 1941.
[86] Letter of Stark to Kimmel, February 10, 1941, and memo of Stark to the President, February 11, 1941 (*Pearl Harbor Attack*, XVI, 2147 ff., 2150 ff.).
[87] *Stimson Diary (MS.)*, February 10, 1941.
[88] *The New York Times*, February 12 and 13, 1941.

with Shigemitsu, and that he send reinforcements to Manila or order a detachment of ships to Singapore.[89]

While decisions on the general question were still open, the President, in the presence of Secretary Hull, received Ambassador Nomura on February 14. Mr. Hull had suggested that, though the President might permit the Ambassador side glances at the political, economic and naval "big sticks" available to the United States, he should say nothing that would close the door on a future adjustment. Mr. Roosevelt followed this general line, but in view of the Far Eastern tension he interpreted it broadly. He had decided, as he told Mr. Berle, that the best way to impress on Nomura the seriousness with which the American people regarded Japan's southward advance and Tokyo's ties with the Axis was "to be really emotional about it." Mr. Berle noted the President's own account of his performance:

He pointed out how President McKinley had done his best to avoid war with Spain, but then one of those horrid things they call an episode occurred. Nobody knew whether the *Maine* was sunk by the Spaniards or not, but President McKinley and John Hay were unable to resist the insistence of the American people for war (sob). When the Japanese sunk the *Panay* a wave of indignation had gone over the country. He and Mr. Hull (who was sitting opposite him during the interview) had with great difficulty restrained another wave of indignation, but, thank God, had succeeded (sob). He hoped Admiral Nomura wanted to make it plain to his Government that everybody here was doing their best to keep things quiet, it trembled on the brink of the indignation of the American people, and should the dike ever break (three sobs), civilization would end.[90]

Nothing is known of Ambassador Nomura's reaction to the President's self-confessed ham acting, but one may legitimately doubt whether he was deeply impressed. As it happened, an American-Japanese conversation of very different stamp was taking place on the very same day in Tokyo. Mr. Eugene Dooman, Counselor of the American Embassy, had just returned to his post and had called on Mr. Chuichi Ohashi, the Japanese Vice Minister for Foreign Affairs. Invited to give his impressions of the American scene, Dooman laid great stress on the determination of the American people to aid Britain to the limits of their capabilities. In this connection, said Dooman:

. . . it would be absurd to suppose that the American people, while pouring munitions into Britain, would look with complacency upon the cutting of communications between Britain and the British dominions and colonies overseas. If, therefore, Japan or any other nation were to prejudice the safety of those communications, either by direct

---

[89] Letter of Halifax to Hull, February 11, 1941 (*Pearl Harbor Attack,* XIX, 3445 ff.).

[90] *Berle Diaries (MS.),* February 18, 1941. Naturally the President's facetious account was not strictly accurate. The official record of the interview is printed in *Foreign Relations of the United States: Japan,* II, 387 ff. See also Hull: *Memoirs,* II, 987 ff. Further evidence is provided in Mr. Hull's account as given the British Ambassador and the Ministers of Australia and the Netherlands (memo of conversation, February 15, 1941).

action or by placing herself in a position to menace those communications, she would have to expect to come into conflict with the United States.

Following a long diatribe by Ohashi in defense of Japanese policy and of the Tripartite Pact, Dooman continued:

It was certainly not the intention of the United States to seek a war with Japan, but at the same time I wished to make it clear that it would be idle and extravagant to believe that, so long as Japan remained a partner of Germany and Italy and so long as she was unable to resolve her troubles with China on a mutually satisfactory and equitable basis, a stabilization of relations between the United States and Japan could be hoped for.

To this official record of the conversation, drafted by Mr. Dooman, Ambassador Grew added this significant passage, in his report to Washington: "Upon listening attentively to what Mr. Dooman described as the philosophy of the American position, Mr. Ohashi remained perfectly quiet for an appreciable space of time and then burst forth with the question 'Do you mean to say that if Japan were to attack Singapore there would be war with the United States?' Mr. Dooman replied, 'The logic of the situation would inevitably raise that question.' "[91]

Dooman's statement was by far the frankest and most direct admonition thus far made to the Japanese Government. It provided a clear definition of the limits of American patience, and it is easy to believe that it left Ohashi "greatly agitated and distrait." But it represented an unusual initiative on the part of Ambassador Grew rather than an action by the American Government. It is hardly necessary to point out the striking disparity between the spineless program being discussed in Washington and the hard-hitting words employed by Mr. Dooman, with Ambassador Grew's prior approval. About all that can be said for the President and the State Department is that they did not disavow Dooman. On the contrary, Grew must have had approval from Washington when, on February 26, he told Matsuoka that Dooman had spoken with his approval and when he furnished the Foreign Minister a copy of Dooman's record of his conversation with Ohashi.[92]

Unwittingly, then, the Administration had spoken in Tokyo in the terms advocated by the British. Had Mr. Churchill known this, he might not have felt it necessary to bring heavier diplomatic artillery into action. On February 15 he sent the President a very persuasively-worded message. Many drifting straws, he said, indicated that Japan might make war on Britain or do something that would oblige Britain to make war in the next few weeks or months. It might all be part of a war of nerves, but the naval situation

[91] Tel. from Grew, February 14, 1941, and despatch from Grew, February 26, 1941 (the latter printed in *Foreign Relations of the United States: Japan*, II, 137 ff.).

[92] Tel. from Grew, February 27, 1941 (in *Foreign Relations of the United States: Japan*, II, 143). On this whole episode see further the discussions in *Pearl Harbor Attack*, II, 671 ff., 706, 726 ff.; and III, 1385 ff.

in the Far East was such that Britain might not be able to cope with it. A large military expedition against Singapore did not seem likely, but the Japanese might seize strategic points and oil fields in the Netherlands Indies and elsewhere, preparatory to a later attack on Singapore. They might even raid the Australian and New Zealand coasts. But what was most to be feared were large-scale raids on the shipping routes across the Pacific and Indian Oceans. If these took place, Britain could not stop them without withdrawing its Fleet from the Mediterranean. However, concluded the Prime Minister, he did not believe that Japan would undertake to wage war against both Britain and the United States. Therefore anything the President could do to inspire the Japanese with fears of a double war might serve to avert the danger.[93]

By this time the need for further American intervention had already passed. Putting all things together, even the doughty Matsuoka was driven to the conclusion that he was getting his country on to very thin ice. First had come Eden's warning to Shigemitsu, followed by Dooman's highly undiplomatic language. To these items the Foreign Minister could add President Roosevelt's significant remark that war in the Pacific would not be permitted to interfere with American aid to Britain, and a statement by the Acting Prime Minister of Australia (February 13) that the situation in the Far East was one of the utmost gravity. Matsuoka evidently decided that the time had come for retreat. On February 15 he had a talk with the British Ambassador, Sir Robert Craigie, who added a new warning: that Britain "could not remain indifferent to any serious increase in Japanese forces in Indo-China." The Foreign Minister hastily disavowed all aggressive designs and assured the Ambassador that Japan would not demand a *quid pro quo* for mediation of the Siamese–Indo-Chinese dispute. He admitted the reasonableness of British apprehensions on this score, since the "extremists" were urging such a demand. But, he continued, both he and Konoye were combating adventurous or aggressive schemes and were prepared to enlist the Emperor in their support. Failing that, they would resign.[94]

This was the beginning of what an American correspondent, Hugh Byas, termed a "painless showdown." During the ensuing few days reports reached Tokyo that Britain was about to mine the east coast of Malaya and that the American Congress had voted the reinforcement of Guam, to say nothing of the fact that the Dutch had recalled their ships from Japanese and Chinese ports.[95] When, finally, the newspapers reported alleged conferences

[93] Tel. from Mr. Churchill to the President, February 15, 1941, printed in *Pearl Harbor Attack*, XIV, 3425 ff., and in Churchill: *The Grand Alliance*, 178-79.

[94] Tel. from Grew, February 17, 1941, giving Craigie's account of the interview. Matsuoka's account may be found in his telegram to Shigemitsu (*Tokyo War Crimes Documents*, No. 1339A-3).

[95] Tel. from Grew, February 18, 1941; memo by the Far Eastern Division of the State Department, reviewing the developments, February 20, 1941.

between Secretary Hull and the representatives of Great Britain, Australia and the Netherlands, the Tokyo Foreign Office lost its nerve. In a public statement Mr. Ohashi denounced the false reports of a projected Japanese military advance southward which, he claimed, had originated in London: "Japan's interests in the South Seas are a matter of life and death to us," he declared, "but settlement by force of arms will only cause destruction. Our policy, therefore, is to seek a solution by peaceful means."[96]

Meanwhile Matsuoka addressed himself directly to Foreign Secretary Eden, reiterating his assurances to Craigie and protesting Japan's altruistic motives in mediating between Siam and Indo-China. While calling in question British and American preparations for war, he repudiated all hostile intentions on Tokyo's part. Indeed, he went so far as to offer to mediate a settlement of the European War and to take whatever action might be necessary to restore peace and normal conditions not only in East Asia, but anywhere in the world.[97] Apparently Matsuoka was so impressed with his own generosity that he allowed his offer to leak to the press.[98] The result was a series of questions in the British Parliament and a hasty statement by Mr. Welles that the United States Government was more interested in the deeds than in the words of other governments. In Berlin and Rome, where the press had long since been prophesying the early and effective implementation of the Tripartite Pact, the news of Matsuoka's tender provoked consternation. The Japanese Foreign Minister lamely attempted to explain away his remarks as a mere manifestation of the "general principle" that Japan was ready and willing to mediate "in any dispute anywhere."[99]

Even without perpetrating this *gaffe*, the Japanese Foreign Minister had made it amply clear that he wanted to ring down the curtain on the current "crisis." Mr. Churchill therefore cabled the President that he had better news about Japan. Matsuoka's forthcoming visit to Moscow and Berlin might well be a diplomatic sop to cover failure of action against Britain: "If Japanese attack which seemed imminent is now postponed, this is largely due to fear of United States. The more these fears can be played upon the better, but I understand thoroughly your difficulties pending passage of [Lend-Lease] Bill on which our hopes depend."[100]

Whether the Prime Minister had his tongue in his cheek when he dictated this message can only be conjectured. Apart from the Dooman warn-

---

[96] Statement of February 17, 1941 (*Bulletin of International News,* XVIII (1), 240).

[97] The text of this message, sent on February 17 or 18, 1941, seems never to have been published. The substance of it was revealed by a British Government spokesman in Parliament on February 25, 1941 (*Bulletin of International News,* XVIII (1), 297 ff.). See also Grew: *Ten Years in Japan,* 372.

[98] *The New York Times,* February 19, 1941.

[99] *The New York Times,* February 18-21, 1941; tel. from Matsuoka to Shigemitsu, February 18, 1941 (*Tokyo War Crimes Documents,* No. 1339A-3).

[100] Message from Churchill to the President, February 20, 1941 (text in Churchill: *The Grand Alliance,* 179, and in *Pearl Harbor Attack,* XIX, 3454).

ing, which had not been authorized by Washington, it is not apparent that the United States Government had participated actively in breaking the tension. If Japan recoiled for fear of American power, it was largely because the British exploited that power vicariously. However, Matsuoka had by this time become very mellow. Speaking to the press on February 21, he denied that Japan had taken any measures which could cause concern to Britain and the United States. As for the reported defense talks between British, American, Dutch and Australian representatives, these were wholly unnecessary and due entirely to "hallucinations." On the same day a Japanese Army spokesman at Shanghai bemoaned the fact that Japan was constantly being victimized: "Japan has the heart of a dove; she is anxious to lay the egg of peace, but Britain and America have placed the snake's eggs of Singapore and Guam in the nest."[101]

The war scare may be said to have ended on February 24, 1941, when Mr. Churchill received Japanese Ambassador Shigemitsu and, in Eden's absence, handed him the British reply to Matsuoka's message. This expressed satisfaction with the Foreign Minister's assurances of peaceful intentions and reciprocated them. It then stressed Britain's determination to defeat Germany and rid the world of Nazi lawlessness and violence. While recognizing the lofty motives behind Matsuoka's offer to mediate, the Prime Minister felt sure that "Mr. Matsuoka will understand that in a cause of this kind, not in any way concerned with territory, trade, or material gains, but affecting the whole future of humanity, there can be no question of compromise or parley." In conversation the two men reiterated their assurances, Shigemitsu repeating several times that Japan would not attempt to attack Singapore or Australia, or to gain a foothold in or make encroachments on the Dutch East Indies. Mr. Churchill took the occasion to remind his visitor that the Tripartite Pact was ever in British minds: "I told him the Axis Pact had been a very great mistake for Japan. Nothing had done them more harm in their relations with the United States, and nothing had brought Great Britain and the United States closer together."[102]

It is difficult, even now, to evaluate the strange developments of February, 1941. With respect to Tokyo's note of injured innocence it may be said that Japan had indeed no intention of attacking Singapore at that time.[103] Furthermore, it is unlikely that operations against the Netherlands Indies were envisaged for the immediate future. On the other hand, it is known that the

---

[101] *Bulletin of International News,* XVIII (1), 305.

[102] Churchill notes of the conversation, as given in *The Grand Alliance,* 179-80. A copy of these notes was communicated to the State Department on February 27, 1941. We have used also a tel. from Grew, February 27, 1941, reporting on a cable received from London by the British Ambassador, and Shigemitsu's report to Matsuoka, February 24, 1941 (*Tokyo War Crimes Documents,* Nos. 702, 1592A and 1592C).

[103] The military plans were not to be completed until June, 1941. See tels. from Matsuoka to Shigemitsu, February 14 and 18, 1941 (*Tokyo War Crimes Documents,* Nos. 1339A-1 and 1339A-3).

Tokyo Government had determined on the southward advance and that the mediation imposed on Siam and Indo-China was intended as an important step in the furtherance of its program. It is altogether probable that it was the Japanese purpose to secure air and naval bases from the two countries as the price of mediation. If these demands did not materialize, the explanation is to be sought in what General Tojo euphemistically described as the "easing of the situation."[104] Even so, the terms of the settlement involved substantial gains for the Tokyo Government, for they included the solemn engagement of Siam and Indo-China not to enter into any agreement or understanding with third powers envisaging political, military or economic coöperation against Japan. In short, Japan not only vindicated its vaunted claim to leadership in Greater East Asia, but effectively deprived these small countries of the means of defending themselves against further Japanese penetration and exploitation.[105]

Japan can therefore not be exonerated of intentions and activities endangering British and indirectly American interests. On the other hand it is reasonably clear that London inflated the immediate threat beyond all reasonable proportions, with the obvious purpose of forcing the hand of Washington and provoking an unmistakable warning to Japan. It was the British theory that a strong American stand, far from precipitating war, would effectively forestall it. The President and his advisers had, however, repeatedly refused to declare themselves, holding that such a course would be provocative and that it would be better to keep Japan guessing. It was not Washington's fault that Ambassador Grew, sharing the British view, took matters into his own hands and authorized Mr. Dooman to make his important statement. What the effect of this unexpected intervention may have been, it is impossible to say. However, Mr. Churchill had already undertaken to prove his thesis and had made the most of the more or less artificial crisis to clean the slate so far as Anglo-Japanese relations were concerned. Just as he had replied to the Tripartite Pact by announcing the reopening of the Burma Road, so now he threw down the gauntlet with respect to southeast Asia. No doubt if Britain had stood alone, he might not have ventured on so bold a course and the Japanese might well have accepted the challenge if he had. It was the shadow of American power that probably clinched the matter, with the Dooman statement thrown in for good measure.

The end result, in any case, was all to the good, for the war scare at least served to postpone for a time the final process by which the fate of Indo-

---

[104] "Tojo Memorandum" (*Tokyo War Crimes Documents,* Proceedings, 36, 236 ff.).

[105] The terms of the agreement of March 11, 1941, are given in *Documents on American Foreign Relations,* III, 293 ff. Germany gave qualified approval of the terms discussed above (tel. from the German Foreign Office to Ambassador Ott, February 17, 1941, and tel. from the German Embassy in Tokyo to Berlin, March 12, 1941, both in *Tokyo War Crimes Documents,* Nos. 4037F and 4038A).

China was sealed and that of Singapore anticipated. Thenceforth Matsuoka and his military supporters could not possibly harbor further illusions about the position of Britain or the United States. If the southward advance was to be undertaken in earnest, Japan would have to make doubly sure of its preparations and await the most favorable possible moment. It was all the more important, then, that Matsuoka get under way to Moscow and Berlin, there to buy security for Japan on its northern flank and to coördinate Tokyo's plans with Hitler's grand strategy.

CHAPTER XI

·

The Kremlin and the World Balance

1. Captious Partners: Hitler and Stalin

Mr. Churchill, dealing in his memoirs with Soviet policy in the spring of 1941, wrote scathingly in condemnation of the Kremlin's course. "So far as strategy, policy, foresight, competence are arbiters," he remarked, "Stalin and his commissars showed themselves at this moment the most completely outwitted bunglers of the Second World War."[1] The British statesman based his strictures on the proposition that the Soviet leaders, after Molotov's visit to Berlin, could not possibly have been unaware of the antagonism that had developed between the two partners of August, 1939, and that they must have realized that Hitler's objectives and intentions with respect to the Balkans ran directly counter to Soviet interests. According to Mr. Churchill, nothing would have made better sense, from the Kremlin's standpoint, than for Soviet Russia to have joined the British in a grand effort to unite and strengthen the Balkan states, so as to enable them to resist the anticipated Nazi advance.

It can probably be taken for granted that Stalin and his associates were not entirely oblivious of the reasoning advanced by Mr. Churchill. But they were obviously influenced also by other considerations, which their critic chose to ignore. They seem to have been unwilling to believe that Hitler would disregard Soviet interests to the point of jeopardizing the agreements of August, 1939, which were economically and strategically so advantageous to the Germans. They probably found it even more difficult to credit the idea that the Nazi dictator would provoke armed conflict with the Soviet Union while his chief enemy, Britain, remained undefeated. In any case, it is altogether likely that the Soviet leaders believed the Socialist Fatherland still unprepared to face a major war and that they were intent, above all, on postponing hostilities as long as possible. Their interest was clearly to stand

[1] Churchill: *The Grand Alliance*, 353.

by while the Germans and British wore each other out, and at all costs to avoid drawing the fire upon themselves. Under the circumstances they attempted to gain time by the evasion of open conflict. They therefore maintained the fiction of the Nazi-Soviet Pact and scrupulously fulfilled the provisions of the economic agreements. At the same time they did what they could to protest and oppose German policy in the Balkans, without however allowing these issues to open an unbridgeable rift.

Hitler, it may be recalled, had made his crucial decision upon receiving the Soviet terms on November 25, 1940. There is no evidence that after that date he had any hope or desire of salvaging the Nazi-Soviet alliance. His recorded utterances breathed profound distrust of Stalin and Molotov and expressed his set determination to liquidate the Soviet state before making further efforts to subjugate Britain. Before the end of 1940 the directive for planning the attack had been issued and the date tentatively set for May, 1941. During the succeeding months military details were worked out and instructions issued for the administration and exploitation of the conquered territories. Soviet commissars, Jews and intellectuals were to be ruthlessly liquidated and the Soviet Union dismembered; northern Russia was to be given to Finland, while the Baltic States, the Ukraine and White Russia were to be erected into German protectorates. Few if any items were overlooked in the characteristically German planning for what was regarded as a certain victory. Hitler was convinced that Britain's one remaining hope was to draw the United States and Soviet Russia into the conflict. There was little to be done to influence the course of American policy, but the threat of a British-Soviet alliance could be exorcised by eliminating the Soviet Union. Thereby Germany would be left free and secure to prosecute the war against Britain, and Japan, too, would be relieved of the danger of Soviet attack in the north.[2]

In all his planning Hitler proceeded from the premise that the initiative was his. "Good relations between Russia and Germany are guaranteed by the divisions drawn up on the frontier, rather than by the pacts in operation," he observed to Ciano at the end of March.[3] That being so, he felt no need to modify his Balkan plans so as to spare Soviet sensibilities. No reply whatever was made to Molotov's proposals of November 25, 1940. When the Foreign Commissar, in mid-January, 1941, inquired anxiously as to Berlin's reaction, he was told that the matters in question were being discussed by the Germans with their Italian and Japanese allies, and that a statement

---

[2] Conference of Hitler with his military advisers, January 8 and 9, 1941 (*Fuehrer Conferences,* 1941 [1], 4); see also *Ciano's Diplomatic Papers,* 418 (conference of January 19, 1941). The German military and other preparations are conveniently summarized, on the basis of the Nürnberg documents, in A. Rossi: *Deux ans d'alliance germano-soviétique* (Paris, 1949), 198 ff. The *Halder Diary,* March 30, 1941, also contributes to this subject.

[3] *Ciano's Diplomatic Papers,* 433 (conference of March 25, 1941).

would be made later.[4] Meanwhile German troop movements into Rumania were increased and accelerated, and every kind of pressure was brought to bear upon Bulgaria and Yugoslavia to join the Tripartite Pact. Only when the question of possible German operations in Bulgaria or against the Straits was raised by Moscow did the Berlin Government reply curtly that, for the purpose of preventing the British from securing a foothold on Greek soil, the German Army would march through Bulgaria.[5] Similarly the Kremlin was informed only at the last moment (February 27) that Bulgaria was about to join the Tripartite Pact and that German troops would presently appear on Bulgarian soil.[6] True, the Nazi Government disclaimed any intention of violating Soviet security interests and protested its resolve to withdraw its forces as soon as the British had been expelled. But it is hardly reasonable to suppose that such assurances satisfied the Kremlin.

Throughout these months Stalin and Molotov were scrupulous in their efforts to avoid a crisis. On January 10, 1941, they agreed to a new economic protocol providing for ever greater deliveries of food and raw materials to the Germans. While German deliveries lagged behind schedule, the Soviets were generally in advance with their shipments of grain. Furthermore, they did everything to facilitate the transport, especially of rubber, from the Far East by way of the Trans-Siberian Railroad. It appears that during January, 1941, no less than one hundred carloads of goods destined for Germany passed daily over this crucial line.[7] In the political sphere, too, the Kremlin acted with the utmost circumspection. With regard to Bulgaria it reminded Berlin that it considered that country and the Straits as a security zone of the Soviet Union and that it could not remain indifferent to events which threatened its security interests. But when the Germans nevertheless announced their intention of sending troops into Bulgaria, Molotov contented himself with an expression of regret that the German Government was taking a course involving injury to the security interests of the Soviet Union.[8]

Efforts of the Yugoslavs to enlist Soviet support against Nazi pressures were likewise cautiously evaded. Only after the military coup at Belgrade in late March did the Kremlin offer the Yugoslavs a pact of nonaggression and friendship. This was far less than the military convention desired by the Yugoslavs, yet when the Nazis indicated their displeasure, Stalin and Molotov quickly abandoned their pro-Yugoslav course. It is quite likely, as Am-

[4] *Nazi-Soviet Relations,* 270 (January 17, 1941).

[5] *Nazi-Soviet Relations,* 268 ff.

[6] *Nazi-Soviet Relations,* 276-77.

[7] Tel. from Steinhardt, February 21, 1941, reporting information received indirectly from the German Embassy in Moscow. On Nazi-Soviet economic relations see *Nazi-Soviet Relations,* 318 ff., 326 ff., 339 ff., and the summary in Rossi: *Deux ans d'alliance germano-soviétique,* 208-9. The published communiqués on the economic agreement are printed in *Documents on American Foreign Relations,* III, 344.

[8] *Nazi-Soviet Relations,* 268-69, 278.

bassador Schulenburg believed, that the agreement with Belgrade was intended primarily to register Soviet opposition to the highhanded policy of Hitler with respect to the Balkan states.[9] Certainly there was nothing heroic or defiant about the Kremlin's attitude in the face of Nazi political and military action in the Balkans. German forces were permitted to concentrate in Rumania, to march through Bulgaria, and to invade both Greece and Yugoslavia. Under the circumstances it was difficult to escape the conclusion that the Soviet leaders, conscious of their military weakness, were determined to avoid provocation as long as possible. It is hard to believe that, while Europe was being increasingly flooded with rumors of a coming Nazi assault on the Soviet Union, the Kremlin remained oblivious of the threat. Its prime objective, therefore, must have been to gain time before facing the supreme ordeal.[10]

2. THE WELLES-OUMANSKY CONVERSATIONS

During the summer and autumn of 1940 it was Prime Minister Churchill and especially Sir Stafford Cripps, the British Ambassador to Moscow, who had hoped to turn the Soviet Government against Germany and draw it into the struggle against Nazi aggression. But after his ill-starred advances of October, 1940, even Sir Stafford had become disillusioned. He had convinced himself that appeasement would lead nowhere and that the Kremlin would be more amenable to pressure than to conciliatory gestures. For months on end he made no attempt to see Soviet officials, while in his reports to London he adopted a line of reasoning strangely akin to that of Ambassador Steinhardt. He was persuaded, he said, that Soviet policy hinged on the belief that Germany would ultimately attack the Soviet Union or make far-reaching demands under threat of attack. In view of Soviet weakness, however, the Kremlin could not afford to provoke the Germans by making agreements with the British. The Soviets would try not to lose contact with the British because they might need them in the event of a German attack. But, until Germany had become considerably weaker, no serious move toward Britain was to be expected. In Sir Stafford's opinion the Nazi-Soviet economic agreements of January 10, 1941, simply provided added evidence of the Kremlin's determination to maintain the relationship established in August, 1939, as long as possible. He therefore recommended that his Government respond by tightening its blockade measures so as to prevent the Germans from getting supplies by way of the Soviet Union.[11]

[9] *Nazi-Soviet Relations,* 316 ff., 330 ff. See also Max Beloff: *The Foreign Policy of Soviet Russia,* II, 364 ff.

[10] See the admirable analysis by Leland Stowe in the *New York Post,* February 27, 1941.

[11] Tels. from Cripps to the Foreign Office, December 23, 1940, and January 11, 1941, communicated to the State Department on January 31, 1941. Further, tels. from Steinhardt, December 16, 1940, and January 2, 10, February 5, 8, 1941.

Mr. Anthony Eden, who in December, 1940, had succeeded Lord Halifax as Foreign Secretary, was believed by Hitler to be "pro-Russian."[12] Actually Eden more than agreed with Cripps's analysis, for he doubted whether even further deterioration of Nazi-Soviet relations would produce a *rapprochement* between London and Moscow. The Soviets, he held, desired to see the British and Germans fight it out as long as possible.[13] The British therefore abstained from making further overtures to the Kremlin. Instead, they applied themselves to the task of persuading the United States to cut down exports to the Soviet Union which, directly or indirectly, were finding their way to Germany. Cotton, they pointed out, was a case in point; the Soviet Union was obligated to deliver large quantities of cotton to Germany; since, despite a bumper crop of its own, the Soviets were importing from the United States some 28,000 tons of cotton per quarter, it was clear that they were using American cotton to replace the amount they themselves were providing the Germans.[14]

Secretary Hull's initial reaction to the British proposal was definitely unpromising. Pointing out that the United States Government did not desire to see Soviet-British relations deteriorate further, he gently chided Lord Halifax for British lack of disposition to improve relations with the Kremlin. In truth, Washington had decided to try where London had failed. Faced with the Tripartite Pact, the growing danger of Japanese expansion to the south, and particularly the threat that the Soviet Union might in fact adhere to the German-Japanese alliance, it seemed highly expedient to make an effort to dissuade the Kremlin from so baleful a commitment. If successful, the effort might lead farther, to the consolidation of Balkan resistance against the Nazi advance, and thereby contribute to relieve pressure on the British position in the Near East.

The conversations between Mr. Welles and Ambassador Oumansky were, to be sure, nothing new but, as they followed their desultory course, they seemed to produce little more than new grievances and fresh recriminations. Only in January, 1941, did they begin to suggest somewhat more substantial progress. This new departure was no doubt attributable to the considerations outlined above, but these in turn must have been greatly fortified by intelligence which reached the State Department early in January, 1941. As Secretary Hull has recounted in his memoirs, Mr. Sam E. Woods, the American Commercial Attaché in Berlin, had for some time been cultivating relations with a highly placed though anti-Nazi German official. Through this source Woods had been receiving valuable items of information, passed

---

[12] *Fuehrer Conferences,* 1941 (1), 4 (Hitler's remarks of January 8, 1941).

[13] Memo of conversation between Mr. Henderson and Mr. Hayter of the British Embassy, January 31, 1941.

[14] Hull: *Memoirs,* II, 970 ff.; letter from Halifax to the President, February 11, 1941 (*Roosevelt Papers:* Secretary's File, Box 73). See also Beloff: *The Foreign Policy of Soviet Russia,* II, 358.

to him in the darkness of a motion-picture theater. The report which came from Woods in January, however, was of truly staggering import. It transmitted what was obviously a copy of Hitler's directive for the attack on Soviet Russia in the spring of 1941. This directive was dated December 18, 1940, and was therefore still fresh when it reached Washington.[15] Mr. Hull has told of the care taken to verify the reliability of Wood's contact. Everything pointed to the authenticity of the document, with the result that it was accepted by the President and his advisers as entirely genuine.

The question at once arose whether the Soviet Government should be warned of the impending danger. According to Mr. Welles the decision was in the affirmative and, at Secretary Hull's request, the Under Secretary imparted the vital information to Ambassador Oumansky almost at once, that is, before the end of January. It seems likely, however, that on this point Mr. Welles's memory has deceived him. No record of such action has been found. The internal evidence of later documents indicates that it was only at the beginning of March that Welles warned Oumansky.[16] This episode should probably be viewed in the context of the new American policy of trying to influence the Soviet Government and may therefore be best treated as part of the continuing Welles-Oumansky conversations.

In mid-December, 1940, the two men were still wrestling with the question of Soviet orders for machine tools. In value these were of the order of four million dollars. Oumansky made no effort to conceal the importance which his Government attached to them and was insistent that as many as possible be released. The Ambassador and his superiors undoubtedly believed that these tools were being purposely withheld for political reasons, but the American records prove that such was by no means wholly the case. Many of them had been requisitioned by the American services and most of the others had been put under the licensing system. The great majority were as important for the American rearmament effort as for the Soviet, and Mr. Welles had to deal with the Administrator of Export Control as well as with Mr. Oumansky. However, in a conversation of December 16, 1940, the Under Secretary had suggested to the Ambassador that, if the Soviet Government would accept compensation for the requisitioned machine tools, the American Government might consider lifting the moral embargo of December, 1939, which precluded Soviet purchases of planes and parts.[17]

[15] The text of the directive is now printed in *Nazi-Soviet Relations*, 260-64.

[16] See Welles: *The Time for Decision* (New York, 1944), 170 ff.; Hull: *Memoirs*, II, 967 ff. Mr. Hull carefully avoids mentioning specific dates and Mr. Welles, in conversation with the authors, was unable to add anything concrete. The wording of a memo of conversation of March 20, 1941, suggests that Oumansky had been told only at the beginning of the month. The first reference to a supposed conversation between Welles and Oumansky on this subject in January appears in a memo of June, 1941, and may well be due to a slip.

[17] Memo of conversation between Mr. Welles and Ambassador Oumansky, December 16, 1940, and a background memo by Mr. Henderson, of the same date.

While the Soviet decision on this crucial though by no means unique issue was still pending, Commissar Molotov on December 26 raised another sore point in discussion with Ambassador Steinhardt. This had to do with ships and gold in the United States belonging to the various Baltic states prior to their absorption by the Soviet Union. The names and flags of some of these ships, so Molotov complained, were being altered by Baltic representatives in the United States, and with the full knowledge of American authorities. How long would this be permitted to continue?

Mr. Steinhardt knew nothing of the matter; neither could he answer Molotov's suggestion that this question be dealt with separately from the Welles-Oumansky negotiations. The Foreign Commissar took the occasion, however, to make clear that the Soviet Government regarded the question of the Baltic states as the most important problem in American-Soviet relations. While complaining of the lack of progress in the Washington conversations and showing the usual Soviet readiness to indulge in charges of discrimination, Molotov nevertheless answered with an "enthusiastic affirmative" when the Ambassador asked whether the Kremlin really desired cordial relations.[18]

Opinions might vary as to the worth of such asseverations, but Secretary Hull and Under Secretary Welles had made up their minds that in view of the growing tension in the Far East and the importance of keeping the Soviet Government from an agreement with Japan, it was necessary to make some concession. Since the machine-tool problem was so difficult of solution, they induced the President to assent to abolition of the moral embargo, on condition that the matter be given no publicity.[19] In his next interview with Oumansky (January 8, 1941) Mr. Welles had an opportunity to notify the Ambassador of the decision. Oumansky had come with a lengthy "oral statement" from Molotov, replete as usual with strident complaints of American failure to turn over the goods ordered by the Soviets and containing also the warning that the Kremlin did not consider a real adjustment of relations with the United States possible unless the latter recognized the Soviet absorption of the Baltic states. Thereupon the statement took note of the American Government's "intention" to revoke the moral embargo. It declined to accept this concession in lieu of an agreement about the machine tools, but as a practical matter adopted the Welles proposal with certain reservations. On the other hand Oumansky, in keeping with his customary practice, demanded further concessions which his Government never showed any disposition to reciprocate and which it usually relegated to the status of "secondary matters."

Even so, Mr. Welles went ahead with his proposal to lift the embargo. He

[18] Tel. from Steinhardt, December 26, 1940.
[19] Letter of Welles to the President, January 9, 1941, recalling the discussion of "about ten days ago."

showed Oumansky a draft notification which the State Department had decided to send to American plane manufacturers. To this the Ambassador protested that without a public announcement normal trade between the two countries would continue to suffer and that, above all, the stigma upon the Soviet Union would remain. By way of a parting shot he warned Mr. Welles that he did not intend to be silenced in his efforts to discuss the issue of the Baltic states.[20]

In his eagerness to advance toward his larger objective, Mr. Welles controlled his temper and set about satisfying Oumansky's demand for public announcement of the lifting of the embargo. To Mr. Roosevelt he wrote that he and Secretary Hull both felt there was some basis for the Soviet argument, adding the following significant remark: "On the whole, our negotiations with the Soviet Union have progressed favorably up to the present moment, and the more friendly relationship which is beginning to exist is unquestionably of real advantage to this Government insofar as the Far Eastern situation is concerned." He therefore requested and received approval for a letter to be addressed to Oumansky which, together with the Ambassador's acknowledgment, could be given to the press.[21]

Although the announcement of the conclusion of a new trade agreement between Berlin and Moscow (January 10) must have come as something of a blow to American officials, Mr. Welles could derive some satisfaction from the pointed Soviet statement (January 12) that if German troops were entering Bulgaria, such action was being taken without the knowledge or consent of the Kremlin. On January 15 Ambassador Oumansky gave assurance that this disclaimer was "authentic." Even more gratifying was the Ambassador's reply to Mr. Welles's question about recent developments in the Far East. Oumansky said that the Soviet Government planned to send larger quantities of munitions to Chiang Kai-shek and stated that, so far as he knew, no further progress had been made in the negotiations between Moscow and Tokyo. He agreed that the spread of Japanese power in China and the southern areas was as inimical to the Soviet Union as to the United States.[22]

With this music ringing in his ears, the Under Secretary completed arrangements for abrogation of the moral embargo. Oumansky was informed on January 21, and the public announcement was made on January 23. The effect, as Mr. Hull has pointed out, was largely psychological, for licenses would still be required for the export of planes and other war matériel to Soviet Russia. Nonetheless, Mr. Welles continued his efforts to secure the

[20] Memo of conversation between Mr. Welles and Ambassador Oumansky, January 8, 1941. Molotov's "oral statement" (dated January 4) is attached to a memo of Mr. Green to the Administrator of Export Control (January 21, 1941).

[21] Letter of Mr. Welles to the President, January 9, 1941.

[22] Memo of conversation between Welles and Oumansky, January 15, 1941.

release of at least part of the requisitioned Soviet shipments and there can be no doubt that it was the Administration's purpose to provide the Soviets with such machines and other goods as could be spared without weakening the American or British defense efforts. Arthur Krock was not far from the mark when he interpreted the lifting of the moral embargo as an indication that the American Government was prepared to fight fire with fire. The risks of such an undertaking were great, but so also were the stakes.[23]

It was undoubtedly too much to expect Soviet-American relations to run smoothly, even for a short time. The British, who had settled down to a "tough" policy toward the Kremlin, were already complaining that American exports to the Soviet Union were finding their way, directly or indirectly, to Germany. Questions were being asked in Parliament and Lord Halifax was appealing to Secretary Hull and even to the President to ration supplies to the Soviets more carefully.[24] It may be assumed that neither Mr. Hull nor Mr. Welles welcomed the addition of another highly controversial item to their agenda. The Secretary rather pointedly indicated to Lord Halifax his disapproval of the British line, while Mr. Welles contented himself with asking Oumansky whether there were any truth in news reports that the Soviet Government had recently increased its purchases of strategic raw materials in the United States. When the Ambassador crustily denied the charge and proceeded in turn to accuse the American Government of discrimination against the Soviet Union in favor of Britain, the Under Secretary did not pursue the matter further.[25]

The following month produced no significant improvement in the relations of the two countries. In his efforts to secure export licenses for Soviet purchases, Mr. Welles continued to collide with other Government agencies, which were either intent on protecting the claims of American defense or else objected to the shipment of goods which might eventually reach Germany. On February 24 the bustling Soviet Ambassador was back in Mr. Welles's office with the harsh charge that since the lifting of the moral embargo trade relations, far from having improved, had grown worse. In this connection he warmly refuted press reports that the Soviet Union was reëxporting to Germany materials it had procured in the United States.

In the improbable event that Mr. Welles took this statement at face value, he was soon to be disabused, for on March 3 the President sent back to Mr. Hull a document which had reached the State Department from reliable sources in Berlin. This proved beyond a doubt that the Soviet Government

[23] *The New York Times,* January 23, 1941. See also Forrest Davis and Ernest K. Lindley: *How War Came* (New York, 1944), 177 ff.; Hull: *Memoirs,* II, 696. We have used also the memo of conversation between Welles and Oumansky, January 21, 1941.
[24] *Bulletin of International News,* XVIII (1), 168; Hull: *Memoirs,* II, 970 ff.; letter of Lord Halifax to the President, February 11, 1941 (*Roosevelt Papers:* Secretary's File, Box 73). See also Beloff: *The Foreign Policy of Soviet Russia,* II, 358.
[25] Memo of conversation between Welles and Oumansky, January 21, 1941.

was assiduously acquitting its heavy obligations under the trade agreement with Germany of January 10, 1941. Among other things it was shipping the Germans, as the British had suspected, large quantities of cotton.[26] With or without this specific knowledge, the Under Secretary suggested to Oumansky that the Soviet Government might issue a public statement on Soviet-German trade to reassure American opinion and encourage further trade. Though the Ambassador began to argue that such a step would constitute a violation of Soviet "neutrality," he soon changed his tune and promised to forward the suggestion to his Government.[27]

A few days later, when the two men resumed their conversations, Oumansky had nothing to report on the subject of Soviet shipments to Germany. On the contrary, he reverted to the thorny question of the Baltic states, reiterating that no significant improvement in American-Soviet relations could be expected unless and until this issue had been settled to the satisfaction of Moscow. Goaded beyond the limits of endurance by the tactless renewal of this theme, Mr. Welles stated with the greatest emphasis that he "would be remiss if he did not at once make it clear that the American Government had never attempted and would not now attempt to purchase the friendship of any country by recognizing rights which it did not regard as legitimate and justifiable." To this the Ambassador replied scornfully that "the American Government could not purchase Soviet friendship, since the Soviet Government would not sell such friendship."[28]

These exchanges certainly did not contribute to the establishment of closer relations or real confidence between the two governments, but they do reveal the difficulties in the way of even modest progress. It would have been altogether understandable if the State Department had suspended further effort. But the situation in the world was such that the President and his advisers had to look beyond the irritations provoked by Oumansky and his masters. At the end of February the world was just emerging from the Far Eastern war scare. It was well known in Washington that Matsuoka was about to depart for Moscow and Berlin and that his chief objective was to secure an agreement with the Kremlin that would safeguard Japan's rear while the attack on the British-Dutch position in Southeast Asia was taking place. To the United States it was of supreme importance that the Soviet Government not fall in line with Japan and Germany. The President therefore decided that, despite the continuing bad relations between the United States and the Soviet Union, the Kremlin should be warned of the German

[26] Confidential memo of the President to Mr. Hull, March 3, 1941, attached to a lengthy document (now missing) entitled "Strictly Confidential Memorandum II; Status of War Raw Materials, Berlin, January 24, 1941" (*Roosevelt Papers:* Secretary's File, Box 76).

[27] Memo of conversation between Welles and Oumansky, February 24, 1941.

[28] Memo of conversation between Welles and Oumansky, February 27, 1941.

plans to launch an attack. On March 1 Ambassador Steinhardt was instructed to seek out Molotov as a matter of urgency and communicate the State Department's "authentic" information on the German plans.[29]

Mr. Steinhardt was not greatly surprised by the Department's information, for by this time all Europe was breathlessly watching the development of the Nazi-Soviet antagonism in the Balkans and the air was rife with rumors of a coming German attack on the Soviet Union.[30] But the Ambassador was reluctant to carry out his instructions. So cynical, he reported, was the reaction of the Kremlin to "approaches of this character" that his proposed visit to Molotov would probably become the subject of a *Tass* communiqué, while the information itself would in all likelihood be passed on to Berlin. Far from serving American interests, the proposed warning to the Soviet Government might well result in greater Soviet concessions to the Germans, not to mention the conclusion of an agreement with Japan.[31]

The Ambassador was spared what he regarded as both a useless and unwise assignment. On March 4 he was informed by Washington that, in the course of a conversation with Oumansky on March 1, Mr. Welles had himself imparted the information in question. What the Soviet Ambassador's reaction may have been it is impossible to say. He subsequently insisted that he had transmitted the warning promptly to his Government.[32] Later still Oumansky's successor, Litvinov, admitted that the Kremlin had received this warning and the one that followed on March 20, but did not take them seriously "because it considered it would have been madness on his [Hitler's] part to undertake a war in the East . . . before finishing off his war in the West."[33]

Whatever the truth of the matter, the meeting between Welles and Oumansky on March 1 produced at least some evidence of Soviet anxiety over relations with Germany and of desire to do business with the United States. The Ambassador announced that his Government had consented to the publication of the assurances suggested by Mr. Welles regarding the ultimate destination of American exports to the Soviet Union. As it presently appeared, the statement read that "goods which have been and are being purchased in the United States by the Union of Soviet Socialist Republics . . . are destined exclusively for the domestic needs of the Union of Soviet

[29] Tel. to Steinhardt, March 1, 1941.

[30] These reports, from a great variety of sources, are far too numerous to itemize. It so happened that Steinhardt himself had reported one on February 26, and that the subject was very competently analyzed by Leland Stowe in the *New York Post* on February 27, 1941.

[31] Tels. from Steinhardt, March 3, 11, 17, 1941.

[32] Memo of conversation between Welles and Oumansky, June 26, 1941. Mr. Welles found it difficult to credit this statement, made after the fat was in the fire (conversation of the authors with Mr. Welles, May 27, 1947).

[33] Soviet Embassy: *Information Bulletin*, December 15, 1941.

Socialist Republics."[34] This assurance, it will be noted, had nothing to say of the possible use of American materials to replace those shipped by Soviet Russia to Germany. However, it did indicate a greater readiness on the Kremlin's part to meet American requirements and Welles's subsequent talks with the Soviet Ambassador were in a somewhat more cordial vein. On March 20 the Under Secretary warned Oumansky in a friendly way that Matsuoka's trip to Europe was chiefly designed to seek a political agreement with the Kremlin which would assure Japan a free hand in the western Pacific. Welles remarked that the American Government believed "that the policy which it itself had pursued in its relations with Japan during recent years, namely, of leaving Japan in a state of complete uncertainty as to the action which their Government might take in the event that Japan pursued a policy which would be regarded here as directed against the interests of the United States, had been beneficial in its results." He suggested that the United States and the Soviet Union had a common interest in the preservation of peace in the Pacific and in the integrity and independence of China. Oumansky expressed appreciation but also skepticism. He thought it more likely that Germany and Japan would make an agreement against Soviet Russia than that Germany would use pressure on the Kremlin to make a political agreement with Japan. He could not, however, forbear to inquire whether Mr. Welles had any further information to confirm earlier reports of a German attack on the Soviet Union. The Under Secretary replied in the affirmative.[35]

No doubt encouraged by such evidence of Soviet perturbation, Mr. Welles on March 22 made one more effort to clear away the obstacles that still choked the channel of American exports to Soviet Russia. Finding Oumansky in an unusually conciliatory mood, the Under Secretary remarked that he thought the time had come to state bluntly that while the United States Government desired to improve relations with the Soviet Union, it would not facilitate Soviet purchase of materials which directly or indirectly served to benefit Germany. For once the Ambassador did not argue, not even when Welles pointed out the inadequacy of the Soviet statement of March 1, 1941.[36] On the other hand, Oumansky at no time offered to supply the further assurance which the United States Government desired. In the ensuing six weeks the subject was raised on several occasions, the Ambassador complaining bitterly that important goods were being refused the Soviet Government and charging that certain American officials were killing Soviet-American trade for political purposes, that is, in the hope of influencing Soviet foreign policy. To this Mr. Welles replied that "there seemed to be

[34] *Documents on American Foreign Relations,* III, 471 ff. See also Davis and Lindley: *How War Came,* 179.

[35] Memo of conversation between Welles and Oumansky, March 20, 1941; see also Hull: *Memoirs,* II, 968.

[36] Memo of conversation between Welles and Oumansky, March 22, 1941.

little to be gained by the Ambassador and myself sitting down together and making exactly the same statements over and over again." Neither would there be much point in here reviewing all the complicated details of these involved trade negotiations. The upshot was that the Under Secretary reiterated his desire to encourage the trade, but stated that under no circumstances would the United States allow that trade to interfere with its own defense requirements or the needs of the British and other resisting nations. Neither would the United States permit goods to go to the Soviet Union that might conceivably aid the German war economy.[37]

Since the Soviet Government, far from agreeing to curtail supplies to Germany, was intent on staving off disaster by meeting and even exceeding Nazi economic requirements, it follows that Soviet-American trade continued in a most unsatisfactory condition. According to the ever gloomy and pessimistic Oumansky, it sank to near the zero point.[38] Yet for all the bitterness and controversy engendered by this and a number of other issues, there were more than mere hints that politically the two Governments were finding common ground. Oumansky himself suggested that if Soviet trade with Germany were to be an insurmountable obstacle to the development of Soviet-American trade, it might be well to be "good sports" about it. "It is our belief," he added, "that many common denominators may be found in the long-range policy of both the American and Soviet Governments and certainly in the immediate future there should be common denominators in the economic policies of the two Governments."[39]

In the same spirit the Ambassador somewhat later was frank to say that the German invasion of Greece and Yugoslavia must be "profoundly disquieting" to his Government, and to remark how useful it would be for both the United States and the Soviet Union, as well as for the whole world, if the foreign policies of the American and Soviet Governments were "identical." Speaking informally to Mr. Loy Henderson of the State Department, Oumansky expressed appreciation of the American attitude toward the recently concluded Soviet-Japanese Neutrality Pact and stressed the common interest of the United States and the Soviet Union in supporting Nationalist China. The effort of some American officials to influence Soviet foreign policy through economic pressure, he concluded, seemed to him "particularly pointless," since without doubt the Soviet Union and the United States would eventually be on the same side anyway.[40]

[37] Memos of conversation between Welles and Oumansky, March 27, April 9, 1941; memo of conversation between Mr. Henderson and Ambassador Oumansky, April 18, 1941.

[38] Memo of conversation between Welles and Oumansky, April 9, 1941. On the Soviet contribution to Germany see the German memo of May 15, 1941 (*Nazi-Soviet Relations,* 339 ff.), which is borne out by tels. from Heath (Berlin), May 13, and from Steinhardt, May 17, 1941.

[39] Memo of conversation between Welles and Oumansky, March 27, 1941.

[40] Memo of conversation between Welles and Oumansky, April 9, 1941; memo of conversation between Henderson and Oumansky, April 18, 1941.

By the beginning of May, then, the Kremlin had probably convinced itself that Hitler's brilliant campaigns in the Balkans were merely the prelude to the main theme, the attack on the Soviet Union. It would be absurd to contend that this conviction sprang from Mr. Welles's warnings of March 1 and March 20, for the Soviet leaders had the course of events and the compelling evidence of German troop concentrations to instruct them. On the other hand, there is reason to suppose that Welles's efforts to smooth the rocky road of Soviet-American trade relations and his communication of reliable information on Nazi plans provided at least a foundation for closer relations. They may even have influenced important decisions of the Kremlin with respect to broad policy. Welles's great preoccupation, throughout the spring of 1941, was that the Kremlin might fall in with Nazi-Japanese plans and that it might join the front against Britain, if only to save its own skin. The story of Matsuoka's discussions in Berlin and Moscow will show to what maneuvers the Kremlin resorted in its desperate effort to fend off the inevitable.

3. MATSUOKA'S PILGRIMAGE

Hitler and Ribbentrop were greatly pleased to learn of Matsuoka's forthcoming visit to Berlin and Rome, for by March, 1941, they had assigned Japan a place in the panorama of Nazi strategy. Admiral Raeder, in his never-ending search for ways of striking at Britain's world position, had come to the conclusion that Germany's Far Eastern ally could play a useful role. Singapore was the key to British power in the Far East and commanded trade routes essential to Britain's survival. Considering that country's weakness, an attack on the great fortress was clearly indicated and might well prove successful. There was, of course, the possibility that the United States might thereby be brought into the war, but, taking all things into account, Raeder thought such an eventuality might be advantageous for Germany rather than the reverse. The United States was not yet prepared for war and it seemed almost certain that, in the event of hostilities with Japan, American opinion would insist that the major part of the United States Fleet be kept in the Pacific. The result might well be that the United States would not be able to act effectively in the Atlantic and might in fact be obliged to reduce its aid to Britain. Raeder therefore recommended that everything be done to induce the Japanese to strike at Singapore, without waiting, as they seemed to be doing, for Germany to stage an invasion of England. Of course, added Raeder, arrangements must be made to ensure that Japan did not pursue selfish aims in the Pacific, but coördinated its effort with overall Axis strategy.[41]

[41] *Fuehrer Conferences,* 1941 (1), 4, 12 ff., 32 ff. (conferences of January 8-9, February 4 and March 18, 1941). The memos of the Naval Command (pp. 12 ff., 40-41) are highly interesting analyses of broad strategy.

Hitler concurred in this reasoning which, after all, promised the Axis real gains at no expense. The arrival of General Oshima as Japanese Ambassador provided an ideal opportunity to press the matter, since Oshima, as Military Attaché in Berlin, had been one of the great proponents of the German-Japanese military alliance. It was, to be sure, somewhat disconcerting to discover that the Ambassador seemed to accord a higher priority to agreement with Soviet Russia and to settlement of the China Incident than to an attack on Britain in southeast Asia, but Ribbentrop at once invited him to Fuchsl and there employed all his eloquence to prove that the hour of decision had struck for Japan. If the Imperial Government would only act promptly and firmly, the victory over Britain, which the Germans already had within their grasp, would be clinched. An attack on Singapore would probably frighten the United States from participation in the conflict, but in any event America "could not wage war militarily at all." Neither was it necessary to consider the Soviet Union, for if a clash occurred it would end in a gigantic German victory and collapse of the Soviet regime. From every standpoint, then, Japan should launch an immediate attack on Britain:

The decisive blow would be an attack on Singapore, to eliminate England's key position in East Asia and to secure for Japan a position in East Asia which it could only win in war. The occupation of Singapore must take place with lightning speed, if at all possible without a declaration of war and in the middle of peace, to contribute to a speedy termination of the war and to keep America out of the war.[42]

Although Oshima confined his observations to eulogy of the Tripartite Pact and vouchsafed no indication of Japanese decisions, the Nazi Foreign Minister professed great satisfaction with the interview and lost no time in urging the German Ambassador in Tokyo to use all means at his disposal "to the end that Japan take possession of Singapore as soon as possible by surprise."[43] As so often, the Nazis counted their chickens before they were hatched. In a directive of March 5, which was in effect the German agenda for the forthcoming talks with Matsuoka, it was explained that:

It must be the aim of the collaboration based on the Three Power Pact to induce Japan as soon as possible to take active measures in the Far East. Strong British forces will thereby be tied down and the center of gravity of the interests of the United States of America will be diverted to the Pacific. . . . The common aim of the conduct of war is to be stressed as forcing England to the ground quickly and thereby keeping the United States out of the war. Beyond this, Germany has no political, military or economic interests in the Far East which would give occasion for any reservations with regard to Japanese intentions.

[42] Tel. of Weizsäcker to Ribbentrop, after a preliminary talk with Oshima, February 22, 1941 (*Tokyo War Crimes Documents*, No. 4037D). On the Ribbentrop-Oshima conversations see the German records in *Tokyo War Crimes Documents,* Nos. 4037D, 4037E, 531, 531A, and in *Nazi Conspiracy and Aggression,* I, 843 ff.; IV, 469 ff.

[43] Tel. from Ribbentrop to Ott, February 27, 1941, and tel. from Oshima to Matsuoka, February 25, 1941 (*Tokyo War Crimes Documents*, Nos. 1592B and 4037G).

Japan should go after areas that contained raw materials important to all the Axis powers. Germany would provide the necessary technological assistance and operational advice, even without reciprocity.[44]

The Nazi line, then, was perfectly clear and, so far as Hitler and Ribbentrop could know, quite in consonance with Japanese plans. Ambassador Ott had telegraphed from Tokyo that Matsuoka intended to discuss in Berlin diplomatic ways and means of keeping the United States out of the war. If that objective appeared impossible, however, Japan would consider a preventive attack on Singapore.[45] However, the record of the meeting of the Tokyo Liaison Conference of February 3 reveals that the thought of the Japanese Government was turned in a quite different direction. The Conference had informally commissioned Matsuoka to stop in Moscow and attempt to reach an accord with the Soviet Government which would establish harmonious relations between the Kremlin and the members of the Tripartite Pact. The basis for such an accord had been sketched out and great importance attached to it, particularly with respect to the possible cessation of Soviet aid to Nationalist China. As for the Foreign Minister's visits to Berlin and Rome, these were thought of chiefly as "courtesy" calls.[46] The Japanese Ambassador in Moscow was therefore being quite frank when he told his American colleague that the earlier negotiations between Soviet Russia and Japan were deadlocked, that Matsuoka's visit to Berlin was mere camouflage, and that the Foreign Minister's real purpose was to talk Molotov into a political agreement.[47]

Matsuoka and his staff, accompanied by the German Ambassador to Tokyo, set out on their long journey to Moscow by way of the Trans-Siberian Railroad on March 12, the day after the passage of the Lend-Lease Act, which certainly provided the Axis Governments with ample food for thought. He arrived in the Soviet capital on March 23, to be met by Mr. S. A. Lozovsky, Vice Commissar for Foreign Affairs. The reception was described as "correct but reserved."[48]

The Foreign Minister hoped to have an interview with Molotov and perhaps even Stalin himself, but before he met either he had a most disarming talk with Ambassador Steinhardt, who happened to be an old acquaintance. Matsuoka assured his caller that his pilgrimage to Berlin and Rome was designed simply to meet Hitler and Mussolini, to size them up and to hear their plans. He denied most emphatically that Japan would attack Singa-

---

[44] *Nazi Conspiracy and Aggression,* VI, 906 ff.

[45] Tel. from Ott to Ribbentrop, February 10, 1941 (*Tokyo War Crimes Documents,* Exhibit 569).

[46] *Tokyo War Crimes Documents,* Exhibit 3657, and the "Tojo Memorandum" (*ibid.,* Proceedings, 36, 213 ff.).

[47] Tels. from Steinhardt, March 3 and 11, 1941. Ambassador Grew had been given similar information from a Japanese Foreign Office official and rightly regarded it as reliable (tels. from Grew, February 27 and March 12, 1941).

[48] *The New York Times,* March 24, 1941.

pore or any British, Dutch or American possessions in the Far East. Japan, he continued, had no territorial ambitions. Indeed, Tokyo was prepared at any time to join the United States in guaranteeing the territorial integrity and independence of the Philippines. Japan's great objective was to end the China conflict. President Roosevelt could easily help if he would use his influence with Chiang Kai-shek. He, Matsuoka, wished the President and Secretary Hull would trust him, despite the record of past years. Any clash between the United States and Japan, he opined, could only benefit the Soviets and would result in the communizing of China and probably the entire Far East. Nonetheless, he frankly admitted his intention of trying for a political agreement with the Kremlin, though not at an excessive price.[49]

What importance the Kremlin attached to the Foreign Minister's visit can be judged from the fact that Stalin himself deigned to be present at the Molotov-Matsuoka interview. It was the first time since 1928 that he had received a Japanese diplomat. Unfortunately the only records of the discussion are Matsuoka's own accounts, given first to a few foreign diplomats in Moscow and a few days later to Hitler and Ribbentrop. Characteristically he told the Ambassadors that the conversation had lasted two hours, while later he assured Hitler that he had had only about ten minutes with Molotov and then a half hour with Molotov and Stalin together. However, no one need doubt Matsuoka's statement that he treated the Soviet leaders to a disquisition on the "moral communism" of the Japanese which, he explained, had been undermined by the liberalism of the West. Nor should it occasion surprise that Stalin allegedly replied that the Soviet Union had never gotten along well with Great Britain and never would.

After this preliminary palaver, so Matsuoka explained to the Germans, he had proposed to Stalin and Molotov a treaty of friendship and nonaggression, to which Molotov had responded by suggesting a less extensive pact of neutrality. There ensued a brisk discussion of the terms of settlement of various outstanding issues that would first have to be disposed of. Matsuoka proposed that the Soviets sell the northern part of Sakhalin to Japan, which led Molotov to inquire whether he meant this as a joke. Apparently the debate was so little promising that the Japanese Foreign Minister suggested that further consideration of these problems be postponed until his return from Berlin. The Soviet leaders concurred, and therewith the interview came to a close.[50]

Matsuoka was received with great pomp and circumstance when he arrived in Berlin on March 26. The fact that he was accorded two long

[49] Tel. from Steinhardt, March 24, 1941 (printed in part in *Foreign Relations of the United States: Japan,* II, 143 ff.).

[50] Tel. from Schulenburg to the German Foreign Office, March 25, 1941 (*Nazi-Soviet Relations,* 280-81); memos of the conversations of Hitler and Ribbentrop with Matsuoka, March 27 and 29, 1941 (*ibid.,* 289 ff., 303 ff.). See also the still interesting account in Dallin: *Soviet Russia's Foreign Policy,* Chapter XII.

interviews with Hitler and Ribbentrop, in addition to three or four others with the Nazi Foreign Minister alone, is enough to prove the importance which the Germans attached to the future development of Japanese policy. Hitler, no doubt prejudiced by his racial theories, thought his visitor looked like a yellow ape from the primeval jungle, but was sufficiently interested in Japan's capabilities to expend much time and effort on Matsuoka, even in the midst of the crisis precipitated by the unexpected overturn in Yugoslavia. The Fuehrer had been warned, first by Admiral Raeder, then by the German Foreign Office, and finally by Ambassador Ott, that Matsuoka was intent above all on reaching an agreement with the Soviet Union and that Tokyo was unlikely to embark on hostilities against Britain until it had obtained some assurance as to the Kremlin's attitude. Both Raeder and Baron Weizsäcker had strongly recommended that the Japanese Minister be informed of German plans for war against Soviet Russia, partly in order to provide him assurance far beyond anything he could get from Moscow, and partly to spare him a disagreeable surprise later on.[51] But Hitler evidently had too little faith in Japanese policy to be willing to confide in Matsuoka to such a degree.

The German documents on the conversations of the Nazi leaders with Matsuoka (March 27-29, April 4, 1941) fill many closely printed pages. A full analysis of these records is unnecessary for the purposes of this study and would in any event be difficult to construct, because the same ground was covered again and again with only minor variations. It goes almost without saying that first Ribbentrop and then Hitler devoted their initial efforts to demonstrating that Britain was, to all intents and purposes, already done for. The issue therefore was simply how Britain could be brought to acknowledge its defeat . . . that is, how the *coup de grâce* could best be delivered before American aid to Britain became effective or the United States intervened actively in the war. The Nazi argument turned on the proposition that Japan should seize this "unique" opportunity to make war on Britain and assault Singapore. If the operation were executed quickly, there was no chance of America's interfering. Neither were there grounds for apprehending a Soviet attack on Japan. The 160 divisions which the Germans had available would be more than sufficient to keep the Kremlin from taking action and if, by chance, war should develop, the Soviet forces would quickly be defeated by Germany.

Matsuoka was hardly the man to suffer a deluge of Nazi eloquence without opening the floodgates of his own oratory. In general, he declared, he agreed with Nazi views. His personal opinion was that the problem of the

---

[51] *Fuehrer Conferences,* 1941 (1), 32-33; tel. from Ott to Ribbentrop, March 25, 1941, and memo from Weizsäcker to Ribbentrop, March 24, 1941 (*Tokyo War Crimes Documents,* Nos. 4038B and 4038C). See also Ernest von Weizsäcker: *Erinnerungen* (Munich, 1950), 309 ff.

"South Seas" could never be solved without the capture of Singapore. He considered it only a matter of time until Japan undertook that venture. He could not, however, pledge his Government to take the step, for he faced many difficulties at home from "intellectual circles," whose influence was felt in the Cabinet and reached even to the Imperial family. Time was therefore required to bring the opposition into line. Meanwhile he had no other alternative but to feign pro-American and pro-British views so as to deceive his domestic critics, as well as London and Washington. Eventually these "soothing" and "misleading" tactics would come to an end and the operation against Singapore would be launched. The Japanese, he added, had to be shaken up. In the words of an old Japanese maxim: "Open fire, and the Nation will then be united."

There is no reason to suppose that Matsuoka was not fully prepared to adopt the policy urged upon him by the Germans. But, mindful of the pre-occupations of his colleagues, he avoided a definite commitment and exerted himself to discover the German attitude toward an improvement of relations between Tokyo and Moscow. On this subject Hitler was characteristically evasive, confining himself largely to the assertion that, if necessary, the Germans would prevent the Soviets from interfering with the realization of Axis plans. Ribbentrop, however, realized that Matsuoka's repeated feelers could not be entirely ignored. He made it quite clear that there could no longer be any thought of associating Soviet Russia with the Tripartite Pact. Soviet-German relations had deteriorated. In reply to Matsuoka's question whether, on his return to Moscow, he should attempt to arrive at a non-aggression or neutrality treaty with the Kremlin, Ribbentrop advised his interlocutor not to raise the question of Soviet adherence to the Tripartite Pact and in general "not to go into things too deeply with the Russians." A conflict between Germany and the Soviet Union, while not probable, was not inconceivable. Furthermore, there was no reason why Japan should be concerned about Soviet policy, for "if Russia should ever attack Japan, Germany would strike immediately." Japan need therefore have no hesitation about going for Singapore.

Matsuoka interrupted his conferences with the Nazi leaders long enough to pay a brief visit to Rome, where he was received by both Mussolini and the Pope. According to his own account, he had an opportunity to see for himself how complete was the unity between the members of the European Axis. Furthermore, his audience with the Pope gave him an opportunity for high-flown philosophizing about the future of civilization and the prospects or rather lack of prospects for peace. Since the Rome conferences had but little bearing on the major issues of Axis strategy, there would be little point in considering them further. On April 3 the Foreign Minister entrained for Berlin and a final discussion with Hitler and Ribbentrop on the following day.

The ground had by this time been covered so thoroughly that little of significance remained to be said. There was some talk of German assistance to Japan in the fields of intelligence and operational data and in scientific and technical matters, all of which Matsuoka considered important in the event of war with the United States. Hitler held this contingency to be as improbable as it was undesirable, but promised that if it did arise, he would at once "take the necessary steps." In a spirit of *noblesse oblige* Matsuoka replied that he, on his part, would not hesitate a moment "to reply at once to any extension of the war by Russia or America." However, he reminded Hitler that if word of such plans got abroad, political and financial circles in Japan (as well, presumably, as the formerly mentioned intellectual circles) could do him much harm. On his return, so he said, he would admit to the Emperor and the War and Navy Ministers that the "matter of Singapore" had been discussed, but only in a "theoretical" way. Hitler promised complete discretion, whereupon the two parted.

On the final day of the Berlin visit (April 5) the Japanese Foreign Minister had a last, repetitious interview with Ribbentrop, who presented his guest a singularly appropriate gift: a talking film apparatus. In pomp similar to that displayed on his arrival, Matsuoka then took leave of his hosts and embarked on his return journey. What he had seen and heard in Germany and Italy, he assured Ribbentrop, had "exceeded his expectations." He had been more than rewarded for his long pilgrimage.[52]

Although during the Berlin discussions the Japanese Foreign Minister had marched briskly to the very brink of commitment, he had not taken the plunge. His mastery of deception is demonstrated by the fact that he managed to leave the Germans with the impression that all preparations for an attack on Singapore would be complete by May, 1941, and that operations against that fortress would in fact be undertaken in the not too distant future.[53] In return for this impression he had himself secured the vital information which he sought. He had learned that the Germans were unlikely to attempt an invasion of England at an early date, that there could no longer be any question of drawing Soviet Russia into the Tripartite Pact, and that relations between Berlin and Moscow had deteriorated to the point where war was no longer "inconceivable." Despite all Nazi assurances, Matsuoka must have left Berlin with the conviction that Japan would have to shift for itself. If the coveted conquests in Southeast Asia were to be made, the Japanese would have to make what arrangements they could to insure against Soviet attack on their rear. And with respect to Britain and the

---

[52] The German records of the Hitler-Ribbentrop-Matsuoka conversations, and Matsuoka's account of his interviews with Mussolini and the Pope, are all printed in *Nazi-Soviet Relations*, 281-316. The record of the concluding Ribbentrop-Matsuoka meeting is printed in part in *Nazi Conspiracy and Aggression*, IV, 526 ff., and in full in the *Tokyo War Crimes Documents*, No. 528.

[53] *Halder Diary*, March 29, 1941; *Fuehrer Conferences*, 1941 (1), 53.

United States, they would have to rely on their own judgment and finally on their own military prowess.

4. The Soviet-Japanese Neutrality Pact

Notoriously a vain statesman, Matsuoka was doubtless much flattered by the attention lavished upon him by the powerful leaders of Nazi Germany. He would probably have been even more deeply gratified had he known that the British and American Governments would have welcomed him, had he chosen to return home by a western route.[54] Indeed, Mr. Churchill, regarding the forthcoming negotiations between Matsuoka and Molotov as of great importance, drafted and showed to the American Ambassador a message which he proposed to send the Japanese Foreign Minister before the latter became involved in his final discussions with Molotov or Stalin. This message, of which Mr. Churchill was quite proud, consisted entirely of a series of questions which, it was suggested, the Tokyo Government might well consider, and from the answers to which might "spring the avoidance by Japan of a serious catastrophe, and a marked improvement in the relations between Japan and the two great sea powers of the West." The questions all hinged on the problem whether the Germans would be able to defeat the British or even prevent the United States from supplying aid to Britain, and whether, if the United States entered the war, the naval superiority of the English-speaking powers would not enable them to deal effectively with Japan while at the same time disposing of the Axis powers in Europe.[55]

With or without such testimony as to the importance of his role, the Japanese statesman, as he journeyed to Moscow, was certainly aware of the arduousness of the task confronting him when he resumed his discussions with the Soviet leaders. Thus far the negotiations between Japan and the Soviet

[54] In a chit to Welles (February 19, 1941) the President had suggested that, when it became known that Matsuoka was starting for Berlin and Rome, Hull or Welles might "express a slight raising of the eyebrows in surprise that he is not also planning to visit Washington on his way home" (*Roosevelt Papers:* Secretary's File, Box 74). On March 31, Lord Halifax raised the question whether the British should invite Matsuoka to London and how the United States Government would react if the Foreign Minister decided to return home through the United States. The reply was that Matsuoka would be welcomed if he wanted to come, but that the United States Government would take no initiative (State Department memo, March 31, 1941).

[55] Tel. from Winant, April 2, 1941. The full text of the message is given in Churchill: *The Grand Alliance,* 189 ff. It was intended to have the Japanese Ambassador in London deliver the message when he went to confer with Matsuoka in Berlin. When Shigemitsu decided not to go, the message was forwarded to Ambassador Cripps, for transmission to Matsuoka in Moscow. It is interesting to note that the phrase in Question IV, "to deal with Japan while disposing of the Axis Powers in Europe," originally read "to dispose of the Axis Powers in Europe before turning their united strength upon Japan." The change was made when the State Department pointed out that the original version might be misinterpreted (tel. to Winant, April 3; tels. from Winant, April 4 and 7, 1941).

Union had been deadlocked by the Kremlin's insistence that Japan sell its (southern) part of the island of Sakhalin, and by Japanese unwillingness to abandon even the concessions which they held in the Soviet (northern) part of the island. Much as it desired an agreement with Soviet Russia, Tokyo felt unable to pay the price of South Sakhalin and feared that Matsuoka would be driven from office if he entered upon such a deal.[56] So far as known the initial conversations between the Japanese Foreign Minister, Stalin, and Molotov had brought this knotty issue no nearer solution. The question was whether on his return journey Matsuoka would find the Soviet leaders in a more accommodating frame of mind.

On his arrival in Moscow on April 7 the Japanese Foreign Minister was received at once by Molotov in a conference that lasted fully three and a half hours. Since no official record of these conversations has been published, the historian is largely dependent on Matsuoka's account, as given to Ambassador Steinhardt at the time. The Ambassador had arranged to invite the Foreign Minister to lunch on April 8, and on that occasion Matsuoka, after profuse assurances as to what had taken place in Berlin, revealed that Soviet demands on Japan were still so high that there was good reason to doubt whether the Kremlin really desired an agreement. He could not see how he could consent "to major territorial concessions," added the Foreign Minister. From this one can safely conclude that after long argument Molotov was still insisting that Japan sell the southern half of Sakhalin to the Soviet Union.

Of the developments of the next few days little is known. Molotov and Matsuoka had another three-hour session on April 9, during which no substantial progress seems to have been made until the Japanese Foreign Minister accepted the earlier Soviet suggestion that the project for a nonaggression pact be abandoned in favor of a simple neutrality treaty. This, he observed, would involve merely an assurance of mutual friendship, respect for each other's territory, and the maintenance of neutrality in the event of war. Japan was prepared to give up the demand for the sale of North Sakhalin if the Kremlin would drop its corresponding demand for the sale of South Sakhalin. Molotov concurred but continued to insist that Japan surrender its oil and other concessions in Soviet (North) Sakhalin, in return for compensation. On this item Matsuoka felt unable to compromise. He therefore went off on a one-day excursion to Leningrad, to allow a cooling-off period prior to the final attempt to arrive at a settlement.[57]

The Foreign Minister's departure for Tokyo had been fixed for Sunday, April 13, and, according to his own story, he was determined to leave at that

[56] Statement of Ambassador Tatekawa to Ambassador Steinhardt (tel. from Steinhardt, March 3, 1941).

[57] Tels. from Steinhardt, April 8, 9, and 11, 1941, supplemented by the tels. of the German Ambassador to his Government, April 9 and 10, 1941, as printed in *Nazi-Soviet Relations*, 321-22.

time, with or without agreement. In conference with Molotov on April 12 he found the Soviet Commissar still adamant, whereupon he took his leave in deep disappointment. But, as it turned out, the matter was not yet settled. Later in the day Matsuoka paid a farewell call on Stalin, who unexpectedly reopened the question at issue. After some debate, Stalin declared that the Japanese were choking him, and made an appropriate gesture. With this rather heavy jocularity he dropped the Soviet demand in return for Matusoka's promise to do what he could to persuade his Government and people to abandon the Sakhalin concessions. Thereupon the Foreign Minister hastily telegraphed his chief, Prince Konoye, for authority to sign the neutrality agreement. With a speed unprecedented in Japanese history the Prime Minister secured the necessary powers from the Emperor and on the afternoon of April 13, 1941, the Neutrality Pact was signed in Moscow, amid unrestrained rejoicing and the customary heroic consumption of champagne.[58]

One more episode in this stirring drama deserves mention. Sir Stafford Cripps had, in the interval, received Mr. Churchill's message to Matsuoka and was anxious to transmit it before final decisions were made. Through the good offices of Ambassador Steinhardt the two men were brought together during the intermission of a performance at the Moscow Art Theater on the evening of April 12. During a brief conversation the Foreign Minister assured Sir Stafford that Japan had no hostile designs on British territory in the Fast East, but when the Ambassador slipped him the Churchill message, Matsuoka put it in his pocket without even opening it. Not until after his return to Tokyo did he trouble to reply with a message which Mr. Churchill has rightly described as "barren." Having closed with Stalin, Matsuoka was obviously not interested in the sage warnings of the British Prime Minister.[59]

The concluding scene of Matsuoka's visit took place on the evening of April 13 at the Trans-Siberian Railroad Station. Soviet and Japanese dignitaries, in various stages of inebriation, were exchanging farewells amid backslappings, bearhugs and even kisses, when suddenly Stalin and Molotov appeared to join in the send-off. Stalin was remarkably friendly and was overheard to say to Matsuoka: "Now that Japan and Russia have fixed their problems, Japan can straighten out the Far East; Russia and Germany will handle Europe. Later together all of them will deal with America."[60]

---

[58] Tel. from Schulenburg to the German Foreign Office, April 13, 1941 (*Nazi-Soviet Relations,* 322 ff.); tel. from Boltze, at Tokyo, to the German Foreign Office, April 14, 1941 (*Tokyo War Crimes Documents,* No. 4056A); and tel. from Steinhardt, April 13, 1941. Toshikazu Kase: *Journey to the "Missouri"* (New Haven, 1950), 159, is the account of a participant.

[59] The text of Matsuoka's reply is given in Churchill: *The Grand Alliance,* 193-94. For the rest we have used a tel. from Steinhardt, April 13, 1941, and a tel. from Winant, April 15, 1941.

[60] Tel. from Steinhardt, April 16, 1941, who derived his information from newspaper correspondents but added that the substance of Stalin's remark had been confirmed to

The Soviet dictator then inquired for the German Ambassador. On locating him, he threw his arm around his shoulder and declared: "We must remain friends and you must now do everything to that end!" And to the Acting German Military Attaché he exclaimed: "We will remain friends with you—in any event."[61]

The document which was the prize of Matsuoka's dogged perseverance was significantly brief. It contained three major points, providing for (1) maintenance of friendly relations and respect for the integrity of each other's territory; (2) maintenance of neutrality in case either party were attacked by one or more third powers; (3) continuance of the agreement for five years. Attached to the text was a "Frontier Declaration" by which Japan pledged itself to respect the territorial integrity of the Mongolian People's Republic, while the Soviet Government made an identical engagement with respect to Manchukuo. Secretly Matsuoka promised in writing to settle the matter of the Japanese concessions in North Sakhalin within the next months.[62]

5. Final Reckoning

Even at the time of its signature the Soviet-Japanese Neutrality Pact was widely recognized as something "limited," something less than the non-aggression pact which had first been envisaged. So it was, but the difference is hardly to be sought in an abtruse or recondite distinction between the words *nonaggression* and *neutrality*. Even from the scanty records presently available it is quite clear that what was first contemplated was an agreement akin to the Nazi-Soviet Pact of August, 1939, that is, an agreement involving something like the association of the Soviet Union with the Tripartite Pact. Such a transaction would have included mutual recognition of spheres of influence in Asia, settlement of numerous outstanding territorial and other issues, and cessation of Soviet aid to Nationalist China. To all intents and purposes it would have implied alignment of the Kremlin with the Axis and adoption of a frankly anti-British and anti-American policy on the part of the Soviets. On the other hand, the Neutrality Pact as actually signed was modeled on the Soviet-German Treaty of 1926, which was still valid. At bottom it simply involved recognition of respective territorial claims in China and a paper promise to remain neutral in the event of an attack on either party by one or more other powers. The pending issues between the signa-

him by members of the German Embassy, who were present. See also Dallin: *Soviet Russia's Foreign Policy,* 346 ff., and the eyewitness account in Kase: *Journey to the "Missouri,"* 159.

[61] Tel. from Schulenburg, April 13, 1941 (*Nazi-Soviet Relations,* 323-24).

[62] Full text in *Documents on American Foreign Relations,* III, 291 ff. Matsuoka's promise was revealed by the Soviet Government in 1944 (see Beloff: *The Foreign Policy of Soviet Russia,* II, 373-74).

tories remained unresolved and the Kremlin made no promises with regard to Nationalist China. It was a very tenuous accord at best and the mere fact that the agreement was observed by both sides for a period of four years is no reason for attributing to it a value higher than that generally assigned to either neutrality or nonaggression pacts in a morally depraved period.[63]

Yet there can be no doubt that on both sides the conclusion of the agreement was regarded as a matter of major importance. The Japanese had been the suppliants throughout, and had been willing to pay a substantial price for adherence of the Soviet Union to the Tripartite Pact, for Soviet recognition of Japan's claims to a Co-Prosperity Sphere in East Asia, and for the abandonment of Nationalist China to the mercies of the Tokyo militarists. The Neutrality Pact, as finally signed, certainly fell far short of Matsuoka's hopes. But he had learned in Berlin that adherence of the Kremlin to the Axis was out of the question and had therefore decided that there was no chance of securing Soviet recognition of Japan's aspirations. Under these circumstances it is quite understandable that he was unwilling to sacrifice even the North Sakhalin concessions to obtain a mere assurance of neutrality. However, the Neutrality Pact was certainly better than nothing. On paper, at least, it gave Japan a free hand to stage the advance to the south and provided security in the north if as a result Japan became involved in war with Britain or the United States. Official and semiofficial Japanese statements made this point and revealed the expectation that at the very least the agreement was bound to make so great an impression on Chiang Kai-shek as to ease negotiations with him. Ambassador Grew presumed that Soviet aid to China would fall off and was convinced that the agreement would "strengthen the hands of and stimulate those elements in Japan which favor a vigorous prosecution of the southward advance."[64]

The importance attributed to the agreement by Stalin and Molotov was most eloquently demonstrated by the farewell scene at the railroad station. Ribbentrop had been accorded no such send-off. The problem, then, is to explain the phenomenal change in the Soviet attitude from lukewarmness to any agreement that did not promise huge gains, to readiness to conclude a pact involving no gains. Ambassador Steinhardt believed the reversal had taken place within the few weeks between the two sojourns of the Japanese Foreign Minister in Moscow, and even now this reasoning sounds plausible. Steinhardt rightly discounted the idea that the Germans had used their influence to bring the Soviets and Japanese together, and reported home:

[63] Ambassador Grew attempted to establish a distinction between the two varieties of pact (tel. from Grew, April 14, 1941).

[64] Tel. from Grew, April 14, 1941. See also Matsuoka's remarks to the German Ambassador (*Nazi-Soviet Relations*, 322-23), and Ohashi's statement to the German representative in Tokyo (*Tokyo War Crimes Documents*, No. 4056A). See further the press comment assembled in the *Bulletin of International News*, XVIII (1), 527.

I believe that the treaty was brought about much less by German influence or a desire on the part of Japan to prepare itself for eventual collaboration with Germany in hostilities against the United States, than by fear on the part of Japan that it may become involved in hostilities with the United States against its will and the desire on the part of the Soviet Government to prepare itself against a possible attack by Germany.[65]

The Ambassador might have gone even further and fixed the change in Soviet attitude as of April 12-13, 1941. Following the Yugoslav *coup d'état* at the end of March, the Kremlin had hastily concluded an agreement with the new anti-German regime, by all odds the most offensive manifestation, since August, 1939, of Soviet hostility to Hitler's Balkan policy. The Fuehrer had replied by invading Yugoslavia and Greece on April 6. By the time of Matsuoka's departure on April 13, the German armored forces were already riding roughshod over Yugoslavia and hope that the rugged Serbs might hold out in the mountains was rapidly vanishing. It requires no great effort of the imagination to picture the impact of these events on the Kremlin. To foreign observers in Moscow it was perfectly plain that Soviet leaders now saw in all its starkness the likelihood of an early Nazi attack on the Soviet Union. Under the circumstances Stalin and Molotov welcomed a Neutrality Pact with Japan, hoping that if hostilities broke out in Europe they would be spared an attack in the rear and a war on two fronts. The evidence is admittedly fragmentary, but it seems that the Kremlin regarded the agreement with Matsuoka as a gesture of conciliation toward Germany. Ambassador Steinhardt reported the gossip in Moscow that the hidden import of the Soviet-Japanese treaty was that it constituted a first step toward full association of the Soviet Union with the Tripartite powers in a concerted drive to impose their will both on Asia and Europe. Somewhat later he quoted a reliable German source as having told him that the motive of the Soviet leaders was to put themselves in a position to join the Tripartite Pact or at least safeguard themselves against Japanese attack in case of German invasion: "The Soviet Union is now at the crossroads," he added, "and must either shortly join the Axis Pact or face an attack by the German Army along a front from the Baltic to the Black Sea."[66] Lest it be supposed that all this was mere diplomatic tattle, the reader may be reminded of Stalin's pathetically eager efforts to reaffirm the Soviet-Nazi friendship. Perhaps the great send-off accorded Matsuoka was intended less for that vain and mercurial statesman than for the stalwart and impassive German Ambassador.

In this connection it is certainly worth noting that the public statements of the interested parties all harped on this very theme. The official Soviet *Pravda* published a long article reviewing the course of the negotiations and concluding that the Kremlin's motive in signing the agreement was simply

[65] Tel. from Steinhardt, April 13, 1941.
[66] Tels. from Steinhardt, April 16 and 20, 1941.

and solely to support its fixed policy of avoiding war and preserving peace. Care was taken to refer scornfully to Anglo-American comments to the effect that tension between Soviet Russia and Germany explained the pact, and it was scrupulously pointed out that the new agreement was in no way aimed at Germany.[67] Prince Konoye, in turn, emphasized that the new agreement fitted neatly into the framework of the Tripartite Pact, which remained the "axis" of Japanese foreign policy. Both agreements served the same objective of preventing the spread of war and of securing peace in East Asia. According to the inspired Tokyo press, the Neutrality Pact might well pave the way to a new phase in the collaboration of Soviet Russia and Germany. Let Britain and the United States beware.[68]

Even the Nazis hastened to put the best face possible on the matter. Hitler assured his military men that the Soviet-Japanese pact had been concluded with German acquiescence and that it was valuable because it would serve to distract the Japanese from Vladivostok and encourage them to attack Singapore instead.[69] Meanwhile the Nazi press joined in the jubilation of the signatories, asserting that the new agreement complemented the Tripartite Pact, that it would be a staggering blow to Britain and the United States, and that, in effect, Soviet Russia had agreed to hold Japan's coat while the latter fought it out with the democracies.[70]

How sincere these paeans were, the reader may judge for himself. From the evidence adduced above he will probably conclude that on the part of the Soviet Union, at least, it was a case of whistling in the dark. It would be hard, in fact, to imagine a more complete reversal of role than that imposed on the Kremlin in the few months from November, 1940, to April, 1941. At the time of Molotov's visit to Berlin the Soviet leaders clearly believed that the Tripartite Pact had so divided the capitalist world that the Kremlin could set its own terms for coöperation, even with its Nazi partner. At that time, and indeed through the spring of 1941, the British, the Americans, and the Japanese were all suing for Soviet favor and were all meeting with but little spirit of accommodation. The efforts of the British and Americans to point out that Soviet Russia was undoubtedly on Hitler's list were put aside with incredulity. Only as the dispute between Moscow and Berlin assumed formidable proportions, only when Mr. Welles was able to submit specific evidence of Hitler's plan to attack his partner, only when the German invasion of Yugoslavia and Greece tore to shreds the Kremlin's veil of self-deception, did a change take place.

[67] Bulletin of International News, XVIII (1), 609; tel. from Steinhardt, April 19, 1941.

[68] Konoye's statement as printed in Documents on American Foreign Relations, III, 292 ff. For the rest see the press comment in Bulletin of International News, XVIII (1), 527, 534, 535, 598, 599.

[69] Fuehrer Conferences, 1941 (1), 53 (April 20, 1941).

[70] See the Bulletin of International News, as cited above.

Even then the Soviet policy remained enigmatic. In his talks with Welles, Ambassador Oumansky struck a more cordial note and dropped broad hints that identity of policy between the United States and Soviet Russia might be desirable and eventually necessary. It may be that Molotov, in his initial conversation with Matsuoka, suggested a limited neutrality agreement in preference to a far-reaching settlement so as not to estrange the democracies by seeming to associate the Kremlin with the Tripartite Pact. But the dominant thought of the Soviet leaders seems to have been to make a gesture of conciliation toward Berlin and keep open the prospect that the Soviet Union might yet decide to coöperate with the Axis. The Neutrality Pact, in addition to providing the flimsy assurance of protection against attack in the Far East, was clearly conceived of in Moscow as a move agreeable to Berlin. Actually Hitler seems to have cared little one way or the other. His purpose was fixed and, when the moment came, he was to demonstrate to the Kremlin that its efforts at appeasement, like those of others previously, were utterly futile.

CHAPTER XII

The Threat to North Africa

1. FRANCO THE INTRACTABLE

Adolph Hitler was constitutionally incapable of acknowledging a setback or defeat and therefore never canceled plans upon which he had set his heart. When he saw the impracticality of invading England in the autumn of 1940, he did not abandon the project but merely deferred it. Similarly, when the Spanish dictator, early in December, 1940, categorically refused to enter the war on the Axis side and in addition rejected German requests for permission to attack Gibraltar, the Fuehrer, though obliged to give up his immediate designs, by no means relinquished hope that eventually he might achieve his purpose. He had become converted to Admiral Raeder's thesis that the most effective method of striking at Britain was to cut the supply lines in the Atlantic and Mediterranean, and he was convinced that it was as important to conquer Gibraltar as to secure control of Egypt and Suez. Until he had far greater numbers of submarines he could not hope to interdict the flow of supplies from the United States to Britain which, after the enactment of Lend-Lease, promised to assume immense and quite possibly decisive proportions. The Mediterranean therefore took on added importance. If the British could be effectively barred from that great corridor, they might be forced to surrender before the full weight of American support could make itself felt.

By December, 1940, the prospects for an early Axis victory in the Mediterranean had grown dim. The Italian advance on Egypt had stalled almost at the outset and Mussolini had turned on Greece only to meet with disaster in his effort to subjugate that country. Worse, the British had suddenly launched a counteroffensive from Egypt, had smashed Graziani's army and had embarked on a drive to the west which, in a matter of weeks, was to sweep the Italians out of all Cyrenaica. As Hitler saw it, there was real likelihood that General Weygand would throw in the lot of French North

Africa with that of the British, in which case the Italians might soon be expelled from all Libya. Such a disaster might well bring on the collapse of the Fascist regime and the withdrawal of Italy from the war. Merely to contemplate such dire eventualities was enough to demonstrate to Hitler the urgent need for remedial measures.[1]

The Fuehrer was completely baffled by Franco's refusal to fall in line with Nazi plans, which envisaged the crossing of the Pyrenees by German forces on January 10, 1941, and an attack on Gibraltar early in February. The Caudillo, wrote Hitler to Mussolini on December 31, 1940, was naïve in thinking that Britain and the United States would really provide Spain with food and other essential supplies as a reward for continued nonbelligerency. He, Hitler, could not abandon hope that Franco would reconsider.[2] Discussing the situation with his military advisers, the Fuehrer admitted that there was no prospect of Spain's becoming an ally, yet a week later he ordered further efforts to bring Franco to his senses. Bemoaning to Count Ciano the Spanish dictator's "hesitant and faithless" attitude, he appealed to the Italians to use their influence. The intervention of Spain, he observed, was of fundamental importance: "Once in possession of Gibraltar, we would be in a position to gain a foothold with strong forces in North Africa, and thus put an end to Weygand's blackmail."[3]

Although Ciano lost no time in inviting Franco and his Foreign Minister, Serrano Suñer, to pay a visit to Mussolini, it was not until February 12 that the Italian and Spanish dictators met at Bordighera, on the Italian Riviera. Meanwhile Hitler had already brought his own influence and logic to bear. In a long and outspoken letter of February 6 he had recalled to Franco the community of interest between Germany, Italy and Spain, and had reviewed the understanding arrived at during the Hendaye conference of October 22, 1940. With painstaking care he had dissected the arguments advanced by Franco against entering the war, and had reminded him that Britain would not and could not save Spain from starvation. Germany was and had always been prepared to send grain, but only after Spanish intervention. If only the original plans had been adhered to, Gibraltar would already have been taken. As it was, two months had been lost "which otherwise would have helped to decide world history." Franco must see that his own and his country's future was bound up with the Axis: "I believe that we three men, the Duce, you, and I, are bound to one another by the most rigorous compulsion of history that is possible, and that thus we in this his-

---

[1] For a good brief survey of the Mediterranean problem see F. H. Hinsley: *Hitler's Strategy* (New York, 1951), Chapter VII.

[2] *Les lettres secrètes échangées par Hitler et Mussolini* (Paris, 1946), 103 ff.

[3] Record of the conference of Hitler with his generals, January 8-9, 1941 (*Fuehrer Conferences, 1941* (1), 1 ff.); Ciano's conferences with Ribbentrop and Hitler, January 19, 1941 (*Ciano's Diplomatic Papers*, 417 ff.); record of the same conference, from the German side, in *Nazi Conspiracy and Aggression*, VI, C-134.

torical analysis ought to obey as the supreme commandment the realization that in such difficult times, not so much an apparently wise caution as the bold heart, rather, can save nations."[4]

There was actually little in Hitler's long harangue to induce Franco to abandon his "wise caution." The Fuehrer had nothing to say about Spain's territorial aspirations and his contention that the outcome of the war was already decided, "regardless of what ephemeral successes the British believe they can achieve anywhere on the periphery," can hardly have been convincing. When, at Bordighera on February 12, Mussolini pleaded Hitler's cause and attempted to prove at length the certainty of Axis victory, Franco spoke his mind. His country, he pointed out, was threatened with serious famine and simply could not afford to engage in war. With much bitterness he reflected on the German attitude and declared that Spain would not play second fiddle in the Axis concert. Indeed, he went so far as to question Hitler's military estimates. Gibraltar, he thought, could not be taken by air attack alone. Therefore he, Franco, was concentrating heavy artillery on the coast facing the British fortress. When the time came, the Spaniards would launch the attack themselves. Furthermore, he made it crystal clear that Spain would not participate in the war without explicit assurance that its national claims would be satisfied.[5]

While Franco, on his return journey, stopped at Montpellier to confer with Marshal Pétain, Mussolini at once informed Hitler of the results or lack of results of the Bordighera meeting. The Fuehrer was not surprised. Replying to his Italian colleague, he said that he was expecting a letter from Franco, but added significantly: "In any case, the upshot of the long Spanish palaver and written explanations is that Spain does not want to enter the conflict and will not enter it."[6] The Caudillo's response to Hitler's letter certainly bore out the accuracy of this conclusion. While protesting his absolute loyalty and full appreciation of the community of Spain's interests with those of Germany and Italy, he enlarged upon the economic difficulties faced by his country and the consequent need for time and material aid. He recognized the importance of taking Gibraltar, but now introduced a new idea: "in order that the closing of Gibraltar may have a decisive value it is also necessary that the Suez Canal be closed at the same time." Finally, as to Spain's national claims, the Spanish dictator observed that the Hendaye agreement was too vague: "the facts in their logical development have today left far behind the circumstances which in the month of October had to be taken into consideration with respect to the prevailing situation, and the protocol then existing must at the present be considered outmoded. Franco's letter ended with a courtly, Hispanic flourish:

[4] *The Spanish Government and the Axis* (Washington, 1946), No. 12.

[5] *Ciano's Diplomatic Papers,* 421 ff.

[6] Hitler's letter to Mussolini, February 28, 1941 (*Les lettres secrètes échangées par Hitler et Mussolini,* 115 ff.).

These are my answers, dear Fuehrer, to your observations. I want to dispel with them all shadow of doubt and declare that I stand ready at your side, entirely and decidedly at your disposal, united in a common historical destiny, desertion from which would mean my suicide and that of the cause which I have led and represent in Spain. I need no confirmation of my faith in the triumph of your cause and I repeat that I shall always be a loyal follower of it.[7]

But Hitler was not interested in professions of faith. He wanted Spain in the war and was burning with zeal to launch his carefully prepared assault upon Gibraltar. Franco's letter left no doubt that Spain would not participate or even coöperate unless its national claims were gratified. This, however, could not be done without driving French North Africa into the arms of the British. At bottom, Hitler felt, and probably rightly, that Franco would not move until the British position had already begun to collapse. Clearly the German failure to invade England, the Italian reverses in Greece, and the British victory in Libya had given Franco pause. The Fuehrer realized that there was nothing more to be done for the moment. Again and again he lamented the Caudillo's attitude and the lost opportunity to strike Britain a mortal blow, yet he had no alternative but to reconcile himself to Franco's intractability.[8]

2. IBERIAN ISSUES IN AMERICAN POLICY

It was the well-established British policy to counter Nazi propaganda in Madrid with full and forceful publicity designed to demonstrate not only that Britain was not done for, but that a British victory, with American aid, was inevitable. London hoped that Franco and his Government would stand aloof from the conflict at least until they were assured and reassured that the future belonged irrevocably to Hitler's New Order. The British had no doubt of Franco's intense dislike for them or of his strong sympathy with Fascism and Nazism, but they relied heavily on his shrewdness and caution and firmly believed that in view of Spain's desperate economic situation the Spanish dictator would never intentionally involve his country in anything but a very short conflict. To reinforce their propaganda the British had long since decided to forestall Spanish dependence on Germany for food and supplies by doling out enough support to keep the economy alive, and to use the threat of cutting off supplies in order to hold Franco and Serrano Suñer to a policy of nonbelligerency.

Since the British had very little to spare for other countries, they made continued efforts to induce the United States to support their policy.[9] But Washington followed London's lead only with reluctance. American public opinion was generally hostile to the Franco regime and the State Depart-

---

[7] *The Spanish Government and the Axis,* No. 13 (letter of February 26, 1941).

[8] Hitler's remarks to Ciano, March 25 and April 20, 1941 (*Ciano's Diplomatic Papers,* 431 ff., 434 ff.).

[9] See Chapter III, above.

ment itself was deeply divided on Spanish policy. While Ambassador Weddell pleaded for wholehearted support of the British policy and added his
own reasoning to London's arguments, Secretary Hull and many of his associates were unwilling to take the gamble. They were ready to send Red
Cross and some other relief supplies, but insisted on making larger commitments dependent on explicit Spanish assurances that the policy of nonbelligerency would be maintained.

There was no marked change in either British or American policy during
the early months of 1941. The despatch of Red Cross aid from the United
States was announced on January 8, 1941, but no further relief measures
were undertaken. Though neither London nor Washington could know the
complete story of the German-Spanish negotiations, they rightly suspected
that Franco was resisting Nazi pressure for Spanish intervention.[10] Under
the circumstances there seemed to the State Department no really cogent
reason for retreating from the uncompromising stand previously adopted regarding a larger program of aid to Spain. Repeatedly Ambassador Weddell
urged a course which would be not "appeasement, but a calculated policy
of supporting the Spanish Government to resist German pressure in its
efforts to continue as a nonbelligerent." American policy, he explained,
"should be a careful weighing of what Spanish neutrality is worth to us and
to the common cause, and we should make a flat offer of foodstuffs with the
sole condition and understanding that the spaced deliveries would cease the
moment Spain entered the war or Germany occupied the Peninsula."[11] But
for the reasons mentioned above Secretary Hull turned a deaf ear to all
these appeals. Since Franco and Serrano Suñer showed no disposition to
accept the American terms for a substantial credit, aid to Spain continued
to be insignificant.[12]

It can hardly be argued, then, that American policy had a direct bearing
on Franco's refusal to cast in his lot with Hitler. No doubt the larger American policy of unlimited aid to Britain, as reflected in the Lend-Lease legislation, had much to do with shaping Franco's estimate of the probable outcome of the war, but there remained the possibility that he, like Hitler, might
decide that American power could not be brought to bear in time and that
Spain, by its intervention, could clinch the defeat of Britain. Washington
had to be prepared, therefore, to see Franco yield to German pressure and
to face the consequences of a Nazi attack on Gibraltar and North Africa.
Rumors of such action were rife and may well have been propagated by

---

[10] Tels. from Weddell, January 29 and February 5, 1941; memo of conversation
between Mr. Welles and Lord Halifax, February 19, 1941.

[11] Tel. from Weddell, January 29, 1941.

[12] See Herbert Feis: *The Spanish Story* (New York, 1948), 107 ff. A formal British
request that the United States join in a more inclusive program of assistance (March
20, 1941) brought no result (see William L. Langer: *Our Vichy Gamble,* New York,
1947, pp. 137-78).

both Madrid and Berlin for purposes either of deception or intimidation. President Roosevelt seems to have been more disturbed by these possibilities than Secretary Hull, and had a notion that he might forestall them by a display of power. As early as January 30, 1941, he had suggested to Mr. Hull that a squadron of the Atlantic Fleet, consisting of four or five cruisers and a dozen destroyers, be sent on a courtesy visit to Lisbon and Cadiz, in the hope that such a demonstration would serve to deter the Germans from an attack on England as well as from an advance through Spain.[13]

For the time being nothing came of this project and the American effort to influence Spanish policy remained confined to the repetition of statements of determination to support Britain and of confidence in an ultimate British victory. At the end of February Colonel William J. Donovan, returning from an extended special mission in the Middle East, stopped at Madrid and gave his own vigorous twist to this formula. Serrano Suñer succeeded in preventing an interview between Donovan and Franco, but himself engaged in a two-hour debate with the American emissary. Despite Donovan's altogether unvarnished presentation of his Government's position, Serrano Suñer made no secret of his hope and belief that Germany would win. It was clearly futile to suppose that the Foreign Minister could be swayed by contrary arguments. On the other hand, other Spanish leaders with whom Donovan conferred were by no means certain of Nazi victory and stressed the vital contribution which American aid could make in preventing Hitler from exploiting Spain's economic distress and forcing a hungry people and a reluctant Government to enter the war. The British Ambassador, Sir Samuel Hoare, took the occasion once again to advocate his program. He outlined to Donovan a joint British-American policy calling not only for a concerted propaganda campaign but also for extensive economic assistance, including an American credit of twenty million dollars, and even for military aid in case of need. Sir Samuel thought it mistaken to make aid to Spain conditional on guarantees, and argued that installments of aid could be stopped the very moment Spain evidenced any inclination to yield to Hitler or itself launch an attack against Gibraltar.[14]

The policy so ardently advanced by the British, so persistently supported by Ambassador Weddell and so wholeheartedly espoused by Colonel Donovan was substantially the policy which the United States Government was applying to Vichy France and which, strangely enough, the British were, in the case of France, inclined to obstruct. Since the American public abominated Vichy as well as Madrid, it is hard to explain State Department opposition to the program of aid for Spain except perhaps by its greater distrust

[13] Memo of the President to Secretary Hull, January 30, 1941 (*Roosevelt Papers: Secretary's File*, Box 73).

[14] Donovan's reports of his conferences in Madrid are contained in the *Donovan Papers* (*MS.*), Folder 9. See also Sir Samuel Hoare (Lord Templewood): *Complacent Dictator* (New York, 1947), 107 ff.

of Franco and Serrano Suñer than of Pétain and by its belief that Spanish leaders were constitutionally immune to democratic influence. The State Department continued to evade suggestions for concrete measures of aid to Spain. As late as April 10, when the German armies were already in full career against Greece and Yugoslavia and when Rommel and his Nazi divisions were already threatening to destroy the British position in Libya, Ambassador Weddell was once again instructed to reiterate ("in the strongest terms") the United States Government's faith in ultimate British victory![15]

It remained to be seen how long this ritualistic formula could outweigh Hitler's demonstration of Nazi power, which in April and May promised to resolve all the doubts on which Spanish nonbelligerency had been based. When Ambassador Weddell carried out his instructions on April 19, he found Serrano Suñer sullen and unresponsive. The discussion led to complaints by the Ambassador about the tone of the Spanish press and to his suggestion that some of these press effusions read like translations from a foreign language, possibly German. This was too much for the Foreign Minister, who thenceforth asserted that the Ambassador had insulted him, and through him Spain itself. For months thereafter official relations between the United States and Spain were frigid and Serrano Suñer managed to prevent any interview between the Ambassador and Franco. The initial indications, then, were that the German victories would prove too great a temptation for the Spanish leaders and that presently Nazi successes in the Balkans and Libya would be matched by the conquest of Gibraltar and the occupation of North Africa.[16]

It must be emphasized in this context that during April and May, 1941, there seemed every likelihood that the American Government, to insure arrival of its supplies in Britain, would have to adopt a system of convoy protection, and that naval clashes between American and German ships would presently result in American involvement in the war. This, in turn, meant that control of the Atlantic islands—the Portuguese Azores, Cape Verdes and Madeira, and the Spanish Canaries—became a matter of major importance. Both sides had long been cognizant of the opportunities and dangers involved and both were elaborating plans to frustrate the supposed designs of their opponents. But from the British-American viewpoint the occupation of some of these islands was deemed desirable not only to forestall Nazi seizure, but to deter Hitler from any effort to coerce Spain or Portugal and then advance on North Africa.

Portugal was the traditional ally of Britain and it was obviously in London's interest to afford Portugal all possible aid in the event of a German attack. Unfortunately it was a grave question whether British military and

[15] Tel. to Weddell, April 10, 1941. Cf. Hull: *Memoirs*, II, 940.
[16] Tel. from Weddell, April 19, 1941. See also Feis: *The Spanish Story*, 131 ff.

naval assistance could be given in sufficient amount to save the country from German divisions advancing from Spain. Pointing out the dilemma in a message to the President at the end of March, Mr. Churchill suggested that the visit of an American naval squadron to the Azores and Lisbon might bolster the morale of Dr. Salazar and the Portuguese Government.[17]

This idea, as noted above, had already occurred to the President. He now pursued it with alacrity, but only to find the Lisbon Government unwilling to permit a demonstration which might easily provoke Hitler to make the very attack which the visit was intended to forestall. Secretary Hull pointed out to the Portuguese Minister that the fate of Portugal and its island possessions was of hardly less concern to the United States than to Portugal itself. But he could do little more than reserve the right to revive the proposal if the circumstances required it.[18]

The Prime Minister was unwilling to let the matter rest, for he had long since realized that if Franco refused to coöperate with Hitler the latter might force his way into Spain and Portugal as soon as the weather permitted, in April or May. To meet such a contingency the British had held in readiness a strong brigade and four transports for the occupation of some of the Atlantic islands.[19] By mid-April it appeared to the Prime Minister highly probable that Hitler would follow up his successes in the eastern Mediterranean by making a sudden thrust through Spain at Gibraltar. From Vichy Ambassador Leahy reported that Pétain himself had become convinced of the imminence of a German advance through Spain, while Ambassador Weddell, who was anything but an alarmist, cabled from Madrid that the opinion was widespread in diplomatic quarters that "important decisions concerning Spanish-Axis relations would shortly be made." Sir Samuel Hoare, it is true, believed Franco would try to maintain his attitude of "nonbelligerency in an atmosphere of nebulous inaction," but that was no guarantee that Hitler would not break the deadlock whenever it suited his book.[20]

In some apprehension Mr. Churchill therefore cabled the President that if Spain yielded to German pressure or were attacked by Germany the British would at once despatch expeditions to seize the Azores and Cape Verde Islands. Since these operations would, however, take some eight days and might be anticipated by German action, it would, he suggested, be of

[17] Tel. from the Foreign Office to the British Embassy in Washington, for communication to the State Department, March 28, 1941; memo of conversation between Mr. Welles and Lord Halifax, March 31, 1941.

[18] Memo of conversation between Mr. Hull and the Portuguese Minister, April 18, 1941; Hull: *Memoirs,* II, 940.

[19] Churchill: *Their Finest Hour,* 625; *The Grand Alliance,* 7-8.

[20] Tel. from Leahy, April 17, 1941; tel. from Weddell, April 19, 1941; Hoare's despatch of May 1, 1941 (Hoare: *Complacent Dictator,* 110 ff.), a copy of which was transmitted to Secretary Hull on May 5, 1941. See also Langer: *Our Vichy Gamble,* 144 ff.

great advantage if an American squadron could be sent for a friendly cruise in those regions at the earliest moment. This would probably warn off Nazi raiders and "keep the place warm."[21]

In view of the firm attitude already assumed by Lisbon, it was impossible for the President to comply with the Prime Minister's proposal without antagonizing the Portuguese authorities. He therefore replied at some length in the following terms:

One. In relation to paragraph 14 of yours of April 23 we received strong protest from the Portuguese Government in regard to a proposed friendly visit to the Azores and Cape Verde Islands at this time. In view of this we deferred proposed visit. We then received recommendation from American Ambassador in Spain that friendly visit planned to Canaries or to Spain be carried out but that no fuel should be taken on locally in the islands or in Spain. In view of this situation the proposed naval visits were cancelled.

The new naval patrol now going into operation will extend to westerly side of both Azores and Cape Verde Islands, but planes will not be flown over the islands themselves. Our patrol is already on way to take positions assigned, and I think liaison work between the two naval services is being established satisfactorily.

Two. It is, of course, of utmost importance, in my judgment, that you send no expedition to either place unless Portugal is attacked or you get definite word of an immediate German attack on the islands. Furthermore, I know you will not mind my saying that in the event of a British expeditionary force you make it very clear to the American people that in case of Azores it is for purpose of British defense and not for permanent occupation. In other words, that Britain will restore islands to Portuguese sovereignty at close of war if Portugal is restored as an independent nation. The reason I suggest this is that, as you know, most of Azores are in Western Hemisphere under my longitudinal map reading.[22]

This message was distinctly disappointing to the Prime Minister, who replied at once, pointing out that the conditions laid down by Mr. Roosevelt in his paragraph II made it almost certain that the British would be forestalled by the Germans. The Nazis, he continued, were undoubtedly infiltrating the islands. There was no way of controlling this activity and the Governments of Spain and Portugal were too intimidated to dare take notice of it. It was virtually certain that any German move against Spain or Portugal would be synchronized with a stroke against the islands. "We have taken no decision yet," added the Prime Minister, "but I am sure you would not wish to prescribe our remaining passive, if we feel we have to act in advance of the conditions set forth in the first sentence of your paragraph II." In that event the British would not only promise the restoration of Portuguese sovereignty at the end of the war, but would be prepared to have

---

[21] Tel. from Churchill to the President, April 23, 1941. In handing this message to Ambassador Winant, Mr. Churchill remarked that it would be of the greatest help if the suggested action could be taken "in the next few days."

[22] Tel. from the President to Mr. Churchill, May 1, 1941.

the United States stand guarantor for the execution of such an engagement. "We are far from wishing to add to our territory," declared Mr. Churchill, "but only to preserve our life and perhaps yours."[23]

Mr. Roosevelt could hardly persist in his veto of emergency action by the British, which would be in the American as well as the British interest. The question of the Portuguese islands was therefore left in abeyance. Meanwhile, on May 14, the President cut short the long debates within his official family as to shifts of American naval forces by ordering three battleships, an aircraft carrier and the appropriate supporting vessels to leave Pearl Harbor and join the Atlantic Fleet.[24] At about the same time he requested Under Secretary Welles to compose a draft message to Congress which, in effect, would have declared all West Africa north of the Equator, as well as the Portuguese and Spanish islands in the Atlantic, as thenceforth falling under the protective provisions of the Monroe Doctrine.[25]

It is reasonably clear that the President at this time planned for the possibility of an occupation of the Azores by American forces, as advocated by Senator Pepper on the floor of the Senate and agitated in the press. Mr. Roosevelt intended to despatch a special emissary to Lisbon to secure Dr. Salazar's assent and on May 23 secretly ordered the Chief of Naval Operations to have ready, within thirty days, a force sufficient to transport 25,000 men to the islands.[26] But in the end nothing came of these projects. Mr. Hull persuaded the President that the threat to Latin America and the Western Hemisphere from a German occcupation of the Atlantic islands or Dakar "could be better stated nakedly without raising a technical Monroe Doctrine issue," so the idea of a message to Congress was abandoned. Similarly, the undiminished opposition of the Portuguese Government and London's desire to conduct the negotiations with Lisbon led Washington to renounce the projected expedition to the Azores.[27] There remained, however, the re-

[23] Tel. from Mr. Churchill to the President, May 3, 1941.

[24] *Pearl Harbor Attack,* I, 122 ff.; V, 2112 ff.; XVI, 2163 ff.; *Stimson Diary (MS.),* May 1 to 13, 1941.

[25] Welles's draft of the message, together with his letter to the President of May 20, setting forth Secretary Hull's objections to the project, are in the *Roosevelt Papers:* Secretary's File, Box 74. See also Hull: *Memoirs,* II, 959.

[26] Letter of Admiral Stark to Admiral Kimmel, May 24, 1941 (*Pearl Harbor Attack,* V, 2113). The Committee to Defend America took the lead in advocating action against the Atlantic islands and Dakar (*The New York Times,* May 17, 1941). On the staff plans for the possible use of expeditionary forces in the Atlantic islands, Dakar, etc., in May, 1941, we have used the account in the MS. study of Dr. Stetson Conn on the *Hemisphere Defense Policy of the United States,* Chapter III, pp. 54 ff., and 64 ff.

[27] Note from the Spanish Embassy in Washington, May 7, 1941; tel. from Fish (Lisbon), May 9, 1941; memo of conversation between Welles and Lord Halifax, May 17, 1941, and between Hull and Lord Halifax, May 21 and 24, 1941; *Roosevelt Papers:* Secretary's File, Box 73 (Hull's memo to the President regarding the message to Congress, May 25, 1941, and a note from the British Embassy, June 4, 1941, outlining a proposed course of action with respect to the Lisbon Government).

inforcement of the Atlantic Fleet and the expanded American patrol of the vital shipping lanes.

The supposed crisis of late April also reacted, albeit sluggishly, on the American policy toward Spain. Following a suggestion of Ambassador Weddell, the State Department cautiously sounded out some of the Latin American Republics on the feasibility of an appeal to Madrid to maintain its nonbelligerency.[28] At the same time it was decided to make at least a halfhearted gesture of aid to Spain. On April 29 Ambassador Weddell was informed that he might tell Franco that the United States was prepared "at once" to broaden and liberalize trade relations and thereby enable Madrid to obtain wheat, corn and cotton without resort to credit transactions. The Ambassador was to warn, however, that the United States might not be able to spare much of these commodities, and he was reminded of the conditions which, since December, 1940, had been attached to the program of assistance.[29]

Precisely what the Administration hoped to achieve in thus restating a position which had already ended in an impasse is by no means clear. It made little difference, however, for Foreign Minister Serrano Suñer saw to it that Mr. Weddell should not present the American offer to the Chief of State. On one pretext or another and with varying degrees of rudeness and insolence the Ambassador was put off. There would be no point in recounting all the details. By May, 1941, the relations between the United States and Spain were as distant and cold as ever. Despite its desperate economic plight, Spain was receiving no aid to speak of from the United States. The British were doing what little they could to prevent the country's falling into dependence on Germany, but there was no knowing whether or not Franco would think it advisable or necessary to align himself with Hitler. If in fact Spain maintained a status of nonbelligerency, the explanation is no doubt to be sought in other factors. For one thing, Hitler hesitated to force the issue of intervention lest he provoke France and drive North Africa into the arms of the British. For another, the British managed, with American support, to hold their position in Egypt until Hitler diverted his immense military power to the campaign against Russia. Finally, American policy played an important, even if indirect role. Franco could hardly overlook the implications of the Lend-Lease Act and must have concluded that the war would probably be a long one in which Spain could not afford to become involved. At the same time the reinforcement of the United States Fleet and the extension of the patrol system made it virtually certain that a German or Spanish move against Gibraltar or North Africa would entail the immediate British

[28] Circular tel. to American representatives in various American capitals, April 29, 1941; memo by the Division of American Republics, May 8, 1941; memo of conversation between Mr. Hull and Lord Halifax, May 21, 1941. Nothing promising came of this *démarche*.

[29] Tel. to Weddell, April 29, 1941; Feis: *The Spanish Story*, 133 ff.

or American occupation of the Atlantic islands, West Africa and possibly North Africa, and perhaps even Portugal. Under these circumstances Franco might well ask himself whether the game was worth the candle. For Hitler the question can scarcely have been less pertinent, particularly since the German High Command continually warned him of the virtual impossibility of seizing and holding the Atlantic islands, desirable though such a move might be.[30]

3. THE SUCCESSION TO LAVAL

On the eve of Pierre Laval's dismissal from his influential position in the Vichy Government (December 13, 1940), Hitler had finally brought himself to the point of accepting the program of collaboration with the French. After the British-Gaullist attack on Dakar in September and the defection to Free France of the French colonies in Central Africa, the Fuehrer was consumed by anxiety lest General Weygand, lately appointed French Delegate-General in North Africa, go over to the British and thereby preclude that Axis control of the Mediterranean which was now recognized as essential to the defeat of the British. Laval and General Huntziger had conducted military conversations with Abetz and General Warlimont on December 10 and the Germans had good reason to believe that the powerful Vice Premier would undertake the reconquest of the dissident colonies. That enterprise, it was thought, would necessarily lead to conflict with the British and so become the prelude to French participation in the war on the Axis side.[31] How important the issue of collaboration with France on African affairs appeared to Hitler is best indicated by the fact that even before Laval's fall, and presumably as a precaution against the failure of the plan outlined above, the Fuehrer issued a directive for Operation *Attila* (December 10, 1940). This provided that if a movement of revolt should develop in parts of the French Empire under Weygand's command, steps should be taken immediately for the occupation of Vichy France and particularly for the seizure or destruction of the French naval forces at Toulon and elsewhere.[32]

The unexpected overthrow of Laval was therefore a severe setback for the Germans. In view of the sudden and successful British attack on the Italian forces in Libya, the collapse of the projected plan for reconquest of the dissident colonies was fraught with serious possibilities. Refusing to be misled by reiterated assurances that the crisis at Vichy was a purely domestic affair and that Pétain and his Government proposed to continue the policy of collaboration, Hitler was deeply convinced that Weygand and his adherents were responsible for Laval's downfall. Under the circumstances the Fuehrer

---

[30] *Fuehrer Conferences,* 1941 (1), 64-73.
[31] For details see Chapter III, Section 8.
[32] This project is discussed in Anthony Martienssen: *Hitler and His Admirals* (New York, 1949), 97, and in F. H. Hinsley: *Hitler's Strategy,* 120-21.

harbored no illusions about the future of collaboration and anticipated the early defection of French North Africa to de Gaulle or the British, with or without the connivance of Pétain. The appointment of Pierre Flandin as Vichy Foreign Minister was regarded as particularly symptomatic, for Flandin, despite occasional past gestures of friendship for Germany, was looked upon as a champion of the Anglo-French Alliance.[33]

Otto Abetz, the German Ambassador to France, had been one of the warmest advocates of collaboration and took the dismissal of his French counterpart, Laval, as a personal affront. Both he and Ribbentrop argued that Pétain should be forced to restore Laval to his position. On December 17, 1940, Abetz appeared at Vichy with ten armed SS officers. After some plain talk between the Ambassador and the aged and obviously unnerved Marshal, Laval was called from his nearby estate for a conference. Heated argument quickly developed between Pétain and Laval, the latter accusing the Chief of State to his face of secret dealings with the British. The Marshal was certainly shaken and did what he could to persuade Abetz that the Montoire policy would be continued without change. Indeed, he suggested that eventually Laval might be recalled, if not as Vice Premier, at least to some office in the Government. Abetz was not satisfied, but could do little more than return to Paris (taking Laval with him) and await further developments.

The complicated details of the struggle between the Germans and the French during the next six weeks are not essential to the present narrative. Abetz continued to exert all possible pressure to compel Laval's restoration. The line of demarcation between Occupied and Unoccupied France was closed to Vichy officials for many months and the collaborationist press of Paris was inspired to launch a systematic campaign of denigration against Pétain, Flandin and other influential figures in the Vichy Government. In mid-January, 1941, Pétain was induced to receive Laval a second time, on which occasion the fallen Minister feigned repentance, declared his loyalty and promised good behavior for the future. Once again the Marshal indicated his intention of letting bygones be bygones, but scrupulously avoided anything like a definite commitment.[34]

It may seem surprising that the Germans, considering their military power and position, did not in fact impose their will on Pétain and his Government. The explanation appears to be a dual one. In the first place Hitler

---

[33] Hitler's remarks to his military advisers, January 8-9, 1941 (*Fuehrer Conferences, 1941* (1), 1 ff.); *Halder Diary*, January 16, 1941; Abetz's testimony, as cited in *Le procès Flandin* (Paris, n.d.), 169 ff.

[34] The Pétain-Laval feud is discussed in great detail in the French postwar literature. See Langer: *Our Vichy Gamble* (New York, 1947), 123 ff., and the following later books: Louis-Dominique Girard: *Montoire, Verdun diplomatique* (Paris, 1948), 306 ff.; *Le procès Flandin*, 169 ff., 191 ff.; *Pétain et les allemands: memorandum d'Abetz* (Paris, 1949), 47 ff.; Fernand de Brinon: *Mémoires* (Paris, 1949), 57 ff.; Yves Boutillier: *Le drame de Vichy* (Paris, 1950), 259 ff.

himself had never been entirely converted to the policy of collaboration. For his purposes Spain and the Gibraltar project were more important than the coöperation of Vichy. He distrusted the French, even Laval, and was all too keenly aware that closer relations between Germany and France would antagonize the Italians and estrange the Spaniards. German sources record his reaction to Laval's downfall as one of fury, but on personal rather than political or military grounds. The Fuehrer was not sure, noted General Halder, that he needed France, for he still cherished hopes of peace with the British at the expense of the French colonial empire.[35] Finally, the Germans were confronted by Pétain's threat to resign if Laval were forced upon him. It is not unlikely that this threat decided Hitler's attitude, for he had to fear that if Pétain, for whom he appears to have had at least a measure of respect and sympathy, abandoned his post, Weygand and the pro-British elements would bring about the defection of French North Africa, no matter what the cost. Abetz discounted the danger of Pétain's resignation, but Hitler evidently took it seriously. While he raised no objection to the efforts of Ribbentrop and Abetz to engineer the return of Laval to power, he refused to force the issue. By the end of January, 1941, he had reached the decision to abandon the attempt and to keep Laval in reserve as a replacement for Pétain in the event of Weygand's desertion to the British. On February 5, 1941, Abetz was told that no arrangement for an agreement between Pétain and Laval was to be made for the present.[36]

Flandin and the other opponents of collaboration suspected the embarrassment of the Germans and frankly gambled on it. Pétain was not so sure. Under German pressure he dismissed a number of high officials and, as recounted above, proliferated assurances and general promises. After the dismissal of Laval he had set up a directorate of Ministers, consisting of Admiral Darlan, Foreign Minister Flandin and Defense Minister Huntziger, to tide the Government over the crisis. Of these men Darlan was certainly the most forceful and influential. While Flandin counseled firmness toward the Germans, Darlan argued that some *modus vivendi* must be found if the return of Laval were to be circumvented. The Admiral had hurried off to see Hitler on Christmas Day, 1940, and had made clear that he favored collaboration. Since his Anglophobia was notorious and since the future conduct of the French naval forces depended largely on his decision, Hitler and his advisers were not disposed to reject his advances out of hand. At the beginning of February, 1941, Darlan again went to Paris to confer with Abetz. It is quite possible that he had something to do with the German decision to drop Laval. In any event Flandin was obliged to resign on February 9 and presently Darlan emerged as the key figure at Vichy. He not

---

[35] *Halder Diary*, December 18, 1940.
[36] *Halder Diary*, January 28, 1941; Ribbentrop's tel. to Abetz, February 5, 1941 (*Pétain et les allemands*, 79).

only succeeded to Laval's position as Vice President of the Council, but added the Ministries of Foreign Affairs and Interior to the Ministry of Marine, which he had occupied since the advent of the Vichy regime.[37]

With Darlan's rise to power a new chapter in Franco-German relations was to open. The first phase of collaboration had ended with Laval's downfall, and the critical period following that dramatic event had been successfully weathered by Pétain and his Government. This was the period when Hitler was champing the bit to get on with his Gibraltar plan and when the British offensive in Libya was being carried to the very border of Tripolitania. Vichy France, for all its apparent weakness, had come to be a key factor in the further development of the Mediterranean situation and consequently in the evolution of the whole European conflict. This being so, the British and American Governments were compelled to take a hand in French affairs and to achieve, if possible, exactly what Hitler so greatly dreaded. Though their efforts and activities may not have decided the attitude and policy of the Vichy regime, they undoubtedly exerted an indirect influence of some magnitude.

4. WEYGAND AND THE NORTH AFRICAN SCENE

London and Washington, though their interest in the position and policy of Vichy France was the same, held rather widely divergent views of the best course to follow. The British, it might be said, pursued a positive line which, in retrospect, appears to have been overambitious. The Americans, on the other hand, approached the problem more negatively and aimed more at prevention than at cure. Mr. Churchill's attitude was based on distrust of the men who had concluded the armistice. He believed a harsh policy most likely to forestall and check collaboration and relied chiefly on pressure to hold the Vichy regime in line. He was prepared to conclude, and did conclude, specific agreements with Vichy, but always with the aim of forcing Pétain and his Government into closer coöperation. By contrast, Mr. Roosevelt and Secretary Hull were from the outset concerned primarily with holding France strictly within the requirements of the armistice and preventing the French Fleet from falling under Axis control. Washington was disposed to regard Pétain with understanding and sympathy and concentrated its efforts on assurances and warnings. While the British objective was to get France back into the war, the Americans were more intent on averting the complete subjection of France to Germany. It was hoped that the maintenance of close contact and the provision of the most essential aid would do more to uphold the traditional friendship than the application of economic pressure or the encouragement of dissident movements.

Mr. Roosevelt and Mr. Churchill shared the conviction of Hitler and

[37] *Halder Diary*, January 28, 1941; *Le procès Flandin*, 195 ff.; *Pétain et les allemands*, 76 ff.; de Brinon: *Mémoires*, 69; Bouthillier: *Le drame de Vichy*, 279 ff.

Admiral Raeder that French North Africa was an area of the greatest strategic importance. Each side was determined to secure control of the region or, at the very least, to deny it to the enemy. While Hitler on the one side was conspiring with Laval for the establishment of German power in French Africa, the democracies took hope from the appointment of General Weygand as the supreme Vichy authority in that region and were naturally elated by Pétain's unceremonious dismissal of the obnoxious and dangerous Laval. Hardly had Weygand arrived at his new post before Churchill began to make proposals to Pétain and, through General Catroux, the chief Free French representative in Cairo, to Weygand himself. Pétain was told that if, in the near future, the French Government decided to move to North Africa and resume the war against the Axis, Britain would send as many as six divisions to aid in the defense of Morocco, Algeria and Tunisia. Pointing out that "the command of the Mediterranean would be assured by the re-union of the British and French Fleets and by our joint use of Moroccan and North African bases," the Prime Minister warned of the danger of German attack through Spain and offered to engage immediately in secret staff conversations.[38] Similarly Catroux sent special emissaries to Weygand to induce him to attack Tripolitania in conjunction with the British offensive in Cyrenaica, even if such action were to entail the occupation of Vichy France and a German advance through Spain.[39]

Nothing came of this frontal attack on the problem. Pétain made no reply at all, even though in January, 1941, Mr. Churchill enlisted the aid of the State Department to impress upon him the seriousness of the British offer and to stress that the British would provide extensive aid, though only North Africa entered the war.[40] Weygand, in turn, explained to Catroux's agent that he and Marshal Pétain were alike determined that there should be no military alliance with Germany and that neither Germany nor Italy should be allowed to acquire bases in North Africa. He had hopes, so he said, of eventually entering the war on the British side, but the time was not yet ripe, for the French forces in North Africa lacked essential equipment and there was no prospect that Britain or the United States could supply planes, tanks and other matériel in the near future. In any event, he made clear that he would not act without authorization from Pétain.[41]

From the British standpoint it was nothing less than a tragedy for Weygand to refuse coöperation. During January, 1941, General Wavell's forces

[38] Churchill: *Their Finest Hour*, 623-24.

[39] General Catroux: *Dans la bataille de Méditerranée* (Paris, 1949), 70 ff.; General Weygand; *Mémoires* (Paris, 1950), 477 ff.; Paul Reynaud: *La France a sauvé l'Europe* (Paris, 1947), II, 457 ff.

[40] Tel. from Mr. Churchill to the President, January 11, 1941; tel. from the President to Mr. Churchill, January 13, 1941; tel. from Mr. Churchill to the President, January 21, 1941; tels. to Leahy (Vichy), January 13, 22, 29, 1941.

[41] Catroux: *Dans la bataille de Méditerranée*, 74 ff.

were driving the Italians back on Tripolitania and some weeks would yet be required before the Germans could send reinforcements to their hard-pressed allies. Catroux drew up a long and most interesting commander's estimate of the situation which he hoped Colonel Donovan, who was then in Cairo, could submit personally to General Weygand. At the same time he despatched his confidential agent, "Richards," with a further message from Churchill. The Prime Minister was now prepared to offer four British divisions, including one armored division, and to promise supplies from the United States. Furthermore, he proposed to reward France with the acquisition of Tripolitania in the event of victory. But Weygand, while expressing interest, refused to yield to temptation and made no formal reply. He told the American representative, Mr. Robert D. Murphy, that he hoped and prayed for a British victory. In fact, he sent a secret message to Wavell congratulating him on his success. But, from the strictly military standpoint, Weygand thought it foolhardy to intervene in the conflict at that time. Furthermore, he still flatly refused to act without instructions from Pétain. The Marshal, in turn, made no reply to the arguments and proposals which Catroux sent through his friend, General Laure. It was the time of greatest crisis in the relations between Vichy and Berlin. To Pétain's mind, no doubt, the sole consequence of the Churchill plan would be the occupation of Vichy France by the Germans. According to Hitler's directive for Operation *Attila* that would, in all probability, have been the outcome.[42]

5. ADMIRAL LEAHY AT VICHY

President Roosevelt's decision to send Admiral William D. Leahy to Vichy as Ambassador was a striking illustration of the American policy of cultivating friendly relations with France and strengthening the influence of the democracies. Leahy's instructions, dated December 20, 1940, comprised a review of United States relations with Vichy France and a careful analysis of the main points at issue. The Ambassador was to stress the President's conviction that the defeat of the Axis was essential to the preservation of the liberty, peace and prosperity of the world, and his determination that the United States should aid all nations defending themselves against aggression. As for France, the Ambassador was to warn Marshal Pétain against collaboration beyond the requirements of the armistice, and to remind him that "it has been a cardinal principle of this Administration to assure that the French Fleet did not fall into German hands and was not used in the furtherance of German aims." Leahy, in his talks with French naval officers, was to convince them "that to permit the use of the French Fleet or naval bases by Germany or to attain German aims would most certainly forfeit the

[42] Catroux: *Dans la bataille de Méditerranée,* 77-78, 85 ff.; Weygand: *Mémoires,* 477 ff.; Murphy's report: *Visit to North Africa,* January 17, 1941, in State Department files.

friendship and good will of the United States, and result in the destruction of the French Fleet, to the irreparable injury of France." Beyond this, he was to state that with regard to the French possessions in the New World, the United States desired nothing but the maintenance of the *status quo,* and to promise that, through the Red Cross, efforts would be made to relieve the food shortage in France itself.[43]

Admiral Leahy reached his post early in January, 1941, and established himself in the cramped and chilly American Embassy. He was by far the most eminent foreign representative in Vichy and his arrival must have been a source of real consolation to Marshal Pétain, whose genuine affection for and trust in the United States appears to have been deep and constant. The new Ambassador took up his duties in the midst of the Franco-German tension resulting from Laval's dismissal, and he was called upon almost at once to exert American influence in support of Churchill's efforts to draw France into the war on the British side. As noted above, neither Pétain nor Weygand proved amenable to the British proposals, but in the course of his conversations Leahy was able to get a fairly full and accurate impression of Vichy personalities and their attitude toward the crucial issues.[44]

The Ambassador found Marshal Pétain remarkably alert considering his age, but struggling with problems almost beyond his powers. He had an intense dislike of Laval, whom he suspected of scheming to replace him as actual head of the Government. The Marshal, reported Leahy, would make every effort to live up to the terms of the armistice and not to go beyond them. But he would not under any conditions abandon continental France and move to North Africa. Like the French people generally, he desired a British victory but could not believe such a victory possible. He was highly sensitive to German pressure, especially when applied to the French war prisoners, to the French food supply, and to the authority of the Vichy Government. Consequently it was to be expected that he would make any necessary compromise with Berlin, even to the extent of taking back Laval.[45]

By and large it seemed that Pétain could be relied upon to do what was possible to resist complete German domination. On the other hand, Leahy's long and apparently frank conversation with Admiral Darlan struck an ominous note. The Ambassador had to listen to Darlan's usual tirade against the British and came away from his conference with highly disturbing thoughts:

Admiral Darlan impressed me as a well-informed, aggressive, and courageous naval

[43] These instructions are printed in full in *Peace and War* (Washington, 1943), 596 ff., and in William D. Leahy: *I Was There* (New York, 1950), Appendix I.

[44] Admiral Leahy's book: *I Was There,* provides a full and vivid account of his mission.

[45] Letter of Leahy to the President, January 25, 1941 (printed in full in Leahy: *I Was There,* Appendix II).

officer, incurably anti-British, who believes that the Hitler regime cannot long survive after the passing of Hitler, and that the French people will then attain a position of great influence or control in a new Europe that will emerge from this war. While he does not believe a successful invasion of the British Islands can be accomplished, even under the existing condition of British inefficiency, he is confident that the Germans will win the war and establish a new order in Europe.

Darlan, concluded the Ambassador, was speculating on a Nazi attack on Soviet Russia which, he believed, would mean Germany's downfall.[46]

For the time being there appeared to be little that Ambassador Leahy and his Government could do to sway the course of Vichy policy. The Ambassador did, however, develop numerous confidential contacts and cherished some hope of building good will and a spirit of resistance in the country at large. To this end he urged Washington to send food and other relief to Unoccupied France. Such a program had been vigorously advocated for some time by Mr. Herbert Hoover and other prominent Americans, but had come to nothing because of the refusal of the British to relax their blockade. However, arrangements were finally concluded for shipments of medical supplies and milk by the American Red Cross, and the first of these shipments was received at Marseilles amid demonstrations of gratitude. There can be little doubt that such contributions, entirely nonpolitical in character, did much to keep alive the tradition of Franco-American sympathy and friendship and, in the gloomy winter of 1940-1941, indicated to the dispirited French people that they were not completely forgotten.[47]

6. THE MURPHY-WEYGAND AGREEMENT

Of greater immediate interest and of profound later significance was the fruition of the American plan to provide economic aid to North Africa. This plan had taken shape in the State Department shortly after the announcement of General Weygand's mission to North Africa and was merely one reflection of the hope that this crucial area could be brought into the war against the Axis. Since its implementation depended largely on British willingness to relax blockade restrictions, the matter had been taken up with the British Embassy in Washington early in December, 1940. At the same time Mr. Robert D. Murphy, formerly Counselor of Embassy in Paris, had been despatched to North Africa to make a firsthand investigation. Murphy had arrived in Algiers on December 18 and had spent the ensuing month in wide travel and extensive conference with French officials, including Weygand and Pierre Boisson, the Governor General of French West Africa. The essence of his observations, as embodied in his detailed and penetrating report, was this:

[46] Tel. from Leahy, January 21, 1941.
[47] Leahy: *I Was There*, 13 ff., 26 ff.; Langer: *Our Vichy Gamble*, 127-28, where the key documents are listed.

General Weygand and his associates are engaged in laying the necessary foundation for substantial military action against Germany and Italy. Their program cannot be termed a dissident movement as it is being formulated with Marshal Pétain's approval. It is based on an ardent desire to retain the control of French Africa in the hands of the duly constituted French Government. Should that Government be captured by the Germans as a result of the occupation of all Metropolitan France or otherwise deprived of its present limited authority, French Africa will unquestionably provide the spring-board for the military rebound which will follow. The Weygand organization is being constructed along sound and substantial lines, but its leaders have no desire to plunge into an ill-prepared adventure. They regard French Africa as France's last trump, which must be cautiously and skillfully played. They are all eager for American sympathy and immediate economic coöperation. I believe they merit our interest and practical support in their determination to resist German domination of French Africa.

Elsewhere in his report Mr. Murphy stressed the urgent need for economic aid and reported Weygand's readiness to give whatever guarantees the Washington Government might desire. In conclusion he observed:

Just as the President's November message to Pétain supported the Marshal in his decision to oust Laval and marked a turning point in French policy, economic support now of French Africa will strengthen Weygand's determination to resist Axis aggression. Translated into action it would mean small shipments immediately of automotive gasoline, kerosene, and gas oil to Dakar and Casablanca under whatever guarantee we wish. Such shipments would go far to counteract German propaganda and would stimulate all those in French Africa working for eventual independent action.[48]

Murphy's report was read with great interest not only in the State Department, but in the White House.[49] The American emissary was instructed to return at once to Algiers and work out the details of an agreement with Weygand. Meanwhile the State Department reopened the matter with the British and pressed for a decision on the blockade question. But London's reply did not arrive until February 7 and then proved rather exasperating. The British observed that "they are not as confident as the United States Government appear to be that General Weygand will enter the war." They were willing to support the American policy, but only on condition that no serious breach in the British blockade were involved, no excessive stocks built up in North Africa, and no risk taken of the supplies falling into enemy hands. They regarded close supervision by American officials as essential and suggested that Washington make an effort to secure the release of British and neutral shipping in Moroccan harbors as a *quid pro quo*. Indeed, they went so far as to state: "His Majesty's Government are also anxious to get some undertakings in writing from General Weygand as to his future atti-

[48] Tel. from Murphy (at Lisbon), January 14, 1941, and his long despatch of January 17, 1941. See, for further details, Langer: *Our Vichy Gamble*, 128 ff., and Weygand: *Mémoires*, 483 ff.

[49] Memo from the President to Mr. Welles, February 12, 1941, doubtless referring to Murphy's despatch (*Roosevelt Papers:* Secretary's File, Box 74).

tude before acquiescing or collaborating in economic assistance to North Africa, and they are instructing their representative to endeavor to obtain such undertaking if he is able to go to Algeria to see General Weygand."[50]

The State Department, fully aware that the British were themselves negotiating with French authorities in Morocco to secure goods needed to support the program of British aid to Spain, lost patience with London's equivocation, which was obviously based on the belief that North Africa's desperate need could be exploited so as to obtain a commitment from Weygand. Secretary Hull spoke plainly to Lord Halifax about the matter and there ensued a lively exchange of notes which was brought to a close by the following forthright memorandum from the State Department to the British Embassy:

> It is the considered opinion of the Department of State that it is urgently necessary to resume trade relations on a restricted basis with French North Africa, if there is to be prevented an economic breakdown in that area which may have far-reaching and perhaps disastrous consequences. It has therefore been decided to authorize at once the unblocking of the necessary funds to permit the shipment of a tanker of petroleum products to Casablanca. This is the first step in a program which this Government proposes to pursue with a view to furnishing minimum and urgently needed supplies to French North Africa.[51]

A further difficulty was presented by Vichy's objection to Murphy's return to North Africa and to the conduct of such important negotiations with local authorities. To this Mr. Welles replied that, while the United States Government appreciated Marshal Pétain's difficult position, it would be impossible to conclude the economic accord unless Murphy could negotiate directly with Weygand.[52] Meanwhile Murphy had conferred with French and British officials at Lisbon and Tangier and had blocked out the terms of an agreement. He eventually proceeded to Algiers, where Weygand approved his draft on February 26. Washington gave its approval immediately and on March 10 the Vichy Government also sanctioned it. In essence the so-called Murphy-Weygand Agreement committed the United States to supply North Africa's economic needs, provided the supplies were currently consumed in that area. American officials were assured control of the shipments both in the ports and on the railroads. Payment, as required, was to be made from French funds frozen in the United States.[53]

[50] British memo of February 7, 1941, quoted at greater length in Langer: *Our Vichy Gamble*, 132-33.

[51] Memo of February 13, 1941. See also Hull: *Memoirs*, II, 950 ff.

[52] Memo of conversation between Mr. Welles and Ambassador Henry-Haye, February 4, 1941; Weygand: *Mémoires*, 483 ff.

[53] Langer: *Our Vichy Gamble*, 135 and 399 ff., where the full text of the agreement is printed. The French texts, including the letters of approval, are printed in "Les accords concernant l'Afrique du Nord française" (*Cahiers d'histoire de la guerre*, October, 1949). See also Weygand: *Mémoires*, 486-88.

One of the most important features of the Murphy-Weygand Agreement was the establishment of American control officers in North Africa. The French had raised no objection to this arrangement; they had, indeed, welcomed it. Obviously the institution of such officials opened up the possibility of intelligence operations as well as of economic supervision. The State Department therefore consulted with the War and Navy Departments and secured the services of certain highly qualified officers, who were sent to North Africa in a civilian capacity, as "technical assistants." Mr. Murphy, while officially still Counselor of Embassy, was assigned to Algiers as a kind of High Commissioner to direct the control organization, maintain contact with French officials, and report on all matters of political and military, as well as economic, interest. Thereby American influence was firmly established in North Africa. Washington had neither asked for nor received commitments from General Weygand, but American interest had been linked with one of the most important strategic areas, and the sequel was to demonstrate how valuable was to be the position created by the Murphy-Weygand Agreement.[54]

7. DARLAN'S DEBUT

The Murphy-Weygand Agreement was negotiated in an atmosphere rife with rumor. Some reported the Germans on the verge of crossing Spain to occupy Morocco, while others forecasted German action from Tripolitania against Tunisia. Nazi forces were in fact being concentrated in Sicily for transfer to Graziani's hard-pressed army in Libya, but there was no knowing whether they might not be turned against Tunisia. Indeed, there was some reason to fear that the Germans would extort from the Vichy Government permission to use the port of Bizerte in Tunisia, or, failing such permission, that they would launch a seaborne operation from Italian ports directly against French North Africa. On February 9, 1941, British naval forces shelled Genoa in the belief that from that port the Germans might embark a force directed against Tunisia or Algeria.[55]

In the light of the intense German preparations to relieve Graziani and particularly of Hitler's desperate efforts to enlist Spain in the struggle, these reports were not implausible. They seemed particularly credible in view of the reorganization of the Vichy Government and the rise of Admiral Darlan to the key position in the Council. Darlan made no secret whatever of his passionate dislike of the British and, as previously recorded, told Ambassador Leahy quite frankly that he was convinced of the inevitability of German

[54] The details of the control system were reviewed in a State Department memo entitled "The Role of the Department of State in the North African Economic and Political Program." See Hull: *Memoirs*, II, 951 ff.

[55] These rumors and reports are discussed in greater detail in Langer: *Our Vichy Gamble*, 125-27.

victory. Like a number of other Frenchmen, probably including Laval, he believed the best course for France was to collaborate with Germany, at least to the extent of assuring itself an important and ultimately perhaps dominant role in the new Europe. Darlan's approach to the problem was that of the opportunist. It is most improbable that he would ever have allowed the Germans to secure control of the French Fleet, which was, after all, a trump card in the game. On the other hand, he appears to have been willing to go a long way toward making concessions and may even have been prepared to accept hostilities with the British, provided the Germans made it worth while. The British were naturally apprehensive and took seriously reports of French collusion with the Germans which eventually proved grossly exaggerated.

The British advance in Libya came to an end in February; in March Wavell's forces were obliged to fall back under pressure of the newly arrived Germans commanded by General Rommel. The commitment of the Nazi divisions in Libya relieved somewhat the British fear of a German attack on French North Africa, but new dangers arose almost at once from the re-ported infiltration of German agents and officials into Morocco and from Darlan's public statement of his determination to use French naval forces to prevent further British interference with the importation of food and other supplies for Vichy France. The story of Darlan's dealings with the Germans is even now not fully known, but it is clear that Vichy made no strong objection to the establishment of Nazi armistice commissions in North Africa in replacement of the ineffectual Italians. Weygand and his associates did what they could to frustrate the designs of the Nazis and, indeed, there never were the thousands of German officials from time to time alleged. But there were at least a few hundred and their objective was clearly to extend German influence and control. Darlan's announced policy of countering the British blockade by force made it appear probable that a Franco-German agreement on North Africa was in the making.[56]

This development produced new tension and led to a lively exchange of messages between London and Washington during the spring of 1941. On March 13 Mr. Churchill appealed to the President anent the Darlan threat, pointing out that if imports were permitted to reach Unoccupied France, many would obviously find their way to Germany and thus contribute to prolonging the war. "Dealing with Darlan," the Prime Minister remarked, "is dealing with Germany, for he will not be allowed to agree to anything they know about which does not suit their book." Nevertheless, Mr. Churchill somewhat incongruously suggested that the President attempt to conclude with Vichy a secret agreement, making the provision of food and other supplies to France and North Africa conditional on restriction of Ger-man infiltration into North Africa and the gradual removal of French

[56] For details see Langer: *Our Vichy Gamble,* 136 ff.

warships from Toulon to Casablanca or Dakar. In a supplementary memorandum the Nazi infiltration was described as "a deadly menace," inasmuch as it threatened to take Spain in the rear and force that country to capitulate to German demands. To forestall it, the British proposed that the United States offer Vichy "reasonable supplies of principal commodities, with guarantees against reëxport and of navicert facilities for five to eight million bushels of wheat for Unoccupied France."[57]

The British were torn between distrust of Darlan and Vichy on the one hand and, on the other, desperate desire to secure some assurance against Franco-German collaboration. Having gone as far as they could to bring economic and other pressures to bear on Pétain, and having attempted to obstruct the American policy as reflected in the mission of Admiral Leahy and the conclusion of the Murphy-Weygand Agreement, they were now proposing a program of aid that exceeded anything envisaged by Washington, contingent on terms which Pétain could hardly accept without openly defying the Germans. As further illustration of London's anxiety and confusion may be mentioned another message from the Prime Minister to the President calling attention to alleged agreements between Darlan and the Germans and to efforts of Vichy to make large purchases of food in Latin America. "If we were to put up with this," cabled Mr. Churchill, "it would mean that French ships, unhampered by the fetters of convoy, would soon be doing a big trade and Germany would secure at least half the import." He was therefore, he added, ordering the Admiralty to tighten up the blockade of Unoccupied France as much as British naval resources and opportunities permitted. On the very next day the Prime Minister reported that British ships had driven a French freighter, laden with rubber, into a Moroccan port. This rubber, he was persuaded, would presently be shipped across the Mediterranean and find its way to the Germans. Accordingly he asked the President whether he felt "inclined" to warn Vichy that it would get not even Red Cross shipments of wheat unless it handed over the rubber or at least promised to keep it in Unoccupied France.[58]

Mr. Hull was disposed to attribute the deterioration of British-French relations in part to British obtuseness. London's proposals went far beyond what the State Department regarded as practical, and therefore no detailed reply was made to them.[59] But at the beginning of April the British did succeed in eliciting American action on another, very sensitive issue. They had, so the Prime Minister cabled the President, received "entirely authentic secret information" that the French battleship *Dunkerque* was to be transferred, under heavy escort, from Oran to Toulon for repairs, and that this

---

[57] Message from Mr. Churchill to the President, March 13, 1941, and memo from the British Embassy (quoted at length in Langer: *Our Vichy Gamble*, 137-39).

[58] Messages from Mr. Churchill to the President, March 29 and 30, 1941.

[59] Hull: *Memoirs*, II, 955.

transfer was to take place within a matter of days. At some length Mr. Churchill explained the "grave danger" involved in such a move. There was a real possibility that once the ship was at Toulon, the Germans would manage to get control of her and add her to their raiding forces. The whole project confirmed the Prime Minister's worst suspicions of Darlan and flew in the face of the President's expressed desire that the French gradually transfer their warships from Toulon to North African ports. Mr. Churchill therefore requested Mr. Roosevelt to warn Pétain that if Darlan persisted in his purpose, all relief supplies would be cut off and France would forfeit American sympathy. If such admonitions remained without effect, the British would have to make an effort to intercept and sink the vessel.[60]

Since one of the main objectives of American policy had all along been to keep the French naval forces from falling into German hands, Mr. Churchill's cable brought an immediate response. Ambassador Leahy was instructed to see Marshal Pétain and, after reviewing the American position and recalling American efforts to aid France, to lodge a stern warning:

> You should report to Marshal Pétain the information received by this Government concerning the transfer of these important units of the French Fleet, as above set forth. You should state that such action on the part of the French Government, under whatever pretext, is not only completely counter to the hopes expressed by your Government as to the policy which the French Government would pursue, but is also unquestionably destined to be of great potential advantage to Germany.
>
> In conclusion you should say that this Government has great personal confidence in Marshal Pétain and would accept, as it has in the past, without question the personal assurances conveyed to the United States Government by him. The Government of the United States cannot believe that the action which the French Government is contemplating, involving the transfer of the French battleship, can have been sanctioned by the Marshal. We feel that the Marshal would understand how such action would eventually alienate public opinion in the United States. However, you should add that your Government finds it necessary in all frankness to state that if such action were taken, the Government of the United States could no longer consider the continuation of the policy which it has desired to pursue of affording in every practical manner relief to French needs in Unoccupied France, or even of further acts of coöperation contemplated. A continuation of such policy could only be predicated upon clear evidence that the French Government, under the direction of Marshal Pétain, was determined to take no steps which could conceivably be of assistance to Germany beyond the bare terms of the armistice agreement itself.[61]

In the temporary absence of Admiral Leahy, who had gone to Marseilles to receive the first American Red Cross shipment, Mr. H. Freeman Matthews, the Counselor of Embassy, took up the matter with Marshal Pétain

[60] Message from Mr. Churchill to the President, April 2, 1941 (full text in Churchill: *The Grand Alliance*, 130-31).

[61] Tel. to Leahy, April 3, 1941; tel. from the President to Mr. Churchill, April 3, 1941, informing him of the action taken.

on April 4. The Marshal at once summoned Darlan, who as usual indulged in anti-British remarks, among others to the effect that the British wanted their fleet to be the only one in the Mediterranean. The *Dunkerque,* he said, could not be repaired at Oran and would not be left there. On the other hand, she would not be moved to Toulon immediately. Both the Marshal and he himself had given the United States Government assurances as to the French Fleet, which he now willingly renewed. Thereupon the Marshal asked Matthews for a memorandum on the matter, to which he promised a written reply.

All this was promptly reported to Mr. Churchill by the President. The Prime Minister expressed gratitude for Mr. Roosevelt's "spirited intervention," but observed that "Darlan's honour about her [the *Dunkerque*] never falling into German hands is rooted in dishonour." He therefore urged continuance of strong pressure on Vichy: "Pétain does not know half what this dirty Darlan does. It would be far better if your pressure deterred Darlan, as it has already, than that we should have to take rough action, with all its dangers." On April 9 the Prime Minister, with the tacit consent of the President, made a forthright statement in Parliament, indicating clearly the Government's intention to prevent the transfer of the *Dunkerque* by force.[62]

Pétain lost no time in complying with the President's request. On April 8 Ambassador Leahy was able to report a note from the Vichy Government explaining that the decision to move the *Dunkerque* had been made without foreign pressure and for purely technical reasons. However, in view of the significance which the American Government attached to it, the French Government promised not to make the transfer without prior agreement. In return it asked Washington to use its good offices to secure from the British a guarantee that as long as the *Dunkerque* remained in North Africa they would not capture any more French ships in trade between North Africa and the mother country.[63] Mr. Roosevelt made no effort to extract such an engagement from the British and contented himself with the achievement of his immediate end. Mr. Churchill, too, was satisfied. He admitted that it was "remarkable how they have conformed to your representations," but added a warning against allowing Darlan's concession to be used as a lever to weaken the British blockade.[64]

April was a black month for the democratic cause. While Hitler's forces were crushing Yugoslavia and overrunning Greece, the German-Italian divisions under Rommel were driving the British back on Egypt. So com-

[62] Message from Mr. Churchill to the President, April 7, 1941 (full text in Churchill: *The Grand Alliance,* 133-134), in response to messages from the President, April 4 and 5, reporting tels. from Matthews and Leahy, April 4, 1941.

[63] Tel. from Leahy, April 8, 1941; tel. from the President to Mr. Churchill, April 11, 1941, repeating Leahy's message (full text in Churchill: *The Grand Alliance,* 134-35).

[64] Tel. from Mr. Churchill to the President, April 13, 1941 (*Roosevelt Papers:* Secretary's File, Box 87).

plete was the German victory in the eastern Mediterranean that it seemed only reasonable to suppose that the Fuehrer would presently attack North Africa also, with or without French or Spanish assent. Washington's solution was to increase its relief shipments to Vichy France and strengthen its naval forces in the Atlantic partly in anticipation of a Nazi descent on the Spanish or Portuguese islands. The British, on the other hand, kept urging a stronger line, a line of warning and threat with regard to Vichy, and a policy of economic aid to Spain. Why the two Governments should have pursued these diametrically opposite courses is hard to explain, for it would seem that what was sauce for the French goose should have been sauce also for the Spanish gander. As it was, the divergence of view provoked much argument and led Secretary Hull to speak plainly to the British Ambassador, while at the same time venting his feelings even more freely to his War and Navy colleagues.[65]

By the end of the month Admiral Leahy was reporting from Vichy that Marshal Pétain was expecting an early move of the Germans through Spain. French officials were pointing out the concentration of German forces on the Spanish frontier and were confessing Vichy's utter inability to resist Nazi action if it came.[66] At this juncture Mr. Churchill again addressed himself to the President. In a long cable he analyzed the situation in the Middle East and expatiated on the danger threatening North Africa. Large and important areas, he argued, might soon be lost and if, at a later period, the United States were to become a belligerent, the democracies would have a much longer road to cover. He therefore appealed to the President to put "the most extreme pressure" on Vichy to break with the Germans if the latter violated Syria, Morocco, Algeria or Tunisia. "I feel," he declared in conclusion, "Hitler may quite easily now gain vast advantages very cheaply and we are so fully engaged that we can do little or nothing to stop him spreading himself." A supplementary note from the British Foreign Office proposed that Britain should warn Pétain that if he allowed the Germans to cross France into Spain and North Africa, Vichy would be considered to have entered the war on the Axis side and the British would no longer be able to make a distinction between Occupied and Unoccupied France. If, on the other hand, Vichy resisted the German demands and broke with Berlin, the British would promise the maximum possible aid—enough, they believed, to prevent the Germans from getting across the Mediterranean. The British Government, according to its note, could do no more than this, but hoped the United States Government, which could speak with authority at Vichy and had a special interest of its own in North and West Africa, would go farther than it had in the past: "Indeed, His Majesty's Govern-

[65] Hull: *Memoirs*, II, 955 ff.; *Stimson Diary* (*MS.*), April 8 and 30, 1941.
[66] Langer: *Our Vichy Gamble*, 144-47.

ment hope that the United States Government will feel able to arrange for some units of the United States Fleet to visit Dakar and Casablanca."[67]

These proposals brought to a head the difference between British and American policy toward Vichy. The projected British message to Pétain, argued Mr. Welles to Lord Halifax, would be known to the Germans within fifteen minutes of its delivery and might precipitate precisely the Nazi action it was intended to forestall. The best thing, from both the American and British standpoints, would be "to try and persuade the Marshal to play for time and to resist at every point, with the hope that eventually the situation, in North Africa at least, could be stabilized and strengthened to our common advantage." Meanwhile Leahy could see Pétain and express once more the hopes of the American Government that Vichy would refuse to go beyond the terms of the armistice.[68]

Although he assented, Halifax raised objection to Mr. Welles's proposal to negotiate for the delivery of further wheat shipments to France. But the Under Secretary stood his ground and took the opportunity to restate the American policy in succinct terms:

It seemed to us wise and desirable to do what we could to demonstrate in a practical way that we desired to assist the Marshal in relieving distress in Unoccupied France, and we believed that thereby we would make it easier for him to maintain his own prestige and position and to resist German pressure because of the support the population would give him. I said that what the British Government in essence proposed was merely for us to continue delivering sharp and frequently menacing messages from the British Government to Marshal Pétain, and that it did not seem to us that our policy would be advanced by limiting ourselves to the transmission of messages of this character.

A cable was therefore despatched to Leahy to see Pétain privately and tell him that the United States was arranging to send two shiploads of food, but would not do so if France yielded to German pressure to exceed the terms of the armistice.[69]

Meanwhile the President conferred with Hull, Stimson, Knox and Morgenthau on how best to cope with Mr. Churchill's evident "misunderstanding" of the French situation.[70] The outcome was Mr. Roosevelt's long and detailed message to the Prime Minister of May 1 in which, as noted earlier in the present chapter, the President took a stand against British plans for an expedition against the Atlantic islands. With respect to Vichy the President outlined his policy as follows, asking the Prime Minister's views:

[67] Tel. from Mr. Churchill to the President, April 29, 1941; memo from the British Embassy, same date.

[68] Memo of conversation between Mr. Welles and Lord Halifax, April 29, 1941.

[69] Memo of conversation between Mr. Welles and Lord Halifax, April 29, 1941; tel. to Leahy, April 30, 1941.

[70] *Stimson Diary (MS.)*, April 30, 1941.

1. Recognize that Vichy is in a German cage, but still issues orders to Weygand, Syria, and Indo-China.

2. That because Vichy has already ordered French colonies to resist British occupation, Vichy can and ought to issue orders to colonies equally to resist German occupation.

3. United States has already started Red Cross shipments with food for children and undertaken to continue this work in Unoccupied France. Two ships with food grains are already en route from the Red Cross to Marseille. Yesterday this Government informed Marshal Pétain that it agrees in principle to permit under certain conditions two food ships a month to go forward to Unoccupied France beginning July 1 and contingent upon British agreement. We have stated furthermore that if the French Government acquiesces in the demands now being made upon it by Germany and agrees to conditions outside the armistice terms, assistance to Unoccupied France cannot be continued. We are also discussing here with British and French representatives supplies for North Africa, likewise under very similar conditions, including close American control. This might be supplemented by an offer of munitions to Weygand, this latter being conditioned, of course, on agreement by Weygand to resist German occupation.

4. At the same time it is at least possible that if Weygand gets orders to resist Germans and agrees to do so, he would put up a strong rear-guard defense, moving slowly southward toward Casablanca.

If Germany crosses Straits of Gibraltar with land forces, she can probably eventually occupy Tunis, Algiers, and Morocco down to Casablanca, but it is of utmost importance to keep Germans out of the Moroccan ports as long as possible, including Villa Cisneros in Rio de Oro. We are willing to help meet such a thrust by stocking material and stores in Freetown and/or Bathurst. We think it almost impossible for Germans to reach Dakar overland, especially with what is left of French Army and Navy concentrated there.[71]

It is easy to understand Mr. Churchill's disappointment with the President's response, and his description of it to Ambassador Winant as a "delaying message" rather than, as the Ambassador had interpreted it, a "supporting message."[72] For while Mr. Roosevelt objected to London's proposal to administer another dose of strong medicine to Vichy, the Prime Minister found little novelty in the American prescription for the rapidly sinking patient. The President merely reiterated the conviction, so often expressed by Secretary Hull to Lord Halifax, that the only practical alternative to the program of encouraging Vichy to resist the Nazis by diplomatic maneuvers was British or joint Anglo-American military intervention in French Africa. While, in fact, Secretaries Knox and Stimson were even then insisting to Mr. Hull that the United States Fleet should be brought immediately into the Atlantic to do what was necessary "particularly in the Azores and Dakar,"

[71] Tel. from the President to Mr. Churchill, May 1, 1941.
[72] Tel. from Winant, May 6, 1941.

all the President held out to Mr. Churchill was an offer to stock materials at Bathurst or Freetown for such a contingency.[73]

In his reply to the President's message, the Prime Minister struck a hurt tone with reference to the American attitude on the Atlantic islands and the Middle East, but did not argue about Washington's Vichy policy, which in all conscience had been debated long enough: "With regard to Vichy," he remarked, "we are more than willing that you should take the lead, and work out how to get the best from them by threats or favors. You alone can forestall the Germans in Morocco. If they are once installed, it will not be necessary for them to go overland; they will soon get airborne troops to Dakar."[74]

Since, in the interval, Ambassador Leahy had conferred with Marshal Pétain and had received anew assurances that French collaboration with Germany would not go beyond the terms of the armistice, the President hastened to console his British friend:

I have now received through Ambassador Leahy a reiteration of Marshal Pétain's assurances that he does not intend to agree to any collaboration by France that is beyond the requirements of the armistice agreement, that he has publicly stated that he will not consent to any offensive action against his former ally. While he states that Germany has no need of a passage for its troops through Unoccupied France to the Spanish frontier, and that he is endeavoring to limit the number of Germans in the African colonies, Leahy points out that it is accepted at Vichy that a refusal of the Marshal to agree to German demands would have little or no deterrent effect upon the Germans. Pétain had no comment to make upon the British Government's offer of assistance, transmitted through Leahy, and I gather that he feels that France can do nothing to prevent the arrival of German troops in Spanish Morocco which he, Pétain, considers imminent. Leahy believes that Pétain has the genuine support of all the French people, but that they do not share the same confidence in Darlan. He further believes that most of the people are openly or secretly supporting your cause. We are sending instructions to Leahy to urge Pétain to issue orders to all French authorities, especially in French colonies, to resist Germany in any attempt to violate French territory or to use it as a base for military operations.[75]

By the time this message went off to London the focus of danger had already shifted from the western Mediterranean to the eastern and Darlan was already negotiating the famous Paris Protocols with the Germans. Little indeed is known of the steps by which the Admiral reached this crucial juncture. The German documents reveal only that while Hitler was just as much exercised about the North African situation as were the British, and while Admiral Raeder was urging the desirability of an accord with Vichy to secure the French colonial empire against Anglo-American attack, the

[73] *Stimson Diary (MS.)*, May 2 and 5, 1941.
[74] Message from Mr. Churchill to the President, May 3, 1941.
[75] Tel. from the President to Mr. Churchill, May 10, 1941; see also Hull: *Memoirs*, II, 958 ff.

Fuehrer continued to harbor deep distrust of the French and came only gradually to believe that perhaps he could rely on Darlan. Only at the end of April had he yielded to the importunities of Abetz and authorized the discussions that threatened to bring on the catastrophe so much dreaded by Mr. Churchill.[76]

These negotiations, though they had some bearing on French North Africa, dealt primarily with the acute situation that had arisen in the Middle East, particularly in Syria, as a result of Hitler's phenomenal successes in the Balkans and Libya. Analysis of that situation will reveal the concatenation of the two aspects of the Mediterranean problem and serve to introduce the acute crisis which immediately preceded Hitler's fateful attack on Soviet Russia.

[76] *Fuehrer Conferences,* 1941 (1), 35 ff. (German naval memorandum of March 18, 1941) and 54 (Hitler's remarks on April 20, 1941); *Ciano's Diplomatic Papers,* 431 ff. (conference of March 25, 1941); *Pétain et les allemands,* 96 ff. (Abetz's report of April 25, 1941).

CHAPTER XIII

The Balkan Crisis and the Middle East

1. British Victories in Africa

General Wavell's attack on the Italian forces at Sidi Barrani (December 7, 1940) began as a limited operation but ended in Britain's first resounding victory in the war. Graziani's forces, ill-equipped and poorly led, collapsed in the face of greatly inferior numbers. Driven from Egypt, they were soon obliged to surrender Bardia and Tobruk and fall back in confusion to the west. The British took Benghazi on February 7, 1941, and two days later stood at El Agheila, on the frontier of Tripolitania. Never using more than two divisions and suffering fewer than two thousand casualties, they had advanced five hundred miles, destroyed an army of nine to ten divisions, taken 130,000 prisoners, and captured 400 tanks, 1290 guns and heaps of other equipment. By the beginning of February, 1941, Egypt was no longer threatened from the west and the British had already embarked upon campaigns against Eritrea, Abyssinia, and Somaliland which, in the course of the next few months, were to wipe out Italian rule in all Africa.[1]

The repercussions of this unexpected success were certainly far-reaching. The British themselves took new heart, while their friends in America were greatly cheered. Revived confidence in the British cause no doubt facilitated the passage of the Lend-Lease legislation, for Wavell's victory was due at least in part to the arrival of American equipment and could therefore be cited as conclusive evidence of the value of American aid. The Spaniards and French were similarly impressed with the developments in Africa. The relief of Egypt and the triumphant drive of the British demonstrated that Axis hopes of dominating the Mediterranean had been temporarily frus-

[1] The basic account is the despatch, dated June 21, 1941, by General Sir Archibald P. Wavell: *Operations in the Western Desert from December 7, 1940 to February 7, 1941* (Supplement to the *London Gazette*, June 26, 1946), but see also Churchill: *The Grand Alliance*, Book I, Chapter I, and Field Marshal Lord Wilson of Libya: *Eight Years Overseas* (London, 1948), 57 ff.

trated and that Hitler was much farther from victory over his chief enemy than he had pretended to be. Following on the failure of the Nazis to invade England or subjugate the British by air attack, Wavell's successes increased the likelihood that the war would continue for some time. It was inevitable, in these circumstances, that what Mr. Churchill has called "the rivetted audience" of powers yet uninvolved in the conflict should avoid commitment to the Axis side as long as possible.

Hitler was quick to grasp the implications of the African campaign. He saw at once that the Italian disaster in Libya, coming hard upon the failure of the Duce's offensive against Greece, would rock the Fascist regime to its foundations. Mr. Churchill's radio broadcast of December 23, 1940, a violent attack on Mussolini and an appeal to the Italian people to take a hand in shaping their own fortunes, was a clear indication of coming British attempts to exploit their victory.[2] Hitler could not ignore the fact, underlined by the British Prime Minister, that the Italian court, the Catholic Church, and other influential elements in Italy had been opposed to the war and were now utterly disgusted with its course. Discontent, wrote Ambassador Phillips to Under Secretary Welles, was open, and even members of the Foreign Office were expressing the hope that President Roosevelt would mediate or otherwies help Italy make a separate peace before it fell entirely under Nazi control.[3]

While recognizing the foolhardiness and ineptitude of the Fascist Government, the Fuehrer refused to risk the loss of face involved in the defection of his partner. He determined to bolster Mussolini's position and help the Italians forestall further reverses. Long before the catastrophe in Libya was complete he had therefore decided to send planes, tanks, antitank and antiaircraft equipment, with the appropriate personnel, to enable the Italians to hold Tripolitania. The matériel was to be sent by sea and the personnel by air, beginning in February, 1941. Because of shortage of transports, the operation, he calculated, would take five weeks to complete, which meant that the relief of the Italians would be a matter of nip and tuck.[4]

In accordance with the supreme directive, the Tenth German Air Army, consisting of some 400-500 aircraft, was established in Sicily, with the mission of protecting communications with Tripoli and, if possible, taking Malta and so preventing the despatch of British convoys from Gibraltar to Alexandria. Early in February General Erwin Rommel, dashing Nazi tank leader, was appointed to command the two armored divisions (the *Afrika Korps*) which were to buttress the Italian reinforcements in Tripoli.

[2] Churchill: *Their Finest Hour*, 620-21.

[3] Letter of Phillips to Welles, which the latter transmitted to the President, January 28, 1941 (*Roosevelt Papers:* Secretary's File, Box 74).

[4] Conference of January 8-9, 1941 (*Fuehrer Conferences*, 1941 [1], 1 ff.); Hitler's directive of January 11, 1941 (*Trial of War Criminals*, X, Washington, 1951, pp. 903 ff.); letter of Hitler to Mussolini, February 28, 1941 (*Les lettres secrètes échangées par Hitler et Mussolini*, 115 ff.); *Halder Diary*, February 3 and 7, 1941; Raymond de Belot: *The Struggle for the Mediterranean* (Princeton, 1951), 94 ff.

Hitler's objective at this time was a strictly defensive one. He saw no possibility of resuming the offensive against Egypt before 1942 and intended the German forces only for the protection of Tripolitania. Nonetheless, the German military were soon taking over control of crucial posts in Sicily and throughout Italy. Rommel, while officially subordinate to the Italian High Command, was not long in securing direction of all Axis operations in North Africa. In a remarkably short time Nazi interference was making itself felt everywhere. From mid-January until May the British were unwilling to risk sending convoys through the central Mediterranean. The German *Luftwaffe* subjected Malta to incessant and merciless bombardment and obliged the British to abandon plans for the seizure of the Italian base on Pantelleria Island. By March Nazi air attacks on Benghazi had made it impossible to utilize that port as a base for supplies. Under the circumstances, the British abandoned all thought of a further advance from Cyrenaica against Tripolitania. For the moment the situation in Libya remained precariously stable.[5]

2. THE BALKAN SITUATION AND THE DONOVAN MISSION

British plans had not envisaged the reconquest of Cyrenaica but merely the expulsion of the Italians from Egypt and the safeguarding of the British position on the west. The offensive strategy of Mr. Churchill and his military advisers was directed at the Balkans rather than at North Africa, for the Italian attack on Greece had opened the prospect of reviving the plan of 1939 for a campaign against Germany based on Saloniki. It was clearly the Prime Minister's hope that if British forces could secure a foothold in the Balkans, at least the Turks and Yugoslavs could be induced to join the Greeks in a common front, while the Soviet Government too might be encouraged to take a more determined stand against Axis expansion to the southeast. As early as November, 1940, the British Ambassador at Ankara had been instructed to urge the Turkish Government to warn Bulgaria that any hostile movement against Greece, or any move by Germany through Bulgaria to attack Greece, would lead to an immediate declaration of war by Turkey. The instructions continued:

We should like Turkey and Yugoslavia now to consult together so as, if possible, to have a joint warning ready to offer Bulgaria and Germany at the first sign of a German movement towards Bulgaria. In the event of German troops traversing Bulgaria with or without Bulgarian assistance, it is vital that Turkey should fight there and then. If she does not, she will find herself left absolutely alone, the Balkans will have been eaten up one by one, and it will be beyond our power to help her.[6]

This was the British plan in a nutshell. It led to the application of strong

---

[5] Churchill: *The Grand Alliance,* 56 ff.; Desmond Young: *Rommel* (London, 1950), 82-86; *Halder Diary,* February 7, 1941; De Belot: *The Struggle for the Mediterranean,* 94 ff.

[6] Churchill to the Foreign Secretary, November 26, 1940 (Churchill: *Their Finest Hour,* 547).

pressure on Turkey and Yugoslavia throughout the winter of 1940-1941, and to the use of argument and suasion in Moscow. The details have not been revealed, even by Mr. Churchill, but for the purposes of this narrative they are relatively unimportant, the more so as they met with failure. The British did, however, afford such assistance as they could to the hard-pressed Greeks. A naval base was established at Suda Bay on the island of Crete and several squadrons of British planes were sent to support the Greek forces on the Albanian front. Airfields were developed in Greece and Turkey, from which strikes could be made at Italy and, if necessary, at the Rumanian oil fields, so important to the German war economy.[7] Futhermore, it was planned to send ground forces as well as additional air forces to Greece just as soon as the Italian threat to Egypt had been mastered. "It is quite clear to me," wrote Mr. Churchill in January, 1941, "that supporting Greece must have priority after the western flank of Egypt has been made secure." He thought it likely that the Germans, in coming to the aid of the Italians, would advance through Bulgaria rather than through Yugoslavia. In that case it would be essential that the Turks enter the war. Indeed, it was not unreasonable to suppose that such action by the Germans would affect the Soviet attitude also. Since it was thought that the Nazi move might come soon, the British Chiefs of Staff issued instructions to General Wavell to give military aid to Greece priority over further operations in the Middle East as soon as Tobruk had been captured.[8]

The Greeks themselves had never doubted that, following their victories over the Italians, Hitler would rescue his partner as soon as weather conditions permitted. They were determined to resist the Germans as they had the Italians, not because they believed they could save Greece from Germany, but because they were convinced of the ultimate victory of Britain and felt "that the country owed it to its future to keep at least its soul alive."[9] It was certainly no secret that the Fuehrer was preparing for large-scale operations in the Balkans in the spring. There might be some doubt whether he would advance through Yugoslavia or through Bulgaria and whether he would strike only at Saloniki or also at the Turkish Straits, but the threat to Greece was obvious and played an important part in the calculations of all the interested powers.

Just as the British plan to support Greece rested on hidden as well as ostensible motives, so Hitler's determination to carry the war into the Balkans was based on divers considerations. Naturally he felt that he had to uphold the prestige of the Axis by wiping out the presumptuous little Greek state. But he appears to have been even more concerned over the deploy-

---

[7] Churchill: *Their Finest Hour*, 626.

[8] Churchill memorandum of January 6, and instructions to Wavell of January 10, 1941 (Churchill: *The Grand Alliance*, 9-10, 17).

[9] Taken from a lengthy memorandum by Ambassador MacVeagh reviewing the entire Greek situation, after the debacle, and dated June 16, 1941.

ment of British forces in Greece and the establishment of airfields for modern bombers, which he rightly looked upon as a grave menace to the Rumanian oil fields. His objective in crushing Greece, therefore, was primarily to expel the British from the continent. There could be no argument about this and the Fuehrer was prepared to incur even the ill will of his Soviet partner in order to attain his end.[10]

During the winter Germany, Britain, and the Soviet Union all competed for the "souls" of Yugoslavia, Bulgaria, and Turkey. Even if these diplomatic maneuvers were known in all their aspects, to retail them would take this narrative too far afield. Hitler did his utmost to bring all three countries into the Tripartite Pact. All resisted his efforts to the best of their limited abilities. The Turks, being most advantageously situated and bound to Britain by alliance, managed to hold out successfully. The Yugoslavs, though their government was weak and rent by dissension, refused the bait of Saloniki and tried to buy off Hitler with the offer of a nonaggression pact. On the other hand, the Bulgarians, threatened by the presence of strong German forces in Rumania, were unable or unwilling to resist, despite Soviet offers of support. They did not openly adhere to the Tripartite Pact until the end of February, 1941, when the German forces were on the point of crossing the Danube. But long before that time they had invited the Fuehrer to proceed as though Bulgaria were a member of the Axis. In mid-January they had agreed to staff conversations to arrange for the transit of Nazi forces in the direction of Saloniki. On January 21 the Soviet Government had been informed by Berlin that the German Army would march through Bulgaria if operations against Greece proved necessary. The troops would be withdrawn as soon as they had accomplished their objective of preventing British forces from establishing themselves on Greek soil. Molotov's wry reply and his reiteration that the Kremlin considered Bulgaria and the Straits part of the Soviet security zone had no effect whatever on Hitler's plans.[11]

In laying his plans Hitler felt justified in believing that the Soviet Government, for all its "intrigue" and obstruction, would not resort to war to prevent German domination of the Balkans. The Turks, though unfriendly, were too weak to take offensive action against German forces, while the Yugoslavs would be only too happy to be let alone. The main thing was that the Bulgarians had been brought into line and that preparations for the

[10] Directive for Operation *Marita* (the campaign against Greece), December 13, 1940 (*Trials of War Criminals*, X, 899 ff.).

[11] *Nazi-Soviet Relations*, 268 ff. For the rest see the directive for staff conversations with the Bulgarians, January 16, 1941 (*Trials of War Criminals*, X, 906); Hitler's conferences with his military advisers, January 8-9, 1941 (*Fuehrer Conferences*, 1941 [1], 1 ff.); the *Halder Diary*, December 12, 1940; Ribbentrop's conference with Ciano, January 19, 1941 (*Ciano's Diplomatic Papers*, 418); Walter Hagen: *Die geheime Front* (Vienna, 1950), 218 ff. The best systematic account of these issues is that of Max Beloff: *The Foreign Policy of Soviet Russia*, II, 360 ff.

campaign, scheduled for the end of March, could therefore proceed according to schedule.

To Hitler's opponents, however, the future alignment of the Balkan states and Turkey was still an open question. The British, eagerly supported by the United States, redoubled their efforts to establish themselves militarily in the Balkans and to organize a common front before the weather permitted the German divisions to intervene. True, General Wavell was inclined to consider the Nazi moves in the Balkans mere bluff, basing his opinion on Germany's interest in keeping that area quiet and avoiding a war on two fronts.[12] But his Government thought otherwise and, having decided that Greece should have priority over a further advance in Libya, ordered the Commander to betake himself at once to Athens for consultation with the Greeks.

On January 14 and 15, 1941, General Wavell and Air Chief Marshal Sir Arthur Longmore conferred with the King of Greece, Prime Minister Metaxas, and General Papagos. The Greeks expressed skepticism regarding action either by the Yugoslavs or the Turks in the event of German intervention against Greece. Papagos pointed out that if the Thracian-Macedonian front were to be held against Nazi attack, he would require the support of nine British divisions, together with large-scale air forces, and that these reinforcements would have to arrive before the Germans entered Bulgaria. Wavell replied that the British could provide immediately only one artillery regiment, one antitank regiment, and about sixty tanks. At most they might later contribute two or three divisions, but these could not reach Greece in less than two months. In view of these facts the Greeks refused to accept British ground forces, arguing that their establishment in Greece would provoke the Germans without providing assurance of successful resistance.[13] Similarly the Turks, when approached with an offer of British air support, declined to expose themselves to Nazi wrath. In contrast to the British, they firmly believed that Hitler, when he moved, would drive toward the Straits rather than toward Saloniki. They were determined to resist, but they were equally resolved to avoid any action that would precipitate or even hasten the evil day.[14]

It was only after their failure to lay the groundwork for offensive operations based on Saloniki that the British undertook their drive toward Ben-

[12] Churchill: *The Grand Alliance*, 18 ff.; Wavell's remarks to Colonel William J. Donovan in mid-January, 1941, as recorded in the diary of Brigadier Dykes, who accompanied Donovan (*Donovan Papers, MS.*, Folder 35).

[13] General Sir Archibald P. Wavell: *Operations in the Middle East from February 7, 1941 to July 15, 1941;* General Alexander Papagos: *The Battle of Greece* (Athens, 1949), 310 ff.; Churchill: *The Grand Alliance*, 19; Lord Wilson: *Eight Years Overseas*, 68 ff.; despatch from MacVeagh, January 30, 1941.

[14] Wavell's despatch, as cited above; record of the Anglo-Turkish negotiations, January 15-22, 1941, in the *Donovan Papers, MS.*, Folder 6; despatch from MacVeagh, January 30, 1941.

ghazi. The Greeks had promised to call for help as soon as the Germans actually crossed the Danube into Bulgaria. In the interval there was nothing to do but wait.

At this point the furtherance of the British plan was taken over by an American emissary, Colonel William J. Donovan, distinguished soldier of the First World War, prominent Wall Street lawyer, active Republican leader and at the same time vigorous proponent of President Roosevelt's foreign policy. Donovan had contributed notably to the British cause by his report on the defense of England in the summer of 1940. In December of that year he had again visited London, officially as the representative of his close friend, Secretary of the Navy Knox, but in reality as the agent of the President. His mission was to journey to the Middle East, to collect information on conditions and prospects and, more importantly, to impress on everyone the resolution of the American Government and people to see the British through and provide all possible assistance to countries which undertook to resist Nazi aggression.[15]

Colonel Donovan, traveling by air via Gibraltar and Malta, arrived in Cairo on January 7, 1941. He conferred at length with the British commanders, made a tour of inspection in the western desert and then joined the British delegation in Athens (January 15). He was received by the Greek King and consulted with Metaxas and Papagos, learning from them the most urgent needs of the Greek forces and particularly those requirements that could be met only through American aid. Donovan was fully initiated into British plans and negotiations with the Greeks and Turks. Like the British, he was convinced that if the Balkan states and Turkey could be induced to form a united front, Nazi aggression might yet be averted. He therefore readily agreed to postpone his visit to the Albanian front and make the rounds of the Bulgarian, Yugoslav and Turkish capitals in an effort to bring those governments into line. At Sofia (January 20-22) he had an opportunity to talk with the Bulgarian Prime Minister, the Foreign Minister, the Minister of War, and finally for a full hour and a half with King Boris. From the Ministers he learned nothing specific but gained the impression that they were awaiting with folded arms the entry of the German troops. The King struck his American visitor as honest, idealistic and devoted to peace. Having listened to Donovan's forceful presentation of American policy and his stern warning of the consequences of collaboration with Hitler, Boris gave the impression that he was still maneuvering to avoid a head-on collision with the Germans. Donovan tried to pin him down by summarizing his understanding of the Bulgarian position as follows: "That Germany is still uncertain as to what you will do in the event that she demands passage through your country; but that if a decision is forced and

---

[15] Conversations of the authors with General Donovan; *Stimson Diary* (*MS.*), December 2, 1940; Hull: *Memoirs*, II, 928.

you are no longer able to delay, you will then permit Germany to come through, although you will not participate with her." In response the King looked his visitor straight in the eye and smiled. Since, as noted above, the Bulgarians had already committed themselves to Hitler, it is easy to understand why the Sofia Government enjoyed a reputation for duplicity.[16]

Vital to the success of the British plans was the position of Yugoslavia, a country torn by the factional strife of Serbs, Croats and Slovenes and currently governed by a Prime Minister and Foreign Minister who favored appeasement of Germany. During his stay in Belgrade (January 23-25) Colonel Donovan had a long talk with Prince Regent Paul, with his chief Ministers, and with a number of military leaders. He found them all cordial, with the exception of Foreign Minister Cincar-Markovich, who was so preoccupied with fears of the German reaction to Donovan's visit that he tried desperately to keep all news of it out of the press. Prince Paul thought there was a bare possibility that, under American influence, the Bulgarians might refuse the Germans permission to transit their territory, but, like all other Yugoslavs, he was full of distrust of his neighbor and really expected the Bulgars to yield to Nazi pressure. In the event of a German occupation of Bulgaria, Prince Paul thought the Yugoslavs might fight, but he recognized that they were not united. Donovan had ample opportunity, in his conversations with Belgrade politicians and military men, to realize that the chances of Yugoslav intervention were slim indeed. All agreed that their country would fight rather than allow the Germans transit rights or other concessions that might infringe Yugoslav sovereignty, but a number of them, notably Prime Minister Cvetkovich and Foreign Minister Cincar-Markovich, apparently deluded themselves into thinking that Hitler would not disturb the Balkan breadbasket, while General Simovich, later to lead the coup of March 27, was inclined to believe the Nazis would turn on Soviet Russia rather than on Britain or Turkey. Ambassador Lane reported home that Colonel Donovan's visit and his forceful exposition of American policy had probably bolstered the Yugoslav Government in its determination to resist Nazi encroachment, but Donovan, while not without hope, was deeply impressed with the weaknesses and divisions of the Belgrade regime. It was certainly more than doubtful whether the Yugoslavs would react against a German occupation of Bulgaria.[17]

At this point the American emissary interrupted his tour of the Balkan

[16] Donovan's itinerary and activities were recorded by Brigadier Dykes, who accompanied him (*Donovan Papers, MS.*, Folder 35). The details of his visit to Sofia were reported in a despatch from MacVeagh, February 3, 1941. We have used also telegrams from Earle (Sofia), January 22 and 23, 1941, and a despatch from Earle, January 24, 1941.
[17] The *Dykes Diary*, as cited above; tels. from Lane (Belgrade), January 23, 24, and 25, 1941; despatch from Lane, February 1, 1941; reports in the *Donovan Papers (MS.)*, Folder 5.

capitals to pay a visit to the Greek forces in Albania. He arrived in Istanbul on January 31 and thence proceeded at once to Ankara. There he learned from the British Ambassador that Mr. Churchill had just sent a message to President Inönü urging him to permit the stationing of ten squadrons of fighter and bomber planes on Turkish soil. That having been done, argued Mr. Churchill, it would be possible to threaten the Germans with an attack on the Rumanian oil fields if they advanced into Bulgaria, as well as to deter the Soviets from aiding the German operations. In any case, if Greece went under, Britain could then continue the air war from Turkey.[18]

The Turkish reaction to this daring suggestion was negative. Ankara insisted on about ten times as many aircraft as London had offered and requested an exact statement of what the British proposed to do and of what they expected of the Turks. Donovan was to learn from his conferences with the Prime Minister, the Foreign Minister, the Minister of Defense and the Commander in Chief that the Turks, while determined to resist aggression to the very limit of their capabilities, were unwilling to oppose a German occupation of Bulgaria unless the Bulgars themselves resisted. Since they believed there was only one chance in a hundred that the Bulgars would do so, there was no likelihood that the Turks, hopelessly deficient in the instruments of modern war, would do anything to provoke a German attack which they thought there was still a good chance of avoiding.[19]

In many successive interviews Donovan had done his utmost within the limits of his mandate. He had put all the force of a vivid personality into his exposition of United States policy, assuring his worried listeners of America's intention not only to supply the British but to give all possible aid to small nations that elected to resist Hitler. He promised that American war production, still developing, would be in full swing by September, and reiterated his conviction that if Britain and Greece could only survive another six months, decisive American assistance would reach them. It made no difference, he argued, whether in the process Hitler were provoked. To quote his remarks to King Boris of Bulgaria: "Hitler must be beaten at all costs, even though our peace may be endangered."

Further than this Donovan did not presume to go, but the American chiefs of mission all testified to the tonic effect of his assurances, general though they were. Nonetheless, the Colonel himself recognized that exhortation and promise were not enough—that British capabilities in the Middle East were too limited to induce the smaller countries to defy Hitler as the Greeks had defied Mussolini. The only way to construct a Balkan barrier, he

[18] Letter of Churchill to President Inönü, January 31, 1941 (text in Churchill: *The Grand Alliance*, 33 ff.).

[19] *Dykes Diary*, as cited above; tels. from MacMurray (Ankara), February 3 and 7, 1941; despatch from MacMurray, February 10, 1941; memorandum of conversation between Donovan and General Marshall Cornwall, the British emissary to Ankara, February 17, 1941 (*Donovan Papers, MS.*, Folder 35).

was persuaded, would be through direct intervention by President Roose-velt. Despite the "normal" distrust of the Balkan nations for each other, the prestige of the President was so great that he might yet bring them together. What was needed to spur the desired union was an "outside impulse" from a relatively "disinterested nation," namely, the United States. Under such an impulse the Balkan states might not merely construct a defensive bloc, but might even provide the British the means for mounting offensive action against Hitler's European fortress. Ultimately "Britain must defeat Ger-many in the Balkans." It was a fallacy, according to Donovan, to think of the Mediterranean primarily as a line of communication from west to east, for it was basically also a no man's land between Africa and Europe. If circumstances should eventually bring the United States into the war, he foresaw that the attack on Germany would have to be launched from the south, on a wide front, with American forces probably based in northwest Africa and operating in conjunction with the French.[20]

It is certainly problematical whether any action the United States Gov-ernment could have taken, short of direct intervention in the war, would in fact have influenced the course of Balkan politics. America was far away and not even Donovan could promise immediate, substantial aid. On the other hand, the Nazi divisions were already massed on the frontiers. Con-sidering their military weakness, the Balkan states could not hope success-fully to resist a Blitzkrieg. It was therefore almost inevitable that they should knuckle under when the pressure became great. Promises of favorable treat-ment at the peace settlement, such as Donovan had in mind, could hardly compensate for the material destruction certain to befall them in the event of resistance. To believe in the ultimate victory of the democracies was diffi-cult enough; to face in the meantime military subjugation and years of occupation was too much to ask.

So far as American policy was concerned, these considerations were to a large degree academic. While Donovan was busily collecting and sending to Washington lists of Greek requirements in matériel, the Administration was still wrestling with the problem of finding for the Greeks the thirty modern combat planes which the President, in a moment of misguided generosity, had long since promised. Since the Greeks had refused the obsolete Navy planes offered them and since Secretary Knox would not hear of turning over any of the new planes so desperately needed by both the American and British services, a deadlock was reached at the end of Jan-uary. Mr. Roosevelt and most of his Cabinet were weary of this apparently insoluble issue and suggested telling the Greeks to take the old planes

---

[20] Despatch from MacVeagh, February 3, 1941, reporting Donovan's views on his return from Belgrade; *Dykes Diary*, quoting Donovan's remarks to the British Ambas-sador in Ankara, February 1, 1941; despatch from Fish (Cairo), February 18, 1941, recording Donovan's estimate of the situation on his return to Egypt on February 7-11, 1941.

or leave them. But the State Department insisted that irreparable moral damage would be done throughout the Balkans if the President's promise were not honored. Finally, in mid-February, the Navy Department was induced or ordered to provide the modern planes. At the same time, however, it was decided to delay shipment until the Lend-Lease bill had been approved by Congress. As a result, Greece was overrun by the Germans before this important item of American aid arrived.[21]

Though adamant in his insistence that the President's promises to the Greeks be fulfilled, Secretary Hull had no intention of countenancing further commitments to the Balkan Governments and no inclination to take the lead in the effort to influence their policies. When Ambassador Lane reported Donovan's proposals from Belgrade, the Secretary replied that such a course would be contrary to American policy. Much the same response was made when the British enthusiastically espoused Donovan's ideas and appealed to Washington to support "the line taken by Colonel Donovan during his recent visits to the Balkan countries."[22] Although Mr. Hull does not explain the reasons for his refusal to participate in the effort to forge a joint defense in the Balkans, his attitude derived no doubt from the traditional American aversion to any intervention in European affairs that transgressed the limits of exhortation. Appeals and admonitions were still America's stock in trade. They were to play a part again in the sequel, though it must have been clear to Washington policy makers that mere words were useless where even the efficacy of drastic action was highly dubitable.

3. THE EASTERN COCKPIT

It is an all but impossible task to reduce the complicated developments in the Balkans during February and March, 1941, to a reasonably simple and comprehensible narrative. Hitler, with his many divisions and his firm foothold in Rumania, felt he could afford to ignore the objections of the Kremlin and therefore proceeded to impose his will on the Balkan Governments. On February 8 the military conferences with Bulgaria were completed and ten days later the Fuehrer ordered the construction of a bridge across the Danube to be started on February 28. This would permit the passage of German troops from Rumania into Bulgaria on March 2.[23] Concurrently the Nazis continued and increased their efforts to bring Yugoslavia into the

[21] Morgenthau Diaries (MS.), Vol. 347, pp. 74 ff., 159, and passim; Vol. 353, pp. 184 ff.; Vol. 373, pp. 89 ff.; Berle Diaries (MS.), January 31, February 5, 6, 11, 14, 1941. For the previous history of this troublesome issue see above, Chapter IV, Section 5.

[22] Tel. from Lane, January 25, 1941; tel. to Lane, January 29, 1941; tels. from Hopkins (London) to the President and Secretary Hull, January 28, February 5 and 8, 1941; memo of conversation between Mr. Hull and Lord Halifax, February 5, 1941. See also Hull: Memoirs, II, 928.

[23] Nazi Conspiracy and Aggression, IV, 272 ff.; Trials of War Criminals, X, 908 ff.

Tripartite Pact and to deter Turkey from action against Bulgaria or in favor of Greece. The Yugoslav Prime Minister and Foreign Minister were summoned to Salzburg on February 14, while Prince Paul paid secret visits to Berchtesgaden at the beginning and in the middle of March. On these occasions Hitler and Ribbentrop used every conceivable argument to persuade the Yugoslavs to join the Tripartite Pact, so as to make a united Balkan front once and for all impossible. Their visitors offered instead a nonaggression pact and presented a number of conditions. Hitler professed willingness to respect the sovereignty and integrity of Yugoslavia and asserted that no request for the passage of German troops would be made. But the Yugoslav leaders continued to evade. Eventually the Fuehrer saw no other course save resort to an ultimatum.[24]

Hitler had been obliged to give up his initial hope of drawing Turkey into the Tripartite Pact. Recognizing that the Turks would fight if attacked and having, in fact, no intention for the present of extending the war to the Middle East, the Fuehrer was concerned only to forestall Turkish intervention when the Germans embarked on their operations against Greece. At the very time of the entry of Nazi forces into Bulgaria he therefore wrote President Inönü assuring him that the German moves were not directed against Turkey, but designed solely to prevent British forces from establishing themselves on Greek territory. Turkey would not be disturbed unless the Ankara Government took measures to aid the British.[25]

The question of the hour was whether the British, with such support as they could get from Washington, might yet succeed in building a Balkan barrier comprising Yugoslavia, Greece, and Turkey. On February 8, just as Hitler was completing his military arrangements with the Bulgarians, the Greeks approached the British with the request for all possible aid in resisting the expected German attack. Benghazi having just fallen to the British, General Wavell was at once instructed to defer all plans for further operations in North Africa and prepare to send a large force to the aid of the Greeks. It was of great importance to hold Greece, if only on account of Turkey, wrote Mr. Churchill. So important, indeed, that Mr. Eden, the Foreign Secretary, and General Sir John Dill, the British Chief of Staff,

[24] The details of these complicated negotiations, even so far as they are known, cannot be considered here. See particularly Constantin Fotitch: *The War We Lost* (New York, 1948), 38 ff.; Grégoire Gafenco: *Préliminaires de la guerre à l'est* (Fribourg, 1944), Chapter VI, *passim;* Beloff: *The Foreign Policy of Soviet Russia,* II, 364 ff. Dallin's *Soviet Russia's Foreign Policy,* 277 ff., 301 ff., is still worth reading.

[25] Hitler's letter to Mussolini, February 28, 1941 (*Les lettres secrètes échangées par Hitler et Mussolini,* 118). The Turks communicated the substance of this message to the State Department (memo of conversation between Hull and the Turkish Ambassador, March 15, 1941). On Turkey's position see further C. Açikalin: "Turkey's International Relations" (*International Affairs,* XXIII, 1947), and Harry N. Howard: "Germany, the Soviet Union and Turkey during World War II" (*Department of State Bulletin,* XIX, July 18, 1948).

were despatched to Cairo without delay. Together with Wavell they were to make a last effort to bring Greece, Yugoslavia, and Turkey into a common front. Eden was given wide powers to make decisions if the urgency of the situation was such as to preclude reference to London.[26]

Eden and Dill, delayed by bad weather, arrived in Cairo only on February 19. They found Wavell now ready and eager to move. The Commander had had the satisfaction of finishing off the conquest of Cyrenaica and may well have been influenced by the arguments of Colonel Donovan, recently returned to Cairo after a visit to Baghdad. Donovan sat in on the conferences of the British leaders and seems to have impressed them with his concept of the Mediterranean as an ideal route for attacking the Axis in Europe. At Eden's request he departed almost at once for London to expound his views to the War Cabinet. Meanwhile he promised to do his best to enlist American diplomatic support for the British effort and secure all possible aid in the way of shipping, which was one of the severest limiting factors in all British planning.[27]

Although by this time German reinforcements were already being landed in Tripoli, British intelligence was so faulty that this move was not reported to Wavell. The latter, believing that action by the Germans in North Africa would be impossible before May, therefore left relatively small, untrained and poorly equipped forces to hold Cyrenaica and prepared to throw almost all his fully trained troops into Greece. The dangers of this decision were clearly recognized, but it was thought the gamble might succeed to the extent of checking a further Nazi advance in the Balkans.[28] That, in turn, would depend on the willingness of the Greeks to deploy the major part of their forces on the Bulgarian front and on the degree of coöperation, if any, which the Yugoslavs and Turks might afford.

On February 22 Eden, Dill and Wavell were back in Athens for further conferences with the Greek leaders. Difficulties arose at once. The Greeks were determined to maintain their victorious position in Albania and would promise only a few divisions for action farther east. They recognized that the limited Anglo-Greek forces would probably not be able to hold a line in Thrace or indeed anywhere east of Saloniki. On the other hand, to abandon Saloniki would mean the end of any chance to bring the Yugoslavs into the conflict, for that port was essential to the supply of Belgrade's forces. After much discussion of strategy it was decided that the British should send as many troops and planes as possible, but that these should not land in Greece

[26] Wavell's despatch, as cited above; Churchill: *The Grand Alliance,* 64 ff.; Lord Wilson: *Eight Years Overseas,* 70.

[27] *Dykes Diary,* as cited above (memos of conversations in Cairo between February 19 and 21, 1941). The substance of these memos was reported to Washington in tels. from Fish, February 20, 22, March 1 and 11, 1941.

[28] Wavell's despatch, as cited above; Eden's report to Churchill, February 21, 1941 (Churchill: *The Grand Alliance,* 72).

until the Germans had actually crossed the Danube into Bulgaria. A further attempt was to be made to enlist the support of Turkey and Yugoslavia. Only if and when this attempt failed were the Greeks to fall back from Thrace and join the British in defense of the Aliakhmon Line, to the west of Saloniki.[29]

The Turks had not only rejected earlier British offers of limited aid and coöperation, but had on February 17 concluded a nonaggression pact with Bulgaria which, if it meant anything, signified that Ankara would not take action against a Nazi occupation of Bulgaria unless the Bulgarians or Germans initiated hostilities against Turkey. They had evidently made some effort to come to an agreement with Yugoslavia for joint defense, but had achieved nothing.[30] Although Eden and Dill were well aware that there was little prospect of a change in the Turkish or Yugoslav attitudes, they went on from Athens to Ankara to make doubly sure. Their conferences with the Turkish leaders were cordial but unprofitable. The Turks approved the British decision to aid Greece, but were fearful lest they be next on Hitler's list of prospective victims. In view of Britain's admitted failure to provide the necessary equipment, they could promise no aid to either Greece or Britain. Until supplies reached them they could do nothing but wait until attacked, in which case, of course, they would fight as long as possible.[31]

On their return to Athens (March 2) with this discouraging news, Eden and Dill ran into further trouble. The situation had become tense, for the Germans had begun to cross the Danube and a new Italian offensive was expected in Albania. General Papagos therefore felt that he could not promise as many troops for the eastern front as he had originally indicated. Neither was he willing to fall back to the Aliakhmon Line, since there was still some hope that Yugoslavia would make a favorable decision. Naturally these developments were a severe blow to the British. Mr. Churchill relates that for a time the Cabinet was inclined to leave the Greeks to their fate, since there was in any case little hope that the Germans could be held. But Eden, Dill and Field Marshal Smuts all maintained that, since the Greeks would fight in all circumstances, it would be disastrous for the British to withhold their support. Besides, there was still a chance that the Yugoslavs could be persuaded, in which case their forces could assist the Greeks in driving the Italians out of Albania and then join up with the British-Greek forces to prevent a German advance through the Monastir gap to turn the left flank of the Aliakhmon Line. According to Ambassador MacVeagh,

[29] Wavell's despatch; Churchill: *The Grand Alliance*, 73 ff.; Papagos: *The Battle of Greece*, 320 ff.

[30] Little is known of these *démarches*, but see C. Açikalin: "Turkey's International Relations" (*International Affairs*, XXIII, 1947, p. 483) and Sir Hughe Knatchbull-Hugessen: *Diplomat in Peace and War* (London, 1949), 159 ff.

[31] Eden's report to Churchill, February 28, 1941 (Churchill: *The Grand Alliance*, 97 ff.); Knatchbull-Hugessen: *Diplomat in Peace and War*, 160 ff.

Mr. Eden was not too discouraged, for he felt that despite all slipping and sliding, Yugoslavia and Turkey would eventually be drawn into the conflict. Even if the Germans succeeded in overrunning Greece, it would not help them much, for in the interval the British would have cleaned up the Middle East and would be "sitting pretty" in Africa: "In making war in the Balkans, Germany is only playing football in her own cabbage patch."[32]

Yielding to the opinion of the men on the spot, the British Cabinet decided on March 7 to proceed with the operations as planned and to make another diplomatic assault on the wavering Yugoslavs. On March 10 Mr. Churchill informed President Roosevelt of this decision, stressing the importance of Yugoslavia's position and requesting American aid to Belgrade, Ankara and Moscow in a last effort to effect united opposition to Hitler. Colonel Donovan, whom the Prime Minister praised highly, had already been urging such intervention on the President.[33]

Thanks to Donovan's persuasive reports and Mr. Churchill's eloquent appeals, Washington gradually took a somewhat stronger line in its communications with the Balkan Governments. A message sent to Belgrade and Ankara on February 9 was still of the traditional, purely hortatory variety, stressing American determination to support Britain, pointing out the extent of American preparations, and ending with the warning that peace was to be obtained from Hitler only at the price of complete surrender.[34] But this was followed almost at once by messages of the President to the Yugoslav and Turkish Governments, intended to counteract reports that the Yugoslav Ministers were about to visit the Nazi potentates at Salzburg. These messages reiterated the earlier warnings against concessions to the Nazis, but contained the additional feature of a reference to the forthcoming passage of the Lend-Lease bill, which would permit the President "to supply the materials of war to those nations that are now the victims of aggression or which might be threatened with aggression."[35]

The response to these messages was cordial. Ambassador Lane was able to report from Belgrade that the Prince Regent had stated that Yugoslavia would fight if attacked, though it would be unable to resist for more than a couple of weeks. At the same time the Yugoslav Ambassador in Washington indicated to the State Department that Hitler had made no specific demands

---

[32] Letter of Ambassador MacVeagh to President Roosevelt, March 8, 1941 (*Roosevelt Papers:* Secretary's File, Box 75). For the rest see Wavell's despatch, as cited above; Churchill: *The Grand Alliance,* 99 ff.; Lord Wilson: *Eight Years Overseas,* 72 ff.

[33] Churchill: *The Grand Alliance,* 110; tel. from Fish (Cairo), February 20, 1941, reporting Donovan's recommendations.

[34] Tels. to Lane and MacMurray, February 9, 1941; Hull: *Memoirs,* II, 929; Fotitch: *The War We Lost,* 45.

[35] Memo of Atherton to Welles, reporting a conversation with the Yugoslav Ambassador, February 14, 1941. Tels. to Lane and MacMurray, February 14, 1941, transmitting the President's message to the Yugoslav and Turkish Prime Ministers; Hull: *Memoirs,* II, 929; Fotitch: *The War We Lost,* 46-47.

on the Ministers and that no decisions had been made. Thereupon the President had another message sent to Belgrade, this time addressed to Prince Paul. The final text was essentially that outlined by Mr. Roosevelt himself, pointing out what even brief resistance would mean in terms of American and world sympathy and citing the examples of Abyssinia, China, Norway and Greece. The President wanted it particularly understood that the eventual peace settlements, as they touched any specific nation, would depend on its attitude in the face of aggression.[36]

What effect, if any, the American arguments and warnings may have had in Belgrade it is impossible to say. It should be noted that while the instructions from Washington became firmer and more explicit, while they included promises of Lend-Lease aid and opened the prospect of favorable peace settlements in the event of resistance, the President and his advisers never went so far as to urge either the Yugoslavs or the Turks to join in a common front with the British and Greeks. Since the United States itself was as yet unwilling to become involved in the world conflict, one can understand the Administration's reluctance to urge weaker powers to anticipate aggression by taking steps tantamount to provocation of a Nazi attack. These self-imposed limitations of American action were bound to reduce its effect. To Balkan Governments good will was certainly a matter of consequence. On the other hand, American aid was a hope rather than a reality; for the moment it weighed light in comparison with the incubus of Nazi power.

Continued efforts of the British and Turks to enlist the Yugoslavs in a Balkan front proved utterly futile. A proposal that Mr. Eden and Sir John Dill visit Belgrade for political and military discussions was politely declined and Mr. Eden's personal message to Prince Paul (March 5) bore no fruit. On March 18 the British Foreign Secretary held a secret conference on Cyprus with the Turkish Foreign Minister, at which it was agreed that a last effort should be made to bring Belgrade into line. Mr. Eden therefore proposed to the Yugoslav Government that it send representatives to a secret meeting with himself and Turkish and Greek delegates, to discuss all Balkan problems.[37] But by that time it was already too late to stave off Belgrade's fateful decision. Ambassador Lane had long since concluded, from his conversations with Prince Paul and the Yugoslav Ministers, that Cvetkovich was an opportunist who would yield if necessary, while Foreign Minister Cincar-Markovich was an out-and-out appeaser. Prince Paul was certainly averse to the Tripartite Pact and had promised the Ambassador

---

[36] State Department memos of February 20, 1941, dealing with the advisability of sending a message to Prince Paul; memo from the President to Mr. Hull, outlining the message, February 20, 1941; tel. to Lane, transmitting the message, February 22, 1941. See also Hull: *Memoirs*, II, 930-31; Fotitch: *The War We Lost*, 49 ff.

[37] Churchill: *The Grand Alliance*, 98; Knatchbull-Hugessen: *Diplomat in Peace and War*, 162 ff.; tel. from the Foreign Office, communicated to Mr. Welles on March 21, 1941.

that he would resist both diplomatic and military pressure to accept demands that would infringe his country's sovereignty and integrity. But the Regent was painfully aware of Yugoslavia's political and military weakness. He was pessimistic about his country's ability to resist and his "susceptible nature" made it all too likely that in a crisis he would cave in.[38]

And so it was, for when Hitler summoned Paul to a second secret meeting, about March 17, the game was practically up. The Fuehrer would hear nothing of a nonaggression pact and refused to be satisfied with anything less than Yugoslav adherence to the Tripartite Pact. In order to attain that, he was willing to give all sorts of assurances, including promises not to demand the transit of troops and matériel through Yugoslavia. The whole proposition was tantamount to an ultimatum and was so regarded in Belgrade, where on March 20 a Crown Council decided to yield.[39]

This tragic development was known to the American and British Ambassadors almost at once. Mr. Lane cabled Washington pleading for further word from President Roosevelt in the desperate hope that the Regent might yet elect the heroic course. Unfortunately the President had already left on a Caribbean cruise and Acting Secretary Welles could only instruct Lane to repeat to Prince Paul, as emphatically as necessary, that the President adhered, more strongly than ever, to the statements he had made in earlier messages.[40] Two days later, evidently in response to British appeals for American support in the effort to postpone a decision and induce the Yugoslavs to attend a conference, Ambassador Lane was further instructed to see the Regent and point out to him again that the Italians, after their dismal failure in Albania, were no threat to Yugoslavia; that British troops were landing in Greece in advance of schedule; that the terrain conditions were favorable for defense against German attacks; and that the Turkish position was now clear. Lane was to repeat that the United States was prepared to offer all possible aid under the recent Lend-Lease Law so long as Yugoslavia retained its independence and freedom of action.[41]

There was little chance that these last minute moves, or even Mr. Churchill's personal appeal to the Yugoslav Prime Minister (March 22), would alter the situation. Ambassador Lane was unable to report grounds for hope and was told by the Regent on March 23 that Hitler had given the Belgrade Government only until midnight to accept or reject the German terms.[42] That same day Hitler was informed that the Belgrade Government

[38] Despatches from Lane, February 25, March 19, 1941.

[39] The facts, so far as they are known, are well reviewed in Beloff: *The Foreign Policy of Soviet Russia*, II, 364, whose account should be supplemented by Fotitch: *The War We Lost*, 64 ff.

[40] Tels. from and to Lane, March 19, 1941.

[41] Three telegrams from the Foreign Office, transmitted to the State Department, March 21, 1941; tel. to Lane, March 21, 1941; Fotitch: *The War We Lost*, 67 ff.

[42] Churchill's tel. to Cvetkovich, March 22, 1941 (Churchill: *The Grand Alliance*, 160); Arthur Bliss Lane: "Conquest in Yugoslavia" (*Life*, September 15, 1941); Nicholas

would comply. On March 25 Cvetkovich and Cincar-Markovich signed the Tripartite Pact at a ceremonial meeting in Vienna which the Fuehrer dignified with his presence.

That the submission of the Government to Nazi pressure was unpopular in Belgrade and in the Serbian sections of the country was perfectly well known and seemed to Mr. Churchill to afford some slight hope of organized resistance. He therefore cabled the British Ambassador to "continue to pester, nag and bite," and to neglect no alternative action if the existing Government had actually gone beyond recall.[43] Actually the situation took care of itself, for a group of Serbian Army officers, passionately nationalistic and anti-German, had long been preparing to meet the contingency that had now arisen. On March 27, under the leadership of General Simovich, Chief of the Air Force, they engineered a coup that swept Prince Paul and his pusillanimous ministers from power and installed the young King Peter on the throne.

Hitler, it seems, charged the American Government, acting through Colonel Donovan, with prime responsibility for the spectacular coup which threatened to snatch a bloodless victory from his hands. There is no evidence, however, to show that either American or British influence played an important part in this dramatic overturn. Washington and London certainly knew that plans for a coup were under way and hoped they might succeed. But the conspirators had nothing more to go on than the well-known American and British assurances of general support in resistance to Nazi pressure or aggression, nor were they apparently able to count on anything more from Soviet Russia than vague suggestions that the Kremlin would welcome any obstacle in the path of the Nazi juggernaut.[44] There is nothing in the record to detract in any way from the credit due the Serbian patriots for their daring decision to overthrow the weak Government that had agreed to accept whatever place might be accorded Yugoslavia in the Nazi new order.

4. A Three Weeks' Blitz

In Washington, London, and even Moscow the spectacular overturn in Belgrade came like "a lightning flash illuminating a dark landscape."[45] Everywhere it was assumed that the new regime would reject the Tri-

---

Mirkovich: "Yugoslavia's Choice" (*Foreign Affairs*, October, 1941); Fotitch: *The War We Lost*, 68-69; Ulrich von Hassell: *Vom anderen Deutschland* (Zurich, 1947), 188 ff.

[43] Tel. of March 26, 1941 (Churchill: *The Grand Alliance*, 161).

[44] For Hitler's views we have relied on the State Department interrogation of Dr. Paul Schmidt, but see also *Nazi Conspiracy and Aggression*, VI, 895-96. We have also discussed this matter at length with General Donovan. See further Ambassador Lane's tribute to King Peter in *The New York Times*, April 27, 1948; Fotitch: *The War We Lost*, 75 ff.; Beloff: *The Foreign Policy of Soviet Russia*, II, 366 ff.; Churchill: *The Grand Alliance*, 161 ff.

[45] *The New York Times*, March 28, 1941 (quoted by Fotitch: *The War We Lost*, 80).

partite Pact and brave the shock of the Nazi steam roller. The American people were deeply stirred. Newspapers outdid each other in paeans of praise, while organizations and individuals besieged the Yugoslav Embassy with congratulatory telegrams and floral tributes. Secretaries Knox and Stimson were so elated that they sent a message to President Roosevelt (still cruising in the Bahamas aboard the *Potomac*) urging him to make a public statement and proposing that Yugoslav ships in American ports be loaded at once with munitions for Yugoslavia and Greece, as well as for the British forces in the east. The *Potomac* at once put into a Florida port, where communication with Washington was easier. There, no doubt, the President learned that Ambassador Lane, without awaiting instructions, had sought out the new Yugoslav Foreign Minister, Mr. Ninchich, on the very evening of the coup, and had indicated the approval of the American Government.[46]

The State Department had, in fact, already directed the Ambassador to inform either General Simovich or Foreign Minister Ninchich of the excellent impression made by their determined action and to say that the United States would, under the Lend-Lease Act, provide assistance to Yugoslavia in repelling aggression.[47] Furthermore, the President, acting on a suggestion from Lane, despatched a message of congratulation and good wishes to King Peter, while Acting Secretary Welles informed Ambassador Fotitch and announced to the press that Yugoslavia would be given American food and munitions in the event of a Nazi attack.[48] Preparations were also made to implement the plan advanced by Secretaries Knox and Stimson. The Yugoslav Government was invited to submit a list of its immediate requirements and Mr. Roosevelt, on his return to Washington (April 2), instructed Harry Hopkins, as Administrator of Lend-Lease, to devote all his attention to the aid program. Discussing the situation at length with Ambassador Fotitch, the President said he wanted to demonstrate that democracies could act speedily and effectively. As soon as the first Yugoslav ship was loaded, he proposed to make an appropriate public announcement.[49]

For a brief period, at least, it seemed as though the sudden reversal of the situation in the Balkans might even shake the Kremlin from its cautious reserve. The German occupation of Bulgaria had undoubtedly been a severe blow to the Soviet Government as well as to the Russian people. It had led to sharp but carefully worded protests and to plain-spoken newspaper communiqués, none of which, however, had sufficed to deter Hitler.[50] The British had exerted their best efforts to induce the Kremlin to take a stronger stand

[46] *Stimson Diary (MS.)*, March 27, 1941; tel. from Lane, March 27, 1941.
[47] Tel. to Lane, March 27, 1941.
[48] Fotitch: *The War We Lost,* 81 ff.; the President's message to King Peter, March 28, 1941; Welles's press statement (*The New York Times,* March 28, 1941).
[49] Fotitch: *The War We Lost,* 83 ff., discusses this matter in some detail.
[50] *Nazi-Soviet Relations,* 278 ff.

and above all to secure Soviet support for the projected Balkan front. But Stalin and Molotov advanced only by inches. Early in March they gave the Turks secret assurance that if they became victims of aggression, the Soviet Government would not take advantage of their plight to attack them. Left-handed though this statement was, it could be interpreted only as an encouragement to the Turkes to resist possible German attack. The Soviet message and the Turks' gracious reply were published on March 25, obviously in connection with the announcement of Yugoslavia's adherence to the Tripartite Pact, and were at once accorded public praise by Acting Secretary Welles.[51]

Whether, in addition to this move, the Soviet Government had taken a hand in the *coup d'état* in Belgrade is highly doubtful, though it seems likely that General Simovich and his associates hoped for support and perhaps aid from Moscow. The Kremlin and the Communists throughout the world certainly struck a sympathetic attitude. For example, the official Soviet *Pravda*, while denying that Moscow had congratulated the new regime, stated that it might well have done so.[52] Moreover, the Kremlin permittted General Simovich to send two special emissaries to Moscow to discuss the conclusion of what the Yugoslavs thought was to be a military convention. This was probably a misunderstanding, as Vishinsky explained to the Yugoslav delegates when they arrived in Moscow on April 4. On that very day Molotov had informed the German Ambassador that the Soviet Government was about to conclude a nonaggression pact with the new Yugoslav Government. Naturally Simovich's agents were profoundly disappointed and tried to secure something more substantial than the Kremlin suggested. But the Soviet leaders were obviously not prepared openly to challenge their Nazi partners or run serious risk of involving the Soviet Union in the forthcoming struggle. Stalin himself intervened and in the night of April 5-6, 1941, the Soviet-Yugoslav pact of friendship and nonaggression was signed. For lack of detailed knowledge it is even now difficult to determine what objective the Kremlin may have envisaged in taking this unusual step. The fact that the Soviet press made much ado about the pact and published photographs of Stalin, Molotov and Vishinsky with the Yugoslav Ambassador lends color to the possibility that the prime purpose of Soviet leaders was to throw a sop to their own people.[53]

[51] Tel. from Winant (London), March 12, 1941, reporting the news from the British War Office. Tel. from Steinhardt, March 15, 1941, reporting that the message had been sent to Ankara on that day. The Turks replied on March 17, 1941. The public announcement on March 25 may be found in *Documents on American Foreign Relations*, III, 340, and Welles's statement in *The New York Times*, March 26, 1941. This problem is well discussed in Gafenco: *Préliminaires de la guerre à l'est*, 164 ff.

[52] *The New York Times*, April 2, 1941; see also the *Daily Worker*, March 19, 1941.

[53] Tel. from Steinhardt (Moscow), April 6, 1941, reporting the agreement. See further Fotitch: *The War We Lost*, 91 ff.; Walter Hagen: *Die geheime Front* (Vienna, 1950), 224 ff.; and the discussion of this episode in Gafenco: *Préliminaires de la guerre à l'est*, 167 ff., and in Beloff: *The Foreign Policy of Soviet Russia*, 365 ff.

The Kremlin's attitude and policy were of particular significance because they reopened the prospect that the Soviet Union, itself increasingly threatened with Nazi aggression, might join with Britain in supporting the Balkan states, if only to embroil the Germans and thereby delay their operations against the Soviet Union. To this end Mr. Churchill and Mr. Eden despatched a message to Stalin pointing out that the obvious way for the Kremlin to strengthen its position was to provide aid to Turkey, Greece, and Yugoslavia: "This help might so increase German difficulties in the Balkans as still further to delay the German attack on the Soviet Union, of which there are so many signs." It was clearly in the Soviet interest "to put every possible spoke in the German wheel." Unfortunately Sir Stafford Cripps, the British Ambassador in Moscow, deferred delivery of this message on the plea that he had already presented the same argument at greater length to Vishinsky and that to repeat it would only weaken the impression. The Prime Minister was much annoyed by Cripps's failure to follow instructions and eventually insisted on transmission of his message. But by that time (April 19) the Germans had already overrun Yugoslavia and it was obviously too late for effective action. The Soviet Government, which had not raised a finger to prevent the Balkan catastrophe, has been most severely castigated by Mr. Churchill for its blindness and ineptitude.[54]

The British had not, of course, waited on the Kremlin before taking steps to exploit the favorable turn provided by the upset in Belgrade. The Prime Minister had hailed the Simovich coup with the announcement that the Yugoslav nation had "found its soul." He had cabled at once to President Roosevelt stating that if the new Government showed readiness to share in Greece's heroic resistance, the British would extend the fullest possible aid: "We should encourage the Yugoslavians to roll up the Italians in Albania, which would produce result of prime importance, and give them a good packet of arms. I trust that you will take a similar line and will sustain the new Government with promise of America's powerful support and backing."[55] At the same time he had instructed Mr. Eden to turn back from Malta to Cairo and renew his efforts to construct a united front. An appeal in this sense was despatched also to President Inönü of Turkey. All told, it seemed to Mr. Churchill that, with a large number of Yugoslav divisions thrown into the scales, it might be possible through united action to prevent or at least delay the German advance to the southeast.[56]

For a moment there was a fair chance that the Balkan defenses might be consolidated. Mr. Eden and Sir John Dill were back in Athens, whence the latter hurried off to Belgrade for further discussions. Unhappily his visit

---

[54] Churchill: *The Grand Alliance*, 358 ff.

[55] Message of Mr. Churchill to the President, March 27, 1941 (*Roosevelt Papers: Secretary's File, Box 87*).

[56] Churchill messages to Eden, March 27 and 28, 1941, and to President Inönü, March 27, 1941 (Churchill: *The Grand Alliance*, 169 ff.).

proved disappointing. Simovich was confronted with great domestic difficulties and had not yet succeeded in bringing the Croat leader, Dr. Machek, into his Government. He was still hoping to avoid a clash with the Germans, but agreed to detail a high staff officer for military conferences with the British and the Turks. On April 4 General Yankovich arrived at Florina, where he discussed the situation with Eden, Dill, Wilson, and Papagos. But these conversations brought little more than disillusionment: the Yugoslavs were militarily unprepared, had no specific plan of action, and had an altogether exaggerated idea of British strength in Greece. Furthermore, they were loath to commit their forces in Albania, holding that in the event of a German attack they would have to defend their entire country if only for domestic political reasons. Under the circumstances not even Mr. Churchill's eloquent appeal to General Simovich to act and act quickly in Albania was likely to have much effect.[57]

Within a couple of hours of the signature of the Soviet-Yugoslav pact all argument was cut short by the terrific Nazi air attack on Belgrade (April 6) which signaled the beginning of the German sweep through the Balkans. Hitler had decided to liquidate Yugoslavia almost the moment he learned of the Simovich coup, for he was convinced that it would involve a change of policy entailing serious dangers. He felt he had made great concessions in order to bring Yugoslavia into the Tripartite Pact and had been delighted when his efforts were crowned with succcess. As he explained to his Italian partner, it was almost impossible to undertake the campaign against Greece, much less an eventual campaign against Soviet Russia, with a hostile Yugoslav Army on his flank, to say nothing of the fact that the Yugoslav attitude necessarily influenced that of the Turks.[58]

The Fuehrer therefore disregarded all assurances from Belgrade. Without delay he summoned his generals and explained the reasons which made it imperative to destroy Yugoslavia militarily and nationally, and to do so as soon as possible:

It is of particular importance politically to carry out the blow against Yugoslavia inexorably and ruthlessly and to smash her armed forces by a *Blitz* operation. This is likely to deter Turkey sufficiently and to have a favorable influence on our prospective campaign against Greece. . . . The war against Yugoslavia should be very popular in Italy, Hungary, and Bulgaria, as acquisition of territory can be promised to these states, namely the Adriatic coast to Italy, the Banat to Hungary, and Macedonia to Bulgaria.[59]

[57] Churchill: *The Grand Alliance,* 172-74; General Wavell's despatch on operations in the Middle East, as cited above; Lord Wilson: *Eight Years Overseas,* 80 ff.; Papagos: *The Battle of Greece,* 338 ff.

[58] Hitler's conversation with Ciano, March 25, 1941 (*Ciano's Diplomatic Papers,* 431 ff.), and Hitler's letter to Mussolini, March 28, 1941 (*Nazi Conspiracy and Aggression,* IV, 475 ff.).

[59] Record of conference of March 27, 1941 (*Trials of War Criminals,* X, 917 ff.).

In accord with Hitler's instructions, military plans were hastily drawn and, the weather permitting, the great assault was launched on both Yugoslavia and Greece on April 6, 1941. Along with the military operations came the usual flood of denunciation of the "band of ruffians" and "criminal usurpers" who, in the pay of Churchill, had caused so much trouble.[60]

The present study cannot pretend to review military developments at any length. The Nazis enjoyed a tremendous superiority over the Yugoslavs, British and Greeks, not only in divisions, but in tanks and especially in planes. Yugoslavia was assailed from all directions and forced to abandon organized resistance on April 17. The Greeks were quite unable to hold in Thrace and fell back as best they could to the Aliakhmon Line, which in turn had to be abandoned when the German forces coming from Macedonia through the Monastir gap began to turn the Allied flank. The situation was so hopeless that the decision was made on April 19 to evacuate the British forces. The Greek Army, quite demoralized, surrendered on April 24. In less than three weeks, then, the Nazi hordes had crushed all opposition in the Balkans and had once again driven the British from the continent.

5. ROMMEL'S RAMPAGE

The commitment of British troops in Greece had been recognized from the outset as a gamble. Over and above the moral obligation to support the Greeks, it was thought in London and Cairo that bold action would rally Turkey and Yugoslavia to the British cause. In that happy event the Soviet Government might feel encouraged to translate its opposition to Nazi policy from mere protests into concrete action. There would then be a real possibility of blocking Nazi domination of the Balkans and even some prospect of opening an offensive from Turkey and Greece. At the worst, it was thought, the British and Greeks, fighting alone, might delay or obstruct Hitler's conquest and provide time for the British to consolidate their positions in North and East Africa, and in the Middle East generally. The risks did not appear unacceptable, for there seemed little likelihood that the Italians, supported by the Germans, could resume operations in North Africa before May. It therefore seemed reasonable to employ what forces the British had available in Egypt in the attempt to hold and perhaps extend the foothold on the continent provided by Greek resistance.

The phenomenal sweep of the Nazi armies demonstrated that their power had been greatly underrated. Even the timely association of Turkey and Yugoslavia with Britain and Greece would probably not have sufficed to alter the outcome. But events were to show that the greatest error of the British lay in their faulty estimate of the Libyan situation. They were to

---

The translation of this record in *Nazi Conspiracy and Aggression*, IV, 275 ff., is even more clumsy than the one here quoted.

[60] Fotitch: *The War We Lost,* 94.

suffer inordinately from this error because chance or the perspicacity of the Fuehrer had brought to the North African theater so able and energetic a leader as General Erwin Rommel.

The German commander had arrived in Tripoli on February 12, to be followed soon afterward by an armored brigade. With this force and the 15th Armored Division, which had been promised him, Rommel was to help the Italians hold Tripolitania against further British advances. By early March the British had become aware that German reinforcements were arriving in North Africa, but little intelligence was available and General Wavell concluded that, considering the difficulties of distance and transport, it was improbable that the Axis commanders would attempt an offensive for some time to come. The British forces which had swept Graziani out of Benghazi had already been committed to Greece or were being reformed and refitted in Egypt. The line at El Agheila was being lightly held by inexperienced troops with but few tanks.[61]

On March 21 Rommel received instructions from home to prepare a plan for a limited offensive, the plan to be complete by April 20, at which time it was expected that the 15th Armored Division would have joined him. Quite without orders, however, the General decided to exploit the weakness of the British and on March 31 launched an attack at El Agheila with two Italian divisions and the one German armored division which was already on the scene. The British were unable to hold. They fell back from the front and abandoned Benghazi on April 3. Rommel swept on, taking Bardia on April 12 and reconquering all Cyrenaica well before the date set for the completion of his plan. Except for the fortress of Tobruk, which Wavell had been ordered on April 10 to hold at all costs, there were no serious obstacles to further Axis advance as far and as fast as transportation and supply lines would permit.

This daring drive, concurrent with the Nazi Blitzkrieg in the Balkans, filled the cup of British disaster to the brim. On both sides of the Atlantic something like panic assailed the common man. The Churchill Government was taken severely to task for having embarked upon the Greek venture while leaving North Africa and Egypt exposed to Nazi assault. Apparently Hitler's power was irresistible. How long was it to be before his troops, tanks and planes cleared the British from the eastern Mediterranean and cracked down on Suez in a great pincer movement from Libya on the one side and Turkey and Syria on the other? To many it seemed that Britain was doomed, since the full weight of American supplies could not possibly make itself felt for months to come.

[61] General Sir Archibald P. Wavell: *Operations in the Middle East from 7th February, 1941 to 15th July, 1941.* This despatch, dated September 5, 1941, is published as a supplement to the *London Gazette,* July 3, 1946. See further Churchill: *The Grand Alliance,* 199 ff., and Desmond Young: *Rommel,* 86.

President Roosevelt was doubtless shaken like most of his compatriots, but drew some reassurance from a careful estimate of April 12 prepared by the chief Navy planner, apparently at White House request. This interesting document deserves quotation in full:

1) It has long been my opinion that driving the British out of Egypt, and driving the British Fleet out of the Mediterranean is a MUST for the Germans. When they are out, several of Germany's supply problems will be partially solved, and there will remain no area from which a successful land offensive against Germany can be launched by the British.

2) Sending British troops to Greece has so weakened the British Army in Egypt, that the Germans will have little difficulty in regaining all of Libya. However, it will take considerable time for them to prepare forces and supplies for crossing the desert and attacking the Nile position.

3) It was essential, in my opinion, for the British to send an army to support Greece. There was a chance that Yugoslavia could offer effective resistance; Turkish backs needed stiffening; Russia has been influenced by this move; and finally, abandoning Greece to its fate, after the great help they have already given to Britain, would have been an action so base and immoral that reënforcing them was necessary, regardless of its influence on the future of Britain. It is doubtful if the Greeks and the British can withstand the Germans and hold on to any part of Greece. Nevertheless, it is possible that they can do so for a time, and thus absorb German military energy. The Germans may win within the next ten days; on the other hand, the British and Greeks might even hold out for six weeks.

4) When the Germans have conquered all of Greece, they will then begin to work directly against Egypt with great strength. They will drive the British out of Crete. They will move into the Dodecanese Islands and launch a vigorous air and submarine campaign which will be difficult for Admiral Cunningham's fleet to sustain. They may land troops by air in Egypt and Syria, and doubtless will insist on the transportation of troops and supplies across Turkey. However, I do not believe that they can make the position of British troops untenable before some time in June. Once they drive the British Fleet out of the Mediterranean, however, the German Army will go by sea to Syria, and the end will then be in sight.

5) Because of the present tragic situation of the British Government, I do not recommend troubling them further at this time by informing them as to our opinion on the seriousness of the situation. They realize it pretty well themselves, even though they are somewhat too optimistic. Warning them on this score could have only a bad influence on their morale, and could serve no useful purpose.

6) On the contrary, I believe that a public statement by the President praising the courage and self-sacrificing stand taken by the British in sending troops to Greece would strengthen Mr. Churchill's position, might give some uplift to morale, and might influence neutrals, particularly if coupled with praise of the Greeks themselves. However, I suggest that any such statement not be made until we clearly see the end of hostilities in Greece.[62]

[62] Memo of Admiral R. K. Turner to Admiral Stark, April 12, 1941, approved by Secretary Knox and forwarded by him to the President. See also Sherwood: *Roosevelt and Hopkins*, 275 ff.

This sympathetic appraisal must have struck a responsive chord in the President's heart, as did the news, from Mr. Harriman and from the Prime Minister himself, that, for all the disasters in Greece and North Africa, the British were not without hope and proposed to fight back. In a message to the President (April 16) Mr. Churchill reported that he was not unduly anxious about the situation in Libya, for he was convinced that Rommel's "audacious formations" were working "on very small margins" and that Tobruk could be held. The British were going to launch a naval and air assault on the town of Tripoli in the effort to cut the Axis supply line to North Africa, and were going to try to run a convoy through the Mediterranean with several hundred tanks for Wavell. All available forces in East Africa were to be concentrated in Egypt, while during the last days of April some 80 percent of the troops were being evacuated from Greece, chiefly to Crete. Naturally there was a tremendous need of tanks, antiaircraft and antitank guns, transport vehicles, and other equipment.[63]

In further messages to the President the Prime Minister reiterated his belief that the situation in Libya could be stabilized, the more so as Tobruk was already serving as a magnet for the enemy's forces. On the other hand, he expressed grave concern about the anticipated Nazi assault on Crete and the danger that the Germans might establish themselves in Syria while at the same time launching an attack on Gibraltar.[64] It was in response to these messages that Mr. Roosevelt sent his long cable of May 1, 1941, part of which has been quoted in an earlier chapter.[65] Characteristically, the President's survey of the situation created by the Nazi victories bore largely on the renewed dangers of aggression in the western Mediterranean and on the problems presented by French, Spanish, and Portuguese policy. Anent the Middle East the message revealed a strange equanimity:

In regard to yours of April 29 my thoughts in regard to eastern Mediterranean are: You have done not only heroic but very useful work in Greece and the territorial loss is more than compensated for by the necessity for enormous German concentration and resulting enormous German losses in men and matériel.

Having sent all men and equipment to Greece you could possibly spare, you have fought a wholly justified delaying action and will continue to do so in other parts of eastern Mediterranean including North Africa and the Near East. Furthermore, if additional withdrawals become necessary, they will all be part of the plan which at this stage of the war shortens British lines, greatly extends Axis lines, and compels the enemy to expend great quantities of men and equipment. I am satisfied that both here and in Britain public opinion is growing to realize that even if you have to with-

---

[63] Tel. from Harriman to the President, April 14, 1941 (*Roosevelt Papers:* Secretary's File, Box 78); Churchill: *The Grand Alliance,* 213 ff., 241, 245 ff.; De Belot: *The Struggle for the Mediterranean,* 117 ff.

[64] Tels. of Mr. Churchill to the President, April 25 and 29, 1941 (*Roosevelt Papers:* Secretary's File, Box 87).

[65] *Supra,* Chapter XII, Section 7.

draw further in the eastern Mediterranean you will not allow any great debacle or surrender, and that in the last analysis the naval control of the Indian Ocean and the Atlantic Ocean will in time win the war.[66]

Mr. Churchill was understandably upset by the President's apparent readiness to countenance the loss of the Middle East. He therefore hastened to reply, adjuring Mr. Roosevelt not to underrate the gravity of a collapse in that area. It must be realized, he argued, that the attitude of countries like Spain, Vichy France, Turkey, and even Japan might be determined by the outcome of the struggle in the Middle East theater. He could not, therefore, share the view that the loss of the Middle East and the neighboring area would be merely a preliminary to an arduous but successful oceanic war. Such a war would, at best, be "a hard, long and bleak proposition." The British consequently felt obliged to fight "to the last inch and ounce for Egypt." The situation was extremely grave and the outcome doubtful: "Therefore, if you cannot take more advanced positions now or very soon, the vast balances may be tilted heavily to our disadvantage. . . . The one decisive counterweight I can see to balance the growing pessimism in Turkey, the Near East, and in Spain, would be if the United States were immediately to range herself with us as a belligerent power. If this were possible, I have little doubt that we could hold the situation in the Mediterranean until the weight of your munitions gained the day."[67]

The Prime Minister can hardly have expected a specific reply to his suggestion that the United States enter the war. Very likely he threw out that suggestion more to underline the seriousness of the situation in the Middle East than for any other purpose. That he succeeded in correcting what he must have regarded as mistaken or at least narrow American views seems indicated by the President's reaction. On May 10 Mr. Roosevelt cabled:

In my message of May 1, I did not intend to minimize in any degree the gravity of the situaton, particularly as regards the Mediterranean. I am well aware of its great strategic importance and I share your anxiety in regard to it.

I saw General Whitely [a special representative from the British command in Egypt] while he was here and heard from him the magnificent effort of Wavell's army and Cunningham's and Somerville's fleet. I have issued instructions that supplies in so far as they are available here are to be rushed to the Middle East at the earliest possible moment. Thirty ships are now being mobilized to go within the next three weeks to the Middle East. I want to emphasize we intend to continue the supplies and to get the ships to carry them until there is a final decision in the Mediterranean. I know of

---

[66] Tel. from the President to Mr. Churchill, May 1, 1941, quoted also in Churchill: *The Grand Alliance*, 234-35. Views similar to those in this message were contained in a memo of the State Department's Division of Near Eastern Affairs, April 21, 1941.

[67] Message from Mr. Churchill to the President, May 4, 1941, printed in full in Churchill: *The Grand Alliance*, 235-36. The copy in the State Department files is dated May 3, 1941.

your determination to win on that front and we shall do everything that we possibly can to help you do it.

My previous message merely meant to indicate that should the Mediterranean prove in the last analysis to be an impossible battleground, I do not feel that such a fact alone would mean the defeat of our mutual interests. I say this because I believe the outcome of this struggle is going to be decided in the Atlantic and unless Hitler can win there, he cannot win anywhere in the world in the end.

I cannot speak too highly of the admiration which the American people hold toward your generals, admirals, troops, airmen, and sailors who fought in Greece and are now fighting in the Mediterranean and Africa. I think the feeling in America is that the efforts which your country made to stem the tide in Greece was a worthy effort and the delaying action which you fought there must have greatly weakened the Axis. . . .[68]

This exchange of cables threw a rather harsh light on Anglo-American differences as to the strategic importance of the Middle East, differences which, in the sequel, were to produce further argument. Leaving these matters for later treatment, the point worth emphasis in the present context is that by early May, 1941, the British position in the eastern Mediterranean was truly desperate. On May 1 Rommel, now reinforced by the 15th Armored Division, loosed his forces on Tobruk, only to be turned back by its valiant defenders. There was, as Mr. Churchill calculated, a good chance that the British could hold in Libya, but east of Egypt the prospect was bleak indeed. What was to prevent Hitler from dragooning the Turks into collaboration, from taking Crete and thence establishing himself in Syria and Iraq? These questions, and the related question of possible German action against Gibraltar and North Africa, kept Europe and the world in suspense during May and early June till Hitler's abrupt shift to the offensive against Soviet Russia provided temporary relief of the Mediterranean tension.

[68] Tel. from the President to Mr. Churchill, May 10, 1941. The rest of the message deals with the situation at Vichy, and will be quoted later in that connection.

CHAPTER XIV

The Battle of the Atlantic

1. The Aftermath of Lend-Lease

The enactment of the Lend-Lease Law was extolled in a number of impressive speeches on both sides of the Atlantic. None, however, quite equaled the tribute paid to the American decision by Prime Minister Churchill in the course of an address welcoming Ambassador John G. Winant to London on March 18, 1941. Mr. Churchill compressed into one sentence all the sense of relief and hope which the people of Great Britain had drawn from this "new Magna Carta": "At such a moment and under such an ordeal the words and acts of the President and people of the United States come to us like a draught of life, and they tell us by an ocean-borne trumpet call that we are no longer alone."[1]

Even Mr. Churchill, however, was too cautious to assert, as Mr. Roosevelt did, that the action of Congress constituted recognition by the American people that their country could no longer remain "an island." Yet *The New York Times* expressed the view that March 11, 1941, would be remembered in history as marking "the end of the great retreat which began with the Senate rejection of the Treaty of Versailles and the League of Nations." It may indeed prove to have been the disavowal of the long tradition of American isolationism, though the historian must remain doubtful whether most Americans on March 11 clearly grasped the full import of the more immediate commitment represented by Lend-Lease. This was, to quote President Roosevelt again, "collective responsibility for the kind of life which is going to emerge from the ordeal through which the world is passing today."[2]

[1] Winston S. Churchill: *The Unrelenting Struggle* (Boston, 1942), 61 ff. Mr. Winant's appointment, attributed to the influence of Justice Frankfurter and Harold Laski, and to the alleged view of the President that Labour would eventually govern Britain, was not well thought of generally in the State Department (*Moffat Diary, MS.*, January 31, 1941).

[2] Address to Farmers, March 8, 1941 (*Public Papers and Addresses*, X, 44 ff.).

It is therefore sufficient testimony to the significance of Lend-Lease to observe that it openly pledged America's full economic power and resources to the task of underwriting the victory of the democratic powers over the Axis. In Prime Minister Churchill's judgment the enactment of Lend-Lease ranks with the Fall of France, the Battle of Britain, and the Nazi invasion of Russia as an event which truly shaped the destinies of the warring nations. Whether or not it proves to have marked the end of American isolationism, one must agree with the verdict that Lend-Lease was "on any count among the two or three most far-reaching decisions that have determined the history of our time."[3]

The subsequent history of Lend-Lease, the manner in which it was financed and administered, cannot be treated in detail in this study of policy.[4] It must suffice to point out that the preparations for financing and administering the law were far advanced before its enactment. In the matter of appropriations Mr. Harold Smith, Director of the Budget, and initially Secretary Morgenthau as well, favored asking Congress for a lump sum to cover aid to all eligible foreign governments. Secretary Stimson, however, wanted as far as possible to incorporate Lend-Lease grants with the appropriations for the United States Army and Navy. Morgenthau was persuaded of the wisdom of this plan and eventually Mr. Smith was overborne by sheer force of numbers. Accordingly, Stimson's plan was adopted in the appropriation bill which Mr. Roosevelt and the Budget Director drafted together.[5]

The sum for which the President was to ask likewise occasioned difficulty at the outset. The original British estimate of 1941-1942 requirements totaled upwards of ten billions. Upon American protest this figure was reduced to eight billions' worth of equipment to be delivered by June 30, 1942. Even this the Administration thought too high, and it was ultimately decided that seven billion dollars was the utmost the American economy could carry, a figure which, as Morgenthau noted with some satisfaction, corresponded to the recent increase of the Treasury's debt limit from fifty-eight to sixty-five billions.[6] Despite the magnitude of the figure, the President remarked that Congressional leaders, with whom he conferred before sending his request to

[3] W. W. Riefler: "Turning Points of the War: Our Economic Contribution to Victory" (*Foreign Affairs,* October, 1947).

[4] The reader is referred to the accounts of Edward R. Stettinius, Jr.: *Lend-Lease: Weapon for Victory* (New York, 1944); Robert E. Sherwood: *Roosevelt and Hopkins* (New York, 1948); the official history: *Industrial Mobilization for War,* I (Washington, 1947).

[5] *Stimson Diary (MS.),* February 13, 15, 16, 17, 1941; *Morgenthau Diaries (MS.),* February 13, 15, 18, March 9, 12, 1941. Stimson's letter to the President, February 13, 1941, outlining his views on Lend-Lease organization, is in *Roosevelt Papers: Secretary's File,* Box 81.

[6] *Industrial Mobilization for War,* I, 123; *Morgenthau Diaries (MS.),* March 10, 12 (Vol. 380, pp. 237 ff.; Vol. 381, pp. 94 ff.); *Stimson Diary (MS.),* March 11, 1941.

Capitol Hill, "took it well." Indeed, the hearings on the appropriation bill were rather superficial and perfunctory. The bill was reported out of committee less than a week after its introduction, was rushed through the subsequent stages without amendment, and approved by both Houses on March 27, 1941.[7]

The plan for administering Lend-Lease was also largely the brain child of Secretary Stimson and his War Department assistants. It called for a four-man Advisory Committee (promptly dubbed the "War Cabinet," or, more informally, the "Plus Four"), consisting of the Secretaries of State, Treasury, War and Navy, with an Executive Secretary in charge of actual operations. For this latter all-important task Secretary Stimson initially recommended General James H. Burns, but the President had other ideas. He accepted Stimson's general program on February 25, but selected Harry Hopkins to administer it.[8]

Thus on March 27, 1941, ended what Secretary Morgenthau has aptly described as the "cash on the barrelhead era" of American aid to the warring democracies. With it, too, ended the heavy responsibilities which the Secretary of the Treasury had so signally discharged. These were now to fall upon the frailer shoulders of an individual in whom at the moment even ardent New Dealers had little confidence. Harry Hopkins's career as Administrator (in all but name) of the vast Lend-Lease operation has been skillfully described elsewhere, as has been, incidentally, the abrupt reversal of initial doubts as to his capacities for so exacting and heavy a burden.[9]

The enactment of Lend-Lease had given the Roosevelt Administration, as leading members of it have testified, substantially what was desired for underwriting victory.[10] The price paid, however, was high in point of time. In the course of the long debate the Battle of the Atlantic had entered its crisis stage. Before the debate was concluded, Germany had launched its 1941 spring offensives. Mr. Roosevelt thus found himself in the quandary so freely predicted by friend and foe alike. Having appropriated billions of dollars to provide the resources required for Britain's victory, and having also discussed in staff conversations with the British the wisest allocation of these resources, the Administration was at once confronted with the problem of how to assure their safe and timely delivery. On March 25, 1941, a few days before the staff conversations ended and Congress appropriated the funds for Lend-Lease, Berlin extended the North Atlantic war zone to in-

[7] Stimson Diary (MS.), March 11, 12, 13 and 20, 1941; Documents on American Foreign Relations, III, 723-29.

[8] Stimson Diary (MS.), February 11, 12, 13, 1941; Morgenthau Diaries (MS.), February 13, 17, 19, 25, 26, March 5, 12, 1941; Berle Diaries (MS.), February 27, March 13, 14, 1941; Documents on American Foreign Relations, III, 729-31.

[9] Sherwood: Roosevelt and Hopkins, 265 ff.

[10] Hull: Memoirs, II, 925; Henry L. Stimson and McGeorge Bundy: On Active Service in Peace and War (New York, 1947), 362 ff.

clude not only Iceland, but the entire area westward to the coast of Greenland. With Yugoslavia clearly weakening, with the British presently in full
retreat from Libya, and with Greece bracing itself for the Nazi assault, the
long-predicted crisis of the democracies seemed at hand. Unless the United
States acted promptly, it could discard both Lend-Lease and ABC-1 as dead
letters. How the Administration reacted to the challenge in the Atlantic
throughout the remainder of the spring constitutes an absorbing chapter in
the story of American policy.

2. ALTERNATIVES TO CONVOY

The Fuehrer's decision to extend the North Atlantic war zone to the territorial waters of Greenland represented a partial victory for Admiral Raeder's
thesis that Britain could be brought to its knees if the German High Command permitted full concentration of all available air and sea power upon
Britain's ports and life lines. Throughout the winter, and particularly after
the introduction of the Lend-Lease bill, Raeder had pleaded with Hitler to
cancel the orders requiring his submarines and surface raiders to respect the
Neutrality Zone, the more so as American naval vessels, he charged, were
guilty of various unneutral actions. It seemed to Raeder by early February
at least a debatable question whether Germany's ultimate interests would
not be better served if America were forced to throw off the mask and
become an open belligerent, especially if Japan then entered the war on
Germany's side.[11]

With the passage of the Lend-Lease bill, Admiral Raeder redoubled his
arguments. Promising the Fuehrer that Britain would be brought to its knees
in six months if the tonnage destroyed during that interval equaled the
highest figure of the First World War, the Admiral reported that German
intelligence indicated that American escort of convoys as far as Iceland was
about to commence. Since the United States had not claimed Iceland as
part of the Western Hemisphere, the very least Germany should do to offset
this newest threat to victory in the Atlantic was to extend the combat area
to comprise not only Iceland but the Denmark Strait between Iceland and
Greenland. Thus Germany would establish its right to treat United States
shipping in that area exactly as it treated British or neutral vessels. It could
sink American ships without warning. It would be better yet to end the
whole comedy and cease to respect the American Neutrality Zone, or at least
to limit it to distances of three hundred miles from Western Hemisphere
shores. In his indignation Hitler was almost persuaded, but calmer counsels
prevailed. The upshot was the Berlin decree of March 25, 1941, extending
the combat area of the North Atlantic to Greenland.[12]

[11] *Fuehrer Conferences,* 1941 (1), 5 ff. (February 4, 1941). Cf. Anthony Martienssen:
Hitler and His Admirals (New York, 1949), Part II.
[12] *Fuehrer Conferences,* 1941 (1), 27 ff. (March 18, 1941), 55 ff. (April 20, 1941).

The developments which culminated in Germany's extension of the combat zone were accompanied by ever more urgent British appeals to Washington for assistance, strongly supported by American officials in London, notably Harry Hopkins, Ambassador Winant and Averell Harriman, as well as by Secretaries Knox and Stimson. In the first weeks of 1941 the appeals followed the familiar pattern of requests for additional cargo and escort vessels. On January 9 Prime Minister Churchill hinted broadly that the Royal Navy could use to advantage more American over-age destroyers. "I believe you know," he wrote the President, "we have not been able to bring many of your destroyers into action. As I have seen it stated, this is due to our inability to man them. I should like to tell you that this is not the case. Indeed we could man another thirty destroyers from April next onwards besides your first fifty."[13]

With Lend-Lease about to go to Congress and the American Navy requiring all available vessels for the Neutrality Patrol, this appeal fell on deaf ears. But the Prime Minister soon began to hint at more dangerous expedients. The German battle cruisers *Scharnhorst* and *Gneisenau* had eluded observation by the seriously weakened British Home Fleet and, emerging into the Atlantic, had destroyed 115,000 tons of Allied shipping in less than two months. To these exploits were soon added the signal achievements of the new "wolf-pack" tactics of the German U-boats. The report of the British Admiralty to the Prime Minister on these grave losses was sent by Mr. Churchill to the President on March 20, 1941. Pointing out that British convoys had been attacked five hundred miles southeast of Newfoundland and therefore far to the west of the thirtieth meridian, the report stressed the belief that the enemy was now basing himself on supply ships in the mid-Atlantic. Only the commitment of British battleships could offset the new German tactics and there were too few of them to spare for convoy duty. Accordingly the report recommended that the United States extend the area of the Neutrality Zone: "It would be a very great help if some American warships and aircraft could cruise about in this area, as they have a perfect right to do without any prejudice to neutrality. Their mere presence might be decisive as the enemy would fear that they might report what they saw and we could then despatch an adequate force to try to engage them."[14]

Two days later the Prime Minister was able to underscore the Admiralty's somber appreciation of the situation by a vivid illustration. A further message to the President stated that the presence of the *Gneisenau* and *Scharnhorst* in the Atlantic was forcing the dispersal of the whole British Home Fleet. Not only did this represent a serious danger in case of an invasion

---

On the development of German tactics in the Atlantic in this period, see Churchill: *The Grand Alliance*, 111-28.

[13] Tel. from the Prime Minister to the President, January 9, 1941.

[14] Letter of Lord Halifax to Mr. Welles, March 20, 1941, enclosing a report from Mr. Churchill to the President; Churchill: *The Grand Alliance*, 122 ff.

attempt on the British Isles, but the battleship *Malaya* had already been torpedoed while escorting a convoy. "We should be much obliged," ended the message, "if she could be repaired in United States yards. She is now steaming thither at fourteen knots."[15]

The passage of the Lend-Lease bill on March 11 enabled the President to respond affirmatively to some of the British appeals, the validity of which was amply confirmed by the reports of Mr. Roosevelt's own representatives in London.[16] On March 25 the President cabled Mr. Churchill that he would be "delighted" to have the *Malaya* repaired in Boston, New York, or Norfolk. This was followed in a few days by another message to the Prime Minister: "I have this morning allotted funds for the building of 58 shipping ways and 200 additional ships. I have also made complete arrangements for repairs to merchant ships and for your larger friends."[17]

The request for additional vessels proved more troublesome, since Secretary Knox still insisted that no more destroyers could be spared. But even this difficulty was finally surmounted. Mr. Roosevelt bethought himself of an expedient which the Secretary of the Treasury as head of the Coast Guard had recommended earlier. A telegram to Mr. Churchill on March 28 informed him that the President was arranging for the transfer to Great Britain of ten Coast Guard cutters. The offer was gratefully accepted, along with notice that these vessels would be based on Iceland so as to counter the new German tactics along the twenty-ninth meridian—another reminder of the critical situation created by the German extension of the combat zone.[18]

In the same category of relatively innocuous expedients to meet the Atlantic crisis must be placed the Administration's decision of March 29 to take custody of the thirty Axis and thirty-five Danish vessels interned in United States ports. Secretary Morgenthau had been urging this measure since the summer of 1940 and the legal groundwork had long since been laid. Hitherto, however, the President had withheld his approval. It was impossible to sound out public opinion since, unless the action came as a bolt from the blue, the Axis ships would be sabotaged by their crews. Reports of such sabotage piled up during March. Secretary Knox and Admiral Stark then added their pleas to those of Secretary Morgenthau. Mr. Hull was also

---

[15] Tel. from the Prime Minister to the President, handed to Mr. Welles on March 23, 1941, by Sir Gerald Campbell, British Minister in Washington.

[16] Mr. Hopkins's lengthy cable of January 28, 1941, is reproduced in Sherwood: *Roosevelt and Hopkins*, 257 ff. We have also used tels. from Harriman to the President, March 25, 26, and to Hull and Knox, March 27, 1941.

[17] Tels. from the President to the Prime Minister, March 25 and April 2, 1941; memo of Knox to the President, March 24, and the President's reply, April 1, 1941 (*Roosevelt Papers:* Secretary's File, Box 77). The latter is now printed in *F.D.R.: His Personal Letters*, II, 1137.

[18] Tels. from the President to the Prime Minister, March 28, and from the Prime Minister to the President, March 30, 1941. On the transfer of the cutters we have also used *Morgenthau Diaries (MS.)*, March 4 and April 2, 1941 (Vol. 378, pp. 372 ff., and Vol. 385, p. 202).

induced to recommend seizure of the ships. Finally, on March 29, in the absence of Mr. Morgenthau, the Acting Secretary of the Treasury, Mr. Herbert Gaston, requested White House permission to seize the Axis vessels. When Acting Secretary of State Welles was consulted (Mr. Hull was also on vacation), he recommended inclusion of the Danish vessels. Mr. Roosevelt thereupon authorized the Coast Guard to seize both categories of ships. Quietly in the early morning hours of Sunday, March 30, 1941, Coast Guard personnel boarded the vessels, removed their crews, and formally took the ships into custody. It only remained to seek from Congress legislation which would enable the Government to requisition the ships for its own use—a step which was forthcoming shortly.[19]

Certainly the successive steps which the Administration had taken by the end of March were deemed more than mere gestures by the hard-pressed British Admiralty as well as by the German High Command. Yet even in their totality they added up to no genuine solution of the problem created by German successes in the now extended North Atlantic combat area. In particular no response had been made to London's plea for expansion and intensification of the patrol activities of the American Navy. Mr. Roosevelt's messages to Mr. Churchill at the end of March gave no hint as to the next step. But the President devoted the first ten days of April to hammering out the final increments of an overall program which he hoped would prove sufficient to save the day. Torn between the advice of most of his aides to issue forthright orders to the Navy to escort Allied convoys, and his own uncertainty whether the American public was ready for so drastic a solution, the interval between April 1 and April 10 must have been as heavy a strain on the President as the period which culminated in the launching of the Lend-Lease bill three months before.[20]

Actually little is known of the precise sequence of decisions constituting the program which the President communicated secretly to Prime Minister Churchill on April 11, 1941. Meetings between the President and his leading military and civilian advisers occurred almost daily during this crowded interval. It is clear that Secretary Stimson, still in the vanguard of the all-outers, constantly hammered away at his thesis that the only satisfactory way to confront the menace in the Atlantic was the forthright way: escorting of Allied shipping by United States naval vessels and aircraft. A completed plan to carry out such operations in close coöperation with the Royal Navy

[19] This episode is vividly described in a memo of Mr. Gaston to Secretary Morgenthau (*Morgenthau Diaries, MS.*, Vol. 384, pp. 364 ff.). The problem is discussed by Mr. Hull in some detail in *Memoirs*, I, 759 ff., and II, 927 ff. Cf. *Documents on American Foreign Relations*, III, 621-35.

[20] Although in the sources and literature of the time there is constant reference to "convoy" and "convoying," the issue was really whether U.S. naval forces should be used to escort and protect convoys. We therefore try to avoid the misleading use of the term "convoy."

had been handed to Mr. Roosevelt by Secretary Knox on March 20. Stimson could scarcely conceal his impatience with the President when, at a meeting on April 2 at the White House, with the heads of the major Government departments present, "no concrete decisions" were reached for getting munitions to Britain "both by the northeast route and the southeast."[21]

The President's unwillingness to follow Stimson's advice at this juncture by no means indicated inaction. Mr. Stimson himself was aware that the President had been having "very frank" conferences with Secretary Knox and Admiral Stark. They had informed him that the Atlantic Fleet would soon be prepared for the task of escorting merchant shipping if the President decided to adopt the March 20 plan, but Admiral Stark still insisted on the transfer of a strong force from the Pacific to the Atlantic Fleet as essential to the success of these operations, and bases in Northern Ireland, Scotland, and Iceland as very desirable.[22] The President was, in fact, temporarily converted to the transfer of important naval units to the Atlantic and even authorized Admiral Stark to issue orders to the Navy for reconnaissance as far as Iceland.[23] It is probable that he had also discussed with Knox and Stark his final "alternative" to escort of convoys, that is, extension of the American Neutrality Patrol Zone to approximately longitude 30° west. In any case he had hinted broadly to friends even outside Government circles that convoying involved highly technical problems, to the solution of which he had a new and different approach.[24]

The essential elements of this new approach were actually revealed in the course of an all-day conference at the White House on April 10, 1941, with the President, the four members of the "War Cabinet," and Mr. Hopkins in attendance. The President's first decision was to extend the Neutrality Zone not to the thirtieth meridian, as the British had earlier suggested, but even farther, to longitude 25° west. Mr. Stimson thus described the rapid de-

[21] *Stimson Diary (MS.)*, April 2, 1941. Present at this meeting, in addition to the President and Stimson, were Hull, Morgenthau, Knox, Marshall, Stark, and the Commandant of the Marine Corps.

[22] *Stimson Diary (MS.)*, March 24, 25, 1941; Kittredge MS. study on *United States-British Naval Coöperation;* MS. study by Stetson Conn on the *Hemisphere Defense Policy of the United States,* Chapter III, p. 44; memo of Admiral Stark to the President entitled "Ocean Escort in the Western Atlantic," April, 1941 (*Pearl Harbor Attack,* XVI, 2162 ff.). See also Stark's letters to Admiral Kimmel of April 3 and 4, 1941, the first printed in part in Charles A. Beard: *President Roosevelt and the Coming of the War* (New Haven, 1948), 420-25 (note 24), the second in *Pearl Harbor Attack,* XVI, 2160-61.

[23] Mark Watson: *Chief of Staff: Prewar Plans and Preparations* (Washington, 1950), 382-83.

[24] Note of Mr. Thomas Lamont to the President enclosing a letter of Lamont to Clark Eichelberger, April 8, 1941 (*Roosevelt Papers:* Secretary's File, Box 81). Mr. Lamont's note contains this line: "That other approach to the convoy problem which you touched upon over the telephone Sunday night appeals strongly to me."

termination of the new limits of the Western Hemisphere, a problem which had baffled generations of geographers:

We had the atlas out and by drawing a line midway between the westernmost bulge of Africa and the easternmost bulge of Brazil we found that the median line between the two continents was at about longitude line twenty-five. By projecting that northward, it took into the western hemisphere most of Greenland, running up the east side of Greenland until it finally struck the coast of the most important, in fact almost the only important landing place on the east coast of Greenland. . . .[25]

The President, his four Secretaries, and Harry Hopkins were all in agreement that "every bit" of Greenland must be defended, line or no line, and were plainly concerned over the possibility of German attacks in that area. This required further extension of the zone, but the choice of the twenty-fifth meridian was made primarily with a view to meeting Britain's shipping crisis. Mr. Roosevelt was as frank in expounding this in the bosom of his official family as he was Delphic outside it. Indeed, even as the plan was being adumbrated in Washington, Admiral Le Breton, who was to command the United States patrol vessels, arrived in Canada to confer with Admiral Nelles of the Royal Navy and with the Canadian naval officials in charge of convoys at Halifax.[26]

The President's plan, as Secretary Stimson heard him describe it, was the following:

. . . . We shall patrol the high seas west of the median line, all the way down as far as we can furnish the force to do it, and that the British will swing their convoys over westward to the west side of this line so that they will be within our area. Then by the use of patrol planes and patrol vessels we can patrol and follow the convoys and notify them of any German raiders or submarines that we may see, and give them a chance to escape. Also notify the British warships so they can get at the raider. . . .[27]

This plan did not quite cross the technical line which distinguished patrol and escort. It was not envisaged that United States naval vessels should hunt down and launch attacks on Axis warships. Nevertheless, it was plainly the President's intention in enlarging the Neutrality Zone to answer Hitler's challenge in extending the combat area and to provide maximum assistance for British shipping. What this would mean in practice would depend largely on the precise nature of the orders Mr. Roosevelt would presently authorize the War and Navy Departments to issue respecting action in the enlarged zone.

Extension of the patrol area was the heart of the Administration's program for saving the situation in the Atlantic. Other significant decisions had, however, been made by April 10 in support of the general objective. On

[25] Stimson Diary (MS.), April 10, 1941; Sherwood: Roosevelt and Hopkins, 291 ff.
[26] Moffat Diary (MS.), April 10, 1941.
[27] Stimson Diary (MS.), April 10, 1941; Sherwood: Roosevelt and Hopkins, 291 ff.

that day Mr. Roosevelt sent the Congress a request for legislation which would enable the Government to requisition for its own use the Axis and Danish vessels which had just been taken into custody.[28] No difficulty was anticipated with the Axis vessels, since the extensive sabotage committed by their crews had enabled the American Government to frame a very curt rejection of the protests from Berlin and Rome. The Danish ships, however, occasioned some embarrassment. For Mr. Roosevelt the issue was clear. "The main point," he wrote to former Senator Minton, "is that they are in our waters—or possessions—and ought to be used in the effort to save democracy including the return of democracy to Denmark itself."[29] In June, 1941, Congress granted the required authority and shortly thereafter the Danish vessels became available. While the Axis ships were not put to use until after Pearl Harbor, several of the Latin American Republics followed the example of the United States, thus further increasing the shipping pool ultimately available to wage the Atlantic battle.[30]

Likewise on April 10 it was announced in Washington that the United States had concluded an agreement with the Danish Minister, Mr. Henrik de Kauffmann, which placed Greenland under the temporary protection of the United States and authorized the American Government to construct bases there. The exchange of notes on that date brought to a successful conclusion negotiations which had been going on in desultory fashion since the autumn of 1940 and in earnest since January, 1941.[31]

The quickened American interest in Greenland derived, in the first instance, less from concern over any German threat to this appendage of the Western Hemisphere than from anxiety over Canadian and British plans. The Dominion Government had not receded from its earlier position that if the United States was not prepared to insure Greenland against attack, it ought not oppose Canadian or British measures to this end. The creation of bases in Greenland was desirable not only from the point of view of Canadian and hemisphere defense; there was the additional advantage of using Greenland bases in flying American-made planes to Britain via Iceland.[32]

28 Text in *Public Papers and Addresses,* X (1941), 94 ff.

29 Memo of the President to Senator Sherman Minton, April 23, 1941 (*Roosevelt Papers:* Secretary's File, Box 73). The problem is discussed in Hull: *Memoirs,* I, 759-60, and II, 927-28 and 942-43. The relevant documents are printed in *Documents on American Foreign Relations,* III, 621-35.

30 The resolution of the Inter-American Financial and Economic Advisory Committee (April 26, 1941) on expropriating foreign vessels is printed in *Documents on American Foreign Relations,* III, 116 ff. We have also used a memo from Mr. Welles to the Division of International Communications, March 24, 1941, and a memo of conversation between Mr. Welles and the Ambassadors of Argentina, Colombia, Brazil, Mexico and the Chargé d'Affaires of Chile, dated April 17, 1941.

31 *The Challenge to Isolation,* Chapter XII, Section 5; Hull: *Memoirs,* II, 935 ff. The terms of the agreement are printed in *Documents on American Foreign Relations,* III, 228-40.

32 Memo of conversation between Mr. Hugh Cumming and Mr. Escott Reid of the Canadian Legation, January 6, 1941.

Although the American Government remained firm in its opposition to the establishment of Canadian or British bases in Greenland, the logic of Ottawa's position was irrefutable. Assistant Secretary of State Berle was therefore assigned the task early in 1941 of reformulating the United States position. Initially the accent was heavily on the role of Greenland in the defense of the hemisphere. The Assistant Secretary took the stand that Greenland was within the confines of the Western Hemisphere and therefore subject to the Monroe Doctrine, and that, furthermore, the United States could not, out of considerations of hemisphere defense, permit belligerent activity in the Greenland area.[33]

A fresh survey of Greenland was thereafter authorized with the understanding that if it disclosed the existence of feasible base sites they might be acquired and developed in accordance with existing hemisphere defense plans and policy. Either the Greenland Government would build them with American assistance or the American Government would itself construct them. Failing eventual resumption of sovereignty over Greenland by a liberated Denmark, Washington was unwilling to have Ottawa take control.[34]

The Canadian Government having expressed its readiness to go along, the State Department began negotiating on Greenland in mid-February. Initially it was thought desirable to deal directly with the two Greenland Governors, Messrs. Svane and Brun, who had already expressed willingness to accept American protection against Nazi attack. At it turned out, however, the Danish Minister, Mr. Henrik de Kauffmann, represented Greenland during the critical weeks of the negotiations. He proved himself more effective in defense of his country's real interests than could the unhappy Government of German-occupied Denmark.[35]

Thanks to this decision it was possible to hasten the conclusion of an agreement. The basis for it was completed by Mr. Berle on March 5, by which date the American Government had also reached the conclusion that it would be more practical for it to construct and finance the desired base facilities itself. On March 28 Berle was able to present Minister de Kauffmann with the completed draft of an agreement for his consideration. On April 4, de Kauffmann having signified his acceptance of substantially the whole American position, the news was broken to the Governors of Greenland. They responded favorably, if with some surprise, and Mr. Hull and

[33] *Berle Diaries (MS.)*, February 1, 1941.

[34] *Morgenthau Diaries (MS.)*, February 13, 1941 (Vol. 372, pp. 95 ff.); memo of Berle and Cumming to Hull for discussion with the President, February 11; *Berle Diaries (MS.)*, February 13, 14, 1941; memo of conversation between Messrs. Berle, Cumming, Hickerson of the State Department and Messrs. Merchant Mahoney and Escott Reid of the Canadian Legation, February 13, 1941; conversation of the authors with Mr. John D. Hickerson, 1948.

[35] Memos of conversations between Berle and the Danish Minister, February 7, 18, March 4, 1941.

Mr. de Kauffmann signed the agreement on April 9. While fear of German attack remained real, the Administration was by this time placing new emphasis on Greenland's potentialities for contributing to its plans to keep German warships east of the twenty-sixth meridian. In any case, it was heartening to the President that April 10, 1941, the very day on which the agreement with Greenland was made public, also saw final Congressional approval of the Administration's policy of refusing to recognize the transfer of areas of the Western Hemisphere from one non-American power to another.[36]

The German reaction to the announcement of the agreement between the United States and Minister de Kauffmann was to put heavy pressure on the Copenhagen Government to compel the recall of the offending diplomat. It is clear that Washington was sensitive about the legal status of the agreement. The President himself helped draft the lengthy message sent to the Danish King in explanation. The gist of this was that since Greenland was in the Western Hemisphere, no change of sovereignty from Denmark to another European power could be permitted. In view of the danger of a German assault, the United States was obliged "to take steps which are tantamount to holding Greenland in trust for Denmark until such time as the Royal Danish Government ceases to be subject to duress on the part of an occupying nation and full Danish control over Greenland may be restored."[37] With the despatch of the message to Copenhagen on April 19 the Administration considered the case closed. Mr. Roosevelt, expressing serious concern over possible German operations in Scoresby Sound, had already requested of the Secretaries of State, War, and Navy "recommendation to counteract any possible establishment of military, naval, or weather bases at that point even if it be for the summer months only."[38]

Though the Canadians were doubtless relieved by Washington's long-delayed acceptance of a commitment to defend Greenland, by force if necessary, the potentialities for friction between Washington and Ottawa were

[36] State Department memo: "Respecting the Establishment of Landing Fields in Greenland," March 7; memos of conversation between Mr. Berle and Minister de Kauffmann, March 28, and between Mr. Hull and de Kauffmann (dictated by Berle), April 9; tels. to Penfield (Godhavn), April 4, 10; tels. from Penfield, April 5, 12, 19; despatches from Penfield, April 9, May 17, July 15, 1941. Berle summed up the entire course of the negotiations in a memo to Hull, April 30, 1941 (See Hull: *Memoirs*, II, 936 ff.). The text of the Joint Resolution on the transfer of Western Hemisphere territories, introduced in June, 1940, which became Public Law 32 on April 10, 1941, is printed in *Documents on American Foreign Relations*, III, 94-95.

[37] Memos of the President to Hull and Welles, April 14, 18, 1941, requesting comment on his draft message to the King (*Roosevelt Papers:* Secretary's File, Box 75). The April 18 memo is now printed in *F.D.R.: His Personal Letters*, II, 1142-43. For a critical view of the legality of the Greenland agreement, see Herbert W. Briggs: "The Validity of the Greenland Agreement" (*American Journal of International Law*, July, 1941).

[38] Memo of the President to Hull, Stimson, and Knox, April 18, 1941 (*Roosevelt Papers:* Secretary's File, Box 77).

still visible. That these potentialities never materialized is to be credited in part to the skill and tact with which the United States Minister, Mr. Pierrepont Moffat, explained to the Canadian authorities the exigencies of American policy and public opinion with respect to Greenland, in whose security Ottawa had at least as large a stake as Washington. Even more influential in obviating Canadian resentment was the close and cordial personal relationship between President Roosevelt and Prime Minister Mackenzie King, which assured that the coöperation of the two Governments in defense of their mutual interests would survive almost any strain. The continuing labors of the Permanent Joint Board on Defense were now concentrated upon the completion of a comprehensive American-Canadian plan for protection of the continent, which was ready by early summer. The Royal Canadian Navy not only shared its knowledge and experience of North Atlantic convoy problems with the United States Navy, but, at Admiral Stark's request, rushed to completion before the end of April arrangements permitting American naval vessels to use the ports of Halifax and Shelburne.[39]

The most spectacular public manifestation of Canadian-American coöperation was, however, to come in the economic rather than in the strictly military field. Ten days after the announcement of the American agreement with Greenland Mr. Mackenzie King journeyed to Hyde Park to visit the President. On April 20 the two leaders issued the so-called Hyde Park Declaration, designed to be the economic counterpart of the Ogdensburg Agreement of August, 1940.[40] The Dominion Government had for some months been urging upon Washington the military advantages of closer economic coöperation, particularly in the production of munitions. More than ever after the passage of Lend-Lease the Canadians were apprehensive about paying out scarce American dollars for materials ultimately destined for the United Kingdom. Sensitive, on the one hand, to the difficulties of its economic relations with London, and increasingly concerned with American criticism of Canada's war effort, Ottawa felt that what was really needed was a master plan for coördinated economic defense, analogous in scope and timing to the developing military defense plan. To this end Assistant Secretary Berle and Mr. Keenleyside of the Canadian Legation had, at the end of March, outlined the creation of a long-range Canadian-American economic commission.[41] To their surprise, shared by most of the American and Canadian Government officials concerned, the Prime Minister and the

---

[39] Letters of Admiral Stark to the President, April 25, 1941 (*Roosevelt Papers:* Secretary's File, Box 77). For evidence of American-Canadian military coöperation see the President's memo to Stimson and Knox, May 14, 1941 (*F.D.R.: His Personal Letters,* II, 1155-56).

[40] Text in *Documents on American Foreign Relations,* III, 160 ff.

[41] Memo of Berle to Hull, February 28; *aide-mémoire* of the Canadian Legation, March 17; memo of conversation between Berle and Mr. Hume Wrong, March 17; *Berle Diaries* (*MS.*), March 18, 1941.

President hastily drew up their own terms of reference for Canadian-American economic coöperation and announced them in the course of the Hyde Park visit.[42] While this characteristic example of the President's penchant for conducting affairs of state directly with the heads of foreign governments complicated Mr. Berle's carefully considered plans, Mr. Mackenzie King described the maneuver to Mr. Moffat as "most dramatic and gratifying."[43] Certainly it left no one in doubt of the determination of the United States and Canada to persevere on the road of coöperation in defense on which they had entered with similar éclat at Ogdensburg.

The pressure of events which compelled the United States to clarify its stand on Greenland applied with equal force to other potential or actual base areas in the Atlantic, particularly to those which had been leased from Britain. Contrary to the relatively smooth course of American negotiations with Canada on such matters, the attempt to work out the details of the leased bases occasioned extraordinary delays and difficulties between London and Washington. At the root of much of the misunderstanding was the American contention that the new base facilities in certain British possessions should theoretically be available to all the American Republics for the common defense of the hemisphere, but not to the armed forces of the United Kingdom because it was a belligerent. Not only was this a blow to British pride, but it dashed Britain's hopes of securing advantageous joint arrangements for the defense of areas such as the Caribbean. In reply to this latter argument Washington emphasized the view that such arrangements would invite German attack and do the British cause more harm than good.[44]

When to this standing difference were added new grievances in the shape of War and Navy Department demands for full jurisdiction and far-reaching rights within the base areas, British patience almost reached the breaking point. To complete the confusion the colonial governments were exasperated that London had not consulted with them sufficiently before coming to terms with Washington. In order to avoid a complete impasse it became necessary to establish in January, 1941, a special Base-Lease Commission in London. Prime Minister Churchill, to whom would fall the task of defending the eventual terms before the House of Commons, appealed to the American negotiators to moderate their demands. President Roosevelt, fearing that Congress would presently inquire about the delay, and in any case altogether averse to acquiring sovereignty over Britain's West Indian islands, urged speedy action. Good sense and mutual trust, spurred at the end by sharp realization that procrastination was helpful only to the enemy,

[42] *Moffat Diary* (*MS.*), April 24, 25, 1941.

[43] *Moffat Diary* (*MS.*), April 23, 1941. We have also used a letter of the Canadian Prime Minister to the President, April 24, 1941 (*Roosevelt Papers:* Secretary's File, Box 75).

[44] Memo of conversation between Mr. Welles and the British Chargé d'Affaires, Mr. Butler, January 4, 1941.

eventually brought agreement two days after Berlin enlarged the North Atlantic combat zone. Most of the concessions were, indeed, made by the British, many of them at the direct suggestion of Mr. Churchill himself.[45]

No time was lost in taking advantage of the agreement reached in London on March 27. While small numbers of American forces had already been despatched to some of the bases, the President now desired that additional reinforcements be sent at once, even though facilities and housing were far from complete. On April 7 he sought the Prime Minister's approval, therefore, for stationing additional forces in Newfoundland, Bermuda, and Trinidad, if necessary outside the leased areas. Mr. Churchill replied a day later: "Certainly, go ahead." On April 7 Secretary Stimson sent the President a list of the units which, after careful consideration of the defense requirements of the Atlantic bases, he had determined should be despatched. To his notation of approval Mr. Roosevelt added the words: "Hurry Bermuda. That is a necessary priority. Get planes there as soon as any place can be prepared." Having decided to enlarge the patrol zone and to intensify action within it, the President was resolved to move ahead with all possible speed to clear the decks for action, whether offensive or defensive.[46]

The last of the President's measures short of convoy escort was his proclamation of April 10, 1941, removing the Red Sea region from the list of combat areas forbidden to United States shipping since June, 1940.[47] This move was aimed not only at reducing the inordinate strain on British shipping generally, but specifically at getting matériel to the British forces for their last-ditch defense of Egypt and the Middle East. It had been under consideration by Mr. Harriman in London at least as early as March.[48] It was the latter's opinion that one obvious way to reduce the terrific pressure on Britain's pool of merchant vessels was to have the United States assume full responsibility for supplying the British forces in North Africa and the Middle East.[49] At one stroke this would eliminate the wasteful process by

---

[45] Memo of conversation between Welles and Halifax, February 25; tel. to the President's Base-Lease Commission, March 8; tel. from the Commission, March 12; tel. from the President to Welles, March 24, 1941. The text of the final agreement of March 27, 1941, is printed in *Documents on American Foreign Relations*, III, 215-28. Mr. Churchill put particular store by the fourth clause of the Preamble, which embodied for him the true spirit of the agreement and saved it from being a "capitulation." On the general subject, see Watson: *Chief of Staff: Prewar Plans and Preparations*, 477-79.

[46] Tel. to Winant, April 7; tels. from Winant, transmitting Churchill's approval, April 8, 9; tel. from Harriman to Hopkins, April 8 ("First base Bermuda; second base Iceland."); memo of Secretary Stimson to the President, April 8, 1941 (*Roosevelt Papers: Secretary's File, Box 74*); Watson: *Chief of Staff: Prewar Plans and Preparations*, 477-94.

[47] Text in *Documents on American Foreign Relations*, III, 654-55.

[48] Tels. from Hopkins to Harriman and to the Prime Minister, March 19; tel. from Harriman to Hopkins, April 10, 1941.

[49] Engaged with Mr. Forrestal in coördinating Lend-Lease supplies with production in the United Kingdom, Harriman recommended the same plan for supplying other distant areas, such as Singapore, Colombo, and Capetown, and urged that British naval

which munitions for these areas were often carried from the United States to the United Kingdom and transshipped thence to their final destination.

The idea was well received at the American end. On April 5 Mr. Oscar Cox, who had helped write the Lend-Lease bill and was now a member of Harry Hopkins's staff, completed a study of ways and means by which Lend-Lease supplies could be shipped to the Middle East without violating the neutrality legislation. Among several possibilities the simplest and most practical called for a redefinition by the President of the 1940 combat zone so as to reopen the Arabian and Red Seas to American shipping.[50] This solution was strongly advocated by Secretary Morgenthau, who had been in frequent touch with Sir Arthur Salter, Mr. Churchill's newly arrived representative for shipping problems. Mr. Roosevelt was quickly won over and at his press conference on April 4 hinted that a proclamation opening up these waters to American shipping awaited only the completion of British mopping-up operations against the defeated Italians in East Africa and Ethiopia.[51]

Accordingly, the groundwork had already been completed when Mr. Harriman cabled Harry Hopkins on April 10 stating that the London War Cabinet had appointed a committee to develop plans for Basra as a base for the delivery of aircraft, particularly from America, and that the Cabinet wanted to know if the President would approve American flag vessels carrying planes to that area.[52] In a few hours, replied Hopkins, an important message on the subject would be sent to London.[53] The President indeed discerned no further dangers of combat in the Red Sea area and at once issued his proclamation removing it from the list of forbidden zones. Actually American vessels were at that time already en route to Middle Eastern ports. By the end of May forty cargo ships and fifty tankers were assigned to this shuttle service. Thus began the process by which this country gradually took over the supply of Britain's forces in Egypt.[54]

With these decisions—of equal significance for the outcome of the Battle of the Atlantic and for the ultimate defense of Egypt and the Middle East—President Roosevelt exhausted for the moment the reservoir of expedients

---

vessels in United States ports take on the supplies and equipment they needed "in exactly the same manner as if they were units of our own fleet."

[50] Memo of Oscar Cox to Harry Hopkins: "Shipments under the Neutrality Act," April 5, 1941 (*Morgenthau Diaries, MS.,* Vol. 386, pp. 148 ff.).

[51] Mr. Roosevelt's concern for Italian civilians in East Africa manifested itself in a telegram to Mr. Churchill, April 3, 1941, transmitting suggestions from Count Sforza for taking psychological advantage of Mussolini's defeat. The Prime Minister's answer of April 4 is printed in *The Grand Alliance,* 87.

[52] Tels. from Harriman to Hopkins, April 10, 14, 1941.

[53] Tel. from Hopkins to Harriman, April 11, 1941.

[54] Tels. from the President to the Prime Minister, and from Hopkins to Harriman, May 27, 1941; memo of the President to Admiral Emory S. Land, May 10, 1941 (*F.D.R.: His Personal Letters,* II, 1152-53).

which he felt public opinion and the country's resources permitted him to invoke. The totality of these alternatives to naval protection of convoys he outlined to Mr. Churchill in a message of April 11 as follows:

1. We propose immediately to take the following steps in relation to the security of the Western Hemisphere, which will favorably affect your shipping problem. It is important for domestic political reasons which you will readily understand that this action be taken by us unilaterally and not after diplomatic conversations between you and us. Therefore, before taking this unilateral action I want to tell you about the proposal.

2. This Government proposes to extend the present so-called security zone and patrol areas which have been in effect since very early in the war to a line covering all North Atlantic waters west of about west longitude twenty-five degrees. We propose to utilize our aircraft and naval vessels working out from Greenland, Newfoundland, Nova Scotia, the United States, Bermuda, and the West Indies, with possible later extension to Brazil if this can be arranged. We will want in great secrecy notification of movement of convoys so our patrol units can seek out any ships or planes of aggressor nations operating west of the new line of the security zone. We will immediately make public to you position aggressor ships or planes when located in our patrol area of west longitude twenty-five degrees.

3. We propose to refuel our ships at sea where advisable. We suggest your longer shipping hauls move as much as possible west of new line up to latitude of the Northwest Approaches.

We have declared Red Sea area no longer a combat zone. We propose sending all types of goods in unarmed American flag ships to Egypt or any other nonbelligerent port via Red Sea or Persian Gulf. We think we can work out sending wheat and other goods in American ships to Greenland or Iceland through the next six months.

We hope to make available for direct haul to England a large amount of your present shipping which is now utilized for other purposes. We expect to make use of Danish ships very soon and Italian ships in about two months.

4. I believe advisable that when this new policy is adopted here no statement be issued on your end. It is not certain I would make specific announcement. I may decide to issue necessary naval operations orders and let time bring out the existence of the new patrol area.[55]

3. Limits and Limitations of Nonbelligerency

The President's request that Mr. Churchill refrain from any public statement about the measures outlined in the April 11 message makes it plain that he thought his program represented the ultimate in practicable American assistance to Britain at this stage. Both initially, in devising the strategic program, and afterward, in selecting the means to carry it out, Mr. Roosevelt and his advisers continually found themselves confronting the limitations inherent in the concept and practice of nonbelligerency. On the one hand, Great Britain's steadily worsening situation on land as well as on sea

[55] Tel. from President to Prime Minister, April 11, 1941.

called for ever more strenuous and risky measures of assistance if catastrophe was to be avoided. On the other, the Administration deemed it impossible, in view of the relatively slow pace of American arms production, the unreadiness of the Army, and the inability of a one-ocean Navy to police both the Atlantic and Pacific, to do for Britain what its desperate situation demanded.

Moreover, even if these hard economic and military facts had not beset him, the President felt, rightly or wrongly, that his freedom of action was rigidly circumscribed throughout the spring of 1941 by the allegedly unfavorable climate of American public sentiment, particularly on the issue of escorting convoys. Opinions, both inside and outside the President's official family, differed widely on the cause and cure of the disease which, all admitted, afflicted the nation's rearmament effort. Still more lively was the controversy over the degree of public support for measures adequate to assure the flow of munitions to Britain and its allies. Since these factors determined the course which Mr. Roosevelt had just outlined to Mr. Churchill, a glance at each is essential to an understanding of how American policy developed prior to June 22, 1941, when the German invasion of the Soviet Union afforded at least temporary relief from the dilemma.

By mid-April it had already become painfully apparent that the Arsenal of Democracy, for which the President had so eloquently pleaded at the end of 1940, was not producing sufficient weapons to support the objectives of the Administration's policy. This conclusion became inescapable when, thanks to the enactment of Lend-Lease, it finally became possible to estimate what the American arsenal would have to produce. At this date the statisticians of the Office of Production Management calculated that the total cost of providing the armed forces of the United States, Britain, and other foreign beneficiaries the matériel they professed to require in the calendar years 1941 and 1942 would amount to some fifty billion dollars. In submitting this estimate, Mr. Stacy May, its chief author, observed that it would place an unprecedented burden on American industry and that the goal could not be reached at the existing production rate. Billions of dollars of additional capital would be required at once for the construction and expansion of defense plants. Immense increases in the existing labor force would have to be envisaged. Serious shortages in certain critical materials had already emerged. Finally, "some curtailment of consumer income or the production of durable nondefense goods or both" was essential.[56]

Massive as was this first unified estimate of the dollar cost of assuring the security of the United States, the British disasters of April and May caused a steady upward revision until, at the end of May, Secretaries Stimson and Knox were proposing that the March total be trebled. It was, of course, impossible to contemplate such a goal unless the nation were prepared to

[56] *Industrial Mobilization for War*, I, 133 ff. .

convert at once to a full wartime economy. The prospects for this were faint indeed in the spring of 1941. Most business executives persisted in their conviction that while rearmament was necessary, it could and should be carried on with minimum disruption of the normal economy.[57] For labor, also, if strikes and work stoppages are sound criteria, the urgency of the task was not such as to require notable sacrifices. The first walkouts in defense plants had occurred in January, 1941, before the echoes of the President's appeal for an all-out industrial effort had altogether died away. They broke out sporadically throughout the winter and spring and, in some instances, such as the Allis-Chalmers strike at Milwaukee, dragged on for many weeks. The climax of all these woes occurred at the beginning of April, when Mr. John L. Lewis chose to call out his soft coal miners. For the rest of the month the country was obliged to carry on in the face of a threat that not merely specific defense industries but the entire economy would be paralyzed by a coal shortage.[58]

These and a profusion of less spectacular symptoms of normalcy continued to manifest themselves in the face of the deepening crisis in the Atlantic and overseas. Tempers grew shorter, but production still lagged. Labor accused management of undue concern for profits. Management charged the Administration with undue partiality toward labor. Congress talked ominously of legislation to outlaw strikes in defense industries. Everybody was sure that someone else was responsible for the failing effort to produce, and the final charge usually took the form of indiscriminate castigation of the public's lamentable refusal to face the facts. Mr. Knudsen, the target of many critics, stormed with fine impartiality against both labor and management. The nation had "got to get over this strike epidemic we have had since January." It was "no time to ask for quotations on the defense of the United States. . . . This job cannot be handled with money. It must be handled with our hearts."[59] By mid-April, according to columnists whose statements had often in the past reflected the views of important Administration officials: "Every informed person in Washington agrees that the result may be tragedy if the all-out American effort is put off much longer."[60]

Certainly this statement summed up with complete accuracy the views of men such as Knudsen, Stimson, and Knox. If it was also intended to include the President, there is but slight evidence that he was preparing to attack the roots of the problem, described by Mr. William L. Batt, one of Knudsen's ablest deputies, as the "fiction that we can perform a miracle of industrial transformation without hurting anybody."

[57] *Public Opinion Quarterly,* V (1941), 493.
[58] *Stimson Diary (MS.),* February 27, 28, March 19, April 2, 4, 1941; O. T. Barck, Jr.: "Labor Disputes and Defense" (*Events,* June, 1941).
[59] *Vital Speeches,* VII (1941), 410 ff.
[60] Alsop and Kintner in the *New York Herald Tribune,* April 23, 1941.

In the Office of Production Management (OPM), created in January, 1941, to provide stronger leadership for the national rearmament program, authority continued to be divided between Mr. Hillman and Mr. Knudsen, with the President himself as the final court of appeal. In consequence the initial misgivings entertained by Secretary Stimson and others about the efficiency of the new organization were all too quickly confirmed. Within three months of its birth OPM had already begun to manifest "the same overlapping of functions, multiplication of liaison groups, delays, contradictions, and general confusion" that had hastened the demise of the Advisory Commission.[61] Though aware of this, the President, hostile as ever to centralized authority in the OPM, opposed any reorganization of the defense production agency and manifested scant sympathy with proposals for a thorough investigation of the defense effort. When Senators Byrnes and Barkley urged him not to resist the passage of Senator Harry S. Truman's resolution calling for a continuing Senate investigation of the national defense program, Mr. Roosevelt agreed. But his reasons appear to have been largely political. It was wise "to keep the investigation in friendly hands."[62]

Left to itself, the OPM did manage to make some progress in overcoming its worst faults and in groping its way toward more centralized authority. By May the system of priorities had reached a point where manufacturers were being compelled, not merely encouraged, to fill defense orders first. Not until the summer, however, was the President at last prevailed upon to permit a major reorganization of the OPM, the first of several efforts to prolong the life of an agency which was chronically sick and which ultimately had to go the way of its predecessor.[63]

The same reluctance to resort to drastic remedies characterized Mr. Roosevelt's handling of the strike epidemic and the relations between labor and management in defense industry. In view of the President's record over the years, and of what Secretary Stimson delicately described as his "sensitivity to the danger of antagonizing labor," it is no surprise that he was unalterably opposed to legislation outlawing strikes in defense plants.[64] Mr. Knudsen himself shared the view that such legislation was unnecessary and unenforceable.[65] What really disturbed Knudsen and others who believed that, in the existing emergency, production was more important than the grievances of labor or management, was Mr. Roosevelt's disinclination to admit the need for any significant change in the established procedures for settling labor disputes. Not until March 19, after Knudsen and Stimson

[61] *Industrial Mobilization for War,* I, 101; cf. Donald M. Nelson: *Arsenal of Democracy* (New York, 1946), 118-20.

[62] Letter of the President to Senator Sherman Minton, February 27, 1941 (*Roosevelt Papers:* Secretary's File, Box 73).

[63] *Industrial Mobilization for War,* I, 91 ff.

[64] *Stimson Diary (MS.),* March 19, 1941.

[65] *Vital Speeches,* VII (1941), 410 ff.

had repeatedly stressed the necessity, did the President agree to establish a special agency to handle such disputes. Even so, the new National Defense Mediation Board could not take jurisdiction until the normal conciliation agencies, the Department of Labor and the National Labor Relations Board, had certified their inability to achieve a settlement.[66]

Although Secretary Stimson did finally induce the President to let him serve a twenty-four-hour ultimatum in the critical Allis-Chalmers strike, after which period the Navy would take over the plant and Army troops would maintain order, Mr. Roosevelt was generally reluctant to employ rough treatment when special interests clearly obstructed production, or even, as in the Allis-Chalmers strike, when Stimson was convinced of Communist inspiration.[67] He did not, to be sure, compel Mr. Knudsen to adopt Secretary Morgenthau's formula for ending labor disturbances—that is, in effect, to withhold defense contracts from manufacturers who did not abide by the Federal Labor laws. Yet he apparently sympathized with Morgenthau's view that there were "higher considerations than quick delivery."[68] Similarly, he was not easily induced to forget his long-standing hostility to monopolies, even after critical shortages of aluminum became manifest early in 1941.[69]

Lastly, for one who must have sensed that the strife between labor and management was but a specific reflection of a general and widespread failure to grasp the magnitude of the task and the lateness of the hour, Mr. Roosevelt moved with notable circumspection in preparing the public at large for the prospect of sacrifice or discomfort. In April, it is true, he surprised his advisers by establishing the Office of Price Administration and Civilian Supply. Appointed to head it was Mr. Leon Henderson, who in February had first presented the President with a blueprint of the powers and functions of such an agency.[70] Even moderate rationing and a mild degree of price control would probably have occasioned some grumbling in the spring of 1941, but either would have had a salutary effect in relieving shortages in critical materials as well as in bringing home to the American people the realities of the situation. Unhappily the first effect of the new agency was to enhance confusion, thanks to a protracted controversy with the OPM over control of civilian priorities. The President permitted this feud to continue into the late summer before finally intervening to end it. It was to be later still before Americans began to feel the first real pinch and to experience some slight difficulty in procuring new refrigerators, cars, and tires.[71] It may also be noted, anent Mr. Roosevelt's distaste for knocking

[66] *Stimson Diary* (*MS.*), March 7, 19, 1941.

[67] *Stimson Diary* (*MS.*), April 2, 3, 4, 1941.

[68] *Morgenthau Diaries* (*MS.*), April 4, 6, 16, 18, 1941 (Vol. 386, pp. 3 ff.).

[69] *Stimson Diary* (*MS.*), February 14, 1941.

[70] *Morgenthau Diaries* (*MS.*), February 17, April 11, 1941 (Vol. 373, p. 134; Vol. 388, p. 138); *Stimson Diary* (*MS.*), April 3, 1941.

[71] *Industrial Mobilization for War*, I, 90 ff.

official heads together, that another family row, this time between the Secretaries of State and of the Treasury, still prevented the imposition of general foreign funds control and impeded effective coördination of the various measures which came to be known collectively as economic warfare. The President inquired from time to time about progress in this important field, but was unwilling to force the issue. Early in May Mr. Hull and Mr. Morgenthau, with the assistance of Attorney General Jackson, were finally able to report agreement on the text of a memorandum recommending the creation of an Economic Defense Committee. But some months were to elapse before the final emergence of the Board of Economic Defense. Unwilling to the last to make a choice between rival claimants, Mr. Roosevelt ended by vesting authority over the new board in Vice President Henry A. Wallace.[72]

Except for a few measures, of which a notable one was the creation in the late spring of the Office of Civilian Defense under Mayor La Guardia of New York, it seems clear that Mr. Roosevelt had done but little since the Arsenal of Democracy speech to challenge public apathy or kindle the imagination of the American people over the rearmament program. It was almost inevitable that the civilian defense agency, established for the praiseworthy purpose of stimulating "affirmative patriotism," should have encountered general indifference and have been denounced in the isolationist press as just another "phony,"the latest example of the President's "campaign of deception, of false alarms, and of cunning manipulation of fears and emotions."[73]

The manifest survival within the Administration itself of wishful thinking that the ever higher and more distant goals of national rearmament might yet be reached without hurting anybody very much testifies to the virtual impossibility of fully rearming a democratic nation in the absence of the psychology begotten of actual war. Remarkable progress (considering the point of departure) had been achieved in rearming the country and in assisting the British, but progress was not nearly rapid enough to keep pace with the commitments made in Lend-Lease, which themselves had continually to be increased to meet the demands imposed by the latest string of Nazi successes. There was much truth in the resigned judgment expressed by the Secretary of War at the end of April: "Considering that we are not at war and cannot invoke war measures, conditions are better than one might expect."[74]

[72] *Morgenthau Diaries* (*MS.*), February 14, 18, 26, March 3, May 5, 1941 (Vol. 372, p. 208; Vol. 373, pp. 218 ff.; Vol. 376, p. 83; Vol. 378, pp. 144 ff.; Vol. 395, pp. 27 ff.) ; *Berle Diaries* (*MS.*), February 26, 1941. We have also used an undated note of February from the President to Mr. Hull, and a memo of the President to Hull, Morgenthau, and Attorney General Jackson, dated February 26, 1941 (*Roosevelt Papers:* Secretary's File, Box 78).

[73] *Stimson Diary* (*MS.*), April 17, May 27, 1941; *Chicago Tribune,* May 26, 1941.
[74] *Stimson Diary* (*MS.*), May 1, 1941.

The checks imposed on the President's eagerness to accede to Mr. Churchill's pleas by the simple lack of the material means to do so were matched, in his own mind at least, by uncertainty as to whether American public opinion at this stage of the conflict would back him in the dangerous course of action which he believed the circumstances required. An apparently genuine if somewhat rash indication of Mr. Roosevelt's despair of convincing his fellow countrymen of the dangers confronting them is provided by his response to a letter from Norman Thomas, one of the most capable of the isolationists and one whose opposition the President respected. Thomas had warned the President against getting the country into war "crabwise" by the protection of convoys or "similar devices." If he did the country might follow him but their hearts would not be in it. The reply read:

> The trouble with 99% of us Americans—who are not very different from other people in the world—is that we think of modern war in terms of the conduct of war in 1812, or in 1861, or in 1898. It takes several generations to understand the type of "facts of life" to which I refer. Very few people really came to understand the lessons of the World War—even though twenty years went by.
>
> The lessons of *this* war constitute such a complete change from older methods that less than 1% of our people have understood. I wish you could be here for a week sitting invisibly at my side. It would not be a pleasant experience for you because you would get a shock every ten minutes.[75]

The accuracy of this estimate of the public's understanding of the somber situation and, therefore, of its willingness to contemplate warlike measures, including escort of convoys, is open to serious doubt, even if allowance be made for the exaggerated pessimism of the above statement. Though the President was skeptical of their value, the verdicts on mass opinion registered by the innumerable polls were by no means uniformly unfavorable to the Administration view that measures involving far greater risk of war were now required if British defeat in the Atlantic, North Africa, and the Middle East were to be avoided. The number of Americans who believed it more important for the United States to see Britain through than to keep out of war rose slowly but steadily during the winter until it reached 68 percent in May. By that time an even larger majority (73 percent) professed to believe that an Axis victory would constitute, if not an immediate military threat, at least a "serious danger" to the United States.[76]

Against the President's contention that the vast majority of his fellow-countrymen had not yet grasped the "facts of life" about the current conflict may also be noted the growing dissent from the so recently cherished belief that this war was merely another sordid struggle for power into which

[75] Letter from Norman Thomas to the President, May 12; the President's reply, May 14, 1941 (*Roosevelt Papers:* Secretary's File, Box 82).

[76] *Public Opinion Quarterly,* V (1941), 481-85. On the President's attitude toward opinion polls see *F.D.R.: His Personal Letters,* II, 1158.

America must not let itself be tricked. In April, 1937, approximately two out of every three Americans took this speciously realistic line. By April, 1941, the proportion was well on the way to being reversed. Hard-boiled Americans were embracing instead the fashionable proposition that the country would enter the war, willy-nilly, at some stage before it ended. A bare majority professed this belief after the fall of France. By May, 1941, the number had grown to 85 percent.[77] It is true that the majority of Americans persisted in a not very surprising desire to have their cake and eat it, too, and responded to the point-blank question whether or not they favored immediate American entry into the war with an overwhelming negative. Yet it was the judgment of experts in the analysis of public opinion that, after making due allowance for the shadings represented by personal values and interests, the American people were at this juncture prepared to accept the harsh fact that if Britain could not win without American participation, America would have to intervene.[78]

To those who were really convinced of the truth of this judgment, the vital factor in the equation of public opinion once again appeared to be Mr. Roosevelt's own leadership. Pointing to the great victory he had achieved with the Arsenal of Democracy speech, which had solidified opinion in favor of the Lend-Lease program, the all-outers clamored throughout the spring for another dramatic display of the President's capacity for leadership. The state of public opinion was, they insisted, ripe for the effort, but Mr. Roosevelt was deliberately failing to catalyze the elements of opinion by his refusal to make some dramatic gesture such as a major speech on policy. Secretary Stimson summed up this sentiment when in mid-April he warned his chief that "without a lead on his part it was useless to expect the people would voluntarily take the initiative in letting him know whether or not they would follow if he did take the lead."[79]

The President's estimate of public opinion and the effect it had on the conduct of his program may well be open to the unfavorable interpretation which the Secretary of War had formed and which led to a temporary coolness in his relations with the White House. Nevertheless, the difficulties which Mr. Roosevelt actually encountered on the specific issue of naval escort of convoys were sufficiently serious to exonerate him of the charge of being merely the victim of an attack of nerves. In a real sense the Administration's highly effective tactics in presenting the Lend-Lease bill as certain to assure a British victory without serious risk of American involvement in hostilities had boomeranged. As its enemies had predicted throughout the long debate,

[77] *Ibid.*, p. 476.

[78] *Public Opinion Quarterly*, V (1941), 483; Professor Hadley Cantril of Princeton University in *The New York Times*, May 11, 1941.

[79] *Stimson Diary (MS.)*, April 22, 1941; Stimson and Bundy: *On Active Service in Peace and War*, 369 ff. See also Basil Rauch: *Roosevelt, from Munich to Pearl Harbor* (New York, 1950), 323-28.

the measure had no sooner become law than its proponents began to clamor for all the dangerous expedients required to deliver Lend-Lease materials safely across the Atlantic. "I realized from the first," Senator Wheeler was quoted as saying, "after the Lend-Lease bill was passed, that the next step would be that the warmongers in this country would cry for convoys, and everyone recognizes the fact that convoys mean war."[80]

Amid a flood of rumor that the Administration was on the point of ordering the recently organized Atlantic "Support Force" to commence escorting operations, the interventionists and isolationists resumed their battle. The Committee to Defend America by Aiding the Allies, now under more daring if less stable leadership, promptly came out in favor of naval escort. Colonel Donovan, fresh from his adventurous mission to Britain, the Balkans, and the Middle East, painted a dark picture of the odds Britain faced and called on his fellow countrymen to provide the requisite assistance at all costs. In a notable address (March 27) before the Inter-American Bar Association at Havana, Attorney General Jackson denounced nineteenth century legal argument that a neutral must treat all wars alike and that all warring powers are possessed of equal rights. Mr. Jackson warmly defended the Administration's aid-to-Britain program not only on earlier concepts of international law, but on the Kellogg-Briand Pact and, finally, as a wholly legitimate application of the doctrine of self-defense.[81]

True to form, the America First Committee denounced its rival's plea for immediate naval escort as just another of the Administration's trial balloons. This time, moreover, the opposition did not confine itself to a battle of words. On March 31, 1941, Senator Charles W. Tobey of New Hampshire and Congressman Harry Sauthoff of Wisconsin introduced into Congress a joint resolution to prohibit the use of American merchant vessels to transport cargo to belligerents and of American naval craft to escort them.[82]

This was a move which the President had long dreaded and which he had been at great pains to avoid having written into the Lend-Lease Law. However favorably he might construe the verdict of the opinion polls, he was clearly more influenced by his own personal estimate of public sentiment, and, above all, by the words and actions of the isolationists in Congress. The Tobey Resolution therefore abruptly applied the brakes to whatever enthusiasm the President had generated for a direct challenge to his opponents. Through Mr. Thomas Lamont word was quietly passed to Clark Eichel-

[80] *Christian Science Monitor*, April 2, 1941.

[81] Walter Johnson: *Battle Against Isolation* (Chicago, 1944), 210 ff. Donovan's report of March 26 is printed in *Vital Speeches*, VII, 386 ff. Mr. Jackson's speech is printed in the *American Journal of International Law*, April, 1941. The October, 1941, issue of the same journal contains a rebuttal by Professor Borchard of Yale University, the gist of which was that "international law has no criteria for passing on moral issues."

[82] Text in *The New York Times*, April 1, 1941. See Beard: *President Roosevelt and the Coming of the War*, 72 ff.

berger, the new head of the Committee to Defend America, "not to wave the red flag of immediate convoy."[83] Five weeks later Mr. Eichelberger was still complaining to Secretary of the Interior Harold Ickes that his appeals to the White House had been "without result."[84] The reasons for the silence are clear enough. Mr. Roosevelt had become increasingly uncertain of his hold over public opinion and correspondingly reluctant to risk his leadership in a test of vital issues either in foreign policy or domestic rearmament. The details may safely be left for consideration in the context of the actual measures he took or failed to take as the so-called "May Crisis" set in. Though one may agree with interventionist critics that the dilemma which confronted Mr. Roosevelt throughout the rest of the spring was partly of his own making, it was real enough to him and goes far to explain the halting and secretive fashion with which, prior to June 22, 1941, he developed his strategy to frustrate the apparently impending victory of the Axis powers.

4. The "May Crisis"

With the threat of the Tobey Anti-Convoy Resolution hanging over him, and in genuine anxiety about the degree of public approval he might expect, the President had begun in early April to consider with his chief military and civilian advisers the ways and means to implement the program outlined to the Prime Minister in the "momentous" message of April 11. In defining the mission of United States naval vessels and aircraft assigned to operate in the enlarged Atlantic patrol zone he was confronted with the most significant of the many decisions he was required to make. He could choose between two strategic plans, both of which had been discussed with the British during the recent staff conversations in Washington.[85] The more dynamic of the two, Hemisphere Defense Plan No. 1, not only encompassed the minimum objectives outlined to Mr. Churchill, but went well beyond them. It provided for denial of the newly defined waters of the hemisphere to Axis vessels and aircraft by force if necessary. It frankly envisaged naval escort for merchant shipping along the Atlantic sea lanes as far as the twenty-sixth meridian of longitude. This was the plan initially selected by the President when, early in April, he authorized Admiral Stark to issue orders transferring three battleships, an aircraft carrier, four cruisers and supporting destroyer squadrons from the Pacific to the Atlantic. Without this vital

---

[83] Letter of Thomas Lamont to Clark Eichelberger, April 8, 1941 (*Roosevelt Papers: Secretary's File*, Box 81). The words quoted were Mr. Lamont's. On the President's high opinion of Mr. Lamont's services see his letter to Vice President Wallace, April 26, 1941 (*F.D.R.: His Personal Letters*, II, 1142).

[84] Letter of Secretary Ickes to the President, May 13, 1941 (*Roosevelt Papers: Secretary's File*, Box 73).

[85] Kittredge MS. study on *United States-British Naval Coöperation;* "Digest of Hemisphere Defense Plans" (*Pearl Harbor Attack*, V, 2293 ff.); Conn MS. study on *Hemisphere Defense Policy*, Chapter III, 44 ff.

increment of force Admiral King would be unable to escort shipping effectively over so extended an area.[86]

Before these orders could be carried out, however, various considerations had induced Mr. Roosevelt to reëxamine the arguments in favor of the more cautious course of action set forth in the alternative Hemisphere Defense Plan No. 2. Secretary Hull's long-standing opposition to the transfer of any significant part of American naval power from Pearl Harbor was given new force by the conclusion on April 13, 1941, of the Soviet-Japanese Neutrality Pact. This was certainly not the moment, argued the Secretary of State, to make a move which Foreign Minister Matsuoka might easily interpret as a sign of weakness. Possibly of equal force in raising doubts in the President's mind was the report that the USS *Niblack*, which had recently undertaken an armed reconnaissance mission to Iceland, had depth-bombed a German submarine, thereby raising concretely the danger of an incident involving war with the Axis powers, or lending substance to the isolationist charge that the President sought to provoke war.

With all this in mind Mr. Roosevelt summoned his advisers to a meeting at the White House on April 15 to make the final choice between operating orders to the Navy to carry out full-fledged escort of shipping within the confines of the hemisphere, and new orders, prepared by Admiral Stark, calling only for intensified naval patrolling. The Secretary of War stood firmly by his earlier conviction that naval escort was the only sure solution and urged the President not only to authorize it but to explain his decision to the American people. Secretary Morgenthau warned that it would in any case be impossible to maintain secrecy and that to try was only to court future embarrassment. Although Admiral Stark wavered, Secretary Knox argued that "if the Navy were turned loose, they would clean up the Atlantic in thirty days." Harry Hopkins likewise threw his support in favor of whatever course of action was necessary to get supplies safely to Britain. Most influential, perhaps, on the side of caution, apart from Mr. Hull, was the reasoning of General Stanley D. Embick, whose professional advice was made available to the President by special arrangement.[87]

The upshot of the debate was the President's decision to abandon, for the time being at least, plans for forthright naval escort of merchant shipping as far as longitude 26° west. Calling Admiral Ernest J. King to Hyde Park, whither he had gone to receive the visit of the Canadian Prime Minister, Mr. Roosevelt on the week-end of April 19-21 countermanded his previous directive and instructed the Admiral to conduct his operations in accordance with Hemisphere Defense Plan No. 2. American escort vessels were still to

[86] Kittredge MS. study on *United States-British Naval Coöperation;* testimony of Admiral Stark (*Pearl Harbor Attack*, V, 2292 ff.).

[87] *Stimson Diary (MS.)*, April 15, 1941; Conn MS. study on *Hemisphere Defense Policy*, Chapter III, pp. 47-51; Watson: *Chief of Staff: Prewar Plans and Preparations*, 386-91; Sherwood: *Roosevelt and Hopkins*, 291 ff.

assume that the entry of Axis ships into the waters of the Western Hemisphere was motivated by possible "unfriendly interest." However, such vessels were not to be deliberately pursued and destroyed on sight. Instead, American craft were to follow Axis warships along the shipping lanes, broadcasting their positions to the British and generally rendering their operations as hazardous as possible within the limits imposed by the rule that American ships were not to shoot first."[88]

On April 24, 1941, the day on which Admiral King's forces began to operate on this basis, the President also gave his approval to the companion directive which Secretary Stimson had prepared to guide Army commanders in the base areas to which American troops had been sent (Newfoundland, Bermuda, Trinidad). As originally submitted to the President this directive was quite as forceful as the initial orders to Admiral King. It stated bluntly that Axis vessels "which approached within twenty-five miles . . . of any British possession on which a United States base is located, will be viewed as having the intention immediately to attack such possessions and so threaten the safety of United States bases." Such Axis craft were first to be warned. If they failed to heed the warning they were to be attacked forthwith by "all available means."[89] Subsequently, as a result of Secretary Hull's intervention, the Army's orders, like the Navy's, were toned down. Even so, the directive which actually went out on May 10, 1941, was a strongly worded document.[90]

Still more convincing evidence of the caution with which Mr. Roosevelt was now proposing to carry out his strategy in the Battle of the Atlantic is provided by yet another change of the presidential mind. The orders issued early in April to transfer important units of the Fleet from Pearl Harbor to the Atlantic were abruptly canceled. Without additional forces the Atlantic Fleet was incapable of successfully carrying out even the less extensive patrol operation. "What will be done about convoying," wrote Admiral Stark to the bewildered Admiral Kimmel in Hawaii, "is pure guess," though the Chief of Naval Operations warned the Commander in Chief of the Pacific Fleet to be "mentally prepared" for the eventual transfer. This proved shrewd advice. For the next three weeks the transfer of the Fleet was debated as never before since the issue had arisen in the early stages of the conflict. Those who had lately insisted on strong action in the Pacific, complained Stark, now clamored for all-out action in the Atlantic.

[88] Letters of Admiral Stark to Admiral Kimmel, April 19, 26, 1941 (*Pearl Harbor Attack*, V, 2292 ff., and XVI, 2163-65); Watson: *Chief of Staff: Prewar Plans and Preparations*, 390-91. We have also used the detailed account in the Kittredge MS. study on *United States-British Naval Coöperation*.

[89] Text in *Roosevelt Papers:* Secretary's File, Box 74.

[90] Watson: *Chief of Staff: Prewar Plans and Preparations*, 384. The text of the order of May 10, 1941, is given, *ibid.*, 383. On the changes urged by Mr. Hull we have used *Stimson Diary (MS.)*, May 10, 1941, and Stimson's letter to Hull, May 12, 1941.

With the receipt on April 24 of Mr. Churchill's considered reply to the President's program of April 11, still other tasks were suggested for the already overextended Atlantic Fleet.[91] Conceding some progress in dealing with the submarine menace around the Northwest Approaches, Mr. Churchill nevertheless warned that the U-boats were already operating out of Lorient and Bordeaux as far west as the thirtieth meridian, and predicted that they would soon push even farther into the waters of the Western Hemisphere. The area west of longitude $35°$ and south of Greenland was the immediate danger spot. Unescorted ships in the Newfoundland region offered the enemy a comparatively easy target. A new source of threat to the shipping lanes from the South Atlantic and Mediterranean had likewise arisen from the heavy pressure currently exerted by Berlin on Spain and Portugal. Should these countries give way, Britain would find itself obliged to attempt occupation of their Atlantic islands or else stand by while the Germans added them to their own list of available bases. Concluded the Prime Minister: "It would be a very great advantage if you could send an American squadron for a friendly cruise in these regions at the earliest moment."[92]

A few hours later the Prime Minister, having just learned the nature of the patrol operations under Hemisphere Defense Plan No. 2, again cabled the White House his relief and satisfaction over a decision which had "almost entirely covered the points" made in his earlier message. He particularly welcomed the significant news that the President had authorized the use of Lend-Lease funds to commence immediate construction of United States bases in Scotland and Northern Ireland.[93] It may be observed parenthetically that the Roosevelt Administration had spared no effort to influence the Eire Government to abandon its position of neutrality and provide the hard-pressed British desperately needed bases in Eire's ports. In addition to regular channels for stressing to Dublin America's growing alarm over developments which threatened its own as well as Eire's security, special emissaries like Ambassador Winant, Colonel Donovan, and Mr. Wendell Willkie all made efforts to soften Mr. De Valera, but all confessed total failure to move that proud and sensitive statesman. Not only did he refuse, publicly at least, to take sides between the democracies and the Germans, but he complained in his St. Patrick's Day broadcast (March 17) that he was being blockaded by both sides. Under the circumstances Washington, where

[91] Tel. from the Prime Minister to the President (Churchill: *The Grand Alliance,* 143-45). A preliminary message on the April 11 program was sent by Mr. Churchill to the President on April 16 (*ibid.,* 142).

[92] The contemporary German plans for intensifying attacks on Atlantic shipping are set forth in *Fuehrer Conferences,* 1941 (1), 50 ff. (Conference on April 20, 1941). It is to be noted that Admiral Raeder still regarded Hitler's concessions in favor of more aggressive tactics insufficient.

[93] Tel. from the Prime Minister to the President, April 24, 1941 (Churchill: *The Grand Alliance,* 145-46).

this remark created a painful impression, saw no alternative to refusing Eire both vitally needed armament and highly desirable wheat. Both might have been made available under Lend-Lease if Eire's policy could have been described as contributing to the national security of the United States.[94] Mr. Roosevelt's personal atittude toward this vexed problem is perhaps best revealed by a paragraph in his letter to Representative James F. O'Connor of Montana: "When will you Irishmen ever get over hating England? Remember that if England goes down, Ireland goes down too. Ireland has a better chance for complete independence if democracy survives in the world than if Hitlerism supersedes it."[95]

In the light of these developments it doubtless seemed to Mr. Churchill only a matter of time before the President would authorize the United States Navy to escort Allied merchant shipping at least within the limits of hemisphere waters. Mr. Roosevelt, however, was still pursuing a cautious course and insisting that his aides do likewise. But once the decision against naval escort was firmly made and the Atlantic Fleet actually commenced instead its intensified patrolling activities (April 24), it was possible to break the secrecy in which the program had thus far been shrouded. Something of the alternatives to convoy protection which had finally been adopted was revealed to the public by the Secretary of the Navy's speech of April 24. It is noteworthy, however, that when Mr. Knox submitted his text to the President for approval prior to delivery, the latter deleted two "brash sentences," one of which described certain Administration measures as "acts of war," while the other stated that "we are now at war with the Axis powers."[96] Secretary Hull's address of the same date, before the American Society of International Law, effectively set forth the country's stake in the Battle of the Atlantic. Yet on the crucial point of how to assure the safe delivery of American munitions to the British, Mr. Hull took refuge in generalities. "Such aid," he proclaimed, "must reach its destination in the shortest possible time and in maximum quantity. So ways and means must be found to do this."[97]

[94] Among the mass of materials on Irish-American relations for this period, the following contain the essentials: tels. from Winant, March 11, 26, April 6, May 26; despatch from Gray (Dublin), February 6; tels. from Gray, May 1, 17; tels. to Gray, April 10, 25; memos of conversation between Berle and the Irish Minister (Mr. Brennan), January 29, and between Welles and Brennan, March 20, April 29, May 15, 1941. We have also used items on Irish problems in the *Donovan Papers* (MS.), Folder 11. On British policy toward Eire at this point see Churchill: *The Grand Alliance*, 725, 729, 731-32.

[95] Letter of the President to James F. O'Connor, May 19, 1941, in reply to the Congressman's letter of May 6 (*Roosevelt Papers:* Secretary's File, Box 79), now printed in *F.D.R.: His Personal Letters*, II, 1159.

[96] *Morgenthau Diaries* (MS.), April 22, 1941 (Vol. 390, pp. 230 ff.); memo of the President to Knox, April 21, 1941 (*F.D.R.: His Personal Letters*, II, 1144-45). The pertinent portions of Knox's speech are printed in *Documents on American Foreign Relations*, III, 43 ff.

[97] Hull: *Memoirs*, II, 941-43.

Taking their cues from these speeches, reporters besieged the President with pointed questions at his press conference the following day. Despite the skillful evasion of the Chief Executive, the newsmen contrived to ferret out bits and pieces of his secret and gave him a most uncomfortable few minutes of questioning on the essential differences between escorting and patrolling. In reply to this question, Mr. Roosevelt observed:

I think some of you know what a horse looks like. If, by calling a cow a horse for a year and a half, you think that makes the cow a horse, *I* don't think so. You can't turn a cow into a horse by calling it something else; calling it a horse it is still a cow. Now this is a patrol, and has been a patrol for a year and a half, still is, and from time to time it has been extended, and is being extended, and will be extended—the patrol—for the safety of the Western Hemisphere.[98]

The general effect of the President's elliptical language, of which the above excerpt is characteristic, was to confirm the suspicions of his enemies that he was courting war in the Atlantic, without reassuring his friends that the goods would really be delivered to Britain.

So determined had the President now become to avoid further discussion of the escort issue that he was even unwilling to accept the normally welcome support of the titular head of the Republican Party. When Mr. Willkie in a Pittsburgh speech exhorted the Administration to take whatever steps its military experts believed necessary to insure that supplies to Britain should not be sunk and, further, to tell the American people what these steps would be, he received the same cryptic advice earlier given to Clark Eichelberger. Word was sent to him, this time through Mr. Lauchlin Currie, that "our experts were not at all sure that convoys were the answer; that the problem was tougher than in 1918, and that perhaps what was needed was more aerial observation and more scattering of ships." Mr. Willkie presently relapsed into silence lest he seem to "snatch leadership from the Commander in Chief to whom he had sworn fealty."[99] The President's Democratic friends were left equally in the dark as to his real views. To Senator Josiah Bailey of North Carolina, who wrote to express his anxiety lest escort lead to war, the President replied in terms as disingenuous as those he had used in his press conference:

In regard to convoys, I wish to God I could make out what all this full-dress debate they are talking about in the Senate relates to. Why not change the subject to the maintenance by the American Army and Navy of a guaranteed aircraft route to Central Africa in 1951?

[98] Text in the *Public Papers and Addresses*, X, 132-38. For a harsh criticism of the President's performance see Beard: *President Roosevelt and the Coming of the War*, 82 ff., 420 ff. Cf. Rauch: *Roosevelt, from Munich to Pearl Harbor*, 318-20.

[99] Memo of Lauchlin Currie to the President, April 25, 1941 (*Roosevelt Papers*: Secretary's File, Box 73), now printed in *F.D.R.: His Personal Letters*, II, 1146. Letter of Secretary Ickes to the President, May 13, 1941 (*Roosevelt Papers*: Secretary's File, Box 73).

This whole thing is, of course, a matter of military and naval strategy in its relationship to the defense of the Western Hemisphere. . . . Frankly I do not think it is much of a subject for laymen like you or I [sic] to waste much time about in public.[100]

Perhaps Mr. Roosevelt held the failure of the Tobey Anti-Convoy Resolution in Congress at the end of April as proving the wisdom of his cautious tactics. Secretary Stimson had urged him to take a clear-cut stand, either by supporting Congressman Wadsworth's proposal to introduce into the House a resolution authorizing escort of convoys or at least by permitting the Tobey Resolution to reach the floor of the Senate.[101] Mr. Roosevelt shied away from these suggestions, preferring to have the resolution die in the Foreign Relations Committee and personally approving Secretary Hull's letter to that body stating that "if there were no other reasons against consideration of the proposed Resolution, it is manifest that its passage would be misunderstood abroad."[102] Thus vanished Stimson's hope that the death of the Anti-Convoy Resolution in Congress would provide a mandate for immediate naval escort.

Meanwhile, unless the Atlantic Support Force were built up by significant additions from the Fleet at Pearl Harbor, it was likely to prove unequal to the task of patrolling the Atlantic, not to mention the protection of convoys. The President had himself complained to Mr. Stimson of the extent of the new area to be covered and of how "thinly spread out he was." Stimson and Knox, bitterly disappointed by the reversal of the order of early April, now redoubled their pressure on Mr. Roosevelt and Mr. Hull to authorize the transfer of a sizable detachment from Admiral Kimmel's Pacific Fleet. Their basic argument remained the futility of continuing to maintain so heavy a preponderance of American naval power in the Pacific where, even if war did break out, the United States planned to maintain a defensive posture for some time. The weight of naval power belonged in the Atlantic where all authorities, including the President himself, agreed that the ultimate decision rested. "I believe," wrote Mr. Roosevelt to Mr. Churchill, "that the outcome of this struggle is going to be decided in the Atlantic and unless Hitler can win there he cannot win anywhere else in the world in the end."[103]

To bolster their established position Stimson and Knox could, of course, adduce a number of new arguments drawn from the alarming record of Nazi successes in the Mediterranean as well as in the Atlantic during the course of April. The probability that the Germans would presently establish themselves at Dakar or in the Atlantic islands, or both, posed a grave threat

---

[100] Letter of the President to Senator Bailey, May 13, 1941 (*Roosevelt Papers: Secretary's File,* Box 81), now printed in *F.D.R.: His Personal Letters,* II, 1156-57.

[101] *Stimson Diary (MS.),* April 22, 25, 1941.

[102] *Roosevelt Papers:* Secretary's File, Box 73 (April 29, 1941); Hull: *Memoirs,* II, 943-44.

[103] Tel. from the President to the Prime Minister, May 10, 1941. The entire message is now printed in *F.D.R.: His Personal Letters,* II, 1148-50.

not only to British survival in the Battle of the Atlantic, but to the ultimate safety of the Western Hemisphere. In an all-out effort to gain their point the two Secretaries enlisted the services of all and sundry who seemed likely to exert influence on their stubborn State Department colleague: old personal friends of Mr. Hull, like Norman Davis, as well as Dean Acheson, Robert Sherwood, Harry Hopkins, and others. When all these failed to break the impasse, it was decided to solicit the views of British and Commonwealth leaders. The first response (from the military) supported the view that at least six capital ships should be retained in the Pacific. Subsequently, however, Prime Minister Churchill overruled his subordinates and advocated the transfer of the American Navy's main strength to the Atlantic.[104]

But Mr. Hull soon marshaled fresh arguments to justify his basic conviction that the Fleet at Pearl Harbor, strength unimpaired, constituted a significant deterrent to any resumption of Japan's southward advance. Inasmuch as he was at this juncture eagerly anticipating news of Tokyo's reaction to the proposals which Admiral Nomura had forwarded to his Government, the Secretary of State begged the President to delay. It seemed most ill-advised to transfer warships to the Atlantic at the very moment when Tokyo might be deciding to renounce its commitment under the Tripartite Pact to enter the war on Germany's side if the latter became involved in hostilities with the United States. If this happy issue came to pass, Mr. Hull would breathe easier over the danger of incidents in the Atlantic.[105]

Although the Japanese reply of May 12 brought no such assurance, the mere fact that the Imperial Government had made a seemingly conciliatory move finally brought Secretary Hull to agree to a transfer. Accordingly the solution of this long controversy was in sight. Characteristically, however, the President compromised between the extremes represented by Stimson and Hull and ordered a force consisting of three battleships, an aircraft carrier and appropriate supporting vessels to leave Pearl Harbor for the Atlantic. While this amounted to only about a quarter of the strength of the Pacific Fleet, it was a welcome addition to Admiral King's forces, strained as they were to carry out their assigned tasks. This time, moreover, the order stuck, and at the end of May the new contingent took its place in the ever-extending activities of the Atlantic patrol.[106]

In the course of the long-drawn debate on the transfer of these units from the Pacific to the Atlantic, Britain's position in the Mediterranean and

---

[104] A detailed record of this phase of the controversy is given in *Stimson Diary* (*MS.*), April 29, 30, May 1-14, 1941. See Stimson and Bundy: *On Active Service in Peace and War,* 386-87; Samuel E. Morison: *The Battle of the Atlantic* (Boston, 1947), 56-57; Watson: *Chief of Staff: Prewar Plans and Preparations,* 391. We have also used the exchange of letters between the President and Mr. Averell Harriman, April 10 and 22, 1941 (*Roosevelt Papers:* Secretary's File, Box 75).

[105] *Supra,* Chapter XI, Section 5.

[106] *Pearl Harbor Attack,* I, 122 ff.; V, 2112 ff.; XVI, 2163 ff.

North Africa had declined so catastrophically as, for the moment, to center American attention less on the convoy issue than on the disasters which might well lead to German attacks on Iceland, Dakar, the Canaries, and the Cape Verdes, and, thereafter, to possible attempts to launch an assault on the bulge of Brazil. For the first time since the summer of 1940 an Axis attack on the Western Hemisphere itself seemed both a real and a present danger. In some confusion and agitation Washington set about the task of sealing off the remaining chinks in the armor of the Western Hemisphere.

Iceland's fate had been a cause of concern ever since the Germans occupied Denmark in the spring of 1940. When, however, British and Canadian forces landed on the island in May of that year and succeeded in maintaining themselves, the alarm had gradually subsided.[107] Though it had been determined by the Washington staff conversations that United States forces should take over responsibility for Iceland from the British in the event of American entry into the war, Icelandic overtures, resumed in earnest in December, 1940, evoked little response from Washington prior to April, 1941.[108] At that time Berlin's extension of the war zone to Iceland and subsequent reports of German submarine and air activity there, as well as rumors of concentrations of German shipping and troops in Norway, reawakened latent fears of a Nazi attack. Washington's detached attitude changed abruptly.[109] Although Iceland lay beyond the Western Hemisphere, as defined by longitude 25° west, the USS *Niblack* was hastily despatched in early April on a mission of armed reconnaissance in Icelandic waters. Its subsequent engagement with a German submarine not only confirmed American suspicions, but marked, so far as known, the first hostilities between United States and Axis naval vessels in the course of the war. Mr. Roosevelt hastened to entrust Harry Hopkins and the American naval authorities with the reopening of negotiations with the Icelandic Consul General in Washington, Mr. Thor Thors. These continued throughout the spring and ultimately proved satisfactory to both sides. They were, however, conducted with such secrecy by the President's naval advisers that both Secretary Hull and the British Ambassador were long unaware of their purport.[110]

As in the case of Greenland, the President's objectives in Iceland were based on considerations of hemisphere defense, active as well as passive. In the category of active defense, American assumption of Britain's responsi-

---

[107] See *The Challenge to Isolation,* 429-35, 687-88.

[108] Memo from Berle to Hull and Welles, January 17; tel. to Kuniholm (Reykjavik), January 18; despatch from Kuniholm, February 7, 1941.

[109] Tels. from Kuniholm, May 10, and to Kuniholm, May 22; letter from Mr. Forrestal to Secretary Hull, May 31, 1941.

[110] *Stimson Diary (MS.),* April 16, 1941; Sherwood: *Roosevelt and Hopkins,* 290-91; memos of conversation between Mr. Hull and Lord Halifax, May 7, 1941; Hull: *Memoirs,* II, 945 ff.

bilities in Iceland, already agreed to in ABC-1 in case of war and set forth in the newly developed joint war plan, Rainbow V (May 14, 1941), would contribute enormously to ease the strain on the Royal Navy. Specifically, it promised early realization of the hope expressed by the President in his April 11 message to Mr. Churchill that it might be possible to send supplies to Greenland and Iceland in American ships. If United States forces replaced the British, the logical corollary would be escort by United States naval vessels of shipping (Icelandic and American, if not British) between American ports and Iceland.

Similarly, Iceland played an important role in the Administration's efforts to provide more effective ferry service for military aircraft between the United States and the United Kingdom. Secretary Stimson felt that the best solution of this problem was to have the United States Army take over and deliver the planes to the British at the new United States air base in Newfoundland. In broaching this plan to Mr. Churchill the President pointed out that "later and depending on developments we might be able to deliver them to your people in Iceland."[111]

While appreciating the advantages which possession of secure bases in Iceland would confer on the American effort to help the British, the President was plainly worried by the possibility that the Germans might secure a lodgment at Scoresby Sound in northeast Greenland (if they did not try instead to reach the bulge of Brazil). Secretaries Knox and Stimson were inclined to be skeptical of a German attempt on Greenland, at least at this time, but Mr. Roosevelt overruled them. "I think," he replied, "Germany will probably seek to get a definite foothold even if this foothold can only defend its own location."[112] Inspection flights from Iceland to Greenland were authorized at once and plans made for an expedition to Greenland in July. When it became apparent that the Navy had no vessels suitable for operations in Greenland waters, the resources of the Coast Guard were enlisted. On May 7, 1941, Secretary Knox announced that the transfer of the oceanic functions of the Coast Guard to the Navy had been orally authorized by the President and would soon be formalized in written

[111] Tel. from the President to the Prime Minister, May 29, 1941. The last paragraph of the lengthy message from which these words are quoted was written by the President himself longhand. A subsequent British request that American pilots be permitted to fly 50 heavy bombers from the United States all the way to England was rejected as beyond the limits of neutrality (memo of conversation between Welles and Lord Halifax, June 5, 1941). On the plane ferry service: *Stimson Diary (MS.)*, March 7, April 8, 11, 25, May 22, 1941; Winant: *Letter from Grosvenor Square*, 243. Closely related to this problem was the President's offer to Churchill, through General Arnold, of one third of the capacity for pilot training in the U. S. for the use of British trainees (tel. from the Prime Minister to the President, May 10, 1941). See also the President's letter to Secretary Stimson, May 28, 1941 (*F.D.R.: His Personal Letters*, II, 1161-62).

[112] Memo of the President to Secretaries Stimson and Knox on "Prevention of German Activity in the Scoresby Sound Region, Greenland," April 30, 1941 (*Morgenthau Diaries MS.*, Vol. 395, pp. 347-48).

orders.[113] On May 10 Mr. Roosevelt cabled Mr. Churchill: "Our patrols are pushing farther out into the Atlantic. I have just added all our heavier units of the Coast Guard to the Navy for the purpose of implementing that patrol. Other steps to strengthen that patrol will be taken soon."[114]

With respect to Iceland the termination of that island's ancient connection with the Danish crown on May 17, 1941, promised to obviate the complications encountered earlier by Washington in its negotiations with Greenland. The British Government was naturally delighted when at last President Roosevelt sounded out Mr. Churchill at the end of May. The Prime Minister replied in these words:

We cordially welcome your taking over Iceland at the earliest possible moment, and we will continue to hold ourselves and all our resources there at your disposal as may be found convenient. It would liberate a British division for defence against invasion or the Middle East. If it could be done in the next three weeks or less, or even begun, it would have a moral effect even beyond its military importance. You have only to say the word and our staffs can get to work at once.[115]

Unhappily for Mr. Churchill, his enthusiastic message of approval found the Administration utterly perplexed in trying to determine where the Nazis would next strike. As is now quite clear, Hitler had not changed his plans to attack the Soviet Union in June. He had therefore been obliged to renounce all hope of seizing the Azores or other Atlantic islands before autumn at the earliest, desirable though their possession might be for immediate intensified attacks on British shipping or for later long-range air attacks on the Western Hemisphere. Admiral Raeder had convinced him that his present military resources were insufficient to hold these islands even if they could be captured. Hitler, in turn, had refused Raeder permission for unrestricted attacks on shipping in waters of the Western Hemisphere, on the sound ground that to do so would be a mistake so long as President Roosevelt gave evidence of not having made up his mind on America's entry into the war.[116]

The United States Government had, however, no certainty as to the Fuehrer's decisions, despite the increasing evidence of the impending Nazi assault on Russia. As a result plans had to be hastily revived or improvised for the despatch of expeditionary forces to the Azores, Dakar, and northeastern Brazil.[117] In view of the inadequate Army forces available it was manifestly impossible, however, to implement more than one of these operations. Indeed, to mount even one before autumn would involve the greatest

[113] Memo of the Chief of Naval Operations to the Commandant of the Coast Guard, ca. May 7, 1941 (*Morgenthau Diaries MS.*, Vol. 395, pp. 345 ff. and pp. 353 ff.). See *Pearl Harbor Attack*, XVI, pp. 2163 ff.

[114] Tel. from the President to the Prime Minister, May 10, 1941.

[115] Tel. from the Prime Minister to the President, May 29, 1941. See also Churchill: *The Grand Alliance*, 139, 149-50.

[116] *Fuehrer Conferences*, 1941 (1), 65 ff. (Conference of May 22).

[117] *Stimson Diary (MS.)*, April 16, 1941; Conn MS. study on *Hemisphere Defense Policy*, Chapter III, pp. 64 ff.; Hull: *Memoirs*, II, 956.

difficulty. For a time no one in Washington could be certain whether steps would have to be taken to despatch American forces to Iceland, to the Azores, or to Brazil. While the President seriously contemplated drafting a message to Congress declaring West Africa within the scope of the Monroe Doctrine, Ambassador Caffery was urgently instructed to sound out the Brazilian Government on its willingness to invoke the emergency mutual defense arrangements discussed at the staff conversations in 1940 between Brazilian and American officers.[118]

The reluctance of the Lisbon Government to entertain any American proposal for protective custody of its island possessions until it was convinced of the imminence of a German attack has been noted earlier in this narrative.[119] Dr. Salazar showed no disposition to recede from this position despite Washington's evident anxiety. From Brazil, too, the initial response was noncommittal. The Brazilians, moreover, made a point of the impossibility of coöperating in the execution of plans so long as they were ignorant of their purport, and so long as Washington withheld the aircraft or munitions they needed in order to do their share.[120] As the probability that Darlan would commit the Vichy Government to a program of full collaboration with the Germans ushered in the final stages of the May Crisis, Mr. Roosevelt made up his mind that the Atlantic islands, and next in line South America, were the greatest danger points. Accordingly he directed Admiral Stark to be ready in thirty days to transport a force of twenty-five thousand men to the Azores.[121]

This presidential directive, which, like so many of its recent predecessors, was presently to be abandoned, is of interest chiefly as an illustration of the paralysis which gripped official Washington at the height of the May Crisis. In the darkest hour for the democratic cause since the summer of 1940, Mr. Roosevelt seemed no longer capable of selecting a course of action and staying with it. "The situation," complained Secretary Stimson, "has been very trying for the last few days . . . everybody asking what is going to be done and no way of finding out whether anything will be done."[122]

Among those who most earnestly sought to fathom what was in the President's mind was Secretary Morgenthau. Unable to elicit the information directly, Morgenthau approached Harry Hopkins, who had for some time been a guest at the White House and who might be expected to have the facts. At lunch with Hopkins on May 14 the Secretary of the Treasury confided his own conclusion, reached only in the course of the previous week,

[118] Tels. from Caffery (Rio de Janeiro), May 20, June 4, 1941. The War Department also sent Lt. Col. Matthew B. Ridgway, who had participated in the staff conversations with Brazil, to discuss the matter with Brazilian authorities. See also the President's memo to Mr. Hull, May 31, 1941 (*F.D.R.: His Personal Letters,* II, 1162).

[119] *Supra,* Chapter XII, Section 2.

[120] Tel. from Caffery, May 20; tel. to Caffery, May 22, 1941.

[121] Letter of Admiral Stark to Admiral Kimmel, May 24, 1941 (*Pearl Harbor Attack,* V, 2113); Watson: *Chief of Staff: Prewar Plans and Preparations,* 116-17, 333.

[122] *Stimson Diary (MS.),* May 10, 1941; Sherwood: *Roosevelt and Hopkins,* 292 ff.

that "if we are going to save England we would have to get into this war." Hopkins vouchsafing no response to this, Morgenthau shifted his tack: "I said that instead of the President trying in some way to declare us in the war, how about doing something internally first?" As examples the Secretary cited the declaration of a full national emergency, the creation of a Cabinet post for supply, and the establishment of a home-defense organization. At first he felt that Hopkins thought well of these possibilities, but upon reflection framed the following judgment: "I think that both the President and Hopkins are groping as to what to do. They feel that something has to be done but don't know just what. Hopkins said that the President has never said so in so many words, but he thinks the President is loath to get into this war, and he would rather follow public opinion than lead it."[123] No estimate so nearly accords with the existing evidence as to the President's real attitude after the passage of the Lend-Lease Act. None so readily explains his failure thus far to answer Mr. Churchill's appeal of May 3 for immediate American intervention in the war, an appeal provoked by British reverses in the Middle East and discussed at some length in the preceding chapter. None so surely points to the "solution" which the President finally worked out in the two weeks preceding his fireside chat of May 27, 1941.

5. Unlimited National Emergency

The fortnight from May 14 to May 27, 1941, the day when the oft-postponed Pan American Day address was firmly set for delivery, was probably as difficult an interval as Mr. Roosevelt had lived through since the outbreak of the war. The dilemma in which he had been caught throughout the spring was never sharper. The dreary news of British reverses in Crete was climaxed by the shocking report that the *Bismarck* had sunk HMS *Hood*. Breaking the unwritten law that had so long restrained the British press, a London newspaper appealed openly for American entry into the war.[124]

Adolf Hitler, anxious to maximize the divisions in American public opinion and to do everything possible to queer the President's pitch, had issued orders to restrain the German Navy until Mr. Roosevelt's speech had been delivered. A Nazi submarine, presumably by inadvertence, had violated these orders and on May 21 torpedoed the American freighter *Robin Moor* in the middle of the South Atlantic. So long an interval elapsed before the survivors, left in open boats, reached shore and confirmed the barbarous character of the attack that the President could make no use of the incident in his forthcoming fireside chat. The most that Berlin contrived to do to

---

123 *Morgenthau Diaries* (*MS.*), Vol. 397, pp. 301A ff.
124 Reports of the President's difficulties in drafting his speech are typified by the comments of Pearson and Allen in the "Washington Merry-Go-Round," May 27, and in the syndicated column "Capital Parade," same date. On the engagement between the *Hood* and the *Bismarck,* see Churchill: *The Grand Alliance,* Chapter XVII. The President's reactions are outlined in Sherwood: *Roosevelt and Hopkins,* 294.

assist him was an authorization to Admiral Raeder to state, just before the speech, that American vessels carrying Lend-Lease materials were subject to attack according to international law. If escort vessels resisted such attack, "German forces would have to resort to armed force."[125]

Deprived of the help so often inadvertently provided by the enemy, and in his own words "more or less laid up" with a low-grade infection,[126] Mr. Roosevelt steadfastly kept his counsel in the face of a flood of advice, solicited and unsolicited, on the content of his coming speech. On one side were ranged the diminishing advocates of caution like Mr. Hull who, pessimistic to a point which seemed to some defeatist, still believed that an attempt to repeal the neutrality legislation would end in failure. "Everything," he lamented, "was going hellward."[127]

In the opposite camp were ranged by now most of the Cabinet. Secretary Stimson fairly bombarded the President with appeals for forceful words or, better still, for decisive action. With Mr. Roosevelt's approval Stimson himself had delivered a speech on May 6 calling for the immediate introduction of convoy protection. Shortly afterward he and Secretary Knox came out unequivocally for repeal of the neutrality legislation, thus provoking further charges that the Administration spoke out of both sides of its mouth at once. Secretary Stimson's final shot consisted of a draft resolution by Congress authorizing the President to resort to force, which he wanted Mr. Roosevelt to sponsor.[128]

Secretary Morgenthau, as previously noted, had also become a convert to the view that the United States ought to enter the war. Both he and Secretary Ickes appreciated the difficulty the President faced, as Ickes described it, in "cold-bloodedly" going to war with Germany. The least, however, that he felt justified in recommending to the President was that his May 27 address proclaim an unlimited national emergency. Attorney General Jackson, to judge from his conversations with Stimson and Ickes, concurred vigorously in a recommendation for drastic action of some sort by the President.[129] While Secretary of Commerce Jesse Jones refrained from offering precise suggestions on the content of the speech, he stated his belief that "the great majority of the people want you to take a positive position in the present situation. I believe they will follow you in whatever course you outline."[130]

[125] The draft of this planted interview with Raeder is given in the form approved by the Wilhelmstrasse, in *Fuehrer Conferences*, 1941 (1), 74 ff. Cf. *The New York Times*, May 26, 1941.

[126] Letter of the President to Admiral Leahy, June 26, 1941 (*Roosevelt Papers: Secretary's File, Box 75*).

[127] *Stimson Diary (MS.)*, May 27, 1941; Hull: *Memoirs*, II, 943 ff.

[128] *Stimson Diary (MS.)*, May 6, 24, 1941; *The New York Times*, May 7, 23, 1941; *New York World-Telegram*, May 23, 1941. See also Beard: *President Roosevelt and the Coming of the War*, 102.

[129] *Stimson Dairy (MS.)*, May 12, 1941.

[130] Letter of Jones to the President, May 27, 1941 (*Roosevelt Papers: Secretary's File, Box 73*).

Mr. Roosevelt apparently canvassed the views of his Cabinet at the meeting of May 23, preparatory to starting on the drafting process next day. No record of the discussion on this occasion has become available, but it is significant that several members of the Cabinet came away with a feeling that Mr. Roosevelt was hoping for an incident in the Atlantic which would free him from his dilemma. Mr. Stimson expressed anxiety "because the President shows evidence of waiting for the accidental shot of some irresponsible captain on either side to be the occasion of his going to war," when he ought to have been "considering the deep principles" which were at the bottom of the great issues confronting the world.[131] Writing to the President next day, Secretary Ickes expressed the opinion that "the Germans will not create an incident for us until Hitler is ready to strike, and then he will strike, incident or no incident. I know that we cannot cold-bloodedly go to war with Germany, but isn't there something we could do to clarify the issue, such as declaring a general emergency or announcing that all our Pacific Fleet had been ordered to go into the Atlantic? . . ."[132]

The charge of courting hostilities in the Atlantic, so frequently leveled at the President by his isolationist critics, gains in credibility when suggested by his firmest supporters and coworkers. It is altogether likely that in this difficult period the thought or even the hope of an "incident" at intervals crossed the President's mind. It is doubtful however, whether the idea was seriously or continuously entertained. Mr. Roosevelt took no advantage of the opportunity provided in April by the encounter between the USS *Niblack* and a German U-boat. Nor was he to capitalize to the full on the sinking of the *Robin Moor* when the detailed report of her destruction was revealed in June, though it must be admitted that by then Mr. Roosevelt had every reason to suppose that his dilemma would be resolved by Hitler's determination to attack Russia. Until more conclusive evidence comes to hand, therefore, the record of Mr. Roosevelt's caution, coupled with Harry Hopkins's guess that the President was "loath" to get into war, suggests that his hope of a shot by an irresponsible captain expressed a fleeting mood of despair rather than a consistent objective or planned course of action.

On May 24 the President commissioned Robert E. Sherwood and Judge Rosenman to compose the first draft of the fireside chat. Contrary to inveterate habit he gave them no guidance on content or form. Even from Harry Hopkins the drafters got no suggestions except the presumption that the President wanted to end his address with a proclamation of unlimited national emergency.[133] When Sherwood and Rosenman had completed a first draft, they discussed it with Mr. Welles and Mr. Berle, who were sent to the White House by Secretary Hull. To Berle the speech seemed "calculated to scare the daylights out of everyone," but not much else. Even after

---

[131] *Stimson Diary (MS.)*, May 23, 1941.

[132] Letter of Secretary Ickes to the President, May 24, 1941 (*Roosevelt Papers: Secretary's File, Box 73*).

[133] Sherwood: *Roosevelt and Hopkins*, 296 ff.

he had himself gone over the draft and discussed it with Sherwood, Rosenman, Welles and the President—even, indeed, after the latter had rewritten
a large part of it—Berle observed that "the principal problem which is still
unsettled is whether the President proclaims a national emergency and goes
into the whole business of really heavy preparation. It is obvious now that
the German tactic is to keep us clear of this by every means they can."[134]

Up to the very last moment the text was repeatedly altered at the suggestion of Cabinet officers and others. Secretary Stimson pleaded for inclusion
of an announcement of the forthcoming arrival in the Atlantic of the ships
detached from the Pacific Fleet. Mr. Hull not only vetoed this suggestion
but experienced difficulty in bringing himself to recommend the proclamation of unlimited national emergency. This had come at the end to constitute the "real highlight" of the approaching speech.[135] The best the weary
Chief Executive could hope, after seeing his words through at least six versions, was that every one of its authors would find in it something he liked.
To Mr. Churchill the President a few hours before his address confided his
belief that the speech "went further than I thought was possible even two
weeks ago," and his hope that it would receive "general approval from the
fairly large element which has been confused by details and that it will even
enable Hitler to see the simple facts."[136] To the American press Mr. Stephen
Early, the President's secretary, observed: "I think you can say that by Wednesday morning there will be no longer any doubt as to what the national
policy of this Government is."[137]

On the evening of Tuesday, May 27, 1941, while Communist antiwar
pickets plodded up and down the sidewalks in front of the White House, the
President took his plunge. He spoke for some three quarters of an hour from
the East Room. His guests were the Ambassadors and Ministers of the Latin
American Republics and Canada; his audience, one can hardly doubt, a
very large proportion of the adult population of the United States, together
with as many others elsewhere in the world as could somehow manage to
reach a radio. In all, the White House estimated eighty-five million listeners.

As was incumbent on a President who had made no major speech on
policy for almost five months, Mr. Roosevelt launched his fireside chat with
a résumé of the measures he had taken in the face of the "first and fundamental fact," that the European War had developed precisely as Hitler intended it should, into a war "for world domination." Of this review it is
sufficient to remark the President's reasoned and conciliatory efforts to
answer critics who still doubted the wisdom or necessity for all the measures
already adopted. It was only after he had recapitulated the recent developments which had brought this war "to the brink of the Western Hemisphere

---

[134] *Berle Diaries* (MS.), May 26, 1941; Sherwood: *Roosevelt and Hopkins,* 297;
Rauch: *Roosevelt, from Munich to Pearl Harbor,* 344-46; Hull: *Memoirs,* II, 942.
[135] *Berle Diaries* (MS.), May 29, 1941.
[136] Tel. from the President to the Prime Minister, May 27, 1941.
[137] Quoted in the *Christian Science Monitor,* May 27, 1941.

itself" that Mr. Roosevelt went to the heart of the matter. It then became his task to attempt clarification of the vital point in all this reasoning, the point which he himself believed had eluded most of his fellow citizens, namely, that America's security was already gravely endangered and could only be adequately defended by the strategy of anticipating attack.

To this thesis the President devoted his best powers of lucid argument. "Control or occupation by Nazi forces of any of the islands of the Atlantic would jeopardize the immediate safety of portions of North and South America . . . and therefore the ultimate safety of the continental United States itself." That Hitler's forces had thus far failed to achieve their objective, he went on, was to be explained by their inability to obtain control of the seas, thanks to continued British resistance. If Great Britain fell, the Germans would "close in relentlessly on this hemisphere." If, on the other hand, the Axis powers failed to gain control of the seas, "they are certainly defeated." That explained "why they are risking everything they have, conducting desperate attempts to break through the command of the ocean."

Proceeding to reveal the blunt truth that the present rate of Nazi sinkings of merchant ships was "more than three times the capacity of British shipyards to replace" and "more than twice" the current combined British and American output, Mr. Roosevelt saw only two means of meeting the peril: "speeding up and increasing our great shipbuilding program" and "helping to cut down the losses on the high seas." Concluding this phase of the argument, he reminded his audience that he had

. . . said on many occasions that the United States is mustering its men and resources only for the purpose of defense—only to repel attack. I repeat that statement now. But we must be realistic when we use the word "attack"; we must relate it to the lightning speed of modern warfare. . . .

Anyone with an atlas, anyone with a reasonable knowledge of the sudden striking force of modern war, knows that it is stupid to wait until a probable enemy has gained a foothold from which to attack. Old-fashioned common sense calls for the use of strategy which will prevent such an enemy from gaining a foothold in the first place.

Having thus appealed for comprehensive public understanding of the necessity for a strategy which to him and to his chief advisers had virtually ceased to be a matter of debate, the President reached the climax of his message. Enunciating the national policy he proposed to follow in support of the strategy he had been justifying, Mr. Roosevelt was forceful, if not specific:

Our patrols are helping now to insure delivery of the needed supplies to Britain. All additional measures necessary to deliver the goods will be taken. Any and all further methods or combinations of methods which can and should be utilized are being devised by our military and naval technicians who, with me, will work out and put into effect such new and additional safeguards as may be needed.

I will say that the delivery of needed supplies to Britain is imperative. I say this can be done; it must be done; it will be done.

After this it proved difficult for the speaker to maintain his pace. Turning briefly to the domestic scene, Mr. Roosevelt mildly admonished the American people on the unimpressive fashion in which they had acquitted the duty of rearming the nation. "Your Government has the right to expect of all citizens that they take part in the common work of our common defense." Labor and, more especially, capital were dealt sharper rebukes. Both were reminded that the "future of all free enterprise—of capital and labor alike—is at stake." Both were warned that "this Government is determined to use all its powers to express the will of its people, and to prevent interference with the production of materials essential to our nation's security." From what might well have been a decided anticlimax, Mr. Roosevelt saved himself by the solemn words with which he announced the "highlight": "Therefore, with profound consciousness of my responsibilities to my countrymen and to my country's cause, I have tonight issued a proclamation that an unlimited national emergency exists and requires the strengthening of our defense to the extreme limit of our national power and authority."[138]

No one was more pleased and surprised at the enthusiastic reception accorded this address than its author. Mr. Sherwood has noted the President's delight in the fact that 95 percent of the telegrams which he pored over before retiring that night were favorable, whereas he had doubted whether he could expect more than an "even break."[139] Days later he was still congratulating himself on the unexpected vindication of his severely criticized sense of timing. Writing to close personal friends he explained that "it has been possible, as you know, for me to carry the country along slowly, but I think surely, and last week's speech met with far more approval—I should guess at least seventy-five or eighty per cent—than if I had given it even two weeks before."[140]

If, in view of all his last-minute doubts and misgivings, Mr. Roosevelt himself could express undisguised elation over the immediate results, there is no need to document the favorable domestic reaction to the fireside chat. There was, to be sure, a measure of disappointment among those who had hoped the President would be precise in defining the measures by which the Axis was to be defeated and Britain saved. If considerations of security prevented such definition, there was no good reason for the President's failure to specify how he proposed to use his new powers under the unlimited national emergency to spur the pace of rearmament. It was confidently expected by the interventionists, however, that these deficiencies would shortly be remedied by action rather than by words. Even Secretary Stimson, who felt

---

[138] The complete text of the address and of the proclamation of unlimited emergency are printed in *Public Papers and Addresses,* 1941, pp. 181 ff., and in *Documents on American Foreign Relations,* III, 48 ff., 754 ff. On the President's definition of "attack," see Beard: *President Roosevelt and the Coming of the War,* 135.

[139] Sherwood: *Roosevelt and Hopkins,* 298.

[140] Letter of the President to Arthur and Faith Murray, June 2, 1941 (*Roosevelt Papers:* Secretary's File, Box 81).

slightly let down after hearing the speech and noted how it had been "soft-ened down" in delivery, went to bed much relieved. Mr. Roosevelt was still weak on strikes and the labor situation, but on aid to Britain and on free-dom of the seas his speech had been "all right and very praiseworthy."[141]

Significantly, the isolationists were generally gratified that the speech had not been worse. Extremists like Senator Nye commented in characteristic fashion that the "Roosevelt war is surely progressing."[142] Yet the antiwar group in Congress, some thirty-five members of which had immediately after the address met in conclave to determine their course of action, emerged to issue a hopeful statement. They were encouraged, they said, to carry on the fight against war "because the President has not yet been won over by the war party," nor had he quite closed the door on millions of voters "who had preserved their faith in his pre-election pledges."[143]

In general Congress was considerably baffled as to what the speech actually portended. Many members thought it significant that there was no specific reference to escort of convoys or to repeal of the Neutrality Law, and not a single word about Japan. Opinion on the meaning of the proclamation of unlimited emergency was divided. Senator Taft was convinced it was meaningless. The President had had, since September, 1939, all the emer-gency powers he could legally exercise. Senator Carter Glass, on the other hand, was glad that Mr. Roosevelt had proclaimed the full emergency. "I hope," he added, "that we will protect every dollar's worth of stuff that we send to Great Britain and that we will shoot the hell out of anybody who interferes."[144]

Overseas comment, in turn, illustrated the wide variety of constructions the President's words could be made to bear. London consoled itself for the absence of a war declaration or an announcement of convoy protection by assuming that the speech was meant to forecast decisive action.[145] Rome took its cue from Mussolini's remarks to Ciano. Admittedly, thought the Duce, the speech was "a very strong document, even though it is not clear as to plans of action." Privately Mussolini inveighed against the President—"never in the course of history has a nation been guided by a paralytic"—but such brutal notes were not allowed to appear in the controlled Axis press.[146] The objective of Axis propaganda continued unchanged: to maxi-mize disunity in the United States and to forestall as long as possible the formulation of specific plans of action against themselves.

Accordingly, it must have been a matter of self-congratulation to the dic-tators that the very morning after the fireside chat evidence from the highest source apparently justified their tactics. At his press conference of May 28

[141] Stimson Diary (MS.), May 27, 1941.
[142] Quoted in PM, May 28, 1941.
[143] New York Herald Tribune, May 29, 1941.
[144] New York Herald Tribune, May 29, 1941.
[145] Mallory Brown in the Christian Science Monitor, May 28, 1941.
[146] Ciano Diaries, May 28; H. B. Matthews in The New York Times, May 28, 1941.

the President's replies to reporters, who eagerly sought to learn the concrete intentions behind the previous night's brave words, spread consternation among those who had turned off their radios the night before in the conviction that uncertainty was over. Mr. Roosevelt was quoted as stating that he had no plans to ask Congress to repeal the neutrality legislation, or to institute naval escort of shipping which, he implied, was outmoded anyway. Asked what he would do if his appeal to labor and management to compose their differences failed, he turned off the question as "iffy." To complete the debacle of interventionist hopes, the President explained that even his proclamation of unlimited national emergency could be made effective only through a series of executive orders reviving emergency laws enacted over a period of some fifty years. Quite frankly, he concluded, he had no plans for issuing such orders.[147]

The effect of his words and manner on this occasion was inevitably to vitiate much of the leadership offered the nation only a few hours earlier. Secretary Stimson, inveterate critic of Mr. Roosevelt's press conferences, lamented that this was "one of his worst and almost undid the effect of his speech."[148] Opinion analysts agreed with the Secretary's pessimistic judgment. The press conference remarks were being construed generally as capitulation to the reluctance of the minority to run real risks of war.[149]

Even Harry Hopkins was at a loss to explain why the President, who had gone to bed the night before in a mood of exultation over the success of his bid for popular support, should have awakened the next morning prepared to cast aside the gains of many weeks of inner struggle. Intimates were inclined to dismiss the whole performance as one more example of the President's "unaccountability," a lesson that all who worked with him were compelled to learn over and over again.[150] Those who remain dissatisfied with explanations based on vagaries of temperament, or on aberrations induced by illness and exhaustion, are entitled to inquire whether the fireside chat of May 27, 1941, was ever intended by its author to be a springboard for decisive action. It may rather have been the latest and most dramatic of the long series of trial balloons sent up by a President who, whether he preferred to lead or to follow public opinion, was certainly determined not to get too far ahead of it. That Mr. Roosevelt refrained from capitalizing on the success of his speech to repeal the Neutrality Law, to institute escort of convoys, or otherwise to extricate himself from his dilemma is perhaps truly explained by the prospect of at least temporary relief which would shortly be afforded by Hitler's invasion of the Soviet Union.

[147] Quoted by Turner Catledge in *The New York Times*, May 29, 1941.
[148] *Stimson Diary (MS.)*, May 29, 1941.
[149] Report of Mr. Alan Barth to Secretary Morgenthau: "Faltering in the Ranks" (*Morgenthau Diaries, MS.*, June 6, 1941, Vol. 405, pp. 443-44).
[150] Sherwood: *Roosevelt and Hopkins*, 299.

CHAPTER XV

Impasse in the Far East

1. Strange Interlude

Not even the huge stacks of Japanese and German documents that have come to light since the end of the Second World War suffice to solve the problem of Tokyo's policy during Yosuke Matsuoka's incumbency of the Foreign Office. In part, at least, the prevailing obscurity must be attributed to the unsystematic way in which Japanese business was conducted. It was not at all unusual for Japanese governments to be rent by dissension or for factions within the same administration to pursue widely divergent courses of action toward the same national objective. During January and February, 1941, Ambassador Grew had reported frequently and in full about the opposition to the pro-German policy of the Foreign Minister and there can be little doubt that criticism of Matsuoka was in fact widespread. Many influential figures, from the Emperor downward, had grave misgivings lest Tokyo's policy eventuate in hostilities with the United States. So far as one can detect, these feelings were particularly characteristic of naval, commercial and banking circles, though they were shared also by prominent politicians and even by certain military leaders. It may be assumed that most opponents of the official policy subscribed to the ultimate Japanese program to secure control of most if not all of East Asia, but they appear to have objected to the employment of force for attainment of the national ends and above all to have believed that to challenge Britain and the United States would lead only to disaster. What does not emerge from the existing evidence is the nature and extent of Matsuoka's following. One hears little of his supporters, yet he seems to have had enough backing to enable him to impose his own views at every crucial turn. It must be supposed, then, that powerful extremist groups, notably military groups, backed him to the hilt and that his opponents were literally in constant danger of annihilation.

In this situation it was impossible to counteract Matsuoka's policy except by secret moves. Such moves had, in fact, been initiated by the Prime Minister, Prince Konoye, in December, 1940, when he commissioned the two American clerics, Bishop Walsh and Father Drought, to carry a message to President Roosevelt and Secretary Hull.[1] Matsuoka had, it is true, taken a hand in this *démarche*, but the evidence is quite conclusive that once the two emissaries had departed, the Foreign Minister lost contact with the negotiation. Toward the end of January, 1941, Bishop Walsh and Father Drought had been received in the White House to transmit their message. Though Mr. Roosevelt and Mr. Hull were skeptical of the project, they decided that contact should be maintained and that any eventual proposals should be communicated to the State Department through the good offices of Postmaster General Walker. Some time in February, 1941, Mr. Tadao Wikawa, a Japanese banker who allegedly spoke for influential business interests, arrived in New York, to be followed a few weeks later by Colonel Hideo Iwakuro, supposedly a spokesman for the Japanese Army. These men had taken part in the original discussions with Bishop Walsh and Father Drought. Working together, the unofficial American and Japanese agents produced, early in March, the basic agenda for further conversations, which were conveyed promptly to Secretary Hull.[2]

The list of "principal items" was a long one, touching almost every aspect of Far Eastern political and economic relations, the Open Door policy, the China Incident, the Tripartite Pact, etc. The general tenor seemed to be that the United States and Japan, having ironed out their difficulties and closed out the China War, should work together to set up some kind of Monroe Doctrine for East Asia and top off their achievement with a grand meeting of President Roosevelt and Prime Minister Konoye at Honolulu. In a supplementary memorandum assurances were given that Wikawa had authority from Konoye and that the Emperor, the Privy Council, and Army and Navy leaders had agreed to a "conditional reversal of policy." If this decision became known in Tokyo, some of the leaders of this reversal would surely be assassinated. On the other hand, if the move succeeded, Matsuoka could be dismissed. Nomura himself was ignorant of the program and it was suggested that Secretary Hull abstain carefully from drawing him into these particular discussions.[3]

The atmosphere of this whole negotiation and the vagueness of the topics suggested were certainly not such as to inspire great hope. Both Mr. Roose-

[1] See above, Chapter X, Section 5.

[2] Memos of February 28 and March 5, 1941, by Father Drought, in the *Walker Papers* (*MS.*). A number of documents bearing on these negotiations may be found in *Pearl Harbor Attack*, XX, 4284 ff., and the episode is discussed in Hull: *Memoirs*, II, 989 ff. We have used also a State Department study of the organization and work of the Division of Far Eastern Affairs, by Harold F. Gosnell. See also the affidavit of Iwakuro in *Tokyo War Crimes Documents*, Defense Document No. 2589.

[3] Memo of March 7, 1941, in *Walker Papers* (*MS.*).

velt and Secretary Hull were profoundly distrustful of all statements originating in Tokyo. Speaking of the Japanese at this period, the President is reported to have said: "They hate us. They come to me and they hiss between their teeth and they say: 'Mr. President, we are your friends. Japan wants nothing but friendship with America,' and then they hiss through their teeth again, and I know they're lying. Oh, they hate us, and sooner or later they'll come after us."[4] It is understandable, then, that the White House and State Department should have continued on the course they had long since charted. Restrictions on trade with Japan were constantly expanded, the policy of aid to China was implemented as rapidly as possible, the Dutch were encouraged to resist Japanese economic and political demands on the Netherlands Indies, the Philippines were reinforced and Guam fortified, and preparations were made for combined action with the British and Dutch in the generally anticipated event of a Japanese move on Malaya or the Netherlands Indies.

At his initial conversation with Ambassador Nomura on February 14 President Roosevelt had suggested that it might be useful for his visitor and Secretary Hull to meet from time to time for discussion of pending issues. Evidently each of the two diplomats waited on the other to make the first move. It was to be three weeks before Admiral Nomura called on Mr. Hull at his apartment in the Carlton Hotel, "by an indirect arrangement based on the equal and joint initiative" of both parties.[5] The Secretary began by expressing appreciation for the efforts of some "responsible, fine and capable citizens" who were seeking to improve relations between the two countries, but hastened to add that he could treat official questions and problems only with the Ambassador and had therefore informed the "good people" from Japan that he could not confer with them unless the Ambassador assumed the responsibility. Nomura was patently mystified by these remarks: "he merely bowed each time I referred to the matter, without saying anything."

As a matter of fact, the Ambassador had nothing in particular to take up with the Secretary and the conversation was therefore of a desultory and inconclusive nature. Mr. Hull expatiated on his favorite theme, the dangers to a healthy political and economic order presented by Axis programs of military conquest and the great desirability of returning to liberal international trade policies. Nomura expressed assent but rejected the implication that any considerable segment of the Japanese public wanted war with the United States. Nor, he added, was the Konoye Government committed to any general program of military expansion, despite the utterances of the "politician" Matsuoka which, according to the Ambassador, were intended

---

[4] Quentin Reynolds: *Only the Stars Are Neutral* (New York, 1942), 170. Mr. Hull expressed similar distrust in a conversation with Lord Halifax on March 3, 1941.
[5] Memo by Mr. Hull (*Foreign Relations of the United States: Japan*, II, 389 ff., conversation of March 8, 1941). See also Hull: *Memoirs*, II, 989 ff.

primarily for home consumption. Tokyo's moves, he went on, had been provoked chiefly by American economic pressure. As for China, Japan would still welcome peace and was still willing to treat, even with Chiang Kai-shek. On what terms he did not say.

Secretary Hull thereupon switched the conversation to the Tripartite Pact and the obstacle it presented to any real improvement in Japanese-American relations. Nomura's meager comments did little to satisfy the Secretary's curiosity about the relations of Tokyo and Berlin. Even when asked point-blank whether reliance could be placed on recent Japanese assurances against an attack on Singapore or the Netherlands Indies, the Ambassador was only "fairly definite" in discounting the danger, provided the United States eschewed the imposition of further embargoes. Clearly the discussion left matters exactly where they were. From the Japanese records it is reasonably certain that Nomura had received no specific instructions and had no program for the settlement of issues between the two countries. Matsuoka was about to depart for Moscow and Berlin in the expectation of concluding agreements that ran completely counter to such a settlement. Meanwhile Konoye appears to have staked his hopes on the informal negotiations carried on in secrecy and as yet unknown to Nomura. Under the circumstances the Ambassador could do little more than mark time and evade concrete questions as best he could.

The President, had he realized the situation, would probably not have tried his own hand, as he did a week later when he had a second conversation with Nomura in Secretary Hull's presence. The rays of Mr. Roosevelt's personality failed to thaw his visitor any more than had the warmth of Mr. Hull's appeal to principle and morality. The President managed to turn the talk to China and to Japan's insistence on maintaining troops in that country to fight communism. He tried to persuade Nomura that the Communists of China were not communist in the same sense as the Russians, and that therefore Japan's fears were unwarranted. But the Ambassador had little to say on the subject and refused to be drawn beyond reassuring generalities with respect to other issues pending between his country and the United States. The conversation, then, was as indecisive as that between Mr. Hull and the Ambassador, and ended with none of the participants much wiser for what had been said.[6]

In the interval Father Drought was sending frequent reports of his dealings with Mr. Wikawa. The latter, he averred, was in constant communication with Prince Konoye, using a secret code. The chances that an agreement could be worked out seemed more promising than ever. Matsuoka's journey to Europe was merely a maneuver to keep the German door open and a device of Konoye's to get the Foreign Minister out of the way so

[6] Memo by the Secretary of State, March 14, 1941 (*Foreign Relations of the United States: Japan*, II, 396 ff.) ; see also Hull: *Memoirs*, II, 990 ff.

that he himself could exercise more direct control over the negotiations with the United States. Wikawa was urging upon his Government the necessity for a decision on the basic principles of the negotiation, in view of the fact that it was becoming more and more difficult to preserve secrecy in Washington.[7]

From all this one might conclude that, considering the good will of Konoye and of those acting for him, there was at least a fair chance of breaking the Japanese-American deadlock. But the memoranda that have survived reflect enthusiasm rather than political acumen. They concerned themselves, even at this early date, with the personnel to be sent to Honolulu for the spectacular conference that was to seal the reconciliation of the two great nations of the Pacific. They dilated on the grand project for a Far Eastern Monroe Doctrine, to be proclaimed jointly by Japan and the United States. By March 17, indeed, the two amateur diplomats had already worked out a preliminary draft setting forth, at some length, the bases for the negotiation of the final settlement.[8]

All aspects of these secret dealings are not known, but on or about March 25 Colonel Hideo Iwakuro arrived in New York. He was supposedly the spokesman of the Imperial Army, whatever exactly that may have meant, and appears to have been despatched from Tokyo at the request of Ambassador Nomura. Iwakuro evidently brought more recent instructions from home and at once initiated the Ambassador into the mysteries of the project. At his behest the Drought-Wikawa preliminary draft was drastically revised and then accepted by Nomura.

As finally presented to Secretary Hull on April 9 the Japanese program was far from justifying the sanguine forecasts of Father Drought.[9] Thus, with respect to the hoped-for disavowal of Japan's commitment under the Tripartite Pact there was nothing but the proposal that Tokyo honor its obligation to Germany only in the event of that power's being attacked by the United States. The solution suggested for the settlement of the China Incident was equally questionable: President Roosevelt was to request Chiang Kai-shek to negotiate peace on the following basis: (1) withdrawal of Japanese troops in accordance with a bilateral agreement between Japan and China, which was to take into account the need for joint defense against communism; (2) return to China of all its territory, without indemnities; (3) resumption of the traditional Open Door policy according to an interpretation to be agreed upon subsequently between Washington and Tokyo; (4) merger of the Chungking and Nanking regimes; (5) restriction

[7] Memos of Father Drought to Postmaster General Walker, March 11, 13, 1941 (*Walker Papers, MS.*).

[8] Memo from Father Drought to Mr. Walker, March 17, 1941 (*Walker Papers, MS.*).

[9] The text is printed in *Foreign Relations of the United States: Japan*, II, 398 ff. See also Iwakuro's affidavit in *Tokyo War Crimes Documents*, Defense Document, No. 2589, and the "Konoye Memoirs" (*Pearl Harbor Attack*, XX, 3985).

of Japanese immigration into China, on condition that China recognize Japan's absorption of Manchuria. Added to all this was a final proviso that in the event of Chiang Kai-shek's failure to respond favorably to the President's request for peace, the United States should discontinue its aid to China. In conclusion the document provided, as anticipated, for a conference between President Roosevelt and Prime Minister Konoye at Honolulu; for restoration of normal trade relations between the United States and Japan; for free access for Japan to the raw materials it needed; and for an American loan to Japan.

Despite Mr. Hull's belief that most of the proposals in the April 9 document were all the Japanese militarists could desire, he recognized that they were not all unacceptable. Moreover, with respect to interpretation and "loopholes," much obviously would depend on the good faith of Prince Konoye and his supporters, and on their ability to fulfill their commitments. All in all the matter seemed worth at least some exploration. Accordingly Mr. Hull invited Ambassador Nomura to discuss the program with him at his hotel apartment on April 14. On this occasion the Secretary first sought assurances that the Ambassador was conversant with the document, that he would assume responsibility for it, and that he would present it officially to the United States Government. Upon receiving affirmative answers and learning that the Ambassador had not yet forwarded the text to Tokyo, Mr. Hull added that he wished to raise certain points and desired that Nomura send them to Tokyo before the Japanese Government finally decided whether or not to accept the program as a basis for negotiation.[10]

Mr. Hull's points, reduced to a written statement and given to Ambassador Nomura on April 16, turned out to be little more than a reformulation of his already well-known recipe for the establishment of better relations between Japan and the United States. The preconditions of a future agreement between the two countries required that Japan pledge itself to respect the integrity and sovereignty of all nations, support the principle of non-interference in their internal affairs, embrace the principle of equality of economic opportunity for all nations and, finally, pledge itself not to change the *status quo* in the Pacific save by peaceful means.

To make assurance doubly sure, Mr. Hull took the occasion to warn the Ambassador that the American Government considered it of paramount importance, in making its own decision as to the initiation of negotiations, to be certain that the Japanese Government not only intended to proceed with the plan, but would be able to carry out the terms agreed upon. He took great pains to impress on Nomura that unless Tokyo underwent a genuine conversion and was prepared to accept in good faith the Secretary's

[10] Memo of conversation between Mr. Hull and Ambassador Nomura, April 14, 1941 (*Foreign Relations of the United States: Japan,* II, 402 ff.). See also Hull: *Memoirs,* II, 993 ff.

four points, nothing would be gained by submitting the April 9 document to the American Government, nor by Mr. Hull's accepting it as a basis for negotiation.[11]

Mr. Hull himself had doubts whether the bluff and slow-thinking Ambassador fully grasped the significance of these admonitions. However, Nomura formally presented the April 9 document and promptly forwarded it, along with the Secretary's four points, to his own Government. On April 17 the Japanese Prime Minister was in possession of these first fruits of the private negotiations. His reaction and that of his associates could be expected to be favorable, since the program undoubtedly reflected the instructions which Iwakuro had taken to Washington. The reception accorded Mr. Hull's four points would, of course, be another matter. Most important of all, assuming acceptance of the terms, was the question whether Konoye would succeed in carrying the Cabinet and the Army with him. Matsuoka was about to arrive home from his triumphal tour and would undoubtedly have much to say. Clearly, a first-class conflict was in the offing.

Quite another question, and one which can hardly be glossed over, concerns the President's and Mr. Hull's handling of the product of the Drought-Wikawa-Iwakuro confabulations. As it turned out later, the Secretary made a rather serious mistake in requesting Nomura to send the informal program to Tokyo with the inquiry whether the Imperial Government would accept it as a basis for negotiation. The Japanese quite naturally took this to mean that the United States Government was prepared so to accept it, particularly since Mr. Hull had asked that the paper be presented to him officially. Yet it is almost certain that neither the President nor the Secretary of State intended any such commitment. The evidence would seem to indicate that they disliked these unofficial proceedings and had but little faith in the Japanese generally. If they tolerated the informal discussions and plans, it was undoubtedly because they thought there was at least a slight chance that in Matsuoka's absence Prince Konoye and his supporters might succeed in undermining the Foreign Minister's position and adopt a different policy. At the end of March the Anglo-American staff conferences at Washington had reaffirmed the principle that in the event of war the chief effort should be made in the Atlantic and that therefore everything possible should be done to forestall hostilities in the Pacific. As yet there was no knowing what the outcome of Matsuoka's pilgrimage might be, but his objectives were public knowledge and from the American standpoint it seemed worth while at least to explore the possibilities of reaching a settlement by circumventing him.

Connected with the informal negotiations and particularly with Matsuoka's journey to Europe was the mission of small American naval

[11] Memo of conversation between Mr. Hull and Ambassador Nomura, April 16, 1941 (*Foreign Relations of the United States: Japan,* II, 406 ff.).

forces to New Zealand and Australia, ostensibly for good will and recreation purposes. These visits were in accord with the President's idea of having American ships "popping up here and there and keep the Japs guessing." Although Admiral Stark disapproved of using the Navy "for popping up purposes in aid to diplomacy," he consoled himself with the thought that this "childish" performance did not involve the dangers of sending American warships to Singapore or permanently weakening the flanking threat to Japan represented by the stationing of the Fleet at Pearl Harbor.[12] The Chief of Naval Operations was far better disposed toward Admiral Hart's suggestion that the Asiatic Fleet, based on the Philippines, be taken on a cruise through the Netherlands East Indies. Stark liked this idea because such a cruise seemed "about the most positive move we could make" and because "it is in line with our war plans, so if war were to break, we would be with our surface ships where we want them." But even so he felt that the outcome of Matsuoka's negotiations should be awaited. When the State Department decided that the Indies cruise would be inadvisable while the Japanese-Dutch economic conversations were still in progress, the whole proposal was dropped.[13]

These incidents illustrate once again how much importance Washington attached to Matsuoka and his activities. The passage of the Lend-Lease Act (March 11, 1941) was bound to create ever greater tension in American relations with the Axis and to make it almost vital that a crisis in American-Japanese relations be avoided. When Mr. Hull and Ambassador Nomura discussed the informal program on April 14, 1941, the Secretary already knew that Matsuoka had succeeded in concluding a neutrality pact with the Soviet Government. Thereby the chances of a settlement of American-Japanese differences had presumably diminished. But it still remained to be seen whether Konoye and his friends really desired a settlement and if so, whether they would be able either to bring the Foreign Minister into line or to encompass his downfall.

2. THE TRIUMPH OF MATSUOKA

Admiral Nomura's report on the informal "Proposal for Understanding" reached Tokyo on April 18 and was carefully studied during the following three days by Prince Konoye and the Liaison Conference, consisting of the Ministers of War and of the Navy and the Chiefs of Staff of the two services. Both Konoye and War Minister Tojo have since maintained that they and their colleagues regarded the proposals as the beginning of official negotiations, in view of the way in which Mr. Hull had discussed them and

[12] *The New York Times,* March 17, 20, 1941; letters of Stark to Admiral Kimmel, April 19, 1941 (*Pearl Harbor Attack,* XVI, 2163 ff.; see also V, 2413 ff.).

[13] Hart's letter to Stark, March 4, 1941, and Stark's memo to the President, March 28, 1941, with attached note on the State Department decision of April 3, 1941.

Admiral Nomura had reported them.[14] Konoye, having sponsored the informal negotiations and drafted the outlines of the proposals, was delighted that Washington had reacted so favorably. His colleagues, too, were well impressed and conceded that the proposals provided at least a ray of hope for agreement with the United States.

That a settlement of Japanese-American differences was desired by influential circles in Tokyo there can be little doubt. Matsuoka was later to explain to the German Ambassador that there were "Anglophiles" in the Emperor's entourage and that business and financial circles, as well as many high naval officers and even important groups in the Army, favored an agreement with the United States. Contemporary reports bear out this assertion and indicate that there was much dissatisfaction over the continuance of the apparently bootless China policy. Furthermore, American and British trade restrictions were making themselves keenly felt, while the passage of the Lend-Lease Act appeared to bring American participation in the war and therefore Japanese involvement much closer. A long memorandum prepared at this time by the Bureau of American Affairs of the Japanese Foreign Office reviewed in detail the developments of the preceding months and revealed much uneasiness about the American-British-Dutch conversations, both in Washington and Singapore, as well as about American naval movements and the fortification of Guam and other Pacific Islands.[15] Simultaneously Ambassador Grew was reporting that influential newspapers and organizations were emphasizing the peaceful aims of Japan's southward policy and even criticizing Hitler and the Tripartite Pact. The recent Japanese-Soviet Neutrality Pact was being given only guarded approval, while many had frank doubts whether Japan, once it was engaged in the advance to the south, would not be attacked by Soviet Russia, pact or no pact.[16]

It was evidently the Imperial Army that was most divided as to the course of action to be adopted. Distrust and hatred of Communist Russia were certainly widespread in military circles. On the other hand the activist groups, which had long favored a military alliance with Germany, held the Tripartite Pact sufficient assurance that the Kremlin's hand would be stayed, even without Matsuoka's Neutrality Pact. Events in Europe had presented Japan with the opportunity of ages; it would be nothing less than criminal not to seize the golden moment to attack Singapore and realize the Greater East Asia Co-Prosperity Sphere. In these extremist circles it was commonly argued that, in view of the relationship between the United States and

[14] "Konoye Memoirs" (*Pearl Harbor Attack*, XX, 3985); "Tojo Memorandum" (*Tokyo War Crimes Documents:* Proceedings, 218 ff.).

[15] "On the Formation of the Anti-Japanese Joint Encirclement by Great Britain, United States, and the Netherlands," dated April, 1941 (*Tokyo War Crimes Documents,* Defense Document No. 1739).

[16] Tel. from Grew, April 17, 1941.

Britain, America would not fight in the Pacific so long as the Nazi threat in Europe had not been exorcised.[17]

Even those Army circles which hoped to close out the China Incident through agreement with the United States were fearful of the reaction of Berlin to the initiation of negotiations between Tokyo and Washington. Since the outcome of such negotiations could not be foreseen and at best seemed to provide but a "slight ray of hope," it was patently dangerous to jeopardize the Tripartite Pact. Nonetheless, the Liaison Conference on April 21, 1941, made the decision to continue the negotiations with the United States. It was recognized that these might have a "chilling" effect on Japanese relations with Germany, but it was thought that the informal proposals could be harmonized with the Tripartite Pact by putting the proper interpretation on the crucial Article III of that agreement. As for Mr. Hull's four points of principle, the Japanese appear to have taken these not too seriously. In the words of General Tojo, they placed much more emphasis on "the practical solution of existing problems than on statements of general principles."[18]

It was the intention of Konoye and his colleagues to despatch appropriate instructions to Nomura without delay, but at the insistence of Vice Foreign Minister Ohashi they finally agreed to await the arrival of Matsuoka, who had meanwhile reached Dairen. Over the long distance telephone Konoye informed the Foreign Minister of the American "note." According to one of Matsuoka's companions, the latter was elated, believing that the United States had made definite proposals for settling the China Incident and believing further that this auspicious development was the direct result of Ambassador Steinhardt's report of Matsuoka's warning that if the United States entered the war, Japan woud strike.[19] On arriving in Tokyo (April 22) and discovering that the "proposals" were of a very different nature and the product of informal discussions, the Foreign Minister "was extremely annoyed and showed no interest whatever." At a meeting of the Liaison Conference that very evening he insisted on telling in detail of his European trip. Reference to the American negotiations only roiled him and led him to harp further on the need for keeping faith with the Nazis. Only a resolute Japan, he declared, could ward off the danger of open conflict with the United States. As a result of his petulance the conference finally acceded to his request for a two weeks' delay before sending further instructions to Nomura. Repeated efforts were made, by the Army and Navy Ministers as well as by others, to make Matsuoka more favorably disposed and there was

[17] Tel. from Grew, April 17, 1941.
[18] "Tojo Memorandum," as cited above; "Konoye Memoirs" (*Pearl Harbor Attack*, XX, 3986 ff.); "Kido Diary" (*Tokyo War Crimes Documents*, No. 1632W-49).
[19] Toshikazu Kase: *Journey to the "Missouri"* (New Haven, 1950), 45. Matsuoka, though he had in the interval learned better, repeated this hypothesis to the German Ambassador on May 6, 1941 (*Tokyo War Crimes Documents*, No. 4059A).

even some talk of the necessity for dismissing him if he persisted in his opposition. But Matsuoka showed no indication of yielding and evidently had sufficient support to defy the wishes of his colleagues.[20]

Further delay was occasioned by the illness of both Konoye and Matsuoka, because of which there was no further meeting of the Liaison Conference until May 3. At that time the Foreign Minister presented a revision, and a rather drastic one, of the original proposals, and insisted that before even these were submitted to Washington the conclusion of a neutrality treaty should be proposed to the United States as a test. Apparently the conference assented, on the understanding that the Foreign Minister would take prompt action. This he did, in the sense that he instructed Nomura to present the idea of a neutrality pact and submit to Secretary Hull a "tentative reply," which was in effect a statement that Axis leaders were confident of victory, that American participation in the war would lead only to the downfall of civilization, and that Japan would never act in any way injurious to its partners of the Tripartite Pact.

It will be obvious to the reader that Matsuoka, far from pressing on with the original proposals from Washington, was doing his utmost to confuse the issue and sabotage the projected negotiations. On May 6 he promised the German Ambassador to acquaint him with the American proposals as soon as possible. Explaining the opposition which he was encountering among his colleagues, he held forth hope that he could maneuver in such a way as to kill the chances of an understanding. For good measure he assured the Ambassador that in the event of a Nazi-Soviet conflict Japan would be driven by necessity to attack the Soviet Union. No neutrality pact could change the situation.[21]

In Washington Ambassador Nomura had an interview with Secretary Hull on May 7. The latter was no doubt disappointed that no reply to the original program had as yet been forthcoming. When Nomura brought forth the proposal for a neutrality pact, Mr. Hull gave it short shrift, since under existing circumstances it was hard to interpret such a proposition as anything more than a device to permit Japan to pursue its expansionist policy free of American interference. As for Matsuoka's "tentative reply," which Nomura had been instructed to present as an oral statement, the Secretary took but a quick glance at it and then permitted the disconcerted Ambassador to follow his obvious inclination and regard it as undelivered. Thus far it could certainly not be said that the prospect for an American-Japanese settlement had brightened. Matsuoka's return had, as Washington feared, cast a long shadow over the future.[22]

[20] "Tojo Memorandum" and "Konoye Memoirs," as cited above.

[21] Tel. from Ott to the German Foreign Office, May 6, 1941 (*Tokyo War Crimes Documents,* No. 4059A).

[22] Memo of conversation between Mr. Hull and Ambassador Nomura, May 7, 1941

After the failure of Matsuoka's insidious suggestions, Ambassador Nomura urged upon his Government the need for an early reply to the original proposals. Since the passage of the Lend-Lease legislation the question of American naval protection of the supplies intended for Britain had become acute and the likelihood of armed conflict between the United States and Germany correspondingly greater. In Tokyo the battle of the factions increased in tempo. Matsuoka told the Emperor on May 8 that if the United States entered the war, Japan must stand by its allies, and that if the pressure for an agreement with the United States became too strong, he would resign. On the other hand, Konoye and his colleagues were at their wits' end as to how to deal with the Foreign Minister and were deeply concerned by the anticipated German reaction to news of the negotiations with Washington. Konoye was trying to allay the anxiety of the Emperor and was doing his utmost to get on with the negotiations with the United States. He finally succeeded in persuading Matsuoka to authorize Nomura to submit to Mr. Hull the program as revised by the Liaison Conference on May 3, without awaiting the German reply.[23]

The already highly confused situation was now further complicated by the fact that when Nomura presented the Japanese revision of the original proposals, Secretary Hull took this as a Japanese program now being submitted for the first time, while the Tokyo Government had all along assumed that the proposals as received in Japan on April 18 constituted an initial offer by Washington and therefore regarded the reply of May 12 simply as a revision of terms already in the main agreed to by the American Government.[24] All this aside, the Japanese revision represented rather far-reaching modifications of the initial text, clearly revealing Matsuoka's fine hand. On crucial issues of Japan's obligations under the Tripartite Pact and American support of Britain, the new Japanese version proposed the following solutions: Japan would state that its alliance with the Axis was "designed to prevent the nations which are not at present directly affected by the European War from engaging in it"; the United States on its part would declare that "its attitude toward the European War is and will continue to be directed by no such aggressive measures as to assist any one nation against the other."

As for the withdrawal of Japanese troops from China the revised terms were certainly no improvement over the original ones, for it was now stipulated that American proposals to Chiang Kai-shek for peace should be based on the Konoye statement of 1938, the Sino-Japanese treaty of November 30,

---

(*Foreign Relations of the United States: Japan,* II, 411 ff.); Hull: *Memoirs,* II, 997; "Konoye Memoirs," as cited above.

[23] "Konoye Memoirs," as cited above, pp. 3989 ff.

[24] "Tojo Memorandum," as cited above, pp. 225 ff.; Hull: *Memoirs,* II, 1000; memos of conversation between Mr. Hull and Ambassador Nomura, May 11, 12, 1941 (*Foreign Relations of the United States: Japan,* II, 415 ff.).

1940, and the Joint Declaration by Japan-Manchukuo and the Wang Ching-wei Government of the same date. In the event of Chiang Kai-shek's refusal to accept these terms, the United States was to discontinue aid to Nationalist China.

The May 12 proposals further provided for a joint guarantee of Philippine independence, for the resumption of normal trade relations between the United States and Japan, and for the ending of discrimination against Japanese immigration into the United States.[25]

Considered as a whole, the Japanese note of May 12 certainly did not warrant optimism about a settlement. Secretary Hull told Secretary Stimson that he regarded the chances of an agreement as only about one in ten. Yet the President and Mr. Hull decided to accept the Japanese proposals as the basis for further conversations. In the sequel the Secretary was to be scrupulously careful always to remind Ambassador Nomura that there was as yet no question of "negotiations" and that the discussions were merely informal talks or conversations, aimed at finding a basis for genuine negotiations. This matter of definition was probably of no great importance and certainly does not answer the question why the American authorities agreed to continue the discussions when the basic proposals were so unpromising.

The answer to that question can surely not be simple. The President and Mr. Hull were under no illusions about Matsuoka's attitude and must have realized that if the Foreign Minister had his way Japan would spring to Germany's side the moment a naval conflict broke out between the United States and Germany in the Atlantic.[26] But there still seemed a chance that Matsuoka would fall and that more moderate elements would gain the upper hand in Tokyo. Thus, Father Drought reported, evidently from Konoye through Wikawa, that Matsuoka might yet be overthrown. He besought the Secretary not to be misled by the contradictions in which the Prime Minister and his supporters had been obliged to engage in their effort to circumvent the extremist elements.[27]

Furthermore, Ambassador Grew was not without hope that the conflict in Tokyo government circles might yet end favorably. Basing his observations on a careful appraisal of opinion in Japan, he expressed the conviction "that predominant influences, such as the Emperor, the Premier, the majority of the members of the Cabinet, Baron Hiranuma, and the majority of the Japanese Navy would be loath to engage in war with the United States and

[25] The text is given in full in *Foreign Relations of the United States: Japan,* II, 420 ff., and there is an informal translation in Appendix II of the "Konoye Memoirs." In his *Memoirs* (II, 1000 ff.) Mr. Hull has analyzed in some detail the specific points of his dissatisfaction.

[26] Matsuoka restated his position to Ambassador Grew in a conversation of May 14, 1941 (tel. from Grew, same date); Joseph C. Grew: *Ten Years in Japan* (New York, 1944), 388 ff.

[27] Memo from Postmaster General Walker to Mr. Hull, with attached documents, May 12, 1941 (*Walker Papers, MS.*).

would try in every way to discover an interpretation of Article III of the [Tripartite] agreement which would release Japan from going to the assistance of her allies, providing this could be accomplished without losing face vis-à-vis the United States and without sacrificing Japanese honor." The important thing, he held, was that the United States scrupulously avoid firing the first shot in the event of an American-German naval conflict in the Atlantic: "It would appear reasonable to suppose that if a German attack on an American warship or other American vessel should bring about war, the Japanese Government would take the position that Germany had taken provocative action and had given the *casus belli*. On the other hand, the obligation of Japan under Article III might in good faith be made effective if an American warship fired the first shot."[28]

On the very day of Grew's telegram the President and Mr. Hull had finally agreed that to meet the danger of war in the Atlantic at least a part of the United States Fleet would have to be withdrawn from the Pacific.[29] Just because the situation arising from the Lend-Lease legislation threatened to become so acute, they could not afford to overlook the possibility of helping Konoye and his friends get rid of the bellicose Matsuoka. At a minimum there was a chance that through negotiations time could be gained. It must be remembered that Washington had every reason to suppose that in the very near future Hitler would loose his divisions on Soviet Russia and thereby revolutionize the international situation. Time, then, was of the essence. Even though it is probably mistaken to suppose, as General Tojo did later, that the sole objective of the American Government was to delay decisions by drawing out the conversations, that consideration certainly entered into its calculations.[30]

Despite all the obscurities still enveloping the problem, there is good warrant for believing that at this time (mid-May, 1941) there was in fact a better chance for the solution of the American-Japanese issue than at any other point during the pre-Pearl Harbor period. The opposition to Matsuoka was evidently widespread and influential and, if led by a stronger personality than Prince Konoye, might well have imposed its will on the Foreign Minister. It seems indeed to have been true that a majority of the Cabinet, including the military, were unwilling to accept a conflict between the United States and Germany as necessarily involving the *casus belli* for Japan. But Matsuoka stood his ground and drew support not only from General Oshima, the Ambassador in Berlin, but from Ribbentrop himself.

Just after Nomura had been instructed to submit the Japanese proposals to Secretary Hull (May 12) the eagerly awaited German comment on the April 9 program arrived in Tokyo. It revealed the importance which Hitler

[28] Tel. from Grew, May 13, 1941.
[29] *Stimson Diary (MS.)*, May 13, 1941. See also above, Chapter XIV.
[30] "Tojo Memorandum," as cited above, p. 225; Hull: *Memoirs*, II, 999 ff.

attached to Japanese policy, first as a threat and eventually as a counterweight to American action.[31] Consequently the German Foreign Office struck a warning note: "the policy of the American Government is to intensify *de facto* unneutral actions (patrol or convoy) without declaring war, to wait for counteraction by Germany and Italy and, thus, to shift responsibility for starting the war to the Axis side." Accordingly the Germans recommended that Tokyo's reply to Washington emphasize that continued American provocation of Germany and Italy would "force" Japan to enter the war. On the other hand, if the United States abstained from such provocation, Japan would be ready to study the "American proposal."[32]

The Germans were naturally irritated to learn that the Japanese reply to Washington had gone off before they had seen it. On May 18 Ambassador Ott complained to Matsuoka on this score and reminded him that the aim of the Tripartite Pact was to prevent other powers from intervening in the war. In order to avoid a weakening of the Pact its members should not make special agreements outside it, or at any rate fail to ensure recognition of the crucial stipulation of the Pact. The provision on this point, as set forth in the Japanese proposals of May 12, must be regarded as the absolute minimum. The German Government demanded that in future it be permitted to participate fully in the Japanese-American negotiations.

In response to these strong, almost threatening words, Matsuoka gave profuse assurances that he would not "jolt" the Tripartite Pact, that he had insisted that the Cabinet recognize the obligations imposed by the Pact, and that he had no intention of yielding to American pressure. His sole motive in negotiating with the United States, he explained, was if possible to prevent or postpone America's entry into the war and, furthermore, to forestall the increase of American assistance to Britain. He did not expect to succeed, he added, because American involvement appeared imminent, but he had yielded to the pressure of his colleagues, some of whom were convinced that there was no other way to avoid war with the United States. He promised faithfully to show the Ambassador the American reply as soon as it arrived.[33]

As though Ambassador Ott's strictures were not enough, General Oshima reported in detail on the perplexity and vexation of the Germans. Matsuoka had said nothing in Berlin of the projected negotiations with the United States. On the contrary he had given Hitler to understand, as his personal opinion, that Japan would presently attack Singapore, and on May 6 he had assured Ott that in the event of a German-Soviet conflict Japan would intervene on Germany's side. How, then, explain the effort to reach an agree-

---

[31] Hitler's remarks to Ciano, April 20, 1941 (*Ciano's Diplomatic Papers,* 436).

[32] "Summary of the Opinion of the German Government as Told by Ambassador Ott in Tokyo, May 11, 1941" (*Tokyo War Crimes Documents,* Defense Document No. 1659).

[33] Tel. of the German Foreign Office to Ambassador Ott, May 17, 1941 (*Tokyo War Crimes Documents,* Defense Document No. 1658); tel. from Ott to the Foreign Office, May 18, 1941 (*ibid.,* Document No. 4060A).

ment with a power which was an avowed enemy of the Axis? Ribbentrop, continued Oshima, had frankly expressed the fear that a Japanese-American agreement would make the Tripartite Pact meaningless. The Ambassador himself pointed out that the Germans could regard such an agreement only as an effort on Japan's part to evade its obligations under the Tripartite Pact and as a move that would facilitate the American campaign against Germany in the Atlantic.[34]

It is plain that Matsuoka made the most of the German reaction in pursuing his controversy with his colleagues, a controversy which appears to have continued unabated until the German attack on Soviet Russia gave events a new turn. In his altercations with the Prime Minister, Matsuoka refused to retreat even as much as an inch from his position that if American naval escorts were attacked by the Germans, Japan would be obliged to enter the war and help the Germans, since such escort was in itself a form of attack. President Roosevelt, he asserted, was apparently determined to intervene in the war. If that should happen, an American-Japanese agreement would be useless. Japan would simply have to make up its mind as between Britain and America on the one hand and Germany and Italy on the other.[35]

So long as the Japanese Foreign Minister retained his position there was practically no hope that the Hull-Nomura conversations would bear fruit. At intervals of only a few days informal conferences took place for over a month between the Secretary, supported by Mr. Hamilton and Mr. Ballantine of the State Department staff, on the one hand, and the Ambassador, assisted by Mr. Wikawa and Colonel Iwakuro, who had in the meantime been officially attached to the Japanese Embassy, on the other. The records of these talks fill almost a hundred printed pages, yet Mr. Hull, when later writing his memoirs, considered them insufficiently important to warrant more than a brief summary. For endless hours the negotiators went over the familiar ground, asking innumerable questions in their efforts to arrive at some degree of clarity. But no significant progress was recorded. Though the Japanese fervently reiterated that their Government, including Matsuoka, genuinely desired an agreement with the United States, they could adduce no evidence of Tokyo's readiness to yield on any essential point. On various occasions Nomura or his associates would declare that they agreed with the American position, except for "some of the phraseology." They had, so they averred on June 4, "crossed the mountain and valley which separated us, so that only a ditch remained to be bridged." But close scrutiny invariably failed to reveal adequate grounds for optimism.

The discussions all hinged on the Japanese draft of May 12 and more

---

[34] Tel. from Oshima to Matsuoka, May 20, 1941 (*Tokyo War Crimes Documents*, No. 1383B-18).

[35] "Konoye Memoirs," as cited above, pp. 3991-92.

particularly on the three main issues, which Mr. Hull, in conversation with Lord Halifax, summarized as follows: "a satisfactory Chinese settlement, assurances that they [the Japanese] will not go south for purposes of military conquest, and assurances that they will not fight for Germany in case the United States should be drawn into the war."[36] Although on this occasion the Secretary expressed hope that a basis might be found "very soon" for instituting actual negotiations, his conversation with Ambassador Nomura on May 28 yielded little further information on the points at issue. While President Roosevelt had carefully omitted all reference to Japan in his fireside chat of May 27, Mr. Hull took his remarks on the necessity for maintaining freedom of the seas against Hitler as a springboard for an earnest effort to secure from Nomura a clarification of Japan's position under the Tripartite Pact. The Japanese Ambassador offered, as a personal opinion, that in the event of an American-German conflict there would be no war between the United States and Japan, but doubted very much whether his Government would be willing to add anything to what it had already stated regarding such a contingency. He was sure, he added, that whatever decision Japan made, it would be Tokyo's own and not Germany's or Italy's.

Finding himself in this familiar impasse, Mr. Hull took a deep breath and then entered another blind alley by raising the question of how the Japanese proposed to withdraw their troops from China. Nomura would not venture to say "precisely what the Japanese Army had in mind," but was certain that, whatever it was, it would emerge from direct negotiations between Japan and China. These, he thought, might consume six months and the final evacuation might take fully two years. Furthermore, it should be understood that Japanese troops would have to remain in Inner Mongolia and North China "for an indefinite period" to combat the Communists. Mr. Hull, who only a few days ago had assured the Chinese Ambassador that before the initiation of actual negotiations with Japan he would hold "full and exhaustive" conferences with the Chinese Government, felt obliged to call Nomura's attention to the American position in this vital matter.

The Ambassador reacted to the Secretary's statement by remarking blandly that he had no expectation that the United States Government would involve itself in negotiations for the withdrawal of Japanese troops from China. In his view the United States should confine itself to providing "a bridge to bring the Chinese and Japanese together for direct negotiations" unless, indeed, by refusing further assistance to Chiang Kai-shek, the United States should actually compel the Chinese Nationalist Government to accept Tokyo's terms.[37]

[36] Memo of conversation between Mr. Hull and Lord Halifax, May 27, 1941 (*Pearl Harbor Attack*, XX, 4077 ff.).

[37] Memo of conversation between Mr. Hull and Ambassador Nomura May 28, 1941 (*Foreign Relations of the United States: Japan*, II, 440 ff.); Hull: *Memoirs*, II, 1005

This exposition of Tokyo's views, together with similar statements of Nomura's subordinates, undoubtedly clarified Japanese policy with respect to China, but at the same time revealed the depth of the cleavage between the two Governments on this all-important issue. The same may be said of the Japanese reaction to an American draft of May 31, 1941, commenting on Tokyo's proposals of May 12. This draft included a proposed statement of the attitudes of the two parties toward the European War and of Japan's obligations under the Tripartite Pact. "Obviously," it read, "the provisions of the Pact do not apply to involvement through acts of self defense." As a practical matter, Foreign Minister Matsuoka had already reacted to this proposition when, in reply to an inquiry by an American correspondent, he had stated publicly:

> Japan's attitude and policy regarding the obligations of the Tripartite Pact are, as I have repeatedly affirmed, crystal clear, and there is no question that we will faithfully observe them.
>
> Japan will also pursue the course and policy in East Asia which she has been following unwaveringly in the past, namely, establishment of a new order throughout the region of Greater East Asia.
>
> Nothing will alter or influence that course or policy.[38]

It was only natural, therefore, that Ambassador Nomura's assistant, Mr. Wakasugi, should reject the American proposal. Queried by Mr. Hamilton whether or not the American Government was correct in believing that Tokyo desired to disengage itself gradually from its Axis connection, Wakasugi "stated categorically that if we had received any such impressions they were not in accord with fact." Colonel Iawakuro chimed in with the observation that there were two sources of possible conflict between Japan and the United States. One was "matters affecting the Pacific region," the other "circumstances under which the United States might become involved in the European War." At best, he added, "the proposed understanding was designed to take care of the first source."[39]

In view of the fact that discussion seemed only to reveal ever greater differences between Washington and Tokyo, Secretary Hull thought it well to bring "the divergencies to a head" by submitting an "oral statement" on June 6, 1941. "From such study as it has so far been possible to make of the revisions which the associates of the Japanese Ambassador offered on June 4," ran this statement in part, "it is disappointing to note a vast difference between the proposal as it now stands with these revisions and the original document on which earlier discussions were based." Successive

---

ff. On Mr. Hull's assurances to Ambassador Hu Shih we have used memos of conversation between the two, May 23, 1941, and between Mr. Hull and Lord Halifax, May 27, 1941.

[38] Karl von Wiegand, in the *New York Journal-American,* June 1, 1941.

[39] Memo of conversation, June 4, 1941 (*Foreign Relations of the United States: Japan,* II, 455 ff.).

Japanese revisions were described as having carried the proposal away from the essential points which Washington considered involved "in establishing and preserving peaceful conditions in the Pacific area." Before attempting to consider further "phraseological changes" it was therefore important to secure "a meeting of minds and mutual understanding of the underlying purposes of the proposed understanding." Hull's statement concluded with an invitation to Nomura to reconsider his comments on the American draft of May 31, bearing the above observations in mind.[40]

The Ambassador and his associates professed great astonishment on reading this statement. Once again they protested that Matsuoka was really desirous of an understanding and that it had been their impression that the obstacles to agreement were gradually being surmounted.[41] On what they based this impression is not at all obvious. Actually there had been not the slightest indication of Japanese readiness to conform to American views. Indeed, from what has since been learned of developments in Tokyo one can hardly escape the conclusion that Matsuoka and his supporters were determined to stand pat on all vital issues and were, in fact, preparing to embark on a policy which ran even more directly counter to the interests of the western powers.

The impetus to Japan's fateful decision was provided by the final suspension, on June 10, 1941, of the prolonged negotiations with the Netherlands Indies. The Dutch had firmly rejected all proposals involving an increase of Japanese influence, an acceptance of control, or a recognition of the inclusion of the Netherlands Indies in the Greater East Asia Co-Prosperity Sphere. Their final note, dated June 6, was so uncompromising that the Japanese emissary, Mr. Yoshizawa, announced the departure of his mission for June 27. All he could show for many months of effort was the agreement of November 13, 1940, between Dutch petroleum interests and Japanese importers of oil.[42]

The infuriated Japanese blamed the British and Americans for the loss of face and of vital raw materials which they had suffered at the hands of the Dutch. So bitter were the recriminations of the Tokyo press that it seemed highly probable that the Japanese would try to solve the whole issue by making a lunge at the Indies. The British suggested the advisability of a statement in support of a speech by the Netherlands Foreign Minister, delivered in early May, in which Mr. Van Kleffens had warned Tokyo that an attack on any part of a line running from Singapore through the Netherlands Indies

---

[40] Full text in *Foreign Relations of the United States: Japan*, II, 467 ff.

[41] Memo of conversation, June 6, 1941 (*Foreign Relations of the United States: Japan*, II, 465 ff.).

[42] Hubertus Van Mook: *The Netherlands Indies and Japan* (New York, 1944), 80 ff. We have used also tels. from Foote (Batavia), May 18 and 23, 1941, and the fifth memo on the Netherlands-Japanese negotiations, dated May 23, 1941, handed to Mr. Hornbeck by the Netherlands Minister on July 15, 1941.

to Australia would have to be considered and treated as an attack on the whole line, and one equally affecting all the powers concerned. Mr. Hull rejected this proposal, remarking that he made it a practice never to utter threats which he was not prepared to back up. He did, however, publicly reiterate his Government's adherence to the policy of maintaining the *status quo* in the Pacific and eventually authorized Ambassador Grew, at his discretion, to repeat the warning given the Japanese Foreign Office by Mr. Dooman in February, when Tokyo seemed poised for a military move southward.[43]

Actually there was not much danger of a Japanese assault on the Netherlands Indies, for Tokyo military leaders had long since decided that such a move would be too risky while Singapore remained in British hands. Moreover, they considered an attack on Singapore foolhardy until they had secured adequate naval and air bases in southern Indo-China. The real question in Tokyo was, therefore, whether the acquisition of these bases, by fair means or foul, should be undertaken at once and in the face of anticipated opposition from the British and Americans. The plans had long since been laid and were now reviewed in the light of the rupture of negotiations with the Netherlands Indies. General Tojo has testified that at a meeting of the Liaison Conference on June 13 the Supreme Command pressed urgently for the acquisition of the bases, but that Matsuoka succeeded in deferring the decision until June 25.[44]

At first glance the Foreign Minister's attitude may seem incongruous. He had, it will be remembered, promised Hitler and Ribbentrop in the spring that he would do everything possible to secure his Government's assent to an attack on Singapore. Furthermore, he had already taken steps to obtain German support at Vichy for the projected Japanese program anent Indo-China. It can hardly be supposed, therefore, that he was out of sympathy with the policy outlined by the Supreme Command. The explanation of his attitude lies rather in the fact that early in June the Tokyo Government had learned from Ambassador Oshima in Berlin that a German attack on the Soviet Union was likely. Though the report was viewed with some skepticism in Tokyo, it was nonetheless of such significance as to make a temporary postponement of Japanese plans desirable. If the German attack on Soviet Russia materialized, the Tokyo Government might find it expedient to defer

[43] Memo of conversation between Mr. Hull and Mr. Butler, June 3, 1941; memo by the Division of Far Eastern Affairs, June 9, 1941; Hull's press conference statement, June 6, 1941 (*The New York Times,* June 7, 1941); tel. to Grew, June 17, and from Grew, June 18, 1941. Mr. Grew decided against repetition of the Dooman warning.

[44] *Tokyo War Crimes Documents:* the "Tojo Memorandum," 36, 236 ff.; tel. from Matsuoka to Yoshizawa, May 23, 1941 (Document No. 2784A); record of the Liaison Conference, June 25, 1941, referring to the plans for securing the bases (Document No. 2137H).

its advance to the south and first join with Hitler in disposing of Japan's traditional enemy.[45]

Matsuoka at this time quite frankly expounded his position in conversation with the German Ambassador, General Ott, on June 21, 1941. He made no secret of Japan's desire to move into Indo-China and to reject whatever terms Secretary Hull might offer for an understanding with the United States. In order to proceed against the Netherlands Indies, he remarked, naval bases would have to be secured in French Indo-China. He requested German support in obtaining the consent of the Vichy Government, but made it clear that in the event of German refusal he would take the matter up directly with Vichy. As for America, he continued, Nomura's reports indicated that Mr. Hull wanted to include his last anti-German declaration as a constituent part of the American-Japanese agreement. "Such a nonsensical proposal" only proved that the United States wanted the negotiations to fail, while holding Japan responsible for such failure. However, he, Matsuoka, proposed to manage the affair in such a way as to put the blame entirely on the United States.[46]

These remarks leave hardly a shadow of doubt that Matsuoka and his military backers had triumphed in their contest with the less adventurous elements in the Government. By mid-June the Japanese were poised for action—diplomatic action in the first instance, but military action if necessary—to secure a foothold in southern Indo-China, whence they could threaten Singapore and eventually stage operations against the Netherlands Indies. If for the moment they were deferring decision, it was only to await the outcome of the Nazi-Soviet situation. So much, however, was practically certain, that they were going to move, if not to the south, then against Vladivostok and the Soviet Far East. Under the circumstances it was inevitable that attempts to arrive at an American-Japanese understanding should fail. Far from conducting the discussions with sincerity, Matsuoka was doing his utmost to encompass their collapse. So long as he remained in office the situation between Washington and Tokyo could only become worse.

On June 21, 1941, the day before Hitler loosed his *Blitzkrieg* against Soviet Russia and the very day on which Matsuoka and Ambassador Ott were conspiring in Tokyo, Secretary Hull submitted to Ambassador Nomura a long note embodying the American revisions of previous Japanese drafts. This document was the basic statement of the American position and was to be the point of departure for the protracted conversations that ended only with the attack on Pearl Harbor. It marked the beginning of a new

---

[45] "Kido Diary," June, 1941 (*Tokyo War Crimes Documents,* Nos. 1632W-51, 52, 54); memo to Ribbentrop, June 10, 1941 (*ibid.,* No. 4061A).

[46] Tel. from Ott to Ribbentrop, June 21, 1941 (*Tokyo War Crimes Documents,* No. 4081E),

phase of the discussions and will have to be examined in some detail in a later context. In view of the foregoing considerations, however, it is obvious that the American note was at best no more than a forlorn hope.

3. STAFF CONVERSATIONS AT SINGAPORE

Although Washington may have hoped that something would come of the informal discussions set on foot by Catholic missionaries and developed in the Hull-Nomura talks, and may also have been willing to contribute in any possible way to the victory of Konoye over Matsuoka, the American Government at no time staked its Far Eastern position on these diplomatic maneuvers. Throughout the spring of 1941 it maintained close contact with the British, Australians and Dutch, and bent its efforts toward the elaboration of contingent plans for common action in the event of a Japanese attack.

The British, in this regard, required no prodding. On the contrary, the American attitude at all times fell short of what London desired, namely, a strong joint statement of determination to oppose Japanese aggression and the concentration of a substantial American naval force at Singapore. Following the conclusion of the Soviet-Japanese Neutrality Pact, Lord Halifax revived earlier British proposals for such action, which was favored also by the Australians and the Dutch. But once again Secretary Hull advised against a statement. While he steadfastly objected to any diversion of United States naval forces from the Pacific to the Atlantic, he felt that the visit of American squadrons to New Zealand and Australia in March, 1941, had served as a warning to Japan and that further action along the lines suggested by the British would be gratuitously provocative.[47]

On the other hand, Admiral Stark had for some time been encouraging Admiral Hart, the Commander of the Asiatic Fleet at Manila, to use his influence to bring the British, Dutch and Australians together for common planning. They had, in fact, met in conference at Singapore in February, 1941, with Captain William R. Purnell, U.S.N., in attendance as an American observer. But the discussions on that occasion had centered on arrangements for reciprocal reinforcement, the Australian naval authorities insisting on the primacy of defense of the trade routes. Captain Purnell evidently expressed criticism of this concept and left no doubt as to the part the American Asiatic Fleet would probably play in the event of a Japanese attack. But the problem of drafting a common plan for defense against Japanese aggression proved too much for the conferees.[48]

[47] Tel. from Winant (London), April 19, 1941; memos of conversation between Hull, Halifax and Casey, April 22 and 28, 1941, together with an *aide-mémoire* and other documents presented by Lord Halifax. Dutch support for the British suggestion is evidenced in a note from the Minister Counseler, van Botzelaer, to Secretary Hull, April 28, 1941. See also Admiral Stark's memo to the President, April 29, 1941 (*Pearl Harbor Attack*, XIX, 3456 ff.).

[48] Letter of Admiral Hart to Admiral Stark, March 4, 1941, enclosed in a memo from

Admiral Hart was profoundly disappointed by the outcome of the February meeting and Admiral Stark, in transmitting Hart's letter to the President, suggested that a word from Mr. Roosevelt might do much to get the British, Dutch, Australians and New Zealanders together. As a matter of fact Sir Robert Brooke-Popham, Commander in Chief of the British forces in East Asia, visited Manila early in April and conferred with Admiral Hart, General Douglas MacArthur and other military authorities. At about the same time the Dutch Foreign Minister, Mr. E. N. Van Kleffens, stopped at Manila en route to Batavia.[49] By this time the Anglo-American staff conferences at Washington had been concluded and the basic strategy for the event of American participation in the war had been established. In view of the signature of the Soviet-Japanese Neutrality Pact (April 13) it seemed urgent that specific plans for the Far East be devised. Though the Anglo-American strategic plan (ABC-1) provided for maintenance of the defensive in the Pacific, it was not intended that operations in that area should be confined to holding operations. In accord with the Washington agreements, Admiral Stark issued instructions to the American delegates to a new Singapore conference emphasizing that in case of a Japanese attack American forces would assist in the defense of the Malay Barrier by launching offensive operations against the Japanese mandated islands.[50]

The Singapore Conference took place between April 21 and 27, 1941, under the chairmanship of Air Chief Marshal Sir Robert Brooke-Popham. The United States was officially represented by Captain Purnell, while the Dutch, Australian, New Zealand and Indian armed forces were represented by high-ranking officers. Although the discussions and agreements arrived at involved no political commitments whatever, they did eventuate in a definite military plan (the ADB Plan) to meet Japanese aggression against any one of the participating countries. Since no one could predict at which of a number of possible places the Japanese might strike, the planning was of necessity of a local, defensive character. However, recommendations were made for unified command and areas of responsibility were defined. All told, the work of the conference constituted a real achievement and its plan was, in its fundamentals, to be followed in the period just after the Pearl Harbor attack, despite the fact that the American Chief of Staff and Chief of Naval Operations objected to it on the ground that it introduced certain political factors and that the suggested strategy was in some respects faulty.[51]

Stark to the President, March 28, 1941. See also Air Chief Marshal Sir Robert Brooke-Popham: *Operations in the Far East, from 17th October 1940 to 27 December 1941*, dated May 28, 1942, and published as a supplement to the *London Gazette* of January 20, 1948.

[49] *The New York Times*, April 3 and 5, 1941.

[50] The instructions are printed in *Pearl Harbor Attack*, IV, 1933; V, 2387-88. See also Samuel E. Morison: *The Rising Sun in the Pacific* (Boston, 1948), 52 ff., and Mark S. Watson: *Chief of Staff: Prewar Plans and Preparations* (Washington, 1950).

[51] The agreement is summarized in *Pearl Harbor Attack*, XV, 1551-55, and in Brooke-

It may be argued with some cogency that after the Singapore Conference, as before, no one knew what position the United States would take if the Tokyo Government followed Germany's advice in attacking British or Dutch territory while by-passing the Philippines. That was, to be sure, the crucial question, but one which not even the President could have answered at the time. Yet even though the Singapore Conference, like other moves, was inconclusive, it would be a mistake to suppose that it did not have an important bearing on the development of the Far Eastern situation. The Japanese memorandum "On the Formation of the Anti-Japanese Joint Encirclement by Great Britain, the United States and the Netherlands" (April, 1941) shows that the Tokyo Foreign Office kept close watch on all the conversations between the British, Australians, Dutch and Americans, and noted with anxiety all reports of conferences between Secretary Hull, Lord Halifax, Mr. Casey and the Netherlands Minister in Washington.[52] Time and again the Japanese press headlined news that British, American and Dutch representatives had forged a military agreement. Though Secretary Hull publicly denied knowledge of such a pact, his mere admission that staff conversations were being held doubtless strengthened Tokyo's conviction that the western powers were closing ranks in opposition to Japanese plans for the Far East.[53]

This interpretation was certainly not unwelcome in Washington and London, where it was probably hoped that the threat of combined action would serve as yet another deterrent to further Japanese aggression. Anglo-American policy and strategy were to avoid armed conflict with Japan if at all possible, but at the same time to forestall a Japanese advance in Southeast Asia. It was politically impossible for the President to commit the United States in advance to any eventual course of action, and for lack of sufficient military strength in the Far East it was exceedingly difficult for the democracies to lay out even contingent plans to meet so large a variety of possible developments. But if Tokyo could be made to understand that the western nations proposed to do all in their power to support Chinese resistance and reinforce their own possessions in the Far East; if Tokyo could be led to believe that an effort to expand southward would in all probability meet with determined, unified resistance, there was at least a chance that the Japanese war lords would pause and even that the Nazi power in Europe might be broken without the democracies having at the same time to fight a war in the Pacific.

Popham's despatch, as cited above. One of the best accounts of the conference is in the MS. study by Captain Tracy B. Kittredge: *United States-British Naval Coöperation,* but see also Morison: *The Rising Sun in the Pacific,* 54 ff., and Watson: *Chief of Staff: Prewar Plans and Preparations,* 398 ff.

[52] This memo may be found in *Tokyo War Crimes Documents,* No. 1739.

[53] *Washington Post,* April 19; *The New York Times,* April 21 and 22, 1941.

4. THE CHINESE BASTION

The Japanese documents adduced in the course of the Tokyo war crimes trials leave little doubt that by the spring of 1941 the inconclusive war in China was weighing heavily upon Tokyo and that Prince Konoye, in his efforts for an understanding with the United States, was motivated largely by the hope that President Roosevelt would use his influence to bring about a Chinese-Japanese peace settlement. Even the activist elements in Tokyo government circles must have felt that so long as huge forces were bogged down in China it would be difficult if not impossible to mount major operations in Southeast Asia.

For the United States, as for Britain and even the Soviet Union, the trammeling effect upon Japan of the China Incident made the continuance of Nationalist resistance a matter of some moment, and it therefore follows that Washington sustained and increased its endeavors to save the Chungking regime from defeat and collapse. In March, 1941, Mr. Lauchlin Currie, an Administrative Assistant to the President, returned from a two months' visit to China, undertaken at the invitation of Generalissimo Chiang Kai-shek. He had taken with him a member of the U. S. Treasury staff, Mr. Emile Despres, and had concerned himself primarily with the economic situation, which had reached a dangerously critical phase. He brought back the first detailed statistical information on the financial condition of the Nationalist Government, but also reported at some length on the shortcomings of the Chungking Administration and the peculiar problems presented by the Chinese Communists.[54]

Currie concluded that there was little to be done from outside to solve China's acute inflation problem, but his report on other needs unquestionably did much to stimulate Washington's efforts to get supplies to the valiant but distraught country. Matsuoka was known to be renewing his efforts to bring Chiang Kai-shek to terms and there was every reason to suppose that the Japanese Foreign Minister would offer Moscow substantial concessions in return for a promise to discontinue its aid to Chungking. As recounted in an earlier chapter, Under Secretary Welles, in his conversations with Soviet Ambassador Oumansky, made a point of stressing the common American-Soviet interest in the maintenance of Chinese resistance and was much gratified by the Ambassador's indication that his Government would probably maintain and perhaps even increase the level of aid to Chiang Kai-shek.[55]

In the tense state of affairs created by Matsuoka's visits to Moscow and

---

[54] Mr. Currie seems to have reported orally to the President and to have prepared no written record. However, many of his observations were embodied in a long and interesting memo prepared by the Division of Far Eastern Affairs, entitled, "Résumé of the Economic and Political Situation in China and Suggestions for Action," dated April 14, 1941.

[55] Memos of conversation between Welles and Oumansky, March 20 and 22, 1941.

Berlin the American Government thought it particularly important to give Chungking all possible encouragement. Chiang was assured that China would be eligible for aid under the Lend-Least Act and that war supplies would be despatched as quickly as they became available. A transportation expert was put at Chiang's disposal to study ways and means of improving the crucial Burma Road, and much thought was given to meeting the Generalissimo's request for an economic mission to advise him on fiscal and other problems. At the same time Mr. Stimson met Chiang's request for a high-ranking air officer by appointing General Henry B. Clagett, who was to check on the Nationalist Air Force, study the adequacy of airfields, and report on the tactics of the Japanese.[56]

On April 1 the President charged Mr. Currie with the problems of supplies to China under Lend-Lease and that energetic official soon found himself immersed in programs which were, to say the least, impressive. Chinese requests at this time involved goods valued at something like $560,000,000, including 750 pursuit planes, 300 bombers, 80 Beechcraft, 300 Ryan trainers, 30 transports, spare engines, guns and munitions of all kinds, tractors, signal equipment, trucks, steel and other metals, hospital supplies, uniforms and gasoline.[57]

Before much could be done to analyze these requirements Washington like Chungking was shocked by the news of the Soviet-Japanese Neutrality Pact. Even though the published text of the agreement made no mention of China and it seemed unlikely that the Kremlin would abandon Chungking merely in return for a promise of Japanese neutrality, it was generally assumed that the Pact would lead to a gradual reduction of Soviet aid to China. Secretary Hull quickly issued a statement warning against overestimation of the agreement and repeating the idea already expressed with regard to the Tripartite Pact, namely, that it "would seem to be descriptive of a situation which has in effect existed . . . for some time past." Nonetheless Chiang Kai-shek took a gloomy view and predicted that the Soviet-Japanese Pact might sound the death knell of Soviet aid.[58]

Actually Molotov lost no time in dispelling Chinese anxiety. He assured the Chinese Ambassador in Moscow that the Neutrality Pact had nothing to do with China and that in the course of the Soviet-Japanese negotiations China was not discussed—was not even mentioned. Soviet policy toward

[56] *Stimson Diary (MS.)*, March 27, 1941. The provision of an economic mission was strongly favored by the State Department, but appears to have been abandoned in favor of an arrangement by which the U.S. Treasury official designated to serve on a Chinese Currency Stabilization Committee should also serve in the capacity of economic adviser (memo of the Division of Far Eastern Affairs, April 25 and 26, 1941; memo from Adams to Hamilton, May 21, 1941).

[57] Memo on Chinese requirements, March 31, 1941 (copy in the *Donovan Papers, MS.*).

[58] Tel. from Johnson (Chungking), April 16, 1941. For Hull's statement see *Documents on American Foreign Relations*, III, 293; Hull: *Memoirs*, II, 969, 993.

China, he added, would remain unchanged so long as China continued its resistance to Japan.[59] But before these glad tidings could reach Chungking both the President and the Generalissimo had gone into action. On April 15 Mr. Roosevelt, together with Secretary Morgenthau and Mr. Currie, conferred with the Chinese Ambassador, Dr. Hu Shih, and Mr. T. V. Soong, who was serving as Chiang's special emissary. The President's first question was whether the Soviet-Japanese Pact had reduced or ended Soviet aid to China. The question was a bit premature, but Mr. Roosevelt's comment was interesting: if the Soviets continued to send aid, he remarked, it would indicate that the new pact had little meaning. He then discussed ways and means by which supplies could be gotten to China under Lend-Lease and generally renewed his promise to do all in his power to help the Nationalist Government.[60]

On the following day the Generalissimo reviewed the situation with Ambassador Johnson. It was six weeks, he remarked, since Mr. Currie's visit and as yet there had been no manifestations of further American assistance. Meanwhile Soviet officials in China were making great propaganda play of American failure to implement the many professions of sympathy that had been lavished on China. He hoped a schedule of supplies for China could be settled upon and voiced objection to the U.S. Treasury's decision to make only twenty million of the fifty million dollar stabilization loan available initially and dole out the rest in five million dollar installments. The Ambassador reported home that Chiang's pride was obviously hurt, that he and the Chinese generally felt that they had won the right to be treated on a basis of equality among the nations fighting to preserve their rights.[61]

Ambassador Johnson's message, coming at so critical a moment, caused a flurry in Washington. The State Department had just completed a long memorandum reviewing United States policy toward China since 1937 and summarizing the aid thus far provided. The figures were truly depressing: less than $200,000,000 in credits and loans, and only about $25,000,000 in arms and munitions.[62] State Department officials, traditionally favorable to the policy of supporting China, seem to have been shocked by the realization of how little had been done. Mr. Welles at once sent Ambassador Johnson's cable to the White House, with a memorandum for the President:

The telegram under reference appears to raise a very important question. A number of messages from you and from the Secretary of State to General Chiang Kai-shek during past months have conveyed to General Chiang repeated expressions of our friendliness and of general encouragement to the Chinese cause. We could, of course,

[59] Tel. from Steinhardt (Moscow), April 16, 1941; tel. from Johnson, May 10, 1941.
[60] Memo of conversation, April 15, 1941 (*Morgenthau Diaries, MS.*, Vol. 389, pp. 51 ff.).
[61] Tel. from Johnson, April 17, 1941.
[62] Memo of April 17, 1941, prepared by several officers of the Division of Far Eastern Affairs and forwarded to Hornbeck, Welles and Hull.

send General Chiang a further message of that nature. . . . However, in view of the recent conclusion of the Soviet-Japanese Neutrality Pact and its discouraging effect upon Chinese morale, and in view of the indication . . . that some Russians at Chung-king are apparently endeavoring to weaken the confidence of the Chinese Government that the United States will aid China substantially, it is believed important that in such reply as may be sent to Chiang Kai-shek there be given to the extent possible concrete information as to the amount and character of the supplies this country proposes to furnish and as to what material progress is being made toward that end.[63]

Concurrently Secretary Hull enlisted the President's aid to influence the Treasury to strike the installment feature from the stabilization loan, the final agreement for which was signed on April 25. On the following day Mr. Roosevelt let Mr. T. V. Soong know that certain supplies requested under Lend-Lease would be made available at once and others as quickly as possible.[64] Since the Generalissimo was particularly anxious to obtain more planes, the resolution of this issue was especially urgent. On April 15 the President had signed an unpublicized executive order permitting United States Army, Navy and Marine Corps flyers and ground crews to resign from the Services for the specific purpose of joining Colonel Claire L. Chennault's American Volunteer Group (later known as the "Flying Tigers") as civilian employees of the Chinese Government. Chennault, in Chinese service, had been in Washington since the preceding autumn at-tempting to find planes and personnel to reinforce the decrepit Chinese Air Force. Permission to recruit aviators was, of course, a crucial item in the development of his program. Most difficult, however, was the task of finding planes.[65]

The Chinese program of March 31, 1941, had called for some 1500 planes, including 750 pursuit planes, 300 bombers and 300 trainers. Perhaps because the Generalissimo's agents in Washington realized that these figures were hopeless, they began to press for about half the original numbers. Tak-ing advantage of the Soviet-Japanese Pact, they pleaded for the construction of an efficient air force in China that could threaten the flank of the Japanese armies if they moved south. At the same time, they argued, such an air force could protect Chinese airfields and the Burma Road, scout out Japanese

[63] Memo of Welles to the President, April 18, 1941. On April 21 Mr. Welles sent a copy of this memorandum to Mr. Harry Hopkins, the Administrator of Lend-Lease, with a note saying: "It seems to me in the highest degree desirable from the standpoint of our own interest to do what we can to bolster [Chinese] morale as rapidly as possible. One of the most effective things we can do is to send the Generalissimo as quickly as we can some concrete information as to what military equipment we can make available to the Nationalist Government in the near future."

[64] The joint statement on the stabilization loan is printed in *Documents on American Foreign Relations,* III, 243 ff. On the background we have used the *Morgenthau Diaries* (*MS.*), Vol. 390, pp. 73 ff., and Vol. 391, pp. 287 ff. The President's assurances were reported in tels. to Johnson at Chungking, April 26 and 28, 1941.

[65] General Claire L. Chennault: *Way of a Fighter* (New York, 1949), Chapter VII, and General Marshall's testimony in *Pearl Harbor Attack,* III, 1222 ff.

operations, and hamper the movement of troops and supplies. Nothing would be more important for the defense of Singapore.[66] On the basis of this or some similar Chinese program, Currie wrote the President asking that he intervene personally to induce the American Services and the British to divert sufficient planes to the Chinese, partly because of the importance of defending Singapore and partly because "Chinese morale needs a shot in the arm."[67]

Mr. Roosevelt was only too well aware of the desirability of bolstering the Chungking regime. Early in May he personally reassured the Generalissimo that steps were being taken to get munitions to Nationalist China. He even went so far as to hint that he had not altogether ruled out the prospect of another declaration of America's determination to aid China. He merely pointed out that while such a declaration would lift Chinese morale, Chiang would do well to consider its impact on Tokyo and take into account the possibility that it might cause Japan to move faster.[68] Nonetheless, the President on May 6 declared China eligible for Lend-Lease aid and on May 15, after another appeal from Currie, authorized the latter to negotiate with the War Department for planes "or any other thing that the Chinese request." He added, however, the cautious remark: "I don't want to imply that I am at the time in favor of any of the proposals. Obviously that can only be finally worked out in relationship to our whole military problem and the needs of ourselves and the British."[69]

Finally, as a further earnest of the policy of active assistance, the President, in response to the Generalissimo's request for help in finding a competent political adviser, suggested the name of Owen Lattimore. Chiang accepted at once and the necessary arrangements were made. Lattimore was to serve the Chungking Government as a private citizen. However, in the sequel he kept in correspondence with Currie and so with the President, serving thus as an important link in the direct line from the Generalissimo to the White House.[70]

It was still to take some time before war supplies in substantial quantities reached Nationalist China. Indeed, the practical difficulties of transportation remained throughout the war period, as they were during the months before Pearl Harbor, a serious limiting factor. But there can be no doubt that the various steps taken in April and May, 1941, gave the Chinese new

[66] Unsigned and undated memo, written soon after the conclusion of the Soviet-Japanese Pact (copy in the *Donovan Papers, MS.*).

[67] Letter of Currie to the President, April 25, 1941 (*Roosevelt Papers:* Secretary's File, Box 73).

[68] Message from Chiang Kai-shek to the President, sent in a tel. from Johnson, April 25, 1941, and the reply, drafted by Hornbeck and Currie, and approved by the President on May 2, 1941.

[69] *Pearl Harbor Attack,* XX, 4539 ff.

[70] Memo from the President to Secretary Hull, May 19, 1941; tel. to Johnson, May 29, 1941; tel. from Gauss (Chungking), June 1, 1941, conveying Chiang's acceptance.

hope and ensured the continuance of their struggle against Japan. How important Chinese resistance was to the cause of America and Britain need not be restated, but it is worth recalling that in the spring of 1941 Washington regarded prolongation of the hostilities in China as one of the chief levers to bring Japan into line. The State Department memorandum of April 17, reviewing United States policy toward China, recommended aid to Chungking to the fullest extent possible and concurrently the exertion of ever greater economic pressure on Japan, short only of embargoes on materials which Japan regarded as essential to its existence. The objective, continued the memorandum, should be not to drive the Japanese into a war of desperation, but rather to demonstrate to them the dangers of the activist program. The current year, 1941, was a critical year for the war in Europe. If by the end of the year the prospects of an early German victory should have faded, Japan might think twice before plunging into a long and potentially disastrous struggle. Japan might even voluntarily abandon its connection with the Axis.

In retrospect it may be thought that these ideas and hopes were altogether extravagant. Yet in the setting of the period they were by no means unwarranted. Article III of the Tripartite Pact certainly left Japan a loophole for escape from the Axis and it was still a question whether the policy of Matsuoka or that of Konoye would prevail. In June, 1941, the conflict of views in Tokyo was still unresolved, though the odds seemed to be turning against Matsuoka. Only when Hitler turned on Soviet Russia, only when his victorious divisions seemed on the point of striking down the Communist colossus, did the Japanese extremists manage to carry the day. An entirely new situation was then created for Japan. The opportunities and the temptations were too great, and in the atmosphere of exuberant aggressiveness the hopes of peaceful settlement were bound to be stifled.

CHAPTER XVI

The World in Suspense

1. HITLER'S GOLDEN OPPORTUNITY

History may well decide that in May and June, 1941, Adolf Hitler was closer to victory than at any other time in the course of the epic struggle known as the Second World War. While his U-boats wrought havoc on British shipping in the Atlantic, Nazi successes in the Balkans and in Libya provided him an unusual opportunity to overrun the entire Middle East, to attack Egypt from two sides and, by forcing Spain to align itself with the Axis, to seize Gibraltar and occupy North Africa. For a time there were no British, Turkish or Spanish forces capable of stemming the tide of Nazi victory. Consequently it was all too likely that the British would be driven from the Mediterranean, that their vital supply lines in that area would be severed and that, from West Africa, the much longer trade routes by way of the Cape would also be endangered. True, the United States might in such circumstances have intervened in the gigantic duel, but even this would probably not have saved the situation, for the United States had as yet but little military force in being and as an arsenal of democracy was still only in the tooling up stage. Given the six months still needed to gear the American war effort, Hitler might possibly have forced his British opponents to the wall. At the very least he had a better opportunity to do so in the spring of 1941 than at any later date.

Admiral Raeder and his associates of the Naval High Command viewed the situation in this light. They had for months been expounding to the Fuehrer the principles of global war and stressing the supreme need for striking at Britain's supply lines before the full weight of American power could be thrown into the scales. In the hour of Balkan victory they renewed their importunities, pointing out that the crucial German objectives in the Middle East had come within "grasping distance" as a result of the Balkan campaign and urging that "the offensive exploitation of the present favor-

494

able situation must take place with the greatest speed and energy, before Great Britain recovers in the Near East with American aid." They pleaded the necessity for strengthening the French position in Syria and for using that country as a base of operations against Suez. Furthermore, they repeated their arguments for an assault on Malta and for the commitment of more troops and tanks to Rommel's Libyan operation.[1]

The fact that Hitler failed to exploit his opportunity is a source of profound grief to German naval authorities even at the present day.[2] Yet the explanation is not hard to find. The Fuehrer clearly lacked understanding of sea power and had never subscribed to Raeder's Mediterranean plans without reservation. Neither did he take the American threat seriously. If any weight is to be given Ribbentrop's remarks to Mussolini, the Nazis still deluded themselves into thinking that if it were made plain to the United States that naval escort of shipping meant war, they would hesitate, "because American rearmament was the biggest bluff in the world's history."[3] Hitler had long since decided that the solution of his problem lay in knocking out the Soviet Union, an undertaking highly congenial to him and one to which Nazi military men had become converted to such a degree that they bemoaned the loss of time and the diversion of forces entailed by the Balkan campaign.[4] That being so, it cannot be too strongly emphasized that Hitler's objective in proceeding against Greece was basically defensive. He thought it imperative to drive the British from the continent and so remove all threat to the Rumanian oil fields. Having achieved this goal, the Fuehrer was ill-disposed toward further distraction from his grand design for the conquest of Soviet Russia.

His approach to the Middle East problem seemed the more justified since further operations in that area bristled with difficulties. In conversation with Count Ciano on April 20, 1941, he made no attempt to conceal his perplexity. Victory in the Balkans had indeed made life more difficult for the British and had brought the Axis considerably closer to Suez. But how was the assault on Egypt to be delivered? Once again Hitler lamented the recalcitrance of Franco and Serrano Suñer, whom he had patently come to distrust. There was little hope, he thought, that the Spanish could be brought into line or that they would permit the seizure of Gibraltar. As for Libya, Rommel had won a brilliant action and had pointed the way to destruction of the British position in Egypt. But a decisive victory in that

[1] Memo of the Naval High Command, June 6, 1941 (*Fuehrer Conferences*, 1941 [1], 98 ff.). This problem is well discussed in F. H. Hinsley: *Hitler's Strategy* (New York, 1951), 154 ff.

[2] Cf. especially the excellent study of Admiral Kurt Assmann: *Deutsche Schicksalsjahre* (Wiesbaden, 1950), Chapter XI.

[3] Ribbentrop's conference with Mussolini, May 13, 1941 (*Nazi Conspiracy and Aggression*, IX, 1866-PS).

[4] *Halder Diary*, May 22, 1941.

theater would require five more German divisions and it seemed unlikely, on account of the summer heat, that further operations could be undertaken before October. There remained Turkey, but plans for an advance through Asia Minor and Syria held little promise. The Turks would resist and the great distances would make an advance uncertain and dangerous. The Fuehrer saw little prospect of aligning Turkey with the Axis even diplomatically, for there were no obvious political advantages to be offered the Ankara Government. In sum, there was for the present little to be done in the Middle East and the Mediterranean, and Hitler was not greatly disturbed by the temporary stalemate. He explained to Ciano that German victories in the Balkans, together with Japanese pressure, would probably keep the United States from intervention and that American deliveries could not become decisive before 1942. Though he did not say so, he firmly believed that in the interval he could dispose of Soviet Russia and thereby revolutionize the entire international situation.[5]

In consonance with this estimate of the situation, the Germans accorded the complex of Mediterranean problems a decidedly secondary role. In the west nothing of importance was planned or done. Raeder had finally convinced the Fuehrer that German resources were insufficient to capture and hold the Azores and, since Franco's wrongheadedness appeared incorrigible, no further effort was made to convert him to active intervention.[6] Darlan proved not only ready but eager to accommodate the Germans in one way or another, but his advances were received with suspicion, as will appear presently, and his proposals were accepted in only a halfhearted way. Further east Rommel was left to his own devices. The Nazi High Command was not disposed to forgive him for exceeding his instructions and flatly denied him the reinforcements needed to exploit his unexpected victory.[7] To complete the conquest of Greece and deprive the British of their important base on Crete, that island was conquered by a whirlwind airborne operation in late May. But the Germans did not follow up this dramatic success, as the British feared they would. An opportunity was presented them in connection with an anti-British, pro-Axis rising in Iraq, which Hitler felt obliged to support as best he could. But Nazi action in the Middle East was so hesitant and halfhearted that it was almost bound to fail. The net result, therefore, was the British-Free French campaign in Syria which eventually enabled the anti-Axis forces to recover, at least in part, their command of the eastern approaches to Egypt.

[5] Ciano's conversation with Hitler, April 20, 1941 (*Ciano's Diplomatic Papers,* 434 ff.). Ribbentrop's remarks to Ciano on June 2, 1941 (*ibid.,* 441 ff.), were still of the same general tenor.

[6] Conference of Hitler with the High Command, May 22, 1941 (*Fuehrer Conferences,* 1941 [1], 65).

[7] *Halder Diary,* April 14, 23, May 9-11, 1941.

2. THE PARIS PROTOCOLS

It would be difficult indeed to exaggerate the complexity of the situation which confronted General Wavell in April and May, 1941. With the limited forces at his disposal he had to defend the British position in the western desert and complete the conquest of Italian East Africa. The major part of his forces had been sent to Greece and were evacuated only with the loss of their equipment. Meanwhile it was necessary to defend Crete as well as possible and prepare to meet the anticipated Nazi advance either through Turkey or, by way of sea and airborne operations, from Syria. One can readily believe that the British commander was a tired man and seemed to have aged ten years on learning of the disaster in Cyrenaica.[8]

Though Wavell thought it essential to concentrate his efforts on the defense of Egypt, Prime Minister Churchill and the War Cabinet could hardly ignore the developments which now took place elsewhere in the Arab world. In his message to President Roosevelt of April 29, 1941, Mr. Churchill had recounted his fears: the Nazis might make "dangerous" demands on the Turks, who might feel obliged to make concessions, though short of permitting the passage of large numbers of German troops. Syria, on the other hand, was in more immediate danger, for it was likely that the Germans would soon attack Crete and, if they succeeded in that operation, despatch an airborne force to Syria by way of Rhodes: "If the German Air Force and troop carrier planes get installed in Syria, they will soon penetrate and poison both Iraq and Iran and threaten Palestine." The Prime Minister appealed to the President to use his influence at Vichy to prevent French collaboration in such designs and concluded: "I feel Hitler may quite easily now gain vast advantages very cheaply and we are so fully engaged that we can do little or nothing to stop him spreading himself."[9]

The immediate threat came from Iraq, where the Government, despite its treaty obligations, had long been unfriendly to Britain. The Arab-Zionist antagonism had provided the Nazis with admirable propaganda material and had led to the formation at Baghdad of a small but influential pro-Nazi party, inspired by the Grand Mufti of Jerusalem. In March, 1941, when the Iraqi Government was taken over by Rashid Ali al-Gailani, it was virtually certain that trouble would ensue. Before long the pro-British regent fled the country and by mid-April the British felt obliged to land additional Indian forces at Basra. This was too much for the military clique ("The Golden Square") then in control at Baghdad. Inspired, apparently, by the Nazi successes in Greece, Ali al-Gailani decided to precipitate a revolt which originally had been planned for a later date. On May 2 Iraqi forces attacked

[8] Churchill: *The Grand Alliance*, 344.
[9] Message from the Prime Minister to the President, April 29, 1941.

the British air camp at Habbaniya, outside Baghdad, while the Iraqi Government appealed to Hitler for armed support.[10]

The British, long concerned lest the Nazis secure a foothold in the Arab world, acted with great promptness and energy. Operations were at once entrusted to Wavell's command, with instructions to send a flying force to the relief of Habbaniya. While sturdy and courageous British forces repelled the Arab attack on the camp (May 7), an advance column set out from Palestine and arrived on May 18. A combined attack on Baghdad was undertaken immediately. The British took the city on May 30, whereupon the revolt collapsed. Al-Gailani and his supporters fled the country.

Obviously the insurrection in Iraq was in itself of little moment. It had but slight support in the country and its leaders proved utterly inept in their management of the affair. Long before Nazi aid could arrive in significant quantity the British had defeated the insurgents and reëstablished control. Yet the trouble in Iraq was to have larger repercussions, for Hitler felt bound to heed the appeals from Baghdad and felt impelled to turn to Vichy France for staging facilities in Syria, without which it would be difficult if not impossible to fly planes to Iraq. This situation in turn led to the negotiation of the so-called Paris Protocols, which constitute an important chapter in the history of Franco-German collaboration and which, at the same time, profoundly affected the course of American policy toward the Pétain-Darlan regime.

Although the main facts of Darlan's arrangements with the Germans are now known, it is still extremely difficult to determine his motives. It is possible that, as Mr. Churchill believed, the Admiral was simply "a dirty dog" and "an ambitious crook" who detested the British and was therefore an even greater menace to their interests than Laval.[11] But there was probably more to his attitude and policy than mere Anglophobia. His previous record had been long and distinguished and quite untainted by pro-Nazi sentiment. Furthermore, there is nothing in the evidence to suggest that, in order to have his revenge on the British, he desired a German victory. It would seem rather that, as an opportunist and a man notoriously ambitious and thirsty for power, he was above all intent on currying favor with the Germans and convincing them that the restoration of Laval to power was quite unnecessary. He probably held the ultimate victory of Hitler inevitable and therefore believed it important for France to make peace with its traditional enemy before the latter's domination of Europe was complete. From

---

[10] General Sir Archibald P. Wavell: *Despatch on Operations in Iraq, East Syria and Iran from 10th April, 1941 to 12th January, 1942,* dated October 18, 1942 (Supplement to the *London Gazette,* August 14, 1946); Churchill: *The Grand Alliance,* Book I, Chapter XIV; Field Marshal Lord Wilson: *Eight Years Overseas* (London, 1948), Chapter IV.

[11] Memos of the Prime Minister to his subordinates, February 16, 17, 23, 1941 (Churchill: *The Grand Alliance,* 735-36, 740).

his remarks to American diplomats it would seem that, like some other Frenchmen, he was confident that in the long run he could outwit the Germans and bend events to France's advantage.

More immediately Darlan, and indeed the Vichy Government as a whole, were confronted with serious problems arising from the armistice of June, 1940, an agreement which was originally intended as a short-run solution and which over the longer period became extremely onerous. It was essential to do whatever was possible to hasten the return of French war prisoners, to secure a reduction of the heavy occupation charges, to relax the restrictions between the two zones of France, and to regulate innumerable administrative matters. In addition it was urgent to secure German permission to rearm the Fleet and strengthen the colonial military forces. If the empire in North and West Africa was to be preserved, Weygand would need sufficient troops to repel Gaullist or British attacks. At the same time adequate military strength in North Africa would enable the French to resist German encroachment and would provide them a firm basis for military operations if and when they decided to reënter the war on the British side. Darlan's apologists, admittedly few in number, have maintained that one of the Admiral's chief objectives in negotiating with the Germans was to get their sanction for the reinforcement of the North African military establishment.[12]

Hitler's resounding victories in the Balkans and in Libya in April, 1941, led both Pétain and Darlan to apprehend renewed Nazi pressure on France and Spain preparatory to the opening of operations in the western Mediterranean area. If any credence is to be given the Admiral's explanations to his colleagues, he felt that the situation was rapidly coming to a head and that presently Vichy would be confronted with far-reaching Nazi demands. Any French effort to support the British would mean almost immediate disaster, and even an attempt to maintain a balance between the two great contestants would be futile. According to Darlan the only sane course was that of collaboration, short of deliberate participation in the war against Britain. By showing a readiness to make some concessions Vichy might succeed in heading off exorbitant and dangerous demands. Furthermore, by establishing good relations with Germany, France could hope not only to survive as an independent nation but also to cut its territorial losses when the final reckoning was made and even assure itself of an important place in the Nazi new order.[13] As a first step toward collaboration Darlan therefore approved a German request for a certain number of military trucks, to be sent from Tunisia to Rommel's *Afrika Korps*. This step was taken without

[12] Louis-Dominique Girard: *Montoire: Verdun diplomatique* (Paris, 1948), 342 ff.; Amiral Docteur: *La grande énigme de la guerre: Darlan* (Paris, 1949), 116 ff.

[13] Pétain's letter to Weygand, April 25, 1941, and Darlan's communication to his colleagues and to Weygand, May 14, 1941 (Weygand: *Mémoires,* 419-20, 421 ff.).

consulting Weygand, who was told, in reply to his protest, that it was deemed inadvisable if not impossible to refuse the Nazi request.[14]

On the German side the program for collaboration was most ardently championed by Otto Abetz, the German Ambassador in Paris, who was un- remitting in his efforts to persuade Ribbentrop and Hitler of the great possi- bilities inherent in Franco-German friendship. The Fuehrer, however, evinced little interest. He could not reconcile himself to Laval's uncere- monious dismissal and felt in honor bound to secure his reappointment. More importantly, he could not overlook the fact that a *rapprochement* with France would estrange his Italian partner. Above all else, he distrusted the French, individually and collectively. Though Darlan's known Anglophobia was something of a recommendation and Hitler eventually agreed to receive him, he explained to Mussolini and Ciano two days after his conference with the Admiral that he had no faith in French sincerity. Pétain, he said, was "an old fox, whose memory deserted him just at the moments when it best suited him." At bottom, he was convinced, all Frenchmen hoped for a British victory and there was undoubtedly much truth in Ciano's anecdote that while in Paris people said: "Let us hope the British win," in Vichy they put the matter somewhat differently and said: "Let us hope the British swine win."[15] Lest it be thought that the Fuehrer was merely trying to reassure the Duce, it should be noted that the subsequent Franco-German negotiations provided ample evidence of the genuineness of Nazi distrust.

It was the revolt in Iraq and Rashid al-Gailani's appeal for Nazi support that finally obliged Hitler to resume the program of collaboration. On May 3 Abetz was able to inform Darlan that the Fuehrer would receive him and that the Germans were prepared to make various concessions if Vichy would permit the shipment to Iraq of certain military stocks in Syria and the use of Syrian airfields for the staging of Nazi planes. The Ambassador emphasized that the future of collaboration would depend on the extent of French per- formance, in short that Hitler would look for deeds, not words. Darlan, in turn, pointed out that he would have difficulties with his colleagues unless the concessions offered by the Germans were real and substantial.

After further conferences on May 5 and 6, the two men came to agree- ment. Darlan accepted the German demands and in addition promised that officials objectionable to Hitler would be recalled both from Syria and North Africa. French trucks delivered to Rommel were to be loaded with German supplies shipped from French Mediterranean ports to Bizerte in Tunisia. In return the Germans promised to permit the rearmament of six French de- stroyers and seven torpedo boats, to relax the stringent travel and traffic regulations between the two zones of France, to reduce the costs of occupa-

[14] William L. Langer: *Our Vichy Gamble* (New York, 1947), 148; Weygand: *Mémoires,* 420.

[15] Record of conversation between Hitler, Ribbentrop, Mussolini and Ciano, May 13, 1941 (*Nazi Conspiracy and Aggression,* IV, 1866-PS).

tion, and to liberate French prisoners who had fought in the First World War and were required for French war industry.[16]

Darlan appears to have concluded these arrangements without reference to Marshal Pétain or the Vichy Cabinet. By way of extenuation his apologists have explained that the military stocks in Syria were in any case under control of the Italian Armistice Commission and that the Germans could have taken them over without French permission. Furthermore, it has been noted that since international law had nothing to say on the subject of belligerent planes landing and refueling on neutral airfields, Darlan was justified in holding that such planes had rights similar to those of belligerent warships.[17] It was hardly to be expected, however, that the British would countenance such legalisms. General Dentz, the French Commander in Syria, had been instructed at once by Darlan not to resist the landing of German planes but, on the contrary, to provide them all facilities. Dentz was, however, to oppose with force all British attempts at retaliation.[18]

The presence of German planes on Syrian airfields did not escape the attention of the British. Mr. Churchill and his military advisers had long been apprehensive about Syria and had pondered ways and means of securing control of this strategically vital area. General Catroux, the Free French emissary in the Middle East, had made efforts to win over General Dentz, an Alsatian and reputedly bitterly anti-German, to the Free French cause. His attempts had proved futile and consequently Mr. Churchill, under constant pressure from General de Gaulle, had agreed in principle to Free French military action at the opportune moment. If by May, 1941, nothing had been done, it was largely because the Free French leaders insisted on British aid, while the British in turn were so deeply involved in North Africa and Greece that they had no forces available for further operations. Besides, Dentz was constantly assuring the British that he would resist German encroachment.[19]

The problem of action against Syria had been discussed at length by Wavell and Catroux on May 5, 1941. The Free French were eager to march if it turned out that Dentz failed to resist the Germans. Catroux urged the danger of a German air attack and expressed hope that if the British and Free French took a firm stand, the French forces in Syria would defect.

---

[16] Langer: *Our Vichy Gamble*, 148-49, to be supplemented by *Pétain et les allemands: mémorandum d'Abetz* (Paris, 1948), 99 ff.; Jean-Louis Aujol: *Le procès Benoist-Mechin* (Paris, 1948), 118-37; *Halder Diary*, May 7 and 8, 1941.

[17] Aujol: *Le procès Benoist-Mechin*, 127 ff.; Maurice Martin du Gard: *La carte impériale* (Paris, 1949), Chapter X.

[18] Langer: *Our Vichy Gamble*, 149; George London: *L'amiral Esteva et le général Dentz devant la Haute Cour de Justice* (Lyon, 1945), 174-75.

[19] Churchill: *Their Finest Hour*, 687 (memo of November 12, 1940); Vice-amiral Muselier: *De Gaulle contre le gaullisme* (Paris, 1946), 216 ff.; Général Catroux: *Dans la bataille de Méditerranée* (Paris, 1949), 85 ff.; Jacques Soustelle: *De Londres à Alger* (Paris, 1947), 243 ff.; London: *L'amiral Esteva et le général Dentz*, 200 (Dentz's assurances, as late as May 2, 1941).

Wavell, however, felt he could not spare British ground forces for such an operation. He was suspicious of Free French intelligence and discounted Catroux's reports that Dentz was planning to withdraw his troops into the Lebanon and abandon Syria to the Germans. But the London War Cabinet took a different view. Churchill had for some time impressed on his colleagues that nothing was to be hoped from Vichy, that an end should be made of the "cold shouldering" of de Gaulle, and that the Free French should not be tied up too tightly. "I think he [de Gaulle] is much the best Frenchman now in the arena, and I want him taken care of as much as possible," he had written in February.[20] Furthermore, the Prime Minister took a grave view of the threat to Syria and was determined to eliminate it at all costs. Wavell was ordered to permit Catroux and the Free French to go ahead and to give them all possible aid. Although on May 21 Catroux admitted that his reports from Syria had been exaggerated, the War Cabinet instructed Wavell to prepare ground forces for action with the Free French. On May 29 General Spears, Mr. Churchill's special representative, arrived in Jerusalem in the company of General de Gaulle, after which final preparations were made for the forthcoming campaign.[21]

In arriving at his decision, the British Prime Minister was probably not at all deterred by Pétain's assurances to Admiral Leahy that he would in no case give "any voluntary active military aid to Germany."[22] These were words susceptible of various interpretations and in any case seemed completely untrustworthy in the light of news that Darlan had conferred with Hitler at Berchtesgaden on May 11. Mr. Churchill therefore cabled the President:

. . . Syria is a cause of great anxiety. There is no doubt that Darlan will sell the pass if he can, and German aircraft are already passing into Iraq. I have no means of action on that caitiff Government. The more Leahy can do, the better. It is the only hope. We are also sure Vichy is letting transport, etc. go to Tripoli overland from Tunis. The Azores and Cape Verde Islands are always liable to be jumped by the Germans at the same time that they break into Spain or seduce the Spanish Government. It will be very difficult for us to avoid being either too soon or too late.[23]

The Prime Minister's temperament disposed him to be forehanded rather than tardy. Abandoning hope of Ambassador Leahy's influence, he informed Mr. Roosevelt on May 21 of the coming Syrian operation:

I hope you will forgive me if I say there is anxiety here. We are at a climacteric of the war, when enormous crystallizations are in suspense but imminent. The battle for

[20] Churchill: *The Grand Alliance*, 735-36, 740.
[21] Churchill: *The Grand Alliance*, 322 ff.; Catroux: *Dans la bataille de Méditerranée*, 117-26; Wavell's despatch, as cited above; Lord Wilson: *Eight Years Overseas*, 109 ff.; Muselier: *De Gaulle contre le gaullisme*, 224 ff.; Soustelle: *De Londres à Alger*, 246.
[22] Tel. from Leahy, May 13, 1941. See also William D. Leahy: *I Was There* (New York, 1950), 30 ff.
[23] Message of Mr. Churchill to the President, May 14, 1941.

Crete has opened well. I had steps taken to reinforce Egypt which gives me good confidence about the Western Desert. . . . We now have to launch out into Syria with the Free French in the name of Syrian and Lebanon independence. Spain, Vichy and Turkey are a rivetted audience.[24]

Although the British action against Syria threatened to destroy the American Vichy policy, the President raised no objection, partly because the Vichy policy had always been predicated on noninterference with "British war measures" and partly because Darlan's maneuvers seemed to threaten the future of North and West Africa as well as of Syria.[25] Pétain himself admitted to Admiral Leahy that he thought the arrival of German forces in Spanish Morocco imminent and confessed that there was little Vichy could do to stop such German operations. Under the circumstances both Mr. Roosevelt and Mr. Hull felt the time had come for positive action. On May 15 Marshal Pétain had announced in a radio broadcast his approval of Darlan's visit to Hitler: "The new interview permits us to light up the road into the future and to continue the conversations that have been begun with the German Government." In reply Mr. Roosevelt at once issued a public statement which amounted to an appeal to the French people against the Vichy Government:

It is inconceivable they [the French people] will willingly accept any agreement for so-called "collaboration," which in reality will imply their alliance with a military power whose central and fundamental policy calls for the utter destruction of liberty, freedom, and popular institutions everywhere.

The people of the United States can hardly believe that the present Government of France could be brought to lend itself to a plan of voluntary alliance implied or otherwise which would apparently deliver up France and its colonial Empire, including French African colonies and their Atlantic coasts, with the menace which that involves to the peace and safety of the Western Hemisphere.

Mr. Hull, in turn, summoned Ambassador Henry-Haye and warned him once again that if Vichy continued its present course, he would regard it as an indirect attempt "to slit the throat of the United States." To show that he meant business, the President had the Coast Guard take custody of all French ships in American ports, including the ill-fated *Normandie*.[26]

If indeed Vichy was slipping down the inclined plane into military collaboration with the Germans, the one remaining hope seemed to Washington to be Weygand's position in North Africa. "I am not hopeful," cabled the President to Mr. Churchill on May 14, 1941, "of any concrete orders to Weygand to resist, but we may still pull some of the chestnuts out of the

[24] Message from Churchill to the President, May 21, 1941.
[25] Hull: *Memoirs*, II, 958 ff.
[26] Langer: *Our Vichy Gamble*, 151-52; Hull: *Memoirs*, II, 958 ff.; memos of Mr. Hull to President Roosevelt, May 13, 1941, commenting on letters from Admiral Leahy to the President (*Roosevelt Papers:* Secretary's File, Box 75).

fire."[27] There was evidently some doubt in the State Department whether even the Murphy-Weygand Agreement was still worth pursuing, but the War Department urged that the supplies being loaded for North Africa be despatched on schedule, so as to "get a hold on Weygand." Accordingly the terms of the agreement were observed, at least for the time being.[28] It is worth recalling, however, that it was on May 14 that the President finally decided to order three warships, an aircraft carrier and supporting ships from Pearl Harbor into the Atlantic, and that plans were being made for the occupation of the Azores, should such a move become necessary.[29]

British and American apprehensions were, it is now known, only too well founded. Neither London nor Washington had specific information on Darlan's negotiations with Hitler, but sensed correctly that an important and dangerous deal was in the making. On May 11 there had been a two-hour conference on the Berghof, followed the next day by further discussion between Darlan and Ribbentrop. The Frenchman had made clear to the Fuehrer that France was prepared to aid the Axis in its war against Britain, provided adequate concessions were made by the Germans. Hitler, in turn, indicated that if Vichy collaborated sincerely, France might be compensated for inevitable territorial losses in Europe and Africa by receiving part of the British African spoils. However, he added sternly, the time had come for France to take a definite stand; it should be clearly understood that all arrangements must be strictly on the basis of give and take.[30]

The agreement in principle arrived at by Hitler and Darlan was perfected in a series of conferences (May 21 and 28) between Darlan's assistant, M. Benoist-Mechin, and General Huntziger on the French side, and General Warlimont on the German. These conferences eventuated in the three Paris Protocols of May 28, 1941, the first of which dealt with Syria and Iraq, the second with North Africa, and the third with West and Equatorial Africa. In return for the promise of political and economic concessions, the French agreed to make available to the Iraqi insurgents three quarters of the munitions stocked in Syria; to afford German planes the facilities of Syrian airfields; to provide the Germans an air base at Aleppo; and to permit the use of Syrian ports, roads and railroads for the transport of German supplies to Iraq. In North Africa the French were to make available to the Germans the port of Bizerte and the railroad from Bizerte to Gabès; they agreed also to sell trucks and guns to the Germans and to use French ships for the trans-

---

[27] Tel. from the President to the Prime Minister, May 14, 1941.

[28] *Stimson Diary (MS.)*, May 19, 20, 21, 1941.

[29] See above, Chapter XII, Section 2.

[30] For greater detail see Langer: *Our Vichy Gamble*, 149-51, to be supplemented by the record of Ribbentrop's conference with Mussolini and Ciano on May 14, 1941 (*Nazi Conspiracy and Aggression*, IV, 1866-PS), and by the material in *Pétain et les Allemands*, 101 ff.; Aujol: *Le procès Benoist-Mechin*, 150 ff.; and Amiral Docteur: *La grande énigme de la guerre: Darlan*, 116 ff.

port of German supplies across the Mediterranean, these ships to be escorted by French warships. In West Africa, Dakar was to be put at the disposal of the Germans as a supply base for submarines, warships and airplanes.[31]

Several items of these accords call for special attention. In the first place, the terms as they touched Syria and Iraq were almost entirely retrospective. By the end of May the French had already afforded German planes all the facilities specified in the Paris Protocols and about a hundred German planes had actually passed through Syria.[32] Furthermore, General Dentz had sent thousands of rifles, machine guns and ammunition to Iraq, though he claimed later to have despatched less than was promised and to have chosen old and defective stock as far as possible.[33] Finally, by the end of May it had already become clear that the German-French program for Syria and Iraq was futile. The insurrection in Iraq was all but finished. British planes were bombing Syrian airfields and it was reasonably clear that in the near future the British or Free French, or both, would take punitive action against Syria.

With respect to North Africa the same was at least partially true, for French trucks had been going to Rommel's forces for some time, even though French ships and convoys had not as yet been employed in the transport of German supplies to North Africa. Finally, and most important, the French concession of rights to Dakar was very definitely tied to a *protocole complémentaire* to which the Germans had objected vigorously, but on which Darlan had insisted. This additional agreement noted that the use of Dakar by the Germans involved for the French the danger of immediate armed conflict with the British and Americans, and that therefore it could not be implemented until the reinforcements necessary for the defense of West Africa had actually been provided. Furthermore, the German Government would first have to accord the French such political and economic concessions as to enable the Vichy Government to justify to the French public an eventual conflict with the democracies. In brief, the utilization of Dakar by the Germans was conditional and prospective rather than real and immediate.[34]

Pétain and the Vichy Cabinet were informed of Darlan's dealings with the Germans on May 14 and were sufficiently convinced or intimidated to give his program unanimous approval. If Pétain was indeed the old fox the Germans thought him to be it is possible that he subscribed to collaboration in the hope of alleviating the burden of the armistice and in the thought that

---

[31] These detailed and lengthy agreements are printed in full in Langer: *Our Vichy Gamble,* Appendix II, and in the official French version in "Les accords concernant l'Afrique du Nord française" (*Cahiers d'histoire de la guerre,* October, 1949).

[32] London: *L'amiral Esteva et le général Dentz,* 209; Churchill: *The Grand Alliance,* 322.

[33] London: *L'amiral Esteva et le général Dentz,* 175 ff., 212 ff.

[34] On this point see particularly *Pétain et les allemands,* 103, and Aujol: *Le procès Benoist-Mechin,* 182 ff.

the terms of the agreement could always be evaded. One cannot be sure that Darlan himself was not playing a game of rank duplicity, making concessions in Syria and North Africa which he felt could not be resisted anyway, and attempting to tide over a particularly critical period by embarking on protracted negotiations. One need not necessarily accept the contention of Benoist-Mechin that he and Darlan asked so much of the Germans in order later to have a pretext for nonfulfillment of the engagements. Yet it is worth noting that the discussions were spun out so long that important provisions of the protocols were outdated before agreement was reached. It is also to be remarked that the French insisted on substantial concessions which, as Hitler observed to Darlan, involved a weakening of the German position in the war against Britain. Most instructive of all, however, was Darlan's attitude toward his Cabinet colleagues when the time came for approval of the Paris Protocols.

From the very beginning various Ministers—Generals Huntziger and Bergeret, M. Bouthillier and M. Moysset—appear to have felt that Darlan was running too great a risk of conflict with the British, an attitude which may well have derived from the strong stand and unmistakable warnings of Admiral Leahy. Strangely enough, Darlan at no time made much effort to defend his work. Neither did he object when it was proposed to summon General Weygand and General Boisson from Algiers and Dakar. The former reached Vichy on June 2, whereupon a restricted council of ministers was held in Marshal Pétain's presence (June 3). Darlan explained the agreements without reading them and argued that, if France refused to ratify them, the Germans would undoubtedly solve their problem by staging an advance through Spain to North Africa. Thereupon Weygand read a long memorandum he had prepared in advance. This set forth all the objections to military collaboration and the dangers of popular opposition to Vichy in France and North Africa if concessions were made to the enemy. Weygand vigorously objected to the granting of any base rights to the Germans in Africa and warned that if Hitler once had a foothold in that region the British would intervene and presently France would find itself in the war— on the wrong side. He therefore refused flatly to be a party to a policy which he regarded as both dishonorable and dangerous. Announcing his resignation, he stalked out of the council chamber.

General Boisson, who arrived late on the evening of June 4, threw his entire influence on the opposition side. Meanwhile Pétain made every effort to induce Weygand to return to his post and begged him for suggestions as to how the situation could be dealt with. The General suggested a demand on the Germans for written guarantees of the concessions they offered, a suggestion in which Darlan concurred without much ado. The necessary note to Berlin was drafted and in the course of long confabulations Weygand and Boisson were assured that no rights would be accorded the Germans anywhere in French Africa unless they accepted the French demands. These were so extensive as to involve an entire reëxamination of Franco-German relations. Since their rejection was almost a certainty, Weygand agreed to resume his position in North Africa. On June 6 the Cabinet formally adopted the new line.[35]

Darlan's rather ready surrender in the face of Weygand's opposition seemed to reflect a strange acquiescence. Speaking to Ambassador Leahy, who had learned from opponents of the Admiral what was in the wind and who naturally used his influence to wreck the program of collaboration, Darlan remarked in resignation: "France is like a prostrate man with a great stone on his chest which he must seek to push off by all means in his power in order to live." But meek submission to fate was hardly characteristic of Darlan, and one is perhaps justified in surmising, from his conduct, that his dealings with the Germans had some devious purpose. In connection with his easy abandonment of the Paris Protocols it is quite possible that he may have been influenced by the excellent intelligence that reached Vichy in June of Hitler's intention to attack Soviet Russia on the 20th of the month. To be sure, he told Ambassador Leahy that in his opinion the Nazi operations against Russia would take no longer than those against Yugoslavia and Greece, but he must have realized, as did Weygand, that involvement in the east might lead the Fuehrer to lose interest in the Mediterranean and that therefore France might yet weather the storm which was certain to break when Vichy's new demands were submitted to Berlin.[36] Vichy's great and immediate objective must therefore be to prolong the negotiations. To that end Darlan submitted to the Germans a memorandum specifying the concessions required under the *protocole complémentaire* if the Paris agreements were to be implemented. The French terms were as imposing as they were daring, for they included the reëstablishment of French sovereignty over all Metropolitan France, the demarcation line to define merely the limits of German military occupation; a special statute for Alsace-Lorraine, pending the conclusion of a peace treaty; abolition of all costs of occupation; gradual release of all war prisoners; public assurance that the Germans had no designs on Syria, North Africa or West Africa; suppression or drastic reduction of the control commissions in Africa, etc.[37]

It was to be expected and undoubtedly was anticipated that the Germans would reject these extravagant proposals. Discussions dragged on through

---

[35] The most detailed and reliable account is that of Weygand himself, as given in his *Mémoires*, 428 ff., but see also Langer: *Our Vichy Gamble*, 157 ff., and such recent materials as Girard: *Montoire, Verdun diplomatique*, 342 ff.; Aujol: *Le procès Benoist-Mechin*, 195 ff.; Fernand de Brinon: *Mémoires* (Paris, 1949), 70 ff.; Albert Kammerer: *Du débarquement africain au meutre de Darlan* (Paris, 1949), 47 ff.; Leahy: *I Was There*, 30 ff.

[36] Weygand: *Mémoires*, 439; Langer: *Our Vichy Gamble*, 158; Kammerer: *Du débarquement africain*, 47 ff.

[37] Text in Aujol: *Le procès Benoist-Mechin*, 200-201.

June and July, 1941, Ribbentrop becoming more and more furious as they proceeded. On June 2 the Nazi Foreign Minister had told Ciano that the Germans were aware that "if France had the opportunity she would with one accord rush to arms against the traditional enemy." Two weeks later he observed that French demands were becoming more pressing and that the Germans were convinced of France's "fundamental, unalterable aversion to the Axis." But, he added, the Germans lacked all means of effective reaction, for "any gesture of force would have as its immediate effect the separation of North Africa, where Weygand is carrying on activities openly hostile to Pétain and the Axis." In short, the Germans were obliged to wheedle the French as best they could.[38] The details are of no interest in the present context and it must suffice to note that the French continued to stand their ground. Since the Germans had meanwhile embarked upon their great venture in the east, French North Africa became for them distinctly a side show. On July 30 Ribbentrop flatly rejected a French suggestion of July 14 for a review of the whole problem of Franco-German relations. Therewith the Paris Protocols were more or less decently interred and the still baffling episode of Darlan's projected collaboration came to an end.[39]

Two weeks before Ribbentrop cut short the palaver, the British and their Free French allies had closed out the Syrian affair. On June 8, after publicly promising Syria and Lebanon independence, they had begun the invasion "with a piece of sugar in one hand and a gun in the other," to quote Lord Wilson. Vichy ordered General Dentz to resist, on the familiar ground that if France failed to defend its possessions, it would be unable to prevent the Germans from trying to do so. Actually the Germans, after the heavy losses suffered in the battle of Crete, were not in a position to intervene effectively. Although the hoped-for defections from Dentz's forces did not take place, the Vichy troops were no match for the invading forces. When Damascus fell (June 21) the military decision was already clear, though Vichy refused to allow Dentz to request an armistice until July 12. Under the terms of the settlement Syria passed to the administration of the Free French. The defenses of Suez and Egypt had been moved two hundred and fifty miles to the north and direct contact with the Turks had been established by land. Though the British and Free French soon fell to squabbling over the management of Syrian affairs, this did not alter the fact that a vital area had been snatched from potentially hostile forces and that another barrier had been erected against possible Nazi aggression in the Middle East.[40]

[38] *Ciano's Diplomatic Papers*, 441 ff., 445 ff.

[39] The final phases of the negotiation are recorded at some length in Aujol: *Le procès Benoist-Mechin*, 270 ff.

[40] On the Syrian campaign see Wavell's despatch: *Operations in the Middle East*, as cited above; Churchill: *The Grand Alliance*, Book I, Chapter XVIII; Lord Wilson: *Eight Years Overseas*, 113 ff.; and on the French side, London: *L'amiral Esteva et le*

In terms of American policy it might be argued with some cogency that the Paris Protocols demonstrated the bankruptcy of the Administration's Vichy policy, inasmuch as the effort to understand, to conciliate and to aid France had in no way deterred Darlan from embarking upon the course of collaboration. The State Department was in fact subjected to cascades of public criticism, the general tenor of which was that the Vichy policy was clearly a blunder, if not a crime. On many sides demands were raised that the fiasco be recognized and that American support be switched from Pétain to de Gaulle. Failing that, the United States should at least proceed to occupy Martinique and other Vichy-controlled territories in the New World.

Secretary Hull, though inured to such attacks, was much disturbed by the vehemence of public criticism. To make matters worse Lord Halifax had come to him on May 21 with the suggestion for something more "conspicuous" in the way of American recognition of de Gaulle. But the President and Mr. Hull were not yet willing to abandon ship. Even though Pétain and Darlan should prove hopeless, there was still Weygand, commanding the crucial North African area. Since that general's attitude was well known, even to Hitler, and since at this very time he reiterated his determination to defend North Africa against aggression from any quarter, it seemed most inadvisable to estrange him by recognizing de Gaulle. Lord Halifax was therefore told that no change in American policy could be contemplated.[41] Somewhat later, when it was suggested to the President that he receive de Gaulle's emissary, M. René Pleven, who would explain the whole Free French position, Mr. Roosevelt declined. "Frankly," he wrote Mr. Welles, "I think it would be difficult for me to see Mr. Pleven," though he had, so he said, no objection to the latter's being given "a sympathetic reception" by the State Department.[42]

This does not mean that during the critical days of early June Washington was not consumed by anxiety. After talking with the President, Assistant Secretary Berle was inclined to think that Vichy had "caved in completely" and had granted the Germans bases at Casablanca and Dakar. His one consolation was that the American Navy "was pretty well set to do something, if possible, about our Atlantic approaches," and that the "Brazilian shoulder" was being "pretty well cobbled up." Yet, as he sat down next day with Mr. Hull and Mr. Welles to draft another statement against col-

général Dentz, 215 ff.; Catroux: Dans la bataille de Méditerranée, Chapters XVI to XIX. General E. L. Spears's letter commenting on the Catroux book (The Times Literary Supplement, February 10, 1950) is also of some interest.

[41] Memos of conversation between Mr. Hull and Lord Halifax, May 21, 1941, and between Mr. Welles and Lord Halifax, May 23, 1941. See also Langer: Our Vichy Gamble, 154-55; Hull: Memoirs, II, 961 ff.

[42] Letter of Ambassador Biddle to the President, June 9; note of the President to Mr. Welles, June 19, 1941; State Department draft of the President's reply to Mr. Biddle (Roosevelt Papers: Secretary's File, Box 75).

laboraton, Berle thought it likely that before long the United States might have to break relations with the Pétain Government.[43]

A curious episode occurred on June 4, when Ambassador Henry-Haye, evidently in an effort to counter the growing popular demand for the occupation of Martinique, suggested to Mr. Welles that Vichy might provide the United States with base facilities on that island and in French Guiana. The Under Secretary rejected the proposal, saying that Mr. Roosevelt felt that under other circumstances such an offer would have received "the most friendly consideration," but that it could not be entertained so long as it would require the prior approval of the German Government. It would be more to the point, remarked Mr. Welles, if Vichy would inform Washington whether or not it was planning to put France and its colonial possessions under permanent German control.[44]

In the effort to frustrate Darlan's collaborationist policy, Secretary Hull on June 5 and again on June 13 issued statements sternly condemning what appeared to be the Vichy program and warmly defending the British and Gaullist action against Syria as designed "to prevent German actions there which the French, under the direction of the Vichy Government, were permitting if not abetting."[45] Naturally it is impossible to say to what extent the uncompromising stand of the American Government may have influenced the final decision at Vichy. It is not unreasonable, however, to suppose that it reinforced Weygand and his supporters in their opposition to the Darlan program and that, indeed, it made a deep impression on Marshal Pétain, who desired above all to avoid estrangement of the United States. It is even worth pointing out that Darlan himself, assuming he was sincerely committed to military collaboration with the Germans, which is at least debatable, was obliged to draw back in face of the opposition presented by his own colleagues. Mr. Hull is certainly not far off the mark when he asserts that the United States had become "the strongest foreign influence in Vichy."[46] Far from being a failure, then, the American Vichy policy appears to have contributed materially to tiding the democracies over the acute crisis that followed Hitler's victories in the Balkans and Libya.

3. Diplomatic Battle for Turkey

The German occupation of Bulgaria and especially the conquest of Yugoslavia and Greece had brought the Turkish Republic face to face with the danger of Nazi aggression. Despite a plethora of reports and rumors that

[43] *Berle Diaries* (MS.), June 5, 1941.

[44] Memo of conversation between Mr. Welles and Ambassador Henry-Haye, June 4, 1941.

[45] The texts of these statements, and the French replies, may be found in *Documents on American Foreign Policy*, III, 402 ff. See also Hull: *Memoirs*, II, 964, for the Secretary's justification of the invasion to the French Ambassador.

[46] Hull: *Memoirs*, II, 966.

Hitler would turn on Soviet Russia, it was impossible to ignore the likelihood that he would, either by pressure or military action, force the submission of Turkey as a first step in the advance on Suez by way of Syria. The Turks were naturally astounded and awed by the dramatic speed of the Nazi conquest, and completely disheartened by the failure of their British allies, from whom they were now militarily isolated. The Foreign Minister confided to the British Ambassador that he was racking his brains to find a way of getting through the ensuing few months and that he considered it necessary to secure from the Germans, if possible, some kind of reassurance.[47] The British, unable to lend the Turks effective assistance and recognizing the danger of a reversal of Turkish policy, acquiesced in exploratory conversations, on the understanding that the Turks would not demobilize and that they would not, under any circumstances, agree to the passage of German matériel or troops across their territory.

Hitler, who had no intention of abandoning his plans against Soviet Russia and whose aims in the Middle East were distinctly limited, was quite prepared to strike a bargain. He had given up hope of luring the Turks into the Tripartite Pact or even inducing them to scrap their alliance with Britain, but he was genuinely interested in assuring Ankara's neutrality when he launched his attack on Russia and furthermore hoped to secure permission to send matériel and troops across Turkey to Iraq. He had called Ambassador Papen home for conference in early May and had instructed the Nazi press to adopt a tone of good will in its discussions of Turkish affairs.[48]

After his return to his post Papen elatedly reported that a conversation he had just had with President Inönü promised well. The Turkish statesman had indicated that if Germany would promise not to conclude any agreement with another country directed against Turkey, the latter would undertake not to do anything contrary to German interests and never to enter the conflict against Germany. Under the circumstances Papen thought the transit of war material could be easily arranged. There ensued a rapid exchange of telegrams between Ribbentrop and Papen, the Foreign Minister urging the need for haste if German aid to Iraq were to be effective. In order to secure transit rights, for men as well as for matériel, he was prepared to offer the Turks territorial gains in Thrace and in the Aegean Islands.[49]

[47] Tels. from MacMurray (Ankara), April 11, May 19, 1941, and the Ambassador's long, retrospective tel. of July 7, 1941; Sir Hughe Knatchbull-Hugessen: *Diplomat in Peace and War* (London: 1949), 169 ff.

[48] Record of the conference between Hitler and Mussolini on May 13, 1941 (*Nazi Conspiracy and Aggression*, IV, 1866-PS).

[49] Tel. from Papen, May 14, and Ribbentrop's tels. to Papen, May 16, 17, 19, 26, 1941, as printed in *Documents secrets: Turquie* (Paris, 1946), Nos. 1-6. Almost all the official material on the negotiations is contained in these German documents, captured

To Papen's discomfiture, the Turks refused to be hurried. They were ready to promise neutrality in the event of war between Germany and another power and agreed to a treaty of nonaggression and friendship, but they would not desert their British alliance, neither would they take the bait of territorial concessions in return for transit rights. Since the Iraqi insurrection had been suppressed by the end of May, the Germans did not insist on these rights and eventually contented themselves with a treaty of friendship which specifically reserved Turkey's connection with Britain. This treaty was finally signed on June 18, exactly four days before the opening of the Nazi offensive against the Soviet Union.[50]

The Ankara Government was certainly not proud of its achievement, inasmuch as it necessarily appeared to let down Turkey's allies. The Turks consoled themselves, however, with the argument that by the treaty they had erected a barrier against a German advance on Egypt, and that the *furor teutonicus* was to be turned against their traditional enemy, Russia.[51] While the British naturally disliked the whole business and were momentarily panic-stricken, they decided to accept it as inevitable. Recognizing that the Turks might have been subjected to even greater German pressure and influence, they were willing to leave something on the laps of the gods. London therefore decided to continue to provide the Turks with war materials, as called for by the treaty of October, 1939, and requested that the United States Government accord the Turks the same high priority they had thus far enjoyed. It was above all important, the British argued, to avoid the impression that the democracies had lost faith in Ankara. That would be the surest way of driving the Turks into greater dependence on the Germans.[52]

Ambassador MacMurray was convinced that the Turks remained loyal to their British connections and explicit assurances in this sense were given the State Department by the Turkish Ambassador in Washington.[53] But on the issue of continued aid, as on that of assistance to Franco Spain, the regional experts of the State Department were hard to convince. They felt the Ankara

---

and published by the Soviets. However, much of the important data appeared at the time in the press (see David J. Dallin: *Soviet Russia's Foreign Policy* [New Haven, 1942], 312 ff.).

[50] *Documents secrets: Turquie,* Nos. 5-9. For Ribbentrop's disappointment see his remarks to Ciano on June 2 and 15, 1941 (*Ciano's Diplomatic Papers,* 442, 446). Neither Harry N. Howard: "Germany, the Soviet Union, and Turkey during World War II" (*Department of State Bulletin,* XIX, July 18, 1948), nor Cevat Açikalin: "Turkey's International Relations" (*International Affairs,* XXIII, October, 1947), adds materially to what appears in the German documents published by the Soviet Government.

[51] Tel. from MacMurray, July 7, 1941.

[52] Memo of the Division of Near East Affairs to Mr. Welles, May 25, 1941, reporting the request of the British Embassy; memo from the British Embassy, received by the State Department on July 2, 1941; memos of conversation between Mr. Welles and Lord Halifax, June 22, July 8 and 10, 1941.

[53] Tel. from MacMurray, May 23, 1941; memo of conversation between Mr. Welles and the Turkish Ambassador, June 20, 1941.

Government "had behaved none too well lately" and that the best course would be to reduce the flow of supplies. It was not proposed to issue any public statement, but simply to suspend aid, at least temporarily, to reject pending requests for priorities, and to withhold export licenses. Meanwhile the Turks were to be asked to guarantee fulfillment of their contracts to deliver chrome to the United States and to promise not to permit the sale of this important strategic material to the Germans.

Ambassador MacMurray objected warmly to this policy, which, incidentally, was approved by Harry Hopkins. He reasoned that it would be a serious mistake "to do anything that might add to their [i.e., the Turks'] inner turmoil, their demoralizing suspicion that their friends may desert them and leave them to face the German menace by themselves." "I submit," he added, "that if (as I assume) our Government regards as essential the maintenance of the Turkish barrier to German advance in the Near and Middle East, then it is a question of how large a premium we are willing to pay upon insurance policy against Turkey's being manipulated into the mood of seeking safety under Germany's aegis. My own estimate of situation is that with eyes open to possibility of failure, we should nevertheless reckon it worth our while to continue material aid to this Government in degree sufficient to retain so far as possible its confidence in support by democratic cause."[54]

But the State Department refused to be mollified. For fully a month aid to Turkey was suspended, while a warm debate was carried on between Washington and the Ankara Embassy regarding the exact degree of Turkish culpability. When, under continued British prodding, a decision was finally reached, it was that the British should continue to supply Lend-Lease aid to Turkey and that, for purposes of American aid, the Ankara Government should be put on a par with the Latin American Republics. Since the latter were getting little more than token aid, the burden of supporting the Ankara Government was left largely to London.[55]

In part the State Department attitude may be explained by the skepticism prevalent in Washington about Britain's capabilities for holding in the Middle East. The British had sent a special emissary to set forth their requirements in tanks, planes and other equipment, and the President was already laying plans for improving the plane ferry service by way of Natal (Brazil) and the West African coast.[56] But a British effort, several times

---

[54] Tel. from MacMurray, July 7, 1941. For the rest we have used memos from the Division of Near East Affairs to Mr. Welles, June 19 and 25; tels. to MacMurray, June 28 and 30, 1941.

[55] Memos of conversation between Mr. Welles and Lord Halifax, July 10 and 14, 1941; letter of Mr. Noel Hall, of the British Embassy, to Mr. Acheson, July 10, 1941; memos of the Division of Near East Affairs to Mr. Welles, July 15, 1941; tel. from MacMurray, July 12, 1941; tel. to MacMurray, July 18, 1941.

[56] Memo from Mr. Purvis, of the British Purchasing Mission, to Secretaries Knox and Stimson, May 12, 1941 (copy in *Morgenthau Diaries, MS.,* Vol. 397, pp. 318 ff.); tel.

postponed, to drive Rommel from his strong position in the Halfaya Pass failed on June 17, 1941, and the situation in Libya remained critical. Furthermore, Mr. Churchill himself feared an early German drive through the Middle East. On June 21 he relieved General Wavell and replaced him by General Auchinleck. At the same time Mr. Oliver Lyttelton was appointed to the War Cabinet and assigned to handle the coördination of affairs in the Middle East.[57]

The situation remaining so precarious, it seemed to Washington hardly wise to stake valuable supplies on the Turks, who were surely doomed if Hitler decided to exploit his victories in that area. For the British and therefore for the Americans it was a major break of fortune that the Fuehrer's destiny beckoned elsewhere. While the Nazi divisions turned eastward, the British still held at Tobruk, the Free French established control in Syria, Iraq was safe from Nazi domination, and the Turks, though most exposed of all, still held to their alliance. For the future this alignment was to prove of major importance.

4. The Administration and the Emergency

The activist members of Mr. Roosevelt's Cabinet were in high hopes when, on May 27, 1941, the President proclaimed the existence of an unlimited national emergency. There was every reason to suppose that after months of hesitation the White House would face up to the urgent questions raised by the Lend-Lease legislation and that a new impetus would be given the national effort. But Mr. Roosevelt had promptly turned a cold douche on these expectations. At his press conference of May 28 he seemed to take back much of what he had promised the evening before and during the succeeding few weeks nothing spectacular happened. There was no movement in the direction which, either in hope or dread, the American public might have anticipated after hearing the President's fireside chat. It was a period of outward calm, bordering on flat anticlimax, a period of distinct deflation.[58]

The record provides no altogether satisfactory explanation for this striking letdown. In part it was undoubtedly due to the fact that the President was still suffering from a low-grade infection which, though in no sense dangerous, was highly debilitating. More important, however, was probably the impact of recent developments in the war. The British reverses in the Middle East had struck Washington a severe blow and had raised many doubts. Secretary Stimson, remarkably buoyant for a man of his age, looked for a great national upsurge after the fireside chat, but had his enthusiasm dampened by a conference with Secretary Hull:

---

from Hopkins to Winant and Harriman, May 27, 1941; message from the President to Mr. Churchill, June 17, 1941, and the latter's reply, June 20, 1941.

[57] Churchill: *The Grand Alliance*, 338-51.

[58] See above, Chapter XIV, Section 5.

He is so pessimistic over the progress of events in Europe, which of course are not encouraging, that whenever we have these meetings he does nothing but emit sentiments of defeatism and that is not very good for those who are trying to push things along. Today he was about at his worst. "Everything was going hellward" was the expression he kept using again and again.[59]

Though the President may have been less disheartened than Mr. Hull, he too must have struggled with the prevailing uncertainty. There was simply no knowing in what direction the Nazi conqueror would strike next. If Egypt were lost, that would be bad enough, though, as noted earlier, Mr. Roosevelt was inclined to rate that position less important than did Mr. Churchill. From the American standpoint a German advance through Spain into North and West Africa, followed by seizure of the Atlantic islands and possibly by a lunge at northeast Brazil, appeared as a greater threat and one which would be obviated only if and when Hitler turned his divisions against Soviet Russia. There were innumerable reports that the Fuehrer was planning to do so, but it was impossible to give full credence to this intelligence while seemingly more attractive possibilities were available to the Germans. The President's indecision probably stemmed from all these considerations, as well as from the realization that to go on with the naval escort program would involve great risk of conflict with the Germans at sea. This in turn would draw their full forces to the west against Britain and the United States and would, in all likelihood, provoke the intervention of the Japanese. It was certainly the part of wisdom to avoid all provocative moves, to hold the policy of supporting Britain to established procedures, and at the same time to do everything possible to prepare defensively against all conceivable German moves in western Europe and the Atlantic.

The correctness of this interpretation cannot be demonstrated, but American moves in the period between the fireside chat and the German attack on Soviet Russia fit it well enough. None of these moves was in itself of great significance and therefore does not require elaborate treatment. In the category of defense preparations belongs the executive order of June 14 freezing German and Italian assets in the United States and extending the ban to all continental European countries, including the Soviet Union. On June 16 the State Department notified Axis representatives that all their consulates in the United States must be closed by July 10. Included in this order were the German Library of Information and German news and tourist agencies, described in the American note as having engaged in "improper and unwarranted" activities. The Axis countries retaliated at once by closing American consulates. This seemed a small price to pay for eliminating centers of Axis espionage and propaganda in the United States.[60]

[59] *Stimson Diary (MS.)*, May 27, 1941.

[60] The relevant documents are printed in *Documents on American Foreign Relations*, III, 416, 537. We have used also a letter from Mr. Welles to the President, June 14, 1941 (*Roosevelt Papers:* Secretary's File, Box 74), and Hull: *Memoirs,* II, 945.

The issue of freezing foreign funds generally, and in fact the larger issue of organizing American economic warfare under separate direction, had been heatedly debated in official quarters ever since January, 1941. Secretary Morgenthau had insisted on the necessity of thus blocking the financial operations of the Axis powers, but the State Department had offered vigorous opposition, chiefly on the score that such drastic action would lead to complications with Soviet Russia, Japan, Switzerland and other powers. The question had been shelved pending debate on the Lend-Lease bill, but had finally been resolved according to Mr. Morgenthau's recommendations. Although the order of June 14 was undeniably a measure of economic warfare and therefore went beyond the province of defense strictly speaking, the main objective was to prevent the use of Axis funds for subversion. The interests of genuine neutrals were to be safeguarded by the issuance of general licenses for use of foreign currency to such European nations as gave the required assurances.[61]

In the field of military defense these few weeks saw the deferment of plans for occupation of the Azores. Fear of a German move on Spain and Portugal had haunted both London and Washington during the May Crisis and it had been agreed between the two Governments that, since Portugal itself could not be defended, every effort should be made to induce the Lisbon Government to withdraw to the Azores. In any case the British felt that they would have to occupy the islands and had accepted the offer of American assistance. The President had issued orders for the preparation of a joint Marine and Army expeditionary force.[62]

There is no reason to suppose that the temporary shelving of this plan resulted from any diminution of anxiety over the likelihood of Nazi aggression against Portugal. Rather it seemed more urgent to relieve the British of at least part of the responsibility for the defense of Iceland. Above all, President Roosevelt felt strongly that action against the Azores should be taken only on the explicit invitation of the Lisbon Government and there was no present prospect that such an invitation would be extended. In his fireside chat Mr. Roosevelt had referred to the Nazi threat against the Iberian Peninsula, North Africa, and what he called "the island outposts of the New World." "The Azores and the Cape Verde Islands," he had declared, "if occupied or controlled by Germany, would directly endanger the freedom

[61] The development of this issue is very fully recorded in the *Morgenthau Diaries* (*MS.*), as follows: January 7, 1941 (Vol. 345, p. 304); January 10, 1941 (Vol. 346, p. 440); January 14, 1941 (Vol. 347, pp. 246 ff.); January 30, 1941 (Vol. 353, pp. 31 ff.); June 14, 1941 (Vol. 408, pp. 78 ff.); and June 17, 1941 (Vol. 409, pp. 188 ff.). We have used also the *Berle Diaries* (*MS.*), February 7, 11, 13, 14, 17, 1941, and the *Stimson Diary* (*MS.*), February 11, 1941. On this matter see further Hull: *Memoirs*, II, 945; Percy W. Bidwell: "Our Economic Warfare" (*Foreign Affairs*, April, 1942); Herbert Feis: *The Road to Pearl Harbor* (Princeton, 1950), 143 ff.

[62] Tel. from Mr. Churchill to the President, May 29, 1941. See also above, Chapter XII, Section 2.

of the Atlantic and our own physical safety. . . . We insist upon the vital importance of keeping Hitlerism away from any point in the world which could be used and would be used as a base of attack against the Americas."

The Portuguese Government, mortally terrified lest this statement precipitate preventive action on Germany's part and concerned also lest Nazi propaganda succeed in sowing distrust among the Portuguese people, at once lodged a protest against the President's remarks. Pointing out that Portugal had pursued a policy of strict neutrality and that it had done its utmost to fortify the Azores and Cape Verdes against attack, the Portuguese note continued:

> The Portuguese territories have not, therefore, presented any harm, hindrance or menace to any of the belligerents or their allies, in the first place owing to the irreproachable attitude maintained; secondly, because the Portuguese Government declare and manifest their disposition to defend such an attitude against whoever may be; and, in the third place, due to the fact that such territories have not been the object of any threat by any of the belligerents or third power. It is therefore not possible to understand the specific reference by name to those Portuguese possessions which by itself could not fail to surprise the Portuguese people and Government.

Mr. Hull and Mr. Welles expostulated with the Portuguese Ambassador that it could not be supposed that the American Government had aggressive designs against the sovereignty or territorial integrity of Portugal or any other country. In a written note it was explained that

> In referring to the islands in the Atlantic it was the intention of the President to point out the dangers to this hemisphere which would result if these islands were to come under the control or occupation of forces pursuing a policy of world conquest and domination. The strategic importance of these islands, because of their geographical location, was stressed by the President solely in terms of their potential value from the point of view of attack against this hemisphere.

But the Lisbon Government was not satisfied with this statement, which it described as "a generical and vague declaration." Further explanations were given, but the incident, while not of great or lasting importance, clearly precluded any possibility that the Portuguese could then be brought to invite a British or Anglo-American occupation. Since the British felt reasonably sure that, in an emergency, they could count on Lisbon, the President decided to let the responsibility rest with them.[63]

[63] Portuguese note of May 30, 1941; memo of conversation between Mr. Hull and the Portuguese Minister, May 31, 1941; note to the Portuguese Government, June 10, 1941; Portuguese note of June 13, 1941; memo of conversation between Mr. Welles and the Portuguese Minister, June 13, 1941; memo of conversation between Mr. Dunn and the Portuguese Minister, June 17, 1941. Further: memo from the British Embassy, June 4, 1941, reviewing the earlier development of the problem; letters of Mr. Welles to the President, June 4 and 18, 1941, enclosing notes from the British Embassy (*Roosevelt Papers:* Secretary's File, Box 74).

The United States War and Navy Departments had never been enthusiastic about the Azores plan, which presented many difficulties. They were, on the other hand, greatly alarmed by Marshal Pétain's radio broadcast of May 15 and inclined to believe that the Germans would presently establish themselves at Dakar and thereby threaten the security of northeastern Brazil. Ever since May, 1940, the problem of defending the Brazilian bulge had worried the American Services and plans had long since been laid for the despatch of United States troops to aid if necessary. But as yet nothing concrete had been accomplished. There were no American warships within a thousand miles of this crucial area and no military forces within twice that distance. The Brazilian Government had been willing throughout to coöperate with the United States in measures of defense, but had made clear that it could by itself do little unless given equipment and supplies. These had not been forthcoming; even the development of airfield facilities by Pan American Airways was only in its initial stages. There was no possibility that the Brazilian Government could alone defend the bulge against Nazi attack, and there was always a chance that the impressive Nazi victories in the Balkans might provoke pro-Nazi or even Nazi-supported movements in Brazil.[64]

So intent was General Marshall on ensuring the defense of northeastern Brazil that he requested President Vargas and his Chief of Staff, General Goes Monteiro, to permit the United States to undertake an aerial survey of the region, to allow American detachments to take part in the Brazilian maneuvers scheduled for August, and to accept the aid of American staff officers in preparing plans for defense of the bulge. To these requests President Roosevelt added the proposal that Brazil, as a nation of Portuguese ancestry, participate in the protective occupation of the Azores. In return, Washington hoped to make twelve Douglas bombers available to the Brazilian forces in the northeast.[65]

The Brazilian authorities, though frequently complaining of America's failure to provide much-needed matériel and to keep Rio informed of its estimates and plans, nevertheless found Washington's proposals acceptable. Meanwhile, however, the Army-Navy Joint Planners and the Joint Board had approved a proposal that, with Brazilian consent, 9300 men and 43 planes should be despatched to northeast Brazil to bolster its defenses. After consulting the State Department, Secretaries Stimson and Knox submitted this program to President Roosevelt (June 13) and requested him to seek Brazilian approval. Evidently Mr. Roosevelt concurred without question.

---

[64] Many aspects of these matters are treated in some detail in a MS. study of the Department of the Army on *Western Hemisphere Defense Problems,* the work of Dr. Stetson Conn.

[65] Tel. from Caffery (Rio), May 31, 1941, reporting his conversation with President Vargas; tel. and despatch from Brigadier General Miller, Chief of the American military mission, reporting his conversation with General Goes Monteiro, June 2, 1941; tel. from Caffery, June 4, 1941.

Ambassador Caffery was instructed to approach President Vargas and point out the acute danger to northeastern Brazil if the Germans were to gain control of Dakar.[66]

The project for the mission of American forces to Brazil was not actually presented to the Brazilian authorities until June 26, that is, until after the German invasion of Soviet Russia. In Washington it was fully recognized that the proposal was a delicate one in view of the growing opposition in some Brazilian quarters to more extensive coöperation with the United States. The sequel was to show that the plan, like the project for the occupation of the Azores and later the project for relieving the British troops in Iceland, bristled with difficulties. Discussion of these may well be left for later treatment. In the present context it is sufficient to cite the proposal as a reflection of American fears and hopes during the emergency of May and June, 1941.

It should be noted that both the Azores and Brazilian projects were conceived as strictly defensive, that is, as precautionary measures made necessary by the threat of a Nazi advance on the Iberian Peninsula and North and West Africa at a time when the United States was militarily unable to take over Dakar.[67] American capabilities for overseas action were at this time still utterly insignificant. It was therefore essential to avoid provocation of Hitler at least so long as there was a good chance of his turning his main strength against the east. Accordingly nothing further was done to solve the issue of convoy protection or to take advantage of the British offer to make the fully equipped naval base at Londonderry in Northern Ireland available to the American Navy.[68]

Even more illustrative of this circumspect policy was the President's reaction to the news of the sinking of the American ship *Robin Moor* by a German submarine in the South Atlantic at the end of May. On June 11 the President began to receive the first reports of the incident, cabled by the survivors who had finally landed in Brazil. It was the first instance of the torpedoing of an American ship and the circumstances were particularly brutal. In his first flush of anger Mr. Roosevelt thought seriously of retaliating by ordering American naval vessels to seize a German merchant ship, the *Windhuk*, if she should leave her temporary refuge in a Brazilian port.[69]

[66] The fullest treatment of this proposal is to be found in the Conn MS. study on *Western Hemisphere Defense,* but we have used also a memo from General Marshall to Mr. Welles, June 17, 1941, and a telegram from Welles to Caffery, June 26, 1941, referring to a secret airmail letter from Welles to Caffery, June 18, 1941, in which the Ambassador was informed of the proposal.

[67] Conn MS. study. The War Department calculated that a successful American operation against Dakar would require 100,000 men and could not be undertaken before November, 1941, at the earliest.

[68] Kittredge MS. study on *United States-British Naval Coöperation.*

[69] Memo of the President to Mr. Hull and Mr. Welles, June 11, 1941 (*Roosevelt Papers: Secretary's File, Box 73*).

Subsequent reports confirmed the full extent of the outrage and Harry Hopkins, at least, was convinced that the attack on an American vessel so far from any war zone provided exactly the incident the President might require. In a memorandum to Mr. Roosevelt he argued:

The sinking of the *Robin Moor* violated international law at sea; it violates your policy of freedom of the seas.

The present observation patrol of the Navy for observing and reporting the movement of ships that are potential aggressors could be changed to a security patrol charged with the duty of providing security for all American flag ships traveling on the seas outside the danger zone.

It occurred to me that your instructions to the Navy Department could be that the United States Atlantic patrol forces, to be specific, are to, in effect, establish the freedom of the seas, leaving it to the judgment of the Navy as to what measures of security are required to achieve that objective.[70]

But those, like Mr. Purvis, the Chief of the British Purchasing Mission, who hoped there would be "some dividends" from the *Robin Moor* sinking, were doomed to disappointment. The President, for all his indignation, did nothing about Hopkins's suggestion. Instead, he confined himself once again to words. In his message to Congress (June 20) he outlined the facts of the case, pointed out how aptly they illustrated his May 27 analysis of the Nazi threat to the hemisphere, and expressed the belief that "we are warranted in considering whether the case of the *Robin Moor* is not a step in a campaign against the United States analogous to campaigns against other countries." To Hitler's warning that the United States might use the high seas only with Nazi consent, he asserted "we are not yielding and we do not propose to yield." But he carefully refrained from declaring the sinking of the *Robin Moor* an attack on the United States in the sense that clearly released him from his 1940 pledge not to take the United States into the war unless it were actually attacked. Thus, after June 20 as before, the United States Atlantic patrol, however far extended and strengthened, was, to quote Secretary Hull, "still for information only."[71]

No doubt Mr. Roosevelt's circumspection derived in part from realization that the country was not yet willing to approve a more positive policy in the Atlantic. A Gallup poll taken on June 14 revealed that only 55 percent of those queried favored the armed escort of American merchant ships across the ocean. Furthermore, two prominent columnists, Messrs. Alsop and Kintner, had just created a stir by charging publicly that in a recent encounter between an American destroyer and what was believed to be a German

---

[70] Memo of Hopkins to the President, June 14, 1941 (*Roosevelt Papers:* Secretary's File, Box 80); Sherwood: *Roosevelt and Hopkins,* 299. The reports of the American consul at Pernambuco and Mr. Welles's press statement on the sinking (June 12) are printed in *Documents on American Foreign Relations,* III, 417 ff.

[71] Hull: *Memoirs,* II, 945; *Moffat Diary* (*MS.*), June 17, 1941. The President's message may be found in *Documents on American Foreign Relations,* III, 58 ff.

submarine, the destroyer had attacked. According to the two journalists the President and his advisers, while saying nothing, were hoping the Atlantic patrol would produce an incident "to serve as the pretext for really strong action by this country."[72] Secretary Knox, at a press conference, denounced this story, though he would neither confirm nor deny the accuracy of the report. Mr. Roosevelt's own attitude appears from a letter he wrote to Secretary Ickes: " . . . Alsop and Kintner's story about an American destroyer dropping depth charges near a German submarine ought not to have been printed, whether it was true or not."[73]

The truth of the matter was that neither the President nor Secretary Knox was then in a position to know the full facts. Not until July did Knox feel able to deny the charge. The isolationists, however, naturally seized upon it and it is reasonable to assume that fear of further charges tempered Mr. Roosevet's reaction to the *Robin Moor* incident. Over and above these considerations, however, was undoubtedly the further thought that it would be most unwise to precipitate a crisis with Germany until the future course of Nazi operations was clear.

Within the carefully circumscribed framework of a defensive, temporizing policy, the program of supporting Britain in every possible way was, of course, continued with vigor. The limits were rather nicely drawn when Mr. Churchill suggested that the United States participate in a meeting of British, Dominion, and Allied Governments in London on June 12, 1941, to demonstrate "our common tenacity of purpose." The Prime Minister emphasized "what an accession of strength it would be if the United States Government felt it possible to be associated in some form or another with these proceedings." But the President replied that he thought it "inadvisable for domestic considerations for this Government to take any action with regard thereto."[74] It is interesting, however, to note that Mr. Roosevelt as well as other high officials of the Government were even at this critical time continuing to think of the principles and provisions of a future peace settlement. There was even some sentiment for calling a "congress of democracies." But it was quite another thing to participate openly in a meeting of the belligerents. It may be assumed that aside from the probable reaction of the American public, the President had also in mind the effect of such participation upon Hitler.[75]

[72] *Washington Post,* June 9, 1941; cf. Charles A. Beard: *President Roosevelt and the Coming of the War* (New Haven, 1948), 107 ff.

[73] Letter of the President to Secretary Ickes, June 16, 1941 (*Roosevelt Papers: Secretary's File, Box 73*).

[74] Tel. from the Prime Minister to the President, June 8, 1941, and the latter's reply, June 11, 1941.

[75] Memo of conversation between Mr. Hull and the Australian Minister, May 9, 1941, in which the former stressed the need for defining basic principles for a settlement; memo of conversation between Mr. Acheson and Mr. Maynard Keynes, June 20, 1941, from which it becomes clear that Mr. Roosevelt had discussed some of these matters

On concrete issues of aid, however, there was no question. In June regular consultation and planning between American and British military and naval authorities was initiated both in London and in Washington, where the British Joint Staff Mission was still carefully camouflaged as a group of "advisers to the British Supply Council in the United States."[76] On May 29, 1941, it was publicly announced that the United States would make available one third of its flying school capacity for the training of British aviators.[77] On the same day the President sent Mr. Churchill his plan for the complete reorganization under American direction of the North Atlantic plane ferry service, for which the Prime Minister expressed himself as "deeply grateful." Two weeks later Mr. Roosevelt informed the Prime Minister that the southern ferry route, by way of Brazil and West Africa, would be further developed and that the United States would be willing to build facilities at Bathurst, Freetown and Liberia so that American planes could be delivered to the British at West African terminal points. Mr. Churchill was enthusiastic and promptly offered a base at Bathurst "on similar terms to those already given for bases in the Western Atlantic." But this, again, was going too far for the President, who declined the offer as unnecessary. Clearly Mr. Roosevelt, while eager to aid, was also alert to avoid too great commitment.[78]

Leaving these developments of the assistance program with this brief reference, somewhat more extended treatment must be given to the most significant and important new departure in American policy, namely, the decision to despatch American troops to Iceland.

The eventual relief of the British occupation forces in Iceland had been agreed to in the Washington staff conversations (March, 1941) and had been included in the joint Anglo-American program known as ABC-1. But this move, the chief purpose of which was to reduce British military commitments, had not been envisaged for any date prior to September, 1941. What brought the issue to a head in May were the reports of Consul General Kuniholm and the results of the reconnaissance visit of the USS *Niblack* in

with Keynes (*Roosevelt Papers:* Secretary's File, Box 81); letter of the President to Mr. Berle, June 26, 1941, approving Berle's suggestion that he try his hand at outlining a postwar settlement and reminding him that "the elimination of costly armaments is still the keystone" (*ibid.,* Box 78); letter of Welles to the President, June 28, 1941, enclosing a draft reply to a letter from Secretary Ickes to the President, June 23, 1941, in which reference was made to earlier suggestions of Secretary Knox and others.

[76] Kittredge MS. study on *United States-British Naval Coöperation.*

[77] Tel. from the President to Mr. Churchill, May 21, 1941; *Stimson Diary (MS.)*, May 29, 1941.

[78] Tel. from Mr. Churchill to the President, June 11, 1941; tel. from the President to Mr. Churchill, June 17, and the latter's reply, June 20, 1941. The rather interesting details of these arrangements are discussed in Wesley F. Craven and James L. Cate: *The Army Air Forces in World War II* (Chicago, 1948), I, 313 ff. We have used also a memo from the President to Mr. Hull and Mr. Welles, June 11, 1941, and a letter from Mr. Welles to the President, June 18, and the latter's reply, June 19, 1941, these dealing with establishment of a base in Liberia.

April. German submarines were being sighted in Iceland's coastal waters and German planes were flying across the island with impunity. Added to these were the increasingly frequent reports of huge German troop and ship concentrations in northern Norway which, though probably directed against Soviet Russia, might also be intended for an attack on Iceland. By early June the President as well as the Chief of Staff and the Chief of Naval Operations had come to regard Iceland as sharing with the bulge of Brazil the dangerous distinction of being the vulnerable chinks in the armor of the hemisphere.[79]

In view of the growing likelihood that Hitler would follow up his Balkan victories with an attempt to invade Britain, there was every reason for Washington to relieve the British of their Icelandic responsibilities as quickly as possible. The President evidently felt that, whether or not Iceland could be properly construed as being within the confines of the Western Hemisphere, the American public would probably approve assumption of custody over the island, considering the favorable reaction to the extension of the Atlantic patrol. As for the British, it could be presumed that in their straitened circumstances they would be only too glad to relinquish their garrison duties, the more so as the logical consequence of occupation of Iceland by the Americans would be United States Navy escort of convoys as far east as American military commitments extended. As a matter of fact Mr. Churchill, when approached on the subject on the eve of the President's fireside chat, responded enthusiastically:

We cordially welcome your taking over Iceland at the earliest possible moment, and we will hold ourselves and all our resources there at your disposal as may be found convenient. It would liberate a British division for defense against invasion or the Middle East. If it could be done in the next three weeks or less, or even begun, it would have a moral effect even beyond its military importance. You have only to say the word and our staffs can get to work at once.[80]

Secretaries Knox and Stimson, supported by Harry Hopkins, all of them intent on "further and more effective means of pushing up this situation,

[79] Despatches from Kuniholm, April 21 and May 15; memo from Admiral Stark to Mr. Welles, May 7; memo from Mr. Welles to Mr. Hull, May 8; memo of conversation between Mr. Hull and Lord Halifax, May 7; tel. from Stockholm, May 26; despatch from Kuniholm, June 7; tels. presented by the British Embassy, June 14, 1941, reporting German movements in Norway; memo of General Marshall to Mr. Welles, June 17, 1941. These matters are treated at greater length in Captain Tracy Kittredge's MS. study on *United States-British Naval Coöperation* and in Dr. Stetson Conn's MS. study on *Western Hemisphere Defense Problems.*

[80] Tel. from the Prime Minister to the President, May 29, 1941. See also John G. Winant: *Letter from Grosvenor Square* (Boston, 1947), 203. The fact that the negotiations regarding Iceland were kept closely in the hands of the President and the Prime Minister, and their military advisers, is attested by Lord Halifax's ignorance of them and by Mr. Hull's admission that the Navy Department was handling the matter on the American side (memos of conversation between Mr. Hull and Lord Halifax, May 7 and 30, 1941; Hull: *Memoirs,* II, 945 ff.).

particularly by action in the northeast," were keen to undertake the operation and heartily endorsed the Prime Minister's stand, despite the fact that certain high staff officers feared such a move would unduly strain American combat forces.[81] Secretary Hull was persuaded to support the project and on June 5 the President therefore directed that a force of Marines be prepared for despatch within fifteen days. Meanwhile Mr. Roosevelt planned to have the Icelandic authorities request American protection.[82]

At this point the British suggested that, on the arrival of the American forces in Iceland, an announcement be issued stating that the United States Government was acting in full accord with London. This procedure did not, however, suit the President, who insisted that the British representative at Reykjavik first inform the Icelandic Government that London felt unable to continue the defense of the island but that the United States, if invited, would be willing to replace the British forces. As Mr. Welles explained to the British Minister, Mr. Butler, the President felt that since United States relations with the American Republics were based on a policy of nonaggression and nonintervention, the occupation of Iceland without the explicit invitation of its Government would destroy the confidence of the other Republics and give the Axis a welcome opportunity to exploit their distrust. The British having acquiesced, arrangements were made to concentrate the American naval and military forces at Argentia Bay (Newfoundland) by June 22, the very day of Hitler's attack on the Soviet Union.[83]

Though men like Stimson and Knox probably viewed the decision on Iceland as one more step toward naval escort and participation in the war in the Atlantic, the sequel was to show that the President was still determined to make haste slowly on these large and vital issues. So far as one can see, his adoption of the Iceland project was chiefly a reflection of his desire to do something to bolster British morale and afford some measure of relief in the Battle of the Atlantic. In terms of hemisphere defense the occupation of the Azores would have made more sense than the occupation of Iceland. But the former was more risky than the latter and, when the Portuguese raised objections, the President was not too reluctant to abandon the project and turn to another which would serve as a demonstration without at the same time involving serious difficulties or incurring the danger of German retaliation.

5. The Threat to Soviet Russia

While London and Washington were anxiously awaiting possible Nazi moves against Spain, Portugal or the Middle East, Hitler himself seems

---

[81] *Stimson Diary (MS.)*, June 2, 1941, reporting his conversation with Knox and Hopkins; further, the Conn MS. study as cited above.

[82] *Stimson Diary (MS.)*, June 5, 1941; Conn MS. study.

[83] British memo of June 16, 1941; memo of conversation between Mr. Welles and Mr. Butler, June 18, 1941; memo of conversation between Mr. Welles and Lord Halifax, June 22, 1941; tel. from Winant, June 23, 1941; the Kittredge and Conn MS. studies, as noted above.

never to have wavered in his determination to stake everything on his forth-coming offensive against the Soviet Union. Goering and Raeder might lament the failure to exploit a marvelous opportunity to deal Britain, the chief enemy, a mortal blow before American war production could get into high gear. High officials of the foreign service, like Baron von Weizsäcker and Ambassador von der Schulenburg, might warn of a two-front war and question whether even a striking military success would settle the problems of communism and Soviet might. Leading staff officers might express doubts of an easy and early victory. But admonitions and arguments had no effect on the Fuehrer. He was enraged by the maladroit Soviet treaty with Yugoslavia, which he took as conclusive proof that in the long run a conflict over the Balkans was inevitable. While recognizing the vast superiority of the Soviet forces in tanks, Hitler was convinced that the Nazi armies were irresistible and that a decisive victory could be won in a matter of three or four months. Thereafter Germany would have the entire continent at its disposal for the final struggle against Britain and, if necessary, the United States. At the same time he deluded himself into thinking that the British, once they saw that the collapse of Soviet Russia was imminent, would decide to give up the contest and accept a deal with the Germans.[84]

The Nazi campaign against Yugoslavia had obliged Hitler to postpone the opening of the attack on Soviet Russia by about four weeks; rainy weather, which interfered with troop movements, entailed a further delay. But on April 30, 1941, the Fuehrer had fixed June 22 as the day of the offen-sive. This date he adhered to, despite the fact that the Cretan campaign made it impossible fully to concentrate German air power in the east by June 22.[85] Meanwhile over one hundred divisions were being deployed along the Soviet front and all necessary preparations made with customary Ger-man thoroughness.

It is inconceivable that the Soviet authorities were unaware of this ominous turn of events. They had themselves long been concentrating forces along the border, though they were certainly not ready for an offensive. Indeed, when the Germans launched their attack they found that the Soviets had not completed their preparations even for defense.[86] Incredible though it may seem, the Kremlin was evidently unwilling to believe that Hitler would willfully saddle himself with a two-front war. Soviet leaders appear to have

---

[84] It seems unnecessary to document these statements in detail. The most important evidence will be found in *Nazi-Soviet Relations*, 330 ff., and in *The Trials of War Criminals*, X, 917 ff. See also the record of Ribbentrop's conversation with Mussolini, May 13, 1941 (*Nazi Conspiracy and Aggression*, IV, 1866-PS), and Hitler's statement to his generals on June 14, 1941 (*Trials of War Criminals*, X, 953). Good general accounts may be found in Gregoire Gafenco: *Préliminaires de la guerre à l'est* (Fribourg, 1944), Chapters VIII and IX; Max Beloff: *The Foreign Policy of Soviet Russia* (New York, 1949), II, 376 ff.; and Assmann: *Deutsche Schicksalsjahre,* Chapter VII and IX.

[85] *Halder Diary,* May 22 and 30, 1941.

[86] *Trials of War Criminals,* X, 953-54; Assmann: *Deutsche Schicksalsjahre,* 260.

interpreted German troop concentrations as foreshadowing Nazi pressure for concessions and to have believed till the end that Hitler could be appeased. There is no evidence that the reports from their excellent spy ring in Tokyo, which were sent on May 20, 1941, and which stated that the Germans were deploying 170-190 divisions for an attack about June 20, were given credence.[87] Even the last minute efforts of the German Ambassador to warn of the impending onslaught went unheeded, though the Soviet leaders must have known that Count von der Schulenburg was an altogether devoted champion of Soviet-German friendship.

The Kremlin's recipe for dealing with the oncoming crisis was an out-and-out policy of conciliation. Every effort was made to explain away the abortive treaty of friendship with the doomed Yugoslavs and Soviet deliveries under the Soviet-German economic accords were pushed to the point where even the Germans were astonished. On May 6 Stalin took over from Molotov the chairmanship of the Council of People's Commissars, a move generally taken to indicate that the greatest emphasis was to be placed on the maintenance of the Nazi-Soviet partnership. A few days later the Kremlin requested the Norwegian, Dutch, Belgian and even Yugoslav representatives to leave Moscow, which was tantamount to frank recognition of the Nazi conquests. A communiqué was issued on June 13 warmly denying that there had been any deterioration of relations and there is some evidence that on June 18, on the very eve of the Nazi assault, it was suggested that Molotov visit Berlin for conferences. All told, the Soviet effort to avoid a clash was so obvious that the German diplomatic and military representatives in Moscow reported home that the Kremlin would make any concessions short of the sacrifice of territory, and that Soviet Russia would fight only if attacked.[88]

If the Soviet leaders themselves were unwilling to believe in the forthcoming Nazi aggression, it is not altogether surprising that the British and American Governments continued for a long time to have their doubts. The State Department had months before come into possession of the key German directive of December, 1940, and had warned Ambassador Oumansky of what might be in store for his country.[89] But no one could guarantee that Hitler would not change his mind—especially that he would not decide to exploit his phenomenal Balkan successes before turning on the Soviet Union. Neither was it possible to predict that Stalin would not buy off his opponent, at almost any price. Reports, some of which proved astonishingly accurate,

[87] Department of the Army: *The Sorge Spy Ring.*

[88] *Trials of War Criminals,* X, 951; German Naval Diary, entries for May 6, 10, June 4, 6, 1941 (*Nazi Conspiracy and Aggression,* VI, C-170); *Halder Diary,* June 20, 1941; *Nazi-Soviet Relations,* 339 ff., 362 ff.; Gafenco: *Préliminaires de la guerre à l'est,* Chapter IX; Beloff: *The Foreign Policy of Soviet Russia,* II, 356, 381. On Soviet deliveries to Germany we have used also a tel. from Heath (Berlin), May 13, 1941, and a tel. from Steinhardt (Moscow), May 17, 1941.

[89] See above, Chapter X.

continued to reach Washington from foreign capitals, but there was always the chance that these were being floated by the Germans themselves either as part of their war of nerves or as deception for forthcoming operations in the west.[90] Furthermore, intelligence of German plans to attack was invariably counterbalanced by reports that the Germans and Soviets were engaged in secret negotiations which would result in vastly increased Soviet economic assistance to Germany, if not in a military alliance.[91] As late as May 25 Vishinsky was assuring Ambassador Steinhardt that Nazi-Soviet relations were friendly and that, if trouble arose, Soviet Russia was quite capable of defending itself alone and unaided.[92]

Though the British, too, were lost in a fog of doubt, Mr. Churchill personally seems to have convinced himself by April that the tension between the two continental partners would end in armed conflict. He had, therefore, conveyed a personal warning to Stalin. Unfortunately the British Ambassador, Sir Stafford Cripps, had delayed the communication of this message until April 19, on the plea that he had already initiated conversations with Vishinsky and had pointed out the common interest of Britain and the Soviet Union in resisting Hitler. He had, indeed, reinforced his observations with a warning that if the Kremlin chose the course of collaboration with Germany, it could expect nothing from Britain either during or after the war.[93]

It may well be doubted whether Cripps's failure to follow instructions explicitly made any great difference. Molotov would not see him at all and there was not the slightest indication that the Kremlin would consider any policy other than that of appeasing Hitler. Mr. Churchill was probably not far off the mark when he observed: "Nothing that any of us could do pierced the purblind prejudice and fixed ideas which Stalin had raised between himself and the terrible truth."[94]

Under the circumstances the State Department was just about ready to give up the ship. Ambassador Oumansky had appeared in Mr. Hull's office on May 14, but only to discuss the well-worn themes of American failure to meet Soviet requirements for supplies and in general of Amercian "hostility" to the Soviet Union. Although Mr. Hull once again and with some

---

[90] To mention only two examples: a consular report from Vienna, April 22, 1941, on which State Department officials noted that the report bore a striking resemblance to the earlier information on German war plans but might be of German origin; tel. from Chungking, May 12, 1941, reporting Chiang Kai-shek's information that the attack on Russia would come in six weeks.

[91] Tel. from Morris (Berlin), May 21, 1941. See also Dallin: *Soviet Russia's Foreign Policy*, 366 ff.; Beloff: *The Foreign Policy of Soviet Russia*, II, 383.

[92] Tel. from Steinhardt, May 25, 1941.

[93] Churchill: *The Grand Alliance*, 354, 358 ff.; memo of conversation between Mr. Hull and Lord Halifax, May 7, 1941, during which the Ambassador reported on Cripps's démarche. See also Wallace Carroll: *We're in This with Russia* (Boston, 1942), 53.

[94] Churchill: *The Grand Alliance*, 367.

warmth repudiated these charges, he was sick and tired of the interminable and unremunerative debate with Oumansky and had more or less decided that any future steps to improve relations would have to come from the Kremlin, on the theory that "improvement of our relations is more important to them than to us."[95] Until almost the eve of the Nazi offensive Washington continued to be baffled by conflicting intelligence. Reliable and accurate reports came in from Berlin, Stockholm and Bucharest in early June, but Ambassador Steinhardt stuck by his conviction that Stalin was so anxious to avoid war that he would concede anything consonant with Soviet Russia's unimpaired capability to defend its territory. Noting from incoming intelligence that hostilities were about to break out, Secretary Stimson on June 17 confided to his diary that Germany was evidently bringing "gigantic" pressure on its partner in the hope of getting enormous advantages by threatening war: "At present, from all the despatches, it seems nip and tuck whether Russia will fight or surrender. Of course, I think the chances are she will surrender."[96]

It might have been expected that some light would be thrown on German plans by Hitler's deputy, Rudolf Hess, who on May 10, 1941, startled his master as well as the rest of the world by completing a solo flight to Scotland. His hope was that, through the Duke of Hamilton, he could reach King George and convince him that, since German victory was certain, Britain would do well to end the useless bloodshed and accept a peace which he was sure the Fuehrer was prepared to offer. There could be no negotiation with the Churchill Government, but with a suitable Cabinet Hitler would be willing to make a settlement on the basis of a free hand for Germany in Europe and the return to Germany of its lost colonies. Beyond this "crazy idea," as Ribbentrop described it to Mussolini, Hess had nothing to communicate. He denied that an early attack on Soviet Russia was being planned and when, at Mr. Roosevelt's suggestion, he was interrogated on Hitler's designs on the New World, he had only this to say:

The Germans reckoned with American intervention and were not afraid of it. They knew all about American aircraft production and the quality of the aircraft. Germany could outbuild England and America combined.

Germany had no designs on America. The so-called German peril was a ludicrous figment of imagination. Hitler's interests were European.

If we [the British] made peace now, America would be furious. America really wanted to inherit the British Empire.[97]

[95] Hull: *Memoirs*, II, 971 ff.

[96] Tel. from Morris (Berlin), June 8, 1941, reporting that the attack was scheduled for June 22; tel. to Steinhardt, June 9, 1941, transmitting for comment reports from Stockholm and Bucharest; tel. from Steinhardt, June 12, 1941; *Berle Diary (MS.)*, June 5, 1941; *Stimson Diary (MS.)*, June 17, 1941.

[97] Records of the Duke of Hamilton's conversations with Hess (*Nazi Conspiracy and Aggression*, VIII, M-116—M-119); text of the British official statement of September 22, 1943 (*ibid.*, VII, D-614); Ribbentrop's report on the incident to Mussolini, May 13,

Hess had undertaken his mission without Hitler's knowledge and much to his discomfiture. Although nervous and hypochondriacal, he seemed at first to be in his right mind. However, he soon developed symptoms of a psychopathic nature, fearing plots to poison him or force him to commit suicide. By the end of May psychiatrists had convinced themselves that he was indeed psychopathic. Under the circumstances little store could be put by anything he said and the whole incident can therefore be brushed aside as a "completely devoted and frantic deed of lunatic benevolence."[98]

Early in June Mr. Churchill, convinced of the forthcoming German attack on Soviet Russia, decided to make a last effort to establish some form of coöperation with the Kremlin. Ambassador Cripps was recalled from Moscow for consultation, while Foreign Secretary Eden approached the Soviet Ambassador, Mr. Maisky, for a clear statement of his Government's relations with Germany. This first step netted the British nothing more than a repetition of the assurance that the Kremlin was not negotiating with Berlin for any new agreement and that it felt no anxiety about Nazi troop concentrations. Thereupon the Prime Minister himself took over the discussion. He told Maisky that if the Germans invaded the Soviet Union, Britain would be ready to assist the Soviets by continued air bombardment of Germany, by the maximum possible amount of economic aid and, finally, by the immediate despatch of a military mission to Moscow. But even this generous offer failed to evoke an appropriate response. Maisky's rejoinder, that British assistance would be more welcome if preceded by recognition of Soviet absorption of the Baltic states, may indeed be taken as a classic example of Soviet *sang-froid*, even on the verge of disaster.[99]

The British had an obvious interest in prolonging Soviet military resistance to Germany and Mr. Churchill therefore decided to plan on support of the Soviets in the event of attack, with or without prior agreement. Through a personal message to the President and through Lord Halifax he appealed to the American Government to adopt a similar policy. It so happened that these suggestions followed hard upon a State Department formulation of future policy toward the Soviet Union which, to say the least, struck a cool note. This important statement, sent at once to London and to the Moscow Embassy, ran as follows:

1941 (*ibid.*, IV, 1866-PS). We have used also a tel. from Winant, May 13, 1941, reporting information from Mr. Eden, and a message from the President to Mr. Churchill, May 14, 1941, suggesting that Hess be persuaded to talk of Hitler's plans for the United States and the Western Hemisphere, "including commerce, infiltration, military domination, encirclement of the United States, etc." On the entire episode, see Churchill: *The Grand Alliance*, 48 ff.

[98] Churchill: *The Grand Alliance*, 55. The medical side of the case is set forth in great detail by the examining physicians in *The Case of Rudolf Hess*, edited by J. R. Rees (New York, 1948).

[99] Tel. from Johnson (London), June 11, 1941; tel. from the Foreign Office, June 11, 1941, transmitted to the State Department by the British Embassy, June 16, 1941; tel. from Johnson, June 13, 1941.

A. We are making no approaches to the Government of the Soviet Union.

B. If that Government makes such approaches to us, we treat them with reserve until and unless we are certain that the Russian Government is not out to get concessions and advantages from us by a policy of maneuvers.

C. It is our policy to refuse to make concessions to Soviet Russia which that country suggests as a means of bettering United States-Soviet relations. If we do make any, we demand a strict *quid pro quo*.

D. In order to improve relations we will not sacrifice any principles.

E. We make clear to Russia our belief that improvement of our relations is more important to them than to us.

F. The principle of reciprocity governs all our day to day relations with Russia in so far as practicable.[100]

This uncompromising program, inspired perhaps by the reports of Mr. Eden's talks with Ambassador Maisky, was warmly applauded by Ambassador Steinhardt, who reminded the Department of his oft-repeated contention that only a "firm" policy could succeed with the Soviets. The Kremlin, he held, did not react to the customary amenities. Soviet leaders were utterly unresponsive to efforts to create international good will and were apparently quite prepared to sacrifice future for immediate gains. They were blind to ethical or moral principles and if they did react to firmness, that was only a reflection of their primitive instincts. Since they regarded any conciliatory move with suspicion and interpreted it as weakness, the only sensible line to take was that of dignity and firmness.[101]

Considering the official American attitude, it was inevitable that the British proposal should have been rather critically scanned by the State Department. Mr. Welles rehearsed to Lord Halifax the fantastic difficulties he had encountered in his long dealings with Oumansky and pointed out the further consideration that Japan might make it impossible for the United States to get supplies to Soviet Russia. While promising to reëxamine the situation, Welles expressed the hope that Britain, in its anxiety to effect a *rapprochement* with Soviet Russia, would not be tempted to modify its policy toward the Baltic states. Believing that he sensed an unwonted cynicism in the Ambassador's suggestion that the military coöperation of Soviet Russia might be worth recognition of Soviet claims to those states, Welles protested that such a move would undermine Britain's moral position and be a heavy blow to the American public. "What logical distinction," queried Welles, "could be drawn between recognition of the brutal conquest by Russia of the Baltic States and the brutal conquest by Hitler of other independent peoples such as the Dutch and Belgians?"[102]

The British Government hastily informed Washington that it had no in-

---

[100] Tel. to Winant, June 14, 1941; summarized in Hull: *Memoirs,* II, 972 ff.

[101] Tel. from Steinhardt, June 17, 1941.

[102] Memos of conversation between Mr. Welles and Lord Halifax, June 14 and 15, 1941.

tention of offering Soviet Russia unilateral concessions. Mr. Eden declared that he was as firmly opposed to appeasement as ever and that he shared the sentiments of Ambassador Steinhardt, whose report had been submitted to him.[103] Nonetheless, the State Department found it difficult to adopt the British proposal to aid Soviet Russia in the event of a German attack. A memorandum of the Division of European Affairs, dated June 21, 1941, had this to say on the subject:

If the Soviet Government should approach us direct, requesting our assistance, we should, so far as possible, without interfering in our aid to Great Britain and to victims of aggression, or without seriously affecting our own efforts of preparedness, relax restrictions on exports to the Soviet Union, permitting it even to have such military supplies as it might need and which we could afford to spare.

Such aid, however, should be given directly, "on the basis of mutual advantage and not in coöperation with any third power. We should," concluded the memorandum, "steadfastly adhere to the line that the fact that the Soviet Union is fighting Germany does not mean that it is defending, struggling for, or adhering to the principles in international relations which we are supporting." Hence we should make no specific promises in advance or assume any commitments as to our future policy toward the Soviet Union.[104]

Mr. Roosevelt's position, however, was more flexible than that of his professional advisers. It has been remarked earlier that he had more sympathy than most Americans for the Bolshevik experiment, that he regarded the Communist threat as less grave and certainly less immediate than the Nazi menace, and that he fancied that over the years the Soviet and American systems would approximate each other.[105] Above all, he was prone to take the line that the first requirement of American policy, beyond national and hemisphere defense, was to support Britain and that, barring conclusive arguments to the contrary, Mr. Churchill's decisions should be concurred in. He therefore requested Ambassador Winant, who had returned home for conference early in June, to hasten back to his post with a personal message to the Prime Minister. This message included the promise that, in the event of a German attack on Soviet Russia, the President would issue immediately a statement in support of any declaration Mr. Churchill might make welcoming the Soviet Union as an ally. Mr. Winant reached Britain in time to join the Prime Minister, Mr. Eden and Ambassador Cripps at Chequers on Friday, June 20. Though Cripps still felt that the Kremlin would yield to German pressure rather than fight, the Prime Minister was convinced that the attack was imminent and was already working on a statement which he proposed to make at once over the radio. As he explained his policy to Mr.

[103] Tel. from Johnson, June 17, 1941.
[104] Memo of the Division of European Affairs, June 21, 1941.
[105] See particularly Sumner Welles: *Where Are We Heading* (New York, 1946), 38.

Winant: "I have only one purpose, the destruction of Hitler, and my life is much simplified thereby. If Hitler invaded Hell, I would make at least a favorable reference to the Devil in the House of Commons."[106]

When the German onslaught began on the morning of June 22, therefore, there was complete agreement between London and Washington at the highest level. Mr. Churchill proposed to make a statement promising Soviet Russia all possible support and Mr. Roosevelt had undertaken to declare the American position in consonance with the British. The long period of uncertainty and apprehension was drawing to a close and for a brief space, at least, London and Washington could breathe more freely, awaiting the outcome of the titanic struggle that was now to unfold itself in the east.

[106] Churchill: *The Grand Alliance,* 368 ff.; Winant: *Letter from Grosvenor Square,* 203-4. It is interesting to note that Mr. Biddle, in a letter to Mr. Hull of June 20, 1941, reported that General Sikorski had intelligence that the attack would come on June 22 and that the British had received information from Tokyo that about ten days earlier Ribbentrop had confided the German plans to the Japanese Ambassador.

CHAPTER XVII

A Temporary Breather

1. Britain and the Nazi-Soviet Conflict

The Nazi assault on Soviet Russia, launched in the early hours of Sunday, June 22, 1941, was a personal venture of Adolf Hitler. Despite the objections of his military advisers, that great gambler had long since convinced himself that he was safe in risking a two-front war. Despite the disparity in manpower resources, in tanks and even in planes, he had no doubt that German organization, leadership and valor would win the day and that a vigorous kick on the front door would bring down the whole Soviet structure. Within a few months the Communist armies would be beaten and the Soviet regime would collapse. Thereafter Nazi Germany would be relieved of the threat to its rear. With Russian food and raw materials to bolster its war economy, the Reich would be ready to deliver the projected "massive attack in the West." So far, indeed, did Hitler's imagination range that he envisioned the collapse of the Churchill Government as one of the possible results of Nazi victories in the east. The new demonstration of German power would, he believed, deprive the British of all hope of further resistance in conjunction with the Soviets and would lead conservative elements to encompass Churchill's downfall prior to seeking a deal with triumphant Germany. Failing this, Britain would soon be brought to its knees by powerful Nazi offensives in North Africa and the Middle East, combined with submarine warfare and the threat of actual invasion.[1]

Meanwhile, however, the Churchill Government was still firmly in the saddle and able to count not only on undivided support at home but also on aid from the British Commonwealth. So convinced was the British public that Hitler could be decisively defeated only with the active military aid of Soviet Russia that it had pressed for a military alliance in 1939 and had, even after the conclusion of the Nazi-Soviet pact, taken a charitable view

[1] *Halder Diary,* June 22 and 30, 1941, July 3, 1941.

533

of the Kremlin's policy. Indeed, many Englishmen blamed their own Government for the failure of the 1939 negotiations. Ever since the downfall of France, Britons had been watching hopefully for indications of Nazi-Soviet estrangement and praying for the success of the Cripps mission. In June, 1941, the British public was fully aware that "if Hitler goes East, it is only to be in a materially stronger position to come West," to borrow the words of the *Sunday Dispatch* (June 22, 1941). Despite contrary military opinion, it was popularly believed that the Russians would hold out for at least a year and that in all probability the Nazis would not be able to annihilate the Soviet forces. Under the circumstances there was in Britain overwhelming sentiment for agreement with Soviet Russia and for fullest coöperation with Hitler's latest victim.[2]

Mr. Churchill could therefore anticipate an enthusiastic response to his announcement of the Government's proposal to aid the Soviet Union. His carefully prepared broadcast, delivered on the evening of June 22 and listened to attentively by millions of people on both sides of the Atlantic, was one of the most moving, as it was one of the most significant, pronouncements of the war period. Speaking compassionately of the hundreds of millions of human beings who on that day were being sucked into the maelstrom, the Prime Minister made a special point of reminding his audience that in the past no one had been more consistent than he in opposing communism. He would not, he declared, unsay a word of what he had previously uttered on the subject. But all that, he added, in fact the entire past with its follies and crimes and tragedies, was flashing away, and all he could see was the Russian people valiantly defending their country. At this critical juncture the policy of the Government was to be as follows:

We have but one aim and one single, irrevocable purpose. We are resolved to destroy Hitler and every vestige of the Nazi regime. From this nothing will turn us—nothing. We will never parley, we will never negotiate with Hitler or any of his gang. We shall fight him by land, we shall fight him by sea, we shall fight him in the air, until with God's help we have rid the earth of his shadow and liberated its peoples from his yoke. Any man or state who fights on against Nazidom will have our aid. Any man or state who marches with Hitler is our foe. . . . It follows, therefore, that we shall give whatever help we can to Russia and the Russian people. We shall appeal to our friends and allies in every part of the world to take the same course and pursue it, faithfully and steadfastly to the end. . . .

This is no class war, but a war in which the whole British Empire and Commonweath of Nations is engaged without distinction of race, creed, or party. It is not for me to speak of the action of the United States, but this I will say: if Hitler imagines that his attack on Soviet Russia will cause the slightest division of aims or slackening of effort in the great democracies who are resolved upon his doom, he is woefully

---

[2] See particularly Tom Harrison: "Public Opinion about Russia" (*Political Quarterly*, XII, October-December, 1941, 353-66), but also W. P. and Zelda K. Coates: *A History of Anglo-Soviet Relations* (London, 1944), 673 ff.

mistaken. On the contrary, we shall be fortified and encouraged in our efforts to rescue mankind from his tyranny. We shall be strengthened and not weakened in determination and in resources.

Warning the democratic world of Hitler's objectives and the inevitable consequences of his success, the Prime Minister limned the Nazi program in terms that have since been proved altogether accurate:

He wishes to destroy the Russian power because he hopes that if he succeeds in this, he will be able to bring back the main strength of his army and airforce from the east and hurl it upon this Island, which he knows he must conquer or suffer the penalty of his crimes. His invasion of Russia is no more than a prelude to an attempted invasion of the British Isles. He hopes, no doubt, that all this may be accomplished before the fleet and air power of the United States may intervene. He hopes that he may once again repeat, upon a greater scale than ever before, that process of destroying his enemies one by one, by which he has so long thrived and prospered, and that then the scene will be clear for the final act, without which all his conquests would be in vain— namely, the subjugation of the Western Hemisphere to his will and to his system. The Russian danger is therefore our danger, and the danger of the United States, just as the cause of any Russian fighting for his hearth and home is the cause of free men and free peoples in every quarter of the globe.[3]

In keeping with its declared program, the British Government at once offered to send military and economic missions to Moscow and arranged to have Sir Stafford Cripps return to his post immediately. The Kremlin concurred but, as Mr. Eden informed the House of Commons on June 24, "made it plain to us that in the period of military coöperation which now lies ahead, help will be upon a mutual and a reciprocal basis."[4] Actually the Soviet leaders showed remarkably little enthusiasm over the prospect of British aid. They made no official reply to Churchill's broadcast and when, on June 27, Cripps and the military mission arrived in Moscow, they were given a rousing reception but no information, except in the most general terms.[5] True, Stalin, in his eloquent radio address to the Soviet people on July 3, 1941, after explaining away the ill-starred Nazi-Soviet Pact, called for a war of liberation and announced that the Soviet Union would not stand alone:

In this great war we shall have true allies in the peoples of Europe and America, including the German people which is enslaved by Hitlerite misrulers. Our war for the freedom of our country will merge with the struggle of the peoples of Europe and America for their independence, for democratic liberties. It will be a united front of the people standing for freedom and against enslavement and threats of enslavement

[3] Winston S. Churchill: *The Unrelenting Struggle* (New York, 1942), 169 ff. See also Churchill: *The Grand Alliance* (Boston, 1950), 371-72.

[4] Anthony Eden: *Freedom and Order* (London, 1947), 112 ff.

[5] Churchill: *The Grand Alliance*, 381; Eric Estorick: *Stafford Cripps* (London, 1949), 274. We have used also tels. from Steinhardt (Moscow), June 24 and 30, July 2, 1941.

by Hitler's Fascist armies. In this connection the historic statement of the British Prime Minister, Mr. Churchill, regarding aid to the Soviet Union, and the declaration of the United States Government signifying readiness to render aid to our country, which can only evoke a feeling of gratitude in the hearts of the peoples of the Soviet Union, are fully comprehensible and symptomatic.[6]

But on the official level there was only silence, "oppressive" silence, according to Mr. Churchill.

Probably fearing lest, driven backward in headlong retreat, the Red armies collapse and the Soviet Government accept Hitler's terms for peace, the Prime Minister on July 7 addressed Stalin in a personal message, assuring him again that Britain would accord help to the extent permitted by circumstances, telling him of the heavy British air attacks on Germany that should distract the German Air Force from the east, and arguing: "We have only got to go on fighting to beat the life out of these villains."[7]

On July 8 Ambassador Cripps had an interview with Stalin, presumably to transmit the Churchill message. On this occasion the Soviet chief made no effort to conceal the gravity of the military situation, but suggested that wholehearted coöperation between the Soviet Union and Britain would require a political agreement. This would have to include reciprocal promises not to engage in separate peace negotiations with Hitler and to render mutual aid. Cripps recommended this proposal strongly to his Government, holding that such an agreement would give the Soviets the feeling of self-respect which they seemed to crave, and would make them coöperative at an eventual peace conference. Mr. Churchill, too, was anxious to bind the Kremlin and was probably relieved that no territorial issues had been raised. His attitude was well expressed in a contemporary note to the First Lord of the Admiralty:

The advantage we should reap if the Russians could keep the field and go on with the war, at any rate until the winter closes in, is measureless. A premature peace by Russia would be a terrible disappointment to great masses of people in our country. As long as they go on, it does not matter so much where the front lies.[8]

He therefore at once consulted the Dominions and secured their approval, at the same time assuring himself that Washington had no objection provided the agreement involved no secret clauses. Within a few days the road was clear and the declaration, in much the form suggested by Stalin, was signed in Moscow on July 12, 1941. In communicating it to Parliament on July 15 Mr. Churchill pointed out that while the form of a joint declaration had been chosen, "it is, of course, an alliance, and the Russian people

---

[6] Text in the official Soviet publication: *Soviet Foreign Policy during the Patriotic War* (New York, n. d.), I, 21 ff.

[7] Churchill: *The Grand Alliance*, 380-81.

[8] Churchill memo to the First Lord, July 10, 1941 (Churchill: *The Grand Alliance*, 381-82).

are now our allies." Stalin, in a message to the Prime Minister, his first since the Nazi attack, concurred in this interpretation, stating that the two countries "have become fighting allies in the struggle against Hitlerite Germany."[9]

2. THE ISSUE OF AMERICAN AID

The British position toward the Nazi-Soviet struggle was relatively easy to establish, for popular sentiment was united and Britain, deeply involved in what to many seemed a hopeless struggle, was obliged by circumstances to make the most of whatever opportunity offered. In the United States, on the other hand, the issue was far more complicated and presented far greater difficulties. Hostility to communism and to Soviet policy ran deep and strong, and the country was obviously not in such dire straits as to have to grasp at any straw. American like British military opinion was almost unanimous in giving the Soviet armies only a few weeks—at most two or three months—of effective resistance. The general feeling was that, while the Nazi attack would provide what Harry Hopkins called "a temporary breather," Hitler was bound to win and that his victory would serve only to strengthen him for a renewed assault on the west. Under the circumstances it was thought senseless to sacrifice scarce and valuable equipment. It seemed more logical to take advantage of the precious respite afforded by Hitler to redouble aid to Britain and prepare for the crucial contest that appeared inevitable in the near future.

Those who, like Secretaries Stimson and Knox, held that the United States should take a more active part in the European conflict, pressed this argument upon the President. After a luncheon discussion with his colleagues on June 23 Mr. Stimson sent a memorandum to the White House setting forth that Hitler would be fully occupied with Soviet Russia for a minimum of one month and a possible maximum of three months. During that time he would be unable to invade Britain or take action against Iceland. His pressure on West Africa, Dakar and South America would have to be relaxed and any plan he might have to envelop the British flank in Egypt would have to be deferred or abandoned. The democracies should make the most of this "almost providential occurrence." His advisers, continued the Secretary:

. . . were unanimously of the belief that this precious and unforeseen period of respite should be used to push with the utmost vigor our movements in the Atlantic theater of operations. They were unanimously of the feeling that such pressure on our part was

---

[9] Churchill: *The Grand Alliance*, 383-84. The text of the agreement was published at once, and may be found in *Soviet Foreign Policy during the Patriotic War*, I, 77; in *Documents on American Foreign Relations*, IV, 252; and elsewhere. On the negotiations we have used also tels. from Winant (London), July 9, 11, 12; tels. from Steinhardt, July 9, 11, 12; a memo of conversation between Mr. Welles and Lord Halifax, July 10; a memo from the British Embassy, July 12, 1941.

the right way to help Britain, to discourage Germany, and to strengthen our own position of defense against our most imminent danger. . . . By getting into this war with Russia, Germany has relieved our anxiety, provided we act promptly and get the initial dangers over before Germany gets her legs disentangled from the Russian mire.[10]

While Secretary Stimson still veiled his suggestion that the United States seize the golden moment to introduce naval escort and other measures in the Atlantic, Secretary Knox, in a letter to the President on the same day, was less circumspect:

Since I left here Friday, the Russian-German war has begun and I feel very deeply that I ought to say to you that, in my judgment, this provides us with an opportunity to strike and strike effectively at Germany. Hitler has violated his own resolution not to engage in two wars at once on two separate fronts. The best opinion I can get is that it will take anywhere from six weeks to two months for Hitler to clean up on Russia. It seems to me that we must not let that three months go by without striking hard—the sooner the better.[11]

Of the same tenor, and even more outspoken, were Admiral Stark's recommendations to the President on June 24, 1941. As the Chief of Naval Operations reported to one of his subordinates:

Within forty-eight hours after the Russian situation broke, I went to the President, with the Secretary's approval, and stated that on the assumption that the country's decision is not to let England fall, we should immediately seize the psychological opportunity presented by the Russian-German clash and announce and start escorting immediately, and protecting the Western Atlantic on a large scale; that such a declaration, followed by immediate action on our part, would almost certainly involve us in war and that I considered every day of delay in our getting into the war as dangerous, and that much more delay would be fatal to Britain's survival. I reminded him that I had been asking this for months in the State Department and elsewhere, etc., etc., etc. I have been maintaining that only a war psychology could or would speed things up the way they should be speeded up; that strive as we would it just isn't in the nature of things to get results in peace that we would, were we at war.[12]

Secretary Ickes struck the same note in a letter to the President: "It may be difficult to get into this war the right way, but if we do not do it now, we will be, when our turn comes, without an ally anywhere in the world."[13] In a public address at Hartford on June 26 Ickes declared: "If America does not go quickly all out for Britain, she may find herself all in without Britain."

[10] *Stimson Diary (MS.)*, June 22 and 23, 1941. This letter is printed almost in full in Robert E. Sherwood: *Roosevelt and Hopkins* (New York, 1948), 303-4. The original is in the *Roosevelt Papers*: Secretary's File, Box 74.

[11] Letter of Knox to the President, June 23, 1941 (*Roosevelt Papers*: Secretary's File, Box 73).

[12] Letter of Admiral Stark to Captain Charles M. Cooke, Jr., U.S.N., July 31, 1941 (printed in *Pearl Harbor Attack*, XVI, 2175 ff.).

[13] Letter of Secretary Ickes to the President, June 23, 1941 (*Roosevelt Papers*: Secretary's File, Box 73).

To close the circle, Secretary Knox expounded his ideas to the Conference of Governors on June 30:

For the first time since Hitler loosed the dogs of war on this world, we are provided with a God-given chance to determine the outcome of this world-wide struggle. . . . While his back is turned, we must answer his obvious contempt with a smashing blow that can and will change the entire world perspective. If, while Hitler is assaulting Stalin, we can clear the path across the Atlantic and deliver, in safety, the weapons our factories are now producing, ultimate defeat for Hitler is certain.

This program, involving no truck with the Kremlin, was bound to appeal to all who saw in Britain the sheet anchor of hemisphere security. Applauding Knox's courageous speech, the *Christian Science Monitor* agreed (July 1, 1941) that "this is no breathing spell. This is not time to debate aid to Russia; this is a time to aid America and the cause of freedom by throwing every weight into the scales on the Western front." According to *The New York Times* (July 2, 1941), "this is the time to give our ships the protection of our Navy and to throw into the Western front, on Britain's side, every plane that we can spare."

It was not to be expected that the President would quarrel with the general proposition that all possible use should be made of the temporary breather provided by Hitler to press on with the program of assistance to Britain. The question was rather whether he would be willing to throw down the gauntlet to Hitler and seize the opportunity to introduce the system of escorting convoys. At first he seems to have been so disposed. He wrote Prime Minister Mackenzie King of Canada: "I feel that if the Russians should fail to hold out through the summer, there may be an intensified effort against Britain itself, and especially for control of the Atlantic. We may be able to help a good deal more that seems apparent today."[14] Furthermore, he agreed that plans should be drawn for American naval escort in the western Atlantic, to go into effect on July 11, 1941.[15] But, despite all pleading and pressure from Knox, Stimson, Ickes and others, he soon reneged. Secretary Knox's request for the transfer of more warships from the Pacific to the Atlantic was turned down flat and he had "the devil's own time" in getting presidential approval even for the plans to escort American shipping as far as Iceland. Intercepted messages forecasting renewed activity by the Japanese undoubtedly had something to do with the President's hesitation, but it is highly likely that he was concerned above all with the probable reaction of the American public to the introduction of naval escort, with all its implications. On June 30 Senator Wheeler had succeeded in having referred to the Naval Affairs Committee a resolution instructing it

[14] Letter of the President to Mr. Mackenize King, July 1, 1941 (now printed in *F.D.R.: His Personal Letters,* New York, 1950, 1179).
[15] Kittredge MS. study on *United States-British Naval Coöperation,* Chapter XIX.

to investigate rumors that American ships were already engaging in such activities.[16]

While reluctant to challenge Hitler openly, Mr. Roosevelt, apparently supported by Secretary Hull, was quite prepared to join Britain in promising support to Soviet Russia as a victim of Nazi aggression. In the concluding section of the preceding chapter the story has been told of his disregard for the circumspect program of the State Department and his instruction to Ambassador Winant to assure Mr. Churchill that he would, in the event of a Nazi attack on Russia, issue a statement supporting a British announcement welcoming Soviet Russia as an ally. Like Churchill, he seems to have had greater confidence than the military men in Russia's staying power and may well have been influenced in this respect by the arguments of former Ambassador Joseph E. Davies, at that time Secretary Hull's Special Assistant for War Emergency Problems and Policies. Davies had a high opinion of Soviet military strength and contended that before long the Red Army would amaze the world. Therefore, he argued, it was only a matter of common sense to support it.[17]

Mr. Roosevelt could have been under no illusion about the extent of opposition throughout the country to any proposal to aid Communist Russia, not only from the isolationist elements but also from the ranks of the so-called interventionists and especially from the Roman Catholic Church. Furthermore, Mr. Welles, as Acting Secretary during Secretary Hull's illness and absence, voiced reservations about too close relations with the Kremlin. His long and frustrating experience with Ambassador Oumansky had no doubt led him to support the cool and carefully circumscribed policy advocated by the regional specialists of the State Department. On June 22, the very day of Hitler's attack and Churchill's broadcast, Mr. Welles warned Lord Halifax that sooner or later Japan would probably join in the assault on Soviet Russia and that then, if Britain and Russia were allied, Britain would become involved in hostilities in the Far East. He therefore recommended that Britain, like the United States, adopt a policy of pure expediency, based on the recognition of the simple fact that both Britain and Soviet Russia were at war with Germany, but for the present going no farther.[18]

It is hard to believe that neither Mr. Roosevelt nor Mr. Welles heard the Churchill broadcast, delivered on the afternoon of June 22 (Washington time) and eagerly listened to by millions of their countrymen. Nonetheless,

[16] *Stimson Diary (MS.)*, July 3-7, 1941; Kittredge MS. study on *United States-British Naval Coöperation*, Chapter XIX.

[17] On Davies's influence see especially Forrest Davis and Ernest K. Lindley: *How War Came* (New York, 1942), 251; Foster Rhea Dulles: *The Road to Teheran* (Princeton, 1945), 233-34; and in general George Fischer: "Genesis of United States-Soviet Relations in World War II" (*The Review of Politics*, XII, July, 1950, 363-78).

[18] Memo of conversaton between Mr. Welles and Lord Halfax, June 22, 1941.

Mr. Welles has stated that when he conferred with the President on the morning of June 23 neither of them had "seen" the text of the Prime Minister's declaration, though it had been released. Be that as it may, they agreed on a statement drafted by Mr. Welles and approved by the President after the addition of a crucial last sentence. This statement, which Mr. Welles says was intended to forestall confusion of the public mind, was released immediately, as follows:

The immediate issue that presents itself to the people of the United States is whether the plan for universal conquest, for the cruel and brutal enslavement of all peoples, and for the ultimate destruction of the remaining democracies, which Hitler is now desperately trying to carry out, is to be successfully halted and defeated.

That is the present issue which faces a realistic America. It is the issue at this moment which most directly involves our own national defense and the security of the New World in which we live.

In the opinion of this Government, consequently, any defense against Hitlerism, any rallying of the forces opposing Hitlerism, from whatever source these forces may spring, will hasten the eventual downfall of the present German leaders, and will therefore redound to the benefit of our own defense and security.

Hitler's armies are today the chief dangers of the Americas.[19]

This enigmatic statement, at bottom little more than an assertion that successful opposition to Nazism, from whatever source, was in the American interest, committed the American Government to nothing whatever, not even to the kind and degree of aid envisaged by the State Department program in case the Kremlin asked for it. Yet the President undoubtedly intended to lend the Soviets support, in the hope of prolonging their resistance, and planned to lay on as much as American opinion would bear. His first moves were modest and almost shamefaced. On June 24 Soviet funds in the United States (about $40,000,000), which had only recently been frozen, were defrosted, but the President explained at his press conference that American aid to Soviet Russia could be effective only in the event of a long war (in which hardly anyone believed). Furthermore, he remarked, Britain would continue to have first claim on anything that could be made available. He confessed that he was ready to aid Soviet Russia, but quickly added that he had no idea what the Russians needed. Two days later the White House announced, through Mr. Welles, that the President would not invoke the Neutrality Law against Soviet Russia, on the plea that, though Hitler had declared war against the Soviet Union, the war did not imperil the United States or American citizens. The real significance of failure to apply the law was that the Soviet port of Vladivostok, at least, would remain open to American shipping.[20]

[19] Text in *Documents on American Foreign Relations*, III, 364-65. For the background see Sumner Welles: *The Time for Decision* (New York, 1944), 171.

[20] *The New York Times*, June 24, 25, 26, 1941; tel. to Steinhardt, June 28, 1941, recounting the steps that had been taken to date.

The popular reaction, probably influenced more by the Churchill broadcast than by the shifty statements of the Administration, was on the whole more favorable than might have been expected.[21] The isolationists, to be sure, ran true to form. "Let us hope," wrote the *New York Journal-American* (June 23), "that Occidental peace can still be made and Europe united against the expansion of Asiatic Communism." According to the *Chicago Tribune* (June 23), "the news is hardly less welcome in this country than in Britain, for it means that if there ever was any justification for our intervention in arms, that justification no longer exists. The heat is off. The pressure upon us is relaxed. . . ." Continuing on the next day, the same paper wrote: "Mr. Churchill can welcome what Hitler has sent his way. Our war birds here may try also to welcome it as reason for getting into war. To other Americans, to the majority of them, it presents the final reason for remaining out."

Isolationist leaders in Congress lent their voices to the same argument. Senator Bennett C. Clark's remarks were succinct: "It's a case of dog eat dog. Stalin is as bloody-handed as Hitler. I don't think we should help either one. We should tend to our own business, as we should have been doing all along. The whole business shows the absolute instability of European alliances and points to the necessity of our staying out of all of them." Senator Burton K. Wheeler declared: "I don't think the American people will stand for us to tie up with the Communists. . . . Now we can just let Joe Stalin and the other dictators fight it out." To this may be added the following from John T. Flynn: "If Germany wins, Russia will go Fascist. If Russia wins, Germany will go Communist. There is no chance for us at all. The question now is, are we going to fight to make Europe safe for Communism?" Senator Robert A. Taft: "The victory of Communism in the world would be far more dangerous to the United States than a victory of Fascism." Congressman Frederick C. Smith: "Much as we may desire the destruction of Hitlerism, we as free Americans cannot afford to pay the price in money and blood to strengthen and enhance the power of Communistic Russia. . . . There is no doubt that any union between ourselves and Russia will operate strongly to encourage the further development of Communism in this country."[22]

The attitude of the Catholic Church and indeed of many Protestant groups was equally negative. Catholics felt bound by the Papal Encyclical *Divini redemptoris* (March 19, 1937), which stated categorically: "Com-

---

[21] See Jan Ciechanowski: *Defeat in Victory* (New York, 1947), 25-26, 29 ff., reporting the apprehensive statements of Harry Hopkins.

[22] Review of press opinion, in *Morgenthau Diaries* (*MS.*), Vol. 415, pp. 218 ff. See further D. F. Fleming: *While America Slept* (New York, 1944), 191 ff.; Jerome S. Bruner: *Mandate from the People* (New York, 1944), Chapter VI; *The New York Times*, June 24 and 25, 1941; *New York Herald Tribune*, June 24, 1941. On June 29 *The New York Times* published a digest of opinion throughout the country.

munism is intrinsically wrong and no one who would save Christian civilization may give it assistance in any undertaking whatsoever."[23] It was only natural, then, that the *Catholic World* should have roundly denounced in advance all ideas of coöperation with the Soviet Union and warned of the consequences of a pact with the forces of evil. In the event of Hitler's defeat, wrote that influential journal, it was inconceivable that Stalin would not demand a share of the spoils: "Hitler and Nazism may be the chief menace now. But is it unthinkable that after a war in which the Soviets participate and which they help to win, Communism will not become the primary menace?"[24]

Even the supporters of the Administration's foreign policy were uncertain and divided on the issue of aid to the Soviet Union. Not a few expressed hope that the two hated dictatorships would bleed each other white and thus relieve the world of the totalitarian threat. Others held that Stalin, having concluded his nefarious pact with Hitler, was now getting nothing more than his just deserts. Nevertheless, a Gallup poll revealed that in the Nazi-Soviet conflict 73 percent of those queried preferred to see the Russians win, as against 4 percent who favored Germany. Perhaps the decision came easy for the majority, since about 70 percent were convinced that the Soviets would be defeated and forced to conclude a peace that would give Hitler control of Russian resources.[25]

There was certainly little sentiment for positive aid to Hitler's latest victim. The country generally had been outraged by Communist agitation and provocation of strikes in defense industries and could greet only with contempt the latest reversal of the Communist Party line involving the spectacular transformation of the "imperialist war" into a "war of liberation" and a "war for democracy." However, many great metropolitan newspapers concurred with Churchill that a victory of Hitler over Stalin would further endanger the security of the United States. Halfheartedly the idea of associating Soviet Russia with the democracies was accepted, though *The New York Times* for some time continued to warn against sending equipment to the Soviet Union, lest it fall into Hitler's hands. That influential newspaper, along with many others, adopted the line suggested by Stimson, Knox and Ickes, that under the circumstances by far the best policy for the United States would be to utilize the respite afforded by Hitler's diversion to the east in order to strengthen the defenses of the west and aid Britain intensify its air war against Germany. The chance of a Soviet victory was rated low and some consolation was drawn from the notion that the Communists had lost interest in world revolution and would, even in the hour of victory, be so weakened as to be relatively innocuous. "It is now many years," wrote the

[23] Denis Gwynn: *The Vatican and the War in Europe* (Dublin, 1941), 155 ff.

[24] *Catholic World*, August 1941, 513-23. This editorial, entitled "Covenant with Hell," recalled earlier warnings and professed to summarize the Catholic standpoint.

[25] Bruner: *Mandate from the People*, 107; Dulles: *The Road to Teheran*, 233.

New Republic (June 30, 1941), "since Russian Communism abandoned all but the emptiest pretext of continued revolutionary effort abroad." The *Christian Science Monitor* (July 5) made the same point: "Much as we dislike Communism, it is necessary to recognize that Russia has in twenty years shown neither the disposition nor the ability to assail the free peoples." And the *New York Herald Tribune* (July 3, 1941) was even more explicit:

A Hitler victory over Russia and Britain means, in the coldest calculation of probabilities, the triumph of totalitarian barbarism throughout the world. A victory of Great Britain, the United States and Communist Russia holds out no such prospect. Even if Communist totalitarianism survives the strain in Russia, the fact that it would only do so in association with victorious democracy in Britain and the United States would give it no such untrammeled prestige and power as success would bring to Nazi totalitarianism. An essentially democratic world would still be possible. This is not a matter of ethics or ideology or theory; it is a matter simply of the practical facts of the practical situation before us.

That President Roosevelt shared this delusion is eloquently attested by his letter to Admiral Leahy at the time: "Now comes this Russian diversion. If it is more than just that, it will mean the liberation of Europe from Nazi domination,—and at the same time I do not think we need worry about any possibility of Russian domination."[26]

Torn between the desire to see Hitler defeated and the hope that communism would not triumph, the American people raised no strong protest to President Roosevelt's announcement of his intention to give aid to Soviet Russia. After all, the President had made clear that Britain would continue to enjoy priority and, in view of the known shortage of vital equipment, it was unlikely that much material could reach Russia before the anticipated collapse of the Red armies.[27] Furthermore, all still depended on what requests the Soviet Government would submit. On the evening of June 26 Ambassador Oumansky had sought out Mr. Welles and expressed his gratification over the President's press statement, but at the same time had admitted that he had not yet heard from Moscow on the question of aid. Welles had suggested the provision of technicians, industrial experts and engineers, but had urged above all that military attachés and press correspondents be given the opportunity to visit the front and see for themselves what might be done to assist. Oumansky was sympathetic and, strange though it may seem, voiced regret that the conversations of the past year had proved

[26] Letter of President Roosevelt to Admiral Leahy, June 26, 1941 (quoted in Langer: *Our Vichy Gamble*, 161). In addition to the newspapers quoted above, we have drawn on *The New York Times*, June 23, 24, 26, July 2; the *New York Herald Tribune*, June 23; the *New York World-Telegram*, June 23; *PM*, June 23; the *Christian Science Monitor*, June 26, July 1; the *San Francisco Chronicle*, June 25; the *Daily Worker*, June 27, 1941.

[27] Hulen in *The New York Times*, June 23; Krock in *The New York Times*, June 24, 1941.

so unprofitable. Welles suggested that the past be forgotten and all effort concentrated on the current problem.[28]

That problem assumed concrete form only on June 29, when Molotov opened discussions with Ambassador Steinhardt and at the same time forwarded to Washington the first schedule of Soviet requirements. Speaking to the Ambassador, Molotov expressed appreciation of the American offer, but did not conceal his skepticism about the actual provision of war materials. The Soviet program, as submitted by Oumansky to Welles on June 30, listed nine categories, such as antiaircraft guns, fighter planes, short-range bombers, antitank guns, airplane factory equipment, cracking plants for aviation gasoline, machinery for tire manufacture, rolling mills for light alloys, etc. The emphasis on plant equipment was noted at once by the State Department and was taken as an indication of Soviet determination to fight on even if the industrial areas of western Russia were lost. Welles therefore received the Soviet program sympathetically and urged that a more complete breakdown of items be provided as soon as possible. Oumansky promised to do so and inquired about a possible five-year credit, which he thought would be preferable to raising the question of Lend-Lease. This problem, too, Mr. Welles promised to explore with the Secretary of the Treasury.[29]

Measures were taken at once to enable the State Department to deal with the new situation. On June 30 Acting Secretary Welles approved the establishment of a special committee to clear and expedite Soviet orders. This committee was to include representatives of the Office of Defense Aid Reports, the Administrator of Export Control, the Office of Production Management, the Army and Navy Munitions Board, and when necessary the Maritime Commission.[30] Within a week Oumansky appeared with his more detailed schedule, on which occasion Mr. Welles suggested the possibility of an exchange of American equipment, at least in part, for Soviet raw materials needed by the United States.[31]

Despite the desperate military position of the Soviet Union during the first weeks of the war and the prevalent opinion in western military circles that its collapse could not be long delayed, President Roosevelt was determined to furnish as much aid as possible and as quickly as possible. Ambassador Steinhardt reported that the German advance was so rapid that he might not even have time to move the embassy eastward. At the same time he did not share the general fear that Stalin might suddenly make

[28] Memo of conversation between Mr. Welles and Ambassador Oumansky, June 26, 1941.

[29] Tels. from Steinhardt, June 29 and 30, 1941; memo of conversation between Mr. Welles and Ambassador Oumansky, June 30, 1941.

[30] Memo of Charles P. Curtis, Jr., to Mr. Welles, and the latter's note of approval, June 30, 1941.

[31] Memo of Mr. Feis to Mr. Welles, July 3, suggesting such an arrangement; memo of conversation between Mr. Welles and the Soviet Ambassador, July 7, 1941.

peace and expressed hope that the Russians would continue the war even if driven beyond the Urals.[32]

Former Ambassador Davies, too, argued to Harry Hopkins that, though the loss of the rich Ukraine might provoke a revolution against the Communist regime or induce Stalin to make peace, the Soviets could maintain themselves beyond the Urals and that therefore everything possible should be done to encourage them: "Word ought to be gotten to Stalin direct that our attitude is 'all out' to beat Hitler and that our historic policy of friendliness to Russia still exists."[33]

The President's views and policy at this time were well reflected in his remarks to Ambassador Oumansky on July 10. As reported by Mr. Welles to Lord Halifax, the record reads:

The President said that we would undertake to supply urgently to the Soviet Union such of the orders which the Soviet Government desired to place in the United States which it might find it possible to ship and that the President had emphasized the fact that whatever was sent of an urgent character should actually reach the Soviet Union before October 1 at the latest. I added that the President had made clear his own opinion that if the Russians could hold the Germans until October 1 that that would be of great value in defeating Hitler since after that date no effective military operations with Russia could be carried on and the consequent tying up of a number of German troops and machines for that period of time would be of great practical value in assuring the ultimate defeat of Hitler. The President had also stressed his belief that the more machines the Germans were forced to use up in the Russian campaign, the more certain would be the rapidity with which Germany would be defeated, since he did not believe that the ability for replacement on the part of Germany was nearly as great as that which had been supposed. Finally, the President, I said, had laid particular stress upon the fact that whatever it was decided by this Government to send to Russia would be the subject of consultation between this Government and the British Government, since it was a matter of common concern to all three Governments that the supplies which this country might have available be utilized in those particular places where, from the military standpoint, they might prove to be most useful.[34]

Mr. Roosevelt, then, was staking everything on the chance that the Red armies could hold out until the onset of winter. His estimate went well beyond anything the military authorities were willing to subscribe to and seems to reflect the influence of Davies. Lest it be thought that the President's assurances of help were meant only to encourage the Soviets to fight on, it may be pointed out that he tried to impress on his subordinates the need for utmost expedition and took what steps he could to forestall organized opposition to the aid program. He had good reason to suppose that the Catholic hierarchy might issue a declaration against support of Communist

[32] Tels. from Steinhardt, July 1, 2, 3, 1941.
[33] Sherwood: *Roosevelt and Hopkins*, 307-8 (July 8, 1941). See also Joseph E. Davies: *Mission to Moscow* (New York, 1943), 493 ff.
[34] Memo of conversation between Mr. Welles and Lord Halifax, July 10, 1941.

Russia or at least insist on the recognition of the Four Freedoms as a condition for aid. Furthermore, Mr. Harold H. Tittman, who was serving as Myron Taylor's substitute at the Vatican, reported rather ominously that Church circles were maintaining a "strict reserve," equidistant from Communist Russia and Nazi Germany. It was Tittman's impression that in the Curia "the militant atheism of the former is still regarded as more obnoxious than the modern paganism of the latter." There was a real danger that the Nazi "crusade" might make an impression on the Catholic Latin countries.[35]

To counteract unfavorable developments and if possible convert the Vatican to the policy of the democracies, both the American and British Governments on July 8, 1941, submitted notes to the Curia. The American note repeated Welles's statement of June 23 and pointed out that the new conflict "has not in any way affected the present policy of the United States Government, namely to insure that all possible aid and assistance will be furnished the victims of aggression and our program of assistance to Great Britain is going forward with no alteration whatsoever." Tittman was instructed to make clear "that the principles and doctrines of communistic dictatorship are as unacceptable and as alien to the beliefs of the American people as are the principles and doctrines of Nazi dictatorship, and neither one nor the other is tolerated by the American people."[36]

The Vatican made no adverse comment on this note, which, in fact, rather carefully avoided the issue of material aid. The Catholic hierarchy in the United States likewise abstained from publicly announcing an official position. Meanwhile Postmaster General Frank C. Walker, a very influential Catholic layman, made a concerted effort to head off Church opposition. In an important and much noted address at Butte, Montana (July 12, 1941), he argued against the idea of a crusade against communism, on the plea that the Soviets were not fighting to spread communism and that in any case communism could not be defeated by the sword:

> Realistically, is it not absurd for leaders of the opposition to insist that we stand indifferent to Russia's fate—or even worse—hope for her defeat? Do they not realize that a Russian defeat of the character that would bring about her collapse would leave the ports and airfields of Eastern Siberia in the hands of the Axis powers? If, after she was beaten at Moscow, she gave no resistance in Siberia, consider then what would confront us. It is not Stalin and his philosophy that we should consider at this point: it is the safety, security and well-being of a threatened America.

3. FINLAND'S WAR

American sentiment toward Communist Russia was influenced to some extent by the fact that, shortly after the German attack, Soviet planes began to bomb Helsinki and other Finnish towns. Officially these bombings were

---

[35] Tels. from Tittman, June 30 and July 2, 1941.
[36] Tel. to Tittman, July 5, and tel. from Tittman, July 11, 1941.

retaliation for Finland's permitting the Germans to use its airfields for attacks on Leningrad. These allegations were never substantiated, but it may be assumed that the Kremlin had gotten wind of negotiations between Germany and Finland and was fully convinced that the Helsinki Government would presently throw in its lot with Hitler in the hope of recovering the territories lost in the Winter War. On the evening of June 25, 1941, the Finnish Cabinet decided for war in retaliation for the Soviet bombings, but at the same time carefully abstained from alliance with Nazi Germany.

It was perhaps inevitable and was certainly expected in London and Washington that such a contingency would arise. Ever since September, 1940, when Helsinki concluded an agreement with Germany allowing the passage of Nazi troops to and from northern Norway by way of Finland, it had seemed likely that, in the face of continued Soviet pressure, the Helsinki Government would look to Germany for protection and that Hitler would lend Finland support. Molotov had, during his visit to Berlin in November, 1940, made every effort to secure a free hand for further Soviet action against Finland, but the Fuehrer had stated categorically that he would not permit further aggression against that little country. The Germans had lost no time in communicating to Helsinki the Soviet demands and their rejection, and had thereby laid the foundation for closer relations, not to say future coöperation.[37]

Uncertainty over the precise development of German-Finnish relations has by no means been completely dispelled by the materials made available since the end of the war. President Ryti and Marshal Mannerheim were evidently aware of the likelihood of a Nazi-Soviet conflict as early as January, 1941, but scrupulously avoided any commitment to participate.[38] On the other hand, German military authorities, planning their campaign against Soviet Russia, were eager for Finnish coöperation in an attack on Leningrad and the Murmansk Railway. On their initiative military discussions took place on various occasions, notably in February and again in late May, 1941. In the course of these conferences the Finns seem to have been informed of German military plans, which involved the transfer of troops from northern Norway to the Finnish-Soviet border and the mobilization of Finnish forces on the Karelian front. Finnish staff officers, including the Chief of Staff, evidently raised no objections, but the Government insisted throughout that Finland would not make war on the Soviet Union unless actually attacked.[39]

[37] Much of this is based on the reports of the American Minister, Mr. Arthur Schoenfeld, which were conveniently summarized in a long memorandum by Mr. Robert McClintock, the Secretary of Legation, dated October 28, 1941. See also the discussion in John Wuorinen, ed.: *Finland and World War II* (New York, 1948).

[38] Tel. from Schoenfeld, January 28, 1941.

[39] The crucial military conferences took place at Salzburg and Berlin on May 25-26, 1941. On these see the testimony of Buschenhagen and Paulus (*Trials of the Major War Criminals,* VII, Nurnberg, 1947, pp. 258, 309 ff.) and the *Halder Diary,* May 26 and

Sensing the likelihood of Finnish participation in the expected Nazi assault on the Soviet Union, the British Government had on June 13 warned both President Ryti and Marshal Mannerheim that if Finland joined Germany it would forfeit British support and sympathy and would oblige London to subject Finland to every form of economic pressure. At the same time British traffic to Petsamo was temporarily suspended.[40]

When requested by Lord Halifax to support this British policy, Acting Secretary Welles evaded a definite answer. The American Government had, in April, set forth to the Finnish, as to other Governments, its attitude toward the war and its determination to support Britain in every way.[41] Mr. Welles therefore took the stand that Helsinki was already sufficiently aware of the American position.[42] In view of the strong American sympathy for Finland and the legacy of hostility toward the Soviet Union left by the Winter War, the State Department was naturally intent on avoiding any action that might appear as pressure on the Finns in behalf of the Kremlin.

As best it could the Administration continued to sidestep the Finnish issue, even after the outbreak of hostilities was announced by Helsinki. Mr. Procopé, the Finnish Minister in Washington, made this course as easy as possible. He was at great pains to explain the Soviet aggressions and the failure of his Government to obtain a satisfactory explanation from Moscow. In view of the circumstances, he asserted, his Government had no choice but to take defensive measures. But it was Finland's desire to maintain neutrality as between Germany and Great Britain; in any measures it might take it proposed to act quite independently. In other words, while a cobelligerent with Germany against Soviet Russia, Finland was not an ally of Germany, particularly not against Britain.[43]

For the moment this was reassuring, but it presently became known that Marshal Mannerheim, in his order of the day to the Finnish forces, had indicated that his country's objectives were more than merely defensive. The State Department therefore made immediate efforts to secure a more precise definition of Finnish policy and intentions. Mr. Schoenfeld was instructed to point out that the sacrifice of Finnish lives to assist Germany in dominating the world or a formal alliance with Germany would be an ill-conceived policy, unlikely to lead to any lasting gains at the future peace conference.[44] A

June 7, 1941. On the other hand, General Waldemar Erfurth: *Der finnische Krieg* (Wiesbaden, 1950), 26-35, stresses the noncommittal, contingent character of these discussions, and Wuorinen: *Finland and World War II*, 97 ff., also insists that Helsinki refused to make promises.

[40] Tels. from Schoenfeld, June 13, 14, 16, 19, 1941; memo from the British Embassy, June 14, 1941.

[41] Tel. to Schoenfeld, April 25, and tels. from Schoenfeld, April 26, 28, May 20, 1941.

[42] Memo of conversation between Mr. Welles and Lord Halifax, June 14, 1941.

[43] Memos of conversation between Mr. Welles and Minister Procopé, June 26 and 28, 1941.

[44] Tel. to Schoenfeld, June 30, 1941.

few days later the American Minister was directed to call on President Ryti and explain that Finnish policy seemed broader in scope than was necessary merely to protect Finland against foreign attack. Hence the question emerged whether Finnish policy was not in a measure thwarting the declared American policy of resisting the powers of aggression with all available means: "Until the policy of Finland is satisfactorily clarified, the Government of the United States will be unable to decide what further assistance it may be possible to render Finland in the political, economic, and financial fields, should there be occasion to render such assistance."[45]

Washington's note was submitted to President Ryti on July 4, but evoked only an equivocal reply. To quote Mr. Schoenfeld's report:

President Ryti stated and authorized me so to inform the President of the United States, that Finland was a cobelligerent with Germany in those hostilities [against the Soviet Union] and was seeking to achieve purely Finnish aims. The strategic position of Finland after the conclusion in 1940 of the previous hostilities with the Soviet Union was dangerously vulnerable and it would be the purpose of Finland to correct that condition for her own protection only. Aside from necessary military understandings in connection with the parallel operations now proceeding in common with the German forces, no political agreements exist between the Finnish and the German Governments. . . . It is the view of President Ryti that the defeat of the Soviet Army and the complete crushing of Bolshevism as a consequence thereof are in the interest of the whole world, and particularly of Finland. But the Finnish people have not departed and have no intention of departing from their established national system of political and social organizations.[46]

Washington, anxious as ever to avoid aggravation of the Finnish issue, accepted these statements for what they were worth and was probably relieved by the decision of the British Government to maintain relations with Helsinki for the time being. On July 10 the Finnish forces began operations and Marshal Mannerheim, in another order of the day, revealed that their objective was the liberation of eastern Karelia as well as the recovery of the territory lost in 1940: "The freedom of Karelia," he declared, "and a greater Finland stand before us in the mighty avalanche of historical events." Once again Minister Schoenfeld inquired what interpretation was to be put upon these utterances, but when the Finnish Foreign Minister assured him that the Government had had no part in drafting Mannerheim's order of the day and that it was still true that there were no political agreements between Finland and Germany, nothing more was done from the American side.[47]

Washington probably shared the hope of London that after the Finns had reëstablished their territorial security they would be less inclined to continue

---

45 Tel. to Schoenfeld, July 2, 1941.
46 Tels. from Schoenfeld, July 4 and 5, 1941.
47 Tels. from Schoenfeld, July 11, 16, 18, 1941.

coöperation with the Germans. But before that point was reached the Finnish Government, on July 28, itself took the initiative in breaking diplomatic relations with the British. This step was taken on the plea that since Britain had, by its agreement with the Kremlin of July 12, engaged itself to furnish the Soviets all possible aid, no good purpose would be served by the maintenance of regular diplomatic relations. The British on their part attributed the move to German pressure, probably on Finnish headquarters, which evidently demanded the rupture so as to eliminate the danger of military information being passed to the Soviets through British channels. At bottom, however, the Helsinki Government was probably influenced primarily by its faith in an early German victory. The official German press hailed Finland's decision and announced that "Finland's successful participation as a loyal and active member in the struggle for a new Europe insures it in all spheres a claim to a generous reward for its sacrifices. . . . Its position on the most northeasterly wing of the European defense front demands that it be strengthened and consolidated. The fact that as a Nordic state it has tackled the European eastern mission with energy . . . guarantees it a leading place in the Scandinavian area which it is defending."[48] It was not unreasonable to suppose, therefore, that the Germans had baited Finland with the prospect of substantial territorial gains and an important role in the new order.[49]

Undesirable and regrettable though the break of diplomatic relations was from the British standpoint, it had at least this advantage, as seen from Washington: it put Helsinki in the wrong and made it appear that Finland was willingly throwing in its lot with Hitler. As yet the Finns had not recovered even the territory lost in 1940, so that militarily the northern front was still decidedly a secondary theater. There was no immediate occasion for Washington to take action, and none was considered. However, the weakening of American friendship for Finland lowered one of the hurdles confronting the Administration program of aiding the Soviet Union.

4. THE POLISH PROBLEM

One of the most difficult and, as it was to prove, one of the most baleful issues evoked by the Nazi-Soviet war and the alliance of the British with the Soviets was the problem of Poland's position and future status. Poland, a full-fledged ally of Britain, had been the chief victim of the Nazi-Soviet Pact of August, 1939. Defeated by Hitler's armies, it had been divided between the two associated dictators. The Polish state had been liquidated, but a Polish Government-in-Exile had been set up in London, with General

[48] Tel. from Morris (Berlin), July 29, 1941.
[49] On the rupture of relations and the evidence of German pressure see Wuorinen: *Finland and World War II*, 130-32. We have used also tels. from Schoenfeld, July 29, August 1 and 2, 1941; memo of conversation between Mr. Higgs and Minister Procopé, July 29, 1941.

Wladyslaw Sikorski as Prime Minister and Mr. August Zaleski as Foreign Minister. Polish military forces had been organized and by June, 1941, were fighting side by side with their British allies in various theaters of operations. Obviously it was a matter of great and urgent importance to the British Government to effect a reconciliation between Poland and Soviet Russia, if only in order to extricate itself from the impossible position of being allied to each of two mutually hostile powers. In a sense the problem was of almost equal though less direct importance to the United States Government, in view of its oft-reiterated policy of not recognizing territorial changes brought about by aggression and in view of the large Polish population in the country. Polish-Americans were predominantly Catholic and therefore as anti-Communist as they were anti-Russian.

General Sikorski was himself eager for reconciliation and appears to have persuaded himself that if once Poles and Russians fought side by side against a common enemy a new spirit would be engendered which would facilitate the settlement of the thorny issues between the two countries. Hardly had the British policy of supporting Soviet Russia been announced than the Polish Prime Minister, after conferring with Mr. Churchill and Mr. Eden, turned to the radio (June 23) to hail the end of Nazi-Soviet collaboration and express the hope that soon the Polish-Russian question would disappear from international politics. "We are entitled to assume," he said, "that Russia will cancel the pact of 1939, and that should logically bring us back to the position created by the treaty of Riga of March, 1921. The political and moral significance of such an act would be tremendous."[50]

This address was regarded by some prominent Poles as premature and unfortunate. The Prime Minister, they felt, was too sanguine and would have been better advised had he awaited a Soviet offer. Mr. Jan Ciechanowski, the Polish Ambassador in Washington, at once called on Acting Secretary Welles with the suggestion that the United States Government urge upon the Kremlin the restoration of Poland's territory if and when the Soviet Government applied for American aid. Mr. Welles, however, struck a cautious note: the Polish request would be given sympathetic consideration, but he could promise only to keep the matter in mind whenever the opportune moment arose for the United States Government to be useful.[51]

The Kremlin took its time in responding to the Polish advances and there was good reason to doubt whether the Soviet leaders would prove willing to surrender the gains made through their past association with Hitler. Incredible though it may seem, Soviet diplomats in Washington as well as in Lon-

[50] R. Umiastowski: *Poland, Russia and Great Britain, 1941-1945* (London, 1946), 13 ff. We have used also a despatch from Mr. Biddle, the American representative assigned to the Governments-in-Exile, June 24, 1941.

[51] Memo of conversation between Mr. Welles and Ambassador Ciechanowski, June 26, 1941; despatch from Biddle, June 30, 1941; Jan Ciechanowski: *Defeat in Victory*, 29 ff.

don were still trying, even while the Red armies were being driven back by the Nazis, to secure recognition of the Soviet acquisition of the Baltic states.[52] When finally, on July 4, Ambassador Maisky took up the Polish question with Foreign Secretary Eden, he was decidedly shifty on the territorial issue. He stated that the Kremlin was quite prepared to have the Poles, Czechs, and Yugoslavs set up national committees on Soviet soil and organize military forces from among the prisoners of war, which forces the Soviet Government would agree to equip. The ultimate form of government of these peoples should be left to their own decision. As for Poland, the Kremlin favored the establishment of an independent, national state, the boundaries of which "would correspond with ethnographical Poland." Pressed for a more precise definition of terms, the Ambassador would say only that the territorial issue should cause little difficulty if there were good will on both sides.[53]

The measure of good will on the Soviet side was soon to be demonstrated. On July 5 General Sikorski and Foreign Minister Zaleski began discussions with Maisky, in the presence of an official of the British Foreign Office. The Poles at once asked for the abrogation of the Nazi-Soviet agreements of 1939 and return to the *status quo* preceding the German attack on Poland. Furthermore, they proposed the resumption of regular diplomatic relations and the release by the Kremlin of all Polish military and civilian personnel in the Soviet Union. Maisky, however, indicated that his Government would insist on the maintenance of the Ribbentrop-Molotov Line, which did not differ materially from the so-called Curzon Line—the supposedly ethnographic frontier advocated by the British in 1919. In view of this fundamental divergence of view it was natural that the atmosphere of the conference should have been, in Mr. Churchill's words, "frigid." However, Maisky promised to inform Moscow of the Polish position.[54]

While awaiting the Soviet reaction Ambassador Ciechanowski exerted himself further to enlist the support of the American Government. He urged Mr. Welles to indicate to the Kremlin Washington's earnest hope that an arrangement could be arrived at on the basis of the Polish program. While promising to do so, the Acting Secretary added that he felt strongly that the American Government should limit itself to an expression in general terms and should not become involved in the details of the proposed agreements.[55] As a matter of fact the Acting Secretary and other officials of the

---

[52] Memo of conversation (unofficial) between Mr. Loy Henderson of the State Department and Ambassador Oumansky, July 2, 1941.

[53] Tel. from Winant, July 4, 1941.

[54] Churchill: *The Grand Alliance*, 390 ff.; Umiastowski: *Poland, Russia and Great Britain*, 16. We have used also a tel. from Biddle, July 6, and a despatch from Biddle, July 10, 1941, and communications from the Polish Embassy to the State Department, July 7 and 24, 1941.

[55] Memo of conversation between Mr. Welles and the Polish Ambassador, July 8, 1941.

State Department were much disturbed by the raising of territorial questions and by the prospect that agreements might be made that would later jeopardize the conclusion of a just peace. As recently as June 15 Mr. Welles had reiterated to Lord Halifax his hope that the British would not recognize Soviet claims to the Baltic states. He was now apprehensive lest London, in its eagerness to square the Soviets and the Poles, bring pressure on the latter to make territorial concessions. So seriously did he view this situation that he induced the President to admonish Mr. Churchill. In a message to the Prime Minister, Mr. Roosevelt excused himself for referring to an issue "which is not in any way serious at this time but which might cause unpleasant repercussions over here later on." He noted the divergent views and interests of foreign racial groups in the United States and recalled the difficulties that had arisen on this score in the past. Thereupon he expounded the American position:

It seems to me that it is much too early for any of us to make commitments for the very good reason that both Britain and the United States want assurance of future peace by disarming all troublemakers and secondly by considering the possibility of reviving small states in the interest of harmony even if this has to be accomplished through plebiscite methods.

The plebiscite was on the whole one of the few successful outcomes of the Versailles Treaty, and it may be possible for us to extend the idea by suggesting in some cases preliminary plebiscites to be followed a good deal later on by second or even third plebiscites.

For example, none of us know at the present time whether it is advisable in the interest of quiet conditions to keep the Croats away from the throats of the Serbs and vice versa.

I am inclined to think that an over-all statement on your part would be useful at this time, making it clear that no postwar peace commitments as to territories, population or economics have been given. I could then back up your statement in very strong terms. There is no hurry about this, but you might think it over.[56]

Since the President stated explicitly that there was no hurry about this matter, Mr. Churchill made no direct reply. Neither did he make a public statement. Nonetheless, the President's message was a clear enunciation of what was to become a basic American policy and it is unthinkable that the Prime Minister failed to take note of it. So far as the Polish issue was concerned, the British Government counseled deferment of the territorial question. Various Polish writers, evidently reflecting the opinion of a majority of Polish leaders, have argued that if Britain and the United States had, in July, 1941, insisted that Poland be given the frontiers of the Riga Treaty, the Kremlin, in its hour of need, would have had to yield. Far from doing this, they continue, the British Foreign Office exerted what an eminent Polish

---

[56] Message of the President to Mr. Churchill, July 14, 1941. On the background we have used the *Berle Diaries* (*MS.*), July 8, 9, 11, 19, 1941.

diplomat has described as "very strong, not to say even brutal" pressure to have the territorial issue shelved. If this was so, the British Government may well have been acting according to its own lights in an effort to prevent a crisis and bring its two allies into line. At the same time its course met the requirements of the President's message, which may, in fact, have influenced the British policy.[57]

General Sikorski, personally eager to reach agreement with the Soviets, was apparently prepared from the outset to postpone discussion of the frontier question and therefore made no great difficulty so long as the Kremlin showed itself accommodating on other issues, such as the release of Polish prisoners and the formation of a Polish Army.[58] Accepting British advice to trust in the future good faith of the Soviets, he dropped the proposal for a territorial guarantee and, with British aid, came to agreement with Maisky toward the end of July. The Polish-Soviet Pact, signed on July 30, 1941, provided for the resumption of diplomatic relations, mutual support in the war, liberation of the Poles in Russia, and the formation of a Polish Army on Soviet soil. The territorial question was glossed over in the following enigmatic terms: "The Government of the U.S.S.R. recognizes the Soviet-German treaties of 1939 as to territorial changes in Poland as having lost their validity." Nothing, however, was said of the settlement that would be valid in the future.

In protest against this text the Polish Deputy Prime Minister, General Sosnkowski; the Foreign Minister, Mr. Zaleski; and the Minister of Justice, Mr. Seyda, at once resigned. The British Government, on its part, had agreed in advance to provide the Poles a solatium in the form of a statement, published on July 31, assuring General Sikorski "that His Majesty's Government do not recognize any territorial changes which have been effected in Poland since August, 1939." However, this "lullaby" statement was again purely negative. Questions were asked in Parliament, whereupon Mr. Eden felt impelled to state that the British declaration did "not involve any guarantee of frontiers by His Majesty's Government." General Sikorski tried to surmount the crisis in Polish circles by proclaiming that the agreement with Soviet Russia "does not permit even of the suggestion that the 1939 frontiers of the Polish State would ever be in question," but he must have known better and could hardly have been surprised when the official Soviet press (*Izvestia*, August 3, 1941) warmly contended that the Kremlin had committed itself to nothing: "We do not consider immutable the Polish-Soviet frontier established by the Treaty of Riga in 1921."[59]

[57] For the Polish views expressed above see especially Ignacy Matuszewski: *Great Britain's Obligations towards Poland* (New York, 1945), 40-42, and W. W. Kulski: "The Lost Opportunity for Russian-Polish Friendship" (*Foreign Affairs*, July, 1947).

[58] Tel. and despatch from Biddle, July 6 and 10, 1941, respectively; despatch from Biddle, July 27, 1941.

[59] Churchill: *The Grand Alliance*, 390-92. For the official text of the Polish-Soviet

The arrangement arrived at by General Sikorski, with advice and aid from the British, was in consonance with the official American position. Ambassador Ciechanowski, who throughout had shared the objections of Foreign Minister Zaleski, made a last ditch effort to induce the State Department to intercede with the British and secure for the Polish Government permission to issue a statement that in signing the agreement with Soviet Russia it had not in any way "admitted any change in its prewar territorial boundaries or the existence of any basis for the discussion of such changes." But the Ambassador was told that the American Government did not desire to intrude upon the negotiations and that the British note to the Polish Government seemed to cover the matter.[60] The State Department did not look with disfavor on the agreement and Acting Secretary Welles said as much in his statement to the press on July 31:

> The United States position toward Poland was made clear immediately after that country was invaded [by the Germans]. It was one of not recognizing any change in her status as a free, sovereign, and independent nation. That position is maintained and continued. His [Welles's] understanding of the Russian-Polish agreement was that it was in line with the United States policy of nonrecognition of territory taken by conquest.

Here was no reference whatever to the question of Poland's boundaries in the hour of victory. That question, like all other territorial issues, the Administration was anxious to defer till the war was over. Whether or not this was a sound decision will probably long continue to be debated. Those who hold that Britain and the United States should have insisted on specific terms of a territorial settlement will face the question whether in 1945 the Soviets, with their armies in occupation of all Poland, would have honored their engagements. It is, furthermore, highly doubtful whether even in the summer of 1941 the Kremlin would have yielded on this issue, no matter how desperate its military position or its need for aid. Certainly its pertinacity in trying to secure recognition of the absorption of the Baltic states indicates that it would not, under any circumstances, have abandoned its claims to eastern Poland.

From the standpoint of American policy the Polish-Soviet negotiations, like the Anglo-Soviet "alliance" of July 12, 1941, had the effect of reviving and stimulating suspicions and fears of Soviet designs. Among State Depart-

---

agreement see *Polish-Soviet Relations, 1918-1943* (Washington, n.d.), 108-9; *Soviet Foreign Policy during the Patriotic War,* I, 80-81. On the negotiations we have used despatches from Biddle, July 16, 17, 24, 27, 1941. For the disagreements between Polish leaders see Umiastowski: *Poland, Russia and Great Britain,* 18 ff.; Waclaw Jedrzejewicz, ed.: *Poland in the British Parliament, 1939-1945* (New York, 1946), I, 469 ff.; Matuszewski: *Great Britain's Obligations toward Poland,* 40-42; and the article by Kulski, as cited above.

[60] Memo of conversation between Mr. Loy Henderson and the Polish Ambassador, July 31, 1941; tel. from Biddle, August 2, 1941; and a tel. of explanation to Biddle, August 5, 1941, which Acting Secretary Welles decided should not be despatched.

ment officials some were already filled with dire forebodings. They foresaw, even then, that the Kremlin was aiming at the establishment of a sphere of influence comprising Finland, the Baltic States, Poland, Czechoslovakia, Yugoslavia and presumably Rumania and Bulgaria, if not Hungary. Within this sphere, it was thought, the Soviets would absorb Finland or impose upon it a puppet government, while the Baltic states would be incorporated in the Soviet Union and a confederation of Poland, Czechoslovakia and Yugoslavia would be set up under Soviet domination. The whole business, noted Assistant Secretary Berle, was "damned dangerous."[61]

Acting Secretary Welles certainly shared these apprehensions and gave much thought to reorganization of the Department's Advisory Committee on Problems of Foreign Relations so as to advance study of postwar settlements. There was some talk of enlarging the Committee by including a number of qualified outsiders like Norman Davis, Hamilton Fish Armstrong (editor of *Foreign Affairs*) and Isaiah Bowman, the eminent geographer who had played an important role in devising the territorial settlements of 1919. A meeting of the State Department members was held on August 1 and drew up certain broad recommendations: the United States should, on the conclusion of the war, take an active part in European reconstruction; another note should be sent to London suggesting that the British Government abstain from making commitments on issues of peace; arrangements should be made to arrive with the British at a common program of nationality and economic problems. The Committee further expressed the opinion that there was as yet no reason for the United States to sever relations with Finland and that, indeed, the United States was in honor bound to support the independence not only of Finland, but of the Baltic states, Poland, Czechoslovakia, and Yugoslavia, the boundaries of which should be left for future discussion and settlement.[62]

5. THE AID PROGRAM AND THE HOPKINS MISSION

While the British were clearing away political obstacles to full coöperation with Soviet Russia, the problem of military and economic support was rapidly becoming a controlling factor. Once they had overcome their initial distrust, the leaders of the Kremlin showed little hesitation in advancing demands and requirements of an extensive and occasionally unreasonable character. Mr. Churchill has narrated how, on July 19, 1941, the Soviet Ambassador brought him the first message from Stalin, the one recognizing that Britain and the Soviet Union had become "fighting allies" in the struggle against Hitlerite Germany. This same message contained also the earliest Soviet request for a second front, to be formed by the British in northern

---

[61] *Berle Diaries (MS.)*, August 1 and 2, 1941.

[62] *Berle Diaries (MS.)*, July 31 and August 2, 1941; memo from Mr. Dunn to Secretary Hull, August 2, 1941. See especially Harley A. Notter: *Postwar Foreign Policy Preparation, 1939-1945* (Washington, 1949), 41 ff.

France and northern Norway for the purpose of drawing Nazi forces from the east. To this the British Prime Minister could only reply that an invasion of western Europe was for the time being out of the question, but that Britain would intensify its air attack on Germany and provide Russia air support in the north. Knowing that this response would not satisfy Stalin and ignoring the lack of cordiality on the Kremlin's part, Mr. Churchill did what he could to despatch much-needed supplies. He promised his new partner two hundred fighter planes as well as raw materials and military equipment. By the end of September, 1941, the British had already sent to Russia 450 aircraft, 22,000 tons of rubber, 3,000,000 pairs of boots, and varying quantities of tin, aluminum, lead, jute, and wool.[63]

President Roosevelt had equally committed himself to a program of economic aid, but the implementation of his directive proved halting and disappointing. Administrative difficulties had much to do with the constant delays. Since it was not contemplated that Soviet requirements should be handled through Lend-Lease, assistance to Russia devolved upon the State Department, which, naturally, was not adequately equipped to manage large and complicated procurement problems. Furthermore, at least a half dozen Washington agencies were involved in various aspects of the program and coördination between them was practically nonexistent. Consequently the Soviet schedule passed from one agency to another. Each scrutinized the requirements from the standpoint of its own capabilities and almost invariably rejected them. Ambassador Oumansky, who for a few days had been all sweetness and light, soon reverted to his customary complaints and recriminations. His request for a huge credit had been referred to Mr. Jesse Jones and had been agreed to in principle, only to run quickly into the usual snag respecting the provision of adequate security. Such security, according to Jones, could take the form only of shipments of raw materials and these, in turn, were not really needed by the United States.[64]

As for the program of requirements which Oumansky had submitted on July 8, this was laid before the Cabinet by Acting Secretary Welles on July 18, after the reaction of various government agencies had been canvassed. It turned out to be a staggering proposition, for the requirements in terms of value ran to about $1,850,000,000, and included such items as 3000 pursuit planes, 3000 bombers, 20,000 antiaircraft guns, 50,000 tons of toluol, large quantities of aviation gasoline and lubricants, raw materials of many kinds, and some $50,000,000 worth of industrial plant and equipment. In view of the acute shortages in most of these items and in view further of the vast program then being worked out between Washington and London, Mr.

[63] Churchill: *The Grand Alliance*, 384-88; W. K. Hancock and M. M. Gowing: *British War Economy* (London, 1949), 359.

[64] Memo of conversation between Mr. Morgenthau and Ambassador Oumansky, August 15, 1941 (*Morgenthau Diaries, MS.*, Vol. 433, pp. 218 ff.).

Welles, relying on statements made by various agencies, reported that he could recommend only very modest, not to say insignificant, assignments to the Soviets, even over the period of a year.[65]

The President, evidently under the spell of former Ambassador Davies, who in turn relied on the estimates of former Military Attaché Colonel Philip R. Faymonville, had hopes that the Soviet armies might hold out until winter, and was above all intent on encouraging Stalin sufficiently to keep him from considering another deal with Hitler. He was therefore much dissatisfied with the lack of progress and with the generally negative attitude of the executive agencies. Welles suggested the need for an American-British-Soviet commission to survey overall needs and decide on the wisest allocation of available supplies. He also requested the President to write Secretaries Stimson and Knox as well as Mr. Knudsen and General Burns, asking them to review the whole problem of aiding Soviet Russia and calling upon them to report at once such items as might be provided and shipped by October 1. This last suggestion was acted upon at once by Mr. Roosevelt. On July 21 he set a deadline of forty-eight hours for the report in question. Those concerned hastily convened and conferred, after which they recommended that matériel to the value of about $60,000,000 be sent, about a third of which (chiefly machine tools, aviation gasoline, tiremaking equipment and oil-cracking machinery) might be despatched by October 1. The question of planes and munitions was left for further study.[66]

The President approved these proposals at once (July 23) and communicated them to Ambassador Oumansky on July 27. But the all-important question of planes remained open. The War Department was not encouraging: bombers were not available and it was unlikely that more than fifty fighter planes could be provided over and above what the British might be willing to contribute from those on order in the United States. It goes without saying that Oumansky, when given this news, "complained bitterly and in rather unmeasured terms of the delays he was encountering." Happily a Soviet military mission, headed by Lieutenant General Filip I. Golikov, arrived at this time from London. Golikov, a man of attractive personality, exuded confidence that his fellow countrymen would be able to hold out until winter. In the company of Oumansky he called upon all important American officials and stressed the significance of the Soviet front, urged the need for haste in sending supplies, and pleaded for coördination of Soviet with British and American military requirements. Eventually Secretary Stimson agreed to provide a squadron of fighter planes in addition to another 150 which had already been crated and shipped to Britain. But

---

[65] State Department memoranda, July 18 and 19, 1941.

[66] Edward R. Stettinius, Jr.: *Lend-Lease: Weapon for Victory* (New York, 1944), 121 ff.; *Industrial Mobilization for War* (Washington, 1947), I, 130 ff.; *Morgenthau Diaries (MS.)*, Vol. 428, pp. 52 ff. (record of Morgenthau's conference with Cox, Coy and Faymonville, August 5, 1941).

this concession led only to further confusion, for the Russians now insisted that the planes already in England, instead of being despatched to Archangel, be returned to the United States, freighted to the Pacific coast, and there loaded for Vladivostok, whence they were to be flown to the European front. What considerations may have engendered this fantastic proposal it is hard to say. General Marshall and his advisers were convinced that under these conditions the planes would never see battle, but they finally agreed to sacrifice them as a token of good will. Later, incidentally, the Russians saw the error of their ways and the planes were ultimately shipped to Archangel.[67]

What with shortages, confusions and delays, American supplies to Soviet Russia inevitably remained insignificant. For the entire month of July, 1941, exports totaled only $6,521,912 in value, and for the period to October 1 they were estimated to reach only $29,000,000.[68] At this rate the United States would make but a slight contribution to Soviet defense or to ultimate victory on the eastern front.

Secretary Morgenthau, whose authority in these matters had passed largely into other hands, was outraged when he learned the gloomy facts. He told the President that in his opinion the Russians were being given the proverbial Washington "run around." No doubt the President had arrived at the same conclusion, for he had instructed "Pa" Watson to see the appropriate Secretaries and get the mix-up on Soviet deliveries straightened out at once.[69] Furthermore, he had already summoned Mr. Wayne Coy to Washington to tackle the task of clearing up the administrative confusion. During the Cabinet meeting of August 1 the President took no less than forty-five minutes to make his position clear. Secretary Morgenthau noted that his chief "went to town in a way I never heard him go to town before. He was terrific. He said he didn't want to hear what was on order; he said he wanted to hear what was on the water." Most of his remarks were obviously directed at Mr. Stimson, who was much annoyed. The Secretary of War, more interested in aiding Britain than in risking valuable supplies on the eastern front, had long been the most severe critic of the "uncorrelated organization" for handling supply problems. Rather pointedly he remarked to Mr. Roosevelt that to date he had heard nothing of the Soviet program beyond the request for planes, a request which had become completely snarled by Soviet insistence on shipment by way of Vladivostok. But the

[67] Stettinius: *Lend-Lease,* Chapter XI; *Stimson Diary (MS.),* July 21, 22, and 31, 1941; memo of conversation between Mr. Welles and Ambassador Oumansky, July 24, 1941; minutes of a conference of interested agencies at the State Department, July 28, 1941; memo of conversation between Secretary Morgenthau, General Golikov and Ambassador Oumansky, August 1, 1941 (*Morgenthau Diaries, MS.,* Vol. 428, pp. 52 ff.).

[68] Memo prepared for Mr. Harry Hopkins, August 6, 1941.

[69] Memo to General Watson, July 25, 1941 (now printed in *F.D.R.: His Personal Letters,* II, 1189).

President was in no mood for explanations. He insisted that the planes be sent at once: "Get 'em, even if it is necessary to take them from [U.S.] troops." Mr. Stimson had no alternative but to comply, but he entered the following aggrieved note in his diary: "This Russian munitions business thus far has shown the President at his worst. He has no system. He goes haphazard and he scatters responsibility among a lot of uncoördinated men and consequently things are never done."[70]

Belatedly the President now undertook to correct the administrative shortcomings as they affected the problem of supplies for Soviet Russia. He adopted Mr. Welles's suggestion and named a committee to integrate requirements, to consist of Mr. Harry Hopkins (with General Burns as substitute), Mr. Purvis, Chief of the British Purchasing Mission, and Ambassador Oumansky, with Colonel Faymonville as executive secretary. At the same time he wrote Mr. Wayne Coy a strong directive:

I raised the point in Cabinet Friday that nearly six weeks have elapsed since the Russian War began and that we have done practically nothing to get any of the materials they have asked for. Frankly the Russians feel that they have been given the run-around in the United States. Please get out the list and please with my full authority use a heavy hand and act as a burr under the saddle and get things moving. . . . In regard to the bombers, we should make and the British should make small token deliveries. With regard to the P-40's, it is ridiculous to bring any back from England by stealing through the submarine zone, but we should expedite two hundred of them from here. I have told the Russians that I am dividing things into two categories, first materials to be delivered on the Russian western front in time to take part in the battle between September 1 and October 1, and secondly, those materials which physically could not get there before October 1. I have chosen that date because after October 1 we all doubt if there will be very active operations, due to rain, snow, etc. Step on it.[71]

It was at this time, too, that the Administration went on record officially regarding aid to Soviet Russia. Oumansky had been trying for some time to secure far-reaching promises and engagements, but the State Department had held out for a less formal and purely unilateral declaration of support. The exchange of notes, which took place on August 2, stated simply:

. . . that the Government of the United States has decided to give all economic assistance practicable for the purpose of strengthening the Soviet Union in its struggle against armed aggression. This decision has been prompted by the conviction of the Government of the United States that the strengthening of the armed resistance of the Soviet Union to the predatory attack of an aggressor who is threatening the security and independence not only of the Soviet Union but also of all other nations is in the interest of the national defense of the United States.

[70] Stimson Diary (MS.), August 1, 4 and 5, 1941; Morgenthau Diaries (MS.), Vol. 428, pp. 52 ff. (August 5, 1941).

[71] Memo of the President to Mr. Wayne Coy, August 2, 1941 (Roosevelt Papers: Secretary's File, Box 73).

The Soviet Government was therefore assured that its requests would be given friendly consideration and its orders priority. Furthermore, unlimited licenses for export would be granted and all possible shipping made available.[72]

The news of this official commitment, when published a few days later, was received with but little public enthusiasm and indeed provoked a new outburst of isolationist criticism. Representative Tinkham of Massachusetts called for an investigation of the Administration's policy toward Soviet Russia and of the influence of Communists in Washington. "By what authority," he asked, "are we allies of Bolshevism?" Among the newspapers the *Chicago Tribune* objected violently to "an alliance with an Asiatic butcher and his godless crew." Britain, it conceded, had to accept the Soviet alliance in order to save itself, but the United States was under no such compulsion: "We can resist the filthy disease."[73] Even among the nonisolationist newspapers doubts and objections were raised. *The New York Times* noted editorially (August 6):

It is more than a little too bad that Mr. Oumansky's Government is just now discovering the community of interest of the freedom-loving nations. Where was Stalin in the summer of 1938, when the war began, if not playing ball with Hitler? And where was Stalin in the winter of 1940-41 [sic], if not across his own border, making war in Finland?

True, argued *The Times,* Soviet resistance to Hitler was in the interest of the United States, and it was not so much a question of helping Stalin as of stopping Hitler. But the question remained, could the dictator of the Kremlin be trusted?

Stalin is on our side today. Where will he be tomorrow? In the light of his record, no one can say that he will not switch sides again, make a sudden treacherous peace with Germany and become, in effect, Hitler's *Gauleiter* in the East. We should be in a fine state of affairs if we succeeded in landing a hundred bombers on Russian soil just in time for this reconciliation.

The best course, concluded the paper, would be to support America's trusted friends, Britain and China, the more so as to strengthen those powers would serve to divert German power from Soviet Russia.

Despite these anxieties, the country at large appears to have accepted the decision of the President. For what they may be worth, the public opinion polls indicated that by August, 1941, there was much sentiment for selling war materials to Soviet Russia. In fact a majority of those questioned thought that, if they ever reached such a pass, they would prefer to live un-

---

[72] Full text in *Documents on American Foreign Policy,* IV, 600-601. We have used also a memo of Mr. Loy Henderson to Mr. Welles, July 31, 1941.

[73] *Chicago Tribune,* August 16, 1941; see also the *New York Journal-American,* August 4, 1941.

der a Communist system rather than under a Nazi regime.[74] By and large it seems that the country was willing to follow the lead of Mr. Churchill and Mr. Roosevelt and to accept, as in the national interest, the obligation to provide the Soviet Union with material aid. It should be stressed, however, that no one, not even the President, could at that time have foreseen the later Lend-Lease contribution of something like ten billion dollars. In the summer of 1941 it was still generally assumed that Soviet resistance could not last long. It was not a question of supporting a Soviet victory, but rather of prolonging the Nazi-Soviet struggle in order to gain time for Britain and so for the United States. On that basis the American people were willing to do what they could, believing withal that their contribution could not be very substantial.

This first chapter of the story of American aid to Soviet Russia came to a close with the spectacular mission of Mr. Harry Hopkins to Moscow in the last days of July, 1941. It should perhaps be said at the outset that this episode was in a sense accidental and had no demonstrable bearing on the policy decision of August 2. Its significance lay entirely in the future, for the fuller and more accurate report of conditions which Hopkins brought back from Russia provided the basis for the much more extensive and dynamic aid program decided upon in the sequel.

Hopkins had by this time become the confidant and personal adviser of the President, who had appointed him Administrator of Lend-Lease. He had gone to London in mid-July to discuss the consolidated British program then in preparation and to make arrangements for a meeting of the President with Mr. Churchill, long projected and now scheduled to take place during the first half of August. Having completed his conferences on British requirements, Hopkins on July 24 attended a meeting of British and American military authorities under the chairmanship of Mr. Churchill. On this occasion, to be treated at greater length later, there was much discussion of the wisdom of sending further reinforcements and supplies to the Middle East preparatory to launching a limited offensive in that region while Hitler's armies were involved in Russia. The American officers took the stand that, if additional matériel were immediately available, it might be used more effectively in Russia than in the Middle East: "If the Russians could keep the Germans in play nearly to the end of September, then the invasion danger [to England] would recede and further armament could be sent to the Middle East."[75]

Obviously it was important, in connection with these strategic considerations, to know what the prospects of continued Soviet resistance were. According to one inspired account, Mr. Churchill therefore turned to Hopkins

[74] Jerome S. Bruner: *Mandate from the People*, 107.
[75] Churchill: *The Grand Alliance*, 424-25; Kittredge MS. study of *United States-British Naval Coöperation*.

with the remark: "Harry, why don't you go and have a look for all of us?"[76] Hopkins, though in very poor health, evidently received the suggestion with enthusiasm. On July 25 he wired the President:

I have a feeling that everything possible should be done to make certain the Russians maintain a permanent front even though they be defeated in this immediate battle. If Stalin could in any way be influenced at this critical time, I think it would be worth doing by a direct communication from you through a personal envoy. I think the stakes are so great that it should be done. Stalin would then know in an unmistakable way that we mean business on a long-term supply job.[77]

Mr. Roosevelt, quite apart from his faith in Hopkins's ability to get things done, was fond of such dramatic moves. He concurred at once and cabled Hopkins a message for Stalin. In this message, after referring to the assurances already given Oumansky, he went on to say:

The visit now being made by Mr. Hopkins to Moscow will, I feel, be invaluable by clarifying for us here in the United States your most urgent requirements so that we can reach the most practicable decisions to simplify the mechanics of delivery and speed them up. We shall be able to complete during the next winter a great amount of matériel which your Government wishes to obtain in this country. I therefore think that the immediate concern of both Governments should be to concentrate on the matériel which can reach Russia before October 1.

I ask you to treat Mr. Hopkins with the identical confidence you would feel if you were talking directly to me. He will communicate directly to me the views that you express to him and will tell me what you consider are the most pressing individual problems on which we could be of aid.

To this cordial introduction Mr. Churchill added an oral message from the British Government: "Tell him," the Prime Minister asked Hopkins, "that Britain has but one ambition today, but one desire—to crush Hitler. Tell him that he can depend upon us."[78]

Hopkins made the strenuous flight to Archangel and Moscow in one of the American planes assigned to the British. He arrived in the Soviet capital on the morning of July 30 and was given an impressive reception at the airfield. Obviously Stalin had sensed at once the importance of the visit, for the Moscow press for days devoted a large part of its front-page space to the American emissary, of whom it had previously known little or nothing.[79]

[76] Forrest Davis and Ernest K. Lindley: *How War Came,* 253.

[77] Published in *Pearl Harbor Attack,* XX, 4384 ff., but see also Sherwood: *Roosevelt and Hopkins,* 317 ff.

[78] Tel. from the President to Hopkins, July 26, 1941, "highly approving" the visit (*F.D.R.: His Personal Letters,* II, 1189); tel. from Welles to Hopkins, July 27, 1941, communicating the President's message to Stalin. This is given in paraphrase in Sherwood: *Roosevelt and Hopkins,* 321-22. Ambassador Steinhardt was informed by tel. of July 27 of Hopkins's forthcoming visit.

[79] Tels. from Steinhardt, July 30, August 1 and 2, 1941. Hopkins himself published a vivid account of the externals of his mission under the title "The Inside Story of My Meeting" (*American Magazine,* December, 1941).

Stalin himself, usually assisted by Molotov, conferred with Hopkins for hours on end during the latter's three days in the Soviet capital. Hopkins found the Soviet dictator hard, direct and well informed, and reported him a man consumed by hatred of Hitler, whom he was determined to resist to the last. In view of the fact that Hopkins's reports have already been published at length, a summary of the main features will suffice.[80]

At the first meeting on July 30 Hopkins conveyed to Stalin the messages from Mr. Roosevelt and Mr. Churchill, pointing out that the President, since he believed "the most important thing to be done in the world today was to defeat Hitler and Hitlerism," was determined to give the Soviet Union all possible aid and that as quickly as might be. Stalin thereupon launched upon a tirade against Hitler and the Nazi leaders, who, he declared, lacked even the minimum moral standard without which nations could not coexist. He then turned to the problem of Soviet requirements, both immediate and long range, elaborating and justifying the schedules already submitted to Washington.

The most important discussions, however, took place on the following day, when Hopkins explained that what had been bothering both London and Washington was the lack of reliable information on the military situation. Thus far the Soviet authorities had permitted neither the Ambassadors nor the Military Attachés nor even the newspaper correspondents to go to the front, nor had they vouchsafed them any detailed information on the operations. Hopkins made the most of this point and stated that President Roosevelt was eager to learn Stalin's estimate of the situation. The latter showed no embarrassment or hesitancy, but embarked at once upon a detailed and apparently frank exposé of the campaign. He thought his forces probably had a slight superiority in divisions and that ultimately the Red Army could mobilize 350 divisions as against Hitler's 300. He admitted that the Soviets had been taken by surprise, but explained how they had been able to obstruct the German advance and described the difficulties encountered by the Nazi forces as a result of back-of-the-line insurrections and the inadequacies of transportation. Parenthetically it may be remarked that many of Stalin's observations were later confirmed by the testimony of captured German generals: Hitler had underestimated the strength of the Red Army and particularly of the Soviet tank and air forces. Stalin had the impression, so he told Hopkins, that the Germans were already tiring and that they might soon have to pass to the defensive. They had found that "moving mechanized forces through Russia was very different than moving them over the boulevards of Belgium and France." The crucial need of the Soviets was

---

[80] See Sherwood: *Roosevelt and Hopkins*, 327 ff. These reports were addressed to the President personally and copies were not sent to the State Department until September, 1941. The concluding section of the overall report, which was particularly delicate in nature, appears never to have reached the Department.

to obtain tanks and planes during the winter, for even though they could themselves produce 1000 tanks and 1800 planes a month, German production was still higher. Furthermore, the Soviets were in danger of losing much of their plant capacity through capture, though many factories were already being moved eastward. Without in any way underrating the power of the Nazi armies, Stalin was convinced that the Germans would be obliged to go on the defensive by October 1 and that "during the winter months the line would be in front of Moscow, Kiev and Leningrad—probably not more than 100 kilometers from where it is now."

The discussion then reverted to the question of Soviet requirements, especially in antiaircraft guns, machine guns, rifles, and aluminum. Hopkins pointed out that the United States could supply at once only such items as were already in stock and that therefore plans should be made for a long war. The United States and Britain would have to know Soviet needs in detail and it might be well to arrange a conference to study the strategic requirements of all forces opposing aggression, Stalin agreed and promised to make the necessary data available. In short, he showed himself frank and coöperative. For the first time he gave a foreigner a detailed picture of the military situation and explained why the Soviets confidently expected to hold out. In conclusion, however, he asked that a very blunt message be transmitted to the President, a message that struck so close to the heart of the problem that it had to be kept rigorously secret. The salient passages, according to Hopkins's report, were these:

Stalin said Hitler's greatest weakness was found in the vast numbers of oppressed people who hated Hitler and the immoral ways of his Government. He believed these people and countless other millions in nations still unconquered could receive the kind of encouragement and moral strength they needed to resist Hitler from only one source, and that was the United States. He stated that the world influence of the President and the Government of the United States was enormous.

Contrarywise, he believed that the morale of the German Army and the German people, which he thinks is already pretty low, would be demoralized by an announcement that the United States is going to join in the war against Hitler.

Stalin said that he believed it was inevitable that we should finally come to grips with Hitler on some battlefield. The might of Germany was so great that, even though Russia might defend herself, it would be very difficult for Britain and Russia combined to crush the German military machine. He said that the one thing that could defeat Hitler, and perhaps without ever firing a shot, would be the announcement that the United States was going to war with Germany.

Stalin said that he believed, however, that the war would be bitter and perhaps long; that if we did get into the war he believed the American people would insist on their armies coming to grips with German soldiers; and he wanted me to tell the President that he would welcome the American troops on any part of the Russian front under the complete command of the American Army.

Hopkins discreetly avoided discussion of these startling suggestions and reminded his host that his concern was exclusively with the supply problem. To this Stalin replied that "while he was confident that the Russian Army could withstand the German Army, the problem of supply by next spring would be a serious one and that he needed our help."[81]

Hopkins's reports of his conversations in the Kremlin are so vivid and comprehensive as to require no further elaboration or explanation. When the American emissary returned to Scapa Flow, where he joined Mr. Churchill for the sea voyage to the Atlantic Conference, he was able for the first time to give the Prime Minister and subsequently the President a detailed account of Soviet conditions and prospects. Mr. Churchill cabled Washington that "Harry returned dead-beat from Russia," but his mission was certainly worth while and his report most encouraging. The Germans, despite their initial successes, had failed to wipe out the Red armies and were already beginning to bog down. Weeks had passed since the attack was launched, yet Soviet Russia was still far from collapse. It was noteworthy that Stalin had talked almost entirely in terms of long-range needs and of plans for a spring campaign. Nothing could have been more heartening than Hopkins's cable from Moscow: "I feel ever so confident about this front. The morale of the population is exceptionally good. There is unbounded determination to win." Even Ambassador Steinhardt, formerly disposed to be pessimistic, confessed to having changed his mind. He now inclined to the view that the Red Army could hold the bulk of the Nazi forces until winter set in, and that it would eventually be able, if necessary, to withdraw in force to the east and continue hostilities.[82] These estimates gave the outlook an entirely new hue. From having provided merely a "temporary breather," the Nazi attack on Soviet Russia now promised to open wider vistas to Anglo-American strategy.

[81] The above third part of Hopkins's report was first published by Sherwood: *Roosevelt and Hopkins*, 342-43.

[82] Tels. from Steinhardt, August 1 and 5, 1941.

CHAPTER XVIII

The Race Against Time

1. AMERICAN PREPAREDNESS: THE CONSCRIPTION ISSUE

The relative apathy with which the American people accepted the President's decision to aid Soviet Russia was in part a reflection of the marked letdown of feeling toward the European conflict after Hitler's resounding victories in the Balkans and North Africa. Though commentators repeatedly pointed out that the Lend-Lease Act had sounded the death knell of real neutrality and that, to all intents and purposes, the United States had become an active participant in the struggle against Nazism, the country at large still refused to draw the logical conclusions. The opinion was widespread that Britain could never defeat Hitler and that the anticipated liquidation of Soviet power by the Nazis would reduce still further Britain's chances of surviving the enemy's assault. There was general agreement that advantage should be taken of the respite provided by the Nazi-Soviet war to rush supplies to Britain, but there was little sentiment indeed for any extension of the American commitment. Public opinion polls showed an overwhelming majority strongly opposed to involvement of the country in a shooting war and even much suspicion of proposals for protecting in transit to Europe the materials of war which Congress had agreed to supply beleaguered Britain. The establishment of an Office of Civilian Defense (May 20, 1941), under the dynamic leadership of Mayor La Guardia of New York City, and the proclamation of the national emergency by the President were undoubtedly moves designed to arouse the country to keener realization of its danger, but the passivity of the public continued throughout much of the summer, indeed so long as the victory of the Nazis over the Soviets appeared inevitable.[1]

[1] Cf. the President's press conference remarks on August 19, 1941 (*The New York Times*, August 20, 1941), and the comments of Frank L. Kluckhohn (*The New York Times*, August 31, 1941).

Contributing to the hopelessness, not to say the defeatism, of the American people was doubtless the unimpressive record of war production. Some progress, of course, was being made. During the year ending in June, 1941, total industrial production had increased about 30 percent. In certain crucial items the advance was, indeed, quite noteworthy. Aircraft production had risen by 158 percent and shipbuilding by 120 percent. But what were even these achievements in the light of the vast requirements of American defense, of aid to Britain and, more recently, of supply to Soviet Russia? Actually the national effort was still but a halfhearted one, for the expansion of production was as yet based upon the use of idle facilities and unemployed labor. There had been no serious interference with the manufacture of consumer goods, which had actually grown in volume in the course of the year.[2] Furthermore, the administration of the war production program remained chaotic. While alphabetical war agencies were being created in bewildering profusion, coördination and singleness of direction were still lacking. War industry was plagued by strikes and shortages. The programming of national and foreign requirements was in its infancy. The system of priorities was altogether inadequate. Under the circumstances it was hard to believe that the country could actually become the Arsenal of Democracy in time to determine the outcome of the struggle.[3]

Then, as before, the President bore a large share of the responsibility. He still refused to appoint a "czar" of war production, on the plea that he could not find the required "superman" and that, in fact, he knew of no one more competent than Mr. Knudsen.[4] Even when, at this time, he finally concluded that something must be done to coördinate the foreign economic activities of the Government in the interests of defense, he decided against the appointment of a single administrator and established, under Vice President Wallace, an Economic Defense Board (July 30, 1941), of which the Secretaries of State, Treasury, War, Navy, Agriculture, and Commerce, as well as the Attorney General, were members.[5] True, Mr. Roosevelt was coming to admit that if sufficient tanks and other items of war equipment were to be provided, it would be necessary to utilize a substantial number of the durable goods factories still producing consumer goods.[6] Furthermore, he had at last convinced himself that if the confused problems of war pro-

[2] Calvin B. Hoover: "The Requirements of a War Economy" (*The Annals,* November, 1941). See also the figures for 1941 in *Industrial Mobilization for War* (Washington, 1947), I, 169-70.

[3] Eliot Janeway: *The Struggle for Survival* (New Haven, 1951), 232 ff.

[4] Letters of the President to Secretary Ickes, June 23, 1941, and to Ambassador Daniels, July 3, 1941 (*Roosevelt Papers:* Secretary's File, Boxes 73 and 79).

[5] Letter of the President to Vice President Wallace, July 9, 1941 (*Roosevelt Papers:* Secretary's File, Box 74). The executive order is given in full in *Documents on American Foreign Relations,* IV, 179-82.

[6] Letter of the President to Secretary Stimson, July 9, 1941 (*Roosevelt Papers:* Secretary's File, Box 74).

duction were to be solved, it would be necessary to have a clear statement of possible strategic commitments and overall requirements. In a crucial letter to the Secretaries of War and Navy (July 9, 1941), he called upon them to explore at once "the over-all production requirements required to defeat our potential enemies." "I realize," he added, "that this report involves the making of appropriate assumptions as to our probable friends and enemies and to the conceivable theaters of operation which will be required." It was this letter which at long last provided the impetus for the elaboration of strategic estimates and the drafting of consolidated statements of American and British requirements, in short for the formulation of what was later to be called the Victory Program.[7]

Of at least equal importance and of even greater urgency was the question of the future of the American Army. In June, 1941, the Selective Service Act, permitting the Armed Services to conscript up to 900,000 men for the period of a year, was less than nine months old. Heroic efforts had been made since its passage to build up a modern force, but the task was enormous, the time short, and the essential equipment sadly lacking. It has been well said that throughout this period "the American military establishment was to a large extent closed for alterations."[8] Men of the Regular Army and National Guard had to be used to train recruits, which in turn meant that the best units had to be officered and in part manned by reserves or newly trained levies. Lack of equipment made training difficult and unreal, while the absence of actual war induced a sense of futility. By the summer of 1941 many of the so-called "selectees" and even of the National Guardsmen were looking forward eagerly to a return to their homes and their jobs.[9]

It was self-evident that if, in the course of the autumn of 1941, the men conscripted under the Selective Service Act were to be discharged, the new Army would disintegrate and an entirely new start would have to be made. In a period of mounting crisis the country would have had no army in the modern sense; it would hardly have had sufficient trained forces to man the overseas bases. Secretary Stimson and General Marshall were naturally much disturbed by this prospect and urged the President to make a decision on retention of the National Guard in service and the prolongation of the term of the conscripted forces. On June 21 Mr. Roosevelt gave the War Department permission to propose to Congress that the period of service be extended and that the provision of the current law forbidding the use of con-

---

[7] The War Department background of the Victory Program is discussed in detail in Mark S. Watson: *Chief of Staff: Prewar Plans and Preparations* (Washington, 1950), Chapter XI. See also *Industrial Mobilization for War*, I, 132-40, and W. K. Hancock and M. M. Gowing: *British War Economy* (London, 1949), 384 ff.

[8] Walter Millis: *This Is Pearl* (New York, 1947), 56.

[9] The best survey of the state of the new Army is still that of General George C. Marshall, as given in his biennial report for 1941 (*The War Reports*, Philadelphia, 1947, 20 ff.), but see also the extended analysis of the problem in Watson: *Chief of Staff: Prewar Plans and Preparations*, Chapter VII.

scripted troops beyond the confines of the Western Hemisphere be removed. In his noteworthy biennial report, published on July 3, 1941, General Marshall recommended such action, pointing out that the Selective Service Act had provided for extension of the service period "whenever Congress has declared that the national interest is imperilled." That, in July, 1941, a "grave national emergency" existed could not, according to the Chief of Staff, be denied.[10]

The mere suggestion of such action evoked opposition in Congress. In the House even Administration leaders like Speaker Rayburn and Floor Leader McCormack objected, while in the Senate isolationist members protested particularly against lifting the restriction on the use of conscripted men beyond the limits of the hemisphere. Unhappily for the Administration, the newspapers at this very time were featuring ominous statements by two prominent British field commanders, Generals Wavell and Auchinleck. Asked whether he thought the tools called for by Mr. Churchill would suffice to ensure victory, Wavell had replied: "No, undoubtedly we shall need man-power if the war continues long enough, and I have no doubt it will. We shall have to have planes, tanks, munitions, transports and finally, men. . . . The sooner the better. I suppose you will be able to equip any number of men for anywhere in the world." Auchinleck was equally outspoken: "We certainly are going to need American manpower, just as we did in the last war."[11] This was what Mr. Churchill had been privately making clear to the President for some time, but it was another matter to state it bluntly and openly to the American people, as the British commanders in Egypt did. The public was shocked by these confirmations of its worst fears. The isolationists took fullest advantage of the situation, though many who were not isolationist also shrank back as they saw their hopes of victory with American participation "short of war" fade into obscurity. After the Wavell and Auchinleck utterances it was almost impossible to delude oneself any longer that American boys could be drafted, yet kept at home.

The two main arguments against the Marshall proposals were that an extension of the term of service would be tantamount to a breach of contract with the conscripted men and that removal of the restriction on the use of these men abroad would be the entering wedge for a new American Expeditionary Force. It can be readily understood that Congressmen were loath to assume the odium for so unpopular a measure. Early predictions were that the proposals would call forth a bitter controversy cutting across party lines.[12]

[10] *Stimson Diary (MS.)*, June 21, 1941; *The War Reports*, 29 ff.; Watson: *Chief of Staff: Prewar Plans and Preparations*, 218-20.

[11] Harold Denny in *The New York Times*, July 5 and 7, 1941.

[12] *The New York Times*, July 4 and 8, 1941; Henry L. Stimson and McGeorge Bundy: *On Active Service in Peace and War* (New York, 1947), 376 ff.; Watson: *Chief of Staff: Prewar Plans and Preparations*, 223.

General Marshall assumed the chief burden of dealing with Congress. On July 9 he conferred in closed session with the Senate Military Affairs Committee, stressing the fact that the virtual disbandment of two thirds of the trained enlisted strength and three quarters of the officer personnel of the Army might well entail a national tragedy. He assured the Committee that there was no plan for a new A.E.F., which, in fact, could be authorized only by the President and the Congress. Above all, he insisted that the national emergency foreseen by the existing legislation was a reality and that, consequently, there could be no question of a breach of contract with the conscripted men. Two days later he expounded his views to House leaders. On the whole the impression he made was excellent, though Senator Reynolds, Chairman of the Senate Committee, remained unconvinced and Messrs. Rayburn and McCormack felt themselves bound by their previous statements. House leaders thought the period of service for reserve officers and the National Guard might be extended, but considered it impossible to change the terms of service of the conscripted men. They thought that conceivably the President's influence might help and therefore urged that he confer at once with Congressional leaders.[13]

On July 14 a political strategy meeting was held at the White House, with Senators Barkley, George, Reynolds, Hill and Austin, and Representatives Rayburn, McCormack, May and Wadsworth present. Once again General Marshall repudiated all ideas of an A.E.F., though he pleaded the need for task forces on the ground that it would be suicidal not to take protective action in the Azores and Cape Verdes if the Nazis occupied Portugal. He spoke at some length of secret Nazi formations in several Latin American countries and made a distinct impression on his audience by his exposition of the dangers confronting the country. But the political obstacles to his program still stood and there was much discussion of the possibility of meeting the admittedly real need by encouraging voluntary enlistment. In the end the President decided to drop the proposal to lift the restriction on the use of conscripted men overseas, the Congressional leaders on their part promising to work out an acceptable solution to the problem of extending the term of service.[14]

Presently appropriate resolutions were introduced in both Houses and hearings began. Again and again General Marshall appeared before the Military Committees, reviewed the dangers facing the country and explained in detail the problems with which the War Department was grappling.[15]

[13] *Stimson Diary* (*MS.*), July 9, 10, 11, 1941; *The New York Times,* July 13 and 16, 1941.

[14] *Stimson Diary* (*MS.*), July 21, 1941; Watson: *Chief of Staff: Prewar Plans and Preparations,* 221; *The New York Times,* July 15 and 16, 1941 (reporting the President's press conference statement).

[15] Marshall's testimony is analyzed in some detail in Watson: *Chief of Staff: Prewar Plans and Preparations,* 222-31.

Then, on July 21, the President himself took a public stand. In a radio broadcast he recalled the schedule of Nazi conquest, pointed out that the wave of aggression was coming ever closer, and insisted that the country was in the midst of a grave national emergency. He reminded his audience of the urgent need for national defense and of the country's obligations to Latin America: "We Americans cannot afford to speculate with the security of America," he warned, borrowing a phrase of General Marshall's.[16]

The President's appeal was given a friendly reception and led *The New York Times* (July 22, 1941) to remark: "An immediate endorsement of the President's recommendation by overwhelming majorities in both branches of Congress would be worth ten battleships. It would warn Japan, shake Germany, cheer Britain, and give fresh impetus to democracy in every corner of the world." But in reality there was no chance whatever of "overwhelming majorities." The Senate Military Affairs Committee finally accepted a declaration that "the national security is imperilled," and recommended that the term of service be extended and the limit on the number of "selectees" lifted. Even so, Senator Reynolds dissented, arguing that a resolution in these terms would be tantamount to authorizing the President to enter the war "as an active, participating, shooting ally of Russia and Great Britain."[17]

In the country at large opinion continued divided. A Gallup poll of July 29 revealed 51 percent in favor of extension of the term of service, but a digest of newspaper opinion indicated greater support for the resolution once the question of using conscripted men abroad had been eliminated.[18] On the other hand, men in the training camps were reported disgruntled about the projected "dirty double cross," and peace groups, notably the Mothers of America organization, voiced indignant protests. Extreme isolationist newspapers denounced the Administration's alleged equivocation and deceit, though even isolationist members of Congress recognized the need for extension of the service term and were ready to accept some compromise.

The subsequent debate, which *The New York Times* described as the most important since Lend-Lease, began early in August, 1941. In the upper House, Senator Taft rallied wide support for a proposal to extend the term of service by four to six months, which led the Administration leaders to give up their demand for extension for the duration of the emergency and to offer to compromise on a period of eighteen months. On August 7 the Senate, after beating down various amendments, approved this term and

---

[16] Full text in *Public Papers and Addresses of Franklin D. Roosevelt*, 1941 (New York, 1950), 272-76.

[17] *The New York Times*, July 18, 22, 24, 27, 28, 1941. The Military Affairs Committee of the House agreed on a similar recommendation on July 30, 1941.

[18] James S. Twohey: "An Analysis of Newspaper Opinion" (*Public Opinion Quarterly*, V, 1941, 448-55).

provided for a raise in pay after one year's service, as well as for the release, so far as possible, of men over the age of twenty-eight. But in the lower House the opposition was firm and general. When the bill reached the floor on August 9, Democratic leaders had to admit the possibility of defeat. Supporters of the measure made much of the threat of Nazi-Vichy collaboration and the consequent danger to Dakar, but opponents refused to admit that the international situation was more serious than at the time of the enactment of Selective Service. Representative Fish, for example, held the bill "part and parcel of a gigantic conspiracy" to involve the country in European, African and Asiatic wars without the consent of Congress. As the debate continued there was no sign of any slackening of the opposition and when the vote was at last taken, on August 12, 1941, the bill was passed by a majority of exactly one: in favor were 203 members (182 Democrats, 21 Republicans); opposed, 202 members (65 Democrats, 133 Republicans.)[19]

The vote on the extension of the term of Selective Service made a lasting impression on the memory of the country. But for a single vote the nation might have been left with an Army in dissolution, only a few months before the Pearl Harbor attack. This contingency is still terrible to contemplate, for even though there can be little doubt that if the bill had failed other legislation would have been enacted, the loss of valuable time might have been disastrous. On the other hand, it would be a mistake to interpret the vote in the House as reflecting the sentiment of the country with respect to national defense and the international situation in general. The evidence indicates that the opponents of the measure were themselves surprised by the closeness of the tally. Many, including several who had voted for Lend-Lease, appear to have believed that the bill would be passed with a reasonable margin and that therefore they could afford to shirk the responsibility for supporting an unpopular measure. A good many Congressmen were evidently willing to take a long chance to escape the odium of voting to keep their constituents and their constituents' offspring in camp. As one of them wrote to his colleagues before the roll call: "If you don't watch your step, your political hide, which is very near and dear to you, will be tanning on the barn door." On this basis a substantial number of Congressmen came close to outsmarting themselves and only the unremitting efforts of the American Legion appear to have stiffened enough of them to produce even the precarious majority of August 12. The shock to Congress itself was severe, while the impression made on the country was profound and lasting.[20]

[19] *Stimson Diary (MS.)*, August 4, 6, 7, 8, 12, 13, 1941; *The New York Times*, August 9 and 13, 1941.

[20] On the importance of the Legion's efforts see the speech of Secretary Knox to the Legion Convention at Milwaukee, September 15, 1941. For the rest see *The Autobiography of Sol Bloom* (New York, 1948), 243; Carlisle Bargeron: *Confusion on the Potomac* (New York, 1941), 208 ff., 219; *The New York Times*, August 13, 1941; the *Chicago Daily News*, August 14, 1941.

2. ICELAND AND THE ATLANTIC SEA LANES

The mission of an American Marine Brigade of about four thousand men to Iceland, early in July, was the Administration's one overt act of participation in the European conflict during the listless early summer of 1941. Although the decision to make this move had been reached before the Nazi attack on Soviet Russia, that important turn in the war made it less likely that Hitler would react militarily to the American initiative.[21]

According to the arrangements made between Washington and London, the British Minister to Iceland was to inform the Reykjavik Government that the British could no longer spare the troops necessary for the protection of the island, but that the United States, if invited, would be willing to assume the burden of defense. However, when the Minister carried out his assignment on June 24, he found the Icelandic Prime Minister, Mr. Jonasson, ill-disposed toward the suggestion. While admitting that several members of his Government favored American protection and indicating that he himself neither could nor would oppose it actively, he was quite unwilling to "invite" it. Since, for reasons discussed earlier, the President felt that an explicit invitation was indispensable, the British Minister was instructed to return to the charge and put the case as strongly as possible. But no argument would persuade Mr. Jonasson to accept the word "invite." He felt that he could not issue an invitation without consulting Parliament, yet was obviously worried by the prospect of British forces leaving and abandoning Iceland to its fate. In order to secure American protection without asking for it, he therefore suggested that he send President Roosevelt a message in which the issue of "invitation" was adroitly evaded. The crucial passage of this message was to read:

In a conversation of June 24 the British Minister explained that British forces in Iceland are required elsewhere. At the same time he stressed the immense importance of adequate defense of Iceland. He also called my attention to the declaration of the President of the United States to the effect that he must take all necessary measures to ensure the safety of the Western Hemisphere—one of the President's measures is to assist in the defense of Iceland—and that the President is therefore prepared to send here immediately United States troops to replace the British force here. But that he does not consider that he can take this course except at the invitation of the Iceland Government.

After careful consideration of all the circumstances, the Iceland Government, in view of the present state of affairs, admit that this measure is in accordance with the interest of Iceland, and therefore are ready to entrust the protection of Iceland to United States on the following conditions . . .

These conditions included a promise to withdraw American forces at once on conclusion of peace; to recognize the absolute independence and

---

[21] On the earlier phases of the Iceland project see above, Chapter XVI, Section 4.

sovereignty of Iceland; not to interfere in Icelandic internal affairs; and to exchange diplomatic representatives.[22]

The text of Mr. Jonasson's proposed message was satisfactory to Mr. Roosevelt excepting for one important item. The President knew it would be hard to find sufficient Marine or Army forces to provide adequate protection for Iceland, particularly in view of the fact that under the Selective Service Act conscripted men could not be deployed beyond the limits of the Western Hemisphere and it had not yet been determined that Iceland fell within those limits. He therefore notified the British of his desire that no British troops be withdrawn immediately on arrival of the American forces, the more so as he considered the British occupation forces inadequate.[23] That being so, the President objected to Mr. Jonasson's phrase "to send here immediately troops to replace the British force here." Instead he suggested the wording "to supplement and perhaps eventually replace." The Icelandic Prime Minister, in turn, wished to avoid anything like an Anglo-American condominium and stood by his wording until the President agreed to delete the word "perhaps." On July 1 the text of the message was concurred in by both sides and it was agreed that announcement of the change should be made immediately upon the arrival of the American forces.[24]

While the Marine Brigade was en route to its destination a minor conflict developed in Washington over the wording of the President's forthcoming message to Congress. Secretary Stimson proposed that Mr. Roosevelt seize the opportunity to tell the country the whole truth: that American troops were going to Iceland to anticipate possible seizure of the island by Germany and protect the trade routes to Britain; further, that American naval escort of shipping all the way to England would be initiated at once. He suggested further that the President conclude his message by admitting that his hopes of safeguarding the United States without resort to armed force were growing dim:

It has now become abundantly clear that, unless we add our every effort to the efforts of those free nations which are still fighting for freedom in this world, we shall ourselves ultimately be brought to a situation where we shall be fighting alone at an enormously greater danger than we should encounter today if we joined our full efforts to their aid.[25]

This viewpoint, which had been publicly proclaimed by Secretary Knox in his address to the Conference of Governors on June 30, was perfectly

[22] Memos of conversation between Mr. Welles and Lord Halifax and the British tels. from Reykjavik submitted on those occasions, June 25, 26, 28, 1941; memo of conversation between the President and Mr. Welles, June 28, 1941; tel. from Winant, June 28, 1941; *Stimson Diary (MS.)*, June 24, 1941.

[23] Memo of conversation between Mr. Welles and Lord Halifax, June 26, 1941, and letter from Lord Halifax to Mr. Welles, June 28, 1941, giving assurances on this point.

[24] Memos of conversation between Mr. Welles and Lord Halifax, June 28 and July 1, 1941; *Stimson Diary (MS.)*, July 1, 1941.

[25] *Stimson Diary (MS.)*, July 3-7, 1941.

familiar to the President, who probably sympathized with it. But Mr. Roosevelt was definitely unwilling to lay the situation before the country so frankly. The constant agitation against naval escort and the necessity of asking Congress to extend the term of Selective Service suggested caution. Consequently the President's message of July 7 amounted to little more than a restatement of American policy, supplemented by a vague indication of a future program of convoy protection:

The United States cannot permit the occupation by Germany of strategic outposts in the Atlantic to be used as air or naval bases for eventual attack against the Western Hemisphere. We have no desire to see any change in the present sovereignty of those regions. Assurance that such outposts in our defense-frontier remain in friendly hands is the very foundation of our national security and of the national security of every one of the independent nations of the New World.

For the same reason substantial forces of the United States have now been sent to the bases acquired last year from Great Britain in Trinidad and in British Guiana in the south in order to forestall any pincers movement undertaken by Germany against the Western Hemisphere. It is essential that Germany should not be able successfully to employ such tactics through sudden seizure of strategic points in the South Atlantic and in the North Atlantic.

The occupation of Iceland by Germany would constitute a serious threat in three dimensions:

The threat against Greenland and the northern portion of the North American Continent, including the islands which lie off it.

The threat against all shipping in the North Atlantic.

The threat against the steady flow of munitions to Britain—which is a matter of broad policy clearly approved by the Congress.

It is therefore imperative that the approaches between the Americas and those strategic outposts, the safety of which this country regards as essential to its national security, and which it must therefore defend, shall remain open and free from all hostile activity or threat thereof.

As Commander in Chief I have consequently issued orders to the Navy that all necessary steps be taken to insure the safety of communications in the approaches between Iceland and the United States, as well as on the seas between the United States and all other strategic outposts.[26]

Considering all the implications of the American advance to Iceland, the President's message was well received by Congress and the country. A Gallup poll of July 17 reported approval of the President's move by 61 percent of those questioned, while only 20 percent were definitely opposed. Another survey also revealed widespread support for a policy of "dynamic defense."[27] To be sure, the question was raised in some quarters whether Iceland could be considered part of the Western Hemisphere, but since

[26] *Public Papers and Addresses,* 1941, 255-63. The text of this message as well as of the exchange of letters between President Roosevelt and Prime Minister Jonasson is given also in *Documents on American Foreign Relations,* IV, 254-58.

[27] Survey prepared for Secretary Morgenthau, July 11, 1941 (*Morgenthau Diaries, MS.,* Vol. 420, pp. 154 ff.).

there was no official definition of hemisphere limits, the issue was of little practical importance. At a press conference the President refused to commit himself, though he hinted that for purposes of policy the decisive question was whether a particular area was vital for defense of the Americas.[28]

Mr. Roosevelt was agreeably surprised by the public reaction to his latest move, for he had prepared himself for a "vitriolic outburst."[29] The opportunity seemed ideal for yet further action, such as the introduction of escort of convoys. Mr. Churchill had been pressing discreetly for help along this line. Replying to a message from the President announcing an increase in merchant shipping construction, he had remarked:

> This vast expansion opens up the prospects of the future and assures the means of continuing the war in this vital sphere to a victorious conclusion. I know you will feel with me the pain that such vast masses of tonnage have to be sunk before being replaced by colossal American efforts. Any increase in our escorts will produce immediate savings in losses. Forgive me mentioning this when I know all you are doing.[30]

Again, when the Prime Minister received a copy of the American Hemisphere Defense Plan, envisaging American naval escort of British as well as United States shipping as far as longitude 26° west, he replied enthusiastically: "Putting such a plan into immediate operation would give timely and needed aid. At present the strain upon our resources is far too great."[31] It goes without saying that the British leader hailed the American occupation of Iceland with elation: "The military occupation of Iceland by the forces of the United States," he told the House of Commons, "is an event of first-rate political and strategic importance," in fact, "one of the most important things that have happened since the war began." In further remarks he adumbrated his hopes of American naval aid:

> . . . . The position of the United States forces in Iceland will, of course, require their being sustained or reinforced by sea from time to time. These consignments of American supplies for American forces on duty overseas for the purposes of the United States will, of course, have to traverse very dangerous waters and, as we have a very large traffic constantly passing through these waters, I daresay it may be found in practice mutually advantageous for the two navies involved to assist each other, so far as is convenient, in that part of the business.[32]

---

[28] *The New York Times,* July 9, 1941. Admiral King's operations order of April 18, 1941, approved by the President, had defined the hemisphere as that area westward of longitude 26° west, which meant inclusion of at least the western part of Iceland (Kittredge MS. study on *United States-British Naval Coöperation*).

[29] *Knox Papers, MS.*

[30] Message of the President to the Prime Minister, June 25, 1941; reply of Mr. Churchill, July 1, 1941.

[31] Mr. Churchill to the President, July 7, 1941, reviewing in detail Britain's convoy difficulties. At a Liaison Conference in London on July 11, 1941, British officers told their American colleagues quite frankly that there was no hope of stemming the loss of vital imports without American aid (Kittredge MS. study on *United States-British Naval Coöperation*).

[32] Statement of July 9, 1941 (Churchill: *The Unrelenting Struggle,* 176-77).

It was certainly Mr. Roosevelt's desire and probably his plan to extend the scope of American assistance to Britain at this time. The evidence is scanty, but it shows that he was considering a proposal to Congress to eliminate from the Neutrality Act those provisions restricting the arming of American merchant ships and their use in war zones. This idea was shelved when Congressional leaders reported that, even though revision could undoubtedly be put through the legislature, "the debate would be prolonged and the isolationist group would filibuster on the issue."[33] Furthermore, it appears that, after a conference with Admirals Stark and King, the President decided in favor of escorting British as well as American shipping as far as Iceland. Hemisphere Defense Plan IV was issued on July 11 and called for "escort convoys of United States and Iceland flag shipping, including shipping of any nationality which may join such convoys, between United States ports and bases, and Iceland." On July 19 Admiral King issued operations orders to this effect. Yet at the last moment the President drew back. When, on July 25, the Chief of Naval Operations ordered that Defense Plan IV be put into effect on the following day, the provision for escorting ships of other than American or Icelandic nationality was suspended "until necessary arrangements had been made."[34]

Whether the President's decision derived from anxiety over developments in the Far East or from fear of jeopardizing the extension of Selective Service, it is impossible to say, but it is easy to understand that "poor old Knox was quite tired and discouraged."[35] No doubt this was true of all activist members of the Cabinet, and also of Mr. Churchill and his colleagues. Somehow it seemed impossible to induce Mr. Roosevelt to take what appeared to many the logical and essential step. Even so, the occupation of Iceland and the introduction of naval escort for American shipping marked an important advance toward American participation in the war, for henceforth the Atlantic Fleet was under orders not only to trail and report the movements of Axis ships, but to "protect United States and Iceland shipping against hostile attack by escorting, covering, and patrolling, as required by circumstances, and by destroying hostile forces which threaten such shipping."

The President embarked upon this program fully confident that Hitler,

[33] Memo by Mr. Welles, June 28, 1941, and letter of Mr. Welles to the President, July 9, 1941, transmitting the memo and reporting the reaction of Senators George and Connally; memo of the President to the two Senators, July 11, 1941, inquiring further whether they would advise trying "to put over now or hold over" (*Roosevelt Papers: Secretary's File*, Box 74).

[34] Statement of Mr. Hopkins to Mr. Morgenthau, July 10, 1941 (*Morgenthau Diaries, MS.*, Vol. 419, p. 367); Admiral Stark's testimony in *Pearl Harbor Attack*, V, 2294-95; Kittredge MS. study on *United States-British Naval Coöperation;* see also Charles A. Beard: *President Roosevelt and the Coming of the War* (New Haven, 1948), 437-38, and Samuel E. Morison: *The Battle of the Atlantic* (Boston, 1947), 78-79.

[35] *Stimson Diary (MS.)*, July 21, 1941.

while deeply involved in the east, would at all costs avoid further commitments in the west. German records since published bear out this estimate completely. They reveal Admiral Raeder much impressed by the American occupation of Iceland and inquiring of the Fuehrer whether this move should be taken to mean war. But, according to the record, "the Fuehrer explains in detail that he is most anxious to postpone the United States' entry into the war for another one or two months." Hitler was unwilling to divert his Air Force from Russia and felt that his expected victory in the east would prove the most effective deterrent to American intervention. Raeder submitted a memorandum arguing that ever since the Destroyer Deal the United States had abandoned all pretense of neutrality and had taken a long series of actions in support of Britain. He once again stressed the importance of the battle of the Atlantic and the danger that Britain or the United States might seize the Atlantic islands, Casablanca or Dakar: "The presence of United States or British forces in Dakar or Casablanca, especially naval surface forces, would almost suspend warfare in the North Atlantic and would render operation *Felix* [the capture of Gibraltar] largely ineffectual." He begged for permission to answer the occupation of Iceland by attacks without warning on American shipping in the blockade area. At the end of July, 1941, he complained that "the whole situation in the Atlantic has become more unfavorable for all our forces because of the occupation of Iceland and the increasing effect of United States support [of Britain]." But the Fuehrer remained unmoved by argument. He was determined to avoid trouble with the United States until the campaign in the east had been victoriously concluded. "After the eastern campaign," reads the record, "he reserves the right to take severe action against the United States as well." Meanwhile he deluded himself into thinking that the British would not continue to fight once they realized that they no longer had any chance of winning: "Britain is already beginning to have misgivings in view of the United States occupation of Iceland."[36]

3. French Africa and the Atlantic Islands

On July 10, 1941, President Roosevelt despatched a long letter to President Vargas of Brazil, explaining the reasons for the American occupation of Iceland and calling attention to the continuing danger of Nazi action against the Atlantic islands or West Africa. "The gist of the matter," wrote Mr. Roosevelt, "is frankly this":

First. If Germany should eliminate Russia in a few weeks, a very large amount of personnel and matériel would be released for use elsewhere.

Second. In such event it could be used directly against the British Isles, or, should

[36] *Fuehrer Conferences,* 1941 (2), 3 ff., 13 ff., 15 ff. (reporting conferences of July 9 and 25, 1941). See also Anthony Martienssen: *Hitler and His Admirals* (New York, 1949), 115 ff., and F. H. Hinsley: *Hitler's Strategy* (Cambridge, 1951), 172-73.

that seem to the Germans of doubtful outcome, the obvious alternative would be to try to close all access for shipping to Great Britain. The obvious places to cut off shipping would be the narrow portion of the South Atlantic and the northwest approaches to the British Isles. The success of such a move should be forestalled with plenty of preparation. Germany so far has succeeded through the use of surprise tactics and because of the shortness of time for preparation on the part of the countries she has attacked. Therefore, we feel that this summer, even before the Russian venture is settled, the Americas should take all preliminary steps.[37]

Fears of the sequel of a German victory in the east were altogether warranted, for Nazi documents show that Hitler, immediately after the attack on Soviet Russia, issued directives for the preparation of plans to drive the British from the Mediterranean and that, at the end of July, he stated categorically that as soon as the U.S.A. occupied Portuguese or Spanish islands, he would march into Spain and would send Panzer and infantry divisions to North Africa from there, in order to defend North Africa.[38] For the moment the Fuehrer was too deeply involved to consider anything more than retaliatory action in the Atlantic and Mediterranean, but of his ultimate objectives there can be little doubt. It was therefore patently important for the United States as for Britain to take whatever precautionary measures were possible. Since American military capabilities were still extremely limited, the President was obliged to rely on diplomacy to attain his ends.

The situation at Vichy and therefore the probable fate of French North and West Africa continued obscure but ominous. Although the details of the struggle over the Paris Protocols were unknown to Ambassador Leahy and his Government, there seemed good reason to consider Darlan a convinced collaborationist and to expect him to make significant concessions to Nazi demands for base rights at Bizerte and Dakar. That being so, there was some sentiment in Washington for initiating a deal with General Weygand and attempting through him to secure a strong position in North Africa.[39] Others favored greater recognition for General de Gaulle's Free French movement and tried to induce the President to receive M. Pleven, who had been sent to Washington as de Gaulle's representative. The Canadian Government, indeed, favored permitting the Free French to take over the islands of St. Pierre and Miquelon (off the Newfoundland coast), on the plea that the Vichy authorities might be using the local radio station to report ship movements to the Germans.[40]

[37] Letter of President Roosevelt to President Vargas, July 10, 1941. The quoted passage is only the conclusion of the letter, the body of which will be discussed at greater length in a later context.

[38] *Fuehrer Conferences,* 1941 (2), 13 ff. (July 25, 1941); see further Martienssen: *Hitler and His Admirals,* 115-16.

[39] Tel. from Murphy (Algiers), July 14, 1941; *Berle Diary (MS.),* July 16, 1941. Such ideas were voiced also by the British at Liaison Conferences of July 18 and 25, 1941 (Kittredge MS. study of *United States-British Naval Coöperation*).

[40] On the efforts to secure a hearing for M. Pleven we have used the *Morgenthau*

But the President and his advisers preferred to stick by the established Vichy policy, at least until there were further evidence of military collaboration between the French and the Germans. With regard to the Free French representative Mr. Roosevelt noted briefly: "I cannot see Pleven. The matter has been taken up before."[41] Similarly, the Free French claims to St. Pierre and Miquelon were put aside with reference to the fact that any change in the status of those French possessions would open up the larger and more important issue of French territories in the Caribbean. Whatever reasons the British might have for supporting de Gaulle, the President and State Department continued to hold that adoption of the Free French cause would seriously jeopardize American interests in the French possessions without producing corresponding gains. Admiral Leahy and other American officials in France, though admitting the difficulty of determining French popular sentiment, had the impression that while the desire and hope for a British victory were steadily growing, there was as yet little feeling or support for de Gaulle. Resistance movements were being organized in various parts of France, but those known to be Gaullist were still few and unimpressive.[42]

On one point, however, the observations of foreign observers were in general agreement: collaboration with Germany was intensely unpopular among Frenchmen, so much so that Darlan was hated as a traitor and even Pétain was losing public respect and confidence. There was reason to hope, therefore, that Vichy's program of collaboration might be checked by popular sentiment. The American policy was one of wait and see, though at the same time of bringing all possible diplomatic pressure to bear to prevent Darlan from making concessions beyond the requirements of the armistice.

In an earlier context it has been pointed out that the implementation of the Paris Protocols had, thanks to the influence of Weygand and Boisson, been made conditional on extensive concessions by the Germans. Whether Hitler would consent to negotiate on this basis or would use force to secure base rights in North and West Africa remained in doubt. The full details of the discussions of July are even now unknown, but on July 8 Marshal Pétain again summoned Weygand to Vichy. Apparently the Germans were insisting on the use of Bizerte, but on this occasion even Darlan was unwilling to yield. The decision of the Council was to stick by the program agreed on in June and the Germans were so informed on July 14. It was the

Diaries (MS.), Vol. 419, pp. 53, 193, 198 (July 8 and 9, 1941). The Canadian suggestions were made to the American Minister by the Acting Under Secretary for External Affairs (Moffat Diary, MS., June 3, July 8, 15, 31, 1941).

[41] Morgenthau Diaries (MS.), Vol. 419, p. 198 (July 9, 1941).

[42] Fleet Admiral William D. Leahy: I Was There (New York, 1950), 43, 54-55, 460-62; reports of returning American consuls, August, 1941 (Roosevelt Papers: Secretary's File, Box 90). For unofficial testimony in the opposite direction see William L. Langer: Our Vichy Gamble (New York, 1947), 165 ff.

French note of this date which precipitated the acute crisis in Franco-German relations at the end of July. To all intents and purposes the Paris Protocols were dead, but the Germans were so furious that for weeks Vichy lived in anticipation of an ultimatum. That no evil consequences ensued is undoubtedly to be explained by Hitler's desire not to cut the wire to Vichy or provoke the defection of North Africa while the German forces were still committed in the east. This we have on the testimony of Ribbentrop himself.[43]

The Germans attributed their difficulties to a variety of causes: to Darlan's loss of prestige since the conquest of Syria by the British and Free French; to the consequent increase of the influence of Weygand, who was regarded as the soul of the anti-German faction; to French fears that concessions to the Germans would be followed at once by British or American attacks on Africa; and finally, to sustained and heavy American pressure on Pétain. Admiral Leahy was reported to have warned the Marshal that military collaboration with the Germans would result in American recognition of General de Gaulle and support of Free French efforts to take over French possessions in the New World.[44]

Some measure of truth there certainly was in these Nazi calculations. Weygand kept Mr. Robert Murphy, the American Consul General at Algiers, informed of what was going on and thereby provided Washington grounds for recurrent protests to Vichy. Having learned of the July conferences, Mr. Roosevelt sent a memorandum to Acting Secretary Welles to this effect:

> In view of the suggestion in today's despatches that Darlan is again discussing with the Germans the use of Casablanca and Dakar, what would you think of having Leahy tell Pétain and having Murphy simultaneously tell Weygand that if any further German occupation occurs in Morocco or Dakar, the United States would, as a matter of course, be compelled to stop all conversations relating to supplies to North Africa. We would have to do the same in regard to any further American food for unoccupied France. All this could be couched in polite but decisive terms.[45]

This suggestion was translated into instructions to Admiral Leahy to seek an interview with Marshal Pétain and call his attention to the reports reaching Washington. The Ambassador was to explain:

> The President has publicly stated as recently as in his last message to Congress relating to the occupation of Iceland that this Government does not desire to see any change in sovereignty or in jurisdiction over those strategic points in the Atlantic

---

[43] Général Maxime Weygand: *Mémoires: Rappelé au service* (Paris, 1950), 440-41; *Pétain et les allemands: mémorandum d'Abetz* (Paris, 1948), 107-16 (correspondence of Abetz and Ribbentrop); Jean-Louis Aujol: *Le procès Benoist-Mechin* (Paris, 1948), 284 ff. (the situation at Wiesbaden).

[44] *Pétain et les allemands*, 107 ff. (July 15, 1941), 114 ff. (August 8, 1941).

[45] Memo of the President to Mr. Welles, July 11, 1941 (*Roosevelt Papers*: Secretary's File, Box 74).

whose retention in friendly hands is regarded by this Government as vital to the security and defense of the United States. This of course includes the French ports mentioned [Casablanca and Dakar]. Any attempt by Germany at the exercise, direct or indirect, of control over Casablanca and Dakar, or for that matter over other African ports in the Atlantic now under French jurisdiction, would immediately be of the gravest concern to the United States.

The President feels that, while your approach to the Marshal should be entirely friendly and should emphasize the desire of this Government to continue to be as helpful as possible to the French people in their present difficulties, you should nevertheless be completely frank and leave not a shadow of a doubt as to the gravity with which this Government views this question.

Please make it entirely clear beyond any doubt to the Marshal that in accordance with its announced policy, this Government has no desire to see modified or to encroach upon French jurisdiction over these regions provided such jurisdiction remains entirely French and so long as France does not permit German infiltration or German encroachment in those regions. Should, however, such a development take place, the policy of this Government would immediately change. Necessarily, the first change would be complete abandonment by this Government of any and all efforts to continue present trade arrangements with North Africa or to negotiate any commercial arrangements in the interest of metropolitan France. The subsequent steps which would be taken by this Government need not be detailed at this time but will be determined upon without the slightest delay in the light of such developments.[46]

A few days later a similar message was sent to Mr. Murphy for transmittal to General Weygand, who was to be told further that President Roosevelt had spoken of him in the highest terms and was confident that he would not permit German domination of North or West Africa.[47]

The response of Vichy to this *démarche* was not altogether reassuring. Darlan, as usual, insisted on being present when the Marshal received Ambassador Leahy. Indeed, it was Darlan who did most of the talking. According to Leahy's report:

Admiral Darlan stated very clearly that he could not say that Germany has not asked for the use of the bases. He did say that as long as the present political arrangement with Germany based on the Armistice continued, no foreign Power would be permitted to use the bases. He repeated "for so long as the present political arrangement with Germany lasts," indicating and leaving with me an impression that there may soon be a change in the existing Armistice Agreement. I was told in this interview that Japan will in the immediate future occupy bases in Indo-China with the purpose of projecting military operations to the southward.[48]

Vichy's acquiescence in Japanese demands for bases in southern Indo-China was a matter of the utmost moment to American policy, but one that can be more profitably discussed in a later chapter. In the present context it

[46] Tel. to Leahy, July 13, 1941.
[47] Tel. from Welles to Murphy, July 17, 1941.
[48] Leahy: *I Was There,* 54 (a record of his conversation with Pétain and Darlan, July 16, 1941).

is significant insofar as it reinforced American fears for North Africa, fears which were by no means allayed by Darlan's enigmatic remarks. But in Africa there was Weygand, on whom the President placed high hopes. Murphy saw the General soon after his return from Vichy and found him apprehensive about German moves against Africa in September or October. While appreciative of Mr. Welles's message, Weygand made clear that he could not be expected to take military action without authorization of his Government. However, there had been, to the best of his knowledge, no recent action changing the status of French African ports or conceding their use to the Germans. As before, he was determined to resist aggression on the territories under his control, though he indicated that the United States might do more to equip his forces for successful resistance.[49]

Although by August, 1941, nothing of a seriously deleterious nature had occurred in French Africa, Washington could not know that the Paris Protocols had by this time been shelved and could therefore not be sure that Darlan would not yield to German pressure as he had already succumbed to Tokyo's demands. Admiral Leahy reported:

Indications here point to a German move against the Mediterranean upon the completion of the Russian campaign regardless of the outcome. It is practically certain that Germany some time ago demanded the use of French African bases, and that Darlan was unable to deliver them because of the resistance offered by General Weygand. It is generally believed here that the demand will be renewed and that Weygand will at that time not succeed in preventing use of the bases by Germany.[50]

Why Darlan thought it necessary to keep the American Ambassador guessing must remain a matter of conjecture. Happily his evasions were counterbalanced by Weygand's firmly enunciated resolution to resist aggression and by his unqualified assurances to Murphy: "There is no change in our situation in Africa and no concessions have been made to the Germans."[51] For the time being this had to suffice. From the American standpoint the situation in North Africa continued highly precarious. Pétain seemed wholly under the thumb of Darlan, the Admiral himself appeared altogether untrustworthy, and Weygand might at any time be recalled from his post. On the other hand, Hitler's operations in the east made it unlikely that for some weeks or even months he would make an issue of the North African bases. The British and Americans would therefore enjoy a further respite for preparation. Since in the summer of 1941 their available forces were as yet quite inadequate for large scale operations, they had little choice but to hope for the best and trust in the resolution and influence of General Weygand.

[49] Letter from Murphy to Secretary Hull, July 15, 1941; tel. from Murphy, July 21, 1941; letter from Murphy to Mr. Wallace Murray, July 30, 1941.
[50] Letter of Leahy to the President, July 28, 1941 (full text in Leahy: *I Was There,* 460-62).
[51] Tel. from Murphy, August 10, 1941; Weygand: *Mémoires,* 444 ff.

With Madrid even less could be done than with Vichy, for the Spanish Foreign Minister, Serrano Suñer, was engaged in a personal feud with the American Ambassador and relations between the United States and Spain had steadily deteriorated. Hitler's attack on Soviet Russia, with its promise of early success, had made Serrano Suñer more arrogant and outspokenly antidemocratic than ever. "History and the future of Europe demand the extermination of Russia," he shouted to his Falangist cohorts.[52] With great enthusiasm he devoted himself to the recruitment of "volunteers" to serve alongside the Nazi "crusaders." There is no doubt that he did his utmost to persuade Franco to intervene in the war on Hitler's side, and that he felt perfectly safe in snubbing the American and British Ambassadors, whom he prevented from seeing Franco. Popular feeling was whipped up to the point where a mob launched an attack on the British Embassy (July 24), but London and Washington made every effort to avoid a crisis. The British Government, indeed, favored continuation of economic aid to Spain precisely in the hope of forestalling decisions born of desperation. Washington raised no objection, though on one pretext or another it reduced exports to Spain to the barest minimum.[53]

The American Government, like the British, assumed that Franco, despite pressure from Serrano Suñer and the extreme nationalists, would not range himself on the German side and that the Spanish military, too, would oppose any but the "safest" adventures. Yet on July 17 the Caudillo himself seemed to blast these expectations when, in a public address, he denounced the "inhuman blockade" to which the British were subjecting the continent, accused the United States of trying to exploit Spain's need for supplies in order to influence the Madrid Government in a way "incompatible with our sovereignty and dignity as a free nation," and declared that the Allies had already lost the war, despite their association with Communist Russia. London, much disturbed by this outburst, feared it portended a reversal of the policy pursued by Franco since the summer of 1940. Mr. Eden even announced in Parliament that the Government felt obliged to reconsider the program of economic aid. But after further deliberation the British decided not to force the issue. The existing program was maintained, but not expanded. There matters rested while Franco, like most others, awaited Hitler's anticipated victory in the east.[54]

[52] T. J. Hamilton in *The New York Times,* June 25, 1941.

[53] Tel. of the German Ambassador to Madrid, June 28, 1941 (in *Documents secrets du ministère des affaires étrangères d'Allemagne: Espagne,* Paris, 1946), No. 28; tels. from Weddell (Madrid), July 1, 10, 1941; tels. to Weddell, July 3 and 5, 1941; memos of conversation between Mr. Welles and Lord Halifax, July 3 and 8, 1941. See also Sir Samuel Hoare: *Complacent Dictator* (New York, 1947), 100, and Herbert Feis: *The Spanish Story* (New York, 1948), 135 ff.

[54] Franco's charges against the United States were refuted by Mr. Welles in a press conference on July 21, 1941. For the rest we have used a tel. from Winant (London), July 18, 1941; tel. from Johnson (London), July 30, 1941; and a British memo on the Spanish situation, submitted to the State Department by Lord Halifax, July 30, 1941.

So long as Franco's future course remained uncertain, there was always the danger that he might throw open the road to North Africa or turn over bases in the Canary Islands to the Nazis. Neither the British nor the Americans were actually in a position to influence the policy of Madrid as Franco claimed. Aside from military action, for which the resources were not at hand, they had only the instruments of economic warfare, and these could be effective only over the long term. Expectation of Nazi success against Soviet Russia for a time brought the Spaniards to such a degree of exaltation that they willingly risked the loss of much needed supplies. In the summer of 1941 they were immune to pressure by the democracies and London and Washington were practically helpless. To discontinue aid would only aggravate the internal situation in Spain and might well force the Government into complete dependence on Germany. It was therefore the part of wisdom to ignore Franco's provocation, to keep to the established policy, and to trust that the future would bring a favorable turn of events.

Of the Atlantic islands the Azores and the Cape Verdes, possessions of Portugal, were hardly less important strategically than the Spanish Canaries. In June, 1941, more than half the British merchant shipping losses through submarine attack in the Atlantic took place within a radius of a thousand miles from the Cape Verdes. These islands were also the obvious point of departure for eventual Nazi operations against Brazil and South America.[55] The Azores, in turn, could be made a valuable base for German submarine operations and even for Nazi air attacks on the United States. From the discussion in an earlier chapter it will be recalled that the British and American Governments had for some time been considering the protective occupation of these various islands and that the Azores operation, an American assignment, had been shelved in June in favor of the relief of British forces in Iceland.[56] The postponement of the Azores project had stemmed in part from the irritation provoked in Lisbon by certain references to the islands in President Roosevelt's speech of May 27, 1941. Since ordinary diplomatic explanations had failed to appease Prime Minister Salazar and since the Azores issue seemed one of increasing urgency, Mr. Roosevelt felt it necessary to take a personal hand in the matter. No doubt he was much impressed by Mr. Averell Harriman's report, on his return from the Middle East, to the effect that both General Wavell and General Gort (who was in command at Gibraltar) expected a German move on North Africa as soon as Nazi forces could be released from the Russian front.[57]

The President's position with respect to the Atlantic islands was expounded at length in the letter he wrote to President Vargas on July 10, part of which was quoted above. He explained that the acquisition of bases

[55] MS. study by Stetson Conn on *Defense of the Americas.*
[56] See above, Chapter XVI, Section 4.
[57] Harriman's reports of July 5 and 11, 1941, cited in the Conn MS. study referred to above.

from Britain and the measures already taken for the defense of Greenland and Iceland had rendered the outposts of the defense frontier reasonably secure. On the other hand there was still the danger that the Germans might seize Dakar and the Cape Verde Islands and utilize them as bases for naval and air attack against British convoys, if not as concentration points for actual attack against North and South America. If such an attempt were made, the United States forces in Trinidad and British Guiana would not be close enough to provide immediate effective assistance to the Brazilian forces defending Natal. Since it was most unlikely that the Nazis, having suddenly occupied West Africa and the Cape Verdes, would give the Americas time to prepare their defenses, the President, so he wrote his colleague, was considering a proposal to the Netherlands Government to permit the temporary use of base facilities in Surinam (Dutch Guiana) by United States forces. He then inquired whether, in the event of Dutch agreement, Brazil would also send troops as a measure of coöperation in defense of the hemisphere. Furthermore, there was the question of the Azores, which the Germans might also attempt to seize. Considerations of defense would oblige the United States to prevent Nazi control of these strategic islands and it was hoped that in such a contingency the Portuguese Government would request the United States, or Brazil, or both, to assist in defense of its island possessions. In this connection, too, the President wished to know whether Brazil would be willing to share in the task.[58]

Thus Mr. Roosevelt, recalling the historic affinity between Portugal and Brazil, invited the Brazilian Government to associate itself with any military action which the United States might consider necessary for defense of the Americas. The Rio authorities decided that for the time being they could not contribute militarily, but they expressed full sympathy with the President's views and objectives.[59] Mr. Roosevelt therefore felt justified in broaching the matter to Prime Minister Salazar, to whom a long personal letter was despatched by courier on July 14. In order to dispel any residue of misunderstanding he restated, in much the same terms as those he had employed in his letter to President Vargas, the interest of the United States in the maintenance of Portuguese control over the Atlantic islands. Furthermore, he expressed gratification over the steps already taken by Lisbon to strengthen its Atlantic defenses against possible Nazi attack and offered American aid if such were desired.[60]

The President's message, couched in warm personal terms, was delivered on July 21.[61] It evidently gave the Prime Minister much satisfaction, for he presently replied at equal length and with equal cordiality. His message

[58] Letter of President Roosevelt to President Vargas, July 10, 1941.
[59] Ambassador Caffery reported President Vargas's reaction in tels. of July 12, 16, 19 and 28, 1941.
[60] Letter of President Roosevelt to Prime Minister Salazar, July 14, 1941.
[61] Tel. from Fish (Lisbon), July 21, 1941.

(dated July 29) did not, however, reach Washington until August 6. Much of it was of a general nature and need not be considered here. The important point was that, with respect to the Azores issue, Dr. Salazar expressed doubt whether, in view of the inferiority of German sea power in the Atlantic, the danger of Nazi attack was as great as some seemed to suppose. In any event he believed that Portugal, through its own efforts and with the aid of British supplies, would be able to overcome the danger of successful assault. However, he continued, if Britain should find it impossible to provide the necessary munitions and equipment, Portugal would be grateful for American assistance.[62]

This reply, though not as explicit as the President might have desired, did mark the end of the misunderstanding which had prevailed for two months and left no doubt that the Lisbon Government was prepared to coöperate with the British. Since London appeared satisfied, there was no need to pursue the matter further. The President thought of the occupation of the Azores only as a possible contingency. As he wrote Admiral Land, of the Maritime Commission: "The Navy (and the Army) make much of having sufficient ships ready at all times for the carrying of an expedition to the Azores or the Cape Verdes or Brazil. It is my thought that no human being can tell when or if such an expedition will ever be ordered."[63] The likelihood that the Germans would, before long, loose their military power on the west made adequate measures of precaution indispensable. The Portuguese Government was naturally intent on avoiding commitments so extensive that they might draw the Nazi fire. But by August, 1941, there was good reason to suppose that in an emergency Portugal would align itself at once with the democracies.

4. THE MIDDLE EAST

Of all the issues raised by Hitler's expected victory over Soviet Russia and the anticipated renewal of his attack on the west only the defense of the Middle East created a serious difference of opinion between London and Washington. Mr. Churchill, ever disposed to think in offensive rather than defensive terms, was eager to take advantage of the respite provided by the Nazi-Soviet conflict to rush reinforcements to Egypt and launch an attack on Rommel in the hope of driving him out of North Africa before Hitler could make more troops, tanks and planes available to the Libyan theater. Wavell had been replaced by Auchinleck, whom the Prime Minister tried to induce to stage an offensive by the end of September at the latest. In these efforts he was unsuccessful, for the new commander was apprehensive of a

---

[62] Letter of Prime Minister Salazar to the President, July 29, 1941, sent to Washington by courier. See also the references to this letter in the records of the Atlantic Conference (*Pearl Harbor Attack,* IV, 1785 ff.).

[63] Memo of the President to Admiral Land, August 1, 1941 (*Roosevelt Papers: Secretary's File,* Box 80).

Nazi attack through Turkey and in general considered his forces and equipment insufficient to warrant an attack on Rommel before November, 1941. Even this schedule he made conditional on the arrival of substantial reinforcements and supplies.[64]

Mr. Roosevelt appears to have accepted the Prime Minister's estimate of the importance and possibilities of the Middle East, for under his instruction the development of the air ferry route by way of Takoradi was pursued energetically and arrangements made for financing it from Lend-Lease funds. The project was announced publicly on August 19 and by October the first American bombers were flown from the United States directly to Egypt by this route.[65] Meanwhile the shipment of American munitions—planes, tanks, trucks and other items—by the Red Sea route continued unabated. Whatever could be spared was contributed to the build-up of British strength in the eastern Mediterranean.

American military authorities, however, had grave doubts whether in the long run the British would be able to maintain their position in Egypt. They felt "sunk" by the news of British reverses in Libya and quite disheartened by reports from American observers of the shortcomings of the British command. There had been, so it seemed, serious lack of coördination between the ground, naval, and air forces, as well as serious mismanagement in matters of supply. At Takoradi some eighty American fighter planes lay crated and unused; others were stranded at staging points along the route to Khartum. According to American observers, the United States would have to take a much more active part in the management and distribution of supplies if these were to be fully effective.[66]

General Marshall and his staff were particularly disturbed by Mr. Churchill's plans to send additional troops and equipment from England to the Middle East. Since they were persuaded that Hitler, once he had despatched the Russians, would resume his efforts to invade the British Isles, they considered it far more important to concentrate available forces and supplies in that vital bastion. So strongly did they argue their point that the President himself began to have doubts of British capabilities to defend the United Kingdom and to question the wisdom of trying in addition to hold the Middle East. When Mr. Harry Hopkins went to London in mid-July this was one of the chief issues raised by him in discussion with the Prime Minister. The latter was certainly aware of American criticism of the con-

[64] For details see Churchill: *The Grand Alliance*, Book II, Chapter 2.

[65] The most detailed and authoritative account is in Wesley F. Craven and James L. Cate: *The Army Air Forces in World War II* (Chicago, 1948), I, 320 ff., but see also E. R. Stettinius, Jr.: *Lend-Lease: Weapon for Victory* (New York, 1944), 147 ff. We have used further the *Stimson Diary* (MS.), June 30, 1941 (containing General Arnold's report), and the *Morgenthau Diaries* (MS.), Vol. 414, p. 77; Vol. 417, pp. 71 ff.

[66] *Stimson Diary* (MS.), July 30, 1941, recording conversations with American officers recently returned from Egypt. Such reports continued for some time (Watson: *Chief of Staff: Prewar Plans and Preparations, 404-5).

duct of Middle East operations and of the misgivings of American military men over the future of that area. Early in June he had requested the President to permit Mr. Averell Harriman to accompany a British mission to the Middle East in order to see for himself the problems and possibilities of that theater. Harriman was now back in London and Mr. Churchill therefore invited him and Mr. Hopkins, together with the American "Special Observers," Admiral Ghormley and General Chaney, and the Military Attaché, General Lee, to attend a conference with himself and his military advisers.

In the meeting at 10 Downing Street on July 24 the entire problem was examined in detail. Hopkins stated the American position succinctly and forcefully, pointing out that if the campaign in the Middle East were to be resumed, the United States would have to send large quantities of supplies and assign as many as a hundred additional ships to the job. All this, he continued, would have to be done systematically, not on a day-to-day, hit-or-miss basis as theretofore:

Our Chiefs of Staff believe that the British Empire is making too many sacrifices in trying to maintain an indefensible position in the Middle East. At any moment the Germans might take Gibraltar and seal up the western Mediterranean. They might block the Suez Canal. They might concentrate enough air and armored forces to overwhelm the British armies in the Middle East. Our Chiefs of Staff believe that the Battle of the Atlantic is the final, decisive battle of the war and everything has got to be concentrated on winning it. Now, the President has a somewhat different attitude. He shares the belief that British chances in the Middle East are not too good. But he realizes that the British have got to fight the enemy wherever they find him. He is, therefore, more inclined to support continuing the campaign in the Middle East.

In support of the military view General Chaney then expounded the thesis that of the major problems confronting Britain the defense of the United Kingdom and the Atlantic sea lanes came first, the defense of Singapore and the trade routes to Australia and New Zealand second, the defense of the ocean routes in general third, and the defense of the Middle East last.

In view of President Roosevelt's sympathetic attitude, Mr. Churchill's battle was at least half won. His advisers—Admiral Pound, Field Marshal Dill and Air Marshal Portal—all explained that their preparations against invasion were adequate. The Royal Air Force was twice as strong as it had been in 1940. The British had, during the preceding eight months, put almost half of their war production into Middle Eastern operations and considered it essential to continue reinforcement of that theater. To abandon it would have a disastrous moral effect throughout the Moslem world. Mr. Churchill himself made a special point of the danger of a Nazi smash through Spain, past Gibraltar and into North and West Africa, and reminded his American listeners that if the United States were ultimately drawn into the war, North and West Africa might well prove to be areas necessary for American operations. Britain, he promised, would do nothing to jeopardize the defense of the home island, but it was clear to him that by holding the Middle East the British could force the Germans to consume resources that might otherwise be used for the invasion of England.[67]

The Prime Minister had the feeling, at the end of the conference, that he and his staff had convinced their American colleagues. This may have been correct, but General Marshall and many of his advisers continued skeptical about the Middle East. As Hopkins explained to Mr. Churchill: "We in the United States just simply do not understand your problem in the Middle East, and the interests of the Moslem world, and the interrelationship of your problems in Egypt and India." This was certainly not true of responsible officials of the State Department, but it was probably accurate with respect to the military authorities. Their uncertainty, in turn, derived in part from the fact that, as Hopkins pointed out, neither the President nor the American Government had as yet been given a comprehensive exposition of Britain's broad strategy in the Middle East. This was one of many matters urgently demanding solution. Pending further clarification, the American program of supply to the Middle East was maintained without curtailment. If and when Hitler resumed his assaults on the British position in Egypt, he was certain to find that position much stronger than it had been in March, 1941.

[67] Kittredge MS. study on *United States-British Naval Coöperation;* Churchill: *The Grand Alliance,* 424-25; Robert E. Sherwood: *Roosevelt and Hopkins* (New York, 1948), 314 ff.

CHAPTER XIX

The Good Neighbors

1. Economic and Cultural Relations

The Latin American Republics continued to be, throughout the year 1941, a major political and military concern of the United States. The Administration, the Congress and the American people were unanimously agreed that the defense of Central and South America was essential to the national security and that therefore everything possible should be done to provide for the stability, the economic welfare and the military protection of the hemisphere. The Panama and Havana Conferences had been designed to promote solidarity and secure common action in the event of emergency. Programs of economic assistance had been laid down and the initial steps taken to arrange for military collaboration against aggression from overseas. The earlier phases of Washington's policies with respect to the American Republics have already been touched upon.[1] The task remains of tracing their further development, which once more became a matter of urgency when Hitler's victories in the Balkans and the British reverses in Libya revived the threat of Nazi action against North and West Africa and possibly against the New World.

Latin American aspects of United States policy are difficult to present in logical sequence, for there were twenty countries involved, each with its own peculiar conditions and needs, each with its own traditions and objectives. To recount in detail the relations of the United States with each of the American Republics would be an undertaking far beyond what is required in the context of the present study. The effort will therefore have to be made to abstract the issues that were of general importance and to examine in greater detail only those problems which bore directly on the question of hemisphere defense.

In the economic sphere the United States increased its imports from Latin

[1] See above, Chapter VI.

American countries by more than 50 percent during the first nine months of 1941. Extensive loans were made to various countries by the Export-Import Bank and currency stabilization agreements were concluded with Brazil, Cuba, Mexico, and Ecuador. In July, 1941, it was announced that the Federal Loan Agency had made arrangements with Mexico for the purchase of all surplus strategic materials (antimony, copper, graphite, lead, mercury, tungsten, tin, zinc, etc.), after which similar agreements were negotiated for the acquisition of Peru's copper, vanadium and lead, Chile's copper and manganese, and Argentina's tungsten. While relieving Latin American countries of embarrassing surpluses, these arrangements also served the purpose of denying valuable raw materials to the enemy. On July 17, 1941, the United States issued a Proclaimed (Black) List of some 1800 Latin American firms known to be trading with Axis powers, a move that was presently reinforced by the action of various American Governments in instituting export controls akin to those of the United States. In return, Washington made every effort to satisfy essential civilian requirements of the other Republics and to provide manufactured goods at reasonable prices. On April 1, 1941, the State Department informed the Latin American Governments that unless the supply of such goods was "dangerously low" or absolutely indispensable for the defense requirements of the United States, they would be made available for export to Latin American countries at least to the extent of their previous purchases. Even in the case of materials in short supply an attempt would be made to fulfill "the most urgent requirements" if at all possible. Six months later (October 22, 1941) the Economic Defense Board reiterated this policy and undertook a study, item by item, of the minimum requirements of the American Republics with a view to establishing priorities and allocations. Taken by and large, the economic crisis provoked by the war in Europe was much alleviated. Though a certain amount of trade with the Axis, even in strategic materials, persisted, United States imports and loans did much to relieve the most acute situations and at the same time strengthen the American defense effort through the acquisition of crucial raw materials.[2]

In the political field the danger of Nazi or pro-Nazi coups appeared to diminish in the course of 1941, due primarily to the ever more drastic measures taken by Latin American Governments to curb German and Italian propaganda and organization. Bolivia, for example, insisted that the German Minister be recalled, and the Argentine Government, under pressure from the Radical Party, took action against Nazi associations. A special in-

[2] See Percy W. Bidwell: "Self-Containment and Hemisphere Defense" (*The Annals,* November, 1941, 175-85). Much statistical information is given in *Industrial Mobilization for War* (Washington, 1947), I, 123 ff., 155 ff., and also in *The New York Times,* September 19 and November 28, 1941. On the Black List and preclusive buying see David L. Gordon and Royden Dangerfield: *The Hidden Weapon: the Story of Economic Warfare* (New York, 1947), 150 ff.

vestigating committee of the Chamber of Deputies, chaired by the Radical leader Damonte Taborda, was set up in mid-July and reported its findings a few weeks later. The committee discovered that, despite the prohibition of the Nazi Party and the German Labor Front, the Germans had been organized, willingly or unwillingly, in local groups numbering thousands. The entire paramilitary system was directed by the German Embassy, which levied contributions and used them for propaganda purposes. The Government thereupon ordered the arrest of thirty-six persons accused of anti-Argentine activities. A wave of hostility to Germany and Nazism swept the country and for a time it seemed inevitable that the recall of the German Ambassador would be demanded. Yet the Government stopped short of extreme measures, partly no doubt from fear of German reprisals, but partly also from unwillingness to yield to popular pressure. Nonetheless, even in Argentina checks had been imposed upon the free development of Nazi organizations.[3]

The United States Government took no direct part in the campaign against subversive movements in the American Republics, being scrupulous to avoid even the appearance of interference in the internal affairs of its neighbors. Now and again American officials made public reference to the Nazi menace, but without mention of specific situations. In one instance, at least, such reference led only to embarrassment. In a speech of October 27, 1941, President Roosevelt himself stated that he had in his possession a secret map, made in Germany for the Nazi Government, which allegedly revealed a Nazi plan to divide South America into five vassal states, one of which would have included the Republic of Panama. His remarks naturally provoked curiosity and somewhat excited inquiries at the State Department. Hectic researches were undertaken, but apparently the map referred to by the President was never turned up. The chances are that Mr. Roosevelt had before him an item of clumsy propaganda wholly unworthy of the notice he gave it. Berlin at once denied that such a map had ever been produced in Germany, while the Nazi press denounced the President's statement as "an emanation of a crazy and absurd imagination."[4]

Some progress was made, during this period, in the campaign to counter Nazi propaganda throughout Latin America. In July, 1941, the Office for

[3] Tel. and despatch from Tuck (Buenos Aires), June 19, 1941; tels. from Tuck, June 27, July 16, 1941; despatch from Tuck, July 11, 1941; tels. from Armour (Buenos Aires), August 4, 5, 21, 29, September 23, December 26, 1941; despatches from Armour, August 27, September 5, 17, 1941; letter from Armour to Welles, September 5, 1941. See also Secretary Stimson's speech of August 15, 1941, warning of the danger of Nazi *putsches* in South America. The state of Latin American feeling and opinion was well reported by Vera Dean in the *Christian Science Monitor,* November 1, 1941, and by Edward Tomlinson in the *New York Herald Tribune,* November 10, 1941.

[4] Memo from Daniels to Welles, reporting a request for a copy of the map by the Paraguayan Minister, October 28, 1941. For Nazi comment see the *Bulletin of International News,* XVIII (2), 1885 ff.

Coördination of Commercial and Cultural Relations between the American Republics, created in the summer of 1940, was renamed the Office of the Coördinator of Inter-American Affairs (CIAA). In the latter part of 1941 this organization undertook the systematic dissemination of news about the United States and particularly about the American defense effort. It published a biweekly news letter and initiated radio broadcasts, eventually launching a lavishly illustrated periodical called *En Guardia,* which soon attained great popularity wherever it appeared. While it is difficult to appraise the effects of such propaganda activities, it can at least be said that at long last the United States was challenging the influence of German news services, radio broadcasts, moving pictures and propaganda literature. The American program was from the start based on the proposition that the truth was the most effective weapon. Pitched on a dignified factual level, American reporting and cultural programs certainly helped convince the Latin American peoples that their great neighbor to the north took a genuine interest in their problems, their activities and their welfare.[5]

2. THE PROBLEM OF MILITARY COLLABORATION

The principle of military coöperation between the American Republics in the event of an attack on any one of them had been accepted through the signature of the Act of Havana (July, 1940). Therefore the United States Government had initiated staff conversations with its various Latin American neighbors designed to reach agreement on the nature and extent of mutual aid. In conjunction with these conversations most Latin American Governments had submitted to Washington itemized lists of their requirements in armaments for their own defense. Taken together these Latin American requests ran to over a billion dollars in value. How to finance these supplies remained a knotty problem until the passage of the Lend-Lease Act and the President's ensuing declaration that, in view of the importance of hemisphere defense to the security of the United States, the American Republics were eligible to receive Lend-Lease aid. Even this decision, however, did not solve the much more difficult problem of finding the matériel called for by the American Governments.

For a time the question of military requirements was the subject of much argument among Washington agencies. The Armed Services were only too painfully aware of the acute shortages in most items of military equipment and doubted whether significant amounts of matériel could be despatched to Latin American countries before 1942 or even 1943. Clearly the demands of the United States Services came first, and the requirements of Britain next. Civilian agencies in general and the State Department in particular might urge a more generous attitude toward Latin American estimates, in

[5] See the official *History of the Office of the Coördinator of Inter-American Affairs* (Washington, 1947), especially pp. 14 ff.

the interests of securing the very coöperation so ardently desired by the military, but all such pleas inevitably foundered on the rocks of reality.[6]

The passage of the Lend-Lease legislation provided the means to finance Latin American requirements and made it imperative to establish orderly procedures for the allocation of whatever might be available. A Joint Advisory Board on American Republics was therefore created to advise Secretaries Stimson and Knox on problems of hemisphere defense. This Board's eagerly awaited report restated succinctly the approved policies of the United States Government with respect to military assistance:

A. The United States will employ its armed forces to assist any Republic to defeat attacks on it by the armed forces of a non-American state, or by Fifth Column groups . . . when requested to do so by the recognized Government of the Republic concerned.

B. The United States will assist American Republics to acquire armaments, to train their personnel, and to provide the assistance of such advisers as may be desired and available.

C. Arms to be furnished to the various American Republics in accordance with an estimate of their needs. . . .

D. The arms to be provided on financial terms the American Republics could meet.[7]

To carry out these commitments the Board recommended the creation of an Inter-American Defense Fund or some similar mechanism for the procurement and allocation of armaments for the American Republics, basing the transactions either on credits or on Lend-Lease. The maximum sum available for this purpose over the next five years was thought to be $700,000,000, as contrasted with the Latin American requests totaling nearly a billion and a quarter. Assuming that Lend-Lease aid would presently be extended to the American Republics, Secretary Hull signed the report. On April 22, 1941, the three Secretaries jointly addressed to the President a recommendation that over "the next few years" matériel be furnished the other American Republics to the value of $400,000,000, and that such matériel be provided under Lend-Lease. Mr. Roosevelt quickly approved the recommendation, which United States missions were instructed to communicate to the Latin American Governments on May 20, 1941.[8] By the end of June the President had sanctioned also the text of a basic agreement to be negotiated with the various Governments. Discussions began with most of them before the end of July and agreements were signed with a number of Governments during the next few months. However, by

6 Memo of the Division of American Republics to Mr. Welles, January 21, 1941.

7 Report of the Joint Advisory Board on American Republics, as submitted to the State Department, with a memo from Mr. Orme Wilson to Mr. Welles, March 22, 1941.

8 Memos of Mr. Duggan to Mr. Welles, March 29 and April 25, 1941; letter of Secretaries Hull, Stimson and Knox to the President, April 22, 1941 (returned at once with Mr. Roosevelt's O.K.); circular tel. to Chiefs of Mission in the other American Republics, May 20, 1941.

the time of the Pearl Harbor attack the program of military aid to the hemisphere nations was still in a rudimentary stage. Relatively little equipment had been supplied by the United States. Indeed, requisitions for the agreed lists had been filed for only eight or nine countries. As before, the acute shortage of essential munitions made it impossible to meet the requests or even to fill the recognized needs of the American states.[9]

Latin American statesmen, while doubtless ready to admit that nations actually resisting aggression, like Britain and China, should have first call on any munitions the United States might be able to provide, had understandable difficulty in believing that the United States, with its much vaunted industrial capabilities, should find it impossible to supply even the basic needs of the countries involved in hemisphere defense. The importance of that aspect of the defense problem was, of course, fully recognized in Washington, but it seemed clear that none of the Latin American states could hope to defend itself against attack from abroad. The chief burden must fall on the United States. Considering the limited matériel available, the Latin American demands for military equipment involved liabilities. In the discussions carried on with most of these Governments since the autumn of 1940 efforts had been made to arrive at arrangements for making bases available to the United States, but thus far the conversations had produced few concrete results. In most instances the Governments, sensitive of their sovereignty and of popular feeling, took the stand that they should first be helped to defend themselves and that United States support should supplement their own national efforts. This vital problem continued, therefore, to plague the military planners as well as the diplomats.[10]

On June 21, 1941, the Uruguayan Government addressed a note to the other American Governments suggesting the possibility of further progress in the direction of military collaboration. In effect Uruguay proposed that the principles of hemisphere solidarity laid down at the Lima, Panama and Havana Conferences be further implemented. Recalling a Uruguayan decree of June 18, 1917, "that no American country which in defense of its own rights should find itself in a state of war with nations of other continents will be treated as belligerent," Foreign Minister Guani suggested that all American Governments adopt this policy in advance, in view of the fact that situations of extreme urgency might arise and make impossible a timely meeting of the Foreign Ministers of all the Republics.[11]

Dr. Guani's hope that the United States Government would give active

[9] Memo of Mr. Welles to the President, June 28, 1941, transmitting the text of the basic agreement; memo of Mr. Collado to Mr. Welles, July 21, 1941, reporting on the status of negotiations; memo from the War Department, November 26, 1941, summarizing the situation with respect to Lend-Lease.

[10] War Department memo of July 11, 1941 (*Pearl Harbor Attack*, XIV, 1341-42); memo of conversation between Mr. Duggan and the Argentine Ambassador, July 31, 1941.

[11] Tel. from Chapin (Montevideo), June 20, 1941.

support to his proposal and use its influence with other American Governments was fulfilled with enthusiasm and alacrity. Ambassador Chapin was instructed to inform the Foreign Minister that the Uruguayan note had been received in Washington "with the deepest gratification and with a sense of lively satisfaction." United States missions in Latin America were directed to state to the Governments to which they were accredited that the United States viewed the Uruguayan initiative "as an example of enlightened and far-sighted statesmanship, giving content to the oft-repeated pledges of Inter-American solidarity."[12] The Brazilian Government, too, lent vigorous support.[13]

Nonetheless, the response to the Uruguayan note proved disappointing. Following the lead of Argentina and Chile, many Governments replied reaffirming their devotion to the principles of inter-American solidarity and their adherence to the procedures for consultation already agreed upon, but at the same time expressing their conviction that further provisions would be superfluous. In its official reply (July 1, 1941) Washington stated the case for the Uruguayan proposal as strongly as possible:

The safety of the Americas hangs in the balance today. Constructive and far-sighted action now on the part of all the American Republics acting together will ensure the preservation for future generations of those liberties and other blessings which our forefathers so laboriously gained.

The Government of the United States welcomes and wholeheartedly supports the present initiative of the Government of Uruguay, and earnestly hopes that it may secure the common approval of the Governments of all the American Republics.[14]

But even this appeal achieved little more than a softening of some of the Latin American replies. The end result appeared to leave no alternative to individual negotiation with the Latin American states in the effort to secure the use of their ports and other facilities. When, in September, Secretary Knox in a letter to Secretary Hull reverted to the Uruguayan proposal and urged the need for a general agreement enabling United States naval forces to use Latin American bases at once and at any time, Mr. Welles expressed the belief that no useful purpose would be served by renewed efforts to secure the adherence of the other Republics to the Uruguayan note and recommended that the question of bases be taken up separately with the Governments concerned.[15]

[12] Tel. to Chapin, June 21, 1941; circular tel. to the Chiefs of United States missions in Latin America, June 21, 1941.

[13] Tels. from Caffery (Rio de Janeiro), June 27 and 28, 1941.

[14] Full text in Documents on American Foreign Relations, IV, 334-36. The replies of all the American Governments were summarized in a despatch from Chapin, October 3, 1941. On the position of the Argentine and Chilean Governments we have used a despatch from Tuck (Buenos Aires), July 1, 1941, and a tel. from Bowers (Santiago), July 2, 1941.

[15] Letter of Secretary Knox to Secretary Hull, September 19, 1941, and reply of Under Secretary Welles, October 14, 1941.

Discussions and negotiations to this end were in fact conducted with various American Governments in the course of 1941. To review them all would be as tedious as it would be unrewarding. In the following sections the attempt will therefore be made to analyze a few of the more important and instructive situations, with particular reference to special problems affecting the relations of the United States with its southern neighbors.

3. BRAZIL AND DEFENSE OF THE BULGE

From the standpoint of Washington the problem of northeastern Brazil completely overshadowed every other aspect of hemisphere defense except the protection of the Panama Canal. The so-called "bulge" was a critical area not only because it was most exposed to possible Nazi attack from West Africa, but also because it was an essential base for the naval patrol of the South Atlantic and was soon to become an indispensable link in the air ferry route to Africa and the Middle East. In connection with the seemingly imminent threat of a Nazi advance through Spain on West Africa in May and June, 1941, some consideration has already been given in earlier chapters to American military plans for strengthening the defenses of the bulge. Fortunately the Brazilian Government was quite alert to the dangers confronting it and was devoted to the principles of Pan American solidarity and military coöperation with the United States. It had given Pan American Airways permission to expand existing airfields and construct new ones in northern and northeastern Brazil. It had agreed that United States naval vessels might use the ports of Recife and Bahia for purposes of patrol and had accepted American aid to develop Natal and Maceio as bases for the use of both countries. Furthermore, in June, 1941, it had introduced regulations forbidding the export of strategic materials to Axis countries.[16]

Gratifying though these measures were, they contributed but little to the protection of the bulge against overseas attack. General Marshall was so perturbed by the threat of such an attack that in May, 1941, he had despatched Colonel Matthew B. Ridgway posthaste to Rio to canvass the possibility of sending United States forces to northeastern Brazil as reinforcements for the Brazilian troops already stationed there. Ridgway reported, somewhat too optimistically, that the Brazilian authorities would probably agree to such action. Thereupon plans were drawn and Mr. Roosevelt's approval secured for submission of the proposal to Rio, which took place on June 27. Somewhat later Mr. Roosevelt sent a long letter to his Brazilian colleague expounding his views of the situation in the Atlantic and recounting the protective measures taken through the mission of American forces to Iceland, Trinidad, and British Guiana. Although he did not specifically repeat

[16] Tel. to Caffery (Rio de Janeiro), April 17; tels. from Caffery, April 18 and May 12, June 14, 1941. We have used further the MS. study by Stetson Conn on *Defense of the Americas.*

the request for permission to station American troops in northeastern Brazil, he indicated that the American forces in Trinidad and British Guiana would not be close enough to the point, namely Natal, which the Germans would probably attack first. He therefore suggested that if the Netherlands Government would agree to the temporary use of Dutch Guiana by United States air and naval patrols, the Rio Government might share these facilities by also committing troops to that area. Similarly he suggested the eventual participation of Brazilian forces in the occupation of the Azores, should such a move become necessary and should the Portuguese Government invite protective action.[17]

Mr. Roosevelt's letter was cordially received by Senhor Vargas. The various proposals, which Ambassador Caffery thought came too thick and fast, were discussed by the Brazilian President with his Ministers for Foreign Affairs, War and Navy. All appear to have favored the utmost measure of coöperation, though the Minister of War felt that participation in the occupation of Surinam (Dutch Guiana) or the Azores would for some time exceed the capabilities of the Army. Apparently there was some fear of getting too deeply involved in actions obviously inimical to the Germans, whose influence, even in Brazil, was far from negligible. However, President Vargas concurred in the establishment of a Joint United States-Brazilian staff conference which was to be given the task of working out the details of military collaboration. On July 20 it was agreed that this body should function on the explicit understanding that (1) only Brazilian troops should be used on Brazilian territory; (2) Brazil, when it deemed fitting, should, in the event of a positive threat to its territory, feel free to request the aid of United States forces at such points and for such a period of time as the Brazilian authorities might determine; (3) Brazilian forces should maintain and command all bases on Brazilian territory, though these might be occupied by United States forces at Brazil's request; and (4) the Joint Planning Group should determine the technical and material aid to be given by the United States in the preparation of bases.

These arrangements obviously fell short of Washington's requests, though Senhor Vargas, in his reply to Mr. Roosevelt's letter, reiterated that Brazil would continue its policy of complete collaboration. In so doing, he added, his country would provide all means and all forces at its disposal to ensure the common defense of the hemisphere. The American members of the Joint Planning Group were in fact shown the Brazilian plans for defense of the bulge and work was at once undertaken on a program of eventual joint defense of that vital area. On the other hand the Brazilian members of the Group held out little hope that American forces could be sent to Brazil prior to actual attack or at least prior to imminent threat of attack. The Chief of

[17] Letter of President Roosevelt to President Vargas, July 10, 1941. See above, Chapter XVI, Section 4.

Staff of the Brazilian Army and the Foreign Minister reminded the American Ambassador that no Brazilian Government could hope to survive popular indignation if it invited United States troops into the country before the people were convinced that attack was impending. This was a matter of national self-respect and sensibility, and there was no way of circumventing it.[18]

Ambassador Caffery's considered opinion was that the United States was indeed asking a good deal of the Rio Government and that it was unrealistic to expect Brazil to make major concessions unless Washington were able and willing to send the military supplies so often and so urgently requested. He therefore resisted again and again the requests of the Navy Department for permission to make more extensive use of Brazilian ports for naval and air patrols. Only after repeated German ship sinkings within five hundred miles of the Brazilian coast had made the issue even more urgent from the Navy's standpoint, was the request submitted to President Vargas early in November. The latter agreed on November 10, on the understanding that a certain number of planes badly needed by the Brazilian Air Force for training purposes would be delivered without further delay. The final decision permitting use of the ports for United States patrol purposes was made on November 26, 1941, that is, on the eve of Pearl Harbor.[19]

The course of military coöperation, too, was beset with difficulties. While negotiations for a Lend-Lease agreement were pushed with vigor and a generous allocation of $100,000,000 was envisaged for Brazil, the flow of matériel, however financed, left much to be desired.[20] Failing the arrival of planes and other much needed equipment, Brazilian military authorities showed understandable reluctance to make further provision for eventual United States action in Northeast Brazil.[21] In Washington, on the other hand, there were complaints of delays in the submission of Brazilian requirements and of confusion among purchasing agencies.

Fortunately a new and more promising prospect opened up when, on November 10, the Chief of Staff of the Brazilian Army proposed the establishment of a permanent Joint Board for Northeast Brazil, the primary function of which would be to work out problems of construction and supply for the defense of the bulge area. The United States authorities quickly concurred,

---

[18] Despatch from Caffery, July 8, 1941; tels. from Caffery, July 12, 16, 19, 28, 1941 (the last mentioned transmitting President Vargas's reply to President Roosevelt's letter); tel. from Caffery, August 21, 1941, reporting the views of the Chief of Staff and Foreign Minister.

[19] Memo from the Navy Department asking that the State Department submit the request, July 11, 1941; tel. to Caffery, July 17; tels. from Caffery, July 22, August 19; tel. to Caffery, September 7, and his reply, September 9; tels. to Caffery, October 23 and November 7; tels. from Caffery, October 27, November 8, 10, 14, 21, 26, 1941. Minutes of the Liaison Committee, November 12 and 24, 1941.

[20] Tels. from Caffery, August 5, 15, September 9, November 3, 1941.

[21] Tel. from Caffery, September 8, 1941.

but the implementation of this plan was delayed by the spread of rumors in
Brazil that the United States was about to occupy the northeastern part of
the country. This situation created some tension, which was relieved only by
the Japanese attack on Pearl Harbor. The plan for the Joint Board for
Northeast Brazil was not actually approved and put into effect until December 19, 1941.[22]

Even the apparently simple project for stationing United States-Brazilian
troops in Surinam (Dutch Guiana) brought tribulation, though of a somewhat different nature. General Marshall was much exercised by fear lest the
bauxite mines of Surinam, which supplied 65 percent of the raw material
for the American aluminum industry, be destroyed by sabotage or raid.
Dutch defense forces were deemed inadequate and President Roosevelt
therefore decided to approach the Netherlands Government with the suggestion that the United States and Brazil should send forces to assure protection of the mines for the period of the emergency. On August 22, 1941,
President Vargas agreed to coöperate, if invited by the Netherlands Government to do so.[23]

President Roosevelt thereupon laid the proposal before Queen Wilhelmina
of the Netherlands, explaining the danger and stressing the urgent need for
action.[24] The response was prompt and favorable. Her Majesty gladly accepted the President's offer to send American troops, on the understanding
that they be withdrawn not later than the end of the war, that they be
placed under Netherlands command, and that they be paid by the Netherlands Government.[25] In the course of the subsequent discussions Foreign
Minister Van Kleffens suggested that the Brazilian contribution might take
the form of special measures of military vigilance on the Surinam-Brazilian
frontier and of a mission to Paramaribo for the purpose of exchanging information and concerting the requisite measures of defense.[26]

Actually the Brazilian Government had some reservations about sending
its troops to Surinam, fearing that the higher pay of the American forces
might create difficulties. President Vargas was therefore quite agreeable to
the form of Brazilian participation suggested by the Netherlands Government and was ready to act whenever invited by Her Majesty's Government
to do so.[27] On the American side the only objection to the Netherlands
proposals bore on the question of command. This issue it was hoped could
be solved by having the American forces "coöperate" in defense of the mines
under the "general direction" of the local Netherlands authorities. In view

[22] Tel. to Caffery, November 10, 1941; tels. from Caffery, November 13, 15, 19, 21,
December 5, 13, 16, 19, 20, 1941.
[23] Tel. to Caffery, August 18; tel. from Caffery, August 22, 1941.
[24] Message of President Roosevelt to Queen Wilhelmina, September 1, 1941.
[25] Tel. from Biddle, September 5, 1941, transmitting Queen Wilhelmina's reply.
[26] Tels. from Biddle, September 25 and 30, October 1, 1941.
[27] Tels. from Caffery, October 2, 15, 1941.

of Brazil's decision against contributing troops, however, General Marshall favored acceptance of the Netherlands terms in order to avoid further delay of an operation which he regarded as urgently necessary. On the strength of his opinion and of Mr. Welles's recommendation, the President approved the Netherlands proposals and so informed Ambassadors Biddle and Caffery.[28]

By mid-October, then, everything seemed settled. A United States force of a thousand officers and men was ready to embark at Trinidad and nothing remained but to reach agreement on the wording of the public announcement. But at this juncture the Netherlands Government began to make difficulties. Foreign Minister Van Kleffens felt that consideration of Dutch sensibilities made it desirable if not necessary that the American occupation forces be placed under direct Netherlands command and raised a number of other questions of detail.[29] Further time was lost in discussion and negotiation. Finally, on November 1, the Netherlands invitation to Brazil was despatched to Rio, where it was promptly accepted.[30] But the Netherlands Government, involved in a Cabinet crisis and apprehensive of the German reaction as it might affect the people of the occupied Netherlands, still delayed final arrangements for the reception of the American troops. Meanwhile rumors began to spread in Latin America about the alleged American occupation. The State Department urged the need for decision, if only for security reasons. But the last obstacles were not surmounted until the end of November. The joint communiqué was issued on November 24. On the following day United States forces began to disembark in Surinam.[31]

Though the protection of the Surinam bauxite mines provided a good illustration of the difficulties involved in meeting even the most obvious requirements of hemisphere defense, Washington must have noted with satisfaction the complete readiness of the Brazilian Government to coöperate in this cause. It should, in fact, be emphasized that President Vargas and his ministers did everything possible within the limits of national susceptibilities. United States military and naval authorities were understandably oppressed by fear of Nazi operations against Latin American countries. They knew that none of these countries would be able alone to offer effective resistance and that the main burden of defense would devolve upon United

[28] Tels. to Biddle and Caffery, October 13, 1941.

[29] Tel. from Biddle, October 17, 1941.

[30] Tels. to Caffery, October 24 and November 1, 1941; tel. from Caffery, November 4, 1941; tel. to Biddle, November 5, 1941.

[31] Tels. from Biddle, October 31, November 6, 12, 16, 17, 21, 1941; tels. to Biddle, November 5, 15, 19, 1941; tels. from Caffery, November 13, 25, 1941; tels. to Caffery, November 7, 14, 19, 1941; circular tel. to the other American Republics, for later release, November 6, 1941; minutes of the Liaison Committee, October 29, November 12, 1941. The joint communiqué of November 24 is printed in full in *Documents on American Foreign Relations,* IV, 467.

States forces. These forces were, in all conscience, few enough and there was next to no matériel to satisfy Latin American appeals for defense equipment. The inevitable result was that the War and Navy Departments were profuse in their requests for facilities which would enable them to employ their military resources to the greatest effect. But, to quote Ambassador Caffery, matters reached the pass where requests for favors at times came one a day. For Governments like that of Brazil these were tall orders and one need not be amazed that they could not all be met.

With respect to Brazil it cannot be gainsaid that that country stood squarely on the structure of Pan American solidarity and coöperation with the United States. Foreign Minister Aranha gave a final demonstration of his country's position in the last weeks preceding the Japanese attack on Hawaii. The occasion was his visit to Chile, which in turn included two brief stops in Buenos Aires. The Brazilian Foreign Minister, on his arrival in Argentina and Chile, proclaimed publicly and privately that Brazil would not be a party to any special South American defense bloc, that it was the champion of Pan American solidarity in defense, that it proposed to coöperate 100 percent with the United States, and that even if the United States entered the war actively without being directly attacked, Brazil would provide aid such as the United States was already affording Britain. In his statement to the Argentine press he expounded his position in the most unequivocal terms: "We were, are and desire to be Pan Americans. We go along with America and we will follow the destiny of America. We will not remain neutral if an American nation takes part in the war. . . . There is no room for two attitudes or personal sentiments at the present time. Nations must either save themselves united, or perish in face of the threats of the enemy."[32]

According to his own statements the Brazilian Foreign Minister succeeded in dispelling distrust of the United States and in strengthening the forces of Pan Americanism not only in Chile but also in the Argentine. Ambassadors Armour and Caffery, while they suspected the Minister of being somewhat overoptimistic, were disposed to concur. In any case there was no room whatever for doubt as to the general position of President Vargas and his Foreign Minister. For all the arguments and irritations that inevitably flowed from close day to day contacts, Brazil was clearly one of the main pillars of the hemisphere structure.

4. MEXICO AND THE QUESTION OF NAVAL BASES

The Mexican Government had for many months been professing sentiments of solidarity with the United States and the other American Republics, and these professions had fallen most agreeably on Washington ears.[33]

[32] Tels. from Caffery, November 4 and 5, 1941; tel. from Mr. Welles to Caffery, November 6, 1941; tels. from Armour (Buenos Aires), November 10, 24, 1941; despatch from Caffery, November 28, 1941.

[33] Statement of Foreign Minister Padilla, January 14, 1941 (*The New York Times*,

The Mexican Government had agreed with the United States in December, 1940, that a Joint Defense Commission like the United States-Canadian Commission should be established and had, in mid-February, 1941, sent staff officers to Washington to work out defense arrangements with their American colleagues. On April 1 the two Governments signed an agreement for the transit of military aircraft which ensured the United States of an inland route to the Panama Canal and the lower Caribbean.[34] But the project for a Joint Defense Commission was not pressed, since the State Department felt that American claims for compensation arising from Mexico's expropriation of foreign petroleum properties should first be settled and that the issue of naval base rights should also be given precedence. Thus far no progress had been made toward the long-term lease of naval bases on Mexico's Pacific coast, despite the fact that such facilities were regarded by the United States Navy as essential for the common defense.[35]

The reluctance of the Mexican Government to meet in full the program considered by Washington necessary for protection of the hemisphere stemmed in good part from causes common to most of the Republics south of the Rio Grande. Whatever its inclinations, the Avila Camacho Administration could not ignore the feelings of sincere nationalists, zealously intent on safeguarding every last ounce of Mexican sovereignty against the imaginary designs of the Colossus of the North. It had furthermore to deal with a vociferous element composed about equally of confirmed pro-Nazis and of Communists, both factions ready and eager to join forces in sabotaging any concrete program of Mexican-American coöperation. The press announcement of the opening of defense conversations between the United States and Mexico had led at once to close questioning of Foreign Minister Padilla in the Mexican Senate. While approval of his policy was general, loud and sustained applause greeted his categorical promise that in no case would any foreign power be permitted to occupy Mexican bases or in any way infringe Mexico's sovereignty.[36]

The Mexican Government was throughout perfectly willing to construct

January 15, 1941); tels. from Boal (Mexico City), January 14 and 21, 1941; tels. to Boal, January 17 and 25, 1941.

[34] Memo of conversation between Mr. Welles and the Mexican Ambassador, February 13, 1941; letter of Mr. Welles to the President, March 28, 1941. The text of the agreement is printed in *Documents on American Foreign Relations*, III, 142 ff. See also Samuel F. Bemis: *The Latin American Policy of the United States* (New York, 1943), 348.

[35] Memo of General Marshall and Admiral Stark to Mr. Welles, July 3, 1941, reviewing the problem of the Joint Defense Commission. With respect to the projected bases at Magdalena Bay and Acapulco, Ambassador Daniels had, on Mr. Roosevelt's suggestion, broached the question directly to President Avila Camacho early in February, 1941 (letter of Ambassador Daniels to President Roosevelt, February 4, 1941, in *Roosevelt Papers:* Secretary's File, Box 76).

[36] *The New York Times*, March 5, 1941; despatch from Daniels (Mexico City), March 8, 1941.

the necessary naval bases and make them available coöperatively as required for continental solidarity and safety, but only on condition that the United States assume the financial burden of such construction and that the Mexican flag continue to fly over the localities in question.[37] This solution was not satisfactory to the United States Navy, which desired base arrangements with Mexico similar to those concluded with the British Government in September, 1940. However, Secretary Knox on May 7, 1941, advised Mr. Hull that, "due to the present critical situation," the Navy was willing to have the State Department conclude agreements with Mexico for joint use of the naval bases as an emergency measure, deferring until later the effort to secure long-term leases. This concession by the Navy was at once approved by Secretary Hull, since the State Department had long taken the position that the Mexican Government would find it impossible to induce the country to accept the lease program. Yet when the Navy Department on June 6 submitted its revised proposals to the Mexican Ambassador, even the new, attenuated program provoked consternation in Mexico City. The question was discussed by the Liaison Committee (Mr. Welles, General Marshall, and Admiral Stark) on July 1, but no solution to the dilemma could be found. American authorities saw no alternative to awaiting the counterproposals of the Mexican Government.[38]

Toward the end of July the Mexican Ambassador informed the State Department that he was suggesting to his Government the conclusion of an agreement regarding naval vessels similar to the agreement of April 1 concerning the transit of aircraft. Such an arrangement, he thought, would serve to pave the way toward a more ample agreement on the development of naval bases.[39] Having secured official approval, the Ambassador presented his proposals to the State Department about ten days later. In a lengthy "Memorandum concerning Port Facilities" the Mexican Government suggested that the United States provide the funds to enable Mexico to construct the desired facilities, Mexico to retain full title and United States naval vessels to make use of the bases for not more than one week at a time. These terms were described as the utmost concessions possible within the framework of Mexican sovereignty and national dignity.[40]

This memorandum was a profound disappointment to both the State and

[37] Letter of Ambassador Daniels to President Roosevelt, March 11, 1941; memo of conversation between Mr. Welles and the Mexican President's brother, General Maximino Avila Camacho, April 14, 1941.

[38] Letter of Secretary Knox to Secretary Hull, May 7, 1941, and the latter's reply, May 14, 1941; minutes of the Liaison Committee, July 1, 1941; letter of Admiral Stark to Mr. Welles, July 11, 1941, insisting that the Navy's proposals to the Mexicans conformed to the program approved by Mr. Hull, that they were in harmony with President Avila Camacho's announced policies regarding hemisphere defense, and that they contained nothing to cause the Mexican Government "undue perturbation."

[39] Memo of Duggan to Welles, July 28, 1941.

[40] Memo from the Mexican Embassy, undated but referred to later as of about August 6, 1941. A slightly revised version was submitted on August 21, 1941.

Navy Departments, the more so as the proposal to restrict the stay of United States vessels to one week seemed to mark a step backward from accepted practice. The matter was argued to and fro, with much reference to the fact that, far from offering naval bases, the Mexican proposal dealt only with port facilities and that it reflected lack of appreciation of the importance of the bases to Mexican as well as United States defense. In the end Admiral Stark supported Mr. Welles's suggestion that the Mexican offer be declined and the matter allowed to rest until other issues, notably the oil controversy, had been settled. On October 1 Mr. Welles expressed confidence that by the middle of the month these other issues would have been disposed of and that then, in an atmosphere of mutual gratification and good will, the question of naval facilities could be dealt with more easily. Actually the oil issue was not settled until November 19 and it was only after the Pearl Harbor attack that the issue of naval bases was reopened.[41] At that time, of course, Washington renewed its earlier requests as a matter of urgency. President Avila Camacho submitted them to the Mexican Senate on December 16 and secured unanimous approval on December 24, 1941. Thenceforth Mexican ports were, in theory at least, available to ships and hydroplanes of all the American Republics for indefinite periods, subject only to prior notification. Furthermore, the establishment of the United States-Mexican Joint Defense Commission, agreed on late in December, 1940, was at last announced on January 12, 1942, and thereby full provision made for the expeditious settlement of innumerable detailed questions.[42]

Throughout the negotiations for naval base facilities in Mexico it was fully realized in Washington that a satisfactory solution of this problem was dependent upon the settlement of various other issues between the two Governments and above all upon disposition of the protracted dispute over the claims of American oil companies resulting from the nationalization of the petroleum industry by the Mexican Government in 1938.[43] Informal discus-

[41] Memo of conversation between Messrs. Wilson and Bursley of the State Department and Captain Spears of the Navy Department, August 12, 1941; minutes of the Liaison Committee, August 18, 1941; letter of Admiral Stark to Secretary Hull, September 4, 1941; memo of Bursley to Duggan, commenting on the preceding item, September 12, 1941; memo of Bonsal to Bursley, September 22, 1941; memo of Duggan to Welles, September 29, 1941; minutes of the Liaison Committee, October 1, 29, 1941.

[42] Tel. to McGurk (Mexico City), December 10, 1941; tel. from McGurk, December 11, 1941; memo of conversation between Mr. Welles and the Mexican Ambassador, December 17, 1941; memo of Duggan to Welles, December 18, 1941, on establishment of the Joint Defense Commission; tels. from McGurk, December 16, 26, 1941, and January 8, 1942; despatches from McGurk, December 17, 1941, and January 8, 1942. For announcement of the Joint Defense Commission and the relevant executive order see the Department of State Bulletin, January 17, 1941, p. 67, and February 28, 1942, p. 193.

[43] A review of outstanding issues had been presented by the Mexican Government on February 17, 1941, in a twenty-page memorandum. This had been sent by the State Department to the Treasury with a request for coöperation in the forthcoming discussions with the Mexican Ambassador (Morgenthau Diaries, MS., March 18 and 20, 1941—Vol. 384, pp. 75 ff.).

sions were carried on with the Mexican Ambassador during the spring of 1941, when it soon became clear that until a final agreement was reached between the Mexican Government and the American oil companies a completely satisfactory relationship between the United States and Mexico would remain improbable. Ambassador Daniels therefore urged the State Department to induce the companies to accept the terms of the Mexican settlement with the Sinclair interests, which, he reported, the Mexican Government apparently regarded as a model.[44]

While the State Department was ready to adopt this line, there was but slight hope that the companies could be persuaded to go along. The Department of the Interior, on the basis of Mexican statistics, estimated the physical assets of the American companies at $7,165,000, plus net accrued profits of $3,512,000, while American estimates ranged as high as $408,000,000. How to reconcile these widely diverging figures was indeed a difficult question.[45] Nonetheless, the effort had to be made. On July 15, 1941, the State Department produced the proposals which were to become the basis for the eventual settlement. These proposals, involving a down payment by the Mexican Government and a subsequent appraisal of the companies' assets by a mixed commission of experts, were concurred in by the Mexican Government in August and President Avila Camacho, with what proved to be premature optimism, announced publicly on September 1 that in a few weeks, if not in a matter of days, important solutions would be revealed which would reflect the spirit of real comprehension between the two Governments.[46]

Unfortunately Secretary Hull and his colleagues, when they called representatives of the companies into conference, found them altogether uncompromising. Despite the Secretary's emphasis on the importance of a settlement in the interests of general American-Mexican relations, the companies refused to accept compensation which they regarded as tantamount to recognition of the right of the Mexican Government to confiscate foreign properties. Following the first meeting on September 27, a second conference took place on October 28, but to no avail. Meanwhile the Mexican Government was pressing for action. The companies having definitely refused their concurrence (November 13), the State Department decided to close with the Mexican Government on the best terms possible. By the agreement of November 19, 1941, Mexico undertook to pay $40,000,000, over a period of years, in satisfaction of agrarian and other property claims as distinct from the oil claims. With respect to the latter it was to pay $9,000,000 on

[44] Despatch from Daniels, May 1, 1941.

[45] MS. study by Graham H. Stuart of the history of the Office of American Republics Affairs; letter of President Roosevelt to Ambassador Daniels, June 17, 1941 (*Roosevelt Papers:* Secretary's File, Box 76); Hull: *Memoirs,* II, 1140 ff.

[46] Letter of Ambassador Daniels to the President, July 25, 1941; letter of Mr. Welles to the President, August 8, 1941, enclosing the draft of a reply.

account and each of the two Governments was to appoint a commissioner whose recommendation it was hoped would satisfy the companies. In addition the two Governments announced their decision to conclude a trade agreement. The United States engaged itself further to help stabilize the peso, to purchase Mexican silver in large amounts, and to furnish loans for highway construction and similar purposes.[47]

The oil controversy was not finally settled until April 18, 1942, after the involvement of the United States in the war, when the figure of $23,995,000 was established as compensation to the American companies. Nonetheless, the agreement of November 19, 1941, though partial and one-sided, was an important landmark. The Mexicans were naturally delighted with it, and hailed it as a great victory. On the other hand, President Roosevelt and his advisers had the satisfaction of knowing that the chief source of embitterment between the two countries had been eliminated. Mr. Hull, in announcing the agreement, spoke of it as "a new milestone of great importance in the cause of increasingly greater collaboration and solidarity between the countries of the New World." So it undoubtedly was, but even more significant was its effect on strictly American-Mexican relations. No major difference any longer divided the two neighbors and after the Japanese attack on Pearl Harbor the military arrangements so essential to their common defense were readily agreed upon.

5. PANAMA AND PROTECTION OF THE CANAL

Of all strategic areas of Latin America the Panama Canal was of the greatest importance to the security of the United States. Protection of the Canal, to ensure its free and continuous use by the Navy, was a responsibility of the War Department and a heavy one indeed. Ever since September, 1939, reinforcements had been sent to the troops stationed in the Canal Zone, and a chief objective of the Destroyer-Bases Deal of September, 1940, had been to provide additional protection to the Caribbean approaches to this vital area. But the Canal continued vulnerable to sabotage and even to surprise attack, especially from Japan, and its defense was therefore a matter of chronic anxiety to the War Department.[48] Due to the developments of modern warfare, the facilities located within the Canal Zone were no longer deemed sufficient. American military authorities were

[47] Stuart MS. study as cited above; Hull: *Memoirs,* II, 1140 ff.; Josephus Daniels: *Shirt Sleeve Diplomat* (Chapel Hill, 1947), 266 ff. We have used also a tel. from Daniels, November 4, 1941; a letter from President Avila Camacho to President Roosevelt, November 7, 1941, attached to a memo from Mr. Roosevelt to Mr. Hull and Mr. Welles, November 21, 1941 (*Roosevelt Papers:* Secretary's File, Box 76); a memo of conversation between Mr. Hull and the Mexican Ambassador, November 6, 1941; a memo of the Ambassador to Mr. Hull, November 7, 1941. See also Bemis: *The Latin American Policy of the United States,* 348 ff., and *Documents on American Foreign Policy,* IV, 357 ff., 421 ff.

[48] Watson: *Chief of Staff: Prewar Plans and Preparations,* 458 ff.

therefore insistent that arrangements be made with the Panamanian Government for additional base sites, on long term lease and with a large measure of American jurisdiction.[49]

Unfortunately President Arnulfo Arias of Panama, reputed at that time to have totalitarian if not pro-Nazi proclivities, gave evidence of having small sympathy with the needs of the United States in this connection, at least unless substantial concessions were made to Panama. From the very outset the discussions between the two Governments were beclouded by a basic difference of view. The State Department held that, under the Treaty of 1936, the Panamanian Government was obligated to grant the United States further military facilities for defense of the Canal, since the "international conflagration," the "threat of aggression," and the "unforeseen contingency" envisaged in that treaty had unquestionably come to pass. The Arias Administration, on the other hand, refused to acknowledge that the treaty entailed further concession of lands or base sites, and in any event insisted that further military arrangements should be tied in with the satisfaction of various financial and economic demands which had been under negotiation for some time. These dealt with such matters as ownership and control of the water supply, title to real estate properties in Colón and Panama City, the construction and maintenance of roads, the liquidation of loans and kindred matters. The State Department was quite prepared to recognize the validity of many of the claims put forward by Panama in the so-called Twelve Points, but was unwilling to link concessions on these issues to the question of further base rights. Month after month argument on these matters continued without either side indicating readiness to yield. To trace the highly complicated discussions in any detail would require a separate monograph and would in any event add little to a study of the broad lines of American policy. The present account must therefore be restricted to the merest outline of American relations with Panama, with particular emphasis on the defense problem.[50]

No progress whatever having been made in the negotiations of the autumn of 1940, the State Department, under pressure from the military authorities and with the approval of President Roosevelt, requested permission for American military personnel to enter the desired base areas and proposed that the terms of occupancy be left for later determination. In a note of February 18, 1941, which duly invoked Panama's obligations under the Treaty of 1936, that country was requested to make available the tracts of land needed for the protection of the Canal "at the earliest opportunity."[51]

---

[49] See above, Chapter VI, Section 1.

[50] For a detailed analysis of the whole question see the authoritative article by Almon R. Wright: "Defense Sites Negotiations between the United States and Panama, 1936-1948" (*Department of State Bulletin*, XXVII, August 11, 1952).

[51] Letter of General Van Voorhis (Commanding General, Panama Department) to General Marshall, January 3, 1941; despatch from Dawson (Panama City), January 3,

Although at first President Arias threatened to resign if American forces occupied the proposed sites without permission, he finally reconsidered. Grudgingly and under conditions which the State Department found eminently unsatisfactory and to which it had not even agreed, Arias on March 5 issued a manifesto authorizing "North American military authorities" to occupy the sites. Secretary Hull, in turn, contented himself with an expression of gratitude and hope that the details could be worked out to the mutual satisfaction of both Governments.[52] Unhappily this hope proved ill-founded. The Panama Government now pressed its Twelve Point program of concessions, which was discussed in Washington with Ambassador Carlos N. Brin during April and May. Early in June Foreign Minister Raúl de Roux himself visited Washington and on June 3 the Panamanian draft of an agreement was formally submitted. The State Department, in turn, brought forward its proposed text of a lease agreement on June 7. During the ensuing three weeks Under Secretary Welles and Foreign Minister de Roux held a series of conferences, going over individual items seriatim. But nothing much was gained through the long and often acrimonious verbal bouts in which the chief negotiators engaged. De Roux revealed or at least simulated extraordinary obtuseness with respect to interpretation of the Treaty of 1936. He insisted on satisfaction of Panama's requests as set forth in the Twelve Points as a necessary preliminary to the conclusion of the base agreement and advanced the most extravagant demands regarding such items as rentals.

Meanwhile Mr. Welles, though stoutly maintaining his stand on the obligations of the 1936 Treaty, submitted the Panamanian proposals to the War Department for approval. The reaction was generally unfavorable, for the demands were regarded as excessive and certain concessions as definitely undesirable and impracticable. The already difficult situation was in no sense improved by the publication (June 18) of a statement by President Arias, reading in part as follows:

I have blind faith, absolute conviction that . . . the United States will take into account the formal declaration of the [American] Ambassador . . . in Panama, delivered to me last February 10th, to the effect that subsequent upon the compliance by the Government of Panama with its treaty obligations in this respect, the Government of the United States will be glad to give friendly and careful consideration to the suggestions for assistance advanced by the Government of Panama.

I am still confident that . . . the President of the United States . . . will intervene

1941; *Stimson Diary (MS.)*, January 9, 1941, reporting the President's advice to Secretary Hull; memo of Mr. Welles to the President, February 17, 1941, prior to his meeting with Panamanian Ambassador Brin (*Roosevelt Papers:* Secretary's File, Box 74); tel. to Dawson, February 18, 1941.

[52] Note of the Panama Government, enclosed in a tel. from Dawson, February 21, 1941; tel. to Dawson, February 25, 1941, transmitting the American counterproposals. The texts of the statements of March 5 and 6, 1941, are printed in *Documents on American Foreign Relations*, III, 140 ff.

in the current negotiations, in time for them to continue, or that they be directed along such a course that the sacrifices to which the Government and people of Panama have consented shall not have been in vain.

This attempt to represent the State Department as obstructing the will of President Roosevelt proved too much even for Mr. Welles, a most devoted champion of Pan American coöperation. In a note to Mr. Roosevelt he excoriated the tactics of Foreign Minister de Roux and his Government and easily secured the President's permission to make clear to the Panamanian statesman that the views expressed by Mr. Welles represented those of the White House. The Acting Secretary lost no time in taking advantage of this authorization.[53]

The Panamanian Foreign Minister left Washington on June 24, saying that he had no doubt that an agreement would soon be reached and observing that his visit was the best proof of his Government's desire to arrive at an arrangement. Actually the discussions were to drag on for weeks and months, due not only to the recalcitrance of the Arias regime but also to the insistence of the War Department on keeping concessions to an absolute minimum.[54] No good purpose would be served by recounting in detail the further development of the situation. The Panamanian Government replied to the American draft on August 20, but revealed no disposition to retreat from its previous stand. State Department officials were much perplexed by the question of how to get on with the matter, but were unwilling to yield on certain basic points. A new American draft was finally despatched on September 30, to be submitted to Panama on October 8, 1941, but this, again, involved no substantial concessions as compared with the earlier proposals.[55]

At this point a new situation was created by the overthrow of the Arias Administration (October 9, 1941). It was perhaps inevitable that not only the German press, but also some American journals should have at once laid the downfall of the President to the manipulation of American authorities, supposedly convinced that it was impossible to do business with the Arias regime. As a matter of fact, however, there had long been much popular

[53] Tels. from Wilson (Panama City), June 19, 1941; letter of Mr. Welles to the President, June 19, 1941, with the latter's annotation of approval. We have used also the memos of conversation between Mr. Welles and Foreign Minister de Roux, of June 4, 9, 16 and 23, 1941.

[54] The American counterdraft of eight of the Twelve Points was submitted to the Panama Embassy on June 24, and a memo covering all items was despatched to Panama City on July 8, after the War Department had commented on them. Some of the differences between the War and State Departments, particularly with regard to real estate property in Colón, were brought out in a letter from Secretary Stimson to Mr. Welles, June 24, and in the latter's rather pointed reply of June 30, 1941.

[55] Despatches from Wilson, August 20 and 21, 1941; tel. to Wilson, October 8, 1941, transmitting the draft of September 30. We have used also a letter from Bonsal to Wilson, August 30, 1941, and the latter's reply, September 11, 1941. For a detailed analysis of the points at issue see the article by Almon R. Wright, as cited above.

discontent in Panama with the dictatorial methods and allegedly pro-Nazi sympathies of the President, and rumors of plots to despose him had been recurrent. In July, 1941, when Arias departed on a visit to Costa Rica, there was talk among his opponents of taking advantage of his absence. By the end of September the American Ambassador was reporting that the Republic was "rumor ridden," but that so long as the President controlled the police there was little likelihood that his opponents could succeed in driving him from power.[56]

However, when the apparently unsuspecting President on October 7 suddenly departed incognito by plane for Havana, without the required permission of the National Assembly or the Supreme Court, unrest developed to the point where the Cabinet felt it necessary to act, if only to forestall a popular uprising. Early on the morning of October 9 several of the Ministers, including Colonel Fabrega, the Chief of the National Police, called on Ambassador Wilson and explained the situation to him, stressing the popular discontent and the disgust of the Cabinet with Arias's attitude toward the negotiations with the United States. They then inquired as to the American position and the likelihood of early recognition of a new regime. To this Ambassador Wilson replied that he could give no assurances and that the policy of his Government, in accordance with the Good Neighbor Policy, was to refrain from interfering in the internal affairs of the other American Republics. He could not, he added, "deviate an iota from this policy no matter what apparent inducements of gain or advantage might be held out" for his Government.[57]

No evidence has turned up to support the charge that American representatives were privy to the action taken to replace Arias by a new chief executive, Ricardo Adolfo de la Guardia. Under the circumstances Secretary Hull was on safe ground when, on October 16, he issued a press release summarizing Ambassador Wilson's reports and adding: "I state clearly and categorically for the record, that the United States Government has had no connection, direct or indirect, with the recent Governmental changes in the Republic of Panama."[58]

Although the new Panamanian Administration was more favorably disposed toward the United States proposals than its predecessor, agreement on the required base rights was still outstanding at the time of the Japanese attack. The new regime was exceedingly anxious to secure the concessions involved in the Twelve Points but, as Foreign Minister Fabrega explained to Ambassador Wilson, could not for political reasons retreat from the posi-

[56] Report of the Military Intelligence Division of the War Department, March 31, 1941; tels. from Wilson, July 16 and September 25, 1941.

[57] Tels. from Wilson, October 7, 9, 1941. Army and Navy cables of these same dates reported substantially in the same terms.

[58] See *Documents on American Foreign Relations*, IV, 429-30. We have used also the *Stimson Diary (MS.)*, October 9, and the *Berle Diary (MS.)*, October 10, 1941.

tion of the Arias Government, that the lease of bases must go hand in hand with agreement on the concessions. Since action on the Twelve Points would involve approval of the United States Congress, delays seemed inevitable. The State Department therefore gave some consideration, in the days after Pearl Harbor, to the possibility of action on three of the most important concessions by executive order under the President's emergency powers.[59] Eventually this course was abandoned as inadvisable, but the negotiations were pressed with all possible vigor and provision made for prompt Congressional action. The agreements were finally signed on May 18, 1942, though ratification by Panama occasioned further delay (until May 11, 1943) in their execution.[60]

The story of the negotiations between Washington and Panama in 1941 was certainly among the least edifying in the history of the Good Neighbor Policy. The dispute might well have produced dire consequences, had not United States forces occupied the most essential base sites in April, 1941, pending agreement on concessions and details. While militarily prudent and necessary, this step certainly had the effect of depriving the negotiations of the urgency they would otherwise have had. The result was that the Arias Government attempted to exploit American defense requirements to wring extensive, in some instances utterly extravagant, favors from the State Department. For its own part, the latter agency was prepared to pay even an unreasonable price to secure what was needed while still preserving good will and cordial relations. But American military authorities consistently took the stand that the request for base sites was altogether legitimate under the terms of the 1936 Treaty and that there was no excuse for giving up various rights which were still of value to the United States. All the disheartening difficulties in the way of agreement were certainly not occasioned by the Arias regime, but it nevertheless remains true that the effort to provide adequate protection for the vital Panama Canal produced a sad commentary on the limitations of Pan American solidarity when the need arose to translate high-sounding words into concrete measures of action.

6. ECUADOR AND PERU: THE THREAT OF WAR

The boundary dispute between Ecuador and Peru was of long standing and constituted one of the chronic threats to peace in South America. When it flared up anew in the spring of 1941 there was real danger that it might lead to hostilities, thereby damaging the vaunted solidarity of the hemisphere and obstructing the conclusion of mutual defense arrangements. Although

---

[59] Tel. from Wilson, October 29, 1941; personal letter of Wilson to Mr. Welles, December 4, 1941; memo of the Division of American Republics Affairs, December 12, 1941; memos of the Office of the Legal Adviser, December 18 and 24, 1941; tel. from Wilson, December 24, 1941; tel. to Wilson, December 29, 1941; memo by Bonsal, December 29, 1941.

[60] *Executive Agreement Series No. 359: Lease of Defense Sites* (Washington, 1944).

the Ecuadorian Government was perfectly willing to accord the United States naval base rights on its coasts and on the strategically important Galapagos Islands, Washington felt impelled to reject all overtures, lest such arrangements provide substance to Peruvian charges, sure to be echoed elsewhere, of American favoritism or pressure.[61]

When the boundary dispute became acute in May, 1941, the United States, Brazilian and Argentine Governments, acting as mediators, appealed to both sides, reminding them of their obligations under the agreements of Lima and Havana. High and noble sentiments were uttered by all parties, but to no avail.[62] Finally, in July, the long anticipated and much dreaded border hostilities broke out, Quito and Lima each accusing the other of having fired the first shot. Once again the mediating powers made representations, this time proposing that both parties withdraw their troops fifteen kilometers from the so-called *status quo* line, pending an agreement on the boundary. Ecuador accepted the proposal, but Peru did so only with reservations. Before the difficulties could be ironed out further fighting took place on July 23, making necessary renewed pleas for continental unity, solidarity and peace. The disputants eventually agreed to a cessation of hostilities, which President Roosevelt hailed as "a notable triumph for those principles of peace and continental solidarity to which all of the American Republics adhere."[63]

During the July crisis the United States Government was determined to observe the strictest neutrality. Among other things it declined to engage in discussions of Lend-Lease aid with either party pending a settlement of the controversy, and even went so far as to requisition a number of planes destined for Peru so as to make doubly sure that these planes were not used to attack Ecuador.[64]

Despite the agreement to suspend hostilities, skirmishes along the frontiers continued to occur during August and September. The Quito Government begged for action by the mediating powers and Secretary Hull felt obliged to speak firmly to the former Peruvian Foreign Minister, who happened to be visiting Washington. Pointing out the parlous state of the world situation,

[61] Tels. to Lima and Quito, May 8 and 20, 1941; tel. from Quito, May 9 and from Lima, May 13, 1941; memo of conversation between Mr. Welles and the Peruvian Ambassador, May 29, 1941.

[62] The tripartite mediation was undertaken at the suggestion of the Argentine Government. For details see *Department of State Bulletin*, May 17, 1941, and *Documents on American Foreign Relations*, III, 156 ff. We have used also memos of conversation between Mr. Welles and the Argentine Ambassador, May 14 and 15, 1941.

[63] The key documents are printed in *Documents on American Foreign Relations*, III, 156 ff.; IV, 431 ff. We have used also a tel. from Drew (Quito), July 6; a memo from Bonsal to Welles, July 7, reporting a telephone conversation with Norweb (Lima); tels. to Quito and Lima, July 8; tel. from Norweb, July 9; tels. from Caffery (Rio de Janeiro), July 7, 12, 28, 1941.

[64] Memo from Duggan to Welles, August 12, 1941; *Stimson Diary (MS.)*, October 16, 1941.

Mr. Hull observed that, without reference to the merits of the boundary dispute, he knew that it should not exist "in this period of crisis when the fate of civilization is hanging by a thread." The two countries, he continued, simply could not afford the risk of starting a conflagration in the heart of South America at a time when the flames of war from east and west were already so clearly discernible.[65] Yet these appeals seem to have had less effect than a proposal of the Mexican Government (September 18) that all American Republics join in a collective effort to prevent further conflict. The Peruvian Government, understandably intent on avoiding appearance before the bar of Pan American opinion, joined Ecuador in agreeing to the establishment of a neutral zone and discussion of a definitive settlement (October 2). Even so, it was not until after the Pearl Harbor attack that the two disputants signed a protocol of peace and friendship (January 29, 1942).

Meanwhile the growing fear in Washington of Axis raiders appearing in the Pacific made it imperative to secure port facilities for American Navy patrol ships. Consequently appropriate requests were forwarded to both the Ecuadorian and Peruvian Governments, as well as to the Chilean, on September 12, 1941. Peru actually acceded to this request before Ecuador did, and Chile too showed itself coöperative.[66] In December, after the outbreak of war between the United States and Japan, Washington embarked upon Lend-Lease negotiations with both Ecuador and Peru. These were followed by the conclusion of comprehensive understandings for coöperative action in hemisphere defense with Ecuador (February 2, 1942), and with Peru (July 9, 1942). Thus, by impartiality and patience, the United States Government had steered its course through the threatening South American boundary dispute and had paved the way for the conclusion of the requisite defense arrangements.

7. SOUTHERN LATIN AMERICA AND THE ARGENTINE POSITION

The countries along the River Plate, together with Chile, were geographically most remote from the United States, least directly threatened by attack either from Europe or the Far East, and of course least susceptible of American military support in the event of a crisis. Of all these Republics, Uruguay had long been and continued to be the closest friend of the United States and the warmest champion of Pan American solidarity, if only because of the fact that the traditional policy of the Argentine was to assert preëminence in the River Plate area. It will be recalled that Uruguay

[65] Memos of conversation between Mr. Hull and the Ecuadorian Ambassador, August 9 and September 18, 1941; memos of conversation between Mr. Hull and the former Peruvian Foreign Minister, Dr. Carlos Concha, August 14 and September 22, 1941.

[66] Tels. to Ecuador, Peru and Chile, September 12, 1941; tels. from Norweb (Lima), September 14 and 15, 1941; tels. from Long (Quito), October 21 and 26, 1941; tels. from Bowers (Santiago), September 17, 26, October 2; tel. to Bowers, October 17; letter from Bowers to Welles, October 27, and the latter's reply, November 17, 1941.

had, in 1940, readily accepted the United States proposals for staff conversations and had shown readiness to provide the base facilities desired by American naval authorities. Nothing concrete had come of the initial plans, partly because Washington was not in a position to supply the needed armaments, but even more because of the persisting Argentine contention that defense of the River Plate region was primarily its responsibility. Nevertheless, the Montevideo Government continued to raise the issue and eventually, in August, 1941, the United States decided to explore the possibility of constructing a seaplane base at Laguna Negra, in the area adjacent to Brazil and therefore well removed from the sphere of immediate Argentine interest.[67] For the rest, the United States continued to do what it could to help Uruguay through Lend-Lease and kindred arrangements. When, in the days just prior to Pearl Harbor, Montevideo expressed fears of possible Japanese forays into the South Atlantic, arrangements were made to send an American warship to demonstrate the United States' seriousness of purpose in matters of defense.[68]

Relations between the United States and Chile, on the other hand, continued uncertain. Chile suffered severely from the outbreak of war in Europe and remained in grave economic straits. The position of the Government was precarious, exposed as it was to strong pressure from both Nazi and Communist elements. There was much popular criticism of the United States and of the Pan American system for their failure to provide relief and there was much disgruntlement over the fact that Chile was not invited to share with the Argentine, Brazil and the United States in the effort to mediate between Ecuador and Peru. Still, the appointment of a new Foreign Minister, Señor Rossetti, in June, 1941, brought a change for the better. Rossetti was from the outset profuse in declarations of devotion to the United States and to the principles of Pan American coöperation. He declared himself for common action in hemisphere defense and in October, 1941, made no difficulty about affording the United States Navy port facilities for its patrol ships.[69]

In part the more coöperative attitude of the Chileans may have stemmed from their desire to enlist American support for their project to fortify the Straits of Magellan, which lay almost entirely within Chilean territory. Under the terms of the Argentine-Chilean Treaty of 1881 the Straits were to be neutralized forever and were to remain open to the free navigation of all nations; no fortifications or military defenses that might interfere with the freedom of navigation were to be constructed. In 1941, however, there was some danger that in the event of war between the United States and Japan

[67] Minutes of the Liaison Committee, August 18, 1941; despatch from Montevideo, September 24, 1941.
[68] Tel. from Dawson (Montevideo), November 17, 1941; minutes of the Liaison Committee, November 24, 1941.
[69] Minutes of the Liaison Committee, October 29, 1941.

the Panama Canal might be obstructed and that Japanese raiders would attack shipping through the Straits of Magellan. The United States Government, which in 1879 had declared unequivocally against action by any Government that might jeopardize freedom of commerce through the Straits, now recognized the desirability of assuring Chilean military and naval control of the area in the event of hostilities, and was ready to approve fortification of the Straits for the duration of the war.

The crucial question was whether Argentina too would accept a protocol to the 1881 treaty permitting temporary measures of defense. Negotiations were carried on by Chile to this end during November, 1941, and Argentine assent, at least in principle, was secured early in December. On receipt of this news, Washington promptly expressed gratification, which, however, proved premature. The further details of the transaction are obscure, but eventually the whole matter was dropped, possibly because Buenos Aires attached unacceptable conditions to its approval. After some deliberation the United States Government, which was not fully informed of the negotiations, decided against raising the issue at the meeting of American Foreign Ministers at Rio de Janeiro in January, 1942.[70]

So long as agreement on fortification of the Straits still seemed likely, the Chilean Government took care to impress Washington with "the transcendental importance of this step which Chile has given in behalf of continental defense."[71] If indeed it had such significance, this may explain why the Argentine Government eventually withdrew from it. There was, at the time, considerable talk in Argentine conservative and military circles, and particularly in the pro-Nazi press, of the desirability of reviving the old ABC bloc (Argentina, Brazil, Chile), perhaps with the addition of Peru and Colombia and with the avowed objective of combating "unnatural Pan Americanism" and defeating the "rapacious designs" of the United States. How seriously such talk was to be taken it is impossible to say. It does seem likely, however, that some pressure was brought on Chile to align itself wholly with the Argentine.

The mere fact that Argentine authorities, and particularly Dr. Enrique Ruiz Guinazu, could be suspected of machinations so contrary to the spirit of Pan Americanism indicates how uncertain the position of Argentina continued to be down to the very eve of the Pearl Harbor attack. Reference to the traditional Argentine policy may be omitted here, since it has been adequately considered in earlier contexts. It should be noted, however, that the

[70] Tels. from Bowers, November 13, 21, December 2, 8, 1941; tels. from Armour (Buenos Aires), December 5, 15, 26, 27, 1941; tel. to Bowers and Armour, December 16, 1941; chits by Messrs. Baldwin and Bonsal attached to a tel. to the American delegation at Rio, January 17, 1942, which was not sent; memo of Baldwin to Bonsal and Welles, January 29, 1942.

[71] Memo of the Chilean Embassy, December 5, 1941, handed to Mr. Welles on December 6, 1941.

situation in 1941 was much influenced by domestic factors. The President, Señor Ortiz, was incapacitated by failing eyesight, while the Acting President, Señor Castillo, supported by the conservative elements, notably the Senate and the Army, kept the country's policy in strictly nationalist channels. Dr. Ruiz Guinazu, the Foreign Minister, was variously characterized as a muddled thinker and an unimaginative, vacillating statesman.[72] He was certainly a man difficult to deal with and quite unaccountable. In short, there was no reason whatever to expect much coöperation in hemisphere defense from the existing Argentine regime. Liberal and Radical elements, and indeed public opinion generally, appear to have been highly critical of the Government's stand, but the dispute which developed during 1941 over official manipulation of elections led the opposition to adopt a policy of parliamentary obstruction which in turn contributed to the difficulties in the way of even limited collaboration.

Washington was only too well aware of the various facets of the Argentine situation and had long since decided to pursue a patient and conciliatory line. It was discouraging to observe, during the spring of 1941, that the Argentine Congress, though for strictly domestic reasons, refused to pass legislation approving the Export-Import Bank credit of $60,000,000 and the United States Treasury stabilization loan of $50,000,000. Furthermore, it was only in late April that the Senate passed the bill for the appropriation of 650,000,000 pesos ($155,000,000) for the purchase of military equipment, on which the Chamber of Deputies had acted favorably in June, 1940.[73] That is to say, the Argentine Government had thus far not only refused to engage in staff conversations in the interest of continental defense, but had only recently secured approval for the purchase of army equipment essential to its own defense. Meanwhile Buenos Aires continued to oppose the grant of base facilities by Uruguay to the United States and to press for a solution of the hemisphere defense problem through regional arrangements, as, for example, for the River Plate area. Argentine authorities were quite prepared to have the United States finance such arrangements, but it was their aim to reserve for themselves the dominant role in their own vicinity. Naturally the Uruguayan Foreign Minister distrusted and resented this attitude, though the American Ambassador in Buenos Aires thought it might not be objectionable if it were understood that regional arrangements were to complement a broader and more general program of continental defense.[74]

---

[72] Mr. Welles has described him as a "calamitous figure" (Welles: *The Time for Decision,* New York, 1944, 220, 225).

[73] Despatches from Armour, April 2 and 23, May 9, 1941, and from Chargé d'Affaires Tuck, June 17, 1941.

[74] Despatches from Armour, January 15 and June 13, 1941; despatch from Wilson (Montevideo), February 20, 1941, and tel. from Chapin (Montevideo), June 7, 1941; memo from Bonsal to Welles, June 30, 1941.

The astounding victories of the Nazis in the Balkans and North Africa in April and May, 1941, followed by President Roosevelt's proclamation of a national emergency (May 27), brought some indication of a change for the better. The Argentine public, like the rest of the free world, was frightened and became more insistent than ever that its Government take a clear stand with the other American Republics in the interest of common defense measures. On May 13 the Government did, in fact, issue a decree barring from Argentine ports and waters the submarines of belligerent nations.[75] Furthermore, it took the initiative in proposing tripartite mediation (with the United States and Brazil) in the Ecuadorian-Peruvian boundary dispute and somewhat later responded in not altogether uncoöperative fashion to the Uruguayan proposal for further implementation of the agreements of Lima, Panama and Havana. Indeed, Dr. Ruiz Guinazu, the Foreign Minister, set out for Washington to renew negotiations for a trade agreement, the lack of which had been a major obstacle to close American-Argentine relations for almost a century. In the course of his conversations with the Foreign Minister, Mr. Welles made the most of the collaboration between Vichy and Berlin to stress the growing danger to the New World and urge the need for Argentine support of hemisphere defense plans.[76]

Another opportunity to impress the Argentines was afforded by the visit to Washington of Admiral Guisasola, the Argentine Chief of Naval Operations, who had been invited by Admiral Stark to tour American defense industries and convince himself of the progress being made in preparation for all eventualities. The Admiral was agreeably surprised by what he saw and professed himself disturbed by his own country's failure to coöperate with the United States in the military and naval fields. The Argentine Navy, he averred, favored such coöperation and the time had clearly arrived for reopening the whole question of Argentina's role in hemisphere defense.[77]

In view of these signs of greater cordiality, Washington decided that General Marshall should accept the Argentine invitation to attend the celebration of the one hundred and fiftieth anniversary of the country's independence, despite the fact that the invitation was accompanied by a statement that the visit was to be purely of a courtesy character.[78] More important still was the beginning of systematic examination of Argentine needs for military equipment and other goods. Like all American Republics, Argentina was eligible for Lend-Lease aid. The War and Navy Departments

[75] Tel. from Armour, May 13, 1941.

[76] Memos of conversation between Mr. Welles and Dr. Ruiz Guinazu, May 14 and 15, 1941. For the initiation of trade negotiations see *Documents on American Foreign Relations*, III, 459, and Hull: *Memoirs*, II, 1140.

[77] Memo of conversation between Mr. Welles and Admiral José Guisasola, May 30, 1941. See further *Documents on American Foreign Relations*, III, 144 ff.

[78] Tel. to Armour, June 11, 1941; tel. from Armour, June 12, 1941. Actually the international tension made it impossible for General Marshall to attend. He was represented by General Frank M. Andrews.

had in fact agreed that a total of $66,000,000 should be assigned for Argentine military and naval requirements, and the original draft of a Lend-Lease agreement provided that of this sum only $36,000,000 should be repaid, $6,000,000 annually for a period of six years. In the course of June, 1941, the Argentine Government submitted its first lists of requirements, though it declined Lend-Lease aid on the grounds that the appropriations voted by its own Congress were more than enough to permit cash purchase. Following the advice of Ambassador Armour, the State Department had adopted the line that, once the Argentine lists had been presented, Argentine officers should come to Washington to explain how the materials, most of which could ill be spared, were to be used and what military plans had been made by the Argentine within the general framework of continental defense. In keeping with this policy it was therefore suggested, at the end of July, that an Argentine military delegation be sent to Washington to discuss requirements and initiate the staff conversations basic to the requirements.

This proposal at once raised a storm of objection. The Argentine Ambassador protested against this apparent linkage of requirements with staff conversations and refused to transmit the American note to his Government. The State Department had no recourse but to deny all intention of making the supply of military equipment dependent on the resumption of staff conversations and to express readiness to conduct the latter in Buenos Aires.[79] This assurance and the cogent explanations of Ambassador Armour appear to have satisfied Dr. Ruiz Guinazu and his War and Navy Department colleagues, for on August 19 he informed the Ambassador of Argentina's decision to despatch a mission to the United States to discuss requirements and also to initiate staff conversations. At about the same time the State Department accepted the Argentine terms for a Lend-Lease agreement; this was to be on a cash basis and, contrary to all previous practice, was to omit all obligation on the part of Argentina to supply the United States with such defense materials as it might have available.[80]

Lest it be thought that the major obstacles to coöperation in the field of

[79] Letter from Armour, May 21, 1941, with attached chit from Mr. Welles informing the War and Navy Departments of the course he proposed to follow; memo of conversation between Messrs. Wilson, Curtis and American military authorities with Ambassador Espil and Air Attaché Palladino, June 24, 1941; letter of General Marshall to Mr. Welles, July 2, 1941, reporting the War Department attitude toward the Argentine requirements as discussed by the Liaison Committee on July 1, 1941; tels. to Armour, July 25 and August 5, 6, 1941; memo of conversation between Mr. Duggan and the Argentine Ambassador, July 31, 1941; State Department memo by Mr. Collado, November 28, 1941, reviewing the course of negotiations with the American Republics on Lend-Lease; memo by Mr. Wilson, December 23, 1941, reviewing the subject of staff conversations with Argentina.

[80] Tels. from Armour, August 18 and 19, 1941, reporting his conversations with the Foreign Minister; memo of Mr. Collado to Mr. Duggan, August 18, 1941, on the draft of the Lend-Lease agreement; memo of Mr. Collado, November 28, 1941, reviewing the Lend-Lease negotiations.

hemisphere defense had now been surmounted, it must be pointed out at once that weeks and months were to pass before the Argentine delegation actually reached Washington. In fact it did not arrive until after the outbreak of war. Ambassador Armour was at first highly optimistic about the future of Argentine-American relations. It seemed that the military mission would depart at an early date and that the recent discovery of the Nazi organization and activity in the Argentine would induce the Government to draw closer to the other Republics in countering what was clearly a common danger. But before long the Foreign Minister was inquiring for data on the proposed agenda of the staff conversations, as a result of which the State Department was obliged to take time for consultation with the War and Navy Departments. The American proposals appear to have revived Argentine fears of commitment. The military delegation did not depart on October 3, as expected. Indeed, it was only at the end of October that the Argentine Cabinet finally decided on its composition and instructions. November too was to wear away before Ambassador Armour was informed that the mission would leave on November 27.[81]

Meanwhile, as the shooting war developed in the Atlantic, Washington redoubled its efforts to ensure Argentine good will in the event of major hostilities. On October 14, 1941, the trade negotiations, which had so often collapsed, were finally brought to a close by a distinctly one-sided agreement. The United States undertook to reduce import duties on 69 percent of its trade with the Argentine (including canned beef, hides, etc., but excluding the important item of fresh meat). Furthermore, it promised not to raise the tariff on most of the remaining items. The Argentine, by contrast, reduced its duties on only 18 percent of its imports from the United States and engaged itself not to increase the existing tariff on only 12 percent of the remaining items.[82]

There was every reason to hope that this settlement of trade relations, so advantageous to Argentina, would contribute to the establishment of closer and more coöperative relations. In addition to the mission of the military delegation, the Buenos Aires Government early in December despatched to Washington Dr. Irigoyen, a financial expert particularly close to Acting President Castillo. The Argentine Government now expressed its readiness to accept Lend-Lease aid on the terms originally proposed by the United States, and took firmly in hand various questions of a financial nature. At the same time Acting President Castillo assured Ambassador Armour of the

[81] Letter of Armour to Welles, September 5, 1941; tel. from Armour, September 13, 1941; memo by Mr. Wilson, September 18, 1941; reporting his conference with representatives of the War and Navy Departments; Navy Department memo, September 19, 1941, with draft of agenda; tel. to Armour, September 26, 1941, transmitting the suggested agenda; memo of Mr. Ravndal to Mr. Welles, October 4, 1941, reporting a telephone conversation with Mr. Armour; tels. from Armour, October 19, 24, 29, November 5, 14, 27, 1941; despatch from Armour, November 28, 1941.

[82] For details see Bemis: *The Latin American Policy of the United States*, 305-6.

Argentine Government's determination to comply fully with its continental commitments and stated categorically that the United States could count on Argentina's full support.[83]

Viewed individually, the issues in American relations with the Latin American Republics during 1941 are apt to appear magnified. The discussions were often difficult and discouraging and there were frequent occasions when loss of patience might have seemed justified. Yet the attitude of forbearance and conciliation prescribed by the Good Neighbor Policy was steadfastly adhered to. Official Washington was at one in the conviction that in a major crisis friendship, good will and voluntary coöperation would count for more than any advantages secured by pressure or threat. True, little progress was made in obtaining base rights in the Latin American Republics. Even with respect to the crucial defense of northeastern Brazil the United States was unable to get beyond the stage of planning in common. But it was generally understood in Washington that the reluctance of Latin American Governments to make military concessions arose not from opposition or even disapproval of United States policy, but rather from considerations of national pride. In the large, there was throughout Latin America greater trust in the United States in December, 1941, than there had been at any time in the past.[84] Following the Japanese attack on Pearl Harbor, the Republics of Central America and the Caribbean at once declared war, first on Japan and then on Germany and Italy. Colombia, Mexico and Venezuela severed diplomatic relations with those countries, while the remaining Republics proclaimed solidarity and nonbelligerency. Most of them took some form of action in support of the United States; none of them declared neutrality as against the United States. In other words, during the most critical period of the conflict Washington was relieved of serious concern over the attitude of its neighbors. This was sufficient vindication of the Good Neighbor Policy and, in a world of human frailty, was perhaps as much as could have been expected from a community of twenty independent countries.

[83] Tel. to Armour, December 2, 1941; tels. from Armour, December 2 and 5, 1941; memo by Mr. Welles of his first meeting with Dr. Irigoyen.

[84] Memo of the Division of American Republics Affairs, entitled "The Tangible Results of United States policy of Non-Intervention in the other American Republics," November 10, 1941.

CHAPTER XX

Japan's Fateful Gamble

1. TOKYO'S CRUCIAL DECISION

The Nazi attack on Soviet Russia precipitated a shift in Far Eastern affairs more immediate and initially more significant than the shift in the course of the European War. In the west Hitler's assault seemed to provide nothing more than a temporary breather. In the east, on the other hand, it gave the final impetus to the Japanese advance which was, in a matter of months, to result in hostilities with the United States and the other democracies.

When the news of Hitler's betrayal of his pact with Stalin reached Tokyo, the Japanese Government had already been rent by differences over basic policy decisions. One faction, apparently led by Prime Minister Prince Konoye, favored negotiations with the United States in the hope of attaining at least some of Japan's objectives without war. The other, headed by Foreign Minister Yosuke Matsuoka and evidently supported by the Army, advocated complete collaboration with the Axis powers against Britain; in other words, operations toward the south, even at the risk of armed conflict with the United States. Thus far the party of compromise had been able to maintain itself: "informal and exploratory" conversations had been carried on with Washington since April, though in truth they had made no significant progress because of the opposition of Matsuoka and his adherents to any retreat from the Japanese position on the Tripartite Pact and the settlement of the China Incident. By June, 1941, there was every likelihood that Matsuoka and the Army would have their way. The decision to expand and strengthen the Japanese position in French Indo-China, as a prelude to eventual advances against Malaya or the Netherlands East Indies, had been adopted. In mid-June approaches had been made to Berlin for support in extracting new concessions from the Vichy Government.[1]

[1] See above, Chapter XV, Section 2. The first Japanese approach was made on June

625

It was at this point that Japanese officialdom, like the public, was stunned by the news of the Nazi offensive against Soviet Russia. True, there was no good reason why the Foreign Office and the General Staff should have been surprised. During Matsuoka's visit to Berlin in April, 1941, Ribbentrop had made it quite clear that a conflict between Germany and Soviet Russia should not be ruled out of Japanese calculations. Furthermore, the Japanese Ambassador in Berlin, General Oshima, had reported on June 6 that, after a conversation with Hitler, he was convinced that a Nazi assault on the Soviet Union was in the offing. Ten days later the Japanese Military Attaché in Berlin had reported that war was imminent, though the exact timing was not yet known. These items of intelligence had been carefully weighed in Tokyo, but Matsuoka, General Tojo and indeed the whole Liaison Conference discounted them. The Ambassador in Moscow was of the opinion that war was unlikely, despite the obvious tension. Like the officials of many other Governments, the Japanese concluded that the German threat to the east was designed to camouflage a coming assault on Britain and that, even if genuine, the Nazi-Soviet crisis would be resolved by Stalin's acceptance of new and stiffer German demands. When events disproved these estimates, Tokyo was dismayed and shaken. For the second time Hitler had presented his Far Eastern partner with a *fait accompli*. Ambassador Grew and other observers considered the Nazi move such an affront to the Japanese that Matsuoka's resignation seemed inevitable. According to later testimony, Prince Konoye did in fact regard Hitler's action as a betrayal of Japanese confidence and therefore favored withdrawal from the Tripartite Pact.[2]

In the new policy discussions which now ensued the Prime Minister took the stand that Japan had joined the Tripartite Pact on the assumption that Soviet Russia would presently be brought into the Axis combination, thus creating a strong united front against Britain and its allies and friends. By his new aggression Hitler had destroyed the basis of the alliance and had left Japan to face a probable coalition of Britain, Soviet Russia and the United States. But Konoye's arguments carried little weight either with Matsuoka or the military chiefs. Apart from the fact that there were no adequate grounds for surprise at Hitler's move, Matsuoka felt deeply committed to

10, 1941 (German Foreign Office memo, in *Tokyo War Crimes Documents,* Exhibit 586). See also the tels. between Tokyo and Berlin of June 16 and 21, 1941, in *Pearl Harbor Attack,* XIV, 1397-98.

[2] "Kido Diary" (*Tokyo War Crimes Documents,* Nos. 1632W-51 and 1632W-54); "Tojo Memorandum" (*ibid.,* Proceedings, 36254 ff.). It is interesting to note that on June 15 the newspaper *Nichi Nichi* quoted General Yamashita, Chief of the Japanese Military Mission in Berlin, as saying that something great would happen soon (Tolischus, in *The New York Times,* June 16, 1941), and that on June 20, 1941, Ambassador Biddle reported that the British had learned from Tokyo that ten days previously Ribbentrop had told Oshima of the coming attack and had suggested a Japanese assault on Siberia (letter of Biddle to Hull, June 20, 1941). On Grew's reaction we have used tels. from Grew, June 25 and July 27, 1941, and the *Grew Diary (MS.),* summary for June, 1941.

the Germans and was much impressed by the new vistas opened for Japan by the Nazi-Soviet conflict. Early in May, 1941, he had assured the German Ambassador, probably on his own responsibility, that "no Japanese Premier or Foreign Minister would ever be able to keep Japan neutral in the event of a German-Russian conflict. In this case, Japan would be driven, by the force of necessity, to attack Russia at Germany's side. No neutrality pact could change this." In consonance with this conviction, the Foreign Minister now blandly told the Soviet Ambassador that if the Tripartite Pact and Japan's Neutrality Agreement with the Soviet Union should prove at variance with each other, the latter would have to be dropped. Matsuoka, though the father of the Japanese-Soviet Neutrality Pact of April, 1941, had no compunctions about scrapping that agreement if it seemed in Japan's interest to do so. Nothing seemed to him more obvious than that the situation, after June 22, called for such action: the Nazi attack on Japan's traditional enemy clearly presented a golden opportunity to launch an assault on Soviet Siberia to eliminate once and for all the threat of Communist power and realize Nippon's long-cherished objectives in continental East Asia.[3]

By-passing the Prime Minister, Matsuoka hurried to the Imperial Palace to expound his grand design, but only to meet with a cool and skeptical reception. The Emperor questioned whether the Army chiefs would consider their forces adequate for operations in the north as well as in the south and implied that the plans already agreed upon should be adhered to. The military men soon proved the Emperor right. General Tojo opined that an attack on Soviet Siberia should be carefully weighed, and for good reasons. The Japanese Kwantung Army had suffered severe reverses at the hands of the Soviet forces in 1938 and 1939 and was currently inferior to the autonomous Soviet Far Eastern Army in numbers, planes and tanks. In the event of war the Japanese could hardly hope for success in ground operations, while it was almost certain that the Soviets would raise havoc with their submarine fleet, concentrated at Vladivostok, and might even subject Tokyo to heavy air attack. In addition it could be argued that the Germans would soon defeat the Soviet forces singlehanded or at least oblige the Kremlin to withdraw a large part of its forces from East Asia to Europe, thus creating a more favorable opportunity for Japanese operations. Meanwhile there was no prospect of Japan's securing in the north the oil and raw materials it so sorely needed. These could be obtained only in the south, for which reason it seemed most inadvisable to abandon the program already in process of execution.

[3] Tel. from Ott to Berlin, May 6, 1941 (*Tokyo War Crimes Documents*, Exhibit 1068); "Kido Diary" (*ibid.*, Document No. 1632W-55); Kido deposition (*ibid.*, Defense Document No. 2502); Konoye memorandum (*ibid.*, Defense Document No. 1580); diary of K. A. Smetanin, the Soviet Ambassador, June 25, 1941 (*ibid.*, Document No. 1886). See also the "Konoye Memoirs" in *Pearl Harbor Attack*, XX, 3993 ff.

The issue of how best to exploit the situation created by Hitler's new aggression led to Matsuoka's loss of Army support and left him almost alone on one side of the argument. Nevertheless, he could fall back on a lengthy series of cables from Berlin and could plead the danger of jeopardizing the whole Japanese position as established by the Tripartite Pact. Ribbentrop, aided and abetted by Oshima, did his utmost to convince the Japanese that the backbone of Soviet resistance was already broken and the collapse of Communist power imminent. If only Japan would intervene at once, he reasoned, the Soviet defeat could be clinched and the Communist menace disposed of:

The approaching collapse of the military power of Russia and the probable fall of the Bolshevist regime itself offers to Japan the unique opportunity to free herself from the Russian threat and to give the Japanese Empire security in the north, which is a necessary prerequisite to her expansion in the south in accordance with her vital needs. It seems to me, therefore, the requirement of the hour that the Japanese Army should, as quickly as possible, get possession of Vladivostok and push as far as possible towards the west. The aim of such an operation should be that, before the coming of cold weather, the Japanese Army advancing westward should be able to shake hands at the half-way mark with the German troops advancing to the east, that both by way of the Trans-Siberian Railroad and by air uninterrupted communication should be established between Germany and Japan by way of Russian territory, and that finally the whole Russian question should be solved by Germany and Japan in a way which would eliminate the Russian threat to both Germany and Japan for all time.

This once accomplished, added Ribbentrop, Germany's victory over Britain would soon become "an irrevocable fact," while Japan would have less difficulty in settling the China Incident and would secure a perfectly free hand for expansion to the south. For, he argued, the speedy liquidation of Soviet Russia would "probably be the best way to convince the United States of the absolute futility of entering into the war on the side of England, then completely isolated and facing the most powerful alliance of the earth."[4]

Alluring though the prospect, the Japanese military leaders, like the majority of the Cabinet, remained unmoved, even after the Liaison Conference had met six times in five days to canvass the arguments pro and con.[5] In the end the question reduced itself to considerations of capability and priority. Effective military control of all Indo-China was regarded as essen-

[4] Tel. from Ribbentrop to Ott, June 28, 1941 (*Tokyo War Crimes Documents*, No. 4081C); Ribbentrop's personal message to Matsuoka, July 1, 1941 (*Department of State Bulletin*, June 16, 1946, pp. 1040 ff.).

[5] The Liaison Conference, though it had no constitutional position, was of crucial importance. It consisted on the one side of five Cabinet officers (the Prime Minister, the Foreign Minister, the Ministers of War and Navy, and the President of the Cabinet Planning Board), and on the other of the Chiefs of Staff of the Army and Navy, usually with their Assistant Chiefs. No proposal was submitted to the Privy Council before it had been unanimously adopted by the Liaison Conference, whose recommendation, as representing the decision of both civilian and military authorities, was invariably accepted.

tial and urgent. For the rest it was confidently expected that the Germans would soon put an end to the Soviet regime, after which it was thought Britain and the United States would be less disposed to resist the Japanese advance to the south. Meanwhile, in order to be ready to take full advantage of the eventual collapse of Soviet Russia, it was decided to hasten the reinforcement of Japanese troops in Manchuria in the hope that, if the Kremlin were obliged to withdraw part of its Far Eastern Army, Japan would soon attain military superiority over the Soviet forces. Reflecting Japanese military opinion, the German Ambassador reported to Berlin on June 28, 1941, that Tokyo's preparations for an assault on the Soviet Far East could not be completed in less than six weeks unless the Kremlin within the near future reduced the strength of its Far Eastern forces. The majority of the Cabinet, he added, felt that nothing should be done to weaken the Japanese military position in China and was convinced that the wisest course was to proceed with the occupation of Indo-China. Even the extreme nationalist elements supported the policy of prudence toward Soviet Russia and favored energetic prosecution of the advance to the south.[6]

The program arrived at by the Liaison Conference on June 30 was approved by the Privy Council in a fateful meeting on July 2, 1941. Like many Japanese state papers, the policy decision was cautiously, not to say obscurely, worded, in these terms:

1. The Imperial Government is determined to follow a policy which will result in the establishment of the Greater East Asia Co-Prosperity Sphere and world peace, no matter what international developments take place.

2. The Imperial Government will continue its efforts to effect a settlement of the China Incident, and seek to establish a solid basis for the security and preservation of the nation. This will involve an advance into the Southern Regions and, depending on future developments, a settlement of the Soviet Question as well.

3. The Imperial Government will carry out the above program no matter what obstacles may be encountered.

In simpler terms, the Tokyo Government decided to defer operations against Soviet Russia until preparations were complete and the situation favorable. Explanatory notes attached to the decision of July 2 were far more explicit than the basic document itself:

Our attitude with reference to the German-Soviet War will be based on the spirit of the Tripartite Pact. However, we will not enter the conflict for some time, but will steadily proceed with military preparations against the Soviet and decide our final attitude independently. At the same time, we will continue carefully correlated activities in the diplomatic field.

In case the German-Soviet War should develop to our advantage, we will make use

---

[6] Tel. from Ott to Berlin, June 28, 1941 (*Tokyo War Crimes Documents*, No. 4081D); decision of the Liaison Conference, June 25, 1941 (*ibid.*, No. 2137H).

of our military strength, settle the Soviet question, and guarantee the safety of our northern borders.[7]

In execution of this program the Kwantung Army was steadily reinforced by some 200,000 men, bringing its total strength to about 600,000. Equipment was despatched, training accelerated, fortifications built and plans drawn. Everything was to be in readiness within six months (not six weeks, as Ambassador Ott had been led to believe), by which time it was hoped the Soviet forces would have been substantially reduced in number.[8] In this connection it is important to note, however, that the Kremlin was promptly informed by its master spy, Richard Sorge, of the Japanese decisions of July 2 and especially of the postponement of operations against Siberia. The Soviets therefore felt safe in withdrawing some 200,000 men, as well as planes and tanks, from the Far East to Europe, leaving, however, forces which were still superior to those of the Japanese. Whatever the hopes and intentions of the Tokyo General Staff in July, it was obliged to conclude, by the end of August, that an offensive against Soviet Russia would be impossible before the end of the year. Sorge's last report to Moscow before his discovery and arrest in mid-October stated that there was no serious danger of an attack from Manchuria; that the Japanese would move south and that war with the United States and Britain was probable before the end of the year.[9]

To Matsuoka was left the ungrateful task of communicating the decisions of the Privy Council to the Germans and persuading them that these decisions were all for the best. In a personal message to Ribbentrop the Foreign Minister gave assurance that Japan would prepare for all eventualities so far as Soviet Russia was concerned and that Japan was fully determined to destroy the Communist power in the east. Meanwhile, however, the chief Japanese effort would be directed toward acquiring *points d'appui* in Indo-China which would enable it "further to strengthen pressure upon Great Britain and the United States." Matsuoka ended his message on an expression of hope that the Germans would understand and appreciate the vital contribution which Japan would be making to the common cause, a contribution which, he thought, was "no less vital than Japan's intervention in the German-Soviet War." But Ambassador Ott made no secret of his dis-

---

[7] "Tojo Memorandum" (*Tokyo War Crimes Documents,* Proceedings, pp. 36254-58); "Konoye Memoirs," Appendix III (*Pearl Harbor Attack,* XX, 4018-19). Somewhat variant versions of the decision are given in the telegrams sent to Berlin (*Pearl Harbor Attack,* XII, 1-2), and in *Tokyo War Crimes Documents,* No. 1652.

[8] Tel. from Ott to the Foreign Office, July 10, 1941 (*Tokyo War Crimes Documents,* No. 4052A). See also the affidavit of General Tanaka, the Soviet interrogation of General Kita, and the affidavit of General Kasahara (*ibid.,* Exhibits 2676, 835, 2670).

[9] Department of the Army: *The Sorge Spy Ring* (February 10, 1949). For the rest see the Japanese staff paper, the agenda for a meeting of the Liaison Conference in late October, and the Tanaka affidavit (*Tokyo War Crimes Documents,* Exhibits 2681, 1328, 2676).

appointment, which was undoubtedly shared in full by Hitler and Ribbentrop. The course of German-Japanese relations continued to run true to past form: each party attempting to exploit the other and consulting only its own interest.[10]

2. AMERICAN-JAPANESE RELATIONS

The policy debates which rocked Tokyo during the ten days following the opening of the Nazi campaign against Soviet Russia necessarily involved full consideration of Japan's future relations with the United States and Britain. Prince Konoye was subsequently to insist that his Government intended to realize its aims by peaceful methods, but the explanatory notes attached to the decisions of July 2 leave no shred of doubt that Japanese authorities understood that their advance into southern Indo-China might result in hostilities with the democracies. The relevant passages read:

> In case the diplomatic negotiations break down, preparations for a war with England and America will also be carried forward. First of all, the plans that have been laid with reference to French Indo-China and Thai will be prosecuted, with a view to consolidating our position in the southern territories. In carrying out the plans outlined in the foregoing article, we will not be deterred by the possibility of being involved in a war with England and America.

And further on:

> In case all diplomatic means fail to prevent the entrance of America into the European War, we will proceed in harmony with our obligations under the Tripartite Pact. However, with reference to the time and method of employing our armed forces, we will take independent action . . .

In short, the Japanese Government and High Command, having at an earlier date decided to extend Nippon's control to the south, were now more determined than ever to take advantage of the Nazi-Soviet War to attain their objectives in Indo-China, whatever the cost.

In arriving at this significant decision, Tokyo was undoubtedly influenced by the breakdown of the long negotiations with the Netherlands East Indies Government, negotiations which had aimed at securing a much larger supply of oil and raw materials from the Indies than had thitherto been available. It was probably impressed also by the action of the United States Government (June 20, 1941) in prohibiting the export of oil from Atlantic and Gulf coast ports to all countries excepting Britain and the Latin American Republics. This measure was due entirely to the serious oil shortages which had developed in the eastern states and had provoked popular agitation against the continued supply of oil to Japan while important parts of the United States were obliged to curtail their activities for lack of fuel.

[10] Tels. from Ott to Berlin, July 3 and 4, 1941 (*Tokyo War Crimes Documents,* Nos. 4062A, 4062B, 4062E).

Nonetheless, Washington's action must have served to remind Tokyo of the precariousness of its position with respect to normal oil supplies and may have reinforced its determination to drive on toward the establishment of the Greater East Asia Co-Prosperity Sphere.

Even more important in shaping Japanese decisions must have been the long American note of June 21, 1941, which marked the culmination of several months of discussion and finally provided Tokyo with a comprehensive statement of the American position on a settlement of Far Eastern issues. The American note was officially a redraft of previous Japanese proposals, notably those of June 15, 1941. It was accompanied by an "oral statement," read to Ambassador Nomura by Secretary Hull, and by four annexes to the proposed joint statement of policies. One of these annexes defined in detail Japan's course for the settlement of the China Incident and another the American Government's position with regard to future commercial relations with Japan. A third contained a suggested exchange of letters dealing with the attitude of the two powers toward the European War, while the fourth consisted of a proposed letter from Secretary Hull to Ambassador Nomura outlining the former's views as to the future application of the principle of nondiscrimination to the economic relations between Japan and China.[11]

The note of June 21, which was to become basic to all subsequent discussions, revealed no disposition on Washington's part to retreat from the contentions and terms advanced on previous occasions. On the contrary, it was an uncompromising restatement of the principles of international relations, so frequently enunciated by Secretary Hull, and of the American position regarding the peaceful settlement of the China affair, trade relations and economic activities in the Pacific area, the political stabilization of that area, and the neutralization of the Philippine Islands. The "oral statement" was particularly pointed, recapitulating the grounds for American suspicions of Japanese sincerity, insisting that any final agreement must be in accord with the "liberal policies" to which the United States was committed, and warning that further progress in the discussions was contingent upon "some clearer indication than has yet been given that the Japanese Government as a whole desires to pursue courses of peace such as constitute the objectives of the proposed understanding." Indeed, the statement adverted to reports reaching Washington

that some Japanese leaders in influential official positions are definitely committed to a course which calls for support of Nazi Germany and its policies of conquest, and that the only kind of understanding with the United States which they would endorse is one that would envisage Japan's fighting on the side of Hitler should the United States become involved in the European hostilities through carrying out its present policy of self-defense. . . . So long as such leaders maintain this attitude in their

[11] For the full texts see *Foreign Relations of the United States: Japan,* II, 483 ff.

official positions and apparently seek to influence public opinion in Japan in the direction indicated, is it not illusory to expect that the adoption of a proposal such as the one under consideration offers a basis for achieving substantial results along the desired lines?[12]

While this unmistakable reference to Matsuoka and his activities may have been warranted, it certainly stretched diplomatic usage to unwonted lengths. The body of the American note, too, dispensed with the customary circumlocutions. Thus, on the most controversial issue of Japan's obligations to the Axis in the event of America's being drawn into the European War, Washington offered Tokyo an ingenious loophole to wriggle out of its commitments without seeming to repudiate them in dishonorable fashion. More importantly, however, the note made crystal clear that the assumption on which the Washington conversations rested was that Japan did in fact not intend to go to war against the United States if the latter felt impelled to engage in hostilities against Germany. If this assumption were false, it was high time that Tokyo should say so in unequivocal language.

The position taken by the United States Government with regard to China similarly aimed to dispel Japanese illusions and hopes. It by no means envisaged America's playing the role of mediator between Japan and China. On the contrary, it specified that before the President undertook to invite Chiang Kai-shek to embark on peace negotiations with Japan, Tokyo should reveal to Washington the "general terms" which it proposed to submit. The question of how Japan would effect the removal of its armed forces from China and the question of Japan's future economic relationship to that country were to be left for further discussion. So, likewise, was the status of Manchuria (Manchukuo). However, the first and fourth annexes to the American note left no room for doubt that the United States expected the Japanese-Chinese settlement to be based on "mutual respect of sovereignties and territories," and Japan's future position in China to be only such as Tokyo could secure on the basis of nondiscrimination and equality of economic opportunity. These principles, furthermore, were to be applied not only to the southwestern Pacific area, as specified in earlier notes, but to the whole Pacific region.

There is nothing in the record to support the charge that the note of June 21 represented a deliberate hardening of the American position. Almost without exception the terms embodied in the note had been advanced on previous occasions and should therefore have been familiar to Ambassador Nomura and his Government. The comprehensive and unequivocal statement of American terms was merely a reflection of Secretary Hull's conviction, frequently expounded to Nomura, that no useful purpose would be served by further discussions unless each side clarified its position. In the face of widespread official and private skepticism the State Depart-

[12] *Foreign Relations of the United States: Japan*, II, 485.

ment had labored earnestly to produce a program considered capable of reconciling what the two countries regarded as their vital and permanent interests. The idea that the American note was nothing more than a dilatory tactic or even a challenge appears quite unwarranted. The President and his advisers, both civilian and military, had long since decided that the Atlantic should have priority over the Pacific and that, in view of the ever-growing danger of a conflict with Nazi Germany, everything should be done to forestall a crisis in relations with Japan. It would have been utterly pointless to goad the Japanese along the very course from which it was Washington's aim to deflect them. It was certainly no fault of the American Government that, the more clearly the authorities on either side came to understand each other, the more remote became the hope and possibility of adjustment of their differences by diplomatic methods.

At the same time it is not difficult to believe that the Japanese Government took the American note as evidence of unfriendliness and of a sudden and sinister hardening of attitude occasioned by Washington's knowledge that Germany was poised for an attack on Soviet Russia.[13] Although, as aforesaid, there was no basis for the contention that the United States Government had introduced new and more stringent conditions, it cannot be denied that the total impression left by the American note was more unfavorable than that of previous, partial communications. Many Japanese no doubt desired to avoid conflict with the United States and hoped against hope that eventually they could convince the American Government and people of the justice of their claims and aspirations. To them the terms of June 21 were undoubtedly disillusioning, while to others, like Matsuoka, who had long regarded the reconciliation of conflicting interests as impossible, the overall statement of the American position, and particularly the undiplomatic "oral statement," must have provided eloquent proof of their contentions.

In Tokyo the proponents of ruthless action had long since convinced themselves that Japan's "vital" program could be realized only at the cost of American hostility and opposition. Reviewing the events of the months just past, they noted that the United States, far from being deterred by the Tripartite Pact, had continued its aid to Britain even at the risk of becoming involved in hostilities with Germany. American policy in the Far East had been no less positive. Difficult though it was, for geographic reasons, to supply China, everything possible was being done to encourage Chiang Kai-shek and stiffen his resistance to Japan. American transportation experts were making surveys of the Burma Road with a view to increasing its capacity, and American Army and Navy pilots were being permitted to volunteer for service with the Chinese Air Force being organized by an American officer, Colonel Claire L. Chennault. Furthermore, President Roosevelt had

[13] Testimony of General Tojo (*Tokyo War Crimes Documents:* Proceedings, 36228).

extended to China the benefits of Lend-Lease and had allowed Mr. Owen Lattimore to take service with the Nationalist Government as political adviser to the Generalissimo. American officers had participated with the British and Dutch in staff conversations at Singapore and it was no secret that the United States was supplying arms and munitions to the British in Malaya and to the Dutch in the Indies. Finally, Washington had, over the preceding year, laid a series of restrictions on exports to Japan, with the result that trade in most items had been reduced to the merest trickle. All in all, the Tokyo press believed it had ample evidence of hostile encirclement and every reason to call for appropriate counteraction.[14]

It was against the background of such views that the Imperial Conference on July 2 took the decision to press on with its program of southern expansion, at the same time preparing for eventual war with the United States and Britain. For the time being the question of further discussions with Washington remained open and no immediate reply was made to the American note of June 21. Initially American authorities attached no particular significance to this, because they were almost unanimous in thinking that Japan would take advantage of the new situation created by Hitler to loose its forces against Soviet Siberia, meanwhile deferring action to the south.[15] Although such a distraction of Japanese power would provide Britain, the Netherlands and the United States a breathing period and enable them to strengthen the defenses of Malaya, the Indies and the Philippines, any action on Tokyo's part that tended to hasten the collapse of Soviet Russia was obviously not in the British or American interest. In the effort to avert such a calamity President Roosevelt sent a personal message to Prince Konoye (July 4) calling his attention to the reports reaching Washington and expressing his reluctance to believe them, in view of the oft-repeated declarations of the Japanese Government of its desire to preserve peace in the Pacific area. However, the President put Tokyo on notice in these words: "Should Japan enter upon a course of military aggression and conquest, it stands to reason that such action would render illusory the cherished hope of the American Government, which it understood was shared by the Japanese Government, that peace in the Pacific area, far from being further upset, might now indeed be strengthened and made more secure."

Prince Konoye replied by reaffirming Japan's desire for peace in the Pacific and stating that his Government "have not so far considered the possibility of joining the hostilities against the Soviet Union." At the same

---

[14] See particularly the Japanese Foreign Office memorandum entitled "The Anglo-American Policy of Encirclement against Japan in the Southern Pacific Ocean," dated July, 1941 (*Tokyo War Crimes Documents,* Defense Document No. 1482).

[15] Memos of the Far Eastern Division, June 23, 25, 26, 1941; Far Eastern situation summary, July 10, 1941, reviewing numerous reports from abroad forecasting a Japanese attack on Soviet Russia. On the persistence of this conviction in American military and naval circles see Watson: *Chief of Staff: Prewar Plans and Preparations,* 494-96.

time he gave tit for tat by adding: "Incidentally, the Japanese Government would like to avail themselves of this opportunity for definitely ascertaining whether it is really the intention of the President or the American Government to intervene in the European War, as they are naturally and very deeply concerned at the prospect, disturbed as they sincerely are by reports reaching them from a variety of sources." Foreign Minister Matsuoka elaborated in conversation with Ambassador Grew: Japanese policy, he said, would depend on "future developments" such as the conclusion of an Anglo-Soviet alliance or an attempt by the United States to supply the Soviet armies by way of Vladivostok. With his usual mendacity he asserted that he was under great internal pressure to join in the war against Soviet Russia. Eventually this reciprocal effort to probe intentions was closed by an American statement that United States policy was solely one of self-defense against aggressors, who made no secret of their aim to conquer the whole world:

It can hardly be expected, therefore, that the United States Government will stand idly by and permit Germany to obtain control of the seas or any other strategic advantages which would directly threaten the security of the United States. Any intimations or suggestions that the United States should desist from its policy of self-defense and protection would in actual fact range those making such suggestions or intimations on the side of those favoring or facilitating the aims of the aggressor nations to conquer the world by force.[16]

This terse exchange of statements did not dispel Washington's fears that presently the Japanese would turn against their traditional enemy, the Soviet Union. Chinese sources, in fact, continued to asseverate that the Germans, Italians and Japanese had reached agreement on their respective spheres of influence and that the Japanese would soon move against Vladivostok as well as against Indo-China and Siam.[17] However, Ambassador Grew had soon learned of the decisions of the Imperial Conference on July 2, and on July 8 the highest Washington officials had in hand a copy of Tokyo's telegram to Berlin transmitting the larger part of the adopted program. American cryptographers had succeeded, some time before, in breaking the secret Japanese diplomatic code and were now regularly deciphering the telegrams between the Washington Embassy and the Foreign Office, as well as other messages sent by Tokyo to its foreign missions. The all-important intelligence henceforth available to Washington enabled the President and a few of his chief civilian and military advisers to follow closely the evolution and implementation of Japanese policy. Unfortunately it was

[16] *Foreign Relations of the United States: Japan,* II, 502 ff.; Joseph C. Grew: *Ten Years in Japan* (New York, 1944), 396 ff.

[17] Messages from Chiang Kai-shek, July 2 and 8, 1941; tel. from the Chinese Ambassador at Berlin, July 4, 1941; tel. from the Chinese Minister of Communications, July 8, 1941. All these documents were transmitted by Mr. T. V. Soong and are to be found in the *Morgenthau Diaries (MS.),* Vol. 419, pp. 373 ff., 380-82.

decided, for security reasons, not to make this material available to Ambassador Grew, who did not learn until long afterward that Japanese diplomatic correspondence had been intercepted and read. Surely this may be taken as an example of the dilemma created when security is maintained to the point of critically reducing the value of the intelligence obtained.[18]

The unexpected insight thus afforded Washington was bound to affect all further discussions. For one thing the intercepts confirmed reports which had come in on July 5 that Japan was about to seize military control of Indo-China and Siam so as to threaten the Burma Road, Singapore and the Netherlands Indies.[19] Under the circumstances the State Department might well wonder whether Tokyo would further pursue the informal, exploratory conversations. Thus far there had been no response to the American note of June 21 beyond a short statement by Ambassador Nomura on July 4 that he was authorized by his Foreign Minister to assure Mr. Hull "that there is no divergence of views in the [Japanese] Government regarding its fundamental policy of adjusting Japanese-American relations on a fair basis."[20] But this had reference only to the "oral statement" and in any event was overshadowed by the exchange of notes regarding a possible Japanese move against Soviet Siberia. It still remained to be seen how Tokyo would react to the comprehensive American statement of terms.

To this issue the Tokyo Liaison Conference directed its attention as soon as the decisions of July 2 had been accepted by the Privy Council and the Emperor. Once again Matsuoka was provided with ammunition by the Germans, who were profoundly disappointed to learn that Japan would not immediately join in the attack on Soviet Russia and were greatly concerned lest Tokyo make a deal with the United States for attainment of its goals in the south. On July 10 Ribbentrop cabled Ambassador Ott inquiring frantically about American-Japanese relations: "Do you think it possible that . . . Nomura has made any oral assurances—without any written agreement—to the American Government which would have induced Roosevelt to occupy Iceland, knowing that in the rear he has nothing to fear from Japan?" Revealing deep distrust of Germany's ally, the Nazi Foreign Minister inquired whether Ott thought there was any chance of Japan's pursuing a shortsighted policy "by coming to terms with America, thereby

[18] Statement of Mr. Grew to the authors, March 23, 1948. On July 10, 1941, the Ambassador cabled Washington complaining that he was obliged to turn to his British colleague for information about conversations between the State Department and the Japanese Ambassador (*Grew Diary, MS.*). On the breaking of the Japanese code see *Pearl Harbor Attack,* Report, 296. It should be noted that the Japanese message to Berlin, which was deciphered by July 8, omitted that part of the July 2 decisions which bore on Japanese relations with the United States.

[19] Tel. from Winant (London), July 4, 1941; memo of Hamilton to Hull, July 5, 1941; State Department summary of Far Eastern developments, July 10, 1941. Message from Chiang Kai-shek to the President, July 6, 1941 (*Pearl Harbor Attack,* XIX, 3496 ff.).

[20] *Foreign Relations of the United States: Japan,* II, 499.

entangling it [i.e., the United States] in a European war for a long time in order to have a free hand in East Asia without openly clashing with America, to adjust the Chinese question and further expand in the south." Japan, he warned, could never set up the Greater East Asia Co-Prosperity Sphere with the United States and Britain, but only against them. It was difficult for him to understand why Japan did not first solve the question of Soviet Siberia, even though any course of Japanese expansion, to the south as well as to the north, would be welcome to Berlin. As for the United States, said Ribbentrop, Germany could not but regard the despatch of military forces to Iceland as in itself an act of aggression requiring eventual counteraction by Japan under the terms of the Tripartite Pact: "I do not doubt for a moment that in case of the outbreak of hostilities between Germany and America, in which case today already it may be considered as an absolutely established fact that only America will be the aggressor, Japan will fulfill her obligations, as agreed upon in the Three Power Pact."[21]

Ribbentrop was whistling in the dark, for he certainly knew that Japan would not attack Soviet Russia until the Nazi armies had thoroughly softened Soviet resistance. He must also have known that Tokyo desired to avoid war with the United States and Britain and that it was therefore highly doubtful whether Japan would live up to German hopes and expectations as far as the Tripartite Pact was concerned. Ott's reply certainly eliminated any remaining uncertainty. The Ambassador admitted that Japanese-American relations were becoming constantly more strained, but he doubted any Japanese commitment with respect to Iceland and pointed out that "the majority of the Japanese Cabinet and the Japanese Foreign Minister consider the possibility of an American entry into the war with unconcealed concern." He was, so he said, doing everything possible to get Japan into the war against Soviet Russia and was convinced that Tokyo would act as soon as essential preparations were complete. But, he added, "the greatest obstacle against which one has to fight is the disunity of the Activist group which, without unified command, follows various aims and only slowly adjusts itself to the changed situation."[22]

The disunity with which the German Ambassador had to contend led to further dissension on July 10, when the Liaison Conference finally turned to consideration of the American note of June 21. Matsuoka is reported to have objected vigorously to continuance of the Washington discussions and to have described the American proposals as based on ill will, designed "to subjugate Japan or throw her into utter confusion." As proof he pointed to the unfortunate "oral statement," which he interpreted as a demand for his

[21] *Tokyo War Crimes Documents,* No. 571. A partial version is given also in *Nazi Conspiracy and Aggression,* V, No. 2896-PS.

[22] Tel. from Ott to Berlin (*Tokyo War Crimes Documents,* No. 522). A partial version is printed in *Nazi Conspiracy and Aggression,* V, No. 2897-PS.

own dismissal and therefore as an intolerable attempt to interfere in Japanese affairs. Prince Konoye, greatly disturbed by the Foreign Minister's vehemence, consulted privately with the War and Navy Ministers, who, though by no means willing to accept the American terms, agreed that the Washington conversations should be continued and exploited for whatever they might be worth. A reply was thereupon drafted, but only to meet with renewed obstruction on the part of Matsuoka, who refused to despatch it to Washington until some days after the rejection of the "oral statement" as "an impolite and improper document." There was much wrangling about procedure until Matsuoka took matters into his own hands and sent off an indignant rejection of the "oral statement," with instructions to Nomura to secure satisfaction on this item before presenting the Japanese reply to the note of June 21. At the same time he communicated the reply to the German Ambassador.[23]

Contrary to Japanese expectations the rejection of the oral statement caused no difficulty. Mr. Hull, asserting that the statement had been misinterpreted, gave immediate assurance that no interference in Japanese internal affairs had been intended and agreed to the return of the document.[24] Nonetheless, Prince Konoye and his colleagues were outraged by Matsuoka's highhanded procedure, including his continued, unauthorized confabulations with the German Ambassador. They agreed that the obnoxious Foreign Minister must be removed and decided that it would be best for the entire Cabinet to resign so as to avoid the appearance of yielding to American pressure. This action was taken on July 16, while Matsuoka was confined to his bed by illness. On the following day the Senior Statesmen approved the formation of a new Cabinet by Konoye, and this was completed on July 18. In this third Konoye Government Admiral Teijiro Toyoda was assigned the crucial post of Foreign Minister. As a naval officer he was thought to be particularly well posted on the Japanese-American problem. Indeed, he had the reputation of being well disposed toward both the United States and Britain.[25]

According to Prince Konoye it was hoped and expected that the new Cabinet would make a good impression in Washington and facilitate further discussions looking toward an agreement. In this spirit Father Drought, the intermediary in the unofficial negotiations of the spring, cabled Postmaster General Walker: "If our people coöperate immediately with the new man as they expect us to, we can achieve a great, lasting success. The changes have been made from here to suit our desires." And again: "New Minister

---

[23] "Konoye Memoirs" for July 14-15, 1941 (*Pearl Harbor Attack*, XX, 3995-96); "Kido Diary," July 15, 1941 (*Tokyo War Crimes Documents*, No. 1632W-60).

[24] *Foreign Relations of the United States: Japan*, II, 506 ff.

[25] "Konoye Memoirs" (*Pearl Harbor Attack*, XX, 3996-97); "Kido Diary," July 15, 16, 17, 1941 (*Tokyo War Crimes Documents*, Nos. 1632W-60-62); *Grew Diary* (*MS.*), July 16, 1941.

is great personal friend of sailor [Nomura] and his appointment and the reappointment of others friendly to us should be seized upon."[26]

In his postwar memoirs Prince Konoye made a point of bemoaning the failure of the American Government to grasp the significance of the Japanese Cabinet change or appreciate the desire of the new Government to breathe new life into the Washington conversations. With the materials now available, however, it is easy to understand Washington's unresponsiveness. American officials knew from Japanese intercepts that Tokyo was poised for an advance into southern Indo-China. Furthermore, repeated efforts to smoke out Ambassador Nomura on the Japanese reaction to the American note of June 21 had proved futile.[27] Meanwhile it was common knowledge that Japan had begun to call up reservists in large numbers, that it had directed its merchant fleet to leave the Atlantic, that it had imposed strict censorship, and that it had further restricted travel by foreigners. Everything pointed to a serious crisis, the more so as the Government-inspired press of Tokyo was engaging in a vigorous campaign against Britain and the United States. The former was accused of encircling Siam and plotting with the Gaullists to take over Indo-China; the latter of encouraging the British to make an alliance with Chiang Kai-shek and angling for an American-British-Soviet-Chinese-Dutch coalition to check Japan.[28]

As a final demonstration of Japanese duplicity intercepted messages from Tokyo to its Washington Embassy revealed statements such as these: "There is more reason than ever before to arm ourselves to the teeth for all-out war," and "The Cabinet shake-up was necessary to expedite matters in connection with national affairs and has no further significance. Japan's policy will not be changed and she will remain faithful to the principles of the Tripartite Pact."[29] In the same sense Foreign Minister Toyoda assured the German Ambassador that the reconstructed Cabinet would continue the policy based on the spirit and aims of the Tripartite Pact: "As successor of former Foreign Minister Matsuoka, I intend to continue his foreign policy and to strengthen even more the close unity of Japan, Germany, and Italy, and march forward in the common spirit."[30] All told, Washington saw no

[26] Tels. from Father Drought to Mr. Walker, July 16, 18, 1941 (*Walker Papers, MS.*).

[27] Memos of conversation between Mr. Ballantine and Ambassador Nomura, July 14 and 15, 1941 (*Foreign Relations of the United States: Japan,* II, 505-9).

[28] Reports by Tolischus from Tokyo, July 12 and 13, 1941 (*The New York Times,* July 13, 14, 1941), and a report from Shanghai (*ibid.,* July 14, 1941). Through Mr. T. V. Soong, Chiang Kai-shek had in fact inquired whether President Roosevelt would favor a military arrangement between China and Soviet Russia. The reply was that the President could not take the responsibility for such arrangements but thought they would benefit China: "His attitude toward the suggested pact between China, Russia and Great Britain was similar" (memo by Mr. Currie after a conversation with Mr. Welles, July 11, 1941, in *Roosevelt Papers:* Secretary's File, Box 176).

[29] *Pearl Harbor Attack,* XII, 2-5; XIV, 1398-99.

[30] *Tokyo War Crimes Documents,* No. 4052F.

grounds for confidence or optimism. On the contrary, all signs pointed to developments of the most ominous and dangerous kind.

3. INDO-CHINA: THE SECOND CRISIS

Comparatively little is known, even now, of the Japanese-French negotiations concerning Indo-China in July, 1941. Admiral Decoux, the French Governor General, learned early in July of Tokyo's forthcoming demands from General Sumita, commander of the Japanese forces in Tonkin, and warned his Government, which in turn warned its Ambassador in Tokyo. But the Japanese, suspecting the French Ambassador of Gaullist sympathies and of passing on information to his British and American colleagues, decided to negotiate at Vichy. On July 12 Baron Kato was instructed to inform the French Government that, regretfully, the Japanese Government felt obliged to present certain demands. He was to explain that, in order to forestall interference by the British or Americans, Japan required a favorable reply by July 20, failing which force would be employed. The demands, in brief, were these: permission to despatch the "necessary" land, sea and air forces to southern Indo-China; occupation of eight air and two naval bases in the same region; recognition of freedom of movement for Japanese forces in southern Indo-China; withdrawal of French garrisons from the places to be occupied by the Japanese.[31]

This brutal note, submitted to the Vichy Government on July 14, was followed almost at once by a personal appeal from Prince Konoye to Marshal Pétain, couched in quite different language. The Japanese Prime Minister explained that the new demands were due to "the inevitable necessity of self-preservation and defense of Japan and maintenance of her position in the Greater East Asia Sphere." He gave the Marshal solemn assurance that the territorial integrity of Indo-China and the sovereignty of France would be respected, and urged him "to accept our proposal open-mindedly, without a shade of suspicion as to the intention of the Japanese Government."[32]

Pétain could hardly view the matter so ingenuously and had Admiral Darlan inform Ambassador Leahy at once of what was in the wind. Washington, in response, instructed its Ambassador to use all his influence to delay a decision as long as possible. Darlan did temporize, but evidently only long enough to appeal to the Germans to intervene. The precise position assumed by Berlin is not clear. Following earlier Japanese approaches in mid-June, Matsuoka had informed the German Ambassador at once of the demands submitted in July. He explained to Ott that

[31] Admiral Decoux: *A la barre de l'Indochine* (Paris, 1949), 150-51; tel. from Tokyo to the embassy at Vichy, July 12, 1941 (*Tokyo War Crimes Documents,* Nos. 1383C and 1383D).

[32] Message of Prince Konoye to Marshal Pétain, July 15, 1941 (*Tokyo War Crimes Documents:* Proceedings, 36239).

the realization of this plan is the first step for our push to the south. It will undoubtedly play an important part as a diversion of the English-American forces. In this sense the Japanese Government believes that in pursuing this aim she is giving valuable assistance to Germany and Italy, loyal to the spirit of the Tripartite Pact. She therefore believes to be able to assume that the German Government will not only refuse any entreaty of the French Government to mediate a refusal or mitigation of the Japanese proposal, but will also stand at the side of the Japanese Government by endeavoring to convince the French Government of the appropriateness of its acceptance.[33]

Whether the German Government, at that time furious with Vichy over the failure of the Paris Protocols, actually brought pressure on the French to yield cannot be determined. It certainly did nothing to obstruct Tokyo's program and probably gave some support, since the Japanese Foreign Minister subsequently thanked the Germans for their coöperation.[34] In any case, the crisis proved short-lived. Darlan, denied German support, saw no alternative to acquiescence. As he explained to Ambassador Leahy, he had hoped the United States would send warships to Saigon to head off the Japanese forces. Since neither the Americans nor the British held out any prospect of aid, Vichy was helpless: to resist would simply have meant the immediate and complete loss of Indo-China; to accept meant to have at least the paper assurance that French sovereignty would be respected. Germany, he insisted, had nothing to do with it.[35]

A preliminary agreement between France and Japan was signed at Vichy on July 21, to be followed by local arrangements at Hanoi (July 23) and by the definitive exchange of letters between Darlan and Kato (July 29). By the terms of the protocol Japan was to have the use of eight airfields in southern Indo-China, as well as of the naval bases at Saigon and Camranh Bay. No limit was placed on the number of Japanese troops to be stationed in the area, though initially 50,000 were despatched.[36] All in all, the Japanese had taken a very significant step forward. Thenceforth they were in a strategic position not only to interdict the remaining supply routes into China, but to threaten Malaya, the Netherlands Indies and the Philippines. The United States Government, having failed to frustrate or even seri-

[33] Tels. from Ott to Ribbentrop, July 10 and 15, 1941; memo of General Oshima to Ribbentrop, July 17, 1941 (*Tokyo War Crimes Documents*, Nos. 11A [3], 4052C and 1375A). On the American action at Vichy see William L. Langer: *Our Vichy Gamble* (New York, 1947), 177-78; William D. Leahy: *I Was There* (New York, 1950), 44.

[34] Tel. from Ott to Ribbentrop, July 24, 1941 (*Tokyo War Crimes Documents*, No. 4052G). On the German attitude see further the tel. from Schleier (Paris) to Ribbentrop, July 21, 1941 (*ibid.*, No. 4025E[7]).

[35] Langer: *Our Vichy Gamble*, 177-78; Leahy: *I Was There*, 44; Decoux: *A la barre de l'Indochine*, 153 ff. We have used also a tel. from Leahy, August 1, 1941, and a memo from Darlan, August 5, 1941. Darlan remarked to Leahy at this time: "If and when the United States can bring to Marseilles three thousand tanks, five hundred thousand men and six thousand planes, be sure to let me know, for then you will be welcomed."

[36] Details in Decoux: *A la barre de l'Indochine*, 151 ff.

ously delay the Japanese *démarche* at Vichy, was equally unsuccessful in its efforts to influence Tokyo itself. Ambassador Nomura, when questioned by State Department officials, at first disclaimed having any information, though he admitted that the reputed action by Japan was likely:

He explained that Japan was concerned over possible encirclement, and that the Japanese people had been especially alarmed over reports of an alliance between China and Great Britain. He referred also to increased aid by the United States to the Chungking Government and to reported plans for strengthening the Burma Road. He affirmed that Japan was obliged to take appropriate precautionary measures, and he referred to our military occupation of Iceland and to reports that we might take Dakar and the Azores.[37]

This effort to link American measures in the Atlantic to Japanese expansion in the Pacific could hardly impress the State Department or the President, in view particularly of the plans revealed by intercepted Japanese messages. Washington shared Ambassador Leahy's opinion that the whole business was part of the Axis design, that Vichy had yielded under Nazi pressure and that the occupation of southern Indo-China was just another manifestation of Vichy's collaborationist policy.[38] Secretary Hull, still convalescing at White Sulphur Springs, was filled with grim forebodings. Speaking to Mr. Welles over the telephone he expressed fear that Japan might soon "break forth on a general program, not a piecemeal program." It was likely, he thought, that Hitler might go for Gibraltar and that a full-fledged alliance between France and Germany might soon emerge. Nonetheless, he approved of a further conversation with Nomura, if only for the record. He suggested that Mr. Welles tell the Ambassador that if the new Japanese Cabinet were planning to work for a peaceful settlement, it would find the United States patient. On the other hand, "if the new Government is not prepared to move along the lines of a peaceful settlement, but takes action showing the world that it is following a policy of force and conquest, then we want the Japanese Government to be frank with us and say that it cannot discuss with us a peaceful settlement."[39]

It was most unlikely that Tokyo would thus lay its cards on the table, particularly at a time when so much depended on skillful deception. Mr. Welles spoke to Mr. Wakasugi, the Japanese Minister serving under Nomura, on the same day, but without eliciting any important information. Wakasugi still insisted that the Embassy had had no knowledge of its Government's intention to occupy southern Indo-China and inquired whether the new development would jeopardize the American-Japanese conversations. Welles replied to this query as follows:

[37] *Foreign Relations of the United States: Japan,* II, 508.
[38] Leahy: *I Was There,* 44.
[39] Memo of Hamilton to Welles, July 19, 1941; memo of a telephone conversation between Mr. Hull and Mr. Welles, July 21, 1941.

It seemed to me altogether illogical for one party to these conversations to be carrying on discussions on a basis predicated on the maintenance by the parties to the conversations of a policy of peace, no resort to force or conquest, et cetera, and at the same time for the other party to the conversations to be undertaking in practice policies utterly and hopelessly at variance therewith.[40]

Ambassador Nomura, interestingly, had chosen these critical days for a visit to Maine. He now hurried back to the capital and asked to be received by the Acting Secretary. In a meeting on July 23 he explained once again that the Japanese move into Indo-China was necessitated by concern for the food supply and the requirements of national defense in the face of hostile encirclement. He besought the American Government not to rush to "hasty conclusion," but to allow a little time to elapse in the effort to find a friendly adjustment of differences. Mr. Welles, who had telephoned Mr. Hull in advance of the conference, pointed out that any agreement which Japan might have made with Vichy could have resulted only from Nazi pressure on the French. He reasoned further that Japan's food and raw materials supply might have been more effectively assured through the projected agreement with the United States than through the advance into southern Indo-China. As for the issue of encirclement, the Acting Secretary reminded his visitor that the policy of the United States "was the reverse of a policy of encirclement or of a policy which would constitute any threat to Japan." The same, he added, was true of British policy. There was no doubt that if Japan and the United States succeeded in reaching agreement, the Governments of Britain, the Dominions, the Netherlands and China would associate themselves with it. Having thus disposed of Nomura's arguments, Mr. Welles stated the American position in the most explicit terms:

The movement now undertaken by Japan could only be regarded by the United States as having two probable purposes, neither of which purposes this Government could ignore: First, the United States could only assume that the occupation of Indo-China by Japan constituted notice to the United States that the Japanese Government intended to pursue a policy of force and of conquest, and second, that in the light of these acts on the part of Japan, the United States, with regard to its own safety in the light of its own preparations for self-defense, must assume that the Japanese Government was taking the last step before proceeding upon a policy of totalitarian expansion in the South Seas through the seizure of additional territories in that region.

That being so, he concluded, Secretary Hull "could not see that there was any basis now offered for the pursuit of the conversations in which he and the Ambassador had been engaged."[41]

[40] Memo of conversation between Mr. Welles and Mr. Wakasugi, July 21, 1941 (*Foreign Relations of the United States: Japan*, II, 520 ff.).

[41] *Foreign Relations of the United States: Japan*, II, 522 ff.; memo of a telephone conversation between Mr. Hull and Mr. Welles, July 23, 1941; Hull: *Memoirs*, II, 1013 ff.; tel. to Grew, July 24, 1941; tel. from Nomura to Tokyo, July 23, 1941, this last item in *Pearl Harbor Attack*, XII, 5.

Nomura, greatly distressed by this threat to the success of his mission, cabled his Government at once that diplomatic relations might be severed by the United States or that, at a minimum, steps just short of such a rupture might be decided upon. There was a growing feeling in Washington, he reported, that Japan's negotiations were nothing but a stratagem, designed to cloak the advance to the south, and that this advance was merely the prelude to operations against Singapore and the Netherlands Indies.[42] The Ambassador's apprehensions could only have been enhanced by the strong statement released to the public by Mr. Welles on the following day. After a review of past efforts to provide for the maintenance of peace and the *status quo* in the Pacific, it underlined the significance of Japan's most recent step:

By the course which it [Japan] has followed and is following in regard to Indo-China, the Japanese Government is giving clear indication that it is determined to pursue an objective of expansion by force or threat of force.

There is not apparent to the Government of the United States any valid ground upon which the Japanese Government would be warranted in occupying Indo-China or establishing bases in that area as measures of self-defense. . . .

This Government can, therefore, only conclude that the action of Japan is undertaken because of the estimated value to Japan of bases in that region primarily for purposes of further and more obvious movements of conquest in adjacent areas.

In the light of previous developments, steps such as are now being taken by the Government of Japan endanger the peaceful use by peaceful nations of the Pacific. They tend to jeopardize the procurement by the United States of essential materials such as tin and rubber, which are necessary for the normal economy of this country and the consummation of our defense program. . . . The steps which the Japanese Government has taken also endanger the safety of other areas of the Pacific, including the Philippine Islands.[43]

Thus the gravity of the new turn in the Far Eastern situation had been set forth to the Japanese Ambassador and explained in the most forceful terms to the American people.

4. THE EXTENSION OF SANCTIONS

Although Mr. Welles's public statement contained no indication of retaliatory measures, the Japanese Government, like Ambassador Nomura, must have been aware that the American reaction to the occupation of southern Indo-China would, at the very least, involve further economic restrictions. The trade in most critical items had already been drastically reduced, but thus far nothing had been done to curtail seriously the export of oil and oil products from the United States to Japan. As Mr. Roosevelt explained in the simplest terms to a meeting of the Volunteer Participation

[42] *Tokyo War Crimes Documents,* No. 1383E.
[43] *Foreign Relations of the United States: Japan,* II, 315 ff.

Committee on July 24, the American Government had held its hand for fear that the Japanese, cut off from their normal and chief supply of oil, would seize the Netherlands Indies and thereby deprive Britain and the United States of essential sources of raw materials. This policy, argued Mr. Roosevelt, had worked for two years and had prevented the war's spreading to the South Pacific.[44] There had, however, long since developed a strong popular protest against the continued provision to Japan of one of the items essential to its military program, and several influential members of the Cabinet, notably Secretaries Stimson, Morgenthau and Ickes, had frequently agitated for the imposition of an embargo on oil exports. It was almost inevitable that in July, 1941, this issue should be raised again as a matter of vital importance and urgency.

The Cabinet discussions on further economic sanctions were prefaced by one of the not infrequent tiffs between the State Department and other agencies regarding an oil embargo. In June Secretary Ickes, recently appointed Petroleum Coördinator for National Defense, had secured approval for the prohibition of oil exports from the Gulf and Atlantic coast ports to all countries outside the hemisphere except those of the British Commonwealth. In this connection he had requested the Administrator of Export Control to furnish him complete information on the quantities and grades of oil being shipped to Japan. To this the State Department objected and the President wrote Ickes that his writ did not run in the field of export control policy. Nothing daunted, the Petroleum Administrator replied by urging that the moment had arrived to impose an embargo on oil, since Japan was too preoccupied with the Nazi attack on Soviet Russia to venture a move against the Netherlands Indies. Mr. Roosevelt queried whether Mr. Ickes would stick to this judgment "if this were to tip the delicate scales and cause Japan to decide to attack Russia or to attack the Dutch East Indies." But Mr. Ickes stood his ground and eventually offered to resign as Petroleum Coördinator. This offer the President declined in a letter which gives one of the rare insights into the Chief Executive's thinking:

I think it will interest you to know that the Japs are having a real dragdown and knockout fight among themselves and have been for the past week—trying to decide which way they are going to jump—attack Russia, attack the South Seas (thus throwing their lot definitely with Germany), or whether they will sit on the fence and be more friendly with us. No one knows what the decision will be but, as you know, it is terribly important for the control of the Atlantic for us to help keep peace in the Pacific. I simply have not got enough Navy to go round—and every little episode in the Pacific means fewer ships in the Atlantic.[45]

[44] The President's remarks are printed in *Foreign Relations of the United States: Japan*, II, 264-65.
[45] State Department draft of a letter from the President to Mr. Ickes, June 24, 1941, in which reference is made to a letter from the President to Mr. Ickes of June 18, and the latter's reply of June 20. These earlier letters have not turned up. The President

This interesting exchange makes perfectly clear that, pending reliable information on the Japanese Cabinet decisions of July 2, the President was still supporting the policy long since advocated by Secretary Hull. But by July 8 there could no longer be any reasonable doubt that Japan was resolved on expansion to the south. Thereupon both Mr. Roosevelt and Mr. Welles recognized that their previous position had become untenable. On July 10 the Acting Secretary approached Lord Halifax and told him that the President had authorized him to say that if "Japan took any overt step through the exercise of pressure or force to acquire or conquer territories of other nations in the Far East, the Government of the United States would immediately impose various embargoes, both economic and financial, which measures had been under consideration for some time past and which had been held in abeyance for reasons which were well known to the Ambassador." To this notification the British Government responded at once, stating that in the event of a Japanese move into southern Indo-China it contemplated taking these measures: prohibition of the loading of iron ore, etc., off the Malayan coast by night; denunciation of the Anglo-Japanese commercial treaty; closure of the Japanese consulate at Singapore; restriction of exports to and imports from Japan. The British suggested discussions with a view to correlating action and it was agreed that appropriate officials of the Department and the Embassy should explore the situation in a purely informal and entirely confidential fashion.[46]

A series of three conferences between Mr. Hornbeck and the British Minister, Mr. Hall, on July 15 and 16, proved unrewarding, since neither of these officials could say just what his Government proposed to do.[47] From the records it is reasonably clear that the freezing of Japanese funds in the United States as well as extensive embargoes on trade were under consideration, but as yet no one could say how comprehensive the sanctions would be or on what "overt act" by Japan they would depend.[48]

The problem was discussed by the Cabinet on July 18 and the imposition of further sanctions agreed to, at least in principle. On the following day Mr. Welles requested his subordinates to prepare, by July 21, the necessary orders for the freezing of Japanese and, at Chiang Kai-shek's specific re-

---

wrote Mr. Ickes again on June 23 and then on June 25, replying to a letter from Mr. Ickes of June 25. The above quotation is taken from the President's final letter of July 1, 1941. For the full text of Mr. Roosevelt's letters of June 23 and July 1, 1941, see *F.D.R.: His Personal Letters* (New York, 1950), II, 1173-74.

[46] Memo of Mr. Hamilton to Mr. Welles, July 9, 1941; memos of conversation between Mr. Welles and Lord Halifax, July 10 and 14, 1941, the latter with attached memo from the British Embassy; tel. to Grew, July 14, 1941.

[47] Memos of conversation between Mr. Hornbeck and the British Minister, July 15 and 16, 1941.

[48] This statement is based on remarks made by Mr. Hornbeck in the conferences mentioned above, and is borne out by Minister Moffat's conversation with Mr. Norman Robertson of the Canadian Ministry for External Affairs, following Moffat's return to his post from Washington (*Moffat Diary, MS.*, July 15, 1941).

quest, of Chinese funds; for the prohibition or restriction of the import of Japanese silk and perhaps other important items; for the lowering of the specification for the octane content of gasoline and a reduction in the qualities of lubricating oils for export to Japan; and for the establishment of a quota for export of petroleum products based on a period when such exports were not abnormally large.[49]

This memorandum must have reflected the decisions of the Cabinet, of which nothing further has been discovered.[50] It indicates that on July 18 the whole question was still fluid and that a total embargo on oil products was not being contemplated. In consonance with instructions, which were probably given orally, State and Treasury Department officials canvassed proposed measures. The Treasury representative reported that there was agreement on the freezing order, but noted: "This is unquestionably very strong action vis-à-vis Japan, but apparently that is what is desired." For the rest it was planned to work out quotas for export by license of oil, cotton and other products, to be paid for by silk imports of equivalent value. In general it was proposed to reduce the annual export of petroleum products from the current four million barrels to one million.[51]

There matters rested for a few days, despite the fact that intercepted messages left no doubt that the Japanese were determined to attain their ends in Indo-China even if by force. The British reported on July 23 that the question of freezing Japanese funds had been taken up with the Dominions, the Netherlands and the Free French, with London's recommendation that such action be taken. But this news appears to have shocked rather than gratified Assistant Secretary of State Acheson, who was handling the problem on the American side. Mr. Acheson's notes betray something of his dismay:

In accordance with instructions from the Acting Secretary, I stated to Mr. Hall that the exact situation in Indo-China was still not clear to this Government, and that the timetable for putting restrictions into effect by this Government and the order and extent of the restrictions would depend upon the facts as they developed. I warned him that my prior conversation with him was not to be interpreted as meaning that this Government would put all the controls into effect simultaneously or immediately . . .[52]

[49] Memo by Hornbeck, July 19, 1941, transmitting Mr. Welles's request.
[50] This view is supported by a letter of Mr. Welles to the President of July 22, 1941, saying that in connection with the Cabinet discussions he had inquired of General Marshall whether restrictions on the import of Japanese silk would be undesirable from the War Department's standpoint, and had been told that General Marshall had no objection.
[51] Memo by Mr. Foley of the Treasury Department, July 21, 1941 (*Morgenthau Diaries, MS.*, Vol. 423, pp. 194 ff.). Evidently the substance of these recommendations was at once communicated to the British Government, as appears from a memo of conversation between Mr. Acheson and Messrs. Butler and Hall of the British Embassy, July 23, 1941.
[52] Memo of conversation between Mr. Acheson and Messrs. Butler and Hall, July 23, 1941.

The indecision so evident on the American side may have been due to the continued opposition of certain State Department officials to the adoption of extreme measures.[53] It may well have resulted also from a Navy Department memorandum, prepared by Admiral Richmond Kelly Turner, which Admiral Stark forwarded to President Roosevelt on July 21. This memorandum recommended against a trade embargo on the plea that such a step "would probably result in a fairly early attack by Japan on Malaya and the Netherlands East Indies and possibly would involve the United States in early war in the Pacific. If war in the Pacific is to be accepted by the United States, actions leading up to it should, if practicable, be postponed until Japan is engaged in war in Siberia."[54]

The period of uncertainty came to an end only on July 24, when it was definitely known that Vichy had acceded to the Japanese demands. That afternoon the question of American countermeasures was again discussed by the Cabinet. The President was evidently out of patience. With regard to Vichy's surrender he remarked that "of course everyone knew that the orders were issued under pressure from Germany." He insisted that Japanese funds be frozen and that comprehensive provision be made for restrictions on trade. The orders were to be so wide and adaptable as to be changeable without further discussion. When asked whether so drastic a step might not precipitate the very action by Japan which the United States had tried to forestall, Mr. Roosevelt replied that he did not think so: "He was inclined to go ahead with the order in the regular way and grant licenses for the shipment of petroleum as the applications are presented to the Treasury. This policy, he stated, might change any day and from there on we would refuse any and all licenses."[55]

In effect what the President decided to do was to emit a loud and resounding bark, in the hope that Tokyo might yet be frightened away from its prey. If this proved futile, he proposed to bite, as often and as hard as the situation might require. It is quite possible, though it cannot be proved, that he already had in mind a proposal which he expounded to Ambassador Nomura later on the same afternoon. The Ambassador had begged Admiral Stark to arrange a meeting with the President and this took place at 5 P.M., Admiral Stark and Acting Secretary Welles being present. Nomura said what he could to justify his Government's move into southern Indo-China, reiterated that Tokyo was eager for an understanding with the United States and urged the President "to give the matter statesmanlike consideration

[53] MS. study of Harold F. Gosnell of the history of the Division of Far Eastern Affairs of the State Department.

[54] The memorandum was dated July 19, 1941. For the text see *Pearl Harbor Attack,* V, 2382 ff., and for discussion see Admiral Turner's testimony (*ibid.,* IV, 2013-14) and Admiral Stark's letters to Admiral Hart, July 24, 1941, and to Admiral Cooke, July 31, 1941 (*ibid.,* V, 2114 and XVI, 2175).

[55] Notes on the Cabinet meeting of July 24, 1941 (*Morgenthau Diaries, MS.,* Vol. 424, pp. 145 ff.).

from a broad viewpoint with a view to maintaining the peace of the Pacific." Mr. Roosevelt hinted at the possibility of an embargo on oil products and explained once again why thus far nothing had been done to interfere with this traffic. He pointed out "that if Japan attempted to seize oil supplies by force in the Netherlands East Indies, the Dutch would, without the shadow of doubt, resist, the British would immediately come to their assistance, war would result between Japan, the British and the Dutch and, in view of our policy of assisting Great Britain, an exceedingly serious situation would immediately result." He had, so he said, deep sympathy for Japan's problem in obtaining resources. As for Indo-China, it might already be too late to undo Tokyo's move, but he would like to suggest a proposal which had just occurred to him and which he had not yet discussed even with the State Department:

If the Japanese Government would refrain from occupying Indo-China with its military and naval forces or, had such steps actually been commenced, if the Japanese Government would withdraw such forces, the President could assure the Japanese Government that he would do everything within his power to obtain from the Governments of China, Great Britain, the Netherlands, and of course the United States itself a binding and solemn declaration, provided Japan would undertake the same commitment, to regard Indo-China as a neutralized country in the same way in which Switzerland had up to now been regarded by the powers as a neutralized country. . . . He would further endeavor to procure from Great Britain and the other pertinent powers a guarantee that so long as the present emergency continued, the local French authorities in Indo-China would remain in control of the territory and would not be confronted with attempts to dislodge them on the part of de Gaullist or Free French agents or forces.[56]

This important proposal, designed to dispel Japan's alleged fears of encirclement and its suspicions of British-Free French plans for Indo-China, and to assure Japan access to the products of Indo-China, unfortunately failed to impress the Ambassador. Nomura, who was not a professional diplomat and who, in addition, suffered from an altogether inadequate command of the English language, was so concerned by the threat of economic sanctions that he failed to grasp the full import of the President's proposal. He reported it only incidentally to the Tokyo Foreign Office, and in rather garbled form: "After inquiring of me if I had consulted in advance with the State Department, he [the President] stated that he would not hesitate to make efforts if there were a way by which the troops now stationed in French Indo-China might be withdrawn, the neutrality of the area guaranteed (as in the case of Switzerland) and its resources obtained by the Powers freely and equitably."[57] Even so, it is strange that Foreign Minister

56 *Foreign Relations of the United States: Japan*, II, 527 ff.; tel. to Grew, July 25, 1941. See also Nomura's report to Toyoda, July 24, 1941 (*Tokyo War Crimes Documents*, Defense Document No. 1401-D-1).
57 Tel. from Nomura to Toyoda, July 24, 1941 (*Tokyo War Crimes Documents*, De-

JAPAN'S FATEFUL GAMBLE 651

Toyoda, too, seems to have missed the point completely. When Ambassador Grew queried him on the matter, he asserted that he had never heard of it. Conceivably he took this line because he was unable to hold out much hope that his Government would retrace its course. On July 28 the Japanese forces were already disembarking at Saigon.[58]

The evidence indicates that Mr. Roosevelt himself counted more on the threat of comprehensive sanctions than on his neutralization proposal to deter the Japanese Government. The requisite orders had been agreed to in conference between the State Department, the Treasury and the Attorney General and were ready for issuance on the morning of July 26, 1941. On July 25 the War and Navy Departments, with the President's approval, warned American commanders in the Pacific of what was coming. The commanders were told that no immediate hostile action on the part of Japan was anticipated, but that "appropriate precautionary measures" might well be instituted. On the evening of July 25 a press release from Hyde Park announced the forthcoming freeze. In a message to Mr. Harry Hopkins (July 26) the President requested his emissary to inform Mr. Churchill that he thought the Anglo-American action with regard to Japan was already bearing fruit: "I hear their Government much upset and no conclusive future policy has been determined on. Tell him [Mr. Churchill] in great confidence that I have suggested to Nomura that Indo-China be neutralized by Britain, Dutch, Chinese, Japan and ourselves, placing Indo-China somewhat in status of Switzerland. Japan to get rice and fertilizer but all on condition that Japan withdraw armed forces from Indo-China *in toto*. I have had no answer yet. When it comes, it will probably be unfavorable, but we have at least made one more effort to avoid Japanese expansion to South Pacific."[59]

The executive order freezing all Japanese funds and assets in the United States was duly issued on July 26, 1941, and was accompanied, on the same day, by the British and Dominion denunciations of trade treaties with Japan and the imposition of various financial restrictions. The Netherlands Government, not fully posted by London, as had been expected, was much

---

fense Document No. 1401D-1). On Nomura's disabilities it is worth quoting from the *Grew Diary (MS.)*, August 5, 1941: "We have all too much evidence that the Japanese Embassy in Washington is half the time asleep at the switch either in failing to understand statements made by our Government or in failing to report them promptly, accurately and comprehensively. This view, I am confidentially informed, is shared by the Foreign Office here."

[58] *Foreign Relations of the United States: Japan*, II, 318 ff., 534 ff.; *Tokyo War Crimes Documents*, Proceedings, 36,251 ff., and Defense Document No. 1683. The Japanese public announcement of July 26, 1941, is given in *Documents on American Foreign Relations*, IV, 502. See also André Gaudel: *L'Indochine française en face du Japon* (Paris, 1947), 117 ff.

[59] Text in *Pearl Harbor Attack*, XX, 4374, and now in *F.D.R.: His Personal Letters*, II, 1189-90. The joint State-Treasury Department memo, dated July 25, 1941, is in the *Morgenthau Diaries (MS.)*, Vol. 424, pp. 268 ff. For the War and Navy Department warnings, see Mark S. Watson: *Chief of Staff: Prewar Plans and Preparations*, 495.

concerned by the possible Japanese reaction to the American-British program, but fell in line on July 28.[60]

To the American public the new measures did not come as a surprise, for the deliberations of the Government had leaked to the press on July 22.[61] The popular response was generally favorable, even to the extent of approving a complete embargo on trade with Japan. *The New York Times* (July 24) had called for a stiff line:

> The Japanese Government must be made to understand clearly that aggressive action on its part in any one of three possible areas . . . Siberia, the Netherlands East Indies, or Indo-China . . . will be met by prompt retaliation on the part of the United States. We have a direct and legitimate interest in each of these three areas. . . . Any action by Japan that threatens a legitimate American interest in the Far East should be met at once by efforts on our part to deal Japanese finance and industry and trade a deadly blow.

Other newspapers, which had long since been agitating for an embargo, were jubilant over the new orders, assuming that they meant the end of all trade with Japan. They hailed the end of "appeasement" and rejoiced that their Government at last meant business. "Let there be no mistake," wrote the *New York Post*, "the United States must relentlessly apply its crushing strength." "The noose is around Japan's neck at last," crowed a writer in *PM*, pointing out that it was now in America's power to decide how fast Japan should be strangled: "For a time it may bluster and retaliate, but in the end it can only whimper and capitulate."[62]

A contrast to such exuberant utterances was the comment of Wilfrid Fleischer, one of the most careful and responsible observers of Far Eastern developments: "Japan must move quickly to consummate her conquests in Asia or face economic ruin and defeat. . . . The Japanese are now with their backs to the wall and they must carry on with the struggle they have so rashly embarked upon or renounce their dreams of empire in Asia. The die has been cast."[63] This, as events were to prove, was the situation in a nutshell. Even though it was not Mr. Roosevelt's intention to impose at once a full embargo, to include oil products, some of his advisers had grave misgivings about the new sanctions. Secretary Hull, still at White Sulphur Springs, regretted the publicity given the American action, yet saw no alternative to the measures taken. Speaking to Mr. Welles over the telephone he remarked on July 25:

[60] *Foreign Relations of the United States: Japan*, II, 266-67; *Documents on American Foreign Relations*, IV, 506 ff. We have used also memos of conversation between Mr. Acheson and the Netherlands Minister Counselor, July 27, 1941, and between Mr. Welles and the Netherlands Minister, July 29, 1941.

[61] *The New York Times*, July 23, 1941 (dateline Washington, July 22, 1941).

[62] *New York Post*, editorial, July 26, 1941; Kenneth G. Crawford in *PM*, July 27, 1941.

[63] Wilfrid Fleischer in the *New York Herald Tribune*, July 27, 1941.

I am sure Japan is going on unless something happens to stop her. This is a world movement. The Japanese are seeking to dominate militarily practically one half the world and apply the barbarous methods that they are applying to China and that Hitler is applying to Europe, and if they have their way, they will carry out what they are saying of their right to be supreme in that half of the world, by which they mean military supremacy with methods of arbitrary, selfish domination and the Hitler method of piracy and naval control of the seas and commerce.

A few days later, tortured by anxiety, the Secretary was considering the possibility of dispelling Japanese fears of attack from Indo-China by offering to interpose an American naval force; Washington might say to Tokyo: "We would be willing, if they take the right course, to utilize our Navy to help the Japanese, in a way satisfactory to them, to protect themselves from Indo-China. And . . . as we remarked a dozen times to Nomura, we would try to get Britain and the Netherlands and other interested countries to sign an agreement similar to the one we were talking about." On the other hand, Mr. Hull could not overcome his conviction that the military chiefs had taken control in Tokyo and that the United States must be prepared for the worst: "We are making a mistake if we don't look out for other developments instead of clinging too much to our discussions looking toward a settlement." "I think we need to keep a stiff rein and consider making it just as stiff as possible short of actual military activity." He pleaded with his subordinates to formulate "a comprehensive program of action short of war, to be placed into effect as rapidly as circumstances permitted."[64]

These inconclusive observations of the ailing Secretary are of interest chiefly as a reflection of the doubts and hesitancies that persisted even in high circles. If in fact there was any lack of appreciation of the gravity of the American policy decision, it must have been quickly dispelled by the Japanese. Admiral Toyoda remarked to Ambassador Grew that the American move had robbed him of his sleep. After explaining again the purpose and character of the Japanese action with respect to Indo-China, the Foreign Minister handed the Ambassador a memorandum ending on this grave note:

Should any provocative attitude or any concrete step be taken against such measures of joint defense which Japan as well as French Indo-China were compelled to take for the sake of their self-defense, on the exclusively theoretical ground that it contradicts general doctrinarian principles which the American Government embraces, the Japanese Government may not be able, it is feared, in spite of all its efforts (which have succeeded in suppressing them thus far) to suppress an outburst of the national feeling which has unfortunately received an extremely strong impetus from the attitude which the American Government has taken in connection with its aid to the Chiang Kai-shek regime. In such a case, there is a danger that Japan would be forced to take

[64] Memos of conversation by telephone between Mr. Hull and Mr. Welles, July 25, 28, 29, 30, 1941.

some countermeasures, to the destruction of all the hopes of myself as well as the present Cabinet to prevent by all possible efforts the coming about of such a situation. This would be much to be dreaded, indeed, for the maintenance of friendly relations between Japan and the United States and the peace of the Pacific. It is cordially requested, therefore, that Your Excellency as well as your Government give prudent and general consideration thereto.[65]

Well might Mr. Grew note in his private diary: "The vicious circle of reprisals and counter-reprisals is on. . . . Unless radical surprises occur in the world, it is difficult to see how the momentum of this downgrade movement in our relations can be arrested, nor how far it will go. The obvious conclusion is eventual war."[66]

5. THE AFTERMATH

On July 28, 1941, the Japanese Privy Council, after long deliberation and in full appreciation of all that was involved, decided to ratify the agreement with Vichy France.[67] At the same time Tokyo announced the freezing of American, British and Dutch funds in Japan. In a telegram to the Ambassador at Berlin, the Government's iron determination was clearly expressed:

Commercial and economic relations between Japan and other countries, led by England and the United States, are gradually becoming so horribly strained that we cannot endure it much longer. Consequently, the Japanese Empire, to save its very life, must take measures to secure the raw materials of the South Seas. It must take immediate steps to break asunder this ever-strengthening chain of encirclement, which is being woven under the guidance of and with the participation of England and the United States, acting like a cunning dragon seemingly asleep.[68]

Meanwhile the American Government had followed up its order of July 26 with a notification to Japan that the Panama Canal would be closed for repairs. Furthermore, the Philippine military forces were mustered into service with the United States Army under General Douglas MacArthur as Commanding General of American forces in the Far East. In an atmosphere of increasing tension, marked by reports of Japanese demands on the Siamese Government for bases and of substantial troop movements to Manchuria, the State and Treasury Departments, assisted by the office of the Attorney General, worked out the details of the new trade restrictions. The State Department recommended procedure by stages: during the first two weeks no indication should be given of American policy with respect to the

[65] Memo of July 26, 1941 (*Tokyo War Crimes Documents,* Defense Document, No. 1901).
[66] *Grew Diary (MS.),* summary for July, 1941.
[67] *Tokyo War Crimes Documents,* No. 1031.
[68] Tel. to Oshima, July 31, 1941, quoted in Herbert Feis: *The Road to Pearl Harbor* (Princeton, 1950), 249. This message was intercepted and deciphered in Washington on August 4, 1941.

implementation of the freezing order; the Government should continue to accept applications for export and import licenses, but should not act upon them. During the ensuing two or three months it should still avoid any announcement of general policy in these matters. Depending on future political developments it should permit limited exports and imports, keeping the two roughly in balance. The export of petroleum products should be permitted to about the extent of 1935-36 shipments, but none of these products was to be of high octane grade. In the final period, assuming political conditions warranted an expansion of trade, a clearing arrangement might be made allowing sufficient exports to pay for needed imports.[69]

In accordance with the program recommended by the Interdepartmental Committee, the President on August 1, 1941, issued an order prohibiting the export to Japan of certain materials (wood pulp, metals and manufactures, machinery and vehicles, rubber and manufactures, chemicals and related products), and of petroleum products of such grade as to make them usable as aviation gasoline. This new step was greeted with another outburst of approval by the press, which for the most part disregarded the plain wording of the order and assumed that a full embargo was being imposed. The more ardent newspapers proclaimed that Japan was now bound hand and foot, that Japan would either have to put up or shut up. A survey of opinion on the West Coast reported the general sentiment to be: "They are asking for it, let's let them have it." According to public opinion polls at least half the number of those questioned expressed willingness to risk war in order to keep Japan from becoming more powerful. Indeed, the polls revealed a substantial degree of sentiment in favor of American action to defend Singapore, the Netherlands Indies or Australia.[70]

It can hardly be denied that with respect to sanctions against Japan, American public opinion was running well ahead of the President and his Administration. Actually the order of August 1 was little more than a demonstration, since many if not most of the items therein mentioned had long since been under license. This was notably true of high grade gasoline and lubricants. It is no exaggeration, therefore, to say that the President was still barking, not biting. If Tokyo had shown the slightest disposition to desist from its campaign of expansion, there is every reason to suppose that the recently issued American orders would have become dead letters. But the Japanese, far from retreating, were clearly preparing further moves. United States consuls in Manchuria reported three thousand Japanese troops moving through Dairen daily and a continuing concentration of forces on the

[69] Memo of the Office of the Adviser on International Economic Affairs, July 30, 1941; letter of Mr. Welles to the President, July 31, 1941.

[70] Wilfrid Fleischer, in the *New York Herald Tribune*, August 2; *The New York Times*, August 3 (survey of opinion on the West Coast); Joseph G. Harrison in the *Christian Science Monitor*, August 7; tel. to Grew, August 5, 1941, summarizing American press opinion.

Soviet Siberian border. The general feeling, they reported, was that a conflict between Japan and the Soviet Union was impending.[71]

Even more ominous were the indications that Japan would presently assume control of Siam. Diplomatic reports from Bangkok stated that the Japanese were demanding bases and threatening to employ force if the Siamese proved recalcitrant.[72] On July 30 Lord Halifax informed the State Department that the British had learned from the Siamese Prime Minister himself that military and economic concessions were being demanded under threat and that the Bangkok Government had inquired what aid it could expect from Britain and the United States in case it decided to resist.[73]

The State Department was well aware that the Japanese program included the subjection of Siam and that Japanese control of that country would constitute a major threat to the security of Malaya. It was highly skeptical of Bangkok's will to resist and was above all deeply impressed by the inability of either Britain or the United States to aid Siam effectively and in good time. The President therefore attempted to meet the situation by extending his proposal for the neutralization of Indo-China to include Siam. On August 6, 1941, both Foreign Secretary Eden and Secretary Hull publicly warned Japan against any move against Siam. Mr. Eden declared that "any action which would threaten the independence and integrity of Thailand [Siam] would be a matter of immediate concern to this country [Britain], more particularly as threatening the security of Singapore." Mr. Hull, on his part, told the press that a Japanese move into Siam would be regarded by Washington as a menace to American security and a danger to American territory in the Pacific. Apparently these admonitions were enough to decide the Japanese not to overdraw the bow. Tokyo promptly disclaimed all aggressive intentions and declared that British and American fears were "based on no warrantable facts."[74]

Tokyo was naturally much disturbed by the strong American statement with regard to Indo-China, the prompt American action in freezing Japanese funds, and the State Department's notification to Nomura that further discussions of a peaceful settlement were obviously pointless. Nomura reported the strength of popular support for the Government's firm policy, and noted that public interest focused more on Japanese-American than on German-American relations. The Ambassador felt the situation slipping out

[71] State Department, general summary of Far Eastern developments, July 31 and August 7, 1941.

[72] Tels. from Grant (Bangkok), July 25 and 28, 1941.

[73] Memo of conversation between Mr. Welles and Lord Halifax, July 30, 1941.

[74] *Bulletin of International News,* XVIII (2), 1109, 1112, 1116; memo from Hamilton to Hornbeck, July 30, 1941, recommending that no reply be made to the Siamese appeals; memo of a telephone conversation between Mr. Hull and Mr. Welles, July 31, 1941; memo of conversation between Mr. Hamilton and the Siamese Minister, August 7, 1941; tel. from Grant, August 8, 1941, conveying the satisfaction of the Bangkok Government. On this episode see also *Pearl Harbor Attack,* XIX, 3707 ff., and Frank L. Kluckhohn in *The New York Times,* August 7, 1941.

of control and pathetically requested that some senior member of the Japanese diplomatic service (he suggested Mr. Kurusu) be sent promptly to assist him: "I deeply fear lest I should make a miscalculation at this moment, and besides, there is a limit to my ability. . . . I am unable to perceive the delicate shades of the policy of the Government, and am quite at a loss what to do."[75]

One can readily sympathize with the Japanese sailor-diplomat in his quandary. The fact is that within the Tokyo Government the conflict of factions had been reopened. In both Army and Navy circles there were hotheads who demanded that Japan take up the challenge thrown down by Washington. But Admiral Nagano, Chief of the Naval General Staff, was decidedly not one of them. On the contrary, he kept urging upon the Emperor the necessity for avoiding war and made no secret of his conviction that so long as Japan adhered to the Tripartite Pact no adjustment of relations with the United States would be possible. Failing a settlement with Washington, Tokyo would have to reckon with the oil embargo, which would put Japan in a hopeless position. The oil reserves were sufficient for two years at the most and the embargo might thus force Japan to take the initiative in hostilities against the United States, despite the fact that the outcome of war would be extremely doubtful. Marquis Kido, who was present at Nagano's interview with the Emperor, was "filled with trepidation by the Imperial anxiety about the danger of having to wage a desperate war." Nonetheless, he took the view that if Japan dropped the alliance with the Axis, it would earn only the contempt of the United States. Some other solution must be found. Prince Konoye, too, was much exercised by the temerity of the military and threatened to resign unless agreement could be reached on the course of future action.[76]

After several conferences between the civilian and military authorities the Japanese finally concluded that they could not retreat from Indo-China under pressure and that the best course to pursue would be, if possible, to revive the Washington conversations looking toward a general settlement. On August 5, 1941, new proposals were forwarded to Nomura along these lines: (1) Japan would promise not to send troops into territories other than Indo-China; (2) Japan would agree to withdraw its forces from Indo-China as soon as a settlement of the China Incident had been arrived at; (3) Japan would guarantee the neutrality of the Philippines; (4) the United States would suspend military preparations in the southwest Pacific and eventually induce the British and Dutch to do likewise; (5) the United States and Japan would coöperate in securing for each other the raw materials of the southwest Pacific area; (6) the United States would use its

[75] Tel. from Nomura to Toyoda, August 4, 1941 (*Tokyo War Crimes Documents*, Defense Document No. 1401E-1).

[76] "Kido Diary," July 31 and August 2, 1941 (*Tokyo War Crimes Documents*, 1632W-63 and 1632W-64). See also the tel. from Grew, July 30, 1941, in *Pearl Harbor Attack*, XX, 4387 ff.

good offices to bring about direct negotiations between Japan and Chiang Kai-shek; (7) the United States would recognize Japan's special position in Indo-China even after the withdrawal of the Japanese forces.[77]

These proposals were hardly promising and evidently did not appear so to Prince Konoye, who for some time had been genuinely worried by the repercussions of his own policies. The Prime Minister was much impressed by the statement of Japanese naval leaders that in a war the country's oil reserves would at best meet requirements for eighteen months, while military men thought they would suffice for only one year of combat.[78] Under the circumstances Prince Konoye could not see how a war against the United States could be anything but hopeless. The Japanese could not risk an attack on the Netherlands Indies before having reduced Singapore and the Philippines and even if they did attack the Indies, they were sure to find the oil wells destroyed. To restore them to operation would require eighteen months. Meanwhile the United States would probably have declared war and have cut Japanese communications through submarine and air attacks. All in all the Prime Minister thought it essential to revive friendly relations with the United States, if only to gain time for Japan to build up its oil and other reserves and develop synthetic oil and other war industries.[79]

Evidently satisfied that the latest Japanese proposals would not fill the bill, Prince Konoye did not even await the American reaction before telegraphing Nomura a new and personal proposal, namely for a meeting between Mr. Roosevelt and himself. He hoped, so he said, that such a conference might result in at least some alleviation of tension, though it is hard to see on what he based his optimism. His own memoirs, as well as other Japanese records, show that he had no real intention of abandoning Japan's connection with the Axis or Japan's program for a Greater East Asia Co-Prosperity Sphere. Quite possibly he may have calculated that a conference with the President, even though abortive, would enable him to pose before the Japanese public as the man who had done his utmost to find a peaceful solution. Army leaders were highly skeptical of the project from the outset and concurred in it only on the explicit understanding that if it failed Prince Konoye would not throw up his office, but would take responsibility for leading the nation into war.[80]

---

[77] Tel. from Toyoda to Nomura, August 5, 1941 (the American intercept in *Pearl Harbor Attack*, XII, 10, and the official text in *Tokyo War Crimes Documents*, Defense Document No. 1401G-1). See further *Foreign Relations of the United States: Japan*, II, 546-50, the "Konoye Memoirs" (*Pearl Harbor Attack*, XX, 3998) and the "Tojo Memorandum" (*Tokyo War Crimes Documents*, Proceedings, 36268).

[78] In this connection it is interesting to note that American oil companies with interests in the Netherlands Indies estimated the Japanese reserves as sufficient for one year under war conditions, and that independent United States Treasury calculations came to substantially the same conclusion (*Morgenthau Diaries, MS.*, Vol. 424, pp. 73 and 258).

[79] "Kido Diary," August 7, 1941, reporting a talk with Prince Konoye (*Tokyo War Crimes Documents*, No. 1632W-66).

[80] "Konoye Memoirs" (*Pearl Harbor Attack*, XX, 3999-4000); "Tojo Memorandum"

Secretary Hull, who returned to his Washington post on August 4, was hardly in a mood to consider any Japanese proposals sympathetically. He was now firmly convinced that there was little chance of stopping the Japanese in their headlong advance. Speaking to Mr. Welles by telephone just before his departure from White Sulphur Springs, he had remarked:

We have got to keep in mind every day what seems to be the central fact in the situation, so far as the Japanese are concerned, and that is that they are at a point right now where they must either go forward more and more toward Thailand and the Burma Road area—no matter how surreptitiously—by evasion, deceit, and all manner of avowals of friendship and peace—as they have done so many times in the past—or they must turn around and come back toward the road of friendship and peace. They swear every day that they are going forward and they are fitting their acts to their words. The only time they modify their policy of overt, unfriendly acts is when they make false and fraudulent avowals of peace and friendship. This they do until they are ready to go forward. While I am not suggesting anything, we should keep what I think is the central point of the situation in mind every day, otherwise we will find ourselves surprised. Nothing will stop them except force. Unless we figure that they are going to turn back, we should not figure that they are going to be satisfied to stop where they are. The point is how long we can maneuver the situation until the military matter in Europe is brought to a conclusion. . . . You have to keep this in mind— that there is naturally going to continue to be an element of risk and danger in our course, if it is sufficiently firm and extensive to checkmate them. I just don't want us to take for granted a single word they say, but to appear to do so to whatever extent it may satisfy our purpose to delay further action by them. If it can bring about a situation over there responsive to the standpoint we seek and also public opinion at home, it will be fine. Of course, I think they would have stood for cutting off oil entirely as a deserved penalty for going into Indo-China. We must realize that the extreme elements that don't reason much may be poised and ready to take advantage of any attractive slogan to make a break southward.[81]

Secretary Stimson was delighted to find his State Department colleague, on the latter's return to Washington, firm and determined: "He has made up his mind that we have reached the end of any possible appeasement with Japan and that there is nothing further that can be done with that country except by a firm policy and, he expected, force itself." After discussing recently intercepted Japanese messages, the two Secretaries concluded that they provided further examples of duplicity:

They [the Japanese] are trying now to get up a conference between the Japanese Prime Minister and President Roosevelt on a most engaging program of peace, while at the same time they are carrying on negotiations with their Ambassadors throughout the world showing on its face this is a pure blind and that they have already made up their minds to a policy of going south through Indo-China and Thailand. The invitation is merely a blind to try to keep us from taking definite action.[82]

(*Tokyo War Crimes Documents:* Proceedings, 36269); tel. to Nomura, August 7, 1941 (*Pearl Harbor Attack,* XII, 12).

[81] Memo of telephone conversation between Mr. Hull and Mr. Welles, August 2, 1941.
[82] *Stimson Diary* (*MS.*), August 7, 8, 9, 1941.

Knowing as much as he did of Japanese deliberations and plans, it was inevitable that Mr. Hull should have given Ambassador Nomura a cool reception when that gentleman came, on August 6, to present the newest Japanese proposals. The Secretary promised to study them, though he showed little interest. Instead he expressed to Nomura his disappointment over Japan's recent moves and remarked "that, so long as Japan holds to the policy of conquest by force, there is no room left for negotiations and that, so long as the Government authorities of Japan call American actions the encirclement of Japan, he can expect nothing of them." Nomura, reporting home, could not repress a lugubrious note: "Judging from the impression I received today, it seems utterly impossible now by explanation to bring the authorities of the American Government to understand the true intention of Japan, and it was clearly perceived that the United States is already determined to face any situation that may be brought about."[83]

The official American reply (August 8) to the Japanese proposals was hardly more encouraging. It simply recalled the President's offer to neutralize Indo-China and pointed out that the latest Japanese note "was lacking in responsiveness" to that offer. As for the suggested meeting between Mr. Roosevelt and the Japanese Prime Minister, Mr. Hull showed no enthusiasm and held out no hope. The President had already left Washington to attend the Atlantic Conference and a final decision was therefore impossible for the moment.[84]

The foregoing detailed analysis of the crisis in Japanese-American relations in July, 1941, hardly requires much by way of recapitulation. General Tojo, at his trial in 1947, asserted that neither the Japanese Cabinet nor the Supreme Command envisaged the move into southern Indo-China as likely to bring on the rupture of economic relations between the United States and Japan. On the contrary, he maintained, it was believed in Tokyo that the Washington conversations, looking toward a general settlement, would continue. Although the new instructions sent to Nomura on July 25 appear to support this contention, it is difficult to believe that Tokyo could have so completely misread the American reaction. Tojo has argued, as did Toyoda at the time, that the occupation of southern Indo-China was necessary because the speedy conclusion of the China Incident called for the severance of ties between Chungking on the one hand and the Americans, British and Dutch on the other; because the military preparations of these powers in the Southwest Pacific and their alleged maneuvers and activities in Indo-China and Siam constituted a threat of attack upon Japan; and because the rupture of commercial negotiations with the Netherlands Indies

[83] Tel. from Nomura to Toyoda, August 6, 1941 (*Tokyo War Crimes Documents,* Defense Document No. 1401H-1).

[84] *Foreign Relations of the United States: Japan,* II, 550-53; tels. from Nomura to Tokyo, August 7 and 9, 1941 (*Pearl Harbor Attack,* 13-15).

and the increasing economic pressure from the United States made it essential for Japan to ensure its sources of food and raw materials.

But even if one concedes that the Japanese, refusing to recognize that the collaboration of the United States, Britain, China, and the Netherlands was the direct result of Japan's publicly announced policy of expansion, genuinely feared encirclement and possibly an eventual combined attack, one is faced with the question why Tokyo ignored President Roosevelt's offer to neutralize Indo-China and Siam and thereby exorcise its apprehensions. Taking all factors into consideration it is hard to escape the conclusion, firmly supported by the content of the intercepted Japanese messages, that Tokyo, though already deeply involved in the China Incident, was determined to exploit the European War for further gains. The defeat of France had provoked the first move to the south and the German attack on Soviet Russia seemed to provide an additional opportunity for advance toward the realization of the Greater East Asia Co-Prosperity Sphere. To quote the words of one among many Japanese journalists on this point:

Opportunity must be taken by the forelock. Germany's bold and decisive action has put us to shame. Japan has already missed four opportunities: one following the collapse of the Netherlands, Belgium and France in June; second, when Japan signed the Tripartite Pact in September; third, when Japan mediated between Thailand and French Indo-China in February this year; and fourth, at the conclusion of the Russo-Japanese neutrality pact in April. The outbreak of the Soviet-German War now affords us a fifth opportunity. If Japan fails to seize it, it will go like the others.[85]

The Tokyo Government did, to be sure, veto Matsuoka's bold plan for an assault on Soviet Siberia, but only because the chances of success were slim and because it was thought more profitable to take advantage of the respite from the danger of Soviet attack to make the most of the really grandiose opportunity for advances in the south. Britain was reeling from the reverses suffered in the Middle East and the tension between the United States and Germany was such that it was thought Washington would be unwilling to take a strong line in the Pacific. Furthermore, Japanese leaders seem to have reasoned that, in view of the British conquest of Syria and the American occupation of Iceland, they could justify the acquisition of bases and the stationing of troops in southern Indo-China, especially if the matter could be settled quickly and peacefully.

Whatever the pros and cons of the Japanese position, as seen from Washington and London the essential point was that the Japanese were again on the march and that this time they had succeeded in poising themselves for effective action against British, Dutch and American possessions in the Far East. It was inevitable that the United States Government, knowing from intercepted messages that Japan was determined to reach its goals even at

[85] *Miyako*, July 2, 1941 (quoted in Otto D. Tolischus: *Through Japanese Eyes,* New York, 1945, p. 98).

the risk of war, should take a much firmer stand than before. The remarkable thing is that even then American opposition to Japan remained so largely a matter of threats. Mr. Welles's public statement on Indo-China constituted an unmistakable warning, reiterated even more explicitly in his remarks to Minister Wakasugi on the eve of the latter's departure for Japan:

I said that I wished to make it very clear to Mr. Wakasugi that in my considered judgment, if Japan continued on an aggressive policy of force and undertook moves of expansion which would result in acts of aggression upon additional peoples in the Far East, in the south or in other regions of the Pacific, the aim of Japan could only be regarded by the United States as the creation of a military overlordship of the Southern Pacific and perhaps over other areas as well. If this were in reality the objective of the Japanese Government, I thought it necessary at this stage to say that in my judgment such a situation as that would inevitably be regarded as intolerable by the United States and by other peace-minded nations having direct interests in the Pacific and that, consequently, whether it came tomorrow, or next month, or next year, or even later, the pursuit of such an objective by Japan would inevitably result in armed hostilities in the Pacific.[86]

This explicit admonition, reinforced by the likelihood that the freezing order would eventuate in a complete embargo on trade, should have given Tokyo pause. As yet there was still time, for the threat of fatal economic sanctions had not yet materialized. The President and his responsible advisers still lagged behind American public opinion in their response to Japanese moves. Quite obviously they were intent on avoiding or at least deferring military action in the Pacific because of the growing tension in the Atlantic. But Japan's decisions were, as its leaders never tired of repeating, "irrevocable." Not even the dismissal of the obnoxious Matsuoka made any real difference. The Japanese might be divided on the question of what direction and method to choose for expansion and conquest, but there is no evidence that any important figure, civilian or military, was prepared to abandon aspirations which were truly national. Prince Konoye was distinguished from his colleagues only insofar as he posed as a man of good will and hoped, probably sincerely, that he could attain by negotiation what the military men recognized could be won only by force of arms. By and large Japanese leaders seem to have believed, along with statesmen throughout the world, that Hitler's victory over Soviet Russia was imminent and that thereafter the Axis would be so powerful that the United States would be obliged to concentrate all its attention and power on the Atlantic. Under the circumstanecs they felt reasonably safe in risking the imposition of mortal sanctions. If, in the sequel, they felt their country being strangled by American economic pressure, they had largely their own vaulting ambition and their own fateful miscalculations to blame.

[86] Memo of conversation between Mr. Welles and Mr. Wakasugi, August 4, 1941 (*Foreign Relations of the United States: Japan,* II, 543).

CHAPTER XXI

The Atlantic Conference

1. THE SETTING

The suspense with which the New as well as the Old World watched the Nazi-Soviet conflict during the summer of 1941 was broken, in August, by news of the dramatic meeting of President Roosevelt and Prime Minister Churchill aboard the warships *Augusta* and *Prince of Wales* off Argentia, on the coast of Newfoundland. This meeting, prototype of the famous conferences of the war period, was the realization of Mr. Roosevelt's longstanding desire for a personal exchange of ideas with Mr. Churchill, with whom he had been in close correspondence for more than a year. He had been on the point of arranging an interview in February, 1941, and at that time, in connection with Mr. Harry Hopkins's first mission to London, had remarked to Secretary Morgenthau: "I have just got to see Churchill myself in order to explain things to him."[1] No doubt what the President then had in mind were the issues involved in the pending Lend-Lease legislation, on which discussion might well have proved profitable. Developments in the Balkans and North Africa, however, made the plan impracticable and it was not until Hitler's offensive in the east provided temporary respite that another favorable moment arrived for both statesmen to leave their posts for a period of at least ten days. Hopkins was despatched to London in mid-July to make arrangements and Mr. Churchill at once fell in with the President's proposal.

Mr. Roosevelt's original idea envisaged only a meeting *à deux,* but it was finally decided that there would be real advantages in having the highest military and naval authorities of the two nations become acquainted. Almost at the last moment it was further agreed to include diplomatic representatives. The conferring parties therefore comprised, on the military side, the Chiefs of Staff, the commanders of the Air Forces and members of the

[1] *Morgenthau Diaries (MS.),* February 17, 1941 (Vol. 373, p. 77B).

planning divisions. On the civilian side Under Secretary Welles represented the State Department, and Sir Alexander Cadogan the Foreign Office. Thus the projected meeting of the two statesmen was transformed into a full-scale conference.[2]

All arrangements were made in deepest secrecy, some members of the American party not knowing the purpose or destination of their journey until they were already at sea.[3] Not only was Mr. Stephen T. Early, the President's press secretary, left in the dark, but even the chief of the White House secret service was misled as to the President's plans.[4] Mr. Roosevelt doubtless derived innocent pleasure from mystifying his entourage. Officially he embarked on the *Potomac* at New London on August 3 for a midsummer fishing trip along the northeastern coast, but once at sea he transferred to the cruiser *Augusta* (Admiral King's flagship) and, accompanied by the *Tuscaloosa* and a destroyer escort, proceeded to Argentia, which was reached on August 7. Meanwhile Mr. Churchill and the entire British party crossed the Atlantic aboard the new battleship *Prince of Wales,* arriving at the rendezvous on August 9. By this time the absence from Washington of so many high officials had been noticed by the press and rumors of an important meeting had spread on both sides of the Atlantic. There was some consideration of the advisability of announcing the facts, but Mr. Roosevelt insisted that nothing be done to satisfy popular curiosity.[5]

During the four days from August 9 to August 12 the two principals and their subordinates conferred almost continuously, though quite informally. Because of the President's infirmity, Mr. Churchill generally came aboard the *Augusta,* but on the morning of Sunday, August 10, Mr. Roosevelt attended an impressive religious service aboard the *Prince of Wales.* The military men, as well as Mr. Welles and Sir Alexander Cadogan, went to and fro between the two warships as convenience dictated. The only really general session seems to have taken place after dinner on the evening of August 9, on which occasion Mr. Churchill delivered one of his masterly reviews of the world situation and expounded his hopes and plans for the future conduct of the war. The President's son, Elliott Roosevelt, has reported that the Prime Minister pleaded eloquently for immediate intervention: "It's your only chance! You've got to come in beside us!" But this

---

[2] Sumner Welles: *The Time for Decision* (New York, 1944), 175 ff.; Forrest Davis and Ernest K. Lindley: *How War Came* (New York, 1944), 250 ff.; Robert E. Sherwood: *Roosevelt and Hopkins* (New York, 1948), Chapter XVI; Winston S. Churchill: *The Grand Alliance* (Boston, 1950), 427 ff. Good accounts of the externals of the meeting are given in H. V. Morton: *Atlantic Meeting* (London, 1943) and in Elliott Roosevelt: *As He Saw It* (New York, 1946), Chapter II.

[3] General H. T. Arnold: *Global Mission* (New York, 1949), 246 ff.

[4] Grace Tully: *F.D.R., My Boss* (New York, 1949), 246-48. Early was furious when he learned that while American correspondents had been left behind, the British delegation included two or three thinly disguised members of the Ministry of Information.

[5] Morton: *Atlantic Meeting,* 15-16; tel. from Winant, August 5; tel. to Winant, August 6, 1941.

interesting item, unsupported by other evidence, must be viewed with reserve. While it reflects the hope and conviction of the British, more circumspectly expressed in the military discussions, it is highly unlikely that Mr. Churchill adopted so flat-footed an approach in a rather large and open gathering.

2. MILITARY CONVERSATIONS

Since the conference was thought of primarily as providing an opportunity for personal acquaintance and informal exchange of views, no agenda had been drawn up and the discussions for the most part were desultory and inconclusive. This was true particularly of the military conversations, carried on by groups of varying size and composition. The problems considered were largely of a technical nature, such as coördination of requirements, assignment of priorities, and methods of allocation. In response to rather pointed American criticism the British agreed to reorganize their purchasing system and to push on with the drafting of long-term, overall requirements. Among the naval authorities it was recognized that the question of convoy escort, which had been hanging fire for many months and to which Mr. Churchill had again called attention, was most urgent. Discussions of this issue resulted in one of the few definite decisions arrived at during the meeting: arrangements were completed for American escort of British as well as American merchant ships as far as Iceland and the new system was put into operation on August 20.[6]

More interesting and illuminating were the discussions of larger issues of strategy which, on the British side, Mr. Churchill had outlined on the evening of August 9. On the following day the British Chiefs of Staff circulated to their American colleagues a General Strategy Review, dated July 31, 1941, which, in a sense, was the most recent summary of issues and conclusions discussed with the American military representatives in London since the drafting of the ABC-1 plans in March, 1941. Once again the British paper stressed the importance of the defense of the Atlantic islands, North Africa, Egypt and Singapore, but with particular reference to the basic need of American aid and even participation: "The intervention of the United States would revolutionize the whole situation. . . . It is clear, however, that if intervention is to come, the longer it is delayed, the greater will be the leeway to be made up in every direction." As for eventual victory, British plans appeared to focus on the destruction of the German economy and morale, which it was hoped to encompass by blockade, bombing, subversive activity, and propaganda. Particular reliance was placed on a huge bombing offensive, for which the British requested several thousand more heavy

[6] Kittredge MS. study on *United States-British Naval Coöperation.* The most complete account of the military discussions is to be found in Mark S. Watson: *Chief of Staff: Prewar Plans and Preparations* (Washington, 1950), 401-9.

bombers than the United States was then producing. The British chiefs made no secret of their hope that Germany might be knocked out by heavy air attack, thus making an actual invasion of the continent unnecessary. They did not envision the use of huge land armies in any event, but planned, if necessary, to employ only a small number of highly mechanized divisions in operations on the continent. All in all, their review concluded, "United States intervention would not only make victory certain, but might make it swift."[7]

General Marshall and his colleagues made clear to the British that they could not take a position on the strategy review until they had had time to study it. However, in the ensuing discussions they raised a substantial number of detailed questions and objections. Generally speaking they felt strongly that the United States was far from prepared for large-scale military operations and they therefore doubted if American intervention would do much immediate good. Furthermore, they were utterly skeptical of the idea that Germany could be vanquished by a bomber offensive or by anything short of defeat of its armies in ground warfare. They were fully persuaded that, if the United States became involved in the war, it would have to send large forces into combat and they were deeply concerned lest so much matériel be consigned to Britain and Soviet Russia that there would not be enough left for the needs of the projected American armies. While the official American comments on the General Strategy Review were not transmitted to London until September 30, no secret was made at the Atlantic Conference of American doubts and reservations. Indeed, the breadth and depth of the differences dividing the two parties were so manifest as to preclude even tentative agreement on the strategy of victory. Meanwhile American authorities rested their position on the ABC-1 plan, which they held still valid.

3. QUESTIONS OF POLICY AND STRATEGY

Since the further development of the European War depended in large measure on the continuance of Soviet resistance until the onset of winter weather, it was inevitable that the issue of large-scale aid to the Kremlin should come up for discussion at the conference. Six weeks had elapsed since Hitler had loosed his attack. Though the Soviet armies had been driven back and had suffered terrific losses, they still held the field and showed no sign of collapse. At the end of July the Nazi press had first confessed "that the hardships of these battles exceed anything in history," and admitted that the Soviets had been able to throw unexpectedly large numbers of planes and tanks into the struggle.[8] From the point of view of Britain and the

[7] Watson: *Chief of Staff: Prewar Plans and Preparations*, 402-3; Arnold: *Global Mission*, 251, 253.

[8] *Bulletin of International News*, XVIII (2), 1042.

United States the situation in the east was developing more favorably than anticipated and President Roosevelt had taken advantage of one of his press conferences (August 1, 1941) to describe Soviet resistance as "magnificent," as far more effective than the Germans had reckoned on. Meanwhile Mr. Harry Hopkins had made his spectacular flight to Moscow and had reported his conviction that the Soviets could and would hold out. Hopkins's belief that it would be good business for the democracies to support the Kremlin to the utmost of their capabilities could only confirm the President in his faith. He still estimated that if the Red armies could keep the field until October 1, they would have a respite from attack until spring. During the winter it would be possible to do much toward making good their losses in matériel and equipment. On the other hand, the vast requirements of the Kremlin would have to be meshed with those of American national defense and aid to Britain.

Mr. Elliott Roosevelt would have us believe that at the Atlantic Conference not only British military authorities but the Prime Minister himself expressed skepticism of Soviet survival and hesitation about letting supplies go to the Soviets which they (the British) had been eagerly awaiting to fill their own needs. This was true only to the extent that Mr. Churchill and his colleagues dreaded the loss of supplies on which they had counted so heavily. The Prime Minister, it should be recalled, had promised the Kremlin aid immediately after the Nazi assault. He had suggested or at least concurred in Hopkins's mission to Moscow and there is reason to believe that the conclusions at which the American emissary arrived were substantially in accord with those of British Ambassador Sir Stafford Cripps. Hopkins had accompanied the British party to the Atlantic meeting and, though seriously ill, had reported his findings in detail first to the Prime Minister and later to the President. There is no evidence whatever to support the idea that Mr. Churchill opposed the program of large-scale aid to the Soviet Union, as recommended by Hopkins and approved by the President. In a cable to Mr. Atlee, Mr. Churchill spoke of Soviet Russia as "a welcome guest at a hungry table," and acknowledged that Soviet requirements would necessitate a review of production schedules and an expansion of American war production.[9]

By this time Stalin had already started to clamor for the opening of a second front in western Europe and had had to be told that there was no possibility of the British doing anything on a scale likely to be of the slightest use to him.[10] However, the unavoidable rejection of Stalin's request made it all the more desirable to demonstrate in other ways that Britain and the United States meant to provide all assistance within their power. Mr. Roose-

[9] Elliott Roosevelt: *As He Saw It,* Chapter II; Churchill: *The Grand Alliance,* 430, 446-47.
[10] Churchill: *The Grand Alliance,* 383-86.

velt and Mr. Churchill therefore decided that the American and British Ambassadors in Moscow should at once deliver to Stalin a message suggesting a conference in Moscow to block out a long-term program of supply and plan the apportionment of available resources. The message was cabled to the State Department and forwarded to Moscow on August 13. Two days later the Ambassadors had a conference with Stalin, whom they found cordial and appreciative. The Soviet chief at once drafted a reply accepting the proposal for a conference at an early date. In discussion with the Ambassadors he conceded that the position of the Red armies was "very strained" and complained that the Germans were withdrawing troops from the west so as to increase their pressure on the Soviet forces. At the same time he recognized, however, that it would be difficult for the British to open a new front.[11]

As a result of his conversation with Stalin, Ambassador Steinhardt reported his conviction that the Kremlin would not make peace with Hitler "regardless of the course which military developments may take." American and British aid, or at least the promise of such aid, was doing much to maintain Soviet morale and the Ambassador saw no reason to suppose that the Communist regime would prove unable to maintain itself.[12] Mr. Roosevelt evidently felt confident enough about the situation to publish the joint message to Stalin, which was released on August 16, 1941. On his return to Washington he explained to Congressional leaders that Soviet Russia was the key to the immediate situation in Europe and expressed hopes that the Soviets would be able to hold out indefinitely. In brief, aid to Soviet Russia had ceased to be a temporary expedient and had become a long-term project. Mr. Churchill, it is true, still favored a certain circumspection. Though he had decided to send to Moscow no less a personage than Lord Beaverbrook, he was anxious to postpone the Moscow Conference until late September, by which time there would presumably be some indication of where the front would lie for the winter.[13] Whether this particular view had been discussed at the Atlantic Conference and whether Mr. Roosevelt concurred in this procrastination, it is impossible to say. Actually, the Moscow Conference could hardly have been held before late September in any case.

It should be recalled, in connection with the discussion of the problem of aid to Soviet Russia, that the British and Americans were alike convinced that if Hitler succeeded in defeating the Red armies and overthrowing the Communist regime, he would almost at once turn westward, if not to invade England, at least to advance through Spain on North and West Africa. To forestall German seizure of the Atlantic islands of Spain and Portugal,

---

[11] Tel. to Steinhardt, August 13; tels. from Steinhardt, August 15, 1941. See also Davis and Lindley: *How War Came*, 265 ff.; Sherwood: *Roosevelt and Hopkins*, 349 ff.

[12] Tel. from Steinhardt, August 17, 1941.

[13] Churchill: *The Grand Alliance*, 446-47. For the rest see Mr. Roosevelt's press conference of August 18, 1941 (*The New York Times*, August 19, 1941).

London and Washington had long since made preparations for the protective occupation of the Azores, the Canary Islands and the Cape Verdes. There had been grounds for hope that, despite the hostile attitude of Spain, the Portuguese Government would coöperate with the western powers.[14] Lisbon had taken the position that, with British aid, it would be able to defend the Azores against hostile attack and that, failing the delivery of British supplies, it would be glad to turn to the United States for assistance in protecting the islands.

This was not very explicit and not entirely satisfactory. Mr. Harry Hopkins among others feared that if the Germans advanced into Spain and Portugal, the Lisbon Government would offer only token resistance and then abandon the country to the invaders. But the British took the stand that Lisbon clearly intended to remain faithful to its alliance with Britain. Although the existing record is hazy, it seems to have been agreed that the British should inform Dr. Salazar that they could not provide the equipment required for defense of the Azores and suggest that he turn to the United States for support. It was suggested to the British that in the event of an American occupation of the Azores, the Brazilian Government might participate, thereby making the operation more palatable to Portuguese opinion and weakening the chances of a German propaganda success. At one of the last conferences between Mr. Roosevelt and Mr. Churchill it was agreed between them that Lisbon's attitude was "highly satisfactory, and made possible without any difficulty the carrying out of arrangements for the occupation of the Azores as a means of assurance that the islands would not be occupied by Germany." But the whole project was thought of as purely preventive. Since on the American side there was some doubt whether sufficient naval forces and naval aircraft could be made available to protect an expeditionary force, and since the British continued to eschew pressure on Lisbon, the question of the occupation of the Azores was permitted to hang fire. After all, it was agreed that the danger of a German move would become acute only when and if the resistance of the Soviets collapsed.[15]

In connection with the projected protective occupation of the Azores, Mr. Churchill informed the President that the British had completed plans for the occupation of the (Spanish) Canary Islands by September 15, 1941. This again was thought of as a precautionary move, as an alternative to the occupation of Dakar, which was the key to the situation in West Africa and

14 See above, Chapter XVIII, Section 3.

15 State Department records of the conferences between Mr. Welles and Sir Alexander Cadogan on August 9, 1941, and between the President, Mr. Churchill, Welles, Cadogan and Hopkins on August 11, 1941 (the former now printed in *Pearl Harbor Attack*, IV, 1785 ff.). Further, Churchill: *The Grand Alliance*, 438, and a British memo of September 4, 1941, reviewing the discussions and suggesting that action be suspended (*Roosevelt Papers:* Secretary's File, Box 86). We have used also the *Stimson Diary (MS.)*, August 19, 1941,

the crucial base for protection of the shipping coming from the Cape of Good Hope. Both the British and Americans anticipated Darlan's acquiescence in the German demand for base rights at Dakar, but neither felt militarily capable of seizing that vital port in the face of probable French resistance. Accordingly, only the occupation of the Canary Islands and eventually the Cape Verde Islands could give assurance of adequate protection of the Atlantic trade routes. At the time of the Atlantic Conference this whole nexus of questions seemed so pressing that Mr. Churchill thought it might become necessary to seize the Canary Islands even before Hitler actually intervened in the Iberian Peninsula, despite the fact that British action against a Spanish possession would almost certainly involve a Spanish attack on Gibraltar, which in turn would render that fortress untenable by the British Navy. Mr. Roosevelt concurred in the proposed British course of action, noting that operations against the Canaries would make all the more necessary the safeguarding of the Azores. Actually the situation eventually proved less dangerous than it seemed in August and nothing was done about the occupation of either the Azores or the Canaries prior to Pearl Harbor.[16]

4. The Proposed Warning to Japan

The question of future policy regarding Japan was by far the most urgent of the various matters discussed at the Atlantic Conference. Tokyo had just succeeded in extorting from Vichy the right to occupy bases and station troops in southern Indo-China and was known to have submitted similar demands to Siam. Despite the freezing of Japanese funds in the United States, the British Commonwealth and the Netherlands Indies, and despite the public warnings of Foreign Secretary Eden and Secretary Hull as to Siam, there was no knowing whether Japan could be deterred from further aggressive action by these methods. The Dutch, apprehending an early Japanese move against the Indies, had induced the British Government to give assurances of support, in these terms:

We have assumed the duties of safeguarding and restoring the possessions and rights of the Netherlands Government to the best of our ability during the war and after peace. It follows therefore that an attack upon the Netherlands East Indies would lead us to do the utmost in our power. We must, however, remain sole judge of what actions or military measures are practicable and likely to achieve our common purpose. Should the United States be disposed to take supporting action, many things would become possible which we cannot undertake now.

The last sentence of this declaration, of course, struck at the heart of the problem. The British had only weak forces in the Far East and could hardly hope to do much more than defend Singapore. Everything depended on the attitude and action of the United States in response to further Japanese ag-

---

[16] Sources as cited in the preceding footnote. We have used, in this connection, also the Kittredge MS. study on *United States-British Naval Coöperation.*

gression. But all efforts to discover what Washington proposed to do had thus far ended in failure. Mr. Hull firmly declined to commit himself. When approached by the Australian Minister with the question of what the United States would do if Japan started a war in the Pacific, the Secretary replied evasively: "What we might do depended on the situation of the British in their struggle against Hitler and the particular circumstances and conditions both in the Pacific and the Atlantic presenting themselves at the time; that circumstances change so rapidly these days, I would not undertake to be very specific." Lord Halifax, inquiring what aid the United States would provide in the event of a Japanese attack on Singapore or the Netherlands Indies, fared no better. Mr. Hull remarked that he visualized the problem in broader terms and believed that Japanese plans included the invasion of the whole Indian Ocean area, isolating China, probably sailing across to the mouth of the Suez Canal, to the Persian oil region, and to the Cape of Good Hope, thus severing the British trade routes from Asia. What the United States could or would do must depend on the British position in Europe and on American naval requirements in the Atlantic. In the event of further Japanese advances in the south, the British and Americans should, of course, confer at once and determine what further measures to take.[17]

Mr. Hull's altogether noncommittal answers are explainable in part, certainly, by the fact that the President could not promise to commit American military forces without Congressional approval. Equally important, however, was Washington's conviction that it would be disastrous both for the British and Americans if war broke out in the Pacific and obliged the United States to divert large forces and supplies from the struggle against Hitler. In addition there was good reason to fear that the Japanese might direct their energies and forces to the north, joining their Nazi allies in the task of destroying Soviet Russia. Reports of Japanese reinforcements arriving in Manchuria were numerous and all indications ominous. The German records have since revealed that Hitler himself was convinced that a Japanese surprise move against Siberia was merely a matter of time.[18]

While the President and Secretary Hull might hope that the threat of mortal economic sanctions, reinforced by refusal to continue the Washington conversations and by repeated warnings, would give even the Japanese militarists pause, Mr. Churchill was harassed by pleas from the Pacific Dominions and the Dutch that he secure some promise of American military

[17] Tel. from Winant, August 1, 1941, reporting the British statement to the Dutch; memo of conversation between Mr. Hull and the Australian Minister, August 7, 1941; memo of conversation between Mr. Hull and Lord Halifax, August 9, with a tel. from the Foreign Office to the Ambassador, August 5, 1941, attached; tel. from Biddle (London), August 8, 1941.

[18] Tel. from Steinhardt, August 5, 1941, reporting information from the Chinese Ambassador; tel. from Ott to Berlin, August 1, 1941 (*Tokyo War Crimes Documents*, No. 4025D), and August 19, 1941 (*Nazi Conspiracy and Aggression*, VI, No. 3733-PS); *Fuehrer Conferences*, 1941 (2), 27-28.

aid in the event of Japanese attack. It was a foregone conclusion that this issue would loom large in the conferences of the President and Prime Minister.

On the afternoon of August 9, immediately after the arrival of the British party, Mr. Welles and Sir Alexander Cadogan canvassed the situation in a preliminary way. The Under Secretary recounted the suspension of the Washington conversations and recalled Mr. Roosevelt's offer to arrange for the neutralization of Indo-China and Siam. He informed Sir Alexander of the unsatisfactory reply of the Japanese (August 6) and of Mr. Hull's renewed declaration to Nomura that Tokyo's policies made further discussions of a general settlement useless. Finally he related his own conversation with Mr. Wakasugi and his pointed statement that if Japan continued on its course of conquest, war would, sooner or later, become inevitable. Under the circumstances it seemed to him that Tokyo must realize that the patience of the United States Government was wearing thin. Nonetheless, the President and his advisers thought it best to exploit the unsatisfactory Japanese counterproposal as a means for protracting discussion and thereby gaining time; in other words, "in order to put off the showdown (if such was inevitable) until the time that such a showdown was from our standpoint more propitious." The Under Secretary, according to his own notes, added the following:

I said that I also wished by direction of the President to make it clear that the Government of the United States did not believe that even should Thailand [Siam] be occupied by Japan, such occupation should be made a *casus belli* by Great Britain. I said that in the opinion of both the War and Navy Departments of the United States the chief objective in the Pacific for the time being should be the avoidance of war with Japan inasmuch as war between the United States and Japan at this time would not only tie up the major portion of, if not the entire American Fleet, but would likewise create a very serious strain upon our military establishment and upon our production activities, at the very moment when these should be concentrated upon the Atlantic. This applied, of course, even more strongly in the case of the American Fleet.[19]

Although Sir Alexander expressed general agreement, he at once began to expound the British viewpoint, the gist of which was that Japan could be deterred only if the United States took a much stronger stand. Mr. Churchill, he observed, had come to believe that the Japanese were prepared to take on, at one and the same time, all their potential opponents: Soviet Russia, China, the Netherlands Indies, Great Britain, the Dominions, and the United States. To quote Sir Alexander's exact words: "He [Mr. Churchill] felt that only the stiffest warning from the United States could

[19] Memo of conversation between Mr. Welles and Sir Alexander Cadogan, afternoon of August 9, 1941. General Arnold (*Global Mission,* 250) notes that in a conference at sea on August 7 the President had remarked that "he would turn a deaf ear if Japan went into Thailand, but not if they went into the Dutch East Indies."

possibly have any concrete counteracting effect." Cadogan then informed
Welles of the assurances of support recently given the Dutch and spoke of
the insistence of the Australians that the Prime Minister obtain from the
President "a commitment that in the event that Japan attacked the Netherlands East Indies and that Great Britain then went to the latter's assistance
. . . the President would agree that he would then request of the Congress
authority necessary to make possible for the United States to assist the British, the Dominions and the Netherlands East Indies forces to resist Japanese
aggression." Mr. Welles, however, deprecated this suggestion, remarking
that Mr. Roosevelt would wish to avoid the appearance of bringing pressure on Congress. Such a course would, in all probability, react preju-
dicially on American public opinion, which, as a matter of fact, was of its
own accord rapidly and sharply mounting in opposition to Japanese policy.
But, said Mr. Welles, this was a question which the President would have to
decide, whereupon both parties agreed to leave further discussion of the
issue to their principals.[20]

In the course of the evening discussions (August 9) Mr. Churchill, despite the fact that he must have had Cadogan's report of the afternoon conference, returned to the charge. This time, however, he pleaded for joint
action rather than for a unilateral American warning. The United States,
Britain and Soviet Russia, he insisted, must send an ultimatum to Japan to
the effect that if the Japanese advanced into Malaya or the Netherlands
Indies, the three powers would employ such means as were necessary to
force them to withdraw.[21] Whether the Kremlin would have proved amenable to such a suggestion may well be doubted, for obviously it was not in the
Soviet interest to provoke Japan. In conversation with Mr. Hopkins on July
31, 1941, Mr. Molotov had made clear the desire of his Government to
avoid trouble with Tokyo. The Kremlin, he had remarked, did not anticipate a Japanese attack in the immediate future, though it suspected that the
Japanese would strike as soon as they were ready. The one thing that would
keep them from attacking Siberia, he intimated, would be for President
Roosevelt to warn them and perhaps hint to them that the United States
would come to the Soviet Union's aid in the event of a Japanese assault.[22]
This suggestion patently fell short of what Mr. Churchill had in mind.

Mr. Roosevelt refused to fall in with the Prime Minister's proposal. He
left no doubt that his great objective was to gain time, even though the period be short, and that further negotiation was therefore desirable. To quote
Mr. Churchill's version of the President's thought:

[20] Memo of conversation between Mr. Welles and Sir Alexander Cadogan, afternoon
of August 9, 1941.

[21] Arnold: *Global Mission*, 252.

[22] Memo of conversation between Hopkins and Molotov, July 31, 1941; see also Sherwood: *Roosevelt and Hopkins*, 331 ff.

President's idea is to negotiate about these unacceptable conditions [of August 6] and thus procure a moratorium of, say, thirty days in which we may improve our position in Singapore area and the Japanese will have to stand still. But he will make it a condition that the Japanese meanwhile encroach no further, and do not use Indo-China as a base for attack on China. He will also maintain in full force the economic measures directed against Japan. These negotiations show little chance of succeeding, but President considers that a month gained will be valuable. I pointed out of course that the Japs would double-cross him and would try to attack China or cut the Burma communications. However, you may take it that they [the Americans] consider it right to begin the negotiations on these lines, and in view of what has passed between the United States and Japan it will be necessary to accept this fact.[23]

While rejecting the idea of a joint warning and insisting on resumption of conversations with Japan, Mr. Roosevelt did, however, agree to renew his admonitions to the Japanese Ambassador and apparently to employ language as strong as the Prime Minister desired. At the end of a note which he undertook to hand to Ambassador Nomura on his return, he was to say something like this:

1.) Any further encroachment by Japan in the Southwestern Pacific would produce a situation in which the United States Government would be compelled to take countermeasures even though these might lead to war between the United States and Japan.

2.) If any third power becomes the object of aggression by Japan in consequence of such countermeasures or their support of them, the President would have the intention to seek authority from Congress to give aid to such Power.

This was the wording as drafted by the British and submitted by Mr. Churchill on the morning of August 10. While the warning was to emanate from the President, the British plan provided that they and the Dutch should take parallel action, on the theory that

Either the Japanese will refuse the conditions the President prescribes—namely, continuance of the economic sanctions and no movement on the Japanese part and no invasion of Siam—or alternatively they will go on with their military action while lying about it diplomatically.

In this case the conditions indicated by the final passage just quoted [i.e., the warning above] would come into play with great force, and the full effect of parallel declarations could be realized. The Soviet Government should also be kept informed. It might be dangerous to tell the Chinese what we are doing for them, though they might be assured in general terms that we have had their security in mind in all that we have done.

On all these grounds I consider that we should endorse the proposed course of action, and that the Dominions should be told about it and made to see that it is a very great advance towards the gripping of Japanese aggression in united forces.[24]

[23] Churchill's tel. to Foreign Secretary Eden, August 11, 1941 (Churchill: *The Grand Alliance*, 439 ff.).
[24] Tel. of Churchill to Eden, August 11, 1941 (Churchill: *The Grand Alliance*, 440).

The parallel warnings to Japan on the part of Britain, the Netherlands and possibly the Soviet Union were to be identical with the American warning except that, instead of providing for Congressional authority, they were to state simply that the British (or Dutch) Government "would give all possible aid." In presenting the British draft to Mr. Welles, Prime Minister Churchill once again emphasized his position:

He impressed upon me [reported Mr. Welles] his belief that some declaration of the kind he had drafted with respect to Japan was in his opinion in the highest degree important, and that he did not think that there was much hope left unless the United States made such a clear-cut declaration of preventing Japan from expanding further to the south, in which event the prevention of war between Great Britain and Japan appeared to be hopeless. . . . He pled with me that a declaration of this character participated in by the United States, Great Britain, the Dominions, the Netherlands and possibly the Soviet Union would definitely restrain Japan. If this were not done, the blow to the British Government might be almost decisive.[25]

The final discussion of the Far Eastern situation took place on the morning of August 11, when the President and Prime Minister conferred in the presence of Mr. Welles, Mr. Hopkins and Sir Alexander Cadogan. The meeting began with a reconsideration of the Japanese reply (August 6) to the President's proposal to arrange for the neutralization of Indo-China and Siam. Mr. Churchill, having had an opportunity during the previous days to study this reply, held it to be highly unsatisfactory, inasmuch as it implied "that Japan, having already occupied Indo-China, said that she would move no further provided the United States would abandon their economic and financial sanctions and take no further military or naval defensive measures and further agree to concessions to Japan, including the opportunity for Japan to strangle the Chinese Government, all of which were particularly unacceptable." Mr. Roosevelt concurred, but reiterated "that he felt very strongly that every effort should be made to prevent the outbreak of war with Japan." He was determined to negotiate, if only to gain time. In his interview with Ambassador Nomura he proposed, however, to utter an unmistakable warning:

The President stated that in that interview he would inform the Japanese Ambassador that provided the Japanese Government would give the commitment contained in the first paragraph of the proposal of the Japanese Government of August 6, namely that the Japanese Government "will not further station its troops in the Southwestern Pacific areas, except Indo-China, and that the Japanese troops now stationed in French Indo-China will be withdrawn," specifically and not contingently, the United States Government, while making it clear that the other conditions set forth by the Japanese

[25] Memo of conversation between Mr. Welles, Mr. Churchill and Sir Alexander Cadogan, August 10, 1941 (now printed in *Pearl Harbor Attack*, IV, 1784-85). The text of the draft is dated August 15, 1941. As printed in *Pearl Harbor Attack*, XIV, 1255, it is quite illegible, but the crucial last part is quoted in *Pearl Harbor Attack*, II, 460 ff.

Government were in general unacceptable, the United States would, nevertheless, in a friendly spirit seek to explore the possibilities inherent in the various proposals made by Japan for the reaching of a friendly understanding between the two Governments. The President would further state that should Japan refuse to consider this procedure and undertake further steps in the nature of military expansions, the President desired the Japanese Government to know that in such event in his belief various steps would have to be taken by the United States notwithstanding the President's realization that the taking of such measures might result in war between the United States and Japan.[26]

Mr. Churchill assented to this program, convinced, so he said, that while it contained an element of "face-saving" for Japan, it also constituted "a fair United States warning to Japan of the consequences involved in a continuation by Japan of her present course." The two statesmen then discussed the desirability of informing the Kremlin of their decision and of adding to the proposed warning a statement covering possible Japanese moves against the Soviet Union. Mr. Welles suggested that the problem of Japanese expansion was all of a piece and that the warning should therefore not be restricted to moves in the Southwest Pacific. This was agreed and it was further decided that the President should assure Ambassador Nomura that Britain supported the proposal to neutralize Indo-China and Siam, having no aggressive designs against the latter state. In closing the meeting Mr. Roosevelt expressed his belief "that by adopting this course any further move of aggression on the part of Japan which might result in war could be held off for at least thirty days."[27]

Certain members of the Joint Congressional Committee to Investigate the Pearl Harbor Attack were to experience some difficulty in grasping exactly what was decided during the Atlantic Conference. There is, in fact, a margin of uncertainty which the haziness of Mr. Welles's testimony did little to dispel.[28] This touches more particularly Mr. Churchill's original proposal for joint or parallel action by the United States, Britain, the Netherlands and possibly Soviet Russia. Evidently the Prime Minister abandoned this idea in favor of a strongly worded, unilateral warning by the President to Nomura, with which Britain and the other interested powers could then associate themselves. But Mr. Churchill apparently yielded his point only on the understanding that the American warning should be couched substantially in terms of the British draft. His contemporary messages seem to bear

[26] Memo of conversation between the President, Mr. Churchill, Mr. Welles, Mr. Hopkins and Sir Alexander Cadogan, August 11, 1941 (now printed in *Pearl Harbor Attack,* IV, 1785 ff.).

[27] See preceding footnote.

[28] See *Pearl Harbor Attack,* Report, 300-302; II, 477-91, 539 (Welles's testimony); XIV, 1254 ff. See also Hull: *Memoirs,* II, 1017 ff.; George Morgenstern: *Pearl Harbor* (New York, 1947), 124 ff.; Walter Millis: *This Is Pearl* (New York, 1947), 125 ff.; Charles A. Beard: *President Roosevelt and the Coming of the War* (New Haven, 1948), Chapter XV; Herbert Feis: *The Road to Pearl Harbor* (Princeton, 1950), Chapter XXXIII.

this out. Reporting to Mr. Atlee on the last day of the conference, the Prime Minister stated: "We have laid special stress on warning to Japan which constitutes the teeth of the President's communication. One would always fear State Department trying to tone it down, but President has promised definitely to use the hard language." And a few days later, in a message to the Australian Prime Minister:

President promised me to give the warning to Japan in the terms agreed. Once we know this has been done, we should range ourselves beside him and make clear that if Japan becomes involved in war with United States, she will also be at war with Britain and British Commonwealth. I am arranging this with Eden, and you will be advised through the regular channels. You should note that the President's warning covers an attack upon Russia, so that perhaps Stalin will line up too, and of course, the Dutch. If this combined front can be established, including China, I feel confident that Japan will lie quiet for a while. It is however essential to use the firmest language and the strongest combination.[29]

These quotations leave little doubt that in Mr. Churchill's mind the terms and character of the warning were uppermost. Just how explicit the President's promise to use "hard" language may have been, it is impossible to say. Mr. Churchill's messages do not suggest that Mr. Roosevelt bound himself in any formal way to employ the wording of the British draft. Indeed, neither he nor Mr. Welles can have felt committed in this respect, for the Under Secretary hastened back to Washington by plane in order to draft the declaration to Nomura according to the decisions reached at the Atlantic Conference. The President's actual statement to Ambassador Nomura (August 17) was undoubtedly less forceful and explicit than Mr. Churchill had proposed, but there is no evidence that the latter felt let down. The question is still moot, but it should not be allowed to obscure the fact that while to the Prime Minister the decisive thing was the hardness of the language and the strength of the combination behind it, to Mr. Roosevelt the crucial consideration was to gain time. Even thirty days would be of moment. To win them the President was determined to resume conversations which he himself regarded as virtually hopeless. It was almost a foregone conclusion that he would temper his words to Nomura so as not to precipitate the clash which he was intent on deferring and if possible avoiding entirely.

5. The Atlantic Charter

The meeting between President Roosevelt and Prime Minister Churchill will be remembered by posterity chiefly for the joint declaration of policy to which it gave birth. Yet the so-called Atlantic Charter was apparently a by-product of the conference rather than its primary objective. The states-

[29] Churchill: *The Grand Alliance,* 446, 448.

men and military men, both American and British, were more intent on immediate problems of winning the war than on long-range plans for a better future world. Neither London nor Washington appears to have made any systematic preparation for a statement of war and peace aims or to have anticipated the formulation of a basic program. Ever since his advent to power Mr. Churchill had in fact refused to pronounce on the conditions of peace and the future organization of the world, fearing, as he did, that discussion of such issues would divide British opinion without serving any important or useful purpose. When Foreign Secretary Eden, in his Mansion House address of May 29, 1941, ventured to touch upon the future, it was only to recall President Roosevelt's Four Freedoms and give his audience assurance that Britain intended to work for the furtherance of social security.

On the American side the situation was similar. The enthusiasm with which in 1939-1940 the Administration and the public had approached the problem of making peace after a war from which it expected the United States would stand aloof had quickly evaporated after the collapse of France. The State Department's Advisory Committee on Problems of Foreign Relations and its newly organized Research Division continued to function, but only in a perfunctory way. Under the guidance of Dr. Leo Pasvolsky attention was focused largely on questions of international economics, ever dear to Secretary Hull.[30] From time to time the Secretary voiced his concern over these problems, even in public utterances. Thus, on May 18, 1941, he declared in a radio address: "It is none too early to lay down at least some of the principles by which policies must be guided at the conclusion of the war, to press for a broad program of world economic reconstruction and to consider tentative plans for the application of those policies."[31] The passage of the Lend-Lease legislation and the need to draft economic agreements with the recipient Governments also necessitated study of future economic relationships. Mr. Hull, as always, made a great point of nondiscrimination in trade, and Mr. Eden's Mansion House speech, just referred to, was probably intended by the British Government to provide assurance that there would be no conflict between Britain and the United States on this score. Before quoting Mr. Hull's actual words, Mr. Eden had stated: "Let no one suppose that we for our part intend to return to the chaos of the old world. To do so would bankrupt us no less than others. When peace comes we shall make such relaxations of our wartime financial arrangements as will permit the revival of international trade on the widest possible basis.[32]

It is unlikely that the mere resurrection of economic issues which had been debated *ad nauseam* for many years would have resulted in anything

---

[30] *Postwar Foreign Policy Preparation* (Washington, 1949), Chapter III.

[31] The pertinent passages are qoted in *Postwar Foreign Policy Preparation*, 45-46, and in Louise W. Holborn: *War and Peace Aims of the United Nations* (Boston, 1943), I, 39.

[32] Holborn: *War and Peace Aims of the United Nations*, I, 204.

more than the continued expression of high hopes and pious intentions, had it not been for the fact that Lord Keynes, in Washington to negotiate the Lend-Lease agreement, shocked the State Department by his expression of opinion that the postwar world economic structure could only be one of closed economies.[33] At the same time Hitler's attack on Soviet Russia provoked new interest in larger political issues. Certain American isolationists, for instance, urged that the United States mediate between Britain and Germany as the only way of avoiding ultimate involvement in a war at the side of Communist Russia.[34] Others, like former Ambassador John Cudahy, called upon Mr. Roosevelt to raise his voice as the arbiter of peace and democracy, and, with the approval of Congress, to advance an American program: "a peace with a new world order based on an association of nations, the inauguration of a sovereign international government with power to enforce its decrees for the solution of this and all the endless wars of Europe."[35] In this connection it is worth recalling also that a Gallup poll taken in the early summer of 1941 revealed 49 percent of those questioned as favoring some kind of League of Nations after the conclusion of the war.

Mr. Roosevelt was known to be disillusioned about the League of Nations and was by nature not greatly interested in questions of organization. Although Mr. Welles has stated that the President believed passionately that civilization could not survive without some form of international organization, there is no evidence that he had definite ideas on the subject or that he was much engrossed by the problem in the summer of 1941. He was convinced throughout that disarmament was the crux of international peace and reminded Assistant Secretary of State Berle of the fact when the latter asked permission to try his hand at drafting basic terms of peace in June, 1941.[36] If Mr. Roosevelt, in July and August, 1941, began to consider the possibility of publicly declaring war and peace aims, the explanation is probably to be sought in the conclusion of the British-Soviet and Polish-Soviet agreements, which caused much concern in the State Department and raised the specter of the secret treaties of the First World War. It may be remembered that in July the President, at the instigation of Mr. Welles, had warned Mr. Churchill that the United States Government disapproved of territorial settlements prior to the conclusion of the conflict.[37] No doubt this preoccupation in high American quarters led to Mr. Welles's remarks in a speech delivered at the Norwegian Legation on July 22, 1941. Since this

[33] *Berle Diary* (*MS.*), July 17, 1941; memo of the Division of Commercial Treaties, August 4, 1941, analyzing the implications of Keynes's remarks.

[34] For example, President Robert M. Hutchins of the University of Chicago (*New York Journal-American,* July 16, 1941).

[35] John Cudahy: "A Program for Peace" (address delivered on August 10, 1941).

[36] See above, Chapter XVII. See also Welles: *Where Are We Heading?* (New York, 1946), 3 ff.

[37] Above, Chapter XVII, Section 4.

address in a sense foreshadowed the Atlantic Charter, it is worth quoting at least in part:

. . . . What does the future hold for us after this struggle is over?

It seems to me that those of us who are fortunate enough to be able to live as citizens of the free American Republics have our great responsibility in the framing of the answer to that question.

For we all of us now see clearly, if we did not before, that no matter how great our American capacity for defense may be, no matter how perfect our hemispheric system may become, our future welfare must inevitably be contingent upon the existence in the rest of the world of equally peace-minded and equally secure peoples who not only will not, but cannot, become a source of potential danger to us in the New World.

I feel it is not premature for me to suggest that the free governments of peace-loving nations everywhere should even now be considering and discussing the way in which they can best prepare for the better day which must come, when the present contest is ended in the victory of the forces of liberty and of human freedom, and in the crushing defeat of those who are sacrificing mankind to their own lust for power and for loot.

After recalling President Wilson's vision of an ordered world governed by law, and suggesting some reasons for the failure of the League of Nations, the Acting Secretary continued:

Some adequate instrumentality must unquestionably be found to achieve such adjustments when the nations of the earth again undertake the task of restoring law and order to a disastrously shaken world.

But whatever the mechanism which may be devised, of two things I am unalterably convinced:

First, that the abolition of offensive armaments and the limitation and reduction of defensive armaments and of the tools which make the construction of such armaments possible can only be undertaken through some rigid form of international supervision and control, and that without such practical and essential control, no real disarmament can ever be achieved; and

Second, that no peace which may be made in the future would be valid or lasting unless it established fully and adequately the natural rights of all peoples to equal economic enjoyment. So long as any one people or any one government possesses a monopoly over natural resources or raw materials which are needed by all peoples, there can be no basis for a world order based on justice and on peace.[38]

These passages, almost certainly approved by the President, make it easy to understand Mr. Welles's later statement that, for some weeks prior to his meeting with Mr. Churchill, Mr. Roosevelt had been talking about the seriousness of the world situation and remarking "that nothing would be more valuable from the standpoint of keeping alive some principles of international law, some principles of moral and human decency, than for him to make some kind of public statement of the objectives in international rela-

[38] Holborn: *War and Peace Aims of the United Nations,* I, 42-43.

tions in which the Government of the United States believed."[39] Before leaving Washington at the beginning of August he had evidently decided to propose a joint American-British declaration which would keep the London Government from concluding secret agreements and would, at the same time, "hold out hope to the enslaved peoples of the world."[40] From his conversations with Mr. Roosevelt, Mr. Churchill was to gain the impression that the President attached great importance to the proposed declaration and that he believed it would "affect the whole movement of United States opinion."[41]

The way for a joint declaration was prepared in the initial discussion between Mr. Welles and Sir Alexander Cadogan on the afternoon of August 9, in connection with the Under Secretary's query about British secret commitments. Sir Alexander gave "the most specific and positive assurance that the British had entered into no agreements and had made no commitments which had to do with frontiers or territorial readjustments," with one insignificant and extremely vague exception. Mr. Welles expressed himself "very much heartened" by this statement. His notes continue as follows:

I said he would remember what damage had been caused in 1917 by the sudden revelation of the series of agreements which Great Britain had previously entered into at that time with her then Allies and that rumors which had now been current alleging that the present British Government had entered into similar secret agreements created both disquiet and suspicion on the part of the people of the United States, who believed that the United States was rightly concerned in British victory. Sir Alexander said that he fully appreciated this fact, and that Mr. Churchill had it very much in mind. We agreed that consideration might be given to sending out a statement at an appropriate moment by the British Government in regard to this question.

After these preliminaries, the Under Secretary attacked the economic problem, with special reference to the alarming indications given by Lord Keynes. These suggested that at least a segment of British opinion was "directing its energies towards the resumption or continuation by Great Britain after the war of exactly that kind of system which had proved so fatal during the past generation." Mr. Welles ventured the conviction that Sir Alexander saw eye to eye with him regarding "the need, when the time came for world reconstruction to be undertaken, of the freest possible economic interchange without discriminations, without exchange controls, without economic preferences utilized for political purposes and without all of the manifold economic barriers which had in my judgment been so clearly responsible for the

[39] Mr. Welles's testimony (*Pearl Harbor Attack,* II, 536 ff.).

[40] Welles: *Where Are We Heading?,* 6; Davis and Lindley: *How War Came,* 265 ff., who state that Mr. Welles took to the Atlantic Conference various working drafts of such a declaration. Of these nothing has become known.

[41] Mr. Churchill's message to Mr. Attlee, August 11, 1941 (Churchill: *The Grand Alliance,* 441).

present world collapse." Sir Alexander concurred, but eschewed further discussion pending the deliberations of the President and Prime Minister.[42]

That same evening at dinner Mr. Roosevelt suggested to Mr. Churchill a joint declaration "laying down certain broad principles which should guide our policies along the same road."[43] The Prime Minister naturally leaped at this chance to identify the policies of the two nations even more closely. In accord with the British practice of having their own text used as the basis for discussion whenever possible, Sir Alexander Cadogan submitted a draft by noon on August 10. Since this draft was to be in fact the foundation of the final declaration, it may be well to quote it in full:

The President of the United States of America and the Prime Minister, Mr. Churchill, representing His Majesty's Government in the United Kingdom, being met together to resolve and concert the means of providing for the safety of their respective countries in the face of Nazi and German aggression and of the dangers to all peoples arising therefrom, deem it right to make known certain principles which they both accept for guidance in the framing of their policy and on which they base their hopes for a better future for the world.

First, their countries seek no aggrandizement, territorial or other;

Second, they desire to see no territorial changes that do not accord with the freely expressed wishes of the peoples concerned;

Third, they respect the right of all peoples to choose the form of government under which they will live; they are only concerned to defend the rights of freedom of speech and of thought without which such choosing must be illusory;

Fourth, they will strive to bring about a fair and equitable distribution of essential produce not only within their territorial jurisdiction, but between the nations of the world;

Fifth, they seek a peace which will not only cast down forever the Nazi tyranny, but by effective international organization will afford to all states and peoples the means of dwelling in security within their own bounds and of traversing the seas and oceans without fear of lawless assault or need of getting burdensome armaments.[44]

Mr. Welles has provided an admirable and authoritative account of the process by which this original five-point draft was transformed into the final eight-point charter.[45] Consequently nothing more is necessary, in the present context, than to comment on certain aspects of the ensuing debates. On the American side the first three articles of the British version, which so clearly revealed Mr. Churchill's own hand, were regarded as essential and appropriate, though Mr. Welles has recorded his doubts whether Congress would approve a pledge to defend the rights of freedom of speech and thought in view of the fact that those rights had been abrogated in every Axis country. This

[42] Memo of conversation between Mr. Welles and Sir Alexander Cadogan, August 9, 1941.

[43] Churchill: *The Grand Alliance*, 433.

[44] Memo of conversation between Mr. Welles and Sir Alexander Cadogan, August 10, 1941 (printed in *Pearl Harbor Attack*, IV, 1784-85). See also Welles: *Where Are We Heading?* and Churchill: *The Grand Alliance*, 433-34.

[45] Welles: *Where Are We Heading?*

observation seems strange when it is recalled that the Four Freedoms proclaimed by President Roosevelt in January, 1941, specified "freedom of speech and expression—everywhere in the world" as the first of the "four essential human freedoms" which the United States sought to make secure for the future. Equally noteworthy was the omission, from the Atlantic Charter, of Mr. Roosevelt's second essential freedom—"freedom of every person to worship God in his own way." There is no reason to suppose that this omission was anything but an oversight, but it was certainly an astounding one. All told, it would seem that the President's earlier formulation was not very prominently in the minds of the conferees in August, 1941.

According, again, to Mr. Welles, Articles IV and V of the British proposal were thought by the Americans to be either questionable as to meaning or far too limited in scope. Quite possibly the vagueness of those two articles reflected Mr. Churchill's desire to avoid controversial or explosive issues. It would probably be going too far to say, as does Mr. Sherwood in his *Roosevelt and Hopkins,* that the Prime Minister's objective was primarily to provide an effective publicity handout, to appeal to the German people over the head of their Fuehrer, and at the same time to rally the populations of the occupied countries, as he did in Articles II and III of his draft. The crucial consideration respecting Articles IV and V was no doubt Sir Alexander's report of his discussion with Mr. Welles and Mr. Churchill's realization that such issues as postwar economic policy and international organization might provoke dissension rather than promote agreement.

The President and the Under Secretary, however, thought it indispensable to clarify these questions. Mr. Welles therefore redrafted the proposed declaration, omitting the reference to freedom of speech and thought, phrasing Article IV in terms of the liberal, nondiscriminatory trade doctrine, and adding to Article V the principle of disarmament, by which the President set such great store. The President then went over the revision with great care, cutting down the preamble and generalizing it, recasting Article IV, striking "international organization" from Article V, and devoting a separate new article to a much stronger statement on disarmament of the aggressor nations. In rewriting the draft once more, Mr. Welles cast it in seven articles and in this form it was discussed on the morning of August 11 by the two principals, assisted by Mr. Welles, Sir Alexander Cadogan and Mr. Hopkins.

Before attacking matters of substance, Mr. Roosevelt suggested that, as a matter of form, the declaration be issued to the radio and press as a joint statement, probably on August 14. He proposed that it report that the two principals had met at sea, had discussed questions of Lend-Lease aid, had not entered into any further commitments, but had agreed on certain general principles, which would then be listed. This approach, carefully calculated to reassure the American public, was naturally disappointing to Mr. Churchill, who observed that specific reference to the absence of further commitments would be fully exploited by Nazi propaganda while it would necessarily discourage the British and their friends. Since the President, however, thought it essential to spike isolationist charges in advance, Mr. Churchill was unable to achieve more than a restatement of the point in affirmative rather than negative terms: the two principals had discussed only questions relative to the provision of aid under Lend-Lease (certainly a generous interpretation of the conversations that actually took place).[46]

Turning then to consideration of the revised draft, the conferees soon found themselves engaged in rather spirited debate. After suggesting a few minor changes of wording Mr. Churchill came to grips with the most controversial article (IV), dealing with postwar economic policy. He queried whether this was intended, according to the American redraft, to apply also to the Ottawa Agreements, and was told by Mr. Welles that of course it did, but that the phrase "they will endeavor to further" did not imply formal and immediate obligation on the part of the British to abrogate those agreements. The Prime Minister thereupon remarked that while he personally had always been opposed to the policy of Empire Preference and sympathized fully with the American program, the matter was one on which he would have to consult the Cabinet and the Dominion Governments, all of which would take at least a week. At this point Mr. Hopkins, eager as ever to get results even at some sacrifice of principle, suggested that Mr. Welles and Sir Alexander redraft the article in unobjectionable form: "It was inconceivable," he remarked, "that the issuance of the joint declaration should be held up by a matter of this kind." But Mr. Welles, mindful presumably of his State Department chief, stuck to his guns, insisting that the question was not one of phraseology, but of vital principle:

I said that if the British and the United States Governments could not agree to do everything in their power to further, after the termination of the present war, a restoration of free and liberal trade policies, they might as well throw in the sponge and realize that one of the greatest factors in creating the present tragic situation in the world was going to be permitted to continue unchecked in the postwar world.

The Prime Minister had by this time become rather irked by the uncompromising stand taken by Mr. Welles. He reminded the Under Secretary that Britain had followed a policy of free trade for some eighty years but had gotten in return only a series of ever-rising American tariffs. But since Mr. Roosevelt made clear that he did not want to embarrass Britain and was perfectly willing to accept special temporary arrangements if only the British would adopt free-for-all trade policies as an ultimate objective, the Prime Minister suggested a compromise wording to include the phrase "with due regard for our present obligations." This would obviate the need for consulting the Dominion Governments and would make possible the issuance of the joint declaration to which the President attached so much importance.

[46] On this item see especially Churchill: *The Grand Alliance*, 436.

It was then agreed that Mr. Churchill should try his hand at restating the article in acceptable terms.[47]

Further argument developed over the draft of Article VII, from which the President had struck all reference to "effective international organization" so as to forestall public controversy over the League of Nations issue. Mr. Churchill besought his friend to consider restoration of this item. The difference between the two men appears vividly from the record:

The President replied that he did not feel that he could agree to this because of the suspicions and opposition that such a statement on his part would create in the United States. He said that he himself would not be in favor of the creation of a new Assembly of the League of Nations, at least until after a period of time had passed and during which an international police force composed of the United States and Great Britain had had an opportunity of functioning. Mr. Churchill said that he did not feel that he would be candid if he did not express to the President his feeling that point seven would create a great deal of opposition from the extreme internationalists. The President replied that he realized that, but that he felt the time had come to be realistic and that in his judgment the main factor of the seventh point was complete realism. Mr. Churchill then remarked that of course he was wholeheartedly in favor of it and shared the President's view.

From Mr. Churchill's correspondence it would appear that he saw great possibilities in the President's "realistic" approach, for he cabled Mr. Attlee that same day (August 11): "The seventh paragraph is most remarkable for its realism. The President undoubtedly contemplates the disarmament of the guilty nations, coupled with the maintenance of strong united British and American armaments both by sea and air for a long indefinite period."[48] He may well have felt that such an Anglo-American police force held greater promise than an elaborate organization and endless debate. However, it is patent from the Prime Minister's messages that he still hoped to extract some concessions, seeing how anxious the President was to arrive at agreement on a joint declaration.

Following the extended discussion of the morning of August 11, Mr. Welles and Sir Alexander Cadogan resumed their drafting. The Under Secretary's task was somewhat lightened by a note from the President indicating his readiness to compromise on the wording of Article IV to the extent of omitting explicit reference to nondiscrimination in trade. But the Under Secretary must have been even more relieved and gratified to discover that the British, in their redraft of the controversial article, had gone farther than the Americans had dared hope. In this fourth version of the declaration they had inserted a new article expressing the common desire of the two Governments to bring about the fullest collaboration between all nations in the economic field, with the object of securing for all peoples improved

[47] To the American records, as previously listed, should be added Mr. Churchill's account, in *The Grand Alliance,* 436 ff. We have made use also of an interesting account by Lord Halifax, as reported in the *Moffat Diary (MS.),* August 20, 1941.

[48] Churchill: *The Grand Alliance,* 441.

labor standards, economic advancement and social security. On the other hand, they had retained in Article VII some reference to future international organization, in the hope that the President might yet be persuaded to accept it. As Sir Alexander pointed out, Mr. Churchill "thought that it would be a tragic thing to concentrate solely upon the transition period after the war was ended, when some kind of joint police power would have to be exercised by the British and by the United States Governments, and omit any reference to the need of the creation of some effective and practicable international organization which would function after the transition period was concluded."

Mr. Roosevelt did, in fact, refrain from further objections. Doubtless pleased by the compromise text of Article IV, he was willing to subscribe to some form of international organization as an ultimate, far-off goal. "The President said," to quote Welles's report, "that it seemed to him entirely desirable, since the [British] amendment made it clear that once the war was over a transition period would have to take place and that the permanent international organization would only be set up after that experimental period had passed." When queried by Mr. Welles whether he did not anticipate strong opposition to a declaration that the aggressor nations should be disarmed, since this might imply a commitment on the part of the United States to disarm not only Germany but possibly also Japan and at least theoretically the Soviet Union if that power should again embark on aggression against its neighbors, Mr. Roosevelt replied that he thought the American people would recognize the realism of Article VII and enthusiastically support the program of disarming aggressors.

According to Mr. Sherwood, the President had in the interval been persuaded by Mr. Hopkins that the American people not only desired some form of international organization, but would settle for nothing less. This would explain Mr. Roosevelt's statement to Mr. Welles that his disparaging remarks about the League of Nations were intended merely to stress the need for a transition period, during which no organization like the League could possibly assume the prerogatives and powers which had once been assigned to it. Mr. Welles still objected that it would be impossible to exclude from the police force such powers as the American Republics, or even Norway, the Netherlands and Belgium. But the President "felt that a solution for this difficulty could probably be found through the ostensible joining with Great Britain and the United States of these Powers, but it would have to be recognized that it would be ostensible, since none of the nations mentioned would have the practical means of taking any effective or, at least, considerable part of the task involved."

The Prime Minister had, meanwhile, secured the approval of his Cabinet, which had met in nocturnal session in the night of August 11-12. In order to avoid further discussion and delay, Mr. Churchill decided not to raise certain minor proposals suggested by the Cabinet. Agreement was reached on the definitive text of the declaration at noon on August 12. As released to the radio and press on August 14, it read as follows:

The President of the United States and the Prime Minister, Mr. Churchill, representing His Majesty's Government in the United Kingdom, have met at sea.

They have been accompanied by officials of their two Governments, including high ranking officers of their Military, Naval and Air Services.

The whole problem of the supply of munitions of war, as provided by the Lend-Lease Act, for the armed forces of the United States and for those countries actively engaged in resisting aggression has been further examined.

Lord Beaverbrook, the Minister of Supply of the British Government, has joined in these conferences. He is going to proceed to Washington to discuss further details with appropriate officials of the United States Government. These conferences will also cover the supply problems of the Soviet Union.

The President and the Prime Minister have had several conferences. They have considered the dangers to world civilization arising from the policies of military domination by conquest upon which the Hitlerite Government of Germany and other Governments associated therewith have embarked, and have made clear the steps which their countries are respectively taking for their safety in the face of these dangers.

They have agreed upon the following joint declaration:

The President of the United States of America and the Prime Minister, Mr. Churchill, representing His Majesty's Government in the United Kingdom, being met together, deem it right to make known certain common principles in the national policies of their respective countries on which they base their hopes for a better future for the world.

First, their countries seek no aggrandizement, territorial or other;

Second, they desire to see no territorial changes that do not accord with the freely expressed wishes of the peoples concerned;

Third, they respect the right of all peoples to choose the form of government under which they will live; and they wish to see sovereign rights and self-government restored to those who have been forcibly deprived of them;

Fourth, they will endeavor, with due respect to their existing obligations, to further the enjoyment by all States, great or small, victor or vanquished, of access, on equal terms, to the trade and to the raw materials of the world which are needed for their economic prosperity;

Fifth, they desire to bring about the fullest collaboration between all nations in the economic field with the object of securing, for all, improved labor standards, economic advancement and social security;

Sixth, after the final destruction of the Nazi tyranny, they hope to see established a peace which will afford to all nations the means of dwelling in safety within their own boundaries, and which will afford assurance that all the men in all the lands may live out their lives in freedom from fear and want;

Seventh, such a peace should enable all men to traverse the high seas and oceans without hindrance;

Eighth, they believe that all the nations of the world, for realistic as well as spiritual reasons, must come to the abandonment of the use of force. Since no future peace can be maintained if land, sea and air armaments continue to be employed by nations which threaten, or may threaten, aggression outside of their frontiers, they believe, pending the establishment of a wider and permanent system of general security, that the disarmament of such nations is essential. They will likewise aid and encourage all other practicable measures which will lighten for peace-loving peoples the crushing burden of armaments.[49]

6. REPERCUSSIONS OF THE CONFERENCE

The joint declaration, soon to become known as the Atlantic Charter, was not a state paper in the usual sense of the term. Technically it was nothing more than a press release, of which there was no official copy, signed or sealed. As the President explained to a press conference some years later, the joint declaration was scribbled on pieces of paper with many corrections, and the nearest thing to an official copy was the paper distributed to the radio operators.[50] These circumstances led some to contend, rather belatedly, that the document lacked validity, a thesis warmly and rightly rejected by Mr. Welles.[51] As he has pointed out, the form of the declaration was a reflection of the conditions under which it was drawn: "It was precisely as valid in its binding effect as if it had been signed and sealed. It was exactly what it purported to be: notice to the world by the President of the United States and the Prime Minister of the United Kingdom, that in accordance with their constitutional authority to speak for their countries and their Governments, the two nations which they represented would adhere to the great principles set forth in the declaration."

The President's gratification over the joint declaration was somewhat beclouded by the reception accorded it by Secretary Hull, the recognized champion of liberal international trade policies and agreements. The Secretary, already piqued by the prominent part assigned his subordinate in these transactions, was beset by newspaper reporters inquiring whether Article IV meant the continuance of the objectionable Ottawa Agreements after the war. Although, to quote Mr. Welles, it was fully understood at the conference that the reservation "with due respect for their existing obligations" was intended merely to take care of "what it was hoped would be merely temporary impediments to the more far-reaching commitment originally envisaged," the Secretary evidently felt that a vital American position had been surrendered. After discussing the matter with the President, he sent him a long memorandum prepared earlier (August 4) by the Division of Commercial Treaties and Agreements, in which Lord Keynes's contentions

[49] The most important source for the history of the drafting of the charter is the series of memoranda of conversation made by Mr. Welles, most of which are now printed in Pearl Harbor Attack, IV, 1784 ff., and in part in Welles: Where Are We Heading?, 5 ff. Churchill: The Grand Alliance, 436 ff., is the most valuable British account. Additional points are contributed by Davis and Lindley: How War Came, 268 ff.; Sherwood: Roosevelt and Hopkins, 360 ff.; and Elliott Roosevelt: As He Saw It, 35 ff. For a detailed analysis of the charter see Julius Stone: The Atlantic Charter (London, 1943).

[50] The New York Times, December 20, 1944. A search of the Library of Congress and the National Archives bore out the President's statement (Morton: Atlantic Meeting).

[51] Sumner Welles in the New York Herald Tribune, January 3, 1945, and his testimony in Pearl Harbor Attack, II, 523 ff. See also his Where Are We Heading?, 16-17.

were once again reviewed and the great dangers of discriminatory policies set forth.[52] Mr. Hull thought it absolutely essential that some clarifying statement be issued at once. He took up the matter with Lord Halifax, who was about to return to London, and later pursued it further through Ambassador Winant. What he proposed was the addition to Article IV of some clause such as "by means of the reduction of trade barriers and the reduction or elimination of preferences and discriminations." Winant reported that both Mr. Churchill and Mr. Eden had expressed sympathy, but that the Prime Minister was doubtful of Dominion approval and only too keenly aware of the attachment of many members of his own party to the system of Empire Preference. There was real danger, he added, that if the issue were to be debated in Parliament it would create serious divisions and even provoke criticism of the United States. In the end Mr. Hull decided, albeit reluctantly, not to press the matter, though he instructed Ambassador Winant to leave the British under no misapprehension about "the great store our Government sets by the commercial policy which is involved in this issue." There can be no doubt whatever that Article IV was a great blow to the Secretary, whose health in general left much to be desired. A full month later one of his associates found him discouraged and resentful over what had happened; very tired and without fight.[53]

It was almost a foregone conclusion that the news of the Atlantic meeting and the issuance of the joint declaration would evoke loud protest from isolationist leaders and newspapers. The *Chicago Tribune,* in a scathing editorial, denounced the President's theatricality and challenged his right to meet with the leader of a belligerent nation to discuss war and peace plans. "He is the true descendant of that James Roosevelt, his great-grandfather, who was a Tory of New York during the Revolution and took the oath of allegiance to the British King," it added. It was ridiculous, in the editor's opinion, to suppose that the two statesmen had met merely to confer on these "pretentious and meaningless eight points." Mr. Churchill would not have felt justified in making even a luncheon engagement to discuss a bit of rhetoric. What the Prime Minister wanted to know was "when are you coming across?" No doubt he had now gotten the President to pledge himself to the destruction of the Nazis but, so the *Tribune* warned, the American people would repudiate the commitment.[54]

The Chicago editorial sounded the keynote for the general isolationist offensive. The *New York Journal-American* protested against the President's

[52] Memo of Mr. Hull to the President, August 18, 1941, enclosing the memorandum mentioned in the text (*Roosevelt Papers:* Secretary's File, Box 78).

[53] *Moffat Diary (MS.),* September 24, 1941, reporting on his visits in Washington. For the rest we have used a letter of Mr. Hull to the President, August 25, 1941; tels. to Winant, August 25 and September 9, 1941; a draft tel. to Winant, September 26, 1941, which was not sent; tels. from Winant, September 1, 2, 25, 1941; memo by the Adviser on International Economic Affairs, September 27, 1941; *Stimson Diary (MS.),* August 19, 1941. See further Hull: *Memoirs,* II, 975, and *The New York Times,* August 15, 1941.

[54] *Chicago Tribune,* August 15, 1941.

independent action which, it thought, might involve the country in a war which it did not want: "President Roosevelt is retracing, one by one, all of the steps toward war taken by President Woodrow Wilson—steps which the American people later and in the light of calm reflection and sober judgment overwhelmingly stamped as mistakes."[55] Following the same line Senators Hiram Johnson, Bennett Champ Clark and Robert A. Taft charged the President with having made an alliance and with planning an expeditionary force to invade continental Europe. Article VI, they argued, obviously constituted a commitment, for its objective could be attained only through war. More specifically, criticism was leveled also against Article IV, and the story was put about that freedom of religion had not been mentioned in the Charter out of deference to Soviet sensibilities.[56]

Mr. Roosevelt, having anticipated isolationist protests, had been scrupulous in phrasing the Charter to make it as unobjectionable as possible. He had evidently hoped that publication of the joint declaration would help distract attention from the conference in general. But certain commentators at once noted that there must have been more to the Atlantic meeting than the drafting of the Charter and on his return home (August 16) the President himself let the cat out of the bag when he told reporters that there was not a single section of a single continent that he and Mr. Churchill had not discussed. They had, he continued, reached "a complete understanding on all aspects of the war situation," but this did not mean that the United States was any nearer to war than it had been when he set out on his journey.[57] On his arrival in Washington, Mr. Roosevelt at once called in the Democratic leaders of Congress and gave them a fairly complete account of what had taken place. He spoke of Soviet Russia as the key to the immediate situation in Europe and expressed hope that the Soviets would be able to hold out indefinitely. Soviet resistance, he pointed out, had already precluded Hitler from invading England before the end of the year, though admittedly Britain could not hope for victory without invading the continent. He assured his listeners that he had made no new commitments and volunteered the opinion that the greatest danger of a shooting war lay not in the Atlantic, but in the Pacific. The chances of Japan's embarking on further aggression he thought were about fifty-fifty.[58]

It may well be that on this occasion his Congressional visitors suggested to Mr. Roosevelt the desirability of sending a message to the Legislature, if only to explain the oversight committed in failing to include freedom of religion in the Charter. This he did on August 21, when he transmitted the radio release of August 14 to Congress with the following explanatory remarks:

The Congress and the President having heretofore determined through the Lend-

[55] New York Journal-American, August 17, 1941.
[56] The New York Times, August 20, 1941, summarizing the debate in the Senate.
[57] Crider, in The New York Times, August 17, 1941 (Rockland, Maine, August 16).
[58] Turner Catledge, in The New York Times, August 18, 1941.

Lease Act on the national policy of American aid to the democracies in the war which East and West are waging against dictatorships, the military and naval conversations at these meetings made clear gains in furthering the effectiveness of this aid.

Furthermore, the Prime Minister and I are arranging for conferences with the Soviet Union to aid it in its defense against the attack made by the principal aggressor of the modern world—Germany.

Finally, the declaration of principles at this time presents a goal which is worth while for our civilization to seek. It is so clear cut that it is difficult to oppose in any major particular without automatically admitting a willingness to accept compromise with Nazism; or to agree to a world peace which would give Nazism domination over large numbers of conquered nations. Inevitably such a peace would be a gift to Nazism to take breath—armed breath—for a second war to extend the control of Europe and Asia to the American Hemisphere itself.

It is perhaps unnecessary for me to call attention once more to the utter lack of validity of the spoken or written word of the Nazi Government.

It is also unnecessary for me to point out that the declaration of principles includes of necessity the world need for freedom of religion and freedom of information. No society of the world organized under the announced principles could survive without these freedoms, which are a part of the whole freedom for which we strive.[59]

Notwithstanding isolationist attacks and a certain amount of criticism of Article IV of the Charter, the popular reaction to news of the Atlantic Conference was generally favorable in the United States and throughout the American Republics. The American people had a notorious weakness for high-sounding principles and were definitely more willing to participate in the making of peace than in the waging of war. For the most part they saw in the Charter a means of giving "new heart to the oppressed nations" and were quite prepared to support a new system of collective security based on Anglo-American coöperation.[60]

Mr. Churchill, though probably less enamored of statements of peace aims than the President, was undoubtedly delighted to join in any action, even verbal, that proclaimed the close association of the two great democracies. Mr. Roosevelt's acceptance of the reference to "the final destruction of the Nazi tyranny" was, to his mind, a challenge which ordinarily would imply military action, while the idea of joint Anglo-American police forces after the war appealed to him strongly. All this was expressed in his message to Mr. Attlee, suggesting that the British press would surely see "that Joint Declaration proposing final destruction of Nazi power and disarmament of aggressive nations while Britain and United States remain armed is an event of first magnitude."[61] But the response of the British public was rather dis-

[59] Text in *Documents on American Foreign Relations,* IV, 13. See also Mark Sullivan in the *New York Herald Tribune,* August 25, 1941.

[60] *The New York Times,* August 15, 1941, surveying the initial editorial comment throughout the nation. We have used also an admirable digest of press opinion prepared for Secretary Morgenthau (*Morgenthau Diaries, MS.,* Vol. 434, pp. 213 ff.). The Latin American reaction was reviewed by the London *Times,* August 16, 1941, and in a long State Department memorandum of August 20, 1941.

[61] Churchill: *The Grand Alliance,* 444, 448.

appointing, probably because Englishmen had for so long been looking forward to a definite American commitment to enter the war. The "piteous platitudes" of the Charter seemed a poor substitute for such a commitment and many newspaper commentators tried to console themselves with the thought that Mr. Churchill would never have run the risks of crossing the ocean simply to join in a declaration of principles. They found further comfort in the realization that the meeting had strengthened Anglo-American solidarity. The United States, it was argued, could not, after all, hope to shape the future peace without first taking part in the war.[62]

It goes without saying that the press of Berlin, Rome and Tokyo greeted the generalities of the Charter with ridicule and did their utmost to revive memories of Wilson's "dishonest" and ill-fated Fourteen Points. But the fact that the Axis Governments preferred to treat their peoples to floods of vituperation rather than supply them with the official text of the joint declaration may be taken as an indication of the Charter's propaganda value. The sequel was to show that, despite the earlier tragedy of the Fourteen Points, the Atlantic Charter made a profound impression on the conquered nations and provided a foundation for the United Nations organization, thereby contributing substantially to ultimate victory.

In the more immediate sense it should be remembered that the Atlantic Conference was more concerned with the war situation of the summer of 1941 than with the distant future. From the discussions that eventuated in the Charter the President obtained explicit assurance that the British had made no secret territorial or other agreements and that they would not make any without prior consultation with the United States. Furthermore, the Charter itself published to the whole world the community of interest and purpose of Britain and the United States and, by spiking all ideas of a compromise peace with Hitler, strengthened the relationship of the democracies with Soviet Russia. Beyond these considerations lay the imponderables, such as the value derived from the personal contact and growing trust between the President and the Prime Minister, and between the highest military authorities on both sides. For fully four days the leading personages of the two nations had been able to sit together, to exchange ideas and to discuss plans. They found themselves far from agreement and they made no commitments. But they became more familiar with each other's reasoning and capabilities, with the result that in the months to come there was to be greater understanding and easier resolution of differences. The Atlantic Conference remained in a class by itself, inasmuch as it took place at a time when one party to the discussions was still nonbelligerent. But it was to become the model for the great conferences of the war period and, seen in historical perspective, clearly ranks with the important international gatherings of modern times.

[62] *The New York Times*, August 15, 1941. It is worth noting that later British comment was much more guarded.

CHAPTER XXII

Konoye's Last Chance

1. RESUMPTION OF CONVERSATIONS WITH JAPAN

As the President and the Prime Minister were bidding each other farewell off the Newfoundland coast, Secretaries Hull, Stimson, and Knox resumed their informal weekly meetings in Washington. This so-called "War Council" was the nearest approximation to a clearing house for national security problems which the Administration could offer. Of the meeting on August 12, the first since Mr. Hull's return from White Sulphur Springs, Secretary Stimson noted in his diary: "We are now back again on the same ground— appeasement is over and Hull, with his analytical mind, is asking searching questions of the Navy what they'll do next in case any of these issues that he has been handling brings up an impasse and the necessity for force." The burning questions, as Stimson listed them, all touched the Far East:

Thailand: What do we say when the British ask us whether we will fight with them if they tell the Japs not to advance into Thailand?

Netherlands East Indies: Same question in N.E.I. Dutch are bound to ask what we will do if Japan marches into these islands.

Northwestern Pacific: Vladivostok. What do we do if Japs attempt to prevent us from shipping supplies into Vladivostok?

South Atlantic: We have insufficient naval strength to cover the danger that would occur should the Germans march on Dakar as they are now preparing to do. Shall we move more of the Fleet from Pacific to Atlantic?[1]

The answers to these questions are not recorded but at best they could have been no more than tentative. Much depended on the outcome of the discussions at Argentia, known in full only after Mr. Welles's return to Washington on August 15. The President had already notified Mr. Hull that he desired to see the Japanese Ambassador immediately upon his own return and Mr. Welles at once began drafting the text of a warning to Japan

[1] *Stimson Diary (MS.)*, August 12, 1941.

in accordance with the understanding between the President and Prime Minister Churchill. The Under Secretary's draft emerged as a lengthy review of the situation resulting from Japan's move into southern Indo-China and the consequent suspension of the Japanese-American conversations. It did, however, hint at the possibility of resumption of the discussions if the Japanese Government were willing to give assurances of peaceful intent. But all this was merely a prelude to the vital last paragraph comprising the warning: If Japan persisted in its program of domination by force, the United States would be compelled to take forthwith "all steps of whatsoever character it deems necessary in its own security, notwithstanding the possibility that such further steps on its part may result in conflict between the two countries."[2]

Though in anything but a conciliatory mood, Secretary Hull deemed this formulation "dangerously strong" and likely to incite the Japanese extremists at the very moment when the United States was most anxious to avoid war. He and his advisers on Far Eastern affairs therefore toned down the words of warning and even added an offer to resume the conversations with Japan. In part the Secretary was probably influenced in this direction by his conversation with Ambassador Nomura on August 16. The latter appeared genuinely worried over the existing impasse and assured Mr. Hull that his Government was so desirous of reaching peaceful relationships that he believed it ready to make concessions. Nomura then repeated his suggestion for a meeting between Prince Konoye and President Roosevelt and asked if the Japanese-American conversations could not be resumed. Though Mr. Hull was cool and took the occasion to restate seriatim the American objections to Japan's course of action, he agreed to discuss the envoy's proposals with the President.[3]

Mr. Roosevelt arrived in Washington on the morning of Sunday, August 17. He conferred at once with Secretary Hull and accepted the changes made in the warning document. On the afternoon of the same day the two men received Nomura at the White House for one of the most significant of the protracted conversations. Mr. Roosevelt was in unusually good spirits, evidently refreshed by his two weeks at sea and much gratified by the results of his meeting with Mr. Churchill. After some amiable introductory remarks he commented upon the well-known policies and principles of the United States relative to Japan and by contrast pointed up the Japanese course of aggression. The Ambassador, invited to comment, seized the initiative to pull out of his pocket what he professed were instructions from Tokyo and then proceeded to reiterate his Government's desire for peaceful relations—a desire so strong that Prince Konoye was prepared to meet the President

[2] *Pearl Harbor Attack*, XIV, 1255 ff.

[3] *Foreign Relations of the United States: Japan*, II, 553; tel. from Nomura to Tokyo, August 16, 1941 (*Tokyo War Crimes Documents*, No. 1457); Hull: *Memoirs*, II, 1017 ff.

halfway for a personal conference. This put Mr. Roosevelt at something of a tactical disadvantage but, on the plea that it was necessary to bring matters up to date, he began to recite the prepared statement of warning, the final passage of which now read:

. . . if the Japanese Government takes any further steps in pursuance of a policy or program of military domination by force or threat of force of neighboring countries, the Govermnent of the United States will be compelled to take immediately any and all steps which it may deem necessary toward safeguarding the legitimate rights and interests of the United States and American nationals and toward insuring the safety and security of the United States.

Having allowed time for this to sink in, the President turned to the proposal for a meeting with Prince Konoye and for resumption of the American-Japanese conversations. He read the Ambassador another, much longer statement rehearsing the circumstances under which the earlier talks had been suspended and outlining the principles upon which further discussions would have to be based. Stress was laid particularly upon an economic program for the Pacific area which, if adopted, would give Japan everything it needed. The paper closed with this paragraph:

In case the Japanese Government feels that Japan desires and is in position to suspend its expansionist activities, to readjust its position, and to embark upon a peaceful program for the Pacific along the lines of the program and principles to which the United States is committed, the Government of the United States would be prepared to consider resumption of the informal exploratory discussions which were interrupted in July and would be glad to endeavor to arrange a suitable time and place to exchange views. The Government of the United States, however, feels that, in view of the circumstances attending the interruption of the informal conversations between the two governments, it would be helpful to both governments, before undertaking a resumption of such conversations or proceeding with plans for a meeting, if the Japanese Government would be so good as to furnish a clearer statement than has yet been furnished as to its present attitude and plans, just as this Government has repeatedly outlined to the Japanese Government its attitude and plans.[4]

These two statements, then, carried out the President's commitment, made at the Atlantic Conference, to warn the Japanese Government of the consequences of further aggression or expansion. Mr. Roosevelt at once despatched a message to the Prime Minister in which he said: "The statement I made to him [Nomura] was no less vigorous than and was substantially similar to the statement we had discussed."[5] Mr. Welles testified subsequently in the same sense, expressing the view that the two versions came to much the same thing. Others who were closely concerned with the

[4] Foreign Relations of the United States: Japan, II, 554 ff.; Hull: Memoirs, II, 1019; tels. of Nomura to Tokyo (Pearl Harbor Attack, XV, 1682 ff.; XVII, 2750 ff.).

[5] Tel. from the President to the Prime Minister, August 18, 1941 (Pearl Harbor Attack, IV, 1694 ff.).

President's statement, including Secretaries Hull and Stimson, did not even hesitate to describe it as an "ultimatum."[6] Nevertheless it remains true that the concluding paragraph of the warning handed to Nomura was decidedly less pointed than the language of the original draft. It was, indeed, weaker than the warning handed Minister Wakasugi by Mr. Welles a few weeks earlier, or the "ultimatum" which the British Government was on the point of sending to Tokyo at the end of August.[7] Above all, it was pitched in a minor key as compared with Mr. Churchill's excoriation of Japan's conduct in a public statement on August 24. "It is certain," concluded the Prime Minister, "that this has got to stop. Every effort will be made to secure a peaceful settlement. The United States are labouring with infinite patience to arrive at a fair and amicable settlement which will give Japan the utmost reassurance for her legitimate interests. We earnestly hope these negotiations will succeed. But this I must say: that if these hopes should fail we shall of course range ourselves unhesitatingly at the side of the United States."[8]

The toning down of the American warning to Japan was due in large measure to Secretary Hull's constitutional aversion to strong or decisive action. Evidence of this appeared again when the British Chargé d'Affaires, Sir Ronald Campbell, sought out the Secretary on August 30 and informed him that the London Government, in accordance with the agreements arrived at during the Atlantic Conference, was about to associate itself with the President's warning and submitted for consideration two variant drafts, both of which contained the statement as originally suggested by Mr. Churchill to Mr. Roosevelt: "The British are compelled to warn Japan that any further encroachment in the Southwest Pacific would compel His Majesty's Government to take countermeasures even if these should lead to war." Mr. Hull at once began to dilate on the "explosive" nature of the situation in Japan and recommended that any such "ultimatum" should be presented confidentially, so as not to upset the Konoye Government. He made clear that he thought enough had already been done and, so far as one can judge from the very fragmentary record, either he or Mr. Hornbeck subsequently talked the British out of sending any official warning whatever.[9]

[6] For Mr. Welles's testimony see *Pearl Harbor Attack*, II, 485. Mr. Stimson's judgment is recorded in *Stimson Diary* (*MS.*), August 19, 1941. Mr. Hull referred to the "President's ultimatum" in his memo of a conversation with Sir Ronald Campbell of the British Embassy, August 31, 1941. See also Admiral Schuirman's characterization (*Pearl Harbor Attack,* II, 644 ff.).

[7] Memo of conversation between Mr. Hull and the British Chargé d'Affaires, Sir Ronald Campbell, August 31, 1941, to which are appended drafts of the British warning to Japan.

[8] Churchill: *The Unrelenting Struggle*, 235; *The Grand Alliance,* 446.

[9] Memo of conversation between Mr. Hull and Sir Ronald Campbell, August 30, 1941, with the attached British drafts and with a chit by Mr. Hornbeck, dated September 2, 1941, stating that he had taken up the matter informally with Sir Ronald later on August 30, 1941.

In this connection it should be remembered, however, that Mr. Roosevelt himself had had compunctions about the drastic warning urged upon him by Mr. Churchill. While he had agreed, at the Atlantic Conference, to submit to Nomura an unequivocal warning, he had made no secret of his desire and hope of deferring the crisis by reviving and prolonging the discussions with Japan. When, on his return to Washington, he learned of Nomura's advances, he was no doubt eager to make the most of them and quite ready to fall in line with Mr. Hull's recommendations. There is no reason to doubt Ambassador Nomura's report that Mr. Roosevelt was extremely cordial and expressed regret at having to admonish Japan at all. Furthermore, the evidence of the President's effort to minimize the significance of his statement is unmistakable. In the American records the warning appears in the form of an "oral statement." But Nomura's account explicitly denies it even this status. "After reading them," wrote the Ambassador, "he [the President] requested me to relay the contents to my home Government. He added that the two papers were not to be considered as oral statements, but were to be given the status of only reference material. I accepted the papers on condition that they would be only for my information."[10]

In sum, discretion triumphed over valor and the warning to Japan, envisaged at Argentia as a major state paper, a virtual ultimatum, was reduced to a statement for the information of the Japanese Ambassador. Certainly Nomura left the interview with the impression that it was intended to relate primarily to the possibilities of a resumption of the Japanese-American conversations and a meeting between the President and Prince Konoye. Mr. Roosevelt had given the Ambassador to understand that despite his admonition he was not averse to a personal conference with the Japanese Premier. He had even suggested as a possible date and locality: Juneau, Alaska, in mid-October. A preliminary statement of Tokyo's attitude and plans was not made a prerequisite. The United States Government felt merely that "it would be helpful" if the Japanese Government "would be so good as to furnish" such information. Little, indeed, remained of the stern resolve of the Atlantic Conference. The President, who had there talked of gaining perhaps thirty days, now saw larger vistas opening before him.[11]

Even if allowances be made for Ambassador Nomura's failings as an accurate reporter of the nuances of diplomatic intercourse, and for the fact that all his professional assistants were en route to Tokyo, he seems in this instance to have reported his conversation with Mr. Roosevelt fully and correctly. Moreover, for all his momentary optimism, he left his superiors no doubt about the underlying gravity of relations between the United States

---

[10] Tel. from Nomura to Tokyo, August 17, 1941 (*Pearl Harbor Attack*, XV, 1682).

[11] Tel. from Nomura to Tokyo, August 19, 1941 (*Pearl Harbor Attack*, XVII, 2755). In keeping with the above, Nomura reported that a Cabinet officer (probably the Postmaster General) had assured him that the President was not anti-Japanese and that his readiness to reconsider conversations with Japan was unprecedented (*ibid.*, 2757).

and Japan. These now "hung on a hair," he cabled on August 16. The next Japanese step, especially into Siam, would probably precipitate matters. American opinion, he added, might be divided with regard to the war in Europe, but it was united on the Far East.[12]

2. A ROOSEVELT-KONOYE MEETING?

In later years Prince Konoye described the events of 1941 as essentially a race between his Cabinet and the military. He and his Cabinet colleagues were attempting to make progress in the diplomatic conversations with the United States, while the military extremists were trying to discredit the motives of the United States and rush to completion the preparations for war. Failure to make headway with the conversations was seized upon by the extremists as an argument for further deployment of force.[13]

There was evidently a large measure of truth in this generalization. Certainly Konoye's Government was, as the race entered its final stages in the late summer, being subjected to the heaviest pressures by its activist opponents. The Japanese press rang with denunciations of British-American encirclement and with threats of war if the United States sent munitions to the Soviets through Vladivostok. An attempt was made to assassinate Baron Hiranuma on August 14. Political figures as respected as Marquis Kido felt they could move about safely only under heavy guard. Yet the Cabinet as a whole was not yet prepared to throw in the sponge. Aware of the plight into which his own weakness had led the country, Konoye staked his hopes of achieving a peaceful settlement on a meeting with the President of the United States. In the face of economic strangulation, made imminent by the orders freezing Japanese assets abroad, there remained but two alternatives: conclusion of an agreement, or war with the United States. When Nomura's assistants from the Washington Embassy reached Tokyo about August 20 and reported to a Liaison Conference on the dangers of the American situation, Konoye knew that if peace were to be saved, he must make a supreme effort to talk personally with Mr. Roosevelt.

The stage had already been set. On August 18, probably before Nomura's reports reached Tokyo, Konoye's Foreign Minister, Admiral Toyoda, sat down with Ambassador Grew. For two and a half hours of an insufferably

[12] Tel. from Nomura to Tokyo, August 16, 1941 (*Tokyo War Crimes Documents*, No. 1457; *Pearl Harbor Attack*, XII, 17-18). In an extraordinary telephone interview from Los Angeles with the Japanese newspaper *Nichi Nichi*, Nomura's assistant, Minister Wakasugi, had already warned that the United States desired good relations and would never initiate hostile action, but that it was determined to meet action with action and had already decided on its countermeasures (Tolischus in *The New York Times*, August 12, 1941).

[13] Memo of conversation between Prince Konoye and Mr. Max Bishop, Department of State, entitled "Background of Political Developments in Japan before Pearl Harbor," November 6, 1945. See also Toshikazu Kase: *Journey to the "Missouri"* (New Haven, 1950), 49-50.

hot evening and while Mr. Grew swabbed himself with wet towels, Toyoda
defended Japan's course of action, pleaded for a relaxation of American
economic pressure, and urged the meeting between the Premier and the
President. He felt certain, he said, that such a personal conference would
produce an equitable agreement, but begged for the utmost secrecy so as to
avoid a flare-up of popular passions. The Ambassador was deeply moved by
the Japanese proposal. In his telegram to Washington he urged that it not
be rejected "without very prayerful consideration." Emphasizing that the
project was without precedent in Japanese history, he added that it was "an
indication that Japanese intransigence is not crystallized completely owing
to the fact that the proposal has the approval of the Emperor and the highest authorities in the land. The good that may flow from a meeting between
Prince Konoye and President Roosevelt is incalculable. The opportunity is
here presented . . . for an act of highest statesmanship, such as the recent
meeting of President and Prime Minister Churchill at sea. . . ."[14]

The last week of August certainly confronted the Konoye Government
with serious obstacles to the achievement of the desired resumption of the
conversations and the meeting of the chiefs of government. Two American
tankers loaded with oil for the Soviets were approaching the Straits leading
to Vladivostok. In Japan indignation ran high over the fact that the United
States, while cutting off vital exports to Japan, was supplying oil to the
Soviet forces in the Far East and thereby strengthening them for an eventual
attack on Japan. Obliged to make a gesture, the Japanese Government
lodged rather mild protests on August 26 in both Moscow and Washington.
These were promptly rejected. The *Tass* Agency declared that any attempt
to interfere with the tankers would be regarded as "an act unfriendly to the
USSR," while Secretary Hull dismissed the suggestion that the tankers be
recalled as "too preposterous." The Soviet and American Governments did,
however, explain that the supplies were intended primarily for the Red
armies in Europe. With this Tokyo had to be content.[15]

Prince Konoye did not permit even this ominous development to distract
him from his main objective. Nomura was pleading that "if the Japanese
Government is determined to adjust Japanese-American relations, this is
the time." Convinced that the President was well disposed to a conference,
the Ambassador suggested that a ship be made ready and the Japanese delegation selected. In a long telegram of August 20 he proposed a reply to the
recent United States notes by which Japan would subscribe to a policy of

[14] *Foreign Relations of the United States: Japan*, II, 559-65; Joseph C. Grew: *Ten
Years in Japan* (New York, 1944), 416 ff.

[15] *Foreign Relations of the United States: Japan*, II, 565-70; *Bulletin of International News*, XVIII (2), 1178-79, 1187, 1189; memo of conversation between Mr. Hull
and Ambassador Oumansky, August 27, reporting Molotov's reply to the Japanese protest. On August 19 Secretaries Hull, Stimson, and Knox had agreed that if the Japanese
attacked the tankers, it would constitute an act of war (*Stimson Diary, MS.*, August 19,
1941).

peaceful methods, accept the principle of equality of economic opportunity and treatment, disclaim any intentions of territorial aggrandizement and disavow any alliance or policy of aggression, all this to be confirmed at the so-called "leaders' conference."[16]

The Prime Minister required no prodding. An appropriate ship was commandeered and fitted with special radio and other devices.[17] At the same time Nomura was instructed to inquire about rumors of the forthcoming British-American-Soviet meeting in Moscow and press for an earlier date for the leaders' conference so as to avoid the impression that Japan had yielded only under pressure of a coalition.[18] Finally, on August 26, the Liaison Conference decided on the text of a message from the Prime Minister to the President and also on a reply to the American note of August 17. The message to the President was replete with good will, deploring past misunderstandings and stressing the desirability of open and frank discussion, the results of which could afterward be worked out by subordinate officials. Prince Konoye repeated that he was looking forward eagerly to his conference with the President and again suggested that it take place somewhere near Hawaii. As for the formal reply to the American notes of August 17, no particular reference was made to the first, warning note, but the second, dealing with resumption of conversations, was covered in great detail. After a long disquisition on the fact that certain measures to which the United States Government objected had been taken by Japan in the interests of national defense and that, *pari passu,* countermeasures taken by the Washington Government on the same plea frequently appeared threatening to the Japanese, the Tokyo note expressed full willingness to embark upon conversations looking toward lasting peace in the Pacific area. More concretely:

The Japanese Government is prepared to withdraw its troops from Indo-China as soon as the China Incident is settled or a just peace is established in East Asia.

Furthermore, in order to remove all possible doubt in this regard, the Japanese Government reaffirms herewith its repeated declaration that its present action in Indo-China is not a preparatory step for military advance into neighboring countries. The Japanese Government believes the above pledge will suffice to clarify also Japan's intentions toward Thailand.

As regards Soviet-Japanese relations, the Japanese Government declares likewise that Japan will take no military action as long as the Soviet Union remains faithful to the Soviet-Japanese neutrality treaty and does not menace Japan or Manchukuo or take any action contrary to the spirit of the said treaty. On the other hand, the Japanese Government sincerely hopes that the United States Government will avoid any

[16] Tels. of Nomura to Tokyo, August 20, 1941 (*Pearl Harbor Attack,* XVII, 2759 ff.).
[17] Affidavits of Admirals Oikawa, Takata and Oka (*Tokyo War Crimes Documents,* Defense Documents Nos. 2691, 2761, 2828).
[18] Tel. from Tokyo to Nomura, August 23; tel. from Nomura to Tokyo, August 23 (*Pearl Harbor Attack,* XVII, 2772-73); memo of Mr. Hull, August 23, 1941 (*Foreign Relations of the United States: Japan,* II, 568).

action that might give rise to a fear of menace to Japan through collaboration with the Soviet Union.

In a word, the Japanese Government has no intention of using, without provocation, military force against any neighboring nation.

And, on the more general level, the Tokyo Government offered this assurance as to its attitude and policy:

Regarding the principles and directives set forth in detail by the American Government and envisaged in the informal conversations as constituting a program for the Pacific area, the Japanese Government wishes to state that it considers these principles and the practical application thereof, in the friendliest manner possible, are the prime requisites of a true peace and should be applied not only in the Pacific area but throughout the entire world. Such a program has long been desired and sought by Japan itself.[19]

The Japanese Ambassador presented Konoye's message and the accompanying note to President Roosevelt on August 28. The latter once more demonstrated great cordiality and complimented the Ambassador on the tone and spirit of Prince Konoye's message. He conveyed the impression that he was looking forward to a conference of several days and objected only to the selection of Hawaii. On rather flimsy grounds he renewed his suggestion that Juneau be chosen. As for the accompanying Japanese note, he promised careful consideration, but remarked, "smilingly and cynically," that though he was looking forward to his meeting with Prince Konoye, he wondered "whether invasion of Thailand can be expected during those conversations just as an invasion of Indo-China occurred during Secretary Hull's conversations with your Excellency."[20]

At this point the proposal ran into formidable obstacles. Secretary Hull saw the Ambassador later in the day and promptly began to throw cold water on Prince Konoye's project. There can be little doubt that Mr. Hull and most of his advisers had been cool to the idea of a conference from the very beginning and that they deprecated the President's cordial reaction to the plan. In a memorandum to the Secretary, the Division of Far Eastern Affairs had reminded him of the familiar Japanese strategy of putting through an agreement in very general terms and then evading or rejecting specification. It therefore suggested that the President lay down as conditions precedent to a general settlement that Japan (1) indicate its intention of withdrawing from close association with the Axis; (2) abandon its in-

---

[19] *Foreign Relations of the United States: Japan,* II, 572 ff.; "Konoye Memoirs" (*Pearl Harbor Attack,* XX, 4002). The text of the instruction to Nomura, as intercepted and reprinted in *Pearl Harbor Attack,* XVII, 2779 ff., is almost entirely illegible. So far as one can detect, it was more strongly worded than the text Nomura left with the President, but the form was left to the Ambassador's discretion (*Pearl Harbor Attack,* XII, 20).

[20] Memo by Hull, August 28 (*Foreign Relations of the United States: Japan,* II, 571); tel. from Nomura to Tokyo, August 28, 1941 (*Pearl Harbor Attack,* XVII, 2794).

tention of retaining troops in China to combat communism; and (3) clarify its proposed program of economic coöperation with China. Finally it was argued that before the President agreed to meet with Konoye, there should be a genuine meeting of minds between the two governments "on fundamental principles."[21]

Secretary Hull followed this traditional line in his conversation with Nomura, who was already indulging in agreeable speculations as to details of the meeting. The Secretary brushed aside such talk and characteristically enlarged upon the need for a preliminary agreement in principle on all major questions involved in a settlement. Nomura himself listed these as Japan's relations to the Axis, the retention of Japanese troops in North China and Inner Mongolia, and application of the principle of nondiscrimination in commercial relations. He thought that only the second might cause difficulty, since the Japanese people regarded their adherence to the Axis "as merely nominal" and "he could not conceive of his people being prepared to go to war with the United States for the sake of Germany." Mr. Hull in reply stressed the need for doing something to reassure the American people on this score and then turned to consideration of the China problem. Japan, he remarked, could not expect the United States to mediate between Tokyo and Chungking unless it knew the terms to be offered Chiang Kai-shek. Neither could Washington risk provoking an explosion of indignation in Chungking by a meeting between the President and Konoye. The China problem was one of "the pivotal questions" in American-Japanese relations, and unless settled to everyone's satisfaction "there would remain the roots of future instability and trouble."[22]

Strong justification for Secretary Hull's caution was presently provided by an intercepted telegram sent to Nomura by the Japanese Foreign Office on the same August 28. This explained that the reference to withdrawal of troops from Indo-China on the settlement of the China Incident really meant "when the Chiang regime has become merely a local regime as a result of the closing of routes used to aid that regime." Other points in the Japanese offer were interpreted in such a way as to leave no doubt that Japan intended to stand firmly by its claim to leadership in the East Asia Co-Prosperity Sphere.[23] To add to the customary difficulties in fathoming the real intentions of Tokyo came a cable, also on August 28, from Bishop Walsh to Postmaster General Walker. Presumably passed on at once to Mr. Hull, this message emphasized that the latest Japanese proposal came "straight from the horse's mouth" and that no power could offer more, as no wise architect of policy could expect more than the proposal contained.[24]

[21] Memo to Hull, August 28, 1941 (*Pearl Harbor Attack*, XX, 4406 ff.).

[22] Memo of Mr. Ballantine, August 28, 1941 (*Foreign Relations of the United States: Japan*, II, 576 ff.); tel. of Nomura to Tokyo, August 29, 1941 (*Pearl Harbor Attack*, XII, 21-22).

[23] Tel. to Nomura, August 28, 1941 (*Pearl Harbor Attack*, XVII, 2791).

[24] Telegram, August 28, 1941 (*Walker Papers, MS.*).

If this last item was indeed an accurate description of Konoye's intent, it is not hard to imagine the shock the Prince must have received on reading Nomura's report of Secretary Hull's reaction to the projected leaders' conference. Harsher yet must have been the impact of the news that Ambassador Nomura, on leaving the White House, had disregarded the all-important injunction of secrecy and told newspaper reporters that he had just delivered a message from the Japanese Prime Minister to the President. While neither the Ambassador nor Mr. Hull revealed the contents of the message, the mere fact of its delivery loosed a flood of speculation.[25]

The Tokyo press, already dangerously excited by Mr. Churchill's speech of August 24, by Washington's announcement of an American military mission to Chiang Kai-shek, and by the approach of American tankers to Vladivostok, burst forth in a chorus of defiant vituperation and threats.[26]

Moreover, the cat having been let out of the bag, Prince Konoye's Government was faced with searching questions from its German partner. One of the considerations behind the Premier's desire to meet the President was doubtless the growing Japanese disillusionment about an early Nazi victory over Soviet Russia.[27] It looked increasingly as though Germany would have to face a winter of bitter yet indecisive fighting. Accordingly Prince Konoye and his Foreign Minister had already shown themselves cool to oft-repeated German suggestions for a Japanese attack on Siberia.[28] Ambassador Ott got little satisfaction when, on August 29 and 30, he inquired pointedly about the significance of Konoye's message to the President and warned of American duplicity. The Japanese reply was simply that there had been no change in policy. The purpose of the Tripartite Pact had been to keep the United States out of war. This objective was still being pursued by the Imperial Government. However, Matsuoka had demonstrated that the United States could not be bluffed by threats and so now an effort was being being made to gain the same end by a move toward appeasement so as to "bring about a domestic disintegration rather than to excite and unify them."[29]

Beset by all these woes, Japanese statesmen could only plead with Nomura

[25] Tel. from Nomura to Tokyo, August 28; tels. from Tokyo to Nomura, August 29 (*Pearl Harbor Attack*, XVII, 2796 ff.); tels. and memos from Ambassador Grew, August 29, 30 (*Foreign Relations of the United States: Japan*, II, 579 ff.); Mowrer in the *Chicago Daily News*, August 28; Hulen in *The New York Times*, August 29, 1941.

[26] Reports of Tolischus from Tokyo (*The New York Times*, September 1, 2, 1941).

[27] Report of Newman from Tokyo (*New York Herald Tribune*, September 2). The same view was forcefully expressed by the German Ambassador in Tokyo on September 4, 1941 (*Tokyo War Crimes Documents*, No. 4080A).

[28] Tel. from Ott to Berlin, August 19, 1941 (*Nazi Conspiracy and Aggression*, VI, No. 3733-PS). Soviet spies also reported to Moscow at the end of August that the German Embassy in Tokyo had abandoned all hope of a Japanese attack on the USSR in 1941 unless the Germans decisively defeated the Soviets (Department of the Army Report: *The Sorge Spy Ring*, Washington, 1949).

[29] Tels. from Ott to Berlin, August 29, 30, 1941 (*Nazi Conspiracy and Aggression*, VI, 3733-PS); *Pearl Harbor Attack*, XVIII, 2948 ff.; *Tokyo War Crimes Documents*, Defense Document No. 1641.

and the American Government to avoid further leaks and hasten the leaders' meeting. The situation in Tokyo being extremely tense and Prince Konoye's life in danger, it was suggested to Ambassador Grew that Washington postpone sending further tankers to Vladivostok pending the outcome of the conference and that, during the same period, it suspend the operation of the freezing order.[30] But on September 2 a well-known newspaper correspondent reported publicly that he had learned authoritatively in Washington that Konoye had proposed to the President a meeting on a warship in the Pacific. The White House spokesman, Stephen Early, at once issued a denial: "The President has no invitation. . . . The only plan the President has involving a trip on the water in the immediate future is a cruise from Annapolis on the Chesapeake Bay and on the Potomac River." Similarly Tokyo made light of the story: "It sounds very dramatic—it makes a good newspaper headline."[31] But the report was too plausible to be brushed aside and the Japanese Government therefore began to urge that the best solution would be to issue a joint announcement that the meeting would take place about September 20.[32]

Secretary Hull replied evasively to all these importunate proposals, but could not indefinitely avoid an official response to Prince Konoye's August 28 message. The question had been discussed at length in the State Department for several days. Mr. Hull, in keeping with his temperament and convictions, was firmly opposed to any meeting prior to an agreement on fundamentals. He was reinforced in his stand by the arguments of his chief adviser on the Far East, Mr. Stanley Hornbeck, who maintained that Japan was torn by dissension, shaken, and fearful; in short, in no position to attack. While America should take no unfair advantage, it had everything to gain and little or nothing to lose by standing on its principles and policies.[33]

Against this reasoning could be adduced an urgent appeal from Bishop Walsh, transmitted by the Postmaster General. This argued that the only possibility of success lay precisely in the resumption of the conversations and a simultaneous meeting between the President and the Prime Minister. The vital issues could be settled only at the highest level and the time element was "agonizingly crucial."[34]

Disregarding this message, Mr. Hull clung to his course and Mr. Roose-

---

[30] Tel. from Tokyo to Nomura, August 29, 1941 (*Pearl Harbor Attack,* XVII, 2798); memo by Grew, August 29, 1941 (*Foreign Relations of the United States: Japan,* II, 579 ff.).

[31] Fleischer in the *New York Herald Tribune,* September 3; *The New York Times,* September 4, 1941.

[32] Tels. from Tokyo to Nomura, September 3 (*Pearl Harbor Attack,* XII, 25-26); memo of Ambassador Grew, September 3, 1941 (*Foreign Relations of the United States: Japan,* II, 586 ff.).

[33] Memo of Mr. Hornbeck, September 2, 1941; Hull: *Memoirs,* II, 1023 ff.

[34] Tel. from Bishop Walsh to Mr. Walker, September 3, 1941, sent at once to Mr. Hull (*Walker Papers, MS.*).

velt, despite his initial enthusiasm for the meeting, now veered toward complete agreement with the Secretary. The two men saw Nomura on September 3, when the President handed the Ambassador a reply to Prince Konoye's message together with another "oral statement" of explanation. In these papers, as well as in Mr. Roosevelt's remarks to Nomura, the refrain was always the same: The President favored the meeting and was eager to get on with it; he realized the domestic political difficulties confronting Konoye, but he in turn had to consider the feelings of the American public and the reaction of the Chinese people; he appreciated the assurances of agreement to American principles given by Konoye, but there remained unresolved differences of view. These would have to be cleared up in advance if a meeting were to result in the "collaboration between you and me along the line I am sure we both earnestly desire to follow."[35]

It may be observed that the Japanese Government was well aware that it would have to offer Washington more detailed specifications than those contained in Konoye's original message. On September 4, before Nomura's report of his latest conversation with the President reached Tokyo, the Foreign Office handed Ambassador Grew and transmitted to Nomura a draft of the concessions Japan was prepared to make, as well as of those it asked in return. This draft was intended as an agenda for the Roosevelt-Konoye meeting, in lieu of a preliminary agreement on general principles. It reaffirmed Japan's readiness to concur in the points agreed upon earlier and reiterated the proposals of August 28. On issues still outstanding it provided "that the attitudes of Japan and the United States toward the European War will be decided by the concepts of protection and self-defense, and, in case the United States should participate in the European War, the interpretation and execution of the Tripartite Pact by Japan shall be independently established." The other items in the draft were designed either to make more explicit previous proposals or to pin down the United States to specific concessions, particularly engagements to abstain from measures prejudicial to Japan's effort to reach a settlement with China, to suspend military measures in the Far East, and to abrogate the freezing order.[36]

Even if this amplification of Japan's offer had reached Washington before Mr. Roosevelt replied to Konoye's August 28 note, it is unlikely that it would have influenced the Administration's decision. Whatever its merits, it did not meet the firm requirements advanced by Mr. Hull and approved by the

[35] *Foreign Relations of the United States: Japan*, II, 588 ff.; tel. from Nomura to Tokyo, September 3, 1941 (*Tokyo War Crimes Documents*, Defense Document No. 1401N-1).

[36] Memo by Ambassador Grew, September 4, 1941 (*Foreign Relations of the United States: Japan*, II, 593, 608); tel. from Tokyo to Nomura, September 4 (*Pearl Harbor Attack*, XII, 25-26). On September 4 Nomura submitted a draft document of his own which he later withdrew in favor of the official document (text in *Foreign Relations of the United States: Japan*, II, 597 ff.).

President. The project for a Pacific meeting was not quite dead after September 3, but it had manifestly fallen into a coma. Prince Konoye's hopes were running up against the familiar obstacles that had shattered past hopes and would destroy others in the future: the insistence of the United States on concrete proof that Japan had indeed abandoned its aggressive course and insistence also that agreement on fundamental principles must precede specific adjustments in relations between the two powers. Opinion on the wisdom of advancing these prerequisites, widely divergent throughout the course of Japanese-American negotiations, was nowhere more divided than at this point.

Ambassador Grew has not abandoned his original contention that the President would have done well to accept Prince Konoye's proposal for a meeting. Others, like Postmaster General Walker, who was a colleague of Secretary Hull and himself involved in the unofficial negotiations, share this conviction. Hostile critics of the President's foreign policy have naturally made the most of the disagreement within Mr. Roosevelt's own official family. Their argument can be stated briefly: Japan had reached an advanced state of tension and felt that it was being encircled militarily and strangled economically; Konoye saw as the only alternative a possible agreement with the United States; he was entirely sincere in his efforts and was prepared to make substantial concessions; considering the President's great personal magnetism and political astuteness, he could probably have induced Konoye to accept a reasonable settlement; finally, if the Premier had returned to Japan with an agreement, popular relief and Imperial support would have been sufficient to enable him to quell the opposition of the extremists.

The view of an experienced diplomat like Ambassador Grew can not be set aside lightly. Yet there are great difficulties in the way of accepting at face value the argument that the Pacific meeting might have paved the way to a settlement. The essential elements in this complicated equation were three in number: the real intentions of Prince Konoye; his ability to force through whatever agreement he might have reached with the President; and, finally, the willingness of the United States to make concessions to Konoye substantial enough to achieve agreement.

While Konoye's intentions have been clarified to some degree with the passage of time, they are still far from certain. It would seem impossible to doubt his personal anxiety to reach an agreement that would forestall war with the United States, or his genuine conviction that a meeting with the President would produce it. It is, furthermore, probable that he envisaged making additional concessions to Washington, including concessions on the crucial issue of the withdrawal of Japanese troops from China. According to his own subsequent account, he intended, after meeting with Mr. Roosevelt, to communicate directly with the Emperor and request him to take the decisive step of ordering the Japanese troops out of China. While Konoye professed to believe that he himself would be assassinated soon after his return to Japan, he was sure that such direct intervention by the Emperor would insure fulfillment of his plan.[37]

The Premier's confidence in a *fait accompli* was shared by Bishop Walsh, who was in frequent touch with him and with other members of the Cabinet.[38] Nevertheless, even if Konoye's good faith be accepted without question, it remains very doubtful whether he could have induced the Japanese military to accept the concessions he would have had to make to secure American agreement. Japanese records which became available after the war reinforce this doubt. They reveal that Army circles were highly skeptical of success and wholly unwilling to yield on the really important issues. It is likely enough that the Japanese Government was prepared to give some assurance that if the United States became involved in war with Germany, the Japanese decision would be taken independently. As Nomura kept repeating in Washington, Japan would not go to war with the United States merely to please its German ally. Beyond this, however, there is little to suggest willingness on the part of the military to accept significant concessions to the American position. The German Ambassador at Tokyo, who can scarcely be accused of deluding his Government, may be profitably quoted in this connection: "The impossibility of maintaining the present state of tension with the United States psychologically and materially, without reaching a clash, has induced the circles influencing Konoye to make the attempt of approaching Roosevelt directly." Konoye, he continued, was telling the activist elements that this would be the last and not even a serious effort to convince Japan of the hopelessness of a settlement. The real objective, according to Ambassador Ott, was some sort of *modus vivendi* to tide the Government over a period of serious internal ferment: "The negotiations with the United States could possibly drag on for some time, but a compromise, which can be had only by maximum concessions on the part of Japan, would at once result in grave inner convulsions."[39]

Certainly there was nothing to suggest that Washington, on its part, would yield on any essential issue or principle. Leaving aside for the moment the general principles of international relations to which the United States had been so long committed and which Secretary Hull rarely lost an opportunity to proclaim, and leaving aside also such problems as equality of trade and access to markets, there still remained the vital issue of China and the

[37] Memo of conversation between Prince Konoye and Mr. Max Bishop of the State Department, November 7, 1945. On Konoye's motives see also Herbert Feis: *The Road to Pearl Harbor* (New York, 1948), 252-54.

[38] Memo of Bishop Walsh, October 18, 1941, based on almost daily conferences between August 15 and October 13, 1941 (*Walker Papers, MS.*).

[39] Tel. from Ott to Berlin, September 4, 1941 (*Tokyo War Crimes Documents*, No. 4080A).

related problem of Japanese expansion by aggressive methods. Washington was as determined as ever to ensure the independence and integrity of China and equally determined not to allow the vast and populous Asiatic mainland to fall under Japanese hegemony. When, in July, 1941, the Japanese marched into southern Indo-China, Washington had taken the bit in its teeth. The freezing order was probably the crucial step in the entire course of Japanese-American relations before Pearl Harbor. It was not initially intended to end all American trade with Japan, but rather to serve as a means of exerting pressure as the circumstances warranted. But in practice no exports of any consequence reached Japan after August, nor was Japanese silk or any other commodity imported into the United States. Thanks to the coöperation of the nations of the British Commonwealth and of the Netherlands Indies, the ensuing economic blockade of Japan was all but complete. If one thing was more certain than another, it was that Japan could not continue under such pressure for more than a few months. American officials were well aware that Japan had been given a choice between climbing down or fighting it out. Many believed that Japan was in no condition to fight and would have to climb down. Others, including a majority of the Cabinet, expected that Japan would fight, but one and all felt that Japan's chances of success in war were slim. It was therefore largely a matter of postponing the evil day as long as possible so as to gain time for further American preparations. Spiritually as well as economically the United States was already at war and already exulting in its easy successes. "Japan," wrote one influential editor, "is encircled by the consequences of her own outrages and she is getting desperate. There is just one thing to do about this and that is to draw the circle a little tighter every time she perpetrates a desperate act."[40]

It need not be maintained that this was the universal American attitude, but it was certainly the prevalent one. If the Administration had already decided to take a strong stand, most of the press clamored for an even stronger one. If the Japanese press was bellicose, so was the American. The truth of the matter was that the policies of the two powers were no longer reconcilable. Whether the discussion rose to high levels of moral principle or dipped to mundane consideration of concrete issues, the conflict persisted. While the possibility cannot be entirely excluded that a meeting between Prince Konoye and the President might have achieved a *modus vivendi*, it remains highly dubious whether such a stopgap arrangement could have been translated subsequently into an agreement. It can always be argued that little or nothing would have been lost by giving Prince Konoye the benefit of the doubt, and that as long as there was even a faint chance that the leaders' meeting might avoid hostilities, the gamble was worth taking.

[40] *New York Herald Tribune,* August 20, 1941. Cf. *Fortune,* September 1, and *The New Republic,* September 8, 1941.

On the other hand it should be remembered that at the time it was far from clear to Washington that the game was worth the candle or that the leaders' conference offered even a chance of slowing up Japan's preparations for war. In addition, there was always the danger that failure of the conference would exacerbate feelings on both sides and hasten the unwanted conflict.

3. American Preparations for the Worst

In assessing the Japanese-American problem it must always be borne in mind that Washington officials were regularly receiving transcripts of Japanese diplomatic correspondence and that they could scarcely mistake the difference between what they read in these secret messages and the broad assurances proffered by the Konoye Government. Since these messages plainly indicated that the Japanese had no serious intention of drawing back but, on the contrary, would soon resume their advance, it was incumbent on Washington to take all possible precautionary measures. These cannot be treated in detail, but a few specific examples will illuminate the general program.

For one thing it was decided to keep the Japanese guessing as to the application of the freezing order. Suggestions that oil be released in return for gold shipments or for Japanese payments in Latin America were evaded. Secretary Hull explained to the appropriate officials of the State, Treasury and Justice Departments that he did not want "any clear statement made on the question of oil exports to Japan, but rather prefers that a direct answer be delayed as long as possible." Actually neither oil nor anything else of significance was released.[41] On the contrary, Washington indicated discreetly to the Latin American Governments that the best way to defeat the trend toward Axis world domination was to institute effective export controls. A number of other Republics introduced systems of restrictions while the larger states, like Mexico, Brazil, Argentina and Chile, established controls over the export ef strategic items.[42]

On the military side the War Department began to speed up reinforcement of the Philippines. In August the first Flying Fortresses were despatched in the hope that enough of them could be sent in the next three or four months to serve as a real deterrent to further Japanese action. Secretary Stimson and General Marshall were very optimistic on this score, though the program throughout was beset with technical difficulties.[43]

---

[41] Memo of meeting of State, Treasury and Justice representatives, October 2, 1941 (*Morgenthau Diaries, MS.,* Vol. 447, pp. 128 ff.).

[42] Memo from Welles to Hamilton, asking that a circular telegram be sent to the American Governments, July 28; memo by the Division of Controls, September 9, 1941.

[43] *Stimson Diary (MS.),* August 4, October 8, 1941; Marshall testimony (*Pearl Harbor Attack,* III, 1243 ff.). The reinforcements destined for the Philippines between August and December 14 are summarized in a memo from General Marshall to Admiral Stark, September 12, 1941 (*ibid.,* XVI, 2211-12). See also Wesley F. Craven and James L. Cate: *The Army Air Forces in World War II,* Vol. I (Chicago, 1948), 176 ff.,

Along the same line the Administration continued to do everything possible to strengthen the positions of the friendly powers in the Southwest Pacific. As much material as could be spared was sent to the Dutch in the East Indies and to the British at Singapore. American military and naval officers met with representatives of these nations at Manila and Singapore to coördinate plans and work out the details of coöperation. Siam being the nation most immediately threatened, Washington did what it could, in conjunction with the British, to encourage Bangkok to resist Japanese demands, and American officials tried hard to come to some satisfactory agreement by which the British and Americans would take the bulk of Siam's tin and rubber exports in return for shipments of oil. Nonetheless, it was difficult to put complete trust in the Siamese Government or rely on its assurances of intention to resist. The Administration therefore avoided advance commitments to give aid, though it indicated clearly enough that if the Siamese Government actually did resist, support would be forthcoming as it had been to China and other powers.[44]

Of greater importance, naturally, was the American relationship with Nationalist China and the development of the policy of aiding China in its resistance to Japan. On this issue popular sentiment was well-nigh united, while the Administration too was full of good will. Yet the material contribution remained extremely slight. Added to the physical difficulties of getting supplies into China was the chronic shortage of munitions and the continuing feeling, especially in the War Department, that what little could be spared would do more good in Britain than in China. Statistics compiled in mid-June, 1941, showed that American exports to China were insignificant: during the first three months of the year they amounted to only about one fourteenth of the shipments to Britain.[45]

On all sides it was thought highly important to remedy this situation if Chinese morale were to be sustained. Consequently Mr. Lauchlin Currie had been sent out on special mission to Chungking early in 1941 and on his return had been given a vaguely defined position as adviser to the President on Chinese affairs. He proved a vigorous exponent of assistance to Chungking and an equally determined opponent of any American agreement with Japan which, he argued, "would do irreparable damage to the good will we have built up in China . . . and would largely nullify the effect of lend-lease aid to China."[46]

and Mark S. Watson: *Chief of Staff: Prewar Plans and Preparations* (Washington, 1950), Chapter XIII.

[44] The highly complicated negotiations with Siam cannot be analyzed in detail here, but the crucial period was covered in tels. from Grant, July 17, August 9, 11, 12, and by State Department memoranda, July 25, August 8, 12, 14, 18, 1941 (some of which are printed in *Pearl Harbor Attack,* XIX, 3707 ff.).

[45] Memo by Hornbeck, June 12; letter of the President to Chiang Kai-shek, June 23, and the latter's reply, July 27, 1941.

[46] Memo of Currie to the President, September 13, 1941, enclosing several comments

In further efforts to buttress Chinese morale and counter Chungking's resentment over the failure of the democracies to accept China as a full-fledged ally in the struggle against the totalitarian states, the Administration took a number of additional steps. Professor Owen Lattimore was permitted to take service as the Generalissimo's political adviser. A mission of transportation experts was sent out to study ways and means of improving the Burma Road. The Chungking regime was formally admitted to the benefits of Lend-Lease with an allocation of $166,000,000. Even more significant, American Army and Navy pilots were allowed to volunteer for service with the new Chinese Air Force which Colonel Claire L. Chennault was organizing—a timely move in view of the desperation induced by the persistent Japanese air attacks on the Chinese capital.[47]

Following the Nazi attack on Russia the Chinese situation became even more acute, in view of the likelihood that the Japanese would at once exploit Soviet preoccupation in Europe to press their own campaign in China. Acting Secretary Welles wrote Harry Hopkins pleading that all practicable measures be taken to avert a possible collapse of the Chinese will to resist and arguing that the best method of doing this was "to make available to China urgently needed supplies and to see that these supplies reach China promptly."[48] This, however, was a policy more easily advocated than executed. As late as mid-September Mr. Currie was still obliged to report to the President that shipments to China to date remained "quite small," though he believed they "should step up more rapidly from now on."[49] Not even the frantic efforts of Mr. T. V. Soong, aided by Colonel William J. Donovan, Harry Hopkins, and James Roosevelt, were sufficient to pry loose from the British or American Services the fighter aircraft for which Chiang Kai-shek felt a special need. "We have stuck for five years," pleaded Mr. Soong, "please help us to stick now." But with the Soviets now adding their claims to those of the British, there were simply not enough planes to go around.[50]

As a pledge of something more than mere gestures and to counter the Generalissimo's feeling of isolation, it was decided to follow the British example and send to Chungking a military mission under Brigadier General John Magruder, a former American Military Attaché to China. But, like so many other projects for China, this one made slow progress. From June

by Owen Lattimore, Major McHugh, Naval Attaché at Chungking, and others, on the situation in China (*Roosevelt Papers:* Secretary's File, Box 73).

[47] For a vivid, detailed account see Claire L. Chennault: *Way of a Fighter* (New York, 1949), 95 ff.

[48] Memo of Welles to Hopkins, with copies to Marshall and Stark, July 7, 1941.

[49] Memo of Currie to the President, "On Defense Aid Program for China," September 17, 1941 (*Roosevelt Papers:* Secretary's File, Box 73).

[50] Summary of an interview between T. V. Soong and Colonel Donovan, August 16, 1941, subsequently transmitted to the President (*Roosevelt Papers:* Secretary's File, Box 73).

to August complicated discussions took place between the State and War
Departments as to the exact status of Magruder, his relation to the Embassy,
and the purport of his instructions. In view of Chiang Kai-shek's feeling of
political isolation and his repeated requests for inclusion in the staff conferences between the powers opposed to Japan, it was originally planned to
authorize Magruder

. . . to consult with the Chinese military authorities on the extent and forms of
collaboration to be adopted should the Chinese and American Governments find themselves engaged in hostilities with a common enemy, and to consult with the British,
Dutch, Russian and other military authorities in the Far East on the extent and forms
of collaboration to be adopted should American, British, Dutch and Russian Governments find themselves engaged in hostilities with a common enemy.

But in the end this was deemed too compromising and the provision was
dropped. General Magruder's instructions, as finally drawn, directed him
merely to help the Chinese Government obtain appropriate Lend-Lease aid
and ensure that the most effective use was made thereof.[51]

The Atlantic Conference ushered in a new phase of American relations
with China. At that time the question arose between Mr. Welles and Sir
Alexander Cadogan whether the Chungking Government should be informed of the President's projected warning to Japan. Nothing was done
because of Mr. Welles's fear that the Chinese Government might leak the
news and thereby inflame feeling in Japan.[52] The inevitable result was to
enhance the conviction of the Chinese that they were being neglected and
forgotten while the United States and British Governments flaunted their
aid and support of the Soviet Union. Everybody, complained Chiang Kai-
shek in the presence of the American and British Ambassadors, is making
pacts with everybody else—except with China.[53] Nevertheless, the Chinese
at once announced their adherence to the Atlantic Charter, while Secretary
Hull in response reiterated to the Chinese Ambassador his country's "deep
and abiding interest in aiding China" and assured him that everything was
being done to increase this aid. On August 26 General Magruder's mission
was publicly announced and other occasions were seized upon to emphasize
Washington's determination to support China to the hilt. After news of the
projected Roosevelt-Konoye meeting had transpired, the Chinese professed

[51] The Magruder Mission went back to a tel. from the Military Attaché at Chung-
king, June 15, 1941, suggesting that a general officer with China experience be sent out.
On its further development: memo by Welles, July 24; memo by the Far Eastern Divi-
sion, July 25; memo from Currie to Welles, August 4; memo from Welles to Hornbeck,
August 5; letter of Stimson to Welles, August 5 and reply, August 8; instructions to
Magruder, August 26; *Stimson Diary* (*MS.*), July 29, August 7, 1941.

[52] Memo of conversation between Welles and Cadogan, August 11, 1941 (*Pearl Harbor
Attack*, IV, 1790 ff.).

[53] Tel. from Lattimore to Currie, August 2, 1941, and memo from Currie to Welles,
August 3, 1941; letter from Lattimore to Currie, August 20, 1941, this last item in the
Roosevelt Papers: Secretary's File, Box 73.

great anxiety lest they be sold out in the interests of an American-Japanese settlement. Secretary Hull responded with the most explicit assurances that the conversations with Japan had thus far been merely exploratory and that Chungking would be consulted if ever the talks progressed to the point of formal negotiations.[54]

4. RESTATEMENT OF THE JAPANESE TERMS

Returning to the narrative of the American-Japanese conversations, it may be stated with confidence that high military circles in Tokyo shared the view, expressed earlier in these pages, that Washington's prerequisites (September 3) for a meeting between the President and Prince Konoye killed any hope of its being successfully staged. In his memoirs Prince Konoye makes no bones about saying: "It would seem that from about August, 1941, the [Japanese] Army General Staff, even including the highest quarters, began advocating an immediate breaking off of negotiations and an opening of American-Japanese hostilities." The Liaison Conference was in almost permanent session, working on an "Outline for the Execution of the National Policy." Of the details little is known except that on September 5, shortly after receipt of the American reply, Prince Konoye discussed the Outline with the Emperor, preparatory to the convocation of an Imperial Conference on the following day. The Emperor was impressed by the fact that the document submitted to him appeared to put military preparations before diplomatic negotiations and therefore insisted on calling in the Chiefs of Staff of the Army and Navy to learn their intentions. Both assured him that they proposed to continue negotiations and would proceed with military preparations only when the diplomatic effort appeared hopeless. The Emperor then asked the Chief of Staff of the Army how long he thought hostilities with the United States might last. General Sugiyama replied that operations in the South Pacific might be wound up in three months. In biting words Hirohito then reminded him that he (Sugiyama) had been Minister of War at the time of the outbreak of the China Incident and that he had promised the Throne that the affair would be over in a month. Four years had now passed and it was still unsettled. Continuing, in Konoye's own words:

In trepidation the Chief of Staff went to great lengths to explain that the extensive hinterland of China prevented the consummation of operations according to the

[54] Memo of Mr. Hornbeck, August 11, 1941, urging greater support for the Chinese; memo of the Far Eastern Division, August 16, suggesting possible action; memos of conversations between Mr. Hull and the Chinese Ambassador, August 19, September 4, October 1; despatch from Gauss (Chungking), September 11; tel. to Gauss, September 12; despatch from Gauss, September 18; memo of Mr. Hamilton, October 9, 1941. We have also used material illustrating the efforts of Mr. T. V. Soong to obtain aircraft and other supplies for China in the summer of 1941 (*Roosevelt Papers:* Secretary's File, Box 73).

scheduled plan. At this the Emperor raised his voice and said that if the Chinese hinterland was extensive, the Pacific was boundless. He asked how the General could be certain of his three-month calculation. The Chief of Staff hung his head, unable to answer. At this point the Navy Chief of General Staff lent a helping hand to Sugiyama by saying that to his mind Japan was like a patient suffering from a serious illness. He said the patient's case was so critical that the question of whether or not to operate had to be determined without delay. Should he be let alone without an operation, there was danger of a gradual decline. An operation, while it might be extremely dangerous, would offer some hope of saving his life. The stage was now reached, where a quick decision had to be made one way or the other. He felt that the Army General Staff was in favor of putting hope in diplomatic negotiations to the finish, but that in case of failure a decisive operation would have to be performed. To this extent, then, he was in favor of the negotiation proposals. The Emperor, pursuing the point, asked the Chiefs of the Supreme Command if it was not true that both of them were for giving precedence to diplomacy, and both answered in the affirmative.[55]

The reluctance of the Army High Command to commit itself to further negotiation was explained later by General Tojo, the then Minister of War. A conclusion, he said, had to be reached by mid-October because of technical considerations. November would be the best month for landing operations; December would be possible but difficult; January would be impossible because of the northeast monsoons.[56] That being so, the High Command was in a difficult position, in view of the great desire of the Emperor to continue negotiations as long as possible. When the Imperial Conference assembled on the morning of September 6, Mr. Hara, President of the Privy Council, posed the same question the Emperor had raised the day before. The Minister of the Navy gave the desired reply, but the Chief of Staff remained silent. Thereupon the Emperor took the floor (a most unusual occurrence), expressed his regret and expatiated on his desire for peace. "Everyone was struck with awe, and there was silence throughout the hall." In the end Admiral Nagano, Chief of the Naval Staff, saved the situation by saying that he thought the Minister of the Navy was speaking for the whole Government and that therefore he had remained silent: "He assured the Emperor that the Chiefs of the Supreme Command most certainly concurred with the Navy Minister's answer; that they were conscious of the importance of diplomacy, and advocated a resort to armed force only when there seemed no other way out. The meeting adjourned in an atmosphere of unprecedented tension."[57]

Actually there was little reason why the Army High Command should be so hesitant about continuing negotiations, for the Outline, approved by the

[55] "Konoye Memoirs" (*Pearl Harbor Attack,* XX, 4004-5).

[56] "Tojo Memorandum" (*Tokyo War Crimes Documents,* Proceedings, 36,281 ff.).

[57] "Konoye Memoirs" (*loc. cit.*), which are borne out by the "Kido Diary," September 6, 1941 (*Tokyo War Crimes Documents,* No. 1632W-68). On the September 6th meeting we have also used the memo of conversation between Prince Konoye and Mr. Max Bishop, dated November 7, 1945.

Imperial Conference on September 6, made success along diplomatic lines patently improbable. The salient passages of the plan as adopted were as follows:

Determined not to be deterred by the possibility of being involved in a war with America (and England and Holland) in order to secure our national existence, we will proceed with war preparations so that they can be completed approximately toward the end of October.

At the same time we will endeavor by every possible diplomatic means to have our demands agreed to by America and England. Japan's minimum demands in these negotiations with America (and England), together with the Empire's maximum concessions, are embodied in the attached document.

If by the early part of October there is no reasonable hope of having our demands agreed to in the diplomatic negotiations mentioned above, we will immediately make up our minds to get ready for war against America (and England and Holland).

Japan's minimum demands provided, in brief, that (1) the United States and Britain should not intervene in or obstruct a settlement of the China Incident by Japan. They should close the Burma Road and cease all military, political or economic aid to the Nationalist Government. Japan would adhere rigidly to the plan for stationing troops in specified areas of China, but would agree to withdraw forces from the rest of China on conclusion of the Incident. (2) The United States and Britain should take no action in the Far East which would constitute a threat to Japan; they should not establish military bases in Siam, the Netherlands Indies, China or Far Eastern Russia, and should not increase their forces in the Far East beyond existing strength. Demands for the liquidation of Japan's special relations with Indo-China should not be considered. (3) The United States and Britain should coöperate with Japan in her attempt to secure needed raw materials; they should restore trade relations with Japan and assist Japan in establishing close economic ties with Siam and the Netherlands Indies. If all these terms were accepted by the United States, Japan would undertake (1) not to use Indo-China as a base for operations against any neighboring country except China; (2) to withdraw troops from Indo-China as soon as a just peace were established in the Far East; (3) to guarantee the neutrality of the Philippine Islands. Furthermore, Japan would promise not to take action against Soviet Russia so long as that power adhered to the Neutrality Pact of April, 1941. As for the Tripartite Pact, Japan would be willing to affirm that there would be no changes in the execution of its obligations under the Axis Agreement.[58]

This program speaks for itself and serves as a valuable commentary on the proposals which Nomura was to submit to Secretary Hull on the same

[58] "Konoye Memoirs" (Pearl Harbor Attack, XX, 4022-23); Tokyo War Crimes Documents, No. 1652. The provision regarding the Tripartite Pact is curiously omitted from the version given by Konoye.

day. In view of its approval by the Imperial Conference it became, in Japanese eyes, "immutable," the fixed basis of policy and negotiation. Some idea of the dubious position of Prince Konoye and of the scant chance of success for his projected meeting with the President may be derived from his statements to Ambassador Grew and Mr. Dooman, with whom he dined at a private house and in utmost secrecy on the evening of the same eventful September 6. On that occasion the Prime Minister assured the Ambassador that Japan "conclusively and wholeheartedly" agreed to the four principles enunciated by Secretary Hull and that personally he was determined to spare no effort to reach a peaceful settlement. He had, so he said, "the strongest concurrence from the responsible chiefs of both the Army and the Navy," who had agreed to send high officers to the projected leaders' meeting: "He admitted that there are certain elements within the armed forces who do not approve his policies, but he voiced the conviction that since he had the full support of the responsible chiefs of the Army and Navy it would be possible for him to put down and control any opposition which might develop among those elements."[59]

The Ambassador was undoubtedly much impressed by Konoye's explicit assurances. According to the Prime Minister, Mr. Grew promised to send a message directly to the President and felt that his report would be "the most important cable to go from his hand since the start of his diplomatic career." Unhappily the Ambassador knew nothing of the decisions of the Imperial Conference, nothing of the content of the intercepted messages to and from the Tokyo Foreign Office, and relatively little of what was happening in Washington. With the benefit of all this knowledge the historian is justified in discounting heavily Prince Konoye's hopes, even if it be conceded that the Prime Minister as a person, having worked himself into an impasse, was now eager to stake his career and perhaps his life on the outcome of the meeting with the President.

With this background there is no need for a detailed account of the exchanges which filled the ensuing weeks. It will be recalled that the Japanese offer had been communicated to Ambassador Grew on September 4. Grew had sent it on to Washington with favorable comment:

Since it is presumed that a detailed formulation of a general plan of reconstruction of the Far East could not probably be worked out in advance [of the leaders' conference], it would be eminently desirable that the military and economic measures of the United States which are now inexorably pressing on Japan be relaxed point by point *pari passu* with the actions of the Japanese Government in the direction of implementing its proposed commitments. If our Government followed this suggested

[59] Memo by Grew, September 6, 1941 (*Foreign Relations of the United States: Japan,* II, 604 ff.); Grew: *Ten Years in Japan,* 425; "Konoye Memoirs" (*Pearl Harbor Attack,* XX, 4005-6). Konoye states that this secret meeting was arranged with the full cognizance of the War and Navy Ministers, which casts some doubt on the sincerity of his professions.

course it would always retain in its hands the leverage which would contribute to Japanese implementation of its commitments. If an adjustment of relations is to be achieved, some risk must be run, but the risk taken in the pursuance on our part of a course which would not only provide inducements to the Japanese to honor their undertakings but would also leave to the United States Government a certain leverage of compulsion, would appear to be relatively less serious than the risk of armed conflict entailed in the progressive application of economic sanctions which would result from a refusal to accept these proposals.[60]

The Ambassador had obviously become worried as he observed the impact of economic sanctions on Japan. He favored making the most of the Japanese offer, which he rightly judged to be more extensive than any previous one. But the State Department was less well impressed. On receipt of Mr. Grew's telegram the Japanese terms were at once analyzed. In a memorandum to the Secretary, Mr. Ballantine emphasized that the new Japanese note seemed to differ both in spirit and in letter from the principles for which the United States stood and which Konoye himself professed to support. More concretely, the note involved no commitment as to the terms Japan would offer China. There was no indication of respect for the integrity and sovereignty of China, of promise to refrain from interference and to treat China as an equal, or of conformity to a policy of economic nondiscrimination. The Japanese, he continued, appeared to reserve to themselves the decision as to how American trade should be conducted. Their proposals further implied that Japan and the United States could decide the fate of the western Pacific without reference to other countries. All told, it was hard to escape the conclusion that the Japanese aimed at cessation of American aid to China, after which they would be free to impose upon Chungking any terms they chose.[61]

These criticisms were made the basis of a long telegram to Grew, consisting of a number of questions to be submitted to the Japanese Foreign Office. Concurrently these questions were discussed at great length between high officials of the State Department and members of the Japanese Embassy in Washington. The end result was that Tokyo, while objecting to getting involved in a mass of detail and while stressing the urgency of the leaders' conference, did restate its readiness to stand by any specific agreements reached in previous conversations, did reaffirm its willingness to have the United States mediate the settlement between Japan and China, and did deny any intention of excluding discussions between the United States and other powers interested in the southwest Pacific.[62]

[60] Memo of Ambassador Grew, September 5, 1941 (*Foreign Relations of the United States: Japan*, II, 601 ff.).

[61] Memo of Mr. Ballantine, September 5, 1941. We have also used a memo of Mr. Ballantine, in a similar vein, dated September 23, 1941.

[62] These discussions, extending from September 10 to 13, are recorded in *Foreign Relations of the United States: Japan*, II, 610-24.

At this point it will be more profitable to examine certain collateral material rather than flounder in the tides of argument. On September 13 the Tokyo Liaison Conference, after many meetings, finally arrived at Japan's basic conditions of peace with China. These included provisions for joint defense to check Communist and other subversive movements:

The stationing of Japanese Army units for a necessary period in prescribed areas in Inner Mongolia and North China for the above purpose, as well as the placing of Japanese warships and units for a necessary period in Hainan Island, Amoy, and other localities on the basis of previous agreements and practices.

Withdrawal of troops. The Army units which have been sent to China for the prosecution of the China Incident shall, with the exception of those mentioned in the preceding item, be withdrawn attendant upon the settlement of the Incident.

In the economic sphere, activities of other powers in China were not to be restricted "if conducted on an equitable basis." Finally, the regime of Chiang Kai-shek was to be "merged" with that of the Japanese puppet Wang Ching-wei and, though there were to be no annexations by Japan, China was to recognize the loss of Manchukuo.[63]

It can hardly be maintained that the suspicions of the State Department were unwarranted. When, on September 11, newspaper rumors got afloat that negotiations for a far-reaching settlement were under way, Mr. Arthur Krock could report that he had been unable to find any responsible official in Washington who was optimistic, though all continued to cherish a spark of hope and to appreciate every bit of time gained.[64] At the same time several subordinate officials of the Far Eastern Division of the State Department, after conferring among themselves, submitted a memorandum to their chief, asking that it be brought to the attention of higher officers. This memorandum argued that, though there was no knowing whether an accord was in fact being contemplated, any agreement with Tokyo would tend to weaken Chinese resistance and relieve Japan of its present difficulties, thereby giving Tokyo a chance to regain strength. It warned against any betrayal of China and insisted that any guarantees given by the Japanese Government short of immediate withdrawal of troops from China would not provide effective protection to American interests.[65]

Much the same reaction to the current rumors was provoked in the press. The New York Post, in an editorial, declared roundly: "Japan's plans for conquest can be shattered by firm, collective opposition from the United States and Great Britain. We know, because we see it happening. We know, too, by the same pragmatic test, that appeasement of Japan only adds to her aggressive hunger. The democracies have gained the advantage by being firm; it would be the height of folly to fail to secure lasting peace by becom-

[63] Pearl Harbor Attack, XVIII, 2952.
[64] Krock in The New York Times, September 12, 1941.
[65] Memo from members of the Far Eastern Division, September 13, 1941.

ing soft too soon . . . Freedom for China, in the concrete form of complete withdrawal of Japanese troops, must be our minimum demand."[66]

More and more the issue was being narrowed to the question of China, the more so as the Japanese Government made no move after the United States began to escort British convoys and even after the episode of the *Greer,* thereby relieving Washington of anxiety lest a shooting war in the Atlantic bring Japan into the conflict. This is not to say that the Konoye Government was not concerned by these developments. It is altogether likely that it was exposed to renewed pressure and attack by the pro-Axis elements. Nonetheless, on the first anniversary of the Pact (September 27) there was no flamboyant celebration in Tokyo. On the contrary, the press as well as the Foreign Minister went out of its way to stress the pacific character of Japan's alliance.[67]

But coolness toward the Axis did not signify Japanese readiness to abandon the national program. On the tenth anniversary of the Manchurian Incident the Japanese opened a new offensive in Hunan Province and General Tojo, the War Minister, proclaimed anew in a public speech Japan's determination to realize the Greater East Asia Co-Prosperity Sphere. Warning other powers against interference, he called upon a hundred million Japanese to rise to full stature "to perform the national mission set forth at the founding of the Empire and to secure a guarantee for a life sphere."[68] And yet, despite the uncompromising attitude of the military activists, Konoye and Toyoda still struggled to clinch the leaders' conference before the deadline for ending negotiations was reached. They were both irritated with Nomura, partly because they felt he was not reporting fully and accurately and partly because he had confused the issue by submitting to Mr. Hull proposals and comments of his own. The first complaint was largely unjustified. As for the second, it was certainly true that no one in either capital was quite clear about the relationship of the Japanese notes of August 28 and September 4 to the American note of June 21 and the undelivered Japanese reply of July 15. The Konoye Government therefore decided, in the hope of preventing the indefinite prolongation of confusion, to submit to Washington its program for a peace settlement with China and also a new synthesis of its proposals for a Japanese-American agreement. The first was handed to Mr. Grew on September 22 and the second on September 25, in both instances accompanied by urgent pleas for an early decision on the Roosevelt-Konoye meeting.[69]

[66] The *New York Post,* September 13; see also the *New York Herald Tribune,* September 16, 1941.

[67] Memo of Ambassador Grew, September 8; memo of Mr. Ballantine, September 12 (*Foreign Relations of the United States: Japan,* II, 609, 613); Tolischus in *The New York Times,* September 28, 29, 1941.

[68] Newman in the *New York Herald Tribune,* September 20, 1941.

[69] *Foreign Relations of the United States: Japan,* II, 631 ff.; and the Japanese telegrams in *Pearl Harbor Attack,* XII, 28 ff.; further, "Konoye Memoirs" (*ibid.,* XX, 4006-7).

The new Japanese note was an effective restatement of the position which Tokyo had gradually reached but, since it contained nothing really new on the critical issues, the language remained broad and open to varying interpretation. It was intended by Konoye and Toyoda to hasten the American reply, with particular reference to the leaders' conference, and did in fact oblige Washington finally to make up its mind. From Tokyo Ambassador Grew cabled and wrote recommending in the strongest terms that Konoye's proposal be accepted. He realized that it involved risks, but it seemed to him that it would be better to face these risks than face the greater danger of war. He remained convinced that Konoye, whatever his previous shortcomings, was now in dead earnest and would probably be able to carry the Army and the country with him. This, Mr. Grew was persuaded, was the last chance and should be taken for what it was worth. In Washington Nomura went over the same arguments again and again, but there was nothing in the reasoning of either of the Ambassadors that would induce Secretary Hull and his advisers to modify their conviction that a conference without previous agreement on broad principles might prove disastrous and so do more harm than good. This was the advice given the President by Mr. Hull. It rested, no doubt, in part on the conviction that the Japanese would not yield on essential points, but in part also on the thought that through the prolongation of the discussions valuable time was being gained.[70]

On this issue there was little difference of opinion among responsible American officials. Secretaries Stimson, Knox, Morgenthau and Ickes were all advocates in varying degrees of the strong line against Japan and were much gratified with the results of the economic sanctions. Mr. Stimson thought the Japanese "rattled and scared" and attributed their changed attitude to America's stiff stand on Siam and the despatch of bombers to the Philippines. He was particularly anxious that the newly created Economic Defense Board recommend against any relaxation of the economic stranglehold. When the Chief of the Military Intelligence Divison of the General Staff submitted the view that neither a leaders' conference nor economic concessions should be considered unless Japan definitely committed itself to withdraw from the Axis, Stimson's concurrence was all but complete. "I believe however that during the next three months, while we are rearming the Philippines, great care must be exercised to avoid an explosion by the Japanese Army. Put concretely this means that while I approve of stringing out negotiations during that period, they should not be allowed to ripen into a personal conference between the President and the Prime Minister. I greatly fear that such a conference if actually held would produce conces-

[70] *Foreign Relations of the United States: Japan*, II, 641 ff.; Grew: *Ten Years in Japan*, 436 ff.; Hull's note to the President (*Pearl Harbor Attack*, XX, 4424 ff.); the Japanese correspondence in *Pearl Harbor Attack*, XII, 39 ff.; "Konoye Memoirs" (*ibid.*, XX, 4006-7).

sions which would be highly dangerous to our vitally important relations with China."[71]

In this connection it must be emphasized that even the most responsible newspapers were dinning into the ears of the Administration the impossibility and immorality of any retreat from its established position vis-à-vis Japan, or of any settlement made at the expense of China. "Such a 'settlement' would be a flat betrayal of our best friend in Asia. It would ridicule our moral position in the war."[72] If anything more were needed to clinch the American attitude, it was supplied by a series of reports of further Japanese moves in Indo-China. The first of these, which arrived on September 29, made a powerful impression on Administration officials, tending to confirm the prevailing view that no agreement with Japan was worth the paper on which it was written.[73] On a visit to Washington from his post in Ottawa, Minister Moffat found Secretary Hull highly skeptical. An agreement with Japan might eventually be reached, said Mr. Hull, but this would depend more on the circumstances than on the conversations. He would never depart from American principles for the sake of appeasement, but meanwhile "every day's grace is so much to the good."[74] In these views the Secretary was supported by his chief departmental advisers. On balance the Far East Division judged it best not to agree to the meeting between the President and Prince Konoye. If Soviet resistance continued, Japan might yet be induced to make concessions.[75]

Such was the despairing atmosphere in which the American note to Tokyo was formulated. This formal reply, finally completed on October 2, turned out to be a long document covering six closely printed pages. Most of it was devoted to another extensive review of previous exchanges, with particular reference to the Japanese note of September 6 and later comments. No mention whatever was made of the summary Japanese note of September 27. In the main the United States Government complained that while Tokyo agreed in a general way with the broad principles set forth by Washington, the effort was being constantly made to narrow and restrict the application of those principles by what appeared "unnecessary qualifying phrases." Consequently it was still not clear what the Japanese Government intended in matters of freedom of trade, the continued occupation of parts of China, and the Tripartite Pact. "Renewed consideration of these fundamental principles may be helpful." The President still hoped earnestly that his

[71] Pearl Harbor Attack, V, 2092; Stimson Diary (MS.), October 6, 1941; Morgenthau Diaries (MS.), Vol. 442, pp. 45 ff. (conversation between Morgenthau and Stimson, September 18, 1941).

[72] The New York Times, September 23, 1941.

[73] Tel. from Leahy (Vichy), September 29, 1941.

[74] Moffat Diary (MS.), September 24, 1941. See also the President's memo to Secretary Hull, September 28, 1941, in F.D.R.: His Personal Letters, II, 1217.

[75] Memo of Mr. Ballantine, recording the consensus of the Far East Division, September 23, 1941.

meeting with Konoye could take place, but only after the uncertainties about the application of the general principles had been dispelled.[76]

In transmitting this document to his Government Ambassador Nomura expressed the opinion that it still left a ray of hope, though it was clear to him that unless there were a radical change in the world situation the United States would not alter its stand. He himself appears to have felt that the American Government had reason to complain of the confused and evasive statements made by the Tokyo Foreign Office.[77] But on their side Prince Konoye and Foreign Minister Toyoda recognized the impending failure of their policy. The Prime Minister had been losing confidence for some time and, in view of the early October deadline for implementing war plans set by the Imperial Conference of September 6, had come to feel "that there was no choice for him but to consider his resignation if the military insisted on starting a war on October 15."[78] He had gone as far as circumstances would permit and that was not far enough. Public opinion was extremely wrought up; the Army was protesting against the Government's treatment of the Tripartite Pact; the Germans themselves were becoming irritable. From Berlin Ambassador Oshima reported that Ribbentrop "expressed great dissatisfaction with Japan's attitude" and that the whole German Foreign Office staff was "thoroughly disgusted with Japan." In great anxiety Oshima concluded: "If Japan takes a wishy-washy attitude and goes ahead with her negotiations without consulting Germany, there is no telling what steps Germany may take without consulting Japan."[79]

Of decisive importance was the stand of the Japanese military leaders. They were convinced that the conversations with Washington held no hope of success and that the United States was simply playing for time, perhaps even preparing to attack. They pointed to the Magruder Mission to China, which, they insisted, meant virtual participation by the United States in China's war against Japan. They noted also the ominous conferences which began on October 5 at Manila between General MacArthur, Admiral Hart, General Magruder, and the British Commander at Singapore, Sir Robert Brooke-Popham.[80] Konoye and Toyoda met with them again and again and argued that since there was little prospect of victory in war, further efforts should be made by diplomatic methods. The Prime Minister tried to persuade the military men to agree to evacuation of troops from China on the

[76] Text in Foreign Relations of the United States: Japan, II, 656 ff.

[77] Tel. from Nomura to Tokyo, October 3, 1941 (Pearl Harbor Attack, XII, 51 ff.).

[78] "Kido Diary," September 26, 1941 (Tokyo War Crimes Documents, No. 1632W-71).

[79] Tel. from Oshima to Tokyo, October 1, 1941 (Pearl Harbor Attack, XII, 48-49). On Konoye's reaction see also his "Memoirs" (ibid., XX, 4007).

[80] The New York Herald Tribune, August 29, quoting the semiofficial Japan Times and Advertiser on the Magruder Mission; The New York Times, October 6, on the Manila meeting; Tolischus in The New York Times, October 7, on the reaction in Japan; tel. from Ott to Berlin, reporting views of the military leaders, October 4, 1941 (Tokyo War Crimes Documents, No. 4065A).

understanding that some arrangement would be made for the occupation of certain key localities later on. The Naval High Command, which was opposed to a war with America, supported him in his efforts and even General Hata, the Commander in Chief of the China Expeditionary Forces, sent a messenger to urge this course, but all to no avail. The War Minister, General Tojo, declared that the Army could not accept such a program and insisted that the decisions of September 6 be adhered to. The extremist press, too, demanded an end to talk. Japan, wrote *Miyako,* was choking under the blockade: "Diplomacy under frozen assets is like defense of a castle without a supply of food. There is a limit to patience in such diplomacy. It is as plain as daylight that the New Order in East Asia cannot be constructed without eliminating the challenge of third powers and that peace through a new world order cannot be achieved without a victory of the Triple Alliance."[81]

5. KONOYE'S FALL

During the ten days in which this battle raged within the Japanese Government, Prime Minister Konoye and Foreign Minister Toyoda tried desperately to get on with the Washington conversations. According to Bishop Walsh they faced virtually hopeless odds in that it was impossible for them even to communicate with Washington without having their correspondence intercepted and read by the military opposition.[82] Great indignation was engendered in Japanese Army circles over the assertion in the American note of October 2 that Prince Konoye, in conversation with Ambassador Grew, had "subscribed fully" to the famous four principles (respect for the territorial integrity and sovereignty of all nations; support of the principle of noninterference in the internal affairs of other countries; support of the principle of equality, including equality of commercial opportunity; nondisturbance of the *status quo* in the Pacific, excepting by peaceful means). Toyoda was obliged to make clear that reference to the Prime Minister's remark was inappropriate and that in any case he had accepted the four principles "only in principle." These principles, argued the Japanese, were "inherently good," as were the Ten Commandments and other moral precepts. But, as a practical matter, there were occasions when it was necessary to discuss their application to concrete problems.

This, however, was peripheral. The main effort of the Foreign Office was directed toward inducing the American Government to say more explicitly what it wished the Japanese Government to provide in the way of assurances. Mr. Ushiba, private secretary to Prince Konoye, told Mr. Dooman

---

[81] Tolischus in *The New York Times,* October 7, 8, 9, 1941; further, "Konoye Memoirs" (*Pearl Harbor Attack,* XX, 4008-9) and "Kido Diary" (*Tokyo War Crimes Documents,* Nos. 1632W-75, 76). On General Hata's appeal, the affidavits of Admiral Oikawa and of General Tanaka (*ibid.,* Defense Documents Nos. 2605, 2637).

[82] Memo of Bishop Walsh, October 18, 1941 (*Walker Papers, MS.*).

frankly though unofficially that the future had grown dark and that official circles were extremely pessimistic because of Washington's failure "to lay its cards on the table." "Although several months had elapsed since the conversations began, the great care apparently being taken by the American Government not to give the Japanese any specifications was extremely discouraging." An increasing number of officials, he continued, had come to feel that Japan had fallen into a trap and were arguing: "The United States never had any intention of coming to any agreement with Japan; it has now got from Japan an exposition of Japanese policies and objectives; those policies and objectives are not in line with American policies and objectives; and there is therefore justification for refusing to make an agreement with Japan and for continuing to maintain an attitude of quasi-hostility against Japan." The American note, complained Mr. Ushiba, was "extremely disagreeable." "It was argumentative and preceptive, it contained no suggestion or indication calculated to be helpful to the Japanese Government toward meeting the desires of the American Government." Tokyo had no other recourse but to ask Washington to specify the precise undertakings it desired of Japan and, "if a clear-cut reply was not forthcoming, to bring the conversations to an end."[83]

The disheartening effect of the American note was also underscored by Bishop Walsh, who wrote that it "shook the confidence of the entire Japanese Government" and "put them back at the starting point." He likewise warned that the Japanese Government "would be glad to consider once more—and once more only—any set of terms or conditions the American Government may declare essential prerequisites to an agreement and/or meeting, provided they are specific, complete, final and prompt." If, however, Washington refused to submit its specifications, the Japanese would conclude that they were being hoodwinked and "proceed almost immediately with the military and naval plans that constitute their only alternative to a meeting." Bishop Walsh was ignorant of the nature of these plans but stated that the Japanese plainly expected them to lead to war.[84]

In numerous and very long-winded conferences in both Washington and Tokyo all possible variations on this theme were sounded. Toyoda became more and more irritated with the "senseless procrastination" and took out his irritation on Nomura, who was certainly doing his best. As the days passed the Foreign Minister became more and more insistent. On October 13 he cabled Nomura that "circumstances do not permit even an instant's delay." But at no time could any further statement be elicited from Mr. Hull or his subordinates. The American stand was briefly this: that Washington's views and requirements had been laid down in the note of June 21

[83] Memo by Mr. Dooman, October 7, 1941 (*Foreign Relations of the United States: Japan*, II, 662-63).

[84] Memo of Bishop Walsh, October 18, 1941 (*Walker Papers, MS.*).

and more recently in the note of October 2. Let Japan study these documents further and decide what it could do toward meeting the American program. After all, it was not America's business to determine what Japan should do.[85]

Convinced, rightly or wrongly, that Ambassador Nomura had confused the issues, the Tokyo Foreign Office had tried, though in vain, to have the conversations transferred to the Japanese capital. It had then decided to send Minister Wakasugi back to Washington posthaste and have him make a last supreme effort. On October 13 that Japanese diplomat had a long talk with Under Secretary Welles in which he reported his conversations with high civilian and military officials in Tokyo and stated that he had found them unanimous in their desire for the maintenance of peace and for the success of the Washington conversations. He admitted that there were younger elements in the Army, and even in the Navy and in other government circles, who were determined "to move heaven and earth to prevent the reaching of any understanding between Japan and the United States and to bring Japan squarely into full activity on the side of Germany." German representatives and agents were exerting themselves to the utmost toward the same end. However, Konoye had the bulk of public opinion and the controlling elements in the Army and Navy behind him in his attempts to reach a settlement. But he could not continue conversations indefinitely unless they showed results. If his Government were overthrown, "in all probability it would be replaced by a Cabinet composed of military representatives responsive solely to German pressure." This would end any hope of a settlement. Under the circumstances he, Wakasugi, hoped that at least unofficially the Under Secretary would tell him what further clarification was desired of the Japanese Government.

In reply Mr. Welles simply went over familiar ground and stressed the recent reports of Japanese reinforcement of its troops in Indo-China as another illustration of the basic contradiction between Japanese assurances and Japanese actions.[86] The American Government, he said, was sincerely desirous of reaching an agreement and had made its position perfectly clear in the diplomatic exchanges to date. There followed some desultory argument, but finally Wakasugi came out with Japan's latest assurances, designed to meet the American request for further clarification: "The Japanese Government was entirely willing to commit itself to undertake no aggressive moves either to the south or to the north," or for that matter "anywhere else in the

---

[85] These lengthy discussions may be followed in *Foreign Relations of the United States: Japan,* II, 663 ff., and in the Japanese diplomatic correspondence (*Pearl Harbor Attack,* XII, 54 ff.); see also Grew: *Ten Years in Japan,* 448 ff.; Hull: *Memoirs,* II, 1033 ff.; Kase: *"Journey to the "Missouri,"* 50 ff.

[86] Reports had come in that the Japanese had demanded of Vichy the right to send 50,000 more troops, but that the French had resisted (tels. to Grew, October 2, 11; tel. from Grew, October 10; tels. from Leahy, October 2, 11, 1941).

Pacific region." On the issue of equal treatment and nondiscrimination in trade with China, "the Japanese Government would be entirely willing to undertake to reach an agreement along the broad and general lines which we had in mind." Touching Japan's obligations under the Tripartite Pact, he asked "whether this Government could not agree to leave the 'discretion' of Japan as to the interpretation of its obligations under such pact to the determination of the Japanese Government," hinting that the Konoye Government was one which "would desire to maintain peace with the United States should the United States go to war [with Germany]."

Finally Mr. Wakasugi reached the crucial question, namely the evacuation of Japanese troops from China. He said "that the Japanese Government was willing to evacuate all of its troops from China." Mr. Welles thought he must have misunderstood and asked his visitor to repeat the statement, which Wakasugi did twice. By way of elaboration, however, the Japanese diplomat pointed out that after four years of military operations, it would be impossible to withdraw all Japanese forces in twenty-four hours. To this Mr. Welles replied that no one expected miracles. He did make it clear, however, in answer to a further question, that the United States could not undertake to mediate between Japan and China if the Japanese terms were, in its judgment, "inequitable and not conducive to the maintenance of a stable peace in the Pacific region." The conversation ended with Wakasugi's expressing belief "that the underlying principles as set forth by this Government on June 21 could be accepted by the Japanese Government." At the same time he remarked that in his opinion "within twenty-four or forty-eight hours his Government must reach a final decision on the basic questions involved." Once more he reiterated "that all of the controlling Generals in the Japanese Army and all of the controlling Admirals in the Japanese Navy were supporting fully the position of the Japanese Government in desiring to conclude a comprehensive and satisfactory agreement with the United States."[87]

This was the last gasp of the Konoye Cabinet. The Foreign Minister had telegraphed to Nomura on the same October 13: "The situation at home is fast approaching a crisis and it is absolutely essential that the two leaders meet if any adjustment of the Japanese-United States relations is to be accomplished." He had, in fact, set up a special code to be used in telephone conversation between Tokyo and the Washington Embassy.[88] But it was already too late. While Wakasugi was conferring with Welles the fate of

---

[87] Memo of Welles, October 13, 1941 (*Foreign Relations of the United States: Japan*, II, 680-86); tels. from Nomura to Tokyo, October 13, 1941 (*Pearl Harbor Attack*, XII, 66-68). This version of the attitude of Tokyo is supported by Bishop Walsh's memo of October 18, 1941 (*Walker Papers, MS.*), but it conflicts with Konoye's account of the pressure exerted by General Tojo (memo of conversation between Prince Konoye and Mr. Max Bishop, November 7, 1945).

[88] Tels. to Nomura, October 13, 1941 (*Pearl Harbor Attack*, XII, 64-65).

Konoye's Government was being decided. From the record of the Cabinet crisis one can certainly learn much about the value of the blanket assurances which Wakasugi was giving the American Under Secretary.

According to the decisions of the Imperial Conference of September 6 the Japanese Government was to prepare to wage war if the negotiations with Washington had come to nothing by early October. This deadline had now been reached. The projected Roosevelt-Konoye meeting had not materialized and Japan's economic situation was becoming desperate. Oil supplies were rapidly sinking and there was an acute shortage even of rubber.[89] Perhaps it was chiefly because of Japan's parlous economic condition that Konoye and Toyoda still felt that everything possible should be done to maintain peace, even at the expense of considerable concessions to the United States. The Navy Minister took much the same view and let Konoye know that the Navy wanted to avoid war. The hitch here, however, was that the Navy did not feel it could openly state its position, lest it appear unequal to its responsibilities. It therefore insisted that Konoye himself make the decision, the idea being that if negotiations were continued, they would have to be carried through to a conclusion, no matter what the price.

On October 12, his fiftieth birthday, Konoye conferred with the Foreign Minister, the War and Navy Ministers and the President of the Cabinet Planning Board at his country home. In a discussion that lasted more than four hours all angles of the situation were examined. Toyoda pointed out that there was no chance of success in the Washington conversations unless Japan made concessions on the stationing of troops in China. The Prime Minister argued for acceptance of the American demand in principle, with the idea that later troops could be kept at crucial points through agreement with China. But General Tojo was unyielding. He was convinced that there was no prospect of success in the negotiations and that the favorable time for fighting was being allowed to slip by. As for withdrawing from China, he pointed out that the Army could not agree: after four years of fighting, abandonment of the China Incident under American pressure would break the morale of the Army and earn for Japan the contempt of the Chinese.

Under the circumstances there was little likelihood of a meeting of minds. Yet Konoye renewed his efforts to convert Tojo. Before the Cabinet meeting on October 14 he pleaded once more for concessions, stressing particularly the fact that war, if it came, would be a real world war and might last five to ten years. Japan would be obliged to strike at the Philippines and thereby arouse American opinion to the point that its anti-German bias would be submerged in a deluge of anti-Japanese feeling. But Tojo was adamant: the Army simply could not yield on the China issue and besides, since the ob-

---

[89] Report of the American Commercial Attaché at Tokyo, October 13, 1941 (*Pearl Harbor Attack*, XX, 4041 ff.); memo of J. G. Liebert, October 3, 1946 (*Tokyo War Crimes Documents*, No. 9030).

jective of the United States was to control the Far East, if Japan were to begin to make concessions, Washington would probably make more and more demands, without limit. At the Cabinet meeting the War Minister expressed himself so forcefully and excitedly that no one ventured to contradict him and no decision was reached.

By this time matters had reached the point where Tojo was unwilling to continue discussions with the Prime Minister, "as he was not sure that he could stifle his feelings." Nonetheless, sensing that the Navy was supporting Konoye in his opposition to dropping the negotiations, Tojo made an effort to shift responsibility in that direction. He therefore suggested to the chief secretary of the Cabinet "that since war with America, in the first place, is a naval matter, it cannot be carried out, no matter how persistent the Army may be, if the Navy does not approve of it and that if the Navy would say she can't do it, then we can find a way to dissuade our subordinates and bring order within the service; but order can't be brought about within the service with only the Premier stating it." But this move also came to naught, since the Navy refused to make such an avowal. As the only other alternative, Tojo on the evening of October 14 suggested to Konoye through an intermediary that the entire Cabinet resign and that new men reëxamine the situation and reach a decision. He proposed that a new Government be formed under Prince Higashikuni. This solution appealed to Konoye, who was all too ready to resign and had reason to believe that Higashikuni would favor continued negotiations with the United States. The proposal was debated throughout the day but was finally dropped because of objection from the Palace. The Emperor feared that Higashikuni, considering his lack of political experience, might fall an easy victim to Army pressure and soon be driven into war. Since Japanese prospects in such a case were anything but promising, it was thought inadvisable to compromise the Imperial family by having one of its members assume responsibility for a possible disaster.

As a last desperate move Prince Konoye called in Bishop Walsh on the evening of October 14 and asked him to go at once to Washington with an oral message for President Roosevelt. The Bishop was to reiterate on Konoye's behalf that the Prime Minister and his Government entertained nothing but "a sincere and wholehearted desire to conclude an agreement that would result in the peace of the Pacific." Konoye expressed regret over the delays and misunderstandings, some of which, he believed, were due "to the maneuvers of third powers." But he still entertained hopes of success and would continue to work for it. "Now that the terms have been discussed as completely as is practicable under present conditions, it is my confident belief that a meeting between the heads of the respective Governments would readily bring about a completely satisfactory understanding that would insure the great objectives we mutually seek."

Nonetheless, the Konoye Cabinet resigned on October 16, when the

Prime Minister submitted to the Emperor a long letter explaining the differences that had developed within the Government. By this time the Emperor had decided to solve the problem by appointing either the War Minister, Tojo, or the Navy Minister, Oikawa, to Prince Konoye's post. The choice finally fell on Tojo, because he alone could hope to control the Army and because, at the last minute, he had taken a more reasonable view of further negotiation. Impressed by detailed reports of the country's economic unpreparedness for war and even more by the fact that the Navy was opposed to a conflict with the United States, Tojo was not wholly averse to reconsidering the question. He accepted the Emperor's command that the Army and Navy coöperate and agreed to the Imperial instruction that the decisions of September 6 be reviewed. On October 17 the Senior Statesmen met in conference and gave approval to the formation of a Tojo Cabinet on the terms laid down by the Emperor.[90]

The fall of Konoye and the advent of the Tojo Cabinet did not surprise Washington except by its suddenness. Ever since September 29 Ambassador Grew had warned that if the Konoye-Roosevelt meeting failed to materialize, the Government would fall and be replaced by a "military dictatorship which will lack either the disposition or the temperament to avoid colliding head-on with the United States."[91] The newspapers meanwhile had been predicting the same eventuality.[92] But during the critical days from October 14 to 17 the situation remained obscure so far as Washington was concerned. On the one hand Wakasugi continued to take up hours of Welles's and even of Hull's time mainly in what the Secretary described as a "rehash" of the previous conversations with Nomura, though on the American side it was noted that the Japanese diplomat was "hedging" on some of the assurances he had given in his initial conversation with Welles on October 13.[93] On the other hand, Japanese messages were being intercepted which demonstrated that at the heart of the crisis in Tokyo was disagreement on

[90] "Konoye Memoirs," together with Konoye's letter of resignation and his memorandum on the crisis submitted to the Senior Statesmen (*Pearl Harbor Attack*, XX, 4008-11, 4025-29); also a memorandum of Konoye entitled "Facts Pertaining to the Resignation of the Third Konoye Cabinet" (*Tokyo War Crimes Documents*, No. 497A); interrogation of Tojo (*ibid.*, No. 2501A); testimony of Tojo (*ibid.*, Proceedings, 36,294); deposition of Marquis Kido (*ibid.*, Defense Document No. 2502); "Kido Diary" (*ibid.*, Nos. 1632W-77 to 81); testimony of Suzuki (*ibid.*, Defense Document No. 2902); statement of Prince Higashikuni (*ibid.*, Defense Document No. 2900); affidavit of Tomita (*ibid.*, Defense Document No. 1902); memorandum by Toyoda, October 13, 1941, entitled: "Opinion of the Foreign Minister Concerning the Japanese-American Negotiations" (*ibid.*, Defense Document No. 1891); memo of conversation between Prince Konoye and Mr. Max Bishop, November 7, 1945; memo of Bishop Walsh, October 18, 1941 (*Walker Papers, MS.*).

[91] *Foreign Relations of the United States: Japan*, II, 645 ff.

[92] E.g., Karl von Wiegand, from Shanghai (*New York Journal-American*, October 11, 1941).

[93] *Foreign Relations of the United States: Japan*, II, 687 ff.; Nomura's reports of October 16, 17, 1941 (*Pearl Harbor Attack*, XII, 73 ff.).

the evacuation of China and that the Army did not propose "to yield an inch" on this matter. Other telegrams revealed the fact that Germany was bringing great pressure to bear on the Japanese to declare themselves with regard to the "shooting war" in the Atlantic and that the Tokyo Government was in fact planning to send a warning note to Washington.[94] To top it all, the newspapers reported on October 16 a public statement by Captain Hideo Hiraide, Director of Naval Intelligence, to this effect:

America . . . is carrying out naval expansion on a large scale. But at present America is unable to carry out naval operations in both the Atlantic and Pacific simultaneously. The Imperial Navy is prepared for the worst and has completed all necessary preparations. In fact, the Imperial Navy is itching for action, when needed. In spite of strenuous efforts by the Government, the situation is now approaching a final parting of the ways.[95]

In the midst of the general uncertainty the President, immediately on learning of Konoye's resignation, canceled the regular Cabinet meeting and instead conferred for two hours with Secretaries Hull, Stimson, Knox, General Marshall, Admiral Stark and Harry Hopkins. Unfortunately there is no record of these discussions beyond the note in Mr. Stimson's diary, referring to Hiraide's statement as quoted above: "The Japanese Navy is beginning to talk almost as radically as the Japanese Army, and so we face the delicate question of the diplomatic fencing to be done so as to be sure that Japan was put in the wrong and made the first bad move—overt move."[96] This entry need not be interpreted to mean that the President and his advisers were scheming to force Japan into making an overt move. On the contrary, they were more interested than ever in postponing the day of reckoning so as to secure time for American preparations. In a message to Mr. Churchill (October 15) the President observed: "The Jap situation is definitely worse and I think they are headed North—however, in spite of this you and I have two months of respite in the Far East."[97] These remarks, reflecting the persistent belief in Washington that Tokyo's next move would be against Soviet Russia, indicate that Mr. Roosevelt believed the policy of procrastination was bearing fruit. Thus far the conversations with Nomura had proved well worth while. The question on October 16 was necessarily what line should be taken now that Konoye had been swept away and an activist Japanese general had taken control. Either the White House or the State Department—it is not clear which—conceived the idea that the

[94] Memo by Grew of a talk with the Japanese Vice Minister for Foreign Affairs, October 15 (Foreign Relations of the United States: Japan, II, 686); tel. from Nomura, October 15; tels. to Nomura, October 16, 1941 (Pearl Harbor Attack, XII, 70-71).
[95] Tolischus in The New York Times, October 16, 1941. It is not improbable that this statement was made primarily to blast rumors in Tokyo that the Navy was unable or unwilling to fight.
[96] Stimson Diary (MS.), October 16, 1941; The New York Times, October 17, 1941.
[97] F.D.R.: His Personal Letters, II, 1223.

President might take the unusual step of addressing a message to Emperor Hirohito. Several drafts are still extant. One of them combined a promise to resume normal trade relations if Japan would abandon the policy of conquest with a stern warning that the United States would "be very seriously concerned" if Japan were to start new military operations. Another reviewed the history of the projected Roosevelt-Konoye meeting and suggested that, since time pressed, Roosevelt, Tojo and Chiang Kai-shek should meet in the hope of maintaining peace in the Pacific.[98]

In the end nothing was done, for Ambassador Grew transmitted a letter from Prince Konoye urging the United States not to attach too great importance to the outward appearance of the new Cabinet and assuring Washington that the Tojo Government would do its utmost to carry the conversations to a successful conclusion. Intercepted messages from Tokyo also indicated that the new Administration intended to resume discussions. Before long it was being argued in Washington that after all Tojo, as a member of the Konoye Cabinet, must have approved the policy to date and that possibly it might be easier to deal with a representative of the Japanese Army which, in the last count, was the decisive element. At all events it seemed the part of wisdom to wait and see; so Washington marked time in anticipation of further developments, though with little real hope.[99]

[98] Drafts of October 16, 17, 1941 (*Pearl Harbor Attack*, IV, 1700 ff.; XV, 1727 ff.); Welles's testimony (*ibid.*, II, 530 ff.).

[99] *Foreign Relations of the United States: Japan*, II, 689 ff.; Tolischus in *The New York Times*, October 18, 1941; see also the appreciations of the situation by Captain Schuirmann of Admiral Stark's staff, and by the American Military Attaché in Tokyo (Sherwood: *Roosevelt and Hopkins*, 419); Grew: *Ten Years in Japan*, 456 ff.

CHAPTER XXIII

The Shooting War

1. The Great Dilemma

By the autumn of 1941 the American public had gone far toward identifying itself with the opposition to Nazism and the Axis. It was united in its desire and determination to see Nazism destroyed and was all but unanimous in holding that Britain must be sustained, if only in the interest of American and hemisphere defense. Under Lend-Lease seven billion dollars had been appropriated to provide the opponents of Hitler with the tools of victory. In October, 1941, another six billion dollars was voted for the same purpose, almost without opposition. But the American people, while willing to supply material aid and even prepared to accept measures for ensuring the safe arrival of munitions in Britain, still clung to the hope that material sacrifice would spare them the horror of full-fledged hostilities. Public opinion polls showed that some 75 to 80 percent of the population still strenuously opposed direct participation in the war.[1]

If the man in the street persisted in his self-delusion, it was certainly not for want of enlightenment or admonition. Individuals and newspapers in ever increasing numbers pleaded with the public to face the facts. William C. Bullitt, among others, argued for an immediate declaration of war on Germany, a step which, he pointed out, was inevitable sooner or later: "We are going to war, whether you like it or not. . . . We are doing a job that is really not good enough. Why? We are caught in a conflict of emotions so deep we cannot resolve it. We want to defeat Hitler, but we do not want to go to war. These viewpoints are incompatible. . . . It's a sad thing to say, but the only way we can defeat Hitler is by the United States putting all its resources into this fight and going to war now."[2] Similarly, newspapers like the *New York Post* reasoned that a declaration of war would have a devastating psychological effect on the Germans:

[1] See particularly the editorial in *The New York Times,* October 1, 1941.
[2] *The New York Times,* October 24, 1941.

It would be an icy hand to snatch hope from every soldier in Hitler's line. It would install despair as a permanent guest in every German home. It would uphold the bleeding hands of Russia certainly until the snow flies—more effectively than swarms of planes and fresh divisions of troops. It would enable Britain to pour out her hoarded reserves. And in the resentful lands under conquest, what a backfire it would kindle![3]

But the American public, generally speaking, refused to be persuaded. True, isolationism had long been on the wane and some of its leaders were being discredited by their anti-Semitic utterances and by the revelations of abuse of the franking privileges of Congressmen for the benefit of Nazi propaganda.[4] Nevertheless, many Americans, intent above all on avoiding involvement in war, were prone to heed the positive assertions of Colonel Lindbergh and his ilk and to suspect the President of maneuvering the country into war without the approval of Congress. Senator Robert A. Taft quickly seized upon the Atlantic Charter to argue that the pledge to destroy the Nazi tyranny could be fulfilled only "by sending our soldiers to Berlin." On balance, it appears that the country at large, while firmly committed to almost any move "short of war," hardened in opposition to intervention as the implications of current policies became ever more obvious. Lord Beaverbrook, after visiting Washington in August, was unable to send any but the most discouraging reports to London: there was not the slightest chance of the United States entering the war unless forced to do so by direct attack, which would probably not occur until after Soviet Russia and Britain were already defeated.[5]

The British Government and people, sensing the trend of American sentiment, were much disheartened, especially when it appeared that the dramatic Atlantic Conference had produced nothing but a declaration of general principles. Mr. Mackenzie King, returning from a visit to England, reported the Government absolutely confident that Hitler could not defeat Britain, but quite unable to see how Britain could defeat Germany without the active participation of the United States.[6] Mr. Churchill and his associates had tried to dispel misapprehensions on this score during the At-

---

[3] Editorial, October 10, 1941.

[4] On September 26, 1941, a Federal Grand Jury exposed the mechanism of Nazi agitation. See also the *Chicago Daily News,* October 13 and 14, 1941, on the publication of *Scribner's Commentator* and other ostensibly isolationist but clearly pro-Nazi tracts at Geneva, Wisconsin. On October 6, 1941, the *New Republic* called for a Congressional investigation of America First, charging that organization with having become the general staff of all Fascist, semi-Fascist and proto-Fascist elements in America, as well as the focal point of anti-Semitism. President Roosevelt shared suspicions of the organization (*F.D.R.: His Personal Letters,* II, 1241-42).

[5] Robert E. Sherwood: *Roosevelt and Hopkins* (New York, 1948), 368. Secretary Ickes, after a long tour around the country, wrote the President, September 17, in despair over the popular lack of a wish to fight or will to victory (*Roosevelt Papers:* Secretary's File, Box 73).

[6] *Moffat Diary (MS.),* September 18, 1941, reporting a talk with the Canadian Prime Minister.

lantic meeting, but to no avail. Doubtless the Prime Minister, like Lord Halifax, thought and hoped that more positive leadership by Mr. Roosevelt would carry the American public along the desired course. Mr. Churchill's speech in the House on September 30, 1941, suggests that he had become impatient with the tides of public opinion, for he remarked: "Nothing is more dangerous in wartime than to live in the temperamental atmosphere of a Gallup poll, always feeling one's pulse and taking one's temperature. . . . There is only one duty, only one safe course, and that is to try to be right and not to fear to do or say what you believe to be right."[7] Privately he wrote Mr. Harry Hopkins that a "wave of depression" had come over British Government circles and warned that "if 1942 opens with Russia knocked out and Britain left again alone, all kinds of dangers may arise."[8]

Mr. Hopkins took this opportunity to remind the President that if the British lost hope of American intervention, a critical moment might come and the appeasers might stage a comeback. Mr. Roosevelt may well have discounted this argument, but it is altogether probable that he too was profoundly concerned by the dilemma confronting him. Mr. Churchill has recorded his conviction that after the Atlantic Conference the President desired above all things to bring the United States into the fight for freedom, but was unable to see how this could be encompassed.[9] Others, mostly hostile critics, have made the same assertion, usually with the addition that Mr. Roosevelt was at a loss as to how to deceive his countrymen and circumvent Congress. It seems hardly necessary, however, to ascribe such ignoble motives to the President. It may safely be assumed that from countless conferences with his own military advisers, as well as from his correspondence and discussion with Mr. Churchill, he had been driven to abandon his earlier hopes that America's role could be confined to that of the Arsenal of Democracy. His military advisers, in their contemporary strategic estimates, were at one in stating that Britain might well be defeated unless the United States intervened militarily and that Germany could almost certainly not be defeated without the commitment of American forces on a large scale. It should be noted at once, however, that these same experts were unequivocally of the opinion that early entry of the United States into the war would serve no useful purpose, since the new Army as yet consisted of only two or three divisions ready for action and was therefore far too weak to undertake significant operations.[10]

[7] Winston S. Churchill: *The Unrelenting Struggle* (Boston, 1942), 272. For Lord Halifax's opinion we rely on the *Moffat Diary* (*MS.*), August 20, 1941, reporting the Ambassador's observations at lunch.

[8] Sherwood: *Roosevelt and Hopkins,* 373.

[9] Winston S. Churchill: *The Grand Alliance* (Boston, 1950), 539.

[10] The military view was expressed most comprehensively in the American comments on the British General Strategy Review, which were sent to London on September 25, 1941. For a detailed discussion see Watson: *Chief of Staff: Prewar Plans and Preparations,* 354 ff., 406 ff.

It is impossible to speak with certainty of Mr. Roosevelt's views and intentions, but the evidence, fragmentary though it is, suggests that he was reluctant to accept the thesis that Hitler could be defeated only by a large-scale Anglo-American invasion of the Continent. Secretary Stimson noted in his diary that Mr. Roosevelt "was afraid of any assumption of the position that we must invade Germany and crush Germany."[11] This impression would seem to be bolstered by the fact that in late September the President reviewed with Secretary Stimson and General Marshall the planned strength and organization of the Army in the hope of finding ways and means to allot more equipment to Britain and Soviet Russia through reduction of United States combat forces and overseas garrisons. Such reduction appeared inadvisable, but the very fact that it was considered reflects the trend of Mr. Roosevelt's thought at this time.[12] It is probably not far from the mark to say that by September, 1941, he realized that the defeat of Hitlerism, so ardently desired by the American people, could not be achieved without active military participation on the part of the United States, but that he still hoped the American contribution could be restricted to naval and air support and material assistance. Had he not still deluded himself with the idea that heavy loss of American lives might be avoided, he would hardly at so critical a juncture have reconsidered the 1940 plans for building a large, modern Army. It is certainly worth noting that the President at no time prior to Pearl Harbor suggested further increase of the Army which, according to the existing program, was designed for national and hemisphere defense rather than for overseas operations against Nazi Germany.

2. THE VICTORY PROGRAM

The hopes of the President and his fellow citizens of escaping complete involvement in the war against Hitlerism depended in large measure on the scope and pace of war production. By the summer of 1941 it was common knowledge that the flow of munitions from American factories was far from satisfactory. Deliveries to Britain were still on a relatively modest scale and the new program of supporting Soviet Russia involved commitments which, under existing conditions, were impossible of fulfillment. In certain critical items the failure was so glaring that the President intervened personally to ensure better results. For example, the British shortage of tanks threatened the loss of the entire Middle East and, under pressure from the White House, plans had to be made for doubling tank production within the next nine months. With obvious gratification Mr. Roosevelt kept Prime Minister Churchill informed of his efforts which, needless to say, evoked enthusiasm

[11] *Stimson Diary* (*MS.*), September 25, 1941.
[12] For details see Watson: *Chief of Staff: Prewar Plans and Preparations,* 362 ff., which, however, requires some correction in the light of the Conn MS. study on *Defense of the Americas.*

and gratitude in London. Similarly Mr. Roosevelt insisted repeatedly on the assignment of more four-engine bombers to the British to further their plan for heavy air bombardment of Germany. The War Department objected, arguing that the British were not making good use of the twenty B-17's already supplied them, that the United States would be better able to stage a huge air offensive and should therefore retain the planes for its own program, and, finally, that such planes as became available should be devoted in the first place to the reinforcement of the Philippines. But the President was adamant and many B-24's, which the British seemed to prefer and which the Army Air Forces were more willing to surrender, were in fact allocated to the Royal Air Force.[13]

But action on such individual items was merely to skirt the complex problem of American war production, which continued to be plagued by questions of raw material supplies, priorities and allocations of materials in short supply, conversion of plants, curtailment of civilian consumption, the division of the national product between domestic and foreign requirements, and similar issues. Secretary Stimson, like his Navy colleague and others, was convinced that many of these difficulties stemmed from lack of adequate psychological motivation: it was impossible to get the country to make the requisite effort and sacrifice, to act as though the nation were at war, so long as the American people was still hoping to escape involvement. In Mr. Stimson's opinion it would in any case prove impossible to defeat Hitler simply by supplying arms for the use of others. He therefore relentlessly urged the President to provide courageous leadership, that is, to declare the existence of a war which was inevitable anyway and thereby arouse the people to greater productive effort. At the very least he thought Mr. Roosevelt should put an end to the administrative confusion that was aggravating the difficulties in the way of efficient war production. He and others found it impossible to understand why Mr. Roosevelt still refused to put the whole vast war production program under the direction of one man and one organization, as Mr. Bernard Baruch had been urging for more than a year.[14]

The President continued to turn a deaf ear to all such arguments and pleas. He would not entertain the notion of declaring war, neither would he set up a production "czar."[15] While acknowledging that the Office of Production Management, and particularly the Priorities Board of that agency, lacked sufficient authority and power, he preferred to seek a solution through the familiar device of setting up (August 28) yet another organization, the Supply Priorities and Allocations Board (SPAB), which, in effect, was merely an enlargement of the old Priorities Board of the Office of Pro-

[13] Messages from the President to Mr. Churchill, September 17 and 25, 1941, and the Prime Minister's replies, September 22 and 30, 1941; *Stimson Diary* (*MS.*), September 17, 23, October 15, 22, 23, 1941; General H. H. Arnold: *Global Mission* (New York, 1949), 264 ff.

[14] *Stimson Diary* (*MS.*), August 19, 28, September 25, October 15, 1941.

[15] *Stimson Diary* (*MS.*), August 15, 1941, reporting a statement of Judge Rosenman.

duction Management (consisting of Messrs. Knudsen, Hillman, Stimson and Knox) by the addition of Vice President Wallace, Mr. Harry Hopkins and Mr. Leon Henderson. The Vice President was to serve as chairman and Mr. Donald Nelson as executive director. Administratively the line of authority between this new agency and the Office of Production Management remained hazy. Indeed, there were now very curious kinks in the line of command. In the Supply Priorities and Allocations Board Messrs. Knudsen and Hillman were technically subordinate to Mr. Nelson, while the latter, as continuing Director of Priorities in the Office of Production Management, was subordinate to Messrs. Knudsen and Hillman when it came to implementing the decisions of the new board. Still, the new agency was more representative and more powerful than the old. All its members were deeply impressed with the need for firm, drastic and far-reaching action and went at their assignment in a vigorous and coöperative spirit. In the months before Pearl Harbor they accomplished much more than could have been reasonably expected. The new board made the vital decision to plan and organize for all-out war production; instituted effective control of priorities and allocations as between civilian, defense, and foreign requirements; and in general cut through enough of the administrative jungle to open the way to more effective production efforts.[16]

Those chiefly responsible for planning and organizing war production had long been afflicted by the prevailing uncertainty concerning the objectives of American policy and strategy. Obviously American requirements depended largely on whether and when the country intervened in the conflict and whether the building of a huge Army for overseas use was or was not to be envisaged. By the same token Britain's needs would vary according to the strategy adopted by London, and Soviet requirements would hinge very largely on whether military operations continued beyond the onset of winter. Ever since April, 1941, the General Staff of the War Department had been wrestling with the problem of establishing overall production objectives based on strategic plans and indeed with the larger issue of drafting a supply plan to ensure victory. The Joint Board had approved War Department proposals for the requisite studies (May 17) and had instructed the Joint Planning Committee to prepare the needed strategic estimates, using the ABC-1 and Rainbow V plans as a basis. This work was in progress and the Office of Production Management had been asked for assistance when, on July 3, 1941, Mr. Knudsen went to the President to discuss a War and Navy Department proposal for a threefold increase in the war production program.

[16] Donald M. Nelson: *Arsenal of Democracy* (New York, 1946), 156 ff.; Elliot Janeway: *The Struggle for Survival* (New Haven, 1951), *passim; Industrial Mobilization for War,* I, 109 ff.; *Stimson Diary (MS.),* August 12, 15, 19, September 9, 1941. See also Arthur Krock on Mr. Baruch's testimony before a Congressional Committee, in *The New York Times,* June 27, 1947.

It was presumably as a result of these discussions that the President on July 9, 1941, requested the Secretaries of War and Navy, with the assistance of Mr. Hopkins, to explore at once "the over-all production requirements required to defeat our potential enemies." "I realize," he stated in his letter, "that this report involves the making of appropriate assumptions as to our probable friends and enemies and to the conceivable theaters of operation which will be required. I wish you would explore the munitions and mechanical equipment of all types which in your opinion would be required to exceed by an appropriate amount that available to our potential enemies. From your report we should be able to establish a munitions objective indicating the industrial capacity which this nation will require."[17]

The President's letter paved the way to the formulation of what was to become known as the Victory Program, the first basic study of national requirements to ensure victory over the Axis. Intense effort was devoted to the study of the complex problems involved and to the drafting of essential strategic concepts, without which it was impossible to determine requirements. Concurrently discussions were initiated with the British looking toward a consolidated statement of common or joint needs. Inevitably progress on this great undertaking was hampered by the differences between American and British military men, particularly with respect to grand strategy. From the account previously given of the Atlantic Conference it will be recalled that the British General Strategy Review presented on that occasion reflected the hope that Germany could be defeated by heavy air attacks and by systematic campaigns of propaganda and subversion. These ideas ran counter to those of General Marshall and his colleagues, who were firmly convinced that Hitler could be vanquished only through a large-scale invasion of the continent. Since the American military authorities were further persuaded that such an invasion was beyond the capability of the British, they believed it necessary to plan for eventual American forces of some eight million men, of whom some five million (five field armies, organized in 215 divisions) might be required in Europe.

It is impossible and unnecessary in the present context to examine all aspects of these intricate questions. By the end of August the President had become impatient and called upon the Secretaries of War and Navy to provide him by September 10 with "recommendations of distribution of expected United States production of munitions of war, as between the United States, Russia and the other countries to be aided—by important items, quantity time schedules and approximate values, for the period from the present time until June 30, 1942." "I also desire," he wrote, "your general conclusions as to the over-all production effort of important items needed

[17] Watson: *Chief of Staff: Prewar Plans and Preparations*, 338-39. Watson's book (especially Chapter XI) is the most detailed and authoritative account of these matters, but we have made use also of the Kittredge MS. study on *United States-British Naval Coöperation*.

for victory, on the general assumption that the reservoir of munitions power available to the United States and her friends is sufficiently superior to that available to the Axis powers, to ensure defeat of the latter."[18]

This information, as the President pointed out, was urgently needed for the forthcoming Moscow Conference on aid to Soviet Russia. But the task was so complex and the differences between the War and Navy Departments so difficult to reconcile that the joint Army-Navy estimates did not reach the White House until September 25, 1941. The report was a formidable document or rather collection of documents, among which was a Joint Board strategic estimate based on earlier plans. Since this estimate was the most concise statement of strategic concepts in this period, it is essential to consider and even quote some of the salient passages. The result of long and arduous study, the paper was utterly devoid of false hope or self-delusion:

> It is believed that the overthrow of the Nazi regime by action of the people of Germany is unlikely in the near future, and will not occur until Germany is upon the point of military defeat.
>
> It is the opinion of the Joint Board that Germany and her European satellites cannot be defeated by the European powers now fighting against her. Therefore, if our European enemies are to be defeated, it will be necessary for the United States to enter the war, and to employ a part of its armed forces offensively in the Eastern Atlantic and in Europe or Africa.

The report went on to state that the British and Dutch could not withstand the Japanese advance in Southeast Asia without American assistance. Therefore, it argued, the United States must plan for war simultaneously against Germany and Japan, and in conjunction with friendly powers. After a careful, sober review of German and Japanese strategy and capabilities, the paper continued:

> The Joint Board is convinced that the first major objective of the United States and its associates ought to be the complete military defeat of Germany. If Germany were defeated, her entire European system would collapse, and it is probable that Japan could be forced to give up much of her territorial gains, unless she had already firmly established herself in such strength that the United States and its associates could not afford the energy to continue the war against her.
>
> An inconclusive peace between Germany and her present active military enemies would be likely to give Germany an opportunity to reorganize continental Europe and to replenish her strength. Even though the British Commonwealth and Russia were completely defeated, there would be important reasons for the United States to continue the war against Germany, in spite of the greatly increased difficulty of attaining final victory.
>
> From this it follows that *the principal strategic method employed by the United States in the immediate future should be the material support of present military*

---

[18] Watson: *Chief of Staff: Prewar Plans and Preparations,* 348. The President's letter, dated August 30, 1941, is printed in full in *F.D.R.: His Personal Letters,* II, 1201-2.

operations against Germany and their reënforcement by active participation in the war by the United States, while holding Japan in check pending future developments.

Except in the case of Russia, the principal strength of the Associated Powers is in naval and air categories. Naval and air power may prevent wars from being lost, and by weakening enemy strength may greatly contribute to victory. By themselves, however, naval and air forces seldom, if ever, win important wars. It should be recognized as an almost invariable rule that only land armies can finally win wars.

Since it was clear, according to the Joint Board estimate, that the United States and its friends were not in a position to undertake successful land offensives against Germany in the near future, the emphasis at first would have to be on blockade, bombing, subversion, and operations in areas where the Germans could bring only fractions of their power to bear. Similarly, a strong defensive would have to be maintained against Japan both on the Siberian and Malaysian fronts. Succeeding paragraphs of the report examined the conditions of hemisphere defense, the security of the United Kingdom, the British position in the Middle East, the support of Soviet operations, and finally ways and means of checking Japan.[19]

There was no need for the President officially to approve or disapprove this strategic estimate and there is no evidence that he took action upon it. As set forth in the preceding section, there is reason to believe that, despite the unvarnished statements of his highest military advisers, he still cherished the hope that the United States could escape with something less than complete participation. However, he seems to have raised no objection to the transmission of the substance of the memorandum to the British as constituting the American comment on the General Strategy Review. This was done on September 25 and subsequently led to further Anglo-American conferences in London. During these discussions a reconciliation of conflicting viewpoints was effected without too great difficulty. It is sufficiently clear that Mr. Churchill had never been completely convinced that Germany could be defeated without invading the continent, though he liked to think that a few highly trained mechanized divisions would suffice for the purpose.[20] After receipt of the American comments he apparently used his influence to bring British military men into line. Writing to the Chief of the Air Staff on October 7, 1941, he acknowledged his hopes for the success of an air offensive against Germany, but warned against exaggerated claims and expectations: "If the United States enters the war, it [the air offensive] would have to be supplemented in 1943 by simultaneous attacks by ar-

---

[19] This report was printed in large part in Sherwood: *Roosevelt and Hopkins,* 410-18. It is quoted and discussed at length in Watson: *Chief of Staff: Prewar Plans and Preparations,* 354 ff. The requirements aspects are considered in *Industrial Mobilization for War,* I, 139-40. For the attendant circumstances we have used the *Stimson Diary (MS.),* August 28, September 13, 22, 23, 25, 1941.

[20] This becomes clear from Mr. Churchill's messages to the President, July 25, 1941 (Churchill: *The Grand Alliance,* 806-7), and from his remarks during the Atlantic Conference.

moured forces in many of the conquered countries which were ripe for revolt. Only in this way could a decision certainly be achieved. Even if all the towns of Germany were rendered largely uninhabitable, it does not follow that the military control would be weakened or even that war industry could not be carried on."[21] These were prophetic views and unquestionably had much to do with the eventual acceptance by the British military authorities of the American thesis that ultimately major operations on the continent would be indispensable to ensure the final defeat of the Nazi power.[22]

Although the considerations of strategy set forth above are of prime importance for American policy, it must be remembered that the afore-mentioned report to the President was intended chiefly as an estimate of munitions requirements, basic to the establishment of an overall war production program. Founded, as it was, on the idea of eventually building an American Army of some eight million men, it is understandable that the estimate struck even Mr. Stimson and the War Department as "staggering." The Consolidated Statement of British-American requirements, worked out during the visit to London of Mr. Stacy May, Director of the Bureau of Research and Statistics of OPM and presented to Mr. Roosevelt by Secretary Stimson on September 23, 1941, produced a similar shock. Investigation had shown that under existing rates British and Canadian war production would continue to exceed that of the United States until the end of 1942. Obviously the prevailing plans for continuing business as usual and relying for war production almost exclusively on new facilities would have to be abandoned. On the very eve of the Pearl Harbor attack, when the computations were finally completed, it was evident that for the period until September 30, 1943, previous programs of production would have to be at least doubled, at an expense of something like 150 billion dollars. One can readily understand that Washington was appalled by the results of its research on the Victory Program and the Anglo-American Consolidated Statement.[23] Yet these studies were obviously of crucial significance. For the first time the objectives of the United States had been systematically analyzed and the requirements for their attainment established. The President and his advisers now had before them sober and extremely realistic appraisals of what was needed to encompass the defeat of Hitlerism. To quote Mr. Donald Nelson, the Victory Program as it emerged in September, 1941, "revolutionized our production and may well have been a decisive turning point."[24]

[21] Churchill: *The Grand Alliance,* 508-9.

[22] Watson: *Chief of Staff: Prewar Plans and Preparations,* 406 ff. Agreement was reached only on November 21, 1941, for reasons which, according to Watson, are still obscure.

[23] On the Consolidated Statement see *Industrial Mobilization for War,* I, 139-40; Watson: *Chief of Staff: Prewar Plans and Preparations,* 352; W. K. Hancock and M. M. Gowing: *British War Economy* (London, 1949), 384 ff.

[24] Nelson: *Arsenal of Democracy,* 132 ff.

3. Shoot on Sight

At the time of the enactment of the Lend-Lease legislation Hitler had announced that he would frustrate the program of American aid to Britain by sinking every ship carrying supplies to British ports. The havoc which was in fact raised by Nazi submarines during the spring of 1941 was eloquent proof of the Fuehrer's determination. It left the American Government and people little doubt that if their support of Britain were to be fully effective, something would have to be done sooner or later to ensure the safe arrival abroad of the war materials produced at such expense. The question of using American naval vessels to escort convoys across the Atlantic was an obvious corollary of the Lend-Lease program. As the preceding narrative has indicated, the issue was publicly debated again and again and was of deepest concern to the President. Realizing the full implications of American naval escort, Mr. Roosevelt had repeatedly recoiled from a clean-cut decision. However, a number of battleships had been withdrawn from the Pacific so as to strengthen the patrol system in the Atlantic and after the occupation of Iceland early in July American naval escort of United States and Icelandic shipping as far as Iceland had been initiated. Secretary Knox, Admiral Stark and others had at that time hoped fervently that the President would put an end to the uncertainty by extending the new escort system to all friendly shipping, but they had once again been disappointed. Not until the Atlantic Conference was the decision made to permit American warships to escort other than American shipping as far as Iceland. Although the official orders were not issued until September 13 (effective September 16), the new system had in fact been introduced by August 26, 1941.[25]

It may be observed that this important departure took place at a time when the British had fairly well mastered the submarine menace in the North Atlantic. Mr. Churchill was stating publicly that sinkings had dropped to one third the figure reached in the spring and that, in view of the increased construction of new shipping, the net loss was only one fifth.[26] It should be remembered, however, that the Nazi wolf packs had carried their attacks far into the western Atlantic and that, when effectively opposed there, they had begun to shift their operations to the vicinity of the Cape Verdes and Canaries. In order to hold in check their depredations in the North Atlantic the British Navy was obliged to employ all available destroyers and corvettes, many of which were badly needed elsewhere and

[25] See above, Chapters XVIII and XX. For the implementation of the new system we have used the MS. study by Captain Tracy Kittredge on *United States-British Naval Coöperation*. See also Samuel E. Morison: *The Battle of the Atlantic* (Boston, 1947), 79 ff.

[26] Churchill's speeches in the House, September 9 and 30, November 12 and December 11, 1941 (*The Unrelenting Struggle,* 246 ff., 264 ff., 300 ff., 345). See also Churchill: *The Grand Alliance,* 516-18, and the statistical table on p. 522.

would indeed be essential for countering the submarine menace off the African coasts. By the summer of 1941 yet another aspect of the situation had emerged: if supplies were to be sent to the Soviet Union, the British and other shipping required would have to be escorted northward along the Norwegian coast to Archangel or Murmansk. This additional mission would be beyond British naval capabilities unless some measure of relief were provided in the Atlantic.[27]

President Roosevelt was, of course, kept fully informed by Mr. Churchill of all important features of the situation. Being unable or unwilling to satisfy British expectations of full-scale participation in the war, he was evidently eager to do what he could to relieve the strain on British naval forces and in general to bolster British morale. Hoping still to avoid the commitment of large American expeditionary forces, he could at least press for greater war production and ensure that American supplies reached their destinations safely. Furthermore, he may by this time have convinced himself that Hitler would not accept the challenge presented by American escort of British shipping, at least before Soviet Russia were defeated. In short, Mr. Roosevelt may have concluded that substantial additional support could be given to Britain without entailing serious consequences.

Having made his decision, the President had no alternative but to inform the country and try to justify the grave measure he had now adopted. His Labor Day address (September 1) was clearly a preparatory move, for it referred to Hitler openly as the enemy and warned Americans in these words:

> We are engaged on a grim and perilous task. Forces of insane violence have been let loose by Hitler upon this earth. We must do our full part in conquering them. For these forces may be unleashed on this nation as we go about our business of protecting the proper interests of our country. . . . I know that I speak the conscience and determination of the American people when I say that we shall do everything in our power to crush Hitler and his Nazi forces.

But Mr. Roosevelt was to be spared the unpleasant task of springing on his countrymen the announcement of the new system of escort. On September 4 there occurred a German submarine attack on the *USS Greer* which provided him a perfect opportunity to underline the above-quoted passage of his Labor Day speech.

The facts of the *Greer* episode were briefly as follows: the American destroyer was en route to Iceland with passengers and mail when it was notified by a British patrol plane that a Nazi submarine lay submerged some ten miles ahead. The *Greer* thereupon located and trailed the submarine for several hours, periodically broadcasting its position. Eventually the harassed submarine commander fired two torpedoes, both of which missed their

[27] We rely here chiefly on the Kittredge MS. study cited above.

mark. In reply the *Greer* dropped depth bombs, with unknown effect. The incident had occurred about 175 miles southwest of Iceland, within the zone proclaimed by the Germans as a war zone, but also well within the area in which American warships had been ordered to attack and destroy surface raiders. The *Greer's* commander could not reasonably be blamed for reacting, once the submarine had fired its torpedoes. On the other hand, it is difficult to appreciate the indignation with which news of the episode was received in American official and private circles. Considering that the *Greer* had sought out the submarine, had trailed it doggedly for hours, and had given British planes information to facilitate their attack, it would have been astounding if the prospective victim had not finally turned on her pursuers.[28]

The President seized on the incident with alacrity, even before all the facts were known. In a statement to the press on September 5 he emphasized that the attack on the *Greer* was deliberate, and revealed that orders had been issued to "eliminate" the guilty submarine. On the same day he conferred with Secretary Hull and Mr. Hopkins about an important speech which he proposed to make on the subject. Mr. Hull was duly outraged by the attack and made appropriately stern comments. Thereupon the President requested him to write out his remarks for use in the speech, only to find, on receiving the text, that Mr. Hull had quickly lost his ardor and made no recommendation for specific action.

At this point delay was occasioned by the President's unavoidable absence at Hyde Park to attend the funeral of his mother. Meanwhile, however, Mr. Hopkins, Judge Rosenman and Assistant Secretary of State Berle tried their hands at a draft, keeping in touch with Mr. Roosevelt by telephone. The text was finally completed after the President's return to Washington (September 10) and included important passages from Mr. Roosevelt's own pen. After dinner on the evening of September 10 the address was read to Secretaries Hull, Stimson and Knox, all of whom concurred heartily in thinking it "the most decisive one which he [the President] had made." On the following morning Mr. Roosevelt read it again, this time to a group of Congressional leaders, who evidently took no exception to it. To be sure, at the last moment Secretary Hull was again beset by qualms and urged the omission of all reference to shooting. But the President's mind was made up; on the evening of September 11 he delivered his address over a worldwide radio hookup.[29]

The speech took its departure from the *Greer* incident. Despite what the Nazi propaganda machine might assert, said the President, the facts were

---

[28] The facts, as presented to a Congressional committee by Admiral Stark on September 20, 1941, are given in *Documents on American Foreign Relations*, IV, 93 ff., and in Morison: *The Battle of the Atlantic*, 79 ff.

[29] Sherwood: *Roosevelt and Hopkins*, 370 ff.; Hull: *Memoirs*, II, 1046 ff.; *Stimson Diary (MS.)*, September 9, 10, 11, 1941; *Berle Diary (MS.)*, September 9, 10, 11, 1941, containing various drafts of the speech.

"that the German submarine fired first upon this American destroyer without warning, and with deliberate design to sink her." This, he concluded, was "piracy, legally and morally." Recalling the earlier sinking of the *Robin Moor* and of other American or Panamanian vessels, he argued that these episodes were all part of a Nazi plan to abolish freedom of the seas and acquire control of the oceans as a prelude to domination of the United States and the Western Hemisphere. It was time, declared the President, for all Americans in all the Americas to stop deluding themselves with the romantic notion that the Americas could go on living happily and peacefully in a Nazi-dominated world: "No tender whisperings of appeasers that Hitler is not interested in the Western Hemisphere, no soporific lullabies that a wide ocean protects us from him—can long have any effect on the hard-headed, farsighted and realistic American people." The time had come to call a halt. Diplomatic notes and protests were patently useless. But the United States would refuse to be intimidated:

No act of violence or intimidation will keep us from maintaining intact two bulwarks of defense: first, our line of supply of matériel to the enemies of Hitler, and second, the freedom of our shipping on the high seas.

No matter what it takes, no matter what it costs, we will keep open the line of legitimate commerce in these defensive waters.

We have sought no shooting war with Hitler. We do not seek it now. But neither do we want peace so much that we are willing to pay for it by permitting him to attack our naval and merchant ships while they are on legitimate business.

The next was one of the passages drafted by Mr. Roosevelt himself:

Do not let us split hairs. Let us not ask ourselves whether the Americas should begin to defend themselves after the fifth attack, or the tenth attack, or the twentieth attack.

The time for active defense is now.

Then, continuing:

If submarines or raiders attack in distant waters, they can attack equally well within sight of our own shores. Their very presence in any waters which America deems vital to its defense constitutes an attack.

In the waters which we deem necessary for our defense, American naval vessels and American planes will no longer wait until Axis submarines lurking under water, or Axis raiders on the surface of the sea, strike their deadly blow—first.

Upon our naval and air patrol now operating in large number over a vast expanse of the Atlantic Ocean—falls the duty of maintaining the American policy of freedom of the seas—now. That means, very simply and clearly, that our patrolling vessels and planes will protect all merchant ships—not only American ships but ships of any flag— engaged in commerce in our defensive waters.

At this point the President made reference to the attitude and action of some of his predecessors in like situations and then denounced the idea that his decision involved an act of war: "It is not an act of war on our part when we decide to protect the seas which are vital to American defense. The aggression is not ours. Ours is solely defense." The speech concluded with a crucial warning, again in the President's own language: "But let this warning be clear. From now on, if German or Italian vessels of war enter the waters the protection of which is necessary for American defense, they do so at their own peril."

The official orders to the Commander in Chief of the Atlantic Fleet (September 13) were only the logical implementation of the President's statement. Thenceforth the Fleet was to protect not only American convoys to Iceland, but also "shipping of any nationality which may join such convoys between United States ports and bases and Iceland." Furthermore, American warships were authorized to escort convoys which included no American ships, and American ships, in turn, were permitted to sail under Canadian escort. The Atlantic Fleet was instructed to assure "protection against hostile attack of United States and foreign flag shipping (other than German and Italian shipping) by escorting, convoying and patrolling as circumstances may require, or by destroying German and Italian naval, land, and air forces encountered."[30]

Thus was the long-standing issue of American naval escort resolved by the declaration of the shooting war. The immediate effect was to relieve some forty British destroyers and corvettes for use elsewhere.[31] This in itself was an important contribution to Britain's war effort. But in a larger sense the President's speech and the subsequent orders to Admiral King constituted the proclamation of a naval war between the United States and the two European members of the Axis. Neither the President nor his advisers were under any misapprehension about the implications of the "shoot-on-sight" orders. Indeed, in concluding his address Mr. Roosevelt had made a point of saying: "I have no illusion about the gravity of this step. I have not taken it hurriedly or lightly. It is the result of months and months of constant thought and anxiety and prayer." Similarly Secretary Knox, in his speech to the American Legion Convention at Milwaukee (September 15), took pains to underline the fact that Hitler had now been left with "the grim choice" of leaving the bridge of ships intact or adding the American Navy to his foes. The attack on the *Greer* had dispelled all doubt as to the Fuehrer's decision and the American response was therefore inevitable:

Beginning tomorrow, the American Navy will provide protection as adequate as we can make it for ships of every flag carrying lend-aid supplies between the American Continent and the waters adjacent to Iceland. The Navy is ordered to capture or destroy by every means at its disposal Axis-controlled submarines or surface raiders encountered in these waters. That is our answer to Mr. Hitler.

[30] Kittredge MS. study on *United States-British Naval Coöperation;* Morison: *The Battle of the Atlantic,* 79 ff.

[31] Mr. Churchill's letter to Field Marshal Smuts, September 14, 1941 (Churchill: *The Grand Alliance,* 517).

In a letter to Admiral Kimmel a few days later (September 22) the Chief of Naval Operations made the same point in even fewer words: "So far as the Atlantic is concerned, we are all but, if not actually in it. The President's speech of September 11, 1941, put the matter squarely before the country, and outlined what he expected of the Navy. We were ready for this; in fact our orders had been issued."[32] Finally, this was also Mr. Churchill's understanding, as expressed in a letter to Field Marshal Smuts (September 14): "Hitler will have to choose between losing the Battle of the Atlantic or coming into frequent collision with United States ships and warships."[33]

It was inevitable that isolationist leaders, who had long anticipated the likelihood of American naval escort and had done their utmost to forestall the final decision, should have lodged vigorous protests against the President's words and deeds. Former President Herbert Hoover, in a radio broadcast of September 16, objected violently to Mr. Roosevelt's "edging our warships into danger zones" without the approval of Congress, and Senator Tobey of New Hampshire declared at an America First rally in New York City (September 17) that the American people was "being deceived in a gigantic conspiracy to drive them into war." The Chicago Tribune openly charged the President and "the belligerent old men in his Cabinet" with hoping to create an incident that would bring about war without the need of Congressional action.[34] These and kindred indictments have been repeated by a number of postwar writers who would have their readers believe that Mr. Roosevelt deceived the American people, bypassed Congress, violated his election pledge of 1940, and purposely maneuvered an unwilling and unsuspecting country into war.

The historian can hardly evade the responsibility of pronouncing on this crucial and controversial matter. Basically his opinion will depend on whether or not he agrees with Mr. Roosevelt's conclusion that Hitlerism constituted a menace to the United States and to the principles on which the nation was founded, and that therefore it was in the national interest to support the opponents of Nazism and contribute to Hitler's defeat. The policy of aid to the victims of aggression having been accepted by Congress at the time of the Lend-Lease debates, the conclusion was almost inescapable that sooner or later steps would have to be taken to ensure the safe delivery of the aid which was then thought of as America's contribution to the common cause. Approaching the issue from this angle, posterity is likely to be surprised not so much that the decision to escort was taken, but that it was taken so late.

Viewing the problem in a narrower context, the reader should remember

[32] Pearl Harbor Attack, V, 2217. For Admiral Stark's testimony to the same effect see ibid., pp. 2292 ff., 2310 ff.

[33] Churchill: The Grand Alliance, 517.

[34] Chicago Tribune, September 24, 1941; similarly the New York Journal-American, September 25, 1941.

that Mr. Roosevelt, before delivering his radio broadcast, had read it to Democratic leaders of Congress and had secured at least their tacit assent. Furthermore, public opinion polls throughout the summer of 1941 had indicated at least a slight majority as favoring the introduction of naval escort.[35] Following the *Greer* incident and the President's speech a Gallup poll revealed that 62 percent of those queried approved the stand taken by the President, while a survey conducted by *The New York Times* indicated wide and growing support of the Administration policy throughout the country. It is hardly fair, therefore, to charge Mr. Roosevelt with having acted without reference to the Congress and the country. No doubt the American people were still opposed to involvement in the war and particularly averse to having their boys sent overseas. But the evidence would suggest that they were agreeable to the steps taken by the President to defeat Hitler, even though acceptance of those steps meant that the line between "short of war" and actual war now became so blurred as to lose all significance.

On the other hand it can hardly be gainsaid that Mr. Roosevelt's devious procedure exposed him to criticism. Whether he honestly believed that, in attributing the "attack" on the *Greer* to the Germans, he was released from his election pledges, it is, in the present state of the evidence, impossible to say. However, the strained interpretation put upon the *Greer* incident gives color to the charge. Certain newspapers unfriendly to the Administration were at the time quick to seize upon the discrepancies between Mr. Roosevelt's statements on September 11 and Admiral Stark's account to a Congressional committee on September 20. Secretary Knox attempted to explain by stating that the President based his remarks of September 11 on the best information available to the Navy Department at that time, and that this information had proved incomplete.[36] This does not, however, exonerate the President of the charge of having exploited the incident without awaiting a detailed report.

Some reservation must also be made with respect to the assertion by the President and Secretary Knox, an assertion repeated in Secretary Hull's memoirs, that the "attack" on the *Greer* revealed a systematic Nazi plan to sink American vessels. While it is true that Hitler had publicly threatened to do so, the President by September, 1941, must certainly have been convinced that Hitler, deeply involved in his campaign in the east, was intent on avoiding provocation of the United States. The astounding thing was not that there had been a few sinkings of American ships, but that there had not been many more. Actually it has now been established, from the German

[35] Gallup polls: May 30, 52 percent in favor; June 14, 55 percent; September 2, 52 percent.

[36] Memo of the President to Admiral Stark, September 18, 1941, commenting on the Admiral's proposed answers to questions submitted by the Congressional committee (*Roosevelt Papers:* Secretary's File, Box 77), and Secretary Knox's report to the President on his correspondence with the *New York Daily News* apropos of an editorial of October 29, 1941 (*ibid.,* Box 73).

records, that Hitler steadfastly rejected all pleas of Admiral Raeder for all-out operations against the Anglo-American supply lines. Even after the President's declaration of September 11 Raeder failed to move his chief. In a concise memorandum the Nazi Chief of Naval Operations had stressed the point that thenceforth there would be no difference between British and American ships, and that "the order to fire signifies that the U.S.A. has gone over from silent partnership and only indirect assistance to open participation in the war." Raeder therefore urged that all restrictions on the operations of German submarines be lifted and that the Pan American Safety Zone be ignored except for a strip twenty miles wide along the American coasts. But Hitler remained adamant. He was firmly convinced that Soviet Russia would soon be defeated and that, pending that happy event, trouble with the United States should at all costs be avoided. He therefore requested that care be taken "to avoid any incidents in the war on merchant shipping before the middle of October."[37] These statements on Hitler's part cannot, of course, be taken as demonstrating that the United States and the Western Hemisphere were in no danger from Nazism. The Fuehrer's naval decisions were based squarely on the assumption that Soviet Russia would soon be defeated. Had the Nazis succeeded in liquidating opposition in the east, it is all but certain that they would soon have turned in full force on Britain and probably also on West Africa and South America.

In the introductory paragraphs of the present section an effort was made to determine President Roosevelt's motives in finally making the decision to employ American naval forces to escort not only American but belligerent British shipping over a major part of the Atlantic trade routes. By way of summary it may be noted that in so doing he was in full accord with the highest military opinion. The significant Joint Board Estimate of September 11, the very date of Mr. Roosevelt's speech, put the major considerations in these succinct terms:

The sea communications can continue to support the United Kingdom only if the damage now being inflicted upon them is reduced through increases in the strength of the protective sea and air forces based in the British Isles, Iceland, and positions in the central and eastern Atlantic. Unless the losses of British merchant ships are greatly reduced, or unless there is an internal collapse in Germany, it is the opinion of the Joint Board that the resistance of the United Kingdom can not continue indefinitely, no matter what industrial effort is put forth by the United States. Therefore, the immediate and strong reënforcement of British forces in the Atlantic by United States naval and air contingents, supplemented by a large additional shipping tonnage, will be required if the United Kingdom is to remain in the war. These contingents must be manned by Americans, since the reserves of British manpower for employment in Europe are practically exhausted.[38]

[37] *Fuehrer Conferences,* 1941 (2), 33 ff.; Anthony Martienssen: *Hitler and His Admirals* (New York, 1949), 118.
[38] Sherwood: *Roosevelt and Hopkins,* 416.

It is quite possible, however, that to these compelling reasons should be added a further one deriving from the rapid deterioration of the situation in the Far East. By the terms of the Tripartite Pact Japan was obliged to come to Germany's assistance in the event of the latter's being attacked by the United States. True, this provision left open the question of what constituted an attack. Therefore one of the main issues in dispute between Tokyo and Washington was whether or not what the United States Government regarded as defensive action against German submarines in the Atlantic would be interpreted by Japan as constituting an attack upon Germany. No doubt Japanese authorities were themselves unable to answer the question if put in general terms, but obviously the President and his advisers had to reckon with the possibility that Japan might resort to war while Hitler continued to stand aloof. Since American military authorities had long since decided that Germany was the primary enemy and that American offensive action should be centered in the Atlantic while maintaining a strategic defensive in the Pacific, it was essential to avoid involvement with Japan and the commitment of America's main strength in the Far East.

Considering this problem, Admiral Stark's Plan Dog of November, 1940, had already developed the idea that if war eventuated from a Japanese attack, the United States should initiate steps to bring Germany also into the war. This concept had been reaffirmed by the Joint Board in December, 1940, and had been tacitly accepted by the President as well as by the Secretaries of War and the Navy. There is little if anything in the presently available records to show whether this aspect of the problem was considered in reaching the decision on American naval escort in September, 1941, but in view of the acuteness of the Far Eastern situation and particularly of the discussions at the Atlantic Conference, it seems improbable that it was far from the minds of the President and his military advisers. It may well be that the introduction of American naval escort was intended in part to keep relations with Germany at least one step ahead of relations with Japan. The President made his decision in his capacity as Commander in Chief and there can be little doubt that the crucial departure of September, 1941, was based primarily on strategic considerations.[39]

4. REVISION OF THE NEUTRALITY ACT

The revision of the Neutrality Act in November, 1941, came as a distinct anticlimax to the "shoot-on-sight" orders and the introduction of naval escort of convoys. Like the question of escort, the issue of revising the existing neutrality legislation had been under consideration for many months. President Roosevelt and Secretary Hull had long been convinced that those

[39] On this aspect of the matter see the testimony of Admiral Richmond K. Turner, in *Pearl Harbor Attack*, VI, 2842. We have made use also of notes provided by Captain Tracy Kittredge, U.S.N.R.

sections of the law which excluded American shipping from proclaimed combat areas and forbade the arming of American merchantmen were major and now altogether illogical obstacles to the implementation of the Lend-Lease program. But they could not bring themselves to submit the matter to Congress, lest it provide the isolationists a new springboard for attack.[40]

Within the general framework of American policy the neutrality legislation had certainly become anachronistic, for the country was no longer neutral except in the most rigorously legalistic sense. With the Lend-Lease Act the last tatters of neutrality had been discarded, as everyone recognized. On the very eve of the *Greer* incident *The New York Times* could write editorially (September 3): "The United States is no longer a neutral in this war. It is no longer on the sidelines. It has made its choice. It is a belligerent today, in the sense, and to the degree that it has become a part of the service of supply that leads from its own factories to the battlelines."

Yet the Neutrality Act of 1939 remained on the statute books and from the President's viewpoint its revision had become progressively more urgent. The *Greer* incident seemed to provide an ideal opportunity to dispose of this issue as well as to put over the decision on naval escort. On September 5 the press was already reporting that the President would soon request Congress to amend the existing law and after the noteworthy radio address of September 11 it soon became known that Mr. Roosevelt had already discussed the matter with Congressional leaders.[41] The news was received with jubilation by the interventionists. *The New York Times* hastened to point out once again the contradiction between the law and the Lend-Lease policy approved by Congress: "These self-denying ordinances," it concluded, "are worth as much as a thousand submarines to Hitler. From his point of view they accomplish the same purpose." The *New York Post* likewise demanded that "this hoary and decrepit antique" be scrapped, while the *New York Herald Tribune* insisted that "the Neutrality Act . . . has ended its usefulness; it has ended its reason for being, and has become a stench in the nostrils of anyone for whom two and two still add up to four. It should be repealed *in toto* and at once."[42]

By the last week in September the issue, so far as the President was concerned, was simply whether to ask for total repeal, for the repeal of Sections II, III and VI, or only for the abolition of Section VI. Total repeal was unnecessary and in some ways actually undesirable, for the Act contained several provisions (restrictions on the solicitation and collection of funds, control of munitions export, regulation of financial transactions, etc.) which the Administration itself desired to retain. Total repeal would, of course,

---

[40] Hull: *Memoirs*, II, 943, 1046 ff.
[41] *The New York Times*, September 5 and 6, 1941.
[42] *The New York Times*, September 17; the *New York Post*, September 17; the *New York Herald Tribune*, September 24, 1941.

make a deep impression, both at home and abroad, but it might also provoke unnecessary opposition. The essential thing was the elimination of Sections II, III and VI, among which the repeal of Section VI could be almost certainly counted on. This section prohibited the arming of American merchant ships. Now that naval escort had been introduced it was patently absurd not to arm for self-defense the very ships which the American Navy was assigned to protect.

Mr. Roosevelt was for some time undecided as to how comprehensive to make his request. After numerous conferences with Secretary Hull and Congressional leaders he concluded that it would be best to take no chances with the opposition in Congress, for which he continued to have profound respect. Senate leaders were optimistic about the chances for repeal of all three of the sections in question, but sentiment in the House appeared less favorable. Evidently the President and his Congressional advisers finally arranged that if the repeal of Section VI were carried in the House by a strong majority, a request for repeal of all three sections should be laid before the Senate, in the hope that after favorable action in that body the House too could be brought to accept it.[43]

Meanwhile the issue had become the subject of public debate. The American Legion Convention passed a resolution favoring total repeal and Secretary Knox, speaking at the launching of the battleship *Massachusetts* (September 23), pleaded for immediate action: "The time is now for all of us to face facts which no longer can be ignored. The time has come to do away with the Neutrality Law. We can waste no time in repealing that law. It must be repealed. We must remove the restrictions upon our Chief Executive. Our Army must be used wherever and whenever it is needful." Many leading newspapers chimed in, calling for total repeal and an end to "the whole outworn farce of American neutrality." In an editorial the influential *New York Times* argued (October 3):

> Our relationship with the European war has passed the stage when it can be affected by "incidents." We are not formally at war with Hitler. We may never be formally at war with him. But we are already at war with him in the sense that we are mobilizing our entire economy in order to beat him. The remnants of "neutrality" now on our statute books do not make us less his enemy by one period or comma. They merely hamper our defense and our lend-lease activities—which unavoidably has now become a single activity.

There was evidently considerable sentiment throughout the country for total repeal or at the very least for drastic amendment of a law which, for whatever reasons, had become completely incongruous. According to a Gallup poll of October 5 some 70 percent of those consulted thought it more important to defeat Hitler than to keep the country out of war.

[43] Hull: *Memoirs,* II, 1046 ff.; *Berle Diary (MS.),* September 23, 30 and October 2-6, 1941; *The New York Times,* October 1, 2, 3, 8, 9, 1941.

Though public opinion seems to have been more ready than the Congress to support the President's policy, it was thought by some that even on Capitol Hill there was a strong tendency to line up behind the President, the more so in view of the stand taken by the American Legion.[44] Democratic leaders were certainly optimistic. Senator Connally came out publicly in favor of the abolition of combat zones and the arming of American merchant ships, while Senator McKellar introduced a resolution calling for complete repeal on the theory that the whole Neutrality Act had been a mistake and contravened the principle of freedom of the seas.[45]

But the isolationists were not to be silenced. Following a well-reasoned radio address by former President Hoover (September 16), the opposition in the Senate began to mobilize. Senator Robert A. Taft took the stand that repeal of the Neutrality Act would be tantamount to a declaration of war or would at least authorize the President to carry on an undeclared war. Senator Robert La Follette railed at the Administration for not knowing "whether to bury it completely or leave a skeleton hanging up." The veteran isolationist leader, Senator Hiram Johnson, supported his colleagues in his usual vehement fashion. Before long the whole anti-interventionist group was in full cry. As a result the outlook, even in the Senate, became less favorable. According to an informal poll of Senate opinion early in October only twenty-nine members were well disposed toward total repeal or the elimination of Sections II, III and VI, and only thirty-five were prepared to vote even for the arming of merchantmen. Twenty were opposed to any change and the remainder expressed themselves as undecided. When one remembers that relatively few Senators were needed to kill the bill by filibuster, one can hardly escape the conclusion that Mr. Roosevelt was well advised in trying to make progress slowly.[46]

On October 9 the President laid his proposals before the Congress. His message recalled the erroneous assumptions on which the Neutrality Act had been based and noted that once the war in Europe had broken out the American people had ceased being neutral in thought or indifferent to the fate of Hitler's victims. On the contrary, the country had become increasingly aware of the threat to its traditions and institutions, to its territory and to the entire hemisphere. It had become the nation's policy to defend itself wherever defense appeared necessary:

Therefore it has become necessary that this Government should not be handicapped in carrying out the clearly announced policy of the Congress and of the people. We must face the truth that the Neutrality Act requires a complete reconsideration in the light of the known facts.

The revisions which I suggest do not call for a declaration of war any more than

[44] Arthur Krock in *The New York Times*, September 21, 1941.
[45] *The New York Times*, September 25 and 26, 1941.
[46] *The New York Times*, September 26 and 28, October 5, 1941.

the Lend-Lease Act called for a declaration of war. This is a matter of essential defense of American rights.

In the Neutrality Act are various crippling provisions. The repeal or modification of these provisions will not leave the United States any less neutral than we are today, but will make it possible for us to defend the Americas far more successfully, and to give aid far more effectively against tremendous forces now marching towards conquest of the world.

The message then remarked on the futility of combat zones but, without pursuing that issue, asked specifically only for repeal of Section VI so as to permit the arming of American merchant ships:

The arming of our ships is a matter of immediate necessity and extreme urgency. It is not more important than some other crippling provisions in the present act, but anxiety for the safety of our crews and of the almost priceless goods that are within the holds of our ships leads me to recommend that you, with all speed, strike the prohibition against arming our ships from the statute books.

There are other phases of the Neutrality Act to the correction of which I hope the Congress will give earnest and early attention. One of these provisions is of major importance. I believe it is essential to the proper defense of our country that we cease giving the definite assistance which we are now giving to the aggressors. For, in effect, we are inviting their control of the seas by keeping our ships out of the ports of our own friends.

It is time for this country to stop playing into Hitler's hands and to unshackle our own.

. . . .

I earnestly trust that the Congress will carry out the true intent of the Lend-Lease Act by making possible for the United States to help deliver the articles to those who are in a position effectively to use them. In other words, I ask for Congressional action to implement Congressional policy. Let us be consistent.

. . . .

Hitler has offered a challenge which we as Americans cannot and will not tolerate.

We will not let Hitler prescribe the waters of the world on which our ships may travel. The American flag is not going to be driven from the seas either by his submarines, his airplanes, or his threats.

We cannot permit the affirmative defense of our rights to be annulled and diluted by sections of the Neutrality Act which have no realism in the light of unscrupulous ambition of madmen.

We Americans have determined our course. . . .[47]

The President's message left no doubt that the abolition of combat zones and the employment of American ships for the transport of supplies to friendly ports were just as much at issue as the arming of American merchantmen. As noted, the request for repeal only of Section VI was intended to spearhead the larger program, for even avowed opponents of the Pres-

[47] *Documents on American Foreign Relations,* IV, 23 ff.

ident's policies, like Senator Taft and Representative Fish, were ready to accept the arming of American ships as an obviously defensive measure.

The Administration proposals were given preferred and urgent treatment by Congress. The House Foreign Affairs Committee heard testimony from Secretary Hull on October 13 and thereafter from Secretaries Stimson and Knox. Before appearing on the Hill, Mr. Hull took the precaution of obtaining from Admiral Stark a memorandum analyzing the advantages and disadvantages of the combat zones, of naval escort all the way across the Atlantic, and of a declaration of war by the United States. This memorandum, dated October 8, is of some interest as reflecting current thinking in naval circles. The Chief of Naval Operations referred to the obvious advantages of being able to send American ships to Great Britain and noted the moral effect to be expected from the operation of American warships in British waters. On the other hand he pointed out that a declaration of war could not be followed immediately by major operations and that it might bring Japan into the conflict, which would be a highly undesirable development. Nonetheless, he reiterated his firm conviction that Hitler could not be defeated until the United States was "wholeheartedly in the war" and therefore favored intervention as soon as possible, even at the cost of hostilities with Japan: "I might finally add that I have assumed for the past two years that our country would not let Britain fall; that ultimately in order to prevent this we would enter the war and as noted above I have long felt and have stated that the sooner we get in, the better." After all, he concluded, there was little chance that Hitler would attack until he had calculated coldly that it would be to his advantage to do so. He already had all the pretexts he needed.[48]

Little if any of this reasoning was reflected in Mr. Hull's testimony, which was a carefully worded statement of the weakness of the existing law and of the factors making its modification imperative. The Secretary emphasized that "the Neutrality Acts did not remotely contemplate limiting the steps to be taken by this country in self-defense, especially were there to develop situations of serious and immediate danger to the United States and to this hemisphere." His argument culminated in the assertion that "the theory of the neutrality legislation was that by acting within the limitations which it prescribed we could keep away from danger. But danger has come to us— has been thrust upon us—and our problem now is not that of avoiding it, but of defending ourselves against a hostile movement seriously threatening us and the entire Western hemisphere."[49]

Though Secretaries Hull, Stimson and Knox all expressed themselves in favor of repeal of Section II as well as Section VI, the House was called upon to vote only on the latter. Just before the termination of the limited

[48] Text in *Pearl Harbor Attack*, XVI, 2216 ff. See also Hull: *Memoirs*, II, 1049.
[49] *Documents on American Foreign Relations*, IV, 102 ff.

debate, on the night of October 16-17, the United States destroyer *Kearny* was struck by a German torpedo and suffered many casualties. The *Kearny*, together with other American destroyers and one British destroyer, had been despatched to the aid of a westbound convoy which was under heavy attack by a pack of German submarines about four hundred miles south of Iceland. The escorting warships were dropping depth bombs indiscriminately, while the submarines were taking an impressive toll of the merchant ships. A full-scale naval action was in progress and there was nothing surprising in the fact that the *Kearny* was struck. But this made little difference to the American public, for whom the important fact was that an American warship had been "attacked." Congress was clearly impressed. On October 17 the House voted repeal of Section VI of the Neutrality Act of 1939 by a majority (259-138) larger than had been expected. Only 21 Democrats opposed the measure, while the Republicans voted 39 in favor and 113 in opposition.[50]

The stand of the Republicans in the House outraged Mr. Willkie and that wing of the party which supported the Administration in matters of foreign policy. Willkie promptly appealed for an end of "the shame and deception of the hypocritical Neutrality Laws" and on October 20 three Republican Senators (Bridges, Austin and Gurney) introduced an amendment calling for outright repeal of the Act. On the following day Mr. Willkie and a hundred leading Republicans from some forty states called on their colleagues in Congress to abolish the neutrality legislation as "hypocritical and degrading." Their message declared:

The requirement of America today is for a forthright, direct, international policy, designed to encompass the destruction of totalitarianism by whatever means necessary. This policy should be presented to us by our elected leader frankly and not by doses as though we were children. . . . Millions upon millions of Republicans are resolved that the ugly smudge of obstructive isolationism shall be removed from the face of their party so that it may not be hampered in forwarding these high and important purposes.[51]

The relatively favorable outcome of the vote in the House on repeal of Section VI and the revolt of the nonisolationist wing of the Republican Party encouraged Senators Glass and Pepper to come out openly for total repeal of the Neutrality Law, described by Mr. Glass as "a craven piece of poltroonery." But the Democratic leaders of the Senate, no doubt following advice from the White House, contented themselves with a resolution to repeal only Sections II, III and VI, the only sections really objectionable from the Administration's standpoint. On October 25 the Senate Foreign Relations Committee voted thirteen to ten in favor of the resolution. Two

---

[50] *The New York Times*, October 18, 1941. For the facts of the *Kearny* incident see Admiral Stark's letter to Admiral Kimmel in *Pearl Harbor Attack*, XVI, 2214 ff., and Morison: *The Battle of the Atlantic*, 92-93. We have used also a tel. from MacVeagh (Reykjavik), October 19, 1941, addressed to the President.

[51] *The New York Times*, October 19, 21, 22, 1941.

days later, just as the resolution came to the floor, Mr. Roosevelt delivered a Navy Day address in which he made the most of the *Kearny* incident, as he had previously exploited the "attack" on the *Greer:*

We have wished to avoid shooting. But the shooting has started. And history has recorded who fired the first shot. In the long run, however, all that will matter is who fired the last shot.

America has been attacked. The *USS Kearny* is not just a Navy ship. She belongs to every man, woman and child in this nation. . . .

The forward march of Hitler and Hitlerism can be stopped—and it will be stopped.

Very simply and very bluntly—we are pledged to pull our own oar in the destruction of Hitlerism. . . .

I say that we do not propose to take this lying down.

Our determination not to take it lying down has been expressed in the orders to the American Navy to shoot on sight. These orders stand.[52]

These fighting words no doubt helped further to arouse the country, but they made the isolationist elements all the more angry and irreconcilable. In the course of a ten days' debate in the Senate the opposition rang all possible variations on the basic theme that the decision of Congress would necessarily settle the question "whether America deliberately and consciously shall go all the way into a 'shooting war'—probably upon two oceans."[53] Much was made of the argument that American security would not be directly threatened even if Soviet Russia and Britain went under and that, even if the menace were real, it would be better to cut through all subterfuges and declare war at once. One member of the opposition after another charged the President with willful deceit and with making arrangements for an American Expeditionary Force because he knew that Hitler could not be defeated without the active military aid of the United States. Senator Wheeler embroidered this theme for almost nine hours and Senator Brooks, urging his colleagues not to overlook the implications of the resolution, declared: "You cannot shoot your way a little bit into war any more than you can go a little bit over Niagara Falls."[54]

It is unlikely that the pleas of the isolationists influenced the supporters of the Administration policy any more than the appeals of Willkie and his followers impressed the old guard Republicans. When the tally was taken on November 7 it turned out that the resolution had passed the Senate by a vote of only fifty to thirty-seven. Six Republicans voted in its favor, while twenty-one registered opposition. The Senate majority was smaller than on any major foreign policy issue since the beginning of the war in Europe.

[52] *Documents on American Foreign Relations,* IV, 27 ff.

[53] *The New York Times,* October 28 and 29, 1941, reporting the remarks of Senators Vandenberg and Taft.

[54] *The New York Times,* October 30, November 6 and 7, 1941. The debates on the resolution are summarized in Charles A. Beard: *President Roosevelt and the Coming of the War* (New Haven, 1948), Chapter VI.

What deductions to draw from this fact it is hard to say. Mr. Roosevelt, writing to King George on October 15, expressed the opinion that public sentiment was distinctly "better" than it had been six months before and that it was more strongly with the Administration than was the Congress.[55] A Gallup poll published early in November pointed in the same direction, for it showed that 81 percent favored the arming of American merchant ships and 61 percent the use of American ships in transporting supplies to Britain. In the opinion of many newspaper editors Congress was lagging behind the public, which was thought to be more determined than ever to see the crisis through. The inescapable fact, however, was that in both houses of Congress there was still formidable opposition to the Administration's policy. An out-and-out proposal to declare war would certainly have been defeated even on the very threshold of the Pearl Harbor attack.

A lurid light was thrown on this situation when the House reopened debate on the Senate resolution, which was much more comprehensive than the measure originally passed by the House. Irritated no doubt by the previous efforts of the White House to put over the larger program and evidently incensed by the President's lenient attitude toward labor disputes in key war industries, many members of the House let themselves go in bitter criticism. While isolationists argued that the resolution meant war at a time when the country was still woefully unprepared, others accused the British of wanting to push the United States into action while they themselves were unwilling to risk opening a second front to relieve the Soviet forces. To quote Representative Charles L. South of Texas: "Let's tell England: 'We know you're in distress and we're sorry for you. But get in there and fight like hell for yourself for a while and then we'll see if anything else should be done.'"

Representative Eaton (Republican) did his utmost to combat this simpleminded view, but the House became more and more intractable. Even Democrats showed an inclination to defect until their leaders induced the President to send Congress a message reminding it that "the world is obviously watching the course of this legislation," and to follow this up with another message promising early action to quell labor troubles. When the issue was finally brought to vote (November 13), the majority again proved alarmingly small. The vote was 212 in favor and 194 opposed. Of the Republican members only 22 approved the bill, as against 137 who opposed it. Even more noteworthy was the fact that more Democrats voted in opposition than at the time of the Lend-Lease bill. An analysis of the vote revealed that while the southern states were strong in support of the resolution, the Midwest was generally hostile and the Far West rather evenly divided. Even the large industrial states of the East split their votes in a most unusual fashion: Massachusetts, 7-6; New York, 25-20; New Jersey, 5-9; Pennsyl-

[55] F.D.R.: His Personal Letters, II, 1223 ff.

vania, 10-20. Clearly the President was justified in refusing to share the easy optimism of many of his advisers, both inside and outside Congress. Nevertheless, it would probably be a mistake to ascribe the strength of the opposition solely to the realization that retreat from the neutrality legislation might lead to war, or to strong sentiment against involvement on any terms. If there is reason to suppose that the vote in the House did not accurately reflect the sentiment of the country, there are also grounds for thinking that many members opposed the resolution because of their disgust with the Administration's labor policy and their fear that the country might be dragged into war long before it was economically or militarily prepared.

Despite the closeness of the vote, the essential features of the ill-starred Neutrality Law had now gone into the discard. "No decision of greater importance has been made in this country since the beginning of the war," declared *The New York Times* (November 14), while its London counterpart pronounced revision of the Neutrality Act "the greatest contribution to the defeat of Hitlerism since the passing of the Lend-Lease Act." Surely no one could look back with real satisfaction on the effort to legislate neutrality. According to one eminent student of international law:

It can fairly be said that there was no instance of the application of this theory of neutrality in which it contributed to maintaining the peace of the United States, the peace of the world, respect for international law, or the interests of a free and stable world order. Its effect, as anticipated by most informed observers, was to give American opinion a sense of frustration inducing belligerency, to encourage aggression by the despots in Europe and Asia, and to thwart the democracies from achieving a unity of purpose in the defense of their interests and principles.[56]

In terms of international law the repeal of the key sections of the Neutrality Law meant return to the principle of freedom of the seas. The United States now resumed its traditional right to send its ships wherever it pleased and to arm and protect them in every way possible. There was nothing novel or revolutionary about the revision and it would therefore be misleading to attach too much importance to it. The really significant decision was the one to employ American naval forces in the escort not only of American but of belligerent shipping. The revision of earlier legislation merely indicated a turn in the road already chosen. Such significance as it had derived chiefly from the fact that, unlike the introduction of naval escort, it required Congressional approval. Though the vote was extremely close, the fact remains that that approval was given. To that extent one can say that the country, through its elected representatives, accepted the President's policy, despite the general realization that the arming of merchantmen, the escort of convoys, and the despatch of American ships to the ports of belligerent powers would inevitably result in armed clashes with German submarines.

[56] Quincy Wright: "Repeal of the Neutrality Act" (*American Journal of International Law*, XXXVI, 1942, 8-23).

It may well be argued, then, that by November 13, 1941, the President, the Congress and the country had made the decision to accept war. No doubt, if Mr. Roosevelt had taken up the challenge thrown down by his opponents and had asked Congress for a formal declaration of war, he would have been voted down. As it was, the revision of the Neutrality Act gave him substantially what he and his advisers had come to regard as essential in view of the world situation, namely, acceptance by the nation of genuine involvement in the world conflict. Although one can rarely be apodictic about such matters, the evidence suggests that the American people, perhaps more surely than their representatives, "knew the score." Generally speaking they had come to realize that they could not permit a Nazi victory and must therefore sustain Britain at all costs. They did not want war and shunned that ugly word as much as ever. But they were willing to accept the reality in thin disguise and probably found the President's gradualism and artifice more palatable than the frank and forthright leadership for which Mr. Roosevelt's friends so often clamored.

By way of epilogue it may be well to repeat that in shaping the national policy the President, like many leaders of American opinion, probably calculated that Hitler would not react with a declaration of war or the initiation of hostilities against the United States. By this time it had become sufficiently clear that he would move against the United States whenever it suited his purposes, but not before. In the autumn of 1941 the evidence indicated that the Fuehrer would stay his hand until he had finally subjugated Soviet Russia. The Nazi press denounced the *Kearny* affair as "a clumsy swindle on the part of Mr. Roosevelt" and accused the President of rigging incidents in order to put through the revision of the Neutrality Law. But there was no suggestion that Hitler intended, for the moment, to take reprisals. In his long address of October 3, 1941, the Fuehrer spoke at length about the campaign in the east but made only a few oblique references to the United States. On October 18, the day after the Senate vote on revision, he delivered a great annual address at Munich but again confined himself to defensive and on the whole noncommittal remarks: "President Roosevelt has ordered his ships to shoot as soon as they sight German ships. And I have ordered German ships, upon sighting American vessels, not to shoot but to defend themselves as soon as attacked. . . . If, therefore, an American ship shoots . . . it will do so at its own peril. The German ship will defend itself, and our torpedoes will find their mark."

It may be taken as certain that the President and for that matter most Americans were not deceived by Hitler's proclamation of virtuous self-restraint. It is more likely that they pondered another passage in Hitler's October 3 address, a remark made not with reference to the United States but easily applicable to the relationship between the two countries: "When I see the enemy levelling his rifle at me, I am not going to wait till he presses the trigger. I would rather be the first to press the trigger."

CHAPTER XXIV

The Mediterranean Front

I. THE FENCE-SITTERS OF MADRID

The immediate and perhaps the main purpose of Hitler's assault on the Soviet Union was to break the only military power that could threaten his position on the Continent and so hamper his efforts to subdue Britain. Although the Fuehrer's hopes of quickly eliminating the Red armies and destroying the Soviet regime were being disappointed, both friend and foe recognized that during the summer of 1941 the Nazis were achieving notable successes. Soviet losses in men and matériel and above all in war production were so great that Hitler seemed likely to attain his objectives before the end of the year. Alternatively, he might decide to suspend operations during the winter months, redeploy most of his divisions and air forces in the west, and resort either to an attack on England or to diversionary operations against North Africa or the Middle East. In any case the western powers could hardly afford to run risks. They had to be prepared for a sudden swing of the pendulum. Consequently their plans to anticipate or meet eventual attacks in the west and the Mediterranean were at all times as important or even more important than their programs for bolstering Soviet resistance. The mere restatement of this basic proposition is sufficient reminder of the continuing British and American concern with that twilight zone of doubtful neutrality and nonbelligerency situated between Hitler's Europe and the Atlantic Ocean, that area which, with its North African adjuncts, barred the Nazi advance to key bases athwart the British trade routes and at the same time constituted the only remaining gateway for an eventual attack on *Festung Europa*.

The various aspects of this situation were so numerous as to defy logical analysis, leaving the historian no choice but to treat them seriatim and attempt to set forth their close interrelationship. Still foremost among them was the threat of a Nazi invasion of England, a project to which Hitler

761

referred frequently, though without specifying plans or dates. The Fuehrer and his military advisers had by this time convinced themselves that British resistance could probably not be broken without a successful invasion of the island, but they were more keenly aware than ever of the difficulties in the way of such an operation. For the time being they had no alternative but to expand the submarine campaign against British supply lines and intensify the air attacks on Britain as soon as the situation on the Russian front made possible the release of the *Luftwaffe*. They still hoped that Spain and France might be brought into the war on the Axis side, thus providing naval and air bases which, according to the Naval High Command, were essential for the successful prosecution of the war on British shipping. In any event they saw no possibility of mounting a full-scale invasion of England prior to the late summer of 1942, which meant that this grand design was no longer a part of Hitler's immediate calculations.[1]

British estimates did not differ materially from those of the enemy. Mr. Churchill was convinced that British defenses had now been strengthened to the point where they would necessarily give the Germans pause. Unconfirmed reports of huge concentrations of Nazi shipping in western ports left the Prime Minister skeptical. On the other hand, he had to contend with the apprehensions of his American friends and supporters, some of whom were beset with doubts whether the British were not underestimating the dangers of invasion and sending too many men and supplies to the Middle East. In September, 1941, General Stanley D. Embick, one of the senior American strategists and an officer by whose judgment General Marshall set great store, arrived in England to review the situation. He was concerned over the possibility of an early Nazi attempt at invasion and convinced that British defenses were still inadequate and defective. General Chaney, the American Military Observer, and General Lee, the Military Attaché, reported in similar vein. So disturbed was Secretary Stimson by these military judgments that he brought them to the attention of the President and, with the latter's consent, raised the issue in discussion with Lord Halifax. Under pressure from the War Department, Mr. Roosevelt eventually struck a warning note in a message to Mr. Churchill. The Prime Minister, however, found little difficulty in persuading his American friend that General Embick and his colleagues tended to view the problem too much in terms of passive defense and so underestimate the element of vigorous counterattack. He was, so he said, "resolutely convinced" that England could be successfully defended against invasion.[2]

---

[1] Hitler's remarks to Mussolini, August 25, 1941, and to Ciano, October 25, 1941 (*Ciano's Diplomatic Papers,* 447 ff., 455 ff.); memo of the German High Command, approved by Hitler (*Halder Diary,* September 13, 1941).

[2] *Stimson Diary (MS.),* October 1, 2, 3, 10 and November 6 and 8, 1941; tel. from London, November 12, 1941, reporting Mr. Churchill's conversation with Mr. William Whitney, representing the office of the Coördinator of Information. See on this matter also Churchill: *The Grand Alliance,* 514 ff.

More real and immediate seemed the danger of a Nazi invasion of the Iberian Peninsula, with or without the assent of Madrid. To counter this London and Washington had laid plans for the protective occupation of the Azores and for the seizure of the Canary and Cape Verde Islands. The Portuguese Prime Minister, Dr. Salazar, was much concerned lest entry of the United States into the conflict serve only to prolong it. He was above all anxious to keep his country neutral as " a reservoir of peace" in a war-torn Europe, but if the worst came to the worst he was clearly determined to stand by Portugal's traditional alliance with Britain.[3]

While Portugal envisaged eventual coöperation with the democracies, Spain continued hostile. Accordingly the British had considered the necessity of seizing the Canary Islands even before the Nazis attempted an advance through Spain on Gibraltar and North Africa. But this idea, though accepted by President Roosevelt at the Atlantic Conference, was abandoned almost at once and the British contented themselves with organizing and maintaining in readiness an expeditionary force for emergency use.[4] At the same time, however, both London and Washington continued their efforts to keep Madrid from throwing in its lot with Hitler. The outlook was not bright, for it was known that the Germans were helping the Spaniards fortify the Canaries and were steadily increasing their influence in Spain itself. Madrid's reply to Mr. Churchill's announcement of aid to Soviet Russia was a mob attack on the British Embassy and the formation of a "volunteer" legion to fight alongside the Nazis in the anti-Communist crusade. Señor Serrano Suñer, the fanatical leader of the Falange, continued as Foreign Minister and took every occasion to voice his hatred of the democracies and his confidence in a Nazi victory.[5]

Despite the difficulties of the British position in Madrid, Mr. Churchill and his associates remained firm in their belief that Franco and the military leaders were intent on remaining aloof from the struggle and that they would actually resist an attempt by Hitler to invade their country.[6] In this they were probably right, though actually there was much less danger of Nazi action than London and Washington were led to suppose. Hitler had learned his lesson in Spanish evasion and obstinacy. Again and again he gave vent to bitter criticism of Franco's attitude during the winter of 1940–1941, but he obviously recognized that added pressure would be futile. Spain would not participate actively in the war until the Axis position in the Mediterranean was secure, and any Nazi effort to coerce Madrid would

[3] Report of Mr. Myron Taylor's conversation with Dr. Salazar in September, 1941. This was sent in full in a despatch from the United States Embassy in Lisbon, December 8, 1941.

[4] Message of Mr. Churchill to the President, August 29, 1941.

[5] W. Horsfall Carter: "Spain and the Axis" (*Foreign Affairs*, October, 1941, 175-83); Herbert Feis: *The Spanish Story* (New York, 1948), Chapters XX and XXI. On the fortification of the Canaries see *Fuehrer Conferences*, 1941 (2), 23 ff.

[6] Churchill: *The Grand Alliance*, 550.

almost certainly provoke British seizure of the Canary and Cape Verde Islands. So far as Berlin was concerned, therefore, the Spanish question was left in abeyance. Late in November Serrano Suñer again visited the Nazi capital to join in the anniversary celebrations of the Anti-Comintern Pact. In conversation with Hitler, Ribbentrop and Ciano he again expatiated on Franco's good intentions: Spain would intervene in the conflict because circumstances required it, but the necessary preparatory work was as yet far from completed. The Fuehrer listened to these well-worn assurances with resignation and derived what satisfaction he could from renewing his complaints of Madrid's past attitude.[7]

The British Government continued to supply Spain with enough food, petroleum and other crucial materials to keep the acute economic crisis from becoming desperate. Officially the United States Government followed the same line, though with reluctance and aversion. It will be recalled that Foreign Minister Serrano Suñer had chosen to engage in a personal feud with Ambassador Weddell and that, during the summer of 1941, relations between Spain and the United States were, for all practical purposes, suspended. Under the circumstances American supplies for Spain were curtailed or delayed on one pretext or another. During July, August and September only about half the usual supply of oil was sent.[8]

Meanwhile the Spanish economic crisis was indeed approaching the breaking point. Señor Carceller, Minister of Industry and Commerce, felt impelled to take matters into his own hands. In a series of talks with members of the American Embassy he did not hesitate to make disparaging remarks about Serrano Suñer, gave assurances of Franco's friendly sentiments, suggested that the Caudillo was cultivating the Nazis only to forestall a German invasion, and begged for economic support to enable Spain to maintain its nonbelligerency.[9] When these efforts failed to produce results, Señor Cárdenas, the Spanish Ambassador in Washington, was called home for consultation, in the hope that he might have more success in dealing with the Americans. At regular intervals Cárdenas conferred with Ambassador Weddell, exerting himself to heal the breach between the Ambassador and the Foreign Minister and to pave the way for more extensive economic aid. But Mr. Weddell firmly refused to make the first move, insisting that he was the aggrieved party. It was not until the Papal Nuncio, on instructions from the Vatican, took a hand in the matter that a reconciliation was finally effected. On September 30 the Ambassador and the Foreign Minister were brought together. Both parties scrupulously avoided a revival of past differences. On the contrary, they agreed to regard these differences as water

---

[7] Hitler's remarks to Mussolini, August 25, 1941, and Ciano's notes on the Berlin meeting, November 24-27, 1941 (*Ciano's Diplomatic Papers*, 447 ff., 460 ff.); memo of the German High Command, in *Halder Diary*, September 13, 1941.

[8] Tel. to Weddell, August 23; tel. from Weddell, September 16, 1941, restating what he understood to be the American policy. See also Feis: *The Spanish Story*, 138-39.

[9] Despatch from Weddell, August 14, 1941; Feis: *The Spanish Story*, 139 ff.

over the dam and thereupon turned to a discussion of Spain's economic needs. Serrano Suñer made the explicit statement that there had been no change in his Government's foreign policy and promised to arrange a personal interview between the Ambassador and General Franco.[10]

The conference between the Caudillo and the Ambassador (October 6) was cordial but otherwise of little note. After the usual amenities Franco dilated on Spain's difficulties in obtaining cotton, wheat, oil and other products and indicated that if the United States were unwilling to supply them, he might have to turn to other sources. Mr. Weddell repeated that there was no desire on the part of his Government to strangle Spain and that Madrid's failure to secure certain materials was due largely to the restriction of American exports in the interests of national defense. He suggested that so long as Spain adhered to its nonbelligerency it might be possible to supply its needs in return for certain strategic materials required by the United States. Franco agreed that the details of such an exchange should be worked out in negotiations between the Ambassador and the Foreign Minister.[11]

Despite this official reconciliation and mutual agreement to reopen economic negotiations, various obstacles still prevented a genuine improvement in relations between the two countries. These impediments were analyzed in detail in a masterly memorandum prepared by the Madrid Embassy and forwarded to Washington on October 14, 1941. Starting with a reëxamination of the forces working for Spanish coöperation with the Axis and a review of the factors making for continued nonbelligerency, the memorandum restated the British policy of counteracting Axis influences by supplying limited economic aid and then pointed out the advantages to the United States of maintaining trade relations, so far as possible in coördination with the British. It pleaded above all for reinforcement of the embassy staff and for the delegation of greater authority to the embassy in formulating the economic program. It should be remembered, said the writer, that the Spanish Foreign Office enjoyed but little respect even in Spanish official quarters and that there was but little coördination among Madrid Government agencies, each of which tended to follow its own line. So long as the American Government dealt only with the Spanish Embassy in Washington it was unlikely to make much progress. The Madrid Embassy should be given greater latitude in making such arrangements as seemed wise, the more so as the establishment of the new Economic Defense Board in Washington threatened to complicate policy formulation on the American side also.[12]

[10] Tel. from Tittman (the Vatican), August 18, 1941; tels. from Weddell, September 16, 23, 24, 30, 1941; Feis: *The Spanish Story,* 140 ff.

[11] Tels. from Weddell, October 1 and 6, 1941; Feis: *The Spanish Story,* 141.

[12] Despatch from Mr. Beaulac, Counselor of the Embassy at Madrid, enclosing a memorandum of recommendations, October 14, 1941.

The Madrid Embassy sent copies of this memorandum in personal letters to Under Secretary Welles and Assistant Secretaries Berle and Acheson in the desperate hope that the current halfhearted and ineffectual American procedure could be systematized and strengthened. But the response of Washington was not encouraging. The root of the difficulty was division within the State Department itself on policy toward Spain. Many officials were certain that Spain's hostility to the democracies was insurmountable and suspected Madrid of allowing American supplies to find their way to Germany. Added to this was the confirmed dislike of the Franco regime and a deeply rooted aversion to anything smacking of appeasement, not to mention the fear of public protest against any move to aid the hated Spanish dictatorship. Lastly, in determining its policy the Department could not ignore the new Economic Defense Board, the creation of which had reduced the Department, in matters of economic policy, to the status of one among various agencies participating on a basis of equality. All things considered, it was probably inevitable that the eloquent pleas of the Madrid Embassy should fall on deaf ears. On October 31 Secretary Hull ruled that economic negotiations with Spain should continue to be conducted in Washington. Ambassador Weddell was instructed to avoid binding himself in any way to the British program.[13]

It was not until November 18, when the Vichy Government's recall of General Weygand from North Africa provoked consternation in Washington, that the Spanish question was given more sympathetic consideration. Mr. Welles conferred with Ambassador Cárdenas on the very next day, at which time the Ambassador pleaded once again for a more understanding attitude and expressed the conviction that "the policy of his own Government had been modified considerably in recent months, and both General Franco and his Foreign Minister were playing for time in order to prevent actual occupation [by Germany]." To this Mr. Welles replied that the United States "could only make the earnest plea that the Spanish Government, should Germany undertake measures of expansion in North Africa, would not be tempted by German offers to extend their own sphere of occupation in North Africa." Such a move, he added, could be interpreted by the United States only as an indication that "Spain was definitely pursuing Hitler's strategy and was thereby endangering legitimate interests of the United States."[14]

This exchange, though essentially negative, was nevertheless to produce some slight result, for the situation had become ominous, not only in the Far East but also in Europe. Serrano Suñer was off to Berlin for the grand

[13] Tel. to Weddell, October 31, 1941; replies to the embassy's letter of October 14 were sent by Mr. Welles (November 7), Mr. Acheson (November 7) and Mr. Berle (November 14). We have used also a memo by the Division of European Affairs, October 18, 1941.

[14] Memo of conversation between Mr. Welles and Ambassador Cárdenas, November 19, 1941.

assemblage of anti-Comintern statesmen, and, in a public address, almost outdid the Nazis in his denunciations of Communist Russia.[15] It seemed imperative that something be done to keep Franco in line, so on November 27 Secretary Hull submitted to the Spanish Ambassador a proposal for a new economic accord. Washington had finally, but only after much bickering, arrived at a program, though one that still provided only the barest minimum of aid and reflected no trace of friendship. As Mr. Hull pointed out, in a telegram to Ambassador Weddell, its primary purpose was strategic—to fill Spain's minimum needs and prevent that country from falling into complete dependence on Germany. The United States offered to supply just enough oil to cover essential requirements, and only in return for such strategic materials as mercury, tungsten and cork. Furthermore, Washington demanded that American officials be permitted to make periodic surveys of Spanish stocks and supervise the delivery, distribution and consumption of American supplies. On these conditions the United States would deliver also small quantities of rubber, tractors, trucks, electrical supplies, machinery and metals, but only for civilian use.[16]

It goes without saying that the Spaniards, renowned for their pride and their resentment of the foreigner, balked at such suggestions for supervision and took some time to make up their minds. Consequently the relations between Washington and Madrid were hardly better, at the time of the Pearl Harbor attack, than they had been during the preceding six months. In retrospect and in the light of evidence published since the end of the war, one can hardly say much in praise of the American policy toward Spain in 1940 and 1941. The British, it would seem, had arrived at a fairly accurate estimate of Franco's position and intentions and had shaped their policy to fit a highly precarious situation. But they had never succeeded in persuading the State Department of the wisdom of their policy and had for the most part met only with resentment when they tried to induce Washington to follow their line. If the American Government made some gestures in the direction suggested by London, it made them without conviction and with obvious ill will. Fear of popular opposition and suspicion and dislike of the Franco regime were so strong that nothing more than an evasive and inconclusive course was ever adopted. The American policy was throughout stamped by emotion, confused thinking, indecision and lack of coördination. It reduced Ambassador Weddell to despair and still strikes the historian as one of the least impressive chapters in the history of American foreign relations.

2. FRANCE: THE VICISSITUDES OF COLLABORATION

The problem presented by Vichy France and more specifically by the danger of French military collaboration with Nazi Germany was at bottom

[15] *Ciano Diaries*, November 24, 1941; Feis: *The Spanish Story*, 150.
[16] Tel. to Weddell, November 27, 1941; Feis: *The Spanish Story*, 149 ff.

not unlike the problem posed by Spanish policy, yet the American position was much more clearly defined and the American policy much more positive with respect to the former than with respect to the latter. Doubtless the difference is to be explained not only by the traditional friendship between the American and French peoples, and by the intimate relations that existed between the two Governments before the war, but also by the much greater importance of France in the balance of power. Whether Hitler invaded Spain depended in large measure on whether he succeeded in first squaring the Vichy Government. Furthermore, France still possessed formidable naval power and held most of North and West Africa, so important for control of the Mediterranean and the overseas approaches to the New World. The Spanish question was a marginal one, while the French problem was crucial. That being so, it is necessary to examine more closely the unfolding of what Mr. Churchill has characterized as the "sad and sorry and squalid tale" of developments at Vichy.

Before retracing the course of American policy toward France it may be well to recall that the position of Vichy, with its control of the Fleet and its command of North and West Africa, was as much a matter of concern to Hitler as to Mr. Churchill and Mr. Roosevelt. Admiral Raeder, Nazi Chief of Naval Operations, was forever impressing upon the Fuehrer the immense significance of North Africa and Dakar and more particularly the absolute necessity of preventing these strategic areas from falling into the hands of the British or Americans. Unremittingly he urged help for the Spanish and French in strengthening the defenses of the Atlantic Islands, Casablanca and Dakar, and called attention to the danger of a dissident movement in North Africa which would result in Vichy's loss of that region. To forestall such an eventuality he pleaded for concessions to France that would bring that country into the Axis. Gravely he warned that "loss of the French African colonies to Britain and the United States would entail the great danger that it would no longer be possible to *overthrow* the British," and that *"in order to win the war as a whole,* the loss of North and West Africa to Britain and America must be prevented."[17]

The arguments of Raeder were reinforced by those of Otto Abetz, the German Ambassador in Paris, a determined champion of collaboration with France and of ultimate reconciliation between the two traditional enemies. Abetz was able to point to the freely avowed hostility of Admiral Darlan to the British and to his alleged readiness to coöperate in furthering a German victory. But Hitler had scant faith in the prospects of sincere collaboration. He disliked and distrusted the French and was only too well aware that a deal with them would estrange both Italy and Spain, countries which had designs on France's African possessions. Furthermore, he seems to have

---

[17] *Fuehrer Conferences,* 1941 (2), 3 ff. (July 9); 13 ff. (July 25); 47 (September 17, 1941).

cherished a forlorn hope that some day he might be able to make peace with the British at France's expense.[18]

True, the Fuehrer had finally been talked into the negotiations with Darlan that eventuated in the famous Paris Protocols of May, 1941, but only to find that these agreements netted him little and that the French set a very high price on genuine collaboration. This phase of Franco-German relations had come to an end with the French note of July 15, 1941, which outraged Hitler and blasted any hope he may still have had of securing French military aid. By this time the assault on Soviet Russia was already well under way. The Fuehrer attributed the boldness of the French to the withdrawal of German forces from France and to Vichy's realization that the attention of the Nazis was focused on the east. So indeed it was. Hitler, expecting an early victory over his erstwhile partner, was determined to hold all other issues in suspense until his hands were free. He knew he was taking a chance, for he realized that Britain and the United States were intent on getting control of the North African coast and the Mediterranean, and on securing access to Europe by way of Dakar and Casablanca. He was perfectly aware also that General Weygand, commanding in North Africa, had wrecked the Paris Protocols and might at any time throw in his lot with the democracies. But what could he do? To insure North Africa against conquest by his enemies involved strengthening the French forces in that area, which in turn increased the danger that Weygand might decide to reënter the war on Britain's side. Similarly any Nazi attempt to coerce Spain and move on North Africa, even with Vichy's consent, would precipitate British or American action against the Atlantic islands and Spanish Morocco before the Germans could hope to reach the Straits of Gibraltar. All told, the Fuehrer saw no alternative to gambling. Admiral Raeder was unable to get from him more than the assurance that if the United States occupied the Portuguese or Spanish islands, the Nazis would march into Spain and from there send their divisions into North Africa. Pending the expected victory in the east, the German posture vis-à-vis the west was to be strictly defensive.[19]

Since it takes two parties to make collaboration a reality, it is of more than academic interest to note Hitler's distrust and disillusionment with Vichy. Manifestations of French friendship, he observed, rose and fell with the tide of German successes in the east. The real French attitude, he thought, was best reflected in the assassinations of German officers in France, which became all too frequent after the withdrawal of a large part of the Nazi

---

[18] *Halder Diary*, November 5, 1941 (Colonel Speidel's report of his conversation with Hitler), and December 7, 1941 (Von Etzdorf's statement of Hitler's views).

[19] *Halder Diary*, July 26 and August 4, 1941; the memo of the German High Command, September 13, 1941 (*ibid.*); *Fuehrer Conferences*, 1941 (2), 13 ff. (July 25, 1941). Although Hitler's references to France in his discussions with his Italian allies were apt to be colored, his remarks, as recorded in *Ciano's Diplomatic Papers*, 450 (August 25), 455 ff. (October 25), 460 ff. (November 24-27), are borne out by the strictly German references noted above.

forces. Even the recall of Weygand from North Africa did not completely satisfy him: "There are so many Weygands in France," he remarked to Ciano, "that any one of them could take the role of the old retired general tomorrow."[20]

The question remains, then, whether Pétain or Darlan were more sincere in their desire for collaboration than Hitler believed them to be. The question can probably never be answered categorically. As for Pétain, the evidence thus far adduced is not sufficient to demonstrate that his heart was in collaboration. Plainly he hoped, through negotiation and a measure of concession, to alleviate the burdens of the armistice and more particularly to secure the return of the French prisoners of war. Quite probably he felt that, so long as British chances of victory were slim and so long as the United States remained aloof from the war, it was essential to keep the line to Berlin open. Darlan, on the other hand, was so influenced in his judgment by his hatred and disdain of the British that he had evidently convinced himself of the inevitability of German victory and considered it the part of wisdom to ensure an appropriate role for France in Hitler's new order. But even with respect to Darlan it may be observed that he was willing to collaborate only at a price, and a high price at that. It is unlikely that much more will be learned of his motives and it is impossible, on the strength of present evidence, to document his policy in full. That he made gestures and real concessions to the Germans no one can deny. At the same time it is only fair to add that at every step he tried to drive a hard bargain. Among the many demands that drove the Germans to fury was the persistent one for permission to strengthen the French forces in North Africa, supposedly for defense against British or American attack, but not improbably also for defense against a German move. Such, at any rate, was the understanding of General Weygand, whose motives are hardly open to question. Such was also the suspicion of the Germans.

Some light on these matters may be derived from the story of the St. Florentin meeting between Marshal Pétain, Admiral Darlan and Field Marshal Goering (December 1, 1941), graciously agreed to by Hitler as a reward for Vichy's recall of Weygand from North Africa. The meeting, intended by the Germans merely as a courtesy visit of two distinguished soldiers, turned into a heated political discussion, for Pétain seized the initiative and all but accused the Germans of having failed to live up to the promises made at the time of the Montoire meeting (October, 1940). He read Goering a long memorandum, carefully prepared by the Vichy Foreign Office under Darlan's direction, which rehearsed these German promises, pointed out that none of them had materialized, and argued that consequently it was impossible for the Vichy Government to convert France to the program of collaboration. Darlan in turn reminded the Nazi leader that

[20] *Ciano's Diplomatic Papers,* as cited above.

French concessions to the Germans in Syria had led to the loss of that territory and pleaded the need for strengthening the defenses of North Africa.

Goering was infuriated by the tone struck by his visitors. He accused them of having done nothing to further the cause of collaboration, charged Vichy with hostility to the Germans, and refused to submit the French memorandum to the Fuehrer. Why had not the French Fleet been thrown into the struggle against Britain? What had Vichy done to aid Germany in the fight against communism? These were questions to which he required an answer. The trouble was, he added, that French intellectuals were still hoping for a British victory and deluding themselves with the "fantastic idea" that the United States might yet play a decisive role. As for North Africa, he claimed to know that "Weygand was eager for a strengthening of the North Africa forces only so that he might build up a relatively strong army and put it at the disposal of the British when the opportune moment arrived." To the French complaints and demands he could only say: "Well, Monsieur le Maréchal, who are the victors, you or we?"[21] Obviously the tide of collaboration had reached a low ebb on the eve of the Pearl Harbor attack.

3. AMERICAN PRESSURE ON VICHY

For reasons of his own, not yet wholly clear, Admiral Darlan did little or nothing to relieve American uneasiness about Vichy's policy. On the contrary he appears to have thought it well to have Washington put more stock in the program of collaboration than it deserved. He did not contradict the prevalent rumors of the coming conclusion of a peace treaty between France and Germany and in July, 1941, announced to Ambassador Leahy the impending Japanese occupation of Indo-Chinese bases with such equanimity that Washington felt justified in expecting Vichy to yield to German pressure for North African bases. Furthermore, Darlan's easy compliance with Japanese demands so outraged American opinion that the long-smoldering hostility toward Vichy soon broke into flames of indignation. The American public was inclined to blame the French almost more than the Japanese for the untoward developments in the Far East. Everywhere the question was raised why the United States should continue to "toady" to the Vichy "Fascists" who were so obviously the lackeys of the Axis. There was a widespread demand that relations with Vichy be severed and American interests safeguarded by the occupation of French possessions vital to the national defense, such as Martinique and Dakar. Isolationist newspapers might rail at the proliferating Dakar projects and call Dakar a "sunscorched little dump," but public opinion generally was deeply concerned by

[21] William L. Langer: Our Vichy Gamble (New York, 1947) and the sources there cited, to be supplemented by Jean-Louis Aujol: Le procès Benoist-Mechin (Paris, 1948), 302 ff., and Fernand de Brinon: Mémoires (Paris, 1949), 95 ff.

reports, emanating largely from Free French sources in London, that all West Africa was being flooded by Germans.[22]

The State Department knew there were no Germans in Dakar and only a few in West and North Africa, for the American Consul at Dakar had reported unequivocally on the matter and it was well known that General Weygand was doing everything possible to hinder the activities and expansion of the Nazi armistice commission.[23] There was therefore no disposition in official Washington to jeopardize the future of the French Fleet and the French Empire by throwing over Vichy and openly recognizing General de Gaulle and his Free French organization. No objection was raised to the British practice of passing on to de Gaulle such Lend-Lease materials as he required for his forces and for the defense of the colonial areas which had rallied to his cause. Nothing more seemed required and there was no apparent advantage in official recognition of the Free French movement. The British were finding de Gaulle increasingly difficult and during July and August became involved in so much friction over the handling of the Syrian situation that relations came dangerously close to actual rupture. Within the ranks of the Free French the situation had by September become quite chaotic. Admiral Muselier, in command of the Free French naval forces, had never been on good terms with de Gaulle and evidently tried to take over leadership of the resistance movement. It was decided, perhaps with British encouragement, to set up a National Council to serve as a check on the General's power. Muselier made a desperate effort to secure the presidency of this Council and relegate de Gaulle to a purely honorific position. The result was a conflict so bitter that the British had to intervene. When the Council was established on September 24, de Gaulle remained in the saddle, but according to the testimony of the General's own closest collaborators the movement was in a sorry plight, torn by suspicion and dissension between the leading figures.[24]

Washington had little reason, furthermore, to believe that de Gaulle and his organization enjoyed widespread support in France itself. Reliable information was hard to come by and the situation was obscure then as it is even now. Resistance movements of various kinds had sprung up in France in the late summer and autumn of 1940, as soon as it seemed likely that Britain might withstand the German attack. Some of these movements were fairly well organized and some, indeed, were led by members of Marshal Pétain's own entourage. They were not directed against Vichy, but were

[22] On the isolationist argument see the *New York Daily News,* August 14, 1941, and the *Saturday Evening Post,* September 6, 1941.

[23] Langer: *Our Vichy Gamble,* 187. On August 27, 1941, the Vichy Government issued a public statement denying that there were Germans in West Africa.

[24] Vice-Amiral Muselier: *De Gaulle contre le Gaullisme* (Paris, 1946), Chapter XX; Passy: *Souvenirs* (no place or date), I, 214 ff.; Jacques Soustelle: *De Londres à Alger* (Paris, 1947), 265 ff. On the aftermath of the Syrian campaign see especially General Catroux: *Dans la bataille de Méditerranée* (Paris, 1949), Chapters XX-XXIII.

designed, rather, to strengthen the Marshal's position in resistance to German pressure. There may have been other groups hostile to the Pétain regime, the more so as British radio broadcasts were widely listened to and both the British and the Free French, often in competition with each other, were organizing intelligence networks and sabotage groups on French soil. By the summer of 1941 London was already getting a fairly steady flow of information from agents in France.

After Hitler's attack on Soviet Russia there appears to have been a rapid development of resistance activity throughout France, due in large part, no doubt, to the heavy withdrawals of German troops. The French Communists, having violently opposed the "imperialist" war, had promptly reversed themselves and now embarked upon widespread sabotage. Attacks on German officers and soldiers became frequent and led to large-scale Nazi reprisals which shocked the civilized world. Marshal Pétain, in a radio address of August 12, complained bitterly of the existing state of affairs, for which he blamed the Communists, the British and other subversive influences. On the same occasion he reaffirmed his own authority and announced the institution of rigorous police measures, which before long resulted in a veritable dragonnade against Communists, Jews, Freemasons and other undesirables.

The natural reaction was the growth of opposition and resistance groups and a growing tendency to accept de Gaulle as the symbol of resistance. It is said that in August, 1941, the chiefs of the three strongest resistance groups (Libération, Libération Nationale, and Liberté) met and agreed to recognize de Gaulle as leader. Yet Colonel Passy, who was de Gaulle's agent in these matters, states that none of the resistance leaders sent liaison officers to London and suggests that their moves in the direction of the Free French were made chiefly with an eye to securing financial support. Although it is impossible to speak with assurance on the subject, it would seem that in the period before Pearl Harbor resistance in France, while certainly on the increase and certainly more hostile to Vichy than before, was still quite amorphous and far from being committed to General de Gaulle.[25]

Although for the British, after their rupture of relations with France in July, 1940, there were obvious advantages in aiding the Free French movement, even Mr. Churchill was glad to have both the Canadian and American Governments continue their contacts with Vichy.[26] It would indeed

[25] Langer: *Our Vichy Gamble,* 165 ff., to be supplemented by Passy: *Souvenirs,* I, 166 ff., 212 ff., 231 ff.; Rémy: *Mémoires d'un agent de la France Libre* (Paris, n.d.), *passim;* Georges Loustauneau-Lacau: *Mémoires d'un français rebelle* (Paris, 1948), Chapter VII; Louis-Dominique Girard: *Montoire: Verdun diplomatique* (Paris, 1948), 357 ff. Nonetheless René Cassin, one of the prominent Free French leaders, argued, in "Vichy or Free France?" (*Foreign Affairs,* October, 1941), for recognition of de Gaulle's movement as alone representing the will of the French people.

[26] *Moffat Diary* (*MS.*), September 18, 1941, reporting a talk with Prime Minister Mackenzie King; memo of Mr. Churchill to Mr. Eden, November 30, 1941 (Churchill: *The Grand Alliance,* 837).

have been the height of folly for Washington to precipitate a crisis with Vichy at a time when the world was anxiously awaiting the outcome of Hitler's venture in the east. Uncertainty over Vichy's course had continued now for more than a year. In one way or another disastrous developments had been avoided, even during the Laval period. Darlan might be unscrupulous and unreliable, but it was thought that Pétain did not trust him and it was known that there was no love lost between Weygand and Darlan. Thus far Nazi efforts to secure bases in North and West Africa had been foiled and in late August, 1941, Ambassador Leahy could report to the President: "Since the German invasion of Russia with its slow progress to date, since the American occupation of Iceland, since your conference with Mr. Churchill, and with a growing realization of the power of the American industrial effort, we sense a definite softening of the attitude of even the collaborationists toward America and a revival of hope among the people for an early release from bondage." While it was recognized that Vichy's attitude would probably change if the Germans succeeded in subjugating Soviet Russia, it was the part of wisdom to continue a policy of watchful waiting.[27]

President Roosevelt rated his personal influence high and in the past had relied heavily on his direct appeals to Marshal Pétain. He therefore readily adopted Mr. Welles's suggestion that, in order to forestall unfavorable developments in the North African situation, he again address the Marshal. In a letter dated August 21 and delivered to Vichy by courier, Mr. Roosevelt said:

The Government of the United States recognizes the limitations imposed on the French Government in Metropolitan France by the Armistice provisions. It is, however, of the utmost importance to the United States that the continued exercise by France of jurisdiction over the territory of French North Africa and over all French colonies remain unimpaired inasmuch as only in such manner can there be afforded complete assurance of security to the Western Hemisphere in so far as the regions mentioned are concerned.

It, therefore, remains the consistent desire of the United States that there be no infringement of French sovereign control over these territories, provided of course that such control remains in reality French, and completely unimpaired.

I repeat that so long as these conditions obtain, the Government of the United States has no desire to see existing French sovereignty over French North Africa or over any of France's colonies changed or infringed.

. . . .

For all of the reasons I have mentioned above, this Government will view with lively

[27] Letter of Ambassador Leahy to Mr. Roosevelt, August 26, 1941 (William D. Leahy: *I Was There* [New York, 1950], 463 ff.); Myron Taylor's report of his talks with Ambassador Leahy on September 7, 1941 (*Roosevelt Papers:* Secretary's File, Box 82).

gratification any steps which have been or may be taken by your Government to prevent German penetration into French North Africa or other French possessions and to strengthen their defense so as to render any surprise attack by Germany, or powers coöperating with Germany, less likely of success.[28]

The Marshal's reply, drafted under Darlan's supervision, was delivered in due course and contained the usual assurances: "As concerns the maintenance by France of the exercise of its rights of sovereignty over the territories of French North Africa and of French colonies, I repeat to you in the most categorical manner that the French Government has always been, and is always, determined to assure the respect thereof against any attack. Its determination in this respect remains as strong as ever; and it has given unquestionable proof thereof in several instances." However, the letter also reminded the President that thus far attacks had been made only by the British and Free French, and that the United States Government had done nothing to condemn them. Furthermore, Darlan suggested to Ambassador Leahy that American activities in North Africa were arousing German suspicions and left the Ambassador with the impression that if the Germans renewed their demands he would endeavor to induce Pétain to concede at least commercial facilities at Bizerte, which concession could not be regarded as a relinquishment of sovereign rights.[29]

Since Darlan took pains to attenuate Pétain's assurances and evidently thought it desirable to keep alive American apprehensions about North Africa, Washington could hardly view the situation with equanimity. On November 1 Mr. Roosevelt wrote Ambassador Leahy: "Should the Germans change the direction of their main activities from Russia to the Mediterranean we are fearful that France will not be able to hold out much longer against increasing German demands for what would correspond to military assistance on the part of the French."[30] Only a few days later Marshal Pétain, for once talking with the Ambassador in the absence of Darlan, indicated that if the Russian front were stabilized, the Germans would make further demands on France, and that he would be unable to resist their pressure.[31] Neither Ambassador Leahy nor the President and his State Department advisers were disposed to question the Marshal's sincerity. Aggrieved though Pétain might feel toward the British and de Gaulle, the "viper that he had warmed in his bosom," there was no reason to doubt

[28] Letter of the President to Marshal Pétain, August 21, 1941, delivered by Ambassador Leahy on September 12, 1941 (full text in *Roosevelt Papers: Secretary's File*, Box 75). See also Leahy: *I Was There*, 56.

[29] Letter of Pétain to the President, September 17, 1941, delivered to Mr. Roosevelt only on October 27, 1941 (*Roosevelt Papers:* Secretary's File, Box 75). The substance of the reply and Pétain's and Darlan's comments were transmitted by Leahy in a tel. of September 18, 1941.

[30] Full text in Leahy: *I Was There*, 467-68.

[31] Leahy: *I Was There*, 57, reporting his conversation with Pétain on November 4, 1941.

his devotion to the traditional friendship between the United States and France or his readiness to oppose and obstruct the Germans so far as lay in his power. The trouble was that Pétain was a failing old man, not fully informed and not entirely aware of the activities of his entourage. He had rid himself of Laval only to find himself dependent on Darlan who, in a remarkably short time, had succeeded in subjecting all important activities of the Vichy Government to his own authority. Since Darlan postured as the advocate of collaboration and apparently went out of his way to fan the flame of American suspicion, nothing was more natural than Washington's chronic apprehensions about Vichy's course and more particularly about the fate of North and West Africa.

4. North African Mirage

With Pétain confessing his helplessness and Darlan capable of any chicanery, both Washington and London derived their only consolation from the fact that General Weygand was in control of the French forces in North Africa. Of the General's opposition to collaboration with the Germans there could be no shadow of doubt. Indeed, it was known that he had been chiefly instrumental in nullifying the Paris Protocols in June, 1941. Ever since his appointment as Delegate General of the Vichy Government, Weygand had devoted himself to the restoration of morale throughout North and West Africa and to the rebuilding of the military forces still remaining in that area. He had negotiated with Mr. Robert D. Murphy the economic accord of February, 1941, which it was hoped would save the French possessions from want and unrest. Weygand and his entourage maintained close and confidential relations with Murphy, now serving as Consul General at Algiers, and through him kept Washington posted on the situation not only in North Africa but also in Vichy, insofar as Weygand himself was informed on that enigma.

The General never encouraged illusions as to his role or intentions. On every suitable occasion he made perfectly clear that he proposed to hold North and West Africa for the legitimate French Government at Vichy and that he was determined to resist attack not only from the Germans or Italians but also from the Free French, the British, and even the Americans. He left no room for doubt that he was loyal to Marshal Pétain and intended to follow the orders of the Chief of State. His was not the temperament to play the dissident. On his return from Vichy after the crucial decisions of July 15, he told Mr. Murphy in so many words "that he would not enter into a commitment regarding the general policy of his Government without authorization, neither had he any intention of taking independent military action."[32]

Nevertheless, Weygand was eager to secure from the United States all

[32] Langer: *Our Vichy Gamble,* 181-83.

possible military supplies and equipment to strengthen the defenses of North Africa against Nazi attack. On the same occasion, in July, Mr. Murphy reported:

General Weygand believes that he may be faced with a crisis in September or October next, on the theory that the Germans will turn their attention to this area, especially the Atlantic bases, by then. . . . His close associates suggest that if the United States is interested in military support of Weygand, it is important that I tell him what military aid the United States could give him for the purpose of resisting Axis aggression, and when this could be done. . . . If I could inform the General that there is under study in Washington a program of *substantial* military aid,—that factor alone would have an important effect.

This passage is of particular importance because it suggests the hopes of several high officers on Weygand's staff that, if sufficient equipment could be secured, the General might after all be induced to take action if a favorable situation were to develop. These men were in close touch with a small but energetic group of army officers and civil officials who had already organized a resistance group in North Africa and, as Mr. Murphy discovered on making contact with the group, had already drawn tentative plans for military action, contingent on the provision of American munitions. Mr. Murphy was much intrigued by the prospect opened by this group and hastened to transmit its ideas to Washington.[33]

This and similar reports from Algiers reached Washington at a time when public as well as official opinion was much exercised by the fear of German aggression against North Africa following the expected collapse of Soviet Russia. There was much popular sentiment for the seizure of Dakar and even for preventive occupation of North Africa. Major George Fielding Eliot, among the best known of the military commentators, thought a move on Dakar from the land side not too difficult.[34] Evidently former Ambassador William C. Bullitt shared this view and brought the whole issue of military action in Africa to the President, who in turn requested that a study be made of various possibilities. The result was a flurry of excitement in the War Department, which, while fully appreciative of the importance of West and North Africa, was painfully conscious of the shortage of trained troops even for such operations as the occupation of Iceland or possible action against the Azores. Secretary Stimson implored Mr. Roosevelt not to let his mind wander off to "side shows" and pleaded that "our real interest

[33] Langer: *Our Vichy Gamble*, 180 ff., 228 ff., to be supplemented by Loustaunau-Lacau: *Mémoires d'un français rebelle*, Chapter VIII; Marcel Aboulker: *Alger et ses complots* (Paris, 1945), especially pp. 72 ff.; Albert Kammerer: *Du débarquement africain*, etc. (Paris, 1949), 28 ff., 54 ff.

[34] Unpublished memorandum on "The Politico-Military Situation in West Africa," prepared for the Council on Foreign Relations, August 25, 1941. For a well-balanced analysis of Dakar's defensive strength see Paul M. Atkins: "Dakar and the Strategy of West Africa" (*Foreign Affairs*, January, 1942).

lies in preserving the line of communications and of gradual fortification through the Northeast, including the British Isles." Nonetheless the President insisted on a careful examination of the problem and Mr. Stimson saw no alternative but to follow instructions. Meanwhile, however, he did his utmost to forestall support for the project from other quarters. He emphasized to Mr. Hull "that strategy demanded that we should not get bogged down in any of the side issues such as West Africa, the Azores, or sending all our mercantile marine to the Middle East until the Northeast situation was clear and settled . . ." At the same time he detailed Generals Marshall and Embick to convert Secretary Knox, who appears to have been fascinated by the Bullitt proposals. The two Generals pointed out to Colonel Knox that a North African operation would require 150,000 men and would tie up an immense amount of shipping. The scheme, they argued, was in any case "hopeless," because the Germans were nearer at hand, Weygand would be unable to give much help, and the Germans could easily "do us up" if the attempt were made to land.[35]

Having thus prepared the ground, Mr. Stimson on October 8 reported to the President that the War Department's estimate was ready but that the General Staff was firmly opposed to the North African project "on the ground of getting bogged down on a side track which was not on the direct line of our strategical route towards victory." On the following day the Secretary found Mr. Roosevelt "quite on the defensive about it and apologetic." He assured Mr. Stimson "that he had no present intention of making any such effort." But, to make doubly sure, the Secretary invited Mr. Bullitt to a conference and spent an hour and a half explaining to him why the scheme was not practicable. His visitor seemed impressed and admitted that the Secretary "had completely upset the premises on which his thoughts had been based and completely changed his view."[36]

Mr. Stimson was relieved to think that he had succeeded in exploding one more harebrained project, but the President evidently continued to toy with the idea and entrusted Lord Louis Mountbatten with a message to Mr. Churchill suggesting study of a scheme to send American forces to North Africa, but "only if Pétain goes and Weygand plays with us."[37] If nothing more was heard of the Bullitt project it was probably because Mr. Churchill, banking on Mr. Roosevelt's particular interest in North Africa, Dakar and the Atlantic islands, at this very time advanced plans of his own. These were communicated to the President in a letter, dated October 20, which was brought to Washington by Mr. Attlee on the occasion of an official visit. The Prime Minister's thoughts turned on the situation in Libya, where

[35] *Stimson Diary (MS.)*, September 29, October 3, 6, 7, 1941. We have discussed this matter also with General Embick (April 12, 1946).

[36] *Stimson Diary (MS.)*, October 8, 9, 10, 1941.

[37] Message of the President to Mr. Churchill, October 15, 1941 (*F.D.R.: His Personal Letters*, II, 1223).

Rommel's headlong advance had been providentially stopped in June, though only in the nick of time and by the narrowest margin. With even modest reinforcements in men and supplies it was generally agreed that the Nazi *Afrika Korps* could take Tobruk and resume the offensive against Egypt and the Suez Canal. Fortunately for the British, Hitler in this as in other matters refused to be diverted from his main purpose, which was to liquidate the Red armies. The British were given time to reorganize the Middle East command and improve the system of supply and transport, and to rush tanks, planes and other matériel as well as additional forces to the Egyptian front. Tobruk was held with the aid of British naval forces, while air and naval units operating from Malta took advantage of the withdrawal of German air forces from Sicily, and of the Italian Fleet's lack of fuel oil, to sink the major part of the supplies despatched to Rommel.[38]

Mr. Churchill was convinced that the respite provided by Hitler should be exploited to the full. While recognizing that if the Germans succeeded in driving the Soviet forces back to the Caucasus, they would probably launch an offensive on Turkey, Iraq, Syria and Egypt, he did not believe such operations possible before the spring of 1942. To meet such a contingency, and perhaps also to draw the United States a bit further along the road to active participation, he requested the President (September 1) to provide fast American shipping for the transport of two additional British divisions to the Middle East during the winter. Mr. Roosevelt discussed the matter with Mr. Hopkins and with his naval advisers and decided to assign some of the fastest American liners (already converted to troop transports) to make the run with twenty thousand troops. At the same time the Maritime Commission was directed to assign another ten or twelve American ships to the North Atlantic route so as to release more British bottoms for Middle East supply. The final dispositions were not made until the revision of the Neutrality Law was assured and even then it was thought best to have the British forces sent to Halifax for embarkation on the American transports, which were to follow the American coasts southward as far as possible before cutting across the Atlantic. On November 10, 1941, the convoy left Halifax, thus marking yet another step toward active American participation in British operations.[39]

Meanwhile the Prime Minister brought pressure to bear on General Sir Claude Auchinleck to stage an offensive against Rommel at the earliest possible moment, in the hope of driving the Axis forces not only from Cyre-

---

[38] The losses were 38 percent in September, 63 percent in October and 77 percent in November. See Churchill: *The Grand Alliance,* 488, 554-55, and Kurt Assmann: *Deutsche Schicksalsjahre* (Wiesbaden, 1950), 350.

[39] Messages from Mr. Churchill to the President, September 1, 7, October 5, 1941; from the President to Mr. Churchill, September 6, 1941. See Churchill: *The Grand Alliance,* 491-92; Sherwood: *Roosevelt and Hopkins,* 374 ff.; Morison: *The Battle of the Atlantic,* 109 ff.

naica but also from Tripolitania. Mr. Churchill's fertile imagination already envisaged that Weygand, once the British had appeared on the frontier of Tunisia, would throw in his lot with them. He arranged to have one armored and three field divisions held in readiness in England for commitment at any crucial point in the western Mediterranean, and figured that if Weygand refused to play the game, the British could employ their forces in an invasion of Sicily. These were the plans communicated to the President on the occasion of Mr. Attlee's visit.[40]

In certain American quarters there was still doubt of the ability of the British even to hold Egypt. Mr. Alexander Kirk, the American representative in Cairo, was still complaining of the deficiencies of the British supply services and Secretary Stimson thought that at best the British could fight only a delaying action.[41] But the President and his professional military advisers had by this time adopted entirely the British view of the Middle East situation and favored using American shipping to send out whatever supplies could be made available.[42] Following Mr. W. Averell Harriman's visit to Egypt in June, Major General George H. Brett, of the Army Air Corps, arrived in Cairo on September 10. During a stay of several weeks he made a detailed survey of the organization of the theater, the command relationships, the receiving facilities, the provision for assembling and repairing American equipment, and kindred matters. Among other things he arranged for the establishment of a regular United States Military North African Mission under Brigadier General Russell L. Maxwell and proposed that a number of heavy bombers be sent to the Middle East to take part in the operations against Rommel's supply lines. The fact that the first of these bombers left the United States on November 20 may be taken as an indication of the importance attached to the British plans by the War Department and the President.[43]

Despite all possible support from London and Washington, General Auchinleck was reluctant to launch an offensive against Rommel in view of what he considered the serious threat of a Nazi attack through Turkey and Syria. Much to the distress of Mr. Churchill the operation had, in mid-October, to be postponed till November 18, thereby anticipating by only a

[40] Churchill: *The Grand Alliance,* 540 ff., 551 ff.

[41] Tel. from Kirk, September 18, 1941; *Stimson Diary (MS.),* September 30, October 1, 1941, reporting Secretary Hull as equally pessimistic.

[42] Cf. especially the Joint Board Estimate of September 11, 1941, as quoted in Sherwood: *Roosevelt and Hopkins,* 417.

[43] On the Brett Mission, tels. from Kirk, September 12, 13, 28, 1941; tel. from Brett to Harriman, September 16; tels. from Winant, October 6 and 18, 1941; tels. from Mr. Churchill to the President, October 5, and to Mr. Hopkins, October 8. See also Craven and Cate: *The Army Air Forces in World War II,* Vol. I, 326 ff.; Mark S. Watson: *Chief of Staff: Prewar Plans and Preparations,* 327-28. On the establishment of the military mission we have used a memo from the President to Secretary Stimson, September 13; a letter of instruction to General Maxwell, October 21; and a letter from Mr. Stimson to Mr. Hull, October 29, 1941.

few days the Nazi attack on Tobruk for which Rommel had finally, after much heated argument, obtained authorization. By mid-November Auchinleck was able to take the field with superior numbers of men and tanks, and with adequate air support, but by that time the situation in the Mediterranean had already begun to turn to the disadvantage of the British. For Hitler, appalled by the heavy losses of supplies, had overruled his naval advisers and had begun the transfer of submarines and air forces to the Mediterranean. By mid-December no less than thirty-six U-boats, about half the total number at sea, were already in the Mediterranean or en route to that theater. The British carrier *Ark Royal* was sunk on November 13, the *Barham* on November 25. Before long the approaches to Malta were effectively mined and the British naval forces in the eastern Mediterranean so severely reduced and damaged as to alter completely the situation in that area.[44]

It was last call, then, for the British offensive which, though it took Rommel by surprise, met with vigorous resistance from the *Afrika Korps*. For some days the decision was in doubt, but the outnumbered Axis forces were finally obliged to fall back. On November 29 the British reached Benghazi and by January 5, 1942, they had cleared all of Libya to the Tripolitanian frontier. The victory was a heartening one, coming as it did at the very time of the Japanese attack on the United States. But Mr. Churchill is undoubtedly right in bemoaning Auchinleck's four and a half months' delay as "alike a mistake and a misfortune." For the victory certainly came too late and was much too tenuous to make possible the realization of the larger hopes attached to it. Among other things the 18th of November, which saw the opening of the British offensive, saw also the recall of General Weygand from North Africa and therewith the disappearance from the political scene of the man on whom, rightly or wrongly, both London and Washington had placed high expectations.

5. WEYGAND'S FALL

The records which have become available since the end of the war leave no doubt that the Germans were fully aware of Weygand's views and purposes and that for many months before November, 1941, they had been trying to encompass his downfall. Aside from his association with Foch and his role in the armistice negotiations of November, 1918, Weygand had made himself obnoxious by the conclusion of the economic accord with the United States, by his obstruction of the work of the German control com-

---

[44] Churchill: *The Grand Alliance,* 408-9, 576-77; Sir Claude Auchinleck's despatch *Operations in the Middle East, 1 November, 1941 to 15 August, 1942,* dated January 13, 1948 (Supplement to the *London Gazette,* January 13, 1948); Desmond Young: *Rommel* (London, 1950), 99 ff.; Assmann: *Deutsche Schicksalsjahre,* 350-53; F. H. Hinsley: *Hitler's Strategy* (Cambridge, 1951), 157-59.

mission in North Africa, and by his opposition to the Paris Protocols. By the autumn of 1941 the Germans had become so impatient with him that Field Marshal Keitel ordered his assassination. Pending this solution, however, increasing pressure was brought on Vichy to get rid of this man, who made all talk of collaboration appear farcical.

In view of the fact that Darlan resented Weygand's independent position and attitude and was himself scheming to get rid of his potential rival, it is astonishing that the General retained his position as long as in fact he did. Apparently Marshal Pétain was unwilling to abandon a loyal supporter and thereby strengthen the position of Darlan. Moreover, he evidently hoped to extract concessions from the Germans by delaying the dismissal even if he could not forever avoid it. The details are unimportant. Suffice it to say that by November, 1941, the "Affaire Weygand" had reached the critical stage. Darlan had declared that either he or Weygand must go. Weygand, in turn, had declined the offer of other positions and had flatly refused to resign his post voluntarily. The Germans, finally, had announced that unless Weygand were promptly dismissed, Hitler would take such measures as seemed indicated. Pétain saw no alternative but to yield, which he did on the assurance that he would be invited to meet with Ribbentrop or some other high Nazi functionary, and on some vague promise of the release of North African prisoners of war. Weygand was summoned to Vichy and told of the decision. He was to retire and not to return to North Africa, not even to pack his belongings and make his adieus. His position as Delegate General was to be abolished and the military command in North and West Africa divided. A new position, that of General Secretary for French Africa, was created and assigned to Admiral Fénard, who was made directly responsible to Darlan.[45]

Weygand's recall, though not unexpected, was a severe blow to Washington and London, where little satisfaction could be derived from Pétain's explanations. In conversation with Ambassador Leahy the Marshal pleaded feebly that he was a prisoner of the Germans and unable to resist. The Nazis had long pressed for Weygand's removal and had finally presented Vichy with a "brutal ultimatum," threatening to occupy all France and quarter so large an army on the country that the population would be reduced to starvation. The Ambassador was not convinced. He pointed out that by no stretch of the imagination could Weygand's dismissal be considered as necessitated by the armistice agreement, beyond which Pétain had promised not to go. To quote Leahy's own words:

I told him that in my opinion such an unnecessary surrender to Axis demands, particularly at a time when Germany is so thoroughly involved in Russia, would have a

---

[45] Langer: *Our Vichy Gamble,* 192 ff., to be supplemented by Général Maxime Weygand: *Mémoires: Rappélé au service* (Paris, 1950), 522 ff.; *Pétain et les allemands: mémorandum d'Abetz* (Paris, 1948), 117 ff.; Aujol: *Le procès Benoist-Méchin,* 288 ff.; Kammerer: *Du débarquement africain,* etc., 61 ff.

definitely adverse effect on the traditional amity between our two peoples, that it would probably bring about an immediate suspension of the economic assistance that is being given to the French colonies, and that it might very possibly cause America to make a complete readjustment of its attitude toward the Government of France.

Reporting home, the Ambassador, in hot indignation, declared that "this abject surrender to a Nazi threat at a time when Germany is completely occupied in Russia is the kind of jellyfish reaction that justifies the stoppage of all assistance to France." And, writing to the President a few days later, he observed:

In view of his [Pétain's] willingness under German and collaborationist pressure to sacrifice Weygand, who is a very close and loyal personal friend, it is not reasonable to expect him in the future to refuse under the same pressure the use of African bases, or the employment of the Fleet for the Axis account, or any other demand that Germany may consider of sufficient importance to its military effort.[46]

The President and his advisers took no less serious a view than the Ambassador. The news from Vichy, coming at a time when negotiations with Japan were entering upon their final phase and the British were launching their hopeful Libyan offensive, was grave indeed. It seemed altogether likely that the Pétain-Darlan regime, now completely under the thumb of Hitler, would grant the Germans bases in Tunisia through which Rommel's army could be reinforced. Speaking to the French Ambassador on November 19, Mr. Welles made this very point: "I said that this new step agreed upon by France implied that Germany would now rapidly increase its practical and effective control throughout North Africa and that a situation of this kind was regarded by the United States as a direct threat to the security and national defense requirements of the United States." This, the Under Secretary continued, made necessary "a complete change" in American policy. On the following day the Department announced that United States policy toward Vichy France was being reviewed and that, in the interval, all economic aid to North Africa was being suspended.[47]

It is possible that this announcement was influenced by a message received that day from Mr. Churchill, who cabled the President expressing his hopes for success in Libya and pointing out the significance of the Weygand affair:

It would be disastrous if Weygand were to be replaced by some pro-Hun officer just at the moment when we are likely to be in a position to influence events in North Africa both from the East and from home. I hope you will try your utmost at Vichy to preserve Weygand in his command. . . . Anyhow, Mr. President, Tunis and all

---

[46] Tel. from Leahy, November 19, 1941, and letter from Leahy to the President, November 22, 1941 (text in Leahy: *I Was There*, 468-70).

[47] Memo of conversation between Mr. Welles and Ambassador Henry-Haye, November 19, 1941, and State Department press release of November 20, 1941.

French North Africa might open out to us if we gain a good victory in Libya and we must be ready to exploit success. I am afraid, on the other hand, lest Hitler may demand to occupy Bizerta in view of possible danger to Tripoli. It is now or never with the Vichy French and their last chance of redemption.[48]

There was, of course, no possibility of reversing the decision to recall Weygand, or even of influencing the appointment of his successor. Actually the assignment of General Juin, released from imprisonment by the Germans, to the command in North Africa proved more than satisfactory from the standpoint of the United States and Britain. For the moment, however, all the President could do was assure Mr. Churchill that he was taking steps "to bring forcibly before Pétain the disastrous consequences of any action with regard to the authorities in North Africa which would result in aid to Germany," and transmit to the Prime Minister the substance of Ambassador Leahy's reports.[49] The announcement of the suspension of the aid program for North Africa was one such step; another was the State Department release of November 24, 1941, stating that the President had authorized direct Lend-Lease aid to the Free French forces on the ground that the territories they controlled were vital to the defense of the United States.

There matters stood on the eve of the Pearl Harbor attack. As the British drove Rommel and his *Afrika Korps* out of Cyrenaica and it became known that Pétain and Darlan had met in conference with Goering at St. Florentin, there seemed to be great danger that Vichy would succumb completely to Nazi pressure for facilities in North Africa. Rumors were rife that such demands were being made, that the Germans were on the point of despatching troops and munitions through France, that France and Spain were about to sign a mutual pact for the defense of North Africa against the British, and that Germany would presently take over all naval and air bases in that strategic area.

Under the circumstances the question was bound to arise whether suspension of the North African economic accord, involving the withdrawal of the American vice consuls, would be in the American or British interest. Weygand had pleaded against such a move and Murphy likewise used all his influence to oppose it. Eventually the European Division of the State Department also warned that "any severance of these relations, unless it follows upon an overt act on the part of Vichy, nullifying its assurances, would so affect the already discouraged French public, whose sole hope for the future lies in the United States, as to leave it no alternative but complete collaboration with the Axis." The result was that on December 6, the very day before Pearl Harbor, a telegram was despatched to Ambassador Leahy instructing him to tell Pétain that if he (the Marshal) would once again

[48] Message of Mr. Churchill to the President, November 20, 1941 (full text in Churchill: *The Grand Alliance,* 570).

[49] Message of the President to Mr. Churchill, November 20, 1941.

renew his assurances with respect to the French Fleet and the French colonies, and state that Weygand's recall involved no change in France's North African policy, the United States Government would consider resumption of the economic program. This message was communicated to Pétain on December 11 and the desired assurances were given on the following day. Thereupon Washington returned to its previous policy, the policy of uneasy reliance on Vichy and limited aid to North Africa.[50]

Thus ended the "squalid" tale of Vichy in the period prior to American involvement in the great conflict. Harsh things were said about American policy at the time and the subject has since remained one for heated debate. In this connection it is certainly worth quoting Hitler's remarks to Ciano within a few days of Weygand's recall and on the eve of the St. Florentin meeting. According to Ciano's notes: "Distrust of France has grown in proportion to the disappointments experienced. . . . There is no belief in the sincerity of Vichy, and even the recall of Weygand is considered to be merely a gesture of passing opportunism under continual pressure of Berlin."[51] To the Germans, French collaboration was far from what Darlan supposedly aimed at, far from what London and Washington feared.

To what extent American policy contributed to this result can no more be determined with accuracy than can the motives and purposes of Darlan. All one can say is that eighteen months after the collapse of France a substantial part of the country and most of the empire remained under French rule, that Pétain was still in power, that the Fleet was still in French hands, and that there was no significant military coöperation with Germany. It is inconceivable that this situation would have obtained if the United States had broken off relations with Vichy and thrown its whole weight to de Gaulle and the Free French movement. No responsible member of the Administration, from the President down, had a high opinion of the Vichy regime or staked great hopes upon it. The brutal fact of the matter was, however, that Vichy controlled forces and territories of vital interest to the United States. Prior to Pearl Harbor neither the United States nor Britain had the military power to safeguard these interests against Vichy or against Nazi Germany. The only practical solution seemed to be to secure all possible paper promises and exploit the political and economic influence of the United States to the limit. To combat the worst danger presented by Laval or Darlan there was no other course but to encourage men like Pétain and Weygand.

The aged Marshal seemed on many occasions to be playing the sorry role of a feeble and frightened dotard, but somehow he managed to stay afloat and on occasion proved himself equal to an acute crisis such as that pro-

[50] Langer: *Our Vichy Gamble,* 195 ff.; Leahy: *I Was There,* 61.

[51] *Ciano's Diplomatic Papers,* 460 ff. (record of the Berlin conversations, November 24-27, 1941).

voked by Laval. His authoritarian paternalism was thoroughly obnoxious to most Americans, inside the Government as well as outside, but there was no ground for doubting Pétain's attachment to the United States and it is reasonably clear that he understood full well the weight and significance of the American war potential. He sensed that, whatever the collaborationists might say, the ultimate hope of the French people for deliverance depended not only on the defeat of Hitler but equally on the continued friendship and solicitude of America. He was certainly shrewd enough to realize that a break with the United States would not be understood or accepted by the French people. His policy was therefore to cultivate relations with the United States as best he could without precipitating punitive action by the Germans. The position of France was certainly weak, but not as weak as many have thought. For in 1941 neither the democracies nor Hitler could bring undue pressure on Vichy without provoking undesirable counteraction from their opponents. In the last analysis Pétain appears to have made the most of this situation to assure the survival of his Government and his country. One can hardly deny that in large measure he succeeded and that, in the circumstances of 1941, his achievement was of real, not to say crucial, importance to the interests of the United States.

CHAPTER XXV

Strange Bedfellows

1. RUSSIA'S ORDEAL AND THE ISSUE OF AID

The six weeks that intervened between the Atlantic Conference and the Moscow Conference were decisive for the outcome of Hitler's campaign to destroy the Soviet Union. It has been frequently argued, and with some cogency, that the four to six weeks' delay in launching the Nazi offensive occasioned by the operations against Yugoslavia and Greece jeopardized the success of the Fuehrer's plans at the very outset. Others have maintained that if Hitler had successfully exploited the widespread opposition to the Moscow regime found to exist in the western parts of the Soviet Union, he might have been able to encompass its collapse. Yet the crucial aspect seems to have been the strategic one. During the first few weeks of the conflict the Nazi forces succeeded in attaining their objectives, though the strength of the enemy, especially in armor, surprised them. Fighting with dogged determination, the Red armies were obliged to fall back all along the front, suffering losses of hundreds of thousands of men, thousands of tanks, and vast quantities of other matériel. The grand strategy of the Soviet commanders was to trade men and territory for time. There is good reason to suppose that, had the Nazi armies during August and September driven eastward toward Moscow, their opponents would have had too little time to prepare the defense of the capital and would probably have been unable to prevent the collapse of the regime before the onset of winter.

In this situation Hitler's military conceptions became decidedly confused. While willing to subscribe to the classic proposition that the chief aim must be the destruction of the enemy forces, the Fuehrer had, from the very beginning, tended to assign the highest priority to political and economic rather than to purely military objectives. Rejecting the arguments of his military staffs and freely voicing his lack of interest in the capture of Moscow, he insisted on the importance of taking the industrial complex of

Leningrad in the north and of overrunning the Ukraine and the Donetz Basin in the south preliminary to the advance on the oil fields of the Caucasus. Thereby he hoped to destroy the Soviet war potential and at the same time transform the most valuable parts of the Soviet Union into a modern "India" for German exploitation and colonization.

After weeks of heated dispute Hitler on August 21 overruled his protesting generals and ordered the transfer of the central army's Panzer divisions to the northern and southern armies. During the ensuing six weeks desperate attempts were made to complete the investment and reduction of Leningrad. These efforts proved unsuccessful, but in the south huge Soviet forces were cornered in Kiev. That key center fell on September 20, the Germans taking over half a million prisoners and immense booty. Hitler declared the victory "the greatest battle in world history" and promptly ordered the advance into the Donetz Basin. By the beginning of October the Germans were approaching Kharkov and Rostov and Soviet resistance in the south appeared more and more hopeless. On the other hand the Kremlin had been given what it needed most—further time to build up the forces to defend Moscow. On September 30, when Hitler ordered the return of the Panzer divisions to the central front, Marshal Timoshenko's position was infinitely better than it had been in mid-August. Furthermore, winter could not be long delayed and Hitler, failing a speedy and decisive victory, would either have to suspend operations or face the rigors of a campaign for which the German forces were not prepared and for which the engines of modern war were not well fitted.[1]

The British and Americans knew nothing of Nazi strategy beyond what could be deduced from day to day developments. They were, in fact, kept in the dark as to the military situation even by the Kremlin. So far as London or Washington could determine during the critical weeks of August and September, Hitler seemed unlikely to attain his objectives by October. On the other hand the Red armies were being constantly driven back, were losing huge numbers of men and vast quantities of equipment, and were being forced to abandon many of the economically most important regions of their country. Whether Hitler would elect to continue operations into the winter, whether the Soviets would be able to keep the field much longer, whether Stalin would persist in defense or decide to make another deal

---

[1] One of the best and most concise accounts is that of Kurt Assmann: *Deutsche Schicksalsjahre* (Wiesbaden, 1950), Chapter IX, which is a reprint of an article first published in *Foreign Affairs,* January, 1950. See also Herbert Rosinski: "Hitler's Strategy in Russia" (*Infantry Journal,* June, 1948); Erich Kordt: *Wahn und Wirklichkeit* (Stuttgart, 1947), Chapter XV; and B. H. Liddell Hart: *The German Generals Talk* (New York, 1948), Chapter XIII. Hitler's objectives in Russia appear from the record of the conference of July 16, 1941 (*Nazi Conspiracy and Aggression,* VII, L-221); Rudolf Semmler: *Goebbels, the Man Next to Hitler* (London, 1947), 52-53; and *Hitlers Tischgespräche* (Bonn, 1951).

with Hitler, these were all vital questions to which there was no prospect of obtaining adequate answers.

Following Mr. Harry Hopkins's visit to Moscow at the end of July, Mr. Churchill and Mr. Roosevelt had decided that the chances of continued Soviet resistance were sufficiently good to warrant a commitment to provide large-scale aid over a long term. They had notified Stalin of their decision and had proposed a conference at Moscow to discuss Soviet requirements and decide the apportionment of common resources. Stalin had replied with unwonted enthusiasm and had declared his readiness to do everything possible to facilitate the conference.[2]

When the President and the Prime Minister made their commitment, it was with full realization of all that was involved. Considering the state of British and American war production, it was clear that whatever munitions were allocated to Soviet Russia would have to come from British stocks and American supplies already assigned to the British. One can readily understand, therefore, that Mr. Churchill made his decision with a heavy heart and that the British Services felt it was all "like flaying off pieces of their skin."[3] Yet the game seemed worth the candle and the British Cabinet was prepared to make serious sacrifices on the theory succinctly stated by Mr. Churchill: "If the Russians stay in, it is worth it. If they quit, we don't have to send it."[4]

As though to make the British policy more difficult, the Soviets continued to show themselves, in Mr. Churchill's words, "surly, snarly, grasping," and in general seemed to take the attitude that their plight was the fault of the British. Even in the light of postwar developments the Churchill-Stalin correspondence of this period cannot fail to strike the reader as strange and wondrous. The British had despatched their first convoy to Murmansk on August 12 and were scraping the bottom of the barrel to provide a few hundred additional fighter planes for immediate use at the front. To the Prime Minister's message announcing this painful sacrifice, Stalin replied coldly that aid on this scale was quite inadequate in a conflict of such magnitude. The position of the Red armies, he pointed out, was deteriorating, chiefly because the Germans had been able to withdraw a further thirty or forty divisions from the west, to say nothing of large numbers of tanks and aircraft. The Germans considered the danger in the west a bluff and obviously hoped to defeat their adversaries one by one. The only remedy, as Stalin saw it, was to open a second front in the Balkans or in France before the end of the year, as well as to provide the Soviet Union with matériel to compensate for the loss or disruption of its war production facilities:

[2] Tel. to Steinhardt, August 13, 1941, and reply, August 15, 1941. See above, Chapter XXI, Section 3.

[3] Churchill: *The Grand Alliance*, 453.

[4] Churchill: *The Grand Alliance*, 453, 497.

30,000 tons of aluminum by the beginning of October and monthly delivery of some 400 airplanes and 500 tanks. Without such help the Soviet Union would "either suffer defeat or be weakened to such an extent that it will lose for a long period any capacity to render assistance to its allies by its actual operations on the fronts of the struggle against Hitlerism." Though Stalin recognized that his message might cause Mr. Churchill dismay, the Soviet Ambassador in London saw fit to enhance the dismay by using "language of vague import about the gravity of the occasion and the turning point character that would attach to our reply." "Although nothing in his language warranted the assumption," reported Mr. Churchill to President Roosevelt, "we could not exclude the impression that they might be thinking of separate terms."[5]

This ominous message was discussed at length by the Cabinet and the reply was explained to Ambassador Maisky in conference with Foreign Secretary Eden and the British Chiefs of Staff. In substance it stated that there was no possibility of British action in the west, except air action, before the onset of winter. Furthermore, there was no chance of opening a second front in the Balkans without the help of Turkey. Though the British would shrink from no exertions, "action, however well meant, leading only to costly fiascoes, would be no help to anyone but Hitler." The British, so Mr. Churchill's reply continued, would do everything possible to make good Soviet losses of matériel. He himself would cable President Roosevelt asking him to expedite the Moscow Conference and would try, even before the conference, to tell Stalin how many planes and tanks could be supplied him. The British were prepared to send one half the number required and hoped the United States would undertake to provide the other half. Meanwhile the British forces in the Middle East were being strengthened so as to strike a severe blow at the Germans and Italians in Libya. In a concurrent message to Sir Stafford Cripps, the Ambassador at Moscow, Mr. Churchill explained in detail why the Soviet demands for a second front were impracticable and pointed out that nothing Britain could do or could have done could affect the current battle: "neither sympathy nor emotion will overcome the kind of facts we have to face." The only possibility was to make provision for the operations of the coming year.[6]

Though due allowance be made for the fact that in September the plight of the Soviets was desperate, it is hard to understand how Stalin, after Mr. Churchill's frank explanations, could have cabled again (September 15) requesting the British to land twenty-five or thirty divisions at Archangel, or transport them to southern Russia by way of Iran. Such proposals were so patently beyond British capabilities that Mr. Churchill could describe them

[5] Full texts in Churchill: *The Grand Alliance,* 454-60. We have used also tels. from Winant, September 5 and 6, 1941.

[6] Churchill: *The Grand Alliance,* 458 ff.

only as "absurdities." On the other hand it was evidently impossible to convince Stalin that his British allies were doing as much as they could. Consequently relations between the two Governments continued to be highly unsatisfactory.

President Roosevelt's problem was of a somewhat different nature. He was kept fully informed of the Churchill-Stalin correspondence and should therefore have had few illusions about the partnership with the Kremlin. Indeed, Ambassador Oumansky had no compunctions about giving American officials a taste of the medicine administered to the British. The most important point at issue at the time was the financing of Soviet purchases of American supplies. Soviet funds in the United States were reaching the point of exhaustion and negotiations for a loan of five hundred million dollars were snagged on the legal requirements for adequate security. By mid-August things had reached such a pass that Secretary Morgenthau could save the situation only by purchasing ten million dollars' worth of Russian gold against delivery within ninety days.[7] But this was at best only a stopgap. Oumansky was bitter in his comments on the failure of the American Government to provide the needed funds, one way or another. Eventually the President, aided by Mr. Hopkins, himself took a hand in the matter. On September 11 he conferred with Oumansky in the presence of Secretary Hull and Mr. Hopkins, on which occasion arrangements were worked out to extend the Soviets a credit of $100,000,000, to be repaid through future shipments of Russian manganese, chromite, asbestos and platinum. It was hoped that this credit would suffice for the next couple of months, by which time the President expected to be able to extend the Lend-Lease aid for which Oumansky was now clamoring.[8]

Lend-Lease was the obvious answer to the Soviet financial problem and certainly the key to the program of large-scale aid which the President was planning to launch. Mr. Roosevelt was evidently favorably impressed by Mr. Hopkins's report of his talks with Stalin and was prepared to make specific and far-reaching commitments in the effort to sustain Soviet resistance. In his letter to Secretary Stimson calling for estimates of requirements to serve as a basis for the forthcoming Moscow discussions, he stated explicitly:

[7] Memo of conversation between Mr. Morgenthau and Ambassador Oumansky, August 15, 1941 (*Morgenthau Diaries, MS.,* Vol. 344, pp. 218 ff.); letter of Acting Secretary of the Treasury Gaston to the President, August 16, 1941 (*Roosevelt Papers: Secretary's File,* Box 76).

[8] Memo of conversation between Mr. Hull and Ambassador Oumansky, September 5, 1941; record of telephone conversation between Mr. Hopkins and Secretary Morgenthau, September 5, 1941 (*Morgenthau Diaries, MS.,* Vol. 438, p. 190); memo of Mr. Hopkins to the President, September 5, 1941 (*Roosevelt Papers:* Secretary's File, Box 76); memo of conversation between the President, Secretary Hull, Mr. Hopkins and Ambassador Oumansky, September 11, 1941. See also Hull: *Memoirs,* II, 976 ff., and Turner Catledge, in *The New York Times,* September 17 and 18, 1941. On the final arrangements we have used the *Morgenthau Diaries (MS.),* Vol. 440, pp. 168 ff.

I deem it to be of paramount importance for the safety and security of America that all reasonable munitions help be provided for Russia, not only immediately but as long as she continues to fight the Axis powers effectively. I am convinced that substantial and comprehensive commitments of such character must be made to Russia by Great Britain and the United States at the proposed conference.[9]

On the understanding that the munitions allocated to the Soviet Union would for the most part be taken from the supplies originally earmarked for the British, and not from production for American defense, the War Department supported the President's view without reservation, as may be seen from the passage dealing with Russia in the significant Joint Board estimate of September 11, 1941:

The maintenance of an active front in Russia offers by far the best opportunity for a successful land offensive against Germany, because only Russia possesses adequate manpower, situated in favorable proximity to the center of German military power. For Russia, ground and aviation forces are most important. Predictions as to the result of the present conflict in Russia are premature. However, were the Soviet forces to be driven even beyond the Ural Mountains, and were they to continue an organized resistance, there would always remain the hope of a final and complete defeat of Germany by land operations. The effective arming of Russian forces, both by the supply of munitions from the outside and by providing industrial capacity in the Volga Basin, or to the east of the Ural Mountains, would be one of the most important moves that could be made by the Associated Powers.[10]

It was plain enough that aid to the Soviet Union on the scale envisaged could not be paid for in cash. Yet popular opposition to support of the Kremlin was so strong and widespread that the extension of Lend-Lease aid seemed hardly feasible. The isolationist press, which included some of the most important newspaper chains and a number of the most influential columnists, was loud in its protests against such a policy. The *New York Journal-American,* for example, wrote on September 5, 1941:

If we are fighting against totalitarianism as a foul and oppressive policy, why in the name of high heaven should we not desire to see the two totalitarian powers exterminate each other and destroy not only the principle but the practice of despotic government? . . . Is our free country piling up deficits, bleeding its citizens white with confiscatory taxation, rushing headlong into national bankruptcy, shovelling out our wealth abroad, and shipping our war materials to alien nations to bolster Bolshevism in Russia, to spread it over all Europe including Britain, and to breed it and broadcast it in our own America? We may not think that this is what we want to do, but this is exactly what we are doing with our Bolshevist Alliance and no smoke screen of fine phrases can obscure that outstanding fact.

[9] Letter of the President to Secretary Stimson, August 30, 1941, printed in full in Watson: *Chief of Staff: Prewar Plans and Preparations* (Washington, 1950), 348-49, and in *F.D.R.: His Personal Letters* (New York, 1950), II, 1201-3.
[10] Quoted in Robert E. Sherwood: *Roosevelt and Hopkins* (New York, 1948), 417.

Similarly the *Chicago Tribune* wrote (September 17): "The Nazi-Communist War is the only one of the last century that civilized men can regard with complete approval. They hope it will persist until both brutal antagonists have bled to death. To talk of aiding either of the contestants is treachery to the American people. They are equally our enemies, and the enemies of all free men." Former President Hoover summed up the opposition attitude when he delivered an address at Chicago on September 17:

I hold, and ninety-nine percent of Americans hold, that totalitarianism, whether Nazism or Communism, is abominable.

Both forms are unmoral because they deny religion and there is no sanctity of agreement with them.

They are abhorrent because of their unspeakable cruelty and their callous slaughter of millions of human beings.

I abhor any American compromise or alliance with either of them. . . .

Russia is rightly defending herself against aggression. But when it comes to sending our sons into this war we are confronted with something else. We need to take a long look. Russia is also an aggressor nation against democracies. And what happens to millions of enslaved people of Russia and to all Europe and to our own freedoms if we should send our sons to win this war for communism?

The worst aspect of the situation, from the viewpoint of the Administration, was the fact that religious groups, particularly Roman Catholic groups, supported the isolationist position on aid to Soviet Russia. Mr. Roosevelt felt impelled to overcome the religious opposition if possible, and must have deeply regretted the oversight committed when freedom of religion was left unmentioned in the Atlantic Charter. It may be assumed that it was at his request that Justice Frank Murphy, a prominent Catholic layman, addressed the Supreme Council of the Knights of Columbus (August 19) and attempted to explode the idea that the Nazi attack on Soviet Russia was a crusade against communism. Mr. Justice Murphy made much of the violently anti-Christian doctrine and policy of the Nazi Government. While conceding that for the adherents of Christianity and democracy there was little to choose between Nazism and communism, he added: "We know that Nazism, with its superior competence and perverted intelligence, its extraordinary energy and missionary zeal, its profound belief in racial superiority and destiny, its fanatical intolerance and, above all, its tremendous military power and skill, is by far the greatest menace to free nations and free institutions." He therefore concluded that "in present circumstances any nation resisting the might and aggression of Nazi Germany is, whether intentionally or not, advancing our interest as well as its own."

Such arguments left journals like the *Brooklyn Tablet* and *Social Justice* completely cold. Irreconcilable Catholic elements continued to take their stand squarely on the encyclical of Pius XI (*Divini Redemptoris*), which declared communism intrinsically wrong and forbade collaboration with it in any undertaking whatsoever. Members of the Catholic hierarchy who supported the President's policy were in despair and urged constant emphasis on the fact that aid to Soviet Russia in no sense implied approval or support of communism. The only real solution of the problem, as they saw it, would be for His Holiness himself to make an announcement explaining his predecessor's position.[11]

Apparently Mr. Roosevelt had already decided to send Mr. Myron Taylor on a second mission to the Vatican to enlist the Pope's support for the Atlantic Charter and at the same time explain the necessity for assisting Communist Russia. Mr. Taylor's attention had been called to the fact that Article 124 of the Soviet Constitution of 1936 provided guarantees of freedom of religion and suggested that it "should be quite easy for your mission [to Moscow] to persuade Mr. Stalin to make some kind of declaration quoting Article 124, which could be broadcast all over the world, and might change opinions on this question in some places."[12] Here, then, were two possible lines of approach to the problem of reconciling Catholic opinion to the policy regarded by the President as vital.

The instructions to Mr. Taylor are of interest as an elucidation of the President's thought in proclaiming the Atlantic Charter and are therefore worth summarizing. The American envoy was to stress disarmament: "I put this first in a postwar world because German, Italian and Japanese official policy and also psychology places control of other nations and peoples on the basis of armed force." Mr. Roosevelt admitted that disarmament might take years, possibly generations, to achieve by voluntary methods and therefore argued: "Hence, for some time, the nonaggressor nations must be in a position to enforce nonaggression by the Axis Powers." Secondly, "the self-determination of boundaries and forms of government was the most substantial contribution made by the Versailles Treaty—i.e., the plebiscite method which, on the whole, was successful," and could therefore be extended and developed so as to eliminate war. Thirdly, "in world economics the thought is that freedom to trade in all parts of the world will encourage self-sufficiency and a greater general prosperity . . . and assure general access to the necessary raw materials of the world." Fourthly, "with practically no thought of restoring the mandate principle adopted at Versailles, it seems possible to substitute the trustee principle. . . . In the present complete world confusion, it is not thought advisable at this time to reconstitute a League of Nations which, because of its size, makes for disagreement and inaction. There should be a meeting place of the nations for the purpose of full discussion, but for management there seems no reason

[11] Letter of Mr. Welles to the President, reporting his conversation with two Catholic prelates, August 25, 1941 (*Roosevelt Papers:* Secretary's File, Box 76); memo of Mr. Myron Taylor to the President, August 30, 1941 (*ibid.*).

[12] Memo from Mr. Taylor to the President, August 30, 1941, as cited above.

why the principle of trusteeship in private affairs should not be extended to the international field."

"In all of this," continued the instruction to Mr. Taylor, "freedom of religion and freedom of expression are necessary parts. The objectives are based on the teachings of the New Testament, and call for spiritual leadership." In the case of Russia, the attack on the churches in 1918 was aimed chiefly at removing the Church from politics: "It is worth noting that our best information is that Russian churches are today open for worship and are being attended by a very large percentage of the population." In conclusion the instructions read: "The President is definitely bearing in mind the possibility of persuading the Government of Russia ultimately to accept freedom of religion—but it must be remembered that the Russian Government is essentially a dictatorship, and that Russia is defending its own soil. At the present time Russia is in no sense the aggressor nation—Germany is."[13]

Mr. Taylor was the bearer of a personal letter from the President to the Pope, a letter devoted exclusively to the problem presented by Soviet Russia and the Kremlin's attitude toward religion. Since it was drafted by Mr. Roosevelt personally, it may well be quoted at length:

In so far as I am informed, churches in Russia are open. I believe there is a real possibility that Russia may as a result of the present conflict recognize freedom of religion in Russia, although, of course, without recognition of any official intervention on the part of any church in education or political matters within Russia. I feel that if this can be accomplished it will put the possibility of the restoration of real religious liberty in Russia on a much better footing than religious freedom is in Germany today.

There are in the United States many people in *all* churches who have the feeling that Russia is governed completely by a communistic form of society. In my opinion, the fact is that Russia is governed by a dictatorship, as rigid in its manner of being as is the dictatorship in Germany. I believe, however, that this Russian dictatorship is less dangerous to the safety of other nations than is the German form of dictatorship. The only weapon which the Russian dictatorship uses outside its own borders is communist propaganda which I, of course, recognize has in the past been utilized for the purpose of breaking down the form of government in other countries, religious belief, et cetera. Germany, however, not only has utilized, but is utilizing, this kind of propaganda as well and has also undertaken the employment of every form of military aggression outside of its borders for the purpose of world conquest by force of arms and by force of propaganda. I believe that the survival of Russia is less dangerous to religion, to the church as such, and to humanity in general than would be the survival of the German form of dictatorship. Furthermore, it is my belief that the leaders of all churches in the United States should recognize these facts clearly and should not close their eyes to these basic questions and by their present attitude on this question directly assist Germany in her present objectives.[14]

[13] Memo from the President to Mr. Taylor, September 1, 1941 (*Roosevelt Papers: Secretary's File, Box 76*).

[14] Letter of the President to Pope Pius XII, September 3, 1941 (printed in full in

Mr. Taylor presented the President's message to the Holy Father on September 9 and during the ensuing days had several further conferences with both His Holiness and the Papal Secretary of State. He explained at length the American position with regard to the war, stressing the fact that the American people could not and would not permit the victory of Hitlerism. He transmitted also the President's comments on the Atlantic Charter and requested the Pope to make a declaration supporting it. This His Holiness agreed to do as soon as a fitting occasion presented itself. The main issue, however, was the Soviet problem, with particular reference to the attitude of the Catholic Church toward aid to the Soviet Union. Mr. Taylor argued that the encyclical of Pius XI was clearly not intended to condemn the Russian people, but only Soviet attacks on individual liberties. He enlarged on the condition of the Russian people under the Tsarist regime and on their probable fate should the Nazis conquer them. Now that religion had been divorced from the state, he continued, the Russian people might welcome a religious revival in which the Catholic Church might play a part. In any case he pleaded with His Holiness to issue an interpretation of the troublesome encyclical.

The American emissary felt that his reasoning produced a "sympathetic reaction" and had "a definitely heartening effect upon the Pope." It is hardly likely, however, that the Holy Father was fully convinced by the President's letter or by Mr. Taylor's explanations. He certainly knew, as did Mr. Roosevelt and Mr. Taylor, that if the Soviet Constitution accorded religious freedom, it also recognized full freedom for antireligious propaganda. He must surely have been aware also that the churches in Russia were not "open" in the usual sense of the term, and that of the non-Orthodox churches those that were "open" could be readily counted on the fingers of one hand. Even though he may have agreed that for the moment Nazism was stronger than communism, he probably considered that communism, if victorious, would be as great if not a greater menace to religion. To quote the prophetic remarks of a high Papal official to Mr. Taylor.

If the war now in progress were to mean the end of both dangers, a period of tranquillity would be possible for Europe. If even one of these evils—Communism, for example—were to remain an active force, Europe would, within a few years, be in a situation identical with that in which it finds itself today. In fact, Communism, once victorious, would find no further resistance in Continental Europe and would spread among the Germanic peoples, the Slav races and finally among the Latins. In consequence, within the space of a few years there would be an enormous Communistic

Wartime Correspondence between President Roosevelt and Pope Pius XII [New York, 1947], 61 ff., and in *F.D.R.: His Personal Letters*, 1204-5). A memo from Mr. Welles to Mr. Atherton, August 29, 1941, transmitted the President's draft, which was almost identical with the final text.

bloc, whose inevitable destiny would be to provoke a war with England and America, regarded by the Communists as a capitalistic bloc.[15]

Nevertheless, the Holy Father decided to comply with the President's request to the extent of sending the Apostolic Delegate in Washington an interpretation of the encyclical *Divini Redemptoris* in the sense suggested by Mr. Taylor. The effect was soon noticeable, as prominent members of the Catholic hierarchy began to advance the argument that the encyclical, far from condemning the Russian people, actually expressed affection for them. The United States, they reasoned, was not aiding communism, but was supporting the Russian people. Even though communism might profit thereby, the policy was a laudable one and the evil would have to be taken with the good.[16]

Concurrently with Mr. Taylor's discussions at the Vatican, Mr. Roosevelt was pursuing another tack by raising the issue in conversation with Ambassador Oumansky (September 11). In reply to the Ambassador's plea for Lend-Lease aid, Mr. Roosevelt explained in some detail "the extreme difficulty of getting the necessary authority from Congress on account of the prejudice or hostility to Russia and the unpopularity of Russia among large groups in this country who exercise great political power in Congress." He then suggested that the Soviet Government itself do something to alleviate this antagonism: "He suggested that if Moscow could get some publicity back to this country regarding the freedom of religion during the next few days without waiting for the Harriman Mission to reach Moscow, it might have a very fine educational effect before the next Lend-Lease Bill comes up in Congress."[17] The Ambassador promised to raise the question with his Government, but nothing further was heard from him and the President was therefore obliged to rely on the Harriman Mission to further the good cause. Meanwhile Mr. Roosevelt felt it altogether unwise to broach the issue of Lend-Lease for the Soviet Union. Mr. Hopkins waxed indignant and even profane at the thought that extensive promises might be made to the Kremlin without any real prospect of honoring them because of financial considerations. But not even Mr. Hopkins could move the President, who kept insisting that he "could not handle it now on the

[15] Report of Mr. Taylor to the President, September 21, 1941, transmitted to the President by Mr. Welles with a letter of September 28, 1941, the date of receipt by special State Department courier. We have used also tels. from Mr. Taylor to the President, September 10 and 16, 1941, and a letter from Mr. Tittman to Mr. Welles, October 7, 1941. The Pope's reply to the President's letter, dated September 20, 1941, revealed nothing of his views. For the full text see *Wartime Correspondence between President Roosevelt and Pope Pius XII,* 63 ff.

[16] This note was first sounded by a long editorial in the *Florida Catholic* of September 26, 1941, and was later openly proclaimed in a pastoral letter by Archbishop McNicholas of Cincinnati, October 30, 1941. These and other records bearing on the subject are assembled in the *Roosevelt Papers:* Official File, 220-26.

[17] Memo of conversation between the President, Secretary Hull, Mr. Hopkins, and Ambassador Oumansky, September 11, 1941.

Hill." Pending a change in public opinion he discerned nothing better than a devious course of procedure. An amendment had been offered to the second Lend-Lease bill, then before Congress, which prohibited explicitly the use of Lend-Lease funds for aid to Russia. If this amendment could be defeated, it would be possible to cite its rejection as proof of the intent of Congress not to debar the Soviet Union from the benefits of the program. But this, too, was still in the future. Mr. Harriman, despite protests that he would be seriously handicapped at the Moscow Conference unless he had detailed instructions as to the financing of the projected aid to Soviet Russia, was obliged to set out on his mission empowered to make vast commitments but utterly unable to state how payment was to be arranged.

2. THE TURKISH BULWARK

The Nazi campaign against Soviet Russia immediately enhanced the importance of Turkey and Iran to all the combatants. If Hitler were able to enlist the support of the Turks against their traditional Russian enemy, the Nazi drive into the Ukraine and in the direction of the Caucasus oil fields could be reinforced by a concerted Turkish advance through Armenia to join forces with the German divisions. Furthermore, alliance with the Turks, even if they remained militarily inactive, would ensure the Germans against British operations, especially air operations, from the Middle East and would eventually enable Hitler to stage a campaign against Egypt by way of Anatolia and Syria. The diary notes of General Halder, the Nazi Chief of Staff, reveal the profound anxiety of the Germans about the position of the Turks. The Nazi High Command attached immense importance to Turkish participation in the war against Soviet Russia, partly in order to block the British, partly in order to relieve the German forces in south Russia, and partly to provide eventual passage for an advance on Egypt.[18]

In the spring of 1941 the Ankara Government had been so impressed by the spectacular Nazi conquest of the Balkans and by the huge concentration of German forces in Bulgaria that it had yielded to Hitler's pressure to the extent of signing a treaty of friendship and nonaggression. This treaty, under which the Turks reserved their obligations to the British as laid down in the alliance of October, 1939, was certainly less than the Fuehrer wanted, but was as much as he could get unless he were willing to jeopardize his plans for the Russian campaign by diverting large forces to the conquest of Turkey.[19] Pending the defeat of the Red armies during the succeeding six months Hitler and his generals, while constantly speculating on the desirability of Turkish participation, were all too painfully aware that Ankara would continue to temporize. For the present they could not afford to

[18] *Halder Diary*, July 9, 13, September 11, 1941. On the German plans see also Churchill: *The Grand Alliance*, 553-54, and *Ciano's Diplomatic Papers*, 460 ff. (discussions with Hitler on November 24-27, 1941).

[19] See above, Chapter XVI, Section 3.

employ military force to compel Turkish coöperation. Failing to win the Turks by political promises, they could only make the best of what was for them a thoroughly unsatisfactory situation.[20]

Mr. Churchill and his colleagues understood the position and attitude of Ankara and did their best to persuade their skeptical American friends of the loyalty of the Turks to the anti-Nazi cause. In principle the Prime Minister would have been delighted to have the Turkish Government throw in its lot with the British but he realized that in that case the British would have to commit to Turkey's support men and matériel they could ill spare. He rightly believed that the Germans would be unwilling to take military action against the Turks until the Red armies had been vanquished and therefore held it most immediately important to strengthen the Turks and so induce them to resist Nazi political pressure. To quote one of his messages to Mr. Roosevelt: "We do not require Turkey to enter the war aggressively at the present moment, but only to maintain a stolid, unyielding front to German threats and blandishments. As long as Turkey is not violated or seduced, this great oblong pad of poorly developed territory is an impassable protection for the eastern flank of our Nile Army."[21]

In accordance with this strategy Mr. Churchill induced the Kremlin to join in the note to Ankara of August 10, 1941, which promised respect for Turkey's territorial integrity and even stated that "the two powers would be prepared to send Turkey every help and assistance in the event of her being attacked by a European power." Furthermore, the British transferred to the Turks a share of the Lend-Lease munitions supplied them by the United States and, in September, 1941, engaged to send four divisions and one armored brigade as well as four to twelve squadrons of fighter planes to aid in resisting a Nazi attack if such occurred after December 1, 1941, by which time it was hoped the British would have driven Rommel from Libya and would be able to commit part of the Nile Army elsewhere.[22]

Unfortunately the American Government, despite its conversion to the British view of the importance of the Middle East, continued to have compunctions about supporting the Turks. Neither Ambassador MacMurray nor the British Embassy had succeeded in dispelling the distrust which the State Department felt after the conclusion of the German-Turkish treaty of friendship of June 18, 1941. It was only with great reluctance that Wash-

---

[20] *Halder Diary*, September 11, 1941 (memo of the German High Command).

[21] Mr. Churchill's message to the President, October 20, 1941 (full text in Churchill: *The Grand Alliance*, 546). Much the same ideas were expressed in Mr. Churchill's letter to the Australian Prime Minister, September 7, 1941; in his letters to Stalin, September 17 and 21, 1941; in his memo to the Chief of Staff, September 18, 1941; and in his letter to Field Marshal Smuts, September 20, 1941 (*The Grand Alliance*, 464, 467, 496, 497, 846 ff.). In this connection see also the despatch of General Sir Claude Auchinleck: *Operations in the Middle East, 5 July-31 October, 1941*, dated March 8, 1942 (Supplement to the *London Gazette*, August 20, 1946).

[22] Churchill: *The Grand Alliance*, 536, 546, 846 ff.

ington agreed to the provision of aid by the British from American Lend-Lease supplies. Repeated efforts on the part of London to secure a higher priority for Turkish requirements were firmly rejected.[23] Eventually, and as though to reinforce the viewpoint of the State Department, it became known in September that Dr. Clodius, chief trade negotiator of the Nazi Government, had arrived in Ankara to discuss a new economic deal with the Turkish authorities. His mission was of particular importance since he was intent on arranging the sale of Turkish chrome to the German Government. The Turks had bound themselves to sell their entire production of this essential strategic material to the British and French at least until the end of 1942. It soon transpired that Clodius was attempting to induce the Ankara Government to assign to the Germans that share of their production which was to have gone to the French. The Turks refused but, after long and involved negotiations, agreed to sell the Germans ninety thousand tons of chrome in 1943. This was the most important item in the trade agreement concluded on October 9, 1941.

Once again the British took a sympathetic attitude, realizing that the Turks could not afford to be uncompromising and judging that much water would flow over the dam before 1943. By and large they considered the Clodius mission a failure and British correspondents in Ankara celebrated the Nazi emissary's departure by singing "Chrome, sweet chrome" in the coffeehouses.[24] But the Americans, even the perspicacious Ambassador Mac-Murray, took the matter much to heart. MacMurray complained of the "levity" of the Turks in taking all they could get, as though by right. He thought his Government should, in the future, make aid to the Turks conditional on an explicit understanding that Ankara would in a crisis make common cause with the democracies.[25]

As a result there were more disputes between London and Washington until finally the State Department agreed that everything possible should be done to hold the Turks in line. Even so, there was continued argument about procedure. The Lend-Lease Administration, for bookkeeping if for no other reasons, was insistent that American supplies to Turkey be handled directly through the usual channels. The British, on the other hand, pleaded that Turkish requirements should be viewed in the larger Middle Eastern context and pointed out that they could not hope to maintain their position in Ankara unless they could appear as the purveyors of American munitions. Ultimately Secretary Hull was brought to admit that American policy "was based on the general proposition that such steps should be taken as would give the British the maximum of influence in regard to Turkey, if and when

[23] Tel. from MacMurray, August 25, 1941; tel. to MacMurray, August 30, 1941; memo of conversation between Mr. Welles and Sir Ronald Campbell, August 27, 1941.
[24] Sir Hughe Knatchbull-Hugessen: *Diplomat in Peace and War* (London, 1949), 172.
[25] Tel. from MacMurray, October 15, 1941.

a Turkish-German crisis threatened," and that therefore it was nonsensical to make an issue of ways and means. The previous arrangements were therefore reaffirmed, except for the provision that in future the State Department should notify Ankara of what was being done by America in its behalf. Prior to the American involvement in the war, then, the Turks maintained their precarious neutrality, their alliance with Britain, and their "friendship" with Nazi Germany. Pending a German victory over Russia no acute crisis was anticipated and the British were enabled to employ this providential breathing spell to equip the Turkish Army with American supplies and so prepare it for effective resistance in the event of a Nazi attack.[26]

3. The Occupation of Iran

The Turks were able to impose circumspection on both the Germans and the British because they were intensely patriotic and fully determined to resist aggression, and because they had a substantial army which, though not modernized, was recognized as a valiant and formidable fighting force. Iran, the gateway to the Caucasus from the south, could boast no such potential. A vast country, still predominantly feudal, it was governed autocratically by a corrupt ruler and was notoriously powerless to resist aggression. The Teheran Government, like that of Ankara, had been trying to maintain rigid neutrality with respect to the European War, but the British had long been uneasy about the important oil fields in southwestern Iran, which were controlled by the Anglo-Iranian Oil Company and constituted one of the most important sources of oil supply to the British Fleet and military forces. The Iranian ruler, Reza Shah Pahlevi, suspicious alike of British and Soviet interest in his country, had long looked to the Germans for technical and other aid. This Hitler had been only too ready to provide. Germans had taken a leading part in the construction of the important Trans-Iranian Railway, running from the Persian Gulf in the south to the Caspian coast in the north. They had likewise played a prominent role in developing industry and trade, with the result that by 1939 Iran's trade with Germany exceeded that with any other country. As technical advisers or under the guise of tourists some two thousand Germans had established themselves in the country. It is therefore understandable that the British were apprehensive of fifth column activities, directed either at seizure of the

[26] Memo of conversation between Mr. Hull and Lord Halifax, October 22, 1941, with an attached restatement of the British position; record of a meeting between members of the Near East Division of the State Department and members of the British Embassy, October 24, 1941; memo from Mr. Wallace Murray to Mr. Welles, October 28, 1941; record of a second meeting of State Department officials with members of the British Embassy, November 4, 1941; tel. to MacMurray, November 25, 1941; memo of the Near East Division reviewing the American policy toward Turkey, November 25, 1941.

Government or at sabotage of the vital Iranian oil wells and the huge re-
finery at Abadan.[27]

The British Government had protested and warned against German
activity as early as February, 1941, but to no avail. Meanwhile the pro-Nazi
uprising in Iraq in May, 1941, reëmphasized the danger and suggested the
extent to which German subversive action in Iran might go. Rashid Ali
Gailani, leader of the Iraq rebellion, as well as the Grand Mufti of Jerusalem, pro-Nazi antagonist of the British among the Arabs, took refuge in
Teheran, where the popular attitude became increasingly sympathetic to
Germany as Hitler added his Balkan victories to earlier conquests. Once the
Nazis had turned on Soviet Russia there was every reason to suppose that
they would stage a coup in Iran and use that country as a base for attack
on the Caucasus. In that event it was unlikely that Turkey would be able
to maintain its neutrality. As early as July 10, 1941, General Wavell had
warned his Government that failure to clear the Germans out of Iran would
mean a repetition of the Iraqi affair: "It is essential we should join hands
with Russia through Iran, and if the present Government is not willing to
facilitate this, it must be made to give way to one which will."[28]

British interests in Iran were so patent that Mr. Churchill scarcely needed
instruction. In addition to forestalling a possible Nazi coup in Teheran and
safeguarding the Anglo-Iranian oil fields, the Prime Minister thought it of
highest importance to ensure control of the Trans-Iranian Railway as one
of the most practicable routes for the supply of the Soviet armies, and to
establish contact with Soviet Russia so as to aid militarily in the defense of
the Caucasus if the German advance were pressed that far. Since these
interests in large measure coincided with those of the Kremlin, the British
Government met no difficulty in arranging for joint action. On July 16,
immediately following the conclusion of the Anglo-Soviet "alliance," the
two powers submitted parallel notes to Teheran, demanding the expulsion
of the Germans by September 15. But again they obtained no satisfaction.
The Shah's Government contended that the number of Germans in the
country had been grossly exaggerated, that German activities were being
carefully watched, that there was no danger whatever of a fifth column move,
and that, finally, the Iranian Government, intending to observe strict neutrality, could not take the action desired. Although the Shah's Government
appears to have removed a certain number of Germans on its own initiative,
it refused to assume any obligation toward Britain and Russia.[29]

[27] Thomas P. Brockway: "The Purge of Iran" (*Current History*, October, 1941);
Edwin M. Wright: "Iran as a Gateway to Russia" (*Foreign Affairs*, January, 1942);
and the excellent accounts in L. P. Elwell-Sutton: *Modern Iran* (London, 1941) and
in George Lenczowski: *Russia and the West in Iran* (Ithaca, 1949), 152 ff. A. H.
Hamzawi: *Persia and the Powers* (London, n.d.) contributes little on these matters.

[28] Tel. of General Wavell to the Foreign Office, July 10, 1941 (Churchill: *The Grand
Alliance*, 477).

[29] Official statement of the Iranian Government, July 31, 1941, in *Bulletin of Inter-*

The Iranian reply, no doubt substantially what was expected, provided the British and Soviets with an excuse to employ force and thereby secure a measure of control over the country far beyond anything that would have been achieved by the mere expulsion of the Germans. There was, however, the danger that military action might be resisted and that in the process the Iranian oil fields be destroyed. The first objective of the British was therefore the occupation of the Kuzistan region in the south. The decision to act was taken on July 24 and the concentration of troops in Iraq was begun immediately, to be completed by mid-August. By August 13 Foreign Secretary Eden and Soviet Ambassador Maisky had reached agreement on the text of a new note to Teheran. Since its rejection was fully expected, the new note was probably intended chiefly as the prelude to invasion.[30]

By this time Washington had become deeply concerned about the Iranian situation. Initially there had been disturbing reports of an impending division of the country into British and Soviet spheres, and more particularly of Soviet demands for control of the northern provinces.[31] Not until August 8 did the British confide their plans to the American Ambassador. Reviewing recent developments and stressing the urgent need for the expulsion of the Germans from this critical area, Mr. Eden permitted Ambassador Winant to read the proposed Anglo-Soviet note to Teheran and assured him that both the British and Soviet Governments would give assurances of respect for the independence and integrity of Iran. Thereupon he advanced the suggestion that the United States use its influence to induce the Shah to accept the Anglo-Soviet note as just and necessary, and that Washington indicate to the Turkish Government that it approved the action against Iran. Knowing that Ankara, deeply suspicious of Soviet designs, would not relish the presence of Red forces on its eastern frontiers, London and Moscow had already arranged to submit to the Turks the note of August 10, 1941, repudiating all aggressive intentions, promising respect for Turkish independence and integrity, and even promising to aid Turkey in the event of an attack by the Nazis.[32]

Ambassador Winant's telegram came as a distinct shock to the State Department, which rightly suspected that the impending Anglo-Soviet demand for the expulsion of the Germans was merely a blind for military action to secure control of the country. The situation, awkward at best, was particularly embarrassing in view of the President's plan to issue a

---

national News, XVIII (2), 1050. These developments were reviewed at length in a long memorandum of November 1, 1941, prepared by Harold B. Minor of the American Embassy at Teheran.

[30] Churchill: *The Grand Alliance,* 478-80, and the despatch of General Sir Archibald P. Wavell: *Operations in Iraq, East Syria and Iran,* dated October 18, 1942 (Supplement to the *London Gazette,* August 13, 1946).

[31] Tel. to Ankara, July 4, 1941, inquiring about these reports; tel. from Van Engert, July 18, 1941, reporting alleged Soviet demands.

[32] Tel. from Winant, August 8, 1941.

declaration of high principles, to be discussed at the Atlantic Conference. The Near East Division of the Department therefore counseled caution and urged Secretary Hull not to jeopardize the high prestige of the United States in Iran without first securing further light on Anglo-Soviet intentions. To this end the American representative at Teheran was instructed to provide additional information.[33]

There is no evidence that the Iranian problem was discussed by Mr. Roosevelt and Mr. Churchill during their famous meeting at Argentia, though it seems hardly likely that it should have been wholly ignored. In any event nothing was done to modify or defer the Anglo-Soviet plans. Without active American support the two powers submitted their note to Teheran on August 17 and four days later received the anticipated unsatisfactory reply. The movement of troops, intended to take place immediately, was somewhat delayed by lack of adequate Soviet preparation, but on August 25 forty thousand Soviet troops began the occupation of the north, while nineteen thousand British (mostly Indian) troops moved in from the west and south. At the same time explanatory notes were handed the Iranian Government. The British note confined itself to discussion of the danger of German activity, not only to Britain and Soviet Russia, but to Iran itself. Reviewing past efforts to impress this danger on the Shah's Government, it set forth the need for solving the problem by other means. Teheran was assured that the British Government had "no designs against the independence and territorial integrity of Iran, and any measures they may take will be directed solely against the attempts of the Axis Powers to establish their control of Iran." The Soviet note, on the other hand, was a much longer and more detailed document. It consisted of a survey of Soviet-Iranian relations since the conclusion of the treaty of 1921 and of an analysis of German plans and activities, with much factual information or allegation. After a restatement of earlier efforts to deal with the problem, the Soviet note announced its military measures and attempted to justify them on the basis of Article VI of the 1921 treaty. It stated in conclusion that

These measures are in no wise directed against the Iranian people. The Soviet Government has no designs on the territorial integrity and state independence of Iran. The military measures taken by the Soviet Government are directed solely and exclusively against the danger created by the hostile activity of the Germans in Iran. As soon as this danger threatening the interests of Iran and of the USSR has been removed, the Soviet Government, in discharge of its obligations under the Soviet-Iranian Treaty of 1921, will at once withdraw the Soviet troops from the confines of Iran.[34]

[33] Memos of the Near East Division, August 13 and 16, 1941; tel. to Dreyfus (Teheran), August 16, 1941.

[34] For the full texts of these notes see *Documents on American Foreign Relations*, IV, 674 ff., and *Soviet Foreign Policy during the Patriotic War*, I, 89 ff. They are discussed at some length by Lenczowski: *Russia and the West in Iran*, 170 ff. On the military

The military occupation of Iran put the State Department in a serious quandary, the more so as reports were being allowed to circulate in London that Washington fully approved the Anglo-Soviet action.[35] It was difficult to subscribe to this action, for Minister Dreyfus reported from Teheran that while the danger of Nazi fifth column activity was real, the Shah's Government was simply too weak to control the Germans and resented being "pushed around" by the British. Furthermore, the Minister was convinced that the real reason for the invasion was "the overwhelming military necessity" of establishing contact between the British and the Soviets.[36] Mr. Churchill's postwar memoirs leave no doubt whatever that this was so, yet at the time Mr. Eden was still insisting to Ambassador Winant that British fears of German activity were genuine and that Teheran's replies to the Anglo-Soviet notes were being inspired by the German representative.[37]

Whatever the circumstances, the State Department was confronted with the dilemma of upholding the principles so recently restated in the Atlantic Charter and at the same time avoiding anything that might obstruct the British-Soviet war effort. Even before the initiation of military action the Iranian Minister had asked Secretary Hull in so many words what the United States was disposed to do to prevent such "aggression." Mr. Hull, obviously embarrassed, could reply only that his Government could not discuss hypothetical situations, but that in any event the British were intent only on defending themselves against Nazi aggression.[38] Once the Anglo-Soviet action was under way it was hard to know which way to turn. The Near East Division proposed that a rather pointed telegram be sent to London suggesting that the British, instead of resting their case on the presence of the Germans in Iran, attempt to persuade Teheran of their urgent military requirements and perhaps offer Iran an alliance. It was even thought that London might arrange for a purely British occupation, thus sparing the Iranians the tribulations deemed inevitable under Soviet control.[39]

This proposal can hardly be said to have offered a practicable solution. In any event it came too late to be useful. Mr. Welles noted, in a memorandum to the Secretary: "With all sympathy for the situation of the Iranian Government and much as I regret what might appear to be precipitate action on the part of the British Government, I question the wisdom or expediency of sending such a message as this." It may be assumed that the

operations see Wavell's despatch, as cited above, and the official British history: *PAI Force: the Official Story of the Persia and Iraq Command* (London, 1948).

[35] Tel. to Winant, August 23, 1941; tels. from Winant, August 24, 1941.

[36] Tel. from Dreyfus, August 21, 1941.

[37] Tel. from Winant, August 23, 1941. On British motives see especially Churchill: *The Grand Alliance*, 476 ff., 483.

[38] Memo of conversation between Mr. Hull and the Iranian Minister, August 22, 1941.

[39] Memo of the Near East Division, with attached draft tel. to London, August 25, 1941.

Administration, deeply committed to the British cause, would have been content to accept the accomplished fact with as little commotion as possible, had not the situation been further complicated at this point by a personal protest and appeal addressed by the Shah to the President:

Your Excellency has surely been informed that the Russian and British forces have crossed brusquely and without previous notice the boundaries of this country, occupying certain localities and bombarding a considerable number of cities which were open and without defense. The old pretext which the Russian and British Governments raised consisted in the concern which those countries claimed to feel because of the sojourn of certain Germans in Iran, despite the assurances given by my Government that those Germans will soon leave Iran. No subject for concern could longer exist and I no longer can see for what reason they proceeded to those acts of aggression and to bombarding our cities without reason. I consider it my duty, on the basis of the declarations which Your Excellency has made several times regarding the necessity of defending principles of international justice and the rights of peoples to liberty, to request Your Excellency to be good enough to interest yourself in this incident, which brings into war a neutral and pacific country which has had no other care than the safeguarding of tranquillity and the reform of the country. I beg Your Excellency to take efficacious and urgent humanitarian steps to put an end to these acts of aggression. Being assured of the sentiments of good will of Your Excellency, I renew to you the assurance of my sincere friendship.[40]

This appeal was exactly what Mr. Hull called it: "A red-hot iron." It was debated at length in the Department on the morning of August 26, on which occasion the Near East Division urged that even at this late hour the endeavor be made to induce the British to negotiate with the Iranians so as to secure their friendly collaboration and, if possible, their agreement to an alliance for common defense. Mr. Welles, on the other hand, took the stand that the United States should at all costs avoid interference. At most, he thought, the British should be notified of the Shah's appeal and asked whether the United States could be of assistance in resolving the difficulty. Eventually it was agreed to follow still another tack, namely, to suggest to Teheran that it attempt to arrive at an amicable settlement with the British, and at the same time to inquire of London whether it were true that the British and Russians had at no time made an effort to secure the friendly coöperation of the Shah's Government; what were the precise measures which the British proposed to take in implementation of their general guarantee of Iranian independence and integrity; what were British and Russian intentions with regard to the extent of military occupation; what assurances had the British secured for the protection of the upper classes in Soviet-occupied territory; whether, if Teheran showed a disposition to meet British requirements, London could induce the Soviets to withdraw their forces?[41]

[40] Tel. from Shah Reza Pahlevi to the President, August 25, 1941; tel. from Dreyfus, August 25, 1941; memo of conversation between Mr. Wallace Murray and the Iranian Minister, August 26, 1941.
[41] Memo by Mr. Wallace Murray, August 26, 1941.

On the basis of these State Department deliberations, Secretary Hull on August 27 conferred with the Iranian Minister and later with the British Chargé d'Affaires and the Soviet Ambassador. The first of these interviews was necessarily the most painful, for the Iranian representative made no secret of his disappointment over the failure of the United States to do something "to carry out its preachments of the eight principles underlying peaceful and free nations, and to aid Iran in securing relief from military occupation." Mr. Hull could promise nothing more than an effort to secure further information. He therefore indulged in denunciations of Hitlerism and attempted, without much success, to persuade his visitor to view Iran's problem in the light of the larger struggle against aggression, to the success of which the United States was committed.[42]

In his discussions with Sir Ronald Campbell, on the other hand, Mr. Hull complained of his lack of information and stressed his Government's need for full data on the British-Soviet agreement with Iran as well as for details of their future plans. He suggested to Sir Ronald and also to Ambassador Oumansky that their Governments issue a joint statement, addressed to all peaceful nations and to those opposed to or actively opposing aggression, to the effect that the occupation of Iran was purely temporary and that the occupying troops would be withdrawn as soon as conditions permitted. The two diplomats evinced interest and promised to submit the proposal to their Governments. Meanwhile Mr. Hull, who evidently put much store by this innocuous proposition, had it transmitted to the American Ambassador in London by telephone and to Moscow by cable.[43]

These embarrassed but assiduous American efforts were soon overtaken by events. Iranian resistance to the invaders collapsed almost at once and Teheran had no choice but to accept the inevitable. A new Cabinet was formed on August 28 and Mr. Churchill was able to report to the President in some elation: "The good results which have been so smoothly obtained in Persia put us in touch with the Russians and we propose to double or at least greatly improve the railway from the Persian Gulf to the Caspian, thus opening a sure route by which long-term supplies can reach the Russian reserve positions in the Volga Basin." The danger of serious military complications having passed, the Prime Minister thenceforth proclaimed quite frankly that the chief objective of the Anglo-Soviet action had been control of the railway and establishment of year-round communications with Russia. "Even more than safeguarding the oil fields," he wired Stalin, "our object in entering Persia has been to get another through route to you which cannot be cut." Speaking in the House of Commons, Mr. Churchill asked

---

[42] Memo of conversation between Mr. Hull and Minister Schayesteh, August 27, 1941.

[43] Memo of Mr. Wallace Murray for the Secretary, August 27, 1941; memo of conversation between Mr. Hull and Sir Ronald Campbell, and between Mr. Hull and Ambassador Oumansky, August 27, 1941; memo of telephone conversation between Mr. Atherton and the American Embassy in London, August 27, 1941. See further, Hull: *Memoirs*, II, 976.

approval of "the somewhat drastic measures" that had been taken, explaining that the German fifth column threatened "not only to seize or destroy the oil fields, which are of the highest consequence, but—a fact to which I attach extreme importance—close the surest and shortest route by which we could reach Russia. We thought it necessary, therefore, to make sure that these machinations did not succeed. . . . We must have the unquestioned control and maintenance of the through communications from the warm-water port of Basra to the Caspian Sea."[44]

Once the trick had been turned, President Roosevelt readily fell in line. The invasion of Iran did not provoke the anticipated unfavorable reaction in the American press, for even liberal organs took a realistic view. According to *The New York Times* (August 26) the action against Iran was inevitable: "To beat Germany to a position which she was obviously plotting to seize at the first possible moment is reason enough for the joint action of Britain and Russia." The Iranians ought to consider themselves fortunate that the British and not the Germans had gotten there first. Furthermore, the United States had a great interest in the opening of the Iranian route, the more so as the line to Russia by way of Vladivostok might soon be cut by the Japanese. According to the *New Republic* (September 1) all the British and Soviet troops had done was to prevent Hitler from taking over the country. The *Nation,* in turn (September 6), recalled Britain's past errors in respecting the neutrality of small nations and thus leaving them to fall victims to the Germans: "Self-preservation forbids the taking of any more such chances."

Since such influential journals were willing to forgive and forget, there was no reason for the President to hang back. In reply to the Shah's appeal he merely gave assurance that he was paying close attention to the course of events. He expressed the hope that the Shah would agree "that the situation must be viewed against the entire background of present and developing world events." After reviewing Hitler's known ambitions and once again stressing the imperative need for checking them, the President concluded:

The Government of the United States have taken note of the statement made by the British and Soviet Governments to the Iranian Government that the independence and territorial integrity of Iran will be respected by them. Because our two countries have enjoyed a long-standing friendship, my Government has asked the British and Soviet Governments about their plans and intentions in Iran, both immediate and long range. We have also suggested to them both that a public statement to all the free peoples of the world renewing the assurances they have already made to Your Majesty's Government would be advisable.[45]

[44] Mr. Churchill's message to the President, September 1, 1941; further, his messages to Stalin, August 29, 1941, September 17, 1941 (these last in Churchill: *The Grand Alliance,* 454, 464), and his statement in the House of Commons on September 9, 1941 (Churchill: *The Unrelenting Struggle,* 258 ff.).

[45] Tel. to Teheran, September 2, 1941. The message was conveyed to the Shah on September 6, 1941.

Actually little came of the proposal put forward by Secretary Hull. Ambassador Oumansky opined that enough had already been done in the way of assurance and the British continued to keep the matter under advisement. Despite repeated efforts by the State Department to revive the proposal it eventually passed into oblivion. Both London and Moscow expressed deep appreciation for the President's treatment of the Shah's protest and declared themselves ever ready to restate their intention to respect the independence and integrity of Iran. But the idea of a public commitment to the nations of the world went by the board.[46]

Meanwhile Mr. Harry Hopkins, acting for the President, inquired of Mr. Churchill what the United States could do to help in developing the Iranian Railway. Needless to say, the British responded at once with a request for locomotives and freight cars. Their plans, they stated, were to raise the capacity of the railroad from two hundred to two thousand tons a day by the spring of 1942 and to construct a motor highway in addition. The project was bound to be congenial to Americans. The Government threw itself into the work and at the end of September appointed Colonel Raymond A. Wheeler as Chief of the United States Military Iranian Mission, to handle American supplies and in general support the British operations.[47] The Americans, at first left in the dark and highly embarrassed by the action of the British and Soviets, presently found themselves parties at interest and willing participants. The importance of the Trans-Iranian route, once the policy of aid to Soviet Russia had been decided on, was such as to overshadow further considerations of principle.

The first phase of the Iranian problem may be said to have closed with the deposition of the Shah on September 17, 1941. His opposition and obstruction had been anticipated from the outset and Mr. Churchill had warned the British representative in Teheran early in September that, unless the full Anglo-Soviet requirements were met, there would be an occupation of the capital and action against the ruler. Since the new Iranian Cabinet showed little energy in implementing the Allied terms (which included the closing of the German, Italian, Hungarian, and Rumanian legations, and the surrender of all German nationals), the British radio soon launched a propaganda campaign against Reza Shah. This culminated in the occupation of Teheran by British and Soviet troops on September 17 and the abdication of the Shah in favor of his youthful son, who promptly agreed to fulfill the Allied demands and even to introduce extensive reforms. There-

[46] Memo of conversation between Mr. Hull and Ambassador Oumansky, September 4, 1941; tels. to Winant and Steinhardt, September 4, 1941; memo of conversation between Mr. Hull and Sir Ronald Campbell, September 17, 1941.

[47] Tel. from Hopkins to Churchill, September 4, 1941; tel. from Beaverbrook to Hopkins, September 6, 1941 (the latter in T. H. Vail Motter: *The Persian Corridor and Aid to Russia* [Washington, 1952], p. 15). On the British plans see also Churchill's messages to Stalin, September 4 and 17, 1941 (Churchill: *The Grand Alliance,* 459, 464, 816).

upon the Allied forces were withdrawn from the capital (October 18) and the two occupying forces drafted a treaty of alliance with Iran which, however, was not signed until January 29, 1942.[48]

The alliance project, ostensibly putting Iranian coöperation on a voluntary basis, at least soothed the American conscience. But long before the dawn of the new year Washington had reason for further misgivings, particularly about the future of Soviet-occupied northern Iran. According to official Soviet press releases the native population had received the Red forces with jubilation: "City and village streets were crowded with inhabitants who had come out to welcome our forces, anxious to say a few words to our men and shake their hands."[49] But these rosy reports were soon outweighed by intelligence of Soviet propaganda and intrigue, and of Soviet support of a separatist movement in Azerbaijan. The State Department felt there was good reason to believe these reports and referred them at once to the British Foreign Office. Mr. Eden stated that he had already queried the Kremlin about them and suggested that Washington do likewise. This was done and occasion taken to remind the Soviet Government of its promises and of the adverse effect of political activity in Iran on the attitude of Turkey. But Mr. Vishinsky, at that time Deputy Commissar for Foreign Affairs, put the matter aside with the observation that the reports must have originated with the Germans. They were not in accord with the facts, he added, for the Soviet occupation authorities were interested solely in the maintenance of law and order.[50] This equivocal reply may be taken as the prelude to later, postwar developments, but at the time there was little more to be done. In terms of the campaign against Hitlerism the alliance between Britain and Soviet Russia assumed transcendent importance and the United States was committed to support of both partners. The Kremlin was notoriously difficult to deal with and expediency dictated the avoidance of controversy. The ultimate fate of Iran had therefore to be left on the laps of the gods.

4. The Moscow Conference

During the month of September the military position of the Soviets continued to deteriorate rapidly: Kiev was being surrounded and the Nazi

[48] Churchill's message to the British Minister, September 3, 1941 (*The Grand Alliance*, 484); memo of conversation between Mr. Hull and Sir Ronald Campbell, September 17, 1941, and between Mr. Welles and Sir Ronald, September 22 and 23, 1941; tel. from Winant, September 23, 1941, transmitting the text of the proposed alliance. See further Lenczowski: *Russia and the West in Iran,* 170 ff., and on military developments the despatch of General Wavell, as cited above, and *PAI Force: The Official Story of the Persia and Iraq Command.*

[49] *Soviet Information Bulletin,* August 30 and September 24, 1941.

[50] Tel. from Teheran, September 26, 1941; tel. to London, October 3, 1941; tel. from London, October 4, 1941; tel. to London, October 8 and reply, October 9, 1941; tel. to Moscow, October 8, and reply, October 11, 1941.

armies were on the point of overrunning the industrially important Donetz Basin. Unless the Soviet forces could make good their losses in matériel, reported Ambassador Steinhardt, they might be obliged to abandon the struggle.[51] Under the circumstances it was a matter of the utmost urgency that arrangements be completed for the long-term provision of military supplies, if only to maintain Soviet morale in such desperate straits. Mr. Churchill did what he could by publicly praising the resistance of the Red armies, forecasting the continuance of the conflict into the winter, and declaring that "the veriest simpleton can see how great is our interest, to put it no higher, in sustaining Russia by every possible means."[52]

President Roosevelt and his military advisers shared the Prime Minister's confidence that the Soviets could and would hold out if only they could secure the needed supplies. The War Department went the limit in allocating munitions, even to the extent of sacrificing some of the much-prized four-engine bombers.[53] But the main task was to block out the larger program which would enable the Kremlin to plan its future operations in the full knowledge of what it could or could not count on in the way of munitions. To this end the American Special Mission for War Supplies to the USSR, under the chairmanship of Mr. W. Averell Harriman, spent a large part of September in London discussing with the corresponding British mission under Lord Beaverbrook what proportion of American war production London would be willing to contribute to the Soviets. By dint of hard and continued effort the conferences were concluded by September 22, on which date the two delegations left for Archangel aboard a British cruiser. They arrived in Moscow on September 28 and at once embarked on negotiations with the highest Soviet authorities.

The outcome of the Moscow discussions was naturally awaited with great interest on both sides of the Atlantic. Among the British there was little dissent from the Government's policy, but in America opinion continued seriously divided, despite the fact that the Kremlin was making some effort to overcome the deep-seated suspicion and hostility which had developed over the years. Thus the official organs, *Pravda* and *Izvestia,* hailed the Atlantic Charter as an expression of determination to crush Hitlerism and declared: "The whole Soviet public acclaims the decisions adopted at the conference of the leaders of the United States and Great Britain, seeing in them a pledge of further and stronger struggle against Hitlerite oppression which should immediately be embodied into broad practical measures for the final annihilation of Nazi tyranny."[54] Furthermore, the Soviet Government had agreed to attend an Inter-Allied Council in London on

[51] Tels. from Steinhardt, September 13 and 25, 1941.
[52] Speeches of September 9 and 30, 1941 (*The Unrelenting Struggle,* 256 ff., 269 ff.).
[53] *Stimson Diary (MS.),* September 8, 9, 10, 11, 1941.
[54] *Soviet Information Bulletin,* August 18 and 19, 1941.

September 24, the purpose of which was to obtain the adherence of the Governments-in-Exile to the Charter and lay the foundations for postwar relief and reconstruction. On this occasion Mr. Maisky, the Soviet Ambassador in London, made a pronouncement which overshadowed all other speeches in importance. After expressing his firm conviction that through united action the Nazi aggressors would be defeated, the Ambassador made the two following significant remarks:

> Our countries face also the most important problem of laying the basis for the organization of international relations, and of constituting the postwar world in such a way as to spare our peoples and our future generations the monstrous crimes of Nazism, incompatible with human culture. The USSR is firmly convinced that this task will be successfully accomplished and that as a result of complete and final victory over Hitlerism there will be laid the true foundations of international coöperation and friendship, corresponding to the aspirations and ideals of freedom-loving peoples. . . . .
>
> The Soviet Union was, and is, guided in its foreign policy by the principle of self-determination of nations. It is guided by the same principle which, in fact, embodies recognition of the sovereignty and the equality of nations in its dealings with various nationalities embraced within the frontiers of the Soviet Union. Indeed, this principle forms one of the pillars on which the political structure of the USSR is built. Accordingly, the Soviet Union defends the right of every nation to the independence and territorial integrity of its country, and its right to establish such a social order and to choose such a form of government as it deems opportune and necessary for the better promotion of its economic and cultural prosperity.[55]

But not even this unequivocal declaration in favor of international coöperation, the independence and integrity of all countries, the equality of nations and the right of every people to determine its own form of government and social order sufficed to convince all Americans or to reconcile them to the program of supporting the homeland of communism. "Interventionist" newspapers like the *New York Herald Tribune* (September 21) might argue that the Soviets were obviously contributing most to the destruction of the Nazi military machine and that therefore "it is sheer pettifogging to split hairs about American aid to Russia—to say that this country should send some war material to the eastern front, but not too much, for fear the Russians might waste it, or lose it in action, or surrender it. Such eventualities are the risks of war; they must be taken into account, but cannot be permitted to paralyze action." Similarly *PM* (September 30) might reason that the question at issue was one of self-interest and not of ideology: "What do we care what the Communists think and stand for if they are willing to die to stop the Fascists? Who are we to complain about who does the fighting for us?" But the opposition press continued its denunciations of

---

[55] Full text in *Documents on American Foreign Relations,* IV, 214 ff., and in *Soviet Foreign Policy during the Patriotic War,* I, 96 ff. A digest of the proceedings of the Inter-Allied Council may be found in the *Bulletin of International News,* XVIII (2), 1275 ff.

communism and stuck by the conviction that the Red armies would soon be defeated or surrender. According to the *New York Journal-American* (September 29), "There is not much sense in giving Russia the tools with which to surrender. . . . Why send more arms and munitions and planes and equipment to treacherous and dangerous Russia, either to be surrendered to Germany or retained to defend Communism?" The *Chicago Tribune* (September 30) hailed the Moscow Conference in these words:

Joe Stalin is host in the Kremlin to some distinguished Americans and Britishers who have come to aid his form of Government to overthrow their own. He may be a master of the deadpan, but a tigerish smile is somewhere behind it. . . . If American and British aid should by any chance enable the Red armies to overrun Europe, the British and American Governments will see a different expression on Joe's face when they endeavor to tell him what he shall do with the countries he has taken.

In the face of this opposition it took courage on the President's part to assume the huge commitments involved in really effective support of the Soviet war effort. Mr. Harriman was the bearer of a message from Mr. Roosevelt to Stalin which read in part:

I am very sure that Hitler made a profound strategic mistake when he attacked your country. I am confident that ways will be found to provide the material and supplies necessary to fight him on all fronts, including your own. I want particularly to take this occasion to express my great confidence that your armies will ultimately prevail over Hitler and to assure you of our great determination to be of every possible material assistance.[56]

But the President refused throughout to commit his Government to any program beyond June 30, 1942, which made it necessary for Mr. Churchill to explain to Stalin that no doubt even larger quotas could be furnished after that date and that British war production as well as the American would be developed to the limit.

Both the British and the American missions were staffed with outstanding experts, equipped with detailed facts and figures, and instructed to arrive at a satisfactory agreement if humanly possible. Yet, according to Mr. Churchill, their reception was "bleak" and the discussions not at all friendly. Initially the Soviet leaders approached the conference with skepticism if not distrust. They appear to have been particularly suspicious of the British and quite unconvinced by Mr. Churchill's reasons for refusing to open a second front in Europe. General Sir Hastings Ismay, Chief of Staff to Mr. Churchill, had been included in the British mission in the hope that he

---

[56] Letter of the President to Stalin, dated September 17, 1941 (full text in *F.D.R.: His Personal Letters*, II, 1210). This letter appears to have been cabled to Mr. Harriman only on September 29, 1941, after his arrival in Moscow. The corresponding letter of Mr. Churchill to Stalin, transmitted by Lord Beaverbrook, was much more specific (text in Churchill: *The Grand Alliance*, 465 ff.).

might discuss with his Russian colleagues various possibilities of military coöperation, but he was given no opportunity to do so.[57]

On the other hand, Stalin began to thaw after Mr. Harriman had made his introductory remarks, which emphasized the peculiar character of his mission, considering that the United States was not as yet a belligerent, though it had a vital interest in the outcome of the conflict. The Soviet chief gave a full exposition of his country's original resources, set forth the extent of Russian losses, and explained the prospects of war production for the future. He made much of the fact that the war was essentially a tank war and that the Germans had a marked superiority in tanks as well as planes. Mr. Harriman and Lord Beaverbrook promised to make up the Soviet losses in these important items and to provide other needed munitions, as well as food and raw materials. Stalin in turn agreed to furnish strategic materials needed by Britain and the United States. The key problem of transportation was considered at length, the American and British missions promising to do their utmost to develop the available routes.

The details were worked out by the respective staffs during two days of strenuous work and agreement was reached by the evening of September 30. For the nine month period until June 30, 1942, the British and Americans undertook to send Soviet Russia about one and a half millions tons of supplies, valued roughly at one billion dollars. The program included 400 planes per month (100 bombers and 100 fighters from the United States and 200 fighters from Britain), 500 tanks per month (250 each from the United States and Britain), 1256 antitank guns, 5000 jeeps and substantial quantities of other key items. In view of these generous commitments it is quite understandable that Stalin beamed like sunshine after rain. The conference ended in an atmosphere of optimism and even enthusiasm, the Soviet leader expressing great gratification and requesting Mr. Harriman to convey his personal thanks to President Roosevelt. In bringing the conference to a close, Molotov remarked:

During these days we were completely able to convince ourselves of the degree in which the decisive, vital interests and common aspirations of our great, liberty-loving countries have brought them together and have led them into close coöperation in the historic struggle now being waged against Hitlerite Germany. . . . We do not doubt that our great anti-Hitler front will rapidly gain strength, that there exists no force which could break this anti-Hitler front. A combination of states has at last been formed against Hitlerism which will find ways and means to erase from the face of the earth the Nazi blot on Europe and the threat it carries to all peoples who love their independence and freedom.[58]

---

[57] Churchill: *The Grand Alliance,* 465 ff., 524-25.

[58] *Soviet Information Bulletin,* October 3, 1941, and, for similar remarks in *Izvestia,* October 4, 1941. The best general account of the conference is that of Sherwood: *Roosevelt and Hopkins,* 387 ff., but see also Churchill: *The Grand Alliance,* 468 ff., and Motter: *The Persian Corridor and Aid to Russia,* 23 ff. Lord Beaverbrook's speech in

Mr. Harriman felt that Stalin was entirely satisfied that in the matter of supplies the Americans and British "meant business," and that "if we came through as had been promised and if personal relations were retained with Stalin, the suspicion that has existed between the Soviet Government and our two Governments might well be eradicated."[59] This estimate was surely overoptimistic, for Soviet Russia presented problems far beyond the mere question of material aid. Stalin made clear to Lord Beaverbrook that he still thought the British should despatch forces to Russia to participate in the fighting. Furthermore, he indicated that he would like to see the agreement of July 12, 1941, transformed into an alliance covering the postwar as well as the war period. He desired discussion of war aims, with particular reference to Germany and the question of indemnities.

The British carefully evaded debate on these sensitive matters, fearing that Stalin's proposals were designed to introduce a program of territorial changes that might provoke serious dissension and create major differences between London and Washington. Those who have since criticized President Roosevelt and Mr. Churchill for not having made the supply of munitions to Soviet Russia contingent on hard and fast agreements regarding the future peace settlement should take note that in September, 1941, it was not at all a question of extracting engagements from Stalin, but rather of warding off pressure for such commitments from the Soviet side. The President and Mr. Churchill appear to have been of one mind on these matters and were probably right in thinking that discussion of political issues would end by blowing the program of collaboration with Soviet Russia sky-high.[60]

On the American side the First Supply Protocol was signed without any financial provision. Pending Congressional action on further Lend-Lease appropriations, the Administration could only arrange *ad hoc* deals to tide the Russians over. Thus, an additional agreement was signed on October 10 advancing the Soviets a further thirty million dollars against future deliveries of gold bullion.[61] The President still faced the problem of reconciling public sentiment and especially Congress to the policy of large-scale support of the Socialist Fatherland. The evidence seemed to suggest that opinion was veering in a favorable direction and the idea gaining currency that close association with the democracies in a life and death struggle would overcome the

---

the House of Lords, October 23, 1941, summarized in *Bulletin of International News,* XVIII (2), 1806 ff., is also of value. We have used further, tels. from Steinhardt, September 29 and 30, October 1 and 3, 1941. The terms of the agreement, embodied in the so-called First Protocol, are printed in *Soviet Supply Protocols* (Washington, n.d.), 3 ff.

[59] Sherwood: *Roosevelt and Hopkins,* 391.

[60] Tel. from Steinhardt, October 28, 1941; tel. from Winant, December 4, 1941. For criticism of the President see William C. Bullitt: "How We Won the War and Lost the Peace" (*Life,* August 30, 1948). Sherwood: *Roosevelt and Hopkins,* 387 ff., discusses this issue.

[61] *Morgenthau Diaries* (*MS.*), October 7 (Vol. 448, pp. 254 ff.) and October 10, 1941 (Vol. 450, p. 118); letter of Hopkins to Loy Henderson of the State Department, October 15, 1941.

suspicion and hostility of the Kremlin and eventuate in a close alignment of Soviet Russia with the west. But one issue, that of religious freedom, was regarded by the American public as the touchstone; by October it had become the subject of lively and widespread discussion.

It will be recalled that Mr. Roosevelt had stressed the importance of this question in conversation with Ambassador Oumansky and had pointed out that some public assurance from Moscow would ease the problem of financial and other aid. This *démarche* had borne no fruit and presently Mr. Roosevelt found himself involved in a public controversy that threatened to do his cause more harm than good. It appears that on the very eve of the Moscow Conference Mr. Jan Ciechanowski, the Polish Minister in Washington, received reports that the Soviet Government had permitted the assignment of Roman Catholic chaplains to the Polish forces being organized on Russian soil. This information was communicated to the President and to the State Department, and was at once released to the press. Thereupon Mr. Roosevelt rather precipitately raised the question of religious freedom in the Soviet Union at one of his press conferences. He cited the provisions of the Soviet Constitution of 1936 and intimated that in his opinion the Christian religion was tolerated and protected in Russia.[62]

The President's remarks immediately provoked a storm of protest, not only from Catholic but also from Protestant leaders and organizations. Professor Matthew Spinka of the Chicago Theological Seminary wrote the White House that a careful analysis he had made of the Soviet Constitution did not support the statement that it provided substantially the same freedom of religion as the American Constitution: "The [Soviet] Constitution leaves to religious communions only the bare right of holding personally to their religious view, without the right of testifying publicly to it with the purpose of either conveying it to their children or to non-members. The right of propaganda is restricted specifically only to anti-religious groups."[63] The Secretary of the Catholic Laymen's Committee for Peace likewise lodged a vigorous protest, while the Very Reverend Edmund Walsh, well-known authority on Russian affairs, promptly denounced the Soviet Constitution as a "hollow shell." Representative Martin Dies wrote the President objecting to "any effort in any quarter to dress the Soviet wolf in the sheep's clothing of the four freedoms," and the redoubtable Representative Hamilton Fish, particular *bête noire* of Mr. Roosevelt, suggested publicly that the President invite Stalin to Washington "so that he might be baptized in the swimming

[62] For the background see Jan Ciechanowski: *Defeat in Victory* (New York, 1947), 54-55. We have used also an unsigned memo to the President, September 29, 1941, conveying this information, and a copy of a letter from Ambassador Ciechanowski to Secretary Hull, which the latter sent to the White House on September 30, 1941 (*Roosevelt Papers:* Secretary's File, Boxes 75 and 76). For the President's press conference see *The New York Times,* October 1, 1941.

[63] Letter of Professor Spinka to the President, October 9, 1941 (*Roosevelt Papers:* Official File, 220-26).

pool at the White House." "It could be a fine, big ceremony," he added, "with all the members of Congress there to see that it was done properly. And then afterward I suggest that all of us join the Stalin Sunday School."[64]

In the hope of quieting the uproar Mr. Roosevelt at once released the official text of his remarks, which he claimed had been misunderstood. At the same time he cabled Mr. Harriman at Moscow: "In view of the outstanding importance of this question from the standpoint of public opinion in the United States, the President earnestly hopes that you may be able to secure from the highest authorities of the Soviet Government some statement which can be sent to the press in this country. . . ."[65] Mr. Harriman and Ambassador Steinhardt did their best. They talked to almost all members of the Soviet delegation, including Molotov and eventually Stalin. All nodded assent and Stalin promised to attend to the matter. Yet Harriman was left with the impression "that the Soviet Government will give lip service and make a few gestures to meet the President's wishes, but is not prepared to give freedom of religion in the sense that we understand it."[66]

This impression proved correct, for while the President was revealing to the public that he had been making efforts in behalf of religious freedom in Russia and was being applauded therefor by Father Walsh and other Catholic leaders, the Soviet press chief on October 4 released a statement that went no further than this:

There is freedom of worship in the USSR. This means any Soviet citizen may adhere to any religion, which is a matter for the conscience of each citizen. . . . Religion is a private affair for the Soviet citizen in which the State does not interfere and considers it unnecessary to interfere. . . . The Soviet Constitution provides not only the right to practice this or that religion, but also the right of the Soviet citizen not to belong to any church and to conduct anti-religious propaganda.[67]

Father Walsh at once denounced this statement as "shadow-boxing" and declared: "This is tantamount to a scotching of President Roosevelt's hopes that true freedom of religion might be recognized in Russia." He urged reconsideration of the whole program of aid to Soviet Russia, while Mark Sullivan wrote sanguinely: "Mr. Harriman is now in Moscow with, so to speak, a Bible in one hand and in the other a billion dollars or so of lease-lend material. One feels that Stalin will see the light. Soon he'll be singing *Onward Christian Soldiers* and saying grace before his meal of borsch."[68]

[64] Tel. to the President from the Secretary of the Catholic Laymen's Committee, October 4, 1941 (*Roosevelt Papers:* Official File, 220-26) ; editorial in *The New York Times,* October 2, 1941; article by Reverend Edmund Walsh in the *New York Herald Tribune,* October 2, 1941; article by Arthur Krock in *The New York Times,* October 3, 1941.

[65] Tel. to Harriman, October 2, 1941.

[66] Tel. from Harriman, October 4, 1941; see also the Harriman memorandum printed in Sherwood: *Roosevelt and Hopkins,* 391-93.

[67] Tel. from Steinhardt, October 4, 1941; *The New York Times,* October 5, 1941; *Soviet Information Bulletin,* October 6, 1941.

[68] *The New York Times* and the *New York Herald Tribune,* October 6, 1941.

This was to misread the character of the Soviet dictator, who neither saw the light nor took to saying grace at table. Conceivably some further meaningless and insincere assurance might have been extracted from him, but the prospect of even that was dim and both Ambassador Steinhardt and Mr. Harriman were convinced that further pressure was inadvisable. The President made no further excursions into the realm of spiritual values, though he took care to forward to Catholic dignitaries incoming reports of Nazi plans to de-Christianize Germany and all the lands under its control.[69]

Considering the storm over the religious issue, it is astounding that the Administration should have succeeded in picking its way between the shoals of public opinion and the rocks of Congressional opposition. On October 10 the House, voting on the second Lend-Lease Appropriations Bill, rejected by 217-162 the amendment forbidding the use of such funds for aid to Soviet Russia. The Senate took like action on October 23, from which one is probably justified in concluding that public sentiment in favor of support of Russia, while less articulate, was markedly stronger than the clamor of protest would lead one to suppose. At any rate the President felt that the vote in Congress could be taken to imply approval of Lend-Lease aid to the Soviet Union if such were necessary. It was of considerable import also that on October 16 the American Federation of Labor endorsed "all material and assistance possible" to Soviet Russia as well as to Britain and other nations resisting Nazi aggression.

By the end of October Mr. Roosevelt considered the moment opportune for announcing his vital decision. Mr. Harriman and his staff had returned from Moscow and had made a profound impression by publicly reporting the excellence of Soviet morale and voicing their conviction that the Soviets would fight on. They furthermore assured the public that Soviet industry was highly efficient and that the Russians would make good use of whatever was supplied them.[70] On October 29 the First Protocol was formally approved by the Supplies, Priorities and Allocations Board and on the following day Mr. Roosevelt informed Stalin of his decision to make available to the Soviet Government up to one billion dollars of Lend-Lease aid, to be repaid without interest over a period of ten years, beginning five years after the conclusion of the war. Stalin replied accepting the offer "with sincere gratitude . . . as unusually substantial aid" in the struggle against the common enemy. On November 6 the American offer and its acceptance

---

[69] Tel. from Zurich, October 15, 1941, reporting Rosenberg's thirty-point program for a Reich National Church. The President had copies of this cable sent to prominent members of the Catholic hierarchy and, through Mr. Myron Taylor, to the Vatican (*Roosevelt Papers:* Secretary's File, Box 75).

[70] Harriman's broadcast from London, October 13, and his statement to the press (*The New York Times,* October 22, 1941); similarly the radio speech of Mr. William Batt, one of the economic experts of the mission (*The New York Times,* October 30, 1941). Harriman's formal report to the President, October 29, 1941, was brief and general, and of the same tenor (*Roosevelt Papers:* Secretary's File, Box 76).

were made public and on November 7 Soviet Russia was declared eligible for Lend-Lease aid.[71]

The last obstacle to the full implementation of the program to support Soviet Russia had thus been surmounted, but only in the teeth of continued and highly vocal opposition. According to the *Chicago Tribune* (October 17): "It is ridiculous that sane men should have the slightest faith that Stalin [described by the *Tribune* as 'Bloody Joe' and 'the supreme monster'], who brought on the war by selling out the democracies, will not sell them out again and make another deal with Hitler." Or, to quote the *New York Journal-American* (November 5):

A voluminous, luxurious and snow-white suit of sheep's clothing, with some touches here and there of ecclesiastical style, is being feverishly tailored to make Josef Stalin presentable to the American public. . . . There is something infinitely comic in the stumbling haste with which Stalin's admirers are seeking to transform the bloody-handed persecutor of religion, the merciless extorter of false confessions, the granite-hearted lord of the Cheka and Ogpu, into a benevolent and lovable kind of homespun Foxy Grandpa.

It would be supererogation to point out the extent to which these misgivings and forebodings were vindicated in the sequel. With regard to the decision to extend large-scale aid to the Soviets it is unnecessary to say more than that American policy was based squarely on immediate military considerations. The President was doubtless overconfident in thinking that the leopard could or would change his spots, while many others subscribed to his policy without possibly being able to foresee the extent of the Soviet victories and the growth of Soviet power. Few, however, either inside or outside the Government, deluded themselves into thinking that collaboration with the Kremlin was to be either easy or pleasant. Though perhaps less ungracious toward the United States than toward Britain, the Soviet Government thought nothing of taking a high and mighty attitude and demanding, as its just due, whatever had been promised or requested. Long before the Moscow Conference, in connection with a dispute over spare parts for airplanes, General Marshall had urged Secretary Stimson to make clear to the President "that Mr. Oumansky will take everything we own if we submit to his criticism."[72] Later on the Moscow Government flatly refused to permit American experts and technicians to supervise the assembling and operation of American equipment after its unloading. Neither would it accept the United States Military Mission under General John N.

[71] The full text of the letters is given in *Documents on American Foreign Relations,* IV, 605 ff. On the background see Sherwood: *Roosevelt and Hopkins,* 396-97; Stettinius: *Lend-Lease,* 130 ff.; *Industrial Mobilization for War,* I, 129 ff.; and Motter: *The Persian Corridor and Aid to Russia,* 24 ff. We have used also the *Morgenthau Diaries (MS.),* Vol. 455, p. 267.

[72] Watson: *Chief of Staff: Prewar Plans and Preparations,* 329 (note of August 29, 1941).

Greely, appointed to handle military Lend-Lease problems at the Russian end. Finally, the Kremlin made no move toward granting the United States the use of air bases in eastern Siberia for defense against Japan, and after Pearl Harbor rejected American proposals that it participate in the Far Eastern War.[73] Though at the time these matters were only straws in the wind, they augured little good for the future. But in the strain and stress of the pre-Pearl Harbor days there seemed no alternative to taking the bad with the good.

5. An Exigent Partner

In the first days of October, 1941, just as the Moscow Conference was completing its labors, the Nazi armies opened their great drive to smash the core of Soviet resistance and capture the historic capital. In a grandiloquent order of the day Hitler announced that the enemy already lay defeated and could not rise again; the offensive against Moscow was to be merely "the last stroke which will smash our foe before winter sets in." And so at first it seemed. In a couple of weeks the Panzer divisions, closely followed by the infantry, advanced upward of fifty miles, executing tremendous pincer movements that netted them over half a million prisoners and corresponding quantities of guns, tanks and other equipment. The Moscow population, which was not informed of the new offensive until October 8, was panic-stricken, especially when, on October 15, orders were issued to move government offices and foreign embassies eastward to Kuibyshev. For the moment it seemed as though nothing could stop the German advance. Both the American and British missions were utterly pessimistic and fully expected the fall of the capital within a few weeks.[74]

It was to be expected that in this hour of trial the Soviets would renew their pleas for early assistance in the way of supplies and also their demands on the British for the opening of a front in western or southern Europe. Among the British, voices favoring some such action began to be raised in public. Sir Stafford Cripps, the Ambassador in Moscow, appears to have been sympathetic and even Lord Beaverbrook chafed at the Chiefs of Staff, who "would have us wait until the last button has been sewn on the last gaiter before we launch an attack." But Mr. Churchill refused to be drawn into rash adventures and stood by the decision of the military authorities that no large-scale operations could be undertaken for some time to come.

---

[73] *Stimson Diary (MS.)*, October 22, 23, 30, November 24, 28, 1941; memo of conversation between Mr. Hull and the new Soviet Ambassador, Maxim Litvinov, December 11, 1941. For the story of the Greely Mission see especially Motter: *The Persian Corridor and Aid to Russia,* 65 ff.

[74] Tels. from Steinhardt, October 11, 15, 22, 1941; Sherwood: *Roosevelt and Hopkins,* 395; Quentin Reynolds: *Only the Stars Are Neutral* (New York, 1942), 131 ff. On the German offensive see Liddell Hart: *The German Generals Talk,* Chapter XIII; Herbert Rosinski: "Hitler's Strategy in Russia" (*Infantry Journal,* June, 1948); and Kurt Assmann: *Deutsche Schicksalsjahre,* 273 ff.

In Parliament a Government spokesman remarked: "I cannot imagine anything which would suit Hitler's game better than if we adopted the Chinese method of committing suicide on our enemy's doorstep." Mr. Eden reiterated the Government's determination to aid in every way possible, but insisted that the decision as to what was or was not feasible must be left to the War Cabinet.[75]

Short of opening a second front the British strained every nerve to relieve their allies. The departure of convoys to Murmansk was hastened; an offer was made to the Kremlin to assume full responsibility for the occupation of Iran, so that the five or six Soviet divisions committed there might be used at the front; a proposal was advanced to send General Wavell to Moscow or Kuibyshev to discuss other possibilities of military collaboration.[76] But none of this would satisfy Stalin, who, in a significant address commemorating the anniversary of the October Revolution (November 6), charged that the Soviets were being left to carry on the war singlehanded against the combined forces of Germans, Finns, Rumanians, Italians and Hungarians and once again insisted on the need for a second front.[77] Furthermore, the Soviet dictator expressed himself with brutal frankness in his reply to a message from Mr. Churchill:

> I fully agree with you that clarity should be established in the relations between the USSR and Great Britain. Such a clarity does not exist at present. The lack of clarity is the consequence of two circumstances: a) There is no definite understanding between our two countries on war aims and on plans for the postwar organization of peace. b) There is no agreement between the USSR and Great Britain on mutual military assistance against Hitler in Europe. As long as there is no accord on both these questions there can be no clarity in Anglo-Soviet relations. More than that: to be frank, as long as the present situation exists there will be difficulty in securing mutual confidence.

If General Wavell were to come to Moscow to solve these questions, added Stalin, he would be welcome. But if he were to come merely for information and for discussion of secondary matters, it would not be worth while to have him intrude on the Soviet generals; neither would he (Stalin) be able to find time for conversations.[78]

This exchange took place at a time when the Soviet military position, despite a lull in the fighting due to heavy rains, was becoming increasingly desperate. In mid-November the Nazis began their final surge to envelop

[75] Churchill's letter to Ambassador Cripps, October 28, 1941, restating the case against the Soviet demands (Churchill: *The Grand Alliance*, 472 ff.); Sherwood: *Roosevelt and Hopkins*, 393-94 (for Beaverbrook's remarks); *Bulletin of International News*, XVIII (2), 1839-40 (statements in Parliament on October 22 and 25, 1941).

[76] Churchill: *The Grand Alliance*, 471, 485, 527-28, 546.

[77] Full text in the *Soviet Information Bulletin*, November 6, 1941, and in *Soviet Foreign Policy during the Patriotic War*, I, 24 ff.

[78] Message from Stalin to Churchill, November 8, 1941 (Churchill: *The Grand Alliance*, 528-30).

Moscow, which seemed almost certainly doomed by early December, when the Germans were within twenty miles of the city. These facts illustrate Stalin's persistence and obduracy even in the hour of desperation. Come what may, he stood by his contention that a healthy relationship between the Kremlin and the democracies depended on a settlement of political issues. His position was further reflected in the Soviet treatment of the Polish problem, which was marked by unremitting pressure to force recognition of Soviet claims to eastern Poland. Despite the Soviet-Polish agreement of July 30, the Kremlin's proclamation of an amnesty for all Polish captives, and the conclusion of a military agreement on August 14, 1941, Moscow showed little inclination either to liberate Polish civilians or reconstitute an army from among the Polish war prisoners. There was every indication that large numbers of Poles were being hurriedly sent to labor camps and that the Kremlin was obstructing the formation of a Polish Army of more than a couple of divisions on the plea that equipment for a larger force was lacking. Polish efforts to secure information about the large number of Polish officers who had disappeared were systematically evaded; suggestions for investigations by the Red Cross were turned down. In desperation the Polish Ambassador in Moscow made repeated representations and eventually the Government-in-Exile suggested that General Sikorski, the Prime Minister, pay a visit to Moscow to discuss with Stalin the possibility of concentrating the Polish forces in the Caucasus or Iran, where they could be equipped by the British and Americans and then, if desired, returned to Russia. President Roosevelt was induced to take an interest in this plan and at his suggestion Mr. Harriman cabled an appropriate suggestion to Stalin. But within a week the latter replied that he had not had time to examine the matter, and added: "There is no doubt in my mind that the Soviet Government will take into consideration definitely the Polish desires and the interests of Soviet-Polish friendly relations."[79]

Throughout the painful discussions of the Polish question Soviet leaders alternated evasive replies and vague assurances. Stalin, in his address of November 6, reiterated that the Soviets had no such war aims as the seizure of foreign territories and the subjugation of foreign peoples: "Our aim is to help these nations in their struggle for liberation against Hitler's tyranny and then to leave it to them quite freely to organize their life in their lands as they think fit. No interference in the internal affairs of other nations!"[80] But such promises were small consolation to the Poles, for the root of their dif-

[79] Tel. from Biddle, October 24, 1941; memo from the Polish Ambassador in Washington, October 31, 1941; tel. from Harriman to Stalin, November 7, 1941, and the latter's reply, November 14, 1941; tel. from Steinhardt, November 11, 1941; memo from the Polish Ambassador, November 17, 1941. For a detailed discussion see Ciechanowski: *Defeat in Victory*, 59 ff. On the larger issue of Polish-Soviet relations see the official publication *Polish-Soviet Relations, 1918-1943* (Washington, n.d.), Chapter II-V, and Stanislaw Mikolajczyk: *The Rape of Poland* (New York, 1948), 17 ff.

[80] *Soviet Foreign Policy during the Patriotic War*, I, 32.

ferences with the Kremlin lay in the Soviet claim that all eastern Poland was Russian territory and that the Poles must recognize that claim. General Sikorski did in fact go to Moscow early in December and, after some pointed discussion, convinced Stalin that the Poles were eager to fight at Russia's side if given the opportunity. Stalin finally agreed to the organization of an additional five or six Polish divisions and permitted the departure of some 25,000 Polish soldiers from the country. Furthermore, he and Sikorski signed a new agreement of friendship and mutual assistance, envisaging the postwar period as well as the duration of hostilities. This agreement provided that

After the victorious war and the appropriate punishment of the Hitlerite criminals, the task of the Allied States will be to assure a lasting and just peace. This can be attained only by a new organization of international relations, an organization which is based upon the unification of the democratic countries in a lasting alliance. In the creation of such organization the decisive factor should be respect for international law supported by the collective armed forces of all Allied States.[81]

But even these fair words connoted no retreat from the basic Soviet claims. Stalin did his utmost to persuade Sikorski to agree to an adjustment of the frontier, even if only a minor one. The Prime Minister, however, refused to do so on the plea that the 1921 frontier was sacred to the Poles and that he had no constitutional authority to discuss territorial changes, however insignificant. This vital issue therefore remained open, but the Polish Prime Minister was left in no doubt that the Soviets did not recognize the populations of the western Ukraine as Poles and that, so far as the Kremlin was concerned, "the question of the frontiers between the USSR and Poland has not been settled and is subject to settlement in the future."[82]

Soviet territorial claims on Poland not only conditioned the relations of the two Governments during the war, but also cast a long and ominous shadow over the association of Britain and the United States with Soviet Russia. Polish leaders then and since have bewailed the fact that while London and Washington used their influence to alleviate the lot of the Poles in Russia and to further the project for a Polish Army, they refused to meet squarely the issue of Soviet political and territorial demands. As a matter of fact neither the British nor the Americans failed to recognize that the Kremlin aspired to some form of hegemony in eastern Europe, but they were haunted by the specter of a possible deal between Hitler and Stalin and fearful of raising any issue that might split the common front against Hitlerism. The Poles realized this, but were powerless in the face of circumstances.

[81] *Soviet Foreign Policy during the Patriotic War*, I, 112. A full account of the Stalin-Sikorski conversations is given in Ciechanowski: *Defeat in Victory*, Chapter VII, and in Mikolajczyk: *The Rape of Poland*, 22 ff. We have used also a tel. from Thurston (Kuibyshev), December 11, 1941.

[82] Ciechanowski: *Defeat in Victory*, Chapter VIII. See also *Polish-Soviet Relations*, Chapter VI.

They knew they were running the danger of being sacrificed in the interests of victory but had no choice but to stake their hope of salvation on British-American influence and power when the time came to sit down at the peace conference table.

From the foregoing review of the Soviet attitude one can only conclude that Stalin and his associates were convinced that Moscow could be held and that presently the Red Army would be able to launch a counteroffensive against the exhausted Nazis, as it did on December 4, a few days before Pearl Harbor. Mr. Churchill shared their confidence and as early as November 12 had confided to an American emissary that he thought the chances in the titanic struggle were five to four in favor of the Soviets.[83] But judging from the stiff tone of Stalin's messages and from the harsh Soviet treatment of the Polish issue, the Prime Minister evidently decided that something more had to be done to overcome the Kremlin's distrust. Possibly he may have feared the conclusion of a Nazi-Soviet settlement, such as Hitler in fact dreamed of.[84] He therefore proposed to Stalin that Foreign Secretary Eden, accompanied by military experts, visit Moscow for the purpose of discussing "every question relating to the war," including the despatch of at least some British forces to the Caucasus and South Russia. Above all, Mr. Eden was to be authorized to discuss the postwar organization of peace, a subject which no degree of military stress had banished from the Soviet dictator's thoughts. It was almost a foregone conclusion that Stalin would accept this British surrender with alacrity and enthusiasm. "I fully agree with you," he replied, "that the difference of the State organization between the USSR on the one hand and Great Britian and the United States of America on the other hand should not, and could not, hinder us in achieving a successful solution of all the fundamental questions concerning our mutual security and our legitimate interests."[85]

Mr. Churchill certainly knew, when he made his proposal to Stalin, that he was running the risk of complications with the American Government, which had set its face against discussion of postwar settlements and commitments on territorial issues. On December 4, fully ten days after receipt of Stalin's reply, Mr. Eden finally broached the matter to Ambassador Winant, making it appear as innocent as possible. He first rehearsed the difficulties which had developed between London and Moscow since the beginning of October. The Kremlin, he explained, seemed annoyed that it had not been consulted beforehand on the Atlantic Charter. It appeared to harbor suspicions that the British were scheming to exclude Russia from the final peace

[83] Report of Mr. William Whitney to Colonel William J. Donovan, the Coördinator of Information, November 12, 1941. See also Churchill's speech in Parliament on December 11, 1941 (Churchill: *The Unrelenting Struggle*, 345 ff.).

[84] Assmann: *Deutsche Schicksalsjahre*, 277, quoting remarks of Hitler on November 9, 1941.

[85] Message from Churchill to Stalin, November 21, 1941, and the latter's reply, November 23, 1941 (Churchill: *The Grand Alliance*, 531 ff.).

settlement and evidently feared that the British would not agree to a sufficiently drastic treatment of defeated Germany. The purpose of his visit, said
Mr. Eden, would be to dispel Soviet distrust and, without entering upon
definite commitments, to give Stalin maximum satisfaction. Among other
things he would try to secure a reaffirmation of Soviet acceptance of the
Atlantic Charter and an official restatement of the assurances in Stalin's
speech of November 6, as well as Soviet approval of the eventual disarmament of Germany and of federative agreements among the weaker European
states.[86]

The British decision, even in the attenuated form presented by Mr. Eden,
startled the American Ambassador and created consternation in the State
Department. It clearly threatened to jeopardize American policy, to which
the British had subscribed, albeit with some reluctance. Some officials had
long feared a Soviet maneuver to get the British to agree "to certain territorial adjustments on the European Continent and other arrangements
which would make the Soviet Union the dominating power of Eastern
Europe, if not of the whole Continent," while others suspected that London
had already made concessions to Soviet demands.[87] But these were the tense
and critical last days of the negotiations with Japan and, with the approval
of the President, it was finally decided to let London off with a restatement
of the American position. Ambassador Winant was instructed to read this to
Secretary Eden, but not to leave a written copy.

The telegram to the Ambassador repeated the determination of the
United States Government to aid Soviet Russia to the end and took the line
that the test of British and American good faith should be not the willingness
to recognize extensions of the Soviet frontiers, but loyalty in carrying out
their commitments to furnish supplies. With regard to postwar settlements,
these had been delineated in the Atlantic Charter, which reflected the
position of Britain and Soviet Russia as well as of the United States. Consequently, "in our considered opinion it would be unfortunate for any of
the three Governments . . . to enter into commitments regarding specific
terms of the postwar settlements." Discussions looking toward ultimate
agreement should of course be continued, with full knowledge of the public,
and Soviet Russia would, naturally, join in the final settlement along with
all nations which contributed to Hitler's defeat. But no commitments should
be made with respect to any specific country, lest the common aim of
achieving a lasting peace be jeopardized: "Above all, there must be no
secret accords" to hamper the freedom of later decision.[88]

Mr. Eden, when informed of the American reaction, expressed complete

[86] Tel. from Winant, December 4, 1941.

[87] *Berle Diary* (*MS.*), December 7, 1941; memo by the European Division of the
State Department, February 4, 1942, reviewing the development of Anglo-Soviet relations.

[88] Tel. to Winant, December 5, 1941.

agreement and presently set out on his momentous journey.[89] The story of his discussions in Moscow falls beyond the scope of the present study, though it may be observed that, probably as a result of American representations, the Foreign Secretary did what he could to evade or defer political engagements. Nonetheless, the grievous problems arising from the hoped-for success of the Soviets in resisting the Nazi onslaught were already clearly discernible and were of necessity to become increasingly acute as the great conflict entered upon its later phases.

6. FINLAND'S PREDICAMENT

Among the diverse elements contributing to the tension in Anglo-Soviet relations during the autumn of 1941 the Finnish question was one of the most troublesome and, for the democracies, one of the most embarrassing. In retrospect it would appear that the Helsinki Government, in declaring war on the Soviet Union, embarked on a hopeless task. Its objective was to take advantage of the German attack on Soviet Russia to regain the territories lost as a result of the Soviet-Finnish War of 1939–1940. While, almost of necessity, it permitted its military operations to be coördinated with those of the Germans, the Finnish Government refused to associate itself with Hitler as an ally and attempted to maintain the position that its war against Soviet Russia was a conflict altogether separate from the larger war. From the official statements of the Finns it was reasonable to deduce that once they had reconquered their lost territories they would terminate hostilities.

Since the Finnish operations, in conjunction with those of the Germans using Finland as a base, entailed the commitment of numerous Soviet divisions to that front, it was a matter of major importance to the Kremlin to close out the conflict with Finland as quickly as possible. To that end it authorized the American Government, in mid-August, 1941, to inform Helsinki of its readiness to make peace, even at the cost of territorial concessions to Finland. Since the Soviets were particularly anxious to avoid the impression that they were suing for peace out of weakness, the advances to the Finns had to be couched in suggestive rather than specific terms. However, Under Secretary Welles on August 18 informed the Finnish Minister, Mr. Hjalmar Procopé, that the State Department had received reports "that, should the Government of Finland be so disposed, the Soviet Government was prepared to negotiate a new treaty of peace with Finland which would involve the making of territorial concessions by the Soviet Union to Finland." While Mr. Welles stressed that he was acting merely as a transmitting agent and that the United States was taking no official position with respect to the proposal, he mentioned the Soviet Government by name and told the Minister that the information was authoritative. It was inconceiv-

[89] Tel. from Winant, December 9, 1941.

able that an experienced diplomat should have misunderstood and, indeed, Mr. Procopé conceded later that he had gotten the point correctly.[90]

Minister Procopé's immediate reaction to Mr. Welles's statement was to inquire what guarantees the United States and Britain could offer Finland that the Soviet Government would respect such an agreement in the hour of victory and that the Kremlin "would not again undertake to seize Finland and deprive the Finnish people of their independence." The Under Secretary thought such questions might well be deferred until Helsinki's reaction to the general proposition were known, but he added that he wondered "what guarantees or assurances Finland thought she would have of retaining her own independence and autonomy if Germany succeeded in winning and were then overlord of Europe." "I said," noted Mr. Welles, "that in such event Finland could look to no one for assistance, whereas if Germany were defeated, she would have many extremely powerful friends on her side."

Much to the surprise and disappointment of the State Department no reply was ever made by Helsinki to the proposal of August 18, 1941. Speaking to an official of the Department on September 3, Mr. Procopé referred to the offer as vague and left the impression that his Government thought it held few possibilities. Eventually the Department began to suspect that the Minister, for whatever reason, had never transmitted the proposal to his Government. This was almost certainly not so. On the contrary, the matter, obviously of major importance, was probably considered with great care in Helsinki and finally dropped as either undesirable or impracticable. The Finns had been fighting with customary valor and had already reconquered most of their lost territories. Furthermore, they were evidently convinced that the Germans would soon dispose of the Soviet menace once and for all. The golden moment had clearly arrived to recover the Finnish part of the Soviet province of Karelia and Field Marshal Mannerheim proclaimed publicly (August 30, September 4) that Finland must continue the struggle until final victory, that Finland could not be satisfied with the old, inadequate frontiers, and that "new days are dawning ever brighter before our eyes." On the other hand, Finland was rapidly falling into dependence on Germany, especially for food supplies, and was being subjected to ever greater German pressure for participation in Nazi operations against Leningrad. Early in September the decision was made to reject German demands

[90] Mr. Welles's record of this conversation was published by the State Department early in November, 1941, to cut short further argument about the character of the démarche (text in Documents on American Foreign Relations, IV, 642-43). We have used also a memo of conversation between Mr. Welles and Mr. Procopé, November 13, 1941, reviewing the matter. Official Soviet denials in November that the Kremlin had taken any such initiative in August are probably to be explained by the almost pathological anxiety of the Soviets to avoid the appearance of ever having yielded. On these denials see The New York Times, November 12, 1941, and John H. Wuorinen, ed.: Finland and World War II (New York, 1948), 146 ff.

for direct military coöperation, but it is understandable that, in the circumstances, the Finnish Government was unwilling to defy the Germans to the extent of engaging in peace negotiations with the Kremlin.[91]

Lured on by national aspirations and enmeshed in its relations with Germany, the Finnish Government had passed up a most favorable opportunity for an advantageous settlement with the Kremlin. Stalin was naturally furious and, in connection with his demands for the opening of a second front, began to insist that the British declare war on Finland unless the Finns desisted from an advance beyond their 1939 frontiers. Mr. Churchill, though convinced that such action would merely drive the Finns into Hitler's arms, felt obliged to yield to Soviet importunity, the more so as he felt unable to satisfy Soviet demands for a second front. Indeed, he cabled Stalin that he would ask the United States Government to use its influence to deter the Finns.[92]

It was probably in response to an appeal from the Prime Minister that Mr. Roosevelt on September 6 wrote Secretary Hull:

I have been more and more inclined to the view that the field losses of Finland have been so heavy during the past two and a half months that they cannot afford to continue in battle more than a couple of months longer.

I wonder, therefore, if you should not see Procopé "off the record" and tell him that wholly unofficially and wholly as an old friend of Finland and a strong supporter of her independence, you feel it only fair to say to him:

The United States is taking no part and no action in bringing about a termination of the war between Finland and Russia and is sending no word to the Government of Finland as to our position and desires.

But, for his own information, he should know that in our view sympathy for the cause of Finnish independence lost ground in the United States because of General Mannerheim's rather bombastic speech; that public feeling in the United States is all in favor of Finland's regaining the territory she lost to Russia last year, but that American public opinion has been much upset by the thought that Finland will invade Russia proper or, in other words, cross her old boundaries into enemy country. Thousands of well-wishers of Finland will be alienated by such a move but would be made very happy if Finland could regain her old boundaries, and stop there.

You could even say, if you want to, that I have suggested this as a piece of personal information in regard to American public opinion which, as an old friend, I think he should have.[93]

Modest and guarded though the President's suggestion was, it was evidently too much for Secretary Hull, if one may judge from the record of the latter's talk with Minister Procopé on September 8. Mr. Hull congratulated

[91] Wuorinen: *Finland and World War II*, 117, and especially Waldemar Erfurth: *Der finnische Krieg* (Wiesbaden, 1950), 198 ff.

[92] Churchill's reply (September 4, 1941) to a message from Stalin (Churchill: *The Grand Alliance*, 454-60).

[93] Letter of the President to Mr. Hull, September 6, 1941 (now printed in *F.D.R.: His Personal Letters*, II, 1207-8).

his visitor on Finland's reconquest of the lost territories and made discreet inquiry as to the meaning of Marshal Mannerheim's recent utterances. But the major part of the colloquy consisted of vigorous and eloquent denunciation of Hitler on the part of the Secretary, and of Stalin on the part of the Minister. Mr. Hull scrupulously avoided even a veiled warning and confined himself to a casual suggestion that if and when Hitler were stopped, the United States might show a far greater and more important interest in Finland than ever before.[94]

Toward the end of September the situation took a distinct turn for the worse, for the German forces in northern Finland and the Finnish troops also had advanced to a point where they were threatening the railroad running south from Murmansk to Leningrad and Moscow. Since Murmansk was the only ice-free port in the Soviet Arctic, the railroad was essential for maintenance of the flow of supplies from the western powers to the Soviet battle front. Through the Norwegian Minister in Helsinki the British Government therefore presented the Finns with a stiff warning (September 22), stating that "if the Finnish Government persist in invading purely Russian territory, a situation will arise in which Great Britain will be forced to treat Finland as an open enemy, not only while the war lasts, but also when peace comes to be made." The Helsinki authorities, however, delayed their reply and in the meantime allowed it to become known that the British were threatening them. The United States Government, it was suggested, was unwilling to support this policy and had therefore refused to transmit the British note.

To counter such maneuvers, London appealed to Washington to make its position clear or at least refute the allegations of Anglo-American differences. It was now impossible even for Mr. Hull to maintain his previous reserve, the more so as the United States was as much concerned with the fate of the Murmansk railroad as were the British. On October 3 the Secretary finally made clear to Minister Procopé that in the opinion of the United States Government the Finnish forces had already advanced too far and that, whatever Helsinki's ultimate decision, the United States Government stood foursquare behind the British. Mr. Welles, returning from a vacation, was even more explicit and told Mr. Procopé that the Finnish Government "must be prepared for a very material change in public opinion in the United States regarding Finland if Finland pursued her present policy, which could only be construed by the American people as a policy of aid and comfort to the present German Government."[95]

[94] Memo of conversation between Mr. Hull and Minister Procopé, September 8, 1941. Mr. Hull was equally guarded in his conversation with the British Chargé d'Affaires when, on the same day, the latter asked what might be done to bring about peace between Soviet Russia and Finland.

[95] Memos of conversation between Mr. Hull and Mr. Procopé, October 3 and 6; between Mr. Welles and Sir Ronald Campbell, September 23; between Mr. Atherton

Neither British nor American representations sufficed to produce a change in the Finnish attitude. Helsinki's reply to London (October 6) denied that the areas being occupied were purely Russian in population and asserted that these areas were necessary for the defense of Finland's 1939 frontiers. The same arguments were made to Mr. Schoenfeld by President Ryti and Foreign Minister Witting, but the American Minister was in addition given the impression that the Finns could not afford to estrange Berlin in these matters.[96] Considerations of this nature undoubtedly determined the position of the Finnish Government. There was certainly official and unofficial sentiment for withdrawing from the war on the plea that Finland lacked the resources to carry on. On the other hand, the food situation had become so desperate that the country was dependent on Germany for relief. Besides, there was a real danger that Hitler, if he lost faith in the Finns, might take over the entire country. Being unable to set forth the situation in such plain terms, the Helsinki authorities fell back on complaints of American inability to understand their position.

As the Germans, during October, renewed their drive on Moscow and redoubled their efforts to take Leningrad, the American Government became more and more alarmed about the Murmansk supply route and tried repeatedly to impress the Finnish Minister with its concern.[97] Eventually, on October 25, Mr. Schoenfeld was instructed to warn the Finnish Government that unless it ceased its offensive operations, they would necessarily influence Finnish-American relations adversely. Continued American friendship for Finland depended on satisfactory evidence that Finnish inroads on Soviet territory would stop and that Finnish troops would be withdrawn promptly. Unfortunately, through an error in transmission, the original draft of the cable to Schoenfeld, calling for "satisfactory assurances" and for withdrawal "from Soviet territory to a line corresponding to the 1939 Soviet-Finnish frontier," was forwarded to Helsinki in place of the attenuated revised version. However, Mr. Schoenfeld was instructed to say further that if United States ships carrying supplies to Russia by the Arctic route were attacked from Finnish bases, the effect would be such as to provoke a crisis in Finnish-American relations. The cable to Schoenfeld recalled the Welles-Procopé conversation of August 18 and Finland's failure to

---

and Mr. Procopé, September 30; between Mr. Atherton and Sir Ronald Campbell, October 6; between Mr. Higgs and Mr. Procopé, October 6; between Mr. Welles and Mr. Procopé, October 9, 1941. Further: tels. from Schoenfeld (Helsinki), September 25, October 1 and 6; tels. to Schoenfeld, October 4, 7, 10; tel. from Winant, October 6, 1941. The entire development of the Finnish problem until the end of October, 1941, was admirably reviewed in a long memorandum prepared by the American Legation in Helsinki entitled "The Second Russo-Finnish War," dated October 28, 1941. See also Hull: *Memoirs*, II, 978 ff., and Wuorinen: *Finland and World War II*, 133 ff.

[96] Tels. to Schoenfeld, October 7, 10; tels. from Schoenfeld, October 5, 6, 7, 8, 1941.

[97] Memos of conversation between Mr. Berle and Mr. Procopé, October 20 and 23, 1941; *Berle Diary (MS.)*, October 20, 24, 26, 1941.

respond, and furthermore raised the question whether the Minister had adequately informed his Government.[98]

Mr. Schoenfeld submitted the American note to President Ryti on October 27. The crucial passage was the following unequivocal warning:

. . . The American Minister is instructed to state to the Finnish Government specifically that, if it is the desire of Finland to retain the friendship of the United States both at present and in the future, satisfactory assurances must be given the Government of the United States that the Finnish Government intends at once to discontinue all operations of an offensive character against the territory of the Soviet Union and that Finnish troops will promptly be withdrawn in principle from territory of the Soviet Union to a line corresponding to the border of 1939 between Finland and the Soviet Union.[99]

Later on there was some feeling in the State Department that the stronger version of the note, mistakenly sent to Mr. Schoenfeld, might have influenced the Finnish Government to reject the American representations. At the time, however, no objection was raised to the text as reported by the Minister. On the contrary, a second telegram was sent asking Mr. Schoenfeld to make very clear to the Finns how seriously the American Government viewed the aid Finland was giving the Germans, inasmuch as such aid was jeopardizing American security.[100]

It is unlikely that the wording of the American note materially affected the decision of the recipients. Mr. Schoenfeld found President Ryti vehement and intractable. Ryti held out no hope that the Finns would give up territory conquered from the Soviets, certainly not before the final peace conference. Indignantly he rejected the idea that Finnish operations were a threat to American security, the more so as he was prepared to promise that American shipping to Russia would not be attacked. In this connection he remarked that Murmansk was presumably too close to German bases to be of much use and that supplies would probably have to be shipped by way of Archangel, which in turn would be useless as a port during the winter. Mr. Schoenfeld was left with the impression that no change in Finnish policy was to be hoped for.[101]

Without awaiting the formal reply to the American note, the State Department on October 30 instructed Mr. Schoenfeld to see the Finnish President again and inform him that "in view of the speed at which matters are now developing," a reply was desired "at the very earliest possible time."

[98] Tel. to Schoenfeld, October 25, 1941; memo of conversation with Minister Procopé, October 26, 1941; memo of the European Division, November 25, 1941, reporting its investigation of the error in transmission.

[99] Tel. from Schoenfeld, October 27, 1941, and despatch of the same date.

[100] Tel. to Schoenfeld, October 28, 1941; memo of the European Division, November 25, 1941.

[101] Tels. from Schoenfeld, October 27 and 30, 1941; despatch from Schoenfeld, October 30, 1941. See also Wuorinen: *Finland and World War II*, 136.

If the statement were delayed or proved evasive, it would "weaken to an immeasurable extent the efforts which are still being made by us with great difficulty to protect the future interests of Finland in so far as this is possible under circumstances that now can be foreseen." But this new *démarche* led only to another outburst from Ryti, who observed that neither the United States nor Britiain had done much to protect Finland's interests during the Winter War and added that he could not understand how Americans could talk, without cynicism, of safeguarding democratic principles while in alliance with Bolshevism. So far as he could see, the Kremlin was now directing Anglo-American diplomacy.[102]

This was apparently the last straw for Mr. Hull, who on November 3 informed the country, through a press statement, that the Finns had ignored the possibility of peace in August, that the United States had warned them repeatedly of the danger of their ultimate subjugation by Hitler, and that recently the Administration had called upon the Finns to withdraw their troops from Soviet territory on pain of losing American friendship. The Helsinki press at once disputed that there had ever been a "peace offer" and unanimously protested against American "pressure." The State Department thereupon (November 7) published the records of the Welles-Procopé conversation of August 18 and the text of the American note of October 3.[103] In short, relations between the two countries sank to the level of petulant recrimination and, in the words of Secretary Hull, were perilously close to a breach.

There were undoubtedly good grounds for President Ryti's suspicion of Soviet influence on the strong American representations, for Lord Halifax had informed the State Department that the Kremlin was insisting on a British declaration of war against Finland.[104] To some extent the American *démarche* was probably intended to forestall the need for such drastic action, while Mr. Churchill was arguing with Stalin that a declaration of war might have an adverse effect on American opinion.[105] But time was now running out, for while Stalin remained deaf to British arguments, the Finns continued obdurate. Little is known of the discussions in Helsinki Government circles, but it would appear that eventually even the Social Democrats, who were strongly in favor of closing out the war, recognized the impossibility of a policy that would antagonize the Germans.[106]

[102] Tel. to Schoenfeld, October 30, 1941; tel. from Schoenfeld, October 31, 1941.

[103] Tels. to Schoenfeld, November 3 and 8, 1941; tels. from Schoenfeld, November 5 and 7, 1941.

[104] Memos of conversation between Mr. Hull and Lord Halifax, October 29 and 31, 1941; and a State Department memo of November 1, 1941, reviewing the pros and cons of such action by the British.

[105] Message of Churchill to Stalin, November 4, 1941 (Churchill: *The Grand Alliance,* 527-28).

[106] Tels. from Schoenfeld, November 4 and 8, 1941. See also the sympathetic observations of Erfurth: *Der finnische Krieg,* 200 ff.

The Finnish reply to the American note, finally submitted on November 11, was a long document. It reviewed the history of Finnish-Soviet relations, recalled Soviet aggression in 1939, and stoutly maintained that the Kremlin had been poised for a new attack in the summer of 1941. Under the circumstances, it argued, the Finns were justified in making war and seizing territory necessary for their future security. They had, they asserted, no agreements with the Germans that might jeopardize their future independence, and their operations in no way threatened the security of other nations. With respect to the peace feeler of August, 1941, they stood by their contention that Mr. Welles had merely given them information, without specification of terms or indication of guarantees. In short, the note merely recapitulated arguments already familiar. By way of comment Mr. Schoenfeld reported that the Finns were almost unanimous in support of their Government's position, that they were sincere in their views, and that they simply could not believe that the United States would ever take drastic action against them. The only chance of getting the Finns out of the war, he thought, would be for the United States and Britain to give them guarantees of the settlement to be made with the Kremlin, but even this chance was slim indeed in view of the obvious determination of the Germans to retain Finland as a northern outpost at all costs.[107]

After some deliberation the State Department decided that no useful purpose would be served by replying to the Finnish note. Presently the situation was still further aggravated by the visit of the Finnish Foreign Minister to Berlin and by Finland's adherence to the Anti-Comintern Pact (November 25). Though this step actually appears to have been imposed on the Finns as a condition for the delivery of much-needed German grain, it could be taken abroad only as conclusive evidence that Finland was completely at Hitler's mercy. As Mr. Schoenfeld had so frequently pointed out, the Finns were not really free to act; in their desire to reconquer lost territory and provide for their national security they had sacrificed their independence. Reviewing the military situation, Secretary Stimson declared (November 25):

Regardless of the laudable ambition of the Finnish nation to recover ground lost to the Russians in the last war between these nations, it is evident that the Finns are now being used by the Germans to further the German efforts to defeat the Russian forces in the Leningrad-Lake Onega theater. It is regrettable that the Finnish Army should

---

[107] Tels. from Schoenfeld, November 8, 12, 14, 1941; memos of conversation with Mr. Procopé, November 12 and 13, 1941; memo by the Division of European Affairs, November 12, 1941; memo by Mr. Atherton, November 17, 1941. The development of affairs was reviewed in a memorandum of the American Legation in Helsinki, entitled "Memorandum on Finnish-American Relations, October, 1941—October, 1942," dated November 30, 1942. The full text of the Finnish note of November 11 is printed in *Documents on American Foreign Relations*, IV, 644 ff. See also Wuorinen: *Finland and World War II*, 138.

allow this condition to continue. It is not only inimical to the final interests of Finland, but it enables Germany to concentrate her efforts on a line harmful to the interests of the United States.

Secretary Hull followed this up by a press release on November 28, in which he pointed out that the last Finnish note had thrown no real light on the extent of Finnish-German coöperation against Soviet Russia nor on the threat to the Anglo-American supply lines. Furthermore:

The recent journey of the Finnish Foreign Minister to Berlin to join with Hitler's puppet governments over Europe in signing the "anti-Comintern Pact," used by Hitler solely as an instrument to wage a war of conquest and domination against free peoples, is highly significant and cannot be camouflaged or explained away by propaganda attacks on nations engaged in defending themselves. . . . The Secretary concluded by saying that every act of the Finnish Government since the delivery of its note has confirmed our apprehensions that it is fully coöperating with the Hitler forces.[108]

By this time the die had already been cast. On November 27 Lord Halifax had informed Under Secretary Welles that the British had failed to convince Stalin that a declaration of war on Finland would only drive that country into the arms of Hitler, and that they felt it necessary to yield to the Kremlin if they desired to retain the confidence of the Soviet Government. The Ambassador therefore requested the United States to transmit a note to Helsinki warning that Government that unless it ceased military operations and withdrew from all active participation in hostilities by December 3 (later changed to December 5), the British Government would have no choice but to declare a state of war.[109] At the same time Mr. Churchill sent a personal message to Marshal Mannerheim, through American channels, arguing that the Finnish forces had advanced far enough and begging him simply to stop fighting on the plea that the weather had become too severe. The Prime Minister reiterated his confidence in British victory and warned that Finland might, in the end, find itself in the same dock with guilty and defeated Nazis.[110]

Although the Finns were by this time exhausted and seem to have already decided to discontinue military operations as soon as a few more immediate objectives had been attained, nothing came of last-minute British or American efforts to induce them to terminate their war against the Soviet Union. Omitting details, their deliberations all led to the conclusion that they could not defy the Germans and that, if it was impossible to avoid hostilities with

---

[108] *Documents on American Foreign Relations,* IV, 652-53; Wuorinen: *Finland and World War II,* 127.

[109] Memo of conversation between Mr. Welles and Lord Halifax, November 27, 1941, with attached British memo of November 26, 1941. The text of the British ultimatum is printed in *Documents on American Foreign Relations,* IV, 640-41. For Mr. Churchill's correspondence with Stalin and for British policy generally see Churchill: *The Grand Alliance,* 531 ff.

[110] Tel. to Schoenfeld, November 29, 1941; Churchill: *The Grand Alliance,* 534-35.

one side or the other, Great Britain and the United States, both at a distance, were less dangerous than the Nazis, whose troops were already in the country. Marshal Mannerheim therefore replied to Mr. Churchill that it would be impossible for him to suspend operations until his troops had reached the positions required for Finland's security. The official reply of the Helsinki Government (December 4) simply repeated that Finland's sole aim was to safeguard its existence and security. The Finnish Army, it pointed out, was not far from the achievement of its strategic aims, "namely the liberation of the parts of Finland's state territory lost under the terms of the Peace of Moscow and the rendering harmless of the areas from where the enemy had been preparing to destroy Finland."[111]

In conversation with the Finnish Minister on December 6, the day of the British declaration of war on Finland, Mr. Welles expressed his unhappiness "that the Finnish people would now cast in their lot with Hitler, with the full knowledge that any ultimate success of Hitler would result in their own enslavement." He ventured the thought that, "were the Government of Finland to cease hostilities in the immediate future and announce its willingness to discuss peace terms with the Soviet Union, a situation might develop which would result in a renewal of relations between Great Britain and Finland and which would most decidedly create a far more favorable and friendly opinion in the United States with regard to Finland."[112] But these were hardly more than expressions of pious hope. The British declaration of war was based on considerations over and above the immediate circumstances. All the evidence indicates that the German forces in Finland were unable to take Murmansk without Finnish help and that the Finns refused to give that help, as they had earlier refused to join in operations against Leningrad. It is almost unthinkable that the Finns themselves would have attacked or even obstructed the Anglo-American supply lines. All this explains why not only the Americans but the British tried to avoid formal hostilities against a nation with which in so many respects they deeply sympathized. But the Kremlin had its own purposes and, in the last analysis, the British action against Finland was one more instance of yielding to Soviet pressure in the interests of preserving the alliance, which at that time seemed vital to ultimate victory.

[111] Tels. from Schoenfeld, December 3, transmitting Mannerheim's reply, and December 4, 1941, transmitting the reply of the Finnish Government. See also Churchill: *The Grand Alliance,* 533 ff., and Wuorinen: *Finland and World War II,* 134. In tels. of November 29, December 1, 3, 4, 5, 7, 1941, Mr. Schoenfeld reported what he could learn of the discussions in Finnish Government circles. His information all pointed to the fact that fear of Germany precluded a satisfactory reply.

[112] Memo of conversation between Mr. Welles and Minister Procopé, December 6, 1941.

CHAPTER XXVI

Around and Around the Same Circle

1. ADVENT OF THE TOJO CABINET

In a conversation with the Japanese emissary, Mr. Saburo Kurusu, shortly after his arrival in Washington in mid-November, 1941, Secretary Hull remarked of his lengthy series of talks with Admiral Nomura that he and the Ambassador always seemed "to come to a certain point and then start going around and around the same circle."[1] No one who has waded through the tedious records of the Hull-Nomura conversations, which Mr. Hull steadfastly refused to classify as more than "exploratory," is likely to challenge the Secretary's statement. Endless hours of patient discussion and fruitless argument had resulted in no measurable progress when Prince Konoye's Government fell on October 16, 1941. It seemed likely at first that the new Prime Minister, General Tojo, who retained the status of an Army officer on active duty, would cut off the talk and resort to action. But information from Ambassador Grew, fortified by knowledge drawn from intercepted Japanese messages to Nomura, revealed cleavages within the new Cabinet and indicated the likelihood that the effort to achieve an agreement would be continued at least for a time.[2]

This initial intelligence kindled a glimmer of hope in Washington, although it was far from clear on what basis the Tojo Cabinet would proceed with the discussion. The root of the Cabinet crisis which led to Konoye's downfall had been the refusal of General Tojo and the Army to consider the evacuation of Japanese troops from China. Of all the issues between Tokyo and Washington this, according to Konoye, was thought crucial for Japan. Nevertheless, the Emperor, in ordering Tojo to form a Government, had told him in effect to reconsider the major issues *de novo* and to continue the conversations at all costs. Konoye himself believed that the new Premier

[1] *Pearl Harbor Attack,* XII, 143.
[2] *Supra,* Chapter XXII, Section 5.

would make an honest effort to carry out this bidding.[3] But, as Ambassador Grew noted in his diary: "If Tojo should succeed, it would indeed be little short of miraculous. . . . On the face of things just now it is difficult to see success in the near future, if ever. In spite of the Emperor's active intervention, I cannot avoid the conviction that the outlook is far less favorable than it was before."[4]

More than two weeks were to pass before Washington obtained any firm information of the new Government's position. Meanwhile officials and the press on both sides of the Pacific indulged in most inauspicious exchanges. In reply to the boast of the Japanese Chief of Naval Intelligence that the Japanese Navy was "ready and itching for action if need be," Secretary Knox declared the situation very strained, adding: "We are satisfied in our own minds that the Japanese have no intention of abandoning their expansion plans. If they pursue that course, a collision is inevitable."[5] Major George Fielding Eliot, the popular commentator on military affairs, even raised the question whether the present might not offer the last chance to eliminate Japan as a nuisance. In the face of combined action by the United States, Britain, Russia, China, and the Netherlands, Japan would have to capitulate or go to war, a course which it could not long sustain.[6]

Tokyo made equally threatening noises. General Tojo declared publicly that his country's policies were "immutable and irrevocable." There could be no going backward: "If a hundred million people merge into one iron solidarity to go forward, nothing can stop us."[7] The official Japanese news agency, *Domei,* followed up the Premier's boast with a warning that unless the United States relaxed its economic pressure, a clash in the Pacific seemed inevitable. Japan simply could not abandon its plans for the Co-Prosperity Sphere. General Tojo, it continued, would announce to Parliament on November 15 the time limit to be set for the negotiations with the United States. In any event, the Cabinet was determined to establish the New Order despite the "arbitrary, dogmatic attitude of the United States."[8]

Records now available point clearly to the conclusion that in neither capital was there genuine hope of successful negotiation. The Japanese yearned to reach an agreement, but only if it could be achieved promptly and without renunciation of well-developed plans for expansion. The United States, in turn, would have welcomed a stabilization of the Far

[3] Memo of conversation between Prince Konoye and Mr. Max Bishop of the State Department, November 7, 1945, subject: "Some Political Developments in Japan in 1941"; Herbert Feis: *The Road to Pearl Harbor* (Princeton, 1950), 286-87; Toshikazu Kase: *Journey to the "Missouri"* (New Haven, 1950), 55-56.

[4] *Grew Diary (MS.)*, summary for October, 1941.

[5] *The New York Times,* October 30, 1941.

[6] *New York Herald Tribune,* October 19, 1941.

[7] *The New York Times,* October 27, 31, 1941.

[8] James B. Reston in *The New York Times,* October 30; Tolischus, reporting from Tokyo, *The New York Times,* November 2, 3, 1941.

Eastern situation so as to devote all its energies to Europe, but not at the expense of China nor at the cost of any sacrifice of fundamental principles. While the flame of hope continued to flicker uncertainly and Mr. Hull doggedly refused to admit failure, each side knew that time was running out.

The significant difference between the two countries was Tokyo's conviction that it could not brook delay, as against Washington's anxiety to forestall a decision. If the Japanese were to resort to war, they must do so before their supplies ran too low and while the weather was still favorable. Washington, however, valued every week's, every day's delay in the hope that if its preparations could be completed, they would be sufficiently formidable to deter its antagonist from hostilities. Secretary Stimson was an enthusiastic supporter of the idea of rushing Flying Fortresses to the Philippines the minute they became available, so convinced was he that if sufficient aircraft could be despatched over the next few months, the Japanese would feel obliged to renounce their southward advance on Singapore and the Indies. At every opportunity he preached this doctrine to the President and to Secretary Hull, urging the need for avoiding a showdown and begging that no effort be spared to secure from the Russians air bases in Siberia which would pose the threat of great bomber sweeps over Japan.[9]

Accordingly, in United States Government circles the question of breaking off negotiations never arose. Washington's problem was to determine whether and when the Japanese Government, under Tojo's pressure, would precipitate a break by fresh aggressions. As Prince Konoye has since confirmed, the Japanese military constantly cited the lack of progress in the negotiations as proof of the necessity for further dispositions in the interest of preparedness.[10] There was always the possibility that the Japanese, inspired by the triumphant surge of the German armies toward Moscow, would fall upon the Soviet Far East whence, Tokyo estimated, the Soviet Command had been obliged to withdraw a third of its forces.[11] Fearful of such an attack, the Soviet Government itself had proposed that Britain and the United Sttaes join in warning Japan against a blockade of Vladivostok or an attack on Siberia. London was willing, but Secretary Hull, always opposed to warnings without adequate backing, determined for the time being to adhere to the policy of treating Japanese aggression as a whole rather than in its isolated manifestations. Nevertheless, Washington decided to ship supplies to Russia for a time via Archangel rather than Vladivostok.[12]

[9] Letter of Secretary Stimson to the President, October 21, 1941 (*Pearl Harbor Attack*, XX, 4442 ff.); *Stimson Diary* (*MS.*), October 21, 28, November 6, 1941 (talks with Harriman, Hull, and the President, respectively); Feis: *The Road to Pearl Harbor*, 300-301; Watson: *Chief of Staff: Prewar Plans and Preparations*, 445 ff.

[10] Memo of conversation between Prince Konoye and Mr. Max Bishop, November 6, 1945, entitled: "Background of Political Developments in Japan before Pearl Harbor."

[11] Japanese Foreign Office memo of early November, 1941 (*Tokyo War Crimes Documents*, 1559A).

[12] Tel. from Winant, October 22, reporting conversations with Eden and Maisky; memos of conversation between Mr. Hull and Lord Halifax, October 29, 31, 1941.

Much more immediate seemed the danger that the Japanese would resume their land advance from Indo-China against Yunnan, the Burma Road, or Siam (Thailand). There were incessant reports of increasing Japanese concentrations in Indo-China. Though it was known that the French were resisting Japanese demands for permission to augment their forces in Tonkin above the figure of twenty-five thousand laid down in the agreement of September, 1940, the French themselves had no confidence that Tokyo would not resort to arbitrary action.[13]

In considerable anxiety the Siamese Government renewed its appeals to London and Washington for aid. It proposed that Britain despatch twenty-four fighter aircraft from Singapore, along with other war supplies. The planes would be replaced by others from the United States. The British, though they did not regard the Bangkok regime as wholly trustworthy, were willing to take the risk and the United States representative in Bangkok vigorously endorsed the proposal. Consequently the issue became the subject of brisk debate in Washington throughout November. In view of the shortage of planes and the unlikelihood that Siam could make good use of them, very little enthusiasm for the proposal was generated. Mr. Hornbeck took the view that a joint British-American warning to Japan against attack on Siam would prove much more effective than odds and ends of matériel. But the question of a warning to Japan clearly transcended specific problems such as Vladivostok or Siam. In addition, the State and War Departments shared the conviction that such planes as the British might send to Siam could not be replaced from American stocks. Aviation gasoline might be made available and consideration might be given to offering Bangkok a loan. If the Japanese actually attacked Siam and the latter resisted, Lend-Lease aid could be furnished on the same basis as to China. Beyond this Washington felt unable to go.[14]

Although the problem of Siam was difficult, its significance was far less than that of China, whose situation by October, 1941, had become little short of desperate. While the Japanese had signally failed to bring the Chungking Government to heel, Nationalist China, almost completely bereft of air power, had virtually exhausted its meager resources. Chungking itself

[13] Tel. from Grew, October 28; tel. from Reed (Hanoi), October 29; tel. from the Naval Attaché at Chungking, October 30, 1941 (this last printed in *Pearl Harbor Attack*, XV, 1479).

[14] Memo of Hornbeck to Welles, October 28, referring to two memoranda from the British Embassy left by Sir Ronald Campbell, October 25, 1941; further, the long list of telegrams from Bangkok and other documents on Siam printed in *Pearl Harbor Attack*, XIX, 3720-44. Something of the British attitude is reflected in Sir Robert Brooke-Popham's despatch: *Operations in the Far East from 17th October 1940 to 27th December 1941* (Supplement to the *London Gazette*, January 20, 1948, pp. 545-56, 550). Lord Halifax's proposal that the United States extend a ten million dollar credit to Siam was finally rejected on the grounds that it would be useless unless combined with stronger measures of support (tels. from Bangkok, November 27, 30, December 1, 1941; memo of Mr. Livesey to Mr. Berle, December 4, 1941).

was being bombed with merciless regularity and complete impunity. Colonel Claire Chennault's Volunteer Air Force, consisting of some hundred American pilots and planes, was still in training at a British base in Burma.[15] Very little indeed of the promised Lend-Lease supplies had actually reached Chungking, and there was acute danger that Japan would cut the Burma Road and thus block the one remaining channel through which a trickle of Anglo-American supplies flowed to the Nationalist forces. The Generalissimo felt neglected and unappreciated. Having had no part either in the Atlantic or the Moscow Conference, he regarded himself as relegated to the periphery of the grand alliance. Meanwhile he was not only fighting to the limit to check Japanese aggression, but was doing so in the expectation that he would have to bear alone the brunt of the forthcoming Japanese attack.

It is understandable that the advent of the Tojo Cabinet should have produced something close to panic in Chungking. The Chinese supposed, with good reason, that the new Government would devote itself first and foremost to the liquidation of the China Incident. Recurrent reports of Japanese troop concentrations in Indo-China and constant rumors of a build-up on Hainan Island pointed to the likelihood of an early Japanese advance into Yunnan with the object of capturing Kunming and severing the Burma Road. At this critical juncture General John Magruder, chief of the American Military Mission and an authority on China, arrived in the Nationalist capital for his first interview with Chiang Kai-shek. The Generalissimo brushed aside talk of future Lend-Lease aid, asserting that the Japanese attack would come before the end of November and that he could resist it successfully only if he were given air power immediately:

The Generalissimo insisted, and rightly [reported General Magruder], that Chinese resistance would end if Kunming were lost. In his analysis he argued that Kunming was the Key to the Pacific; if it fell, China would fall, and the attack on Malay Asia would inevitably follow. War in the Pacific then was a certainty. If China could hold, peace in the Pacific might be saved.

To Chiang Kai-shek the only salvation seemed to lie in commitment of the Royal Air Force at Singapore to the defense of Yunnan. He urged the President to intercede with London to this end, and further suggested that the United States join with Great Britain in warning Japan that an attack on Kunming would be inimical to American and British interests. General Magruder supported the Generalissimo's argument. He agreed on the likelihood of a Japanese attack on Yunnan which, if successful, would spell the end of Chinese resistance. He predicted that the Chinese, unless they had air power, would face defeat. Since the American Volunteer Group was not yet ready for action and since Lend-Lease aid in the immediate future was im-

[15] Major General Claire L. Chennault: *Way of a Fighter* (New York: 1949), 106 ff.

practicable, Magruder could see no other solution than the use of the aircraft at Singapore or "perhaps organized units from the Philippines."[16]

Chiang Kai-shek's appeal to Magruder was but the first of a long series. Presently they came so thick and fast as to engender great confusion among the recipients. General Magruder reported directly to the Secretary of War and the Chief of Staff, who considered the problem without consulting the State Department. On October 29 the Chungking Foreign Office advised Ambassador Gauss of the substance of a message which the Generalissimo was sending to the President. For some reason this message was not sent through the Chinese Embassy in Washington, but to Mr. T. V. Soong, who was in charge of the purchase of supplies for China in the United States. Soong sent the message to the President through Secretary Morgenthau on October 30, but failed to inform the Chinese Ambassador, Dr. Hu Shih, who continued to wait for it. Not until November 4, after the State Department had cabled Chungking for an official text, was another message received from the Chinese Embassy in Washington and the American Embassy in Chungking. This included an appeal which Chiang Kai-shek had meanwhile despatched to Mr. Churchill and which the Prime Minister had promptly relayed to the President on November 5. This confusion thrice compounded testifies to the overwrought atmosphere in Chungking as the axe seemed about to fall.[17]

Fortunately the content of all these messages was so similar that they may safely be treated as one. Of significance, however, was the emphasis in the message of October 30 on the necessity of a warning to Japan against an attack on Yunnan:

This move [wrote Chiang] may possibly be averted if America takes immediate action by informing Japan that an attack on Yunnan through Indo-China would be viewed by America as a definite step in southward expansion and that America cannot remain indifferent. Simultaneously military preparations should be made to meet this eventuality.

In his message of November 2 the Generalissimo suggested that British air units at Singapore could support the American Volunteer Group and the Chinese Air Force, either as part of the latter or as a separate volunteer force. Chiang also pointed out that the United States could make a signifi-

---

[16] Magruder Report, October 28, 1941 (*Pearl Harbor Attack*, XV, 1480-81). We have used also the files of the Magruder Mission in the custody of the Historical Division, Department of the Army.

[17] Note of Mr. Morgenthau to the President, transmitting the message from Soong, October 30 (*Pearl Harbor Attack*, XIV, 1077 ff.; *Morgenthau Diaries, MS.*, Vol. 456, p. 16); tel. from Gauss, October 29; tel. to Gauss, November 3; memo of conversation between Mr. Hornbeck and the Chinese Ambassador, October 31; message from the Generalissimo to the President, November 2, received November 4 (*Pearl Harbor Attack*, XV, 1476-78); tel. from Gauss, November 3; tel. from the Prime Minister to the President, November 5, 1941 (*Pearl Harbor Attack*, XIX, 3467 ff.). See also Winston S. Churchill: *The Grand Alliance* (Boston, 1950), 591-93.

cant contribution by drawing upon its air strength in the Philippines. In both messages much was made of the argument that unless Washington took the initiative, the British would probably not act or at any rate not act in time.

On this latter point the Generalissimo's estimate was mistaken. Mr. Churchill continued to favor a warning to Japan such as he had suggested at the Atlantic Conference. He probably believed that such a joint warning would either deter Tokyo from war or, contrariwise, would draw the United States into the subsequent hostilities. In any case the British took a firm stand on their own. On October 29 the British Ambassador in Tokyo called Foreign Minister Togo's attention to the fact that Japan's activities in Indo-China were adjacent to vital British life lines. A further advance would be regarded in London as a direct threat and would be countered by something more than mere economic measures. Britain, continued Sir Robert Craigie, did not want war, but "it would be a great mistake on the part of the Japanese military authorities to assume that Great Britain was either afraid of Japan or insufficiently prepared to meet any threat to British security in southeastern Asia."[18] This statement was followed on November 2 by Prime Minister Churchill's cable informing Mr. Roosevelt that the great new battleship, *Prince of Wales,* was being despatched to the Indian Ocean. "There is nothing," added Mr. Churchill, "like having something that can catch and kill anything. . . . The firmer your attitude and ours, the less chance of their taking the plunge."[19]

The British, it will be recalled, had already suggested that, in connection with the Siamese issue, the United States join them in a warning to Tokyo. The Chinese crisis provided an opportunity to renew this proposal in even stronger terms. In transmitting to the President the text of Chiang Kai-shek's appeal, Mr. Churchill therefore took occasion to state that, despite the inadequacies of Britain's forces at Singapore, he was ready to make some pilots and even a few aircraft available to the Chinese if they could arrive in time. He then tackled the larger issue:

What we need now is a deterrent of the most general and formidable character. The Japanese have as yet taken no final decision and the Emperor appears to be exercising restraint. When we talked about this at Placentia, you spoke of gaining time, and this policy has been brilliantly successful so far. But our joint embargo is steadily forcing the Japanese to decisions for peace or war.

The Prime Minister therefore expressed the hope that the President would be willing to warn Japan. If so the British would do likewise:

No independent action by ourselves will deter Japan because we are so tied up

[18] *Grew Diary (MS.),* October 29, 1941.
[19] Tel. from the Prime Minister to the President, November 2, 1941. On the considerations behind the build-up of the British Far Eastern Fleet, see Churchill: *The Grand Alliance,* 589-91, 854-59. See also Feis: *The Road to Pearl Harbor,* 301.

elsewhere. But of course we will stand with you and do our utmost to back you in whatever course you choose. I think, myself, that Japan is more likely to drift into war than to plunge in.[20]

There was nothing fuzzy about the British position. Mr. Churchill was prepared to go the limit if the United States decided to do likewise. Momentarily it seemed that Mr. Roosevelt agreed. He had immediately sent Mr. Hull the Generalissimo's message of October 30 with the notation: "Can we do anything along these lines? How about telling Japan a move to close the Burma Road would be inimical?"[21] In a conversation of considerable length with Mr. T. V. Soong on October 31 the President had said that something might be done by way of a warning to Japan, but that in any event he would do what he could to induce the British to send planes from Singapore.[22]

2. A WAR WARNING TO JAPAN?

The opening days of November thus found Administration leaders again debating the merits of a warning to Japan as a means of forestalling an attack on Yunnan or Siam and preventing the collapse of Chinese resistance. Mr. Hornbeck, the most literary if not still the most influential of Secretary Hull's advisers on the Far East, has amply documented his views. "Japan will be disinclined to undertake additional military ventures where she has reason to believe she would be met with vigorous resistance, but will be likely to strike at weak areas capable of being easily conquered."[23] He felt virtually certain that in the final reckoning the Japanese would not fight and that, even if they did, they could not last long. Unless a halt were called to their threats and aggressions, they would go on hoodwinking their opponents no matter in which direction they turned their advance:

The important fact, however, and a *certainty* is that the Japanese are keeping the United States, Russia, China, the British and the Dutch worried, and are keeping immobilized in the western Pacific area a huge aggregate amount of armed forces and associated materials which, were Japan's armed forces hamstrung or sterilized, might be released for use in support of Great Britain and Russia against Nazi Germany.

[20] Tel. from the Prime Minister to the President, November 5, 1941 (*Pearl Harbor Attack,* XIX, 3467 ff.; Churchill: *The Grand Alliance,* 592-93). We have also used the Prime Minister's reply to Chiang Kai-shek to which reference is made in *The Grand Alliance,* 593.

[21] *Pearl Harbor Attack,* XIV, 1077.

[22] The President's sentiments were reported by Soong to the Chinese Ambassador and by him to Mr. Hornbeck (memo of conversation between Hornbeck and the Chinese Ambassador, October 31, 1941). We have also used Soong's memo to the President, November 8, 1941 (*Roosevelt Papers,* Secretary's File, Box 74; *Morgenthau Diaries, MS.,* Vol. 459, p. 237).

[23] Memo of Hornbeck, October 29, commenting on a lengthy memo of the Far East Division, October 25, 1941, entitled: "Observations on the Far Eastern Situation and on American Policy in Relation Thereto."

For Mr. Hornbeck, then, the obvious move was to submit a stiff warning to Tokyo. This would cause Japan either to draw back or resort to war. "If, having taken the risk, we should find armed hostilities between Japan and ourselves thrust upon us, there would then exist a situation than which a good many other conceivable situations might be worse."[24]

In view of the President's attitude and the argumentation of Mr. Hornbeck, Secretary Hull could hardly refuse at least to discuss the case for strong measures. On November 1 he convened a meeting of State Department officials and officers of the Army and Navy War Plans and Intelligence staffs. He explained again his objection to further warnings to Japan unless they could be backed up by military force—a view shared by Mr. Hamilton and Mr. Ballantine of the Far East Division. The military men gave unqualified support to his position. Both Services had just drawn up estimates of the situation in which, while acknowledging the possibility of a Japanese attack on Yunnan, they emphasized their belief that Japanese troops in Indo-China were too few to permit an immediate attack, that it would take the Japanese at least two months to complete their preparations, and that it would be difficult for them to find the additional forces required without seriously weakening themselves elsewhere. Furthermore, terrain difficulties made the success of operations in Yunnan problematical and there was at least a chance that the Chinese could hold out against attack if it came. In any event, the use of American air units would probably lead to war, which at the time was highly undesirable from the point of view of strategy.

Certain State Department officers—presumably including Mr. Hornbeck—were not convinced by this reasoning. They pointed out that strong warnings did not necessarily imply immediate military action and that, even if such action ensued, Japan could be disposed of in a relatively short time. The meeting of minds was thus far from complete and the discussions had to be continued on the following day, again without real agreement between the civilians and the military. Finally the whole issue was canvassed in a meeting of the Joint Board of the Army and Navy, in the course of which General Marshall and Admiral Stark received a detailed briefing on what had occurred, together with the negative recommendations of the Army and Navy planners. These were adopted by the Joint Board and recapitulated in a memorandum to the President (November 5) which was intended as a basic statement of the military position, on which alone the nation's foreign policy could be safely grounded. It may be noted that on the same day, November 5, 1941, the Japanese Government made a vital policy decision. On both sides the stage was being set for the swelling theme.

The Joint Board's memorandum retraced the principles of United States

---

[24] Memos of Hornbeck, October 29, 31, November 3, 1941. The October 29 memo is printed in *Pearl Harbor Attack*, V, 2085 ff.

strategy as agreed upon many months before. The argument presented to Mr. Roosevelt ran as follows:

There is little doubt that a Japanese offensive against the Burma Road would be a very severe blow to the Chinese Central Government. The result might even be the collapse of further effective military resistance by that Government, and thus the liquidation by Japan of the "China Incident." If use of the Burma Road is lost, United States and British Commonwealth aid to China will be seriously curtailed for some months. If resistance by the Chinese Central Government ceases, the need for Japanese troops in China will be reduced. These troops can then be employed elsewhere, after the lapse of time sufficient to permit their withdrawal.

Concentration of Japanese troops for the contemplated offensive, based in northern Indo-China, cannot be completed in less than about two months, although initial offensive operations might be undertaken before that time. The advance towards Kunming over nearly three hundred miles of rough country, with poor communications, will be extremely difficult. The maintenance of supply lines will not be easy. The Chinese, on favorable defense terrain, would have a good chance of defeating this offensive by the use of ground troops alone, provided those troops are adequate in quality and numbers.

The question that the Chief of Naval Operations and the Chief of Staff have taken under consideration is whether or not the United States is justified in undertaking offensive military operations with United States forces against Japan, to prevent her from severing the Burma Road. They consider that such operations, however well disguised, would lead to war.

At the present time the United States Fleet in the Pacific is inferior to the Japanese Fleet, and cannot undertake an unlimited offensive in the western Pacific. In order to be able to do so, it would have to be strengthened by withdrawing practically all naval vessels from the Atlantic except those assigned to local defense forces. An unlimited offensive by the Pacific Fleet would require tremendous merchant tonnage, which could only be withdrawn from services now considered essential. The result of withdrawals from the Atlantic of naval and merchant strength might well cause the United Kingdom to lose the Battle of the Atlantic in the near future.

The current plans for war against Japan in the Far East are to conduct defensive war, in coöperation with the British and Dutch, for the defense of the Philippines and the British and Dutch Indies. The Philippines are now being reinforced. The present combined naval, air, and ground forces will make attack on the islands a hazardous undertaking. By about the middle of December, 1941, United States air and submarine strength in the Philippines will have become a positive threat to any Japanese operations south of Formosa. The United States Army Air Forces in the Philippines will have reached the projected strength by February or March, 1942. The potency of this threat will have then increased to a point where it might well be a deciding factor in deterring Japan in operations in the area south and west of the Philippines. By this time, additional British naval and air reinforcements to Singapore will have arrived. The general defensive strength of the entire southern area against possible Japanese operations will have reached impressive proportions.

Until such time as the Burma Road is closed, aid can be extended to Chiang Kai-shek by measures which probably will not result in war with Japan. These measures are: continuation of economic pressure against Japan, supplying increasing amounts of munitions under the Lend-Lease, and continuation and acceleration of aid to the American Volunteer Group.

The Chief of Naval Operations and the Chief of Staff are in accord in the following conclusions:

a). The basic military policies and strategy agreed to in the United States-British Staff conversations remain sound. The primary objective of the two nations is the defeat of Germany. If Japan be defeated and Germany remain undefeated, decision will still not have been reached. In any case, an unlimited offensive war should not be undertaken against Japan, since such a war would greatly weaken the combined effort in the Atlantic against Germany, the most dangerous enemy.

b). War between the United States and Japan should be avoided while building up the defensive forces in the Far East, until such time as Japan attacks or directly threatens territories whose security to the United States is of very great importance. Military action against Japan should be undertaken only in one or more of the following contingencies:

1). A direct act of war by Japanese armed forces against the territory or mandated territory of the United States, the British Commonwealth, or the Netherlands East Indies;

2). The movement of Japanese forces into Thailand (Siam) to the west of 100° East or south of 10° North; or into Portuguese Timor, New Caledonia, or the Loyalty Islands.

c). If war with Japan cannot be avoided, it should follow the strategic lines of existing war plans; i.e., military operations should be primarily defensive, with the object of holding territory, and weakening Japan's economic position.

d). Considering world strategy, a Japanese advance against Kunming, into Thailand except as previously indicated, or an attack on Russia, would not justify intervention by the United States against Japan.

e). All possible aid short of actual war against Japan should be extended to the Chinese Central Government.

f). In case it is decided to undertake war against Japan, complete coördinated action in the diplomatic, economic, and military fields should be undertaken in common by the United States, the British Commonwealth, and the Netherlands East Indies.

The Chief of Naval Operations and the Chief of Staff recommend that the United States policy in the Far East be based on the above conclusions.

Specifically they recommend:

That the dispatch of United States armed forces for intervention against Japan in China be disapproved.

That material aid to China be accelerated consonant with the needs of Russia, Great Britain and our own forces.

That aid to the American Volunteer Group be continued and accelerated to the maximum practicable extent.

That no ultimatum be delivered to Japan.[25]

[25] The records of the conferences of November 1 and 3, and the letter to the President of November 5, are printed in *Pearl Harbor Attack*, XIV, 1061-67. The Naval Intelligence estimate of November 1 is printed in Vol. XV, 1478-79, and the Military Intelligence estimates of November 1 and 2 in Vol. XIV, 1361-63.

Even this carefully developed statement of strategy apparently did not meet with unreserved or undivided approval in the State Department. There was another conference between Mr. Hull, Mr. Hornbeck, Admiral Stark, and General Marshall on November 5, during which Mr. Hornbeck seems to have argued that the decision of the Joint Board was tantamount to the abandonment of China, which regarded itself as morally an ally of the powers resisting aggression. If, continued Hornbeck, Chinese resistance collapsed, the Japanese would be free to turn their forces to other objectives. "Should it not," he queried, "be a constant object of British and American political, economic and military strategy to keep China's moral and material capacity to resist Japan at a high enough point to *ensure against* a termination of Chinese resistance?"[26]

There was the crux of the disagreement. Although Secretary Hull subsequently testified that he was "in thorough accord" with General Marshall and Admiral Stark that no American forces should be sent to China at this time and that no ultimatum should be despatched to Tokyo, he doubtless shared Mr. Hornbeck's keen sense of moral obligation to China and of the importance of keeping China actively in the war. The War Department planners, on the other hand, held that "from the larger viewpoint, prospective Chinese defeat would not warrant involvement of the United States, at this time, in war with Japan."[27] In the end, however, Mr. Roosevelt accepted the counsel of the military men and, with the exception of the terms of a direct attack on American interests, followed the course outlined by the Joint Board. In his reply to Mr. Churchill on November 7 he expressed doubt whether Japanese preparations were such as to warrant expectation of an attack on Yunnan in the near future. He promised to do his best to increase and expedite Lend-Lease aid to China and to build up the American Volunteer Group. As for the warning to Tokyo, he added:

We feel that measures such as the foregoing and those which you have in mind along the lines we are taking, together with continuing efforts to strengthen our defenses in the Philippine Islands, paralleled by similar efforts by you in the Singapore area, will tend to increase Japan's hesitation, whereas in Japan's present mood, new formalized verbal warning or remonstrance might have, with at least an even chance, an opposite effect.[28]

Two days later Mr. Roosevelt informed Mr. Harold Balfour, British Under Secretary of State for Air, who had come to Washington in the hope of increasing the allocation of heavy bombers to Britain, that he could make

[26] Letter of Hornbeck to Stimson, following the conference (*Pearl Harbor Attack*, III, 1394-95).
[27] Memo of General Gerow to the Chief of Staff, November 3, 1941 (*Pearl Harbor Attack*, XIV, 1067). Testimony of Secretary Hull (*ibid.*, II, 428).
[28] Tel. from the President to the Prime Minister, November 7, 1941 (*Pearl Harbor Attack*, XIV, 1081-82); Churchill: *The Grand Alliance*, 593-94; Feis: *The Road to Pearl Harbor*, 302-3.

no decision on this question until the Far Eastern situation had developed one way or the other:

His present Japanese policy is one of stalling and holding off. If during the next few weeks this policy looks likely to succeed for some months ahead, or alternatively, if the President can sign up for peace with Japan so as to ensure no sudden hostilities, then he will feel able at once to direct a further diversion of heavy bombers to U.K. On the other hand, the Japanese situation may blow up in the very near future, in which case U.S.A. and U.K. Joint Staffs will have to get together and decide in the light of combined war strategy where such equipment as becomes available can best be used.[29]

Under the circumstances nothing could be done for the Chinese but console them with further promises. At the suggestion of the President Mr. Soong had made the familiar rounds of Washington, discussing Chinese requirements with Stimson, Knox, Hopkins, Stettinius, and others. All were sympathetic and coöperative, but none could assure the Chinese emissary of the desired aid in planes. On November 8 Soong appealed again to the President, who was clearly embarrassed and passed on Soong's memorandum to Hopkins with the question: "What do we do about this?"[30] Apparently nothing was done beyond the drafting of a reply to Chiang Kai-shek. This merely assured the Generalissimo that the possibility of an attack on Yunnan had been carefully studied by the State, War and Navy Departments, which had concluded that the Japanese preparations were not sufficiently advanced to indicate imminent operations. After calling attention, no doubt gratuitously, to the difficulties of such an operation, the reply concluded that the most useful contribution the United States could make would be to build up Lend-Lease aid and to strengthen the American Volunteer Group. The text was first sent to Prime Minister Churchill for his information and he, in turn, framed his own reply to Chiang Kai-shek along the same lines. The President's message to the Generalissimo was despatched on November 14, 1941.[31]

3. Tokyo's Deadline

While the American Government, under the impact of Chinese appeals, was reëxamining its policy toward Japan and determining its course of action, precisely the same exercise was engaging Tokyo. It will be remembered that the fall of the Konoye Cabinet was occasioned by the refusal of

[29] Memo by Mr. Harold Balfour, November 9, 1941 (quoted in Robert E. Sherwood: *Roosevelt and Hopkins* [New York, 1948], 420).

[30] Memo of T. V. Soong to the President, entitled "China and the Impending Attack on the Burma Road" (*Roosevelt Papers:* Secretary's File, Box 74; also *Morgenthau Diaries, MS.,* Vol. 459, p. 237).

[31] The State Department draft is reproduced in *Pearl Harbor Attack,* XIV, 1070 ff. The British reply is in the State Department files, undated but stamped as having been received on November 17, 1941. See Churchill: *The Grand Alliance,* 593.

the Navy to endorse wholeheartedly the decision of the Imperial Conference of September 6 and to implement the resultant plans for war. This unexpected reverse had thrown the Army into confusion and had forced a fundamental reconsideration of the program agreed upon early in September.[32] General Tojo, the new Premier, recognized that it might be necessary to continue negotiations with the United States, the more so as the Emperor had ordered him to do so. Considering the urgency of a decision, it is significant that the Cabinet did not arrive at a firm conclusion until November 5. Such was the intensity of disagreement within Japanese Government circles.

While the Cabinet deliberated, all Japan was in suspense. Admiral Nomura, disillusioned and discouraged, asked permission to return home. He could not believe that his mission could accomplish anything worthwhile, felt that he was floundering, and had no heart for continuing what he called "this hypocritical existence, deceiving other people." Assured by telegrams from home that the new Cabinet was sincere in its desire to adjust relations with the United States, the Ambassador finally agreed to stay on.[33]

Meanwhile the American Ambassador in Tokyo was similarly engrossed in probing the recesses of his mind and experience. Though Mr. Grew felt that the slim prospects for peace had faded with the fall of Prince Konoye, he derived some comfort from reports of the Emperor's intervention in favor of further negotiations. On the other hand he could entertain no illusion as to the likelihood of Japan's renouncing its aspirations or dissociating itself from Germany. In a long telegram of November 3 he confessed that the heightened economic pressure, which he himself had recommended in September, 1940, had not achieved its purpose. If carried too far this pressure might drive Toyko into an "all-out, do or die attempt to render Japan impervious to foreign economic embargoes, even risking national harakiri rather than cede to foreign pressure." He strongly opposed precipitation of hostilities by the United States and advocated further negotiations on the ground that, even if they failed, valuable time would have been gained. "Why on earth should we rush headlong into war? When Hitler is defeated, as he eventually will be, the Japanese problem will solve itself." Nevertheless, Mr. Grew opposed "appeasement" or any sacrifice of American principles. The precise meaning of the latter statement was not clear and drew some tart comment from Mr. Hornbeck. Actually, the Ambassador had elucidated his meaning in comments which he omitted from his telegram to the Department. These comments reveal that Mr. Grew still felt the State Department approach to be too far-reaching and too rigid. There was too much discussion of general

[32] *Supra,* Chapter XXII, Section 5; Kase: *Journey to the "Missouri,"* 51-52; Feis: *The Road to Pearl Harbor,* 282-87.
[33] Tels. to and from Tokyo (*Pearl Harbor Attack,* XII, 79-82).

principles and insufficient flexibilty in dealing with the concrete issues which separated Tokyo and Washington.[34]

While Tokyo was making up its mind, Washington saw no alternative but to watch and wait. The intercepted diplomatic messages between the Japanese Embassy and the Tokyo Foreign Office revealed little beyond the fact that the Japanese intended to continue the conversations, that they were in a desperate hurry to achieve a settlement, and that their decision on the content of their own proposals would be reached early in November. There is but scanty evidence of the thinking of Secretary Hull and his subordinates during this interval. Prior to the receipt of Chiang Kai-shek's appeal, Mr. Hull seems to have been momentarily optimistic. Secretary Stimson found him much impressed by the intervention of the Emperor:

Hull thinks he has the Emperor on his side and having announced in the course of the negotiations such cardinal points of American policy, which would be insisted on, as the evacuation of China, the equality of opportunity for commerce to all nations with China, and the cessation by Japan of any movements of aggression, this would indicate that the Emperor would agree to these things.

If so, concluded Mr. Hull, "why we will be in a wonderful position." The Secretary of War threw cold water on the possibility, expressing serious doubts whether "the Japanese Army is much influenced by the high principles which our Government stands for." Stimson preferred, he said, a policy of speaking softly, but carrying a big stick.[35] Within a few days Mr. Hull's hopeful mood had vanished and he was inquiring of the military their views on the issuance of a warning to Japan.

Information on the deliberations of the Japanese Cabinet during this critical period is extremely scant. Intercepted diplomatic messages and the evidence adduced in the postwar trials of Japanese war criminals support the conclusion that General Tojo persevered for a time in his belief that further efforts should be made to reach agreement. Not only had the Emperor directed continuation of the conversations with the United States, but the new Foreign Minister, Shigenori Togo, a professional diplomat, almost certainly insisted that the methods of negotiation be exploited to the very limit. Admiral Shimada, Minister of Marine in the Tojo Cabinet, apparently urged the same course, reflecting the continued hesitancy of the naval authorities to risk measuring their strength with the United States Navy.[36]

[34] The Ambassador's views are developed in his *Ten Years in Japan,* 467 ff. In addition we have used the *Grew Diary (MS.),* October 19, November 3, and a memo by Hornbeck, November 3, 1941. Grew's long telegram of November 3 is paraphrased in *Foreign Relations of the United States: Japan,* II, 701-4. The full text is printed in *Pearl Harbor Attack,* XIV, 1045-57.

[35] *Stimson Diary (MS.),* October 28, 1941.

[36] Togo's testimony (*Tokyo War Crimes Documents,* Defense Document No. 2927); Admiral Shimada's testimony (*ibid.,* Defense Document No. 2892); affidavit of Akoho

Originally Foreign Minister Togo planned to make clear to Washington how urgently Japan required a decision and to press for an early reply to the Japanese proposals of September 25. But Minister Wakasugi, who carried on desultory talks with Mr. Welles, was unable to report progress. On October 29 he sent Tokyo a review of the American position, stressing the unlikelihood that the Government would sacrifice any of its general principles or recede from the stand taken in the note of June 21. It would be impossible, he reported, for the United States "to cruelly impose terms on China which would be almost impossible for the United States herself to endure." In sum and substance:

Her [i.e., the United States'] preparations in the event of the worst have been completed. Therefore, I cannot believe that she is stalling for time. On the other hand, I am of the opinion that she is not so anxious to enter into the agreement that she will sacrifice any of her terms. Therefore, I do not believe that we should expect any further counterproposals from them. They have decided on a course of economic pressure plus watchful waiting.[37]

Togo, who claimed later that on taking office he had known nothing of the top-secret discussions with Washington, was evidently much discouraged after reviewing their course to date. Six months of talk had come to little more than a discussion of general principles. Togo suggested to Ambassador Grew that in order to get forward the United States Government face certain realities and facts. To the British Ambassador he remarked that "the attitude of the United States is entirely too theoretical, and if this continues there will be slight chance of a settlement."[38] Under the circumstances the Foreign Minister decided, in the best traditions of diplomacy, to approach the problem anew and try to find solutions to the most critical items. Since Nomura had reported that agreement on nondiscrimination in the Chinese trade and on an acceptable formula regarding Japan's membership in the Tripartite Pact could probably be reached, Togo concentrated on what he deemed the crucial issue: the withdrawal of Japanese troops from China. Although the first meeting (October 23) of the leading Cabinet officers with the Chiefs of Staff of the Army and Navy (the so-called Liaison Conference) had revealed an uncompromising attitude on the part of the Army High Command, the Foreign Minister set to work on an outline plan which would permit discussion of the concrete issues.[39]

Ishii (ibid., Defense Document No. 2786); memos of conversation between Prince Konoye and Mr. Max Bishop (November 6, 7, 1945).

[37] Pearl Harbor Attack, XII, 86-87.

[38] Tel. from Togo to Nomura, November 2, reporting his talk with Grew; Grew's report of the same conversation, in Foreign Relations of the United States: Japan, II, 699-700; tel. from Togo to Nomura, November 2, reporting his talk with Sir Robert Craigie; and tel. from Grew, November 1, dealing with the same interview.

[39] Foreign Minister Togo's testimony (Tokyo War Crimes Documents, Defense Document No. 2927); Feis: The Road to Pearl Harbor, 291-92; Kase: Journey to the "Missouri," 56-57.

Debate in the Liaison Conference reached its height on November 1 and 2, during sessions that continued throughout the night. Foreign Minister Togo presented two plans (A and B) for submission to Washington. The first, designed to bridge the gap between Tokyo's original proposal of May 12 and the American counterproposal of June 21, 1941, addressed itself to the three major problems still unresolved: nondiscrimination in trade, Japan's association with Germany and Italy, and the evacuation of Japanese troops from China. The second, Plan B, to be presented only if a comprehensive agreement on Plan A could not be achieved, was in the nature of a *modus vivendi:* the Japanese were to promise to desist from further expansion in return for relaxation of American economic pressure. Neither plan appealed to General Sugiyama, Chief of Staff of the Army. The Army had no faith whatever, he declared, in the sincerity of America's professed desire to reach an agreement. Washington was merely playing for time, during which United States and British forces in the Far East would continue to be strengthened until before long they would be superior to Japan's. The Army's argument was based squarely on strategic considerations. To draw back now, the leaders argued, would destroy Japan's bargaining power. Above all, Japanese oil stocks were running low and could not be stretched beyond two years. Synthetic oil, though a possibility, could not be sufficiently developed to meet requirements in less than six or seven years. In Prime Minister Tojo's own words: "To adopt a policy of patience and perseverance under such impediments was tantamount to self-annihilation of our nation. Rather than await extinction, it were better to face death by breaking through the encircling ring and find a way for existence."

Admiral Shimada, speaking for the Navy, seems to have agreed that if war came before the beginning of the northeast monsoon off Formosa and Malaya in December, the prospects for immediate success would be good. Japan would be able to occupy essential areas and thus improve her position in a protracted conflict.

Despite the force of these military arguments, Foreign Minister Togo managed to extract a compromise from the Service chiefs. Having persuaded them of the real possibility that the United States would accept at least Plan B, he induced them to agree that the Washington conversations should be continued, though with a deadline of only a few weeks. In anticipation of failure, plans and preparations were to be rushed forward so that military action, when finally decided upon, could be taken promptly. So commenced the last lap of the long race between the moderates and the military.[40]

[40] "Tojo Memorandum" (*Tokyo War Crimes Documents,* Proceedings, 36, 317 ff.); General Tojo's testimony (*ibid.,* Defense Document No. 2927); Admiral Shimada's testimony (*ibid.,* Defense Document No. 2892); deposition of Kumaichi Yamamoto (*ibid.,* Exhibit 3331); affidavit of Akiho Ishii (*ibid.,* Defense Document No. 2786); "Kido Diary" (*ibid.,* Exhibit 3332).

In the interval certain political questions were propounded for study by the Japanese Foreign Office. The answer to one of these questions, a Foreign Office estimate of the world situation, is of special significance. It stated that the war in Europe would probably be a long one, for even though the bulk of the Soviet forces would presumably be destroyed, the spirit of resistance was still strong and Stalin would in all likelihood retreat to the east and use the winter months to prepare for a resumption of the campaign, relying upon British-American aid. Soviet Russia had been obliged to withdraw about a third of its forces from the Far East and was no longer in a position to attack Japan. On the other hand, if Japan were to advance on Siberia, the British and Americans would come to the Soviets' assistance and might occupy strategic positions in Siberia preliminary to an attack on Japan.

If, on the contrary, Japan were to advance southward, there was no prospect of restricting the war to Britain or to Britain and the Netherlands. While there was no evidence of a formal military alliance between Britain, the United States, the Netherlands, and China, there could be no doubt that there were mutual understandings looking toward joint defense against Japanese aggression. If Japan occupied the Netherlands Indies, the United States might not participate fully and immediately in the war. Nevertheless, it would be dangerous to reckon on the United States intervening only gradually, as it had against Germany. American interest in the Southwest Pacific was direct and the area important to the United States as a source of raw materials. Besides, if the United States delayed, it would risk losing its influence in China and would have to fear for the safety of the Philippines. By way of summary the Foreign Office estimate pointed out that if war were postponed until March, 1942, Russia would be further weakened and Britain would be distracted by fear of German invasion. The United States would be better prepared, but would be faced with greater administrative problems and might have to divide its strength. Japan, on its side, would have time to improve its diplomatic position in Siam and Indo-China, though it would clearly be in much worse economic straits.[41]

The final phase of the Tokyo deliberations was reached on November 5 in a meeting of the Privy Council in the Emperor's presence, lasting from 10:30 A.M. until 3:10 P.M. Although the official record of the conference has been lost, it is clear from other documents that the military situation and the need for early action were carefully explained to the Emperor. The Council agreed that the conversations with Washington should be continued with the submission of Plan A, and if necessary of Plan B, but that if they did not produce results in the near future (by about November 25), all preparations were to be completed so that a decision for war could be taken without further delay. The moment the parleys broke down, as it was ex-

[41] Foreign Office memorandum, undated, but obviously belonging to early November, 1941 (*Tokyo War Crimes Documents*, No. 1559A.)

pected they would, negotiations were to be opened with Germany and Italy to ensure their participation in the war and obtain their agreement not to conclude a separate peace. If, however, the Germans insisted on Japan's participation in the war against Soviet Russia, the Japanese were to decline for the time being, even if this meant postponement of a German declaration of war against the United States. Steps were to be taken to ensure British adherence to any settlement made with the United States and, by way of deception, economic discussions with the Netherlands Indies were to be resumed. Other items on the agenda went so far as to outline the future disposition of Burma, Siam, the Philippines, and the Netherlands Indies.[42]

With respect to the fateful decisions of November 5 it cannot be too strongly emphasized that the Japanese military authorities regarded the submission of Plans A and B to the American Government as little more than a formality, designed to satisfy the Emperor's requirement that nothing be left untried.[43] Japan had been on a war footing for some months and to the military the important thing was to make sure that everything was in readiness by early December. The final preparations for the attack on Pearl Harbor leave no doubt on this score. On November 3 Ambassador Grew warned his Government that "it would be shortsighted for American policy to be based upon the belief that Japanese preparations are no more than sabre-rattling, merely intended to give moral support to the high-pressure diplomacy of Japan." In the strongest terms he pointed out that "action by Japan which might render unavoidable an armed conflict with the United States may come with dangerous and dramatic suddenness."[44] By that time Japanese submarines were already prowling in Hawaiian waters. On the very day of Mr. Grew's message, November 3, Admiral Nagano, the Chief of Naval Operations, finally accepted the plan for the attack on Pearl Harbor which Admiral Yamamoto had been elaborating since January. In self-defense Nagano claimed later that he still favored the traditional strategy of awaiting the United States Fleet in the South Pacific, but the fact remains that he yielded to Yamamoto. On November 5 the necessary operational orders were issued, with the warning: "War with Netherlands, America, England inevitable; general operational preparations to be completed by early December." Two days later the date for the attack was tentatively set for December 8, 1941 (Japanese time).[45]

[42] *Tokyo War Crimes Documents,* Defense Document No. 2946, states that the official record has been lost, but Documents 790 and 1441 give a fairly complete record of the decisions. For the rest, see the "Tojo Memorandum" (Proceedings, 36, 317 ff.) and the "Kido Diary" (Document No. 1632W-83); Feis: *The Road to Pearl Harbor,* 292-97.

[43] Kase: *Journey to the "Missouri,"* 59-60.

[44] *Foreign Relations of the United States: Japan,* II, 704.

[45] On the reports of submarines in Hawaiian waters see Hallett Abend, reporting from Honolulu (*The New York Times,* November 2, 1941), and Richard E. Lauterbach: "Secret Jap War Plans" (*Life,* March 4, 1946). See also the interrogations of Admiral Nagano (*Tokyo War Crimes Documents,* Nos. 2495A and 2496A); the study of Japan's

4. JAPAN'S FINAL OFFER

The task of unraveling the tangled skeins of the final negotiations between Japan and the United States is extraordinarily difficult. The last phase of the transaction produced a spate of proposals, counterproposals, reservations, and conditions on the fundamentals of which there was no meeting of minds. The numerous Japanese messages intercepted by "Magic" between November 3 and December 7 convey a mixed impression of earnest exhortation and sly evasion. It can hardly be doubted that both Foreign Minister Togo and Ambassador Nomura were honestly striving for a settlement, though within limits so narrow as to preclude success. These limits were prescribed by the Japanese military who, convinced of American hypocrisy, despaired of any agreement and opposed all compromise. Throughout their tortuous course the final discussions were punctuated by bellicose articles in the Japanese press and by minatory statements by leading members of the Tokyo Government. Listening to such threats, and reading from day to day the diplomatic traffic between the Japanese Embassy and the Tokyo Foreign Office, American officials, even the long-suffering Secretary of State, could scarcely cherish much hope of a satisfactory settlement. The American public, out of patience with Japan and woefully underestimating Japanese resourcefulness and strength, was on its part quite prepared to face a showdown.

Plans A and B were sent to Nomura on November 4, with instructions to submit Plan A to President Roosevelt and Secretary Hull as soon as the Embassy was notified of its approval by the Imperial Council on November 5. At the same time Nomura was informed of the Cabinet's decision to grant his long-standing request for professional assistance. Saburo Kurusu, a personal friend of Nomura's, formerly Japanese Ambassador at Berlin and one of the signers of the Tripartite Pact, was to be sent to Washington by Trans-Pacific Clipper, arriving about the middle of November.

Thus was added another element of confusion. Considering that the Japanese were allowing only three weeks for the discussions, what good reason could there have been to send a special emissary, without additional instructions, who would arrive at best just before the closing hour? The explanation is probably to be found in Togo's message to Nomura: "To make it sound good, we are telling the public that he is coming to help you quickly compose the unhappy relations between the two nations."[46] In short, the Kurusu Mission was mainly window dressing. It would seem a matter of little importance whether or not Kurusu knew of the plans for Pearl

---

decision to fight, prepared from Japanese sources by General MacArthur's headquarters, December 1, 1945 (*Tokyo War Crimes Documents,* Exhibit 1265; *Pearl Harbor Attack,* I, 177 ff., 219 ff., 237 ff.); and the report of the U.S. Strategic Bombing Survey (Pacific): *The Campaigns of the Pacific War* (Washington, 1946).

[46] *Pearl Harbor Attack,* XII, 101.

Harbor. He himself continued to deny it and it is unlikely that any diplomat was privy to top-secret military plans. On the other hand, the International Tribunal was undoubtedly correct in holding that Kurusu knew when he left Japan that "an" attack was imminent and that it was important to keep the negotiations alive until all was in readiness for its execution. No doubt part of his assignment was to inform Nomura of "the exact situation" in Japan.[47]

In transmitting the final Japanese proposals to Nomura, Foreign Minister Togo prefaced them with a message which, deciphered at once in Washington, proved highly illuminating:

Conditions both within and without our Empire are so tense that no longer is procrastination possible, yet in our sincerity to maintain pacific relationships between the Empire of Japan and the United States of America, we have decided . . . to gamble once more on the continuance of the parleys, but this is our last effort. Both in name and spirit this counterproposal of ours is, indeed, the last. I want you to know that. If through it we do not reach a quick accord, I am sorry to say the talks will certainly be ruptured. Then, indeed, will relations between our two nations be on the brink of chaos. I mean that the success or failure of the pending discussions will have an immense effect on the destiny of the Empire of Japan. In fact, we gambled the fate of our land on the throw of this die.

When the Japanese-American meetings began, who would have ever dreamt that they would drag out so long? Hoping that we could fast come to some understanding, we have already gone far out of our way and yielded and yielded. The United States does not appreciate this, but through thick and thin sticks to the selfsame propositions she made to start with. Those of our people and of our officials who suspect the sincerity of the Americans are far from few. Bearing all kinds of humiliating things, our Government has repeatedly stated its sincerity and gone far, yes, too far, in giving in to them. There is just one reason why we do this—to maintain peace in the Pacific. There seem to be some Americans who think we would make a one-sided deal, but our temperance, I can tell you, has not come from weakness, and naturally there is an end to our long-suffering. Nay, when it comes to a question of our existence and our honor, when the time comes we will defend them without reckoning the cost. If the United States takes an attitude that overlooks or shuns this position of ours, there is not a whit of use in ever broaching the talks. This time we are showing the limit of our friendship; this time we are making our last possible bargain, and I hope that we can settle all our troubles with the United States peaceably.[48]

Nomura was instructed to see Mr. Hull and the President and to keep Tokyo constantly informed of developments. "Lest anything go awry," cabled Togo, "I want you to follow my instructions to the letter. In my

[47] *Pearl Harbor Attack*, XII, 101; Kurusu's denial, in an interview with Fred C. Opper of the American Broadcasting Company (*The New York Times*, September 7, 1945). The judgment of the International Tribunal, reported in *The New York Times*, November 11, 1948. The origin and nature of the Kurusu Mission is discussed in detail by Immanuel C. Y. Hsu: "Kurusu's Mission to the United States and the Abortive Modus Vivendi" (*Journal of Modern History*, September, 1952, 301-7).

[48] Tel. from Togo to Nomura, November 4, 1941 (*Pearl Harbor Attack*, XII, 92-93).

instructions, I want you to know there will be no room for personal interpretations."[49] There followed the text of Plan A, which Togo himself described as "our revised ultimatum," though this term was so loosely used on
both sides as to be almost meaningless. Plan A could hardly have been an
ultimatum in view of the fact that Plan B was being held in reserve in case
Plan A proved unacceptable. Plan A, it will be recalled, dealt with the
three key items: nondiscrimination in trade, Japan's association with the
Tripartite Pact, and the evacuation of Japanese troops from China. With
regard to the first item, the Japanese Government was prepared to accept
the principle of nondiscrimination in the entire Pacific area, including
China, provided the same principle were applied to the rest of the world.
As for the Tripartite Pact, Nomura was to make clear that Japan intended
no extension of its "sphere of self-defense" and that it desired to avoid the
extension of the European War to the Pacific. Finally, in the matter of
evacuation:

Japanese troops which have been sent to China will be stationed in North China, on
the Mongolian border regions, and on the Island of Hainan after the establishment of
peace between Japan and China, and will not be evacuated until the lapse of a suitable
interval. The evacuation of other troops will be carried out within a period of two
years. (Note: Should the American authorities question you in regard to "the suitable
period," answer that such a period should encompass twenty-five years.)

The stationing and evacuation of troops in Indo-China. The Japanese Government
respects the territorial integrity of the French possession, Indo-China. In the event that
a just peace is established, or that the China Incident is brought to a successful conclusion, Japanese troops which have been despatched to French Indo-China and are
there now shall be evacuated.

By way of explanation, Togo expressed confidence that agreement could
be reached on the question of nondiscrimination in trade and that the
United States would be satisfied with the Japanese statement regarding the
purpose of the Tripartite Pact. The really difficult issue would be the evacuation of troops from China, on which Togo made the following comments:

In view of the fact that the United States is so much opposed to our stationing
soldiers in undefined areas, our purpose is to shift the regions of occupation and our
officials, thus attempting to dispel their suspicions. We will call it evacuation; but
although it would please the United States for us to make occupation the exception
rather than the rule, in the last analysis this would be out of the question. Furthermore,
on the matter of duration of occupation, whenever pressed to give a clear statement we
have hitherto couched our answers in vague terms. I want you in as indecisive yet as
pleasant language as possible to euphemize and try to impart to them the effect that
unlimited occupation does not mean perpetual occupation.

Summing this up, Proposal A accepts completely America's demands on two of the
three proposals mentioned in the other proposal, but when it comes to the last point

[49] *Pearl Harbor Attack,* **XII,** 94.

concerning the stationing and evacuation of forces, we have already made our last possible concession. How hard, indeed, have we fought in China for four years! What tremendous sacrifices have we made! They must know this, so their demand in this connection must have been only "wishful thinking." In any case, our internal situation also makes it impossible for us to make any further compromise in this connection.[50]

It seems incredible that Togo and particularly Nomura should have deceived themselves into imagining that their proposals on trade and on the Tripartite Pact would be acceptable. The Ambassador, who had chronic and quite understandable trouble in keeping the various threads of the negotiation straight, was evidently further misled by another message from Togo (November 5), saying that the Japanese Government assumed that its statement of September 25 on the Tripartite Pact was satisfactory to the United States Government and that no exchange of notes would be necessary. The Government, Togo added, would refuse to consider such an exchange of notes and Nomura was to bear this in mind. As a result, when the Ambassador, accompanied by Minister Wakasugi, visited Secretary Hull on November 7, he handed him not the complete text of Plan A, but only the two items concerning the stationing of troops and the principle of non-discrimination in trade. Mr. Hull was cordial but noncommittal. He did not even challenge the Ambassador's suggestion that it would not be difficult to reconcile the differences of view on trade and the Tripartite Pact. Instead, he threw out a new idea, which he described as a personal inspiration. According to the American record he said:

. . . . Supposing the Chinese were now to say that they desired a real friendship with Japan and would do everything in their power to work together along peaceful ways, would not this be a wonderful opportunity for Japan to launch forth on a real new order, an order in which Japan would gain her real moral leadership in the Far East? At a time when Hitler was leading his people over a precipice and when Europe was threatened with anarchy, would not the adoption by Japan of a new policy of conciliation and friendship with China now maintained at a sword's point provide Japan with a real opportunity for progressive leadership in which Japan and the United States could collaborate to save the world?

The Japanese record puts the matter more briefly but more concretely:

Hull asked me, as his own personal idea, what Japan would think if China's highest authority pledged to the government and people of Japan China's sincere friendship and confidence and desired the restoration of friendly relations between Japan and China.

Wakasugi asked whether China's intentions had already been ascertained with respect to the matter. In reply, Hull said that China had not yet been consulted on the matter, it being entirely his own personal idea, but that, if it was carried into effect, it would constitute a good example of the maintenance of peace in the Pacific and have a favorable influence on the world. There is some reason to think, however, that it may

[50] Tel. from Togo to Nomura, November 4, 1941 (*Pearl Harbor Attack,* XII, 94-96).

have been as a result of having ascertained China's intentions in the matter that Hull's idea was brought forward. In any case, Hull asked that the above-mentioned idea be conveyed to the Japanese Government for an expression of its views thereon.[51]

There is no evidence that anything resembling Mr. Hull's inspiration had been discussed with the Chinese Government and it is most unlikely that Chiang Kai-shek would have accepted it even if pressed upon him. The Secretary's gambit was most probably a move to spin out the conversations. This interpretation gains plausibility when the episode is viewed in the setting of the hour. Only two days earlier the American military authorities had firmly ruled out a warning or ultimatum to Japan and had stressed the vital importance of winning time. Furthermore, ever since the end of October the American Government had had good reason to expect that Tokyo would put a deadline on the conversations, perhaps November 15, the day on which the Japanese Diet was to convene in special session.[52] More recently still Washington had read in intercepted messages that on November 25 Japan, Germany, and Italy would renew the Tripartite Pact for another five years, and that the same date had been set for the termination of the Washington negotiations.[53] As an additional warning American officials could read in influential Tokyo newspapers, such as *Nichi Nichi* and the *Japan Times and Advertiser*, that the "Empire approaches its greatest crisis"; "patience has reached the point of exhaustion"; the mission of Kurusu offers "a last opportunity [for the United States] to make amends for aggression and restore the occasion for an amicable settlement." The *Japan Times and Advertiser*, mouthpiece of the Foreign Office, even set forth a seven-point program upon which it urged the American Government to reflect. This reaffirmed in the most uncompromising terms all the major objectives of Japanese policy since 1937. Nomura himself was aghast at the content of these publications.[54]

The only conclusion to be drawn by Washington was that time was running out and war in the offing. No wonder then that Mr. Hull cast about for any expedient which might postpone the evil day, even if it could be used by the Japanese extremists to support their contention that Washington's only objective was delay. At the same time Mr. Roosevelt, likewise

[51] The American account is printed in *Foreign Relations of the United States: Japan,* II, 708. *Pearl Harbor Attack,* XII, 106, gives the translation of Nomura's report, made at the time. The text in *Tokyo War Crimes Documents,* Defense Document No. 1401-F-2, is here used, as being probably the more accurate.

[52] Wilfrid Fleischer in the *New York Herald Tribune,* October 29, 1941.

[53] Tel. from Tokyo to Nanking, October 31 (deciphered in Washington, November 3); tel. from Tokyo to Nomura, November 5 (deciphered the same day). Both are printed in *Pearl Harbor Attack,* XII, 89, 100.

[54] Tel. from Grew, November 1; Grew: *Ten Years in Japan,* 471 ff.; Tolischus in *The New York Times,* November 5; Associated Press report from Tokyo (*The New York Times,* November 7, 1941). On the reaction of Admiral Nomura see *Pearl Harbor Attack,* XII, 100-103.

anxious to stave off the inevitable, came up with a more concrete and some-what more promising suggestion. On November 6 he informed Secretary Stimson that he might suggest to Kurusu, when he arrived, "a truce in which there would be no movement or armament for six months, and then, if the Japanese and Chinese had not settled their arrangement in the mean-while, we could go on on the same basis." Mr. Stimson quickly pointed out the fly in this ointment. It would check American reinforcement of the Philip-pines (precisely what time was needed for). It would, furthermore, estrange the Chinese, whom, in any case, it would be dangerous to leave at the mercy of Japanese terms.[55]

The question of general American strategy was discussed by the President with the Cabinet on the following day (November 7). Mr. Hull began with a review of his conversations with Nomura to date, ending with the flat statement that "relations were extremely critical and that we should be on the lookout for a military attack anywhere by Japan at any time." Mr. Roosevelt then polled the Cabinet individually on the question "whether the people would back us up in case we struck at Japan down there and what the tactics should be." "Down there" could only have meant Southeast Asia, as Secretary Stimson made clear when, in subsequent testimony, he re-phrased the President's question in amplified form: "Whether it was thought the American people would back us up if it became necessary to strike at Japan, in case she should attack England in Malaya or the Dutch in the East Indies?" The President was clearly referring to the recommendations of the Joint Board, which had been forwarded to him on November 5. The Cabinet was unanimous in its belief that the country would support such a move and Mr. Roosevelt himself agreed.[56]

The significance of the Cabinet's verdict on this occasion becomes obvious when one recalls that the Joint Board recommended to the President on November 5 that the United States should go to war against Japan in the event of

1). A direct act of war by Japanese armed forces against the territory or mandated territory of the United States, the British Commonwealth, or the Netherlands East Indies;

2). The movement of Japanese forces into Thailand (Siam) to the west of 100° East or south of 10° North; or into Portuguese Timor, New Caledonia, or the Loyalty Islands.

In view of the low repute in which most Americans then held Japanese military power and the strong sentiment for settling scores with Japan at once so as to be free to deal with Hitler in the Atlantic, it is quite possible

[55] *Stimson Diary (MS.)*, November 6; also printed in *Pearl Harbor Attack,* XI, 5420; Feis: *The Road to Pearl Harbor,* 302-303.

[56] *Stimson Diary (MS.)*, November 7; also printed in *Pearl Harbor Attack,* XI, 5420, in a somewhat different version. On Mr. Hull's statement see *Peace and War,* 136-37; *Pearl Harbor Attack,* XI, 5396; and Hull: *Memoirs, II,* 1058.

that a majority of Americans would have gone along with the Administration in the contingencies envisaged.[57] It is doubtful, however, whether this majority would have been sufficiently impressive to warrant the Administration's believing that entry into war would quickly unify the people in support of its objectives. In any case, the Cabinet concluded its deliberations on November 7 by agreeing that responsible officials of the Government should warn the public of the gravity of recent developments. Armistice Day (November 11) would provide a suitable occasion and both Secretary Knox and Under Secretary Welles set about the preparation of speeches. Prime Minister Churchill, however, still hopeful that the United States would take a firm line, jumped the gun. In an address at the Lord Mayor's banquet (November 9) he announced the despatch to Far Eastern waters of more British warships and added: "The United States . . . are doing their utmost to find ways of preserving peace in the Pacific. . . . Should they fail and the United States become involved in war with Japan, it is my duty to say that the British declaration will follow within the hour."[58]

Hardly less ominous were the ensuing American pronouncements. Mr. Welles, speaking at the tomb of Woodrow Wilson, warned his audience that "at any moment war may be forced upon us by that criminal paranoiac Hitler or by Japan." The Secretary of the Navy, in an address at Providence, was even more explicit. The United States, he said, had been patient with Japan "to a degree almost unmatched in the history of international relations." But, he continued:

There comes a time in the life of every man, and every nation, when principles cannot be sacrificed, and when vital and essential rights can no longer be ignored; a time when to go further would mean that our liberality and forbearance would be misunderstood. Our people must understand that grave questions are about to be decided—that the hour of decision is here. There must be clear realization that we will not shrink from or seek to evade the staggering responsibilities of these days.[59]

5. REJECTION OF PLAN A

In this atmosphere, saturated with despair, Secretary Hull sat down with Ambassador Nomura to pursue the discussion of Tokyo's final terms. It will be recalled that when on November 7 Nomura submitted two of the three points covered in Japan's Plan A, Mr. Hull had replied by interjecting a personal plea that Japan and China now enter upon a new era of friendship. However well intended, this suggestion created new complications in Tokyo, where the situation was already hopelessly confused. Almost at once Foreign Minister Togo replied to Nomura:

[57] Editorials in *Chicago Daily News* and *New York Post,* November 6; T. A. Bisson in the *New Republic,* November 3, 1941; on the public opinion polls see *Fortune,* January, 1942.
[58] Churchill: *The Grand Alliance,* 594.
[59] *The New York Times,* November 12, 1941,

We interpret Secretary Hull's plan to have a Chinese person of the highest integrity give his pledge regarding the China problem to mean that the Secretary wishes to leave the China problem, which has been the stumbling block in the Japanese-U.S. negotiations, up to direct negotiations between Japan and China for settlement. This would lead to having Chiang Kai-shek propose to us that peace negotiations be begun.

We recognize this to be a great contribution toward bringing about friendly relations between Japan and China and for this reason we highly welcome it. We will, of course, follow this message up with another giving this Government's opinions. In the meantime please ascertain and advise us what relation this proposal has upon the Japanese-U.S. negotiations.[60]

A second message from Tokyo revealed even more clearly how completely the Japanese Government had been led astray:

If it is the intention of the United States Government to mediate between Japan and China along the lines proposed by Secretary Hull and also to leave the matter of peace terms to the Japanese and Chinese Governments, this plan harmonizes with what the Japanese Government has been looking forward to since the beginning of ————. It would mean that the question of withdrawing troops from China would, according to Hull's suggestion, be left out for the time being from the negotiations. This would make it possible for us to hasten the settlement by means of negotiations conducted between Japan and China alone and it would also have the advantage of bringing about peace between Japan and China without American interference.

Should we take advantage of this proposal, it goes without saying that it would be necessary to secure a promise or a definite statement that the settlement of the negotiations between Japan and the United States would not make the establishment of peace between Japan and China its condition and that the United States would not interfere with the peace to be established between Japan and China. (This promise includes cessation of activities for aiding Chiang.) Furthermore, it is necessary to make it clear that the agreement between Japan and the United States would be immediately signed and put into effect.[61]

On no fundamental of its Far Eastern policy had the United States been more insistent throughout the course of the altercations with Japan than that Tokyo should not be left free to impose its terms upon China. To this end it had been supporting Chungking's resistance ever since 1937. In November, 1941, the possibility that Washington might cease aiding China, use its good offices to bring China and Japan together, and then abandon Chiang Kai-shek to the mercies of the Japanese could scarcely have been more remote. Yet, it is impossible to blame Foreign Minister Togo for putting some such construction on Secretary Hull's suggestion. It was reasonable to assume that before advancing it Mr. Hull had sounded out Chungking and that he was prepared to use his influence to bring about a solution of the China Incident which might be acceptable to the Japanese. Doubtless Togo's enthusiasm carried him too far. Personally ill-informed of

[60] Tel. from Togo to Nomura, November 9, 1941 (*Pearl Harbor Attack*, XII, 106).
[61] Tel. from Togo to Nomura, November 10, 1941 (*Pearl Harbor Attack*, XII, 107-8).

the course of the negotiations prior to his assumption of the Foreign Ministry, he now leaped to the unwarranted conclusion that the question of the withdrawal of Japanese troops from China, the crucial question for Japan, could be dropped from Plan A. He even envisioned an American undertaking to refrain from any action that might impede the establishment of peace between Japan and China.[62]

Had Nomura received Togo's messages a little sooner, he might possibly have been able to dispel the confusion in the Foreign Minister's mind. But he had already arranged to meet with the President and Secretary Hull on November 10. On that occasion he confined himself to a detailed presentation of Plan A, together with an earnest plea for haste in coming to an agreement. The record of the interview is lengthy on both sides, but it contained nothing new and showed no progress. The President read a brief "oral" statement, presumably prepared by the State Department. This was notable chiefly for the brevity with which it summarized the essentials of the American position, which, despite knowledge of impending Japanese action, remained unaltered:

The entire world has been placed in a precarious position as a result of the havoc wrought by the forces of aggression. Our common sense tells us of the extreme need that the world come back to ways of peace. It is the purpose of this Government to do its best in the spirit of fair play to contribute to establishing a basis for peace, stability, and order in the Pacific area. As a means of achieving these objectives it is essential that emphasis be laid upon giving practical effect to a sound philosophy of human welfare. We have often and quite recently made clear publicly what we have in mind in this regard. We hope that our exploratory conversations will achieve favorable results in the way of providing a basis for negotiations. We shall continue to do our best to expedite the conversations just as we understand that the Japanese Government is anxious to do. We hope that the Japanese Government will make it clear that it intends to pursue peaceful courses instead of opposite courses, as such clarification should afford a way of arriving at the results we seek.[63]

Even to a Government aware of the sinister decision made by Tokyo on November 5 and justly convinced that its only immediate objective should be to gain time, the value of this piece of rhetoric must have seemed doubtful. The chagrin and irritation which the statement occasioned among those officials of the Japanese Government who still hoped to beat the deadline and avoid war is as understandable as the scornful triumph with which it was doubtless greeted by those who were dedicated to war. In reply to their Plan A the Japanese were offered homilies on the beauties of peace, exhortations to heed the cause of human welfare, and vague promises to expedite discussions which Washington still insisted were merely exploratory.

---

[62] Tel. from Togo to Nomura, November 10, 1941 (*Pearl Harbor Attack*, XII, 108).
[63] The American account is in *Foreign Relations of the United States: Japan*, II, 715-19; Nomura's account is in his telegram to Tokyo, November 10, 1941 (*Pearl Harbor Attack*, XII, 113-16).

Foreign Minister Togo did his utmost to impress upon Ambassador Grew the urgency of the situation. On receiving Nomura's report of his interview with the President he became frantic. He cabled Nomura reminding him that the deadline of November 25 was "absolutely immovable," that "it is a definite deadline and therefore it is essential that a settlement be reached by about that time." He tried to make the same thing clear in conversation with the British Ambassador, while one of the highest officials of the Foreign Office renewed the effort to impress the dangers of the situation on Ambassador Grew. The Foreign Minister, said this official, could not agree that the conversations were still of a preliminary character; on the contrary they had not only entered upon the stage of negotiation, but upon the final stage of negotiation.[64]

Meanwhile the harassed Nomura had received Tokyo's reaction to Secretary Hull's suggestion regarding relations between Japan and China. Another interview was arranged and on November 12 the Ambassador and Minister Wakasugi spent an hour with Mr. Hull and Mr. Ballantine. There was the usual desultory talk about the Tripartite Pact and other issues, culminating in Mr. Hull's suggestion that, in view of the change of Cabinet in Japan, the Tokyo Government state anew its adherence to the proposals made on August 28 (those of September 25 being ignored). But the main topic of discussion was the Secretary's cryptic suggestion of November 7, on which the Japanese representatives now sought much-needed light. Little of this was shed either by Mr. Hull's remarks or by a further "oral" statement which he gave his visitors in writing. Wakasugi asked specific questions as to how China was to be brought to make the pledge of friendship and coöperation: "Is it the intention of Secretary Hull to leave this matter up to direct negotiations to be conducted between Japan and China; or is it his intention to have the United States secure the pledge from China, and transmit it to Japan; or is it to be accomplished with Japan, the United States, and China meeting in a conference?"

The efforts of the Japanese were of no avail. Mr. Hull reverted to his familiar observations on the principles of peace and hinted vaguely that these principles would have to apply to the Japanese-Chinese problem. If some satisfactory basis could be arrived at in the "exploratory" Japanese-American discussions, the time might come to approach the Chinese Government. According to the American record, the Secretary said:

He felt that the main thing now was to dispose of basic matters in regard to the provisions of a peace settlement and that questions of procedure could thereafter be more satisfactorily settled. These points were gone over two or three times, as the Japanese appeared to find difficulty in understanding them, possibly because of a

[64] Memo by Grew, November 10, 12, 1941 (*Foreign Relations of the United States: Japan*, II, 710-14, 719-22); tels. from Togo to Nomura, November 10, 11, 1941 (*Pearl Harbor Attack*, XII, 109-11, 117-19).

preconception that the Secretary's suggestion contained more than appeared on its face.

The Japanese would not seem to have been entirely at fault in this preconception. After having had their hopes aroused, they were now driven to the conclusion that the Secretary "had no definite plan in mind regarding the matter." Everything remained as before, everything still depended on Japan's acceptance of the principles of a "constructive, liberal and peaceful world program." As yet there had been no formal reply to Japan's Plan A, though Mr. Hull promised one for November 14. The United States, he said, was moving as fast as possible, "but questions pending over a period of ten years cannot be settled overnight."[65]

In truth the fate of Plan A had already been settled. It merely remained to formalize its rejection by the American Government. After a preliminary talk between Mr. Ballantine and Minister Wakasugi on November 13, at which the latter inveighed against the contention that the current conversations were anything less than full-fledged negotiations, Nomura and Wakasugi met with the Secretary and Mr. Ballantine on November 15 to receive the American verdict on Plan A. Painstakingly Mr. Hull attempted to dispel the accumulated Japanese illusions. He refused to recognize the existence of "negotiations," arguing that only after Japan and the United States had reached agreement on principles would it be possible to begin formal negotiations with other interested nations, which both sides admitted to be desirable and necessary.

Having clarified the American position on this long-disputed issue of procedure, the Secretary turned to matters of substance. He produced a memorandum on nondiscrimination in trade which made it clear that while the United States desired the universal application of this principle, it could not guarantee that other nations would accept it and could not undertake to do more than itself apply it so far as possible. The Secretary then turned to the question of the Tripartite Pact and left no further doubt that previous Japanese interpretations and formulas were inadequate. If there were to be real agreement between the two countries, the United States must have the assurance that Japan's pact with the aggressors would become a "dead letter," that it would "automatically disappear." Otherwise neither the American public nor the British and Dutch could be convinced that Japan was really about to embark upon peaceful courses: "If we went into an agreement with Japan while Japan had an outstanding obligation to Germany which might call upon Japan to go to war with us, this would cause so much turmoil in the country that he [Hull] might well be lynched." Finally, in reaction to the constant pressure from Tokyo for a quick settlement, Mr. Hull commented strongly and pointedly:

[65] The American record is in *Foreign Relations of the United States: Japan*, II, 722-29; Nomura's report is in *Pearl Harbor Attack*, XII, 119-22.

That the new Government in Japan seems to take the attitude that we must reply at once to their points, but that we do not feel that we should be receiving ultimatums of such a character from the Japanese Government under circumstances where the United States had been pursuing peaceful courses throughout and the Japanese Government is the one which has been violating law and order. The Secretary said in conclusion that when we [i.e., the United States] hear from the Japanese Government concerning its position on the points we had raised with them two days ago on their peaceful intentions and when we could clear up the question of nondiscrimination, as suggested in our proposal of today, and also in regard to the Tripartite Pact, he believed we could sit down like brothers and reach some solution of the question of stationing Japanese troops in China.[66]

In vindication of Secretary Hull's seemingly intransigent attitude it must be constantly borne in mind that he was reading regularly the correspondence between the Tokyo Foreign Office and the Japanese Embassy. He knew not only that the Tripartite Pact was to be extended, but also, from a message deciphered on November 14, that "in the event of the United States' participation in the European War, Japan shall automatically carry out what she understands to be the obligations which befall her as a party to the Three Power Agreement." Furthermore, he had increasing evidence that the Tokyo Government was about to strengthen its forces in Indo-China, despite the objections of the Vichy Government. Finally, information reaching Washington from Peiping indicated that though Mr. Saburo Kurusu was bringing conciliatory proposals, these were vigorously opposed by the Japanese military, who were indeed communicating their terms to the Germans. In this connection it may be added that intercepted messages had already revealed that the Germans were bringing pressure on Tokyo to issue a warning to the United States against escorting ships to Britain.[67]

To Ambassador Nomura at least it was perfectly plain that the American Government would not be trifled with. On the eve of his talk with Mr. Hull on November 15 he reported home that the American policy was to stop further Japanese advances at all costs. Military preparations were being rushed and every economic weapon was being employed. Negotiations with other governments were being actively pursued and relations with China were being strengthened. There could be no question of the United States abandoning China for the sake of Japan. In fact, rather than surrender its position, the United States would not hesitate to fight. This, Nomura thought, would be a serious matter, the more so as he believed that the

[66] Foreign Relations of the United States: Japan, II, 729-37; Nomura's reports are printed in Pearl Harbor Attack, XII, 123-25, 131-37. See also Feis: The Road to Pearl Harbor, 304-6.

[67] Tel. from Tokyo to Nomura, November 11, 14 (Pearl Harbor Attack, XII, 117, 126); tel. from Grew, November 12, with reference to Japanese-French negotiations regarding Indo-China; rumors regarding the Kurusu mission are described in Pearl Harbor Attack, XX, 4099 ff.

"apex of German victories" had passed and that Soviet resistance would continue. By way of summary he warned his Government:

If we carry out a venture southward for the sake of our existence and our lives, it naturally follows that we will have to fight England and the United States, and chances are also great that the Soviet will participate. It is inevitable that this war will be long, and this little victory or that little victory, or this little defeat or that little defeat do not amount to much, and it is not hard to see that whoever can hold out till the end will be the victor. . . . I had expected in the past that should the United States start warlike activities in the Atlantic, there would be considerable feeling for a compromise in the Pacific, but there has been no evidence of such an inclination as yet. There are even now many arguments against war with Germany as opposed to internal questions, but there is not the slightest opposition to war in the Pacific. It is being thought more than ever that participation will be carried out through the Pacific area.[68]

These sage observations, however well founded or persuasive, could no longer carry weight in Tokyo. The Japanese Foreign Office was working against an unchangeable military deadline and thus far had failed to register any progress whatever. The last forlorn hope was to abandon the fruitless discussion of major issues, as represented by Plan A, and turn to the alternate program, Plan B, which was now transmitted to Nomura. It is not entirely clear why the Japanese thus divided their final program into two parts, nor why, if they thought the United States might more readily accept Plan B than Plan A, the former was not presented in the first place. However, Plan B was in general a *modus vivendi,* an attempt not so much to solve the outstanding problems as to arrive at a stopgap agreement which would afford further time to negotiate a larger settlement. For the sake of completeness, and because these terms were to be the subject of so much discussion, Plan B is here reproduced at length:

1). The Governments of Japan and the United States agree that neither will militarily invade any area in Southeast Asia and the South Seas with the exception of French Indo-China.

2). The Governments of Japan and the United States will coöperate mutually in guaranteeing the obtention of the materials they need in Netherlands India.

3). The Governments of Japan and the United States will mutually return to the situation prior to the freezing of their respective assets and the Government of the United States will agree to furnish Japan with the petroleum she needs.

4). The Government of the United States will engage in no activity which might put an obstacle in the way of Japan in her efforts to make peace with China.

5). The Japanese Government agrees to withdraw her army, which is at present stationed in French Indo-China, whenever peace shall have been established between Japan and China or a just peace firmly established in the Pacific area.

6). The Japanese Government agrees that if the principle of nondiscriminatory

[68] Tel. from Nomura to Tokyo, November 14, 1941 (*Pearl Harbor Attack,* XII, 127-29).

treatment in trade is to be applied throughout the world the same principle should also be applied to the entire Pacific area, in other words, in China as well.

7). The two Governments shall make world peace their common objective and shall coöperate at a suitable time for speedy realization of world peace. However, in dealing with developments prior to the establishment of world peace, the two Governments shall act in accordance with the viewpoint of protection and self-defense. Furthermore, in the event of the United States' participation in the European War, Japan shall automatically carry out what she understands to be the obligations which befall her as a party to the Three Power Agreement existing between Japan, Germany and Italy.[69]

From the Japanese messages it would appear that Togo had arranged with Kurusu that Plan B should be held in abeyance until the latter's arrival in Washington. It is at least possible, therefore, that Plan A was intended merely to provide material for discussion pending the advent of the special emissary in the American capital, and that both the Foreign Minister and Kurusu himself pinned their hopes on this more concrete program. On the other hand, ten days had passed since the fateful decisions of November 5 and nothing had been accomplished. In the interval the Diet had begun to assemble in special session and the military had become ever more restive. Already plans were being sent to the field for the complete annihilation of British and American power in China, as well as directions for the destruction of diplomatic codes.[70] It is perfectly obvious that the decks were being cleared for action. Indeed, when the Diet met (November 15-18), the tone of its proceedings was distinctly warlike. Foreign Minister Togo, perhaps the most moderate member of the Cabinet, while still expressing hopes for a settlement, ended his address on a warning note: negotiations had been going on for six months and there could not possibly be any excuse for prolonging them. Japan was doing its best, "but there is naturally a limit to our conciliatory attitude. Should an occasion arise such as might menace the very existence of the Empire or compromise the prestige of Japan as a great power, it goes without saying that Japan must face it with a firm and resolute attitude."

Prime Minister Tojo was much plainer spoken. Asserting that the Government was bending all efforts toward peace so as to safeguard the existence and prestige of the Empire and assure the establishment of the New Order in East Asia, he nevertheless spoke of the economic blockade as being hardly less hostile a procedure than armed warfare and accused the United States, Britain and the Netherlands Indies of concerting military measures

[69] Tels. from Togo to Nomura, transmitting items 1 to 4, inclusive, November 4; transmitting items 5 to 7, November 14, 1941 (*Pearl Harbor Attack*, XII, 96-97, 126).

[70] Message from Tokyo to Hongkong and other Chinese centers, November 14; message from Tokyo to Washington and other capitals, November 15, 1941 (*Pearl Harbor Attack*, XII, 126-27, 137). These messages, while intercepted, were not available in translation until November 25, 26, 1941.

against Japan. The Washington negotiations, he continued, depended for success upon three points: (1) Japan would expect that third powers refrain from obstructing the successful conclusion of the China Incident; (2) also that they abstain from direct military threats to the Empire, and that they nullify the economic blockade; and (3) that they make the utmost effort to prevent the European War from spreading to East Asia.[71]

In the spirit of these pronouncements one of the deputies, Toshio Shimada, introduced a resolution in behalf of the Throne Aid League, of which three quarters of the deputies were members. Explaining the purpose of the resolution, Shimada said: "The cancer of the Pacific lies in the minds of arrogant American leaders who are seeking world hegemony for themselves and are meddling even in Europe by assisting Britain." This cancer Japan would have to remove by wielding the big knife. Unhappily American leaders failed to understand Japan's "disinterested holy war," but "there are other ways to make such a party understand." Thereupon the Lower House voted the resolution unanimously. It read in part:

The greatest obstacles to a settlement of the China hostilities are the actions of hostile nations led by the United States. It is clear that the fundamental motivating force for the present conflict between the Axis Powers and the British, American and Soviet nations is the inordinate desire of the United States for world hegemony. . . . The patience of the Japanese is not inexhaustible. There is a strict limit beyond which we cannot go in using prudence. The nation's policy has been fixed. The mind of the people is already made up.

In order to dispel any possible remnant of doubt, the *Japan Times and Advertiser* wrote editorially:

The international situation as regards Japanese and American relations has gone from bad to worse. It is now felt in Japan as never before that the war Japan has waged the past four years has in truth and reality been not with Chungking but with America and Britain. . . . The formidable cordon of naval and air bases which the United States has developed around Japan in concert with Britain, the Dutch East Indies, Australia and Chungking constitutes a direct threat against the Japanese Empire.[72]

Considering the exacerbated temper on both sides of the Pacific it is hardly an exaggeration to say that the two countries were already, to all intents and purposes, at war. Since both stood firmly by the positions they had taken long before, the prospects of an agreement, more particularly of an agreement within a matter of days, were virtually nil. But Kurusu was to make a last desperate move. Arriving at San Francisco on November 14 he told reporters: "I fully realize the difficulty of my task but, making a tight scrum, I wish I could break through the line and make a touchdown." On

[71] *The New York Times,* November 17, 1941.
[72] *The New York Times,* November 16, 18, 19, 1941.

reaching Washington the next day, he stated: "So long as there exists a sympathy on the part of the American people for Japan, I think I have a fighting chance to make a success of my mission."[73] All now depended on the American reaction to Plan B, which was Kurusu's ace in reserve.

[73] *The New York Times,* November 15, 16, 1941.

CHAPTER XXVII

Immovable Object — Irresistible Force

1. Point Counter Point

Though Mr. Saburo Kurusu, as it turned out, brought little to the dead-locked Japanese-American conversations but a fluent command of the English language, it seemed reasonable at the time to suppose that the hard-pressed Tokyo Government would not have sent him without good purpose. The President had accordingly devoted considerable thought to the problem of what to say to the Ambassador on his arrival. One fairly obvious possibility had presented itself early in his ruminations: the possibility of a stopgap arrangement. The President had broached this idea to Secretary Stimson early in November but had gotten anything but an enthusiastic response.[1] Apparently Mr. Roosevelt later suggested the idea to Secretary Hull, for on November 11 the Far East Division of the State Department produced a memorandum which was to become the basis for much of the later discussion of an American *modus vivendi*. This memorandum, carefully considered by the Secretary, left no doubt of the purpose which a truce or *modus vivendi* was expected to serve: "It is hoped that a proposal along the suggested lines might offer a basis which might keep conversations going for some time longer than otherwise, and if accepted by the Japanese might lead to an eventual comprehensive settlement of a nature compatible with our principles." The gist of the scheme was that the United States should propose that Japan and China enter immediately into "direct amicable negotiation for a peaceful settlement of their differences." This would entail an armistice, during which the United States would suspend its military aid to China. While Washington would neither inquire into the terms Japan offered China nor exert any influence on them, it would make clear to Chungking that if the negotiations failed, American aid to China would be resumed. Japan on its part would have to agree not to reinforce its

[1] *Supra, Chapter* XXVI, Section 5.

armies in China or Indo-China during the period of the armistice. In return the United States would assent to the immediate reopening of negotiations with Japan for the resumption of trade in nonmilitary goods.[2]

Intimately related to the nascent American interest in a *modus vivendi* was a contemporary penciled note in Mr. Roosevelt's handwriting, outlining possible terms. This note, which the President submitted to Secretary Hull, is undated. It was subsequently filed in the State Department archives with a notation that it was written shortly after November 20, 1941. This is almost certainly an error. Logic as well as internal evidence makes it more likely that Mr. Roosevelt wrote it just before or just after his first interview (November 17) with Kurusu and Nomura. The first is the more probable. In any event this note offers further significant evidence of the direction in which the President's speculation about a stopgap arrangement with Japan was leading him. It is given here in its entirety:

Six Months

1). U. S. to resume economic relations—some oil and rice now—more later.
2). Japan to send no more troops to Indo-China or Manchurian border or any place south (Dutch, Brit. or Siam).
3). Japan to agree not to invoke tripartite pact if U. S. gets into European war.
4). U. S. to *introduce* Japs to Chinese to talk things over but U. S. take no part in their conversations.

Later on Pacific agreements.[3]

Here, in embryo, was a plan for an *ad hoc* solution which, even if it ultimately failed to achieve a comprehensive agreement, would have the inestimable advantage of postponing decision. The President's hope of gaining six months, the interval he mentioned earlier to Mr. Stimson, was certainly overoptimistic, but even six weeks would have been valuable. In any case the plan was kept in reserve for a time, presumably in the hope that Kurusu himself might come up with new solutions.

The President and Mr. Hull received the Japanese emissary on November 17, after which there were several conferences between the Secretary and the two Ambassadors in the course of the following days. All these conferences, though lengthy, were unproductive. There were eloquent expressions of the desirability of a successful outcome of the talks; lengthy disquisitions on the dangers of Hitlerism; fiery denunciations of policies of aggression; and steady harping on the theme of peace. Substantively, however, the Japanese envoys clung to discussion of their Plan A, referring occasionally to the difficulties of accepting the principle of nondiscrimination in trade when the

[2] State Department memo, November 11, 1941 (*Pearl Harbor Attack*, XIV, 1085-93). The advantages of American mediation in the Sino-Japanese War had earlier been explored in a memo of the Far East Division, October 24, 1941, entitled "Observations on the Far Eastern Situation and on American Policy in Relation Thereto."

[3] *Pearl Harbor Attack*, XIV, 1109. On the dating see Feis: *The Road to Pearl Harbor*, 312 and note.

practice had disappeared from the face of the earth. The issue of evacuation of Japanese troops was also touched upon. In this connection Mr. Roosevelt observed that the United States was not trying to interfere or mediate between Japan and China. "I don't know," added the President, "whether there is such a word in the parlance of diplomats, but the United States' only intention is to become an 'introducer.' "

Japan's relationship to the Tripartite Pact occasioned the warmest debate. Kurusu, as it happened, had personally signed that agreement while Japanese Ambassador at Berlin, though he is said to have disapproved of it. Once again he expounded the Japanese interpretation, emphasizing that the Tokyo Government alone would decide if and when it would support Germany. It would be impossible, he said, for Japan simply to renege on a solemn treaty, but if an agreement between Japan and the United States were reached, such an understanding "would far outshine the Tripartite Pact." To this Secretary Hull replied by ringing every change on the well-worn American theme: "Even if an agreement is reached between Japan and the United States at this time, it would be impossible at this time to shake the general U.S. public's conviction that, as Germany is pursuing a policy of expansion by force of arms, Japan is doing likewise in the Far East." Hitler's policy of unlimited expansion, he continued, was a distinct threat to the United States and the action which had been taken and was to be taken by Washington did not exceed the limits of reasonable self-defense. Under the circumstances, unless Japan too had embarked on a policy of aggression and expansion, there was no need for the Tripartite Pact. Until Tokyo could make clear that it proposed to pursue a peaceful policy there could be little prospect of an agreement.[4]

A review of the conversations between November 17 and 20 thus reveals nothing but the familiar deadlock. It may therefore prove more rewarding to examine the underlying developments, despite the fact that they cannot always be traced in detail. On the evening of November 17, after seeing the President, Nomura and Kurusu paid a call on a certain Cabinet officer, presumably Postmaster General Walker. The latter told them that the President was highly desirous of an understanding and that the Cabinet, with the exception of two members, approved in principle: "If Japan would now do something real, such as evacuating French Indo-China, showing her peaceful intentions, the way would be open for us to furnish you with oil and it would probably lead to the reëstablishment of normal trade relations."[5] From this remark one can only conclude that the Cabinet member in question was insinuating, by prior arrangement, the very scheme which

---

[4] The record of these protracted conversations is given in *Foreign Relations of the United States: Japan*, II, 739 ff., and on the Japanese side in Nomura's telegrams to Tokyo (*Pearl Harbor Attack*, XII, 141 ff.).

[5] Tel. from Nomura to Tokyo, November 18, 1941 (*Pearl Harbor Attack*, XII, 154).

the President had been revolving in his mind. Kurusu took the bait and reported home that his own and Nomura's observation led him to think that the President was "very much in earnest" in his desire for an agreement. Therefore, warned Kurusu:

We must exercise great care just now against forming a hasty conclusion that they are merely deferring in order not to seem to swallow our proposals at a gulp, and also against taking any steps that might prove irretrievable.

As a result of the revision of the Neutrality Act, the attention of the United States has turned more than ever toward the Atlantic of late, and a determination is being strengthened to be ready even for a war with Japan if necessary. However, there seems to be a desire to be reassured as to their rear by negotiations with our country.[6]

Kurusu, despite all that was said of him later, seems to have been genuinely anxious to score his "touchdown." Without awaiting instructions from home, he himself began, in his conversation with Mr. Hull on November 18, to broach the idea of a limited, immediate deal. After a ritual discussion of the Tripartite Pact, he pointed out that a comprehensive settlement could certainly not be envisaged within any short space of time. He therefore suggested a limited agreement involving a return to the *status quo* of July: Japan would withdraw its troops from southern Indo-China and the United States would rescind its order freezing Japanese assets. In the more congenial atmosphere thereby created the discussion of larger issues could continue. Kurusu emphasized to his own Government that the wide divergence of views on the Tripartite Pact made unlikely an early agreement either on Japan's Plan A or Plan B. Therefore the best course would be an attempt to secure the lifting of the all-important freezing order.[7]

Kurusu's proposal ran counter to Japanese military plans and was therefore certain to receive a cool reception in Tokyo. Nevertheless, it appears that the Japanese diplomats—certainly Foreign Minister Togo and Ambassador Nomura—were genuinely eager to stave off war. Even Kurusu, once he had sensed the Washington atmosphere, was disposed to strike almost any bargain. Indeed, throughout the course of the ensuing conversations one of the basic difficulties arose from Nomura's, and subsequently Kurusu's, inclination to exceed instructions and introduce proposals of their own. As evidence of the confusion thus engendered, it may be noted that at this precise moment the Tokyo Foreign Office was bombarding the Washington Embassy with notes explaining the Japanese position on non-discrimination in trade and other matters connected with Tokyo's Plan A. Meanwhile Kurusu had advanced the view that it would be best to shelve

[6] Tel. from Kurusu to Tokyo, November 18, 1941 (*Pearl Harbor Attack*, XII, 150-51).
[7] *Foreign Relations of the United States: Japan*, II, 744-50; Nomura's and Kurusu's telegrams to Tokyo are printed in *Pearl Harbor Attack*, XII, 146-52. Telegram No. 1127 on page 146 is misdated. The date should be November 18 instead of 17, since the telegram comprises a preliminary report of the conversations of November 18. On these conversations see Feis: *The Road to Pearl Harbor*, 307-9.

both Plans A and B and concentrate instead on a simple stopgap arrangement. The Tokyo authorities did not like it. On November 19 Togo cabled
that Hull's reiterated insistence that Japan give concrete evidence of intention to pursue a peaceful policy was a patent reference to the Tripartite Pact.
It was therefore inevitable that the Secretary should raise other questions
before the freezing order was rescinded: "On the other hand, the internal
situation in our country is such that it would be difficult for us to handle it
if we withdraw from southern Indo-China, merely on assurances that conditions prior to this freezing act will be restored. It would be necessary to have
a proposed solution that would come up to the B proposal." The Foreign
Minister then rebuked Kurusu for making a move which had not been discussed in Tokyo and predicted that this could lead only to delay and ultimately to failure of the negotiations. He accordingly instructed Nomura
and Kurusu to submit forthwith to Secretary Hull Plan B, with certain
modifications. "If the United States' consent to this cannot be secured,"
concluded Togo, "the negotiations will have to be broken off; therefore,
with the above well in mind, put forth your best efforts."[8]

2. WASHINGTON'S MODUS VIVENDI

While Tokyo was engrossed by the problem of a stopgap arrangement in
lieu of a full settlement, American officials themselves were reaching the
conclusion between November 17 and 20 that only a limited agreement vis-
à-vis Japan offered any hope of avoiding or postponing war. Kurusu reported to Tokyo that Secretary Hull had reacted coolly to his suggestion
for a *modus vivendi,* pointing out how difficult it would be to relax the
freezing order in the absence of concrete evidence that Japan proposed to
follow a peaceful as opposed to an aggressive policy. Nevertheless, he had
expressed willingness to take up with the British, Chinese, and Dutch any
practicable proposal the Japanese might make. Actually, of course, both the
State Department and the President had been considering for some time the
possibility of offering Tokyo a truce.

In the midst of these deliberations, the Secretary of the Treasury intervened with a blueprint for a full-scale, far-reaching settlement. On November 18 he sent the President and the Secretary of State a lengthy memorandum entitled *Suggested Approach for Elimination of United States-Japa-
nese Tension.* This document was actually the work of Mr. Harry Dexter
White, a high official of the Treasury Department who, besides taking a
keen interest in foreign policy, possessed unlimited confidence in his ability

[8] Tel. from Tokyo to Washington, November 19, 1941 (*Pearl Harbor Attack,* XII,
155). Secretary Hull discussed the Nomura-Kurusu suggestion for a temporary arrangement with Mr. Campbell of the British Embassy on November 18. It was later communicated to the Australian and Dutch Ministers (*Pearl Harbor Attack,* XIX, 3683 ff.).
Mr. Hull also discussed the course of the conversations with the Chinese Ambassador on
November 18, but omitted mention of the Japanese suggestion for a *modus vivendi.*

to cut through diplomatic red tape and reach the heart of the issues between Japan and the United States. White had long manifested irritation over what he regarded as the inept gyrations of American diplomacy which, he thought, had been characterized in the Far East by hesitation, bewilderment, inaction, petty maneuvering, sterile conversations, and diverse objectives. It was White's conviction that American diplomacy must use every modern technique and that the United States should employ all its financial and economic power to solve the Japanese problem. Thereafter all would be sweetness and light in the Pacific area and the United States would be left free to dispose of Adolf Hitler.

White had first drafted a memorandum embodying his views in May, 1941. The document which he handed Secretary Morgenthau on November 17, and which the latter forwarded to the President and Mr. Hull on the next day, was substantially a restatement of his earlier paper. Mr. Morgenthau tactfully deleted the strictures on the conduct of American policy and let the paper take off from the following eloquent exordium:

If the President were to propose something like the appended agreement and the Japs accept, the whole world would be electrified by the successful transformation of a threatening and belligerent powerful enemy into a peaceful and prosperous neighbor. The prestige and the leadership of the President both at home and abroad would sky-rocket by so brilliant and momentous a diplomatic victory—a victory that requires no vanquished, a victory that immediately would bring peace, happiness and prosperity to hundreds of millions of Eastern peoples, and assure the subsequent defeat of Germany.[9]

Since the lengthy White-Morgenthau memorandum has been published, nothing more than a brief summary need be presented here. The United States was to propose to withdraw the bulk of its naval forces from the Pacific; to sign a twenty-year nonaggression pact with Japan; to promote a final settlement of the Manchurian problem; to put Indo-China under a joint British-French-Japanese-Chinese-American Commission, assuring most-favored-nation treatment to these five powers until the end of the European war; to give up extraterritorial rights in China and induce the British to do likewise, including the return of Hongkong to China; to press Congress to repeal the Immigration Act of 1917; to negotiate a trade treaty with Japan granting most-favored-nation treatment and other concessions, including an agreement to keep raw silk on the free list for twenty years; to grant a two billion dollar credit to Japan at 2 percent for twenty years, to be drawn on at a rate not to exceed $200,000,000 per year; to set up a

[9] The text of White's memorandum of May, 1941, is in *Morgenthau Diaries (MS.)*, Vol. 405, pp. 471 ff.; the memorandum of November 17 in Vol. 462, pp. 360 ff.; the revision as sent to the President and Hull in Vol. 463, pp. 137 ff. A copy of the latter is also in the *Roosevelt Papers:* Secretary's File, Box 76, and has been printed in *Pearl Harbor Attack,* XIX, 3668 ff.

stabilization fund of $500,000,000, to which the United States and Japan were each to contribute one half; to remove at once restrictions on Japanese funds in the United States; and to use American influence to eliminate sources of potential friction between Japan and its neighbors.

In return Japan was to undertake to withdraw all forces from China beyond the frontiers of 1931, and from Indo-China and Siam; to discontinue support of any kind for Chinese governments other than that at Chungking; to replace with yen currency all military scrip in China; to give up extraterritorial rights in China; to extend a billion yen loan to China for reconstruction; to withdraw all troops from Manchuria, provided the Soviet Government agreed to withdraw all troops from the "Far Eastern Front"; to sell to the United States up to three quarters of current Japanese output of war material, including naval, air, ordnance, and commercial ships on a cost plus 20 percent basis; to grant the United States and China most-favored-nation treatment throughout the whole Japanese Empire; and to negotiate a ten-year nonaggression pact with the United States, China, Britain, the Dutch Indies, and the Philippines.

This proposition was to be offered the Japanese for a limited time. If they refused it, the offer would at least serve to rally American opinion around the President and to create serious division in Japan. If they accepted, the President could call a conference of the other interested powers in Washington. In summary:

Minimum concessions to be obtained from Japan should be withdrawal of troops from the mainland of Asia and sale to us of the bulk of her current production of armaments. If we do not achieve this we shall not obtain any significant relief to allied military forces in the east while we would be making it possible for Japan to strengthen herself for possible later aggression when the situation is more propitious for aggressive acts on her part. The minimum objectives must be to free the American, British, and Russian forces from the Pacific.

How such a program, based on the proposition that Japan, in return for American financial and economic assistance, should renounce all its aspirations for expansion and content itself with the role of a well-behaved but unpretentious contractor for American rearmament, could have received serious consideration in the State Department remains a mystery. Yet Mr. Maxwell Hamilton, the sober and experienced Chief of the Far East Division, reported to Mr. Hull on November 19 that while the Treasury proposal required some revision, it was "the most constructive one" he had yet seen and all senior officers of the Division concurred in this opinion. He therefore recommended that Mr. Hull discuss with his Army and Navy colleagues the Division's redraft, which was couched in more general terms. Eventually the Treasury memorandum became the basis of the so-called Ten-Point program, which went far beyond any terms previously submitted to Tokyo by the Washington Government. From the records presently available it is quite impossible to determine why, in the tension of the last weeks before Pearl Harbor, the State Department should have wedded itself to proposals which must have been recognized as unacceptable to Japan and which, at least in their original form, strike one as little more than the well-meaning but naïve contribution of a tyro in diplomacy.[10]

By this time events had begun to crowd each other. Before American thinking on a *modus vivendi* had evolved into anything like final form, the Japanese Ambassadors, after vainly lodging further remonstrances with their Government, obeyed instructions and presented to Secretary Hull, at noon on November 20, the Japanese Plan B. This, it will be recalled, was itself in the nature of a *modus vivendi*. In its final form as submitted to Mr. Hull, it read as follows:

1). Both the Governments of Japan and the United States undertake not to make any armed advancement into any of the regions in the Southeastern Asia and the Southern Pacific area excepting the part of French Indo-China where the Japanese troops are stationed at present.

2). The Japanese Government undertakes to withdraw its troops now stationed in French Indo-China upon either the restoration of peace between Japan and China or the establishment of an equitable peace in the Pacific area.

3). The Governments of Japan and the United States shall coöperate with a view to securing the acquisition of those goods and commodities which the two countries need in Netherlands East Indies.

4). The Governments of Japan and the United States mutually undertake to restore their commercial relations to those prevailing prior to the freezing of the assets.

The Government of the United States shall supply to Japan a required quantity of oil.

5). The Government of the United States undertakes to refrain from such measures and actions as will be prejudicial to the endeavors for the restoration of general peace between Japan and China.[11]

To evaluate this proposal accurately it is necessary to take into account certain explanations which Tokyo had forwarded to Nomura and Kurusu and which, for the most part, were already known to the Secretary of State through intercepted Japanese telegrams. In the first place, the items dealing with nondiscrimination in trade and with Japan's position in the Tripartite Pact had been dropped so as to facilitate agreement. The offer to withdraw Japanese troops from southern to northern Indo-China on conclusion of the arrangement was introduced as "an important concession," again in the hope of hastening a settlement. In one of Tokyo's telegrams it was explained to the Ambassadors that the terms Southeastern Asia and Southern Pacific in Article I included the Netherlands Indies and Siam, but not China, and

[10] Memo of Hamilton to Hull, November 19, 1941 (*Pearl Harbor Attack*, XIV, 1097 ff.).
[11] *Foreign Relations of the United States: Japan*, II, 755-56.

that with reference to peace negotiations between Japan and China it was to be understood that the United States would cease all aid to Chiang Kai-shek.[12]

All the evidence points to the conclusion that Foreign Minister Togo believed that in this revised version of Plan B he was offering a program that would prove acceptable for a preliminary agreement. In his messages to Washington he spoke of the possibility of getting President Roosevelt's signature within a week. Indeed, he supplied the Japanese envoys with a suitable preamble and sent them the text of formal notes to be exchanged with the British and Dutch, registering their accession to the agreement. He even induced his Government on November 22 to extend its war deadline from November 25 to November 29, warning the Ambassadors, however, that this was absolutely final: "After that things are automatically going to happen."[13]

What hopes, if any, Nomura and Kurusu may have entertained are unknown. However, when they presented Plan B to Secretary Hull on November 20 they remarked that it constituted "an amplification of the Ambassador's suggestion" for a very limited, preliminary agreement. Mr. Hull made little comment but showed himself "terribly aroused" by the suggestion that the United States should suspend aid to China. Kurusu observed that there had been talk of the United States acting as "introducer" between Japan and China and that it was only reasonable to expect that in such event American aid to China, which impeded the conclusion of peace, would cease. The Secretary replied that the President had meant that the Japanese should first make clear their intention to pursue a peaceful policy. This observation in turn led to renewed discussion of the Tripartite Pact, Mr. Hull emphasizing that the United States was supporting Britain because of the menace of Hitlerism and aiding China because of the threat of Japanese aggression and expansion. It need hardly be added that this acrimonious discussion again proved fruitless. The conversation ended with the Secretary's assurance that he would give the Japanese proposals sympathetic study.[14]

In his *Memoirs* Secretary Hull uses strong language in condemnation of the Japanese proposals of November 20:

The President and I could only conclude that agreeing to these proposals would mean condonement by the United States of Japan's past aggressions, assent to future courses of conquest by Japan, abandonment of the most essential principles of our foreign policy, betrayal of China and Russia, and acceptance of the role of silent part-

<hr />

[12] Tels. from Tokyo, November 19, 1941, intercepted and deciphered November 20 (*Pearl Harbor Attack*, XII, 156-57).

[13] Tels. of November 19, 21, 22, 1941 (*Pearl Harbor Attack*, XII, 156, 163-65).

[14] *Foreign Relations of the United States: Japan*, II, 753-57; tels. from Washington to Tokyo, November 20, 1941 (*Pearl Harbor Attack*, XII, 161-63); Hull: *Memoirs*, II, 1070 ff.

ner aiding and abetting Japan in her effort to create a Japanese hegemony over the western Pacific and eastern Asia.

Acceptance of Japan's proposals would have placed her in a commanding position later to acquire control of the entire western Pacific area. It would have destroyed our chances of asserting and maintaining our rights and interests in the Pacific. It would have meant abject surrender of our position under intimidation. And, in final analysis, it would have meant a most serious threat to our national security.

He therefore concludes that the Japanese proposals "were of so preposterous a character that no responsible American official could ever have dreamed of accepting them."[15]

The validity of this *ex post facto* judgment is open to some question. In the first place, it overlooks the fact that the Japanese proposal was not intended as an all-inclusive, final settlement, but rather as a stopgap arrangement to provide further time for negotiation on the long-term issues. Moreover, it is difficult to understand the depth of Mr. Hull's indignation over Japanese-sponsored suggestions which in many respects resembled ideas current in the State Department itself. Officers of the Far East Division were at that very moment working on the draft of an American *modus vivendi* which drew, in part at least, on suggestions from Mr. Roosevelt. Though no final text had emerged, they were discussing, among other things, suspension of aid to China during the course of negotiations between China and Japan and the rescinding of the freezing order. In short, on their face there was nothing reprehensible in the Japanese proposals. Doubtless they were too general and too susceptible of divergent interpretation to serve as the foundation of a long-term agreement. As the basis for a stopgap arrangement or as a device for gaining time, they were suitable enough.[16]

In support of this reasoning it may be pointed out that the Japanese proposals of November 20 were presented in all seriousness by Mr. Hull to the British, Dutch, and Chinese representatives in Washington. So likewise were the projected American suggestions for a *modus vivendi*, along with the outline for a permanent settlement which came later to be known as the "Ten Points." With regard to the American project for a stopgap arrangement it will be recalled that the White-Morgenthau memorandum had been cordially received by the Far East Division of the State Department. Acting on the recommendation of the Division, Secretary Hull on the morning of November 21, the day after the Japanese Ambassadors had presented Tokyo's Plan B, conferred with high officers of the Army and Navy on a toned-down version of the Treasury memorandum. Admiral Stark and General Gerow (representing General Marshall) expressed the opinion that "the document was satisfactory from a military standpoint." By agreement they subsequently supplied Mr. Hull with written comments on the specific

---

[15] Hull: *Memoirs*, II, 1070.
[16] On this point see Feis: *The Road to Pearl Harbor*, 310-11.

provisions. Since the program as a whole was not destined to be used, these comments need not be analyzed in detail. It is worth noting, however, that General Gerow wrote of the plan that:

The adoption of its provisions would attain one of our present major objectives—the avoidance of war with Japan. Even a temporary peace in the Pacific would permit us to complete defensive preparations in the Philippines and at the same time insure continuance of material assistance to the British—both of which are highly important.[17]

On November 22 and 24 the State Department thereupon produced new drafts of a long-range settlement based on the White-Morgenthau memorandum. Despite the initial enthusiasm aroused by the Treasury's contribution, it was presently to lose its identity and become merged in the final draft of a State Department document containing, first, the terms of an American *modus vivendi,* and second, the outline of a proposed general settlement known as the Ten Points. Impetus toward arranging the scattered ideas on a possible American *modus vivendi* stemmed directly from the Japanese plan of November 20, subsequently so roundly denounced by Mr. Hull. On further consideration this plan proved unsatisfactory, but it was thought to provide at least a basis for further discussion. The Far East Division accordingly set to work to draft counterproposals for a *modus vivendi.* Although produced concurrently with the ultimate draft of the White-Morgenthau project for a general settlement and linked with that draft, the counterproposals for a ninety-day truce were a direct response to Tokyo's Plan B. They began by recalling the efforts to arrive at a settlement of questions touching the entire Pacific area, based upon the principles of law and order and fair dealing among nations. These principles, as laid down in the American note of June 21, were once again set forth as fundamental to a long-range settlement, but the main feature of the document was its recognition of the desirability of a limited, temporary agreement to provide further opportunity for discussion. Since the Japanese proposals of November 20 contained "features which from the point of view of the Government of the United States present difficulties in reference to the broad-gauge principles," the American Government preferred to present its own suggestions. In the interests of accuracy the text of this *modus vivendi* also may be given in full:

1). The Government of the United States and the Government of Japan, both being solicitous for the peace of the Pacific, affirm that their national policies are directed toward lasting and extensive peace throughout the Pacific area and that they have no territorial designs therein. They undertake reciprocally not to make by force or threat of force, unless they are attacked, any advancement, from the points at which they have military establishments, across any international border in the Pacific area.

[17] The military comments are all printed in *Pearl Harbor Attack,* XIV, 1103-7.

2). The Japanese Government undertakes forthwith to withdraw its armed forces now stationed in southern French Indo-China, not to engage in any further military activities there, including the construction of military facilities, and to limit Japanese military forces in northern French Indo-China to the number there on July 26, 1941, which number in any case would not exceed 25,000 and which number would not be subject to replacement.

3). The Government of the United States undertakes forthwith to remove the freezing restrictions which were placed on Japanese assets in the United States on July 26 and the Japanese Government agrees simultaneously to remove the freezing measures which it imposed in regard to American assets in Japan. Exports from each country would thereafter remain subject to the respective export control measures which each country may have in effect for reasons of national defense.

4). The Government of the United States undertakes forthwith to approach the British and the Dutch Governments with a view to those Governments' taking, on a basis of reciprocity with Japan, measures similar to those provided for in paragraph three above.

5). The Government of the United States would not look with disfavor upon the inauguration of conversations between the Government of China and the Government of Japan directed toward a peaceful settlement of their differences nor would the Government of the United States look with disfavor upon an armistice during the period of any such discussions. The fundamental interest of the Government of the United States in reference to any such discussions is simply that they be based upon and exemplify the fundamental principles of peace which constitute the central spirit of the current conversations between the Government of Japan and the Government of the United States.

In case any such discussions are entered into between the Government of Japan and the Government of China, the Government of the United States is agreeable to such discussions taking place in the Philippine Islands, if so desired by both China and Japan.

6). It is understood that this *modus vivendi* is of a temporary nature and shall not remain in effect for a period longer than three months unless renewed by common agreement.[18]

Writing of these developments some years later, Secretary Hull asserted that he thought there was but slight possibility that the Japanese would accept any *modus vivendi* save on their own terms of November 20. He pictured himself and his associates as having reached "a stage of clutching at straws to save the situation."[19] Admittedly Mr. Hull had good grounds for pessimism. He knew that Foreign Minister Togo had recently sent word that if Washington rejected Tokyo's Plan B, the negotiations would end. He also knew that a time limit, now almost at hand, had been placed on Washington's acceptance. Finally, the draft of the American *modus vivendi* was accompanied by terms for a final settlement which had been rejected again and again by the Japanese. Nevertheless, it is possible that Mr. Hull's judg-

---

[18] Text in *Pearl Harbor Attack,* XIV, 1110-15.
[19] Hull: *Memoirs,* II, 1073.

ment reflects his reading of later interpretations into earlier events. It is by no means self-evident that the American provisions for a *modus vivendi* were so far removed from the Japanese as to rule out all possibility of favorable consideration by Tokyo. Secretary Hull himself must have entertained some such view at the time, since he took up the matter in all seriousness with the representatives of the friendly and interested powers. On the same 22nd of November he called in the British and Chinese Ambassadors and the Australian and Netherlands Ministers, reviewed for them the recent developments in the Japanese-American conversations, showed them the Japanese note of November 20, and allowed them to read the American draft reply. The record states that "there seemed to be general agreement that a substitute was more desirable than a specific reply to the Japanese proposal, section for section." The reasons are not given, but the record continues: "Each of the gentlemen present seemed to be well pleased with this preliminary report to them," with the exception of the Chinese Ambassador, and even he did not show "serious concern." Though the Secretary pointed out that there was probably not one chance in three that the Japanese would accept the American reply, the whole proposition was evidently taken earnestly. While the various foreign representatives were referring the matter to their Governments for an opinion, work continued in the State Department, where on November 24 a revised draft was produced. The new version differed from the preceding one only insofar as it specified in greater detail what items of trade were to be permitted after the conclusion of the agreement.[20]

For the moment consideration of the *modus vivendi* appeared to be progressing in orderly fashion. On leaving the conference with Secretary Hull the foreign envoys all expressed themselves to the press as satisfied. The Chinese Ambassador said he had "no fear of anything and no cause for alarm." Lord Halifax stressed the solidarity of the ABCD powers and Australian Minister Casey added: "There is no rift in the alphabetical lute."[21] To Nomura and Kurusu Secretary Hull reported that the British, Dutch, and Chinese would all favor gradual relaxation of the freezing orders if Japan provided satisfactory evidence of peaceful intentions. He further indicated his hope of being in a position to reply formally to the proposals in Japan's Plan B by Monday, November 24.[22]

[20] Memo of conversation between Secretary Hull, Lord Halifax, Mr. Casey, Dr. Loudon, and Dr. Hu Shih on November 22, 1941 (text in *Pearl Harbor Attack*, XIV, 1122-23); text of the revised draft, *ibid.*, 1124-31. The three successive drafts of the so-called *modus vivendi* proposal (November 22, 24, 25, 1941) are filed together in the State Department with a descriptive sheet indicating that the drafts of November 22 and 24 had been discussed by Mr. Hull with the British, Chinese, Dutch, and Australian representatives.

[21] Hulen in *The New York Times*, November 23, 1941; Feis: *The Road to Pearl Harbor*, 312-13.

[22] *Foreign Relations of the United States: Japan*, II, 757-62; tel. from Nomura to Tokyo, November 23, 1941 (*Pearl Harbor Attack*, XII, 167-72).

3. FAILURE OF THE MODUS VIVENDI

The receipt in Washington on November 22, 1941, of an intercepted message from Tokyo to the Japanese Embassy heavily influenced the whole subsequent development of American policy toward Japan. This telegram, deciphered on the day it was received, extended Tokyo's deadline from November 25 to November 29, but warned that thereafter "things are automatically going to happen." Thenceforth, of course, American officials were fully aware that unless some kind of solution were achieved within a week, Japanese military action in one direction or another would ensue. In view of this bald evidence of the victory of the war party over the moderates in Tokyo, Secretary Hull can scarcely be blamed if the impetus to achieve a settlement was blunted by a sense of futility and if subsequent moves were made in a fatalistic spirit. Pessimism pervaded even the White House. On November 24 the President despatched to Mr. Churchill the substance of the Japanese note of November 20, together with the proposed American countersuggestion. Of the latter he observed: "This seems to me a fair proposition for the Japanese, but its acceptance or rejection is really a matter of internal Japanese politics. I am not very hopeful and we must all be prepared for real trouble, possibly soon."[23]

If anything further was required to deepen Mr. Hull's disillusionment, it was provided by his own friends on the occasion of his second meeting with the British, Chinese, and Dutch representatives on November 24. It then emerged that only the Dutch envoy had received instructions from his Government which were, on the whole, favorable to the American project. The Chinese Ambassador, though uninstructed, had received a telegram from Chungking indicating a "rather strong reaction" on the part of the Generalissimo. The latter had inferred from the Ambassador's report of November 22 "that the United States Government has put aside the Chinese question in its conversation with Japan instead of seeking a solution, and is still inclined to appease Japan at the expense of China." Dr. Hu Shih therefore began to object to an agreement by which Japan might keep in northern Indo-China a force of 25,000 men which could be used for an attack upon Yunnan. Mr. Hull pointed out that this force would be inadequate for such an attack and that, besides, the United States Goverment was not proposing to recognize Japan's right to keep any troops whatever in Indo-China. Once again he explained:

We were striving to reach this proposed temporary agreement primarily because the heads of our Army and Navy often emphasize to me that time is the all-important question for them, and that it is necessary to be more fully prepared to deal effectively with the situation in the Pacific area in case of an outbreak by Japan. I also empha-

[23] *Roosevelt Papers:* Secretary's File, Box 76; printed in *Pearl Harbor Attack*, XIV, 1138-42, and in *F. D. R.: His Personal Letters*, II, 1245-46.

sized the point that, even if we agree that the chances of such an outbreak are not great, it must be admitted that there are real possibilities that such an outbreak may occur soon—any day after this week—unless a temporary arrangement is effected that will cause the agitated state of public opinion to become more quiet and thereby make it much more practicable to continue the conversations relative to the general settlement.

But even this plain speaking failed to satisfy the Ambassador, and the conference broke up on a sour note. The exasperated Secretary told his visitors that their countries all seemed to be more interested in the defense of their own immediate regions than in the larger issues of policy, and that they showed little appreciation of the costs, which the United States was expected to bear. In conclusion he remarked that he was not sure that he would present the proposal to the Japanese, not knowing what the views of the other Governments were.[24]

Mr. Hull's irritation was evidently but momentary, for he persisted, on November 25, in going ahead with the stopgap project. At 9:30 in the morning he met with Secretaries Stimson and Knox at one of their regular Tuesday sessions. He showed them the latest draft of the *modus vivendi*, which he proposed to hand the Japanese envoys either on the same or the next day. Secretary Stimson noted that he himself thought the document "adequately safeguarded all our interests," though he considered the chances of acceptance by the Japanese to be slight in view of the limited trade concessions it envisaged. Since the meeting lasted an hour and a half and must have been of considerable interest, it is particularly regrettable that the record of it should be so brief. In any case the three Secretaries adjourned at about 11:00 and at noon met again at the White House where, together with General Marshall and Admiral Stark, they conferred with the President until 1:30 P.M. The discussion, long though it was, dealt exclusively with the Japanese situation and evidently hinged on the intercepted message fixing the November 29 deadline. Though unaware that orders for the Japanese Task Force to rendezvous for the attack on Pearl Harbor had already been issued by Admiral Yamamoto, the White House conferees all agreed that the Japanese might attack as early as Monday, November 30, and concurred in the warnings of Ambassador Grew that Tokyo would probably exploit every possible tactical advantage, such as surprise. It was recalled that the Japanese were notorious for attacking without warning. Secretary Hull suggested that they might well attack at several points simultaneously and reminded his colleagues of what might already have been taken as axiomatic: "that the matter of safeguarding our national security was in the hands of the Army and Navy."

According to Secretary Stimson the immediate question before the con-

---

[24] Memo of conversation between Hull, Halifax, Hu Shih, Loudon and Casey, November 24, 1941 (text in *Pearl Harbor Attack,* XIV, 1143-46); Hull: *Memoirs,* II, 1076-77.

ferees was what should now be done. There follows in his diary a cryptic passage which has given rise to much debate and to widely divergent interpretations:

The question was how we should maneuver them into the position of firing the first shot without allowing too much danger to ourselves. It was a difficult proposition. Hull laid out his general broad propositions on which the thing should be rested—the freedom of the seas and the fact that Japan was in alliance with Hitler and was carrying out his policy of world aggression. The others brought out the fact that any such expedition to the South as the Japanese were likely to take would be an encirclement of our interests in the Philippines and cutting our vital supplies of rubber from Malaysia. I pointed out to the President that he had already taken the first steps toward an ultimatum in notifying Japan way back last summer that if she crossed the border into Thailand she was violating our safety and that therefore he had only to point out [to Japan] that to follow any such expedition was a violation of a warning we had already given. So Hull is to go to work on preparing that.[25]

Major interest in this passage has focused on the first sentence. Mr. Stimson's infelicitous and hurried choice of words has exposed him and the Administration to the charge of having deliberately courted war with Japan. Such an interpretation entirely ignores the accumulation of evidence that the Secretary of War, as well as all other leading officials, was anxious to postpone war with Japan at least until the American military position in the Far East had been strengthened. It further overlooks the fact that all those present at the White House conference were in agreement on the immediate danger of a Japanese surprise attack, quite possibly at a number of points simultaneously. Patently, therefore, neither Mr. Stimson nor his colleagues were intent on inducing a Japanese attack. What did worry them, and with every reason, was their virtual certainty that Japan would presently strike at a point or points of its own choosing, while the United States, in the absence of Congressional authorization, would be debarred from parrying the blow by itself initiating hostilities. At the worst, therefore, Mr. Stimson can be charged with having abandoned hope that the situation could be saved either by further discussions or by speedy Congressional action to deprive the Japanese of the advantage of surprise attack.

The rest of the diary passage addresses itself to the manner in which American intervention should be presented to the Congress and people in the event of the anticipated Japanese assault. Mr. Hull proposed to justify it on the basis of freedom of the seas and Japan's association with Hitler in

[25] Stimson Diary (MS.), November 25, 1941 (quoted, with such other evidence on the meeting as exists, in Pearl Harbor Attack: Report, 374); see also Henry L. Stimson and McGeorge Bundy: On Active Service in Peace and War (New York, 1947), 389; Hull: Memoirs, II, 1080; Feis: The Road to Pearl Harbor, 314-15. For unfavorable interpretations of this passage see Charles A. Beard: President Roosevelt and the Coming of the War (New Haven, 1948), 517 ff.; and George Morgenstern: Pearl Harbor (Chicago, 1947), 152 ff.

a policy of world aggression. Others suggested stressing the threat to the Philippines and to American trade routes to Malaysia. Secretary Hull was apparently assigned the task of drafting a message to Congress. But at the root of the matter lay another problem: how to justify American intervention if the Japanese confined their operations to non-American territory.

It will be recalled that the Joint Board had recommended to the President on November 5 that the United States should take military action if the Japanese attacked British or Dutch possessions in the Southwest Pacific, or if they crossed a certain line into Siam. The Cabinet had agreed with the President on November 7 that if, in such an event, the United States intervened, the country would support the Administration. But this remained doubtful and Secretary Stimson, according to his notes, therefore suggested that the issue be presented in the context of earlier warnings to Japan. Parenthetically it might be remarked that at the "War Council" of November 25 it was clearly the general opinion that the Japanese attack, when it came, would be directed from Indo-China against Siam, Malaysia or the Dutch Indies rather than against the Philippines. This was also the opinion of the British Joint Intelligence Committee, which considered a move against Siam most likely. The Dutch, on the other hand, were concerned about rather flimsy reports of Japanese concentrations in the Pelew Islands, with the supposed objective of seizing the Netherlands Indies or Timor. On November 24 Admiral Stark had cabled London expressing doubts of such a move but adding his anxiety about "southward troop movements from Shanghai and Japan to Formosa and also apparent preparations in China, Formosa and Indo-China for an early aggressive movement of some character." To confirm prevalent expectations, Secretary Stimson on the very afternoon of November 25 received a report from the Military Intelligence Division that a large Japanese force had been assembled at Shanghai and had embarked on some thirty to fifty transports, which had been sighted south of Formosa.[26]

Such then were the deliberations of the "War Council" at midday on November 25. Secretary Hull had warned that there was almost no chance of arriving at agreement with Japan. Since, however, it was so manifestly in the American interest to continue conversations and gain time to "the last split second," work had to be continued on the counterproposals to the Japanese note of November 20. But that very afternoon severe strokes of diplomatic lightning began to hit the *modus vivendi*. The Dutch presented the least difficulty, though even they now began to urge that the relaxation of the freezing orders be made gradual and conditional on the withdrawal of Japanese troops from Indo-China to the point where they would no longer

[26] The British estimate (dated November 21) is given in Sherwood: *Roosevelt and Hopkins*, 421-22; the Dutch reports and the American reaction in *Pearl Harbor Attack*, XV, 1770-72; for the rest: *Stimson Diary (MS.)*, November 25, 1941.

constitute a threat to the Netherlands Indies, Malacca, or the Burma Road.[27] Lord Halifax, on the other hand, at long last produced a memorandum giving the British reaction to the American *modus vivendi*. This document, though expressing willingness to leave the decision to Washington, cast doubt upon the wisdom of allowing the Japanese to force a decision and magnified the dangers of delay. It recommended that, in reply to the Japanese note, the United States Government should pitch its demands high and its price low. In particular it suggested that the United States stipulate not only the total withdrawal of Japanese troops but also of naval and air forces from Indo-China, and the prohibition of further military advances against China or any other region. Secretary Hull was obviously taken aback by these suggestions. Once again he pointed out the advantages China could anticipate from the *modus vivendi* and stressed the military opinion that twenty-five thousand Japanese troops in Indo-China could not constitute a serious threat. It would be utterly impracticable, he observed, to request the suspension of further military operations against China in addition to all the other demands.[28]

Even heavier bolts came from Chungking. Chiang Kai-shek, convinced that the Japanese were poised for an attack on Yunnan and much disappointed by the American response to his appeal for air support, was worried by the Kurusu Mission and fearful of a deal which would abandon China to its fate.[29] Ambassador Hu Shih's report that the proposed *modus vivendi* contained nothing to prevent the Japanese from pressing their attack on China and that it would permit them to keep as many as twenty-five thousand troops in northern Indo-China tended to confirm his suspicions. Supposing the Japanese confined themselves to building up their air power in Indo-China, they could then launch a strong attack on the Burma Road and on Kunming, and could also use Indo-China as a vast air base from which to support operations against Yunnan from other points.[30]

The Generalissimo, worn by anxiety, overrode the advice of his Foreign Minister and at once instructed Dr. Hu Shih to put on record his firm opposition "to any measure which may have the effect of increasing China's difficulty in her war of resistance, or of strengthening Japan's power in her aggression against China." At the same time he raised the question with Owen Lattimore, his political adviser, who had never before seen Chiang Kai-shek so agitated. Lattimore cabled at once to Mr. Lauchlin Currie at the White House, summarizing the Generalissimo's objections as follows:

[27] *Pearl Harbor Attack,* IV, 1692-93.

[28] Memo of conversation between Hull and Halifax and text of the British note of November 25, 1941, printed in *Pearl Harbor Attack,* XIV, 1162-66.

[29] See his statement to the People's Political Council on November 17, 1941 (*Chicago Daily News,* November 17, 1941).

[30] Hu Shih's explanations to Mr. Hornbeck on the evening of November 24, 1941 (memo of conversation, in *Pearl Harbor Attack,* XIV, 1171-74).

Loosening of economic pressure or unfreezing would dangerously increase Japan's military advantage in China. A relaxation of American pressure while Japan has its forces in China would dismay the Chinese. Any "modus vivendi" now arrived at with Japan would be disastrous to Chinese belief in America and analogous to the closing of the Burma Road, which permanently destroyed British prestige. Japan and Chinese defeatists would instantly exploit the resulting disillusionment and urge Oriental solidarity against Occidental treachery. It is doubtful whether either past assistance or increasing aid could compensate for the feeling of being deserted at this hour. The Generalissimo has deep confidence in the President's fidelity to his consistent policy, but I must warn you that even the Generalissimo questions his ability to hold the situation together if the Chinese national trust in America is undermined by reports of Japan's escaping military defeat by diplomatic victory.[31]

Not content with these moves, Chiang Kai-shek sent a message of protest to Mr. Churchill and even overstepped the bounds of diplomatic procedure by appealing directly to Secretaries Stimson and Knox through his brother-in-law, Mr. T. V. Soong. The latter was instructed to point out the gravity of the situation, which was outlined in terms similar to those reported by Lattimore, concluding with this passage:

We could therefore only request the United States Government to be uncompromising, and announce that if the withdrawal of Japanese armies from China is not settled, the question of relaxing of the embargo or freezing could not be considered. If, on the other hand, the American attitude remains nebulous, Japanese propoganda will daily perform its fell purpose, so that at no cost to them this propaganda will effect the breakdown of our resistance. Our more than four years of struggle, with the loss of countless lives and sacrifices unparalleled in history, would have been in vain. The certain collapse of our resistance will be an unparalleled catastrophe to the world, and I do not indeed know how history in future will record this episode.[32]

On the evening of November 25, when the Chinese Ambassador came to Mr. Hull to report the Generalissimo's vigorous reaction, the Secretary must have been weary and discouraged. Nonetheless, he went over the old familiar ground patiently and in detail, and without mincing words:

I replied in the first place the official heads of our Army and Navy for some weeks have been most earnestly urging that we not get into war with Japan until they have had an opportunity to increase further their plans and methods and means of defense in the Pacific area. In the second place, at the request of the more peaceful elements in Japan for conversations with this Government looking toward a broad peaceful settlement for the entire Pacific area, we have been carrying on conversations and making some progress thus far; and the Japanese are urging the continuance of these general conversations for the purpose of a broad Pacific area settlement. The situation, therefore, is that the proposed *modus vivendi* is really a part and parcel of the efforts

[31] Texts in *Pearl Harbor Attack*, XIV, 1160, 1170.
[32] Tel. to T. V. Soong of November 25, 1941 (text in *Pearl Harbor Attack*, XIV, 1161).

to carry forward these general conversations for the reasons that have been fully stated from time to time, and recently to the Chinese Ambassador and to others.

I said that very recently the Generalissimo and Madame Chiang Kai-shek almost flooded Washington with strong and lengthy cables telling us how extremely dangerous the Japanese threat is to attack the Burma Road through Indo-China and appealing loudly for aid, whereas practically the first thing this present proposal of mine and the President does is to require the Japanese troops to be taken out of Indo-China and thereby to protect the Burma Road from what Chiang Kai-shek said was an imminent danger. Now, I added, Chiang Kai-shek ignores that situation which we have taken care of for him and inveighs loudly about another matter relating to the release of certain commodities to Japan corresponding to the progress made with our conversations concerning a general peace agreement. He also overlooks the fact that our proposal would relieve the menace of Japan in Indo-China to the whole South Pacific area, including Singapore, the Netherlands East Indies, Australia and also the United States, with the Philippines and the rubber and tin trade routes. All of this relief from menace to each of the countries would continue for ninety days. One of our leading admirals stated to me recently that the limited amount of more or less inferior oil products that we might let Japan have during that period would not to any appreciable extent increase Japanese war and naval preparations. I said that, of course, we can cancel this proposal, but it must be with the understanding that we are not to be charged with failure to send our Fleet into the area near Indo-China and into Japanese waters, if by any chance Japan makes a military drive southward.[33]

The record of this conversation has been quoted at length less for its refutation of the Chinese objections than for its clear summation of the motives and objectives of the American *modus vivendi*. By the evening of November 25 that plan was well on its way to the discard. In his *Memoirs* Secretary Hull relates that after the visit of the Chinese Ambassador he discussed with his colleagues whether or not to submit the American counterproposals to the Japanese. He pictures himself as still in favor of doing so, in the belief that while the chances of acceptance were slight, the American record would thereby remain clean. This does not conform exactly to what the Secretary told the Dutch Minister a day or two after the event, namely, that he had abandoned, "or practically abandoned," the *modus vivendi* on the evening of the 25th, "when the Chinese had exploded without knowing half the true facts or waiting to ascertain them."[34] Subsequently, in any case, Mr. Hull blamed the shipwreck of the plan on the lukewarm attitude of the British and "the hysterical cables" with which Chiang Kai-shek bombarded Washington. There can be little doubt that the Secretary was chagrined by the lack of understanding of his friends and extremely sensitive to any suggestion that he was preparing to sacrifice basic principles to close a profitable deal. Nevertheless, the United States was in a position to over-

[33] Memo of conversation between Hull and Hu Shih, November 25, 1941 (text in *Pearl Harbor Attack,* XIV, 1167-70).

[34] Memo of conversation between Hull and Dr. Loudon, November 27, 1941 (*Pearl Harbor Attack,* IV, 1693-94).

ride British or Chinese objections if the explanations given did not suffice to quiet anxieties. There must, therefore, have been something more behind the decision to abandon the project.

Several other factors seem to have played a role. Foremost among them was the conviction that the Japanese would not accept the American terms anyway, and that in view of the known deadline of November 29 no further time was to be gained. Secondly, there was the alarming report, relayed by Secretary Stimson on the afternoon of November 25, that Japanese transports had already been sighted off Formosa. And thirdly, powerful considerations of domestic policy were cited by Mr. Hull in a cable to Ambassador Grew as having influenced the decision.[35] These were cast up on the rising tide of public sentiment against any "appeasement" of Japan. Presumably the Chinese, as was their wont, had let it be known that something of the sort was in the wind and the newspapers had quickly taken up the cry. As early as November 21 a despatch from Leland Stowe in Chungking had warned that "Any *modus vivendi* that Washington might reach with Tokyo would mean the risk of arousing sharp disillusionment among the Chinese, since they insist on the withdrawal of the last Nipponese soldier from all occupied territories."[36] This was followed by a rash of appeals not to "sell China down the river." Secretary Hull, already disturbed by charges of appeasement emanating from the corridors and cloakrooms of Congress, could not help noting the hostile reception with which his proposed *modus vivendi* was certain to be greeted by influential segments of the American public.[37]

On the evening of November 25 the future of the *modus vivendi* already hung in the balance. Its ultimate fate was doubtless further influenced by the receipt during the night of Mr. Churchill's views. The Prime Minister commented thus:

Of course, it is for you to handle this business and we certainly do not want an additional war. There is only one point that disquiets us. What about Chiang Kaishek? Is he not having a very thin diet? Our anxiety is about China. If they collapse, our joint dangers would enormously increase. We are sure that the regard of the United States for the Chinese will govern your action. We feel that the Japanese are most unsure of themselves.[38]

As far as Mr. Hull was concerned this message evidently clinched matters.

[35] Tel. to Grew, November 27, 1941 (*Pearl Harbor Attack*, XIV, 1188-93).

[36] *Chicago Daily News,* November 21; cf. *New York Post,* editorial, November 22, 1941.

[37] On the rumblings in Congress see Admiral Stark's testimony in *Pearl Harbor Attack,* V, 2326 ff. Cf. the retrospective editorial in the *Washington Post,* August 12, 1948: "Mr. Hull's *modus vivendi* would have had short shrift from American opinion in 1941."

[38] Tel. of the Prime Minister to the President, November 26, 1941 (*Pearl Harbor Attack,* XIV, 1300). Though this message reached Washington at 12:55 A.M. on the 26th, the substance of it may have been known the previous day (Feis: *The Road to Pearl Harbor,* 318 and note). On Mr. Churchill's views see *The Grand Alliance,* 595-97.

When Secretary Stimson telephoned him on the morning of November 26 to tell him of Chiang Kai-shek's message and to ask what he was to do about it, the Secretary replied "that he had about made up his mind not to give the proposition that Knox and I [i.e., Stimson] passed on the other day to the Japanese, but to kick the whole thing over—to tell them he has no other proposition at all." A few minutes later Mr. Stimson telephoned the President to inquire whether he had received the intelligence report on Japanese troop movements to the south. This report, in turn, may have decided Mr. Roosevelt to drop the *modus vivendi*. For, as Mr. Stimson recorded in his diary, the President

fairly blew up—jumped up into the air, so to speak, and said he hadn't seen it and that that changed the whole situation because it was evidence of bad faith on the part of the Japanese that while they were negotiating for an entire truce—an entire withdrawal—they should be sending this expedition down there to Indo-China.[39]

This was the setting for the decision to drop the *modus vivendi*. The long race between the extremists and the moderates in Tokyo was as good as won by the military. The Japanese war machine was already in motion. Only the flimsiest hope remained that the Japanese could be induced to extend their deadline in order to discuss the American terms. Yet, insofar as these terms might conceivably have altered the outcome, the decision to withhold them marked the point of no return along Japan's road to war. Unhappily it is at present and is likely in the future to remain impossible to reconstruct in the necessary detail what occurred in Washington on November 26, 1941. Neither the mass of evidence accumulated for the Congressional investigation of the Pearl Harbor attack, nor the lengthy testimony, civilian and military, at the subsequent hearings, nor even the private records and diaries of President Roosevelt and other principals have thus far clarified the precise sequence of events which led to the final decision. About all that can be said with assurance is that Mr. Hull conferred with his State Department advisers and assistants in the afternoon and evening of the 25th. Evidently under the impact of the Chinese protests and of Mr. Churchill's views they decided to drop the *modus vivendi*. Subsequently a memorandum was drafted for the President giving the reasons. So far as can be determined no new factors had entered into the situation. As the Secretary testified at the Pearl Harbor investigation and later repeated in his *Memoirs:* "In view of these considerations it became clear that the slight prospects of Japan's agreeing to the *modus vivendi* did not warrant assuming the risks involved

[39] *Stimson Diary (MS.)*, November 26, 1941 (quoted in *Pearl Harbor Attack*—Report, 379). The insertion of the parenthetical "from China" after the phrase "on entire withdrawal" is completely unjustified. It neither appears in the original nor corresponds to the facts of the situation.

in proceeding with it, especially the serious risk of collapse of Chinese morale and resistance and even of disintegration of China."[40]

Early on the morning of November 26th, so Mr. Hull relates, he took his memorandum to the White House and read it to the President. This document recalled the relationship of the *modus vivendi* to the outline of the long-term settlement, the so-called "Ten Points," which accompanied it. The memorandum then continued:

> In view of the opposition of the Chinese Government and either the halfhearted support or the actual opposition of the British, the Netherlands and the Australian Governments, and in view of the wide publicity of the opposition and of the additional opposition that will naturally follow through utter lack of an understanding of the vast importance and the value otherwise of the *modus vivendi*, without in any way departing from my views about the wisdom and the benefit of this step to all of the countries opposed to the aggressive nations who are interested in the Pacific area, I desire very earnestly to recommend at this time that I call in the Japanese Ambassadors and hand to them a copy of the comprehensive basic proposal for a general peaceful settlement, and at the same time withhold the *modus vivendi* proposal.[41]

The time and manner in which this document was communicated to the President, and the details of his reaction to it, cannot be precisely established, though they are of crucial importance in clarifying the fate of the *modus vivendi*. Secretary Hull recalls only that "early" Wednesday morning he took his memorandum to the President and read it to him, and that the President "promptly agreed."[42] The original document, filed in the State Department archives, bears a penciled note reading: "Delivered orally & agreed to by the President—Hull." The Secretary could remember nothing further about this significant interview.[43] In the circumstances, and given the obvious reluctance with which the Secretary abandoned the truce plan, it is inevitable that speculation should arise over the possibility that the President himself was instrumental in shelving the proposal for a *modus vivendi*. Such a possibility would at least explain Mr. Hull's own change of mind, though it would deepen the mystery of Mr. Roosevelt's prompt and complete agreement to kill the plan for a truce in the Far East which he himself had initiated and encouraged.

Until and unless additional evidence comes to light, the role of the President as well as of Secretary Hull will remain a subject of speculation. Mr. Hull's interview with the President must certainly have ended before 10 A.M., for Secretary Stimson had by then telephoned Mr. Hull and had

[40] *Pearl Harbor Attack*, II, 434-35; Hull: *Memoirs*, II, 1081. See also Lord Halifax's report to Mr. Churchill of his interview with Mr. Hull on November 29 (Churchill: *The Grand Alliance*, 599).

[41] The text is printed in *Pearl Harbor Attack*, XIV, 1176-77, from a carbon copy in the State Department files.

[42] Hull: *Memoirs*, II, 1081-82.

[43] *Pearl Harbor Attack*, II, 453, and XI, 5391.

learned of the latter's decision to kick the "whole thing over," a statement
for which presidential approval must surely have been secured. Apparently
the news was conveyed to the Navy Department through Captain (later
Admiral) Schuirman at 10:30 and perhaps also by Mr. Hull directly to
Admiral Stark, with whom he talked on the telephone at 11:05 A.M.[44] The
Joint Army-Navy Board met from about 11:30 until almost 1:00 P.M.
Though there is no record of discussion of the recent decision, the Navy
planning officers had hastily drafted a warning to United States commanders in the Pacific. This warning, which must surely have been
prompted by the news from the State Department, was discussed by the
Joint Board. When it adjourned and General Marshall left Washington to
attend the Army maneuvers in the Carolinas, it had come to be known
generally in high official circles that the *modus vivendi* was dead and that
the crisis was at hand.

4. The American Ten-Point Offer

From the moment of its formulation the *modus vivendi* had been considered by the American Government only as a means of achieving a ninety-
day truce during which it might prove possible for the United States and
Japan to agree on the terms of a basic settlement of Far Eastern problems.
The successive drafts of the *modus vivendi* were therefore accompanied by
an outline for such a settlement, subsequently known as the Ten-Point program, and by a specific statement explaining the relationship of the two
parts. The final draft of both the *modus vivendi* and the accompanying Ten
Points had been completed on November 25, the text of the long-range
agreement having been based on a much attenuated version of the White-
Morgenthau memorandum of November 17.[45]

Though it has been impossible to recapture the tenor of the discussions
on the afternoon and evening of November 25th between Mr. Hull and his
chief advisers, the Secretary's memorandum to the President stated that his
decision to submit the Ten-Point program to the Japanese was made at the
same time as the decision to withhold the *modus vivendi*. Since it can
hardly have been thought that the Japanese would accept the sweeping
American terms for a general settlement even if linked with the truce arrangement, the proffer of the Ten Points must have been intended to keep
the record clean and to relieve Washington of the odium of having rejected
Tokyo's offer of November 20 without putting forward a substitute.

The President gave his blessing to this procedure at the time when he
agreed to the shelving of the *modus vivendi* in his morning interview with

---

[44] Testimony of Admiral Turner (*Pearl Harbor Attack*, V, 1947); the record of telephone calls is given in *Pearl Harbor Attack*, II, 442, and V, 2093.
[45] The texts are printed in *Pearl Harbor Attack*, XIV, 1147-59.

Mr. Hull on November 26.[46] When Mr. Roosevelt received the Chinese Ambassador, Dr. Hu Shih, and Mr. T. V. Soong at 2:15 in the afternoon of the same day, he was therefore in a position to meet the Chinese insistence on assurances that the United States still adhered to its basic principles in the Far East. It is not known whether Secretary Hull was present on this occasion. If so, he was certainly back in his office by 3:45, when Admiral Stark talked with him by telephone. According to newspaper reports Mr. Hull thereafter conferred with his chief advisers, who were still with him when Nomura and Kurusu arrived at five o'clock. Since it was not customary to make records of conferences between the Secretary and his advisers, it can only be assumed that the discussion centered on the final form in which the American terms should be presented to the two Ambassadors. In any case Mr. Hull and his colleagues determined to take over almost the entire preamble of the now defunct *modus vivendi* and to recast it in the form of an "oral statement." This statement rehearsed the previous "conversations" and the Japanese suggestion of a *modus vivendi*. It then pointed out the divergence of the Japanese proposals from some of the fundamental principles held by the United States to be essential to a general settlement, and continued:

The Government of the United States believes that the adoption of such proposals would not be likely to contribute to the ultimate objectives of ensuring peace under law, order and justice in the Pacific area, and it suggests that further effort be made to resolve our divergences of views in regard to the practical application of the fundamental principles already mentioned.

With this object in view the Government of the United States offers for the consideration of the Japanese Government a plan of a broad but simple settlement covering the entire Pacific area as one practical exemplification of a program which this Government envisages as something to be worked out during our further conversations.

The plan therein suggested represents an effort to bridge the gap between our draft of June 21, 1941 and the Japanese draft of September 25 by making a new approach to the essential problems underlying a comprehensive Pacific settlement.

This preface was followed by the text of the Ten-Point program, identical with the Department's final draft of November 25, completed prior to the decision to scrap the *modus vivendi*. In accordance with Mr. Hull's unvarying refusal to enter into "negotiations" as opposed to "exploratory conversations," the document he presented to the two Ambassadors bore the heading "Tentative and without Commitment." The title described the contents as an "Outline of Proposed Basis for Agreement between the United States and Japan." The text follows:

[46] The Secretary informed the Netherlands Minister that the decision to submit the larger program had been made "early Wednesday morning" (Memo of conversation between Hull and Loudon, November 27, 1941, printed in *Pearl Harbor Attack*, IV, 1693).

Section I

Draft Mutual Declaration of Policy

The Government of the United States and the Government of Japan, both being solicitous for the peace of the Pacific, affirm that their national policies are directed toward lasting and extensive peace throughout the Pacific area, that they have no territorial designs in that area, that they have no intention of threatening other countries or of using military force aggressively against any neighboring nation, and that, accordingly, in their national policies they will actively support and give practical application to the following fundamental principles upon which their relations with each other and with all other governments are based:

1) The principle of inviolability of territorial integrity and sovereignty of each and all nations.

2) The principle of non-interference in the internal affairs of other countries.

3) The principle of equality, including equality of commercial opportunity and treatment.

4) The principle of reliance upon international coöperation and conciliation for the prevention and pacific settlement of controversies and for improvement of international conditions by peaceful methods and processes.

The Government of Japan and the Government of the United States have agreed that toward eliminating chronic political instability, preventing recurrent economic collapse, and providing a basis for peace, they will actively support and practically apply the following principles in their economic relations with each other and with other nations and peoples:

1) The principle of non-discrimination in international commercial relations.

2) The principle of international economic coöperation and abolition of extreme nationalism as expressed in excessive trade restrictions.

3) The principle of non-discriminatory access by all nations to raw material supplies.

4) The principle of full protection of the interests of consuming countries and populations as regards the operation of international commodity agreements.

5) The principle of establishment of such institutions and arrangements of international finance as may lend aid to the essential enterprises and the continuous development of all countries and may permit payments through processes of trade consonant with the welfare of all countries.

Section II

Steps to be taken by the Government of the United States and by the Government of Japan

The Government of the United States and the Government of Japan propose to take steps as follows:

1) The Government of the United States and the Government of Japan will endeavor to conclude a multilateral non-aggression pact among the British Empire, China, Japan, the Netherlands, the Soviet Union, Thailand and the United States.

2) Both Governments will endeavor to conclude among the American, British,

Chinese, Japanese, the Netherlands and Thai Governments an agreement whereunder each of the Governments would pledge itself to respect the territorial integrity of French Indochina and, in the event that there should develop a threat to the territorial integrity of Indochina, to enter into immediate consultation with a view to taking such measures as may be deemed necessary and advisable to meet the threat in question. Such agreement would provide also that each of the Governments party to the agreement would not seek or accept preferential treatment in its trade or economic relations with Indochina and would use its influence to obtain for each of the signatories equality of treatment in trade and commerce with French Indochina.

3) The Government of Japan will withdraw all military, naval, air and police forces from China and from Indochina.

4) The Government of the United States and the Government of Japan will not support—militarily, politically, economically—any government or regime in China other than the National Government of the Republic of China with capital temporarily at Chungking.

5) Both Governments will give up all extraterritorial rights in China, including rights and interest in and with regard to international settlements and concessions, and rights under the Boxer Protocol of 1901.

Both Governments will endeavor to obtain the agreement of the British and other governments to give up extraterritorial rights in China, including rights in international settlements and in concessions and under the Boxer Protocol of 1901.

6) The Government of the United States and the Government of Japan will enter into negotiations for the conclusion between the United States and Japan of a trade agreement, based upon reciprocal most-favored-nation treatment and reduction of trade barriers by both countries, including an undertaking by the United States to bind raw silk on the free list.

7) The Government of the United States and the Government of Japan will, respectively, remove the freezing restrictions on Japanese funds in the United States and on American funds in Japan.

8) Both Governments will agree upon a plan for stabilization of the dollar-yen rate, with the allocation of funds adequate for this purpose, half to be supplied by Japan and half by the United States.

9) Both Governments will agree that no agreement which either has concluded with any third power or powers shall be interpreted by it in such a way as to conflict with the fundamental purpose of this agreement, the establishment and preservation of peace throughout the Pacific area.

10) Both Governments will use their influence to cause other governments to adhere to and to give practical application to the basic political and economic principles set forth in this agreement.[47]

There can be no doubt that this document went beyond any previous American statement in the long series of American-Japanese conversations. Points 3 and 4, calling for the evacuation of China and Indo-China and for the abandonment of the Nanking regime, were in themselves stiff enough to

[47] Text in *Foreign Relations of the United States: Japan*, II, 766-70.

put this paper in a class by itself. It is clear that Secretary Hull and his colleagues recognized this. During the hearings of the Pearl Harbor Investigating Committee testimony was given over and over again and from various sides that there was no hope nor expectation that the Tokyo Government would accept such drastic terms. By the end of November, however, even this fact had lost most of its significance. When Mr. Hull presented the Ten-Point program to Nomura and Kurusu it was already known from intercepted messages that the Japanese would not accept even the *modus vivendi*, to say nothing of the additional Ten Points. They regarded their own terms of November 20 as the very minimum.[48] It is highly improbable that they would have consented to discuss any further American terms in view of the approach of their firmly fixed deadline. Mr. Hull's Ten-Point program in fact served only to keep the American record straight.[49]

It remains extraordinary that the decision to reply to Japan's minimum terms by a statement of America's maximum demands should have been taken by Mr. Hull without formal consultation with American military authorities and without discussion with the British, Dutch, and Chinese. While the military were informed of the fate of the *modus vivendi*, they apparently knew nothing of the proposal to submit the Ten Points. It was left for Secretary Stimson to inquire on the morning of November 27 what had actually been done. Mr. Hull replied that the whole matter had been broken off: "I have washed my hands of it and it is now in the hands of you [Stimson] and Knox—the Army and the Navy." Not until the Secretary of War talked to the President on the telephone did he finally get to the end of the story, that the matter had not been broken off, but that the United States had ended up "with a magnificent statement prepared by Hull."[50]

This rather casual procedure with respect to a decision of major significance is further evidence of the fact that Mr. Hull had so little confidence in the practical value of the Ten-Point offer as to consider it hardly worth mention outside his own Department. The military authorities probably shared his opinion. High officers of the Army and Navy had never entertained much hope that even the *modus vivendi* scheme would prove productive. As early as November 24 the Navy, with Army concurrence, had issued a warning to Pacific commanders:

Chances of favorable outcome of negotiations with Japan very doubtful. This situation coupled with statements of Japanese Government and movements their naval and military forces indicate in our opinion that a surprise aggressive movement in any direction including attack on Philippines or Guam is a possibility. Chief of Staff has

[48] Tels. to Washington, November 22, 24, 1941 (*Pearl Harbor Attack*, XII, 166, 172-73).

[49] Hull testimony (*Pearl Harbor Attack*, II, 555); Hull: *Memoirs*, II, 1081; Feis: *The Road to Pearl Harbor*, 320-31. Cf. Beard: *President Roosevelt and the Coming of the War*, 235-38.

[50] *Stimson Diary* (*MS.*), November 27, 1941 (*Pearl Harbor Attack*, XI, 5422 ff.).

seen this dispatch concurs and requests action adees [addressees] to inform senior Army officers their areas. Utmost secrecy necessary in order not to complicate already tense situation or precipitate Japanese action.[51]

Furthermore, on the morning of November 26, probably after learning that the *modus vivendi* had been dropped, the Joint Board, as noted above, considered the first draft of another warning, especially to the Philippines. The increasing reports of Japanese movements southward made the likelihood of attack very real. The Navy warning, sent to the commanders of the Asiatic and Pacific fleets on November 27, almost certainly without knowledge of the Ten-Point program, read as follows:

This despatch is to be considered a war warning. Negotiations with Japan looking toward stabilization of conditions in the Pacific have ceased and aggressive move by Japan is expected within the next few days. The number and equipment of Japanese troops and the organization of naval task forces indicates an amphibious expedition against either the Philippines, Thai or Kra peninsula or possibly Borneo. . . .[52]

The Army warning to General MacArthur was less strongly worded because Secretary Stimson insisted on consulting Secretary Hull and the President before sending it. It read:

Negotiations with Japan appear to be terminated to all practical purposes, with only the barest possibilities that the Japanese Government might come back and offer to continue. Japanese future action unpredictable but hostile action possible at any moment. If hostilities cannot, repeat cannot, be avoided the United States desires that Japan commit the first overt act. . . .[53]

These warnings, which would appear to have been adequate and clear, make it sufficiently obvious that the Army and Navy chiefs, with their foreknowledge of Tokyo's deadline and of Japanese troop movements, had but scant faith in the possibilities of further negotiation. Yet both Services clung to the hope that the proposal for a *modus vivendi* would prolong discussion and afford them desperately needed time to complete their preparations in the Pacific area. There is no doubt, therefore, that the unceremonious dropping of the project produced keen disappointment in high Army and Navy quarters. This was reflected to some degree in the joint memorandum which the Service chiefs sent to the White House on November 27. Drafted in the War Plans Divisions after the meeting of the Joint Board in the forenoon of November 26, the memorandum reëmphasized the Joint Board recommendations of November 5 and warned against the dangers of hasty action

---

[51] Text in *Pearl Harbor Attack*, XIV, 1405; see also Admiral Turner's testimony, *ibid.*, IV, 1946.

[52] Text in *Pearl Harbor Attack*, XIV, 1406; cf. also Admiral Stark's letter to Admiral Kimmel, November 27, 1941 (*ibid.*, V, 2301).

[53] See General Gerow's testimony in *Pearl Harbor Attack*, III, 1020-22, IV, 1663 ff.; also the testimony of Admiral Turner, *ibid.*, IV, 1947-48, and *Stimson Diary (MS.)*, November 27, 1941.

by the United States in the event of a Japanese move. Although the Joint Board was thus stressing the need of the Services for time, Secretary Stimson had made it clear that this plea was not to be construed as a request from the military for the resumption of discussions with the Japanese. Though the Secretary, too, wanted time, he did not want it "at any cost of humility on the part of the United States or of reopening the thing which would show a weakness on our part."

This judgment of the Secretary of War is not impressive either for logical or practical completeness, and one is still entitled to query whether Mr. Stimson expressed precisely the views of his military advisers. In any case, the joint memorandum, in its final form, addressed itself to the problem of determining where the Japanese would strike. In the event that they attacked American, British, or Dutch possessions, this country should go to war. But America should not fight if the Japanese turned against Yunnan or eastern Siam. In the last of these contingencies the United States, Britain, and the Netherlands should confine themselves to warning the Japanese not to go beyond the lines of longitude 100° east and of latitude 10° north, inasmuch as further advance would pose an immediate threat to Burma and Singapore. The Army and Navy, while still anxious to gain time, merely restated and reëmphasized their recommendations of November 5.

The effort to link this Joint Board memorandum directly to the scrapping of the *modus vivendi* and the Ten-Point substitute, and to deduce from it a conflict between foreign policy and military strategy, is certainly unwarranted by the evidence uncovered thus far. Nevertheless, it was both bad strategy and careless administrative procedure for the civilian leaders of the Government to make the momentous decisions of November 26, 1941, without formal consultation with the responsible military leaders. The argument that by this date no practical difference could have been anticipated does not alter the seriousness of this breach of fundamental rules for achieving sound decisions of national security policy.[54]

The State Department's failure to discuss with the British, Dutch and other friendly Governments its decision to offer Japan the Ten Points is likewise open to adverse criticism, even though Mr. Churchill has since written that the Ten Points "not only met our wishes and those of the associated Governments, but indeed went beyond anything we had ventured to ask."[55] Secretary Hull telephoned Lord Halifax only after the Ten-Point program had been submitted to Nomura and Kurusu. On the morning of November 27 both the British and Australian envoys, puzzled by this

---

[54] The text of the Joint Board memorandum to the President, November 27, 1941, is printed in *Pearl Harbor Attack,* XIV, 1083; see further Mr. Stimson's testimony (*ibid.,* III, 1292 ff.), General Marshall's (*ibid.,* III, 1168 ff.; XI, 5127 ff.), Admiral Stark's (*ibid.,* V, 2318 ff.), Admiral Turner's (*ibid.,* IV, 2038 ff.), and Feis: *The Road to Pearl Harbor,* 322-25.

[55] Churchill: *The Grand Alliance,* 597.

"sudden change," hastened to the Department for explanations. Secretary Hull and Under Secretary Welles made it abundantly clear that the lukewarm attitude of the British and their apparent support of Chinese protests had been instrumental in the decision to abandon the *modus vivendi*. In any case, said Mr. Welles to Lord Halifax, the reports of Japanese troop movements left no doubt that large-scale military operations were under way. The gravity of the situation could not be exaggerated. This was to say, in effect, that the fat was now in the fire, and it was futile to argue how it got there.[56]

With the abrupt abandonment of the *modus vivendi,* and the equally sudden decision to substitute for it the most uncompromising statement of American terms for a settlement, the small initiative which the United States had been able to exert to save the peace passed wholly into the hands of Japan. Washington felt that henceforth it could do little more than await what it knew, thanks to intercepted Japanese messages, to be a foregone conclusion. It is to Tokyo that interest therefore shifts as the source of power which called the final moves in the diplomatic game which presently culminated in the surprise attack on Pearl Harbor.

[56] Memos of conversation between Hull and Casey, and between Welles and Halifax, November 27, 1941 (*Pearl Harbor Attack,* XIV, 1179-83).

CHAPTER XXVIII

Day of Infamy

1. Tokyo's Preparations for War

So fascinating is the foreground of the last act of the drama leading to Pearl Harbor that the background is easily overlooked. Yet it is only against the backdrop of an aggressive Japanese leadership, eager to use the war in Europe to realize its ambitious goals in Asia, that the performance of the actors can be rightly judged. Throughout the whole course of their negotiations with Washington, Tokyo leaders never abandoned their conviction that Japan must expand in order to survive as a great power and that its national interests could be assured only through Japanese hegemony over East Asia. The real object of the conversations from Tokyo's viewpoint was to secure American acceptance of the requirements deemed vital to Japan's future. Since Washington never seriously considered abandoning its own principles, policies, and interests in the Far East, there was no real prospect of success after July, 1941. Even if the language of agreement could have been achieved, there would never have been a true meeting of minds on the meaning of the words. This fact was widely recognized in both camps. Tokyo in all probability would have gone to war earlier if its military resources had been greater and its preparations more nearly complete. Washington would probably have been much less interested in a truce, as such, if its own preparations had been more advanced.

On the reasonable assumption that Foreign Minister Togo at least was genuinely desirous of reaching some sort of agreement with the United States, the Japanese Plan B, presented to Mr. Hull on November 20, represented the absolute minimum which the Prime Minister and the Cabinet would accept.[1] Unchangeable, likewise, was the November 29 deadline for American acceptance.

[1] Tel. from Tokyo to Washington, November 24, 1941 (*Pearl Harbor Attack*, XII, 172); memo of conversation between Togo and Grew, November 24, 1941 (*ibid.*, 172-B).

In the interval of nearly a week during which Nomura and Kurusu awaited the American reply to their proposals of November 20, the two Ambassadors learned that a *modus vivendi* was under consideration, but that the Chinese were proving difficult. The two envoys were in despair. There was no hope that their Plan B of November 20 would be accepted, they reported to Tokyo, and the conversations would perforce be broken off. The Americans and British would then take the Netherlands Indies under military protection. Japan would thereafter go to war. Even in the doubtful contingency that Germany supported Japan, the China Incident would still be left unresolved. Dreading the prospect of war, Nomura and Kurusu fell back on the forlorn chance that President Roosevelt might be induced to send a message to the Emperor expressing hope that Japan would coöperate in maintaining peace in the Pacific. In that event the Emperor could reply cordially and so clear the atmosphere for further discussion. The speculations of the Ambassadors extended even to a Japanese proposal for the neutralization of Indo-China (as Mr. Roosevelt had suggested in September), of Siam, and of the Netherlands Indies.[2]

Tokyo made short shrift of these well-intentioned suggestions. Resorting in his agitation to the trans-Pacific telephone, the Chief of the American Division of the Foreign Office informed Kurusu of the insurmountable obstacles, and Kurusu himself confessed that his solution would probably avail nothing.[3] Actually, of course, it was later on the same day that Secretary Hull summoned the Japanese Ambassadors to his office and handed them the Ten Point note. After a cursory reading of its "Oral Statement" and the "Proposed Basis for Agreement," the Japanese were "dumbfounded." Kurusu inquired whether this was the reply to the proposals of November 20 and whether the United States were no longer interested in a *modus vivendi*. Two items in the American note he described as wholly unacceptable, adding that Japan could scarcely be expected to apologize to Chiang Kai-shek. It was doubtful, he remarked, whether any useful purpose would be served in sending the Ten Points to Tokyo.

Against the wave of Japanese consternation Secretary Hull, in Kurusu's words, "remained solid as a rock." He asserted that he had done his best to secure favorable consideration of the *modus vivendi* by the other governments. The Ten Point program was all the United States could now offer. Recent fire-eating pronouncements by Japanese leaders had caused a most unfavorable reaction throughout the United States. In order to clear up the resulting confusion it had become necessary to restate the American position

Illustrating the Japanese demands were telegrams from Tokyo to Washington, November 26, specifying the large Japanese requirements for American petroleum (*Pearl Harbor Attack,* XII, 176-77).

[2] Tel. from Washington to Tokyo, November 26, 1941 (printed in *Pearl Harbor Attack,* XII, 180-81, and in a better text in *Tokyo War Crimes Documents,* No. 1532E).

[3] *Pearl Harbor Attack,* XII, 179-80.

in detail. Mr. Hull did, however, try to soften the harsh impact of this restatement. He stressed its tentative character and suggested that if agreement could be reached it would be possible to make concessions to Japan in the areas of finance and immigration. The United States, moreover, would not expect the "immediate" evacuation of Japan's troops from China. All this, however, was cold comfort to the Ambassadors. Kurusu indicated that the Secretary's statement amounted to termination of the conversations, but requested an opportunity to talk with the President. To this a skeptical Mr. Hull agreed.[4]

Reporting home, Nomura and Kurusu warned their Government of the unfavorable effect on the American public if Tokyo decided to continue the conversations but at the same time resorted to military action, for example against Siam. If such action were to be taken, they recommended that the conversations be terminated formally. This, however, was a matter for governmental decision. In line with the Cabinet decisions of November 5, 1941, Tokyo had been rushing to completion both its military and political preparations for war. Before anything was known in Japan of the Ten Point program, the Vice President of the Cabinet Information Board had declared in a broadcast that the Japanese people "have no other choice but to charge forward on their way, and if we knock our head against a stone wall, we must break through it."[5] Only the miracle of Washington's acceptance of the Japanese terms of November 20 could have suspended the preparations for war. Foreign Minister Togo had himself described these terms as an "ultimatum" and had warned Nomura and Kurusu that they represented the irreducible minimum.

As is now known, the task force which was to attack Pearl Harbor left port at 6:00 A.M. November 26, Japanese time. This was November 25 Washington time and therefore prior to Mr. Hull's presentation of the Ten Points. This fact, while significant, cannot, however, be taken as final evidence of Japan's intentions since, theoretically, the task force could be recalled at any time short of launching its attack. More important were the extensive Japanese preparations for operations in Southeast Asia. These comprised strong political pressure on Indo-China and Siam and the transfer of large forces and landing equipment from mainland China to Hainan Island and southern Indo-China. By November 26 Washington was well aware that, in addition to the agreed level of Japanese forces in northern Indo-China (25,000), Tokyo had built up a force of some 70,000 men and more than 150 aircraft in southern Indo-China. All signs pointed to an early move against Siam. There was very little indeed with which to oppose it.[6]

---

[4] *Foreign Relations of the United States: Japan,* II, 764-66; tels. from Washington to Tokyo, November 26, 1941 (*Pearl Harbor Attack,* XII, 181-85).

[5] *The New York Times,* November 24, 1951.

[6] On the Pearl Harbor operation see General MacArthur's report in *Pearl Harbor*

Moves on the diplomatic front kept pace with Japan's military preparations. Though the Tripartite Pact had not deterred the United States, the Japanese military leaders who had inspired the pact hoped that the Germans and Italians might be induced to cast their lot with Japan if war came. This would distract the United States sufficiently to enable the Japanese to conquer Southeast Asia and the East Indies without serious difficulty. From the moment of General Tojo's advent to power intimate contacts with Berlin had therefore been renewed. It was part of the crucial decisions of the Imperial Council on November 5 that once the negotiations with Washington broke down, no effort should be spared to induce Germany and Italy to enter the war beside Japan and to agree not to conclude a separate peace. While the evidence does not permit a detailed account of Japanese-German relations during these last critical weeks, it is clear that Tokyo successfully resisted German pressure to warn the United States against attacking German vessels in the Atlantic. The Japanese likewise evaded all Berlin's attempts to invoke the Tripartite Pact pending the outcome of the Washington conversations. On the other hand, the Japanese agreed on November 22 to renew the Anti-Comintern Pact for another five years, in the evident hope of inducing Germany to join in an eventual war against the United States. The maneuver promised well. On November 21 Ribbentrop cabled the German Ambassador in Tokyo instructions and the latter forthwith canvassed the matter with General Okamoto, whom he assured that Germany "would not leave Japan in the lurch in case of conflict with the United States." Okamoto revealed nothing of Japan's plans and repeated that the outcome of the conversations in Washington must be awaited. Nevertheless, he remarked that the Japanese Army would soon decide on an advance to the south, since the favorable season for operations was at hand.[7]

The Japanese were thus determined to be ready to move the moment the negotiations with the United States broke down or their deadline was reached. While Tokyo deemed failure of the conversations certain, there is no doubt that the Ten Point note was a heavier blow than was anticipated. The Prime Minister, General Tojo, promptly dubbed the American note, received on November 27, an ultimatum, Washington's final word on the

---

Attack, XIII, 391 ff.; U.S. Strategic Bombing Survey (Pacific): *The Campaigns of the Pacific War* (Washington, 1946); and Richard E. Lauterbach: "Secret Jap War Plans" (*Life,* March 4, 1946). On preparations for operations southward see *Tokyo War Crimes Documents,* No. 1448, describing plans for organizing conquered territories (November 20, 1941); the Japanese diplomatic reports from Hanoi and Bangkok in *Pearl Harbor Attack,* XII, 174-76, 202-4, and the U.S. military intelligence reports of November 26, 27, 1941 (*ibid.,* XIV, 1366-68). Cf. Watson: *Chief of Staff: Prewar Plans and Preparations,* 446 ff.

[7] Tel. from Ribbentrop to Ott, November 21; tel. from Ott to Ribbentrop, November 23, 1941 (*Tokyo War Crimes Documents,* Nos. 4070 and 4070B). For the rest see the telegrams printed in *Pearl Harbor Attack,* XII, 117, 166, and Erich Kordt: *Wahn und Wirklichkeit* (Stuttgart, 1947), 323.

conversations. Tojo failed, however, to win over all members of his Government to this convenient view. Some asked how any document plainly marked "tentative" could be described as an ultimatum. According to Prince Konoye the argument was resolved only by permitting each individual to make his own interpretation.[8]

The ultimative character of the Ten Point note was subsequently to become the subject of equally violent argument in the United States. The finality of the document was certainly diminished by the heading it bore. It was still further qualified when, in handing the note to the two Ambassadors, Mr. Hull stated that "our proposal was as far as we would go *at this time* in reference to the Japanese proposal." Lastly, unlike many historic ultimata, the American note was devoid of any deadline and carried with it no threat of action, elements which have especially contributed to give the term its sinister connotation. Nevertheless, in substance if not in form the Ten Point note did constitute America's final terms for the indefinite future, and this was recognized by those who formulated it.[9] In this very real sense it was an ultimatum and it is understandable that the Japanese should have generally regarded it as America's "last word," a "sort of ultimatum," the more so since the military faction found this description so advantageous.[10]

A Liaison Conference, consisting of the leading Cabinet officers and the military High Command, was called to consider the American note when it arrived in Tokyo on November 27. According to postwar testimony all were "dumbfounded at the severity of the United States proposition" and agreed that it indicated America's determination to go to war against Japan. In the words of Foreign Minister Togo, one of the most moderate members of the Government: "We felt that clearly the United States had no hope or intention of reaching an agreement for a peaceful settlement, for it was plain to us and must have been to the Americans that this document demanded as the price of peace total surrender by Japan to the American position."[11]

Although already concluding that unless the United States were willing to reconsider, war would be its only recourse, the Japanese Government postponed final decision until after the conference of the two Ambassadors with the President on November 27. Secretary Hull, informed by Messrs. Stimson and Knox of the memorandum they had sent the President pleading the need for time and the desirability of avoiding hostilities, spent the

[8] Memo of conversation between Prince Konoye and Mr. Max Bishop of the State Department, November 6, 1945.

[9] On this issue see the discussion involving Ambassador Grew in *Pearl Harbor Attack*, II, 575 ff., 587-95. The problem is discussed in Beard: *President Roosevelt and the Coming of the War*. Cf. Feis: *Road to Pearl Harbor*, 326 ff.

[10] Tolischus in *The New York Times*, November 28, 29, 1941.

[11] "Tojo Memorandum" (*Tokyo War Crimes Documents*: Proceedings, 36, 357 ff.); Foreign Minister Togo's testimony (*ibid.*, Defense Document No. 2927); deposition of Admiral Shimada (*ibid.*, Defense Document No. 2892).

morning of November 27 with his advisers, formulating recommendations
to the President regarding the line to be taken with the two envoys. It would
appear that Mr. Hornbeck again argued for firmness. Discounting the plea
of the Armed Services for more time on the ground that diplomacy had
already gained them six months, he urged that the President tell the Army
and Navy what to do, instead of asking them. In an oft-quoted memorandum of this date Hornbeck expressed his conviction that the Japanese would
indeed resume their advance, perhaps in the direction of Siam or into
Yunnan, but in so doing would avoid armed conflict with the United States.
He was willing to lay bets of five to one that the United States and Japan
would not be at war by December 15; of three to one that they would not
be at war by January 15, 1942; and of even money that they would not be
at war by March 1, 1942. In short, Mr. Hornbeck did not believe that the
United States was then on the verge of war in the Pacific, whatever might
happen eventually.[12]

Secretary Hull and others continued to favor a cautious course in the
hope of somehow postponing the evil day. A memorandum to this effect
was forwarded to the President. It presumably met with his approval, since
he had evinced great sympathy for the earlier plea of the military to gain
time.[13] In any event the visit of the Ambassadors to the White House on the
afternoon of the 27th went off cordially if not profitably. Kurusu inquired
about the defunct *modus vivendi* as well as about Mr. Roosevelt's earlier
suggestion that he act as "introducer" between Japan and China. The reply
was that a *modus vivendi* would be worthless in the absence of an agreement on basic principles. The President remarked that he was disappointed
by the course the discussions had taken. The warlike utterances of Japanese
leaders had created a tense situation and, even though he continued to hope
for a favorable outcome, it would be hard to make progress unless Japan
gave unmistakable indications of readiness to pursue a peaceful policy. In
conclusion he once again warned his visitors that if Japan continued to
follow the course of Hitlerism, it was bound to be the loser in the end.[14]

Despite the President's friendliness, he gave no indication of readiness to
reconsider the note of November 26. Indeed, Secretary Hull, in an unusually long press conference, presently gave the American public for the
first time a detailed account of the conversations, referred to the evidence
of impending Japanese moves in Indo-China and made it clear that the
future course of events now depended on the decisions of the military ex-

[12] Hull: *Memoirs*, II, 1086-87; *Berle Diaries (MS.)*, November 27, 1941. The text of
the Hornbeck memorandum is printed in *Pearl Harbor Attack*, XX, 4487.

[13] Note of Admiral Stark to the President, November 28, 1941 (*Pearl Harbor Attack*,
XX, 4487).

[14] *Foreign Relations of the United States: Japan*, II, 770-72; tel. from Washington to
Tokyo, November 27 (*Pearl Harbor Attack*, XII, 192-95); text of the State Department memorandum to the President (*ibid.*, XX, 4477-78); Hull: *Memoirs*, II, 1086-87.

tremists in Tokyo. Heavily inked headlines announced to the world that the crisis was at hand, that the United States would scorn another Munich, and that it was now up to the Japanese to take or leave the American terms.

Nomura and Kurusu were informed on November 28 that the Japanese Government could not use the American note as a basis of negotiation. With an elaboration of the Japanese position, which would be sent them in two or three days, the discussions would therefore be *"de facto* ruptured." However, the two envoys were to avoid giving that impression.[15] Evidently the two or three days were deemed necessary for drafting the formal reply to Washington and for discharging certain constitutional formalities. It is true that the deadline of November 29 was at hand, but since December 8 (Japanese time) had been fixed for the beginning of operations, there were still some days to spare. So far as events in Tokyo can be reconstructed, they followed this sequence: on November 29 (November 28, Washington time) the Cabinet met with the Senior Statesmen, that is, with all available former Prime Ministers. The latter were given a detailed explanation of why war was inevitable, but few of them were willing to fall in with the Cabinet's reasoning. Anxiety was expressed over the adequacy of Japan's material resources for such a conflict. Prince Konoye regretted the failure of negotiations and added "that there would be no need to resort to a hasty war just because of the rupture of the negotiations, as we might be able to reach a wise solution in some way or other. . . ." Admiral Yonai, who had always opposed the connection with Nazi Germany, warned "that we should be careful not to lose what little we possess by trying to avoid becoming poorer by inches." But the Senior Statesmen had only the right to be consulted, not to make decisions. They reported their reservations to the Emperor, who appears to have queried the Navy Minister and Chief of the Naval Staff as to Japan's chances of success. Having received a favorable reply, he instructed Tojo to proceed with the plans.[16]

On November 30 the Liaison Conference met to hear the draft of the final note to Washington. The Emperor had insisted that this be submitted before the opening of hostilities, though it was left to the Foreign Minister and the Chiefs of Staff to decide on the exact timing. General Tojo maintained later that it was only on this occasion that he learned of the Navy's plan to attack Pearl Harbor. This, he claimed, was an operational matter and would not, therefore, have been communicated to the Prime Minister. In fact, he himself learned of it through the Army Chief of Staff.[17] Under the Japanese

---

[15] Tel. to Washington, November 28, 1941 (*Pearl Harbor Attack*, XII, 195).

[16] "Tojo Memorandum" (*Tokyo War Crimes Documents:* Proceedings, 36, 364 ff.). The fullest account is that in the "Kido Diary" for November 29, 1941 (*ibid.*, Document No. 1632W, 86, 87), but see also Admiral Okada's affidavit (*ibid.*, Defense Document No. 2535). On the meeting of the Senior Statesmen see Kase: *Journey to the "Missouri,"* 63 ff., and Feis: *The Road to Pearl Harbor,* 328.

[17] "Tojo Memorandum" (*Tokyo War Crimes Documents:* Proceedings, 36, 391 ff.).

system of conducting Government affairs this may well have been so. It would at least explain why the adverse psychological repercussions of the surprise attack on Pearl Harbor were so completely overlooked. The plan of attack seemed sound enough militarily and evidently this was the only aspect of the operation considered.

To all intents and purposes the decision for war had now been made and the Japanese leaders felt that they could let themselves go. November 30 was the first anniversary of the treaty between Japan, Manchukuo and the Nanking regime in China. General Tojo sent a message, which, though later explained away, was read at a great public rally and printed in the Tokyo press. Among much else he stated:

If we look around we find that there are still many countries who are indulging in action hostile to us. In fact they are trying to throw obstacles in the way of the construction of the East Asia Co-Prosperity Sphere and are trying to enjoy the dream of exploitation of East Asia at the cost of the 1,000 million populace of the East Asiatic peoples to satisfy their greed of possession.

The fact that Chiang Kai-shek is dancing to the tune of Britain, America, and communism at the expense of able-bodied and promising young men in his futile resistance against Japan is only due to the desire of Britain and the United States to fish in troubled waters of East Asia by pitting the East Asiatic peoples against each other and to grasp the hegemony of East Asia. This is a stock in trade of Britain and the United States.

For the honor and pride of mankind, we must purge this sort of practice from East Asia with a vengeance.[18]

The formal decision for war was reached on December 1 when the Privy Council, meeting in the Emperor's presence at 2:00 P.M., approved, as it invariably did, the prior decision of the Liaison Conference. Tojo initiated the fateful deliberations with the following statement:

In accordance with the decision of the Imperial Conference of 5 November, the Government has taken all possible steps, concentrating all its energies, to adjust the relations with the United States, while the Imperial Army and Navy have made efforts to complete their preparations for operations. The United States, however, has not shown any sign of concession from its past position. Moreover, she served, jointly with Britain, the Netherlands and China, new demands such as the unconditional over-all withdrawal of Japanese troops, the withdrawal of recognition of the Nanking Government, and the nullification of the Tripartite Pact, proposing unilateral concessions by Japan. Should Japan submit to her demands, not only would Japan's pres-

[18] Tel. from Grew, December 1, quoting the version printed in the *Japan Times and Advertiser* (*Foreign Relations of the United States: Japan,* II, 148-49). Cf. the U.P. version (*The New York Times,* November 30, 1941). For the subsequent Japanese explanation—that the message had been drafted for Tojo and that he and the Cabinet had never seen it—see the statement by the Japanese Embassy to the State Department, December 2, 1941 (*Foreign Relations of the United States: Japan,* II, 778). Equally uncompromising was the address of Foreign Minister Togo on the same occasion (*ibid.,* II, 149).

tige be entirely destroyed and the solution of the China Affair rendered impossible, but Japan's existence itself would be endangered. It is now clear that Japan's claims cannot be attained through diplomatic measures. Meanwhile, the United States, Britain, the Netherlands and China have increasingly strengthened their economic and military pressure upon Japan. From the viewpoints both of Japan's national power and of strategy, it is now utterly impossible for Japan to permit the present situation to continue any longer. In such circumstances, Japan has now no other way than to wage war against the Unted States, Britain and the Netherlands in order to achieve a solution of the present critical situation and to secure its existence and self-defense.

We are filled with trepidation to think that it causes much anxiety to His Imperial Majesty to plunge into a great war at the present moment when the China Affair has already lasted for four years. Upon careful consideration, however, it is my belief that our national power is now several times as strong as before the outbreak of the China Affair, that our national solidarity is all the more tightened, and that the morale of the Imperial Army and Navy is exceedingly high. I am convinced that the whole nation, presenting a united front and laying down their lives for the sake of the country, will surely deliver us from the present national crisis. I hope that you will give due deliberation to the subject, placed before you. Concerning matters of diplomatic negotiations and military operations, explanations will be given by the Cabinet ministers concerned and the High Command.[19]

Unfortunately there is no record of the ensuing discussions, in the course of which the Emperor asked each member of the Council for his opinion. The matter is of little consequence, however, since approval of the decision of the Liaison Conference was a foregone conclusion. War against the United States had been decided upon and under Japanese practice this decision was irrevocable. Furthermore, in support of the decision and as though to provide the keystone in the arch of Tokyo's diplomatic preparations for war, came a report from the Japanese Ambassador in Berlin (November 29) that Germany had given virtually all the assurances Japan could have asked. Ribbentrop had once again urged on the envoy the necessity for Japan to seize the opportunity to realize its aspirations. After the usual sanguine forecasts of Nazi success against Russia and Britain, the Foreign Minister had come to the vital point: "Should Japan become engaged in a war against the United States, Germany, of course, would join the war immediately. There is absolutely no possibility of Germany's entering into a separate peace with the United States under such circumstances. The Fuehrer is determined on that point."[20]

As far as Germany was concerned there remained but one last shred of anxiety in Tokyo. Would the Nazis make their promise of participation in the war against the United States contingent upon Japan's simultaneous

---

[19] *Tokyo War Crimes Documents,* Defense Document No. 1886; also the "Kido Diary," December 1, 1941 (*ibid.,* Document No. 2500A).
[20] Tel. from Berlin to Tokyo, November 29, 1941 (*Pearl Harbor Attack,* XII, 200-202). This and the subsequent intercepted messages are printed in *Nazi Conspiracy and Aggression,* I, 866 ff.; V, 566 ff.; VI, 310 ff.

entry into the war against the Soviet Union? Determined not to do so unless attacked first, Tokyo did its utmost to emphasize to Berlin that the present crisis stemmed directly from Japan's loyalty to the Tripartite Pact and from American opposition to the New Order in the Far East as in Europe. Japan allegedly had no choice but to act in self-defense and Foreign Minister Togo instructed Ambassador Oshima to hint to Hitler and Ribbentrop how imminent its action was:

Say to them that lately England and the United States have taken a provocative attitude, both of them. Say that they are planning to move military forces into various places in East Asia and that we will inevitably have to counter by also moving troops. Say very secretly to them that there is extreme danger that war may suddenly break out between the Anglo-Saxon nations and Japan through some clash of arms and add that the time of the breaking out of this war may come quicker than anyone dreams.[21]

2. Washington's Defense Dilemma

On the American side of the stage the ten days before Pearl Harbor, though devoid of excitement in the diplomatic sphere, were dramatic enough in the political. Secretary Hull having reported that relations with Japan had passed from the State Department into military hands, the most pressing problem was how the Army and Navy could best meet what Japan might have in store for them. No one seemed to recall Ambassador Grew's warning telegram about Pearl Harbor. All incoming reports for weeks had stressed the probability, or lately the fact, of Japanese moves in Southeast Asia and the South Pacific. In these contingencies direct attack on American possessions was improbable. But Japanese moves against Siam and the Burma road, or directly south against Singapore and the East Indies, would constitute a serious blow to friendly powers, would pose a threat to the Philippines, and would jeopardize American supplies of such vital war materials as tin and rubber. General Marshall and Admiral Stark had recommended to the President on November 5 and again on November 27 that if the Japanese confined their activities to the occupation of eastern Siam, the United States should bide its time. If, however, they advanced beyond longitude 100° east, or latitude 10° north, the security of the United States would require armed resistance.

The problem was further complicated by the expressed determination of the Siamese Government to regard as aggressor whichever power first invaded the national territory. Accordingly Tokyo had been attempting, with some prospect of success, to inveigle Bangkok into inviting Japanese aid so as to forestall British action. At the same time Tokyo had to weigh the

---

[21] Tel. from Tokyo to Berlin, November 30, 1941 (*Pearl Harbor Attack*, XII, 204); similarly a longer telegram of the same date reviewing the situation (*ibid.*, 205-6); and the record of Togo's talk with the German Ambassador, November 30, 1941 (*Nazi Conspiracy and Aggression*, I, 866 ff.; and V, 566 ff.).

danger that the American reaction to a Japanese occupation of Siam would take the form of protective custody of the Netherlands Indies. Washington, in turn, was faced with questions less of sound strategy than of public support. Recent debates in Congress confirmed the continued vitality of the anti-interventionists, while influential isolationist newspapers were constantly arguing that the interests at stake in the Far East were British and Dutch imperial interests, not American interests. Why should America go to war to save foreign landlords threatened by Japanese military ambitions?[22]

The British, holding the Kra Peninsula of Siam vital to the security of Malaya, had already worked out a plan to invade the Singora area the moment they were convinced that the Japanese were about to occupy it. They tried unsuccessfully to induce the United States to concur in this plan and thereupon shelved it, chiefly out of deference to American opinion.[23] Nonetheless, the issue was so important, even from the strictly American standpoint, that it required painstaking consideration. This it received at the meeting of the War Council at noon on November 28, after Secretary Stimson had discussed in detail with the President the latest reports of Japanese troop movements toward Indo-China.

Mr. Hull opened the conference with a review of the American note of November 26 and the statement that there was "practically no possibility of an agreement being achieved with Japan." He thereupon renewed his warning that the Japanese were likely "to break out at any time with new acts of conquest." The Army and Navy, he added, should bear in mind the probability of a surprise attack. The discussion then turned to the Japanese troop movements toward Indo-China and how to meet this threat. Secretary Stimson had told the President beforehand that as between two possible courses of action—to issue a warning to Japan that advance beyond a certain point would mean war, or to take action against the Japanese forces without warning—he favored the latter. He believed the Japanese move would pose a major threat to American interests and security and that it was for the President, as Chief Executive and Commander in Chief, to take such action as he deemed necessary to defend the United States and its possessions.[24] This forthright approach to the problem apparently met with little support in the War Council. The dilemma was well analyzed by Secretary Stimson in his contemporary diary notes:

[22] *Chicago Tribune,* December 2, 1941.

[23] For the "Matador" Plan see Sir Robert Brooke-Popham's despatch: *Operations in the Far East from 17th October, 1940 to 27th December 1941* (Supplement to the *London Gazette,* January 22, 1948), 545, and Sir Paul Maltby's despatch: *Report on the Air Operations during the Campaigns in Malaya and the Netherlands East Indies from 8th December, 1941 to 12th March, 1942* (Supplement to the *London Gazette,* February 26, 1948), 1361 ff. For the American position see the testimony of Admiral Turner in *Pearl Harbor Attack,* IV, 2048 ff. See also Churchill: *The Grand Alliance,* 600-601.

[24] *Stimson Diary (MS.),* November 28, 1941 (quoted in *Pearl Harbor Attack,* XI, 5435); Stimson's statement (*ibid.,* 5456 ff.).

It was the consensus that the present move—that there was an expeditionary force on the sea of about 25,000 Japanese troops aimed for a landing somewhere—completely changed the situation when we last discussed [i.e., on November 25] whether or not we could address an ultimatum to Japan about moving the troops which she already had on land in Indo-China. It was now the opinion of everyone that if this expedition was allowed to get around the southern point of Indo-China and to go off and land in the Gulf of Siam, either at Bangkok or further west, it would be a terrific blow at all of the three Powers, Britain at Singapore, the Netherlands and ourselves in the Philippines. It was the consensus of everybody that this must not be allowed. Then we discussed how to prevent it. It was agreed that if the Japanese got into the Isthmus of Kra, the British would fight. It was also agreed that if the British fought, we would have to fight. And it now seems clear that if this expedition was allowed to round the southern point of Indo-China, this whole chain of disastrous events would be set on foot of going.

It further became the consensus of views that rather than strike at the Force as it went by without any warning on the one hand, which we didn't think we could do; or sitting still and allowing it to go on, on the other, which we didn't think we could do— that the only thing for us to do was to address it a warning that if it reached a certain place, or a certain line, or a certain point, we should have to fight.[25]

From the foregoing it might be inferred that the idea was to issue a warning to the Japanese expeditionary force, but that was certainly not envisaged and would, indeed, have been a most unusual procedure. Secretary Stimson's notes go on to state that the President actually had in mind a special telegram to Emperor Hirohito, such as he had sent at the time of the *Panay* incident and had had under consideration in October, 1941.[26] But Mr. Stimson argued that one could not explicitly warn an Emperor and that, furthermore, it was more important to inform the American public of the danger through a message to Congress. Although the President wished to include in such a Congressional message the substance of his warning to Hirohito, he was finally persuaded to keep the two items separate. It was accordingly agreed that Secretaries Hull, Stimson and Knox should draft both a message to Congress and one to Hirohito.[27]

Immediately after the War Council meeting the President went to Warm Springs for a short vacation. His absence in these critical days is difficult to explain, but his decision to go may have been bolstered by a Japanese message from Tokyo, deciphered on November 28, stating that the reply to the American Ten Point note would be sent in two or three days. Mr. Roosevelt

[25] *Stimson Diary (MS.),* November 28, 1941 (quoted in *Pearl Harbor Attack,* XI, 5435-36).

[26] A White House draft of such a message was sent to the State Department on October 16, 1941 (*Pearl Harbor Attack,* XV, 1727-33).

[27] *Stimson Diary (MS.),* November 28, 1941. On this very day the Nomura-Kurusu telegram to Tokyo, suggesting the possibility of getting the President to address the Emperor, was deciphered in Washington, but it seems unlikely that it was available at the time of the War Council meeting or that it inspired the President's idea, which was of long standing.

promised his worried advisers that he would return at once if the situation required it.[28]

The weekend of November 29–30 was devoted largely to the drafting of the messages to the Congress and to the Japanese Emperor. Mr. Stimson had assumed that the Secretary of State would take the initiative in this urgent task, but to his surprise Mr. Hull was nowhere to be found. Secretaries Knox and Stimson thereupon undertook the first drafts. With help from Admiral Stark and Admiral Turner, Knox presently produced a direct and succinct statement of a few hundred words for the President to send to Congress. His argument emphasized that Japan was confronting the United States in the Pacific with a repetition of the strategy Hitler was pursuing in Europe. In order to defeat the Nazis, the United Kingdom must be preserved. "Were Japan established in Singapore, or the Netherlands Indies, the security of the British Isles themselves would be endangered, and thus the security of the United States threatened." The President was therefore to tell Congress and the people:

Information has reached us of dependable character that Japan contemplates further measures of aggression. She has assembled both land, sea and air forces for new conquests. She can go no further without seriously threatening the vital interests of Great Britain, the Netherlands Indies, Australia and ourselves. Unless Japan renounces such purposes and withdraws this threat of further conquest by force, the four nations involved must resort to force to prevent this aggression, since arguments appear to have failed.[29]

Secretary Stimson's draft concentrated on clarifying the threat to the Philippines and to the American position in the Far East. After recalling past American policy on the Philippines and China, it pointed out that Japan had already largely ruined what had been achieved in China and was now encircling the Philippines and menacing American interests there as well as in the Dutch Indies and Malaya. Mr. Stimson did not undertake to draft the warning to Japan which was to follow. Like many other high Government officials, he was worn out by the pressure of the past few days. Late in the afternoon he finally succeeded in reaching Mr. Hornbeck and learned from him that Secretary Hull had turned over his drafting responsibilities to his political adviser. The latter, however, had as yet done nothing. At Mr. Hornbeck's request, both Mr. Stimson and Mr. Knox sent him their drafts. They also forwarded suggested texts to the President on the following morning.[30]

[28] *Stimson Diary (MS.)*, November 28, 1941.

[29] *Stimson Diary (MS.)*, November 28, 1941; text of the Knox draft in *Pearl Harbor Attack*, XIX, 3509-10.

[30] *Stimson Diary (MS.)*, November 28, 29, 1941; text of the Stimson draft for the President in *Pearl Harbor Attack*, XIX, 3513-19. According to the *Stimson Diary* both Mr. Stimson and Mr. Knox made some revision of their drafts before sending them to the President on the morning of November 29. The drafts were subsequently sent by Mr. Roosevelt to Mr. Hull.

At this point the story becomes decidedly obscure. It appears that not only Secretary Hull but also Mr. Hornbeck became puzzled and discouraged. The latter complained that he could not draft a message without knowing what was to go into it: was it peace, war, or what? Apparently he spent the night working on the problem and emerged with a nineteen-page paper of markedly academic character. It reviewed American aims and policies in the Far East over more than a century and dwelt in some detail on Japan's past misdeeds and their implications for American interests. But despite its length the paper did not come to grips with the issue of a warning.[31]

Although this long draft also seems to have been sent to the President on November 29, further work was done on the problem that day (Saturday) and the following. The details remain unclear, but there are indications that Mr. Hull himself was dissatisfied with the Hornbeck document and wanted greater emphasis on his familiar argument as to the essential harmony of American and Japanese interests. Secretary Stimson found the State Department draft "very long and meticulous," and felt that "it had no punch for the requirements for which we had suggested it." Mr. Hornbeck, unhappy and disgruntled, passed the problem to one of his colleagues. Consequently little progress was made with the drafting on Sunday. Since Congress was to meet on Monday morning and was likely then to adjourn for some time, Mr. Stimson and Mr. Knox decided on the evening of the 30th to take the bull by the horns. Together they drew up a "finale" for whatever message was to be sent to Congress. The text has not been found, but in his diary Mr. Stimson noted that it was "in the shape of a virtual ultimatum to Japan that we cannot permit her to take any further steps of aggression against any of the countries in the southwestern Pacific including China."[32]

Detailed discussion of these matters would have little value unless it reflected something of significance about American policy. What emerges is the War Council's conviction that further Japanese advance from Indo-China would endanger American interests and security and that a warning to Japan was therefore necessary. Plainly Secretary Stimson favored a strong line, as did Secretary Knox. Mr. Hornbeck, convinced that the Japanese would avoid war with the United States, was also inclined to take a firm stand. On the other hand Secretary Hull, who had strained every nerve for months to find a peaceful solution, apparently continued to lament the un-

---

[31] Text in *Pearl Harbor Attack*, XIV, 1202-3. We have also used the text marked "second revised copy" (*ibid.*, XIX, 3523-33), which is apparently the War Department's file copy of the revision sent to the President by Stimson on November 29. It is more rudimentary in form than the document analyzed above and is based more clearly upon the Stimson and Knox drafts.

[32] *Stimson Diary* (*MS.*), November 29, 30, 1941; we have used also the *Berle Diary* (*MS.*) for these days. The latter is incomplete.

timely end of the *modus vivendi*.[33] Accordingly, he was reluctant to face the harsh realities which the failure of the truce attempts had thrust in his path. On the morning of December 1 he complained to Mr. Berle that everybody was trying to run the nation's foreign policy: "Stimson, who felt bitterly about the Far East; Knox; and pretty much everyone else. They all come at me with knives and hatchets." It is reasonably clear that Mr. Hull was still trying to temper the arguments of his War and Navy colleagues by frequent reference to the Navy's desire for more time.

While this confusion of objectives sufficiently explains the failure to achieve a satisfactory draft of the message to Congress, it must be acknowledged that not even the high officials of the War Department could agree on the precise line at which the Japanese advance must be halted. Before leaving for Warm Springs the President had confidentially informed his press conference that the United States could not permit a Japanese move in the Pacific which would jeopardize its own position. The *status quo* must be maintained and, added Mr. Roosevelt, "by *status quo* I mean peace in the Pacific with a retraction of aggressions perpetrated in China."[34] Secretary Stimson fully supported the President's line, but General Marshall was doubtful about including China. Apart from this evidence of indecision regarding the limit to be set on Japanese aggression, there was always the lingering doubt whether the American public would back a warning involving commitments to defend any but strictly American territory.[35]

This, of course, was the very kernel of the nut Washington had to crack. At the time it was altogether logical to anticipate that the Japanese would avoid attacking the Philippines, Guam, or Hawaii. By turning on Siam, or at least restricting their attacks to British and Dutch territory, the Japanese would enormously magnify the dilemma facing the United States Government. All the known preparations pointed to such an eventuality and it must be realized that the assault on Pearl Harbor, however dramatic and successful, was intended only as a feint. The main drive came where it had been feared and anticipated by the United States.

To add to the complications of an already difficult problem, London felt that Japanese occupation of the Kra Isthmus would pose an intolerable threat to Singapore. The British, though intent on anticipating a Japanese move in that area by beating them to the draw, were reluctant to do so if the American reaction were likely to be unfavorable. At the least they sought assurances that if the Japanese moved against the Isthmus, the United

---

[33] Conversation of Ambassador Moffat with Mr. Hull, December 1, 1941 (*Moffat Diary, MS.*, December 1-4, 1941).

[34] Text of a memo on the President's press conference of November 28, 1941, in the *Walker Papers (MS.)*.

[35] The evidence in support of these differences of view comes chiefly from the manuscript diaries of Stimson, Berle, and Moffat, but see Harry Hopkins's notes on Mr. Hull's attitude and especially the President's complaints that the Secretary consistently evaded the definition of any line (Sherwood: *Roosevelt and Hopkins*, 428-29).

States would react militarily against Japan. This well-known position was again explained to Secretary Hull by Lord Halifax on Sunday, November 30, apparently after receipt by the President of another message from Prime Minister Churchill urging once again the crucial importance of warning Japan on the consequences of further aggressive moves:

It seems to me [wrote Mr. Churchill] that one important method remains unused in averting war between Japan and our two countries, namely, a plain declaration, secret or public as may be thought best, that any further act of aggression by Japan will lead immediately to the gravest consequence. I realize your constitutional difficulties but it would be tragic if Japan drifted into war by encroachment without having before her fairly and squarely the dire character of a further aggressive step. I beg you to consider whether, at the moment which you judge right, which may be very near, you should not say that "any further Japanese aggression would compel you to place the gravest issues before Congress," or words to that effect. We would, of course, make a similar declaration or share in a joint declaration, and in any case arrangements are being made to synchronize our action with yours. Forgive me, my dear friend, for presuming to press such a course upon you, but I am convinced that it might make all the difference and prevent a melancholy extension of the war.[36]

Mr. Churchill was recommending the very course of action which Washington was in the throes of debating. It may be assumed that London would have rejoiced in the entry of the United States into the war by the Pacific route if not by the Atlantic. On the other hand, Britain's parlous situation in Malaya made Mr. Churchill's Government appreciative of American military views as to the value of time. Secretary Hull could only tell the British Ambassador that he would discuss the problem again with the President on the latter's return.

At Mr. Hull's urging Mr. Roosevelt left Warm Springs on the afternoon of November 30. The passage of the Japanese deadline and the provocative statement of General Tojo to the rally celebrating the birthday of the Nanking regime left little doubt that the crisis was at hand. Before the President's arrival in Washington late Monday morning, Mr. Hull had an interview with the Japanese envoys at their request. This was necessarily fruitless, since Nomura and Kurusu were, according to instructions, merely trying to string out the conversations for a few days by raising again the American rejection of Japan's November 20 note. The Secretary reported to Mr. Berle that he had talked to the Ambassadors "with a good deal of bark and had given them the devil for what Japan was doing particularly in view of Tojo's statement and their moves in Indo-China."[37] The record bears witness to the truth of this report, but nothing useful emerged from the interview except information that the Japanese Government expected to reply to the Ten

[36] *Pearl Harbor Attack*, XIV, 1249 ff., 1300. Also printed in Churchill: *The Grand Alliance*, 599.
[37] *Berle Diaries* (*MS.*), December 1, 1941.

Points within a few days. Intercepted Japanese messages show clearly that the two Ambassadors were themselves panic-stricken by Tojo's violent statement. They were, furthermore, baffled by Toyko's orders to procrastinate, since until now they had been under terrific pressure to achieve results. It is difficult to doubt that the two diplomats were still working in the dark and striving, according to their own dim lights, to resolve the impasse. By December 1 they had become so desperate as to revive the idea of a meeting of high officials of the two Governments in Honolulu. The suggestion was, of course, promptly vetoed by Tokyo.[38]

Upon arrival at the White House Mr. Roosevelt conferred immediately with Secretary Hull and then with Admiral Stark. In the absence of any record of these conversations, it can only be surmised that the Secretary of State briefed the President on his morning interview with Nomura and Kurusu. There may also have been discussion of Mr. Churchill's latest message and of Lord Halifax's memorandum on the Kra Isthmus and Siam. Presumably Mr. Hull also informed the President of the snarled state of the message to Congress. Secretary Stimson, exasperated by Mr. Roosevelt's failure to call in Knox and himself (thus constituting with Hull a meeting of the War Council), was alarmed by the prospect that the "appeasers" might gain the upper hand with the President. He was relieved to learn from Harry Hopkins, who left his hospital bed to lunch with the President in order to get assurances on the same subject, that Mr. Roosevelt was "all right," that "he had not himself weakened at all."[39]

It is perhaps a safe conjecture that in the course of his White House conversation Mr. Hull persuaded the President to defer any message to Congress until the last minute, on the probable ground that it would create dissension at home and give aid and comfort to the Japanese militarists. He at any rate counseled against despatching a message to the Emperor at this time. To appeal over the heads of the Japanese leaders, he argued, was certain to give offense. But the President, always confident of his personal influence, refused to follow Mr. Hull on this issue.

As to the contents of Mr. Churchill's message, the President ruled out a warning to Japan such as the Prime Minister had proposed, at least until the effect of his message to the Emperor could be appraised. He would, however, discuss personally with Lord Halifax the dilemma which would confront the British when the Japanese moved against the Kra Isthmus. Actually it was Under Secretary Welles who conferred with the British Ambassador later that day, while Mr. Roosevelt, postponing the despatch of his message to the Emperor, suddenly took a new tack. After talking with Mr.

[38] Messages from Washington to Tokyo, December 1, 1941 (*Pearl Harbor Attack*, XII, 206-15); memo of conversation between Mr. Hull and the Japanese Ambassadors, December 1, 1941 (*Foreign Relations of the United States: Japan*, II, 772-77).

[39] *Stimson Diary* (*MS.*), December 1, 1941.

Welles (Secretary Hull was so exhausted that he had taken to his bed), the President issued instructions to the State Department to inquire of the Japanese Government why it was maintaining a much larger force in Indo-China than was permitted under the agreement with Vichy. After pointing up the threat presented by these forces to the Philippines, the Netherlands Indies, Burma, and Siam, the President's instructions directed that Tokyo be asked for a statement of its intentions.[40]

On the following morning (December 2) Mr. Welles transmitted the President's inquiry to the Japanese Ambassadors almost exactly as Mr. Roosevelt had drafted it. Nomura and Kurusu disclaimed all knowledge of troop movements in Indo-China, choosing instead to bewail again the fate of the Japanese proposals of November 20. These, they reminded Mr. Welles, had included a Japanese promise to withdraw their forces from Indo-China. The ensuing exchange followed the familiar pattern. Kurusu complained that there was no time "to argue the *pros* and *cons* of this question or the rights and wrongs. The people of Japan are faced with economic pressure, and I want you to know that we have but the choice between submission to the pressure or breaking the chains that it invokes." In rebuttal Mr. Welles pointed out that if the American Ten Point note were accepted, Japan's problems would be solved. Although the conversation was as inconclusive as its predecessors, it did leave the Ambassadors with the distinct impression that America still desired a settlement. Since they sought the same objective, Nomura and Kurusu urged their Government to bear this in mind in drafting the reply to Mr. Roosevelt's inquiry.[41]

At noon on December 2 the President conferred with Secretaries Stimson and Knox and with Mr. Welles. Mr. Roosevelt described his latest *démarche* but also indicated that he was still considering a message to Hirohito, a message to Congress, and perhaps even a speech to the country.[42] So far as one can deduce, therefore, the inquiry as to Japanese concentrations in Indo-China was merely an addition to the program for postponing a decision for war. From intercepted Japanese messages the President knew by this time of Tokyo's warnings to Berlin that war might break out sooner than anyone dreamed. He knew further of the orders from Tokyo to burn diplomatic codes and use emergency code words. There could be no doubt whatever that the ax was about to fall, but Washington certainly manifested no interest in hastening the fatal moment. On the contrary, everything was being done to gain every possible second.

[40] Memo of the President to Hull and Welles, December 1, 1941 (*Roosevelt Papers:* Secretary's File, Box 76); Hull: *Memoirs,* II, 1091-92; and Hull's testimony in *Pearl Harbor Attack,* II, 552 ff.

[41] Memo of conversation between Welles, Nomura and Kurusu, December 2, 1941 (*Foreign Relations of the United States: Japan,* II, 778-81); tel. from Washington to Tokyo, December 2, 1941 (*Pearl Harbor Attack,* XII, 221-23).

[42] *Stimson Diary* (MS.), December 2, 1941 (quoted also in *Pearl Harbor Attack,* XI, 5437).

One important aspect of the situation, however, remains unclear. The President still evaded any commitment with regard either to Siam or Britain. In response to Bangkok's pleas for supplies the United States had agreed only to the provision of small quantities of aviation gasoline and oil. Otherwise it stood on its earlier promises to treat Siam on the same basis as China in the event that the Bangkok Government resisted Japanese aggression.[43] The British were equally unsuccessful in securing American support for their plans. This phase of the pre-Pearl Harbor crisis is so poorly documented that it has invited very compromising interpretations. From such scraps of evidence as are available it is plain that Mr. Roosevelt yielded to the British request for coöperation in patrolling the South China Sea and the Gulf of Siam. Before midnight on December 1 orders were issued to the Commander of the Asiatic Fleet to charter three small vessels for this purpose. One was to cruise off Hainan Island, another off the southeast coast of Indo-China, and the third off the entrance to the Gulf of Siam. Actually this "defensive patrol" did not operate before December 7, 1941.[44]

The United States was, however, less amenable to other British requests. London had long since suggested the desirability of instituting a special high-priority code system which would enable any commander in the Far East to inform London as well as other Far East commanders of any sudden Japanese move which might necessitate military counteraction. The United States War Department recommended against joining in any agreement "whereby its authorities should report directly to London." The British were so informed on December 2.[45]

More obscure is the nature of the reply which, on instructions from the President, Mr. Welles made to Lord Halifax on December 1 respecting the British plan for protective occupation of southeastern Siam. No record of this conversation has been found and Mr. Welles has been unable to recall its tenor. The only known reference to it occurs in an ambiguous sentence in a telegram from Ambassador Winant of December 6, 1941, reading as follows:

> British feel pressed for time in relation to guaranteeing support Thailand, fearing Japan might force them to invite invasion on pretext protection before British have opportunity to guarantee support but wanting to carry out President's wishes in message transmitted by Welles to Halifax.[46]

It can certainly be deduced from this text that the British, as late as December 6, had not obtained the desired assurances from Washington. The President apparently still opposed any commitment regarding American action

---

[43] The relevant documents are assembled in *Pearl Harbor Attack,* XIX, 3760 ff.

[44] *Pearl Harbor Attack,* II, 955 ff.; VI, 2873.

[45] Tel. from Winant, October 18; War Department memorandum, November 26; tel. to Winant, December 2, 1941.

[46] *Pearl Harbor Attack,* II, 493 ff.

in the event of a Japanese invasion of Siam. Yet Admiral Hart received on December 6 the following mysterious telegram from the United States Naval Attaché at Singapore:

Brooke-Popham [British Commander in Chief, Far East] received Saturday from War Department London quote: "We have now received assurance of American armed support in cases as follows: 1) We are obliged to execute our plans to forestall Japs landing Isthmus of Kra or take action in reply to Nips invasion any other part of Siam. . . . "

This message immediately impelled Admiral Hart to telegraph Washington pointing out that he had not been informed of any such commitment. Years later the Naval Attaché testified that he could not remember the source of his information and thought that what he reported was "really nothing more than a rumor." If so, it remains inexplicable that a message of such gravity should have been transmitted by a responsible officer on the basis of mere talk. The truth or falsity of this telegram is among the important problems relating to Pearl Harbor which have yet to be verified. If the British War Office had in fact received the assurances it had sought from Washington, it will still be difficult to explain why Mr. Welles had no recollection of them and, moreover, why Ambassador Winant should have sent a telegram on December 6 implying precisely the contrary American response to London.[47] Until further evidence to the contrary is forthcoming, it must be assumed that only the launching of Japanese attacks on American as well as on British and Dutch territory on December 7, 1941, finally resolved the dilemma which consistently plagued the Roosevelt Administration in its efforts to reconcile the demands of national security with the limitations imposed by the Constitution, the Congress, and public opinion.

3. The Sword of Damocles

The three succeeding days, Wednesday the 3rd of December through Friday the 5th, marked an interval of *détente*. Having completed their preparations, the Japanese had merely to defer their reply to the Ten Points until the hour set for attack. They lost no time, therefore, in replying to the President's inquiry about their intentions. On December 3 Nomura and Kurusu were instructed to say that the forces in northern Indo-China had been increased in order to counter unusual Chinese activity along the frontier. The movements in northern Indo-China had had repercussions in southern Indo-China, though reports of Japanese activity in that area had

---

[47] On this see the Welles testimony (*Pearl Harbor Attack*, II, 493, and relevant material, *ibid.*, X, 4803, 5080-89; XI, 5514 ff.). The question is analyzed in some detail in Beard: *President Roosevelt and the Coming of the War*, 537 ff., and in George Morgenstern: *Pearl Harbor* (New York, 1947), 113. Cf. Feis: *The Road to Pearl Harbor*, 322, 334-38 and notes 11, 12; and Churchill: *The Grand Alliance*, 601 ff.

been exaggerated. In any case, Japanese forces were not in excess of the limit set in the agreement with Vichy France.

This directive dismayed the two Ambassadors, who hastened to point out to Tokyo the significance which Washington would necessarily attach to the Japanese reply:

> There is no saying but what the United States Government will take a bold step depending on how our reply is made. If it is really the intention of our Government to arrive at a settlement, the explanation you give, I am afraid, would neither satisfy them nor prevent them taking the bold step referred to—even if your reply is made for the mere purpose of keeping the negotiations going. Therefore . . . I would like to get a reply which gives a clearer impression of our peaceful intentions.

Nothing could have been further from the thoughts of the Tokyo Government. On December 4 the Ambassadors were ordered to proceed in accordance with the previous instruction.[48]

In Washington there was little to do but await the Japanese statement. The President held a press conference on December 2 and Secretary Hull did likewise on the following day, both doing their best to prepare public opinion by explaining the efforts of the Government to arrive at a just settlement and the unwillingness of the Japanese to yield on any essential. The impression was conveyed that even though there was little hope of an accord, efforts would be continued. The public was also apprised of the request for information as to Japanese troop concentrations in Indo-China, but it knew nothing of the details of the Japanese note of November 20 nor of the American Ten Point note of November 26. Washington correspondents certainly received the impression that if Japan advanced further it would probably mean war, since American interests in the Philippines and elsewhere would be threatened. On the other hand, the notion was also prevalent that even if the negotiations broke down the Japanese would not move immediately. There might be a cooling-off period—no war, no peace—of some weeks. Many were sure that the arrival of the great British warships, *Prince of Wales* and *Repulse,* at Singapore on December 2 would give the Japanese pause.[49]

As to the state of American public opinion on the eve of the conflict, it is difficult to generalize with any assurance. The press, always inclined to treat Japan in cavalier fashion, grew somewhat more circumspect as the crisis deepened. While still overwhelmingly opposed to any form of appeasement, most editors were reluctant to renounce all hope of a peaceful settlement. Tabulations of public reaction, submitted to the President, revealed the

[48] Tels. to and from Tokyo, December 3, 4, 1941 (*Pearl Harbor Attack,* XII, 224, 227-28, 232).
[49] Edgar A. Mowrer in the *Chicago Daily News,* December 4; Joseph G. Harrison in the *Christian Science Monitor,* December 1, 3; Wilfrid Fleischer in the *New York Herald Tribune,* December 3, 1941.

usual inconsistencies. To the question whether the United States should, even at the risk of war, take steps to prevent Japan from growing more powerful, 69 percent replied in the affirmative, 20 percent in the negative, and 11 percent expressed no opinion. Yet, to the question "Do you think the United States will go to war against Japan some time in the near future?" 51 percent answered "yes," 27 percent "no," and 22 percent had no opinion.[50]

It is not much easier to form a judgment on the vitally important factor of Congressional opinion. Secretary Hull was evidently worried to the end by the strength of isolationist sentiment in Congress. The President, too, had not forgotten the heated debates of recent months. Although Representative May, Chairman of the Armed Services Committee, declared publicly on December 2 that Congress would "support a declaration of war now if Japan moves southward," Mr. Roosevelt knew that there were few members of Congress as bellicose as Mr. May. On December 4 he conferred with Vice President Wallace and several other leaders of the Democratic Party: Senator George, Senator Hill, Speaker Rayburn, and Representatives Sol Bloom and McCormack. The President concluded the two-hour conference with a request that Congress not recess for intervals of more than three days. The Congressional leaders left the White House "with the impression that the situation is critical but will not necessarily come to a show-down with the presentation of Japan's reply" (to the inquiry on its intentions in Indo-China).[51]

Surely the most striking evidence of the hostility of the extreme isolationists to the Administration's policies was offered by the surprise publication in the Chicago Tribune on December 4 of the nation's estimated production requirements in the event of global war, the so-called Victory Program. This reckless revelation of vital military secrets astounded and dismayed all who had any comprehension of the value of such intelligence to potential enemies. Though the Attorney General believed that publication of the information violated the Espionage Act and Mr. Stimson urged prosecution in order "to shake our American people out of their infernal apathy," nothing was actually done. Quite possibly Mr. Roosevelt decided that this was not the moment to exchange broadsides with the heaviest batteries of the isolationist fortress. If he seriously contemplated legal proceedings, as all members of his Cabinet recommended, the idea evaporated in the heat of the Pearl Harbor disaster three days later. Meanwhile, the action of the Chicago

[50] On the press we have used the valuable analysis prepared for Secretary Morgenthau by Mr. Alan Barth (Morgenthau Diaries, MS., December 5, 1941, Vol. 469, pp. 119 ff.); on public opinion we have drawn on the report which Professor Hadley Cantril sent to the President on December 5, 1941 (Roosevelt Papers: Secretary's File, Box 81).

[51] J. G. Harrison in the Christian Science Monitor, December 4; B. D. Hulen in The New York Times, December 5; Washington Post, December 5, 1941.

Tribune was a warning that the people of the United States were not yet united in desiring a showdown with totalitarian aggression.[52]

While Nomura and Kurusu awaited final instructions on the reply to the President's inquiry, cryptic references indicate that the two Ambassadors were continuing their effort to revive the defunct *modus vivendi*. Through Cabinet members, presumably Postmaster General Walker, and other influential people, probably the Reverend E. Stanley Jones, they strove particularly to induce the American Government to act as intermediary between Japan and China. Though the persons concerned reached Mr. Roosevelt, they effected no change in his attitude.[53] Nevertheless, even at this late hour sentiment for reviving the proposal for a ninety-day truce was not quite dead in Washington. This emerges from the appearance in the draft of the President's December 6 message to Emperor Hirohito of references to a possible truce. Further light is thrown on these otherwise obscure references by two unsigned notes on plain paper, dated December 5, which were turned up in the archives of the State Department. These notes are attached to the copy of Chiang Kai-shek's message to Secretary Stimson of November 25, which the latter sent to the State Department on December 2. The inspiration and authorship of the notes are unknown, but they were plainly designed to overcome the Generalissimo's objections to the proposed *modus vivendi*. That they were backed by some authority is demonstrated by their reappearance in the aforementioned draft of Mr. Roosevelt's message to Hirohito. Pending further evidence as to their real significance, it is impossible to do more than reproduce the texts. The first note reads:

Proposal: A truce or standstill arrangement whereby the countries actually or potentially engaged in hostilities in the Pacific Area undertake each to refrain for ninety days from any movement or use of armed force against any of the other parties.

It is assumed that along with this proposal there goes proposal of a provision that Japan shall reduce her armed forces in Indo-China to the number which she had there on July 26, 1941, and shall not send new contingents of armed forces or matériel to that area.

It is understood that the plan also contemplates an undertaking by the United States to suggest to the Government of Japan and to the Government of China that those governments enter into direct negotiations with a view to ascertaining whether there exists a basis for peaceful settlement of the difficulties existing between them.

It is further understood that the proposal outlined in the first paragraph above is not to be construed as calling for discontinuance by the United States of aid to China.

Comment: It is our belief that if such plan is offered for the consideration of the Japanese Government the matter should be handled by the Department of State rather than as a project personally put forward by the President to the Emperor.

The second note raised the question whether the project should be sub-

---

[52] *Stimson Diary (MS.)*, December 4, 5, 1941.

[53] Tel. from Washington to Tokyo, December 6, 1941 (*Pearl Harbor Attack*, XII, 247).

mitted to the British, Chinese, Australians, Dutch and Canadians, and advised against such action on the plea that it would produce delay, confusion and contradictory suggestions. "If we decide among ourselves," it read, "that the project has within itself sufficient of possible advantage and any substantial chance of being accepted by the Japanese, it would probably be better for us to proceed with it without consultation with other powers." The second note concluded, however, that consultation with the Chinese alone might be feasible and desirable in view of all they had at stake.

Whatever merit these last-minute suggestions may have had, they could scarcely have interested Tokyo, where all the crucial decisions had now been made. In accordance with the earlier assurances of Ribbentrop to Oshima, the Japanese Government on December 3 submitted to Berlin and Rome its formal request for intervention and for agreement not to conclude a separate peace. Count Ciano, the Italian Foreign Minister, was staggered by the prospect now opening before his hard pressed country, but Mussolini was not "at all surprised" by the report he received from the Japanese Ambassador, "in view of the utter bull-headedness of the United States and the meddlesome nature of President Roosevelt." The Duce readily promised everything Japan asked, reserving final agreement only until he had consulted with Hitler.[54]

Little is known of Berlin's reaction except that at the moment of the Pearl Harbor attack formal agreement had not been reached. Ribbentrop evidently favored spurring the Japanese on, but the Fuehrer may have entertained some misgivings about assurances so heavily weighted in Japan's favor. It is reasonably certain that for all their close contact with the Japanese military, the German representatives in Tokyo knew nothing specific about Japan's war plans. There is even some evidence that Hitler opposed a sudden attack which would make Japan appear the aggressor.[55]

The Japanese Government in any case had good reason to believe that when it launched the war, the Germans, like the Italians, would promptly fall in line. And so they did. While considerations of prestige may have hastened Hitler's decision to declare war on the United States first, the significant element was the fact that Germany and the United States were already for all practical purposes at war in the Atlantic. Once the United States decided to escort convoys, no further purpose was served by the Fuehrer's efforts to avoid provoking American intervention. While he failed

[54] Tel. from Rome to Tokyo, December 3, 1941 (*Pearl Harbor Attack*, XII, 228-29); *The Ciano Diaries*, December 3, 4, 1941; *Ciano's Diplomatic Papers* (London, 1948), 465 ff.
[55] Tel. from Ott to Ribbentrop, December 5, 1941 (*Tokyo War Crimes Documents*, 1374); affidavit of Alfred F. Kretschmar, German Military Attaché in Tokyo (*ibid.*, Exhibit 2751); diary of the German Naval Attaché in Tokyo (*Nazi Conspiracy and Aggression*, Supplement A, 991); tel. from Tokyo to Berlin, December 6, 1941 (*Pearl Harbor Attack*, XII, 245-46).

to associate Japan in hostilities against the Soviets, it was no small satisfaction to have Japan come in on her own terms, since these certainly promised to divert American and British power from the European theater.[56]

Thanks to intercepted messages, the main steps in Tokyo's preparations for war were known in Washington shortly after they were taken. Mr. Hull was well aware of the order to the Japanese Embassy to destroy its code books. He knew the contents of Tokyo's reply to the President's inquiry on Indo-China before Nomura and Kurusu handed him the document on the morning of December 5. Thus prepared, he could ridicule the Japanese contention that the troop concentrations in Indo-China were designed to guard against Chinese attack from Yunnan. He could likewise cut off all attempts of the Ambassadors, acting under instructions from Togo, to revive discussion of the Japanese proposals of November 20. Whatever the hope of the envoys, and even of Foreign Minister Togo, that some eleventh hour concession by the United States might yet save the situation, their American counterparts knew too much of Japanese intentions and decisions to interpret the continued talk as anything more than a means of gaining time. As the German Naval Attaché noted in his diary, Japanese military leaders were convinced that war was inevitable "even if the United States, at the last minute, should make still greater concessions."[57]

Washington might have been reasonably content with Tokyo's stalling tactics if it could have gauged their time limit and if its own preparations to parry the impending blow had been further advanced. As the matter stood, American authorities had known for a full week that large Japanese convoys were steaming down the China coast. They did not, however, know the precise destination of the convoys nor had they yet fixed on a course of action to follow if, as generally anticipated, the Japanese attack fell on British, Dutch or Siamese territory, but not on American. On December 4 the Netherlands Government suggested that the Japanese Government be warned not to cross the line between Davao and Waigeo in the direction of the Indies. Bangkok was similarly appealing for an Anglo-American statement that a Japanese invasion of Siam would meet with armed resistance.[58] Washington remained silent, even though on December 5 reports placed the Japanese transports and warships in Camranh Bay. By noon on

---

[56] Kordt: *Wahn und Wirklichkeit*, 323-24; DeWitt C. Poole: "Light on Nazi Foreign Policy" (*Foreign Affairs*, October, 1946).

[57] *Nazi Conspiracy and Aggression*, Supplement A, 991. Also significant is the attack by the *Domei* press agency on Mr. Hull's press conference statements (*The New York Times*, December 5, 1941), and Ambassador Grew's tel. to Hull (*Pearl Harbor Attack*, II, 686-87). For the Japanese reply to the inquiry of December 1 see the memo of conversation between Hull and the Ambassadors (*Foreign Relations of the United States: Japan*, II, 781-84). The Nomura-Kurusu version is given in their telegram to Tokyo, December 5, 1941 (*Pearl Harbor Attack*, XII, 235-36).

[58] On the Dutch inquiry see *Pearl Harbor Attack*, XI, 5215 ff.; the Siamese request is in the tel. from Bangkok, December 4, 1941 (*Pearl Harbor Attack*, XIX, 3774-75).

December 6 (December 5, Washington time), British reconnaissance aircraft from Malaya, flying at their extreme range, sighted three Japanese convoys rounding Cape Cambodia and entering the Gulf of Siam. The first of the three was an insignificant force, but the other two were imposing. Together they comprised forty-six transports, convoyed by a battleship, seven cruisers and a number of destroyers. It could not be determined whether these convoys were about to turn westward toward Malaya or northwest to the coast of Siam. With the northeast monsoon blowing full force, accompanied by torrential rains, British reconnaissance forces lost contact with the Japanese convoys for thirty hours. At the end of that interval the convoys had almost reached the coast of Malaya.[59]

This alarming information, relayed from London to Washington on the morning of December 6, underlined Lord Halifax's remarks to Secretary Hull on the previous day that the British thought "the time has now come for immediate coöperation with the Dutch East Indies by mutual understanding. This relates to the matter of defense against Japan."[60] There could now be virtually no doubt that the Japanese attack would fall either on Siam or Malaya within a mere matter of hours. At Mr. Roosevelt's request the State, War, and Navy Departments hastily compiled an estimate of Japanese military forces and equipment in Indo-China, including the additional forces thought to be aboard the convoys. The figures, totaling 25,000 troops in northern Indo-China, 80,000 in southern Indo-China, and 18,000 on transports in Camranh Bay, were promptly released to the press, doubtless in order to alert the country.[61]

The British informed Washington that they believed the Japanese convoys were heading for the coast of Siam.[62] If so, the President's problem would be aggravated. The American public might approve a decision to initiate hostilities in defense of Britain's position in the Far East, but accept-

---

[59] Despatch of Marshal Sir Robert Brooke-Popham: *Operations in the Far East from 17th October 1940 to 27th December 1941* (Supplement to the *London Gazette*, January 22, 1948), 555; despatch of Sir Paul Maltby: *Air Operations during the Campaigns in Malaya and the Netherlands East Indies from 8th December, 1941 to 12th March, 1942* (*ibid.*, February 28, 1948), 1363-64; despatch of General A. E. Percival: *Operations of Malaya Command from 8th December, 1941 to 15th February, 1942* (*ibid.*, February 26, 1948), 1267-68.

[60] Memo of conversation between Mr. Hull and Lord Halifax, December 5, 1941 (*Pearl Harbor Attack*, XI, 5472); tel. from Winant, December 6, 1941, received in Washington at 10:40 A.M. (*Pearl Harbor Attack*, XIV, 1246). Cf. Churchill: *The Grand Alliance*, 601.

[61] *Pearl Harbor Attack*, XX, 4115-20; *The New York Times*, December 7, 1941.

[62] Information similar to that from London arrived also from American officials in Singapore and Manila (*Pearl Harbor Attack*, XV, 1680-81). The British guessed that the first Japanese objectives might be Koh Kong or Koh Tron, both situated on the west coast of Indo-China but on the route to Bangkok. There were many discrepancies in the contemporary reports concerning the size and composition of the Japanese convoys. We have used the British official despatches published since the war, based on corrected reports.

ance of such action on behalf of Siam was much less likely. The afternoon of December 6 was devoted largely to the discussion of this dilemma.

The receipt at 3 P.M. of Ambassador Winant's telegram, mentioned above,[63] made it plain that London felt it could postpone action no longer. It is impossible, however, to reconstruct completely Washington's reaction to this renewal of the British plea, now bulwarked by evidence that the Japanese would strike at any moment. Only this much is certain: in the late afternoon Mr. Casey, the Australian Minister, conferred with the President, inviting his comment on a note of warning which the British and Dominion Governments proposed to send Japan and which London had submitted to the Dominion Governments for concurrence. The draft of this warning was not formally presented by the British until the following day, but it seems likely that the Australian Minister had been commissioned to take soundings. The paper was a strong one. It began by expressing dissatisfaction with the Japanese explanations of their troop movements, especially in southern Indo-China, and closed on this unmistakable note of warning:

His Majesty's Governments have no designs on Thailand [Siam]. On the contrary, preservation of full independence and sovereignty of Thailand is an important British interest. Any attempt by Japan to impair that independence or sovereignty would affect the security of Burma and Malay and His Majesty's Governments could not be indifferent to it. They feel bound therefore to warn the Japanese Government in the most solemn manner that if Japan attempts to establish her influence in Thailand by force or threat of force, she will do so at her own peril and His Majesty's Governments will at once take all appropriate measures. Should hostilities unfortunately result, the responsibility will rest with Japan.[64]

From a telegram sent by the Australian Government to London on the basis of Mr. Casey's report it is clear that the President withheld approval of this message for the time being and reserved the right to specify the time of its submission to Tokyo. Mr. Casey reported:

1) President has decided to send message to Emperor
2) President's subsequent procedure is that if no answer is received by him from the Emperor by Monday evening,
   a) he will issue his warning on Tuesday afternoon or evening,
   b) warning or equivalent by British or others will not follow until Wednesday morning, i.e., after his own warning has been delivered repeatedly to Tokyo and Washington.[65]

Preserved in this oblique fashion is the procedure finally decided on by the President to meet the problem of preventing or parrying a surprise Japanese attack—a matter of acute anxiety to Mr. Roosevelt and his advisers

[63] *Supra*, p. 920.
[64] *Pearl Harbor Attack*, XI, 5165-66,
[65] *Ibid.*, 5166,

ever since Tokyo's war deadline had become known. The first element in the President's program was to revive the dormant message to the Emperor. Despite the mixed reception accorded the November 29-30 drafts of this message, the President had never abandoned the idea of sending it, but had held it in reserve for the moment when Japan's intentions had become clear. Secondly, and only in the event that he received no reply from the Emperor, did Mr. Roosevelt plan to address Congress and the country. Not until both these steps had been taken were the British and other Governments to issue their own warnings.[66]

4. A Bolt from the Blue

In accordance with Mr. Roosevelt's last minute decision the remainder of the afternoon of December 6 was devoted to completion of the President's message to the Emperor. The earlier draft (November 29) served as the point of departure for a fresh start, but at the end of the day two entirely different versions were still under consideration. Their relationship to each other in terms of timing and content cannot be established precisely. One version, drafted in the Far East Division of the State Department but subsequently rejected, is nonetheless significant as showing that even at this late hour consideration was still being given to a *modus vivendi* with Japan.[67] It seems that the President himself favored a last effort to revive this proposal, which had been scrapped on November 26. It was hoped to overcome Chinese opposition by a message from the President to Chiang Kai-shek as well as by his explanations to the Chinese Ambassador and Mr. T. V. Soong. This much may be derived from Secretary Hull's memorandum to Mr. Roosevelt transmitting the draft message. It reads in part:

I understand that, prior to sending the message to the Emperor, you have in mind sending a message to Chiang Kai-shek in which you would, without quoting the text of the message to the Emperor, outline to him the substance of the "stand-still" arrangement which you contemplate proposing to Japan.

From the point of view of ensuring the confidential nature of your message to Chiang Kai-shek, it is suggested that you might care to call in the Chinese Ambassador and Dr. Soong, to impress upon both of them the urgency and secrecy of the matter, and to ask the Ambassador to communicate to Chiang Kai-shek, by his most secret code, your message.

There followed the proposal for a truce, which it was hoped would avert hostilities. The salient passages are given in full, since this aspect of the final phase of the crisis has been generally slighted:

With the foregoing considerations in mind I propose now the conclusion of a tem-

[66] Feis: *The Road to Pearl Harbor,* 337-39.
[67] The original of this draft was presumably sent to the White House. The official file copy remains in the State Department. It is reproduced in *Pearl Harbor Attack,* XIV, 1231-35.

porary arrangement which would envisage cessation of hostilities for a period of ninety days between Japan and China and an undertaking by each of the Governments most concerned in the Pacific area to refrain from any movement or use of armed force against any of the other parties during the period of the temporary arrangement. If the Japanese Government is favorably disposed toward the conclusion of such an arrangement I would be glad promptly to approach the other Governments concerned with a view to obtaining their assent and commitment.

In order to give those Governments an incentive to enter into this arrangement, I further propose that, toward relieving existing apprehensions, Japan reduce her armed forces in French Indo-China to the number which Japan had there on July 26, 1941, and that Japan agree not to send new contingents of armed forces or matériel to that area during the ninety-day period of the temporary agreement.

If the commitments above envisaged can be obtained, I would undertake as a further part of the general arrangement to suggest to the Government of Japan and to the Government of China that those Governments enter into direct negotiations looking to a peaceful settlement of the difficulties which exist between them. Such negotiations might take place in the Philippine Islands should the Japanese and Chinese Governments so desire.

In as much as the Chinese Government has been cut off from its principal industrial areas, I believe it equitable that during the temporary period of the proposed arrangement the United States should continue sending material aid to China. I may add that the amount of matériel which China is able under present conditions to obtain is small in comparison with the amount of material that Japan would save through discontinuance of operations for a period of three months.

It is my thought that while this temporary arrangement would be in effect our two Governments could continue their conversations looking to a peaceful settlement in the entire Pacific area. The kind of solution I have had and continue to have in mind is one in which Japan, on the basis of application of the principles of equality, would be provided through constructive and peaceful methods opportunity for the freer access to raw materials and markets and general exchange of goods, for the interchange of ideas, and for the development of the talents of her people, and would thus be enabled to achieve those national aspirations which Japan's leaders have often proclaimed.[68]

Here was the *modus vivendi* reduced to the simplest possible terms. No clue exists as to why the President changed his mind, but for whatever reason he discarded this draft of the message to the Emperor and made no further reference to the "stand-still" idea. Since Tokyo's reply to the American note of November 26 had already been transmitted to Washington, no truce could have been arranged in any case. That it was even seriously considered in the State Department at this stage casts further doubt on the wisdom of the decision of November 26 to withhold the American draft of the *modus vivendi* when there was still a glimmer of hope that Tokyo might accept it.

The presidential message actually sent to Ambassador Grew for transmission to the Emperor went out over the wires at 9 P.M. December 6. It

[68] *Pearl Harbor Attack,* XIV, 1231-35. See Hull: *Memoirs,* II, 1092.

was drafted in the White House and was in essence a strongly reinforced revision of the original text of November 29. Though duly sent to the State Department, where minor emendations were made, the final text bore little resemblance to the Department's rejected draft containing the stand-still proposal.[69]

Beginning with a review of the past friendship and peaceful relations between the United States and Japan, the message took up the war in China and the recent developments in Indo-China. These, it was pointed out, were such as to create a reasonable doubt in the minds of the peoples of the Philippines, the Indies, Malaya and Siam whether an attack upon them was not being planned:

I am sure that Your Majesty will understand that the fear of all these peoples is a legitimate fear inasmuch as it involves their peace and their national existence. I am sure that Your Majesty will understand why the people of the United States in such large numbers look askance at the establishment of military, naval and air bases manned and equipped so greatly as to constitute armed forces capable of measures of offense.

It is clear that a continuance of such a situation is unthinkable.

None of the peoples of whom I have spoken above can sit either indefinitely or permanently on a keg of dynamite.

The message closed with assurance that no other power would invade Indo-China even if the last Japanese soldier were withdrawn therefrom, and appealed to the Emperor to take action to dispel the clouds of war.[70]

The warning was unmistakable, but it came too late. Despite the pleadings of the British and others, the President had held off and had in the end chosen his own procedure. So far as known, he made his decision in consultation with Secretary Hull alone, though the message, when finally sent, was communicated at once to the British Ambassador and sent also to the Chungking Embassy for transmission to Chiang Kai-shek. The telegram to Chungking, incidentally, sounded as though it referred to the discarded version of the message to the Emperor, for it read in part:

This message, as the situation now stands, would seem to represent very nearly the last diplomatic move that this Government can make toward causing Japan to desist from its present course; that if the slender chance of acceptance by Japan should materialize, a very effective measure would have been taken toward safeguarding the Burma Road; and that it is very much hoped that Chiang Kai-shek will not make or allow to be spread in Chinese Government circles adverse comment.[71]

[69] The original sent by the White House to the State Department contains the Department's penciled corrections and a substitute third page. These corrections are illegible in the photostat reproduced in *Pearl Harbor Attack*, XIV, 1240-45.

[70] Text in *Foreign Relations of the United States: Japan*, II, 784-86; *Pearl Harbor Attack*, XIV, 1240-45. See Hull: *Memoirs*, II, 1094.

[71] *Pearl Harbor Attack*, XI, 5473.

This passage is incomprehensible if related to the message actually sent to the Emperor. It was obviously drafted to head off Chinese objections to the ninety-day truce projected in the rejected version.

The news that Mr. Roosevelt had sent a message to Emperor Hirohito was quickly revealed to the press and radio. The message itself was transmitted in nonconfidential code, since the President had no objection to its becoming known. This mode of transmission may in turn have had some bearing on the fact that in Tokyo the cable was held for more than ten hours before being delivered to Mr. Grew. It is uncertain whether the Japanese deliberately delayed the cable, but in any case the Ambassador was unable to present it to Foreign Minister Togo until after midnight (December 8, Tokyo time), on which occasion Mr. Grew insisted upon an audience with the Emperor. Next morning the Foreign Minister informed him that negotiations had been broken off and that this was the Emperor's reply to the President. More accurately, the surprise attack on Pearl Harbor, launched several hours earlier, constituted Japan's response to the message by which Mr. Roosevelt had set such store.[72]

It will be recalled that Mr. Roosevelt, anticipating the possibility that the Emperor would not reply to his message, planned to address Congress on Monday, December 8, or Tuesday. His address, which was to contain a further warning to Japan, was considered crucial. On the generally accepted assumption that the Japanese attack would fall on Siam or Malaya and not on American territory, it was thought vitally important to convince Congress and the public that such attacks constituted an unacceptable threat to the national security and required military counteraction by the United States. Secretary Stimson's diary and Secretary Hull's later testimony reveal that almost until the time of the Pearl Harbor attack it was assumed that Siam was to be Japan's victim. How to deal with the resulting problem was foremost in all thoughts. Drafting of the message to Congress went on concurrently in the State Department with the drafting of the message to the Emperor during the afternoon and evening of December 6. Secretaries Hull, Stimson, and Knox had arranged to meet at 10:30 the next morning (Sunday) to approve the text and forward it to the White House.[73]

Meanwhile Japanese messages, intercepted on the afternoon of December 6, revealed that the reply to the American Ten Point note of November

[72] Joseph C. Grew: *Ten Years in Japan* (New York, 1944), 486, and Mr. Grew's subsequent testimony (*Pearl Harbor Attack*, II, 569-71, 574, 692 ff.). On the Japanese side see the materials in *Pearl Harbor Attack*, XVIII, 2943 ff.; Togo's testimony (*Tokyo War Crimes Documents*, Defense Document No. 2927), and the "Kido Diary," December 8, 1941 (*ibid.*, Document No. 1632W-90).

[73] *Stimson Diary* (*MS.*), December 7 (*Pearl Harbor Attack*, XI, 5437-38); Hull's testimony (*ibid.*, 5393). For Welles's role in drafting this message see his testimony (*ibid.*, II, 522). We have also used the *Berle Diaries* (*MS.*), December 7, 1941. On the lack of any further news on the movements of the Japanese convoys see the despatches of Brooke-Popham, Maltby, and Percival, as cited above.

26 was being transmitted from Tokyo, that it would be lengthy, and that it was not to be presented to Secretary Hull until further notice.[74] Navy cryptographers had deciphered the first thirteen of its fourteen parts by the late afternoon or early evening of December 6. Mr. Berle's diary indicates that the general tenor of the message was known in the State Department by 7:30 that evening. Secretary Knox knew of it by about 9:00 P.M., and the President by about 9:30. Since Secretary Knox talked to Secretaries Hull and Stimson on the telephone at about this time, it is most unlikely that Mr. Hull was not given at least the gist of the message either by his colleague or by State Department officials. Nevertheless, there is no record of the reaction to this momentous cable of anyone except the President. Discussing its contents with Harry Hopkins, Mr. Roosevelt, according to later testimony, quickly reached the conclusion that "this means war." Hopkins commented that the Japanese were going to strike at their own convenience and that it was a pity that "we could not strike the first blow and prevent any sort of surprise." Mr. Roosevelt replied: "No, we can't do that. We are a democracy and a peaceful people." He then added: "But we have a good record."[75]

Except for an attempt to reach Admiral Stark by telephone, Mr. Roosevelt took no action on the intercepted message. The Admiral was at the theater and the President refused to have him paged for fear of causing public alarm. The telephone connection was made later that evening, but nothing is known of the conversation that ensued.[76] Judging from the record, the first thirteen parts of the Japanese reply occasioned no sensation in Washington. In part this is doubtless to be explained by the fact that the thirteen sections consisted of an excessively long and turgid review of the Japanese-American conversations, followed by an analysis of the Japanese proposals of November 20 and the American note of November 26. While all this verbiage could not obscure the fact that Tokyo was rejecting the last American note, Washington had counted this a virtual certainty ever since it read the intercepted messages of November 28. Confirmation of their expectations created no stir among American officials, whose great concern was how best to meet the inevitable Japanese attack.

By 10:00 A.M. on Sunday, December 7, the President and his chief advisers had in hand the fourteenth and final section of the intercepted Japanese message. This was the definitive part. Marked "Very Important," it read:

Obviously it is the intention of the American Government to conspire with Great Britain and other countries to obstruct Japan's efforts toward the establishment of

[74] Tel. from Tokyo to Washington, December 6, 1941 (*Pearl Harbor Attack*, XII, 238-39).

[75] Testimony of Commander Schulz, who brought the Japanese messages to the President (*Pearl Harbor Attack*, X, 4661 ff.).

[76] Testimony of Captain Krick (*Pearl Harbor Attack*, XI, 5555 ff.).

peace through the creation of a New Order in East Asia, and especially to preserve Anglo-American rights and interests by keeping Japan and China at war. This intention has been revealed clearly during the course of the present negotiations. Thus, the earnest hope of the Japanese Government to adjust Japanese-American relations and to preserve and promote the peace of the Pacific through coöperation with the American Government has finally been lost.

The Japanese Government regrets to have to notify hereby the American Government that in view of the attitude of the American Government it cannot but consider that it is impossible to reach agreement through further negotiations.[77]

Here was final confirmation of the rupture, but since even this was not really news, Section XIV of the Japanese note appears to have made little more impression than the earlier parts. The President did not call Mr. Hull or his other advisers into conference, nor did the three Secretaries allow the intercepted note to disturb their deliberations on the message to Congress. They must have discussed it, but so far as the records show most of their efforts were devoted to studying a memorandum prepared for Secretary Knox on the location of American and other naval forces in the Far East, and above all to formulating a statement for the President to present to Congress. Secretary Stimson noted that Mr. Hull was "very certain that the Japs are planning some deviltry, and we are all wondering where the blow will strike." "The main thing," he added, was "to hold the main people who are interested in the Far East together—the British, ourselves, the Dutch, the Australians and the Chinese." To this end Secretary Hull dictated a statement, the salient passage of which read:

At this moment of serious, threatened, and imminent danger, it is manifest that control of the South Sea area by Japan is the key to the control of the entire Pacific area, and therefore defense of life and commerce and other invaluable rights and interests in the Pacific area must be commenced within the South Sea area at such times and places as in the judgment of naval and military experts would be within sufficient time and at such strategic points as would make it most effective. In no other way can it be satisfactorily determined that the Pacific area can be successfully defended.

Secretary Knox's draft was less finished but more outspoken:

1) We are tied up inextricably with the British in the present world situation.

2) The fall of Singapore and the loss to England of Malaya will automatically not only wreck her Far Eastern position but jeopardize her entire effort.

3) If the British lose their position, the Dutch are almost certain to lose theirs.

4) If both the British and the Dutch lose their positions, we are almost certain to be next, being then practically Japanese surrounded.

5) If the above be accepted, then any serious threat to the British or the Dutch is a serious threat to the United States; or it might be stated any threat to any one of the three of us is a threat to all of us. We should therefore be ready jointly to act together

[77] Text in *Pearl Harbor Attack*, XII, 239-45; *Foreign Relations of the United States: Japan*, II, 787-92.

and if such understanding has not already been reached, it should be reached immediately. Otherwise we may fall individually one at a time (or somebody may be left out on a limb).

6) I think the Japanese should be told that any movement in a direction that threatens the United States will be met by force. The President will want to reserve to himself just how to define this. The following are suggestions to shoot at: Any movement into Thailand; or any movement into Thailand west of 100° east and south of 10° north—this in accordance with the recommendation of the British and Dutch and United States military authorities in the Far East; or any movement against British, Dutch, United States, Free French, or Portuguese territory in the Pacific area.[78]

Before the meeting of the Secretaries broke up it became known that the Japanese envoys would present their note to Mr. Hull at one o'clock. There can be no doubt whatever that according to Washington thinking the rupture of negotiations would be followed quickly by some form of "deviltry" and that on Monday the President would address Congress and the country to explain why the United States was menaced by the anticipated Japanese attack on Siam or Malaya. As may be seen from the above, the exact form of the statement was still causing difficulty and one can therefore readily understand why Secretary Stimson and others felt relieved by the first reports of the attack on Pearl Harbor. That attack made it easy for the American Government to do what it felt bound to do anyway: to take military action if necessary to prevent further Japanese expansion. It has often been pointed out, and need not be enlarged upon here, that the Japanese attack on the American Fleet was, even from the standpoint of Japanese interests, an ill-advised move. This Fleet was distinctly inferior offensively to the Japanese and could in no event have offered effective opposition to the Japanese conquest of Malaya and the Indies. If, for the time being at least, the Japanese had confined their operations to British, Dutch or Siamese territory, the United States undoubtedly would have intervened, but there would have been a serious division of opinion in the country, in contrast to the nationwide upsurge of indignation and determination provoked by the surprise assault. The attack on Pearl Harbor, while notably successful from a military viewpoint, fell far short of returns commensurate with the price paid.

The story of Pearl Harbor Day is now so well known that little can be added by this account. It is practically certain that the delivery of the Japanese reply at 1:00 P.M. was precisely timed to precede by a matter of minutes the beginning of the attack (actually 1:25 P.M., Washington time). But evidently the Japanese Embassy took longer to decode the message than did the American cryptographers. Nomura and Kurusu had to ask for a postponement of their appointment with Secretary Hull until 1:45. They were not in fact received until 2:20 P.M. By that time the first tentative

[78] Stimson Diary (MS.), December 7, 1941 (Pearl Harbor Attack, XI, 5437-40).

reports of the Japanese attack had reached the President and his advisers and there was little doubt that the reports were reliable. Nonetheless, on the merest chance that they might not be, Mr. Hull decided to receive the Ambassadors, though he could not refrain from giving them a piece of his mind. After reading through the Japanese reply (with which he was already well acquainted), he told his visitors: "In all my fifty years of public service I have never seen a document that was more crowded with infamous falsehoods and distortions—infamous falsehoods and distortions on a scale so huge that I never imagined that any Government on this planet was capable of uttering them." Nomura, who had apparently envisaged nothing more than a rupture of diplomatic relations and was evidently unaware of the Japanese attack, was incapable of speech. Mr. Hull simply nodded toward the door and the two envoys departed without another word.[79]

Responsibility on the American side for the disaster at Pearl Harbor has been the subject of protracted debate and extensive investigation. It constitutes a complicated and highly technical problem beyond the competence of the present authors to judge and, unless new evidence comes to light, beyond the scope of a study of American policy. Nonetheless, in view of the critical developments in Japanese-American relations from the summer of 1941 to December 7, not to mention the specific warnings and alerts, it remains inexplicable that responsible American military authorities should have been taken so completely by surprise.[80]

As for the architects of American policy, it seems beyond controversy that the President, Secretary Hull, and their associates were all acutely aware of the probability of a surprise attack. It is equally patent, however, that none of them expected it at Pearl Harbor. That position was deemed too strong. Furthermore, to attack American territory seemed senseless from the standpoint of Japanese interests. Finally, the leading officials of the Government had been living from hour to hour with the problem of how to meet the virtual certainty of a Japanese attack in Southeast Asia. So intense was their preoccupation with this thorny issue that they overlooked not only Ambassador Grew's earlier warning about Pearl Harbor but Secretary Hull's more recent predictions of simultaneous Japanese attacks in several different directions. Less than half an hour before the Japanese struck at Pearl Harbor the President informed the Chinese Ambassador, Dr. Hu Shih, that he anticipated "foul play" within a day or two in Siam, Malaya, the East Indies and

[79] Memo of conversation between Hull and the Japanese Ambassadors, December 7, 1941 (*Foreign Relations of the United States: Japan,* II, 786-87); Hull's press statement late that afternoon, at which time the American note of November 26 and the Japanese reply of December 7 were also made public (*ibid.,* 793); see also Nomura's subsequent account of the meeting given to Ray Falk (*The New York Times,* February 22, 1948).

[80] Walter Millis: *This Is Pearl!* (New York, 1947), 58 ff., 65, offers a succinct resumé of earlier anxiety over Japanese attack. On the general problem see Sherman Miles: "Pearl Harbor in Retrospect" (*Atlantic Monthly,* July, 1948).

"possibly" the Philippines. Of Hawaii there was apparently no thought.[81] This tragic oversight may be a classic example of human frailty, but it provides no evidence whatsoever to support the thesis that the President or any other responsible American official courted a Japanese attack on the Pearl Harbor base in order to enable them to lead the country into the European War by the Pacific back door.

5. THE DECLARATIONS OF WAR

The die having been cast by Tokyo, nothing remains but to review briefly the steps which led to the formal declarations of war. During the afternoon of December 7 reports of heavy casualties and serious damage at Pearl Harbor flowed into Washington. Along with them came the news that the Japanese were indeed attacking in several other directions at once: in Siam, Malaya, and the Philippines. At three o'clock the President summoned into conference Secretaries Hull, Stimson, and Knox, General Marshall, Admiral Stark, and Harry Hopkins. After listening to Mr. Hull's account of his final interview with Nomura and Kurusu, those present concentrated their attention on the immediate steps to be taken. Mr. Hull reports that the President's demeanor and words on this occasion were solemn, but according to the contemporary notes of Harry Hopkins, "The conference met in not too tense an atmosphere because I think that all of us believed that in the last analysis the enemy was Hitler and that he could never be defeated without force of arms; that sooner or later we were bound to be in the war and that Japan had given us an opportunity. Everybody, however, agreed on the seriousness of the war and that it would be a long, hard struggle."[82]

Most pressing among the subjects discussed by the President at this meeting was his message to Congress, which he had now decided to deliver on the following day. To quote the Hopkins notes: "The President expressed himself very strongly that he was going to submit a precise message and had in mind submitting a longer message later. Hull urged that the President review the whole history of the Japanese relations in a strong document that might take half an hour to read. The President objected." Disagreement on this subject continued throughout the day and was aggravated by differences of opinion on whether the President should ask for a declaration of war not only against Japan but also against Germany. Throughout the late afternoon the issue was debated in both the State and War Departments. Meanwhile the President was writing his own draft of the message to Con-

---

[81] Feis: *The Road to Pearl Harbor,* 340.

[82] Sherwood: *Roosevelt and Hopkins,* 431; Hull: *Memoirs,* II, 1097. Curiously Secretary Stimson's diary omits any reference to this meeting, while the White House record of presidential appointments does not list the presence of Secretary Hull, General Marshall, and Admiral Stark. Mr. Hull states that the meeting lasted forty minutes. Hopkins's notes relate that it adjourned about 4:30. This indicates how contradictory the evidence can be on even the most important matters.

gress. In the evening, at 8:30, he met with the entire Cabinet for about an hour. At this time he read his draft, only to meet with further objection. Secretary Stimson recorded:

It was based wholly upon the treachery of the present attack in view of his efforts at peace. For that line of thought it was very effective, but it did not attempt to cover the long-standing indictment of Japan's lawless conduct in the past. Neither did it connect her in any way with Germany. Some of us in the Cabinet thought that this last should be done even at the first presentation tomorrow. Hull took this view particularly and I supported it. I pointed out that we knew from the interceptions and other evidence that Germany had pushed Japan into this and that Germany was the real actor, and I advocated the view that we should ask for a declaration of war against Germany also. But no one backed me in this, although when I got in a few words with the President at the close of the meeting and urged on him the importance of a declaration of war against Germany before the indignation of the people was over, he told me that he intended to present the whole matter two days later. But the feeling among the Cabinet was quite strong in support of Hull's view that the message should be broader.

Nonetheless, the President stuck to his guns and determined to make his message a short and direct one which everyone would read. Late that evening he evaded a State Department draft which Hopkins described as "a long-winded dissertation on the history of Japanese relations leading up to the blow this morning."[83]

Following the Cabinet meeting the President invited the leaders of both parties in Congress to join the group. These included Vice President Wallace, Senators Barkley, McNary, Connally, Austin, and Hiram Johnson, and Congressmen Rayburn, Jere Cooper, Joseph Martin, Sol Bloom, and Charles Eaton. The President reviewed the news as it had come in and arranged for his address to Congress on the following day. Secretary Stimson noted that the effect was tremendous: "They sat in dead silence and even after the recital was over they had very few words." Only Senator Connally expressed what most of those present probably felt. "Well," he remarked, "they were supposed to be on the alert, and if they had been on the alert . . . I am amazed at the attack by Japan, but I am still more astounded at what happened to our Navy. They were all asleep. Where were our patrols? They knew these negotiations were going on."[84] In response to questions, the President refused to say what he meant to tell Congress, pleading that much might happen before noon next day. He did, however, say without reserve: "The fact is that a shooting war is going on today in the Pacific. We are in it."[85]

At four o'clock on December 7 (Washington time) Japanese Imperial

[83] *Stimson Diary* (*MS.*), December 7, 1941 (quoted in *Pearl Harbor Attack*, XI, 5437-39); Sherwood: *Roosevelt and Hopkins*, 433.

[84] Stenographic record of the meeting, printed in *Pearl Harbor Attack*, XIX, 3503-7.

[85] *Ibid.*, 3507; *Stimson Diary* (*MS.*), as noted above.

Headquarters declared that a state of war existed with both the United States and the British Empire. This news reached Washington either in the evening or early next morning, in any case before the President appeared before Congress. According to a telegram from Ambassador Winant which arrived during the night and was handed to the President at 8:00 A.M. Monday, Mr. Churchill wanted to know whether he should ask Parliament for a declaration of war that very afternoon, or wait until the President had addressed Congress. To this Mr. Roosevelt replied at once saying that in view of the American psychology it would be better to wait.[86] Just after noon on Monday Mr. Roosevelt appeared before a joint session of Congress and delivered his message substantially in the form he had himself drafted. Recalling that the Japanese attack had come while the Japanese envoys were still talking negotiations and pointing out that the attack on Pearl Harbor must have been planned long before, he rehearsed the latest assaults on Malaya, Hongkong, Guam, the Philippines, Wake Island and Midway Island, and concluded: "Hostilities exist. There is no blinking at the fact that our people, our territory, and our interests are in grave danger. . . . I ask that the Congress declare that since the unprovoked and dastardly attack by Japan on Sunday, December seventh, a state of war has existed between the United States and the Japanese Empire."[87] Within an hour both houses of Congress, with only one dissenting vote (in the House of Representatives), passed a resolution to that effect. The declaration of war was signed by the President at 4:10 P.M. that afternoon. Great Britain and the members of the British Commonwealth followed suit immediately.

There remained the question, on which Secretary Stimson felt so strongly, of declaring war on Germany and Italy, on the theory that it was well known that Germany had pushed Japan into war. This theory was true only to the extent that Ribbentrop had egged the Japanese on, not to the extent that the Japanese had paid much attention to the desires of their allies. It is practically certain that neither the German Ambassador in Tokyo nor the Japanese Ambassador in Berlin knew anything definite about the timing of the attacks, let alone about the Pearl Harbor plan itself. On the contrary, the Japanese felt so sure of themselves that they took the final step before they were absolutely certain of German intervention against the United States. They were in fact determined that, if the Germans insisted on Japanese intervention in the war against Soviet Russia, they would dispense completely with European Axis aid.[88] In any event, it was not until noon of

[86] Tel. from Winant, sent at 4:00 P.M., December 7 (London time) and received at Washington at 4:00 A.M. (Washington time); tel. to Winant, December 8, 1941; Churchill: *The Grand Alliance*, 605-6.

[87] Text in *Foreign Relations of the United States: Japan*, II, 793-94.

[88] Tel. from Tokyo to Berlin, December 6, 1941 (*Pearl Harbor Attack*, XII, 245-46); for the rest see the affidavit of the German Military Attaché in Tokyo (*Tokyo War Crimes Documents*, Exhibit 2751), and the affidavit of Ribbentrop (*ibid.*, Exhibit 2762).

December 8 that General Oshima officially requested the German Government to declare war on the United States.[89]

In Washington the President was evidently in no hurry to take action. After all, undeclared war already existed in the Atlantic and from the intercepted messages it was almost a foregone conclusion that Germany and Italy would fall in line with Japan. If that were so, it would be far better from the standpoint of public reaction to have Hitler and Mussolini take the initiative. The Fuehrer was not slow to oblige. He was evidently delighted by the news of Pearl Harbor and forgot all else in his relief that at last the Japanese had taken the plunge. On December 8 Ribbentrop told the Japanese Ambassador that orders had already been given the German Navy to attack American ships whenever and wherever they might be met. It seems that Hitler's immediate objective, as a matter of prestige, was to declare war before it could be declared upon him. On the morning of December 11 a note was handed the American Chargé d'Affaires in Berlin recalling the American policy of shooting on sight and putting the declaration of war solely on the basis of German-American relations:

> Although Germany on her part has strictly adhered to the rules of international law in her relations with the United States during every period of the present war, the Government of the United States from initial violations of neutrality has finally proceeded to open acts of war against Germany. The Government of the United States has thereby virtually created a state of war.
>
> The German Government, consequently, discontinues diplomatic relations with the United States of America and declares that under these circumstances brought about by President Roosevelt, Germany too, as from today, considers herself as being in a state of war with the United States of America.

When the German Chargé d'Affaires in Washington appeared at the State Department to deliver the same note, Secretary Hull avoided receiving him and directed the Chief of the European Division, Mr. Ray Atherton, to do so. In accepting the note Mr. Atherton remarked that "he was merely formalizing the realization that the Government and people of this country had faced since the outbreak of war in 1939 of the threat and purposes of the German Government and the Nazi regime toward this hemisphere and our free American civilization."

Italy followed the German pattern. Thereupon the President appealed to Congress to recognize the state of war: "The long known and the long expected has thus taken place. The forces endeavoring to enslave the entire world now are moving towards this hemisphere." At 3:05 P.M. on the same day (December 11) the Senate unanimously and the House without record

---

In a telegram from Ott to Ribbentrop on December 5 (*ibid.*, Exhibit 608), the Ambassador reported that the Japanese tended to feel that, for reasons of internal politics, it was essential to declare war simultaneously with or immediately after the opening of hostilities.

[89] Tel. from Berlin to Tokyo, December 8, 1941 (*Pearl Harbor Attack*, XII, 253).

vote passed a Joint Resolution "that the state of war between the United States and the Government of Germany (or Italy) which has been thrust upon the United States is hereby formally declared."[90]

Thus was closed the circle which enveloped the United States in global war. Of Adolf Hitler it need only be said that his immediate concern was to make this bitter cup as palatable as possible to the apprehensive German people. He therefore avoided all reference to Japan and based his fateful decision solely on the shooting war in the Atlantic. This was indeed an undeclared war and it could only have been a matter of time before it was formalized. Nevertheless, the Fuehrer's initiative, following close on the heels of the Pearl Harbor attack, gave immeasurable aid and comfort to his opponents and his victims. The President of the United States was relieved of the odium which would inevitably have attached to his taking the necessary but still controversial final step from undeclared to declared war.

Ever since the outbreak of the war in Europe, and indeed before it, most Americans had contemplated with resignation the day when the United States would join in hostilities against the Axis powers. In response to the logic of events, at least as much as to the leadership of the President, an ever increasing number had come to feel that it was not merely their country's hapless fate but its bounden duty to enter the great conflict. The dimensions of America's stake in the outcome had been measured by its Government and by its citizens over a period of more than two years. The significance of each momentous step taken along the road which from the start so many believed destiny would compel the country to follow had been debated in Congress, over the air, in the press, and from the platform. Whatever, therefore, the final judgment on the wisdom of America's involvement in the global war, the indictment or the vindication must encompass the whole American people. It was not only the swift disaster of Pearl Harbor which explains the sobriety and even the grimness with which the United States now set its wartime course. The steadfastness and valor of all those warring peoples who were presently to become the United Nations had afforded the American democracy a unique opportunity, by democratic processes, to appraise and at long last to respond to the appeal for leadership in the struggle. Without the elation of 1917, but surely with profounder understanding of the values it sought to preserve, the New World again advanced to the rescue of the Old.

[90] The texts are printed in *Documents on American Foreign Relations*, IV, 118-22; for the rest see Erich Kordt: *Wahn und Wirklichkeit*, 325-26, and DeWitt C. Poole: "Light on Nazi Foreign Policy" (*Foreign Affairs*, October, 1948).

INDEX

943